ADMINISTRATIVE LAW AND PROCESS: CASES AND MATERIALS

Second Edition

Alfred C. Aman, Jr.
Roscoe C. O'Byrne Professor of Law
Indiana University School of Law—Bloomington
and
Director, Institute for Advanced Study, Indiana University

ISBN#: 0-8205-5992-X

Library of Congress Cataloging-in-Publication Data

Aman, Alfred C.
    Administrative law and process: cases and materials / Alfred C. Aman, Jr.--2nd ed.
      p. cm.
    Includes index.
    ISBN 0-8205-5992-X (hard cover)
    1. Administrative law--United States--Cases. I. Title.
KF5402.A4A45 2006
344.4101—dc22   2005035317

This publication is designed to provide accurate and authoritative information in regard to the subject matter covered. It is sold with the understanding that the publisher is not engaged in rendering legal, accounting, or other professional services. If legal advice or other expert assistance is required, the services of a competent professional should be sought.

LexisNexis and the Knowledge Burst logo are trademarks of Reed Elsevier Properties Inc, used under license. Matthew Bender is a registered trademark of Matthew Bender Properties Inc.

Copyright © 2006 Matthew Bender & Company, Inc., a member of the LexisNexis Group.
All Rights Reserved.

No copyright is claimed in the text of statutes, regulations, and excerpts from court opinions quoted within this work. Permission to copy material exceeding fair use, 17 U.S.C. § 107, may be licensed for a fee of 10¢ per page per copy from the Copyright Clearance Center, 222 Rosewood Drive, Danvers, Mass. 01923, telephone (978) 750-8400.
of the LexisNexis Group.

Editorial Offices
744 Broad Street, Newark, NJ 07102 (973) 820-2000
201 Mission St., San Francisco, CA 94105-1831 (415) 908-3200
701 East Water Street, Charlottesville, VA 22902-7587 (804) 972-7600
www.lexis.com

Dedication

To the memory of my father, Alfred Aman, whose sense of decency, fairness and compassion were an inspiration to all who knew him.

2nd EDITION PREFACE

This book is about power and principles. Administrative law is the law governing the legal means by which executive, legislative and judicial powers are exercised and allocated to, among, and within administrative agencies. The principles underlying administrative law have been the subject of controversy, as the de-and anti-regulatory trends of the 1970s and 1980s yielded the neoliberalism of the 1990s and 21st century. In this edition, we examine administrative law in this context of market-oriented reform, emphasizing the connections to some of the broader societal issues of our times, especially the trend towards privatization of governmental services. Public/private partnerships are pervasive and raise new issues for administrative law. A state-centric approach to administrative law no longer suffices: administrative law mediates public and private power in novel ways, the implications of which can be far reaching. This raises new and important issues for administrative law teaching. This edition of Administrative Law adds emphasis on areas where private actors are now playing a greater role in providing services heretofore treated exclusively as governmental.

The book is divided into two parts.[1] An introductory Chapter 1 provides students with an overview of such key administrative law concepts as rules and orders as well as some of the various ways they might conceptualize administrative processes generally. Part I (Chapters 2 to 5) deals with the procedures agencies use to exercise their adjudicatory and rulemaking powers. It focuses on the exercise of power within the walls of administrative agencies. Chapters 2 and 3 explore the constitutional and statutory issues that arise when agencies adjudicate. More specifically, Chapter 2 is concerned with the constitutional law that governs the law-applying functions of agencies. It focuses on the constitutional requirements of the Due Process Clause of the 5th and 14th Amendments as applied to agency adjudication. Chapter 3 examines in detail the Administrative Procedure Act's requirements for formal adjudication. Chapter 4 then focuses on rules and rulemaking processes under the Administrative Procedure Act. Chapter 5 addresses informal agency actions and various alternative dispute resolution approaches. These institutional arrangements, introduced in Part I, are then set into motion in Part II.

Part II (Chapters 6 to 10) examines how various actors outside of agencies attempt to influence and control the exercise of agency discretion. Chapter 6 deals with the constitutional issues that arise when Congress seeks to delegate legislative power to unelected agency administrators. Chapter 7 involves executive controls over agency discretion as well as various legislative or political attempts to influence agency behavior. Chapter 8 examines judicial controls over agency discretion and the scope of judicial review provided when a case is properly before a court. Chapter 9 addresses the question of which litigants can bring a lawsuit to challenge agency discretion, as well as when and where they can do so. Chapter 10 then examines other means of

---

[1] Throughout this book, we have often omitted citations from the cases and articles excerpted.

controlling agency discretion. In particular, Chapter 10 focuses on agencies' and citizens' power to obtain and withhold information.

One could legitimately view each agency as a culture, as Howard Westwood argued over 45 years ago—each agency being "a law unto itself, with its own way of doing things."[2] There is a need for this kind of appreciation of each agency's character as a social system. A more detailed knowledge of agency law in action would greatly advance our overall understanding of bureaucracies in general, and administrative law in particular. At the same time, administrative law has always been subject to wider societal and political pressures that affect the system as a whole, particularly in contexts where a shift in the public's needs, expectations or attitude generates political energy for reform. Thus, there is also a need for a more general, synthetic approach to administrative law, especially for students encountering the basic principles of this field of law for the first time. Most agencies, despite their significant differences, perform a number of common administrative functions. They gather information, formulate policy and then seek to implement and enforce that policy. Moreover, as already pointed out, they carry out these functions in the context of general historic and political forces that affect all institutions.

While acknowledging the importance of particular, substantive agency differences, this book focuses primarily on procedural issues that transcend individual agencies. It focuses on the more general context in which the key cases have arisen and been resolved. Indeed, administrative law must be historically sensitive. Different historic eras are typified by different regulatory problems, different attitudes vis-à-vis the role government should play in dealing with these problems and, consequently, different approaches to substantive regulation and procedure.

Individual agencies have unique histories and ongoing, developing characters that are significantly affected by a number of contextual factors. Primary among these is the historical background that gave rise to the creation of the particular agency in the first place. Second, context includes the regulatory politics generated by an agency's ongoing attempts to carry out its statutory mandates in ever changing political and economic contexts. Closely related to these broad contextual factors, and perhaps most important of all, is the nature of the agency' particular substantive task. As Professors Gellhorn and Robinson long ago noted, "administrative procedures and the administrative process are ultimately related to the substance of administrative regulation."[3] Or, to paraphrase Ben Shahn, form is "the shape of content."[4]

Shahn states an ideal. But in striving for that ideal, we cannot ignore the complex political realities of which administrative law is but a part. The administrative process and the law that it spawns are very much products

---

[2] Westwood, *The Davis Treatise: Meaning to the Practitioner*, 43 MINN. L. REV. 607, 611 (1959).

[3] Gellhorn & Robinson, *Perspectives in Administrative Law*, 75 COLUM. L. REV. 771, 787 (1975).

[4] Ben Shahn, *The Shape of Content* 62 (Harv. Univ. Press 1957).

of dialectical tension between timeless constitutional doctrines and rational administrative principles, on the one hand, and the demands for pragmatic governmental action constrained by politics in the historic context of the moment, on the other. It is a complex mixture of rational political theories and raw political hopes and fears. It reflects various attempts to deal collectively with a wide range of societal problems, some of which may or may not be capable of resolution by market processes. Administrative law often is a bundle of contradictions—thereby expressing the substantive and procedural contradictions in our own culture. In this book, several key contradictions are in play: our love of political process and our seeming inability to accept any finality when it comes to the political results that that process produces; our respect for the market but, at the same time, our continuing belief in the efficacy of collective, pragmatic legal approaches to societal problems; our concern that the common good of the group be achieved, but not at the expense of certain basic individual rights.

Readers should not look to administrative law to resolve these contradictions. Its primary role has been to give vent to their expression and the primary product of the administrative system has been more obviously procedural than substantive. However, procedure often encodes substantive values and agendas, and debates over administrative procedures are a means by which substantive conflicts are played out within agencies and in courts long after the law Congress passes has been signed by the President.

Understanding the interplay between substance and procedure is crucial to understanding the role administrative law plays in our present neoliberal era, including the impact a neoliberal conception of globalization has on domestic law. Privatization, deregulation and regulatory cost consciousness, and regulatory forbearance—introduced in the 1980s and the 90s—will be with us in their present forms for the foreseeable future. Privatization and deregulation are fueled increasingly by global competition and a deepening global regulatory discourse. This global context has intensified and has fueled a new kind of regulatory politics—a politics of efficiency. Regulatory ends are now traded off against cost efficiency, and cost-consciousness pervades the implementation of most regulatory programs today, particularly those administered by the President and subject to Office of Management and Budget review. At the same time, there is, now, more than ever, a willingness to experiment with and to rely increasingly upon private actors to carry out public functions. From welfare to prisons, from snow removal to garbage collection, from military services to social services, private providers now play a much greater role than ever before. What is and what should be the role of administrative law in these contexts? Do we need a new administrative law? These are the central questions this book is designed to help students answer for themselves.

Given the major changes occurring in our political global economy, administrative law today is truly entering a new era. As we adapt to changing times, creative and imaginative approaches towards law and policy will be evermore necessary. Understanding the basic principles set forth in this book will help students build the intellectual foundation for their own future innovations, as legal professionals, thereby devising a new public law appropriate for sustaining democratic government in a global era.

Bloomington, Indiana
June, 2005

ACKNOWLEDGMENTS

This book has benefited enormously from many of my colleagues at IU, especially Professors Robert Fischman, John Applegate, Paul Craig and Yvonne Cripps. I am deeply grateful for their comments, suggestions and insights. I also wish to thank Dean Lauren Robel for the institutional support provided to me by the Indiana University School of Law — Bloomington throughout this project.

This book has also benefited from the various student research assistants who have worked on this project over the year. As the book neared its conclusion, several students played a very important role: Jason Clagg,'03, Russell Menyhart,'03, Anthony Molet,'04, Martin Lee,'05, Adam Greivell,'05, Lucas Carscadden,'05, and Helen Yu,'06 all contributed importantly to the outcome of this book. I especially wish to thank Howard Anderson,'05, who contributed significantly throughout this project, right up to the very end when so many details needed to be addressed. Moreover, I am particularly indebted to Marian Conaty who managed this whole process and entered the numerous changes we made. Her careful and meticulous work has greatly improved this book.

There are also those who assist an endeavor like this by providing the understanding, patience and, at times, crucial encouragement that such a long project demands. In this regard, I am deeply grateful to my wife, Carol Greenhouse, without whose help, encouragement and love this book would not have been possible.

TABLE OF CONTENTS

Page

Chapter 1 The Relationship of the Individual to the State 1

§ 1.01 Three Questions 1

§ 1.02 Rules or Orders? 4

    Londoner v. City and County of Denver 4

    Bi-Metallic Investment Co. v. State Board of Equalization of Colorado 8

    Notes and Questions (1-1 to 1-8) 9

    Problem 1-1 10

    Problem 1-2 11

    Bowles v. Willingham 12

    Notes and Questions (1-9 to 1-14) 15

    Problem 1-3 16

§ 1.03 Rules, Orders and Theories of Procedure — Some Preliminary Reflections 17

    [A] Introduction 17

    [B] Red Light Theories of Administrative Law 19

    [C] Green Light Theories of Administrative Law 21

    [D] Context 24

        Aman, *The Democracy Deficit: Taming Globalization Through Law Reform* 26

§ 1.04 Public/Private Partnerships: From Government to Governance 27

    Aman, "The Limits of Globalization and the Future of Administrative Law: From Government to Governance" 28

    Aman, "Administrative Law for a New Century" 29

    Richardson v. McKnight 30

    Notes and Questions (1-15 to 1-19) 39

    Problem 1-4 41

    Problem 1-5 42

PART ONE: WITHIN AGENCY WALLS

Chapter 2 Due Process and Administrative Adjudication 49

§ 2.01	Introduction	49
§ 2.02	The Right/Privilege Distinction	49
	Bailey v. Richardson	50
	Notes and Questions (2-1 to 2-7)	57
	Cafeteria &amp Restaurant Workers Union v. McElroy	60
	Notes and Questions (2-8 to 2-10)	65
§ 2.03	The Demise of the Right/Privilege Distinction	65
§ 2.04	Due Process, the War on Poverty and the New Property	69
	Reich, *The New Property*	69
	Goldberg v. Kelly	72
	Notes and Questions (2-11 to 2-23)	82
§ 2.05	Refining the Due Process Methodology: Property and Liberty Interests	88
	Board of Regents of State Colleges v. Roth	88
	Perry v. Sindermann	95
	Notes and Questions (2-24 to 2-30)	100
	Sandin v. Conner	105
	Notes and Questions (2-31 to 2-32)	114
	Problem 2-1	114
	Problem 2-2	116
§ 2.06	Due Process and Welfare Reform	116
	Reynolds v. Giuliani	117
	Notes and Questions (2-33 to 2-36)	122
§ 2.07	How Much Process Is Due and When Should It Be Provided?	124
	Mathews v. Eldridge	124
	Notes and Questions (2-37 to 2-42)	134
	Hamdi v. Rumsfeld	138
	Notes and Questions (2-43 to 2-48)	148
	Problem 2-3	152
	Problem 2-4	153

			Page
§ 2.08	Confining the Due Process Explosion		154
	Goss v. Lopez		154
	Ingraham v. Wright		160
	Notes and Questions (2-49 to 2-53)		169
	Walters v. National Association of Radiation Survivors		169
	Notes and Questions (2-54 to 2-57)		176
§ 2.09	Public and Private		177
	[A]	Due Process and Negative Rights	177
		DeShaney v. Winnebago County Department of Social Services	177
		Notes and Questions (2-58 to 2-61)	186
	[B]	Due Process and Healthcare	187
		Schweiker v. McClure	187
		Blum v. Yaretsky	190
		Notes and Questions (2-62 to 2-67)	196
	[C]	Due Process and Welfare	196
		Problem 2-5	198
	[D]	Due Process and Whistleblowers	199
		Brock v. Roadway Express	199
		Notes and Questions (2-68 to 2-70)	208

Chapter 3 Formal Adjudication and the Administrative Procedure Act **211**

§ 3.01	Introduction	211
§ 3.02	The New Deal and the APA: An Overview	212
	Ellis W. Hawley, *New Deal and the Problem of Monopoly*	212
	Walter Gellhorn, *The Administratuve Procedure Act: The Beginnings*	217
	Martin Shapiro, *APA: Past, Present, Future*	220
§ 3.03	Formal Adjudication and the APA	221
	Wong Yang Sung v. McGrath	222
	Notes and Questions (3-1 to 3-6)	227
	Seacoast Anti-Pollution League v. Costle	228
	Buttrey v. United States	231

		Page
	Chemical Waste Management, Inc. v. U.S. Environmental Protection Agency	235
	Notes and Questions (3-7 to 3-18)	240
	Problem 3-1	244
	Citizens Awareness Network, Inc. v. Nuclear Regulatory Commission	245
§ 3.04	Party Status and Intervention in an APA Proceeding	250
	Office of Communication of United Church of Christ v. Federal Communications Commission	250
	Notes and Questions (3-19 to 3-23)	254
§ 3.05	Evidence	257
	[A] Rules of Evidence	258
	Calhoun v. Bailar	258
	Notes and Questions (3-24 to 3-27)	262
	[B] Official Notice	263
	Castillo-Villagra v. Immigration and Naturalization Service	263
	Notes and Questions (3-28 to 3-31)	269
	[C] Burden of Proof	270
	Director, Office of Workers' Compensation Programs, Department of Labor v. Greenwich Collieries	270
	Notes and Questions (3-32 to 3-35)	276
§ 3.06	The Administrative Structure of Formal Adjudication — Combination of Functions and the Constitution	277
	Withrow v. Larkin	277
	Notes and Questions (3-36 to 3-38)	283
	Problem 3-2	284
	Problem 3-3	284
	Problem 3-4	285
	Weiss v. United States	286
	Notes and Questions (3-39 to 3-40)	290
§ 3.07	The Administrative Law Judge and an Unbiased Decisionmaker	290
	Grolier, Inc. v. Federal Trade Commission	291
	Notes and Questions (3-41 to 3-45)	297
	Problem 3-5	299
§ 3.08	*Ex Parte* Communications	299
	Professional Air Traffic Controllers Org. (PATCO) v. Federal Labor Relations Authority	299

		Page
	Notes and Questions (3-46 to 3-49)	312
§ 3.09	Pre-Judgment	312
	Cinderella Career and Finishing Schools, Inc. v. Federal Trade Commission	312
	Notes and Questions (3-50 to 3-54)	316
	Problem 3-6	316

Chapter 4 Agency Rulemaking ... 319

§ 4.01	What Is a Rule?	319
	Shauer, "A Brief Note on the Logic of Rules, with Special Reference to *Bowen v. Georgetown*"	320
	Bowen v. Georgetown Univ. Hospital	323
	Industrial Safety Equipment Ass'n, Inc. v. EPA	329
	Notes and Questions (4-1 to 4-9)	332
	Sugar Cane Growers Cooperative of Florida v. Veneman	333
§ 4.02	Formal and Informal Rules and Rulemaking Processes	337
	[A] Overview	337
	[B] Informal Rulemaking Processes — Notice and Comment	339
	Chocolate Mfrs. Ass'n of United States v. Block	339
	Notes and Questions (4-10 to 4-12)	345
	United States v. Nova Scotia Food Products Corp.	346
	Notes and Questions (4-13 to 4-15)	352
	Problem 4-1	353
	[C] Administrative Common Law	354
	Vermont Yankee Nuclear Power Corp. v. Natural Resources Defense Council	355
	Notes and Questions (4-16 to 4-21)	364
	Problem 4-2	365
	[D] Hybrid Rulemaking Procedures	365
	Industrial Union Department, AFL-CIO v. Hodgson	366
	Notes and Questions (4-22 to 4-32)	373
	United Steelworkers of America v. Marshall	376

			Page
	[E]	Exceptions to Section 553 Rulemaking Procedures	388
		American Hospital Assoc. v. Bowen	388
		Hoctor v. United States Department of Agriculture	396
		Notes and Questions (4-33 to 4-43)	402
		Problem 4-3	405
		Problem 4-4	406
§ 4.03	Choosing Rulemaking or Adjudication		407
	[A]	Introduction	407
	[B]	The Power to Choose	408
		SEC v. Chenery Corp.	408
		National Labor Relations Board v. Bell Aerospace Company	417
		Notes and Questions (4-44 to 4-49)	419
	[C]	The Need For and Agency Use of Rules	422
		Heckler, Secretary of Health and Human Services v. Campbell	422
		Allison v. Block	428
		Notes and Questions (4-50 to 4-55)	433

Chapter 5 Informal Agency Action and Alternatives to Dispute Resolution **435**

§ 5.01	Introduction	435
§ 5.02	Informal Agency Adjudication	436
	Citizens to Preserve Overton Park v. Volpe	436
	Camp v. Pitts	441
	Notes and Questions (5-1 to 5-8)	443
	Pension Benefit Guaranty Fund v. LTV Corp.	445
	Notes and Questions (5-9 to 5-13)	450
§ 5.03	Administrative Equity	451
	Aman, "Administrative Equity: An Analysis of Exceptions to Administrative Rules"	452
	Chemical Manufacturers Association v. Natural Resources Defense Council. Inc.	454
	Notes and Questions (5-14 to 5-17)	459
	Kixmiller v. SEC	460

			Page
		Notes and Questions (5-18 to 5-21)	463
		Problem 5-1	464
		Problem 5-2	465
		Problem 5-3	466
§ 5.04		Conditions and Commitments	466
		Aman, "Bargaining for Justice"	467
		First Bancorporation v. Board of Governors of the Federal Reserve System	471
		Notes and Questions (5-22 to 5-24)	474
		Aman & Mayton, *Administrative Law*	474
		Problem 5-4	476
§ 5.05		Alternative Dispute Resolution Techniques	476
	[A]	Overview	476
	[B]	Settlement	477
		United Municipal Distributors Group v. FERC	478
		Notes and Questions (5-25 to 5-32)	482
	[C]	Arbitration	483
		Thomas v. Union Carbide Agr. Products Co.	484
		Notes and Questions (5-33 to 5-36)	490
		Devine v. Pastore	491
		Notes and Questions (5-37 to 5-39)	496
	[D]	Other ADR Approaches and Their Critics	496
		Harter, "Points on a Continuum: Dispute Resolution Procedures and the Administrative Process"	496
		Edwards, "Alternative Dispute Resolution: Panacea or Anathema"	498
	[E]	Negotiated Rulemaking	501
		USA Group Loan Services, Incorporated, USA v. Riley	502
		Notes and Questions (5-40 to 5-42)	505

PART TWO: LEGISLATIVE, EXECUTIVE AND JUDICIAL CONTROL OF AGENCY DISCRETION: OUTSIDE THE WALLS OF THE AGENCY

Chapter 6 Legislative Control of Agency Discretion **515**

§ 6.01   Introduction   515

		Page
§ 6.02	Legislative Influence Over Agency Discretion	515
	Pillsbury Co. v. FTC	516
	Notes and Questions (6-1)	521
§ 6.03	Article I of the Constitution	521
	Immigration and Naturalization Service v. Chadha	522
	Notes and Questions (6-2 to 6-10)	536
§ 6.04	The Delegation Doctrine	540
	A.L.A. Schechter Poultry Corp. v. United States	540
	Notes and Questions (6-11 to 6-17)	545
§ 6.05	The Delegation Doctrine Since *Panama* and *Schechter*	547
§ 6.06	Delegation Doctrine Revival?	550
	Industrial Union Department, AFL-CIO v. American Petroleum Institute	550
	Notes and Questions (6-18 to 6-21)	563
	Problem 6-1	563
	Problem 6-2	566
	Mistretta v. United States	567
	Notes and Questions (6-22 to 6-25)	574
	Whitman v. American Trucking Associations, Inc.	575
	Notes and Questions (6-26 to 6-29)	582
§ 6.07	Delegation and Privatization	582
	Aman, "Privatization, Democracy and Human Rights"	584
	Problem 6-3	585
§ 6.08	The Delegation of Judicial Power: Article III	586
	Pound, "Administration of Justice in the Modern City"	587
§ 6.09	*Crowell v. Benson*	588
§ 6.10	Administrative Adjudication and Jury Trials	590
	Atlas Roofing, Inc. v. Occupational Safety and Health Review Comm'n	590
	Notes and Questions (6-30 to 6-32)	596
	Problem 6-4	597
§ 6.11	The Return of *Crowell v. Benson*	597
	Northern Pipeline Construction Co. v. Marathon Pipe Line Co.	597
	Notes and Questions (6-33 to 6-40)	605

		Page
	Commodity Futures Trading Commission v. Schor	608
	Notes and Questions (6-41 to 6-48)	616

Chapter 7 Executive Control of Agency Discretion 621

§ 7.01	Introduction	621
	Aman, *Administrative Law in a Global Era*	622
§ 7.02	Controlling Spending: The Line Item Veto	625
	Clinton v. City of New York	625
	Notes and Questions (7-1 to 7-2)	638
§ 7.03	The Power to Appoint	638
	Buckley v. Valeo	638
	Morrison v. Olson	645
	Notes and Questions (7-3 to 7-10)	650
§ 7.04	The Power to Remove	652
	Humphrey's Executor v. United States	652
	Notes and Questions (7-11 to 7-14)	656
	Bowsher v. Synar	657
	Notes and Questions (7-15 to 7-19)	670
	Morrison v. Olson	671
	Notes and Questions (7-20 to 7-25)	679
§ 7.05	Executive Oversight: Executive Orders and the Office of Management and Budget	680
	Aman & Mayton, *Administrative Law*	681
	Croley, "White House Review of Agency Rulemaking: An Empirical Investigation"	683
	Executive Order 12,866	687
§ 7.06	The Limits of Executive Control and the Role of OMB	693
	Environmental Defense Fund v. Thomas	693
	Farmworker Justice Fund, Inc v. Brock	698
	Notes and Questions (7-26 to 7-28)	703
§ 7.07	Executive and Congressional Participation in Agency Rulemaking Proceedings	704
	Sierra Club v. Costle	704
	Notes and Questions (7-29 to 7-35)	710
§ 7.08	OMB and the Data Quality Act	712
§ 7.09	OMB and Privatization	714

Page

Chapter 8 Judicial Control of Agency Discretion 719

§ 8.01	Overview	719
§ 8.02	Judicial Review of Questions of Fact	721
	O'Leary v. Brown-Pacific-Maxon	722
	Notes and Questions (8-1 to 8-6)	724
§ 8.03	Judicial Review of Findings of Fact — The Substantial Evidence Standard	726
	Universal Camera Corp. v. NLRB	726
	Notes and Questions (8-7 to 8-13)	734
§ 8.04	Questions of Law	636
	National Labor Relations Board v. Hearst Publications, Inc.	737
	Notes and Questions (8-14 to 8-17)	744
	Chevron v. NRDC	745
	Notes and Questions (8-18 to 8-25)	751
	Immigration and Naturalization Service v. Cardoza-Fonseca	757
	Notes and Questions (8-26 to 8-30)	762
	Rust v. Sullivan	764
	Notes and Questions (8-31 to 8-33)	768
	Food and Drug Administration v. Brown & Williamson Tobacco Corporation	769
	Notes and Questions (8-34 to 8-35)	784
§ 8.05	Degrees of Deference	784
	Skidmore v. Swift	784
	Notes and Questions (8-36 to 8-38)	787
	United States v. Mead Corporation	787
	Notes and Questions (8-39 to 8-46)	800
	Problem 8-1	802
§ 8.06	The Scope of Judicial Review of Agency Rules	804
	[A] The Arbitrary and Capricious Standard of Review and the Rational Basis Test	804
	[B] The Hard Look Doctrine	805
	Aman, *Administrative Law in a Global Era*	805
	Motor Vehicle Mfrs. Assn. v. State Farm Mutual	807
	Notes and Questions (8-47 to 8-51)	820

			Page
		Baltimore Gas & Electric Co. v. NRDC	820
		Notes and Questions (8-52 to 8-56)	823

Chapter 9 The Availability and Timing of Judicial Review 825

§ 9.01	Introduction	825
§ 9.02	APA Exclusions from Judicial Review	826
	Heckler v. Chaney	827
	Notes and Questions (9-1 to 9-4)	833
	Webster v. Doe	834
	Lincoln v. Vigil	840
	Notes and Questions (9-5 to 9-10)	845
§ 9.03	Who Has Standing to Seek Judicial Review?	845
	Association of Data Processing Service Organizations v. Camp	846
	Notes and Questions (9-11 to 9-16)	849
	Allen v. Wright	851
	Notes and Questions (9-17 to 9-20)	858
	Problem 9-1	859
	Lujan v. Defenders of Wildlife	860
	Notes and Questions (9-21 to 9-28)	871
	Friends of the Earth, Incorporated v. Laidlaw Environmental Services (TOC), Inc.	873
	Notes and Questions (9-29 to 9-32)	881
	Problem 9-2	882
§ 9.04	When Should Judicial Review Occur?	882
	[A] Finality	882
	Federal Trade Commission v. Standard Oil Co. of California	883
	Notes and Questions (9-33 to 9-34)	886
	Problem 9-3	887
	[B] Exhaustion of Administrative Remedies	888
	Myers v. Bethlehem Shipbuilding Corp.	888
	Notes and Questions (9-35)	891
	[C] Ripeness	892
	Abbott Laboratories v. Gardner	892
	Toilet Goods Association v. Gardner	897

			Page
		Notes and Questions (9-36 to 9-37)	901
	[D]	Primary Jurisdiction	904
		Nader v. Allegheny Airlines, Inc.	904
	[E]	Mootness	910
§ 9.05	The Proper Forum		912
	Telecommunications Research & Action Center v. F.C.C.		912
	Notes and Questions (9-38 to 9-41)		916

Chapter 10 Open Government **919**

§ 10.01	Open Government — Introduction		919
	Aman & Mayton, *Administrative Law*		919
§ 10.02	The Freedom of Information Act		921
	[A]	Overview	921
	[B]	Defining Agency and Agency Records	922
		Forsham v. Harris	922
		United States Department of Justice v. Tax Analysts	928
		Notes and Questions (10-1 to 10-5)	931
		Problem 10-1	934
	[C]	FOIA Exemptions	935
		King v. U.S. Dept. of Justice	935
		Wolfe v. Department of Health and Human Services	942
		Center for National Security Studies v. U.S. Department of Justice	950
		Notes and Questions (10-6 to 10-15)	962
	[D]	Reverse FOIA Suits	964
		Chrysler Corp. v. Brown	964
§ 10.03	The Federal Advisory Committee Act		970
	Natural Resources Defense Council v. Herrington		970
	Notes and Questions (10-16 to 10-17)		975
	Byrd v. United States Environmental Protection Agency		975
	Notes and Questions (10-18 to 10-20)		980
	Problem 10-2		981
§ 10.04	Government in the Sunshine Act		982

		Page
	Common Cause v. Nuclear Regulatory Commission	982
	Notes and Questions (10-21 to 10-24)	989
§ 10.05	The Privacy Act	990
	Tijerina v. Walters	992
	Notes and Questions (10-25 to 10-31)	1001

APPENDIX A   Constitution of the United States of America (Selected Provisions) A-1

APPENDIX B   Federal Administrative Procedure Act (Selected Provisions) B-1

APPENDIX C   Freedom of Information Act C-1

APPENDIX D   Privacy Act D-1

APPENDIX E   Government in the Sunshine Act E-1

APPENDIX F   Administrative Dispute Resolution Act F-1

APPENDIX G   Negotiated Rulemaking Act G-1

TABLE OF CASES TOC-1

INDEX I-1

Chapter 1

THE RELATIONSHIP OF THE INDIVIDUAL TO THE STATE

§ 1.01 Three Questions

Administrative law governs the procedures by which a variety of governmental entities — local, state and federal — exercise their power. Like constitutional law, administrative law deals with some of the basic machinery of government and it embodies an important expression of our legal culture. Since administrative agencies represent the state and their actions affect individuals, a fundamental theme raised throughout this book is what the individual's relationship to the state should, in fact, be.

Individuals, of course, have many, varied relations to a variety of governmental bodies, the totality of which may constitute their overall relationship to the state. The relationship of individuals to the state, as represented by administrative agencies, is but one such relationship; it is, however, a very important one. The theory of administrative law that underlies this relationship can tell us much about ourselves and our legal system.

In this book, we shall often return to administrative law's considerations of the individual — both as a distinct person or entity with a unique perspective on an issue, and as part of a larger group, without regard to any characteristics necessarily unique to that person or entity. The administrative law texts we shall examine in this course will serve as rich sources of data for our analysis. They will not only teach us the law, but provide the basis for sustained reflection on the larger societal and jurisprudential issues that they embody. As we shall see at the end of this chapter, these questions also involve consideration of the role administrative law can and should play when public functions are delegated to private providers.

En route to that level of reflection, our analysis of most administrative law cases in this book begins with three far more basic questions: (1) What is the governmental action that gives rise to the issues in the case before us? (2) How does the law characterize those actions? (3) What are the legal consequences of those characterizations?

The first question assumes that traditional administrative law is always concerned with some form of governmental action. Governmental action can take a variety of forms and involve a wide-ranging body of actors. The governmental entities we shall call administrative agencies include, for example, municipal and local bodies such as tax assessors, zoning boards, planning commissions and school boards; state actors such as public service commissions, departments of motor vehicles, the environment or consumer affairs; and federal administrative agencies such as the Securities and Exchange Commission, the Internal Revenue Service, the Department of Labor or the Environmental Protection Agency.

The members of these various kinds of local, state or federal entities may be appointed or elected, and they may exercise their power as a body consisting of either several members or a single, head administrator. For analytical purposes, it is important first to be very clear on just what the governmental action is that gives rise to the procedural claims in the case before you. Is it a school board's decision to suspend a student? A highway commission's decision to build a highway? A warden's decision to place a prisoner in solitary confinement? A health commissioner's determination to ban smoking in public places? An environmental agency's decision to ban the emission of certain chemicals into the air or water?

Having identified the governmental decision or action involved, our second task is to determine how the law does or should characterize this action. Agency action can and does take many forms. Agencies can issue rules, orders, variances, rulings, ordinances, planning documents, tax assessments, expulsions or suspensions. Some of these actions will affect individuals directly. Others will be more general and their specific impact on individuals more remote. As we shall see, the procedural characterization used often will have significant legal consequences.

Two broad procedural categories will be particularly important because they encompass a wide variety of agency action. They are rules and orders. Rules are general, prospective statements of law that apply to a class of persons or entities. Their formulation usually involves legislative-like processes. Orders are more specific, particularized statements of law that usually apply to a single individual or entity and involve the determination of facts that have already occurred. The issuance of orders usually involves adjudicatory processes. We shall examine, define and analyze the underlying concepts of a rule and an order and the kinds of procedures that they require throughout these materials. At this point, it is important to realize that these concepts are by no means air-tight categories; they represent the ends of a spectrum, and there are any number of governmental actions that fall in between rules and orders, having attributes of both.

Determining when certain governmental action is best characterized as a rule rather than an order (or vice versa) or something in between is rarely an easy task, but important procedural consequences can turn upon this characterization. Our third basic question concerns what these procedural consequences are or should be. Once we have identified and characterized the governmental action in question, what procedures must an agency use to exercise its power legally? This inquiry involves larger issues concerning the nature of administrative agencies. If an agency is engaged in issuing what we are sure is an order, and some kind of adjudicatory process is appropriate, does it follow that adjudicative processes similar to those used in a federal court must be employed? How do agencies differ from courts when they adjudicate? How are and how should those differences be reflected in the procedures that they use? Similarly, if an agency is engaged in action more on the rulemaking end of the spectrum, does it follow that the same rules applicable to a legislature are equally applicable to an administrative agency? How do agencies differ from legislatures when agencies are formulating rules and how should these differences be reflected in the procedures they use?

As we pursue these questions in the cases that follow, it will be important to step back and evaluate not only the legal questions they resolve, but also their underlying assumptions and approaches. What do these answers tell us about ourselves and our legal culture? Many other issues are implied in this question. What do the terms "rule" and "order" connote? Are they merely labels or do these concepts involve more fundamental issues? Given the fact that a complete theory of democracy might involve the totality of a number of relationships an individual may have to a variety of entities of the state, what theory of administrative law can we, nevertheless, derive from this analysis? What theory of democracy underlies these administrative law categorizations and the responses they trigger? What does the relationship of the individual to administrative agencies tell us about our theory of democracy in this context?

The issues inherent in these questions are theoretical in nature, and they are important in and of themselves. They also have important practical implications. Their dual relevance is mandated by the realities of law practice. As attorneys, you will have occasion to handle cases in which you will not only want to apply the law, but to change it. To do this, you will need to understand the broad theoretical structure within which the law is framed. You will undoubtedly draw many of your arguments from your attempts either to reconceptualize or to work within the basic structure of the body of law you seek to apply or change.

More important, hopefully, as lawyers you will have the opportunity — over a very long career — to see a variety of cases and issues. The ability to see these cases and issues in terms of a larger perspective will not only make you better lawyers, it will make you more interesting and more interested in your work. Law is an intensely human undertaking and it can teach us a great deal about ourselves and our culture. It is an oversimplification to say that law reflects society, for society has too many faces for a single mirror. At best, law reflects only certain aspects of our culture. It hears some, but usually not all, of society's many voices, and to varying degrees. Your ability to probe and determine the underlying theoretical assumptions of the response of the law to various issues will better enable you to assess both the limits and the potential capabilities of the law, as well as the need for and direction of constructive reform.

Finally, reflecting on the larger societal context of which your corner of the law is but a small part may help you discover, in the words of Justice Holmes, the "universal in the particular." This will help ensure not only a successful practice, but an interesting, and maybe even an ennobling, one.

4 ADMINISTRATIVE LAW AND PROCESS § 1.02

§ 1.02 Rules or Orders?

LONDONER v. CITY AND COUNTY OF DENVER

United States Supreme Court
210 U.S. 373 (1908)

Mr. Justice Moody delivered the opinion of the court.

The plaintiffs in error began this proceeding in a state court of Colorado to relieve lands owned by them from an assessment of a tax for the cost of paving a street upon which the lands abutted. The relief sought was granted by the trial court, but its action was reversed by the Supreme Court of the State, which ordered judgment for the defendants. . . . The Supreme Court held that the tax was assessed in conformity with the constitution and laws of the State, and its decision on that question is conclusive. . . .

The tax complained of was assessed under the provisions of the charter of the city of Denver, which confers upon the city the power to make local improvements and to assess the cost upon property specially benefited. It does not seem necessary to set forth fully the elaborate provisions of the charter regulating the exercise of this power, except where they call for special examination. The board of public works, upon the petition of a majority of the owners of the frontage to be assessed, may order the paving of a street. The board must, however, first adopt specifications, mark out a district of assessment, cause a map to be made and an estimate of the cost, with the approximate amount to be assessed upon each lot of land. Before action notice by publication and an opportunity to be heard to any person interested must be given by the board.

The board may then order the improvement, but must recommend to the city council a form of ordinance authorizing it, and establishing an assessment district, which is not amendable by the council. The council may then, in its discretion, pass or refuse to pass the ordinance. If the ordinance is passed, the contract for the work is made by the mayor. The charter provides that "the finding of the city council, by ordinance, that any improvements provided for in this article were duly ordered after notice duly given, or that a petition or remonstrance was or was not filed as above provided, or was or was not subscribed by the required number of owners aforesaid shall be conclusive in every court or other tribunal." The charter then provides for the assessment of the cost. . . .

It appears from the charter that, in the execution of the power to make local improvements and assess the cost upon the property specially benefited, the main steps to be taken by the city authorities are plainly marked and separated: 1. The board of public works must transmit to the city council a resolution ordering the work to be done and the form of an ordinance authorizing it and creating an assessment district. This it can do only upon certain conditions, one of which is that there shall first be filed a petition asking the improvement, signed by the owners of the majority of the frontage to be assessed. 2. The passage of that ordinance by the city council, which is given authority to determine conclusively whether the action of the board was duly taken. 3. The assessment of the cost upon the landowners after due notice and opportunity for hearing.

In the case before us the board took the first step by transmitting to the council the resolution to do the work and the form of an ordinance authorizing it. It is contended, however, that there was wanting an essential condition of the jurisdiction of the board, namely, such a petition from the owners as the law requires. The trial court found this contention to be true. But, as has been seen, the charter gave the city council the authority to determine conclusively that the improvements were duly ordered by the board after due notice and a proper petition. In the exercise of this authority the city council, in the ordinance directing the improvement to be made, adjudged, in effect, that a proper petition had been filed. . . . The state Supreme Court held that the determination of the city council was conclusive that a proper petition was filed, and that decision must be accepted by us as the law of the State. The only question for this court is whether the charter provision authorizing such a finding, without notice to the landowners, denies to them due process of law. We think it does not. The proceedings, from the beginning up to and including the passage of the ordinance authorizing the work did not include any assessment or necessitate any assessment, although they laid the foundation for an assessment, which might or might not subsequently be made. Clearly all this might validly be done without hearing to the landowners, provided a hearing upon the assessment itself is afforded. . . . The legislature might have authorized the making of improvements by the city council without any petition. If it chose to exact a petition as a security for wise and just action it could, so far as the Federal Constitution is concerned, accompany that condition with a provision that the council, with or without notice, should determine finally whether it had been performed. This disposes of the first assignment of error, which is overruled. . . .

The fifth assignment, though general, vague and obscure, fairly raises, we think, the question whether the assessment was made without notice and opportunity for hearing to those affected by it, thereby denying to them due process of law. The trial court found as a fact that no opportunity for hearing was afforded, and the Supreme Court did not disturb this finding. The record discloses what was actually done, and there seems to be no dispute about it. After the improvement was completed the board of public works, in compliance with § 29 of the charter, certified to the city clerk a statement of the cost, and an apportionment of it to the lots of land to be assessed. Thereupon the city clerk, in compliance with § 30, published a notice stating, *inter alia,* that the written complaints or objections of the owners, if filed within thirty days, would be "heard and determined by the city council before the passage of any ordinance assessing the cost." Those interested, therefore, were informed that if they reduced their complaints and objections to writing, and filed them within thirty days, those complaints and objections would be heard, and would be heard before any assessment was made. . . . Resting upon the assurance that they would be heard, the plaintiffs in error filed within the thirty days the following paper:

Denver, Colorado, January 13, 1900

"To the Honorable Board of Public Works and the Honorable Mayor and City Council of the city of Denver:

"The undersigned, by Joshua Grozier, their attorney, do hereby most earnestly and strenuously protest and object to the passage of the contemplated or any assessing ordinance against the property in Eighth Avenue Paving District No. 1, so called, for each of the following reasons, to wit:

1st. That said assessment and all and each of the proceedings leading up to the same were and are illegal, voidable and void, and the attempted assessment if made will be void and uncollectible.

2nd. That said assessment and the cost of said pretended improvement should be collected, if at all, as a general tax against the city at large and not as a special assessment.

3d. That property in said city not assessed is benefitted by the said pretended improvement and certain property assessed is not benefitted by said pretended improvement and other property assessed is not benefitted by said pretended improvement to the extent of the assessment; that the individual pieces of property in said district are not benefitted to the extent assessed against them and each of them respectively; that the assessment is arbitrary and property assessed in an equal amount is not benefitted equally; that the boundaries of said pretended district were arbitrarily created without regard to the benefits or any other method of assessment known to law; that said assessment is outrageously large. . . .

8th. Because the city had no jurisdiction in the premises. No petition subscribed by the owners of a majority of the frontage in the district to be assessed for said improvements was ever obtained or presented. . . ."

This certainly was a complaint against and objection to the proposed assessment. Instead of affording the plaintiffs in error an opportunity to be heard upon its allegations, the city council, without notice to them, met as a board of equalization, not in a stated but in a specially called session, and, without any hearing, adopted the following resolution:

Whereas, complaints have been filed by the various persons and firms as the owners of real estate included within the Eighth Avenue Paving District No.1, of the city of Denver against the proposed assessments on said property for the cost of said paving, the names and description of the real estate respectively owned by such persons being more particularly described in the various complaints filed with the city clerk; and

Whereas, no complaint or objection has been filed or made against the apportionment of said assessment made by the board of public works of the city of Denver, but the complaints and objections filed deny wholly the right of the city to assess any district or portion of the assessable property of the city of Denver; therefore, be it

Resolved, by the city council of the city of Denver, sitting as a board of equalization, that the apportionments of said assessment made by said board of public works be, and the same are hereby, confirmed and approved.

Subsequently, without further notice or hearing, the city council enacted the ordinance of assessment whose validity is to be determined in this case. The facts out of which the question on this assignment arises may be compressed into small compass. The first step in the assessment proceedings was by the certificate of the board of public works of the cost of the improvement and a preliminary apportionment of it. The last step was the enactment of the assessment ordinance. From beginning to end of the proceedings the landowners, although allowed to formulate and file complaints and objections, were not afforded an opportunity to be heard upon them. Upon these facts was there a denial by the State of the due process of law guaranteed by the Fourteenth Amendment to the constitution of the United States?

In the assessment, apportionment and collection of taxes upon property within their jurisdiction the Constitution of the United States imposes few restrictions upon the States. In the enforcement of such restrictions as the Constitution does impose this court has regarded substance and not form. But where the legislature of a State, instead of fixing the tax itself, commits to some subordinate body the duty of determining whether, in what amount, and upon whom it shall be levied, and of making its assessment and apportionment, due process of law requires that at some stage of the proceedings before the tax becomes irrevocably fixed, the taxpayer shall have an opportunity to be heard, of which he must have notice, either personal, by publication, or by a law fixing the time and place of hearing. . . . It must be remembered that the law of Colorado denies the landowner the right to object in the courts to the assessment, upon the ground that the objections are cognizable only by the board of equalization.

If it is enough that, under such circumstances, an opportunity is given to submit in writing all objections to and complaints of the tax to the board, then there was a hearing afforded in the case at bar. But we think that something more than that, even in proceedings for taxation, is required by due process of law. Many requirements essential in strictly judicial proceedings may be dispensed with in proceedings of this nature. But even here a hearing in its very essence demands that he who is entitled to it shall have the right to support his allegations by argument however brief, and, if need be, by proof, however informal. . . . It is apparent that such a hearing was denied to the plaintiffs in error. The denial was by the city council, which, while acting as a board of equalization, represents the State. . . . The assessment was therefore void, and the plaintiffs in error were entitled to a decree discharging their lands from a lien on account of it. . . .

Judgment reversed.

BI-METALLIC INVESTMENT CO. v. STATE BOARD OF EQUALIZATION OF COLORADO

United States Supreme Court
239 U.S. 441 (1915)

MR. JUSTICE HOLMES delivered the opinion of the court.

This is a suit to enjoin the State Board of Equalization and the Colorado Tax Commission from putting in force, and the defendant Pitcher as assessor of Denver from obeying, an order of the boards increasing the valuation of all taxable property in Denver forty per cent. The order was sustained and the suit directed to be dismissed by the Supreme Court of the State. . . . The plaintiff is the owner of real estate in Denver and brings the case here on the ground that it was given no opportunity to be heard and that therefore its property will be taken without due process of law, contrary to the Fourteenth Amendment of the Constitution of the United States. That is the only question with which we have to deal. . . .

For the purposes of decision we assume that the constitutional question is presented in the baldest way — that neither the plaintiff nor the assessor of Denver, who presents a brief on the plaintiff's side, nor any representative of the city and county, was given an opportunity to be heard, other than such as they may have had by reason of the fact that the time of meeting of the boards is fixed by law. On this assumption it is obvious that injustice may be suffered if some property in the county already has been valued at its full worth. But if certain property has been valued at a rate different from that generally prevailing in the county the owner has had his opportunity to protest and appeal as usual in our system of taxation . . . so that it must be assumed that the property owners in the county all stand alike. The question then is whether all individuals have a constitutional right to be heard before a matter can be decided in which all are equally concerned — here, for instance, before a superior board decides that the local taxing officers have adopted a system of undervaluation throughout a county, as notoriously often has been the case. The answer of this court in the *State Railroad Tax Cases,* 92 U.S. 575, at least as to any further notice, was that it was hard to believe that the proposition was seriously made.

Where a rule of conduct applies to more than a few people it is impracticable that every one should have a direct voice in its adoption. The Constitution does not require all public acts to be done in town meetings or an assembly of the whole. General statutes within the state power are passed that affect the person or property of individuals, sometimes to the point of ruin, without giving them a chance to be heard. Their rights are protected in the only way that they can be in a complex society, by their power, immediate or remote, over those who make the rule. If the result in this case had been reached as it might have been by the State's doubling the rate of taxation, no one would suggest that the Fourteenth Amendment was violated unless every person affected had been allowed an opportunity to raise his voice against it before the body entrusted by the state constitution with the power. In considering this case in this court we must assume that the proper state machinery has been used, and the question is whether, if the state constitution had declared that Denver had been undervalued as compared with the rest of the State and had decreed that for the current year the valuation should be forty per cent higher, the objection now urged could prevail. It appears to us that to put the question is to answer it. There must be a limit to individual argument in such matters if government is to go on. In *Londoner v. Denver,* 210 U.S. 373, 385, a local board had to determine "whether, in what amount, and upon whom" a tax for paving a street should be levied for special benefits. A relatively small number of persons was concerned, who were exceptionally affected, in each case upon individual grounds, and it was held that they had a right to a hearing. But that decision is far from reaching a general determination dealing only with the principle upon which all the assessments in a county had been laid.

Judgment affirmed.

NOTES AND QUESTIONS

1-1. Is it the government's decision to pave a street that is being challenged in *Londoner v. Denver*? What governmental decision *is* being challenged? How does it differ from a decision to pave a street?

1-2. How should the action being challenged in *Londoner* be characterized for purposes of the Fourteenth Amendment? What kinds of procedures are appropriate for making the kinds of assessments involved in this case? How do the individuals who front on the street differ? Are those differences relevant to the Board's decision in this case? How would a hearing help to decide that?

1-3. Is it fair to assume in *Londoner* that the papers plaintiffs filed challenging their tax assessments were read by the members of the city council? If so, why is a "hearing" on the assessment papers not enough? Does the Court explain why an oral hearing is necessary? What do you think accounts for the Court's decision?

1-4. Would the outcome of *Londoner* have been different if Colorado law allowed the plaintiff to object to his assessment in court? Would a hearing at that time in that forum satisfy the demands of the Due Process Clause?

1-5. Based on *Londoner,* how would you describe the characteristics of a governmental action that triggers the Due Process Clause?

1-6. What is the governmental decision that gives rise to the dispute in *Bi-Metallic*? What governmental action results and how does the Court characterize this action? How does *Londoner* differ from *Bi-Metallic* in terms of the nature of the issue to be decided? In terms of the kinds of procedure best able to resolve such an issue?

1-7. What reasons does Justice Holmes give for denying the claim of the petitioners for a hearing in this case? Is it the number of cases or the numbers of litigants involved that make the dispute in *Bi-Metallic* inappropriate for a trial-type hearing? Is it conceivable that a large number of individuals all might have a *Londoner* interest in the outcome of a single proceeding? How should defendant class actions be handled?

1-8. Quite apart from the number of potential litigants involved, what other factors account for the Court's decision in *Bi-Metallic*? What does this case hold?

PROBLEM 1-1

Assume you are practicing law in Chicago. The Illinois Code has a number of provisions that apply to liquor licenses. The most important provisions from your point of view state that "Illinois liquor licenses, once granted, are operative for a term of two years." The statute goes on to state that "liquor licenses are renewable as a matter of right by the Illinois Liquor Licensing Board when the term expires unless the licensee is unqualified or his premises unsuitable." Another provision in the Illinois Code provides that "if 40 percent of the registered voters in a precinct petition the board of elections for a vote on whether to prohibit the sale of liquor at a particular street address, the question shall be put to the precinct electorate at the next election. If a majority votes in favor of the prohibition the license of the establishment located at that address shall become void thirty days after the election." There are approximately 400 citizens in each precinct.

Eakin Rhodes has owned and operated a bar called the Tequila Roadhouse in a precinct in Chicago for over twenty years. It is a very popular bar, frequently crowded and often quite noisy. It is one of five bars in the precinct; one of the others is located just a few doors away.

One night Eakin Rhodes observed a man at his bar who clearly had had a number of drinks. He was totally inebriated and was demanding yet another. Eakin nicely told him he had had his limit and gave him a cup of coffee instead. The customer became incensed. He demanded to be served, but Eakin refused, suggesting strongly it was time for him to leave. As the customer was leaving, he said "you'll pay for this!" The customer was a local alderman and was, of course, politically well known. He went to the bar up the street, the Sundowner, and told his story of outrage to the owner, Dewey Cheatam, another well connected politician. They vowed to get the votes they needed to shut this guy down and organized a petition to close the Roadhouse. The neighbors in the area were already upset with five bars in their precinct and were happy to try to get rid of one of them, if they could. Also, many others who signed the petition were political allies of the alderman and the bar owner and were happy to "give democracy a chance."

The revocation of Eakin Rhodes's liquor license is on the ballot and set to be voted on in two months. Rhodes comes to you and asks you to represent him in court.

(a). What relief do you seek? Set forth the legal theory upon which your case for Eakin Rhodes will be based. What arguments do you anticipate against you and how do you plan to counter them?

(b). At oral argument in Court, the judge says: "Counsel, we have already decided a case very similar to this one and it went against you. In *Philly's v. Byrne*, we upheld the part of the Illinois Code that would allow the voters in a precinct to go dry if they wished. Doesn't that precedent decide your case?" How do you respond?

(c). The judge also asks: "Counsel, are you suggesting that direct democracy is unconstitutional?" What is your answer? What result? *See Club Misty, Inc. v. Laski*, 208 F.3d 615 (7th Cir. 2000).

PROBLEM 1-2

Phil's Porterhouse Deli is the only drive-in deli or take-out restaurant in town. It serves its take-out customers with plastic plates, cups and take-out containers. Recently, the county council passed a law banning the use of all plastic bags and take-out containers in all restaurants in town. The law is to take effect next month. The county council believed that by banning some of the non-degradable plastic products filling up landfills, it was being environmentally aware and helping to cut back on the excesses of the "throwaway society." The members of the council were so sure they were on solid political and moral ground here that they did not hold any hearings at which the public could speak to these issues. They did debate the language of the bill and their rationale for passing it in open session, but no one other than the elected members of the county council spoke. The bill passed unanimously.

Phil and Camille Porter own Phil's Porterhouse Deli, the only restaurant in town that uses plastic plates, cups and containers; thus, theirs is the only establishment directly affected by this new law. They are outraged that they never had the chance to speak directly to the council about their concerns with this legislation. They argue that replacing the plastic cups will not only mean higher costs for them but, they maintain, for society as well. Plastic, they contend, can be recycled, and heavy cardboard coffee cups and plates cannot. It is not at all clear that landfills can accommodate paper and cardboard waste as easily as they can the thinner and re-usable plastic products.

(a) Were the Porters entitled to a hearing?

(b) Assume you serve as the attorney for the county council. How would you draft the plastic ban ordinance they now propose in order to minimize any constitutional problems you might anticipate?

(c) Quite apart from what you perceive to be the constitutional hearing requirements for passing this law, how would you have advised the county to proceed on these issues? If you concluded that no hearings were constitutionally necessary, does that mean that no hearing *should* be provided? What considerations would you take into account in making a judgment concerning whether or not to hold a hearing? What kind of hearing would it be?

BOWLES v. WILLINGHAM

United States Supreme Court
321 U.S. 503 (1944)

Mr. Justice Douglas delivered the opinion of the Court.

Appellee, Mrs. Willingham of Macon, Georgia, sued in a Georgia court to restrain the issuance of certain rent orders under the Emergency Price Control Act of 1942 . . . on the ground that the orders and the statutory provisions on which they rested were unconstitutional. The state court issued, *ex parte,* a temporary injunction and a show cause order. Thereupon appellant, Administrator of the Office of Price Administration, brought this suit in the federal District Court pursuant to § 205(a) of the Act and § 24(1) of the Judicial Code to restrain Mrs. Willingham from further prosecution of the state proceedings and from violation of the Act, and to restrain appellee Hicks, Bibb County sheriff, from executing or attempting to execute any orders in the state proceedings. The District Court . . . dismissed the Administrator's suit on bill and answer, holding that the orders in question and the provisions of the act on which they rested were unconstitutional. The case is here on direct appeal. . . .

Sec. 2(b) of the Act provides in part that, "Whenever in the judgment of the Administrator such action is necessary or proper in order to effectuate the purposes of this Act, he shall issue a declaration setting forth the necessity for, and recommendations with reference to, the stabilization or reduction of rents for any defense-area housing accommodations within a particular defense-rental area." Pursuant to that authority the Administrator on April 28, 1942, issued a declaration designating twenty-eight areas in various parts of the country, including Macon, Georgia, as defense-rental areas. . . . That declaration stated that defense activities had resulted in increased housing rents in those areas[1] and that it was necessary and proper in order to effectuate the purposes of the act to stabilize and reduce such rents. It also contained a recommendation pursuant to § 2(b) that the maximum rent for housing accommodations rented on April 1, 1941, should be the rental for such accommodations on that date; and that in case of accommodations not rented on April 1, 1941, or constructed thereafter provisions for the determination, adjustment, and modification of maximum rents should be made, such rents to be in principle no greater than the generally prevailing rents in the

---

[1] The declaration recited that the designated areas were the location of the armed forces of the United States or of war production industries, that the influx of people had caused an acute shortage of rental housing accommodations, that most of the areas were those in which builders could secure priority ratings on critical materials for residential construction, that new construction had not been sufficient to restore normal rental markets, that surveys showed low vacancy ratios for rental housing accommodations in the areas, that defense activities had resulted in substantial and widespread increases in rents affecting most of these accommodations in the areas, and that official surveys in the areas had shown a marked upward movement in the general level of residential rents.

particular area on April 1, 1941. The declaration also stated in accordance with the provisions of § 2(b) that if within sixty days after April 28, 1942, such rents within the areas in question had not been stabilized or reduced by state or local regulation or otherwise in accordance with the Administrator's recommendation, the Administrator might fix the maximum rents.

On June 30, 1942, the Administrator issued Maximum Rent Regulation No. 26, effective July 1, 1942, establishing the maximum legal rents for housing in these defense areas, including Macon, Georgia. . . . It recited that the rentals had not been reduced or stabilized since the declaration of April 28, 1942, and that defense activities had resulted in increases in the rentals on or about April 1, 1941, but not prior to that date. The maximum rentals fixed for housing accommodations rented on April 1, 1941 were the rents obtained on that date. . . . As respects housing accommodations not rented on April 1, 1941, but rented for the first time between that date and the effective date of the regulation, July 1, 1942 — the situation involved in this case — it was provided that the maximum rent should be the first rent charged after April 1, 1941 . . . but in that case it was provided that the Rent Director . . . might order a decrease on his own initiative on the ground, among others, that the rent was higher than that generally prevailing in the area for comparable housing accommodations on April 1, 1941. . . . By Procedural Regulation No. 3 . . . provision was made that when the Rent Director proposed to take such action he should serve a notice upon the landlord involved stating the proposed action and the grounds therefor. . . . Within 60 days of the final action of the Rent Director the landlord might file an application for review by the regional administrator for the region in which the defense-rental area office was located and then file a protest with the Administrator for review of the action of the regional office . . . or might proceed by protest immediately. . . . As we develop more fully hereafter, the Act provides in § 203(a) for the filing of protests with the Administrator. The machinery for a hearing on a protest and a determination of the issue by the Administrator was designed to provide the basis of judicial review by the Emergency Court of Appeals as authorized by § 204(1) of the Act.

In June, 1943, the Rent Director gave written notice to Mrs. Willingham that he proposed to decrease the maximum rents for three apartments owned by her, and which had not been rented on April 1, 1941, but were first rented in the summer of 1941, on the ground that the first rents for these apartments received after April 1, 1941, were in excess of those generally prevailing in the area for comparable accommodations on April 1, 1941. Mrs. Willingham filed objections to that proposed action together with supporting affidavits. The Rent Director thereupon advised her that he would proceed to issue an order reducing the rents. Before that was done she filed her bill in the Georgia court. The present suit followed shortly, as we have said. . . .

It is finally suggested that the Act violates the Fifth Amendment because it makes no provision for a hearing to landlords before the order or regulation fixing rents becomes effective. Obviously, Congress would have been under no necessity to give notice and provide a hearing before it acted, had it decided to fix rents on a national basis the same as it did for the District of Columbia. . . . We agree with the Emergency Court of Appeals . . . that Congress need not make that requirement when it delegates the task to an administrative agency. In *Bi-Metallic Investment Co. v. State Board,* 239 U.S. 441, a suit was brought by a taxpayer and landowner to enjoin a Colorado Board from putting in effect an order which increased the valuation of all taxable property in Denver 40 per cent. Such action, it was alleged, violated the Fourteenth Amendment as the plaintiff was given no opportunity to be heard. Mr. Justice Holmes, speaking for the Court, stated: "Where a rule of conduct applies to more than a few people it is impracticable that every one should have a direct voice in its adoption. The Constitution does not require all public acts to be done in town meeting or an assembly of the whole. General statutes within the state power are passed that affect the person or property of individuals, sometimes to the point of ruin, without giving them a chance to be heard. Their rights are protected in the only way that they can be in a complex society, by their power, immediate or remote, over those who make the rule." We need not go so far in the present case. Here Congress has provided for judicial review of the Administrator's action. To be sure, that review comes after the order has been promulgated; and no provision for a stay is made. But as we have held in *Yakus v. United States,* 321 U.S. 414, that review satisfies the requirements of due process. As stated by Mr. Justice Brandeis for a unanimous Court in *Phillips v. Commissioner,* 283 U.S. 589, 596-597: "Where only property rights are involved, mere postponement of the judicial enquiry is not a denial of due process, if the opportunity given for the ultimate judicial determination of the liability is adequate. . . . Delay in the judicial determination of property rights is not uncommon where it is essential that governmental needs be immediately satisfied."

Language in the cases that due process requires a hearing before the administrative order becomes effective . . . is to be explained on two grounds. In the first place, the statutes there involved required that procedure.

Secondly, as we have held in *Yakus v. United States,* Congress was dealing here with the exigencies of wartime conditions and the insistent demands of inflation control. Congress chose not to fix rents in specified areas or on a national scale by legislative fiat. It chose a method designed to meet the needs for rent control as they might arise and to accord some leeway for adjustment within the formula which it prescribed. At the same time, the procedure which Congress adopted was selected with the view of eliminating the necessity for "lengthy and costly trials with concomitant dissipation of the time and energies of all concerned in litigation rather than in the common war effort." S. Rep. No. 931, 77th Cong., 2d Sess., p. 7. To require hearings for thousands of landlords before any rent control order could be made effective might have defeated the program of price control. Or Congress might well have thought so. National security might not be able to afford the luxuries of litigation and the long delays which preliminary hearings traditionally have entailed.

We fully recognize, as did the Court in *Home Bldg. & Loan Ass'n v. Blaisdell,* 290 U.S. 398, 426, that "even the war power does not remove constitutional limitations safe-guarding essential liberties." But where Congress has provided for judicial review after the regulations or orders have been made effective it has done all that due process under the war emergency requires. . . .

Reversed.

[JUSTICE RUTLEDGE's concurring opinion and JUSTICE ROBERTS' dissent are omitted.]

NOTES AND QUESTIONS

1-9. What are the various governmental actions that give rise to the legal concerns in *Bowles*? How should they be characterized for purposes of the Due Process Clause? How does Justice Douglas characterize them? Do you agree with the result reached by Justice Douglas? Do you agree with his reasoning? Is this a *Londoner* or *Bi-Metallic* case?

1-10. What procedural protections are provided for landlords under the Emergency Price Control Act? Are they sufficient? Why does Mrs. Willingham object?

1-11. *Bowles* arose during wartime and it involved the application of the Price Control Act to literally thousands of cases. To what extent, if any, should the Constitution be applied differently to deal with mass justice situations? Does the fact that this was wartime also affect the outcome in this case? Should it?

1-12. As we shall see more fully in Chapter 2, the Due Process Clause applies in a variety of contexts, including Social Security, welfare, and other benefit programs that involve hundreds of thousands of individual claims. How do you answer the question posed long ago by Professor Jones in *The Rule of Law and the Welfare State*:*

> Mass-produced goods rarely have the quality of goods made in far smaller quantity by traditional hand craftsmanship; an analogous problem challenges the welfare state. In an era when rights are mass produced, can the quality of their protection against arbitrary official action be as high as the quality of the protection afforded in the past to traditional legal rights less numerous and less widely dispersed among the members of society?

1-13. Is Justice Holmes' numbers analysis relevant in mass justice contexts? Does it follow that due process rights in such contexts must be applied in the same way they are applied when only a few claimants are involved? Does this still mean we have a "constitution for all seasons"?

1-14. Quite apart from the due process clause, can the equal protection clause protect against a "class of one"? In *Willowbrook v. Olech*, 527 U.S. 562 (2000), Olech, a homeowner, sued his village, alleging that the village's demand for a 33-foot easement was more than the standard 15-foot required of everyone else. He alleged that the village demand was motivated by ill will resulting from a previous unrelated and winning lawsuit he filed against this same village. The Court stated, in a *per curiam* opinion that:

---

* Copyright © 1958 by Columbia Law Review. All rights reserved.

Our cases have recognized successful equal protection claims brought by a "class of one," where the plaintiff alleges that she has been intentionally treated differently from others similarly situated and that there is no rational basis for the difference in treatment. . . .

. . . Olech's complaint can fairly be construed as alleging that the Village intentionally demanded a 33-foot easement as a condition of connecting her property to the municipal water supply where the Village required only a 15-foot easement from other similarly situated property owners. . . . The complaint also alleged that the Village's demand was "irrational and wholly arbitrary" and that the Village ultimately connected her property after receiving a clearly adequate 15-foot easement. These allegations, quite apart from the Village's subjective motivation, are sufficient to state a claim for relief under traditional equal protection analysis. 528 U.S. 564-565.

PROBLEM 1-3

Under the provisions of the Federal Meat Inspection Act, 21 U.S.C. § 601 *et seq.*, the Department of Agriculture is empowered to police the safety of most of this country's beef supply by creating rules to regulate the processing of beef, by monitoring compliance with these regulations at meat packing plants, and by inspecting and grading beef produced in meat processing plants. Section 673 of the act also empowers the USDA to institute an *in rem* action in U.S. District Court where beef is found that fails to conform to the standards of the Act. Any party to this proceeding may request a trial by jury.

One power that Congress did *not* give the USDA is the power to order a meat processor to recall beef that it has already shipped into the stream of commerce — for example, that which has been sold to grocery stores. *In rem* actions to seize beef are relatively rare; typically, the meat processor will engage in negotiations with the USDA as to the potential scope of the problem and will voluntarily recall the tainted beef. If these negotiations break down, the USDA can stop inspecting further meat produced at the plant, which has the effect of shutting down the facility, and/or initiating the *in rem* actions to condemn the beef in the stream of commerce.

On December 23, 2003, the USDA issued the following press release:

> Verns Moses Lake Meats, a Moses Lake, Wash., establishment, is voluntarily recalling approximately 10,410 pounds of raw beef that may have been exposed to tissues containing the infectious agent that causes bovine spongiform encephalopathy (BSE) [otherwise known as mad cow disease]. . . .
>
> The beef subject to this Class II recall was produced on Dec. 9 and was shipped to several establishments where it was further processed. FSIS is continuing its investigation to ensure that all distribution of the beef products is correctly identified.

[The] designation of this recall as Class II is due to the extremely low likelihood that the beef being recalled contains the infectious agent that causes BSE. According to scientific evidence, the tissues of highest infectivity are the brain, spinal cord, and distal ileum, which were removed from the rest of the carcass at slaughter. Therefore, the meat produced were cuts that would not be expected to be infected or have an adverse public health impact, but are being recalled out of an abundance of caution.

While Verns Moses Lake Meats was a relatively small-scale meat processor, some meat processors can package more than 400,000 pounds of beef in a single day's shift. Suppose 1) that Vern Moses had been one of those large meat processors; 2) that the voluntary recall negotiations broke down when Verns Moses scoffed at the USDA's demand that it recall 2,000,000 pounds of beef; 3) that the possibly tainted beef had been shipped to hundreds of grocery stores throughout Alaska, Washington, Oregon, Arizona, and New Mexico; and 4) that Verns Moses responded to the USDA's threat to institute *in rem* proceedings to seize the beef by saying "I guess we'll see you in court."

If the USDA were concerned that it would not be able to obtain a preliminary injunction against the sale of the beef in every district court in which it brought suit because of the admitted "extremely low likelihood" that the beef contained the agent that causes mad sow disease, could it simply issue a press release that — "out of an abundance of caution" — the public should not consume the meat that Verns Moses packaged? Should it? What effect does the fact that Congress could have given the USDA the power to order an involuntary recall, but Congress instead chose to require the USDA to engage in *in rem* condemnation actions? Suppose, as was common in the industry before the mad cow scare, Verns Moses did not keep detailed records of which lot of beef went to which grocery outlet. Could the USDA issue a press release warning the entire country of a possible problem with contaminated beef? Does Verns Moses have any procedural rights?

§ 1.03 Rules, Orders and Theories of Procedure — Some Preliminary Reflections

[A] Introduction

Determining whether and where governmental action falls on the rule-order conceptual spectrum is often difficult. Moreover, the rule-order discourse itself is limited and, thus, limiting. Are there some exercises of governmental power that are not easily captured by this discourse? As you begin to formulate for yourselves what constitutes a rule or a legislative action as opposed to an order or adjudicative governmental action, you may find that some rules have order-like qualities and some orders have distinct, rule-like characteristics as well. For example, a rule may theoretically apply to a potentially large number of individuals or entities, but as our environmental ordinance banning plastic cups illustrates, some rules initially may, in reality, affect only one individual or entity. Certainly from the point of view of the entity affected, the government's rulemaking processes have a distinct adjudicative character. On the other hand, some orders, such as injunctive decrees issued by courts in the course of resolving a dispute brought as a class action, have prospective as well as retrospective effects. They may also apply directly to a large number of individuals or entities, especially if the suit involves a defendant class action, or the precedent established may have rule-like effects. The Supreme Court's decision in *Grutter v. Bollinger*, 123 S. Ct. 2325 (2003), which generally reaffirmed the constitutionality of certain affirmative action programs while striking down others, had an effect on affirmative action policy in general that went far beyond the actual parties to that case. Sixty-four amicus briefs — representing some 300 different organizations including Fortune 500 companies like Microsoft, Boeing, and American Express, and including a group of retired military officers — voiced support of affirmative action in higher education, in part because of its effects on business and industry. Similarly, fifteen amicus briefs urged the court to strike down race-conscious admissions.

We shall examine such aspects of rules and orders further in Chapter Four, when we assess the appropriateness of an agency choosing rulemaking or adjudicative procedures in certain contexts. Nevertheless, it is important at this point to understand the basic differences (and similarities) between these two categories, the legal consequences of concluding that you are dealing with one category as opposed to another, and, more important, the limits of this discourse.

One of the most prominent attempts to provide this kind of guidance was that of Professor K.C. Davis. He focused on the differences between what he called adjudicative facts as opposed to legislative facts:

> Adjudicative facts usually answer the questions of who did what, when, how, why, with what motive or intent; adjudicative facts are roughly the kind of facts that go to a jury in a jury case. Legislative facts do not usually concern the immediate parties but are general facts which help the tribunal decide questions of law and policy and discretion. . . .
>
> [Adjudicative facts] are intrinsically the kind of facts that ordinarily ought not to be determined without giving the parties a chance to know and to meet any evidence that may be unfavorable to them, that is, without providing the parties an opportunity for trial. The reason is that the parties know more about the facts concerning themselves and their activities than anyone else is likely to know, and the parties are therefore in an especially good position to rebut or explain evidence that bears upon adjudicative facts. Because the parties may often have little or nothing to contribute to the development of legislative facts, the method of trial often is not required for the determination of disputed issues about legislative facts.

2 K.C. Davis, *Administrative Law Treatise* § 12.3 (2d ed. 1979) (currently in 4th edition).*

This approach, while helpful, may not necessarily take us very far, as Professor Roger Cramton points out below. Does Professor Cramton's approach

---

* Copyright © 1979 by K.C. Davis Publishing Co. Reprinted with permission of Aspen Publishers.

provide any more guidance to determining when we have an order or a rule, or does it suggest an altogether different approach for choosing the appropriate procedures to resolve a particular dispute? Is that approach more helpful? How can courts implement the balancing approach he suggests?

> The distinction between rulemaking and adjudication . . . provides little help. While the idea that trials are appropriate only for "adjudicative facts" is suggestive, it begs the hard question because the identification of "adjudicative facts" is so subjective and flexible. We are reduced to a basic notion that in a society committed to a representative form of government, private persons should have a meaningful opportunity to participate in governmental decisions which directly affect them, especially when governmental action is based on individual rather than on general considerations.
>
> Beyond the fundamental principle of meaningful party participation, any evaluation of administrative procedure must rest on a judgment which balances the advantages and disadvantages of each procedural system. In striking this balance I believe that the following formulation of competing considerations is more helpful than "fairness" or "due process:" the extent to which the procedure furthers the *accurate* selection and determination of relevant facts and issues, the *efficient* disposition of business, and, when viewed in the light of the statutory objectives, its *acceptability* to the agency, the participants and the general public.

Cramton, *A Comment On Trial-Type Hearings in Nuclear Power Plant Siting*, 58 VA. L. REV. 585, 591-92 (1972) (emphasis added).*

Whatever approach one takes to determining the type of governmental action involved and the procedures necessary for the government to act, it is important to recognize that these procedural choices have political, economic and cultural significance. Whether the decision involved relates to a plaintiff's standing to attack a governmental decision, the procedures used to make that decision or the role that a court should play in reviewing it, such questions are an important source of data that can tell us a good deal about the kind of political and administrative theory that underlies administrative law. In *Law and Administration,* Professors Harlow and Rawlings discuss below a number of administrative law theories and categorize them as being red light, green light or enven amber light theories. Though their focus is primarily on English law, their description and categorization of these theories has relevance to the American public law system as well. Their comments make a useful starting point for the more theoretical aspects of your analysis.

[B] Red Light Theories of Administrative Law

Red light theories assume the role of administrative law is essentially to protect the individual from an interventionist state. As Harlow and Rawlings note:

> Behind the formalist tradition, we can often discern a preference for a minimalist state. It is not surprising, therefore, to find many authors believing that the primary function of administrative law should be to

---

* Copyright © 1972 by Virginia Law Review Association. All rights reserved.

control any excess of state power and subject it to legal, and more especially judicial, control. It is this conception of administrative law that we have called 'red light theory'.

C. Harlow and R. Rawlings, *Law and Administration* 37 (2d ed. 1997)*

The question of what role government should or should not play and the red light procedural consequences that flow from how that question is answered are reflected in American administrative law, especially its very early stages. Consider Professor Paul Verkuil's historical account of the early resistance of the organized bar to administrative agencies and administrative solutions to problems:

> The substantive values of the nineteenth-century liberal, non-interventionist state and the procedural values of the common-law, adversary model of decisionmaking have a common core and are mutually supportive. Both sets of values reflected a common philosophical premise that the correct result would be achieved by the free clash of competing forces in the marketplace, or courtroom. As Jerome Frank noted, the "fight or adversary theory of justice is a sort of legal laissez-faire." If this connection is accepted, then the consequence of undermining one would be naturally to jeopardize the other, and conversely, to support one would be to reinforce the other. Substantive tyranny thus possessed an exact procedural counterpart. The administrative tribunal did in effect double injury to traditional values. It undermined laissez faire by enforcing the substantive mandates of regulation, and it compromised the adversary system by resorting to non-adversary administrative procedures.
>
> The lawyers of the time fought hard, therefore, to keep decision-making in the courts for two reasons. First, the adversary system with its opportunity for jury trials and other procedural protections meant less control by the decisionmaker over the process. Second, the judiciary's antipathy to government programs provided a favorable environment for decision. Thus, the adversary system held its place as an important value of classical liberalism even as the definition of liberalism was changing.
>
> This connection between adversary procedures and laissez faire had much to do with the bar's initial resistance to administrative solutions. The events surrounding Roscoe Pound's controversial address to the ABA in 1906 emphasize this phenomenon. Pound shocked the lawyers of that time by speaking derisively of the cherished adversary system as the "sporting theory of justice" and documenting its inefficiencies and intricacies. He also advocated a removal of certain matters from the courts to administrative tribunals where they could be subjected to disposition in more efficient, inquisitorial fashion. This attack upon the "scientific" adversary system was vigorously rejected by the bar. . . .

Paul Verkuil, *The Emerging Concept of Administrative Procedure,* 78 COLUM. L. REV. 258, 264-65 (1978).**

Consider Professor Stewart's description of what he calls the traditional model of administrative law and its gradual transformation:

---

* Copyright © 1997 Weidenfeld & Nicolson.

** Copyright © 1978 by Columbia Law Review. All rights reserved.

The traditional model of administrative law, developed out of judicial decisions and legislative enactments during the first six decades of this century, has sought to reconcile the competing claims of governmental authority and private autonomy by prohibiting official intrusions on private liberty or property unless authorized by legislative directives. To promote this end, the traditional model affords judicial review in order to cabin administrative discretion within statutory bounds, and requires agencies to follow decisional procedures designed to promote the accuracy, rationality, and reviewability of agency application of legislative directives.

Two fundamental criticisms have been levied against the traditional model. First, it has been asserted that the limitation of the traditional model's protections to recognized liberty and property interests is no longer appropriate in view of the seemingly inexorable expansion of governmental power over private welfare. Second, it has been argued that agencies have failed to discharge their respective mandates to protect the interests of the public in given fields of administration, and that the traditional model has been unable to remedy such failure.

In response to these criticisms, judges have greatly extended the machinery of the traditional model to protect new classes of interests. In the space of a few years the Supreme Court has largely eliminated the doctrine of standing as a barrier to challenging agency action in court, and judges have accorded a wide variety of affected interests the right not only to participate in, but to force the initiation of, formal proceedings before the agency. Indeed, this process has gone beyond the mere extension of participation and standing rights, working a fundamental transformation of the traditional model. Increasingly, the function of administrative law is not the protection of private autonomy but the provision of a surrogate political process to ensure the fair representation of a wide range of affected interests in the process of administrative decision. Whether this is a coherent or workable aim is an open issue. But there is no denying the importance of the transformation.

Stewart, *The Reformation of American Administrative Law,* 88 HARV. L. REV. 1667, 1669-70 (1975).*

[C] Green Light Theories of Administrative Law

The transformation to which Professor Stewart refers coincides with the rise and eventual acceptance of a much more activist state. A watershed in American administrative legal history was the New Deal. The activist role the state then commenced to play meant that administrative law involved not only issues that focused on the protection of the individual from the state and the control of state power, but the implementation of federal programs designed to help the public. Green light theories of the administrative process take as a given the appropriateness of state intervention. They then try to ensure that these programs are implemented as fairly and efficiently as possible.

Perhaps the best example of this approach to administrative law was that embodied in the 1941 report of the Attorney General's Committee on Administrative Procedure, described by Professor Verkuil as follows:

---

* Copyright © 1975 by the Harvard Law Review Association. All rights reserved.

Procedures were seen as means to the end of fair implementation of government programs and their efficacy was to be measured by their contribution to that end. This functional view of procedure argued for flexibility and informality along with a recognition of adversary hearings. Thus the report considered the "informal" method of adjudication first because it recognized that "informal procedures" constitute the vast bulk of administrative adjudication and are truly the lifeblood of the administrative process. Informal procedures (including settlement conferences, use of stipulations, inspections, and tests) were seen as indispensable methods for achieving the efficient operation of government business. As for the formal process, the report recommended the use of hearing commissioners, with enhanced independence and status, to conduct formal adjudications. Concerning rulemaking, the report emphasized the importance of outside participation prior to the issuance of rules, but urged against rigidifying the rulemaking process. Finally, the report proposed the creation of an Office of Federal Administrative Procedure to "study and coordinate administrative procedures" and "to achieve and stimulate practical improvements in a manner not possible through omnibus legislation."

The report's ultimate significance rests in its moving discussion about administrative law into its third and mature phase: concern with administrative procedure as an independent model. Automatic and unexamined reliance upon the judicial model would never again satisfactorily resolve debate.

Verkuil, *supra,* 78 COLUM. L. REV. 275-76.*

As we shall see, *infra,* the Administrative Procedure Act, which was passed in 1946, tried to set forth a statutory, procedural framework for the implementation of agency actions. It was not, however, totally unaffected by so-called red light conceptions of administrative law from previous eras. Yet, as Professor Stewart has documented, a transformation was occurring in administrative law, one that now sought not only to facilitate the implementation of governmental programs, but to provide a kind of procedural legitimization for them as well. Public participation in the decision-making process became an important means of legitimizing increased governmental action by unelected agency officials. In 1975, Professor Stewart was able to describe and assess this transformation as follows:

The expansion of the traditional model to afford participation rights in the process of agency decision and judicial review to a wide variety of affected interests must ultimately rest on the premise that such procedural changes will be an effective and workable means of assuring improved agency decisions. Advocates of extended access believe that an enlarged system of formal proceedings can, by securing adequate consideration of the interests of all affected persons, yield outcomes that better serve society as a whole. The credibility of this belief must now be considered.

Although the courts have displayed caution in expanding and reworking administrative law doctrine to ensure the representation of all affected interests, the thrust of decisions over the past decade supports the assessment of the Court of Appeals for the District of Columbia Circuit that: "In

---

* Copyright © 1978 by the Columbia Law Review Association. All rights reserved.

recent years, the concept that public participation in decisions which involve the public interest is not only valuable but indispensable has gained increasing support." The principle of interest group representation in agency adjudication has been warmly endorsed by commentators and by the Administrative Conference of the United States. Such participation, it is claimed, will not only improve the quality of agency decisions and make them more responsive to the needs of the various participating interests, but is valuable in itself because it gives citizens a sense of involvement in the process of government, and increases confidence in the fairness of government decisions. Indeed, litigation on behalf of widely shared "public" interests is explicitly defended as a substitute political process that enables the "citizen to cast a different kind of vote, [which] informs the court that . . . a particular point of view is being ignored or underestimated" by the agency. Its ultimate aim is seen as "a basic reordering of governmental institutions so that access and influence may be had by all."

Not only is the expansion of participation rights applauded, but it is urged that resources be made available to facilitate the representation of otherwise unrepresented interests by private attorneys and by governmental agencies such as a proposed federal consumer advocate agency. Such proposals follow logically from the premise that justice results when all interests are considered.

Stewart, *The Reformation of American Administrative Law,* 88 HARV. L. REV. 1667, 1760-61 (1975).*

Another view of this approach to administrative law has been described by Professor Paul Craig:

The traditional pluralist vision is that derived from Bentley, Truman, and, more recently, from the public-choice theorists. This can be summarized 'thematically' in the following way. First, emphasis is placed upon the political market, which functions similarly to the ordinary market. Legislation is a product which will be 'produced' by the legislature in response to demand from the 'consumers', who vote and who exercise influence on the legislature. *Homo economicus* who inhabits the ordinary market-place also inhabits the political arena and behaves in much the same way, operating so as to maximize his own individual preferences. Groups emerge because this is often the most efficient organizational form in which gains can be won from the legislature. Group interaction thus characterizes political society, and entry and exit from the political market are relatively easy. There is no conception of the public interest which is truly separate from the preferences of individuals within society. Much (some would say all) intervention by the state on distributive grounds is itself no more and no less than a reflection of the current power alignments between groups within society. These groups will seek to maximize their own position. Either they can do so by, for example, producing their goods more efficiently and hence reaping greater profits; or they can attain the same financial goal by winning special treatment from the legislature in the form of subsidies, preferential tax rates, etc.

---

* Copyright © 1975 by the Harvard Law Review Association. All rights reserved.

Secondly, the role of the state within this pluralist vision should be narrowly confined for the two related reasons. On the one hand, it is argued that the ordinary 'private-market' is often 'better' at reaching the optimally efficient solution than is the political market. Even when there is some species of ordinary market failure, the problem may well be exacerbated rather than cured by governmental regulatory intervention. Moreover, much legislative intervention is regarded as a 'front' to mask wealth-transfer and rent-seeking behavior by particular interest groups. On the other hand, the role of the state should be limited because governmental intervention via redistributive policies may well be 'illegitimate'. Such legislative action can infringe individual entitlements.

Paul Craig, *Public Law and Democracy in the United Kingdom and the United States of America*, 80–81 (Oxford University Press, 1990).*

The administrative process need not be viewed only as a clash of competing interest groups. Consider Professor Sunstein's approach in *Interest Groups*, 38 STAN. L. REV. 29, 31:**

When the proposed Constitution was debated, the country faced a choice between two different conceptions of politics. The first conception was republican; the prerequisite of sound government was the willingness of citizens to subordinate their private interests to the general good. Politics consisted of self-rule by the people; but it was not a scheme in which people impressed their private preferences on the government. It was instead a system in which the selection of preferences was the object of the governmental process. Preferences were not to be taken as exogenous, but to be developed and shaped through politics.

To the republicans, the role of politics was above all deliberative. Dialogue and discussion among the citizenry were critical features in the governmental process. Political participation was not limited to voting or other simple statements of preference. The ideal model for governance was the town meeting, a metaphor that played an explicit role in the republican understanding of politics.

The republican conception carries with it a particular view of human nature; it assumes that through discussion people can, in their capacities as citizens, escape private interests and engage in pursuit of the public good. In this respect, political ordering is distinct from market ordering. Moreover, this conception reflects a belief that debate and discussion help to reveal that some values are superior to others. Denying that decisions about values are merely matters of taste, the republican view assumes that "practical reason" can be used to settle social issues. . . .

[D] Context

In addition to considering the underlying theoretical basis of the administrative process, we must also consider the context in which this process occurs.

---

* Copyright © Paul Craig 1990.

** Copyright © 1985 by The Board of Trustees of Leland J. Stanford University. All rights reserved.

Context can mean many things, from the substance of the actual statutes being administered and the values and goals those laws embody to the overall political economy in which these statutes are administered. In determining the kinds of procedures appropriate to the substance of the regulation involved, consider the words of the artist, Ben Shahn, in *The Shape of Content* 62 (Harvard Univ. Press 1957). To what extent do form and content in art correspond to procedure and substance in law?

> I would not ordinarily undertake a discussion of form in art, nor would I undertake a discussion of content. To me, they are inseparable. Form is formulation — the turning of content into a material entity, rendering a content accessible to others, giving it permanence, willing it to the race. . . .
>
> It is the visible shape of all man's growth; it is the living picture of his tribe at its most primitive, and of his civilization at its most sophisticated state. Form is the many faces of the legend — bardic, epic, sculptural, musical, pictorial, architectural; it is the infinite images of religion; it is the expression and the remnant of self. Form is the very shape of content.

Form and content, procedure and substance go hand in hand. Similarly, the means and ends of regulation are often indistinguishable from each other. The regulatory means by which substantive statutory goals are carried out have much to do with what those goals are and how successfully they are achieved. For example, some regulatory approaches may try to specify directly how a company should ensure a safe working place or a clean environment. Other regulatory approaches, however, may try to rely on market forces to provide incentives for the kinds of behavior regulators seek to encourage. The choice of regulatory means often affects not only how well the regulatory ends are achieved, but what these regulatory ends will be. In some contexts, it is important to ask when the market can function effectively as a regulatory tool or when the use of market means is, in fact, an attempt to alter the regulatory ends of the statute involved.

Perhaps among the most significant factors affecting not only the substance of regulation, but the way we view the entire enterprise are the changes that have occurred and continue to occur in the overall global context in which domestic regulation now takes place. We are now in a new era of our regulatory history, a global era. In this era, we are witnessing not only the globalization of politics and markets, but law as well. Changes in the political economy at the global level can encourage profound contextual changes at the domestic level. How should we view agency deregulation in the 1980s and 1990s? Is the desire to substitute market approaches for regulation a return to a red light conception of administrative law or simply the use of new, more efficient regulatory means to achieve long-standing regulatory goals? Can the market be used as a regulatory tool? Does it allow us to do more with less when it comes to regulation in times of budgetary crises or do these new regulatory means introduce new regulatory ends as well? Consider the following:

> Global competition drives deregulatory forces more vigorously than regional or national markets can. It places the costs of domestic regulation in stark relief, whether or not new competition-encouraging technologies are involved or true market failure, in fact, persists. A global perspective on domestic

regulation encourages a more cost conscious regulatory perspective and often reinforces the increasingly global, market oriented perspective of the regulated. Moreover, whether a regulation deals primarily with economic conflicts of interest rather than fundamental conflicts of value is of less importance when a global perspective is involved. The inability of regulators to impose regulation on producers world wide emphasizes the domestic impact of regulatory costs. . . .

Global competition creates pressure for a least common denominator regulatory approach. Such pressure is similar to the political forces that affected state and local regulation before the regulatory nationalism of the New Deal. National regulation came about, in part, because certain problems were beyond the jurisdiction of individual states. In addition, states often had significant incentives to avoid regulation that would increase manufacturing costs and put local industry at a competitive disadvantage. Moreover, it was perhaps easier for opponents to block regulatory attempts at the state or local level than at the national level. Global pressures favoring a more economical, cost-conscious form of regulation need not necessarily translate into a return to laissez faire, but they can encourage an identification of deregulation with "the public interest."

Alfred C. Aman, Jr., *Administrative Law in a Global Era,* 78-79 (Cornell Univ. Press 1992).*

As we proceed with this course and examine various kinds of regulation, deregulation and privatization, and especially the procedures used to achieve these ends, it is important to ask what actually is the role of the state in the global era in which we now live. Similarly, it is important to ask whether a new theory of the state's role and, consequently, administrative law is now developing. Should we continue to rely on an interest-group model of politics in assessing recent developments in administrative law? Is this model best suited for the global era in which we now live? What is the regulatory role of the market in the global era? What political theory best describes these changes? Is it a form of neo-corporatism? Consider the following:

Aman, THE DEMOCRACY DEFICIT: TAMING GLOBALIZATION THROUGH LAW REFORM
143–44 (New York University Press 2004) **

Corporatist theory involves several aspects of regulatory actions that are relevant to our analysis of the democracy deficit and the potential for addressing it through law reform. First, corporatism denies the basic pluralist idea that policy emerges from the free and voluntary interaction of multiple interest groups. It, in effect, advocates government bargaining with selected, representative interest groups or "peak organizations" with subsequent deal-making among those groups with respect to public policy in key areas.

Corporatist theory holds during the bargaining that ensues, the state is operating with a public interest goal in mind. It is not a captured entity,

---

* Copyright © 1992 Cornell University Press. All rights reserved.
** Copyright © 2004 by New York University Press. All rights reserved.

but an independent player with a very important seat at the policymaking table. Thus the state does more than simply reflect the sum total of the preferences of its constituents, but rather seeks to assert its view of the public interest in the bargaining that ensues.

As a result of these state approaches, corporatist theory holds the state is, by definition, elitist — democratic neither in purpose nor result. From a corporatist perspective, the state enters into bargaining in an attempt to avoid confrontation and to maintain a politics of accommodation. For this degree of consensus to occur, however, normal political processes are usually sidestepped or undermined. Traditional democratic processes are replaced by technocratic and managerial solutions.

Each of these three aspects of corporatist theory describes an important aspect of the current globalizing state, especially in privatized contexts. Neocorporatism also illustrates clearly the risks to democracy in globalization. Correspondingly, it underscores the importance of Administrative Law as a context where hybrid approaches to government are forged. . . .

What aspects of the political economy of the global era are reflected in the privatization approaches now being taken? What are the procedural consequences of these substantive changes? What should these changes be? What should administrative law for the global era be? Consider the next section.

§ 1.04 Public/Private Partnerships: From Government to Governance

At the constitutional level, the Supreme Court, at least since the *Civil Rights Cases*, 109 U.S. 3 (1883), has long enforced a public/private distinction. Due process protections apply to state actors, not private, non-governmental actors. Of course, private actors can, in effect, become state actors if they are sufficiently connected to the state. Moreover, common law processes or federal and state statutes mandating certain procedures may apply. Nevertheless, public and private usually are legally constructed as two very different universes.

There has always been a great deal of interplay between public and private entities as they go about their respective tasks. But the relationship of public and private has been changing significantly of late. Globalization, and global processes more generally, are changing the nature of the state and the ways in which states now operate. Markets and market approaches are taking the place of more traditional, command and control forms of agency regulation. Public/private partnerships are increasingly common in various contexts, as the state delegates authority to private actors who then carry out what heretofore — at least for most of the 20th Century — have been thought of as the public responsibilities of public bodies. Consider the following:

Aman, THE LIMITS OF GLOBALIZATION AND THE FUTURE OF ADMINISTRATIVE LAW: FROM GOVERNMENT TO GOVERNANCE

8 IND. J. GLOBAL LEGAL STUD. 379, 379–382 (2001)*

One of the hallmarks of regulation in the global era has been the shift from state-centered, command-control approaches to market forms of regulation. This trend goes well beyond the use of market incentives in rules issued by administrative agencies. It also includes partial and sometimes wholesale delegation of certain public functions and responsibilities to the private sector. Prisons, welfare, healthcare, and education, as well as municipal services such as snow removal and garbage collection, now often involve the private sector directly in a variety of public/private partnerships.

Delegation to the private sector represents an important aspect of more general ways in which global processes encourage and accelerate what has been called 'third party government' whereby 'crucial elements of public authority are shared with a host of nongovernmental or other governmental actors.' The seemingly borderless nature of telecommunications and intellectual exchange, and the relatively easy flow of goods, capital, pollution, and disease across jurisdictional lines, increasingly requires a global conception of both problems and opportunities. The same fluidity with which borders can be crossed expands the need for cooperation, but also the intensity of the competition likely to occur among governmental entities that are territorially based. For example, private entities, in deciding where to locate their businesses or where to make their investments, can choose among many locations, generating competition among various localities for the jobs and opportunities for economic growth that certain private actors can help provide. Such problems often require multi-jurisdictional responses.

For state entities to conceptualize problems on a global basis, or to contemplate solutions or actions across domestic and international borders, they must often cooperate with other governmental units or form partnerships with nongovernmental actors that are not similarly tied to any fixed place. The end result of such collaborations is a growing body of international law that seeks to further both mutually beneficial cooperation among states and new forms of domestic and international governance that rely extensively on nongovernmental (private) actors to carry out public responsibilities.

In short, the effects of globalization are not limited to the international level of policymaking and law. The same forces that make cooperation necessary and fuel competition at the international level are at work at all levels of domestic governance. Administrative agencies share issues and approaches through increased contact and involvement. States, municipalities, and local governing units also compete for investments of various kinds in their jurisdictions. They, too, are limited in their extraterritorial powers and must cooperate with various entities — governmental and nongovernmental. The importance of the role that nongovernmental organizations now

---

* Copyright © 2001 by Trustees of Indiana University. Reprinted with the permission of the Indiana University Press, all rights reserved.

play at the international level is matched by private actors at the local level. The need to extend international law to some nongovernmental actors is linked to a similar need to understand and, in many instances, reconceptualize the role of administrative law at the domestic level. Private actors can more easily conceptualize and implement solutions for problems without regard to any single territory. This creates an important incentive for cooperation between private actors and states that are eager to solve their problems in an effective and efficient fashion.

How one reconceptualizes domestic administrative law significantly depends on how one regards the effects of globalization on law and markets. Public/private partnerships are seen mainly in two ways. One way of seeing such partnerships is as a step away from the state. Increased reliance on markets and the private sector provides opportunities to minimize the role of the state, by emphasizing bright-line distinctions between the public and the private — and by casting the market as essentially voluntary in nature and an end in itself. This is a laissez-faire approach, one that underscores a long-standing debate in administrative law between those who see the role of administrative law as protecting the individual from the state and those who see its role instead as facilitating legislative policies and goals. Another way of viewing public/private partnerships, however, is as an extension of the state. Rather than directly resisting global processes, the delegation of public functions to private actors represents new ways for states to carry out their responsibilities. From this perspective, markets are a form of regulation and not simply the substitution of a wholly private regime for what once was public. Public law values such as transparency, participation, and fairness remain relevant, even though private actors now carry out various tasks that can be appropriately called governmental.

Private prisons are a case in point:

Aman, ADMINISTRATIVE LAW FOR A NEW CENTURY
The Province of Administrative Law, 99-100, (Michael Taggart, ed., Hart Publishing, 1997) *

Privatising prisons differs from deregulating airlines or ending price controls on the price of oil or gas at the wellhead. The airline industry as well as the oil and gas industries are private industries with a substantial number of competitors. Markets can work in setting prices in all of these areas. Prisons, at least in modern times, generally have been thought of as a public function. This does not mean that the "services" associated with running a prison cannot be provided by private companies, but the overall responsibility of providing for prisons has generally been viewed as a governmental responsibility. The implications of privatization of such a function are different from those involved when an industry such as the gas or

---

* Copyright © 1997 by Hart Publishing. All rights reserved.

oil industry is deregulated. When that occurs, public law procedures no longer apply to how the price is set by market competitors. The antitrust laws usually suffice. In such industries, what once was public and the subject of elaborate ratemaking hearings, is now private. But when responsibility for prisons is delegated to the private sector, important constitutional questions persist: can the government delegate these responsibilities and, if so, what are the constitutional rights of prisoners in a private institution?

Courts have begun to resolve these issues, usually in favor of extending some aspects of the public sphere to what is now the private sector. This is accomplished, however, through the application of the state action doctrine, a doctrine that is hardly clear and is highly fact specific. Clearly, this is a doctrine on which much will turn, if there is to be a role for public law in the future. Quite apart from the important legal questions involved, the very nature of this new partnership between the public and private sectors is instructive for at least three reasons. First, it suggests that a major source of regulatory reform by means of privatization is driven by the need to lower the costs of government. Competition among private providers of prison services will enable these services to be provided efficiently. Second, by implication, privatization of a public function suggests that government is *not* as good or, at least, not as efficient as it needs to be. Third, the equation of market approaches and efficiency with the public interest suggests that even a function such as imprisoning violators of the law is not so different in its mechanics from a traditional market activity as to exclude the private sector. It is important to emphasise, however, that privatizing prisons in this way enlists the private sector in a way that does more than arguably save money. It also mixes the private and public sectors in a new way and one that is not isolated, but part of a larger, emerging pattern of governmental attempts to accomplish essentially public responsibilities in cost efficient ways. The question that does arise and which will continue to do so, is the extent to which public law applies to the private side of these partnerships. On a more philosophical level, the question that also arises is whether the kinds of values protected by public law are capable of being translated primarily into an efficiency discourse. Is there anything lost in translation? . . .

RICHARDSON v. McKNIGHT

United States Supreme Court
521 U.S. 399 (1997)

BREYER, J., delivered the opinion of the Court, in which STEVENS, O'CONNOR, SOUTER, and GINSBURG, JJ., joined.

SCALIA, J., filed a dissenting opinion, in which REHNQUIST, C.J., and KENNEDY and THOMAS, JJ., joined.

The issue before us is whether prison guards who are employees of a private prison management firm are entitled to a qualified immunity from suit by prisoners charging a violation of 42 U.S.C. § 1983. We hold that they are not.

I

Ronnie Lee McKnight, a prisoner at Tennessee's South Central Correctional Center (SCCC), brought this federal constitutional tort action against two prison guards, Darryl Richardson and John Walker. He says the guards injured him by placing upon him extremely tight physical restraints, thereby unlawfully "subject[ing]" him "to the deprivation of" a right "secured by the Constitution" of the United States. Rev. Stat. § 1979, 42 U.S.C. § 1983. Richardson and Walker asserted a qualified immunity from § 1983 lawsuits, and moved to dismiss the action. The District Court noted that Tennessee had "privatized" the management of a number of its correctional facilities, and that consequently a private firm, not the state government, employed the guards. The court held that, because they worked for a private company rather than the government, the law did not grant the guards immunity from suit. It therefore denied the guards' motion to dismiss. The guards appealed to the Sixth Circuit. That court also ruled against them. The Court of Appeals conceded that other courts had reached varying conclusions about whether, or the extent to which, private sector defendants are entitled to immunities of the sort the law provides governmental defendants. . . . But the court concluded, primarily for reasons of "public policy," that the privately employed prison guards were not entitled to the immunity provided their governmental counterparts. We granted certiorari to review this holding. We now affirm.

II

A

We take the Court's recent case, *Wyatt v. Cole,* 504 U.S. 158 (1992), as pertinent authority. The Court there considered whether private defendants, charged with § 1983 liability for "invoking state replevin, garnishment, and attachment statutes" later declared unconstitutional were "entitled to qualified immunity from suit." It held that they were not. We find four aspects of *Wyatt* relevant here.

First, as *Wyatt* noted, § 1983 basically seeks "to deter *state* actors from using the badge of their authority to deprive individuals of their federally guaranteed rights" and to provide related relief. It imposes liability only where a person acts "under color" of a state "statute, ordinance, regulation, custom, or usage." 42 U.S.C. § 1983. Nonetheless, *Wyatt* reaffirmed that § 1983 can *sometimes* impose liability upon a private individual.

Second, *Wyatt* reiterated that . . . a distinction exists between an "immunity from suit" and other kinds of legal defenses. As the *Wyatt* concurrence pointed out, a legal defense may well involve "the essence of the wrong," while an immunity frees one who enjoys it from a lawsuit whether or not he acted wrongly.

Third, *Wyatt* specified the legal source of § 1983 immunities. It pointed out that although § 1983 "'creates a species of tort liability that on its face admits of no immunities,'" this Court has nonetheless accorded immunity where a

"'tradition of immunity was so firmly rooted in the common law and was supported by such strong policy reasons that "Congress would have specifically so provided had it wished to abolish the doctrine."'" 504 U.S., at 164 (quoting *Owen v. Independence,* 445 U.S. 622, 637 (1980).

Wyatt majority, in deciding whether or not the private defendants enjoyed immunity, looked both to history and to "the special policy concerns involved in suing government officials." 504 U.S., at 167. And in this respect — the relevant *sources* of the law — both the *Wyatt* concurrence and the dissent seemed to agree.

Fourth, *Wyatt* did not consider its answer to the question before it as one applicable to *all* private individuals — irrespective of the nature of their relation to the government, position, or the kind of liability at issue. Rather, *Wyatt* explicitly limited its holding to what it called a "narrow" question about "private persons . . . who conspire with state officials," and it answered that question by stating that private defendants "faced with § 1983 liability for invoking a state replevin, garnishment, or attachment statute" are *not* entitled to immunity.

Wyatt, then, did not answer the legal question before us, whether petitioners — two employees of a private prison management firm — enjoy a qualified immunity from suit under § 1983. It does tell us, however, to look both to history and to the purposes that underlie government employee immunity in order to find the answer.

B [History of gov't employee immunity]

History does *not* reveal a "firmly rooted" tradition of immunity applicable to privately employed prison guards. Correctional services in the United States have undergone various transformations. *Government*-employed prison guards may have enjoyed a kind of immunity defense arising out of their status as public employees at common law. But correctional functions have never been exclusively public. Private individuals operated local jails in the 18th century, and private contractors were heavily involved in prison management during the 19th century.

During that time, some States, including southern States like Tennessee, leased their entire prison systems to private individuals or companies which frequently took complete control over prison management, including inmate labor and discipline. Private prison lease agreements (like inmate suits) seem to have been more prevalent after § 1983's enactment, but we have found evidence that the common law provided mistreated prisoners in prison leasing States with remedies against mistreatment by those private lessors. Yet, we have found no evidence that the law gave purely private companies or their employees any special immunity from such suits. The case on which the dissent rests its argument, *Williams v. Adams,* 85 Mass. 171 (1861) (which could not — without more — prove the existence of such a tradition and does not, moreover, clearly involve a private prison operator) actually supports our point. It suggests that no immunity from suit would exist for the type of intentional conduct at issue in this case.

Correctional functions in England have been more consistently public, but historical sources indicate that England relied upon private jailers to manage the detention of prisoners from the Middle Ages until well into the 18th century. The common law forbade those jailers to subject "'their prisoners to any pain or torment,'" whether through harsh confinement in leg irons, or otherwise. And it apparently authorized prisoner lawsuits to recover damages. Apparently the law *did* provide a kind of immunity for certain private defendants, such as doctors or lawyers who performed services at the behest of the sovereign. But we have found no indication of any more general immunity that might have applied to private individuals working for profit.

Our research, including the sources that the parties have cited, reveals that in the 19th century (and earlier) sometimes private contractors and sometimes government itself carried on prison management activities. And we have found no conclusive evidence of a historical tradition of immunity for private parties carrying out these functions. History therefore does not provide significant support for the immunity claim.

C  [purposes of govt employee immunity]

Whether the immunity doctrine's *purposes* warrant immunity for private prison guards presents a closer question. *Wyatt,* consistent with earlier precedent, described the doctrine's purposes as protecting "government's ability to perform its traditional functions" by providing immunity where "necessary to preserve" the ability of government officials "to serve the public good or to ensure that talented candidates were not deterred by the threat of damages suits from entering public service." 504 U.S., at 167. Earlier precedent described immunity as protecting the public from unwarranted timidity on the part of public officials by, for example, "encouraging the vigorous exercise of official authority," . . . by contributing to "'principled and fearless decision-making,'" and by responding to the concern that threatened liability would, in Judge Hand's words, "'dampen the ardour of all but the most resolute, or the most irresponsible,'" public officials.

The guards argue that those purposes support immunity whether their employer is private or public. Since private prison guards perform the same work as state prison guards, they say, they must require immunity to a similar degree. To say this, however, is to misread this Court's precedents. The Court has sometimes applied a functional approach in immunity cases, but only to decide which type of immunity — absolute or qualified — a public officer should receive. And it never has held that the mere performance of a governmental function could make the difference between unlimited § 1983 liability and qualified immunity, especially for a private person who performs a job without government supervision or direction. Indeed a purely functional approach bristles with difficulty, particularly since, in many areas, government and private industry may engage in fundamentally similar activities, ranging from electricity production, to waste disposal, to even mail delivery.

Petitioners' argument also overlook certain important differences that, from an immunity perspective, are critical. First, the most important special government immunity-producing concern — unwarranted timidity — is less likely present, or at least is not special, when a private company subject to competitive market pressures operates a prison. Competitive pressures mean not only that a firm whose guards are too aggressive will face damages that raise costs, thereby threatening its replacement, but also that a firm whose guards are too timid will face threats of replacement by other firms with records that demonstrate their ability to do both a safer and a more effective job.

These ordinary marketplace pressures are present here. The private prison guards before us work for a large, multistate private prison management firm. The firm is systematically organized to perform a major administrative task for profit. It performs that task independently, with relatively less ongoing direct state supervision. It must buy insurance sufficient to compensate victims of civil rights torts. And, since the firm's first contract expires after three years, its performance is disciplined, not only by state review, but also by pressure from potentially competing firms who can try to take its place.

In other words, marketplace pressures provide the private firm with strong incentives to avoid overly timid, insufficiently vigorous, unduly fearful, or "nonarduous" employee job performance. And the contract's provisions — including those that might permit employee indemnification and avoid many civil-service restrictions — grant this private firm freedom to respond to those market pressures through rewards and penalties that operate directly upon its employees. To this extent, the employees before us resemble those of other private firms and differ from government employees.

This is not to say that government employees, in their efforts to act within constitutional limits, will always, or often, sacrifice the otherwise effective performance of their duties. Rather, it is to say that government employees typically act within a *different* system. They work within a system that is responsible through elected officials to voters who, when they vote, rarely consider the performance of individual subdepartments or civil servants specifically and in detail. And that system is often characterized by multidepartment civil service rules that, while providing employee security, may limit the incentives or the ability of individual departments or supervisors flexibly to reward, or to punish, individual employees. Hence a judicial determination that "effectiveness" concerns warrant special immunity-type protection in respect to this latter (governmental) system does not prove its need in respect to the former. Consequently, we can find no *special* immunity-related need to encourage vigorous performance.

Second, "privatization" helps to meet the immunity-related need "to ensure that talented candidates" are "not deterred by the threat of damages suits from entering public service." It does so in part because of the comprehensive insurance-coverage requirements just mentioned. The insurance increases the likelihood of employee indemnification and to that extent reduces the employment-discouraging fear of unwarranted liability potential applicants face. Because privatization law also frees the private prison-management firm from many civil service law restraints, it permits the private firm, unlike a government department, to offset any increased employee liability risk with higher pay or extra benefits. In respect to this second government-immunity-related purpose then, it is difficult to find a *special* need for immunity, for the guards' employer can operate like other private firms; it need not operate like a typical government department.

Third, lawsuits may well "'distrac[t]'" these employees "'from their . . . duties,'" but the risk of "distraction" alone cannot be sufficient grounds for an immunity. Our qualified immunity cases do not contemplate the complete elimination of lawsuit-based distractions. And it is significant that, here, Tennessee law reserves certain important discretionary tasks — those related to prison discipline, to parole, and to good time — for state officials. Given a continual and conceded need for deterring constitutional violations and our sense that the firm's tasks are not enormously different in respect to their importance from various other publicly important tasks carried out by private firms, we are not persuaded that the threat of distracting workers from their duties is enough virtually by itself to justify providing an immunity. Moreover, Tennessee, which has itself decided not to extend sovereign immunity to private prison operators (and arguably appreciated that this decision would increase contract prices to some degree), can be understood to have anticipated a certain amount of distraction.

D

Our examination of history and purpose thus reveals nothing special enough about the job or about its organizational structure that would warrant providing these private prison guards with a governmental immunity. The job is one that private industry might, or might not, perform; and which history shows private firms did sometimes perform without relevant immunities. The organizational structure is one subject to the ordinary competitive pressures that normally help private firms adjust their behavior in response to the incentives that tort suits provide — pressures not necessarily present in government departments. Since there are no special reasons significantly favoring an extension of governmental immunity, and since *Wyatt* makes clear that private actors are not *automatically* immune (*i.e.*, § 1983 immunity does not automatically follow § 1983 liability), we must conclude that private prison guards, unlike those who work directly for the government, do not enjoy immunity from suit in a § 1983 case.

III

We close with three caveats. First, we have focused only on questions of § 1983 immunity and have not addressed whether the defendants are liable under § 1983 even though they are employed by a private firm. . . . Second, we have answered the immunity question narrowly, in the context in which it arose. That context is one in which a private firm, systematically organized to assume a major lengthy administrative task (managing an institution) with limited direct supervision by the government, undertakes that task for profit and potentially in competition with other firms. . . . Third, *Wyatt* explicitly stated that it did not decide whether or not the private defendants before it might assert, not immunity, but a special "good-faith" defense. . . .

For these reasons the judgment of the Court of Appeals is

Affirmed.

JUSTICE SCALIA, with whom THE CHIEF JUSTICE, JUSTICE KENNEDY, and JUSTICE THOMAS join, dissenting.

In *Procunier v. Navarette,* 434 U.S. 555 (1978), we held that state prison officials, including both supervisory and subordinate officers, are entitled to qualified immunity in a suit brought under 42 U.S.C. § 1983. Today the Court declares that this immunity is unavailable to employees of private prison management firms, who perform the same duties as state-employed correctional officials, who exercise the most palpable form of state police power, and who may be sued for acting "under color of state law." This holding is supported neither by common-law tradition nor public policy, and contradicts our settled practice of determining § 1983 immunity on the basis of the public function being performed.

I

The doctrine of official immunity against damages actions under § 1983 is rooted in the assumption that that statute did not abolish those immunities traditionally available at common law. I agree with the Court, therefore, that we must look to history to resolve this case. I do not agree with the Court, however, that the petitioners' claim to immunity is defeated if they cannot provide an actual case, antedating or contemporaneous with the enactment of § 1983, in which immunity was successfully asserted by a private prison guard. It is only the absence of such a case, and not any explicit rejection of immunity by any common-law court, that the Court relies upon. The opinion observes that private jailers existed in the 19th century, and that they were successfully sued by prisoners. But one could just as easily show that government-employed jailers were successfully sued at common law, often with no mention of possible immunity. . . .

The truth to tell, *Procunier v. Navarette, supra,* which established § 1983 immunity for state prison guards, did not trouble itself with history, as our later § 1983 immunity opinions have done, but simply set forth a policy prescription. At this stage in our jurisprudence it is irrational, and productive of harmful policy consequences, to rely upon lack of case support to create an artificial limitation upon the scope of a doctrine (prison-guard immunity) that was itself not based on case support. I say an artificial limitation, because the historical *principles* on which common-law immunity was based, and which are reflected in our jurisprudence, plainly cover the private prison guard if they cover the nonprivate. Those principles are two: (1) immunity is determined by function, not status, and (2) even more specifically, private status is not disqualifying. . . .

Private individuals have regularly been accorded immunity when they perform a governmental function that qualifies. We have long recognized the absolute immunity of grand jurors, noting that like prosecutors and judges they must "exercise a discretionary judgment on the basis of evidence presented to them." "It is the functional comparability of [grand jurors'] judgments to those of the judge that has resulted in [their] being referred to as 'quasi-judicial' officers, and their immunities being termed 'quasi-judicial' as well."

Likewise, witnesses who testify in court proceedings have enjoyed immunity, regardless of whether they were government employees. "[T]he common law," we have observed, "provided absolute immunity from subsequent damages liability for all persons — *governmental or otherwise* — who were integral parts of the judicial process." I think it highly unlikely that we would deny prosecutorial immunity to those private attorneys increasingly employed by various jurisdictions in this country to conduct high visibility criminal prosecutions. There is no more reason for treating private prison guards differently.

II

Later in its opinion, the Court seeks to establish that there are policy reasons for denying to private prison guards the immunity accorded to public ones. As I have indicated above, I believe that history and not judicially analyzed policy governs this matter — but even on its own terms the Court's attempted policy distinction is unconvincing. The Court suggests two differences between civil-service prison guards and those employed by private prison firms which preclude any "special" need to give the latter immunity. First, the Court says that "unwarranted timidity" on the part of private guards is less likely to be a concern, since their companies are subject to market pressures that encourage them to be effective in the performance of their duties. If a private firm does not maintain a proper level of order, the Court reasons, it will be replaced by another one — so there is no need for qualified immunity to facilitate the maintenance of order.

This is wrong for several reasons. First of all, it is fanciful to speak of the consequences of "market" pressures in a regime where public officials are the only purchaser, and other people's money the medium of payment. Ultimately, one prison-management firm will be selected to replace another prison-management firm only if a decision is made by some *political* official not to renew the contract. This is a government decision, not a market choice. If state officers turn out to be more strict in reviewing the cost and performance of privately managed prisons than of publicly managed ones, it will only be because they have *chosen* to be so. The process can come to resemble a market choice only to the extent that political actors *will* such resemblance — that is, to the extent that political actors (1) are willing to pay attention to the issue of prison services, among the many issues vying for their attention, and (2) are willing to place considerations of cost and quality of service ahead of such political considerations as personal friendship, political alliances, in-state ownership of the contractor, etc. Secondly and more importantly, however, if one assumes a political regime that *is* bent on emulating the market in its purchase of prison services, it is almost certainly the case that, short of mismanagement so severe as to provoke a prison riot, *price* (not discipline) will be the predominating factor in such a regime's selection of a contractor. A contractor's price must depend upon its costs; lawsuits increase costs;[3] and

---

[3] This is true even of successfully defended lawsuits, and even of lawsuits that have been insured against. The Court thinks it relevant to the factor I am currently discussing that the private prison-management firm "must buy insurance sufficient to compensate victims of civil rights torts." Belief in the relevance of this factor must be traceable, ultimately, to belief in the existence of a free lunch. Obviously, as civil-rights claims increase, the cost of civil rights insurance increases.

"fearless" maintenance of discipline increases lawsuits. The incentive to downplay discipline will exist, moreover, even in those States where the politicians' zeal for market emulation and budget cutting has waned, and where prison-management contract renewal is virtually automatic: the more cautious the prison guards, the fewer the lawsuits, the higher the profits. In sum, it seems that "market-competitive" private prison managers have even greater need than civil-service prison managers for immunity as an incentive to discipline.

The Court's second distinction between state and private prisons is that privatization "helps to meet the immunity-related need to ensure that talented candidates are not deterred by the threat of damages suits from entering public service" as prison guards. This is so because privatization brings with it (or at least has brought with it in the case before us) (1) a statutory requirement for insurance coverage against civil-rights claims, which assertedly "increases the likelihood of employee indemnification," and (2) a liberation "from many civil service law restraints" which prevent increased employee risk from being "offset . . . with higher pay or extra benefits." As for the former (civil-rights liability insurance): surely it is the *availability* of that protection, rather than its actual presence in the case at hand, which decreases (if it does decrease, which I doubt) the *need* for immunity protection. (Otherwise, the Court would have to say that a private prison-management firm that is not required to purchase insurance, and does not do so, is more entitled to immunity; and that a government-run prison system that *does* purchase insurance is *less* entitled to immunity.) And of course civil-rights liability insurance is no less *available* to public entities than to private employers. But the second factor — liberation from civil-service limitations — is the more interesting one. First of all, simply as a philosophical matter it is fascinating to learn that one of the prime justifications for § 1983 immunity should be a phenomenon (civil-service laws) that did not even exist when § 1983 was enacted and the immunity created. Also as a philosophical matter, it is poetic justice (or poetic revenge) that the Court should use one of the principal economic benefits of "prison out-sourcing" — namely, the avoidance of civil service salary and tenure encrustations — as the justification for a legal rule rendering out-sourcing more expensive. Of course the savings attributable to out-sourcing will not be wholly lost as a result of today's holding; they will be transferred in part from the public to prisoner-plaintiffs and to lawyers. It is a result that only the American Bar Association and the American Federation of Government Employees could love. But apart from philosophical fascination, this second factor is subject to the same objection as the first: governments *need not* have civil service salary encrustations (or can exempt prisons from them); and hence governments, no more than private prison employers, have any *need* for § 1983 immunity.

There is one more possible rationale for denying immunity to private prison guards worth discussing, albeit briefly. It is a theory so implausible that the Court avoids mentioning it, even though it was the primary reason given in the Court of Appeals decision that the Court affirms. It is that officers of private prisons are more likely than officers of state prisons to violate prisoners' constitutional rights because they work for a profit motive, and hence an added degree of deterrence is needed to keep these officers in line. The Court of Appeals offered no evidence to support its bald assertion that private prison guards operate with different incentives than state prison guards, and gave no hint as to how prison guards might possibly increase their employers' profits by violating constitutional rights. One would think that private prison managers, whose § 1983 damages come out of their own pockets, as compared with public prison managers, whose § 1983 damages come out of the public purse, would, if anything, be more careful in training their employees to avoid constitutional infractions. And in fact, States having experimented with prison privatization commonly report that the overall caliber of the services provided to prisoners has actually improved in scope and quality. Matters Relating to the Federal Bureau of Prisons: Hearing before the Subcommittee on Crime of the House Committee on the Judiciary, 104th Cong., 1st Sess., 110 (1995).

. . . .

In concluding, I must observe that since there is no apparent *reason*, neither in history nor in policy, for making immunity hinge upon the Court's distinction between public and private guards, the precise *nature* of that distinction must also remain obscure. Is it privity of contract that separates the two categories — so that guards paid directly by the State are "public" prison guards and immune, but those paid by a prison-management company "private" prison guards and not immune? Or is it rather "employee" versus "independent contractor" status — so that even guards whose compensation is paid directly by the State are not immune if they are not also supervised by a state official? Or is perhaps state supervision alone (without direct payment) enough to confer immunity? Or is it . . . the formal designation of the guards, or perhaps of the guards' employer, as a "state instrumentality" that makes the difference? Since, as I say, I see no sense in the public-private distinction, neither do I see what precisely it consists of.

Today's decision says that two sets of prison guards who are indistinguishable in the ultimate source of their authority over prisoners, indistinguishable in the powers that they possess over prisoners, and indistinguishable in the duties that they owe toward prisoners, are to be treated quite differently in the matter of their financial liability. The only sure effect of today's decision- and the only purpose, as far as I can tell — is that it will artificially raise the cost of privatizing prisons. Whether this will cause privatization to be prohibitively expensive, or instead simply divert state funds that could have been saved or spent on additional prison services, it is likely that taxpayers and prisoners will suffer as a consequence. Neither our precedent, nor the historical foundations of § 1983, nor the policies underlying § 1983, support this result.

I respectfully dissent.

NOTES AND QUESTIONS

1-15. How do you characterize the majority's approach in this case? Does it treat the prison provider as a purely private entity? A mixed or hybrid entity? Contrast this with the dissent's functional approach. Describe that approach. Is this case about cost or prisoner's rights? What underlies the majority's approach? What underlies the functional approach of the dissent?

1-16. Contrast these approaches to that taken by an English court in *R. v. Panel on Take-overs and Mergers, ex parte Datafin plc.* in the U.K. The Take-over Panel carries out important financial regulatory functions, but it does so as part of a self-regulatory framework and "without any visible means of legal support." (1987) QB 815, 824. The English Court of Appeals held its decisions to be subject to judicial review, even though the Panel "has no statutory, prerogative or common law powers and is not in contractual relationship with the financial market or with those who deal in the market." The court reasoned as follows:

> The picture which emerges is clear. As an act of government it was decided that, in relation to take-overs, there should be a central self-regulatory body which would be supported and sustained by a periphery of statutory powers and penalties wherever non-statutory powers and penalties were insufficient or non-existent or where EEC requirements called for statutory provisions.
>
> No one could have been in the least surprised if the panel had been instituted and operated under the direct authority of statute law, since it operates wholly in the public domain. Its jurisdiction extends throughout the United Kingdom. Its code and rulings apply equally to all who wish to make take-over bids or promote mergers, whether or not they are members of bodies represented on the panel. Its lack of a direct statutory base is a complete anomaly, judged by the experience of other comparable markets world wide. The explanation is that it is an historical 'happenstance', to borrow a happy term from across the Atlantic. Prior to the years leading up to the 'Big Bang', the City of London prided itself on being a village community, albeit of an unique kind, which could regulate itself by pressure of professional opinion. As government increasingly accepted the necessity for intervention to prevent fraud, it built on City institutions and mores, supplementing and reinforcing them as appeared necessary. It is a process which is likely to continue, but the position has already been reached in which central government has incorporated the panel into its own regulatory network built up under the Prevention of Fraud (Investments) Act 1958 and allied statutes, such as the Banking Act 1979.
>
> The issue is thus whether the historic supervisory jurisdiction of the Queen's courts extends to such a body discharging such functions, including some which are quasi-judicial in their nature, as part of such a system. Counsel for the panel submits that it does not. He says that this jurisdiction only extends to bodies whose power is derived from legislation or the exercise of the prerogative. Counsel for the applicants submits that this is too narrow a view and that regard has to be had not only to the source of the body's power, but also to whether it operates as an integral part of a system which has a public law character, is supported by public law in that public law sanctions are applied if its edicts are ignored and performs what might be described as public law functions.

1-17. How does this approach in *Datafin* compare to Justice Scalia's approach in *McKnight*? Is the Court concerned with the source of the power or with the function it performs? Both?

1-18. See also, *Correctional Services Corp. v. Malesko*, 534 U.S. 61 (2001) (the Court held that *Bivens v. Six Unknown Narcotics Agents*, 403 U.S. 388 (1971), did not confer a private right of action against a private corporation operating a halfway house for federal prisoners); *U.S. v. Thomas*, 240 F.3d 445 (5th Cir. 2001) (guard employed by private prison is a "public official" for purposes of the federal bribery statute).

1-19. For an excellent collection of essays dealing with public/private issues on a comparative basis, see *The Province of Administrative Law* (Michael Taggart ed., Oxford, U.K.: Hart Pub. 1997). For other in depth analyses of governance issues, see Alfred C. Aman, Jr., *The Democracy Deficit: Taming Globalization Through Law Reform*, Chapters 3 and 4 (N.Y.U. Press, 2004); *The Tools of Governance: A Guide to the New Governance* (Lester Salamon ed., New York: Oxford Univ. Press 2002); Martha Minnow, *Partners, Not Rivals: Privatization and the Public Good* (Beacon Press, 2002); Jody Freeman, *The Private Roles in Public Governance*, 75 N.Y.U. L. REV. 543 (2000); Jody Freeman, *The Contracting State*, 28 FLA. ST. U. L. REV. 155 (2000); Alfred C. Aman, Jr., *Administrative Law in a Global Era* (Cornell University Press, 1992).

PROBLEM 1-4

As in the United Kingdom, entirely "private" organizations can wield enormous "public" power in the United States. Consider the American Bar Association (ABA), a purely voluntary professional association of attorneys and judges. As part of its activities, the ABA maintains a list of law schools that meet its accreditation standards. For example, Accreditation Standard 503 reads as follows: "A law school shall require each applicant to take a valid and reliable admission test to assist the school in assessing the applicant's capability of satisfactorily completing the school's educational program." The ABA interprets this standard to require that the law school either use the Law School Admission Test (LSAT) or establish that "such other test is a valid and reliable test to assist the school in assessing an applicant's capability to satisfactorily complete the school's educational program." Interpretation 503-1.

In many jurisdictions, a student who has graduated from a non-ABA accredited law school cannot be admitted to the bar. The Indiana Supreme Court's requirements for bar admission are typical in this regard.

> Each applicant for admission to the bar of this Court by written examination shall be required to establish to the satisfaction of the State Board of Law Examiners that the applicant is . . . a graduate of a law school located in the United States which at the time of the applicant's graduation was

on the approved list of the Council of Legal Education and Admission to the Bar of the American Bar Association. . . .

Burns Ind. Rule 13(4)(A) (2004).

(1) Suppose that an ABA-accredited law school in Indiana concludes in January 2004 that the LSAT is not very helpful in determining whether a particular student will succeed in law school. Instead, the law school concludes that the Graduate Record Examination ("GRE") — the test that many graduate school programs require of their applicants — is a better test to predict law student performance. Suppose further that when the law school comes up for re-accreditation in 2005, the ABA decides that the GRE does not satisfy Accreditation Standard 503 and refuses to grant accreditation to the law school until the law school abandons the GRE. Finally, suppose that the law school can offer conclusive statistical proof that the GRE is in fact a better predictor of law student success if given the opportunity. Should the law school be allowed to obtain a hearing in a court to prove its case? On what grounds?

(2) Assume it is not clear whether the GRE or the LSAT is the better predictor. An applicant for law school is denied admission because she has a low LSAT, but a very high GRE score. Does she have a case against the law school? Against the ABA?

(3) *See generally*, *National Collegiate Athletic Association v. Tarkanian*, 488 U.S. 179 (1988) (NCAA found not to be a state actor).

PROBLEM 1-5

Consider the following in A. Michael Froomkin, *Wrong Turn in Cyberspace: Using ICANN to Route Around the APA and the Constitution*, 50 DUKE L.J. 17, 20 (2000):*

> The United States government is managing a critical portion of the Internet's infrastructure in violation of the Administrative Procedures Act (APA) and the Constitution. . . . [T]he Internet Corporation for Assigned Names and Numbers (ICANN) has been making domain name policy under contract with the Department of Commerce (DoC). ICANN is formally a private nonprofit California corporation created, in response to a summoning by U.S. government officials, to take regulatory actions that DoC was unable or unwilling to take directly. If the U.S. government is laundering its policymaking through ICANN, it violates the APA; if ICANN is, in fact, independent, then the federal government's decision to have ICANN manage a resource of such importance and to allow — indeed, require — it to enforce regulatory conditions on users of that resource violates the nondelegation doctrine of the U.S. Constitution. In either case, the relationship violates basic norms of due process and public policy designed to ensure that federal power is exercised responsibly.

---

* Copyright © 2000 by A. Michael Froomkin. All rights reserved.

(a) As you proceed through this book, ask yourself what criteria are relevant in determining whether or not Congress is, in fact, "laundering" its policymaking through a private body, thereby avoiding the APA? *See* Chapters Three and Four, *infra* especially § 4.02[E], dealing with exceptions to rulemaking procedures.

(b) On a constitutional basis, is Congress delegating its policymaking power to a private body without sufficient guidance and protections? *See* Chapter Six, § 6.07. Is there a statute involved?

Consider Froomkin's arguments:*

Depending on the precise nature of the DoC-ICANN relationship, not all of which is public, DoC's use of ICANN to run the DNS [domain name service] violates the APA and/or the U.S. Constitution. On the one hand, DoC may retain substantial control, either directly or by review, over ICANN's policy decisions. In that case, DoC's use of ICANN to make rules violates the APA. On the other hand, if DoC has ceded temporary policy control to ICANN, that violates the Constitution's nondelegation doctrine.

There is substantial evidence, discussed below, that DoC has directly instructed ICANN on policy matters. Furthermore, as ICANN is utterly dependent on DoC for ICANN's continuing authority, funding, and, indeed, its reason for being, it would be reasonable to conclude that the corporation is currently so captive that all of ICANN's decisions can fairly be charged to the government. If so, the DNS has not, in fact, been privatized at all, even temporarily. At least in cases where ICANN does what DoC tells it to do, and arguably in all cases, DoC's use of a private corporation to implement policy decisions represents an end run around the APA and the Constitution. To the extent that DoC launders its policy choices through a cat's paw, the public's right to notice and meaningful comment; to accountable decisionmaking; to due process; and to protection against arbitrary and capricious policy choices, self-dealing, or ex parte proceedings are all attenuated or eliminated; so, too, is the prospect of any meaningful judicial review. The result is precisely the type of illegitimate agency decisionmaking that modern administrative law claims to be most anxious to prevent.

If, on the other hand, ICANN is making its policy decisions independently of DoC, as ICANN's partisans tend to argue, then even a partial transfer of DoC's policymaking authority over the DNS violates an even more fundamental public policy against the arbitrary exercise of public power, the constitutional doctrine prohibiting the delegation of public power to private groups. . . .

The ICANN issue is unique in a number of ways. Modern federal cases implicating the nondelegation doctrine are quite rare; the Supreme Court does not seem to have considered the issue in the context of a delegation to a private group since the New Deal, and the lower court cases are few and often very technical. In any event, nondelegation cases usually involve a contested statute. The issue then is whether Congress's attempt to vest power in an agency or a private body is constitutional. In the case of ICANN,

---

* Copyright © 2000 by A. Michael Froomkin. All rights reserved.fu

there is no statute. Congress at no time determined that the DNS should be privatized, or, indeed, legislated anything about national DNS policy. Instead, DoC itself chose to delegate the DNS functions to ICANN, relying on its general authority to enter into contracts. ICANN is also a very unusual corporation. There are many government contractors, both profit-making and nonprofit. But it is unusual for a nonprofit corporation to be created for the express purpose of taking over a government regulatory function.

Froomkin, *supra*, 50 DUKE L.J. 27-29.

PART ONE
WITHIN AGENCY WALLS

ADMINISTRATIVE AGENCY ADJUDICATION, RULEMAKING AND INFORMAL ACTION

Chapter One introduced the basic concepts of rules and orders. Like many legal categories, these terms effectively capture governmental actions that occur at either end of the rules-orders continuum. They do not, however, do justice to the complexity that results from governmental actions that have elements of both rules and orders. These materials shall explore these more complex actions. Specifically, Part One shall explore the legal requirements necessary for agencies to exercise power. What must an agency do before it can issue orders, rules, or take informal actions that often embody elements of both rules and orders? Chapter Two focuses on orders and adjudication. It examines the constitutional requirements of the Due Process Clause of the Fifth and Fourteenth Amendments. Chapters Three and Four then focus primarily on the statutory requirements to which agencies must adhere as they engage in formal adjudication and informal and various other types of rulemaking. Chapter Five then examines various informal agency actions and the use of various alternative dispute resolution techniques in the administrative process.

Part One starts at the adjudicatory end of the conceptual framework we began to develop in Chapter One. Part of the reason for this is to enable you to analyze an aspect of the administrative process that your first-year courses are dealing with or already have acquainted you with — adjudication. But as you examine these adjudicatory materials, ask yourself to what extent adjudication in the administrative setting differs from adjudication in state or federal courts. Do administrative agencies have an opportunity to be more procedurally flexible and innovative than state or federal courts? Do they effectively take advantage of those opportunities? Do you expect there to be procedural differences between agency adjudicators and federal or state courts? Why? If there are differences, what are they? Chapter Four then explores the other end of the spectrum: rules. How do these processes compare with legislative processes? And in Chapter 5, when agencies act informally, are they issuing orders, rules, or amendments to rules? What procedures should agencies use when they act informally?

Chapter 2
DUE PROCESS AND ADMINISTRATIVE ADJUDICATION

§ 2.01 Introduction

Chapter One introduced us to the Due Process Clause of the Fifth and Fourteenth Amendments. Chapter Two will now examine, in depth, the application of the Due Process Clause to various kinds of governmental actions taken by a variety of governmental actors. We shall assume that the governmental action giving rise to the case before us has properly been characterized as an order. We shall now focus on the *constitutional* significance of that categorization. What kinds of procedures does the Constitution require before an agency can take this kind of action? The answer to this question requires the analysis of three additional questions: (1) Is there a constitutional, due process *right* to a hearing? (2) If so, *how much process* is constitutionally due and (3) *When* must this process be provided? The last section in this chapter will explore when, if ever, such an analysis might be applied to private entities.

§ 2.02 The Right/Privilege Distinction

The first question to be decided in any due process case is whether the Fifth or Fourteenth Amendment applies. We have already seen that the Court in *Londoner v. Denver* found that the Fourteenth Amendment applied to a state board of tax assessors. But not all governmental action that could be characterized as an order necessarily triggers the Due Process Clause. This was particularly true in the early stages of administrative law development. Courts required the application of the Due Process Clause to the government only if an interest protected by the common law was at stake. For purposes of the Due Process Clause, the government was, in effect, treated like any other private actor. As Professor Richard B. Stewart has explained in *The Reformation of American Administrative Law:*[*]

> Traditionally, the only interests entitled to protection against government interference were those that would enjoy protection at common law against invasion by private parties. Thus a government order for an individual to pay money, or to perform certain acts intruded on the domain of "liberty or property" protected by due process because the common law would protect against similar intrusions by private actors. In contrast, the interest in eligibility for a gift, or the opportunity to work for a given employer, or the opportunity to enter into contractual relations with a given firm was not ordinarily subject to common law protection against the donor, employer,

---

[*] 88 HARV. L. REV. 1667, 1717–18 (1975). Copyright © 1975 by the Harvard Law Review Association. All rights reserved.

or contractor. It was therefore held that no due process safeguards apply to similar advantageous relations with the government. Thus no due process protection traditionally attended the government's denial of noncontractual retirement benefits or termination of government employment. Such advantageous relations with the government were mere "privileges" or "gratuities," not legally protected rights.

These parallels between private and public law appear ultimately to stem from a contractarian view of the state as an artificial person. An individual enjoys against the state a protected sphere of interests equivalent to that which he enjoys against every other person. This sphere may be infringed with the individual's consent. In the case of intrusions by private individuals, one gives consent through contract, and the question whether a given consent authorizes what would otherwise be an unlawful intrusion is decided by judicial procedures. With the government, one's consent is given through a duly constituted elected assembly. Accordingly, when a government official intrudes upon a person's common-law protected interests, that person may require the official to demonstrate that the intrusion is authorized by statute. So long as the protected sphere of individual interests is not infringed, however, the state enjoys as much freedom of action as any other person and need not surmount any procedural hurdles before acting.

Consider the right/privilege distinction in the following case. What is a privilege as far as the court is concerned? How does it differ from a right? Is this case an example of a national security exception to the Constitution or would the right/privilege distinction compel this result no matter what the historic context?

BAILEY v. RICHARDSON

Court of Appeals District of Columbia
182 F.2d 46 (1950),
aff'd by an equally divided Court, 341 U.S. 918 (1951)

PRETTYMAN, CIRCUIT JUDGE.

This is a civil action brought in the United States District Court for the District of Columbia for a declaratory judgment and for an order directing plaintiff-appellant's reinstatement in Government employ. . . .

The Facts

Appellant Bailey was employed in the classified civil service of the United States Government from August 19, 1939, to June 28, 1947. Upon the latter date she was separated from the service due to reduction in force. On March 26, 1948, she was given a temporary appointment, and on May 28, 1948, she was reinstated under circumstances to be related.

§ 2.02   DUE PROCESS AND ADMINISTRATIVE ADJUDICATION   51

The regulations of the Civil Service Commission in effect at the time of appellant's reinstatement made reinstatements subject to the condition that removal might be ordered by the Commission if investigation of the individual's qualifications, made within eighteen months, disclosed disqualification. The regulations listed as a disqualification:

(7) On all the evidence, reasonable grounds exist for belief that the person involved is disloyal to the Government of the United States.

On July 31, 1948, two months after her reinstatement, Miss Bailey received from the Regional Loyalty Board of the Commission a letter and an enclosed interrogatory. The letter said in part:

During the course of an investigation of your suitability for appointment, information was received which the Commission believes you should be given an opportunity to clarify. Consequently, there are inclosed an original and copy of an interrogatory to be answered by you under affirmation or oath.

"Your cooperation in this matter will be appreciated." The interrogatory said in part:

As part of the process of determining your suitability for Federal Employment, an investigation of you has been conducted under the provisions of Executive Order 9835, which established the Federal Employees Loyalty Program. This investigation disclosed information which, it is believed, you should have an opportunity to explain or refute.

The questions in the attached Interrogatory are based on the information received, and are to be answered in writing in sufficient detail to present fairly your explanation or answers thereto. . . .

You are further advised that you have the right, upon request, to an administrative hearing on the issues in the case before the Regional Loyalty Board. You may appear personally before the Board and be represented by counsel or representative of your own choice; and you may present evidence in your behalf. Such evidence may be presented by witnesses or by affidavit.

The Commission has received information to the effect that you are or have been a member of the Communist Party or the Communist Political Association; that you have attended meetings of the Communist Party, and have associated on numerous occasions with known Communist Party members.

The Commission has received information to the effect that you are or have been a member of the American League for Peace and Democracy, an organization which has been declared by the Attorney General to come within the purview of Executive Order 9835.

The Commission has received information to the effect that you are or have been a member of the Washington Committee for Democratic Action, an organization which has been declared by the Attorney General to come within the purview of Executive Order 9835.

Are you now, or have ever been, a member of, or in any manner affiliated with, the Nazi or Fascist movements or with any organization or political party whose objective is now, or has ever been, the overthrow of the Constitutional Government of the United States?

Miss Bailey answered the interrogatories directly and specifically, denying each item of information recited therein as having been received by the Commission, except that she admitted past membership for a short time in the American League for Peace and Democracy. She vigorously asserted her loyalty to the United States. She requested an administrative hearing. A hearing was held before the Regional Board. She appeared and testified and presented other witnesses and numerous affidavits. No person other than those presented by her testified.

On November 1, 1948, the Regional Board advised the Federal Security Agency, in which Miss Bailey was employed, that:

> As a result of such investigation and after a hearing before this Board, it was found that, on all the evidence, reasonable grounds exist for belief that Miss Bailey is disloyal to the Government of the United States.
>
> Therefore, she has been rated ineligible for Federal employment; she has been barred from competing in civil service examinations for a period of three years, and your office is instructed to separate her from the service.

On the same day, a letter was sent by the Board to Miss Bailey, reading in part:

> As shown in the attached copy of a letter to your employing agency, it has been found that, on all the evidence, reasonable grounds exist for belief that you are disloyal to the Government of the United States.
>
> Your application for or eligibility from each of the examinations mentioned below has been canceled and you have been barred from civil service examinations in the Federal service for a period of three years from October 29, 1948. When the period of debarment has expired the Commission will, upon request, consider the removal of the bar.
>
> If you wish to appeal the Board's decision, the Loyalty Review Board, U.S. Civil Service Commission, Washington 25, D.C., should be notified within 20 days from the date of receipt by you of this letter.

Miss Bailey appealed to the Loyalty Review Board and requested a hearing. Hearing was held before a panel of that Board. Miss Bailey appeared, testified, and presented affidavits. No person other than Miss Bailey testified, and no affidavits other than hers were presented on the record.

On February 9, 1949, the chairman of the Loyalty Review Board advised the Federal Security Agency that the finding of the Regional Board was sustained, and he requested that the Agency remove Miss Bailey's name from the rolls. . . .

Miss Bailey's position from May 28, 1948, to November 3, 1948, was that of a training officer (general fields) CAF 13.

The Question

The rights claimed by and for appellant must be discovered accurately and defined precisely. The events with which we are concerned were not accidental, thoughtless or mere petty tyrannies of subordinate officials. They were the deliberate design of the executive branch of the Government, knowingly supported by Congress.

The case presented for Miss Bailey is undoubtedly appealing. She was denied reinstatement in her former employment because Government officials found reasonable ground to believe her disloyal. She was not given a trial in any sense of the word, and she does not know who informed upon her. Thus viewed, her situation appeals powerfully to our sense of the fair and the just. But the case must be placed in context and in perspective.

The Constitution placed upon the President and the Congress, and upon them alone, responsibility for the welfare of this country in the arena of world affairs. It so happens that we are presently in an adversary position to a government whose most successful recent method of contest is the infiltration of a government service by its sympathizers. This is the context of Miss Bailey's question.

The essence of her complaint is not that she was denied reinstatement; the complaint is that she was denied reinstatement without revelation by the Government of the names of those who informed against her and of the method by which her alleged activities were detected. So the question actually posed by the case is whether the President is faced with an inescapable dilemma, either to continue in Government employment a person whose loyalty he reasonably suspects or else to reveal publicly the methods by which he detects disloyalty and the names of any persons who may venture to assist him.

. . . .

The presentation of appellant's contentions is impressive. Each detail of the trial which she unquestionably did not get is depicted separately, in a mounting cumulation into analogies to the Dreyfus case and the Nazi judicial process. Thus, a picture of a simple black-and-white fact — that appellant did not get a trial in the judicial sense — is drawn in bold and appealing colors. But the question is not whether she had a trial. The question is whether she should have had one.

If the whole of this case were as appellant pictures it, if we had only to decide the question which she states and as she states it, our task would indeed be simple and attractively pleasant. But is not so. We are dealing with a major clash between individual and public interests. We must ascertain with precision whether individual rights are involved, and we must then weigh the sum of those rights, if there be any, against the inexorable necessities of the Government. We must examine not only one side of the controversy but both sides.

. . . .

Fifth Amendment

. . . It is next said on behalf of appellant that the Due Process clause of the Fifth Amendment requires that she be afforded a hearing of the quasi-judicial type before being dismissed. The Due Process Clause provides: "No person shall . . . be deprived of life, liberty, or property without due process of law. . . ." It has been held repeatedly and consistently that Government employ is not "property" and that in this particular it is not a contract. We are unable to perceive how it could be held to be "liberty". Certainly it is not "life". So much that is clear would seem to dispose of the point. In terms the Due Process Clause does not apply to the holding of a Government office.

Other considerations lead to the same conclusion. Never in our history has a Government administrative employee been entitled to a hearing of the quasi-judicial type upon his dismissal from Government service. That record of a hundred and sixty years of Government administration is the sort of history which speaks with great force. It is pertinent to repeat in this connection that the Lloyd-La Follette Act, sponsored and enacted by advocates of a merit classified government service, expressly denies the right to such a hearing. Moreover, in the acute and sometimes bitter historic hundred-year contest over the wholesale summary dismissal of Government employees, there seems never to have been a claim that, absent congressional limitation, the President was without constitutional power to dismiss without notice, hearing or evidence; except for the question as to officials appointed with the advice and consent of the Senate. . . .

The Constitution makes the President responsible for the execution of the laws and makes the Congress responsible for the vesting of appointments in the executive branch. Those two authorities are, therefore, responsible for the ability, the integrity, and the loyalty of the personnel of the executive branch. That responsibility necessarily includes the power to choose employees for executive duty, and the power to remove those deemed not qualified is a correlative power. No function is more completely internal to a branch of government than the selection and retention or dismissal of its employees. So it has been held many times that the power of removal is an incident of the power of appointment.

In the absence of statute or ancient custom to the contrary, executive offices are held at the will of the appointing authority, not for life or for fixed terms. If removal be at will, of what purpose would process be? To hold office at the will of a superior and to be removable therefrom only by constitutional due process of law are opposite and inherently conflicting ideas. Due process of law is not applicable unless one is being deprived of something to which he has a right.

Constitutionally, the criterion for retention or removal of subordinate employees is the confidence of superior executive officials. Confidence is not controllable by process. What may be required by acts of the Congress is another matter, but there is no requirement in the Constitution that the executive branch rely upon the services of persons in whom it lacks confidence. . . .

We hold that the Due Process of Law Clause of the Fifth Amendment does not restrict the President's discretion or the prescriptive power of Congress in respect to executive personnel.

We do not reach the question whether, if the Due Process of Law Clause does apply, it requires more than this appellant was given. Miss Bailey was not summarily cut off the rolls. She was advised in writing that information concerning her qualifications for Government employ had been received; she was asked specific questions; and she was told that those questions reflected the information received. The questions revealed the nature of the alleged activities giving rise to the inquiry and the names of the organizations in which she was alleged to have been active. Everything that she wished to present was received; all affidavits offered by her were accepted, and all witnesses presented by her testified. She was twice heard orally. She was represented at all stages by competent counsel. Her case was considered by two separate groups of executive officials. On the other hand, she was not told the names of the informants against her. She was not permitted to face or to cross-examine those informants. She was not given the dates or places at which she was alleged to have been active in the named alleged subversive organizations. So the claim in her behalf necessarily goes farther than an abstract claim for due process of law. The claim must be that the Due Process clause requires, in dismissals of subordinate Government employees, specificity in charges equivalent to that of valid criminal charges, confrontation by witnesses, cross examination of them, and hearing upon evidence openly submitted. Even if the Due Process Clause applies, we would think it does not require so much. . . . [The Court also rejected appellant's First Amendment claims.]

EDGERTON, CIRCUIT JUDGE (dissenting).

Without trial by jury, without evidence, and without even being allowed to confront her accusers or to know their identity, a citizen of the United States has been found disloyal to the government of the United States.

For her supposed disloyal thoughts she has been punished by dismissal from a wholly nonsensitive position in which her efficiency rating was high. The case received nation-wide publicity. Ostracism inevitably followed. A finding of disloyalty is closely akin to a finding of treason. The public hardly distinguishes between the two. . . .

I. *Executive Order 9835[3] requires evidence and an opportunity for cross-examination.* The Executive Order provides that "the standard for the refusal of employment or the removal from employment in an executive department or agency on grounds relating to loyalty shall be that, on all the evidence, reasonable grounds exist for belief that the person involved is disloyal to the Government of the United States."[4] Despite the plain words "all the evidence", the court rules that the Order requires no evidence and authorizes findings based on unsworn confidential reports of unsworn statements of anonymous informants as to their beliefs concerning an employee's affiliations. I think the Order does no such thing. . . .

II. *Dismissal for disloyalty is punishment and requires all the safeguards of a judicial trial.* Most dismissals, including among others dismissals for colorless or undisclosed reasons and dismissals for incompetence, are plainly not punitive. . . .

Punishment is infliction of harm, usually for wrong conduct but in appellant's case for wrong views. Dismissals to provide jobs for persons of certain

---

[3] 12 Fed. Reg. 1935.

[4] Part V, 1.

affiliations, whatever else may be said of such dismissals, are not punitive. But dismissals for disloyal views are punitive. . . .

. . . Appellant was dismissed from a nonsensitive position. She was a staff training officer in the United States Employment Service. In the case of such an officer, no way is apparent and none has been suggested in which "suspicion of disloyalty indicates a risk" to the security of the United States. *Appellant's dismissal for wrong thoughts has nothing to do with protecting the security of the United States.* . . .

Appellant's dismissal attributes guilt by association, and thereby denies both the freedom of assembly guaranteed by the First Amendment and the due process of law guaranteed by the Fifth. The appellant was dismissed as disloyal because she was believed to be a member or associate of the Communist Party. Undoubtedly many such persons are disloyal in every sense to the government of the United States. But the Supreme Court has held that a particular member of the Communist Party may be "attached to the principles of the Constitution" within the meaning of those words in a naturalization act: "As Justice Holmes said, 'Surely it cannot show lack of attachment to the principles of the Constitution that . . . [one] thinks it can be improved. . . .' If there is any principle of the Constitution that more imperatively calls for attachment than any other it is the principle of free thought — not free thought for those who agree with us but freedom for the thought that we hate." "Under our traditions, beliefs are personal and not a matter of mere association, and . . . men in adhering to a political party or other organization notoriously do not subscribe unqualifiedly to all of its platforms or asserted principles." As was said more recently, "To condemn or to interdict all members of a named political party is an abridgment of free speech, press and assembly. The Communist Party in this country is recognized as a political party."[39]

The court thinks Miss Bailey's interest and the public interest conflict. I think they coincide. Since Miss Bailey's dismissal from a nonsensitive job has nothing to do with protecting the security of the United States, the government's right to preserve itself in the world as it is has nothing to do with this case. The ominous theory that the right of fair trial ends where defense of security begins is irrelevant.

On this record we have no sufficient reason to suppose that an unpatriotic person in her job could do substantial harm of any kind. Whatever her actual thoughts may have been, to oust her as disloyal without trial is to pay too much for protection against any harm that could possibly be done in such a job. The cost is too great in morale and efficiency of government workers, in appeal of government employment to independent and inquiring minds, and in public confidence in democracy. But even if such dismissals strengthened the government instead of weakening it, they would still cost too much in constitutional rights. We cannot preserve our liberties by sacrificing them.

---

[39] Prettyman, Circuit Judge, dissenting, in *National Maritime Union of America v. Herzog,* D.C., 78 F. Supp. 146, 177, 178. The Supreme Court affirmed the decision of the court on other grounds, saying: "We do not find it necessary to reach or consider the validity of § 9(h)" of the National Labor Relations Act as amended, 29 U.S.C.A. § 159(h), which required non-Communist affidavits. *National Maritime Union of America v. Herzog,* 334 U.S. 854-855.

NOTES AND QUESTIONS

2-1. What is the basis of the right/privilege distinction as expressed by the court in *Bailey*? Why does the majority of the court decide that the public interest takes precedence over Dorothy Bailey's individual rights? Why does the dissent take an individual rights approach? What values does the Due Process Clause further? Can these be balanced against the public interest? Does the majority engage in balancing, or does the designation of what is at issue as a privilege rather than a right preclude any such balancing?

2-2. Dorothy Bailey was 39 when she was fired in 1949 from her $8,000-a-year job as a training officer in the U.S. Employment Service of the Federal Security Agency. Is this the kind of executive branch official the President is expected to control directly? What do you think her chances of securing future employment were?

2-3. Consider the following account of this case in Laura Kalman's biography of Abe Fortas,* recounting how the firm of Arnold, Fortas and Porter had represented Dorothy Bailey:

> When the Court of Appeals upheld the trial court, Arnold swung his attention toward persuading the Supreme Court to grant certiorari. Despite Paul Porter's fear "that this is the kind of issue the majority may want to duck," the Court decided to hear the case.
>
> "The Dorothy Bailey argument went very well," Porter reported after presenting the case to the Supreme Court. "What the press refers to as 'veteran court observers' told me privately that they had never seen a Solicitor General take the pummelling which Perlman got from Felix [Frankfurter], Jackson and Black. . . . When Perlman rose to argue it was a question of who was going to get him first." When Solicitor General Perlman maintained that the loyalty boards had not forever barred Bailey from federal employment, because she could take the competitive examinations for a government position again, Justice Jackson interrupted. He did not mind being amused, Jackson said, but he did not want to be made a laughing stock. Did Perlman mean that Bailey could ever again get a federal job? As a practical matter she could not, the solicitor general conceded, but in theory she remained eligible. Did the government really wish to win the case on that point, Jackson asked? Perlman replied that the government had other points.
>
> But the Court received the solicitor general's other points equally unenthusiastically. Perlman contended, for example, that the character of loyalty board members ensured any accused of a fair hearing. Justice Frankfurter replied that, although he appreciated the board members' high character, they had exercised no judgment of their own in this particular case. Hugo Black then intervened. He forced the solicitor general to admit that since

---

* L.Kalman, *Abe Fortas: A Biography* (1990). Copyright © 1990 by Yale University Press. All rights reserved.

loyalty board members had not seen the unknown informant against Bailey, the FBI agent who interviewed the informant, or the FBI agent who certified the informant's reliability, they were in no position to evaluate the evidence. "It was really quite a clam bake," Porter concluded. He was cautiously optimistic after the argument. Douglas, Frankfurter, Black, and Jackson seemed sympathetic. Porter believed that the outcome depended largely on Justice Reed and thought "that the triumvirate of Frankfurter, Black and Jackson was needling Perlman primarily for the purpose of educating their brethren on the bench. I am optimistically placing great hope on Reed's innate sense of fairness." Nor had Porter given up on Fred Vinson, though he did not think that the chief justice "would be too upset if an affirmance resulted."

Porter's hoped-for majority did not materialize. Only four justices voted to reverse. As Justice Tom Clark had disqualified himself because he had been attorney general when the loyalty program took effect, a Court equally divided upheld the government's decision to fire Bailey without giving her the right to confront her accusers. Because it was tied, the Court issued no opinion in Bailey. On the same day, the Court released its opinion in *Joint Anti-Fascist Refugee Committee v. McGrath*. There Justice Burton, who had never figured in Porter's calculations, joined Douglas, Black, Jackson, and Frankfurter in extending due process rights to organizations. The Court ruled that the attorney general could not label an organization subversive without first giving it the opportunity to prove the falseness of such a classification at a hearing. Since membership in an organization on the attorney general's subversive list often proved the basis for a loyalty board investigation, the two cases were linked. "So far as I recall, this is the first time this Court has held the rights of individuals subordinate and inferior to organized groups," Justice Jackson said in his *Joint Anti-Fascist Refugee Committee* concurrence. "It is justice turned bottom-side up." Douglas used his concurrence to attack *Bailey*. "I do not see how the constitutionality of this dragnet system of loyalty trials which has been entrusted to the administrative agencies of government can be sustained." Still, his outrage did little to help Dorothy Bailey. Since she could not find a job, Arnold, Fortas & Porter hired her as office manager.

2-4. For purposes of Article II of the Constitution, was Dorothy Bailey an "officer of the United States"? An "inferior officer"? We will examine the removal powers of the executive in detail in Chapter 7, § 7.03, *infra*.

2-5. As Professor Van Alstyne has noted, *Bailey v. Richardson* was, perhaps, the last gasp of the right/privilege distinction. *See Cracks In "The New Property": Adjudicative Due Process in the Administrative State,* 62 CORNELL L. REV. 445, 446 (1977). The result in this case, nevertheless, coincided with a period in which governmental suspicion concerning membership in or affiliation with the Communist Party reigned supreme. Consider the following editorial cartoon from the *New York Times*, March 26, 1950, IV 3:1:*

---

* From the Buffalo Courier-Express Collection courtesy of Buffalo State Archives and the Buffalo and Erie County Historical Society.

'SIFTING THEM OUT'

Roche in The Buffalo Courier-Express

2-6. To what extent do you think the "times" influenced the outcome of this case? National security in general? The logic of the right/privilege distinction?

2-7. The right/privilege distinction has a long history in American law. Perhaps one of its most famous applications was by Justice Holmes in *McAulife v. Mayor of New Bedford,* 155 Mass. 216, 29 N.E. 517 (1892), in which a policeman challenged his dismissal from the force because, he claimed, it was based on the exercise of his First Amendment rights. Holmes stated that "the petitioner may have a constitutional right to talk politics, but he has no constitutional right to be a policeman." 155 Mass. at 220, 29 N.E. at 517. Holmes went on to explain:

> There are few employments for hire in which the servant does not agree to suspend his constitutional right of free speech, as well as of idleness by the implied terms of his contract. The servant cannot complain, as he takes the employment on the terms which are offered him.

155 Mass. at 229, 29 N.E. at 517-18.

What are the implications of this logic when applied to the variety of roles the government plays today? Was this doctrine a product of a time when one could say that the role of government was, relative to today, minimal? Consider Professor Van Alstyne's analysis in *The Demise of the Right-Privilege Distinction in Constitutional Law:**

---

* 81 HARV. L. REV. 1439, 1441 (1968). Copyright © 1968 by the Harvard Law Review Association. All rights reserved.

If [the right/privilege distinction] were uniformly applied the devastating effect it would have on any constitutional claims within the public sector can be readily perceived. A public housing tenant summarily evicted without a hearing or any stated reason should have no basis for complaint: surely one no more has a right to public housing than to public employment; in either case he simply takes the benefit on the terms offered him. An impoverished couple actually domiciled in a state should still have no complaint against a one-year residence requirement for welfare recipients: one may have a right to equal protection, but he has no right to public welfare. . . .

As we examine the breakdown of this doctrine and the "due process explosion" that followed, note how the constitutional logic of the Court's more modern approaches to these issues seems to create a need to limit their applicability. Will the right/privilege distinction appear in a new form? Stay tuned.

CAFETERIA & RESTAURANT WORKERS UNION v. McELROY

United States Supreme Court
367 U.S. 886 (1961)

Mr. Justice Stewart delivered the opinion of the Court.

In 1956 the petitioner Rachel Brawner was a short-order cook at a cafeteria operated by her employer, M & M Restaurants, Inc., on the premises of the Naval Gun Factory in the city of Washington. She had worked there for more than six years, and from her employer's point of view her record was entirely satisfactory.

The Gun Factory was engaged in designing, producing, and inspecting naval ordnance, including the development of weapons systems of a highly classified nature. Located on property owned by the United States, the installation was under the command of Rear Admiral D.M. Tyree, Superintendent. Access to it was restricted, and guards were posted at all points of entry. Identification badges were issued to persons authorized to enter the premises by the Security Officer, a naval officer subordinate to the Superintendent. In 1956 the Security Officer was Lieutenant Commander H.C. Williams. Rachel Brawner had been issued such a badge.

The cafeteria where she worked was operated by M & M under a contract with the Board of Governors of the Gun Factory. Section 5(b) of the contract provided:

> . . . In no event shall the Concessionaire engage, or continue to engage, for operations under this Agreement, personnel who . . .
>
> (iii) fail to meet the security requirements or other requirements under applicable regulations of the Activity, as determined by the Security Officer of the Activity.

On November 15, 1956, Mrs. Brawner was required to turn in her identification badge because of Lieutenant Commander Williams' determination that she had failed to meet the security requirements of the installation. The Security Officer's determination was subsequently approved by Admiral Tyree, who cited § 5(b)(iii) of the contract as the basis for his action. At the request of the petitioner Union, which represented the employees at the cafeteria, M & M sought to arrange a meeting with officials of the Gun Factory "for the purpose of a hearing regarding the denial of admittance to the Naval Gun Factory of Rachel Brawner." This request was denied by Admiral Tyree on the ground that such a meeting would "serve no useful purpose."

Since the day her identification badge was withdrawn Mrs. Brawner has not been permitted to enter the Gun Factory. M & M offered to employ her in another restaurant which the company operated in the suburban Washington area, but she refused on the ground that the location was inconvenient.

The petitioners brought this action in the District Court . . . seeking, among other things, to compel the return to Mrs. Brawner of her identification badge, so that she might be permitted to enter the Gun Factory and resume her former employment. The defendants filed a motion for summary judgment . . . . The motion was granted . . . . This judgment was affirmed by the Court of Appeals for the District of Columbia, sitting *en banc*. . . .

As the case comes here, two basic questions are presented. Was the commanding officer of the Gun Factory authorized to deny Rachel Brawner access to the installation in the way he did? If he was so authorized, did his action in excluding her operate to deprive her of any right secured to her by the Constitution?

I.

[The Court concluded that the commanding officer had the authority to deny Rachel Brawner access to the installation.]

II.

The question remains whether Admiral Tyree's action in summarily denying Rachel Brawner access to the site of her former employment violated the requirements of the Due Process Clause of the Fifth Amendment. This question cannot be answered by easy assertion that, because she had no constitutional right to be there in the first place, she was not deprived of liberty or property by the Superintendent's action. "One may not have a constitutional right to go to Baghdad, but the Government may not prohibit one from going there unless by means consonant with due process of law." *Homer v. Richmond,* 110 U.S. App. D.C. 226, 229, 292 F.2d 719, 722. It is the petitioners' claim that due process in this case required that Rachel Brawner be advised of the specific grounds for her exclusion and be accorded a hearing at which she might refute them. We are satisfied, however, that under the circumstances of this case such a procedure was not constitutionally required.

The Fifth Amendment does not require a trial-type hearing in every conceivable case of government impairment of private interest. "For, though 'due process of law' generally implies and includes *actor, reus, judex,* regular allegations, opportunity to answer, and a trial according to some settled course of judicial proceedings, . . . yet, this is not universally true." *Murray's Lessee v. Hoboken Land and Improvement Co.,* 18 How. 272, 280. The very nature of due process negates any concept of inflexible procedures universally applicable to every imaginable situation. . . . " '[D]ue process,' unlike some legal rules, is not a technical conception with a fixed content unrelated to time, place and circumstances." It is "compounded of history, reason, the past course of decisions. . . ." *Joint Anti-Fascist Comm. v. McGrath,* 341 U.S. 123, 162-163 (concurring opinion).

As these and other cases make clear, consideration of what procedures due process may require under any given set of circumstances must begin with a determination of the precise nature of the government function involved as well as of the private interest that has been affected by governmental action. Where it has been possible to characterize that private interest (perhaps in oversimplification) as a mere privilege subject to the Executive's plenary power, it has traditionally been held that notice and hearing are not constitutionally required. . . .

What, then, was the private interest affected by Admiral Tyree's action in the present case? It most assuredly was not the right to follow a chosen trade or profession. . . . Rachel Brawner remained entirely free to obtain employment as a short-order cook or to get any other job, either with M & M or with any other employer. All that was denied her was the opportunity to work at one isolated and specific military installation.

Moreover, the governmental function operating here was not the power to regulate or license, as lawmaker, an entire trade or profession, or to control an entire branch of private business, but, rather, as proprietor, to manage the internal operation of an important federal military establishment. . . . In that proprietary military capacity, the Federal Government, as has been pointed out, has traditionally exercised unfettered control.

. . . This case . . . involves the Federal Government's dispatch of its own internal affairs. The Court has consistently recognized that an interest closely analogous to Rachel Brawner's, the interest of a government employee in retaining his job, can be summarily denied. It has become a settled principle that government employment, in the absence of legislation, can be revoked at the will of the appointing officer. . . .

It is argued that this view of Rachel Brawner's interest is inconsistent with our decisions in *United Public Workers v. Mitchell,* 330 U.S. 75, and *Wieman v. Updegraff,* 344 U.S. 183. In those two cases an individual's interest in government employment was recognized as entitled to constitutional protection, and it is contended that what the Court said in deciding them would require us to hold that Rachel Brawner was entitled to notice and hearing in this case. In *United Public Workers* the Court observed that "[n]one would deny" that "Congress may not 'enact a regulation providing that no Republican, Jew or Negro shall be appointed to federal office, or that no federal employee shall attend Mass or take any active part in missionary work.'" 330 U.S., at 100. In *Wieman* the Court held unconstitutional a statute which excluded persons from state employment solely on the basis of membership in alleged "Communist-front" or "subversive" organizations, regardless of their knowledge concerning the activities and purposes of the organizations to which they had belonged. In the course of its decision the Court said, "We need not pause to consider whether an abstract right to public employment exists. It is sufficient to say that constitutional protection does extend to the public servant whose exclusion pursuant to a statute is patently arbitrary or discriminatory." 344 U.S., at 192.

Nothing that was said or decided in *United Public Workers* or *Wieman* would lead to the conclusion that Rachel Brawner could not be denied access to the Gun Factory without notice and an opportunity to be heard. Those cases demonstrate only that the state and federal governments, even in the exercise of their internal operations, do not constitutionally have the complete freedom of action enjoyed by a private employer. But to acknowledge that there exist constitutional restraints upon state and federal governments in dealing with their employees is not to say that all such employees have a constitutional right to notice and a hearing before they can be removed. We may assume that Rachel Brawner could not constitutionally have been excluded from the Gun Factory if the announced grounds for her exclusion had been patently arbitrary or discriminatory — that she could not have been kept out because she was a Democrat or a Methodist. It does not follow, however, that she was entitled to notice and a hearing when the reason advanced for her exclusion was, as here, entirely rational and in accord with the contract with M & M.

Finally, it is to be noted that this is not a case where government action has operated to bestow a badge of disloyalty or infamy, with an attendant foreclosure from other employment opportunity. . . . All this record shows is that, in the opinion of the Security Officer of the Gun Factory, concurred in by the Superintendent, Rachel Brawner failed to meet the particular security requirements of that specific military installation. There is nothing to indicate that this determination would in any way impair Rachel Brawner's employment opportunities anywhere else.[10] As pointed out by Judge Prettyman, speaking for the Court of Appeals, "Nobody has said that Brawner is disloyal or is suspected of the slightest shadow of intentional wrongdoing. 'Security requirements' at such an installation, like such requirements under many other circumstances, cover many matters other than loyalty." . . . For all that appears, the Security Officer and the Superintendent may have simply thought that Rachel Brawner was garrulous, or careless with her identification badge.

For these reasons, we conclude that the Due Process Clause of the Fifth Amendment was not violated in this case.

Affirmed.

Mr. Justice Brennan, with whom The Chief Justice [Warren], Mr. Justice Black and Mr. Justice Douglas join, dissenting.

---

[10] In oral argument, government counsel emphatically represented that denial of access to the Gun Factory would not "by law or in fact" prevent Rachel Brawner from obtaining employment on any other federal property.

I read the Court's opinion to acknowledge that petitioner's status as an employee at the Gun Factory was an interest of sufficient definiteness to be protected by the Federal Constitution from some kinds of governmental injury. . . . In other words, if petitioner Brawner's badge had been lifted avowedly on grounds of her race, religion, or political opinions, the Court would concede that some constitutionally protected interest — whether "liberty" or "property" it is unnecessary to state — had been injured. But, as the Court says, there has been no such open discrimination here. The expressed ground of exclusion was the obscuring formulation that petitioner failed to meet the "security requirements" of the naval installation where she worked. I assume for present purposes that separation as a "security risk," if the charge is properly established, is not unconstitutional. But the Court goes beyond that. It holds that the mere assertion by government that exclusion is for a valid reason forecloses further inquiry. That is, unless the government official is foolish enough to admit what he is doing — and few will be so foolish after today's decision — he may employ "security requirements" as a blind behind which to dismiss at will for the most discriminatory of causes.

Such a result in effect nullifies the substantive right — not to be arbitrarily injured by Government — which the Court purports to recognize. What sort of right is it which enjoys absolutely no procedural protection? I do not mean to imply that petitioner could not have been excluded from the installation without the full procedural panoply of first having been subjected to a trial, with cross-examination and confrontation of accusers, and proof of guilt beyond a reasonable doubt. I need not go so far in this case. For under today's holding petitioner is entitled to no process at all. She is not told what she did wrong; she is not given a chance to defend herself. She may be the victim of the basest calumny, perhaps even the caprice of the government officials in whose power her status rested completely. In such a case, I cannot believe that she is not entitled to some procedures. "[T]he right to be heard before being condemned to suffer grievous loss of any kind, even though it may not involve the stigma and hardships of a criminal conviction, is a principle basic to our society." *Joint Anti-Fascist Refugee Comm. v. McGrath,* 341 U.S. 123, 168 (1951) (concurring opinion). . . . In sum, the Court holds that petitioner has a right not to have her identification badge taken away for an "arbitrary" reason, but no right to be told in detail what the reason is, or to defend her own innocence, in order to show, perhaps, that the true reason for deprivation was one forbidden by the Constitution. That is an internal contradiction to which I cannot subscribe.

One further circumstance makes this particularly a case where procedural requirements of fairness are essential. Petitioner was not simply excluded from the base summarily, without a notice and chance to defend herself. She was excluded as a "security risk," that designation most odious in our times. The Court consoles itself with the speculation that she may have been merely garrulous, or careless with her identification badge, and indeed she might, although she will never find out. But, in the common understanding of the public with whom petitioner must hereafter live and work, the term "security risk" carries a much more sinister meaning. . . . It is far more likely to be taken as an accusation of communism or disloyalty than imputation of some small personal fault. Perhaps the Government has reasons for lumping such a multitude of sins under a misleading term. But it ought not to affix a "badge of infamy," . . . to a person without some statement of charges, and some opportunity to speak in reply.

It may be, of course, that petitioner was justly excluded from the Gun Factory. But, in my view, it is fundamentally unfair, and therefore violative of the Due Process Clause of the Fifth Amendment, to deprive her of a valuable relationship so summarily.

NOTES AND QUESTIONS

2-8. What test does the majority set forth to determine whether due process protections are in order? How does this test differ from the right/privilege approach?

2-9. How does the Court frame the issue in this case? Specifically, what does it balance against the security interests of the U.S.? Ms. Brawner's reputation? Her ability to get another job as a short-order cook? Does a balancing approach provide much guidance in cases like these? Is the Court clear on just what should be balanced and how this is to be done? Through whose eyes is this case viewed?

2-10. Of what relevance should Rachel Brawner's future employability be? The newspaper accounts of this case when it reached the Supreme Court noted that though "her union . . . did not know whether she is presently employed," she had "worked off and on at non-government cafeterias." *Wash. Post,* June 20, 1961, A4, col. 1. Should this affect the outcome of the case? What is the significance of footnote 10? If you were Ms. Brawner's lawyer, how would you frame the issue in this case? What kind of trial record would you try to create?

§ 2.03 The Demise of the Right/Privilege Distinction

The right/privilege distinction and legal doctrine that it triggered may have been appropriate for a period in our history when the role of government was relatively minimal. It failed, however, to provide any individual protections from arbitrary governmental action when the role of government expanded considerably. A new conceptualization of both the problem and its legal solution was necessary. The common law did not fully take into account the fact that the ownership of private property did not necessarily include property provided by the government in the form of benefits or largesse of some kinds. For the Due Process Clause to apply, such benefits would have to be considered a form of property. Similarly, other aspects of day-to-day life such as education needed to be seen not as a privilege, but as a right.

Cafeteria Workers was the beginning of an important shift in the law. *Cafeteria Workers* opened the door for new doctrinal developments such as those in the Fifth Circuit Court of Appeals that were linked with the civil rights movement. In *Dixon v. Alabama State Board of Education,* 294 F.2d

150 (5th Cir. 1961), for example, the question presented to the court was "whether due process requires notice and some opportunity for hearing before students at a tax-supported college are expelled for misconduct." *Id.* at 151. The alleged misconduct involved was taking part in a civil rights demonstration, though, as the court noted, the notice of expulsion "assigned no specific ground for expulsion, but referred in general terms to this problem of Alabama State College." *Id.* at 152. In applying the Due Process Clause to these events, the court reasoned:

> Whenever a governmental body acts so as to injure an individual, the Constitution requires that the act be consonant with due process of law. The minimum procedural requirements necessary to satisfy due process depend upon the circumstances and the interests of the parties involved. As stated by Mr. Justice Frankfurter concurring in *Joint Anti-Fascist Refugee Committee v. McGrath,* 341 U.S. 123, 163, 1951:
>
>> Whether the *ex parte* procedure to which the petitioners were subjected duly observed "the rudiments of fair play,". . . cannot . . . be tested by mere generalities or sentiments abstractly appealing. The precise nature of the interest that has been adversely affected, the manner in which this was done, the reasons for doing it, the available alternatives to the procedure that was followed, the protection implicit in the office of the functionary whose conduct is challenged, the balance of hurt complained of and good accomplished — these are some of the considerations that must enter into the judicial judgment.

> Just last month, a closely divided Supreme Court held in a case where the governmental power was almost absolute and the private interest was slight that no hearing was required. *Cafeteria and Restaurant Workers Union v. McElroy et al.,* 1961, 81 S. Ct. 1743. . . . So, too, the Due Process Clause does not require that an alien never admitted to this Country be granted a hearing before being *excluded. United States ex rel. Knauff v. Shaughnessy,* 1950, 338 U.S. 537, 542, 543. . . . In such case the executive power as implemented by Congress to *exclude* aliens is absolute and not subject to the review of any court, unless expressly authorized by Congress. On the other hand, once an alien has been admitted to lawful residence in the United States and remains physically present here it has been held that, "although Congress may prescribe conditions for his expulsion and deportation, not even Congress may expel him without allowing him a fair opportunity to be heard." *Kwong Hai Chew v. Colding,* 1953, 344 U.S. 590, 597, 598. . . .

> It is not enough to say, as did the district court in the present case, "The right to attend a public college or university is not in and of itself a constitutional right." 186 F. Supp. at page 950. That argument was emphatically answered by the Supreme Court in the *Cafeteria and Restaurant Workers Union* case, *supra,* [81 S. Ct. 1748] when it said that the question of whether ". . . summarily denying Rachel Brawner access to the site of her former employment violated the requirements of the Due Process Clause of the Fifth Amendment . . . cannot be answered by easy assertion that,

because she had no constitutional right to be there in the first place, she was not deprived of liberty or property by the Superintendent's action. 'One may not have a constitutional right to go to Baghdad, but the Government may not prohibit one from going there unless by means consonant with due process of law.'" As in that case, so here, it is necessary to consider "the nature both of the private interest which has been impaired and the governmental power which has been exercised. . . ."

The precise nature of the private interest involved in this case is the right to remain at a public institution of higher learning in which the plaintiffs were students in good standing. It requires no argument to demonstrate that education is vital and, indeed, basic to civilized society. Without sufficient education the plaintiffs would not be able to earn an adequate livelihood, to enjoy life to the fullest, or to fulfill as completely as possible the duties and responsibilities of good citizens.

There was no offer to prove that other colleges are open to the plaintiffs. If so, the plaintiffs would nonetheless be injured by the interruption of their course of studies in mid-term. It is most unlikely that a public college would accept a student expelled from another public college of the same state. Indeed, expulsion may well prejudice the student in completing his education at any other institution. Surely no one can question that the right to remain at the college in which the plaintiffs were students in good standing is an interest of extremely great value.

Turning then to the nature of the governmental power to expel the plaintiffs, it must be conceded, as was held by the district court, that that power is not unlimited and cannot be arbitrarily exercised. Admittedly, there must be some reasonable and constitutional ground for expulsion or the courts would have a duty to require reinstatement. The possibility of arbitrary action is not excluded by the existence of reasonable regulations. There may be arbitrary application of the rule to the facts of a particular case. Indeed, that result is well nigh inevitable when the Board hears only one side of the issue. In the disciplining of college students there are no considerations of immediate danger to the public, or of peril to the national security, which should prevent the Board from exercising at least the fundamental principles of fairness by giving the accused students notice of the charges and an opportunity to be heard in their own defense. Indeed, the example set by the Board in failing so to do, if not corrected by the courts, can well break the spirits of the expelled students and of others familiar with the injustice, and do inestimable harm to their education. . . .

Id. at 155-157.

What test does this court propose for dealing with such issues? What do you think of its balancing approach? Did the court provide any guidance as to what goes into that balance and, specifically, the criteria used to make such determinations? At the hearing the court orders, what do you think the state will give as its reasons for expulsion? If those reasons involve the participation in constitutionally protected activities, can its decision be upheld? Can students, implicitly, agree to waive their constitutional rights by attending a state college?

The right/privilege distinction also had a long history of application in various licensing contexts. A license from the state was a privilege, not a right. This requirement, however, provided those in authority with the power to issue or deny issuance of licenses for a variety of reasons, some of them corrupt. Indeed, could the political party that wins an election issue licenses to reward its friends and punish its enemies? Was that likely to occur? The Fifth Circuit, speaking through Chief Judge Tuttle, confronted this issue in *Hornsby v. Allen*, 326 F.2d 605 (1964), where Mrs. Hornsby, an unsuccessful applicant for a license to operate a retail liquor store in Atlanta, filed suit against the Mayor, the City Clerk and the Aldermen of Atlanta.

In her complaint, Mrs. Hornsby alleges that although she met all the requirements and qualifications, as to moral character of the applicant and proposed location of the store, prescribed for the holder of a retail liquor dealer's license, her application was denied "without a reason therefore" by the Mayor and Board of Aldermen. This action is characterized as "arbitrary, unreasonable, unjust, capricious, discriminatory" and in contravention of the due process and equal protection clauses of the 14th Amendment. The complaint also charges that a system of ward courtesy was followed in the issuance of liquor licenses; under this system licenses allegedly would be granted only upon the approval of one or both of the aldermen of the ward in which the store was to be located. This too is said to constitute a violation of the 14th Amendment. . . .

The appellees here, however, seek to place liquor in a special category, and argue that since Georgia has declared a license to sell spirituous liquor to be a privilege, the licensing authority has an unreviewable discretion to grant or deny licenses. It is firmly established, of course, that the state has the right to regulate or prohibit traffic in intoxicating liquor in the valid exercise of its police power . . . but this is something quite different from a right to act arbitrarily and capriciously. Merely calling a liquor license a privilege does not free the municipal authorities from the due process requirements in licensing and allow them to exercise an uncontrolled discretion. There is no suggestion here that Georgia has sought to declare the sale of retail liquor to be a public business which can be franchised by the state and treated as devoted to a public use, as the State of Oklahoma did with cotton ginning. . . . To the contrary, the State of Georgia has limited municipalities in the exercise of their authority over liquor businesses to those *reasonable* rules and regulations which fall within their police powers. . . .

We find in this case that Mrs. Hornsby's allegations, if borne out by the evidence, are sufficient to show a violation of her 14th Amendment rights. If her application actually was denied because the delegation from her ward decided, from their own knowledge of the circumstances, that Mrs. Hornsby should not be issued a liquor license, then she was deprived of the hearing which due process requires, since she could not discover the claims of those opposing her and subject their evidence to cross-examination. In addition, Mrs. Hornsby was not afforded an opportunity to know through reasonable regulations promulgated by the board, of the objective standards which had to be met to obtain a license. Next, the alleged failure of the board to reveal the basis for denying her application would, if true, be a denial of her right to have the board make findings based on the evidence adduced at a hearing. Moreover, appellees themselves indicate that the mandates of equal protection were not observed in the awarding of liquor licenses: "[I]n granting a mere privilege, appellant cites no authority which would prevent the defendants [appellees] from arbitrarily accepting one eligible application while denying others; otherwise they would, of necessity, be forced to grant licenses to every eligible citizen upon application." Brief for Appellees, p. 7. If there are too many qualified applicants, then the proper remedy is for the Board of Aldermen to adopt reasonable rules and regulations which will raise the standards of eligibility or fix limits on the number of licenses which may be issued in an area; the solution is not to make arbitrary selections among those qualified. . . .

How does this case compare to the one set forth in Problem 1-1, in Chapter One?

§ 2.04 Due Process, the War on Poverty and the New Property

As both the perception and the reality of an increasingly active governmental role took hold, the inadequacies of the right/privilege distinction became apparent. A broader conceptualization of property and property rights was suggested by Professor Charles Reich in a very influential law review article entitled *The New Property,* 73 YALE L.J. 733 (1964). As you consider his approach and the Supreme Court's adoption of it in *Goldberg v. Kelly,* 397 U.S. 254 (1970), which follows, consider whether the common law would have protected the property rights involved in *Goldberg.* Can you distinguish the issues in contention in *Dixon* and *Hornsby* from those in *Goldberg?* Were the governmental benefits of education in *Dixon* and a liquor license in *Hornsby* being revoked or denied for reasons that raised constitutional issues, quite apart from the Due Process Clause? Was a hearing likely to reveal these reasons or force the government to recognize that it had no public interest reasons for taking the action it took? What is the purpose of the hearing mandated in *Goldberg,* as conceptualized by Professor Reich in *The New Property?*

Reich, THE NEW PROPERTY

73 YALE L.J. 733, 733-38 (1964)*

The institution called property guards the troubled boundary between individual man and the state. It is not the only guardian; many other institutions, laws, and practices serve as well. But in a society that chiefly

---

* Reprinted by permission of The Yale Law Journal Company and William S. Hein Company from The Yale Law Journal, Vol. 73, 733-787.

values material well–being, the power to control a particular portion of that well–being is the very foundation of individuality.

One of the most important developments in the United States during the past decade has been the emergence of government as a major source of wealth. Government is a gigantic syphon. It draws in revenue and power, and pours forth wealth: money, benefits, services, contracts, franchises, and licenses. Government has always had this function. But while in early times it was minor, today's distribution of largess is on a vast, imperial scale.

The valuables dispensed by government take many forms, but they all share one characteristic. They are steadily taking the place of traditional forms of wealth — forms which are held as private property. Social insurance substitutes for savings; a government contract replaces a businessman's customers and goodwill. The wealth of more and more Americans depends upon a relationship to government. Increasingly, Americans live on government largess — allocated by government on its own terms, and held by recipients subject to conditions which express "the public interest."

The growth of government largess, accompanied by a distinctive system of law, is having profound consequences. It affects the underpinnings of individualism and independence. It influences the workings of the Bill of Rights. It has an impact on the power of private interests, in their relation to each other and to government. It is helping to create a new society. . . .

How important is governmentally dispensed wealth in relation to the total economic life of the nation? In 1961, when personal income totalled $416,432,000,000, governmental expenditures on all levels amounted to $164,875,000,000. The governmental payroll alone approached forty-five billion dollars. And these figures do not take account of the vast intangible wealth represented by licenses, franchises, services, and resources. Moreover, the *proportion* of governmental wealth is increasing. Hardly any citizen leads his life without at least partial dependence on wealth flowing through the giant government syphon.

In many cases, this dependence is not voluntary. Valuables that flow from government are often substitutes for, rather than supplements to, other forms of wealth. Social Security and other forms of public insurance and compensation are supported by taxes. This tax money is no longer available for individual savings or insurance. The taxpayer is a participant in public insurance by compulsion, and his ability to care for his own needs independently is correspondingly reduced. Similarly, there is no choice about using public transportation, public lands for recreation, public airport terminals, or public insurance on savings deposits. In these and countless other areas, government is the sole supplier. Moreover, the increasing dominance of scientific technology, so largely a product of government research and development, generates an even greater dependence on government.

Dependence creates a vicious circle of dependence. It is as hard for a business to give up government help as it is for an individual to live on a reduced income. And when one sector of the economy is subsidized, others are forced to seek comparable participation. . . .

The prospect is that government largess will necessarily assume ever greater importance as we move closer to a welfare state. Such a state, whatever its particular form, undertakes responsibility for the well-being of those citizens who, because of circumstances beyond their control, cannot provide minimum care, education, housing, or subsistence for themselves. This responsibility can only be carried out by means of what we have defined as government largess.

This reconceptualization of the relationship between citizens and their government was based on the fact that the new dependencies that Reich pointed out were now to be considered entitlements. Legal entitlements to certain governmental relationships were now to be considered as property. Presumably, they would provide the same kind of protection for the individual that traditional forms of private property provided in earlier eras. Thus, Reich notes, *id.* at 773-74[*] that property was now coming full circle:

> During the first half of the twentieth century, the reformers enacted into law their conviction that private power was a chief enemy of society and of individual liberty. Property was subjected to "reasonable" limitations in the interests of society. The regulatory agencies, federal and state, were born of the reform. In sustaining these major inroads on private property, the Supreme Court rejected the older idea that property and liberty were one, and wrote a series of classic opinions upholding the power of the people to regulate and limit private rights.
>
> The struggle between abuse and reform made it easy to forget the basic importance of individual private property. The defense of private property was almost entirely a defense of its abuses — an attempt to defend not individual property but arbitrary private power over other human beings. Since this defense was cloaked in a defense of private property, it was natural for the reformers to attack too broadly. Walter Lippmann saw this in 1934:
>
>> But the issue between the giant corporation and the public should not be allowed to obscure the truth that the only dependable foundation of personal liberty is the economic security of private property. . . .
>>
>> For we must not expect to find in ordinary men the stuff of martyrs, and we must, therefore, secure their freedom by their normal motives. There is no surer way to give men the courage to be free than to insure them a competence upon which they can rely.
>
> The reform took away some of the power of the corporations and transferred it to government. In this transfer there was much good, for power was made responsive to the majority rather than to the arbitrary and selfish few. But the reform did not restore the individual to his domain. What the corporation had taken from him, the reform simply handed on to government. And government carried further the powers formerly exercised by the corporation. Government as an employer, or as a dispenser of wealth, has used the theory that it was handing out gratuities to claim a managerial power as

---

[*] Reprinted by permission of The Yale Law Journal Company and William S. Hein Company from The Yale Law Journal, Vol. 73, 733-787.

great as that which the capitalists claimed. Moreover, the corporations allied themselves with, or actually took over, part of government's system of power. Today it is the combined power of government and the corporations that presses against the individual.

From the individual's point of view, it is not any particular kind of power, but all kinds of power, that are to be feared. This is the lesson of the public interest state. The mere fact that power is derived from the majority does not necessarily make it less oppressive. Liberty is more than the right to do what the majority wants, or to do what is "reasonable." Liberty is the right to defy the majority, and to do what is unreasonable. The great error of the public interest state is that it assumes an identity between the public interest and the interest of the majority.

The reform, then, has not done away with the importance of private property. More than ever the individual needs to possess, in whatever form, a small but sovereign island of his own.

To what extent does the Court in *Goldberg v. Kelly* accept Professor Reich's approach? By providing a legal entitlement to welfare benefits, does the Court create a "small but sovereign island" for the individual? On what basis does the Court conclude that welfare benefits constitute "property"? What procedural approaches protect this property? Does this case involve substantive as well as procedural due process?

GOLDBERG v. KELLY

United States Supreme Court
397 U.S. 254 (1970)

Mr. Justice Brennan delivered the opinion of the Court.

The question for decision is whether a State that terminates public assistance payments to a particular recipient without affording him the opportunity for an evidentiary hearing prior to termination denies the recipient procedural due process in violation of the Due Process Clause of the Fourteenth Amendment.

This action was brought in the District Court for the Southern District of New York by residents of New York City receiving financial aid under the federally assisted program of Aid to Families with Dependent Children (AFDC) or under New York State's general Home Relief program.[1] Their

---

[1] AFDC . . . is a categorical assistance program supported by federal grants-in-aid but administered by the States according to regulations of the Secretary of Health, Education and Welfare. . . .

Home Relief is a general assistance program financed and administered solely by New York state and local governments.

complaint alleged that the New York State and New York City officials administering these programs terminated, or were about to terminate, such aid without prior notice and hearing, thereby denying them due process of law.[2] At the time the suits were filed there was no requirement of prior notice or hearing of any kind before termination of financial aid. However, the State and city adopted procedures for notice and hearing after the suits were brought, and the plaintiffs, appellees here, then challenged the constitutional adequacy of those procedures.

The State Commissioner of Social Services amended the State Department of Social Services' Official Regulations to require that local social services officials proposing to discontinue or suspend a recipient's financial aid do so according to a procedure that conforms to either subdivision (a) or subdivision (b) of § 351.26 of the regulations as amended. The City of New York elected to promulgate a local procedure according to subdivision (b). [This was done in an attempt to settle this lawsuit]. That subdivision, so far as here pertinent, provides that the local procedure must include the giving of notice to the recipient of the reasons for a proposed discontinuance or suspension at least seven days prior to its effective date, with notice also that upon request the recipient may have the proposal reviewed by a local welfare official holding a position superior to that of the supervisor who approved the proposed discontinuance or suspension, and, further, that the recipient may submit, for purposes of the review, a written statement to demonstrate why his grant should not be discontinued or suspended. The decision by the reviewing official whether to discontinue or suspend aid must be made expeditiously, with written notice of the decision to the recipient. The section further expressly provides that "[a]ssistance shall not be discontinued or suspended prior to the date such notice of decision is sent to the recipient and his representative, if any, or prior to the proposed effective date of discontinuance or suspension, whichever occurs later."

Pursuant to subdivision (b), the New York City Department of Social Services promulgated Procedure No. 68-18. A case worker who has doubts about the recipient's continued eligibility must first discuss them with the recipient. If the caseworker concludes that the recipient is no longer eligible, he recommends termination of aid to a unit supervisor. If the latter concurs, he sends the recipient a letter stating the reasons for proposing to terminate aid

---

[2] Two suits were brought and consolidated in the District Court. The named plaintiffs were 20 in number, including intervenors. Fourteen had been or were about to be cut off from AFDC, and six from Home Relief. During the course of this litigation most, though not all, of the plaintiffs either received a "fair hearing" . . . or were restored to the rolls without a hearing. However, even in many of the cases where payments have been resumed, the underlying questions of eligibility that resulted in the bringing of this suit have not been resolved. For example, Mrs. Altagracia Guzman alleged that she was in danger of losing AFDC payments for failure to cooperate with the City Department of Social Services in suing her estranged husband. She contended that the departmental policy requiring such cooperation was inapplicable to the facts of her case. The record shows that payments to Mrs. Guzman have not been terminated, but there is no indication that the basic dispute over her duty to cooperate has been resolved, or that the alleged danger of termination has been removed. Home Relief payments to Juan DeJesus were terminated because he refused to accept counseling and rehabilitation for drug addiction. Mr. DeJesus maintains that he does not use drugs. His payments were restored the day after his complaint was filed. But there is nothing in the record to indicate that the underlying factual dispute in his case has been settled.

and notifying him that within seven days he may request that a higher official review the record, and may support the request with a written statement prepared personally or with the aid of an attorney or other person. If the reviewing official affirms the determination of ineligibility, aid is stopped immediately and the recipient is informed by letter of the reasons for the action. Appellees' challenge to this procedure emphasizes the absence of any provisions for the personal appearance of the recipient before the reviewing official, for oral presentation of evidence, and for confrontation and cross-examination of adverse witnesses. However, the letter does inform the recipient that he may request a post-termination "fair hearing."[5] This is a proceeding before an independent state hearing officer at which the recipient may appear personally, offer oral evidence, confront and cross-examine the witnesses against him, and have a record made of the hearing. If the recipient prevails at the "fair hearing" he is paid all funds erroneously withheld. HEW Handbook, pt. IV, §§ 6200-6500; 18 NYCRR §§ 84.2-84.23. A recipient whose aid is not restored by a "fair hearing" decision may have judicial review. . . . The recipient is so notified. . . .

I.

The constitutional issue to be decided, therefore, is the narrow one whether the Due Process Clause requires that the recipient be afforded an evidentiary hearing *before* the termination of benefits. The District Court held that only a pretermination evidentiary hearing would satisfy the constitutional command, and rejected the argument of the state and city officials that the combination of the post-termination "fair hearing" with the informal pre-termination review disposed of all due process claims. The court said: "While post-termination review is relevant, there is one overpowering fact which controls here. By hypothesis, a welfare recipient is destitute, without funds or assets. . . . Suffice it to say that to cut off a welfare recipient in the face of . . . 'brutal need' without a prior hearing of some sort is unconscionable, unless overwhelming considerations justify it." *Kelly v. Wyman,* 294 F. Supp. 893, 899, 900 (1968). The court rejected the argument that the need to protect the public's tax revenues supplied the requisite "overwhelming consideration." "Against the justified desire to protect public funds must be weighed the individual's overpowering need in this unique situation not to be wrongfully deprived of assistance. . . . While the problem of additional expense must be kept in mind, it does not justify denying a hearing meeting the ordinary standards of due process. Under all the circumstances, we hold that due process requires an adequate hearing before termination of welfare benefits, and the fact that there is a later constitutionally fair proceeding does not alter the result." *Id.* at 901. Although state officials were party defendants in the action, only the Commissioner of Social Services of the City of New York appealed. . . . We affirm.

Appellant does not contend that procedural due process is not applicable to the termination of welfare benefits. Such benefits are a matter of statutory

---

[5] . . . In both AFDC and Home Relief the "fair hearing" must be held within 10 working days of the request, . . . with decision within 12 working days thereafter. . . . It was conceded in oral argument that these time limits are not in fact observed.

§ 2.04   DUE PROCESS AND ADMINISTRATIVE ADJUDICATION   75

entitlement for persons qualified to receive them.⁸ Their termination involves state action that adjudicates important rights. The constitutional challenge cannot be answered by an argument that public assistance benefits are " 'a privilege' and not a right." . . . Relevant constitutional restraints apply as much to the withdrawal of public assistance benefits as to disqualification for unemployment compensation, *Sherbert v. Verner,* 374 U.S. 398 (1963); or to denial of a tax exemption, *Speiser v. Randall,* 357 U.S. 513 (1958); or to discharge from public employment, *Slochower v. Board of Higher Education,* 350 U.S. 551 (1956).⁹ The extent to which procedural due process must be afforded the recipient is influenced by the extent to which he may be "condemned to suffer grievous loss," *Joint Anti-Fascist Refugee Committee v. McGrath,* 341 U.S. 123, 168 (1951) (Frankfurter, J., concurring), and depends upon whether the recipient's interest in avoiding that loss outweighs the governmental interest in summary adjudication. Accordingly, as we said in *Cafeteria & Restaurant Workers Union, etc. v. McElroy,* 367 U.S. 886, 985 (1961), "consideration of what procedures due process may require under any given set of circumstances must begin with a determination of the precise nature of the government function involved as well as of the private interest that has been affected by governmental action. . . ."

It is true, of course, that some governmental benefits may be administratively terminated without affording the recipient a pre-termination evidentiary hearing.¹⁰ But we agree with the District Court that when welfare is

⁸ It may be realistic today to regard welfare entitlements as more like "property" than a "gratuity." Much of the existing wealth in this country takes the form of rights that do not fall within traditional common-law concepts of property. It has been aptly noted that

"[s]ociety today is built around entitlement. The automobile dealer has his franchise, the doctor and lawyer their professional licenses, the worker his union membership, contract, and pension rights, the executive his contract and stock options; all are devices to aid security and independence. Many of the most important of these entitlements now flow from government: subsidies to farmers and businessmen, routes for airlines and channels for television stations; long term contracts for defense, space, and education; social security pensions for individuals. Such sources of security, whether private or public, are no longer regarded as luxuries or gratuities; to the recipients they are essentials, fully deserved, and in no sense a form of charity. It is only the poor whose entitlements, although recognized by public policy, have not been effectively enforced." Reich, *Individual Rights and Social Welfare: The Emerging Legal Issues,* 74 YALE L.J. 1245, 1255 (1965). *See also* Reich, *The New Property,* 73 YALE L.J. 733 (1964).

⁹ *See also Goldsmith v. United States Board of Tax Appeals,* 270 U.S. 117 (1926) (right of a certified public accountant to practice before the Board of Tax Appeals); *Hornsby v. Allen,* 326 F.2d 605 (5th Cir. 1964) (right to obtain a retail liquor store license); *Dixon v. Alabama State Board of Education,* 294 F.2d 150 (5th Cir.), *cert. denied,* 368 U.S. 930 (1961) (right to attend a public college).

¹⁰ One Court of Appeals has stated: "In a wide variety of situations, it has long been recognized that where harm to the public is threatened, and the private interest infringed is reasonably deemed to be of less importance, an official body can take summary action pending a later hearing." *R.A. Holman & Co. v. SEC,* 112 U.S. App. D.C. 43, 47, 299 F.2d 127, 131, *cert. denied,* 370 U.S. 911 (1962) (suspension of exemption from stock registration requirement). *See also for example, Ewing v. Myringer & Casselberry, Inc.,* 339 U.S. 594 (1950) (seizure of mislabeled vitamin product); *North American Cold Storage Co. v. Chicago,* 211 U.S. 306 (1908) (seizure of food not fit for human use); *Yakus v. United States,* 321 U.S. 414 (1944) (adoption of wartime price regulations); *Gonzalez v. Freeman,* 118 U.S. App. D.C. 180, 334 F.2d 570 (1964) (disqualification of a contractor to do business with the Government). In *Cafeteria & Restaurant Workers Union, etc. v. McElroy,* 367 U.S. at 896, summary dismissal of a public employee was upheld because "[i]n [its] proprietary military capacity, the Federal Government . . . has traditionally exercised unfettered control," and because the case involved the Government's "dispatch of its own internal affairs." . . .

discontinued, only a pre-termination evidentiary hearing provides the recipient with procedural due process. . . . For qualified recipients, welfare provides the means to obtain essential food, clothing, housing, and medical care.[11] . . . Thus the crucial factor in this context — a factor not present in the case of the blacklisted government employee, the taxpayer denied a tax exemption, or virtually anyone else whose governmental entitlements are ended — is that termination of aid pending resolution of a controversy over eligibility may deprive an *eligible* recipient of the very means by which to live while he waits. Since he lacks independent resources, his situation becomes immediately desperate. His need to concentrate upon finding the means for daily subsistence, in turn, adversely affects his ability to seek redress from the welfare bureaucracy.

Moreover, important governmental interests are promoted by affording recipients a pre-termination evidentiary hearing. From its founding the Nation's basic commitment has been to foster the dignity and well-being of all persons within its borders. We have come to recognize that forces not within the control of the poor contribute to their poverty. This perception, against the background of our traditions, has significantly influenced the development of the contemporary public assistance system. Welfare, by meeting the basic demands of subsistence, can help bring within the reach of the poor the same opportunities that are available to others to participate meaningfully in the life of the community. At the same time, welfare guards against the societal malaise that may flow from a widespread sense of unjustified frustration and insecurity. Public assistance, then, is not mere charity, but a means to "promote the general Welfare, and secure the Blessings of Liberty to ourselves and our posterity." The same governmental interests that counsel the provision of welfare, counsel as well its uninterrupted provision to those eligible to receive it; pre-termination evidentiary hearings are indispensable to that end.

Appellant does not challenge the force of these considerations but argues that they are outweighed by countervailing governmental interests in conserving fiscal and administrative resources. These interests, the argument goes, justify the delay of any evidentiary hearing until after discontinuance of the grants. Summary adjudication protects the public fisc by stopping payments promptly upon discovery of reason to believe that recipient is no longer eligible. Since most terminations are accepted without challenge, summary adjudication also conserves both the fisc and administrative time and energy by reducing the number of evidentiary hearings actually held.

We agree with the District Court, however, that these governmental interests are not overriding in the welfare context. The requirement of a prior hearing doubtless involves some greater expense, and the benefits paid to ineligible recipients pending decision at the hearing probably cannot be recouped, since these recipients are likely to be judgment-proof. But the State is not without weapons to minimize these increased costs. Much of the drain on fiscal and administrative resources can be reduced by developing procedures for prompt pre-termination hearings and by skillful use of personnel

---

[11] Administrative determination that a person is ineligible for welfare may also render him ineligible for participation in state-financed medical programs. . . .

and facilities. Indeed, the very provision for a post-termination evidentiary hearing in New York's Home Relief program is itself cogent evidence that the State recognizes the primacy of the public interest in correct eligibility determinations and therefore in the provision of procedural safeguards. Thus, the interest of the eligible recipient in uninterrupted receipt of public assistance, coupled with the State's interest that his payments not be erroneously terminated, clearly outweighs the State's competing concern to prevent any increase in its fiscal and administrative burdens. As the District Court correctly concluded, "[t]he stakes are simply too high for the welfare recipient, and the possibility for honest error or irritable misjudgment too great, to allow termination of aid without giving the recipient a chance, if he so desires, to be fully informed of the case against him so that he may contest its basis and produce evidence in rebuttal."

II.

We also agree with the District Court, however, that the pre-termination hearing need not take the form of a judicial or quasi-judicial trial. We bear in mind that the statutory "fair hearing" will provide the recipient with a full administrative review.[14] Accordingly, the pre-termination hearing has one function only: to produce an initial determination of the validity of the welfare department's grounds for discontinuance of payments in order to protect a recipient against an erroneous termination of his benefits. . . . Thus, a complete record and a comprehensive opinion, which would serve primarily to facilitate judicial review and to guide future decisions, need not be provided at the pre-termination stage. We recognize, too, that both welfare authorities and recipients have an interest in relatively speedy resolution of questions of eligibility, that they are used to dealing with one another informally, and that some welfare departments have very burdensome caseloads. These considerations justify the limitation of the pre-termination hearing to minimum procedural safeguards, adapted to the particular characteristics of welfare recipients, and to the limited nature of the controversies to be resolved. We wish to add that we, no less than the dissenters, recognize the importance of not imposing upon the States or the Federal Government in this developing field of law any procedural requirements beyond those demanded by rudimentary due process.

"The fundamental requisite of due process of law is the opportunity to be heard." *Grannis v. Ordean,* 234 U.S. 385, 394 (1914). The hearing must be "at a meaningful time and in a meaningful manner." *Armstrong v. Manzo,* 380 U.S. 545, 552 (1965). In the present context these principles require that a recipient have timely and adequate notice detailing the reasons for a proposed termination, and an effective opportunity to defend by confronting any adverse witnesses and by presenting his own arguments and evidence orally. These rights are important in cases such as those before us, where recipients have challenged proposed terminations as resting on incorrect or

---

[14] Due process does not, of course, require two hearings. If, for example, a State simply wishes to continue benefits until after a "fair" hearing there will be no need for a preliminary hearing.

misleading factual premises or on misapplication of rules or policies to the facts of particular cases.[15]

We are not prepared to say that the seven-day notice currently provided by New York City is constitutionally insufficient *per se,* although there may be cases where fairness would require that a longer time be given. Nor do we see any constitutional deficiency in the content or form of the notice. New York employs both a letter and a personal conference with a caseworker to inform a recipient of the precise questions raised about his continued eligibility. Evidently the recipient is told the legal and factual bases for the Department's doubts. This combination is probably the most effective method of communicating with recipients.

The city's procedures presently do not permit recipients to appear personally with or without counsel before the official who finally determines continued eligibility. Thus a recipient is not permitted to present evidence to that official orally, or to confront or cross-examine adverse witnesses. These omissions are fatal to the constitutional adequacy of the procedures.

The opportunity to be heard must be tailored to the capacities and circumstances of those who are to be heard. It is not enough that a welfare recipient may present his position to the decision maker in writing or second-hand through his caseworker. Written submissions are an unrealistic option for most recipients, who lack the educational attainment necessary to write effectively and who cannot obtain professional assistance. Moreover, written submissions do not afford the flexibility of oral presentations; they do not permit the recipient to mold his argument to the issues the decision maker appears to regard as important. Particularly where credibility and veracity are at issue, as they must be in many termination proceedings, written submissions are a wholly unsatisfactory basis for decision. The second-hand presentation to the decisionmaker by the caseworker has its own deficiencies; since the caseworker usually gathers the facts upon which the charge of ineligibility rests, the presentation of the recipient's side of the controversy cannot safely be left to him. Therefore a recipient must be allowed to state his position orally. Informal procedures will suffice; in this context due process does not require a particular order of proof or mode of offering evidence. . . .

In almost every setting where important decisions turn on questions of fact, due process requires an opportunity to confront and cross-examine adverse witnesses. . . . What we said in *Greene v. McElroy,* 360 U.S. 474, 496-497 (1959), is particularly pertinent here:

> Certain principles have remained relatively immutable in our jurisprudence. One of these is that where governmental action seriously injures an individual, and the reasonableness of the action depends on fact findings, the evidence used to prove the Government's case must be disclosed to the individual so that he has an opportunity to show that it is untrue. While this is important in the case of documentary evidence, it is even more important where the evidence consists of the testimony of individuals whose

---

[15] This case presents no question requiring our determination whether due process requires only an opportunity for written submission, or an opportunity both for written submission and oral argument, where there are no factual issues in dispute or where the application of the rule of law is not intertwined with factual issues. . . .

memory might be malice, vindictiveness, intolerance, prejudice, or jealousy. We have formalized these protections in the requirements of confrontation and cross-examination. They have ancient roots. They find expression in the Sixth Amendment. . . . This Court has been zealous to protect these rights from erosion. It has spoken out not only in criminal cases . . . but also in all types of cases where administrative . . . actions were under scrutiny.

Welfare recipients must therefore be given an opportunity to confront and cross-examine the witnesses relied on by the department. . . . We do not say that counsel must be provided at the pre-termination hearing, but only that the recipient must be allowed to retain an attorney if he so desires. Counsel can help delineate the issues, present the factual contentions in an orderly manner, conduct cross-examination, and generally safeguard the interests of the recipient. We do not anticipate that this assistance will unduly prolong or otherwise encumber the hearing. . . .

Finally, the decision maker's conclusion as to a recipient's eligibility must rest solely on the legal rules and evidence adduced at the hearing. . . . To demonstrate compliance with this elementary requirement, the decision maker should state the reasons for his determination and indicate the evidence he relied on . . . though his statement need not amount to a full opinion or even formal findings of fact and conclusions of law. And, of course, an impartial decision maker is essential. . . . We agree with the District Court that prior involvement in some aspects of a case will not necessarily bar a welfare official from acting as a decision maker. He should not, however, have participated in making the determination under review.

Affirmed.

Mr. Justice Black, dissenting.

In the last half century the United States, along with many, perhaps most, other nations of the world, has moved far toward becoming a welfare state, that is, a nation that for one reason or another taxes its most affluent people to help support, feed, clothe, and shelter its less fortunate citizens. The result is that today more than nine million men, women, and children in the United States receive some kind of state or federally financed public assistance in the form of allowances or gratuities, generally paid them periodically, usually by the week, month, or quarter.[1] Since these gratuities are paid on the basis of need, the list of recipients is not static, and some people go off the lists and others are added from time to time. These ever-changing lists put a constant administrative burden on government and it certainly could not have reasonably anticipated that this burden would include the additional procedural expense imposed by the Court today. . . .

---

[1] This figure includes all recipients of Old-age Assistance, Aid to Families with Dependent Children, Aid to the Blind, Aid to the Permanently and Totally Disabled, and general assistance. In this case appellants are AFDC and general assistance recipients. In New York State alone there are 951,000 AFDC recipients and 108,000 on general assistance. In the Nation as a whole the comparable figures are 6,080,000 and 391,000. U.S. Bureau of the Census, *Statistical Abstract of the United States: 1969* (90th ed.), Table 435, p. 297.

The more than a million names on the relief rolls in New York, and the more than nine million names on the rolls of all the 50 States were not put there at random. The names are there because state welfare officials believed that those people were eligible for assistance. Probably in the officials' haste to make out the lists many names were put there erroneously in order to alleviate immediate suffering, and undoubtedly some people are drawing relief who are not entitled under the law to do so. Doubtless some draw relief checks from time to time who know they are not eligible, either because they are not actually in need or for some other reason. Many of those who thus draw undeserved gratuities are without sufficient property to enable the government to collect back from them any money they wrongfully receive. But the Court today holds that it would violate the Due Process Clause of the Fourteenth Amendment to stop paying those people weekly or monthly allowances unless the government first affords them a full "evidentiary hearing" even though welfare officials are persuaded that the recipients are not rightfully entitled to receive a penny under the law. In other words, although some recipients might be on the lists for payment wholly because of deliberate fraud on their part, the Court holds that the government is helpless and must continue, until after an evidentiary hearing, to pay money that it does not owe, never has owed, and never could owe. I do not believe there is any provision in our Constitution that should thus paralyze the government's efforts to protect itself against making payments to people who are not entitled to them. . . .

I would have little, if any, objection to the majority's decision in this case if it were written as the report of the House Committee on Education and Labor, but as an opinion ostensibly resting on the language of the Constitution I find it woefully deficient. Once the verbiage is pared away it is obvious that this Court today adopts the views of the District Court "that to cut off a welfare recipient in the face of . . . 'brutal need' without a prior hearing of some sort is unconscionable," and therefore, says the Court, unconstitutional. The majority reaches this result by a process of weighing "the recipient's interest in avoiding" the termination of welfare benefits against "the governmental interest in summary adjudication." Today's balancing act requires a "pre-termination evidentiary hearing," yet there is nothing that indicates what tomorrow's balance will be. Although the majority attempts to bolster its decision with limited quotations from prior cases, it is obvious that today's result doesn't depend on the language of the Constitution itself or the principles of other decisions, but solely on the collective judgment of the majority as to what would be a fair and humane procedure in this case.

This decision is thus only another variant of the view often expressed by some members of this Court that the Due Process Clause forbids any conduct that a majority of the Court believes "unfair," "indecent," or "shocking to their consciences." *See, e.g., Rochin v. California,* 342 U.S. 165, 172 (1952). Neither these words nor any like them appear anywhere in the Due Process Clause. If they did, they would leave the majority of Justices free to hold any conduct unconstitutional that they should conclude on their own to be unfair or shocking to them. Had the drafters of the Due Process Clause meant to leave judges such ambulatory power to declare laws unconstitutional, the chief value of a written constitution, as the Founders saw it, would have been lost. In fact, if that view of due process is correct, the Due Process Clause could easily swallow up all other parts of the Constitution. And truly the Constitution would always be "what the judges say it is" at a given moment, not what the Founders wrote into the document. A written constitution, designed to guarantee protection against governmental abuses, including those of judges, must have written standards that mean something definite and have an explicit content. I regret very much to be compelled to say that the Court today makes a drastic and dangerous departure from a Constitution written to control and limit the government and the judges and moves toward a Constitution designed to be no more and no less than what the judges of a particular social and economic philosophy declare on the one hand to be fair or on the other hand to be shocking and unconscionable.

The procedure required today as a matter of constitutional law finds no precedent in our legal system. Reduced to its simplest terms, the problem in this case is similar to that frequently encountered when two parties have an ongoing legal relationship that requires one party to make periodic payments to the other. Often the situation arises where the party "owing" the money stops paying it and justifies his conduct by arguing that the recipient is not legally entitled to payment. The recipient can, of course, disagree and go to court to compel payment. But I know of no situation in our legal system in which the person alleged to owe money to another is required by law to continue making payments to a judgment-proof claimant without the benefit of any security or bond to insure that these payments can be recovered if he wins his legal argument. Yet today's decision in no way obligates the welfare recipient to pay back any benefits wrongfully received during the pretermination evidentiary hearings or post any bond, and in all "fairness" it could not do so. These recipients are by definition too poor to post a bond or to repay the benefits that, as the majority assumes, must be spent as received to insure survival.

The Court apparently feels that this decision will benefit the poor and needy. In my judgment the eventual result will be just the opposite. While today's decision requires only an administrative, evidentiary hearing, the inevitable logic of the approach taken will lead to constitutionally imposed, time-consuming delays of a full adversary process of administrative and judicial review. In the next case the welfare recipients are bound to argue that cutting off benefits before judicial review of the agency's decision is also a denial of due process. Since, by hypothesis, termination of aid at that point may still "deprive an *eligible* recipient of the very means by which to live while he waits." . . . I would be surprised if the weighing process did not compel the conclusion that termination without full judicial review would be unconscionable. After all, at each step, as the majority seems to feel, the issue is only one of weighing the government's pocketbook against the actual survival of the recipient, and surely that balance must always tip in favor of the individual. Similarly today's decision requires only the opportunity to have the benefit of counsel at the administrative hearing, but it is difficult to believe that the same reasoning process would not require the appointment of counsel, for otherwise the right to counsel is a meaningless one since these people are too poor to hire their own advocates. . . . Thus the end result of today's decision may well be that the government, once it decides to give welfare benefits, cannot reverse that decision until the recipient has had the benefits of full administrative and judicial review, including, of course, the opportunity to present his case to this Court. Since this process will usually entail a delay of several years, the inevitable result of such a constitutionally imposed burden will be that the government will not put a claimant on the rolls initially until it has made an exhaustive investigation to determine his eligibility. While this Court will perhaps have insured that no needy person will be taken off the rolls without a full "due process" proceeding, it will also have insured that many will never get on the rolls, or at least that they will remain destitute during the lengthy proceedings followed to determine initial eligibility.

For the foregoing reasons I dissent from the Court's holding. The operation of a welfare state is a new experiment for our Nation. For this reason, among others, I feel that new experiments in carrying out a welfare program should not be frozen into our constitutional structure. They should be left, as are other legislative determinations, to the Congress and the legislatures that the people elect to make our laws.

NOTES AND QUESTIONS

2-11. Does the Government contest the fact that welfare benefits are property rights? Does the Court give a rationale for why it holds that welfare benefits are property? What is it?

2-12. What does the Court mean by the term "brutal need"? What constitutes "brutal need" in this case? What is at stake in this case for welfare recipients, as far as the Court is concerned? Is this more of a substantive due process approach to the issue? How do you distinguish between procedural and substantive due process?

2-13. Consider the Court's reference to the dignity of the individual as an underlying basis for the procedural protection provided. Professor Jerry L. Mashaw has expanded on this theme and the inevitable tensions it creates with notions of substantive due process in *The Supreme Court's Due Process Calculus for Administrative Adjudication in* Matthews v. Eldridge: *Three Factors in Search of a Theory of Value:*[*]

> The increasingly secular, scientific, and collectivist character of the modern American state reinforces our propensity to define fairness in the formal, and apparently neutral language of social utility. Assertions of "natural" or "inalienable" rights seem, by contrast, somewhat embarrassing. Their ancestry, and therefore their moral force, are increasingly uncertain. Moreover, their role in the history of the Due Process Clause makes us apprehensive about their eventual reach. It takes no peculiar acuity to see that the tension in procedural due process cases is the same as that in the now discredited substantive due process jurisprudence — a tension between

---

[*] 44 U. CHI. L. REV. 28, 49-50 (1976). Copyright © 1976 University of Chicago. All rights reserved.

the efficacy of the state and the individual's right to freedom from coercion or socially imposed disadvantage.

Yet the popular moral presupposition of individual dignity, and its political counterpart, self-determination, persist. State coercion must be legitimized, not only by acceptable substantive policies, but also by political processes that respond to a democratic morality's demand for participation in decisions affecting individual and group interests. At the level of individual administrative decisions this demand appears in both the layman's and the lawyer's language as the right to a "hearing" or "to be heard," normally meaning orally and in person. To accord an individual less when his property or status is at stake requires justification, not only because he might contribute to accurate determinations, but also because a lack of personal participation causes alienation and a loss of that dignity and self-respect that society properly deems independently valuable.

Are there any limits to the procedural claims that this theory may elicit? Taken to an extreme, does this theory lead to a conclusion that all decisions should be made only by procedures devised by the person affected? If so, would you agree with that conclusion?

2-14. What role should passion play in judicial decisionmaking? Consider the following contrasting points of view, one by Justice Brennan, reflecting on his decision in *Goldberg v. Kelly,* and the other, a response by Professor Owen Fiss:

Many may wonder at this point: how exactly does due process jurisprudence take account of concepts as abstract as reason and passion? What does it mean for a court to be sensitive to the need for both these qualities? I would like to use the case of *Goldberg v. Kelly* to answer these questions. Goldberg, as many of you know, has been described as the opening shot in a modern "due process revolution." In that case, the Court held that a hearing was required before a welfare recipient's benefits could be terminated. The case required the Court to confront an issue that the framers could not have specifically foreseen: the requirements of due process in a bureaucratized society. Some have characterized *Goldberg* as an effort to make the welfare system more rational. They see the Court's insistence that certain trial-type procedures be used in pretermination hearings as a spur to greater formality in welfare administration. From this perspective, *Goldberg* appears as a triumph of the model of reason, holding the welfare system to a demanding standard of rationality that only an even more advanced bureaucracy could satisfy.

I certainly have no regrets about the extent to which *Goldberg* may have made the welfare system more rational. I want to suggest, however, that *Goldberg* can be seen in another way. I believe that the decision can be seen as an expression of the importance of passion in governmental conduct, in the sense of attention to the concrete human realities at stake. From this perspective, *Goldberg* can be seen as injecting passion into a system whose abstract rationality had led it astray.

W.J. Brennan, Jr., *Reason, Passion and "The Progress of the Law."*[*]

---

[*] 10 CARDOZO L. REV. 3, 19–20 (1988). Copyright © 1988 by Cardozo Law Review. All rights reserved.

Allowing passion to play a role in the decisional process of the Supreme Court — even if the passion be the most beneficent imaginable or even if the role be a modest or partial one — is inconsistent with the very norms that govern and legitimate the judicial power and constitute its central disciplining mechanism: impartiality and the obligation of the judiciary to justify its decisions openly and on the basis of reasons accepted by the profession and the public. These features of the judicial process are not infallible, obviously, but they do at least place the judiciary under a discipline that is gone once passion becomes an appropriate basis of decision. Why, we are left to ask, should the passions of those who happen to be justices rule us all?

O.M. Fiss, *Reason in All Its Splendor.**

2-15. What are the fatal flaws in the state's procedures as far as the majority of the Court is concerned? How does the Court conceive of the group of individuals affected by these governmental decisions? Does the Court take an individual rights perspective on this issue or a group rights perspective? Are they, in this case, the same?

2-16. What procedures does the Court, in effect, require before the demands of the Due Process Clause are met in this case? How do these requirements differ from adjudication in a federal court? Are they similar? Should they be? Is that the only way to ensure fairness and individual dignity? Is this approach centered too much on the individual and not enough on the group of welfare recipients, both actual and potential? Are there remedies between those provided by the Court in *Goldberg* and those advocated by Justice Holmes in *Bi-Metallic*? See Mashaw, *The Management Side of Due Process: Some Theoretical and Litigation Notes on the Assurance of Accuracy, Fairness and Timeliness in the Adjudication of Social Welfare,* 59 CORNELL L. REV. 772 (1974).

2-17 Is Justice Black correct in analogizing this case to one involving a debtor and a creditor? Is he correct in suggesting that the cost of more procedure is likely to come out of a pot of money earmarked for benefits for those that duly qualify? Given that, after *Goldberg,* it is more difficult to remove welfare recipients from the rolls, how do you think administrators are likely to resolve close cases in the first instance? By denying benefits at the outset and thereby avoiding the difficulties of correcting any mistakes after the fact?

2-18 Is Justice Black's reference to the intentions of the Founding Fathers convincing? Does he see the majority's approach to these issues as a form of substantive due process?

2-19. How do the issues in *Goldberg* differ from those in *Dixon* and *Hornsby*? What was the purpose of the hearings mandated in *Dixon* and *Hornsby*? To determine whether essentially unconstitutional reasons motivated the decision makers?

2-20. What is the purpose of the hearing provided in *Goldberg v. Kelly*? To assess the accuracy of the agency's decision? To ensure that the affected

---

* 56 BROOK. L. REV. 789, 801 (1990). Copyright © 1990 Brooklyn Law Review. All rights reserved.

individual is treated with appropriate respect? Is Justice Black correct in suggesting such determinations are best left to the legislature? Why or why not?

2-21. It is important to recall the broad historic, legal context in which *Goldberg v. Kelly* first arose:

> The due process explosion begun by *Goldberg*, particularly as applied in cases involving the poor and the powerless was very much of a piece with the civil rights movement that preceded and overlapped it. While courts were able, on constitutional grounds, to void statutes and state practices that discriminated on the basis of race, wealth never achieved the status of a suspect class. Challenges to statutes based primarily on their wealth distribution effects were not appropriate for courts and were treated more as a legislative issue. The due process approach to dealing with recalcitrant state bureaucracies, however, allowed a federal court to assess at least the procedural fairness of these wealth redistributive programs. The glare of publicity, the fact that, perhaps for the first time, some state agencies had to deal with their recipients as legal equals had a profound political impact. But the procedural implications of these decisions were not without cost. Procedures cost money to implement, and . . . particularly in social programs involving hundreds of thousands of recipients, providing more process necessitated tradeoffs with actual substantive benefits and thus raised important fiscal allocation questions. Moreover, procedural due process claims were on occasion abused and courts were undoubtedly subject to their share of frivolous due process cases.

Alfred C. Aman, Jr., *Administrative Law in the United States — Past, Present and Future,* 16 QUEEN'S L.J. 179, 193 (1991).*

2-22. It is also important to recall that when *Goldberg* was first decided, it was enormously influential in determining the procedures to be applied not only to welfare claimants, but, eventually, in a wide variety of other governmental contexts as well:

> [*Goldberg v. Kelly*] became the rallying cry for a new breed of poverty lawyers. Legal Aid clinics and Public Interest law firms, armed with *Goldberg v. Kelly,* were now able to challenge the procedural practices of a number of state bureaucracies in federal court. The battle was procedural, but the substantive and political overtones of some of these cases were clear. Nor did the applications of *Goldberg* stop with welfare bureaucracies. The case was applied in a wide variety of contexts &mdash on behalf of government employees who lost their jobs, prisoners involved in discipline cases or parole revocation or parole granting cases, students involved in school disciplinary proceedings and teachers challenging tenure denials. It became a potent weapon, particularly for those whose legal aid lawyers could constitutionally question the administration of state bureaucracies; invoke the scrutiny of federal courts and provide, if nothing else, bargaining chips for the broad based substantive and procedural negotiations that usually also were involved. *Goldberg v. Kelly* was the foundation for law reform cases designed, for example, to reform a state penitentiary system or provide

---

* Copyright © 1991. Reprinted by permission.

some bargaining power to individuals who usually had little. In the process, there is no question that some procedural abuses were exposed and corrected. There also is little question that federal courts began to feel, at times, quite uneasy about their ever expanding role.

Aman, *supra,* 16 QUEEN'S L.J. at 192–93.*

2-23. The economic and political context in which welfare programs were administered has now changed considerably. In the 1980s legislative welfare reform, budget deficits and increased concern with global competition, economic efficiency and market solutions to societal problems, put welfare policy in a different light. As Professor Joel Handler has noted, *Goldberg v. Kelly* and, more specifically, the theory of entitlements on which it and the New Property was based, was attacked by both the left and the right.** Consider, for example, the position of William Simon in *Rights and Redistribution in the Welfare System*, 38 STAN. L. REV. 1431, 1487–88 (1986):***

> *The New Property* is a curious product. While it sought to transform the classical idea of right more drastically than the liberal Social Security jurisprudence had, it diluted the classical rhetoric much less. As in classicism, the dominant image of right was a sanctuary for the independent individual against the dangerous power of the state. In order to expand the classical category of specific rights, Reich pushed the classical property notion to a higher level of abstraction. At this level, almost every material interest of the individual could be seen as a potential right, since all potentially afford independence and all, unless turned into rights, remain vulnerable to state power. Thus, Reich proposed that all substantial interests in "economic status" be regarded as rights.
>
> In retrospect, Reich's analysis involves a paradox. Although it was clearly designed to legitimate the redistributive activities of the then expanding welfare state, and in particular to incorporate public assistance into the liberal rights catalogue, it had curiously conservative and antiredistributive implications. Reich's analysis tended to legitimate all the established economic practices constituting the prevailing distribution of wealth, but precisely for that reason, it seemed to preclude any further redistribution. If all forms of "economic status" were to be turned into entitlements, there could be no subsequent redistribution. In Reich's analysis, as in classicism, the idea of right serves as a defense *against* redistribution.
>
> This situation results from Reich's refusal to address the issue of distribution directly. He dispensed with classicism's insistence on the primacy of the distributive principles of effort and exchange, but unlike the New Deal social workers and the natural rights lawyers of the 1970s, Reich did not argue in favor of need as a distributive principle. He simply ignored the distributive issue entirely. The rhetorical advantage of doing so was to make it easier to appropriate the individualist rhetoric of classicism. To defend

---

* Originally published in (1991) 16 Queen's Law Journal 179. Reproduced with permission.

** Handler, *"Constructing the Political Spectacle": The Interpretation of Entitlements, Legalization, and Obligations in Social Welfare History*, 56 BROOK. L. REV. 899 (1990).

*** Copyright © 1986. By The Board of Trustees of Leland J. Stanford University. All rights reserved.

need against the primacy of effort and exchange would have required acknowledging conflicts within the liberal tradition. It would have made the analysis more clearly political and controversial. Through bypassing distributive concerns, Reich created the impression of a distinctively legal program that stood above political conflict.

Despite its problems, Reich's rhetoric and imagery, rather than that of the social workers or the natural law lawyers, came to dominate liberal discourse about welfare reform. Part of the reason the paradoxical nature of his analysis was not perceived may relate to the economic circumstances of the decade of welfare expansion that followed the publication of the article in 1964. This was a period of large and sustained economic growth followed by inflationary public finance. Both phenomena tended to facilitate the sublimation of distributive issues by permitting welfare expansion in ways that did not require explicit forms of redistribution through tax increases. It was only with the advent of the stagflation or "zero sum" society of the later 1970's that the rhetorical power of *The New Property* diminished. Once the New Property rights of welfare recipients were perceived to conflict drastically with the old property rights of investors and taxpayers, the distributive issue returned with a vengeance. Having nothing to say about the issue, Reich's analysis was impotent against conservative arguments that the welfare rights had to yield to old property rights.

Professor Handler notes criticism came also from the right: ". . . conservatives, such as Lawrence Mead, have used entitlements to justify the new efforts in social control in welfare, namely 'workfare.'" He goes on to argue that:

> For a long time now, welfare has taken a bad turn. Benefits have declined substantially. It has been extensively tightened by detailed rules designed to reduce administrative errors; the result has been that massive numbers of applicants are denied aid or benefits are terminated through "paper" errors. For almost twenty-five years, the Federal Government has been trying to impose work requirements. The latest welfare reform consensus, the Family Support Act of 1988, has workfare as its centerpiece. Has the concept of entitlements helped chart this path? Has the reconstruction of the welfare relationship provided the ideological grounding for these developments? Simon and Mead say "yes." While Mead, of course applauds this development, Simon harshly condemns *The New Property*.

Handler, *supra* at 900-01.[*]

The materials that follow will now trace the development of modern procedural due process law in the administrative agency context. As we shall see, the logic of *Goldberg v. Kelly* is difficult to contain. Once a property or liberty interest is recognized, claimants can contest the procedures provided as constitutionally deficient. Even if a court disagrees with them, such cases usually are not dismissed for failure to state a claim. They must go forward and that can take time and money.

Given the fact that *Goldberg* assumed a property right in existence, it is important that we begin with the leading cases that set forth the Court's

---

[*] Copyright © 1990 Brooklyn Law Review. All rights reserved.

methodology in determining just what is and what is not a property or liberty interest. We shall then explore what kind of process is due when such an interest is recognized and when that process is due. As we go through the following materials, note the various ways that courts eventually attempt to contain the logic of *Goldberg v. Kelly*. Some cases seemingly try to re-invent the right/privilege distinction. Others focus on when the process is due and still others define liberty and property narrowly. What should the role of the court be in these cases? Should the Due Process Clause provide the minimum of procedure necessary for government to act constitutionally? If so, what should that be and how much, if at all, should the Court defer to legislative and administrative determinations of what those constitutionally required minimum procedures in fact are?

§ 2.05 Refining the Due Process Methodology: Property and Liberty Interests

BOARD OF REGENTS OF STATE COLLEGES v. ROTH

United States Supreme Court
408 U.S. 564 (1972)

MR. JUSTICE STEWART delivered the opinion of the Court.

In 1968 the respondent, David Roth, was hired for his first teaching job as assistant professor of political science at Wisconsin State University-Oshkosh. He was hired for a fixed term of one academic year. The notice of his faculty appointment specified that his employment would begin on September 1, 1968, and would end on June 30, 1969.[1] The respondent completed that term. But he was informed that he would not be rehired for the next academic year.

The respondent had no tenure rights to continued employment. Under Wisconsin statutory law a state university teacher can acquire tenure as a "permanent" employee only after four years of year-to-year employment. Having acquired tenure, a teacher is entitled to continued employment "during efficiency and good behavior." A relatively new teacher without tenure, however, is under Wisconsin law entitled to nothing beyond his one-year appointment.[2] There are no statutory or administrative standards

---

[1] The respondent had no contract of employment. Rather, his formal notice of appointment was the equivalent of an employment contract.

The notice of his appointment provided that: "David F. Roth is hereby appointed to the faculty of the Wisconsin State University Position number 0262. (Location:) Oshkosh as (Rank:) Assistant Professor of (Department:) Political Science this (Date:) first day of (Month:) September (Year:) 1968." The notice went on to specify that the respondent's "appointment basis" was for the "academic year." And it provided that "[r]egulations governing tenure are in accord with Chapter 37.31, Wisconsin Statutes. The employment of any staff member for an academic year shall not be for a term beyond June 30th of the fiscal year in which the appointment is made."

[2] Wis. Stat. § 37.31(1) (1967), in force at the time, provided in pertinent part that:

All teachers in any state university shall initially be employed on probation. The employment shall be permanent, during efficiency and good behavior after 4 years of continuous service in the state university as a teacher.

§ 2.05   DUE PROCESS AND ADMINISTRATIVE ADJUDICATION   89

defining eligibility for re-employment. State law thus clearly leaves the decision whether to rehire a nontenured teacher for another year to the unfettered discretion of university officials.

The procedural protection afforded a Wisconsin State University teacher before he is separated from the University corresponds to his job security. As a matter of statutory law, a tenured teacher cannot be "discharged except for cause upon written charges" and pursuant to certain procedures. A nontenured teacher, similarly, is protected to some extent *during* his one-year term. Rules promulgated by the Board of Regents provide that a nontenured teacher "dismissed" before the end of the year may have some opportunity for review of the "dismissal." But the Rules provide no real protection for a nontenured teacher who simply is not re-employed for the next year. He must be informed by February 1 "concerning retention or non-retention for the ensuing year." But "no reason for non-retention need be given. No review or appeal is provided in such case."

In conformance with these Rules, the President of Wisconsin State University-Oshkosh informed the respondent before February 1, 1969, that he would not be rehired for the 1969-1970 academic year. He gave the respondent no reason for the decision and no opportunity to challenge it at any sort of hearing.

The respondent then brought this action in Federal District Court alleging that the decision not to rehire him for the next year infringed his Fourteenth Amendment rights. He attacked the decision both in substance and procedure. First, he alleged that the true reason for the decision was to punish him for certain statements critical of the University administration, and that it therefore violated his right to freedom of speech.[5] Second, he alleged that the failure of University officials to give him notice of any reason for nonretention and an opportunity for a hearing violated his right to procedural due process of law.

The District Court granted summary judgment for the respondent on the procedural issue, ordering the University officials to provide him with reasons and a hearing. 310 F. Supp. 972. The Court of Appeals, with one judge dissenting, affirmed this partial summary judgment. 446 F.2d 806. We granted certiorari. 404 U.S. 909. The only question presented to us at this stage in the case is whether the respondent had a constitutional right to a statement of reasons and a hearing on the University's decision not to rehire him for another year. We hold that he did not.

I.

The requirements of procedural due process apply only to the deprivation of interests encompassed by the Fourteenth Amendment's protection of liberty

---

[5] While the respondent alleged that he was not rehired because of his exercise of free speech, the petitioners insisted that the non-retention decision was based on other, constitutionally valid grounds. The District Court came to no conclusion whatever regarding the true reason for the University President's decision. "In the present case," it stated, "it appears that a determination as to the actual bases of [the] decision must await amplification of the facts at trail. . . . Summary judgment is inappropriate." 310 F. Supp. 972, 982.

and property. When protected interests are implicated, the right to some kind of prior hearing is paramount.⁷ But the range of interests protected by procedural due process is not infinite.

The District Court decided that procedural due process guarantees apply in this case by assessing and balancing the weight of the particular interests involved. It concluded that the respondent's interest in re-employment at Wisconsin State University-Oshkosh outweighed the University's interest in denying him re-employment summarily. 310 F. Supp., at 977-979. Undeniably, the respondent's re-employment prospects were of major concern to him — that we surely cannot say was insignificant. And a weighing process has long been a part of any determination of the *form* of hearing required in particular situations by procedural due process.⁸ But, to determine whether due process requirements apply in the first place, we must look not to the "weight" but to the *nature* of the interest at stake. . . . We must look to see if the interest is within the Fourteenth Amendment's protection of liberty and property.

"Liberty" and "property" are broad and majestic terms. They are among the "[g]reat [constitutional] concepts . . . purposely left to gather meaning from experience. . . . [T]hey relate to the whole domain of social and economic fact, and the statesmen who founded this Nation knew too well that only a stagnant society remains unchanged." *National Ins. Co. v. Tidewater Co.*, 337 U.S. 582, 646 (Frankfurter, J., dissenting). For that reason, the Court has fully and finally rejected the wooden distinction between "rights" and "privileges" that once seemed to govern the applicability of procedural due process rights.⁹ The Court has also made clear that the property interests protected by procedural due process extend well beyond actual ownership of real estate, chattels, or money. By the same token, the Court has required due process protection for

---

⁷ Before a person is deprived of a protected interest, he must be afforded opportunity for some kind of a hearing, "except for extraordinary situations where some valid governmental interest is at stake that justifies postponing the hearing until after the event." *Boddie v. Connecticut*, 401 U.S. 371, 379. "While '[m]any controversies have raged about . . . the Due Process Clause,' . . . it is fundamental that except in emergency situations (and this is not one) due process requires that when a State seeks to terminate [a protected] interest . . ., it must afford 'notice and opportunity for hearing appropriate to the nature of the case' *before* the termination becomes effective." *Bell v. Burson*, 402 U.S. 535, 542. For the rare and extraordinary situations in which we have held that deprivation of a protected interest need not be preceded by opportunity for some kind of hearing, *see, e.g., Central Union Trust Co. v. Garvan*, 254 U.S. 554, 566; *Phillips v. Commissioner*, 283 U.S. 589, 597; *Ewing v. Mytinger & Casselberry, Inc.*, 339 U.S. 594.

⁸ "The formality and procedural requisites for the hearing can vary, depending upon the importance of the interests involved and the nature of the subsequent proceedings." *Boddie v. Connecticut, supra*, at 378. *See, e.g., Goldberg v. Kelly*, 397 U.S. 254, 263; *Hannah v. Larche*, 363 U.S. 420. The constitutional requirement of opportunity for *some* form of hearing before deprivation of a protected interest, of course, does not depend upon such a narrow balancing process. . . .

⁹ In a leading case decided many years ago, the Court of Appeals for the District of Columbia Circuit held that public employment in general was a "privilege," not a "right," and that procedural due process guarantees therefore were inapplicable. *Bailey v. Richardson*, 86 U.S. App. D.C. 248, 182 F.2d 46, *aff'd, by an equally divided Court*, 341 U.S. 918. The basis of this holding has been thoroughly undermined in the ensuing years. For, as MR. JUSTICE BLACKMUN wrote for the Court only last year, "this Court now has rejected the concept that constitutional rights turn upon whether a governmental benefit is characterized as a 'right' or as a 'privilege.'" *Graham v. Richardson*, 403 U.S. 365, 374. . . .

deprivations of liberty beyond the sort of formal constraints imposed by the criminal process.

Yet, while the Court has eschewed rigid or formalistic limitations on the protection of procedural due process, it has at the same time observed certain boundaries. For the words "liberty" and "property" in the Due Process Clause of the Fourteenth Amendment must be given some meaning.

II.

"While this Court has not attempted to define with exactness the liberty . . . guaranteed [by the Fourteenth Amendment], the term has received much consideration and some of the included things have been definitely stated. Without doubt, it denotes not merely freedom from bodily restraint but also the right of the individual to contract, to engage in any of the common occupations of life, to acquire useful knowledge, to marry, establish a home and bring up children, to worship God according to the dictates of his own conscience, and generally to enjoy those privileges long recognized . . . as essential to the orderly pursuit of happiness by free men." *Meyer v. Nebraska,* 262 U.S. 390, 399. In a Constitution for a free people, there can be no doubt that the meaning of "liberty" must be broad indeed. . . .

There might be cases in which a State refused to reemploy a person under such circumstances that interests in liberty would be implicated. But this is not such a case.

The State, in declining to rehire the respondent, did not make any charge against him that might seriously damage his standing and associations in his community. It did not base the nonrenewal of his contract on a charge, for example, that he had been guilty of dishonesty, or immorality. Had it done so, this would be a different case. For "[w]here a person's good name, reputation, honor, or integrity is at stake because of what the government is doing to him, notice and an opportunity to be heard are essential." . . . In such a case, due process would accord an opportunity to refute the charge before University officials.[12] In the present case, however, there is no suggestion whatever that the respondent's "good name, reputation, honor, or integrity" is at stake.

Similarly, there is no suggestion that the State, in declining to re-employ the respondent, imposed on him a stigma or other disability that foreclosed his freedom to take advantage of other employment opportunities. The State, for example, did not invoke any regulations to bar the respondent from all other public employment in state universities. Had it done so, this, again, would be a different case. For "[t]o be deprived not only of present government employment but of future opportunity for it certainly is no small injury. . . ." *Joint Anti-Fascist Refugee Committee v. McGrath, supra,* at 185 (Jackson, J., concurring). . . . The Court has held, for example, that a State, in regulating eligibility for a type of professional employment, cannot foreclose a range of opportunities "in a manner . . . that contravene[s] . . . Due Process," *Schware*

---

[12] The purpose of such notice and hearing is to provide the person an opportunity to clear his name. Once a person has cleared his name at a hearing, his employer, of course, may remain free to deny him future employment for other reasons.

v. Board of Bar Examiners, 353 U.S. 232, 238, and, specifically, in a manner that denies the right to a full prior hearing. *Willner v. Committee on Character,* 373 U.S. 96, 103. *See Cafeteria Workers v. McElroy, supra,* at 898. In the present case, however, this principle does not come into play.[13]

To be sure, the respondent has alleged that the non-renewal of his contract was based on his exercise of his right to freedom of speech. But this allegation is not now before us. The District Court stayed proceedings on this issue, and the respondent has yet to prove that the decision not to rehire him was, in fact, based on his free speech activities.[14]

Hence, on the record before us, all that clearly appears is that the respondent was not rehired for one year at one university. It stretches the concept too far to suggest that a person is deprived of "liberty" when he simply is not rehired in one job but remains as free as before to seek another. *Cafeteria Workers v. McElroy, supra,* at 895-896.

III.

The Fourteenth Amendment's procedural protection of property is a safeguard of the security of interests that a person has already acquired in specific benefits. These interests — property interests — may take many forms.

Thus, the Court has held that a person receiving welfare benefits under statutory and administrative standards defining eligibility for them has an interest in continued receipt of those benefits that is safeguarded by procedural due process. *Goldberg v. Kelly,* 397 U.S. 254. . . . Similarly, in the area of public employment, the Court has held that a public college professor dismissed from an office held under tenure provisions, *Slochower v. Board of Education,* 350 U.S. 551, and college professors and staff members dismissed during the terms of their contracts, *Wieman v. Updegraff,* 344 U.S. 183, have

---

[13] The District Court made an *assumption* "that non-retention by one university or college creates concrete and practical difficulties for a professor in his subsequent academic career." 310 F. Supp., at 979. And the Court of Appeals based its affirmance of the summary judgment largely on the premise that "the substantial adverse effect non-retention is likely to have upon the career interests of an individual professor" amounts to a limitation on future employment opportunities sufficient to invoke procedural due process guarantees. 446 F.2d, at 809. But even assuming, *arguendo,* that such a "substantial adverse effect" under these circumstances would constitute a state-imposed restriction on liberty, the record contains no support for these assumptions. There is no suggestion of how nonretention might affect the respondent's future employment prospects. Mere proof, for example, that his record of nonretention in one job, taken alone, might make him somewhat less attractive to some other employers would hardly establish the kind of foreclosure of opportunities amounting to deprivation of "liberty." . . .

[14] . . . The Court of Appeals, nonetheless, argued that opportunity for a hearing and a statement of reasons were required here "as a *prophylactic* against non–retention decisions improperly motivated by exercise of protected rights." 446 F.2d, at 810 (emphasis supplied). While the Court of Appeals recognized the lack of a finding that the respondent's non-retention was based on exercise of the right of free speech, it felt that the respondent's interest in liberty was sufficiently implicated here because the decision not to rehire him was made "with a background of controversy and unwelcome expressions of opinion." . . .

In the respondent's case, however, the State has not directly impinged upon interests in free speech or free press in any way comparable to a seizure of books or an injunction against meetings. Whatever may be a teacher's rights of free speech, the interest in holding a teaching job at a state university, *simpliciter,* is not itself a free speech interest.

interests in continued employment that are safeguarded by due process. Only last year, the Court held that this principle "proscribing summary dismissal from public employment without hearing or inquiry required by due process" also applied to a teacher recently hired without tenure or a formal contract, but nonetheless with a clearly implied promise of continued employment. *Connell v. Higginbotham*, 403 U.S. 207, 208.

Certain attributes of "property" interests protected by procedural due process emerge from these decisions. To have a property interest in a benefit, a person clearly must have more than an abstract need or desire for it. He must have more than a unilateral expectation of it. He must, instead, have a legitimate claim of entitlement to it. It is a purpose of the constitutional right to a hearing to provide an opportunity for a person to vindicate those claims.

Property interests, of course, are not created by the Constitution. Rather, they are created and their dimensions are defined by existing rules or understandings that stem from an independent source such as state law — rules or understandings that secure certain benefits and that support claims of entitlement to those benefits. Thus, the welfare recipients in *Goldberg v. Kelly, supra,* had a claim of entitlement to welfare payments that was grounded in the statute defining eligibility for them. The recipients had not yet shown that they were, in fact, within the statutory terms of eligibility. But we held that they had a right to a hearing at which they might attempt to do so.

Just as the welfare recipients' "property" interest in welfare payments was created and defined by statutory terms, so the respondent's "property" interest in employment at Wisconsin State University-Oshkosh was created and defined by the terms of his appointment. Those terms secured his interest in employment up to June 30, 1969. But the important fact in this case is that they specifically provided that the respondent's employment was to terminate on June 30. They did not provide for contract renewal absent "sufficient cause." Indeed, they made no provision for renewal whatsoever.

Thus, the terms of the respondent's appointment secured absolutely no interest in re-employment for the next year. They supported absolutely no possible claim of entitlement to re-employment. Nor, significantly, was there any state statute or University rule or policy that secured his interest in re-employment or that created any legitimate claim to it.[16] In these circumstances, the respondent surely had an abstract concern in being rehired, but he did not have a *property* interest sufficient to require the University authorities to give him a hearing when they declined to renew his contract of employment.

---

[16] To be sure, the respondent does suggest that most teachers hired on a year-to-year basis by Wisconsin State University-Oshkosh are, in fact, rehired. But the District Court has not found that there is anything approaching a "common law" of re-employment, *see Perry v. Sindermann, infra,* so strong as to require University officials to give the respondent a statement of reasons and a hearing on their decision not to rehire him.

IV.

Our analysis of the respondent's constitutional rights in this case in no way indicates a view that an opportunity for a hearing or a statement of reasons for nonretention would, or would not, be appropriate or wise in public colleges and universities. For it is a written Constitution that we apply. Our role is confined to interpretation of that Constitution.

We must conclude that the summary judgment for the respondent should not have been granted, since the respondent has not shown that he was deprived of liberty or property protected by the Fourteenth Amendment. The judgment of the Court of Appeals, accordingly, is reversed and the case is remanded for further proceedings consistent with this opinion.

It is so ordered.

[MR. JUSTICE POWELL took no part in the decision of this case. MR. JUSTICE DOUGLAS' dissenting opinion is omitted.]

MR. JUSTICE MARSHALL, dissenting.

. . . While I agree with Part I of the Court's opinion setting forth the proper framework for consideration of the issue presented, and also with those portions of Parts II and III of the Court's opinion that assert that a public employee is entitled to procedural due process whenever a State stigmatizes him by denying employment, or injures his future employment prospects severely, or whenever the State deprives him of a property interest, I would go further than the court does in defining the terms "liberty" and "property."

The prior decisions of this Court, discussed at length in the opinion of the Court, establish a principle that is as obvious as it is compelling — *i.e.,* federal and state governments and governmental agencies are restrained by the Constitution from acting arbitrarily with respect to employment opportunities that they either offer or control. Hence, it is now firmly established that whether or not a private employer is free to act capriciously or unreasonably with respect to employment practices, at least absent statutory or contractual controls, a government employer is different. The government may only act fairly and reasonably. . . .

In my view, every citizen who applies for a government job is entitled to it unless the government can establish some reason for denying the employment. This is the "property" right that I believe is protected by the Fourteenth Amendment and that cannot be denied "without due process of law." And it is also liberty — liberty to work — which is the "very essence of the personal freedom and opportunity" secured by the Fourteenth Amendment. . . .

Employment is one of the greatest, if not the greatest, benefits that governments offer in modern-day life. When something as valuable as the opportunity to work is at stake, the government may not reward some citizens and not others without demonstrating that its actions are fair and equitable. And it is procedural due process that is our fundamental guarantee of fairness, our protection against arbitrary, capricious, and unreasonable government action. . . .

It may be argued that to provide procedural due process to all public employees or prospective employees would place an intolerable burden on the machinery of government. *Cf. Goldberg v. Kelly, supra.* The short answer to that argument is that it is not burdensome to give reasons when reasons exist. Whenever an application of reemployment is denied, an employee is discharged, or a decision not to rehire an employee is made, there should be some reason from the decision. It can scarcely be argued that government would be crippled by a requirement that the reason be communicated to the person most directly affected by the government's action. . . .

It might also be argued that to require a hearing and a statement of reasons is to require a useless act, because a government bent on denying employment to one or more persons will do so regardless of the procedural hurdles that are placed in its path. Perhaps this is so, but a requirement of procedural regularity at least renders arbitrary action more difficult. Moreover, proper procedures will surely eliminate some of the arbitrariness that results, not from malice, but from innocent error. . . . When the government knows it may have to justify its decisions with sound reasons, its conduct is likely to be more cautious, careful, and correct. . . .

PERRY v. SINDERMANN

United States Supreme Court
408 U.S. 593 (1972)

Mr. Justice Stewart delivered the opinion of the Court.

From 1959 to 1969 the respondent, Robert Sindermann, was a teacher in the state college system of the State of Texas. After teaching for two years at the University of Texas and for four years at San Antonio Junior College, he became a professor of Government and Social Science at Odessa Junior College in 1965. He was employed at the college for four successive years, under a series of one-year contracts. He was successful enough to be appointed, for a time, the co-chairman of his department.

During the 1968-1969 academic year, however, controversy arose between the respondent and the college administration. The respondent was elected president of the Texas Junior College Teachers Association. In this capacity, he left his teaching duties on several occasions to testify before committees of the Texas Legislature, and he became involved in public disagreements with the policies of the college's Board of Regents. In particular, he aligned himself with a group advocating the elevation of the college to four-year status — a change opposed by the Regents. And, on one occasion, a newspaper advertisement appeared over his name that was highly critical of the Regents.

Finally, in May 1969, the respondent's one-year employment contract terminated and the Board of Regents voted not to offer him a new contract for the next academic year. The Regents issued a press release setting forth allegations of the respondent's insubordination.[1] But they provided him no official statement of the reasons for the nonrenewal of his contract. And they allowed him no opportunity for a hearing to challenge the basis of the nonrenewal.

The respondent then brought this action in Federal District Court. He alleged primarily that the Regents' decision not to rehire him was based on his public criticism of the policies of the college administration and thus infringed his right to freedom of speech. He also alleged that their failure to provide him an opportunity for a hearing violated the Fourteenth Amendment's guarantee of procedural due process. The petitioners — members of the Board of Regents and the President of the college — denied that their decision was made in retaliation for the respondent's public criticism and argued that they had no obligation to provide a hearing.[2] On the basis of these bare pleadings and three brief affidavits filed by the respondent,[3] the District Court granted summary judgment for the petitioners. It concluded that the respondent had "no cause of action against the [petitioners] since his contract of employment terminated May 31, 1969, and Odessa Junior College has not adopted the tenure system."

The Court of Appeals reversed the judgment of the District Court. 430 F.2d 939. First, it held that, despite the respondent's lack of tenure, the nonrenewal of his contract would violate the Fourteenth Amendment if it in fact was based on his protected free speech. Since the actual reason for the Regents' decision was "in total dispute" in the pleadings, the court remanded the case for a full hearing on this contested issue of fact. . . . Second, the Court of Appeals held that, despite the respondent's lack of tenure, the failure to allow him an opportunity for hearing would violate the constitutional guarantee of procedural due process if the respondent could show that he had an "expectancy" of re-employment. It, therefore, ordered that this issue of fact also be aired upon remand. . . . We granted a writ of certiorari, 403 U.S. 917, and we have considered this case along with *Board of Regents v. Roth.* . . .

I.

The first question presented is whether the respondent's lack of a contractual or tenure right to re-employment, taken alone, defeats his claim that the nonrenewal of his contract violated the First and Fourteenth Amendments. We hold that it does not.

For at least a quarter-century, this Court has made clear that even though a person has no "right" to a valuable governmental benefit and even though the Government may deny him the benefit for any number of reasons, there are some reasons upon which the government may not rely. It may not deny

---

[1] The press release stated, for example, that the respondent had defied his superiors by attending legislative committee meetings when college officials had specifically refused to permit him to leave his classes for that purpose.

[2] The petitioners claimed, in their motion for summary judgment, that the decision not to retain the respondent was really based on his insubordinate conduct. . . .

[3] The petitioners, for whom summary judgment was granted, submitted no affidavits whatever. The respondent's affidavits were very short and essentially repeated the general allegations of his complaint.

a benefit to a person on a basis that infringes his constitutionally protected interests — especially, his interest in freedom of speech. For if the government could deny a benefit to a person because of his constitutionally protected speech or associations, his exercise of those freedoms would in effect be penalized and inhibited. This would allow the government to "produce a result which [it] could not command directly." *Speiser v. Randall*, 357 U.S. 513, 526. Such interference with constitutional rights is impermissible.

. . . [T]he respondent's lack of a contractual or tenure "right" to re-employment for the 1969-1970 academic year is immaterial to his free speech claim. . . .

In this case, of course, the respondent has yet to show that the decision not to renew his contract was, in fact, made in retaliation for his exercise of the constitutional right of free speech. The District Court foreclosed any opportunity to make this showing when it granted summary judgment. Hence, we cannot now hold that the Board of Regents' action was invalid.

But we agree with the Court of Appeals that there is a genuine dispute as to "whether the college refused to renew the teaching contract on an impermissible basis as a reprisal for the exercise of constitutionally protected rights. . . ."

For this reason we hold that the grant of summary judgment against the respondent, without full exploration of this issue, was improper.

II.

The respondent's lack of formal contractual or tenure security in continued employment at Odessa Junior College, though irrelevant to his free speech claim, is highly relevant to his procedural due process claim. But it may not be entirely dispositive.

We have held today in *Board of Regents v. Roth*, . . . that the Constitution does not require opportunity for a hearing before the nonrenewal of a nontenured teacher's contract, unless he can show that the decision not to rehire him somehow deprived him of an interest in "liberty" or that he had a "property" interest in continued employment, despite the lack of tenure or a formal contract. In *Roth* the teacher had not made a showing on either point to justify summary judgment in his favor.

Similarly, the respondent here has yet to show that he has been deprived of an interest that could invoke procedural due process protection. As in *Roth*, the mere showing that he was not rehired in one particular job, without more, did not amount to a showing of a loss of liberty.[5] Nor did it amount to a showing of a loss of property.

But the respondent's allegations — which we must construe most favorably to the respondent at this stage of the litigation — do raise a genuine issue as to his interest in continued employment at Odessa Junior College. He alleged that this interest, though not secured by a formal contractual tenure

---

[5] The Court of Appeals suggested that the respondent might have a due process right to some kind of hearing simply if he *asserts* to college officials that their decision was based on his constitutionally protected conduct. . . . We have rejected this approach in *Board of Regents v. Roth*. . . .

provision, was secured by a no less binding understanding fostered by the college administration. In particular, the respondent alleged that the college had a *de facto* tenure program, and that he had tenure under that program. He claimed that he and others legitimately relied upon an unusual provision that had been in the college's official Faculty Guide for many years:

> *Teacher Tenure:* Odessa College has no tenure system. The Administration of the College wishes the faculty member to feel that he has permanent tenure as long as his teaching services are satisfactory and as long as he displays a cooperative attitude toward his co-workers and his superiors, and as long as he is happy in his work.

Moreover, the respondent claimed legitimate reliance upon guidelines promulgated by the Coordinating Board of the Texas College and University System that provided that a person, like himself, who had been employed as a teacher in the state college and university system for seven years or more has some form of job tenure. Thus, the respondent offered to prove that a teacher with his long period of service at this particular State College has no less a "property" interest in continued employment than a formally tenured teacher at other colleges, and had no less a procedural due process right to a statement of reasons and a hearing before college officials upon their decision not to retain him.

We have made clear in *Roth* . . . that "property" interests subject to procedural due process protection are not limited by a few rigid, technical forms. Rather, "property" denotes a broad range of interests that are secured by "existing rules or understandings." . . . A person's interest in a benefit is a "property" interest for due process purposes if there are such rules or mutually explicit understanding that support his claim of entitlement to the benefit and that he may invoke at a hearing. . . .

A written contract with an explicit tenure provision clearly is evidence of a formal understanding that supports a teacher's claim of entitlement to continued employment unless sufficient "cause" is shown. Yet absence of such an explicit contractual provision may not always foreclose the possibility that a teacher has a "property" interest in re-employment. For example, the law of contracts in most, if not all, jurisdictions long has employed a process by which agreements, though not formalized in writing, may be "implied." 3 A. *Corbin on Contracts* §§ 561-572A (1960). Explicit contractual provisions may be supplemented by other agreements implied from "the promisor's words and conduct in the light of the surrounding circumstances." *Id.*, at § 562. And, "[t]he meaning of [the promisor's] words and acts is found by relating them to the usage of the past." *Id.*

A teacher, like the respondent, who has held his position for a number of years, might be able to show from the circumstances of this service — and from other relevant facts — that he has a legitimate claim of entitlement to job tenure. Just as this Court has found there to be a "common law of a particular industry or of a particular plant" that may supplement a collective-bargaining agreement, . . . so there may be an unwritten "common law" in a particular university that certain employees shall have the equivalent of tenure. This is particularly likely in a college or university, like Odessa Junior College, that has no explicit tenure system even for senior members of its faculty, but that nonetheless may have created such a system in practice. *See* C. Byse & L. Joughin, *Tenure in American Higher Education* 17-18 (1959).[7]

In this case, the respondent has alleged the existence of rules and understandings, promulgated and fostered by state officials, that may justify his legitimate claim of entitlement to continued employment absent "sufficient cause." We disagree with the Court of Appeals insofar as it held that a mere subjective "expectancy" is protected by procedural due process, but we agree that the respondent must be given an opportunity to prove the legitimacy of his claim of such entitlement in light of "the policies and practices of the institution. . . ." Proof of such a property interest would not, of course, entitle him to reinstatement. But such proof would obligate college officials to grant a hearing at his request, where he could be informed of the grounds for his nonretention and challenge their sufficiency.

Therefore, while we do not wholly agree with the opinion of the Court of Appeals, its judgment remanding this case to the District Court is

Affirmed.

[Mr. Justice Powell took no part in the decision of this case. Justices Burger, White, Blackmun and Rehnquist joined Justice Stewart's opinion. Justices Brennan, Douglas and Marshall agreed with Part I, and voted "to direct the District Court to enter summary judgment for respondent entitling him to . . . reasons why his contract was not renewed. . . ."]

Mr. Chief Justice Burger, concurring.[*]

I concur in the Court's judgments and opinions in *Sindermann* and *Roth,* but there is one central point in both decisions that I would like to underscore since it may have been obscured in the comprehensive discussion of the cases. That point is that the relationship between a state institution and one of its teachers is essentially a matter of state concern and state law. The Court holds today only that a state-employed teacher who has a right to re-employment under state law, arising from either an express or implied contract, has, in turn, a right guaranteed by the Fourteenth Amendment to some form of prior administrative or academic hearing on the cause for nonrenewal of his contract. Thus, whether a particular teacher in a particular context has any right to such administrative hearing hinges on a question of state law. . . .

---

[7] We do not now hold that the respondent has any such legitimate claim of entitlement to job tenure. For "[p]roperty interests . . . are not created by the Constitution. Rather, they are created and their dimensions are defined by existing rules or understandings that stem from an independent source such as state law. . . ." *Board of Regents v. Roth, infra,* at 87. If it is the law of Texas that a teacher in the respondent's position has no contractual or other claim to job tenure, the respondent's claim would be defeated.

[*] This concurring opinion applies also to No. 71-162, *Board of Regents of State Colleges et al. v. Roth, infra,* p. 87

NOTES AND QUESTIONS

2-24. How does the Supreme Court's due process approach in *Roth* and *Sindermann* compare with its approach in *Bailey v. Richardson*? In *Cafeteria Workers v. McElroy*? At what point does the Court employ a balancing test?

2-25. For purposes of the Court's due process methodology, what is a property interest? Why does the Court reach different conclusions in *Roth* and *Sindermann*? How much discretion does the Court have in making these determinations?

2-26. Are there liberty interests at stake in *Roth* and *Sindermann*? What are they? How does the Court go about making these decisions?

2-27. Consider the application of the *Roth* and *Sindermann* approach in *Bishop v. Wood,* 426 U.S. 341 (1976):

Petitioner was employed by the city of Marion as a probationary policeman on June 9, 1969. After six months he became a permanent employee. He was dismissed on March 31, 1972. He claims that he had either an express or an implied right to continued employment. . . .

. . . The North Carolina Supreme Court has held that an enforceable expectation of continued public employment in that State can exist only if the employer, by statute or contract, has actually granted some form of guarantee. *Still v. Lance,* 279 N.C. 254, 182 S.E.2d 403 (1971). Whether such a guarantee has been given can be determined only by an examination of the particular statute or ordinance in question.

On its face the ordinance on which petitioner relies may fairly be read as conferring such a guarantee. However, such a reading is not the only possible interpretation; the ordinance may also be construed as granting no right to continued employment but merely conditioning an employee's removal on compliance with certain specified procedures. We do not have any authoritative interpretation of this ordinance by a North Carolina state court. We do, however, have the opinion of the United States District Judge who, of course, sits in North Carolina and practiced law there for many years. Based on his understanding of state law, he concluded that petitioner "held his position at the will and pleasure of the city. . . ." [The Court concluded that it would defer to the District Court's interpretation and that no property interest existed. It went on to note its unease with the kind of case it was asked to decide].

The federal court is not the appropriate forum in which to review the multitude of personnel decisions that are made daily by public agencies. We must accept the harsh fact that numerous individual mistakes are inevitable in the day-to-day administration of our affairs. The United States Constitution cannot feasibly be construed to require federal judicial review for every such error. In the absence of any claim that the public employer was motivated by a desire to curtail or to penalize the exercise of an employee's constitutionally protected rights, we must presume that official

§ 2.05   DUE PROCESS AND ADMINISTRATIVE ADJUDICATION   101

action was regular and, if erroneous, can best be corrected in other ways. The Due Process Clause of the Fourteenth Amendment is not a guarantee against incorrect or ill-advised personnel decisions. . . .

Is it right for the Supreme Court to defer to a state law interpretation by a lower federal court? Is this approach too rigid? Too formalistic? Or is it an attempt to be objective? On the other hand, was the Court in *Bishop* particularly concerned with both the volume and the appropriateness of personnel decisions in Federal Court?

2-28. Consider Justice Rehnquist's approach to determining whether a property interest exists in *Arnett v. Kennedy*, 416 U.S. 124 (1974):

Prior to the events leading to his discharge, appellee Wayne Kennedy was a nonprobationary federal employee in the competitive Civil Service. He was a field representative in the Chicago Regional Office of the Office of Economic Opportunity (OEO). In March 1972, he was removed from the federal service pursuant to the provisions of the Lloyd-LaFollette Act, 5 U.S.C. § 7501, after Wendell Verduin, the Regional Director of the OEO, upheld written administrative charges made in the form of a "Notification of Proposed Adverse Action" against appellee. The charges listed five events occurring in November and December 1971; the most serious of the charges was that appellee "without any proof whatsoever and in reckless disregard of the actual facts" known to him or reasonably discoverable by him had publicly stated that Verduin and his administrative assistant had attempted to bribe a representative of a community action organization with which the OEO had dealings. The alleged bribe consisted of an offer of a $100,000 grant of OEO funds if the representative would sign a statement against appellee and another OEO employee.

Appellee was advised of his right under regulations promulgated by the Civil Service Commission and the OEO to reply to the charges orally and in writing, and to submit affidavits to Verduin. He was also advised that the material on which the notice was based was available for his inspection in the Regional Office, and that a copy of the material was attached to the notice of proposed adverse action.

Appellee did not respond to the substance of the charges against him, but instead asserted that the charges were unlawful because he had a right to a trial-type hearing before an impartial hearing officer before he could be removed from his employment and because statements made by him were protected by the First Amendment to the United States Constitution. On March 20, 1972, Verduin notified appellee in writing that he would be removed from his position at the close of business on March 27, 1972. Appellee was also notified of his right to appeal Verduin's decision either to the OEO or to the Civil Service Commission.

Appellee then instituted this suit in the United States District Court for the Northern District of Illinois. . . . In his amended complaint, appellee contended that the standards and procedures established by and under the Lloyd-LaFollette Act for the removal of nonprobationary employees from the federal service unwarrantedly interfere with those employees' freedom of expression and deny them procedural due process of law. . . . [The Court summarized the statute and regulations involved].

That Act, as now codified, . . . together with the administrative regulations issued by the Civil Service Commission and the OEO, provided the statutory and administrative framework which the Government contends controlled the proceedings against appellee. The District Court, in its ruling on appellee's procedural contentions, in effect held that the Fifth Amendment to the United States Constitution prohibited Congress, in the Lloyd-LaFollette Act, from granting protection against removal without cause and at the same time — indeed, in the same sentence — specifying that the determination of cause should be without the full panoply of rights which attend a trial-type adversary hearing. We do not believe that the Constitution so limits Congress in the manner in which benefits may be extended to federal employees.

Appellee recognizes that our recent decisions in *Board of Regents v. Roth,* 408 U.S. 564 (1972), and *Perry v. Sindermann,* 408 U.S. 593 (1972), are those most closely in point with respect to the procedural rights constitutionally guaranteed public employees in connection with their dismissal from employment. Appellee contends that he had a property interest or an expectancy of employment which could not be divested without first affording him a full adversary hearing.

In *Board of Regents v. Roth,* we said:

"Property interests, of course, are not created by the Constitution. Rather, they are created and their dimensions are defined by existing rules or understandings that stem from an independent source such as state law — rules or understandings that secure certain benefits and that support claims of entitlement to those benefits." 408 U.S., at 577.

Here appellee did have a statutory expectancy that he not be removed other than for "such cause as will promote the efficiency of [the] service." But the very section of the statute which granted him that right, a right which had previously existed only by virtue of administrative regulation, expressly provided also for the procedure by which "cause" was to be determined, and expressly omitted the procedural guarantees which appellee insists are mandated by the Constitution. Only by bifurcating the very sentence of the Act of Congress which conferred upon appellee the right not to be removed save for cause could it be said that he had an expectancy of that substantive right without the procedural limitations which Congress attached to it. In the area of federal regulation of government employees, where in the absence of statutory limitation the governmental employer has had virtually uncontrolled latitude in decisions as to hiring and firing, *Cafeteria Workers v. McElroy,* 367 U.S. 886, 896-897 (1961), we do not believe that a statutory enactment such as the Lloyd-LaFollette Act may be parsed as discretely as appellee urges. Congress was obviously intent on according a measure of statutory job security to governmental employees which they had not previously enjoyed, but was likewise intent on excluding more elaborate procedural requirements which it felt would make the operation of the new scheme unnecessarily burdensome in practice. Where the focus of legislation was thus strongly on the procedural mechanism for enforcing the substantive right which was simultaneously conferred, we decline to conclude that the substantive right may be viewed wholly apart from the procedure provided for its enforcement. The employee's statutorily defined right is not a guarantee against removal without cause in the abstract, but such a guarantee as enforced by the procedures which Congress has designated for the determination of cause.

The Court has previously viewed skeptically the action of a litigant in challenging the constitutionality of portions of a statute under which it has simultaneously claimed benefits. . . .

This doctrine has unquestionably been applied unevenly in the past, and observed as often as not in the breach. We believe that at the very least it gives added weight to our conclusion that where the grant of a substantive right is inextricably intertwined with the limitations on the procedures which are to be employed in determining that right, a litigant in the position of appellee must take the bitter with the sweet.

To conclude otherwise would require us to hold that although Congress chose to enact what was essentially a legislative compromise, and with unmistakable clarity granted governmental employees security against being dismissed without "cause," but refused to accord them a full adversary hearing for the determination of "cause," it was constitutionally disabled from making such a choice. We would be holding that federal employees had been granted, as a result of the enactment of the Lloyd-LaFollette Act, not merely that which Congress had given them in the first part of a sentence, but that which Congress had expressly withheld from them in the latter part of the same sentence. Neither the language of the Due Process Clause of the Fifth Amendment nor our cases construing it require any such hobbling restrictions on legislative authority in this area. . . .

What do you think of this approach? How does it differ from the right/privilege distinction?

2-29. In *Cleveland Board of Education v. Loudermill,* 470 U.S. 532 (1985), a majority of the Supreme Court specifically rejected the "bitter with the sweet" approach. In that case, a security guard was dismissed from his job by the Cleveland Board of Education "because of his dishonesty in filling out the employment applications." Under Ohio law, Loudermill was a "classified civil servant" and was entitled to administrative review after discharge. The statute made no provisions for process prior to discharge and it was this that Loudermill challenged. In response to the argument that Loudermill's property right under Ohio law was only as good as the process that statute provided, the Court stated:

. . . it is settled that the "bitter with the sweet" approach misconceives the constitutional guarantee. If a clearer holding is needed, we provide it today. The point is straightforward: the Due Process Clause provides that certain substantive rights — life, liberty, and property — cannot be deprived except pursuant to constitutionally adequate procedures. The categories of substance and procedure are distinct. Were the rule otherwise, the Clause would be reduced to a mere tautology. "Property" cannot be defined by the procedures provided for its deprivation any more than can life or liberty.

The right to due process is conferred, not by legislative grace, but by constitutional guarantee. . . .

The *Loudermill* Court went on to hold that due process compelled some form of pretermination hearing. Do you agree that "substance and procedure are distinct"? If the state can create a property right, why can it not determine its weight or significance?

2-30. In *Paul v. Davis,* 424 U.S. 693 (1975), for example, the Court, speaking through Justice Rehnquist, narrowly construed the liberty interest at stake in that case. Plaintiff complained that he had been defamed by a circular distributed by the police to various stores describing him as an "active shoplifter." He argued that his Fourteenth Amendment due process rights had been violated because he was never given notice of this circular nor an opportunity for a hearing to determine whether this characterization of him was accurate before the flyer was circulated. The majority of the Court noted that this complaint "would appear to state a classical claim for defamation actionable in the courts of virtually every State." But, the Court also noted, respondent brought this action in federal court, not state court. Though the real remedy might lie in a tort suit in a state court, the majority went on to address his federal claim and assess the liberty interest at stake in this case. For this Court, damage to Paul's reputation was not enough of a liberty interest to trigger Due Process Clause protections. In a critical view of the Court's reasoning, one commentator has noted:

> The Court of Appeals upheld [Paul's] claim, relying upon the Supreme Court's decisions in *Roth* and *Wisconsin v. Constantineau* to support the proposition that state defamation of a private person implicated a constitutional "liberty." In *Constantineau* the Court had invalidated on due process grounds a state statute that allowed a sheriff to label publicly an individual an alcoholic by posting his name in a public place, without giving him prior notice and a hearing. The Court noted that the challenged procedure denied the individual more than just the opportunity to purchase alcoholic beverages within city limits: the posting was an act of defamation. In language subsequently quoted with approval in *Roth,* the Court said that "[w]here a person's good name, reputation, honor, or integrity is at stake because of what the government is doing to him, notice and an opportunity to be heard are essential."
>
> But in *Paul,* the Court characterized this same language as ambiguous and supportive of the respondent's claim only if "read that way." The majority then proceeded to distinguish a long line of decisions which had recognized the standing of a plaintiff to complain about governmental defamation. The Court concluded that in all those cases the defamation standing alone was insufficient to implicate a liberty interest; instead, all involved an interference with some specific constitutional guarantee *or with some other "more tangible" interest created by state law.* The Court cavalierly distinguished *Constantineau* by noting that the state defamation there involved — posting by the sheriff — had the legal effect of cutting off the plaintiff's prior state-created right to buy liquor, a factor which, the Court failed to add, played an obviously trivial role in the decision of that case. The Court's re-rationalization of the earlier cases is wholly startling to

§ 2.05   DUE PROCESS AND ADMINISTRATIVE ADJUDICATION   105

anyone familiar with those precedents. In many ways I find this *Paul's* most disturbing aspect. Fair treatment by the Court of its own precedents is an indispensable condition of judicial legitimacy.

Monaghan, *Of Liberty and Property,* 62 CORNELL L. REV. 405, 424–25 (1977).*

Perhaps the Court was trying too hard to limit the application of the Due Process Clause. Could it alternatively have held that the Due Process Clause applied, but that the process due was a state court tort action that could occur after the fact? Contrast the approaches the Court takes to the due process issues in the following cases with *Paul v. Davis, Goldberg, Roth* and *Sindermann.* How does the Court treat the liberty strand of the Due Process Clause, as compared to Property? Do these approaches provide both courts and agencies with more flexibility in deciding due process issues or do they, in effect, undermine the basic premises of *Goldberg v. Kelly*?

SANDIN v. CONNER

Supreme Court of the United States
515 U.S. 472 (1995)

REHNQUIST, C.J., delivered the opinion of the Court, in which O'CONNOR, SCALIA, KENNEDY, and THOMAS, JJ., joined. GINSBURG, J., filed a dissenting opinion, in which STEVENS, J., joined. BREYER, J., filed a dissenting opinion, in which SOUTER, J., joined.

CHIEF JUSTICE REHNQUIST delivered the opinion of the Court.

We granted certiorari to reexamine the circumstances under which state prison regulations afford inmates a liberty interest protected by the Due Process Clause.

I

DeMont Conner was convicted of numerous state crimes, including murder, kidnaping, robbery, and burglary, for which he is currently serving an indeterminate sentence of 30 years to life in a Hawaii prison. He was confined in the Halawa Correctional Facility, a maximum security prison in central Oahu. In August 1987, a prison officer escorted him from his cell to the module program area. The officer subjected Conner to a strip search, complete with an inspection of the rectal area. Conner retorted with angry and foul language directed at the officer. Eleven days later he received notice that he had been charged with disciplinary infractions. The notice charged Conner with "high misconduct" for using physical interference to impair a correctional function,

---

* Copyright © 1977 by Cornell Law Review. All rights reserved.

and "low moderate misconduct" for using abusive or obscene language and for harassing employees.[1]

Conner appeared before an adjustment committee on August 28, 1987. The committee refused Conner's request to present witnesses at the hearing, stating that "[w]itnesses were unavailable due to move [sic] to the medium facility and being short staffed on the modules." At the conclusion of proceedings, the committee determined that Conner was guilty of the alleged misconduct. It sentenced him to 30 days' disciplinary segregation in the Special Holding Unit[2] for the physical obstruction charge, and four hours segregation for each of the other two charges to be served concurrent with the 30 days. Conner's segregation began August 31, 1987, and ended September 29, 1987.

Conner sought administrative review within 14 days of receiving the committee's decision. Nine months later, the deputy administrator found the high misconduct charge unsupported and expunged Conner's disciplinary record with respect to that charge. But before the deputy administrator decided the appeal, Conner had brought this suit against the adjustment committee chair and other prison officials in the United States District Court for the District of Hawaii based on Rev. Stat. § 1979, 42 U.S.C. § 1983. His amended complaint prayed for injunctive relief, declaratory relief, and damages for, among other things, a deprivation of procedural due process in connection with the disciplinary hearing. The District Court granted summary judgment in favor of the prison officials.

The Court of Appeals for the Ninth Circuit reversed the judgment. It concluded that Conner had a liberty interest in remaining free from disciplinary segregation and that there was a disputed question of fact with respect to whether Conner received all of the process due under this Court's pronouncement in *Wolff v. McDonnell*. The Court of Appeals based its conclusion on a prison regulation that instructs the committee to find guilt when a charge of misconduct is supported by substantial evidence. Haw. Admin. Rule § 17-201-18(b)(2) (1983).[3] The Court of Appeals reasoned from *Kentucky Dept. of*

---

[1] Hawaii's prison regulations establish a hierarchy of misconduct ranging from "greatest misconduct," Haw. Admin. Rule § 17-201-6(a) (1983), to "minor misconduct," § 17-201-10. Section 17-201-7 enumerates offenses punishable as "high misconduct" and sets available punishment for such offenses at disciplinary segregation up to 30 days or any sanction other than disciplinary segregation. Section 17-201-9 lists offenses punishable as "low moderate misconduct" and sets punishment at disciplinary segregation up to four hours in cell, monetary restitution, or any sanction other than disciplinary segregation. In addition to the levels of misconduct which classify various misdeeds, the regulations also define "serious misconduct" as "that which poses a serious threat to the safety, security, or welfare of the staff, other inmates or wards, or the institution and subjects the individual to the imposition of serious penalties such as segregation for longer than four hours." § 17-201-12. Such misconduct is punished through adjustment committee procedures. *Ibid.* The parties apparently concede that the physical obstruction allegation constituted serious misconduct, but that the low moderate misconduct charges did not.

[2] The Special Holding Unit (SHU) houses inmates placed in disciplinary segregation, § 17-201-19(c), administrative segregation, § 17-201-22, and protective custody, § 17-201-23. Single-person cells comprise the SHU and conditions are substantially similar for each of the three classifications of inmates housed there. With the exception of one extra phone call and one extra visiting privilege, inmates segregated for administrative reasons receive the same privilege revocations as those segregated for disciplinary reasons.

[3] The full text of the regulation reads as follows:

"Upon completion of the hearing, the committee may take the matter under advisement and

Corrections v. Thompson that the committee's duty to find guilt was nondiscretionary. From the language of the regulation, it drew a negative inference that the committee may not impose segregation if it does not find substantial evidence of misconduct. It viewed this as a state-created liberty interest, and therefore held that respondent was entitled to call witnesses by virtue of our opinion in *Wolff, supra*. We granted the State's petition for certiorari, and now reverse.

II

Our due process analysis begins with *Wolff*. There, Nebraska inmates challenged the decision of prison officials to revoke good time credits without adequate procedures. Inmates earned good time credits under a state statute that bestowed mandatory sentence reductions for good behavior, revocable only for "'flagrant or serious misconduct.'" We held that the Due Process Clause itself does not create a liberty interest in credit for good behavior, but that the statutory provision created a liberty interest in a "shortened prison sentence" which resulted from good time credits, credits which were revocable only if the prisoner was guilty of serious misconduct. The Court characterized this liberty interest as one of "real substance" and articulated minimum procedures necessary to reach a "mutual accommodation between institutional needs and objectives and the provisions of the Constitution." Much of *Wolff's* contribution to the landscape of prisoners' due process derived not from its description of liberty interests, but rather from its intricate balancing of prison management concerns with prisoners' liberty in determining the amount of process due. Its short discussion of the definition of a liberty interest, led to a more thorough treatment of the issue in *Meachum v. Fano*.

Inmates in *Meachum* sought injunctive relief, declaratory relief, and damages by reason of transfers from a Massachusetts medium security prison to a maximum security facility with substantially less favorable conditions. The transfers were ordered in the aftermath of arson incidents for which the transferred inmates were thought to be responsible, and did not entail a loss of good time credits or any period of disciplinary confinement. The Court began with the proposition that the Due Process Clause does not protect every change in the conditions of confinement having a substantial adverse impact on the prisoner. It then held that the Due Process Clause did not itself create a liberty interest in prisoners to be free from intrastate prison transfers. It reasoned that transfer to a maximum security facility, albeit one with more burdensome conditions, was "within the normal limits or range of custody which the conviction has authorized the State to impose." The Court distinguished *Wolff* by noting that there the protected liberty interest in good time credit had been created by state law; here no comparable Massachusetts law

---

render a decision based upon evidence presented at the hearing to which the individual had an opportunity to respond or any cumulative evidence which may subsequently come to light may be used as a permissible inference of guilt, although disciplinary action shall be based upon more than mere silence. *A finding of guilt shall be made where*:

"(1) The inmate or ward admits the violation or pleads guilty.

"(2) *The charge is supported by substantial evidence*."

Haw. Admin. Rule § 17-201-18(b)(2) (1983) (emphasis added).

stripped officials of the discretion to transfer prisoners to alternative facilities "for whatever reason or for no reason at all."[4]

Shortly after *Meachum*, the Court embarked on a different approach to defining state-created liberty interests. Because dictum in *Meachum* distinguished *Wolff* by focusing on whether state action was mandatory or discretionary, the Court in later cases laid ever greater emphasis on this somewhat mechanical dichotomy. . . .

As this methodology took hold, no longer did inmates need to rely on a showing that they had suffered a " 'grievous loss' " of liberty retained even after sentenced to terms of imprisonment. *Morrissey v. Brewer*, 408 U.S. 471, 481. For the Court had ceased to examine the "nature" of the interest with respect to interests allegedly created by the State. In a series of cases since *Hewitt*, the Court has wrestled with the language of intricate, often rather routine prison guidelines to determine whether mandatory language and substantive predicates created an enforceable expectation that the State would produce a particular outcome with respect to the prisoner's conditions of confinement.

. . . .

By shifting the focus of the liberty interest inquiry to one based on the language of a particular regulation, and not the nature of the deprivation, the Court encouraged prisoners to comb regulations in search of mandatory language on which to base entitlements to various state-conferred privileges. Courts have, in response, and not altogether illogically, drawn negative inferences from mandatory language in the text of prison regulations. The Court of Appeals' approach in this case is typical: It inferred from the mandatory directive that a finding of guilt "shall" be imposed under certain conditions the conclusion that the absence of such conditions prevents a finding of guilt.

Such a conclusion may be entirely sensible in the ordinary task of construing a statute defining rights and remedies available to the general public. It is a good deal less sensible in the case of a prison regulation primarily designed to guide correctional officials in the administration of a prison. Not only are such regulations not designed to confer rights on inmates, but the result of the negative implication jurisprudence is not to require the prison officials to follow the negative implication drawn from the regulation, but is instead to attach procedural protections that may be of quite a different nature. Here, for example, the Court of Appeals did not hold that a finding of guilt could *not* be made in the *absence* of substantial evidence. Instead, it held that the "liberty interest" created by the regulation entitled the inmate to the procedural protections set forth in *Wolff*.

---

[4] Later cases, such as *Vitek v. Jones*, 445 U.S. 480 (1980), found that the Due Process Clause itself confers a liberty interest in certain situations. In *Vitek*, a prisoner was to be transferred involuntarily to a state mental hospital for treatment of a mental disease or defect; the Court held that his right to be free from such transfer was a liberty interest irrespective of state regulation; it was "qualitatively different" from the punishment characteristically suffered by a person convicted of crime, and had "stigmatizing consequences." . . . . *Washington v. Harper* . . . likewise concluded that, independent of any state regulation, an inmate had a liberty interest in being protected from the involuntary administration of psychotropic drugs.

§ 2.05   DUE PROCESS AND ADMINISTRATIVE ADJUDICATION   109

[This approach] has produced at least two undesirable effects. First, it creates disincentives for States to codify prison management procedures in the interest of uniform treatment. Prison administrators need be concerned with the safety of the staff and inmate population. Ensuring that welfare often leads prison administrators to curb the discretion of staff on the front line who daily encounter prisoners hostile to the authoritarian structure of the prison environment. Such guidelines are not set forth solely to benefit the prisoner. They also aspire to instruct subordinate employees how to exercise discretion vested by the State in the warden, and to confine the authority of prison personnel in order to avoid widely different treatment of similar incidents. The approach embraced by [cases prior to *Wolff*] discourages this desirable development: States may avoid creation of "liberty" interests by having scarcely any regulations, or by conferring standardless discretion on correctional personnel.

Second, [this] approach has led to the involvement of federal courts in the day-to-day management of prisons, often squandering judicial resources with little offsetting benefit to anyone. In so doing, it has run counter to the view expressed in several of our cases that federal courts ought to afford appropriate deference and flexibility to state officials trying to manage a volatile environment. Such flexibility is especially warranted in the fine-tuning of the ordinary incidents of prison life, a common subject of prisoner claims. . . .

In light of the above discussion, we believe that the search for a negative implication from mandatory language in prisoner regulations has strayed from the real concerns undergirding the liberty protected by the Due Process Clause. The time has come to return to the due process principles we believe were correctly established and applied in *Wolff* and *Meachum*.[5] Following *Wolff*, we recognize that States may under certain circumstances create liberty interests which are protected by the Due Process Clause. But these interests will be generally limited to freedom from restraint which, while not exceeding the sentence in such an unexpected manner as to give rise to protection by the Due Process Clause of its own force, nonetheless imposes atypical and significant hardship on the inmate in relation to the ordinary incidents of prison life.

Conner asserts, incorrectly, that any state action taken for a punitive reason encroaches upon a liberty interest under the Due Process Clause even in the absence of any state regulation. Neither *Bell v. Wolfish,* 441 U.S. 520 (1979), nor *Ingraham v. Wright,* 430 U.S. 651 (1977), requires such a rule. *Bell* dealt with the interests of pretrial detainees and not convicted prisoners. The Court in *Bell* correctly noted that a detainee "may not be punished prior to an adjudication of guilt in accordance with due process of law." The Court expressed concern that a State would attempt to punish a detainee for the crime for which he was indicted via preconviction holding conditions. Such

---

[5] Such abandonment . . . does not technically require us to overrule any holding of this Court. . . . Although it did locate a liberty interest in *Hewitt*, it concluded that due process required no additional procedural guarantees for the inmate. As such, its answer to the anterior question of whether the inmate possessed a liberty interest at all was unnecessary to the disposition of the case. Our decision today only abandons an approach that in practice is difficult to administer and which produces anomalous results.

a course would improperly extend the legitimate reasons for which such persons are detained — to ensure their presence at trial.

The same distinction applies to *Ingraham,* which addressed the rights of schoolchildren to remain free from arbitrary corporal punishment. The Court noted that the Due Process Clause historically encompassed the notion that the State could not "physically punish an individual except in accordance with due process of law" and so found schoolchildren sheltered. Although children sent to public school are lawfully confined to the classroom, arbitrary corporal punishment represents an invasion of personal security to which their parents do not consent when entrusting the educational mission to the State.

The punishment of incarcerated prisoners, on the other hand, serves different aims than those found invalid in *Bell* and *Ingraham.* The process does not impose retribution in lieu of a valid conviction, nor does it maintain physical control over free citizens forced by law to subject themselves to state control over the educational mission. It effectuates prison management and prisoner rehabilitative goals. Admittedly, prisoners do not shed all constitutional rights at the prison gate, *Wolff,* but " '[l]awful incarceration brings about the necessary withdrawal or limitation of many privileges and rights, a retraction justified by the considerations underlying our penal system.' " Discipline by prison officials in response to a wide range of misconduct falls within the expected perimeters of the sentence imposed by a court of law.

This case, though concededly punitive, does not present a dramatic departure from the basic conditions of Conner's indeterminate sentence. Although Conner points to dicta in cases implying that solitary confinement automatically triggers due process protection, this Court has not had the opportunity to address in an argued case the question whether disciplinary confinement of inmates itself implicates constitutional liberty interests. We hold that Conner's discipline in segregated confinement did not present the type of atypical, significant deprivation in which a State might conceivably create a liberty interest.

Nor does Conner's situation present a case where the State's action will inevitably affect the duration of his sentence. Nothing in Hawaii's code requires the parole board to deny parole in the face of a misconduct record or to grant parole in its absence, even though misconduct is by regulation a relevant consideration. The decision to release a prisoner rests on a myriad of considerations. And, the prisoner is afforded procedural protection at his parole hearing in order to explain the circumstances behind his misconduct record. . . . The chance that a finding of misconduct will alter the balance is simply too attenuated to invoke the procedural guarantees of the Due Process Clause.

We hold, therefore, that neither the Hawaii prison regulation in question, nor the Due Process Clause itself, afforded Conner a protected liberty interest that would entitle him to the procedural protections set forth in *Wolff.* The regime to which he was subjected as a result of the misconduct hearing was within the range of confinement to be normally expected for one serving an indeterminate term of 30 years to life.[11]

---

[11] Prisoners such as Conner, of course, retain other protection from arbitrary state action even within the expected conditions of confinement. They may invoke the First and Eighth Amend-

The judgment of the Court of Appeals is accordingly.

Reversed.

JUSTICE GINSBURG, with whom JUSTICE STEVENS joins, dissenting.

. . . .

Unlike the Court, I conclude that Conner had a liberty interest, protected by the Fourteenth Amendment's Due Process Clause, in avoiding the disciplinary confinement he endured. As JUSTICE BREYER details, Conner's prison punishment effected a severe alteration in the conditions of his incarceration. Disciplinary confinement as punishment for "high misconduct" not only deprives prisoners of privileges for protracted periods; unlike administrative segregation and protective custody, disciplinary confinement also stigmatizes them and diminishes parole prospects. Those immediate and lingering consequences should suffice to qualify such confinement as liberty depriving for purposes of Due Process Clause protection.[1]

I see the Due Process Clause itself, not Hawaii's prison code, as the wellspring of the protection due Conner. Deriving protected liberty interests from mandatory language in local prison codes would make of the fundamental right something more in certain States, something less in others. Liberty that may vary from Ossining, New York, to San Quentin, California, does not resemble the "Liberty" enshrined among "unalienable Rights" with which all persons are "endowed by their Creator." Declaration of Independence.[2]

Deriving the prisoner's due process right from the code for his prison, moreover, yields this practical anomaly: a State that scarcely attempts to control the behavior of its prison guards may, for that very laxity, escape constitutional accountability; a State that tightly cabins the discretion of its prison workers may, for that attentiveness, become vulnerable to constitutional claims. An incentive for ruleless prison management disserves the State's penological goals and jeopardizes the welfare of prisoners.

---

ments and the Equal Protection Clause of the Fourteenth Amendment where appropriate, and may draw upon internal prison grievance procedures and state judicial review where available.

[1] The Court reasons that Conner's disciplinary confinement, "with insignificant exceptions, mirrored th[e] conditions imposed upon inmates in administrative segregation and protective custody," . . . and therefore implicated no constitutional liberty interest. But discipline means punishment for misconduct; it rests on a finding of wrongdoing that can adversely affect an inmate's parole prospects. Disciplinary confinement therefore cannot be bracketed with administrative segregation and protective custody, both measures that carry no long-term consequences. The Court notes, however, that the State eventually expunged Conner's disciplinary record, . . . as a result of his successful administrative appeal. But hindsight cannot tell us whether a liberty interest existed at the outset. One must, of course, know at the start the character of the interest at stake in order to determine then what process, if any, is constitutionally due. "All's well that ends well" cannot be the measure here.

[2] The Court describes a category of liberty interest that is something less than the one the Due Process Clause itself shields, something more than anything a prison code provides. The State may create a liberty interest, the Court tells us, when "atypical and significant hardship [would be borne by] the inmate in relation to the ordinary incidents of prison life." *Ante,* at 2300; *see ante,* at 2301. What design lies beneath these key words? The Court ventures no examples, leaving consumers of the Court's work at sea, unable to fathom what would constitute an "atypical, significant deprivation," *ibid.,* and yet not trigger protection under the Due Process Clause directly.

To fit the liberty recognized in our fundamental instrument of government, the process due by reason of the Constitution similarly should not depend on the particularities of the local prison's code. Rather, the basic, universal requirements are notice of the acts of misconduct prison officials say the inmate committed, and an opportunity to respond to the charges before a trustworthy decisionmaker.

For the reasons JUSTICE BREYER cogently presents, a return of this case to the District Court would be unavoidable if it were recognized that Conner was deprived of liberty within the meaning of the Due Process Clause. But upon such a return, a renewed motion for summary judgment would be in order, for the record, as currently composed, does not show that Conner was denied any procedural protection warranted in his case.

In particular, a call for witnesses is properly refused when the projected testimony is not relevant to the matter in controversy. Unless Conner were to demonstrate, in face of the disciplinary committee's stated reliance on his own admissions, that an issue of material fact is genuinely in controversy, see Fed. Rules Civ. Proc. 56(c), (e), his due process claim would fail.

. . . .

Because I conclude that Conner was deprived of liberty within the meaning of the Due Process Clause, I dissent from the judgment of the Court. I would return the case for a precisely focused determination whether Conner received the process that was indeed due.

JUSTICE BREYER, with whom JUSTICE SOUTER joins, dissenting.

The specific question in this case is whether a particular punishment that, among other things, segregates an inmate from the general prison population for violating a disciplinary rule deprives the inmate of "liberty" within the terms of the Fourteenth Amendment's Due Process Clause. The majority, asking whether that punishment "imposes atypical and significant hardship on the inmate in relation to the ordinary incidents of prison life," concludes that it does not do so. The majority's reasoning, however, particularly when read in light of this Court's precedents, seems to me to lead to the opposite conclusion. And, for that reason, I dissent.

. . . .

II

The Fourteenth Amendment says that a State shall not "deprive any person of life, liberty, or property, without due process of law." U.S. Const., Amdt. 14, § 1. In determining whether state officials have deprived an inmate, such as Conner, of a procedurally protected "liberty," this Court traditionally has looked either (1) to the nature of the deprivation (how severe, in degree or kind) or (2) to the State's rules governing the imposition of that deprivation (whether they, in effect, give the inmate a "right" to avoid it). . . .

If we apply these general pre-existing principles to the relevant facts before us, it seems fairly clear, as the Ninth Circuit found, that the prison punishment here at issue deprived Conner of constitutionally protected "liberty." For one thing, the punishment worked a fairly major change in Conner's conditions. In the absence of the punishment, Conner, like other inmates in Halawa's general prison population would have left his cell and worked, taken classes, or mingled with others for eight *hours* each day. As a result of disciplinary segregation, however, Conner, for 30 days, had to spend his entire time alone in his cell (with the exception of 50 *minutes* each day on average for brief exercise and shower periods, during which he nonetheless remained isolated from other inmates and was constrained by leg irons and waist chains). . . .

III

The majority, while not disagreeing with this summary of pre-existing law, seeks to change, or to clarify, that law's "liberty" defining standards in one important respect. The majority believes that the Court's present "cabining of discretion" standard reads the Constitution as providing procedural protection for trivial "rights," as, for example, where prison rules set forth specific standards for the content of prison meals. It adds that this approach involves courts too deeply in routine matters of prison administration, all without sufficient justification. It therefore imposes a minimum standard, namely, that a deprivation falls within the Fourteenth Amendment's definition of "liberty" only if it "imposes atypical and significant hardship on the inmate in relation to the ordinary incidents of prison life."

I am not certain whether or not the Court means this standard to change prior law radically. If so, its generality threatens the law with uncertainty, for some lower courts may read the majority opinion as offering significantly less protection against deprivation of liberty, while others may find in it an extension of protection to certain "atypical" hardships that preexisting law would not have covered. There is no need, however, for a radical reading of this standard, nor any other significant change in present law, to achieve the majority's basic objective, namely, to read the Constitution's Due Process Clause to protect inmates against deprivations of freedom that are important, not comparatively insignificant. Rather, in my view, this concern simply requires elaborating, and explaining, the Court's present standards (without radical revision) in order to make clear that courts must apply them in light of the purposes they were meant to serve. As so read, the standards will not create procedurally protected "liberty" interests where only minor matters are at stake. . . .

. . . Prison, by design, restricts the inmates' freedom. And, one cannot properly view unimportant matters that happen to be the subject of prison regulations as substantially aggravating a loss that has already occurred. Indeed, a regulation about a minor matter, for example, a regulation that seems to cabin the discretionary power of a prison administrator to deprive an inmate of, say, a certain kind of lunch, may amount simply to an instruction to the administrator about how to do his job, rather than a guarantee to the inmate of a "right" to the status quo. Thus, this Court has never held that comparatively unimportant prisoner "deprivations" fall within the scope of the Due Process Clause even if local law limits the authority of prison administrators to impose such minor deprivations. And, in my view, it should now simply specify that they do not.

I recognize that, as a consequence, courts must separate the unimportant from the potentially significant, without the help of the more objective "discretion-cabining" test. Yet, making that judicial judgment seems no more difficult than many other judicial tasks. It seems to me possible to separate less significant matters such as television privileges, "sack" versus "tray" lunches, playing the state lottery, attending an ex-stepfather's funeral, or the limits of travel when on prison furlough, from more significant matters, such as the solitary confinement at issue here. . . .

The upshot is the following: the problems that the majority identifies suggest that this Court should make explicit the lower definitional limit, in the prison context, of "liberty" under the Due Process Clause — a limit that is already implicit in this Court's precedent. . . .

IV

. . . .

In sum, expungement or no, Conner suffered a deprivation that was significant, not insignificant. And, that deprivation took place under disciplinary rules that, as described in Part II, *supra,* do cabin official discretion sufficiently. I would therefore hold that Conner was deprived of "liberty" within the meaning of the Due Process Clause. . . .

NOTES AND QUESTIONS

2-31. Does *Sandin*, in effect, rewrite entitlement analysis when it comes to prisoner petitions? What is the logic of the decision to so limit liberty interest claims in this way? Does the logic of the case apply to other, non-prison entitlement cases?

2-32. The Court does not rule out all prisoner petitions, but states that valid claims must be "atypical and significant." What kinds of claims might qualify? Claims that impinge on the duration of the sentence? Any others? *See* Julie M. Glencer, *An "Atypical and Significant' Barrier to Prisoners" Procedural Due Process Claims Based on State-Created Liberty Interests*, 100 DICK. L. REV. 861 (1996).

PROBLEM 2-1

Assume that you represent certain state prisoners who present the following cases in which you wish to assert a right to due process. What will be the basis of your claim in each of the following cases? What kind of record would you like to develop to support your claim? What facts would you like to be able to allege to increase your chances of defeating motions for summary judgment? What will be the result of each of these cases? Why?

(a) Assume your client was out on parole when he was accused of violating his conditions of parole. He was returned to prison and his parole was revoked without a hearing. Is your client entitled to a hearing? What are the minimum due process requirements that your client should expect? *Compare Mack v. Purkett*, S.W.2d 851 (1992), *with Morrissey v. Brewer*, 408 U.S. 471 (1972).

(b) Assume your client, while in prison, has been accused of violating certain rules. He has been placed in solitary confinement without a hearing. Does *Sandin* preclude him from having a due process claim? Can a prisoner's visitation privileges be suspended without a hearing? What types of deprivations qualify as "atypical and significant"? If your client has "good-time" credits taken away without a hearing, does your client have a Due Process claim? *See Edwards v. Balisok*, 520 U.S. 641 (1997).

(c) Assume that your client has been transferred for bad behavior from a medium security to a maximum security prison without a hearing. Does the prisoner have any recourse? *See Meachum v. Fano*, 427 U.S. 215 (1976). What if the prisoner was a pre-trial detainee? *See Resnick v. Hayes*, 213 F.3d 443 (2000). Should there be a difference and if so, what reasons are there for the disparity?

(d) Assume that your client is segregated from the prison population. If your client believes that he has been segregated in retaliation for filing a civil rights claim, does this give him a due process claim? *See Allah v. Seiverling*, 229 F.3d 220 (2000).

(e) Assume your client wishes to file a civil rights claim and is denied access to court. Does *Sandin* preclude your client from raising a due process claim? *See Allah v. Seiverling*, 229 F. 3d 220 (2000).

(f) Assume your client believes that he is in danger by remaining within the general prison population. Does he have a right to be transferred? If the prison officials give the prisoner the choice of staying in his current situation or electing administrative detention, is the prisoner being deprived of a liberty interest? *See Babcock v. White*, 102 F.3d 267 (1996).

(g) Assume that your client has served one third of his sentence and, pursuant to statute, is eligible for parole. The parole board denies his application for parole without a hearing. Any recourse? Suppose he is granted a parole. Once a parole release date is set, can it be changed to a later date without a hearing? Are presumptive parolees granted greater due process rights than those seeking parole? Why? *Compare Morrissey, with Green v. McCall*, 822 F.2d 284 (2d Cir. 1987).

(h) Can a prisoner be given antipsychotic drugs against his or her will without a hearing? *See Washington v. Harper*, 494 U.S. 210 (1990).

PROBLEM 2-2

Consider cases like *Roth, Sindermann,* and *Bishop.* Why would someone dismissed by an organization want to have a hearing? What do they expect to gain? Suppose that they do not have another job opportunity and that they wish to return to their original place of employment. Does a due process hearing necessarily achieve this result? Suppose that they have another job and do not wish to return. Is there any reason why they may still bring suit? Why? Are there any financial incentives to file and pursue such lawsuits?

§ 2.06 Due Process and Welfare Reform

On August 22, 1996, President Clinton signed the Personal Responsibility and Work Opportunity Reconciliation Act of 1996, (PRWORA) P.L. 104-193, the first title of which changes the Aid to Families with Dependent Children program into block grants, for "temporary assistance for needy families," known as TANF. In addition, the law provides that all state plans which are submitted for participation in the federal block grant system do not entitle anyone to benefits. It also prohibits courts from interpreting the block grant as creating an entitlement for individuals. What impact does this have on the procedural rights of welfare recipients? The language of "disentitlement" appears at three places in the act:

§ 103(b) NO INDIVIDUAL ENTITLEMENT. — This part shall not be interpreted to entitle any individual or family to assistance under any State program funded under this part.

§ 116(b)(1)(C) SUBMISSION OF STATE PLAN FOR FISCAL YEAR 1996 OR 1997 DEEMED ACCEPTANCE OF GRANT LIMITATIONS AND FORMULA AND TERMINATION OF AFDC ENTITLEMENT. — The submission of a plan by a State pursuant to subparagraph (A) is deemed to constitute—

(i) the State's acceptance of the grant reductions under subparagraph (B) (including the formula for computing the amount of the reduction); and

(ii) the termination of any entitlement of any individual or family to benefits or services under the State AFDC program.

§ 116(c) TERMINATION OF ENTITLEMENT UNDER AFDC PROGRAM. — Effective October 1, 1996, no individual or family shall be entitled to any benefits or services under any State plan approved under part A or F of title IV of the Social Security Act (as in effect on September 30, 1995).

Matthew Diller argues that a significant consequence of welfare reform has been the increase of low-level worker discretion in *The Revolution in Welfare Administration: Rules, Discretion, and Entrepreneurial Government,* 75 N.Y.U. L. REV. 1121 (2000). He notes that "welfare reform has brought a revolution in welfare administration. The model of benefit administration as a hierarchically ordered system of rules that provides predictability and uniformity of treatment is in the process of being abandoned." *Id.* at 1219. Professor Diller concludes that, "accountability emerges as a central concern. Administrative law has developed mechanisms for providing outside input into the formulation of agency policies and decisions. . . . The new modes of welfare administration bypass or render ineffective critical components of this system of accountability." *Id.* Consider the problems posed by the following case.

REYNOLDS v. GIULIANI

35 F. Supp. 2d 331
(S.D.N.Y. 1999)

On December 16, 1998, plaintiffs . . . filed this action under 42 U.S.C. § 1983 against New York City Mayor Rudolph Giuliani and Jason Turner, Commissioner of the New York City Human Resources Administration (the "City defendants"), together with Brian J. Wing, Commissioner of the New York State Office of Temporary and Disability Assistance, and Barbara DeBuono, Commissioner of the New York State Department of Health (the "State defendants"). The class action complaint alleges that the City systematically prevents otherwise eligible individuals from obtaining food stamps, Medicaid and cash assistance by, *inter alia,* imposing unreasonable requirements upon such individuals during the application process.

Plaintiffs seek preliminary and permanent injunctive relief on behalf of a proposed class of all New York City residents who have or will apply for food stamps, Medicaid and/or cash assistance. Presently before the Court is plaintiffs' motion for a preliminary injunction. For the reasons below, plaintiffs' motion is granted in part.

PROCEDURAL HISTORY AND BACKGROUND

A. *Introduction*

New York City's Human Resources Administration ("HRA") is the public agency charged with making food stamps, Medicaid and cash assistance available to needy individuals. At the present time, HRA is re-engineering the way in which its approximately 18,000 employees accomplish that mission. Until recently, HRA processed applications for food stamps, Medicaid and cash assistance at offices known as "Income Support Centers." However, in March 1998 HRA began converting its 31 Income Support Centers to "Job Centers" in an effort to effectuate changes in federal and State welfare policy.

Those policy changes unfolded with the enactment of the Personal Responsibility and Work Opportunity Reconciliation Act of 1996 ("PRWORA"). PRWORA dramatically changed the climate for welfare programs in New York and around the country. Among other things, PRWORA ended the Aid to Families with Dependent Children ("AFDC") program and replaced it with a block grant program known as the Temporary Assistance to Needy Families ("TANF").

One of the express statutory purposes of TANF is to "end the dependence of needy parents on government benefits by promoting job preparation, work and marriage." TANF contains several provisions meant to encourage cash assistance recipients to obtain paid employment. For example, TANF requires that non-exempt parents or caretakers engage in work activities no later than 24 months after receipt of assistance. TANF also establishes a 5-year lifetime limit on benefits, under the expectation that recipients will secure employment to support their children and themselves. To ensure that States require recipients to work, TANF includes escalating "work participation rates" that States must meet to avoid reductions in their block grants. New York participates in TANF through two cash assistance programs: Family Assistance, which is available to pregnant women and families with a minor child, and Safety Net Assistance, which is available to childless adults.

The City defendants maintain that the procedures utilized at job centers implement these policies by focusing on the employment opportunities and responsibilities of applicants, while assuring that assistance is available to those in need. HRA has already converted 14 of its 31 income support centers to job centers. HRA plans to complete the conversions by April 1999.

Apart from providing cash assistance through the Family Assistance and Safety Net Assistance programs, HRA's job centers are responsible for administering the federal food stamps and Medicaid programs. . . .

B. *Factual Background*

. . . .

1. *Application Process Under The Income Support System*

In the income support centers, any individual seeking public assistance is provided with a State-approved joint application form for food stamps, Medicaid, and cash assistance, together with screening forms for domestic violence and alcohol and substance abuse. Such individuals may qualify for either the Family Assistance Program or Safety Net Assistance. During that visit, the application specialist registers the applicant and schedules appointments with Eligibility Verification and Review ("EVR"), the Office of Child Support Enforcement ("OCSE"), and the "I" interview. The "I" interview is the full application interview that generally takes place within five to seven days of the application date. However, if the applicant has emergency needs, the "I" interview will take place on the application date.

2. *Application Process Under The Job Center System*

The application process at job centers is more rigorous. After an initial interview with a Financial Planning Unit Receptionist, the applicant is required to meet with a Financial Planner, an Employment Planner, a Social Services Planner, and to engage in extensive job search activities before the "I" interview.

On arrival at a job center, the applicant is screened by a receptionist who inquires as to the type of assistance sought and the applicant's zip code. The receptionist explains that cash assistance is now subject to a time limit, and

§ 2.06   DUE PROCESS AND ADMINISTRATIVE ADJUDICATION   119

that the applicant will be required to seek employment during the application process. Then the receptionist provides the applicant with a Participant Job Profile and Assessment Form ("PJP"). Completion of the PJP triggers the application process.

After the applicant submits the completed PJP to a receptionist, a Financial Planning Unit Supervisor reviews the PJP, logs the applicant's name into the Job Center Daily Activity Log, and assigns the applicant to a financial planner. While the applicant is waiting for his appointment with the financial planner, receptionists often make announcements informing applicants about the time limits for public assistance.

Applicants are registered in the Welfare Management System ("WMS") on the day the PJP is completed. The agency's timeliness in complying with federal and state mandates with regard to food stamps, Medicaid, and cash assistance applications is measured from the date the PJP is completed. Thus, the formal application process under both the income support centers and the job centers begins on the first day that the applicant enters the office and completes the document required by that office.

After completing the PJP, the applicant meets with a financial planner, who reviews the PJP and interviews the applicant to determine if any emergency needs requiring an immediate response are present. Applicants are customarily handed a form entitled "Information About an Expedited Food Stamp Interview." Applicants are considered for expedited food stamps if they request an expedited food stamp interview on this form.

If there is an emergency need, the financial planner either determines the applicant's eligibility for emergency benefits or arranges to have the applicant evaluated by an emergency assistance team or the Homeless Diversion Unit. After any emergency is addressed, the financial planner explores whether there are any potential alternatives to cash assistance. These alternatives include whether the applicant has relatives who can assist him, access to bank accounts, or other possible sources of government benefits, such as veterans' benefits, pension, social security, and community services. In addition, the applicant is reminded about the time limits relating to cash assistance. At the conclusion of this interview, the financial planner schedules the remaining appointments that the applicant is required to attend, including the Employment Planner interview, the Social Services interview, the "I" interview, and job search orientation activities.

After meeting with the financial planner, the applicant is interviewed by the employment planner. The employment planner is responsible for connecting the applicant with work activities. If the applicant is not exempt from work activities, then the applicant is immediately assigned job search activities. The employment planner reviews with the applicant a calendar called the "35/50 Days to Employment Calendar" which charts the appointments the applicant is expected to keep and outlines the steps that should be taken to search for and obtain employment. Following an orientation, daily job search activities are then scheduled over a six week period.

At some point, after the job search orientation and while the applicant is still performing job search activities, the "I" interview is scheduled. Assuming the applicant has submitted all of the required paperwork and documentation and has appeared for all scheduled appointments, this is the phase where an eligibility determination is made.

When evaluating an applicant's entire application, separate determinations should be made for each type of assistance requested. A separate determination is necessary because the requirements and standards under each program are different. For example, while work requirements exist for cash assistance, they do not affect eligibility for food stamps or Medicaid. If the applicant requests only food stamps and/or Medicaid, job center staff are required to give an immediate referral to a non-public assistance food stamp or Medicaid office. Income support centers and job centers are only authorized to process joint applications for food stamps and/or Medicaid in conjunction with a request for cash assistance.

C. *The Complaint*

Plaintiffs allege that the City defendants are providing applicants with false and misleading information in an effort to prune the welfare rolls. Plaintiffs further allege that the City defendants are impermissibly raising impediments to applications by needy individuals for food stamps, Medicaid and cash assistance. Their 57-page complaint alleges twelve separate claims for relief. Plaintiffs' first seven claims for relief assert private rights of action based on alleged violations of various federal statutes and regulations. . . .

. . . The complaint further alleges violations of plaintiffs' rights under State law, and asserts that the State defendants' failure to adequately monitor the City's administration of the food stamps and Medicaid programs violates plaintiffs' rights under 7 U.S.C. § 2020 and 42 U.S.C. § 1396, respectively. The common thread running through all of plaintiffs' claims is that defendants have and continue to violate plaintiffs' federal due process rights. . . .

DISCUSSION

A. *The Applicable Standard For Preliminary Injunctive Relief*

A party seeking a preliminary injunction generally must establish "(a) irreparable harm and (b) either (1) likelihood of success on the merits or (2) sufficiently serious questions going to the merits to make them a fair ground for litigation and a balance of hardships tipping decidedly toward the party requesting the preliminary relief." . . .

1. *Irreparable Harm*

. . . .

The Supreme Court has observed that denying welfare benefits to an eligible applicant may deprive that person "of the very means by which to live." *Goldberg v. Kelly,* 397 U.S. 254, 264 (1970). "To indigent persons, the loss of even a portion of subsistence benefits constitutes irreparable injury."

Plaintiffs' pre-hearing submissions and the evidence adduced at the hearing establish the risk of immediate and irreparable harm unless a preliminary injunction is issued. The City defendants' practices continue to endanger numerous individuals in need of public assistance, including children, expectant mothers, and the disabled. This Court has received declarations and testimony describing in stark detail the hardships endured by plaintiffs and other individuals who unsuccessfully sought public assistance at job centers. For example, plaintiff Lue Garlick, a homeless, single mother who is pregnant with twins, testified that she attempted to apply for emergency food stamps on November 16, 1998 at the Hamilton Job Center, but did not receive them until December 19, 1998. During that interim period, Ms. Garlick went entirely without food on more than one occasion. Other plaintiffs and witnesses described similar experiences. Based on the record before this Court, there simply is no question that plaintiffs have established the risk of immediate and irreparable harm.

2. *Likelihood of Success*

. . . .

Turning to the facts, plaintiffs have also met their burden of establishing a likelihood of success on these claims. On March 31, 1998, the City opened its first job center as a test bed so that City officials could make ongoing modifications and expand the program incrementally. As Jason Turner, New York City's Human Resources Administration's Commissioner, observed: "[W]e didn't do lengthy planning followed by implementation, instead, we acted first and worried about the consequences later. And that seems to have worked for us." Commissioner Turner acknowledged that errors are inevitable and added that the benefit of proceeding incrementally is the avoidance of "rolling out a major mistake on a city-wide basis."

The evidence presented by plaintiffs in their motion for preliminary relief, as well as the candid assessments of certain City officials, including Commissioner Turner and other high-ranking HRA deputies, demonstrates that additional self-study is necessary to ensure that the City's vision of job centers as a "beautiful system of engagement" and the enthusiasm of HRA employees for workfare do not obscure the underlying statutory requirement to protect the health and well-being of the neediest households in the population. . . .

CONCLUSION

PRWORA represents a legislative sea change in thinking about welfare. Reforming welfare in a large city such as New York presents tremendous challenges. The City embarked on an ambitious plan to implement PRWORA and exercise its managerial prerogatives to redirect the needy from welfare to workfare. Despite this legitimate goal, this Court cannot ignore the evidence presented by plaintiffs concerning individuals whose urgent needs were overlooked by the City in the wake of this transition. The City defendants argue that these problems were isolated incidents that occurred at a few job centers, and are not indicative of a systemic violation. At this stage of the litigation, this Court cannot agree.

While the City defendants have offered evidence that they are in the process of addressing some of the issues raised by plaintiffs' motion, this Court finds that the plaintiffs and other applicants for food stamps, Medicaid and cash assistance will suffer irreparable harm if preliminary injunctive relief is not entered now. . . .

NOTES AND QUESTIONS

2-33. Is there a procedural due process claim in this case? Do *applicants* for welfare benefits have due process rights? On what basis? Is there an expectation of reasonable processes, especially on the part of those in dire need? Is there too much process here?

2-34. Following the issuance of the preliminary injunction, the trial judge granted the City of New York's request to modify the preliminary injunction to permit it to open additional job centers. In order to obtain this modification, the city had to implement a compliance plan, in which the city promised to 1) inform applicants for benefits of their right to apply for them during their initial visit and 2) perform compliance audits and spot checks of the job centers. *See Reynolds v. Giuliani*, 43 F. Supp. 2d 492 (S.D.N.Y. 1999). The judge, after a full trial on the merits, turned the modified preliminary injunction into a permanent injunction. *See Reynolds v. Giuliani*, No. 98 Civ. 8877, 2004 U.S. Dist. LEXIS 26026 (S.D.N.Y. Dec. 30, 2004).

2-35. Professor Frank Munger notes that the focus of attention in welfare law is now not on need, but behavior, specifically dependent behavior.

> Reliance on public or private welfare by those who cannot make ends meet has always been stigmatized as dependency. Now, dependency is the point of attack on the poor and workers alike. Welfare for the poor has been severely restricted, and the number of impoverished, mother-only families aided by public benefits has been cut in half. Similarly, increasing restrictions are placed on private pensions, health insurance, workers compensation, unemployment compensation, and even bankruptcy relief from overburdening debt. The "dependent" poor and the low-wage labor force are increasingly denied social citizenship, immigrants in their own society.

Frank Munger, *Can We Build a Local Welfare State?* 44 SANTA CLARA L. REV. 999 (2004).* Similarly, Christine Cimini notes "The problems identified by Congress included long-term dependency on welfare benefits, large numbers of out-of-wedlock pregnancies, and the lack of two parent families." Cimini, *The New Contract: Welfare Reform, Devolution and Due Process*, 61 MD. L. REV. 246 (2002). *See also* Michael B. Katz, *The Price of Citizenship: Redefining the American Welfare State* (2001); Jon Michaels, *Deforming Welfare: How the Dominant Narratives of Devolution and Privatization Subverted Federal Welfare Reform*, 34 SETON HALL L. REV. 573 (2004). *See generally* Jean Braucher, *Consumer Bankruptcy as Part of the Social Safety Net: Fresh Start or Treadmill?*, 44 Santa CLARA L. REV. 1065 (2004); Deborah Maranville, *Unemployment Insurance Meets Globalization and the Modern Workforce*, 44 SANTA CLARA L. REV. 1129 (2004).

---

* Copyright © 2004 School of Law, Santa Clara University; Frank Munger. All rights reserved.

2-36. The shift in paradigm from a federal entitlement to welfare benefits to a block grant to the states did not necessarily eliminate due process claims in the welfare context. As Carolyn Goodwin argues:

> By statutorily eliminating an entitlement to welfare benefits, it is unclear whether Congress intended to prohibit courts from interpreting TANF as requiring constitutional procedural due process protections, whether it intended to transform the welfare program from a lifetime guarantee of benefits to conditional temporary assistance, or both. Statutory and regulatory language suggest that Congress did not intend to fundamentally alter procedural fairness in administration of benefits. For example, TANF requires states to develop procedural safeguards in their administration of state welfare programs. Under the federal regulations that govern general administration of public assistance programs, states must submit fair hearing plans to the federal government for review. The regulations describe the requirements for a fair hearing and explain that "[u]nder this requirement hearings shall meet the due process standards set forth in the U.S. Supreme Court decisions in *Goldberg v. Kelly*, 397 U.S. 254 (1970) and the standards set forth in this section."

Carolyn Goodwin, Comment, *"Welfare Reform" and Procedural Due Process Protections: The Massachusetts Example*, 48 BUFFALO L. REV. 565, 572–73 (2000).**

States vary considerably in how they carry out their duties, often privatizing various aspects of welfare administration. As Michele Estrin Gilman notes:

> Lockheed Martin, the defense contracting giant, has found a new business niche in an era of declining defense spending: running welfare offices. Private companies like Lockheed Martin, along with various nonprofit organizations, have become an integral part of the massive welfare reform effort started in 1996 with the enactment of the Personal Responsibility and Work Opportunity Reconciliation Act (PRA). . . . State and local governments have eagerly embraced this new opportunity to privatize welfare in the hopes that private organizations can deliver welfare cheaper, faster, and better. . . . While government has relied heavily on contracting with private nonprofit entities for social service delivery since the 1960s, these entities have usually been limited to providing discrete services such as job training or child care. The PRA makes two major changes to this existing scheme of public/private interdependence. First, under the PRA, private entities are allowed to run entire welfare offices. This means that, for the first time, they can perform eligibility determinations and sanction recipients for noncompliance with program requirements. Second, the PRA has opened the door for large for-profit organizations such as Lockheed Martin to enter into welfare delivery. These for-profit entities have different incentives, and more political power, than the nonprofit entities typically engaged in social service delivery in the past. . . .

Michele Estrin Gilman, *Legal Accountability in an Era Of Privatized Welfare*, 89 CAL. L. REV. 569, 571–72 (2001).* For an excellent discussion of how states

---

** Copyright © 2000 Buffalo Law Review; Carolyn Goodwin. All rights reserved.

* Copyright © 2001 California Law Review, Inc. All rights reserved.

can both deliberately and unwittingly undermine federal welfare reform, *see* Jon Michaels, *supra*, **2-35**, at 619–24.

We shall return to the due process implications of privatization in welfare and other aspects of social services at the end of the chapter.

§ 2.07 How Much Process Is Due and When Should It Be Provided?

MATHEWS v. ELDRIDGE

United States Supreme Court
424 U.S. 319 (1976)

MR. JUSTICE POWELL delivered the opinion of the Court.

The issue in this case is whether the Due Process Clause of the Fifth Amendment requires that prior to the termination of Social Security disability benefit payments the recipient be afforded an opportunity for an evidentiary hearing.

I.

Cash benefits are provided to workers during periods in which they are completely disabled under the disability insurance benefits program created by the 1956 amendments to Title II of the Social Security Act. 70 Stat. 815, 42 U.S.C. § 423.[1] Respondent Eldridge was first awarded benefits in June 1968. In March 1972, he received a questionnaire from the state agency charged with monitoring his medical condition. Eldridge completed the questionnaire, indicating that his condition had not improved and identifying the medical sources, including physicians, from whom he had received treatment recently. The state agency then obtained reports from his physician and a psychiatric consultant. After considering these reports and other information in his file the agency informed Eldridge by letter that it had made a tentative determination that his disability had ceased in May 1972. The letter included a statement of reasons for the proposed termination of benefits, and advised Eldridge that he might request reasonable time in which to obtain and submit additional information pertaining to his condition.

In his written response, Eldridge disputed one characterization of his medical condition and indicated that the agency already had enough evidence to establish his disability.[2] The state agency then made its final determination

---

[1] The program is financed by revenues derived from employee and employer payroll taxes. . . . It provides monthly benefits to disabled persons who have worked sufficiently long to have an insured status, and who have had substantial work experience in a specified interval directly preceding the onset of disability. . . . Benefits also are provided to the worker's dependents under specified circumstances. . . . When the recipient reaches age 65 his disability benefits are automatically converted to retirement benefits. . . . In fiscal 1974 approximately 3,700,000 persons received assistance under the program. . . .

[2] Eldridge originally was disabled due to chronic anxiety and back strain. He subsequently was found to have diabetes. The tentative determination letter indicated that aid would be terminated because available medical evidence indicated that his diabetes was under control, that there

§ 2.07   DUE PROCESS AND ADMINISTRATIVE ADJUDICATION   125

that he had ceased to be disabled in May 1972. This determination was accepted by the Social Security Administration (SSA), which notified Eldridge in July that his benefits would terminate after that month. The notification also advised him of his right to seek reconsideration by the state agency of this initial determination within six months.

Instead of requesting reconsideration Eldridge commenced this action challenging the constitutional validity of the administrative procedures established by the Secretary of Health, Education, and Welfare for assessing whether there exists a continuing disability. He sought an immediate reinstatement of benefits pending a hearing on the issue of his disability.[3] 361 F. Supp. 520 (W.D. Va. 1973). The Secretary moved to dismiss on the grounds that Eldridge's benefits had been terminated in accordance with valid administrative regulations and procedures and that he had failed to exhaust available remedies. In support of his contention that due process requires a pretermination hearing, Eldridge relied exclusively upon this Court's decision in *Goldberg v. Kelly*, 397 U.S. 254 (1970), which established a right to an "evidentiary hearing" prior to termination of welfare benefits.[4] The Secretary contended that *Goldberg* was not controlling since eligibility for disability benefits, unlike eligibility for welfare benefits, is not based on financial need and since issues of credibility and veracity do not play a significant role in the disability entitlement decision, which turns primarily on medical evidence.

The District Court concluded that the administrative procedures pursuant to which the Secretary had terminated Eldridge's benefits abridged his right to procedural due process. The court viewed the interest of the disability recipient in uninterrupted benefits as indistinguishable from that of the welfare recipient in *Goldberg*. . . . Reasoning that disability determinations may involve subjective judgments based on conflicting medical and nonmedical evidence, the District Court held that prior to termination of benefits Eldridge had to be afforded an evidentiary hearing of the type required for welfare beneficiaries under Title IV of the Social Security Act. . . . Relying entirely upon the District Court's opinion, the Court of Appeals for the Fourth Circuit affirmed the injunction barring termination of Eldridge's benefits prior to an evidentiary hearing. . . . We reverse.

---

existed no limitations on his back movements which would impose severe functional restrictions, and that he no longer suffered emotional problems that would preclude him from all work for which he was qualified. . . . In his reply letter he claimed to have arthritis of the spine rather than a strained back.

[3] The District Court ordered reinstatement of Eldridge's benefits pending its final disposition on the merits.

[4] In *Goldberg* the Court held that the pretermination hearing must include the following elements: (1) "timely and adequate notice detailing the reasons for a proposed terminating;" (2) "an effective opportunity [for the recipient] to defend by confronting any adverse witnesses and by presenting his own arguments and evidence orally"; (3) retained counsel, if desired; (4) an "impartial" decisionmaker; (5) a decision resting "solely on the legal rules and evidence adduced at the hearing;" (6) a statement of reasons for the decision and the evidence relied on. 397 U.S., at 266-271. In this opinion the term "evidentiary hearing" refers to a hearing generally of the type required in *Goldberg*.

II.

[The Court found that it had jurisdiction over this claim.]

III.

A.

Procedural due process imposes constraints on governmental decisions which deprive individuals of "liberty" or "property" interests within the meaning of the Due Process Clause of the Fifth or Fourteenth Amendment. The Secretary does not contend that procedural due process is inapplicable to terminations of Social Security disability benefits. He recognizes . . . that the interest of an individual in continued receipt of these benefits is a statutorily created "property" interest protected by the Fifth Amendment. . . . Rather, the Secretary contends that the existing administrative procedures, detailed below, provide all the process that is constitutionally due before a recipient can be deprived of that interest.

This Court consistently has held that some form of hearing is required before an individual is finally deprived of a property interest. . . . The "right to be heard before being condemned to suffer grievous loss of any kind, even though it may not involve the stigma and hardships of a criminal conviction, is a principle basic to our society." *Joint Anti-Fascist Comm. v. McGrath,* 341 U.S. 123, 168 (1951) (Frankfurter, J., concurring). The fundamental requirement of due process is the opportunity to be heard "at a meaningful time and in a meaningful manner. . . ." Eldridge agrees that the review procedures available to a claimant before the initial determination of ineligibility becomes final would be adequate if disability benefits were not terminated until after the evidentiary hearing stage of the administrative process. The dispute centers upon what process is due prior to the initial termination of benefits, pending review.

In recent years this Court increasingly has had occasion to consider the extent to which due process requires an evidentiary hearing prior to the deprivation of some type of property interest even if such a hearing is provided thereafter. In only one case, *Goldberg v. Kelly,* 397 U.S., at 266-271, has the Court held that a hearing closely approximating a judicial trial is necessary. In other cases requiring some type of pretermination hearing as a matter of constitutional right, the Court has spoken sparingly about the requisite procedures. . . . More recently, in *Arnett v. Kennedy,* . . . we sustained the validity of procedures by which a federal employee could be dismissed for cause. They included notice of the action sought, a copy of the charge, reasonable time for filing a written response, and an opportunity for an oral appearance. Following dismissal, an evidentiary hearing was provided. 416 U.S., at 142-146.

These decisions underscore the truism that " '[d]ue process,' unlike some legal rules, is not a technical conception with a fixed content unrelated to time, place and circumstances." *Cafeteria Workers v. McElroy,* 367 U.S. 886, 895 (1961). . . . Accordingly, resolution of the issue whether the administrative procedures provided here are constitutionally sufficient requires analysis of

§ 2.07   DUE PROCESS AND ADMINISTRATIVE ADJUDICATION   127

the governmental and private interests that are affected. . . . More precisely, our prior decisions indicate that identification of the specific dictates of due process generally requires consideration of three distinct factors: First, the private interest that will be affected by the official action; second, the risk of an erroneous deprivation of such interest through the procedures used, and the probable value, if any, of additional or substitute procedural safeguards; and finally, the government's interest, including the function involved and the fiscal and administrative burdens that the additional or substitute procedural requirement would entail.

We turn first to a description of the procedures for the termination of Social Security disability benefits, and thereafter consider the factors bearing upon the constitutional adequacy of these procedures.

B.

The disability insurance program is administered jointly by state and federal agencies. State agencies make the initial determination whether a disability exists, when it began, and when it ceased. The standards applied and the procedures followed are prescribed by the Secretary . . . who has delegated his responsibilities and powers under the Act to the SSA.

In order to establish initial and continued entitlement to disability benefits a worker must demonstrate that he is unable

"to engage in any substantial gainful activity by reason of any medically determinable physical or mental impairment which can be expected to result in death or which has lasted or can be expected to last for a continuous period of not less than 12 months. . . ." 42 U.S.C. § 423(d)(1)(A).

To satisfy this test the worker bears a continuing burden of showing, by means of "medically acceptable clinical and laboratory diagnostic techniques," § 423(d)(3), that he has a physical or mental impairment of such severity that

"he is not only unable to do his previous work but cannot, considering his age, education, and work experience, engage in any other kind of substantial gainful work which exists in the national economy, regardless of whether such work exists in the immediate area in which he lives, or whether a specific job vacancy exists for him, or whether he would be hired if he applied for work." § 423(d)(2)(A).

The principal reasons for benefits terminations are that the worker is no longer disabled or has returned to work. As Eldridge's benefits were terminated because he was determined to be no longer disabled, we consider only the sufficiency of the procedures involved in such cases.

The continuing-eligibility investigation is made by a state agency acting through a "team" consisting of a physician and a nonmedical person trained in disability evaluation. The agency periodically communicates with the disabled worker, usually by mail — in which case he is sent a detailed questionnaire — or by telephone, and requests information concerning his present condition, including current medical restrictions and sources of treatment, and any additional information that he considers relevant to his continued entitlement to benefits.

Information regarding the recipient's current condition is also obtained from his sources of medical treatment. . . . If there is a conflict between the information provided by the beneficiary and that obtained from medical sources such as his physician, or between two sources of treatment, the agency may arrange for an examination by an independent consulting physician. . . . Whenever the agency's tentative assessment of the beneficiary's condition differs from his own assessment, the beneficiary is informed that benefits may be terminated, provided a summary of the evidence upon which the proposed determination to terminate is based, and afforded an opportunity to review the medical reports and other evidence in his case file.[18] He also may respond in writing and submit additional evidence. . . .

The state agency then makes its final determination, which is reviewed by an examiner in the SSA Bureau of Disability Insurance. . . . If, as is usually the case, the SSA accepts the agency determination it notifies the recipient in writing, informing him of the reasons for the decision, and of his right to seek *de novo* reconsideration by the state agency. . . .[20] Upon acceptance by the SSA, benefits are terminated effective two months after the month in which medical recovery is found to have occurred.

If the recipient seeks reconsideration by the state agency and the determination is adverse, the SSA reviews the reconsideration determination and notifies the recipient of the decision. He then has a right to an evidentiary hearing before an SSA administrative law judge. The hearing is nonadversary, and the SSA is not represented by counsel. As at all prior and subsequent stages of the administrative process, however, the claimant may be represented by counsel or other spokesmen. . . . If this hearing results in an adverse decision, the claimant is entitled to request discretionary review by the SSA Appeals Council . . . and finally may obtain judicial review.

Should it be determined at any point after termination of benefits, that the claimant's disability extended beyond the date of cessation initially established, the worker is entitled to retroactive payments. . . . If, on the other hand, a beneficiary receives any payments to which he is later determined not to be entitled, the statute authorizes the Secretary to attempt to recoup these funds in specified circumstances.[22]

C.

Despite the elaborate character of the administrative procedures provided by the Secretary, the courts below held them to be constitutionally inadequate, concluding that due process requires an evidentiary hearing prior to

---

[18] The disability recipient is not permitted personally to examine the medical reports contained in his file. This restriction is not significant since he is entitled to have any representative of his choice, including a lay friend or family member, examine all medical evidence. . . . The Secretary informs us that this curious limitation is currently under review.

[20] The reconsideration assessment is initially made by the state agency, but usually not by the same persons who considered the case originally. R. Dixon, *Social Security Disability and Mass Justice* 32 (1973). Both the recipient and the agency may adduce new evidence.

[22] The Secretary may reduce other payments to which the beneficiary is entitled, or seek the payment of a refund, unless the beneficiary is "without fault" and such adjustment or recovery would defeat the purposes of the act or be "against equity and good conscience."

termination. In light of the private and governmental interests at stake here and the nature of the existing procedures, we think this was error.

Since a recipient whose benefits are terminated is awarded full retroactive relief if he ultimately prevails, his sole interest is in the uninterrupted receipt of this source of income pending final administrative decision on his claim. His potential injury is thus similar in nature to that of the welfare recipient in *Goldberg, see* 397 U.S., at 263-264, [and] the nonprobationary federal employee in *Arnett.*

Only in *Goldberg* has the Court held that due process requires an evidentiary hearing prior to a temporary deprivation. It was emphasized there that welfare assistance is given to persons on the very margin of subsistence:

> "The crucial factor in this context — a factor not present in the case of . . . virtually anyone else whose governmental entitlements are ended — is that termination of aid pending resolution of a controversy over eligibility may deprive an *eligible* recipient of the very means by which to live while he waits." 397 U.S., at 264 (emphasis in original).

Eligibility for disability benefits, in contrast, is not based upon financial need.[24] Indeed, it is wholly unrelated to the worker's income or support from many other sources, such as earnings of other family members, workmen's compensation awards,[25] tort claims awards, savings, private insurance, public or private pensions, veterans' benefits, food stamps, public assistance, or the "many other important programs, both public and private, which contain provisions for disability payments affecting a substantial portion of the work force. . . ." *Richardson v. Belcher,* 404 U.S., at 86-87 (Douglas, J., dissenting).

As *Goldberg* illustrates, the degree of potential deprivation that may be created by a particular decision is a factor to be considered in assessing the validity of any administrative decisionmaking process. . . . The potential deprivation here is generally likely to be less than in *Goldberg,* although the degree of difference can be overstated. As the District Court emphasized, to remain eligible for benefits a recipient must be "unable to engage in substantial gainful activity. . . ." Thus, in contrast to the discharged federal employee in *Arnett,* there is little possibility that the terminated recipient will be able to find even temporary employment to ameliorate the interim loss.

As we recognized last Term in *Fusari v. Steinberg,* 419 U.S. 379, 389 (1975), "the possible length of wrongful deprivation of . . . benefits [also] is an important factor in assessing the impact of official action on the private interests." The Secretary concedes that the delay between a request for a hearing before an administrative law judge and a decision on the claim is currently between 10 and 11 months. Since a terminated recipient must first obtain a reconsideration decision as a prerequisite to invoking his right to an evidentiary hearing, the delay between the actual cutoff of benefits and final decision after a hearing exceeds one year.

---

[24] The level of benefits is determined by the worker's average monthly earnings during the period prior to disability, his age, and other factors not directly related to financial need. . . .

[25] Workmen's compensation benefits are deducted in part in accordance with a statutory formula. . . .

In view of the torpidity of this administrative review process, . . . and the typically modest resources of the family unit of the physically disabled worker,[26] the hardship imposed upon the erroneously terminated disability recipient may be significant. In addition to the possibility of access to private resources, other forms of government assistance will become available where the termination of disability benefits places a worker or his family below the subsistence level.[27] . . . In view of these potential sources of temporary income, there is less reason here than in *Goldberg* to depart from the ordinary principle, established by our decisions, that something less than an evidentiary hearing is sufficient prior to adverse administrative action.

D.

An additional factor to be considered here is the fairness and reliability of the existing pretermination procedures, and the probable value, if any, of additional procedural safeguards. Central to the evaluation of any administrative process is the nature of the relevant inquiry. . . . Friendly, *Some Kind of Hearing*, 123 U. Pa. L. Rev. 1267, 1281 (1975). In order to remain eligible for benefits the disabled worker must demonstrate by means of "medically acceptable clinical and laboratory diagnostic techniques," 42 U.S.C. § 423(d)(3), that he is unable "to engage in any substantial gainful activity by reason of any *medically determinable* physical or mental impairment. . . ." § 423(d)(1)(A) (emphasis supplied). In short, a medical assessment of the worker's physical or mental condition is required. This is a more sharply focused and easily documented decision than the typical determination of welfare entitlement. In the latter case, a wide variety of information may be deemed relevant, and issues of witness credibility and veracity often are critical to the decisionmaking process. *Goldberg* noted that in such circumstances "written submissions are a wholly unsatisfactory basis for decision." 397 U.S., at 269.

By contrast, the decision whether to discontinue disability benefits will turn, in most cases, upon "routine, standard, and unbiased medical reports by physician specialists," *Richardson v. Perales*, 402 U.S., at 404, concerning a subject whom they have personally examined.[28] In *Richardson* the Court

---

[26] *Amici* cite statistics compiled by the Secretary which indicate that in 1965 the mean income of the family unit of a disabled worker was $3,803, while the median income for the unit was $2,836. The mean liquid assets — *i.e.*, cash, stocks, bonds — of these family units was $4,862; the median was $940. These statistics do not take into account the family unit's nonliquid assets — *i.e.*, automobile, real estate, and the like. Brief for AFL-CIO, et al. as *Amici Curiae* App. 4a.

[27] *Amici* emphasize that because an identical definition of disability is employed in both the Title II Social Security Program and in the companion welfare system for the disabled, . . . the terminated disability-benefits recipient will be ineligible for the SSI Program. There exist, however, state and local welfare programs which may supplement the worker's income. In addition, the worker's household unit can qualify for food stamps if it meets the financial need requirements. . . . Finally, in 1974 480,000 of the approximately 2,000,000 disabled workers receiving Social Security benefits also received SSI benefits. Since financial need is a criterion for eligibility under the SSI program, those disabled workers who are most in need will in the majority of cases be receiving SSI benefits when disability insurance aid is terminated. And, under the SSI program, a pretermination evidentiary hearing is provided, if requested. . . .

[28] The decision is not purely a question of the accuracy of a medical diagnosis since the ultimate

recognized the "reliability and probative worth of written medical reports" emphasizing that while there may be "professional disagreement with the medical conclusions" the "specter of questionable credibility and veracity is not present. . . ." To be sure, credibility and veracity may be a factor in the ultimate disability assessment in some cases. But procedural due process rules are shaped by the risk of error inherent in the truth-finding process as applied to the generality of cases, not the rare exceptions. The potential value of an evidentiary hearing, or even oral presentation to the decisionmaker, is substantially less in this context than in *Goldberg*.

The decision in *Goldberg* also was based on the Court's conclusion that written submissions were an inadequate substitute for oral presentation because they did not provide an effective means for the recipient to communicate his case to the decisionmaker. Written submissions were viewed as an unrealistic option, for most recipients lacked the "educational attainment necessary to write effectively" and could not afford professional assistance. In addition, such submissions would not provide the "flexibility of oral presentations" or "permit the recipient to mold his argument to the issues the decision maker appears to regard as important." 397 U.S., at 269. In the context of the disability-benefits-entitlement assessment the administrative procedures under review here fully answer these objections.

The detailed questionnaire which the state agency periodically sends the recipient identifies with particularity the information relevant to the entitlement decision, and the recipient is invited to obtain assistance from the local SSA office in completing the questionnaire. More important, the information critical to the entitlement decision usually is derived from medical sources, such as the treating physician. Such sources are likely to be able to communicate more effectively through written documents than are welfare recipients or the lay witnesses supporting their cause. The conclusions of physicians often are supported by X-rays and the results of clinical or laboratory tests, information typically more amenable to written than to oral presentation.

A further safeguard against mistake is the policy of allowing the disability recipient's representative full access to all information relied upon by the state agency. In addition, prior to the cutoff of benefits the agency informs the recipient of its tentative assessment, the reasons therefor, and provides a summary of the evidence that it considers most relevant. Opportunity is then afforded the recipient to submit additional evidence or arguments, enabling him to challenge directly the accuracy of information in his file as well as the correctness of the agency's tentative conclusions. These procedures, again as contrasted with those before the Court in *Goldberg,* enable the recipient to

---

issue which the state agency must resolve is whether in light of the particular worker's "age, education, and work experience" he cannot "engage in any . . . substantial gainful work which exists in the national economy. . . ." 42 U.S.C. § 423(d)(2)(A). Yet information concerning each of these worker characteristics is amenable to effective written presentation. The value of an evidentiary hearing, or even a limited oral presentation, does not appear substantial. Similarly, resolution of the inquiry as to the types of employment opportunities that exist in the national economy for a physically impaired worker with a particular set of skills would not necessarily be advanced by an evidentiary hearing. *Cf.* 1 K. Davis, *Administrative Law Treatise* § 7.06, p. 429 (1958). The statistical information relevant to this judgment is more amenable to written than to oral presentation.

"mold" his argument to respond to the precise issues which the decisionmaker regards as crucial.

Despite these carefully structured procedures, *amici* point to the significant reversal rate for appealed cases as clear evidence that the current process is inadequate. Depending upon the base selected and the line of analysis followed, the relevant reversal rates urged by the contending parties vary from a high of 58.6% for appealed reconsideration decisions to an overall reversal rate of only 3.3%. Bare statistics rarely provide a satisfactory measure of the fairness of a decisionmaking process. Their adequacy is especially suspect here since the administrative review system is operated on an open file basis. A recipient may always submit new evidence, and such submissions may result in additional medical examinations. Such fresh examinations were held in approximately 30% to 40% of the appealed cases in fiscal 1973, either at the reconsideration or evidentiary hearing stage of the administrative process.... In this context, the value of reversal rate statistics as one means of evaluating the adequacy of the pretermination process is diminished. Thus, although we view such information as relevant, it is certainly not controlling in this case.

E.

In striking the appropriate due process balance the final factor to be assessed is the public interest. This includes the administrative burden and other societal costs that would be associated with requiring, as a matter of constitutional right, an evidentiary hearing upon demand in all cases prior to the termination of disability benefits. The most visible burden would be the incremental cost resulting from the increased number of hearings and the expense of providing benefits to ineligible recipients pending decision. No one can predict the extent of the increase, but the fact that full benefits would continue until after such hearings would assure the exhaustion in most cases of this attractive option. Nor would the theoretical right of the Secretary to recover undeserved benefits result, as a practical matter, in any substantial offset to the added outlay of public funds. The parties submit widely varying estimates of the probable additional financial cost. We only need say that experience with the constitutionalizing of government procedures suggests that the ultimate additional cost in terms of money and administrative burden would not be insubstantial.

Financial cost alone is not a controlling weight in determining whether due process requires a particular procedural safeguard prior to some administrative decision. But the Government's interest, and hence that of the public, in conserving scarce fiscal and administrative resources is a factor that must be weighed. At some point the benefit of an additional safeguard to the individual affected by the administrative action and to society, in terms of increased assurance that the action is just, may be outweighed by the cost. Significantly, the cost of protecting those whom the preliminary administrative process has identified as likely to be found undeserving may in the end come out of the pockets of the deserving since resources available for any particular program of social welfare are not unlimited.

But more is implicated in cases of this type than *ad hoc* weighing of fiscal and administrative burdens against the interests of a particular category of claimants. The ultimate balance involves a determination as to when, under our constitutional system, judicial-type procedures must be imposed upon administrative action to assure fairness. We reiterate the wise admonishment of Mr. Justice Frankfurter that differences in the origin and function of administrative agencies "preclude wholesale transplantation of the rules of procedure, trial, and review which have evolved from the history and experience of courts." *FCC v. Pottsville Broadcasting Co.*, 309 U.S. 134, 143 (1940). The judicial model of an evidentiary hearing is neither a required, nor even the most effective, method of decisionmaking in all circumstances. The essence of due process is the requirement that "a person in jeopardy of serious loss [be given] notice of the case against him and opportunity to meet it." *Joint Anti-Fascist Comm. v. McGrath*, 341 U.S., at 171-172 (Frankfurter, J., concurring). All that is necessary is that the procedures be tailored, in light of the decision to be made, to "the capacities and circumstances of those who are to be heard," *Goldberg v. Kelly*, 397 U.S., at 268-269 (footnote omitted), to insure that they are given a meaningful opportunity to present their case. In assessing what process is due in this case, substantial weight must be given to the good-faith judgments of the individuals charged by Congress with the administration of social welfare programs that the procedures they have provided assure fair consideration of the entitlement claims of individuals. . . . This is especially so where, as here, the prescribed procedures not only provide the claimant with an effective process for asserting his claim prior to any administrative action, but also assure a right to an evidentiary hearing, as well as to subsequent judicial review, before the denial of his claim becomes final.

We conclude that an evidentiary hearing is not required prior to the termination of disability benefits and that the present administrative procedures fully comport with due process.

The judgment of the Court of Appeals is

Reversed.

Mr. Justice Stevens took no part in the consideration or decision of this case.

Mr. Justice Brennan, with whom Mr. Justice Marshall concurs, dissenting.

. . . I would add that the Court's consideration that a discontinuance of disability benefits may cause the recipient to suffer only a limited deprivation is no argument. It is speculative. Moreover, the very legislative determination to provide disability benefits, without any prerequisite determination of need in fact, presumes a need by the recipient which is not this Court's function to denigrate. Indeed, in the present case, it is indicated that because disability benefits were terminated there was a foreclosure upon the Eldridge home and the family's furniture was repossessed, forcing Eldridge, his wife, and their children to sleep in one bed. . . . Finally, it is also no argument that a worker, who has been placed in the untenable position of having been denied disability benefits, may still seek other forms of public assistance.

NOTES AND QUESTIONS

2-37. Through whose eyes does the Court view this case? George Eldridge's? The agency's? Society's? Through whose eyes should the Court view this case?

2-38. If *Goldberg v. Kelly* was premised largely on a dignitary approach to due process, *Mathews v. Eldridge* represents more of a utilitarian perspective. Consider Professor Jerry L. Mashaw's analysis in *The Supreme Court's Due Process Calculus For Administrative Adjudication in* Mathews v. Eldridge: *Three Factors In Search of a Theory of Value*:*

Utility theory suggests that the purpose of decisional procedures — like that of social action generally — is to maximize social welfare. Indeed, the three-factor analysis enunciated in *Eldridge* appears to be a type of utilitarian, social welfare function. That function first takes into account the social value at stake in a legitimate private claim; it discounts that value by the probability that it will be preserved through the available administrative procedures, and it then subtracts from that discounted value the social cost of introducing additional procedures. When combined with the institutional posture of judicial self-restraint, utility theory can be said to yield the following plausible decision-rule: "Void procedures for lack of due process only when alternative procedures would so substantially increase social welfare that their rejection seems irrational."

The utilitarian calculus is not, however, without difficulties. The *Eldridge* Court conceives of the values of procedure too narrowly: it views the sole purpose of procedural protections as enhancing accuracy, and thus limits its calculus to the benefits or costs that flow from correct or incorrect decisions. No attention is paid to "process values" that might inhere in oral proceedings or to the demoralization costs that may result from the grant-withdrawal sequence to which claimants like Eldridge are subjected. Perhaps more important, as the Court seeks to make sense of a calculus in which accuracy is the sole goal of procedure, it tends erroneously to characterize disability hearings as concerned almost exclusively with medical impairment and thus concludes that such hearings involve only medical evidence, whose reliability would be little enhanced by oral procedure. As applied by the *Eldridge* Court the utilitarian calculus tends, as cost-benefit analyses typically do, to "dwarf soft variables" and to ignore complexities and ambiguities.

The problem with utilitarian calculus is not merely that the Court may define the relevant costs and benefits too narrowly. However broadly conceived, the calculus asks unanswerable questions. For example, what is the social value, and the social cost, of continuing disability payments until after an oral hearing for persons initially determined to be ineligible? Answers to those questions require a technique for measuring the social

---

* 44 U. CHI. L. REV. 28, 47-49 (1976). Copyright © 1976 University of Chicago. All rights reserved.

value and social cost of government income transfers, but no such technique exists. Even if such formidable tasks of social accounting could be accomplished, the effectiveness of oral hearings in forestalling the losses that result from erroneous terminations would remain uncertain. In the face of these pervasive indeterminacies the *Eldridge* Court was forced to retreat to a presumption of constitutionality.

Finally, it is not clear that the utilitarian balancing analysis asks the constitutionally relevant questions. The Due Process Clause is one of those Bill of Rights protections meant to insure individual liberty in the face of contrary collective action. Therefore, a collective legislative or administrative decision about procedure, one arguably reflecting the intensity of the contending social values and representing an optimum position from the contemporary social perspective, cannot answer the constitutional question of whether due process has been accorded. A balancing analysis that would have the Court merely redetermine the question of social utility is similarly inadequate. There is no reason to believe that the Court has superior competence or legitimacy as a utilitarian balancer except as it performs its peculiar institutional role of insuring that libertarian values are considered in the calculus of decision. . . .

2-39. How precise is the balancing process that *Mathews* suggests? How much does it depend on the vantage point of the decisionmaker involved? Is it an approach that is sympathetic to what Professor Mashaw calls the "bureaucratic perspective"? Consider the following in Jerry L. Mashaw, *Conflict and Compromise Among Models of Administrative Justice*:*

How is the implementing agency to flesh out this substantive and procedural skeleton in a just manner? The critical literature suggests three types of demands upon our disability program to achieve justice: (1) that decisions be accurate and efficient applications of the legislative will; (2) that decisions be appropriate from the perspective of relevant professional cultures; and (3) that decisions be fair when assessed in light of traditional notions for determining individual entitlements. The elaboration of these demands produces three different models of administrative justice, which I denominate respectively "bureaucratic rationality," "professional treatment," and "moral judgment. . . ."

Given the legislatively approved task of paying disability benefits to eligible persons, the administrative goal from the perspective of bureaucratic rationality is to develop, at the lowest possible cost, a system for distinguishing between true and false claims. If we term the societal cost of reaching incorrect results "error costs," the goal is to minimize the sum of error costs and administrative costs. . . .

From the perspective of bureaucratic rationality, administrative justice is accurate decision-making carried on through processes that take account of costs. The legitimating force of this conception flows both from its claim of correct implementation of legislative decisions about social welfare and from its attempt to conserve social resources for the pursuit of other valuable ends. . . .

---

* 1981 Duke L. Rev. 181, 184-89 (1981). Copyright © 1981 by Jerry L. Mashaw. All rights reserved.

Like the bureaucratic-rationality model, the professional-treatment model requires the collection of information that can be manipulated in accordance with standardized procedures. The professional-treatment model recognizes, however, the incompleteness of facts, the distinctiveness of clients' problems, and the ultimately intuitive nature of judgment. Disability decisions from this perspective are not attempts to establish the truth or falsity of some fact, but rather are prognoses of the likely effects of disease or trauma on the client's ability to work, and efforts to counsel and support the client while pursuing therapeutic and vocational prospects. . . .

An administrative system based on a professional-treatment model would thus have different characteristics than a system based on bureaucratic rationality. Its basic approach is to use the appropriate professional for the problem at hand. Because these allocation decisions, involving assessment of need or ability to help, are themselves professional judgments, they are best made by the relevant professionals in conjunction with claimants. The administrative structure therefore need only funnel claimant-clients to multi-professional centers for examination and counseling. Administration of the disability program would include the facilitation of these contacts, coordination of multiprofessional teams, and implementation of professional judgments about particular cases. Substantive and procedural rules, hierarchical controls, and efficiency considerations would all be subordinated to the norms of the profession.

Administration based on professional treatment differs in one other important aspect from that based on bureaucratic decision-making. Both the professional and the bureaucrat master an arcane body of knowledge and support their judgments by appeals to expertise. But whereas the bureaucrat displays his knowledge through instrumentally rational routines designed to render transparent the connection between concrete decisions and legislative policy, the professional's art remains opaque to the layman. The mystery of professional judgment is nevertheless acceptable because of the service ideal of professionalism. The element of mystery and charisma in the office of physician, priest, or lawyer is combined with the trusteeship implicit in professional-client relations. Justice, in this model, lies in having the appropriate professional judgment applied to one's particular situation. . . .

This entitlement-awarding goal of the moral-judgment model gives a distinctive cast to the basic issue for adjudicatory resolution: the deservedness of the parties in the context of the events, transactions, or relationships that give rise to a claim. The focus on deservedness implies certain things about a just process of proof and decision. For example, fair disposition of charges of culpability or lack of deservedness requires that claims be specifically stated and that any affected party be given an opportunity to rebut or explain. In order for this exploration of individual deservedness to be meaningful, the decisionmaker must be neutral — that is, not previously connected with the relevant parties or events in ways that would bias his judgment. . . .

The goals of the moral-judgment model of justice may suggest additional decisional techniques and routines designed to preserve party equality and

§ 2.07   DUE PROCESS AND ADMINISTRATIVE ADJUDICATION   137

party control of the dispute, promote settlement, and protect the authority of the decision-maker. These details need not detain us; the important point is that the justice of this model inheres in its promise of a full and equal opportunity to obtain one's entitlements. Its authority rests on the neutral application of commonly held moral principles within the contexts giving rise to entitlements claims. . . .

2-40. How has the *Mathews v. Eldridge* calculus been applied in subsequent cases? Consider *Missouri v. Horowitz*, 435 U.S. 789 (1978), where the Court found that the Due Process Clause was not violated when a student at the University Missouri-Kansas City Medical School was dismissed for academic deficiencies. Respondent Horowitz had spent her final year in medical school on academic probation. At the end of that year the school's Council of Evaluation decided to drop her as a student, but allowed her to "appeal" that decision by taking her final exams before seven practicing physicians. After these exams, the Council of Evaluation decided that she should be dropped from school and not allowed to re-enroll. Horowitz sued, alleging that her Fourteenth Amendment due process rights had been violated. The Supreme Court, through Justice Rehnquist, noted that dismissal from a graduate medical school was more severe than the 10-day suspension to which high school students were subjected in *Goss v. Lopez*, the next principal case. The Court went on, however, to dismiss Horowitz's claim, and distinguish *Goss*, by applying *Mathews v. Eldridge*:

> . . . a relevant factor in determining the nature of the requisite due process is "the private interest that [was] affected by the official action." *Mathews v. Eldridge*, 424 U.S. 319, 335 (1976). But the severity of the deprivation is only one of several factors that must be weighed in deciding the exact due process owed. *Id.* We conclude that considering all relevant factors, including the valuative nature of the inquiry and the significant and historically supported interest of the school in preserving its present framework for academic evaluations, a hearing is not required by the Due Process Clause of the Fourteenth Amendment. 435 U.S. at 86, n.3.

JUSTICE MARSHALL, in his partial dissent and concurrence, used a different balancing approach based on *Mathews*:

> In the instant factual context the "appeal" provided to respondent . . . served the same purposes as, and in some respects may have been better than, a formal hearing. In establishing the procedure under which respondent was evaluated separately by seven physicians who had had little or no previous contact with her, it appears that the Medical School placed emphasis on obtaining "a fair and neutral and impartial assessment." In order to evaluate respondent, each of the seven physicians spent approximately half a day observing her as she preformed various clinical duties and then submitted a report on her performance to the Dean. It is difficult to imagine a better procedure for determining whether the school's allegations against respondent had any substance to them. *Cf. Mathews v. Eldridge, supra*, at 337-38, 344 (use of independent physician to examine disability applicant and report to decisionmaker). I therefore believe that the appeal procedure utilized by respondent, together with her earlier notices from and meetings with the Dean, provided respondent with as much procedural protection as the Due Process Clause requires.

2-41. Does *Mathews v. Eldridge* give a court more flexibility in the way it evaluates a procedural due process claim? How do Justice Marshall's and Justice Rehnquist's approaches in *Horowitz* differ? Would Justice Rehnquist's approach allow the case to be dismissed for failure to state a claim? Does Justice Marshall's approach require a more elaborate judicial trial? Does *Mathews v. Eldridge* solve the *Goldberg v. Kelly* "procedural due process explosion problem"? Does it allow the court to dismiss a number of cases that do not seem appropriate for a federal court at the initiation of the lawsuit or can this occur only after a court has taken a reasonably close look at the process claims in question?

2-42. Does the *Mathews v. Eldridge* calculus make particularly good sense for programs involving hundreds of thousands of claimants? Should it be applied to situations that do not involve such numbers?

HAMDI V. RUMSFELD

United States Supreme Court
542 US 507 (2004)

O'CONNOR, J., announced the judgment of the Court and delivered an opinion, in which REHNQUIST, C.J., and KENNEDY and BREYER, JJ., joined.

At this difficult time in our Nation's history, we are called upon to consider the legality of the Government's detention of a United States citizen on United States soil as an "enemy combatant" and to address the process that is constitutionally owed to one who seeks to challenge his classification as such. The United States Court of Appeals for the Fourth Circuit held that petitioner's detention was legally authorized and that he was entitled to no further opportunity to challenge his enemy-combatant label. We now vacate and remand. We hold that although Congress authorized the detention of combatants in the narrow circumstances alleged here, due process demands that a citizen held in the United States as an enemy combatant be given a meaningful opportunity to contest the factual basis for that detention before a neutral decisionmaker.

I

On September 11, 2001, the al Qaeda terrorist network used hijacked commercial airliners to attack prominent targets in the United States. Approximately 3,000 people were killed in those attacks. One week later, in response to these "acts of treacherous violence," Congress passed a resolution authorizing the President to "use all necessary and appropriate force against those nations, organizations, or persons he determines planned, authorized, committed, or aided the terrorist attacks" or "harbored such organizations or persons, in order to prevent any future acts of international terrorism against the United States by such nations, organizations or persons." Authorization for Use of Military Force ("the AUMF"), 115 Stat 224. Soon thereafter, the

President ordered United States Armed Forces to Afghanistan, with a mission to subdue al Qaeda and quell the Taliban regime that was known to support it.

This case arises out of the detention of a man whom the Government alleges took up arms with the Taliban during this conflict. His name is Yaser Esam Hamdi. Born an American citizen in Louisiana in 1980, Hamdi moved with his family to Saudi Arabia as a child. By 2001, the parties agree, he resided in Afghanistan. At some point that year, he was seized by members of the Northern Alliance, a coalition of military groups opposed to the Taliban government, and eventually was turned over to the United States military. The Government asserts that it initially detained and interrogated Hamdi in Afghanistan before transferring him to the United States Naval Base in Guantanamo Bay in January 2002. In April 2002, upon learning that Hamdi is an American citizen, authorities transferred him to a naval brig in Norfolk, Virginia, where he remained until a recent transfer to a brig in Charleston, South Carolina. The Government contends that Hamdi is an "enemy combatant," and that this status justifies holding him in the United States indefinitely — without formal charges or proceedings — unless and until it makes the determination that access to counsel or further process is warranted.

In June 2002, Hamdi's father, Esam Fouad Hamdi, filed the present petition for a writ of habeas corpus under 28 USC § 2241 in the Eastern District of Virginia, naming as petitioners his son and himself as next friend. . . . The habeas petition asks that the court, among other things, (1) appoint counsel for Hamdi; (2) order respondents to cease interrogating him; (3) declare that he is being held in violation of the Fifth and Fourteenth Amendments; (4) "[t]o the extent Respondents contest any material factual allegations in this Petition, schedule an evidentiary hearing, at which Petitioners may adduce proof in support of their allegations"; and (5) order that Hamdi be released from his "unlawful custody." Although his habeas petition provides no details with regard to the factual circumstances surrounding his son's capture and detention, Hamdi's father has asserted in documents found elsewhere in the record that his son went to Afghanistan to do "relief work," and that he had been in that country less than two months before September 11, 2001, and could not have received military training. The 20-year-old was traveling on his own for the first time, his father says, and "[b]ecause of his lack of experience, he was trapped in Afghanistan once that military campaign began."

The District Court found that Hamdi's father was a proper next friend, appointed the federal public defender as counsel for the petitioners, and ordered that counsel be given access to Hamdi. The United States Court of Appeals for the Fourth Circuit reversed that order, holding that the District Court had failed to extend appropriate deference to the Government's security and intelligence interests. It directed the District Court to consider "the most cautious procedures first," and to conduct a deferential inquiry into Hamdi's status. It opined that "if Hamdi is indeed an 'enemy combatant' who was captured during hostilities in Afghanistan, the government's present detention of him is a lawful one."

On remand, the Government filed a response and a motion to dismiss the petition. It attached to its response a declaration from one Michael Mobbs (hereinafter "Mobbs Declaration"), who identified himself as Special Advisor to the Under Secretary of Defense for Policy. Mobbs indicated that in this position, he has been "substantially involved with matters related to the detention of enemy combatants in the current war against the al Qaeda terrorists and those who support and harbor them (including the Taliban)." He expressed his "familiar[ity]" with Department of Defense and United States military policies and procedures applicable to the detention, control, and transfer of al Qaeda and Taliban personnel, and declared that "[b]ased upon my review of relevant records and reports, I am also familiar with the facts and circumstances related to the capture of . . . Hamdi and his detention by U. S. military forces."

Mobbs then set forth what remains the sole evidentiary support that the Government has provided to the courts for Hamdi's detention. The declaration states that Hamdi "traveled to Afghanistan" in July or August 2001, and that he thereafter "affiliated with a Taliban military unit and received weapons training." It asserts that Hamdi "remained with his Taliban unit following the attacks of September 11" and that, during the time when Northern Alliance forces were "engaged in battle with the Taliban," "Hamdi's Taliban unit surrendered" to those forces, after which he "surrender[ed] his Kalishnikov assault rifle" to them. The Mobbs Declaration also states that, because al Qaeda and the Taliban "were and are hostile forces engaged in armed conflict with the armed forces of the United States," "individuals associated with 'those groups' were and continue to be enemy combatants." Mobbs states that Hamdi was labeled an enemy combatant "[b]ased upon his interviews and in light of his association with the Taliban." According to the declaration, a series of "U. S. military screening team[s]" determined that Hamdi met "the criteria for enemy combatants," and "a subsequent interview of Hamdi has confirmed that he surrendered and gave his firearm to Northern Alliance forces, which supports his classification as an enemy combatant."

. . . The District Court found that the Mobbs Declaration fell "far short" of supporting Hamdi's detention. It criticized the generic and hearsay nature of the affidavit, calling it "little more than the government's 'say-so.'" It ordered the Government to turn over numerous materials for *in camera* review, including copies of all of Hamdi's statements and the notes taken from interviews with him that related to his reasons for going to Afghanistan and his activities therein; a list of all interrogators who had questioned Hamdi and their names and addresses; statements by members of the Northern Alliance regarding Hamdi's surrender and capture; a list of the dates and locations of his capture and subsequent detentions; and the names and titles of the United States Government officials who made the determinations that Hamdi was an enemy combatant and that he should be moved to a naval brig. The court indicated that all of these materials were necessary for "meaningful judicial review" of whether Hamdi's detention was legally authorized and whether Hamdi had received sufficient process to satisfy the Due Process Clause of the Constitution and relevant treaties or military regulations.

The Government sought to appeal the production order, and the District Court certified the question of whether the Mobbs Declaration, "'standing alone, is sufficient as a matter of law to allow meaningful judicial review of

[Hamdi's] classification as an enemy combatant.'" The Fourth Circuit reversed, but did not squarely answer the certified question. It instead stressed that, because it was "undisputed that Hamdi was captured in a zone of active combat in a foreign theater of conflict," no factual inquiry or evidentiary hearing allowing Hamdi to be heard or to rebut the Government's assertions was necessary or proper. Concluding that the factual averments in the Mobbs Declaration, "if accurate," provided a sufficient basis upon which to conclude that the President had constitutionally detained Hamdi pursuant to the President's war powers, it ordered the habeas petition dismissed.

II

The threshold question before us is whether the Executive has the authority to detain citizens who qualify as "enemy combatants." There is some debate as to the proper scope of this term, and the Government has never provided any court with the full criteria that it uses in classifying individuals as such. It has made clear, however, that, for purposes of this case, the "enemy combatant" that it is seeking to detain is an individual who, it alleges, was "'part of or supporting forces hostile to the United States or coalition partners'" in Afghanistan and who "'engaged in an armed conflict against the United States'" there. We therefore answer only the narrow question before us: whether the detention of citizens falling within that definition is authorized.

The Government maintains that no explicit congressional authorization is required, because the Executive possesses plenary authority to detain pursuant to Article II of the Constitution. We do not reach the question whether Article II provides such authority, however, because we agree with the Government's alternative position, that Congress has in fact authorized Hamdi's detention, through the AUMF. . . .

The AUMF authorizes the President to use "all necessary and appropriate force" against "nations, organizations, or persons" associated with the September 11, 2001, terrorist attacks. There can be no doubt that individuals who fought against the United States in Afghanistan as part of the Taliban, an organization known to have supported the al Qaeda terrorist network responsible for those attacks, are individuals Congress sought to target in passing the AUMF. We conclude that detention of individuals falling into the limited category we are considering, for the duration of the particular conflict in which they were captured, is so fundamental and accepted an incident to war as to be an exercise of the "necessary and appropriate force" Congress has authorized the President to use.

. . . .

III

Even in cases in which the detention of enemy combatants is legally authorized, there remains the question of what process is constitutionally due to a citizen who disputes his enemy-combatant status. Hamdi argues that he is owed a meaningful and timely hearing and that "extra-judicial detention [that] begins and ends with the submission of an affidavit based on third-hand hearsay" does not comport with the Fifth and Fourteenth Amendments. The Government counters that any more process than was provided below would be both unworkable and "constitutionally intolerable." Our resolution of this dispute requires a careful examination both of the writ of habeas corpus, which Hamdi now seeks to employ as a mechanism of judicial review, and of the Due Process Clause, which informs the procedural contours of that mechanism in this instance.

A [No suspension of Habeas]

Though they reach radically different conclusions on the process that ought to attend the present proceeding, the parties begin on common ground. All agree that, absent suspension, the writ of habeas corpus remains available to every individual detained within the United States. U.S. Const., Art. I, § 9, cl. 2 ("The Privilege of the Writ of Habeas Corpus shall not be suspended, unless when in Cases of Rebellion or Invasion the public Safety may require it"). Only in the rarest of circumstances has Congress seen fit to suspend the writ. . . . At all other times, it has remained a critical check on the Executive, ensuring that it does not detain individuals except in accordance with law. . . . All agree suspension of the writ has not occurred here. Thus, it is undisputed that Hamdi was properly before an Article III court to challenge his detention under 28 U.S.C. § 2241 [28 USCS § 2241]. . . . Further, all agree that § 2241 and its companion provisions provide at least a skeletal outline of the procedures to be afforded a petitioner in federal habeas review. Most notably, § 2243 provides that "the person detained may, under oath, deny any of the facts set forth in the return or allege any other material facts," and § 2246 allows the taking of evidence in habeas proceedings by deposition, affidavit, or interrogatories. . . .

C

. . . .

[A] tension . . . often exists between the autonomy that the Government asserts is necessary in order to pursue effectively a particular goal and the process that a citizen contends he is due before he is deprived of a constitutional right. The ordinary mechanism that we use for balancing such serious competing interests, and for determining the procedures that are necessary to ensure that a citizen is not "deprived of life, liberty, or property, without due process of law," U.S. Const., is the test that we articulated in *Mathews v. Eldridge*, 424 U.S. 319 (1976). *Mathews* dictates that the process due in any given instance is determined by weighing "the private interest that will be affected by the official action" against the Government's asserted interest, "including the function involved" and the burdens the Government would face in providing greater process. The *Mathews* calculus then contemplates a judicious balancing of these concerns, through an analysis of "the risk of an erroneous deprivation" of the private interest if the process were reduced and the "probable value, if any, of additional or substitute safeguards." We take each of these steps in turn.

1

It is beyond question that substantial interests lie on both sides of the scale in this case. Hamdi's "private interest . . . affected by the official action," is the most elemental of liberty interests — the interest in being free from physical detention by one's own government. . . . "We have always been careful not to 'minimize the importance and fundamental nature' of the individual's right to liberty," and we will not do so today.

Nor is the weight on this side of the *Mathews* scale offset by the circumstances of war or the accusation of treasonous behavior, for "[i]t is clear that commitment for *any* purpose constitutes a significant deprivation of liberty that requires due process protection," and at this stage in the *Mathews* calculus, we consider the interest of the *erroneously* detained individual. Indeed, as *amicus* briefs from media and relief organizations emphasize, the risk of erroneous deprivation of a citizen's liberty in the absence of sufficient process here is very real. Moreover, as critical as the Government's interest may be in detaining those who actually pose an immediate threat to the national security of the United States during ongoing international conflict, history and common sense teach us that an unchecked system of detention carries the potential to become a means for oppression and abuse of others who do not present that sort of threat. Because we live in a society in which "[m]ere public intolerance or animosity cannot constitutionally justify the deprivation of a person's physical liberty," our starting point for the *Mathews v. Eldridge* analysis is unaltered by the allegations surrounding the particular detainee or the organizations with which he is alleged to have associated. We reaffirm today the fundamental nature of a citizen's right to be free from involuntary confinement by his own government without due process of law, and we weigh the opposing governmental interests against the curtailment of liberty that such confinement entails.

2

On the other side of the scale are the weighty and sensitive governmental interests in ensuring that those who have in fact fought with the enemy during a war do not return to battle against the United States. . . . [T]he law of war and the realities of combat may render such detentions both necessary and appropriate, and our due process analysis need not blink at those realities. Without doubt, our Constitution recognizes that core strategic matters of warmaking belong in the hands of those who are best positioned and most politically accountable for making them.

The Government also argues at some length that its interests in reducing the process available to alleged enemy combatants are heightened by the practical difficulties that would accompany a system of trial-like process. In its view, military officers who are engaged in the serious work of waging battle would be unnecessarily and dangerously distracted by litigation half a world away, and discovery into military operations would both intrude on the sensitive secrets of national defense and result in a futile search for evidence buried under the rubble of war. To the extent that these burdens are triggered by heightened procedures, they are properly taken into account in our due process analysis.

3

Striking the proper constitutional balance here is of great importance to the Nation during this period of ongoing combat. But it is equally vital that our calculus not give short shrift to the values that this country holds dear or to the privilege that is American citizenship. It is during our most challenging and uncertain moments that our Nation's commitment to due process is most severely tested; and it is in those times that we must preserve our commitment at home to the principles for which we fight abroad. . . .

With due recognition of these competing concerns, we believe that neither the process proposed by the Government nor the process apparently envisioned by the District Court below strikes the proper constitutional balance when a United States citizen is detained in the United States as an enemy combatant. That is, "the risk of erroneous deprivation" of a detainee's liberty interest is unacceptably high under the Government's proposed rule, while some of the "additional or substitute procedural safeguards" suggested by the District Court are unwarranted in light of their limited "probable value" and the burdens they may impose on the military in such cases. *Mathews*, 424 U.S., at 335.

We therefore hold that a citizen-detainee seeking to challenge his classification as an enemy combatant must receive notice of the factual basis for his classification, and a fair opportunity to rebut the Government's factual assertions before a neutral decisionmaker. "For more than a century the central meaning of procedural due process has been clear: 'Parties whose rights are to be affected are entitled to be heard; and in order that they may enjoy that right they must first be notified.' It is equally fundamental that the right to notice and an opportunity to be heard 'must be granted at a meaningful time and in a meaningful manner.'" *Fuentes v. Shevin*, 407 U.S. 67 (1972). These essential constitutional promises may not be eroded.

At the same time, the exigencies of the circumstances may demand that, aside from these core elements, enemy combatant proceedings may be tailored to alleviate their uncommon potential to burden the Executive at a time of ongoing military conflict. Hearsay, for example, may need to be accepted as the most reliable available evidence from the Government in such a proceeding. Likewise, the Constitution would not be offended by a presumption in favor of the Government's evidence, so long as that presumption remained a rebuttable one and fair opportunity for rebuttal were provided. Thus, once the Government puts forth credible evidence that the habeas petitioner meets the enemy-combatant criteria, the onus could shift to the petitioner to rebut that evidence with more persuasive evidence that he falls outside the criteria. A burden-shifting scheme of this sort would meet the goal of ensuring that the errant tourist, embedded journalist, or local aid worker has a chance to prove military error while giving due regard to the Executive once it has put forth meaningful support for its conclusion that the detainee is in fact an enemy combatant. In the words of *Mathews*, process of this sort would sufficiently address the "risk of erroneous deprivation" of a detainee's liberty interest while eliminating certain procedures that have questionable additional value in light of the burden on the Government.[1]

We think it unlikely that this basic process will have the dire impact on the central functions of warmaking that the Government forecasts. The parties agree that initial captures on the battlefield need not receive the process we have discussed here; that process is due only when the determination is made to *continue* to hold those who have been seized. The Government has made clear in its briefing that documentation regarding battlefield detainees already is kept in the ordinary course of military affairs. Any factfinding imposition created by requiring a knowledgeable affiant to summarize these records to an independent tribunal is a minimal one. Likewise, arguments that military officers ought not have to wage war under the threat of litigation lose much of their steam when factual disputes at enemy-combatant hearings are limited to the alleged combatant's acts. This focus meddles little, if at all, in the strategy or conduct of war, inquiring only into the appropriateness of continuing to detain an individual claimed to have taken up arms against the United States. While we accord the greatest respect and consideration to the judgments of military authorities in matters relating to the actual prosecution of a war, and recognize that the scope of that discretion necessarily is wide, it does not infringe on the core role of the military for the courts to exercise their own time-honored and constitutionally mandated roles of reviewing and resolving claims like those presented here. . . .

In sum, while the full protections that accompany challenges to detentions in other settings may prove unworkable and inappropriate in the enemy-combatant setting, the threats to military operations posed by a basic system of independent review are not so weighty as to trump a citizen's core rights to challenge meaningfully the Government's case and to be heard by an impartial adjudicator.

D

In so holding, we necessarily reject the Government's assertion that separation of powers principles mandate a heavily circumscribed role for the courts in such circumstances. Indeed, the position that the courts must forgo any examination of the individual case and focus exclusively on the legality of the broader detention scheme cannot be mandated by any reasonable view of separation of powers, as this approach serves only to *condense* power into a single branch of government. We have long since made clear that a state of war is not a blank check for the President when it comes to the rights of the Nation's citizens. *Youngstown Sheet & Tube Co. v. Sawyer.* 343 U.S. 579 (1952).. Whatever power the United States Constitution envisions for the Executive in its exchanges with other nations or with enemy organizations in times of conflict, it most assuredly envisions a role for all three branches when individual liberties are at stake. . . . [U]nless Congress acts to suspend it, the Great Writ of habeas corpus allows the Judicial Branch to play a necessary role in maintaining this delicate balance of governance, serving as

---

[1] Because we hold that Hamdi is constitutionally entitled to the process described above, we need not address at this time whether any treaty guarantees him similar access to a tribunal for a determination of his status.

an important judicial check on the Executive's discretion in the realm of detentions. Thus, while we do not question that our due process assessment must pay keen attention to the particular burdens faced by the Executive in the context of military action, it would turn our system of checks and balances on its head to suggest that a citizen could not make his way to court with a challenge to the factual basis for his detention by his government, simply because the Executive opposes making available such a challenge. Absent suspension of the writ by Congress, a citizen detained as an enemy combatant is entitled to this process.

Because we conclude that due process demands some system for a citizen detainee to refute his classification, the proposed "some evidence" standard is inadequate. Any process in which the Executive's factual assertions go wholly unchallenged or are simply presumed correct without any opportunity for the alleged combatant to demonstrate otherwise falls constitutionally short. As the Government itself has recognized, we have utilized the "some evidence" standard in the past as a standard of review, not as a standard of proof. That is, it primarily has been employed by courts in examining an administrative record developed after an adversarial proceeding — one with process at least of the sort that we today hold is constitutionally mandated in the citizen enemy-combatant setting. This standard therefore is ill suited to the situation in which a habeas petitioner has received no prior proceedings before any tribunal and had no prior opportunity to rebut the Executive's factual assertions before a neutral decisionmaker.

Today we are faced only with such a case. Aside from unspecified "screening" processes, and military interrogations in which the Government suggests Hamdi could have contested his classification, Hamdi has received no process. An interrogation by one's captor, however effective an intelligence-gathering tool, hardly constitutes a constitutionally adequate factfinding before a neutral decisionmaker. . . . Plainly, the "process" Hamdi has received is not that to which he is entitled under the Due Process Clause.

There remains the possibility that the standards we have articulated could be met by an appropriately authorized and properly constituted military tribunal. Indeed, it is notable that military regulations already provide for such process in related instances, dictating that tribunals be made available to determine the status of enemy detainees who assert prisoner-of-war status under the Geneva Convention. In the absence of such process, however, a court that receives a petition for a writ of habeas corpus from an alleged enemy combatant must itself ensure that the minimum requirements of due process are achieved. Both courts below recognized as much, focusing their energies on the question of whether Hamdi was due an opportunity to rebut the Government's case against him. The Government, too, proceeded on this assumption, presenting its affidavit and then seeking that it be evaluated under a deferential standard of review based on burdens that it alleged would accompany any greater process. As we have discussed, a habeas court in a case such as this may accept affidavit evidence like that contained in the Mobbs Declaration, so long as it also permits the alleged combatant to present his own factual case to rebut the Government's return. We anticipate that a District Court would proceed with the caution that we have indicated is necessary in this setting, engaging in a factfinding process that is both prudent and incremental. We have no reason to doubt that courts faced with these sensitive matters will pay proper heed both to the matters of national security that might arise in an individual case and to the constitutional limitations safeguarding essential liberties that remain vibrant even in times of security concerns.

IV

Hamdi asks us to hold that the Fourth Circuit also erred by denying him immediate access to counsel upon his detention and by disposing of the case without permitting him to meet with an attorney. Since our grant of certiorari in this case, Hamdi has been appointed counsel, with whom he has met for consultation purposes on several occasions, and with whom he is now being granted unmonitored meetings. He unquestionably has the right to access to counsel in connection with the proceedings on remand. No further consideration of this issue is necessary at this stage of the case.

. . . .

The judgment of the United States Court of Appeals for the Fourth Circuit is vacated, and the case is remanded for further proceedings.

It is so ordered.

[JUSTICE SCALIA dissented, and was joined by JUSTICE STEVENS. In his dissent, JUSTICE SCALIA criticized the Court for its use of the *Mathews v. Eldridge* test, pointing out that that case involved withdrawal of disability benefits, and the detention here was of a much more serious character. Scalia argued that there were only two options for detaining Hamdi. The U.S. could either bring full criminal proceedings against him, or Congress could suspend the writ of habeas corpus. JUSTICE SCALIA pointed out that non-criminal detention of citizens is limited to very narrow and concrete categories, such as temporary quarantine to prevent the spread of infectious diseases, or civil commitment of the dangerously mentally ill. In cases that fell out of these narrow categories, the criminal process was the only constitutionally acceptable procedure for detention, whether it was intended to punish, or merely to incapacitate.]

JUSTICE SOUTER, with whom JUSTICE GINSBURG joins, concurring in part, dissenting in part, and concurring in the judgment.

. . . .

Because I find Hamdi's detention forbidden by § 4001(a) and unauthorized by the Force Resolution, I would not reach any questions of what process he may be due in litigating disputed issues in a proceeding under the habeas statute or prior to the habeas enquiry itself. For me, it suffices that the Government has failed to justify holding him in the absence of a further Act of Congress, criminal charges, a showing that the detention conforms to the laws of war, or a demonstration that § 4001(a) is unconstitutional. I would therefore vacate the judgment of the Court of Appeals and remand for proceedings consistent with this view.

Since this disposition does not command a majority of the Court, however, the need to give practical effect to the conclusions of eight members of the Court rejecting the Government's position calls for me to join with the plurality in ordering remand on terms closest to those I would impose. Although I think litigation of Hamdi's status as an enemy combatant is unnecessary, the terms of the plurality's remand will allow Hamdi to offer evidence that he is not an enemy combatant, and he should at the least have the benefit of that opportunity.

It should go without saying that in joining with the plurality to produce a judgment, I do not adopt the plurality's resolution of constitutional issues that I would not reach. It is not that I could disagree with the plurality's determinations (given the plurality's view of the Force Resolution) that someone in Hamdi's position is entitled at a minimum to notice of the Government's claimed factual basis for holding him, and to a fair chance to rebut it before a neutral decision maker, nor, of course, could I disagree with the plurality's affirmation of Hamdi's right to counsel. On the other hand, I do not mean to imply agreement that the Government could claim an evidentiary presumption casting the burden of rebuttal on Hamdi, or that an opportunity to litigate before a military tribunal might obviate or truncate enquiry by a court on habeas, . . .

Subject to these qualifications, I join with the plurality in a judgment of the Court vacating the Fourth Circuit's judgment and remanding the case.

NOTES AND QUESTIONS

2-43. *Hamdi* was one of three "war-on terrorism" cases decided by the Supreme Court in 2004. The other two cases dealt with issues involving the jurisdiction of the federal courts to review the detentions of suspected terrorists. In *Rasul v. Bush,* 124 S. Ct. 2686 (2004), the Court, with Justice Stevens writing the majority opinion, ruled that U.S. courts have jurisdiction under the same habeas corpus statute involved in *Hamdi* to consider challenges to the legality of the detentions of foreign nationals captured abroad and imprisoned at a U.S. naval base at Guantanamo Bay, Cuba. Three justices dissented. *Rumsfeld v. Padilla,* 124 S. Ct. 2711 (2004), held that an American citizen seized in the U.S. and held as an enemy combatant had brought his legal challenge in the wrong federal district court. It thus left open the question of whether an American citizen who, unlike Hamdi, was captured in the U.S. and not on a foreign battlefield can bring such a claim.

2-44. Hamdi was eventually released, under the condition that he relinquish his U.S. citizenship. Additionally, Hamdi was required to renounce terrorism, agree to live in Saudi Arabia for five years and not sue the U.S. government over his captivity. *See* newswww.bbc.net.uk/1/hi/world/americas/3733942.stm.

2-45. The New York Times' Neil A. Lewis reported on November 8, 2004, in *Guantanamo Prisoners Getting Their Day, But Hardly in Court*, p. A–1,[*] as follows:

---

[*] Copyright © 2004□by The New York Times Co. Reprinted with permission.

§ 2.07   DUE PROCESS AND ADMINISTRATIVE ADJUDICATION   149

Each day, several shackled detainees are marched by their military guards into a double-wide trailer behind the prison camp's fences and razor wire to argue before three anonymous military officers that they do not belong here.

One, a 27-year-old Yemeni, spent more than an hour on Saturday telling a panel that he was not a member of Al Qaeda or a sympathizer, saying that he had never fought against the United States and should never have been detained here as an unlawful enemy combatant.

The Yemeni, a scraggly-bearded man bound hand and foot, sat in a low chair, his shackles connected to a bolt in the floor, frustrating his efforts to gesture with his hands to make his arguments. Inside the small, harshly lighted room, he alternated between pleading his case and angrily criticizing the process as unfair. Although he spoke Arabic that had to be translated by a woman sitting beside him, there was no mistaking his contempt for the panel members, who sat on a raised platform about 10 feet away and whose questions he ridiculed frequently.

These briskly conducted proceedings, which have received little notice, constitute the Bush administration's principal answer to a pair of Supreme Court rulings in June regarding the rights of detainees who have been held since the administration began its fight against terrorism after the Sept. 11 attacks . . . .

2-46. What procedures should apply when making the determination of whether or not someone was or was not an enemy combatant? What procedures are mandated by the Supreme Court? Is the kind of hearing the Court envisions clear?

2-47. Following *Rasul*, the 9th Circuit held that the proper venue for *habeas* actions involving non-resident aliens detained at Guantanamo was the Washington, D.C. District. *Gherebi v. Bush*, 374 F.3d 727 (9th Cir. 2004). In April of 2005, two D.C. District Court judges reached very different conclusions on the question of whether such aliens would have any substantive rights under U.S. law on which a *habeas* action could be based.

In *Khalid v. Bush*, a D.C. District Court judge concluded that, although *Rasul* had given non-citizen detainees a procedural right to file *habeas* actions, there were no substantive laws that applied to them, on which a habeas action could be based. *Khalid v. Bush*, 355 F. Supp. 2d 311 (D.D.C. 2005). The judge in *Khalid* concluded that non-resident aliens being held outside the U.S. had no rights under the Constitution, including due process rights, that no U.S. statute (including the Alien Tort Claims Act, and the Administrative Procedure Act) rendered their detention unlawful, and that no international law or treaties disallowed their detention. In addition, the judge rejected the idea that the Guantanamo base was sovereign U.S. territory, pointing out that the lease with Cuba expressly states that the area is the sovereign territory of Cuba. Practically, this ruling would mean that a non-resident alien detained at Guantanamo could file a *habeas* action (under *Rasul*), but could never win, unless Congress passed a new law giving them substantive rights.

In *In re Guantanamo Detainees*, 355 F. Supp. 2d 443 (D.D.C. 2005), however, a different District Judge refused to read *Rasul* so narrowly. She pointed out that the *Rasul* court had found it significant that the United States exercised "exclusive jurisdiction and control" over Guantanamo, and that a U.S. Citizen would unquestionably have substantive constitutional rights there. The court also points out that the *Rasul* court specifically stated in a footnoted comment that what the petitioners in that case alleged "unquestionably describe 'custody in violation of the Constitution or laws or treaties of the United States.'" *Rasul* at 2698 n. 15. The court also noted that application of due process to the Guantanamo detainees would implicate none of the concerns generally present in extraterritorial cases. The American authorities there are in full control of the detainees, and there would be no interference from the Cuban government, since Guantanamo is immune from Cuban law.

Having determined that the detainees are entitled to the protection of the Due Process Clause, the judge in *In re Guantanamo Detainees* went on to describe the procedural requirements for detention, applying the *Mathews v. Eldridge* analysis, as used in *Hamdi*. Adopting the requirements laid out in *Hamdi*, specifically notice of factual basis for classification as an enemy combatant, an opportunity to rebut such evidence as well as an impartial decisionmaker, the court found several defects in the Combatant Status Review Tribunal (CSRT) procedures. The court found that the CSRT's substantial reliance on classified information, not shared with detainees, in making determinations failed to provide the detainee with "sufficient notice of the factual bases for which he is being detained." *In re Guantanamo Detainees* at 468. Although the classified material may be obtained and utilized by the detainee's Personal Representative, the court found this insufficient because the Personal Representative is not a lawyer, nor an advocate for the detainee. The court also noted that, in practice, the Personal Representative was not an adequate substitute for counsel, and that the prohibition of counsel also violated Due Process Requirements.

The court also found that the definition of "enemy combatant" contained in the CSRT order is overly broad and vague. The order states that an "enemy combatant"

> shall mean an individual who was part of or supporting Taliban or al Qaeda forces, or associated forces that are engaged in hostilities against the United States or its coalition partners. This *includes* any person who has committed a belligerent act nor has directly supported hostilities in aid of enemy armed forces.

In re Guantanamo Detainees at 475, quoting July 7, 2004 Order at 1, (emphasis added by court).

This definition is significantly broader than that used by the Supreme Court in *Hamdi*. The court also points out that use of the word "includes" suggests that an "enemy combatant" could mean a person who had neither committed a belligerent act or directly supported hostilities.

Finally, in some of the pleadings, allegations were made that information supporting the classification of the detainee was obtained by the use of torture or other coercive methods. Due Process, according to the court, requires at least an "inquiry into the accuracy and reliability of statements alleged to have been obtained through torture." *In re Guantanamo Detainees* at 473.

As of June 10, 2005, both of these cases were being considered on appeal to the D.C. Circuit, and other *habeas* petitions were stayed pending appellate resolution of these issues.

2-48. Several other detainees, whose *habeas* petitions were before district courts, also motioned for preliminary injunctions to enjoin the government from transferring them from Guantanamo to another country unless they were given 30 days notice prior to the transfer. Again, different judges of the D.C. District Court came to different conclusions.

A majority of the district courts granted the preliminary injunctions, finding that there would be irreparable harm to the petitioners on two grounds. First, there was a substantial risk of detainees being transferred to countries which may subject them to torture, or to indefinite detention. Second, the transfer of the detainee may remove jurisdiction for the detainee's active *habeas* action.

The courts also suggested that there was a substantial likelihood of success on the petitioner's *habeas* claims, in light of the conclusion reached in *In re Guantanamo Detainees*. Although it was impossible to determine a "mathematical probability of success," the likelihood was enough to grant the injunction. *Al-Marri v. Bush*, 274 F. Supp. 2d 1003 (D.D.C, 2005).

The court also considered the interest of the government in facilitating transfer without delay. The government argued that having to provide notice could hamper diplomatic negotiations with foreign governments. Most courts, in weighing these interests, found the detainees' interests far more significant and persuasive. *See Al-Marri v. Bush, Kurnaz v. Bush*, 2005 WL 839542 (D.D.C. 2005) (applying only to detainees who are not being transferred for release) *Abdah v. Bush*, U.S. Dist. LEXIS 6417 (D.D.C. 2005); *Al-Joudi v. Bush*, 2005 WL 774847 (D.D.C. 2005).

Other district court judges, however, rejected similar petitions. In *Al-Anazi v. Bush*, 377 F. Supp. 2d 102 (D.D.C. 2005), the court dismissed the concerns of the detainee about being transferred to a country where he would be treated inhumanely, pointing out that there was no evidence that transferees from Guantanamo were being tortured, and even if the government was sending detainees to countries where they may be tortured, there was no legal basis for the U.S. judiciary to protect them from the actions of a foreign state, and, in any event, a 30 day notice period would not prevent an eventual transfer.

The court differentiated the transfers at issue here from the alleged "rendition" practice in which the foreign governments were expected to "carry out the will of the United States." *Al-Anazi* at 2. In these cases, the government no longer exercises any control over the transferred detainees, and, indeed, a majority of them are transferred for the purpose of release.

As to the issue of maintaining district court jurisdiction over habeas claims, the *Al-Anazi* court argued that there was no evidence that the transfers were being effected with the purpose of defeating jurisdiction. Also, by transferring the detainees, the U.S. was relinquishing its control over them, which is precisely the relief that a successful *habeas* action would grant.

This court also pointed out that the questions raised by *Khalid* and *Guantanamo Detainees* involve the detention of the petitioners, not their transfer. The relevant question for the purposes of the preliminary injunction, according to the *Al-Anazi* court, is whether detainees would have a substantial likelihood of success in a challenge of their transfer. The court pointed out that there was no legal authority preventing such transfer, and no evidence that the U.S. was transferring detainees for illicit purposes (such as torture, or to remove *habeas* jurisdiction).

The *Al-Anazi* court also gave significant weight to the government's interest in having effective negotiations with foreign governments without judicial interference. The court argued that any agreements for transfer would have to be contingent on judicial review, making them less valuable, and impeding the president's ability to speak effectively for the nation on foreign policy. These interests were found to be substantial enough to defeat the motion for preliminary injunction. *See also Almurbati v. Bush*, 377 F. Supp. 2d 102 (D.D.C. 2005).

PROBLEM 2-3

After the court's decision in *Hamdi*, the government established a Combatant Status Review Tribunal (CSRT) to determine whether the detainees held at Guantanamo were, in fact, enemy combatants. In these procedures, detainees are appointed an officer as a "Personal Representative" to assist them at their tribunal. This Personal Representative is not a lawyer, or an advocate for the detainee. In order to be qualified as a Personal Representative, an officer must have a security clearance of at least TOP SECRET. This officer will inform the detainee of the detainee's opportunity to contest his status as an enemy combatant. The detainee may decide to participate or not participate in the tribunal. If the detainee elects not to participate, then the tribunal will be held in his absence.

Prior to the tribunal, the detainee is provided with an unclassified summary of the Government's Evidence, which is presented at the hearing. If material is classified, the Personal Representative will be given the opportunity to review it, but it will not be shared with the detainee. The government evidence is presumed to be genuine and accurate, but this presumption may be rebutted.

After the Government presents its evidence, the detainee is permitted to question reasonably available witnesses, and present his evidence. The Personal Representative assists him in this and may, outside of the presence of the detainee, present classified information. The detainee may testify, but cannot be compelled to testify, may elect whether or not to testify under oath, and may not be compelled to answer any specific questions. The tribunal is not bound by rules of evidence, and is free to consider any evidence, including hearsay, that it believes is relevant. The standard of proof is a preponderance of the evidence.

Following the presentation of the evidence, the members of the tribunal confer and vote in a closed session. The record of the tribunal is then checked by the CSRT Legal Advisor for its legal sufficiency. Assuming the proceedings

§ 2.07   DUE PROCESS AND ADMINISTRATIVE ADJUDICATION   153

are legally sufficient, the record is then sent to the Director of CSRT for final disposition, and the detainee is either released, or continues to be detained.[*]

(a) Are these procedures constitutional under *Hamdi* and *Mathews v. Eldridge*?

(b) Whether or not you believe they are constitutional, are there any changes you would recommend?

PROBLEM 2-4

After a detainee has been found to be an enemy combatant by the CSRT, an Administrative Review Board (ARB) reviews cases annually to determine whether detainees continue to pose a threat to the Unites States, or if they may be released. The procedures for the ARB are similar in some ways to those of the CRST, but differ in several important aspects.

A Designated Civilian Official (DCO) identifies detainees who are eligible for review by the ARB. Unless it would be inconsistent with national security, the detainee's home country is invited to submit relevant information, and to notify the detainee's relatives, allowing them to submit information as well. Several U.S. agencies, such as the Department of State, the CIA, the Department of Homeland Security and others, are also invited to submit information.

A Designated Military Officer (DMO) gathers and compiles all the information relevant to the detainee, and provides this information to the ARB, and to the Assisting Military Officer (AMO), who assists the detainee, in a role similar to the "Personal Representative" in the CSRT context. The DMO also prepares an unclassified summary of the information for the detainee. This summary includes the primary reasons for continued detention, as well as the primary reasons for release or transfer.

At the ARB Session, the detainee may make a statement, but witnesses are not present or questioned. The detainee may be present, but only for the portions of the session involving unclassified information. The ARB may, following the session, submit requests for further information in the forms of questions to the DMO and AMO, behavioral assessments, questions to other detainees (if consistent with intelligence collection), or other such measures. The ARB then consults and votes. Following the ARB session, the proceedings are reviewed for legal sufficiency, and the DCO makes the final disposition.[*]

(a) Are these procedures constitutional? How does this context differ from the one set forth in Problem 2-3?

---

[*] The implementation guidance may be found at: www.defenselink.mil/news/jul2004/d20040730comb.pdf.

[*] The administrative review implementation directive may be found at: www.defenselink.mil/news/Sep2004/d20040914adminreview.pdf.

§ 2.08 Confining the Due Process Explosion

There are various ways to limit the due process logic implied by *Goldberg, Roth,* and *Sindermann.* As we have seen, the *Mathews v. Eldridge* calculus gives courts a good deal of flexibility when reviewing the procedural and timing choices made by agencies and legislative bodies. A court can defer to the balance struck by these other bodies. This, however, occurs only after the court has involved itself deeply enough to conclude that reasonable procedural choices have been made. Narrowly defining what a property or liberty interest is, however, allows such cases to be dismissed before any elaborate balancing analysis of the procedures used (or not used) occurs. The United States Supreme Court has, on occasion, used this approach. It has also, on occasion, been quite creative when it comes to determining what, when, and especially *where* the process due has been provided.

GOSS v. LOPEZ

United States Supreme Court
419 U.S. 565 (1975)

MR. JUSTICE WHITE delivered the opinion of the Court.

This appeal by various administrators of the Columbus, Ohio, Public School System (CPSS) challenges the judgment of a three-judge federal court, declaring that appellees — various high school students in the CPSS — were denied due process of law contrary to the command of the Fourteenth Amendment in that they were temporarily suspended from their high schools without a hearing either prior to suspension or within a reasonable time thereafter, and enjoining the administrators to remove all references to such suspensions from the students' records.

I.

Ohio law, Rev. Code Ann. § 3313.64 (1972), provides for free education to all children between the ages of six and 21. Section 3313.66 of the Code empowers the principal of an Ohio public school to suspend a pupil for misconduct for up to 10 days or to expel him. In either case, he must notify the student's parents within 24 hours and state the reasons for his action. A pupil who is expelled, or his parents, may appeal the decision to the Board of Education and in connection therewith shall be permitted to be heard at the board meeting. The board may reinstate the pupil following the hearing. No similar procedure is provided in § 3313.66 or any other provision of state law for a suspended student. Aside from a regulation tracking the statute, at the time of the imposition of the suspensions in this case the CPSS itself had not issued any written procedure applicable to suspensions. Nor, so far as the record reflects, had any of the individual high schools involved in this case.² Each, however, had formally or informally described the conduct for which suspension could be imposed.

The nine named appellees, each of whom alleged that he or she had been suspended from public high school in Columbus for up to 10 days without a hearing pursuant to § 3313.66, filed an action against the Columbus Board of Education and various administrators of the CPSS under 42 U.S.C. § 1983. . . .

The proof below established that the suspensions arose out of a period of widespread student unrest in the CPSS during February and March 1971. Six of the named plaintiffs . . . were students at the Marion-Franklin High School and were each suspended for 10 days on account of disruptive or disobedient conduct committed in the presence of the school administrator who ordered the suspension. One of these, Tyrone Washington, was among a group of students demonstrating in the school auditorium while a class was being conducted there. He was ordered by the school principal to leave, refused to do so, and was suspended. Rudolph Sutton, in the presence of the principal, physically attacked a police officer who was attempting to remove Tyrone Washington from the auditorium. He was immediately suspended. The other four Marion-Franklin Students were suspended for similar conduct. None was given a hearing to determine the operative facts underlying the suspension, but each, together with his or her parents, was offered the opportunity to attend a conference, subsequent to the effective date of the suspension, to discuss the student's future.

Two named plaintiffs, Dwight Lopez and Betty Crome, were students at the Central High School and McGuffey Junior High School, respectively. The former was suspended in connection with a disturbance in the lunchroom which involved some physical damage to school property.⁵ Lopez testified that at least 75 other students were suspended from his school on the same day. He also testified below that he was not a party to the destructive conduct but was instead an innocent bystander. Because no one from the school testified with regard to this incident, there is no evidence in the record indicating the official basis for concluding otherwise. Lopez never had a hearing. . . .

On the basis of this evidence, the three-judge court declared that plaintiffs were denied due process of law because they were "suspended without hearing prior to suspension or within a reasonable time thereafter," and that Ohio

---

² According to the testimony of Phillip Fulton, the principal of one of the high schools involved in this case, there was an informal procedure applicable at the Marion-Franklin High School. It provided that in the routine case of misconduct, occurring in the presence of a teacher, the teacher would describe the misconduct on a form provided for that purpose and would send the student, with the form, to the principal's office. There, the principal would obtain the student's version of the story, and, if it conflicted with the teacher's written version, would send for the teacher to obtain the teacher's oral version — apparently in the presence of the student. Mr. Fulton testified that, if a discrepancy still existed, the teacher's version would be believed and the principal would arrive at a disciplinary decision based on it.

⁵ Lopez was actually absent from school, following his suspension, for over 20 days. This seems to have occurred because of a misunderstanding as to the length of the suspension. A letter sent to Lopez after he had been out for over 10 days purports to assume that, being over compulsory school age, he was voluntarily staying away. Upon asserting that this was not the case, Lopez was transferred to another school.

Rev. Code Ann. § 3313.66 (1972) and regulations issued pursuant thereto were unconstitutional in permitting such suspensions. It was ordered that all references to plaintiffs' suspensions be removed from school files.

Although not imposing upon the Ohio school administrators any particular disciplinary procedures and leaving them "free to adopt regulations providing for fair suspension procedures which are consonant with the educational goals of their schools and reflective of the characteristics of their school and locality," the District Court declared that there were "minimum requirements of notice and a hearing prior to suspension, except in emergency situations." In explication, the court stated that relevant case authority would: (1) permit "[i]mmediate removal of a student whose conduct disrupts the academic atmosphere of the school, endangers fellow students, teachers or school officials, or damages property;" (2) require notice of suspension proceedings to be sent to the student's parents within 24 hours of the decision to conduct them; and (3) require a hearing to be held, with the student present, within 72 hours of his removal. Finally, the court stated that, with respect to the nature of the hearing, the relevant cases required that statements in support of the charge be produced, that the student and others be permitted to make statements in defense or mitigation, and that the school need not permit attendance by counsel.

The defendant school administrators have appealed the three-judge court's decision. . . . We affirm.

II.

At the outset, appellants contend that because there is no constitutional right to an education at public expense, the Due Process Clause does not protect against expulsions from the public school system. This position misconceives the nature of the issue and is refuted by prior decisions. The Fourteenth Amendment forbids the State to deprive any person of life, liberty, or property without due process of law. Protected interests in property are normally "not created by the Constitution. Rather, they are created and their dimensions are defined" by an independent source such as state statutes or rules entitling the citizen to certain benefits. *Board of Regents v. Roth*, 408 U.S. 564, 577 (1972). . . .

Here, on the basis of state law, appellees plainly had legitimate claims of entitlement to a public education. Ohio Rev. Code Ann. §§ 3313.48 and 3313.64 (1972 and Supp. 1973) direct local authorities to provide a free education to all residents between five and 21 years of age, and a compulsory-attendance law requires attendance for a school year of not less than 32 weeks. . . .

Although Ohio may not be constitutionally obligated to establish and maintain a public school system, it has nevertheless done so and has required its children to attend. Those young people do not "shed their constitutional rights" at the schoolhouse door. . . .

Appellants proceed to argue that even if there is a right to a public education protected by the Due Process Clause generally, the Clause comes into play only when the State subjects a student to a "severe detriment or grievous loss."

The loss of 10 days, it is said, is neither severe nor grievous and the Due Process Clause is therefore of no relevance. Appellants' argument is again refuted by our prior decisions; for in determining "whether due process requirements apply in the first place, we must look not to the 'weight' but to the *nature* of the interest at stake." *Board of Regents v. Roth, supra,* at 570-571. Appellees were excluded from school only temporarily, it is true, but the length and consequent severity of a deprivation, while another factor to weigh in determining the appropriate form of hearing, "is not decisive of the basic right" to a hearing of some kind. . . . The Court's view has been that as long as a property deprivation is not *de minimis*, its gravity is irrelevant to the question whether account must be taken of the Due Process clause. . . . A 10-day suspension from school is not *de minimis* in our view and may not be imposed in complete disregard of the Due Process Clause.

A short suspension is, of course, a far milder deprivation than expulsion. But, "education is perhaps the most important function of state and local governments," *Brown v. Board of Education,* 347 U.S. 483, 493 (1954), and the total exclusion from the educational process for more than a trivial period, and certainly if the suspension is for 10 days, is a serious event in the life of the suspended child. Neither the property interest in educational benefits temporarily denied nor the liberty interest in reputation, which is also implicated, is so insubstantial that suspensions may constitutionally be imposed by any procedure the school chooses, no matter how arbitrary.[8]

III.

"Once it is determined that due process applies, the question remains what process is due." *Morrissey v. Brewer,* 408 U.S., at 481. . . .

. . . The student's interest is to avoid unfair or mistaken exclusion from the educational process, with all of its unfortunate consequences. The Due Process Clause will not shield him from suspensions properly imposed, but it deserves both his interest and the interest of the State if his suspension is in fact unwarranted. The concern would be mostly academic if the disciplinary process were a totally accurate, unerring process, never mistaken and never unfair. Unfortunately, that is not the case, and no one suggests that it is. Disciplinarians, although proceeding in utmost good faith, frequently act on the reports and advice of others; and the controlling facts and the nature of the conduct under challenge are often disputed. The risk of error is not at all trivial, and it should be guarded against if that may be done without prohibitive cost or interference with the educational process.

The difficulty is that our schools are vast and complex. Some modicum of discipline and order is essential if the educational function is to be performed. Events calling for discipline are frequent occurrences and sometimes require immediate, effective action. Suspension is considered not only to be a necessary tool to maintain order but a valuable educational device. The prospect

---

[8] Since the landmark decision of the Court of Appeals for the Fifth Circuit in *Dixon v. Alabama State Board of Education,* 294 F.2d 150, *cert. denied,* 368 U.S. 930 (1961), the lower federal courts have uniformly held the Due Process Clause applicable to decisions made by tax-supported educational institutions to remove a student from the institution long enough for the removal to be classified as an expulsion. . . .

of imposing elaborate hearing requirements in every suspension case is viewed with great concern, and many school authorities may well prefer the untrammeled power to act unilaterally, unhampered by rules about notice and hearing. But it would be a strange disciplinary system in an educational institution if no communication was sought by the disciplinarian with the student in an effort to inform him of his dereliction and to let him tell his side of the story in order to make sure that an injustice is not done. . . .[9]

We do not believe that school authorities must be totally free from notice and hearing requirements if their schools are to operate with acceptable efficiency. Students facing temporary suspension have interests qualifying for protection of the Due Process Clause, and due process requires, in connection with a suspension of 10 days or less, that the student be given oral or written notice of the charges against him and, if he denies them, an explanation of the evidence the authorities have and an opportunity to present his side of the story. The Clause requires at least these rudimentary precautions against unfair or mistaken findings of misconduct and arbitrary exclusion from school.

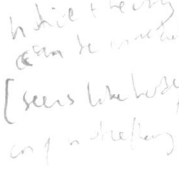

There need be no delay between the time "notice" is given and the time of the hearing. In the great majority of cases the disciplinarian may informally discuss the alleged misconduct with the student minutes after it has occurred. We hold only that, in being given an opportunity to explain his version of the facts at this discussion, the student first be told what he is accused of doing and what the basis of the accusation is. . . . Since the hearing may occur almost immediately following the misconduct, it follows that as a general rule notice and hearing should precede removal of the student from school. We agree with the District Court, however, that there are recurring situations in which prior notice and hearing cannot be insisted upon. Students whose presence poses a continuing danger to persons or property or an ongoing threat of disrupting the academic process may be immediately removed from school. In such cases, the necessary notice and rudimentary hearing should follow as soon as practicable, as the District Court indicated.

In holding as we do, we do not believe that we have imposed procedures on school disciplinarians which are inappropriate in a classroom setting.

---

[9] The facts involved in this case illustrate the point. Betty Crome was suspended for conduct which did not occur on school grounds, and for which mass arrests were made — hardly guaranteeing careful individualized fact finding by the police or by the school principal. She claims to have been involved in no misconduct. However, she was suspended for 10 days without ever being told what she was accused of doing or being given an opportunity to explain her presence among those arrested. Similarly, Dwight Lopez was suspended, along with many others, in connection with a disturbance in the lunchroom. Lopez says he was not one of those in the lunchroom who was involved. However, he was never told the basis for the principal's belief that he was involved, nor was he ever given an opportunity to explain his presence in the lunchroom. The school principals who suspended Crome and Lopez may have been correct on the merits, but it is inconsistent with the Due Process Clause to have made the decision that misconduct had occurred without at some meaningful time giving Crome or Lopez an opportunity to persuade the principals otherwise.

We recognize that both suspensions were imposed during a time of great difficulty for the school administrations involved. At least in Lopez' case there may have been an immediate need to send home everyone in the lunchroom in order to preserve school order and property; and the administrative burden of providing 75 "hearings" of any kind is considerable. However, neither factor justifies a disciplinary suspension without at any time gathering facts relating to Lopez specifically, confronting him with them, and giving him an opportunity to explain.

Instead we have imposed requirements which are, if anything, less than a fair-minded school principal would impose upon himself in order to avoid unfair suspensions. Indeed, according to the testimony of the principal of Marion-Franklin High School, that school had an informal procedure, remarkably similar to that which we now require, applicable to suspensions generally but which was not followed in this case. . . .

We stop short of construing the Due Process Clause to require, countrywide, that hearings in connection with short suspensions must afford the student the opportunity to secure counsel, to confront and cross-examine witnesses supporting the charge, or to call his own witnesses to verify his version of the incident. Brief disciplinary suspensions are almost countless — to impose in each such case even truncated trial-type procedures might well overwhelm administrative facilities in many places and, by diverting resources, cost more than it would save in educational effectiveness. Moreover, further formalizing the suspension process and escalating its formality and adversary nature may not only make it too costly as a regular disciplinary tool but also destroy its effectiveness as part of the teaching process.

On the other hand, requiring effective notice and informal hearing permitting the student to give his version of the events will provide a meaningful hedge against erroneous action. At least the disciplinarian will be alerted to the existence of disputes about facts and arguments about cause and effect. He may then determine himself to summon the accuser, permit cross-examination, and allow the student to present his own witness. In more difficult cases, he may permit counsel. In any event, his discretion will be more informed and we think the risk of error substantially reduced.

Requiring that there be at least an informal give-and-take between student and disciplinarian, preferably prior to the suspension, will add little to the fact finding function where the disciplinarian himself has witnessed the conduct forming the basis for the charge. But things are not always as they seem to be, and the student will at least have the opportunity to characterize his conduct and put it in what he deems the proper context.

We should also make it clear that we have addressed ourselves solely to the short suspension, not exceeding 10 days. Longer suspensions or expulsions for the remainder of the school term, or permanently, may require more formal procedures. Nor do we put aside the possibility that in unusual situations, although involving only a short suspension, something more than the rudimentary procedures will be required. . . .

Affirmed.

Mr. Justice Powell wrote a dissenting opinion in which The Chief Justice, Mr. Justice Blackmun, and Mr. Justice Rehnquist joined.

INGRAHAM v. WRIGHT

United States Supreme Court
430 U.S. 651 (1977)

Mr. Justice Powell delivered the opinion of the Court.

This case presents questions concerning the use of corporal punishment in public schools: First, whether the paddling of students as a means of maintaining school discipline constitutes cruel and unusual punishment in violation of the Eighth Amendment; and, second, to the extent that paddling is constitutionally permissible, whether the Due Process Clause of the Fourteenth Amendment requires prior notice and an opportunity to be heard.

I.

. . . Petitioners' evidence may be summarized briefly. In the 1970–1971 school year many of the 237 schools in Dade County used corporal punishment as a means of maintaining discipline pursuant to Florida legislation and a local School Board regulation. The statute then in effect authorized limited corporal punishment by negative inference, proscribing punishment which was "degrading or unduly severe" or which was inflicted without prior consultation with the principal or the teacher in charge of the school. . . . The regulation, Dade County School Board Policy 5144, contained explicit directions and limitations. The authorized punishment consisted of paddling the recalcitrant student on the buttocks with a flat wooden paddle measuring less than two feet long, three to four inches wide, and about one-half inch thick. The normal punishment was limited to one to five "licks" or blows with the paddle and resulted in no apparent physical injury to the student. School authorities viewed corporal punishment as a less drastic means of discipline than suspension or expulsion. Contrary to the procedural requirements of the statute and regulation, teachers often paddled students on their own authority without first consulting the principal.

. . . The evidence, consisting mainly of the testimony of 16 students, suggests that the regime at Drew was exceptionally harsh. The testimony of Ingraham and Andrews, in support of their individual claims for damages, is illustrative. Because he was slow to respond to his teacher's instructions, Ingraham was subjected to more than 20 licks with a paddle while being held over a table in the principal's office. The paddling was so severe that he suffered a hematoma requiring medical attention and keeping him out of school for several days. Andrews was paddled several times for minor infractions. On two occasions he was struck on his arms, once depriving him of the full use of his arm for a week.

The District Court made no findings on the credibility of the students' testimony. Rather, assuming their testimony to be credible, the court found no constitutional basis for relief. . . .

§ 2.08   DUE PROCESS AND ADMINISTRATIVE ADJUDICATION   161

A panel of the Court of Appeals voted to reverse. . . . Upon rehearing, the en banc court rejected these conclusions and affirmed the judgment of the District Court. . . .

We granted certiorari, limited to the questions of cruel and unusual punishment and procedural due process. . . .

II.

In addressing the scope of the Eighth Amendment's prohibition on cruel and unusual punishment, this Court has found it useful to refer to "[t]raditional common-law concepts," *Powell v. Texas,* 392 U.S. 514, 535 (1968) (plurality opinion), and to the "attitude[s] which our society has traditionally taken." *Id.,* at 531. . . .

The use of corporal punishment in this country as a means of disciplining schoolchildren dates back to the colonial period. It has survived the transformation of primary and secondary education from the colonials' reliance on optional private arrangements to our present system of compulsory education and dependence on public schools. Despite the general abandonment of corporal punishment as a means of punishing criminal offenders, the practice continues to play a role in the public education of schoolchildren in most parts of the country. Professional and public opinion is sharply divided on the practice, and has been for more than a century. Yet we can discern no trend toward its elimination. . . .

III.

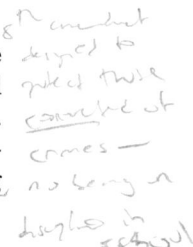

. . . An examination of the history of the [Eighth] Amendment and the decisions of this Court construing the proscription against cruel and unusual punishment confirms that it was designed to protect those convicted of crimes. We adhere to this longstanding limitation and hold that the Eighth Amendment does not apply to the paddling of children as a means of maintaining discipline in public schools. . . .

IV.

The Fourteenth Amendment prohibits any state deprivation of life, liberty, or property without due process of law. Application of this prohibition requires the familiar two-stage analysis: We must first ask whether the asserted individual interests are encompassed within the Fourteenth Amendment's protection of "life, liberty or property;" if protected interests are implicated, we then must decide what procedures constitute "due process of law." . . . Following that analysis here, we find that corporal punishment in public schools implicates a constitutionally protected liberty interest, but we hold that the traditional common-law remedies are fully adequate to afford due process.

A.

"[T]he range of interests protected by procedural due process is not infinite." *Board of Regents v. Roth, supra,* at 570. We have repeatedly rejected "the notion that *any* grievous loss visited upon a person by the State is sufficient to invoke the procedural protections of the Due Process Clause." *Meachum v. Fano,* 427 U.S., at 224. Due process is required only when a decision of the State implicates an interest within the protection of the Fourteenth Amendment. And "to determine whether due process requirements apply in the first place, we must look not to the 'weight' but to the *nature* of the interest at stake." *Roth, supra,* at 570-571.

The Due Process Clause of the Fifth Amendment, later incorporated into the Fourteenth, was intended to give Americans at least the protection against governmental power that they had enjoyed as Englishmen against the power of the Crown. The liberty preserved from deprivation without due process included the right "generally to enjoy those privileges long recognized at common law as essential to the orderly pursuit of happiness by free men." *Meyer v. Nebraska,* 262 U.S. 390, 399 (1923). . . . Among the historic liberties so protected was a right to be free from, and to obtain judicial relief for, unjustified intrusions on personal security.

While the contours of this historic liberty interest in the context of our federal system of government have not been defined precisely, they always have been thought to encompass freedom from bodily restraint and punishment. . . . It is fundamental that the state cannot hold and physically punish an individual except in accordance with due process of law.

This constitutionally protected liberty interest is at stake in this case. There is, of course, a *de minimis* level of imposition with which the Constitution is not concerned. But at least where school authorities, acting under color of state law, deliberately decide to punish a child for misconduct by restraining the child and inflicting appreciable physical pain, we hold that Fourteenth Amendment liberty interests are implicated.[43]

B.

"[T]he question remains what process is due." *Morrissey v. Brewer, supra,* at 481. Were it not for the common-law privilege permitting teachers to inflict reasonable corporal punishment on children in their care, and the availability of the traditional remedies for abuse, the case for requiring advance procedural safeguards would be strong indeed. But here we deal with a punishment — paddling — within that tradition, and the question is whether the common-law remedies are adequate to afford due process. . . .

. . . Whether in this case the common-law remedies for excessive corporal punishment constitute due process of law must turn on an analysis of the competing interests at stake, viewed against the background of "history, reason, [and] the past course of decisions." The analysis requires consideration

---

[43] Unlike *Goss v. Lopez,* 419 U.S. 565 (1975), this case does not involve the state-created property interest in public education. The purpose of corporal punishment is to correct a child's behavior without interrupting his education. That corporal punishment may, in a rare case, have the unintended effect of temporarily removing a child from school affords no basis for concluding that the practice itself deprives students of property protected by the Fourteenth Amendment.

Nor does this case involve any state-created interest in liberty going beyond the Fourteenth Amendment's protection of freedom from bodily restraint and corporal punishment. . . .

of three distinct factors: "First, the private interest that will be affected . . . ; second, the risk of an erroneous deprivation of such interest . . . and the probable value, if any, of additional or substitute procedural safeguards; and finally, the [state] interest, including the function involved and the fiscal and administrative burdens that the additional or substitute procedural requirement would entail." *Mathews v. Eldridge*, 424 U.S. 319, 335 (1976). . . .

1.

Because it is rooted in history, the child's liberty interest in avoiding corporal punishment while in the care of public school authorities is subject to historical limitations. . . .

This is not to say that the child's interest in procedural safeguards is insubstantial. The school disciplinary process is not "a totally accurate, unerring process, never mistaken and never unfair. . . ." *Goss v. Lopez*, 419 U.S. 565, 579-580 (1975). In any deliberate infliction of corporal punishment on a child who is restrained for that purpose, there is some risk that the intrusion on the child's liberty will be unjustified and therefore unlawful. In these circumstances the child has a strong interest in procedural safeguards that minimize the risk of wrongful punishment and provide for the resolution of disputed questions of justification.

We turn now to a consideration of the safeguards that are available under applicable Florida law.

2.

Florida has continued to recognize, and indeed has strengthened by statute, the common-law right of a child not to be subjected to excessive corporal punishment in school. Under Florida law the teacher and principal of the school decide in the first instance whether corporal punishment is reasonably necessary under the circumstances in order to discipline a child who has misbehaved. But they must exercise prudence and restraint. For Florida has preserved the traditional judicial proceedings for determining whether the punishment was justified. If the punishment inflicted is later found to have been excessive — not reasonably believed at the time to be necessary for the child's discipline or training — the school authorities inflicting it may be held liable in damages to the child and, if malice is shown, they may be subject to criminal penalties.[45]

---

[45] . . . Both the District Court . . . and the Court of Appeals, . . . expressed the view that the common-law tort remedy was available to the petitioners in this case. And petitioners conceded in this Court that a teacher who inflicts excessive punishment on a child may be held both civilly and criminally liable under Florida law. . . .

In view of the statutory adoption of the common-law rule, and the unanimity of the parties and the courts below, the doubts expressed in Mr. Justice White's dissenting opinion as to the availability of tort remedies in Florida can only be viewed as chimerical. The dissent makes much of the fact that no Florida court has ever "recognized" a damages remedy for unreasonable corporal punishment. . . . But the absence of reported Florida decisions hardly suggests that no remedy is available. Rather, it merely confirms the common sense judgment that excessive corporal punishment is exceedingly rare in the public schools.

Although students have testified in this case to specific instances of abuse, there is every reason to believe that such mistreatment is an aberration. . . . Moreover, because paddlings are usually inflicted in response to conduct directly observed by teachers in their presence, the risk that a child will be paddled without cause is typically insignificant. . . .

In those cases where severe punishment is contemplated, the available civil and criminal sanctions for abuse — considered in light of the openness of the school environment — afford significant protection against unjustified corporal punishment. . . . Teachers and school authorities are unlikely to inflict corporal punishment unnecessarily or excessively when a possible consequence of doing so is the institution of civil or criminal proceedings against them.[46]

It still may be argued, of course, that the child's liberty interest would be better protected if the common-law remedies were supplemented by the administrative safeguards of prior notice and a hearing. . . . But where the State has preserved what "has always been the law of the land," *United States v. Barnett,* 376 U.S. 681 (1964), the case for administrative safeguards is significantly less compelling.[47] . . .

3.

But even if the need for advanced procedural safeguards were clear, the question would remain whether the incremental benefit could justify the cost. Acceptance of petitioners' claims would work a transformation in the law governing corporal punishment in Florida and most other States. Given the impracticability of formulating a rule of procedural due process that varies with the severity of the particular imposition, the prior hearing petitioners seek would have to precede *any* paddling, however moderate or trivial.

Such a universal constitutional requirement would significantly burden the use of corporal punishment as a disciplinary measure. Hearings — even

---

[46] The low incidence of abuse, and the availability of established judicial remedies in the event of abuse, distinguish this case from *Goss v. Lopez,* 419 U.S. 565 (1975). The Ohio law struck down in *Goss* provided for suspensions from public school of up to 10 days without "any written procedure applicable to suspensions." . . . Although Ohio law provided generally for administrative review, Ohio Rev. Code Ann. § 2506.01 (Supp. 1973), the Court assumed that the short suspensions would not be stayed pending review, with the result that the review proceeding could serve neither a deterrent nor a remedial function. 419 U.S., at 581 n. 10. In these circumstances, the Court held the law authorizing suspensions unconstitutional for failure to require "that there be at least an informal give-and-take between student and disciplinarian, preferably prior to the suspension. . . ." *Id.,* at 584. The subsequent civil and criminal proceedings available in this case may be viewed as affording substantially greater protection to the child than the informal conference mandated by *Goss.*

[47] "[P]rior hearings might well be dispensed with in many circumstances in which the state's conduct, if not adequately justified, would constitute a common-law tort. This would leave the injured plaintiff in precisely the same posture as a common-law plaintiff, and this procedural consequence would be quite harmonious with the substantive view that the fourteenth amendment encompasses the same liberties as those protected by the common law." Monaghan, *Of "Liberty" and "Property,"* 62 CORNELL L. REV. 405, 431 (1977) (footnote omitted). . . .

We have no occasion in this case, to decide whether or under what circumstances corporal punishment of a public school child may give rise to an independent federal cause of action to vindicate substantive rights under the Due Process Clause.

informal hearings — require time, personnel, and a diversion of attention from normal school pursuits. School authorities may well choose to abandon corporal punishment rather than incur the burdens of complying with the procedural requirements. Teachers, properly concerned with maintaining authority in the classroom, may well prefer to rely on other disciplinary measures — which they may view as less effective — rather than confront the possible disruption that prior notice and a hearing may entail.[50] Paradoxically, such an alteration of disciplinary policy is most likely to occur in the ordinary case where the contemplated punishment is well within the common-law privilege.[51]

Elimination or curtailment of corporal punishment would be welcomed by many as a societal advance. But when such a policy choice may result from this Court's determination of an asserted right to due process, rather than from the normal processes of community debate and legislative action, the societal costs cannot be dismissed as insubstantial.[52] We are reviewing here a legislative judgment, rooted in history and reaffirmed in the laws of many States, that corporal punishment serves important educational interests. This judgment must be viewed in light of the disciplinary problems commonplace in the schools. As noted in *Goss v. Lopez*, 419 U.S., at 580: "Events calling for discipline are frequent occurrences and sometimes require immediate, effective action."[53] Assessment of the need for, and the appropriate means of maintaining, school discipline is committed generally to the discretion of school authorities subject to state law. . . .[54]

"At some point the benefit of an additional safeguard to the individual affected . . . and to society in terms of increased assurance that the action is just, may be outweighed by the cost." *Mathews v. Eldridge*, 424 U.S., at

---

[50] If a prior hearing, with the inevitable attendant publicity within the school, resulted in rejection of the teacher's recommendation, the consequent impairment of the teacher's ability to maintain discipline in the classroom would not be insubstantial.

[51] The effect of interposing prior procedural safeguards may well be to make the punishment more severe by increasing the anxiety of the child. For this reason, the school authorities in Dade County found it desirable that the punishment be inflicted as soon as possible after the infraction. . . .

[52] It may be true that procedural regularity in disciplinary proceedings promotes a sense of institutional rapport and open communication, a perception of fair treatment, and provides the offender and his fellow students a showcase of democracy at work. But ". . . [r]espect for democratic institutions will equally dissipate if they are thought too ineffectual to provide their students an environment of order in which the educational process may go forward. . . ." Wilkinson, *Goss v. Lopez: The Supreme Court as School Superintendent*, 1975 SUP. CT. REV. 25, 71-72.

[53] The seriousness of the disciplinary problems in the Nation's public schools has been documented in a recent congressional report, Senate Committee on the Judiciary, Subcommittee to Investigate Juvenile Delinquency, *Challenge for the Third Century: Education in a Safe Environment—Final Report on the Nature and Prevention of School Violence and Vandalism*, 95th Cong., 1st Sess. (Comm. Print 1977).

[54] The need to maintain order in a trial courtroom raises similar problems. In that context, this Court has recognized the power of the trial judge "to punish summarily and without notice or hearing contemptuous conduct committed in his presence and observed by him." *Taylor v. Hayes*, 418 U.S. 488, 497 (1974), citing *Ex parte Terry*, 128 U.S. 289 (1888). The punishment so imposed may be as severe as six months in prison. See *Codispoti v. Pennsylvania*, 418 U.S. 506, 513-515 (1974); *cf. Muniz v. Hoffman*, 422 U.S. 454, 475-476 (1975).

348. We think that point has been reached in this case. In view of the low incidence of abuse, the openness of our schools, and the common-law safeguards that already exist, the risk of error that may result in violation of a schoolchild's substantive rights can only be regarded as minimal. Imposing additional administrative safeguards as a constitutional requirement might reduce that risk marginally, but would also entail a significant intrusion into an area of primary educational responsibility. We conclude that the Due Process Clause does not require notice and a hearing prior to the imposition of corporal punishment in the public schools, as that practice is authorized and limited by the common law.[55] . . .

Affirmed.

MR. JUSTICE WHITE, with whom MR. JUSTICE BRENNAN, MR. JUSTICE MARSHALL, and MR. JUSTICE STEVENS join, dissenting.

Today the Court holds that corporal punishment in public schools, no matter how severe, can never be the subject of the protections afforded by the Eighth Amendment. It also holds that students in the public school systems are not constitutionally entitled to a hearing of any sort before beatings can be inflicted on them. Because I believe that these holdings are inconsistent with the prior decisions of this Court and are contrary to a reasoned analysis of the constitutional provisions involved, I respectfully dissent. . . .

II.

The majority concedes that corporal punishment in the public schools implicates an interest protected by the Due Process Clause — the liberty interest of the student to be free from "bodily restraint and punishment" involving "appreciable physical pain" inflicted by persons acting under color of state law. . . . The question remaining, as the majority recognizes, is what process is due.

The reason that the Constitution requires a State to provide "due process of law" when it punishes an individual for misconduct is to protect the individual from erroneous or mistaken punishment that the State would not have inflicted had it found the facts in a more reliable way. . . . In *Goss v.*

---

[55] MR. JUSTICE WHITE's dissenting opinion offers no manageable standards for determining what process is due in any particular case. The dissent apparently would require, as a general rule, only "an informal give-and-take between student and disciplinarian." . . . But the dissent would depart from these "minimal procedures" — requiring even witnesses, counsel, and cross-examination — in cases where the punishment reaches some undefined level of severity. . . . School authorities are left to guess at the degree of punishment that will require more than an "informal give-and-take" and at the additional process that may be constitutionally required. The impracticality of such an approach is self-evident, and illustrates the hazards of ignoring the traditional solution of the common law.

We agree with the dissent that the *Goss* procedures will often be, "if anything, less than a fair-minded school principal would impose upon himself." . . . But before this Court invokes the Constitution to impose a procedural requirement, it should be reasonably certain that the effect will be to afford protection appropriate to the constitutional interests at stake. The dissenting opinion's reading of the Constitution suggests no such beneficial result and, indeed, invites a lowering of existing constitutional standards.

Lopez, 419 U.S. 565 (1975), the court applied this principle to the school disciplinary process, holding that a student must be given an informal opportunity to be heard before he is finally suspended from public school.

> "*Disciplinarians, although proceeding in utmost good faith, frequently act on the reports and advice of others;* and the controlling facts and the nature of the conduct under challenge are often disputed. *The risk of error is not at all trivial,* and it should be guarded against if that may be done without prohibitive cost or interference with the educational process." *Id.,* at 580. (Emphasis added.)

To guard against this risk of punishing an innocent child, the Due Process Clause requires, not an "elaborate hearing" before a neutral party, but simply "an informal give-and-take between student and disciplinarian" which gives the student "an opportunity to explain his version of the facts." *Id.,* at 580, 582, 584.

The Court now holds that these "rudimentary precautions against unfair or mistaken findings of misconduct," *id.,* at 581, are not required if the student is punished with "appreciable physical pain" rather than with a suspension, even though both punishments deprive the student of a constitutionally protected interest. Although the respondent school authorities provide absolutely *no* process to the student before the punishment is finally inflicted, the majority concludes that the student is nonetheless given due process because he can later sue the teacher and recover damages if the punishment was "excessive."

This tort action is utterly inadequate to protect against erroneous infliction of punishment for two reasons.[10] First, under Florida law, a student punished for an act he did not commit cannot recover damages from a teacher "proceeding in utmost good faith . . . on the reports and advice of others," *supra,* at 692; the student has no remedy at all for punishment imposed on the basis of mistaken facts, at least as long as the punishment was reasonable from the point of view of the disciplinarian, uninformed by any prior hearing.[11]

---

[10] Here, as in *Goss v. Lopez,* 419 U.S. 565, 580-581, n. 9 (1975), the record suggests that there may be a substantial risk of error in the discipline administered by respondent school authorities. Respondents concede that some of the petitioners who were punished "denied misconduct" and that "in some cases the punishments may have been mistaken. . . ." . . . The Court of Appeals panel below noted numerous instances of students punished despite claims of innocence, 498 F.2d 248, 256-258 (CA5 1974), and was "particularly disturbed by the testimony that whole classes of students were corporally punished for the misconduct of a few." . . . To the extent that the majority focuses on the incidence of and remedies for unduly severe punishments, it fails to address petitioners' claim that procedural safeguards are required to reduce the risk of punishments that are simply mistaken.

[11] The majority's assurances to the contrary, it is unclear to me whether and to what extent Florida law provides a damages action against school officials for excessive corporal punishment. Giving the majority the benefit of every doubt, I think it is fair to say that the most a student punished on the basis of mistaken allegations of misconduct can hope for in Florida is a recovery for unreasonable or bad-faith error. But I strongly suspect that even this remedy is not available.

Although the majority does not cite a single case decided under Florida law that recognizes a student's right to sue a school official to recover damages for excessive punishment, I am willing to assume that such a tort action does exist in Florida. I nevertheless have serious doubts about whether it would ever provide a recovery to a student simply because he was punished for an offense he did not commit. . . .

The "traditional common-law remedies" on which the majority relies, *ante,* at 672, thus do nothing to protect the student from the danger that concerned the Court in *Goss* — the risk of reasonable, good-faith mistake in the school disciplinary process.

Second, and more important, even if the student could sue for good-faith error in the infliction of punishment, the law-suit occurs after the punishment has been finally imposed. The infliction of physical pain is final and irreparable; it cannot be undone in a subsequent proceeding. There is every reason to require, as the Court did in *Goss,* a few minutes of "informal give-and-take between student and disciplinarian" as a "meaningful hedge" against the erroneous infliction of irreparable injury. 419 U.S., at 538-584.

The majority's conclusion that a damages remedy for excessive corporal punishment affords adequate process rests on the novel theory that the State may punish an individual without giving him any opportunity to present his side of the story, as long as he can later recover damages from a state official if he is innocent. The logic of this theory would permit a State that punished speeding with a one-day jail sentence to make a driver serve his sentence first without a trial and then sue to recover damages for wrongful imprisonment. Similarly, the State could finally take away a prisoner's good-time credits for alleged disciplinary infractions and require him to bring a damages suit after he was eventually released. There is no authority for this theory, nor does the majority purport to find any, in the procedural due process decisions of this Court. Those cases have "consistently held that *some kind of hearing is required at some time before a person is finally deprived* of his property interests . . . [and that] a person's liberty is equally protected. . . ." *Wolff v. McDonnell,* 418 U.S. 539, 557-558 (1974). (Emphasis added.) . . .

I would reverse the judgment below.

Mr. Justice Stevens, dissenting.

Mr. Justice White's analysis of the Eighth Amendment issue is, I believe, unanswerable. I am also persuaded that his analysis of the procedural due process issue is correct. Notwithstanding my disagreement with the Court's holding on the latter question, my respect for Mr. Justice Powell's reasoning in Part IV-B of his opinion for the Court prompts these comments.

The constitutional prohibition of state deprivations of life, liberty, or property without due process of law does not, by its express language, require that a hearing be provided *before* any deprivation may occur. To be sure, the timing of the process may be a critical element in determining its adequacy — that is, in deciding what process is due in a particular context. Generally, adequate notice and a fair opportunity to be heard in advance of any deprivation of a constitutionally protected interest are essential. The Court has recognized, however, that the wording of the command that there shall be no deprivation "without" due process of law is consistent with the conclusion that a post-deprivation remedy is sometimes constitutionally sufficient.

When only an invasion of a property interest is involved, there is a greater likelihood that a damages award will make a person completely whole than when an invasion of the individual's interest in freedom from bodily restraint and punishment has occurred. In the property context, therefore, frequently a post-deprivation state remedy may be all the process that the Fourteenth Amendment requires. . . .

NOTES AND QUESTIONS

2-49. How do the judicial approaches to the question of how much process is due differ in *Goss* and *Ingraham*? Is a state court tort action the same kind of process that the Court provided in *Goss*? Do you agree with the way the Court distinguishes *Goss* in *Ingraham v. Wright*?

2-50. What were the plaintiffs in *Ingraham v. Wright* hoping to achieve with this lawsuit? What would a hearing before a paddling accomplish? Is there a need to provide frustrated teachers with a cooling-off period? Is it appropriate to use constitutionally compelled procedures to accomplish this goal?

2-51. Do you agree with Justice Stevens' reading of *Paul v. Davis* in his dissent?

2-52. For an interesting analysis of these cases, *see* Burt, *The Constitution of the Family,* 1979 SUP. CT. REV. 329; Yudof, *Legalization of Dispute Resolution, Distrust of Authority, and Organizational Theory: Implementing Due Process for Students in the Public Schools,* 81 WIS. L. REV. 891 (1981); and Rosenberg, Ingraham v. Wright, *The Supreme Court's Whipping Boy,* 78 COLUM. L. REV. 75 (1978).

2-53. Consider the adequacy of the balancing act used by the Court in the following case. Is this a new version of the rights/privelege distinction?

WALTERS v. NATIONAL ASSOCIATION OF RADIATION SURVIVORS

United States Supreme Court
473 U.S. 305 (1985)

JUSTICE REHNQUIST delivered the opinion of the Court.

. . . .

I

Congress has by statute established an administrative system for granting service-connected death or disability benefits to veterans. *See* 38 U. S.C. § 301, *et seq.* The amount of the benefit award is not based upon need, but upon service connection — that is, whether the disability is causally related to an injury sustained in the service — and the degree of incapacity caused by the disability. A detailed system has been established by statute and Veterans'

Administration (VA) regulation for determining a veteran's entitlement, with final authority resting with an administrative body known as the Board of Veterans' Appeals (BVA). Judicial review of VA decisions is precluded by statute. 38 U.S.C. § 211(a); *Johnson v. Robinson,* 415 U.S. 361 (1974). The controversy in this case centers on the opportunity for a benefit applicant or recipient to obtain legal counsel to aid in the presentation of his claim to the VA. Section 3404(c) of Title 38 provides:

> The Administrator shall determine and pay fees to agents or attorneys recognized under this section in allowed claims for monetary benefits under laws administered by the Veterans' Administration. Such fees —
>
> . . . .
>
> (2) shall not exceed $10 with respect to any one claim. . . .

Section 3405 provides criminal penalties for any person who charges fees in excess of the limitation of § 3404.

Appellees here are two veterans' organizations, three individual veterans, and a veteran's widow. The two veterans organizations are the National Association of Radiation Survivors, an organization principally concerned with obtaining compensation for its members for injuries resulting from atomic bomb tests, and Swords to Plowshares Veterans Rights Organization, an organization particularly devoted to the concerns of Vietnam veterans. The complaint contains no further allegation with respect to the numbers of members in either organization who are veteran claimants. Appellees did not seek class certification.

Appellees contended in the District Court that the fee limitation provision of § 3404 denied them any realistic opportunity to obtain legal representation in presenting their claims to the VA and hence violated their rights under the Due Process Clause of the Fifth Amendment and under the First Amendment. The District Court agreed with the appellees on both of these grounds, and entered a nationwide "preliminary injunction" barring appellants from enforcing the fee limitation. . . . To understand fully the posture in which the case reaches us it is necessary to discuss the administrative scheme in some detail.

Congress began providing veterans pensions in early 1789, and after every conflict in which the nation has been involved Congress has, in the words of Abraham Lincoln, "provided for him who has borne the battle, and his widow and his orphan." The VA was created by Congress in 1930, and since that time has been responsible for administering the congressional program for veterans' benefits. In 1978, the year covered by the report of the Legal Services Corporation to Congress that was introduced into evidence in the District Court, approximately 800,000 claims for service-connected disability or death and pensions were decided by the 58 regional offices of the VA. Slightly more than half of these were claims for service-connected disability or death, and the remainder were pension claims. Of the 800,000 total claims in 1978, more than 400,000 were allowed, and some 379,000 were denied. Sixty-six thousand of these denials were contested at the regional level; about a quarter of these contests were dropped, 15% prevailed on reconsideration at the local level, and the remaining 36,000 were appealed to the BVA. At that level some 4,500,

§ 2.08   DUE PROCESS AND ADMINISTRATIVE ADJUDICATION   171

or 12%, prevailed, and another 13% won a remand for further proceedings. Although these figures are from 1978, the statistics in evidence indicate that the figures remain fairly constant from year to year.

As might be expected in a system which processes such a large number of claims each year, the process prescribed by Congress for obtaining disability benefits does not contemplate the adversary mode of dispute resolution utilized by courts in this country. It is commenced by the submission of a claim form to the local veterans agency, which form is provided by the VA either upon request or upon receipt of notice of the death of a veteran. Upon application a claim generally is first reviewed by a three-person "rating board" of the VA regional office — consisting of a medical specialist, a legal specialist, and an "occupational specialist." A claimant is "entitled to a hearing at any time on any issue involved in a claim. . . ." Proceedings in front of the rating board "are *ex parte* in nature," no Government official appears in opposition. The principal issues are the extent of the claimant's disability and whether it is service-connected. The panel is required by regulation "to assist a claimant in developing the facts pertinent to his claim," and to consider any evidence offered by the claimant. In deciding the claim the board generally will request the applicant's Armed Service and medical records, and will order a medical examination by a VA hospital. Moreover, the board is directed by regulation to resolve all reasonable doubts in favor of the claimant.

After reviewing the evidence the board renders a decision either denying the claim or assigning a disability "rating" pursuant to detailed regulations developed for assessing various disabilities. Money benefits are calculated based on the rating. The claimant is notified of the board's decision and its reasons, and the claimant may then initiate an appeal by filing a "notice of disagreement" with the local agency. If the local agency adheres to its original decision it must then provide the claimant with a "statement of the case" — a written description of the facts and applicable law upon which the board based its determination — so that the claimant may adequately present his appeal to the BVA. Hearings in front of the BVA are subject to the same rules as local agency hearings — they are *ex parte,* there is no formal questioning or cross-examination, and no formal rules of evidence apply. . . . The BVA's decision is not subject to judicial review.

The process is designed to function throughout with a high degree of informality and solicitude for the claimant. There is no statute of limitations, and a denial of benefits has no formal *res judicata* effect; a claimant may resubmit as long as he presents new facts not previously forwarded. . . . Although there are time limits for submitting a notice of disagreement and although a claimant may prejudice his opportunity to challenge factual or legal decisions by failing to challenge them in that notice, the time limit is quite liberal — up to one year — and the VA boards are instructed to read any submission in the light most favorable to the claimant. . . . Perhaps more importantly for present purposes, however, various veterans' organizations across the country make available trained service agents, free of charge, to assist claimants in developing and presenting their claims. These service representatives are contemplated by the VA statute . . . and they are recognized as an important part of the administrative scheme. Appellees' counsel agreed at argument that a representative is available for any claimant who requests one, regardless of the claimant's affiliation with any particular veterans' group.[4]

In support of their claim that the present statutory and administrative scheme violates the Constitution, appellees submitted affidavits and declarations of 16 rejected claimants or recipients and 24 practicing attorneys, depositions of several VA employees, and various exhibits. The District Court held a hearing and then issued a 52-page opinion and order granting the requested "preliminary injunction."

With respect to the merits of appellees' due process claim, the District Court first determined that recipients of service-connected death and disability benefits possess "property" interests protected by the Due Process Clause, see Mathews v. Eldridge, 424 U.S. 319 (1976) . . . and also held that applicants for such benefits possess such an interest. Although noting that this Court has never ruled on the latter question, the court relied on several opinions of the Court of Appeals for the Ninth Circuit holding, with respect to similar Government benefits, that applicants possess such an interest. . . .

In reaching its conclusions the court relied heavily on the problems presented by what it described as "complex cases" — a class of cases also focused on in the depositions. Though never expressly defined by the District Court, these cases apparently include those in which a disability is slow developing and therefore difficult to find service connected, such as the claims associated with exposure to radiation or harmful chemicals, as well as other cases identified by the deponents as involving difficult matters of medical judgment. Nowhere in the opinion of the District Court is there any estimate of what percentage of the annual VA caseload of 800,000 these cases comprise, nor is there any more precise description of the class. There is no question but what the 3 named plaintiffs and the plaintiff veteran's widow asserted such claims, and in addition there are declarations in the record from 12 other claimants who were asserting such claims. The evidence contained in the record, however, suggests that the sum total of such claims is extremely small; in 1982, for example, roughly 2% of the BVA caseload consisted of "agent orange" or "radiation" claims, and what evidence there is suggests that the percentage of such claims in the regional offices was even less — perhaps as little as 3 in 1,000. . . .

Appellees' first claim, accepted by the District Court, is that the statutory fee limitation, as it bears on the administrative scheme in operation, deprives a rejected claimant or recipient of "life, liberty or property, without due process of law," by depriving him of representation by expert legal counsel.[8] . . .

---

[4] The VA statistics show that 86% of all claimants are represented by service representatives, 12% proceed *pro se*, and 2% are represented by lawyers. . . . Counsel agreed at argument that the 12% who proceed *pro se* do so by their own choice.

[8] The District Court held that applicants for benefits, no less than persons already receiving them, had a "legitimate claim of entitlement" to benefits if they met the statutory qualifications. The court noted that this Court has never so held, although this Court has held that a person receiving such benefits has a "property" interest in their continued receipt. See *Atkins v. Parker*, 472 U.S. 115, 128 (1985); *Mathews v. Eldridge*, 424 U.S. 319 (1976). Since at least one of the claimants here alleged a diminution of benefits already being received, however, we must in any event decide whether "due process" under the circumstances includes the right to be represented by employed counsel. In light of our decision on that question, we need not presently define what class would be entitled to the process requested.

These general principles are reflected in the test set out in *Mathews,* which test the District Court purported to follow, and which requires a court to consider the private interest that will be affected by the official action, the risk of an erroneous deprivation of such interest through the procedures used, the probable value of additional or substitute procedural safeguards, and the government's interest in adhering to the existing system. . . .

The Government interest, which has been articulated in congressional debates since the fee limitation was first enacted in 1862 during the Civil War, has been this: that the system for administering benefits should be managed in a sufficiently informal way that there should be no need for the employment of an attorney to obtain benefits to which a claimant was entitled, so that the claimant would receive the entirety of the award without having to divide it with a lawyer. . . . This purpose is reinforced by a similar absolute prohibition on compensation of any service organization representative. . . . While Congress has recently considered proposals to modify the fee limitation in some respects, a Senate Committee Report in 1982 highlighted that body's concern that "any changes relating to attorneys' fees be made carefully so as not to induce unnecessary retention of attorneys by VA claimants and not to disrupt unnecessarily the very effective network of nonattorney resources that has evolved in the absence of significant attorney involvement in VA claims matters." S. Rep. No. 97-466, p. 49 (1982). Although this same Report professed the Senate's belief that the original stated interest in protecting veterans from unscrupulous lawyers was "no longer tenable," the Senate nevertheless concluded that the fee limitation should with a limited exception remain in effect, in order to "protect claimants' benefits" from being unnecessarily diverted to lawyers.

In the face of this congressional commitment to the fee limitation for more than a century, the District Court had only this to say with respect to the governmental interest:

> The government has neither argued nor shown that lifting the fee limit would harm the government in any way, except as the paternalistic protector of claimants' supposed best interests. To the extent the paternalistic role is valid, there are less drastic means available to ensure that attorneys' fees do not deplete veterans' death or disability benefits.

It is not for the District Court or any other federal court to invalidate a federal statute by so cavalierly dismissing a long–asserted congressional purpose. If "paternalism" is an insignificant Government interest, then Congress first went astray in 1792, when by its Act of March 23 of that year it prohibited the "sale, transfer or mortgage . . . of the pension . . . [of a] soldier . . . before the same shall become due." Ch. 11, § 6, 1 Stat. 245. Acts of Congress long on the books, such as the Fair Labor Standards Act, might similarly be described as "paternalistic;" indeed, this Court once opined that "[s]tatutes of the nature of that under review, limiting the hours in which grown and intelligent men may labor to earn their living, are mere meddlesome interferences with the rights of the individual. . . ." *Lochner v. New York,* 198 U.S. 45, 61 (1905). That day is fortunately long gone, and with it the condemnation of rational paternalism as a legitimate legislative goal.

There can be little doubt that invalidation of the fee limitation would seriously frustrate the oft-repeated congressional purpose for enacting it. Attorneys would be freely employable by claimants to veterans' benefits, and the claimant would as a result end up paying part of the award, or its equivalent, to an attorney. But this would not be the only consequence of striking down the fee limitation that would be deleterious to the congressional plan.

A necessary concomitant of Congress' desire that a veteran not need a representative to assist him in making his claim was that the system should be as informal and nonadversarial as possible. This is not to say that complicated factual inquiries may be rendered simple by the expedient of informality, but surely Congress desired that the proceedings be as informal and nonadversarial as possible. The regular introduction of lawyers into the proceedings would be quite unlikely to further this goal. . . .

Thus, even apart from the frustration of Congress' principal goal of wanting the veteran to get the entirety of the award, the destruction of the fee limitation would bid fair to complicate a proceeding which Congress wished to keep as simple as possible. It is scarcely open to doubt that if claimants were permitted to retain compensated attorneys the day might come when it could be said that an attorney might indeed be necessary to present a claim properly in a system rendered more adversary and more complex by the very presence of lawyer representation. It is only a small step beyond that to the situation in which the claimant who has a factually simple and obviously deserving claim may nonetheless feel impelled to retain an attorney simply because so many other claimants retain attorneys. And this additional complexity will undoubtedly engender greater administrative costs, with the end result being that less Government money reaches its intended beneficiaries.

We accordingly conclude that under the *Mathews v. Eldridge* analysis great weight must be accorded to the Government interest at stake here. The flexibility of our approach in due process cases is intended in part to allow room for other forms of dispute resolution; with respect to the individual interests at stake here, legislatures are to be allowed considerable leeway to formulate such processes without being forced to conform to a rigid constitutional code of procedural necessities. It would take an extraordinarily strong showing of probability of error under the present system — and the probability that the presence of attorneys would sharply diminish that possibility — to warrant a holding that the fee limitation denies claimants due process of law. We have no hesitation in deciding that no such showing was made out on the record before the District Court.

As indicated by the statistics set out earlier in this opinion, more than half of the 800,000 claims processed annually by the VA result in benefit awards at the regional level. An additional 10,000 claims succeed on request for reconsideration at the regional level, and of those that do not, 36,000 are appealed to the BVA. Of these, approximately 16% succeed before the BVA. It is simply not possible to determine on this record whether any of the claims of the named plaintiffs, or of other declarants who are not parties to the action, were wrongfully rejected at the regional level or by the BVA, nor is it possible to quantify the "erroneous deprivations" among the general class of rejected claimants. If one regards the decision of the BVA as the "correct" result in every case, it follows that the regional determination against the claimant is "wrong" in the 16% of the cases that are reversed by the Board.

. . . In this case we are fortunate to have statistics that bear directly on this question, which statistics were addressed by the District Court. These unchallenged statistics chronicle the success rates before the BVA depending on the type of representation of the claimant, and are summarized in the following figures taken from the record.

**Ultimate Success Rates
Before The Board Of Veterans
Appeals By Mode Of Representation**

American Legion	16.2%
American Red Cross	16.8%
Disabled American Veterans	16.6%
Veterans of Foreign Wars	16.7%
Other non-attorney	15.8%
No representation	15.2%
Attorney/Agent	18.3%

The District Court opined that these statistics were not helpful, because in its view lawyers were retained so infrequently that no body of lawyers with an expertise in VA practice had developed, and lawyers who represented veterans regularly might do better than lawyers who represented them only *pro bono* on a sporadic basis. . . . We think the District Court's analysis of this issue totally unconvincing, and quite lacking in the deference which ought to be shown by any federal court in evaluating the constitutionality of an Act of Congress. We have the most serious doubt whether a competent lawyer taking a veteran's case on a *pro bono* basis would give less than his best effort, and we see no reason why experience in developing facts as to causation in the numerous other areas of the law where it is relevant would not be readily transferable to proceedings before the VA. . . .

The District Court's treatment of the likely usefulness of attorneys is on the same plane with its efforts to quantify the likelihood of error under the present system. The court states several times in its opinion that lawyers could provide more services than claimants presently receive — a fact which may freely be conceded — but does not suggest how the availability of these services would reduce the likelihood of error in the run-of-the-mill case. Simple factual questions are capable of resolution in a nonadversarial context, and it is less than crystal clear why lawyers must be available to identify possible errors in medical judgment. . . . The availability of particular lawyers' services in so-called "complex" cases might be more of a factor in preventing error in such cases, but on this record we simply do not know how those cases should be defined or what percentage of all of the cases before the VA they make up. Even if the showing in the District Court had been much more favorable, appellees still would confront the constitutional hurdle posed by the principle enunciated in cases such as *Mathews* to the effect that a process must be judged by the generality of cases to which it applies, and therefore, process which is sufficient for the large majority of a group of claims is by constitutional definition sufficient for all of them. But here appellees have failed to make the very difficult factual showing necessary. . . .

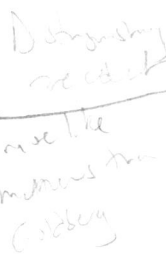

We have in previous cases, of course, held not only that the Constitution permits retention of an attorney, but also that on occasion it requires the Government to provide the services of an attorney. . . .

We think that the benefits at stake in VA proceedings, which are not granted on the basis of need, are more akin to the Social Security benefits involved in *Mathews* than they are to the welfare payments upon which the recipients in *Goldberg* depended for their daily subsistence. Just as this factor was dispositive in *Mathews* in the Court's determination that no evidentiary hearing was required prior to a temporary deprivation of benefits, so we think it is here determinative of the right to employ counsel. . . .

This case is further distinguishable from our prior decisions because the process here is not designed to operate adversarially. While counsel may well be needed to respond to opposing counsel or other forms of adversary in a trial-type proceeding, where as here no such adversary appears, and in addition a claimant or recipient is provided with substitute safeguards such as a competent representative, a decisionmaker whose duty it is to aid the claimant, and significant concessions with respect to the claimant's burden of proof, the need for counsel is considerably diminished. . . .

. . . Especially in light of the Government interests at stake, the evidence adduced before the District Court as to success rates in claims handled with or without lawyers shows no such great disparity as to warrant the inference that the congressional fee limitation under consideration here violates the Due Process Clause of the Fifth Amendment. What evidence we have been pointed to in the record regarding complex cases falls far short of the kind which would warrant upsetting Congress' judgment that this is the manner in which it wishes claims for veterans' benefits adjudicated. . . . The District Court abused its discretion in holding otherwise.

[O'CONNOR, J., filed a concurring opinion in which BLACKMUN, J., joined. BRENNAN, J., filed a dissenting opinion, in which MARSHALL, J., joined. STEVENS, J., filed a dissenting opinion in which BRENNAN and MARSHALL, JJ., joined. These opinions have been omitted.]

NOTES AND QUESTIONS

2-54. Is this Court more deferential to Congress in this case than the *Mathews v. Eldridge* Court? How does the Court characterize the private interest at stake in this case? Do you agree?

2-55. Why, in the Court's view, would the addition of lawyers to these proceedings not necessarily be helpful? Is the Court's view based on a procedural determination or a paternalistic view of what would or would not help veteran benefit claimants?

2-56. Does the nature of the issues in this case differ from those in *Mathews*? If so, how? Is there more need for a lawyer in these cases?

2-57. Is the approach taken by the Court in *Walters* a new version of the right/privilege distinction? How does it compare to the "bitter with the sweet" approach? Have we come full circle? Or are veteran benefits cases different than the cases we have examined thus far? In what way do they differ? In what ways are those differences relevant for due process analysis?

§ 2.09 Public and Private

The public/private distinction plays a major role in our jurisprudence. Indeed, Administrative Law, as we noted in Chapter One, is essentially state-centric in its focus. It seeks to govern the way state bodies and entities carry out their duties. As we have noted, the Due Process Clauses of the 5th and 14th Amendments apply to states and state actors and, as we shall see in Chapters 3 and 10, the Administrative Procedures Act and the Freedom of Information Act, respectively, apply to state agencies, not private entities. Still, it would be wrong to conclude that private actors are not important players in the administrative process, that various forms of non-constitutionally based procedures might not apply, especially at the state level, or that the extension of administrative law principles should not seriously be considered when private actors carry out tasks for the public good. As we also discussed in Chapter One, in the context of private prisons, governance and the use of markets and non-state actors to carry out public functions, is increasingly common.

This section will focus primarily on the Constitution — specifically the relevance and the application of the Due Process Clause to various public/private settings. We begin, first, with a very traditional use of the public/private distinction in *Deshaney v. Winnebago County Department of Social Services* to demarcate the respective responsibilities of the public and private sectors. We then turn to various mixes of public and private especially in the healthcare context, where private actors carry out public responsibilities. And, we revisit the delegation of the public's responsibilities for administering welfare programs, and conclude with an examination of the due process implications of a whistleblower statute. As you consider these various contexts, ask yourself whether the Administrative Procedure Act should be amended so as to apply to various private actors. What changes would you recommend?

[A] Due Process and Negative Rights

DeSHANEY v. WINNEBAGO COUNTY DEPARTMENT OF SOCIAL SERVICES

United States Supreme Court
489 U.S. 189 (1989)

Chief Justice Rehnquist delivered the opinion of the Court.

Petitioner is a boy who was beaten and permanently injured by his father, with whom he lived. Respondents are social workers and other local officials who received complaints that petitioner was being abused by his father and had reason to believe that this was the case, but nonetheless did not act to remove petitioner from his father's custody. Petitioner sued respondents claiming that their failure to act deprived him of his liberty in violation of the Due Process Clause of the Fourteenth Amendment to the United States Constitution. We hold that it did not.

I

The facts of this case are undeniably tragic. Petitioner Joshua DeShaney was born in 1979. In 1980, a Wyoming court granted his parents a divorce and awarded custody of Joshua to his father, Randy DeShaney. The father shortly thereafter moved to Neenah, a city located in Winnebago County, Wisconsin, taking the infant Joshua with him. There he entered into a second marriage, which also ended in divorce.

The Winnebago County authorities first learned that Joshua DeShaney might be a victim of child abuse in January 1982, when his father's second wife complained to the police, at the time of their divorce, that he had previously "hit the boy causing marks and [was] a prime case for child abuse." The Winnebago County Department of Social Services (DSS) interviewed the father, but he denied the accusations, and DSS did not pursue them further. In January 1983, Joshua was admitted to a local hospital with multiple bruises and abrasions. The examining physician suspected child abuse and notified DSS, which immediately obtained an order from a Wisconsin juvenile court placing Joshua in the temporary custody of the hospital. Three days later, the county convened an ad hoc "Child Protection Team" — consisting of a pediatrician, a psychologist, a police detective, the county's lawyer, several DSS caseworkers, and various hospital personnel — to consider Joshua's situation. At this meeting, the Team decided that there was insufficient evidence of child abuse to retain Joshua in the custody of the court. The Team did, however, decide to recommend several measures to protect Joshua, including enrolling him in a preschool program, providing his father with certain counselling services, and encouraging his father's girlfriend to move out of the home. Randy DeShaney entered into a voluntary agreement with DSS in which he promised to cooperate with them in accomplishing these goals.

Based on the recommendation of the Child Protection Team, the juvenile court dismissed the child protection case and returned Joshua to the custody of his father. A month later, emergency room personnel called the DSS caseworker handling Joshua's case to report that he had once again been treated for suspicious injuries. The caseworker concluded that there was no basis for action. For the next six months, the caseworker made monthly visits to the DeShaney home, during which she observed a number of suspicious injuries on Joshua's head; she also noticed that he had not been enrolled in school, and that the girlfriend had not moved out. The caseworker dutifully recorded these incidents in her files, along with her continuing suspicions that someone in the DeShaney household was physically abusing Joshua, but she did nothing more. In November 1983, the emergency room notified DSS that

Joshua had been treated once again for injuries that they believed to be caused by child abuse. On the caseworker's next two visits to the DeShaney home, she was told that Joshua was too ill to see her. Still DSS took no action.

In March 1984, Randy DeShaney beat 4-year-old Joshua so severely that he fell into a life-threatening coma. Emergency brain surgery revealed a series of hemorrhages caused by traumatic injuries to the head inflicted over a long period of time. Joshua did not die, but he suffered brain damage so severe that he is expected to spend the rest of his life confined to an institution for the profoundly retarded. Randy DeShaney was subsequently tried and convicted of child abuse.

Joshua and his mother brought this action under 42 U.S.C. § 1983 in the United States District Court for the Eastern District of Wisconsin against respondents Winnebago County, DSS, and various individual employees of DSS. The complaint alleged that respondents had deprived Joshua of his liberty without due process of law, in violation of his rights under the Fourteenth Amendment, by failing to intervene to protect him against a risk of violence at his father's hands of which they knew or should have known. The District Court granted summary judgment for respondents.

The Court of Appeals for the Seventh Circuit affirmed, 812 F.2d 298 (1987), holding that petitioners had not made out an actionable § 1983 claim. . . .

Because of the inconsistent approaches taken by the lower courts in determining when, if ever, the failure of a state or local governmental entity or its agents to provide an individual with adequate protective services constitutes a violation of the individual's due process rights, and the importance of the issue to the administration of state and local governments, we granted certiorari. We now affirm.

II

[1] The Due Process Clause of the Fourteenth Amendment provides that "[n]o State shall . . . deprive any person of life, liberty, or property, without due process of law." Petitioners contend that the State deprived Joshua of his liberty interest in "free[dom] from . . . unjustified intrusions on personal security," see *Ingraham v. Wright*, . . . by failing to provide him with adequate protection against his father's violence. The claim is one invoking the substantive rather than the procedural component of the Due Process Clause; petitioners do not claim that the State denied Joshua protection without according him appropriate procedural safeguards, . . . but that it was categorically obligated to protect him in these circumstances, see *Youngberg v. Romeo*, 457 U.S. 307, 309 (1982).[12] But nothing in the language of the Due Process Clause itself requires the State to protect the life, liberty, and property of its citizens against invasion by private actors. The Clause is phrased as a

---

[12] Petitioners also argue that the Wisconsin child protection statutes gave Joshua an "entitlement" to receive protective services in accordance with the terms of the statute, an entitlement which would enjoy due process protection against state deprivation under our decision in *Board of Regents of State Colleges v. Roth*, 408 U.S. 564 (1972). Brief for Petitioners 24-29. But this argument is made for the first time in petitioners' brief to this Court: it was not pleaded in the complaint, argued to the Court of Appeals as a ground for reversing the District Court, or raised in the petition for certiorari. We therefore decline to consider it here. . . .

limitation on the State's power to act, not as a guarantee of certain minimal levels of safety and security. It forbids the State itself to deprive individuals of life, liberty, or property without "due process of law," but its language cannot fairly be extended to impose an affirmative obligation on the State to ensure that those interests do not come to harm through other means. Nor does history support such an expansive reading of the constitutional text. Like its counterpart in the Fifth Amendment, the Due Process Clause of the Fourteenth Amendment was intended to prevent government "from abusing [its] power, or employing it as an instrument of oppression," *Davidson v. Cannon, supra,* at 348; *see also Daniels v. Williams, supra,* at 331; ("to secure the individual from the arbitrary exercise of the powers of government," and "to prevent governmental power from being 'used for purposes of oppression'") (internal citations omitted); *Parratt v. Taylor,* 451 U.S. 527, 549 (1981) (Powell, J., concurring in result) (to prevent the "affirmative abuse of power"). Its purpose was to protect the people from the State, not to ensure that the State protected them from each other. The Framers were content to leave the extent of governmental obligation in the latter area to the democratic political processes. Consistent with these principles, our cases have recognized that the Due Process Clauses generally confer no affirmative right to governmental aid, even where such aid may be necessary to secure life, liberty, or property interests of which the government itself may not deprive the individual. . . . As we said in *Harris v. McRae*:

> "Although the liberty protected by the Due Process Clause affords protection against unwarranted government interference . . . it does not confer an entitlement to such [governmental aid] as may be necessary to realize all the advantages of that freedom." 448 U.S., at 317-318. If the Due Process Clause does not require the State to provide its citizens with particular protective services, it follows that the State cannot be held liable under the Clause for injuries that could have been averted had it chosen to provide them.[13] As a general matter, then, we conclude that a State's failure to protect an individual against private violence simply does not constitute a violation of the Due Process Clause.

> Petitioners contend, however, that even if the Due Process Clause imposes no affirmative obligation on the State to provide the general public with adequate protective services, such a duty may arise out of certain "special relationships" created or assumed by the State with respect to particular individuals. Petitioners argue that such a "special relationship" existed here because the State knew that Joshua faced a special danger of abuse at his father's hands, and specifically proclaimed, by word and by deed, its intention to protect him against that danger. Having actually undertaken to protect Joshua from this danger — which petitioners concede the State played no part in creating — the State acquired an affirmative "duty," enforceable through the Due Process Clause, to do so in a reasonably competent fashion. Its failure to discharge that duty, so the argument goes, was an abuse of governmental power that so "shocks the conscience," *Rochin v. California,* 342 U.S. 165, 172 (1952), as to constitute a substantive due process violation.

---

[13] The State may not, of course, selectively deny its protective services to certain disfavored minorities without violating the Equal Protection Clause. *See Yick Wo v. Hopkins,* 118 U.S. 356 (1886). But no such argument has been made here.

We reject this argument. It is true that in certain limited circumstances the Constitution imposes upon the State affirmative duties of care and protection with respect to particular individuals. In *Estelle v. Gamble,* 429 U.S. 97 (1976), we recognized that the Eighth Amendment's prohibition against cruel and unusual punishment, made applicable to the States through the Fourteenth Amendment's Due Process Clause, *Robinson v. California,* 370 U.S. 660 (1962), requires the State to provide adequate medical care to incarcerated prisoners. 429 U.S., at 103-104. We reasoned that because the prisoner is unable "by reason of the deprivation of his liberty [to] care for himself," it is only "just" that the State be required to care for him.

In *Youngberg v. Romeo,* 457 U.S. 307 (1982), we extended this analysis beyond the Eighth Amendment setting, holding that the substantive component of the Fourteenth Amendment's Due Process Clause requires the State to provide involuntarily committed mental patients with such services as are necessary to ensure their "reasonable safety" from themselves and others. As we explained: "If it is cruel and unusual punishment to hold convicted criminals in unsafe conditions, it must be unconstitutional [under the Due Process Clause] to confine the involuntarily committed — who may not be punished at all — in unsafe conditions."

But these cases afford petitioners no help. Taken together, they stand only for the proposition that when the State takes a person into its custody and holds him there against his will, the Constitution imposes upon it a corresponding duty to assume some responsibility for his safety and general well-being. . . . The rationale for this principle is simple enough: when the State by the affirmative exercise of its power so restrains an individual's liberty that it renders him unable to care for himself, and at the same time fails to provide for his basic human needs — *e.g.,* food, clothing, shelter, medical care, and reasonable safety — it transgresses the substantive limits on state action set by the Eighth Amendment and the Due Process Clause. The affirmative duty to protect arises not from the State's knowledge of the individual's predicament or from its expressions of intent to help him, but from the limitation which it has imposed on his freedom to act on his own behalf. In the substantive due process analysis, it is the State's affirmative act of restraining the individual's freedom to act on his own behalf — through incarceration, institutionalization, or other similar restraint of personal liberty — which is the "deprivation of liberty" triggering the protections of the Due Process Clause, not its failure to act to protect his liberty interests against harms inflicted by other means.

The *Estelle–Youngberg* analysis simply has no applicability in the present case. Petitioners concede that the harms Joshua suffered did not occur while he was in the State's custody, but while he was in the custody of his natural father, who was in no sense a state actor. While the State may have been aware of the dangers that Joshua faced in the free world, it played no part in their creation, nor did it do anything to render him any more vulnerable to them. That the State once took temporary custody of Joshua does not alter the analysis, for when it returned him to his father's custody, it placed him in no worse position than that in which he would have been had it not acted at all; the State does not become the permanent guarantor of an individual's safety by having once offered him shelter. Under these circumstances, the State had no constitutional duty to protect Joshua.

It may well be that, by voluntarily undertaking to protect Joshua against a danger it concededly played no part in creating, the State acquired a duty under state tort law to provide him with adequate protection against that danger. . . . A State may, through its courts and legislatures, impose such affirmative duties of care and protection upon its agents as it wishes. But not "all common-law duties owed by government actors were . . . constitutionalized by the Fourteenth Amendment." *Daniels v. Williams, supra,* 474 U.S., at 335. Because, as explained above, the State had no constitutional duty to protect Joshua against his father's violence, its failure to do so — though calamitous in hindsight — simply does not constitute a violation of the Due Process Clause.

Judges and lawyers, like other humans, are moved by natural sympathy in a case like this to find a way for Joshua and his mother to receive adequate compensation for the grievous harm inflicted upon them. But before yielding to that impulse, it is well to remember once again that the harm was inflicted not by the State of Wisconsin, but by Joshua's father. The most that can be said of the state functionaries in this case is that they stood by and did nothing when suspicious circumstances dictated a more active role for them. In defense of them it must also be said that had they moved too soon to take custody of the son away from the father, they would likely have been met with charges of improperly intruding into the parent-child relationship, charges based on the same Due Process Clause that forms the basis for the present charge of failure to provide adequate protection.

The people of Wisconsin may well prefer a system of liability which would place upon the State and its officials the responsibility for failure to act in situations such as the present one. They may create such a system, if they do not have it already, by changing the tort law of the State in accordance with the regular lawmaking process. But they should not have it thrust upon them by this Court's expansion of the Due Process Clause of the Fourteenth Amendment.

Affirmed.

JUSTICE BRENNAN, with whom JUSTICE MARSHALL and JUSTICE BLACKMUN join, dissenting.

"The most that can be said of the state functionaries in this case," the Court today concludes, "is that they stood by and did nothing when suspicious circumstances dictated a more active role for them." Because I believe that this description of respondents' conduct tells only part of the story and that, accordingly, the Constitution itself "dictated a more active role" for respondents in the circumstances presented here, I cannot agree that respondents had no constitutional duty to help Joshua DeShaney.

It may well be, as the Court decides, that the Due Process Clause as construed by our prior cases creates no general right to basic governmental services. That, however, is not the question presented here; indeed, that question was not raised in the complaint, urged on appeal, presented in the petition for certiorari, or addressed in the briefs on the merits. No one, in short, has asked the Court to proclaim that, as a general matter, the Constitution safeguards positive as well as negative liberties.

This is more than a quibble over dicta; it is a point about perspective, having substantive ramifications. In a constitutional setting that distinguishes sharply between action and inaction, one's characterization of the misconduct alleged under § 1983 may effectively decide the case. Thus, by leading off with a discussion (and rejection) of the idea that the Constitution imposes on the States an affirmative duty to take basic care of their citizens, the Court foreshadows — perhaps even preordains — its conclusion that no duty existed even on the specific facts before us. This initial discussion establishes the baseline from which the Court assesses the DeShaneys' claim that, when a State has — "by word and by deed," announced an intention to protect a certain class of citizens and has before it facts that would trigger that protection under the applicable state law, the Constitution imposes upon the State an affirmative duty of protection.

The Court's baseline is the absence of positive rights in the Constitution and a concomitant suspicion of any claim that seems to depend on such rights. From this perspective, the DeShaneys' claim is first and foremost about inaction (the failure, here, of respondents to take steps to protect Joshua), and only tangentially about action (the establishment of a state program specifically designed to help children like Joshua). And from this perspective, holding these Wisconsin officials liable — where the only difference between this case and one involving a general claim to protective services is Wisconsin's establishment and operation of a program to protect children — would seem to punish an effort that we should seek to promote.

I would begin from the opposite direction. I would focus first on the action that Wisconsin has taken with respect to Joshua and children like him, rather than on the actions that the State failed to take. Such a method is not new to this Court. Both *Estelle v. Gamble* and *Youngberg v. Romeo* began by emphasizing that the States had confined J.W. Gamble to prison and Nicholas Romeo to a psychiatric hospital. This initial action rendered these people helpless to help themselves or to seek help from persons unconnected to the government. Cases from the lower courts also recognize that a State's actions can be decisive in assessing the constitutional significance of subsequent inaction. For these purposes, moreover, actual physical restraint is not the only state action that has been considered relevant. *See, e.g., White v. Rochford,* 592 F.2d 381 (CA7 1979) (police officers violated due process when, after arresting the guardian of three young children, they abandoned the children on a busy stretch of highway at night).

Because of the Court's initial fixation on the general principle that the Constitution does not establish positive rights, it is unable to appreciate our recognition in *Estelle* and *Youngberg* that this principle does not hold true in all circumstances. Thus, in the Court's view, *Youngberg* can be explained (and dismissed) in the following way: "In the substantive due process analysis, it is the State's affirmative act of restraining the individual's freedom to act on his own behalf — through incarceration, institutionalization, or other similar restraint of personal liberty — which is the 'deprivation of liberty' triggering the protections of the Due Process Clause, not its failure to act to protect his liberty interests against harms inflicted by other means." This restatement of *Youngberg*'s holding should come as a surprise when one recalls our explicit observation in that case that Romeo did not challenge his commitment to the hospital, but instead "argue[d] that he ha[d] a constitutionally protected liberty interest in safety, freedom of movement, and training within the institution; and that petitioners infringed these rights by failing to provide constitutionally required conditions of confinement." I do not mean to suggest that "the State's affirmative act of restraining the individual's freedom to act on his own behalf" was irrelevant in *Youngberg;* rather, I emphasize that this conduct would have led to no injury, and consequently no cause of action under § 1983, unless the State then had failed to take steps to protect Romeo from himself and from others. In addition, the Court's exclusive attention to state-imposed restraints of "the individual's freedom to act on his own behalf" suggests that it was the State that rendered Romeo unable to care for himself, whereas in fact — with an I.Q. of between 8 and 10, and the mental capacity of an 18-month-old child — he had been quite incapable of taking care of himself long before the State stepped into his life. Thus, the fact of hospitalization was critical in *Youngberg* not because it rendered Romeo helpless to help himself, but because it separated him from other sources of aid that, we held, the State was obligated to replace. Unlike the Court, therefore, I am unable to see in *Youngberg* a neat and decisive divide between action and inaction.

Moreover, to the Court, the only fact that seems to count as an "affirmative act of restraining the individual's freedom to act on his own behalf" is direct physical control (listing only "incarceration, institutionalization, [and] other similar restraint of personal liberty" in describing relevant "affirmative acts"). I would not, however, give *Youngberg* and *Estelle* such a stingy scope. I would recognize, as the Court apparently cannot, that "the State's knowledge of [an] individual's predicament [and] its expressions of intent to help him" can amount to a "limitation of his freedom to act on his own behalf" or to obtain help from others. Thus, I would read *Youngberg* and *Estelle* to stand for the much more generous proposition that, if a State cuts off private sources of aid and then refuses aid itself, it cannot wash its hands of the harm that results from its inaction. . . .

Wisconsin has established a child-welfare system specifically designed to help children like Joshua. Wisconsin law places upon the local departments of social services such as respondent (DSS or Department) a duty to investigate reported instances of child abuse. While other governmental bodies and private persons are largely responsible for the reporting of possible cases of child abuse, Wisconsin law channels all such reports to the local departments of social services for evaluation and, if necessary, further action. Even when it is the sheriff's office or police department that receives a report of suspected child abuse, that report is referred to local social services departments for action; the only exception to this occurs when the reporter fears for the child's immediate safety. In this way, Wisconsin law invites — indeed, directs — citizens and other governmental entities to depend on local departments of social services such as respondent to protect children from abuse.

The specific facts before us bear out this view of Wisconsin's system of protecting children. Each time someone voiced a suspicion that Joshua was being abused, that information was relayed to the Department for investigation and possible action. When Randy DeShaney's second wife told the police that he had "hit the boy causing marks and [was] a prime case for child abuse," the police referred her complaint to DSS. When, on three separate occasions, emergency room personnel noticed suspicious injuries on Joshua's body, they went to DSS with this information. When neighbors informed the police that they had seen or heard Joshua's father or his father's lover beating or otherwise abusing Joshua, the police brought these reports to the attention of DSS. And when respondent Kemmeter, through these reports and through her own observations in the course of nearly 20 visits to the DeShaney home, compiled growing evidence that Joshua was being abused, that information stayed within the Department — chronicled by the social worker in detail that seems almost eerie in light of her failure to act upon it. (As to the extent of the social worker's involvement in, and knowledge of, Joshua's predicament, her reaction to the news of Joshua's last and most devastating injuries is illuminating: "I just knew the phone would ring some day and Joshua would be dead."

Even more telling than these examples is the Department's control over the decision whether to take steps to protect a particular child from suspected abuse. While many different people contributed information and advice to this decision, it was up to the people at DSS to make the ultimate decision (subject to the approval of the local government's Corporation Counsel) whether to disturb the family's current arrangements. When Joshua first appeared at a local hospital with injuries signaling physical abuse, for example, it was DSS that made the decision to take him into temporary custody for the purpose of studying his situation — and it was DSS, acting in conjunction with the corporation counsel, that returned him to his father. Unfortunately for Joshua DeShaney, the buck effectively stopped with the Department.

In these circumstances, a private citizen, or even a person working in a government agency other than DSS, would doubtless feel that her job was done as soon as she had reported her suspicions of child abuse to DSS. Through its child-welfare program, in other words, the State of Wisconsin has relieved ordinary citizens and governmental bodies other than the Department of any sense of obligation to do anything more than report their suspicions of child abuse to DSS. If DSS ignores or dismisses these suspicions, no one will step in to fill the gap. Wisconsin's child-protection program thus effectively confined Joshua DeShaney within the walls of Randy DeShaney's violent home until such time as DSS took action to remove him. Conceivably, then, children like Joshua are made worse off by the existence of this program when the persons and entities charged with carrying it out fail to do their jobs.

It simply belies reality, therefore, to contend that the State "stood by and did nothing" with respect to Joshua. Through its child-protection program, the State actively intervened in Joshua's life and, by virtue of this intervention, acquired ever more certain knowledge that Joshua was in grave danger. These circumstances, in my view, plant this case solidly within the tradition of cases like *Youngberg* and *Estelle*. . . .

As the Court today reminds us, "the Due Process Clause of the Fourteenth Amendment was intended to prevent government from abusing [its] power, or employing it as an instrument of oppression." *Ante,* at 1003, quoting *Davidson,* 474 U.S., at 348. My disagreement with the Court arises from its failure to see that inaction can be every bit as abusive of power as action, that oppression can result when a State undertakes a vital duty and then ignores it. Today's opinion construes the Due Process Clause to permit a State to displace private sources of protection and then, at the critical moment, to shrug its shoulders and turn away from the harm that it has promised to try to prevent. Because I cannot agree that our Constitution is indifferent to such indifference, I respectfully dissent.

JUSTICE BLACKMUN, dissenting.

. . . Poor Joshua! Victim of repeated attacks by an irresponsible, bullying, cowardly, and intemperate father, and abandoned by respondents who placed him in a dangerous predicament and who knew or learned what was going on, and yet did essentially nothing except, as the Court revealingly observes, *ante,* at 1001, "dutifully recorded these incidents in [their] files." It is a sad commentary upon American life, and constitutional principles — so full of late of patriotic fervor and proud proclamations about "liberty and justice for all," that this child, Joshua DeShaney, now is assigned to live out the remainder of his life profoundly retarded. Joshua and his mother, as petitioners here, deserve — but now are denied by this Court — the opportunity to have the facts of their case considered in the light of the constitutional protection that 42 U.S.C. § 1983 is meant to provide.

NOTES AND QUESTIONS

2-58. What is the nature of the petitioner's due process claim in this case? Is it a substantive or procedural claim? What is the liberty interest at stake here? What relief does the petitioner seek?

2-59. How does this case compare with the due process issues presented in *Goldberg v. Kelly*? With those in *Roth* and *Sindermann*? *Goss*? In *Ingraham*? What is the nature of the governmental action under review in this case? How do you characterize it?

2-60. Do you agree with the way the majority characterizes the public as opposed to the private aspects of this case? What makes this a "private" case for the majority? What makes it "public" as far as the dissent is concerned?

2-61. If the Court had granted relief in this case, what would that relief be? What impact would this have on future cases? Should the government be held accountable for such inaction? When? Why?

[B] Due Process and Healthcare

SCHWEIKER v. McCLURE

United States Supreme Court
456 U.S. 188 (1982)

JUSTICE POWELL, delivered the opinion of the Court.

The question is whether Congress, consistently with the requirements of due process, may provide that hearings on disputed claims for certain Medicare payments be held by private insurance carriers, without a further right of appeal.

I

Title XVIII of the Social Security Act, 79 Stat. 291, as amended, 42 U.S.C. § 1395 *et seq*. . . . commonly known as the Medicare program, is administered by the Secretary of Health and Human Services. It consists of two parts. Part A, which is not at issue in this case, provides insurance against the cost of institutional health services, such as hospital and nursing home fees. . . . Part B is entitled "Supplementary Medical Insurance Benefits for the Aged and Disabled." It covers a portion (typically 80%) of the cost of certain physician services, outpatient physical therapy, X-rays, laboratory tests, and other medical and health care. . . . Only persons 65 or older or disabled may enroll, and eligibility does not depend on financial need. Part B is financed by the Federal Supplementary Medical Insurance Trust Fund. This Trust Fund in turn is funded by appropriations from the Treasury, together with monthly premiums paid by the individuals who choose voluntarily to enroll in the Part B program. . . . Part B consequently resembles a private medical insurance program that is subsidized in major part by the Federal Government.

Part B is a social program of substantial dimensions. More than 27 million individuals presently participate, and the Secretary pays out more than $10 billion in benefits annually. . . . In 1980, 158 million Part B claims were processed. In order to make the administration of this sweeping program more efficient, Congress authorized the Secretary to contract with private insurance carriers to administer on his behalf the payment of qualifying Part B claims. . . . (In this case, for instance, the private carriers that performed these tasks in California for the Secretary were Blue Shield of California and the Occidental Insurance Co.) The congressional design was to take advantage of such insurance carriers' "great experience in reimbursing physicians." H.R. Rep. No. 213, 89th Cong., 1st Sess., 46 (1965). . . .

The Secretary pays the participating carriers' costs of claims administration. . . . In return, the carriers act as the Secretary's agents. . . . They review and pay Part B claims for the Secretary according to a precisely specified process. . . . Once the carrier has been billed for a particular service, it decides initially whether the services were medically necessary, whether the charges are reasonable, and whether the claim is otherwise covered by Part B. . . . If it determines that the claim meets all these criteria, the carrier pays the claim out of the Government's Trust Fund — not out of its own pocket. . . .

Should the carrier refuse on behalf of the Secretary to pay a portion of the claim, the claimant has one or more opportunities to appeal. First, all claimants are entitled to a "review determination," in which they may submit written evidence and arguments of fact and law. A carrier employee, other than the initial decisionmaker, will review the written record *de novo* and affirm or adjust the original determination. . . . If the amount in dispute is $100 or more, a still–dissatisfied claimant then has a right to an oral hearing. . . . An officer chosen by the carrier presides over this hearing. . . . The hearing officers "do not participate personally, prior to the hearing [stage], in any case [that] they adjudicate." . . .

Hearing officers receive evidence and hear arguments pertinent to the matters at issue. . . . As soon as practicable thereafter, they must render written decisions based on the record. . . . Neither the statute nor the regulations make provision for further review of the hearing officer's decision.

II

This case arose as a result of decisions by hearing officers against three claimants. The claimants, here appellees, sued to challenge the constitutional adequacy of the hearings afforded them. The District Court for the Northern District of California certified appellees as representatives of a nationwide class of individuals whose claims had been denied by carrier-appointed hearing officers. . . . On cross-motions for summary judgment, the court concluded that the Part B hearing procedures violated appellees' right to due process "insofar as the final, unappealable decision regarding claims disputes is made by carrier appointees. . . ."

III

A

The hearing officers involved in this case serve in a quasi-judicial capacity, similar in many respects to that of administrative law judges. As this Court repeatedly has recognized, due process demands impartiality on the part of those who function in judicial or quasi-judicial capacities. . . . We must start, however, from the presumption that the hearing officers who decide Part B claims are unbiased. . . . This presumption can be rebutted by a showing of conflict of interest or some other specific reason for disqualification. . . . But the burden of establishing a disqualifying interest rests on the party making the assertion.

Fairly interpreted, the factual findings made in this case do not reveal any disqualifying interest under the standard of our cases. The District Court relied almost exclusively on generalized assumptions of possible interest, placing special weight on the various connections of the hearing officers with the private insurance carriers. The difficulty with this reasoning is that these connections would be relevant only if the carriers themselves are biased or interested. We find no basis in the record for reaching such a conclusion. As previously noted, the carriers pay all Part B claims from federal, and not their own, funds. Similarly, the salaries of the hearing officers are paid by the Federal Government. Further, the carriers operate under contracts that require compliance with standards prescribed by the statute and the Secretary. . . . In the absence of proof of financial interest on the part of the carriers, there is no basis for assuming a derivative bias among their hearing officers.

B

Appellees further argued, and the District Court agreed, that due process requires an additional administrative or judicial review by a Government rather than a carrier-appointed hearing officer. Specifically, the District Court ruled that "[e]xisting Part B procedures might remain intact so long as aggrieved beneficiaries would be entitled to appeal carrier appointees' decisions to Part A administrative law judges." . . . In reaching this conclusion, the District Court applied the familiar test prescribed in *Mathews v. Eldridge,* 424 U.S., at 335. . . . We may assume that the District Court was correct in viewing the private interest in Part B payments as "considerable," though "not quite as precious as the right to receive welfare or social security benefits." . . . We likewise may assume, in considering the third *Mathews* factor, that the additional cost and inconvenience of providing administrative law judges would not be unduly burdensome.[13]

We focus narrowly on the second *Mathews* factor that considers the risk of erroneous decision and the probable value, if any, of the additional procedure. The District Court's reasoning on this point consisted only of this sentence:

"In light of [appellees'] undisputed showing that carrier-appointed hearing officers receive little or no formal training and are not required to satisfy any threshold criteria such as having a law degree, it must be assumed that additional safeguards would reduce the risk of erroneous deprivation of Part B benefits." 503 F. Supp., at 416 (footnote omitted).

Again, the record does not support these conclusions. The Secretary has directed carriers to select as a hearing officer

"an attorney or other qualified individual with the ability to conduct formal hearings and with a general understanding of medical matters and terminology. The [hearing officer] must have a thorough knowledge of the Medicare program and the statutory authority and regulations upon which it is based, as well as rulings, policy statements, and general instructions pertinent to the Medicare Bureau." App. 22, quoting Dept. of HEW, Medicare Part B Carriers Manual, ch. VII, p. 12-21 (1980).

---

[13] No authoritative factual findings were made, and perhaps this conclusion would have been difficult to prove. It is known that in 1980 about 158 million Part B claims — up from 124 million in 1978 — were filed. Even though the additional review would be available only for disputes in excess of $100, a small percentage of the number of claims would be large in terms of number of cases.

The District Court did not identify any specific deficiencies in the Secretary's selection criteria. By definition, a "qualified" individual already possessing "ability" and "thorough knowledge" would not require further training. The court's further general concern that hearing officers "are not required to satisfy any threshold criteria" overlooks the Secretary's quoted regulation.[14] Moreover, the District Court apparently gave no weight to the qualifications of hearing officers about whom there is information in the record. Their qualifications tend to undermine rather than to support the contention that accuracy of Part B decisionmaking may suffer by reason of carrier appointment of unqualified hearing officers.[15]

"[D]ue Process is flexible and calls for such procedural protections as the particular situation demands." *Morrissey v. Brewer,* 408 U.S. 471, 481, 92 S. Ct. 2593, 2600, 33 L. Ed. 2d 484 (1972). We have considered appellees' claims in light of the strong presumption in favor of the validity of congressional action and consistently with this Court's recognition of "congressional solicitude for fair procedure. . . ." *Califano v. Yamasaki,* 442 U.S. 682, 693 (1979). Appellees simply have not shown that the procedures prescribed by Congress and the Secretary are not fair or that different or additional procedures would reduce the risk of erroneous deprivation of Part B benefits.

IV

The judgment of the District Court is reversed, and the case is remanded for judgment to be entered for the Secretary.

So ordered.

BLUM v. YARETSKY

Supreme Court of the United States
457 U.S. 991 (1982)

JUSTICE REHNQUIST delivered the opinion of the Court.

Respondents represent a class of Medicaid patients challenging decisions by the nursing homes in which they reside to discharge or transfer patients

---

[14] The District Court's opinion may be read as requiring that hearing officers always be attorneys. Our cases, however, make clear that due process does not make such a uniform requirement. *See Vitek v. Jones,* 445 U.S. 480, 499 (1980) (POWELL, J., concurring in part); *Parham v. J.R.,* 442 U.S. 584, 607 (1989); *Morrissey v. Brewer,* 408 U.S. 471, 486, 489 (1972). *Cf. Goldberg v. Kelly,* 397 U.S. 254, 271 (1970). Neither the District Court in its opinion nor the appellees before us make a particularized showing of the additional value of a law degree in the Part B context.

[15] The record contains information on nine hearing officers. Two were retired administrative law judges with 15 to 18 years of judging experience, five had extensive experience in medicine or medical insurance, one had been a practicing attorney for 20 years, and one was an attorney with 42 years' experience in the insurance industry who was self-employed as an insurance adjuster.

without notice or an opportunity for a hearing. The question is whether the State may be held responsible for those decisions so as to subject them to the strictures of the Fourteenth Amendment.

I

Congress established the Medicaid program in 1965 as Title XIX of the Social Security Act, to provide federal financial assistance to States that choose to reimburse certain medical costs incurred by the poor. As a participating State, New York provides Medicaid assistance to eligible persons who receive care in private nursing homes, which are designated as either "skilled nursing facilities" (SNF's) or "health related facilities" (HRF's). The latter provide less extensive, and generally less expensive, medical care than the former. Nursing homes chosen by Medicaid patients are directly reimbursed by the State for the reasonable cost of health care services.

An individual must meet two conditions to obtain Medicaid assistance. He must satisfy eligibility standards defined in terms of income or resources and he must seek medically necessary services. To assure that the latter condition is satisfied, federal regulations require each nursing home to establish a utilization review committee (URC) of physicians whose functions include periodically assessing whether each patient is receiving the appropriate level of care, and thus whether the patient's continued stay in the facility is justified. If the URC determines that the patient should be discharged or transferred to a different level of care, either more or less intensive, it must notify the state agency responsible for administering Medicaid assistance.

At the time their complaint was filed, respondents Yaretsky and Cuevas were patients in the American Nursing Home, an SNF located in New York City. Both were recipients of assistance under the Medicaid program. In December 1975 the nursing home's URC decided that respondents did not need the care they were receiving and should be transferred to a lower level of care in an HRF. New York City officials, who were then responsible for administering the Medicaid program in the city, were notified of this decision and prepared to reduce or terminate payments to the nursing home for respondents' care. Following administrative hearings, state social service officials affirmed the decision to discontinue benefits unless respondents accepted a transfer to an HRF providing a reduced level of care.

Respondents then commenced this suit, acting individually and on behalf of a class of Medicaid-eligible residents of New York nursing homes. Named as defendants were the Commissioners of the New York Department of Social Services and the Department of Health. Respondents alleged in part that the defendants had not afforded them adequate notice either of URC decisions and the reasons supporting them or of their right to an administrative hearing to challenge those decisions. Respondents maintained that these actions violated their rights under state and federal law and under the Due Process Clause of the Fourteenth Amendment. They sought injunctive relief and damages.

. . . .

The Court of Appeals for the Second Circuit affirmed . . . the District Court's judgment . . . . The court held that URC-initiated transfers from a lower level of care to a higher one, and all discharges and transfers initiated by the nursing homes or attending physicians, "involve state action affecting constitutionally protected property and liberty interests." The court premised its identification of state action on the fact that state authorities "responded" to the challenged transfers by adjusting the patients' Medicaid benefits. Citing our opinion in *Jackson v. Metropolitan Edison Co.*, 419 U.S. 345 (1974), the court viewed this response as establishing a sufficiently close "nexus" between the State and either the nursing homes or the URC's to justify treating their actions as those of the State itself.

We granted certiorari to consider the Court of Appeals' conclusions about the nature of state action. We now reverse its judgment.

II

[The Court first held that plaintiffs had standing to bring the case].

III

The Fourteenth Amendment of the Constitution provides in part that "[n]o State shall . . . deprive any person of life, liberty, or property without due process of law." Since this Court's decision in the *Civil Rights Cases*, "the principle has become firmly embedded in our constitutional law that the action inhibited by the first section of the Fourteenth Amendment is only such action as may fairly be said to be that of the States." *Shelley v. Kraemer*. "That Amendment erects no shield against merely private conduct, however discriminatory or wrongful."

Faithful adherence to the "state action" requirement of the Fourteenth Amendment requires careful attention to the gravamen of the plaintiff's complaint. In this case, respondents objected to the involuntary discharge or transfer of Medicaid patients by their nursing homes without certain procedural safeguards. They have named as defendants state officials responsible for administering the Medicaid program in New York. These officials are also responsible for regulating nursing homes in the State, including those in which respondents were receiving care. But respondents are not challenging particular state regulations or procedures, and their arguments concede that the decision to discharge or transfer a patient originates not with state officials, but with nursing homes that are privately owned and operated. Their lawsuit, therefore, seeks to hold state officials liable for the actions of private parties, and the injunctive relief they have obtained requires the State to adopt regulations that will prohibit the private conduct of which they complain.

A

This case is obviously different from those cases in which the defendant is a private party and the question is whether his conduct has sufficiently received the imprimatur of the State so as to make it "state" action for purposes of the Fourteenth Amendment. It also differs from other "state action" cases in which the challenged conduct consists of enforcement of state laws or regulations by state officials who are themselves parties in the lawsuit; in such cases the question typically is whether the private motives which triggered the enforcement of those laws can fairly be attributed to the State. But both these types of cases shed light upon the analysis necessary to resolve the present case.

First, although it is apparent that nursing homes in New York are extensively regulated, "[t]he mere fact that a business is subject to state regulation does not by itself convert its action into that of the State for purposes of the Fourteenth Amendment." *Jackson v. Metropolitan Edison Co.* The complaining party must also show that "there is a sufficiently close nexus between the State and the challenged action of the regulated entity so that the action of the latter may be fairly treated as that of the State itself." The purpose of this requirement is to assure that constitutional standards are invoked only when it can be said that the State is *responsible* for the specific conduct of which the plaintiff complains. The importance of this assurance is evident when, as in this case, the complaining party seeks to hold the State liable for the actions of private parties.

Second, although the factual setting of each case will be significant, our precedents indicate that a State normally can be held responsible for a private decision only when it has exercised coercive power or has provided such significant encouragement, either overt or covert, that the choice must in law be deemed to be that of the State. Mere approval of or acquiescence in the initiatives of a private party is not sufficient to justify holding the State responsible for those initiatives under the terms of the Fourteenth Amendment. *See Flagg Bros., Inc. v. Brooks*, 436 U.S. 149 at 164–165 (1978); *Jackson v. Metropolitan Edison Co., supra*, at 357.

Third, the required nexus may be present if the private entity has exercised powers that are "traditionally the exclusive prerogative of the State." *Jackson v. Metropolitan Edison Co., supra*, at 353; *see Flagg Bros., Inc. v. Brooks, supra*, at 157–161.

B

Analyzed in the light of these principles, the Court of Appeals' finding of state action cannot stand. The court reasoned that state action was present in the discharge or transfer decisions implemented by the nursing homes because the State responded to those decisions by adjusting the patient's Medicaid benefits. Respondents, however, do not challenge the adjustment of benefits, but the discharge or transfer of patients to lower levels of care without adequate notice or hearings. That the State responds to such actions by adjusting benefits does not render it *responsible* for those actions. The decisions about which respondents complain are made by physicians and nursing home administrators, all of whom are concededly private parties. There is no suggestion that those decisions were influenced in any degree by the State's obligation to adjust benefits in conformity with changes in the cost of medically necessary care.

Respondents do not rest on the Court of Appeals' rationale, however. They argue that the State "affirmatively commands" the summary discharge or transfer of Medicaid patients who are thought to be inappropriately placed in their nursing facilities. Were this characterization accurate, we would have a different question before us. However, our review of the statutes and regulations identified by respondents does not support respondents' characterization of them. . . .

In any case, respondents' complaint is about nursing home decisions to discharge or transfer, not to admit, Medicaid patients. But we are not satisfied that the State is responsible for those decisions either. The regulations cited by respondents require SNF's and HRF's "to make all efforts possible to transfer patients to the appropriate level of care or home as indicated by the patient's medical condition or needs," The nursing homes are required to complete patient care assessment forms designed by the State and "provide the receiving facility or provider with a current copy of same at the time of discharge to an alternate level of care facility or home."

These regulations do not require the nursing homes to rely on the forms in making discharge or transfer decisions, nor do they demonstrate that the State is responsible for the decision to discharge or transfer particular patients. Those decisions ultimately turn on medical judgments made by private parties according to professional standards that are not established by the State. . . .

Respondents next point to regulations which, they say, impose a range of penalties on nursing homes that fail to discharge or transfer patients whose continued stay is inappropriate. One regulation excludes from participation in the Medicaid program health care providers who "[f]urnished items or services that are substantially in excess of the beneficiary's needs." The State is also authorized to fine health care providers who violate applicable regulations. As we have previously concluded, however, those regulations themselves do not dictate the decision to discharge or transfer in a particular case. Consequently, penalties imposed for violating the regulations add nothing to respondents' claim of state action.

As an alternative position, respondents argue that even if the State does not command the transfers at issue, it reviews and either approves or rejects them on the merits. The regulations cited by respondents will not bear this construction. Although the State requires the nursing homes to complete patient care assessment forms and file them with state Medicaid officials, and although federal law requires that state officials review these assessments, nothing in the regulations authorizes the officials to approve or disapprove decisions either to retain or discharge particular patients, and petitioners specifically disclaim any such responsibility. Instead, the State is obliged to approve or disapprove continued payment of Medicaid benefits after a change in the patient's need for services. Adjustments in benefit levels in response to a decision to discharge or transfer a patient does not constitute approval or enforcement of that decision. As we have already concluded, this degree of involvement is too slim a basis on which to predicate a finding of state action in the decision itself.

Finally, respondents advance the rather vague generalization that such a relationship exists between the State and the nursing homes it regulates that the State may be considered a joint participant in the homes' discharge and transfer of Medicaid patients. For this proposition they rely upon *Burton v. Wilmington Parking Authority*, 365 U.S. 715 (1961). Respondents argue that state subsidization of the operating and capital costs of the facilities, payment of the medical expenses of more than 90% of the patients in the facilities, and the licensing of the facilities by the State, taken together convert the action of the homes into "state" action. But accepting all of these assertions as true, we are nonetheless unable to agree that the State is responsible for the decisions challenged by respondents. As we have previously held, privately owned enterprises providing services that the State would not necessarily provide, even though they are extensively regulated, do not fall within the ambit of *Burton*. That programs undertaken by the State result in substantial funding of the activities of a private entity is no more persuasive than the fact of regulation of such an entity in demonstrating that the State is responsible for decisions made by the entity in the course of its business.

We are also unable to conclude that the nursing homes perform a function that has been "traditionally the exclusive prerogative of the State." Respondents' argument in this regard is premised on their assertion that both the Medicaid statute and the New York Constitution make the State responsible for providing every Medicaid patient with nursing home services. The state constitutional provisions cited by respondents, however, do no more than authorize the legislature to provide funds for the care of the needy. . . . Similarly, the Medicaid statute requires that the States provide funding for skilled nursing services as a condition to the receipt of federal moneys. It does not require that the States provide the services themselves. Even if respondents' characterization of the State's duties were correct, however, it would not follow that decisions made in the day-to-day administration of a nursing home are the kind of decisions traditionally and exclusively made by the sovereign for and on behalf of the public. Indeed, respondents make no such claim, nor could they.

IV

We conclude that respondents have failed to establish "state action" in the nursing homes' decisions to discharge or transfer Medicaid patients to lower levels of care. Consequently, they have failed to prove that petitioners have violated rights secured by the Fourteenth Amendment. The contrary judgment of the Court of Appeals is accordingly

Reversed.

JUSTICE WHITE concurred in the judgments with a separate opinion.

JUSTICE BRENNAN, with whom JUSTICE MARSHALL joined, dissented.

NOTES AND QUESTIONS

2-62. How "private" are the Part B adjudicators in *Schweinker v. McClure*? By whom are they paid? How do they differ from ALJ's?

2-63. What finding of fact would have created a due process problem for this Court?

2-64. Why were petitioners concerned about these private adjudicators? Were they qualified?

2-65. Does the Court acknowledge the effect that a nursing home's care determinations have on the access individuals have to those services? Why does it conclude due process does not apply?

2-66. What did the transfer decision in *Blum* ultimately turn on? Who made those decisions? What standards did they use and who established those standards?

2-67. For a discussion of privatization and procedural issues in healthcare, see generally, Gillian E. Metzger, *Privatization as Delegation*, 103 COLUM. L. REV. 1367, 1380–83 (2003); Eleanor D. Kinney, *Behind the Veil Where the Action Is: Private Policy Making and American Health Care*, 51 ADMIN. L. REV. 145 (1999); Jennifer L. Wright, *Unconstitutional or Impossible: The Irreconcilable Gap between Managed Care and Due Process in Medicaid and Medicare*, 17 J. CONTEMP. HEALTH L. & POL'Y 135 (2000).

[C] Due Process and Welfare

We have examined some aspects of due process and welfare reform in § 2.06, *supra*. One major aspect of the changes in welfare has been the willingness of many states to delegate the task of determining eligibility of welfare benefits to private firms. As Jon Michaels has noted in *Deforming Welfare: How the Dominant Narratives of Devolution and Privatization Subverted Federal Welfare Reform*, *supra*, Note **2-35**, at 626–627:*

> How does privatization work? A state, county, or municipality contracts out some or all of its welfare responsibilities. It may contract out simply the billing and accounting work, which raise few welfare-specific concerns; or, it may request bids for vendors to provide aspects of job training and job search responsibilities. More dramatically, states may contract out all the social services, including casework and eligibility determinations. Effectively, then, welfare seekers or recipients might never see the inside of a government building or interact with actual, bona fide civil servants.

> Opportunities to reap efficiency gains motivate privatization. States, counties, and municipalities can reduce the size (and payroll) of government

---

* Copyright © 2004 Seton Hall University School of Law. All rights reserved.

and allow the market to function in its stead. The private sector claims the experience, flexibility, and profit motives to make welfare provisions less wasteful. Indeed, its claims are so persuasive that state and local governments are willing to allow corporate providers to walk away with excess rents in order to promote streamlined welfare governance. The lure of slashing the size of government and the seduction of efficiency gains through private-sector competition supply the one-two combination that the cost-conscious legislator finds so attractive.

Corporations often can outperform state and municipal government through savings in labor costs; they can employ a lower-wage, more flexible (i.e., less secure) labor force that can be augmented or reduced with an ease the public sector could not begin to approach. Of course, corporations may also possess sophisticated delivery and monitoring technologies that give firms such as Andersen Consulting and Lockheed Martin comparative advantages in bidding for contracts. But it also should be appreciated that further cost-savings gains, unrelated to efficiency per se, can be accrued because corporations serve shareholders, not welfare clients, and thus decisions that boil down to a question of serving the shareholders or the clients will be resolved in a manner consistent with the fiduciary duty to the former.

See also Matthew Diller, *Form and Substance in the Privatization of Poverty Programs*, 49 UCLA L. REV. 1739, 1740–41 (2002).

As Professor Kennedy has noted:

It seems quite ironic that the states have urged devolution of welfare policy from the federal government and succeeded on the strength of the argument that local needs are best met by local services, only to vest operational authority in national, if not multinational, corporations. Devolution, after all, was supposed to result in decisions being made in state capitals, rather than corporate boardrooms. Welfare policy is usually the product of different tensions between American values and interest groups. To have these value disputes played out in the political process is one thing; to have a private company definitively resolve them is another. Moreover, when arguably the main function of welfare is to protect people from the market, it seems perverse to allow the market to assume control over welfare policy. Privatization neither balances nor resolves the tension between state and market; it simply surrenders social welfare to the profit motive. As has been noted in the prison context, privatization "is really about privatizing tax dollars, about transforming public money into private profits."

David J. Kennedy, *Due Process in a Privatized Welfare System*, 64 BROOK. L. REV. 231, 266 (1998).*

Jon Michaels also notes that "Charitable Choice" offers another land of privatization:

In tangible ways, Charitable Choice — as compared simply to market privatization . . . — represents a truer departure from government provision. Though they ostensibly operate just like private corporations bidding

---

* Copyright © 1998 Brooklyn Law School. All rights reserved.

for contracts to supply state and local welfare services, Charitable Choice organizations do not simply offer, as an advantage, market-based efficiencies; rather, they promise an altogether different model or methodology to promote personal success and improvement. Faith is trumpeted as the missing element in the welfare reform puzzle. Underlying the impetus for Charitable Choice is the belief that a spiritual awakening can give individuals the moral impetus to succeed in ways that job training and employment preparation alone simply cannot. . . .

In its best light, religion can break through the procedural sterility of the . . . post–*Goldberg* world of entitlements and offer warmth and neighborly authenticity to assist those in need. Since Tocqueville's famous visit, religious institutions in America have been seen as essential mediating social institutions connecting individuals and communities, often in apolitical-but culturally and morally thick-ways. Thus, without having these mediating social institutions "integrated into the political to make policy more meaningful, the political order becomes detached from the values and realities of . . . life. Deprived of its moral foundation, the political order is delegitimized." Concomitantly, however, with that level of intimacy comes the possibility (or opportunity) to judge and degrade. . . .

Jon Michaels, *Deforming Welfare*, supra Note **2-35**, at 642–644.*

PROBLEM 2-5

Assume that a for-profit corporation has been given the task of determining who is and who is not eligible for state welfare benefits. Assume further that this corporation has been accused of "churning," that is that it has placed a variety of obstacles in the path of those who either wish to apply for benefits or those who wish to challenge a decision to terminate their benefits.

Assume that your client has been removed from the welfare roles, but was not given a hearing before this occurred. Moreover, after the benefits ceased, it took nearly six months before they were scheduled for a hearing to contest this decision. Assume your challenge to this action relies on *Mathews v. Eldridge*. What are the interests at stake? How should the relative weights of the interests of the government, the corporation and your client be balanced?

---

* Copyright © 2004 Seton Hall University School of Law. All rights reserved.

[D] Due Process and Whistleblowers

BROCK v. ROADWAY EXPRESS

United States Supreme Court
481 U.S. 252 (1987)

JUSTICE MARSHALL announced the judgment of the Court and delivered an opinion in which JUSTICE BLACKMUN, JUSTICE POWELL, and JUSTICE O'CONNOR join.

Section 405 of the Surface Transportation Assistance Act of 1982, 96 Stat. 2157, 49 U.S.C. App. § 2305, protects employees in the commercial motor transportation industry from being discharged in retaliation for refusing to operate a motor vehicle that does not comply with applicable state and federal safety regulations or for filing complaints alleging such noncompliance. The statute provides for an initial investigation of an employee's discharge by the Secretary of Labor and, upon a finding of reasonable cause to believe that the employee was discharged in violation of the Act, requires the Secretary to issue an order directing the employer to reinstate the employee. The employer may then request an evidentiary hearing and a final decision from the Secretary, but this request does not operate to stay the preliminary order of reinstatement. The issue presented in this appeal is whether the failure of § 405 to provide for an evidentiary hearing before temporary reinstatement deprives the employer of procedural due process under the Fifth Amendment.

I.

Appellee Roadway Express, Inc. (Roadway), is a large interstate trucking company engaged primarily in cargo transportation; it is subject to the requirements of § 405. On November 22, 1983, Roadway discharged one of its drivers, Jerry Hufstetler, alleging that he had disabled several lights on his assigned truck in order to obtain extra pay while waiting for repairs. Hufstetler filed a grievance, contending that he had not been discharged for an "act of dishonesty" as defined in the governing collective-bargaining agreement, but rather had been discharged in retaliation for having previously complained of safety violations. The grievance was submitted to arbitration, which ultimately resulted in a ruling on January 30, 1984, that Hufstetler had been properly discharged.

On February 7, 1984, Hufstetler filed a complaint with the Department of Labor alleging that his discharge had violated § 405. The Occupational Safety and Health Administration notified Roadway of the complaint and began an investigation. An OSHA field investigator interviewed Hufstetler and other Roadway employees and obtained statements substantiating Hufstetler's retaliatory discharge claim. Roadway was afforded an opportunity to meet with the investigator and submit a written statement detailing the basis for Hufstetler's discharge, but it was not provided with the names of the other witnesses or the substance of their statements. Roadway explained the discharge by reiterating that, as found by the arbitration board, Hufstetler had acted dishonestly in fabricating an equipment breakdown.

Following review of the evidence obtained by the field investigator, the Department of Labor Regional Administrator on January 21, 1985, issued a preliminary decision ordering Hufstetler's immediate reinstatement with backpay. Without detailing the evidence relied upon for this decision, the order stated that the Secretary of Labor had found reasonable cause to believe Hufstetler had been discharged in violation of § 405 for having previously complained about the safety of Roadway's trucks. The order characterized Roadway's asserted basis for the discharge as "conjecture." . . .

Roadway then filed the present action in Federal District Court, seeking an injunction against enforcement of the Secretary's order and a declaratory judgment that § 405 was unconstitutional to the extent it empowered the Secretary to order temporary reinstatement without first conducting an evidentiary hearing. The District Court granted Roadway's motion for a preliminary injunction . . . and subsequently granted its motion for summary judgment. . . .

Roadway also filed objections to the reinstatement order with the Secretary and requested an evidentiary hearing and final decision. This hearing took place in March 1985, before an Administrative Law Judge, and the Secretary issued a decision on August 21, 1986, again ordering reinstatement with backpay. Roadway's appeal from this administrative decision is currently pending in the United States Court of Appeals for the Eleventh Circuit, No. 86-8771.

The Secretary brought this direct appeal from the District Court's order granting Roadway summary judgment. 28 U.S.C. § 1252. We noted probable jurisdiction, 476 U.S. 113 (1986), and now affirm in part, agreeing with the District Court that the Secretary's procedures unconstitutionally deprived Roadway of procedural due process by failing to provide Roadway with the substance of the evidence supporting Hufstetler's complaint, and reverse in part, rejecting the District Court's conclusion that § 405 is constitutionally infirm because it empowers the Secretary to order preliminary reinstatement without first conducting an evidentiary hearing and affording Roadway an opportunity to cross-examine witnesses. . . .

III.

Section 405 was enacted in 1983 to encourage employee reporting of noncompliance with safety regulations governing commercial motor vehicles. Congress recognized that employees in the transportation industry are often best able to detect safety violations and yet, because they may be threatened with discharge for cooperating with enforcement agencies, they need express protection against retaliation for reporting these violations. . . . Section 406 protects employee "whistle-blowers" by forbidding discharge, discipline, or other forms of discrimination by the employer in response to an employee's complaining about or refusing to operate motor vehicles that do not meet the applicable safety standards. . . .

Congress also recognized that the employee's protection against having to choose between operating an unsafe vehicle and losing his job would lack practical effectiveness if the employee could not be reinstated pending complete review. The longer a discharged employee remains unemployed, the more devastating are the consequences to his personal financial condition and prospects for reemployment. Ensuring the eventual recovery of backpay may not alone provide sufficient protection to encourage reports of safety violations. Accordingly, § 405 incorporates additional protections, authorizing temporary reinstatement based on a preliminary finding of reasonable cause to believe that the employee has suffered a retaliatory discharge. The statute reflects a careful balancing of the relative interests of the Government, employee, and employer. It evidences a legislative determination that the preliminary investigation and finding of reasonable cause by the Secretary, if followed "expeditiously" by a hearing on the record at the employer's request, provide effective protection to the employee and ensure fair consideration of the employer's interest in making unimpaired hiring decisions. . . .

The statute does not specify procedures for employer participation in the Secretary's investigation, other than to require that the employer be notified of the employee's complaint. . . . The Secretary has assigned the investigative responsibilities to OSHA field investigators . . . who followed standard OSHA procedures until the Secretary issued formal implementing rules for § 405, effective December 22, 1986. . . . The standard procedures which governed the investigation of Hufstetler's complaint against Roadway in this case required that Roadway be notified "of the complaint and of the substance of the allegation" and also that the field investigator consult with Roadway to obtain its explanation for the discharge before the Secretary made any findings and issued a preliminary reinstatement order. . . . The current implementing rules provide for similar participation by the employer, including an opportunity to meet with the investigator and submit statements from witnesses supporting the employer's position. . . .

Neither set of procedures, however, requires that before ordering preliminary reinstatement the Secretary must hold an evidentiary hearing and allow the employer to cross examine the witnesses from whom the investigator has obtained statements supporting the employee's complaint. Nor do the procedures require the Secretary to divulge the names of these individuals or the substance of their statements before the preliminary reinstatement order takes effect. Roadway claims that the lack of an evidentiary hearing and the confidentiality of the investigator's evidence operate to deny employers procedural due process under the Fifth Amendment.

The property right of which Roadway asserts it has been deprived without due process derives from the collective-bargaining agreement between Roadway and its employees' union. It is the right to discharge an employee for cause. Acknowledging that the first step is to identify a property or liberty interest entitled to due process protections, *Cleveland Board of Education v. Loudermill,* 470 U.S. 532, 538-539 (1985); *Board of Regents v. Roth,* 408 U.S. 564, 576-578 (1972), the Secretary concedes that the contractual right to discharge an employee for cause constitutes a property interest protected by the Fifth Amendment.[2] . . .

---

[2] Though we accept the Secretary's concession, we do not accept Roadway's separate assertion that it has a property interest in being able to rely exclusively on the contractually mandated arbitration procedures to determine the propriety of a discharge. The essence of this assertion is that, for purposes of enforcing § 405, the Secretary of Labor and the courts should give collateral

"Once it is determined that due process applies, the question remains what process is due." *Morrissey v. Brewer,* 408 U.S. 471, 481 (1972). Though the required procedures may vary according to the interests at stake in a particular context, . . . "[t]he fundamental requirement of due process is the opportunity to be heard 'at a meaningful time and in a meaningful manner.'" *Mathews v. Eldridge,* 424 U.S. 319, 333 (1976), quoting *Armstrong v. Manzo,* 380 U.S. 545, 552 (1965). . . . Depending on the circumstances, and the interests at stake, a fairly extensive evidentiary hearing may be constitutionally required before a legitimate claim of entitlement may be terminated. *See Goldberg v. Kelly,* 397 U.S. 254, 266-271 (1970). . . . In other instances, however, the Court has upheld procedures affording less than a full evidentiary hearing if "some kind of a hearing" ensuring an effective "initial check against mistaken decisions" is provided before the deprivation occurs, and a prompt opportunity for complete administrative and judicial review is available. . . .

Determining the adequacy of predeprivation procedures requires consideration of the Government's interest in imposing the temporary deprivation, the private interests of those affected by the deprivation, the risk of erroneous deprivations through the challenged procedures, and the probable value of additional or substitute procedural safeguards. *Mathews, supra,* at 335. In the present case, the District Court assessed these factors and determined that § 405 was "unconstitutional and void to the extent that it empowers [the Secretary] to order reinstatement of discharged employees prior to conducting an evidentiary hearing which comports with the minimum requirements of due process." . . . The court concluded that the employer must be given, "at a minimum, an opportunity to present his side and a chance to confront and cross examine witnesses." . . . Our consideration of the relevant factors leads us to a different conclusion.

We begin by accepting as substantial the Government's interests in promoting highway safety and protecting employees from retaliatory discharge. Roadway does not question the legislative determination that noncompliance with applicable state and federal safety regulations in the transportation industry is sufficiently widespread to warrant enactment of specific protective legislation encouraging employees to report violations. "Random inspections by Federal and State law enforcement officials in various parts of the country [had] uniformly found widespread violation of safety regulations," and § 405 was designed to assist in combating the "increasing number of deaths, injuries, and property damage due to commercial motor vehicle accidents." . . .

We also agree with the District Court that Roadway's interest in controlling the makeup of its work force is substantial. In assessing the competing interests, however, the District Court failed to consider another private interest affected by the Secretary's decision: Hufstetler's interest in not being discharged for having complained about the allegedly unsafe condition of

---

estoppel or *res judicata* effect to decisions reached by arbitration boards. Under the Secretary's implementing rules, issues of collateral estoppel and *res judicata* may be raised before the Secretary as part of a § 405 proceeding, and the Secretary's decision may be reviewed by the appropriate Court of Appeals. *See* 51 Fed. Reg., at 42095 (proposed 29 CFR § 1978.112) (interpreting § 405 to allow concurrent jurisdiction over employee complaints before arbitration boards under collective-bargaining agreements and before the Secretary under the statute).

Roadway's trucks. This Court has previously acknowledged the "severity of depriving a person of the means of livelihood." . . . "While a fired worker may find employment elsewhere, doing so will take some time and is likely to be burdened by the questionable circumstances under which he left his previous job." . . . In light of the injurious effect a retaliatory discharge can have on an employee's financial status and prospects for alternative interim employment, the employee's substantial interest in retaining his job must be considered along with the employer's interest in determining the constitutional adequacy of the § 405 procedures. The statute reflects a careful balancing of "the strong Congressional policy that persons reporting health and safety violations should not suffer because of this action" and the need "to assure that employers are provided protection from unjustified refusal by their employees to perform legitimate assigned tasks." . . .

Reviewing this legislative balancing of interests, we conclude that the employer is sufficiently protected by procedures that do not include an evidentiary hearing before the discharged employee is temporarily reinstated. So long as the prereinstatement procedures establish a reliable "initial check against mistaken decisions," *Loudermill, supra,* at 545, and complete and expeditious review is available, then the preliminary reinstatement provision of § 405 fairly balances the competing interests of the Government, the employer, and the employee, and a prior evidentiary hearing is not otherwise constitutionally required.

We thus confront the crucial question whether the Secretary's procedures implementing § 405 reliably protect against the risk of erroneous deprivation, even if only temporary, of an employer's right to discharge an employee. We conclude that minimum due process for the employer in this context requires notice of the employee's allegations, notice of the substance of the relevant supporting evidence, an opportunity to submit a written response, and an opportunity to meet with the investigator and present statements from rebuttal witnesses. The presentation of the employer's witnesses need not be formal, and cross-examination of the employee's witnesses need not be afforded at this stage of the proceedings. . . .

The Secretary represents that it is the practice of Department of Labor investigators to inform employers of the substance of the evidence supporting employees' allegations. . . . Though we do not find this practice expressed in the field manuals for OSHA investigators or in the Secretary's new regulations, we accept the representation as embodying an established, official procedure for implementing § 405 of which employers are specifically made aware. It is undisputed, however, that in this case the procedure was not followed, for Roadway requested and was denied access to the information upon which the Secretary based the order for Hufstetler's preliminary reinstatement. . . . Given this circumstance, the District Court correctly held that Roadway had been denied a due process protection to which it was entitled, and we affirm the order of summary judgment in that respect.

Notice of an employee's complaint of retaliatory discharge and of the relevant supporting evidence would be of little use if an avenue were not available through which the employer could effectively articulate its response. On this score, assuming the employer is informed of the substance of the evidence supporting the employee's complaint, the Secretary's current procedures allowing the employer to submit a written response, including affidavits and supporting documents, and to meet with the investigator to respond verbally to the employee's charges and present statements from the employer's witnesses, . . . satisfy the due process requirements for reliability. Except for the Secretary's failure to inform Roadway of the evidence supporting Hufstetler's complaint, similar procedures were followed in this case.

Roadway contends that, absent an opportunity for the employer to confront and cross-examine the witnesses whose statements support the employee's complaint, the Secretary's preliminary procedures will produce unreliable decisions. We conclude, however, that as a general rule the employer's interest is adequately protected without the right of confrontation and cross-examination, again so long as the employer is otherwise provided an opportunity to respond "at a meaningful time and in a meaningful manner." *Armstrong,* 380 U.S., at 552. Providing the employer the relevant supporting evidence and a chance to meet informally with the investigator, to submit statements from witnesses and to argue its position orally, satisfies the constitutional requirement of due process for the temporary deprivation under § 405. Each of these procedures contributes significantly to the reliability of the Secretary's preliminary decision without extending inordinately the period in which the employee must suffer unemployment. To allow the employer and employee an opportunity to test the credibility of opposing witnesses during the investigation would not increase the reliability of the preliminary decision sufficiently to justify the additional delay. Moreover, the primary function of the investigator is not to make credibility determinations, but rather to determine simply whether reasonable cause exists to believe that the employee has been discharged for engaging in protected conduct. Ensuring the employer a meaningful opportunity to respond to the employee's complaint and supporting evidence maintains the principal focus on the employee's conduct and the employer's reason for his discharge. Final assessments of the credibility of supporting witnesses are appropriately reserved for the administrative law judge, before whom an opportunity for complete cross-examination of opposing witnesses is provided.

Roadway finally argues that requiring an evidentiary hearing as part of the process leading to preliminary reinstatement would not impose a significant additional burden on the Secretary since a subsequent evidentiary hearing must be "expeditiously conducted" in any event. 49 U.S.C. App. § 2305(c)(2)(A). Again, however, Roadway's suggested approach would undoubtedly delay issuance of the Secretary's order of reinstatement.[3] In addition to the extra time required for the hearing itself, this approach would provide an incentive for employers to engage in dilatory tactics. Added delay at this stage of the Secretary's proceedings would further undermine the ability of employees to

---

[3] We do not agree with JUSTICE STEVENS, *post,* at 274-275, that the length of a preliminary investigation deemed necessary by the Secretary in a complex case should become the rationale for extending it even further by making a full evidentiary hearing a constitutional requirement. The record here does not indicate what factors were responsible for the extended investigation. It was certainly not against Roadway's interest to delay the investigation. But even if the delay resulted solely from bureaucratic lethargy, it neither defines nor diminishes the importance of Hufstetler's interest in reinstatement.

obtain a means of livelihood, and unfairly tip the statute's balance of interests against them.

This is not to say, however, that the employer's interest in an expeditious resolution of the employee's complaint can never provide a basis for a due process violation. At some point, delay in holding post-reinstatement evidentiary hearings may become a constitutional violation. . . . The current implementing rules require the evidentiary hearing to take place within 30 days after an employer files objections to a preliminary reinstatement order, unless the employer and employee otherwise agree or good cause is shown. 51 Fed. Reg., at 42093 (proposed 29 CFR 1978.106(b)). The administrative law judge is allowed an additional 30 days to issue a decision, again unless the parties otherwise agree or good cause is shown. . . . The Secretary then must issue a final order within 120 days. . . . The Secretary interprets these time requirements not as mandatory but rather as "directory in nature." . . . Once the Secretary orders preliminary reinstatement, an incentive for delay lies naturally with the employee, and intentional foot-dragging may entitle the employer to challenge the delay. In this case, however, due to the District Court's injunction, the Secretary's preliminary reinstatement order never became effective. Moreover, the record does not reflect why it took the Secretary 19 months to issue a final decision ordering reinstatement. The litigation before the District Court may have been a distraction, Roadway's natural incentive to delay may have played a part, and Labor Department personnel may have acted with extreme inefficiency. Because the procedural posture of this case has not allowed factual development on the issue, we decline to decide whether the delay Roadway has encountered, or the delays authorized in the Secretary's new regulations, are so excessive as to constitute a violation of due process.

IV.

The District Court correctly held that the Secretary's preliminary reinstatement order was unconstitutionally imposed in this case because Roadway was not informed of the relevant evidence supporting Hufstetler's complaint and therefore was deprived of an opportunity to prepare a meaningful response. The court erred, however, in holding § 405 unconstitutional to the extent as interpreted by the Secretary it does not provide the employer an evidentiary hearing, complete with the right to confront and cross-examine witnesses, before the employee's temporary reinstatement can be ordered. Accordingly, the District Court's order of summary judgment is

Affirmed in part and reversed in part.

JUSTICE BRENNAN, concurring in part and dissenting in part.

I agree with the plurality's conclusion that the Secretary's procedures unconstitutionally deprived Roadway of procedural due process by failing to inform Roadway of the substance of the evidence supporting Hufstetler's complaint. I disagree, however, with the plurality's conclusion that the Secretary may order an indefinite preliminary reinstatement of discharged drivers without first affording employers an opportunity to present contrary testimony and evidence and to cross-examine witnesses.

Here Roadway contested the facts underlying the Secretary's preliminary determination that there was reasonable cause to believe that the discharge of Hufstetler was retaliatory. When there are *factual* disputes that pertain to the validity of a deprivation, due process "require[s] more than a simple opportunity to argue or deny." *Cleveland Board of Education v. Loudermill,* 470 U.S. 532, 552 (1985) (BRENNAN, J., concurring in part and dissenting in part). . . .

JUSTICE WHITE, with whom THE CHIEF JUSTICE and JUSTICE SCALIA join, concurring in part and dissenting in part.

I agree that the District Court erred in holding that a full trial-type hearing was necessary prior to termination, so long as the employer was afforded an adequate post-termination hearing at a meaningful time. I also agree that respondent Roadway Express, Inc., was entitled to notice of Jerry Hufstetler's charges and an opportunity to respond to them prior to being ordered to temporarily reinstate him. But with all respect, I disagree with the plurality's conclusion that Roadway was denied due process when it did not have access to the information on which the reinstatement order was based, including the names of witnesses.

The procedures the Due Process Clause requires prior to administrative action such as was taken in this case can vary, depending upon the precise nature of the government function involved, the importance of the private interests that have been affected by governmental action, and the nature of subsequent proceedings. *Cleveland Board of Education v. Loudermill,* 470 U.S. 532, 545 (1985); *Cafeteria Workers v. McElroy,* 367 U.S. 886, 895 (1961). Thus, what may have been required in *Loudermill* or *Arnett v. Kennedy,* 415 U.S. 134, 170 (1974), is not a sure guide to resolving the present case. The plurality ably articulates the Government's purpose underlying § 405: "Section 405 protects employee 'whistle-blowers' by forbidding discharge, discipline, or other forms of discrimination by the employer in response to an employee's complaining about or refusing to operate motor vehicles that do not meet the applicable safety standards." *Ante,* at 258. And the employee himself has substantial interest in not being terminated and in being paid his wages or the remuneration. On the other side of the scale is Roadway's interest in not having an unsatisfactory employee on the job pending a full evidentiary hearing. The interest, however, is protected by requiring a reasonable cause finding by the Secretary prior to the issuance of his order, by notice of the charges, and by the opportunity for Roadway to present its side of the case. That is the balance struck by the statute, and the Secretary's regulations and Due Process require no more, even though in most cases the Secretary may voluntarily reveal the evidence supporting the charge. Given the purpose of § 405, I would not ignore the strong interest the Government may have in particular cases in not turning over the supporting information, including the names of the employees who spoke to the Government and who corroborated Hufstetler's claims, prior to conducting the full administrative hearing.

Because I believe that withholding the witnesses' names and statements prior to ordering temporary reinstatement did not violate respondent's due process rights, I find myself in partial dissent from the plurality's opinion and judgment.

JUSTICE STEVENS, dissenting in part.

Section 405 of the Surface Transportation Assistance Act of 1982, 49 U.S.C. App. § 2305, is an extraordinary piece of legislation. In most organized industries employees are adequately protected against wrongful discharge by the arbitration machinery that has been established pursuant to collective-bargaining agreements, and by their unions. In the motor carrier industry, however, § 405 provides every driver with a special statutory right to reinstatement if an agent of the Secretary of Labor determines that there is "reasonable cause to believe" that the driver was discharged because he reported a safety violation. It was on the basis of this statute that the Department of Labor conducted an 11-month *ex parte* investigation which culminated in its ordering Roadway Express to reinstate Jerry Hufstetler to his job as a driver. The Department heard testimony of witnesses in the course of the investigation, but Roadway was never given a record of the evidence or a list of the witnesses. Yet, based on a "preliminary" decision reached through these procedures, Roadway was required to continue employing Hufstetler, who it claims is a dishonest employee, for an indeterminate period pending an eventual hearing at which the truth might eventually be established.

The Government's compelling interest in highway safety adequately justifies the creation of a special statutory right to protect truck drivers who share the public's vital interest in strict enforcement of motor vehicle safety regulations. That interest, however, does not justify the use of patently unfair procedures to implement that right. Specifically, it does not justify the entry of reinstatement orders on the basis of secret evidence that is neither disclosed to the employer nor tested in an adversary proceeding before the order becomes effective.

The plurality attempts to legitimate this departure from the traditions of due process by asserting that it is essential for the Department of Labor to be able to act swiftly; and delays in reinstatement, it is feared, will deter drivers from reporting safety violations. There are, of course, situations in which the threat of irreparable injury justifies the entry of temporary orders that are not preceded by an adequate hearing. Similarly, government's special interest in the efficient management of programs that it administers sometimes makes it appropriate to briefly postpone an adjudication of the rights of an employee, a program beneficiary, or a licensee, until after an initial determination has been made. In this case, however, it is ludicrous for the Secretary to rely on an "emergency" or "necessity" justification for a reinstatement order entered 14 months after the discharge. . . .

The plurality's willingness to sacrifice due process to the Government's obscure suggestion of necessity reveals the serious flaws in its due process analysis. It is wrong to approach the due process analysis in each case by asking anew what procedures were worthwhile and not too costly. Unless a case falls within a recognized exception, we should adhere to the strongest presumption that the Government may not take away life, liberty, or property before making meaningful hearing available. . . .

NOTES AND QUESTIONS

2-68. What is the property interest in this case that triggers the Due Process Clause on behalf of Roadway Express? Is there also a common law right here as well? What might that be?

2-69. How does Justice Marshall apply the *Mathews v. Eldridge* calculus? What are the private interests at stake? What are the government's interests? Is this what the *Mathews* Court had in mind?

2-70. Consider Professor Rakoff's analysis in Brock v. Roadway Express, Inc. *and the New Law of Regulatory Due Process,* 1987 SUP. CT. REV. 157, 184-85:*

It is of course true that in the course of deciding *Loudermill* under the *Mathews* test, the Court stated: "[T]he significance of the private interest in retaining employment cannot be gainsaid. We have frequently recognized the severity of depriving a person of the means of livelihood." But "depriving" meant, in the context of *Loudermill,* the process of carrying out a constitutional deprivation to which due process constraints were relevant; that is, it referred to a deprivation carried out by a sovereign. To apply the same statement to measure the significance of a nongovernmental employer discharging an employee would appear to be a mistake, for it treats *Loudermill* as being an "employment" case rather than a "governmental process" case, and it has to be the latter to raise a constitutional issue. It would be a mistake, that is, unless the government's "depriving" through an exercise of sovereignty is not different in kind from the employer's "depriving" through an exercise of property. The precise point which this passage exemplifies was stated more than a half-century ago by Morris Cohen. One cannot draw a categorical distinction between the use of property and the exercise of sovereignty, once one views matters in light of the institutional realities of the modern economy.

As the passage also shows, the social understanding which established the analogy between governmental deprivation of a private right and employer deprivation of an employee's job also forms the basis of the fundamental reinterpretation of the *Mathews* test which occurs in *Brock:* "the employee's . . . interest . . . must be considered along with the employer's interest in determining the constitutional adequacy of the . . . procedures." For there is no "must" about this matter if the evil to which the constitutional provision is addressed implicates only one of these interests; if, that is, public deprivation of an interest is different from private deprivation. But Justice Marshall sees them as equal in kind and capable of being offset against each other. Because employees in the transportation industry "may be threatened with discharge for cooperating with enforcement agencies, they need express protection against retaliation

---

* Copyright © 1987 by the University of Chicago. All Rights reserved.

for reporting these violations." Government coercion of employers will prevent employer coercion of employees. Thus, while government may have purely administrative interests of its own in the efficient conduct of its business, or may embrace diffuse public interests in, for example, highway safety, it may also be involved in reallocating rights — including procedural rights — in order to achieve a fair balance between conflicting private interests.

The *Mathews* test, as written, conceived of government as a provider of benefits or organizer of institutions, so that the government's interest, quasi-proprietary at least in part, stood on one side, while the private beneficiary stood on the other. (Indeed, in the past the Court had taken pains to avoid framing cases in a way that would make it adjudicate the procedural claims of two groups of statutory beneficiaries with potentially conflicting interests.) By contrast, the *Mathews* test as rephrased and then applied in *Brock* posits government as having a largely regulatory concern, and supposes that more than one private interest is affected by its decision. The details of Justice Marshall's argument are embraced by only four Justices, but this central point also appears in Justice White's opinion for a total of seven. On its face, the Court shows that it understands itself to be dealing with a different social situation. In this latter role, government is an umpire rather than an interested participant. Despite the effort to use similar words, this is a far different model from the government-versus-private-beneficiary dynamics incorporated by implication in the original *Mathews* test.

Chapter 3
FORMAL ADJUDICATION AND THE ADMINISTRATIVE PROCEDURE ACT

§ 3.01 Introduction

Thus far, we have focused on the administrative procedures required if the Due Process Clause of either the Fifth or the Fourteenth Amendment to the Constitution is applicable. Our focus, in this chapter, will be on the statutory requirements that apply to administrative adjudication. In particular, we shall examine the formal adjudicatory provisions of the Administrative Procedure Act ("APA").

In so doing, we shall examine administrative procedures that are familiar to lawyers and law students whose primary decision-making model is adjudication, usually the adjudicatory procedures of federal and state courts. As we explore the statutory requirements of the APA, we shall also note the explicit and the implicit differences between most agency adjudication and federal or state court adjudication. An important general question throughout this chapter will be the extent to which agency adjudicatory procedures do or *should* differ from those in federal and state trial courts.

Our analysis of the APA's adjudicatory provisions will also allow us to explore more directly a theme we have already raised in Chapter One: the relationship between substance and procedure. We have discussed this theme generally in terms of red light and green light theories of administrative law. We shall now try to explore this theme more fully by trying, first, to understand the historical context within which the APA was ultimately passed. This is not to argue that its provisions are an exact rendering of a political theory or vision; nor is it to take sides on the issue of the extent to which there can be apolitical procedural approaches or whether they all merely reflect some form of political conflict or manipulation. Rather, it is to try to begin to see analytical connections between the political philosophies that drive legislatures and legislation, and the actual substance of the regulation that is produced as well as the procedures and legal doctrines that then develop to carry out the often conflicting substantive goals the legislation represents. As noted in Chapter One, ideally, "form should be the very shape of content." Procedure should provide a means of implementing statutory goals and demands in harmony with the substantive content of the regulation involved. But, especially when the substantive goals of the statutes involve conflict, procedure can also become a vehicle for expressing such substantive uncertainties and doubts in the form of often unnecessary procedural demands. We, thus, begin with excerpts that discuss generally the history of the debate in this country involving the respective roles of the free market and the government in resolving important societal concerns, particularly those relevant to the New Deal. We then shall examine some excerpts dealing with the procedural compromises inherent in the APA. With this as a background, we can understand more fully the legal framework established by the APA to adjudicate disputes at the agency level, as well as explore its applicability to some of today's public/private partnerships.

§ 3.02 The New Deal and the APA: An Overview

The New Deal was the continuation of a long-standing debate on the extent to which the federal government should intervene in the market economy. Consider the following analysis by Ellis W. Hawley.

Ellis W. Hawley, NEW DEAL AND THE PROBLEM OF MONOPOLY 6-14

(Princeton Univ. Press 1966) *

. . . Early attempts to deal with the "monopoly problem" enjoyed little success. Prior to 1900, in spite of considerable agitation on the part of the populists and other protest groups, the only federal measures of any consequence were the Interstate Commerce and Sherman Antitrust Acts, neither of which proved very effective in practice. The Interstate Commerce Commission, in fact, found it virtually impossible to win a case in the federal courts. And the Sherman Act, while it forbade all monopolies and all attempts to monopolize, was laxly enforced, narrowly interpreted, and effective only against loose combines, not against such tight combinations as holding companies and mergers. Ironically, the great era of business consolidation, the years from 1897 to 1904, came after the Sherman Act and not before.

It was not until the progressive era in the early twentieth century that major changes in the political and ideological climate began to take place. Then gradually, as economic independence declined and new and larger consolidations appeared, more and more middle-class Americans became convinced that the new industrial and financial empires amounted to a gross perversion of the American dream. They were increasingly dubious, moreover, about the doctrines of *laissez faire* and Social Darwinism. Man, so they were told by a new generation of intellectuals, could shape his own destiny. He could reform and improve his social and economic institutions, and the place to start was with the "trusts" and the social evils for which they were responsible. When it came to formulating a program, however, there was little agreement. Some reformers, impressed by the productivity of the new corporate institutions, would keep them and then rely upon a strong central government to achieve a more equitable, more humane, and more democratic system. Others, still wary of governmental intervention, hoped that business could reform itself or that non-business groups could develop their own market power. Still others, intent upon returning to a decentralized and automatic economy, favored a program that would limit size, penalize

---

* Copyright © 1966 Princeton University Press, 1994 renewed PUP. Reprinted by permission of Princeton Universioty Press.

bigness, break up the "trusts," remove the unfair advantages of big business, and enforce competitive behavior.

This divergence in reform philosophies was particularly apparent in 1912 in the clash between Woodrow Wilson's New Freedom and Theodore Roosevelt's New Nationalism. As Louis Brandeis and other advocates of the New Freedom saw it, the "trusts" had grown strong because they enjoyed special privileges or because they used unfair practices to crush their rivals, not because of their greater efficiency or productivity. And the solution was to remove these causes of "monopoly," wipe out special privileges, liberate the credit system from Wall Street control, and pass new legislation that would eliminate unfair practices and restore the reign of free competition. In the New Nationalist view, on the other hand, concentration of economic power was the inevitable result of mass production and an advancing technology. In many areas, competition resulted in a gross waste of natural resources, human life, and human energy. And the real solution was to forget about competition and concentrate upon developing national controls, upon establishing a government that could protect underprivileged groups, engage in purposeful planning, supervise the big corporations, and insure that the benefits of modern industrialism were more evenly distributed. The government, so the New Nationalists insisted, could be used to democratize big business. Jeffersonian ends could be achieved through Hamiltonian means.

Some aspects of the New Nationalism also appealed to business leaders. Industrialists like George Perkins and Frank Munsey, for example, would agree that large corporations were both desirable and inevitable, that excessive competition was mainly responsible for child labor, sweat-shop conditions, and other social problems, and that the situation called for some type of regulation and planning. They had their own views, however, about the nature, degree, and type of regulation. Enlightened businessmen, they insisted, were developing a social conscience, a growing awareness of social problems and the need for remedial action; and since these people knew more about the business system than anyone else, business groups should be allowed to govern and discipline themselves with a minimum of government supervision. Along the same line, too, were the theories of the "new competition" expounded by Arthur Jerome Eddy or the idea of government-approved business agreements sponsored by a number of business organizations. Gradually, from these various sources, a third approach to the "monopoly problem" took shape, one that would repeal the Sherman Act, encourage business organization, and allow self-governing trade associations, loosely supervised by federal authorities, to rationalize competition, improve business ethics, and handle the nation's social problems.

By 1912, then, three broad approaches to the "monopoly problem" had emerged, each with its own methods and value configurations, and yet each claiming that it could implement the American dream, narrow the gap between ideal and reality, and achieve an abundant, dynamic, and equitable system. Each approach, moreover, has some influence on progressive reform. Such measures as the Clayton, Federal Trade Commission, Federal Reserve, and Underwood Tariff Acts, for example, were essentially products of the New Freedom. Their sponsors hoped to do away with the causes of monopoly, with unfair practices, special privileges, a rigged credit system, and the various devices by which monopolistic combines were put together and perpetuated; and by doing this, they hoped to restore, strengthen, and preserve a competitive system. Yet alongside these measures came a variety of laws and activities that were basically inconsistent with the New Freedom. The railroads, for example, came under direct regulation. Farm and labor groups received special aid and protection. Action against tight combinations was tempered by the "rule of reason." The job of controlling unfair competitive practices was eventually entrusted to a special trade commission, an agency that resembled the one proposed by the New Nationalists and one that might conceivably sanction cooperative business agreements and carry out the ideas associated with business self-government and the "new competition."

National planning and industrial self-government also moved to the fore during World War I. The emphasis, once the United States became involved in hostilities, shifted from economic reform to maximum war production; and the latter, it seemed, could best be attained under a form of war socialism, a system under which federal agencies directed and controlled broad areas of the economy, business and labor organizations received official encouragement, and industrial leaders cooperated with government officials to plan production, eliminate waste, and organize the nation's resources and energies. The wartime system, moreover, left some permanent marks. The newly organized trade associations remained as a prominent feature of the postwar economy. Business leaders, especially those who had worked in Washington, had caught a new vision of what could be done by economic planning and business-government cooperation. A new breed of public administrators, skilled in the techniques of wartime control, were more prone to reject competitive values and stress the goal of a planned economy. In the crisis of the nineteen thirties a number of business and governmental leaders would remember the war experience and call for action along similar lines.

It was not surprising that the wartime program of industrial self-government should blossom into the Associational Activities of the nineteen twenties. Once again, public officials were equating business interests with the national interest; and in this atmosphere the vision of a business commonwealth, of a benevolent capitalism under which everyone would be happy and prosperous, took on a new and wider appeal. The kind of thinking once characteristic of George Perkins, Frank Munsey, and a few other Eastern businessmen began to seep through the chambers of commerce all over the country. The result was a rapid burgeoning of trade associations, a rationale that justified their anticompetitive activities, and a public policy under which such agencies as the Department of Commerce and the Federal Trade Commission helped these associations to standardize their products, expand their functions, and formulate codes of proper practices, codes that generally regarded a price cutter as a "chiseler" and price competition as immoral. If the official propaganda of these business organizations could be believed, the nation had entered a new era of cooperative activities, an era in which poverty and class conflict would disappear, business would discipline itself, and everyone would benefit from the joint action of enlightened business leaders.

Eventually, the policies and attitudes of the nineteen twenties ended in economic disaster. They concentrated economic and political power in the hands of a business-financial elite that was less altruistic and far less prescient than was generally assumed; and the result was not utopia but economic breakdown, a system that accentuated maldistribution, encouraged speculation, piled up excessive savings, destroyed its own markets, and plunged the nation into the worst depression in its history. Yet so long as prosperity continued, there was little awareness of these underlying defects and little concern about the decline of competition or the growing concentration of wealth and power. The great majority seemed to agree that what was good for business, or at least what businessmen thought was good for them, was by definition good for everyone. If there were troubled consciences left, they could take comfort from the retention of the antitrust laws, the constant praise of "free enterprise," and the fact that the cartels and super corporations usually masked their activities behind a veil of competitive terminology.

The Great Depression, however, with its mass unemployment and declining incomes, brought a new and acute awareness of the monopoly problem, a new consciousness of the gap between ideal and reality. Along with the concern over centralization, injustice, and loss of individual freedom, came a new concern, a growing belief that the misuse of business power was responsible for the economic breakdown and the persistence of depression conditions. Reorganization and reform of the business system, so many Americans felt, had now become an imperative necessity; as one might expect, the approaches to the problem tended to follow the patterns established earlier. Once again, opinion divided along lines that were roughly similar to those which had divided the New Freedom, the New Nationalism, and the "new competition."

Like the advocates of the New Freedom, for example, the antitrusters or neo-Brandeisians favored a policy of decentralizing the business structure and enforcing competitive behavior. They did so both with the idea of implementing democratic and individualistic ideals and with a growing conviction that enforced competition was the best way to achieve sustained prosperity. The Depression, as they saw it, was a product of monopolistic rigidities. The businessmen, because of their market power, had been able to maintain prices even though their costs of production were falling. This had resulted in excessive profits, oversavings, and a failure of consumer purchasing power. And the only real solution, they felt, if such crises were to be averted in the future, was a program that would restore flexible prices and allow competitive forces to keep the economy in balance. They believed, moreover, that these goals were attainable. They could be attained by rigorous antitrust prosecution, by limits on size, by a tax on bigness, by controls over business financing and competitive practices, and by other measures that would encourage more reliance on free markets.

The economic planners, on the other hand, like the New Nationalists of an earlier period, felt that antitrust action was a hopeless anachronism. In a modern economy, they maintained, concentrations of economic power were inevitable. They were necessary for efficient mass production, technical progress, and reasonable security; and while the abuse of this power was largely responsible for the depression, the idea that it could be dispersed was both impractical and dangerous. The only real answer lay in systematic organization and planning, in conscious and rational administrative control of economic processes so as to restore economic balance and prevent future breakdowns.

Again, however, there was strong disagreement as to who should do the planning and the degree and type that would be necessary. On the political left were national economic planners who would deprive businessmen of their power and transfer much of it to the state or to organized non-business groups. In the center were those who felt that some scheme of business-government cooperation could be effective. On the right were industrialists and pro-business planners, men who drew their ideas from the war experience or the Associational Activities of the nineteen twenties, and who felt that an enlightened business leadership, operating through self-governing trade associations, should make most of the decisions. The depression, so some of these business planners argued, was due mostly to irresponsible "chiseling" and "cutthroat competition;" and the government, if it wanted to bring about recovery, should help "responsible and enlightened businessmen" to force the "chiselers" into line.

Under depression conditions, this clash of values and policies became particularly acute. On the one hand, the depression produced insistent demands for planning, rationalization, and the erection of market controls that could stem the forces of deflation and prevent economic ruin. On the other, it intensified antimonopoly sentiment, destroyed confidence in business leadership, and produced equally insistent demands that big business be punished and competitive ideals be made good. The dilemma of the New Deal reform movement lay in the political necessity of meeting both sets of these demands, in the necessity of creating organizations and controls that could check deflationary forces and provide a measure of order and security while at the same time preserving democratic values, providing the necessary incentives, and making the proper concessions to competitive symbols. From a political standpoint, the Roosevelt Administration could ignore neither of these conflicting currents of pressure and opinion; and under the circumstances, it could hardly be expected to come up with an intellectually coherent and logically consistent set of business policies. . . .

This philosophical confusion and the conflicting substantive demands that resulted were reflected in New Deal statutes and the procedures designed to implement New Deal policies. To a large extent, the APA of 1946 sought to institutionalize many of the procedural approaches then developing at various federal agencies. It also, however, sought to implement a general, principled approach to procedural issues, one grounded in the experience of the particular agencies themselves but also applicable to other agencies dealing with similar procedural questions. The APA took an across-the-board procedural approach to all federal agencies as it sought to answer this question: What procedures were necessary to protect individual rights but, at the same time, enable the agency to accomplish its substantive, statutory goals?

Consider the following discussions of the early history of the APA. To what extent do you think one's position on the substance of New Deal reforms affected one's view of the procedures appropriate to implement those reforms? To what extent was it easier or harder to enact a generic approach to procedural issues as opposed to one that sought to provide different procedures for different agencies?

Walter Gellhorn, THE ADMINISTRATIVE PROCEDURE ACT: THE BEGINNINGS

72 VA. L. REV. 219, 224–32 (1986)*

In early 1939 President Roosevelt requested Attorney General Murphy to appoint a Committee to undertake a more particularized examination of administrative functioning. The Committee was to investigate "the need for procedural reform" and to make a "thorough and comprehensive study" of then "existing practices and procedures, with a view to detecting any existing deficiencies and pointing the way to improvements." The Attorney General's Committee on Administrative Procedure, duly appointed, was:

> struck at the outset of its work with the fact that while much criticism is general in language, the thought behind it is specific. As a generality, it may not be sound, but as a specific criticism of a particular agency it may be justified. Accordingly, it was decided, at the beginning of the Committee's work, that criticism and recommendation — both the Committee's own and those of others — arose from and must be tested by knowledge of the practices and procedures of each of the agencies which chiefly affect private interests.

Then began the first intensive and extensive inquiry into the methods of the federal agencies, whose rules and regulations or whose adjudications of rights bore substantially upon persons outside the Government. Altogether, before the Committee concluded its activity, some forty separate agencies and distinct entities within departments were studied; twenty-seven descriptive and valuative "monographs" were prepared for publication; the fruits of the staff's researches were made available to the agencies involved and were discussed by them with the full committee; and, after public notice as well as individual invitations to 100,000 persons whose presence on various lists

---

* Copyright © 1986 by Virginia Law Review Association. All rights reserved.

indicated some measure of interest, public hearings were held to receive oral or written opinions about administrative procedure. Meanwhile, as the Committee remarked with satisfaction, its activities had "stimulated agencies themselves toward the improvement of their own procedures. Some agencies, made conscious of procedural problems by the Committee's inquiries, have already substantially altered existing practices, either as a result of their own thinking or in accordance with informal suggestions of the Committee or its staff." . . .

The Final Report of the Attorney General's Committee on Administrative Procedure and the investigations that preceded it set the stage for the federal Administrative Procedure Act of 1946 even though most of the committee's members had not favored so embracive a legislative approach. At the very least, discussion about next steps tended to become more civil, more pointed, more related to facts than to characterizations. . . .

Vituperation had . . . gone out of style. Factual material describing the methods actually used (rather than supposedly used) by various administrative bodies was now at hand. Moreover, the "war effort" that had so recently united the nation was perceived to have involved civilian administration of massive dimensions, as well as the massive deployment of armed forces. The constrictions of the Logan-Walter bill would have made difficult if not impossible the timely promulgation of rationing regulations that governed the distribution of sugar, coffee, petroleum products, meat, and rubber; it would have rendered unworkable the rent control measures deemed necessary because of sudden population shifts related to war production; it would have encumbered if it had not forestalled the administration of measures to stabilize wage rates and yet to maintain continuity of productive effort without the disruption of work stoppages. These and other administrative activities were not widely perceived at the time to be un-American, absolutist, arbitrary, or otherwise subject to outright condemnation.

At this point an extraordinary development occurred. First, Attorney General Francis Biddle and then his successor Tom Clark apparently "struck a deal" with the chief Congressional proponents of a general statute. Pronunciamentos diminished. Seemingly, all concerned heard the message that agitated advocacy was no longer appropriate. Instead, aides of legislators and Department of Justice attorneys, reinforced by "experts in administrative law," began intensive consultation and collaborative efforts.

Finally, on October 19, 1945, Attorney General Clark wrote to Senator Pat McCarran, chairman of the Senate Judiciary Committee, indicating his conclusion (and presumably the conclusion of the Truman Administration as a whole) that enactment of what is now the Administrative Procedure Act could be recommended. "Previous attempts to enact general procedural legislation," he said,

> have been unsuccessful generally because they failed to recognize the significant and inherent differences between the tasks of courts and those of administrative agencies or because, in their zeal for simplicity and uniformity, they proposed too narrow and rigid a mold. . . . Despite difficulties of draftsmanship, I believe that over-all procedural legislation

is possible and desirable. The administrative process is now well developed. . . . We have in general . . . as we did not have until fairly recently . . . the materials and facts at hand. Since the original introduction of S. 7, I understand that opportunity has been afforded to public and private interests to study its provisions and to suggest amendments. The agencies of the Government primarily concerned have been consulted and their views considered. In particular I am happy to note that your committee and the House Committee on the Judiciary, in an effort to reconcile the views of the interested parties, have consulted officers of this Department and experts in administrative law made available by this Department. . . . The bill appears to offer a hopeful prospect of achieving a reasonable uniformity and fairness in administrative procedures without at the same time interfering unduly with the efficient and economical operation of the Government. Insofar as possible, the bill recognizes the needs of individual agencies by appropriate exemption of certain of their functions. . . . My conclusion as to the workability of the proposed legislation rests on my belief that the provisions of the bill can and should be construed reasonably and in a sense which will fairly balance the requirements and interests of private persons and governmental agencies.

A similar communication went to the House Judiciary Committee, which was working in tandem with the Senate Committee. The House committee had held hearings on June 21, 25, and 26, 1945, chiefly to hear representatives of the American Bar Association and a spokesman for the Interstate Commerce Commission. After these very muted public proceedings, the theater had been closed and work went on quietly behind the scenes.

When Senator McCarran brought his bill before the Senate on March 12, 1946, he declared that it had "the active support of the Attorney General. Not one agency in the executive branch of the Government is on record as opposing it. The American Bar Association has endorsed it wholeheartedly. The bill has, in short, the kind of virtually unanimous support which would be expected in the case of a bill which has received such very lengthy, and very full and meticulous consideration." The measure was passed by the Senate on that day after some desultory questions had been addressed to the committee chairman. No vote was recorded and no dissent was indicated. Proceedings in the House followed the same pattern. The measure was approved on May 24, 1946 without a recorded vote and with no indication of dissent.

Martin Shapiro, APA: PAST, PRESENT, FUTURE

72 VA. L. REV. 447, 452–54 (1986)*

Turning to the APA itself, Professor Gellhorn and most other contributors to this symposium rightly characterize it as a deal struck between opposing political forces. One should consider, however, who struck the deal and what its terms were. The battle of the thirties was between Republicans and conservative Democrats on the one hand and New Deal Democrats on the other, at a time when the New Deal consensus was not yet dominant in American politics. Consequently, the New Dealers were loath to compromise and loath to allow congressional initiatives against the president. The war was still in doubt; every battle had to be fought to the finish. The New Dealers were forced to make the tactical retreat of taking some action on agency procedures, but they then fought the battle out. They won it by blocking congressional action, keeping administrative procedure firmly in the hands of the executive branch itself, and imposing only the thinnest restraints on agency action.

By 1946, the New Deal consensus was absolutely and unassailably established, so the battle was by then really an internal one among New Dealers . . . between conservative and liberal Democrats, both of whom were firmly harnessed to the New Deal vision of the administrative state. At this point, the liberal New Dealers could afford to compromise in a statute that no longer appeared to threaten the strong presidency.

The law of the APA is thus largely a congressional affirmation of the scheme worked out by the executive branch's New Deal lawyers. They formulated a modified and softened version of the prewar vision of Pound and the American Bar Association and fitted it into a basically New Deal plan. It is very important to understand the compromise because it engenders the basic tensions that plague administrative law today.

The APA as originally enacted divided all administrative law into three parts. For matters requiring adjudication, in which government action was directly detrimental to the specific legal interests of particular parties, the compromise was heavily weighted in favor of the conservatives. The Pound-ABA demand for totally separate tribunals was ignored: the agencies themselves adjudicated these matters. But the agencies' processes were to be considered quasi-adjudication and were to be governed by adjudicative-style procedures, presided over by a relatively independent hearing officer, and freely subject to relatively strict judicial review.

The second part, rulemaking, constituted an almost total victory for the liberal New Deal forces. Congress' delegation of vast law-making power to the

---

* Copyright © 1986 by Virginia Law Review Association. All rights reserved.

agencies was acknowledged and legitimated. Rulemaking was to be quasi-legislative, not quasi-judicial. No adjudicatory-style hearings or hearing officers were required. . . .

The third part of administrative law originally conceived by the APA included everything that government did that was neither adjudication nor rulemaking. On this point, the liberal New Dealers won almost complete victory, labeling agency action in this area as "committed to agency discretion." No procedures were prescribed. . . .*

§ 3.03 Formal Adjudication and the APA

The APA draws a bright line between rules and orders. Section 553 provides procedures for informal rulemaking that include notice and an opportunity to comment. These statutory procedures go beyond the due process requirements of the *Bi-Metallic* case examined in Chapter One, and they provide a relatively efficient way of making policy. As we shall see in Chapter Four, § 4.02[D], *infra,* the informal rulemaking provisions of the APA often have been supplemented with more complicated hybrid rulemaking procedures that begin to resemble important aspects of formal adjudication. Our goal at this point is, first, to examine §§ 554, 556 and 557 of the APA and the procedures for formal adjudication (and formal rulemaking) that they provide.

Please read these provisions now with great care (*see* Appendix B). To what extent do the factfinding processes provided for by the APA differ from traditional courtroom proceedings? Does the APA allow for more procedural flexibility than one would encounter in a federal or state court? Is an oral hearing always necessary? Is cross-examination always allowed? As we shall see, rules of evidence in administrative proceedings are usually not very restrictive. More important, agency adjudicators are expected to differ from generalist federal and state judges and juries comprised of laymen. Trial judges or, as they are called in the administrative process, Administrative Law Judges ("ALJ's") as well as Commissioners or the heads of agencies are expected to be highly knowledgeable about the substance of the regulatory fields which they oversee. One of the most important reasons for the creation of administrative agencies is the expertise that they can bring to bear not only on policy questions, but also to the resolution of particular disputes. Agency adjudicators are expected to be very familiar with the law involved and the variety of factual settings to which that law applies. Still another difference between agency adjudication and federal or state court adjudication is that at the agency or commission level, many agencies combine rulemaking, investigatory, and adjudicatory functions. This combination of functions greatly enhances the efficiency of the agency, but it also creates the possibility, both real and apparent, of bias or conflict of interest in the decisionmaking process. As we shall see, the APA attempts to deal with such issues and concerns. Section 554(d) mandates a separation of an agency's investigative and adjudicatory staffs below the Commission or agency head level, and prohibits *ex parte* contacts and undue influence on the decisionmaking process.

---

* For further discussions of and influences upon the history and future of the APA, *see Symposium,* 63 U. CHI. L. REV. 1375-1571 (1996); *Symposium, The Fiftieth Anniversary of the Administrative Procedure Act: Past and Prologue,* 32 TULSA L.J. 185-353 (Winter 1996).

Before exploring these provisions in some detail, we shall begin, first, with the question of when to apply the APA's formal adjudicatory provisions. The APA is a generic statute; that is, it applies generally to most federal agencies. The adjudicatory provisions set forth in sections 554, 556 and 557 must be triggered or activated by an agency's own enabling act. Congress is not always clear on just when or how it intends to trigger the APA. As the cases set forth below reveal, courts have developed a variety of approaches to deal with this issue. Which approach do you find most useful or appropriate? Should the Constitution be able to trigger the APA? How does Justice Jackson's history of the APA mesh with the history of the Act provided by the excerpts from Professors Gellhorn and Shapiro, quoted above?

WONG YANG SUNG v. McGRATH

United States Supreme Court
339 U.S. 33 (1950)

MR. JUSTICE JACKSON delivered the opinion of the Court.

This *habeas corpus* proceeding involves a single ultimate question . . . whether administrative hearings in deportation cases must conform to requirements of the Administrative Procedure Act of June 11, 1946, 60 Stat. 237, 5 U.S.C. §§ 1001 *et seq.*

Wong Yang Sung, native and citizen of China, was arrested by immigration officials on a charge of being unlawfully in the United States through having overstayed shore leave as one of a shipping crew. A hearing was held before an immigrant inspector who recommended deportation. The Acting Commissioner approved; and the Board of Immigration Appeals affirmed.

Wong Yang Sung then sought release from custody by *habeas corpus* proceedings in District Court for the District of Columbia, upon the sole ground that the administrative hearing was not conducted in conformity with §§ 5 and 11 of the Administrative Procedure Act. . . . The Government admitted noncompliance, but asserted that the Act did not apply. The court, after hearing, discharged the writ and remanded the prisoner to custody, holding the Administrative Procedure Act inapplicable to deportation hearings. . . . Court of Appeals affirmed. . . . Prisoner's petition for certiorari was not opposed by the Government and, because the question presented has obvious importance in the administration of the immigration laws, we granted review.

I.

The Administrative Procedure Act of June 11, 1946 is a new, basic and comprehensive regulation of procedures in many agencies, more than a few of which can advance arguments that its generalities should not or do not include them. Determination of questions of its coverage may well be approached through consideration of its purposes as disclosed by its background.

Multiplication of federal administrative agencies and expansion of their functions to include adjudications which have serious impact on private rights has been one of the dramatic legal developments of the past half-century. Partly from restriction by statute, partly from judicial self-restraint, and partly by necessity . . . from the nature of their multitudinous and semilegislative or executive tasks . . . the decisions of administrative tribunals were accorded considerable finality, and especially with respect to fact finding. The conviction developed, particularly within the legal profession, that this power was not sufficiently safeguarded and sometimes was put to arbitrary and biased use.

Concern over administrative impartiality and response to growing discontent was reflected in Congress as early as 1929, when Senator Norris introduced a bill to create a separate administrative court. Fears and dissatisfactions increased as tribunals grew in number and jurisdiction, and a succession of bills offering various remedies appeared in Congress. Inquiries into the practices of state agencies, which tended to parallel or follow the federal pattern, were instituted in several states, and some studies noteworthy for thoroughness, impartiality and vision resulted.

The Executive Branch of the Federal Government also became concerned as to whether the structure and procedure of these bodies was conducive to fairness in the administrative process. President Roosevelt's Committee on Administrative Management in 1937 recommended complete separation of adjudicating functions and personnel from those having to do with investigation or prosecution. The President early in 1939 also directed the Attorney General to name "a committee of eminent lawyers, jurists, scholars, and administrators to review the entire administrative process in the various departments of the executive Government and to recommend improvements, including the suggestion of any needed legislation."

So strong was the demand for reform, however, that Congress did not await the Committee's report but passed what was known as the Walter-Logan bill, a comprehensive and rigid prescription of standardized procedures for administrative agencies. This bill was vetoed by President Roosevelt [on] December 18, 1940, and the veto was sustained by the House. But the President's veto message made no denial of the need for reform. Rather it pointed out that the task of the Committee, whose objective was "to suggest improvements to make the process more workable and more just," had proved "unexpectedly complex." The President said, "I should desire to await their report and recommendations before approving any measure in this complicated field."

The committee divided in its views and both the majority and the minority submitted bills which were introduced in 1941. A subcommittee of the Senate Judiciary Committee held exhaustive hearings on three proposed measures, but, before the gathering storm of national emergency and war, consideration of the problem was put aside. Though bills on the subject reappeared in 1944, they did not attract much attention.

The McCarran-Sumners bill, which evolved into the present Act, was introduced in 1945. Its consideration and hearing, especially of agency interests, was painstaking. All administrative agencies were invited to submit their views in writing. A tentative revised bill was then prepared and interested parties again were invited to submit criticisms. The Attorney General named representatives of the Department of Justice to canvass the agencies and report their criticisms, and submitted a favorable report on the bill as finally revised. It passed both Houses without opposition and was signed by President Truman June 11, 1946.

The Act thus represents a long period of study and strife; it settles long-continued and hard-fought contentions, and enacts a formula upon which opposing social and political forces have come to rest. It contains many compromises and generalities and, no doubt, some ambiguities. Experience may reveal defects. But it would be a disservice to our form of government and to the administrative process itself if the courts should fail, so far as the terms of the act warrant, to give effect to its remedial purposes where the evils it was aimed at appear.

II.

Of the several administrative evils sought to be cured or minimized, only two are particularly relevant to issues before us today. One purpose was to introduce greater uniformity of procedure and standardization of administrative practice among the diverse agencies whose customs had departed widely from each other. We pursue this no further than to note that any exception we may find to its applicability would tend to defeat this purpose.

More fundamental, however, was the purpose to curtail and change the practice of embodying in one person or agency the duties of prosecutor and judge. The President's Committee on Administrative Management voiced in 1937 the theme which, with variations in language, was reiterated throughout the legislative history of the Act. . . .

The Committee therefore recommended a redistribution of functions within the regulatory agencies. "[I]t would be divided into an administrative section and a judicial section" and the administrative section "would formulate rules, initiate action, investigate complaints . . ." and the judicial section "would sit as an impartial, independent body to make decisions affecting the public interest and private rights upon the basis of the records and findings presented to it by the administrative section."

. . . [T]he Attorney General's Committee on Administrative Procedure, which divided as to the appropriate remedy, was unanimous that this evil existed. Its Final Report said:

"These types of commingling of functions of investigation or advocacy with the function of deciding are thus plainly undesirable. But they are also avoidable and should be avoided by appropriate internal division of labor. For the disqualifications produced by investigation or advocacy are personal psychological ones which result from engaging in those types of activity; and the problem is simply one of isolating those who engage in the activity. Creation of independent hearing commissioners insulated from all phases of a case other than hearing and deciding will, the Committee believes, go far toward solving this problem at the level of the initial hearing provided

§ 3.03   ADJUDICATION & THE ADMINISTRATIVE PROCEDURE ACT   225

the proper safeguards are established to assure the insulation. . . ." Rep. Atty. Gen. Comm. Ad. Proc. 56 (1941), S. Doc. No. 8, 77th Cong., 1st Sess. 56 (1941). . . .

Such were the evils found by disinterested and competent students. Such were the facts before Congress which gave impetus to the demand for the reform which this Act was intended to accomplish. It is the plain duty of the courts, regardless of their views of the wisdom of policy of the Act, to construe this remedial legislation to eliminate, so far as its text permits, the practices it condemns.

III. [Application of APA ?purpose to facts of case]

Turning now to the case before us, we find the administrative hearing a perfect exemplification of the practices so unanimously condemned.

This hearing, which followed the uniform practice of the Immigration Service, was before an immigrant inspector, who, for purposes of the hearing, is called the "presiding inspector." Except with consent of the alien, the presiding inspector may not be the one who investigated the case. . . . But the inspector's duties include investigation of like cases; and while he is today hearing cases investigated by a colleague, tomorrow his investigation of a case may be heard before the inspector whose case he passes on today. An "examining inspector" may be designated to conduct the prosecution, . . . but none was in this case; and, in any event, the examining inspector also has the same mixed prosecutive and hearing functions. The presiding inspector, when no examining inspector is present, is required to "conduct the interrogation of the alien and the witnesses in behalf of the Government and shall cross-examine the alien's witnesses and present such evidence as is necessary to support the charges in the warrant of arrest." . . . It may even become his duty to lodge an additional charge against the alien and proceed to hear his own accusation in like manner. . . . Then, as soon as practicable, he is to prepare a summary of the evidence, proposed findings of fact, conclusions of law, and a proposed order. A copy is furnished the alien or his counsel, who may file exceptions and brief . . . whereupon the whole is forwarded to the Commissioner. . . .

The Administrative Procedure Act did not go so far as to require a complete separation of investigating and prosecuting functions from adjudicating functions. But that the safeguards it did set up were intended to ameliorate the evils from the commingling of functions as exemplified here is beyond doubt. And this commingling, if objectionable anywhere, would seem to be particularly so in the deportation proceeding, where we frequently meet with a voteless class of litigants who not only lack the influence of citizens, but who are strangers to the laws and customs in which they find themselves involved and who often do not even understand the tongue in which they are accused. Nothing in the nature of the parties or proceedings suggests that we should strain to exempt deportation proceedings from reforms in administrative procedure applicable generally to federal agencies.

Nor can we accord any weight to the argument that to apply the Act to such hearings will cause inconvenience and added expense to the Immigration

Service. Of course it will, as it will to nearly every agency to which it is applied. But the power of the purse belongs to Congress, and Congress has determined that the price for greater fairness is not too high. The agencies, unlike the aliens, have ready and persuasive access to the legislative ear and if error is made by including them, relief from Congress is a simple matter. . . . We draw, therefore, no inference in favor of either construction of the Act — from the Department's request for legislative clarification, from the congressional committees' willingness to consider it, or from Congress' failure to enact it.

We come, then to examination of the text of the Act to determine whether the Government is right in its contentions: first, that the general scope of § 5 of the Act does not cover deportation proceedings; and, second, that even if it does, the proceedings are excluded from the requirements of the Act by virtue of § 7.

IV.

The Administrative Procedure Act, § 5, establishes a number of formal requirements to be applicable "in every case of adjudication required by statute to be determined on the record after opportunity for an agency hearing." The argument here depends upon the words "adjudication required by statute." The Government contends that there is no express requirement for any hearing or adjudication in the statute authorizing deportation, and that this omission shields these proceedings from the impact of § 5. Petitioner, on the other hand, contends that deportation hearings, though not expressly required by statute, are required under the decisions of this Court, and the proceedings, therefore, are within the scope of § 5.

Both parties invoke many citations to legislative history as to the meaning given to these key words by the framers, advocates or opponents of the Administrative Procedure Act. Because § 5 in the original bill applied to hearings required "by law," because it was suggested by the Attorney General that it should be changed to "required by statute or Constitution," and because it finally emerged "required by statute," the Government argues that the section is intended to apply only when explicit statutory words granting a right to adjudication can be pointed out. Petitioner on the other hand cites references which would indicate that the limitation to statutory hearing was merely to avoid creating by inference a new right to hearings where no right existed otherwise. We do not know. The legislative history is more conflicting than the text is ambiguous.

But the difficulty with any argument premised on the proposition that the deportation statute does not require a hearing is that, without such hearing, there would be no constitutional authority for deportation. The constitutional requirement of procedural due process of law derives from the same source as Congress' power to legislate and, where applicable, permeates every valid enactment of that body. It was under compulsion of the Constitution that this Court long ago held that an antecedent deportation statute must provide a hearing at least for aliens who had not entered clandestinely and who had been here some time even if illegally. . . .

We think the limitation to hearings "required by statute" in § 5 of the administrative Procedure Act exempts from that section's application only those hearings which administrative agencies may hold by regulation, rule, custom, or special dispensation; not those held by compulsion. We do not think the limiting words render the Administrative Procedure Act inapplicable to hearings, the requirement for which has been read into a statute by the Court in order to save the statute from invalidity. They exempt hearings of less than statutory authority, not those of more than statutory authority. We would hardly attribute to Congress a purpose to be less scrupulous about the fairness of a hearing necessitated by the Constitution than one granted by it as a matter of expediency.

Indeed, to so construe the Immigration Act might again bring it into constitutional jeopardy. When the Constitution requires a hearing, it requires a fair one, one before a tribunal which meets at least currently prevailing standards of impartiality. A deportation hearing involves issues basic to human liberty and happiness and, in the present upheavals in lands to which aliens may be returned, perhaps to life itself. It might be difficult to justify as measuring up to constitutional standards of impartiality a hearing tribunal for deportation proceedings the like of which has been condemned by Congress as unfair even where less vital matters of property rights are at stake.

We hold that the Administrative Procedure Act, § 5 does cover deportation proceedings conducted by the Immigration Service. . . .

Reversed.

MR. JUSTICE DOUGLAS and MR. JUSTICE CLARK took no part in the consideration or decision of this case. MR. JUSTICE REED dissented. His opinion is omitted.

NOTES AND QUESTIONS

3-1. How does Justice Jackson's reasoning square with the actual words of section 554(a)? Does section 554(a) say "in every case of adjudication required by statute (*or the Constitution*) to be determined on the record after opportunity for an agency hearing . . ."? Is that the effect of Justice Jackson's interpretation?

3-2. What is the relationship of what the Court believes is required by the Due Process Clause to the Court's view of the immigration statute involved in this case? Could the Court have held that the Constitution independently required the same kind of hearing the APA requires? Is it wise to equate the Constitution with a particular set of statutorily required procedures?

3-3. Alternatively, could the Court have held that the Constitution required more procedure than INS provided, but not as much as the APA?

3-4. Quite apart from the issue of when or how the adjudicatory provisions of the APA are triggered, what kind of procedure is appropriate for a deportation hearing? What are the stakes involved? Might they vary? What if the person to be deported faces political difficulty upon his or her return home? What if his or her life is in danger? Should such facts affect the procedure provided?

3-5. After the decision in *McGrath,* Congress quickly amended the Immigration Act of 1917 to make clear that it did not intend to trigger the APA. Similarly, the Supreme Court, in effect, rejected *McGrath*'s reasoning in *Marcello v. Bonds,* 349 U.S. 302 (1955). Speaking for the Court, Justice Clark found that the history of the Immigration and Nationality Act of 1952 clearly did not indicate any desire on the part of Congress to trigger the APA's adjudicatory provisions.

3-6. The Equal Access to Justice Act (EAJA), 5 U.S.C. § 504, provides that prevailing parties in certain adversary administrative proceedings can recover their attorney's fees and costs from the Government. The EAJA defines "adversary adjudication" as an "adjudication under section 554 of the title in which the position of the United States is represented by counsel or otherwise." Although immigration deportation hearings are not covered by section 554 of the APA, they do require a hearing on the record. Should attorney's fees be available? *See Ardastani v. INS,* 502 U.S. 129 (1991). Writing for the Court, Justice O'Connor held that the meaning of "an adjudication under section 554" is unambiguous in the context of the EAJA and that APA adjudicatory provisions do not apply to immigration hearings.

SEACOAST ANTI-POLLUTION LEAGUE v. COSTLE

First Circuit Court of Appeals
572 F.2d 872, cert. denied, 439 U.S. 824 (1978)

Before COFFIN, CHIEF JUDGE, CAMPBELL and BOWNES, CIRCUIT JUDGES.

COFFIN, CHIEF JUDGE.

This case is before us on a petition by the Seacoast Anti-Pollution League and the Audubon Society of New Hampshire (petitioners) to review a decision by the Administrator of the Environmental Protection Agency (EPA). We have jurisdiction under 33 U.S.C. § 1369(b)(1). The petition presents several important issues relating to the applicability and effect of the Administrative Procedure Act (APA), 5 U.S.C. §§ 501 *et seq.,* and the interpretation of the Federal Water Pollution Control Act of 1972 (FWPCA), 33 U.S.C. §§ 1251 *et seq.* In order to place those issues in context we set forth the procedural and factual background of the case.

The Public Service Company of New Hampshire (PSCO) filed an application with the EPA for permission to discharge heated water into the Hampton-Seabrook Estuary which runs into the Gulf of Maine. The water would be taken from the Gulf of Maine, be run through the condenser of PSCO's proposed nuclear steam electric generating station at Seabrook, and then be directly discharged back into the gulf at a temperature 39° F. higher than at intake. The water is needed to remove waste heat, some 16 billion BTU per hour, generated by the nuclear reactor but not converted into electrical energy by the turbine. Occasionally, in a process called backflushing, the water will be recirculated through the condenser, and discharged through the intake tunnel at a temperature of 120° F. in order to kill whatever organisms may be living in the intake system.

Section 301(a) of the FWPCA, 33 U.S.C. § 1311(a), prohibits the discharge of any pollutant unless the discharger, the point source operator, has obtained an EPA permit. Heat is a pollutant. 33 U.S.C. § 1362(6). Section 301(b) directs the EPA to promulgate effluent limitations. The parties agree that the cooling system PSCO has proposed does not meet the EPA standards because PSCO would utilize a once-through open cycle system . . . the water would not undergo any cooling process before being returned to the sea. Therefore, in August, 1974, PSCO applied not only for a discharge permit under § 402 of the FWPCA, 33 U.S.C. § 1342, but also an exemption from the EPA standards pursuant to § 316 of the FWPCA, 33 U.S.C. § 1326. Under § 316(a) a point source operator who "after opportunity for public hearing, can demonstrate to the satisfaction of the Administrator" that the EPA's standards are "more stringent than necessary to assure the projection [sic] and propagation of a balanced, indigenous population of shellfish, fish, and wildlife in and on the body of water" may be allowed to meet a lower standard. Moreover, under § 316(b) the cooling water intake structure must "reflect the best technology available for minimizing adverse environmental impact."

In January, 1975, the Regional Administrator of the EPA held a non-adjudicatory hearing at Seabrook. He then authorized the once-through system in June, 1975. Later, in October, 1975, he specified the location of the intake structure. The Regional Administrator granted a request by petitioners that public adjudicative hearings on PSCO's application be held. These hearings were held in March and April, 1976, pursuant to the EPA's regulations establishing procedures for deciding applications for permits under § 402 of the FWPCA, 40 C.F.R. § 125.36. The hearings were before an administrative law judge who certified a record to the Regional Administrator for decision. The Regional Administrator decided in November, 1976, to reverse his original determinations and deny PSCO's application.

PSCO, pursuant to 40 C.F.R. § 125.36(n), appealed the decision to the Administrator who agreed to review it. Thereafter, a new Administrator was appointed, and he assembled a panel of six in-house advisors to assist in his technical review. This panel met between February 28 and March 3, 1977, and submitted a report finding that with one exception PSCO had met its burden of proof. With respect to that exception, the effect of backflushing, the Administrator asked PSCO to submit further information, offered other parties the opportunity to comment upon PSCO's submission, and stated that he would hold [a] hearing on the new information if any party so requested and could satisfy certain threshold conditions. . . . Petitioners did request a hearing, but the Administrator denied the request.

The Administrator's final decision followed the technical panel's recommendations and, with the additional information submitted, reversed the Regional Administrator's decision, finding that PSCO had met its burden under § 316. It is this decision that petitioners have brought before us for review.

Applicability of the Administrative Procedure Act

Petitioners assert that the proceedings by which the EPA decided this case contravened certain provisions of the APA governing adjudicatory hearings, 5 U.S.C. §§ 554, 556, and 557. Respondents answer that the APA does not apply to proceedings held pursuant to § 316 or § 402 of the FWPCA.

The dispute centers on the meaning of the introductory phrases of § 554(a) of the APA:

> This section applies . . . in every case of adjudication required by statute to be determined on the record after opportunity for an agency hearing. . . .

Both § 316(a) and § 402(a)(1) of the FWPCA provide for public hearings, but neither states that the hearing must be "on the record". We are now the third court of appeals to face this issue. The Ninth Circuit and the Seventh Circuit have each found that the APA does apply to proceedings pursuant to § 402. *Marathon Oil Co. v. EPA*, 564 F.2d 1253 (9th Cir. 1977); *United States Steel Corp. v. Train*, 556 F.2d 822 (7th Cir. 1977). We agree.

At the outset we reject the position of intervenor PSCO that the precise words "on the record" must be used to trigger the APA. The Supreme Court has clearly rejected such an extreme reading even in the context of rule making under § 553 of the APA. . . . Rather, we think that the resolution of this issue turns on the substantive nature of the hearing Congress intended to provide.

We begin with the nature of the decision at issue. The EPA Administrator must make specific factual findings about the effects of discharges from a specific point source. On the basis of these findings the Administrator must determine whether to grant a discharge permit to a specific applicant. Though general policy considerations may influence the decision, the decision will not make general policy. Only the rights of the specific applicant will be affected. "As the instant proceeding well demonstrates, the factual questions involved in the issuance of section 402 permits will frequently be sharply disputed. Adversarial hearings will be helpful, therefore, in guaranteeing both reasoned decisionmaking and meaningful judicial review. In summary, the proceedings below were conducted in order 'to adjudicate disputed facts in particular cases,' not 'for the purposes of promulgating policy-type rules or standards.'" *Marathon Oil Co., supra* at 1262.

This is exactly the kind of quasi-judicial proceeding for which the adjudicatory procedures of the APA were intended. As the Supreme Court has said, "Determination of questions of [the Administrative Procedure Act's] coverage may well be approached through consideration of its purposes as disclosed by its background." *Wong Yang Sung v. McGrath*, 339 U.S. 33, 36 (1950). One of the developments that prompted the APA was the "[m]ultiplication of federal administrative agencies and expansion of their functions to include adjudications which have serious impact on private rights." *Id.*, 339 U.S. at 36-37. This is just such an adjudication. The panoply of procedural protections provided by the APA is necessary not only to protect the rights of an applicant for less stringent pollutant discharge limits, but is also needed to protect the public for whose benefit the very strict limitations have been enacted. If determinations such as the one at issue here are not made on the record, then the fate of the Hampton-Seabrook Estuary could be decided on the basis of evidence that a court would never see or, what is worse, that a court could not be sure existed. We cannot believe that Congress would intend such a result.

Our holding does not render the opening phrases of § 554 of the APA meaningless. We are persuaded that their purpose was to exclude "governmental functions, such as the administration of loan programs, which traditionally have never been regarded as adjudicative in nature and as a rule have never been exercised through other than business procedures." Attorney General's Manual on the Administrative Procedure Act 40 (1947). Without some kind of limiting language, the broad sweep of the definition of "adjudication", defined principally as that which is not rule making, 5 U.S.C. § 551(6), (7), would include such ordinary procedures that do not require any kind of hearing at all. In short, we view the crucial part of the limiting language to be the requirement of a statutorily imposed hearing. We are willing to presume that, unless a statute otherwise specifies, an adjudicatory hearing subject to judicial review must be on the record. . . .

[The court remanded this decision to the EPA for proceedings in accord with the APA.]

BUTTREY v. UNITED STATES

Fifth Circuit Court of Appeals
690 F.2d 1170 (1982)

Before CLARK, CHIEF JUDGE, POLITZ and RANDALL, CIRCUIT JUDGES.

RANDALL, CIRCUIT JUDGE:

This is an appeal from a district court judgment rejecting the claim of plaintiffs-appellants John Buttrey and John Buttrey Developments, Inc. that the United States Army Corps of Engineers had improperly denied Buttrey's application for a dredge and fill permit under section 404 of the Clean Water Act, 33 U.S.C. § 1344 (Supp. IV 1980). We conclude that the procedures afforded Buttrey in the determination of his permit application violated neither his statutory nor his constitutional rights and that the determination itself was neither arbitrary nor capricious. We therefore affirm the decision of the district court.

I. THE FACTS AND PROCEEDINGS BELOW.

John Buttrey is a land developer who builds residential homes. In November, 1978, he applied to the Mobile, Alabama, district office of the Corps of Engineers for a permit to channelize a half-mile long portion of a small, slow-running stream known as Gum Bayou. The bayou passes near Slidell, Louisiana, before flowing into the West Pearl River. Buttrey accompanied his application with a letter from the Louisiana Stream Control Commission, stating that, having examined a drawing submitted by Buttrey, it was "of the opinion that water quality standards of the State of Louisiana will not be violated provided turbidity during dredging in public waters is kept to a practicable minimum." He also included comments from the St. Tammany Parish Mosquito Abatement District No. 2. The District stated that Buttrey's project would help eliminate potential mosquito breeding areas, provided only that adequate drainage was achieved as per the proposal to avoid the possibility of creating any new breeding sites.

The Corps of Engineers issued a formal public notice of the proposed dredge and fill operation on February 2, 1979. This notice was distributed to all known interested persons to assist in developing facts on which a decision could be based. In the ensuing months, the Corps received numerous comments opposing the issuance of the permit: letters came from the Fish and Wildlife Service of the United States Department of the Interior, the United States Environmental Protection Agency and the National Marine Fisheries Service of the United States Department of Commerce, and from numerous private organizations and individuals. The comments all tended to raise the same objections. The proposed project, they claimed, would destroy natural drainage and sewage treatment capacity, replace a habitat and nursery ground for wildlife with residential homes, perhaps irrevocably damage an aesthetically pleasing wetland area, and, finally, increase the risk of flooding, both downstream and in Buttrey's neighboring Magnolia Forest housing development.

The Corps forwarded copies of all of the comments to Buttrey for review and response. Buttrey requested and received a six-month extension of time for filing his answer. On September 28, 1979, he submitted: (1) a memorandum of law supporting the permit request; (2) an environmental analysis with comments prepared by Dr. Alfred Smalley, Professor of Biology at Tulane University; (3) an engineering discussion with comments prepared by Ivan Borgen, a consulting engineer; (4) a letter supporting the application submitted by the Magnolia Forest Homeowners Association; (5) three other letters, also supporting the application, from downstream property owners; and (6) an aerial photograph of the area. With respect to "any objection which the Corps may feel to be of such a nature as to warrant denial of the permit," Buttrey requested: (1) that he be notified of the specific objection involved, and that he be permitted to provide the Corps a full and detailed response; (2) that he be granted a conference with the Corps in order to resolve any outstanding objections that could not be resolved on the basis of the material furnished; and (3) that, should there exist any objection that might preclude issuance of the permit, he be granted an adversary hearing, and an opportunity to cross-examine witnesses. The responsible official, District Engineer Col. Ryan, responded that Corps regulations precluded the possibility of a full adversary hearing, but that he would be happy to meet with Buttrey informally. Reserving his right to demand a full hearing, Buttrey accepted the invitation, and met with Col. Ryan on February 8, 1980.

The parties remained unable to resolve their differences. On April 2, 1980, the Corps issued an "Environmental Assessment" and an "Evaluation of the Effects of the Discharge of Dredged or Fill Material Into Waters of the U.S.

§ 3.03   ADJUDICATION & THE ADMINISTRATIVE PROCEDURE ACT   233

Using the Section 404(b) Guidelines," and denied Buttrey's permit application. After extensively reviewing the Corps' evaluation process, Col. Ryan made the following "evaluation and findings:"

> Based upon review of the application, conducting an environmental assessment, preparation of a 404(b) evaluation, and consideration of all comments by other agencies and the public, and after weighing all known factors involved in the proposed action, I find in concurrence with national policy, statutes and administrative directives, when the total adverse effects of the proposal are weighed against the benefit to the using public, the public interest would best be served by denial of the requested permit.

The Corps noted particularly that "the environmental effects associated with implementation of the proposal are significant and adverse."

One month later, having exhausted the procedures provided by the Corps of Engineers, Buttrey filed with the United States District Court for the Eastern District of Louisiana an action for damages and declaratory and injunctive relief. . . . On April 1, 1981, the district court issued its opinion denying Buttrey's motion for summary judgment and granting summary judgment for the Corps. . . .

On appeal, Buttrey contends that he was denied his constitutional and statutory rights because the Corps refused to grant him a trial-type hearing, . . .

II. WHAT KIND OF HEARING?

Buttrey's claim that he was wrongfully denied a full trial-type hearing is both statutory and constitutional. The statutory claim is based on a reading of the Administrative Procedure Act, 5 U.S.C. § 554(a) (1976), together with section 404(a) of what is now called the Clean Water Act, 33 U.S.C. § 1344(a) (Supp. IV 1980). The constitutional claim is based on the due process clause. Because the statutory argument is the more straightforward, we shall address it first.

A.   *The Administrative Procedure Act*

The formal trial-type hearing procedures that Buttrey wants are set out in sections 7 and 8 of the Administrative Procedure Act, 5 U.S.C. §§ 556–557 (1976), and are triggered by language at the beginning of section 5: "This section applies . . . in every case of adjudication required by statute to be determined on the record after opportunity for an agency hearing. . . ." 5 U.S.C. § 554(a) (1976). Since in the present case the Corps has acted under the authority of section 404 of the Clean Water Act, the determinative issue is whether section 404 "require[s]" disputes to be "determined on the record after opportunity for an agency hearing." Buttrey claims that it does, and the government claims that it does not. We agree with the government.

Section 404 seems relatively simple. It says, quite plainly, that the Corps of Engineers "may issue permits, after notice and opportunity for public hearings for the discharge of dredged or fill material into the navigable waters at specified disposal sites." 33 U.S.C. § 1344(a) (Supp. IV 1980). Buttrey argues that "public hearings" means the trial-type hearing provided for in the

APA. There are, however, many different kinds of "hearing," and resolution of the issue must turn on "the substantive nature of the hearing Congress intended to provide." *Seacoast Anti-Pollution League v. Costle,* 572 F.2d 872, 876 (1st Cir.), *cert. denied,* 439 U.S. 824 (footnote omitted).

Three other circuits have construed virtually identical language in section 402 of the Clean Water Act, 33 U.S.C. § 1342(a)(1) (1976) ("after opportunity for public hearing"), to require a trial-type hearing, *Seacoast, supra; Marathon Oil Co. v. Environmental Protection Agency,* 564 F.2d 1253 (9th Cir. 1977); *United States Steel Corp. v. Train,* 556 F.2d 822 (7th Cir. 1977). The question, then, is whether section 402 can be distinguished from section 404, despite the similarity of language and despite the fact that both sections are part of the same statutory scheme.

We begin with the observation that none of the three opinions construing section 402 held that the phrase found in both sections . . . "after opportunity for public hearing[s]" . . . was so clear that there was no need to look behind it for other indications of congressional intent. . . . We therefore look to the legislative history for help in determining what Congress meant when it called for "hearings" in section 404.

This is one of those rare instances when a statute's history leaves no room for doubt. Congress did not intend that the "public hearings" called for in section 404 be trial-type hearings on the record. When confronted with a choice between a House version of section 404, which invested permit authority in the Corps of Engineers, and a Senate version, which invested authority in the EPA, Congress consciously chose the House version. The Corps of Engineers had apparently been using its simplified procedures to issue dredge and fill permits (under a related statute) for many years. . . . When Senator Muskie presented the Conference Committee report on the Senate floor, he explained:

> The Conferees were uniquely aware of the process by which the dredge and fill permits are presently handled and did not wish to create a burdensome bureaucracy in light of the fact that a system to issue permits already existed.

118 Cong. Rec. 33,699 (1972) (prepared remarks of Sen. Muskie, presented on behalf of the Conference Committee but not delivered orally). Congress *consciously* chose to use the simplified permit procedures that the Corps had developed in administering its existing dredge and fill permit program. Congress did not intend to burden the implementation of section 404 with a trial-type hearing requirement, and we decline to do so today. . . .

The subsequent history of the Clean Water Act reinforces our conclusion that section 404 does not require trial-type hearings. Congress amended section 404 and several other provisions of the Act in 1977, but again chose to leave the Corps' existing permit granting system intact. The Senate and House reports on the amendments both impliedly approved the Corps' section 404 regulations. S. Rep. N. 370, 95th Cong., 1st Sess. 80. . . . Their only overriding concern about the Corps' section 404 procedures seems to have been for eliminating delay and red tape in processing applications. . . . Indeed, we note that advocates on the "industry" side of the water pollution controversy complain bitterly about the Corps' "complex and unnecessary permit processing procedures." . . . In short, requiring trial-type hearings would do violence

§ 3.03   ADJUDICATION & THE ADMINISTRATIVE PROCEDURE ACT   235

to the obvious congressional purpose of making section 404 processing procedures as simple as possible.

The "public hearings" language in section 404 was, in fact, written into the statute to protect the public, not permit applicants. As Professor Davis has pointed out, "when many are affected, [the term 'public hearing'] usually means a speechmaking hearing rather than a [trial-type] hearing with a determination on the record." 2 K. Davis, *Administrative Law Treatise* § 12:7, at 434 (2d ed. 1979). This circuit has already decided that the "public hearings" referred to in the Corps of Engineers' dredge and fill permit regulations means the kind of "speech-making" hearing described by Professor Davis: "[I]f sufficient public interest is shown in [a] project, then the District Engineer of the Corps is authorized to conduct a public, informal hearing at which both proponents and opponents of the project are allowed to be heard." . . . The current regulations are essentially the same as those construed in *Taylor, see* 33 C.F.R. § 327.8 (1981), and foreclose our reaching any conclusion different from the one reached in *Taylor*:

> Public hearing means a public proceeding conducted for the purpose of acquiring information or evidence which will be considered in evaluating a proposed Department of the Army permit action, or Federal project, and which affords to the public the opportunity to present their views, opinions, and information on such permit actions or Federal projects.

33 C.F.C. § 327.3(a) (1981). It therefore follows that "public hearing[s]" means exactly what the regulation says it means, and that Buttrey is thus not entitled under section 404 of the Clean Water Act and section 5 of the Administrative Procedure Act to insist on a trial-type oral hearing.

[The court also went on to reject Buttrey's due process claim.]

CHEMICAL WASTE MANAGEMENT, INC. v. U.S. ENVIRONMENTAL PROTECTION AGENCY

District of Columbia Court of Appeals
873 F.2d 1477 (1989)

Before WALD, CHIEF JUDGE, and STARR and D.H. GINSBURG, CIRCUIT JUDGES.

Opinion for the Court filed by CIRCUIT JUDGE D.H. GINSBURG.

D.H. GINSBURG, CIRCUIT JUDGE:

Petitioners Chemical Waste Management, Inc. and Waste Management of North America seek review of Environmental Protection Agency regulations, 40 C.F.R. Part 24 (1988), that establish informal procedures for administrative hearings concerning the issuance of corrective action orders under § 3008(h) of the Resource Conservation and Recovery Act (RCRA), as modified by the Hazardous and Solid Waste Amendments of 1984. We conclude that the regulations represent a reasonable interpretation of an ambiguous statutory provision and are not, on their face, inconsistent with the requirement of due process. Accordingly, we deny the petition for review.

I. BACKGROUND

Congress enacted RCRA in 1976 to establish a comprehensive program for regulation of hazardous waste management and disposal. The statute requires generally that the operator of any hazardous waste treatment, storage, or disposal facility obtain a permit, RCRA § 3005, 42 U.S.C. § 6925, but facilities in existence as of 1980 may continue to operate as "interim facilities" pending agency action on their permit applications, RCRA § 3005(3), 42 U.S.C. § 6925(e).

A. *Formal Adjudication under Part 22*

Subsection (a) of RCRA § 3008 authorizes EPA to enter orders assessing civil penalties, including suspension or revocation of permits, for violation of RCRA regulations. 42 U.S.C. § 6928(a). Subsection (b) provides that, upon request made within thirty days of the issuance of a subsection (a) order, EPA "shall promptly conduct a public hearing." Accordingly, the agency is authorized to "issue subpoenas for the attendance and testimony of witnesses and the production of relevant papers, books, and documents, and may promulgate rules for discovery procedures." RCRA § 3008(b), 42 U.S.C. § 6928(b).

In 1978, EPA promulgated procedural regulations to implement the "public hearing" provision of subsection (a). 40 C.F.R. Part 22. These procedures conform to the provisions of the Administrative Procedure Act for formal adjudication. 5 U.S.C. §§ 556 & 557. For example, an Administrative Law Judge presides at the hearing . . . and each party has the right to call and to cross-examine witnesses. . . .

In the preamble accompanying these regulations, EPA explained its selection of formal adjudicatory procedures. Although in EPA's view, there are "many cases" in which the term "public hearing" should not be read to require formal adjudicatory procedures, EPA concluded that "the nature of the decision at issue in [subsection (a)] cases indicates . . . that such formal procedures were probably intended." 43 Fed. Reg. 34738 (1978). In such cases, the agency "will be accusing someone of violating established legal standards through their past conduct, and will be seeking to impose a sanction for it. . . . In addition, the facts at issue will be specific ones involving the past conduct of regulated persons." *Id.*

B. *Informal Adjudication Under Part 24*

In the Hazardous and Solid Waste Amendments of 1984, Congress added to § 3008 a new subsection (h), authorizing the Administrator of EPA to issue "an order requiring corrective action" whenever he "determines that there is or has been a release of hazardous waste into the environment" from an interim facility. RCRA § 3008(h)(1), 42 U.S.C. § 6928(h)(1). Such orders must indicate "the nature of the required corrective action or other response measure, and . . . specify a time for compliance," and may include suspension or revocation of the facility's authorization to operate as an interim facility.

RCRA § 3008(h)(2), 42 U.S.C. § 6928(h)(2). The Administrator may assess a civil penalty of up to $25,000 per day for noncompliance with a corrective action order. *Id.* The 1984 Amendments also modified subsection (b) to make it clear that those subject to corrective action orders under the new subsection (h) have the right to a "public hearing."

To govern subsection (h) hearings, EPA promulgated the procedural regulations here under review. . . . Those rules specifically provide that the formal adjudicatory procedures of Part 22 shall be applicable only to challenges to subsection (h) corrective action orders that include a suspension or revocation of interim status or an assessment of civil penalties for noncompliance. . . . If the order calls upon the interim facility operator merely to undertake an investigation or to do so in combination with interim corrective measures, then, depending upon the burden entailed by such measures, the agency will use either the informal adjudicatory procedures provided in Subpart B of Part 24 (for interim corrective measures that are "neither costly nor technically complex," 40 C.F.R. § 24.80) or those in Subpart C of Part 24.

The procedures in Subparts B and C are substantially similar insofar as is relevant to this case. The crucial point is that both subparts set forth informal rather than formal adjudicatory procedures. Under either subpart, the operator of a hazardous waste facility may submit written information and argument for inclusion in the record . . . ; an oral presentation at the hearing itself . . . ; and be assisted at hearing by legal and technical advisors. . . . Direct examination and cross-examination of witnesses is not permitted, but the Presiding Officer may direct questions to either party. . . . The Presiding Officer is to be either "the Regional Judicial Officer . . . or another attorney employed by the Agency, who has had no prior connection with the case, including performance of any investigative or prosecuting functions." . . . With respect to both Subpart B and Subpart C proceedings, EPA, when issuing a corrective action order, shall deliver to the operator "all relevant documents and oral information (which has been reduced to writing), which the agency considered in the process of developing and issuing the order, exclusive of privileged internal communications." . . .

The Presiding Officer is to review the record and to file a recommended decision with the EPA Regional Administrator. . . . The Regional Administrator, in turn, is to receive comments from the parties and to render a final decision . . . from which an aggrieved party may seek judicial review under the APA.

II. *CHEVRON* ANALYSIS

Petitioners argue initially that the informal procedures of Part 24 are inconsistent with the intent of Congress in enacting and amending § 3008. To this end, petitioners make three specific contentions: first, that the language of subsection (b), as interpreted by EPA in its 1978 implementing regulations, requires formal procedures in all subsection (h) adjudications; second, that the legislative history of the 1984 Amendments demonstrates Congress's intention that EPA use the same formal procedures for the issuance of the new subsection (h) orders as the agency had theretofore established for the issuance of subsection (a) orders; and, third, that precedent in this circuit erects a presumption that when Congress refers to an adjudication as a "hearing," it intends that formal procedures be used.

We approach petitioners' arguments within the framework that the Supreme Court decreed in *Chevron U.S.A. v. Natural Resources Defense Council*, 467 U.S. 837 (1984), for judicial review of an agency's interpretation of a statute under its administration. At the outset, we ask whether "Congress has directly spoken to the precise question at issue," . . . if so, then we "must give effect to the unambiguously expressed intent of Congress" and may not defer to a contrary agency interpretation. . . . If the statute is "silent or ambiguous with respect to the specific issue," however, we proceed to ask "whether the agency's answer is based on a permissible construction of the statute," . . . if so, then we must defer to the agency's construction.

A. *Chevron* Step One

Before turning to petitioners' principal arguments based on the requirement of a "public hearing," we may briefly dispose of a related argument based on the provision in subsection (b) that the EPA "may promulgate rules for discovery procedures." According to petitioners, this nominally permissive statement implies that Congress contemplated, and that the agency must therefore provide, formal procedures in which discovery plays a part. In response to a similar contention at the rule-making stage, EPA read subsection (b) to "suggest that [a] hearing which did not contain this feature most commonly associated with adjudicatory hearings would also be acceptable." . . . Given the implicit but presumably intentional distinction in the statute between things that the agency "shall" do (initiate a "public hearing" upon request) and those that it "may" do (promulgate discovery rules), we reject the argument that the statute compels the use of procedures involving discovery and do not reach the suggested inference from discovery to formal hearing procedures generally.

1. *Prior Agency Interpretation.* As to petitioners' argument based upon the hearing requirement, we observe initially that the statutory language, taken alone, does not show that Congress "has directly spoken to the precise question at issue." Subsection (b) requires a "public hearing" but does not, by its terms, indicate whether Congress intended that formal or informal hearing procedures be used. Petitioners claim, however, that in 1978, EPA interpreted the phrase "public hearing" to require formal adjudication when it promulgated procedures to govern hearings on orders issued under subsection (a). We think they misread the record in this regard.

Although EPA did believe that Congress "intended" it to use formal procedures for hearings on orders under subsection (a), the agency made clear that this conclusion rested upon the particular nature of the issues raised by such orders, not upon the force of the statutory language alone. EPA thus did not adopt the view that the reference to a "public hearing" in subsection (b) necessarily or always imposes a requirement of formal procedures. Even if EPA had taken that position, moreover, it would remain free to change its interpretation in order to permit the use of informal procedures to implement the 1984 Amendments, provided that its new interpretation is otherwise legally permissible and is adequately explained. *See United Technologies Corp. v. EPA*, 821

F.2d 714, 723 (D.C. Cir. 1987). We therefore turn to petitioners' argument based upon the 1984 Amendments.

2. *The 1984 Amendments.* When Congress authorized EPA to issue corrective action orders under subsection (h), it also extended the right to a "public hearing" under subsection (b) to encompass such orders. According to petitioners, Congress's decision to apply the existing hearing provision of subsection (b) — at a time when EPA had only formal adjudicatory procedures in effect — shows that Congress wished also to apply those formal procedures to hearings on orders issued pursuant to the new subsection (h). To support this inference, petitioners rely heavily on a statement by Senator Chafee, a sponsor of the 1984 Amendments, indicating that the "procedures set forth in subsection (b) are made applicable to orders issued under this new subsection [(h)]." 130 Cong. Rec. S39175 (daily ed. July 16, 1984).

The short answer to petitioners' argument is that the Senator referred not to the procedures set forth in Part 22 of EPA's regulations implementing subsection (b), but to the "procedures set forth in" the statutory subsection itself. Absent a more specific reference to the formal procedures of Part 22, we may not infer that Senator Chafee and his colleagues intended to engraft those regulations onto § 3008. See *AFL-CIO v. Brock,* 835 F.2d 912, 915 (D.C. Cir. 1987) ("express congressional approval of an administrative interpretation [is required] if it is to be viewed as statutorily mandated").

Without distinguishing the AFL-CIO case, petitioners maintain that Senator Chafee's failure to refer expressly to Part 22 is "immaterial," since he did cite "the dispositive statutory [sub]section." This contention would be relevant if the language of the statute made clear the type of procedures intended. As we have seen, however, that is not the case. Absent a reference to Part 22, Senator Chafee's statement remains, at best, ambiguous.

3. *Circuit Precedent.* Petitioners point to our statement in a footnote in *Union of Concerned Scientists v. U.S. NRC,* 735 F.2d 1437, 1444 n. 12 (D.C. Cir. 1984) (*UCS*), that "when a statute calls for a hearing in an adjudication the hearing is presumptively governed by 'on the record' procedures," notwithstanding omission of the phrase "on the record" in the statute. See also *Seacoast Anti-Pollution League v. Costle,* 572 F.2d 872, 877 (1st Cir. 1978); *Marathon Oil v. EPA,* 564 F.2d 1253, 1264 (9th Cir. 1977). For the reasons set out below, however, we decline to adhere any longer to the presumption raised in *UCS.*

For perspective, we note first that the very footnote cited by petitioners makes clear that the issue in that case was "whether the NRC can, in its discretion, bypass [a statutory] hearing requirement altogether on issues material to its licensing decisions," and that "we refrain[ed] from holding outright that [the hearing provision in question there] requires 'on the record' hearings." 735 F.2d at 1444 n. 12. Our statement about the presumption to that effect was therefore dicta. We did not actually rely on the presumption we announced, but rather inferred that Congress intended the use of formal adjudicatory procedures based both upon NRC's unsuccessful efforts to convince Congress to do away with such procedures and upon NRC's consistent position, over a twenty year period, that the statute required formal procedures. . . . No such contextual circumstances exist here.

More important, *UCS* and its kin, *Seacoast* and *Marathon,* all predate the Supreme Court's decision in *Chevron*. Under that decision, it is not our office to presume that a statutory reference to a "hearing," without more specific guidance from Congress, evinces an intention to require formal adjudicatory procedures, since such a presumption would arrogate to the court what is now clearly the prerogative of the agency, *viz.,* to bring its own expertise to bear upon the resolution of ambiguities in the statute that Congress has charged it to administer. In effect, the presumption to *UCS* truncates the *Chevron* inquiry at the first step by treating a facially ambiguous statutory reference to a "hearing" as though it were an unambiguous constraint upon the agency. We will henceforth make no presumption that a statutory "hearing" requirement does or does not compel the agency to undertake a formal "hearing on the record," thereby leaving it to the agency, as an initial matter, to resolve the ambiguity.

While an agency might not be able reasonably to read a requirement that it conduct a "hearing on the record" to permit informal procedures in the converse situation to that presented here, an agency that *reasonably* reads a simple requirement that it hold a "hearing" to allow for informal hearing procedures must prevail under the second step of *Chevron*. As usual in cases involving *Chevron*'s second step, the court will evaluate the reasonableness of the agency's interpretation using the normal tools of statutory interpretation . . . such as legislative history, structural inferences, or exceptional circumstances of the type presented in *UCS*. . . .

[The court also rejected arguments to the effect that the agency failed to provide adequate reasons for its choice of procedure and that these procedures violated the Due Process Clause].

NOTES AND QUESTIONS

3-7. Given that the Court in *Seacoast* concludes that the adjudicatory provisions of the APA apply, what was wrong with the procedures used by EPA? If you were arguing the case, to what specifically would you point?

3-8. What is the basis of the court's opinion for concluding that the APA applies in *Seacoast*? To what extent should the court focus on the rights of intervenors? Are these procedures necessary to achieve an accurate and fair decision or are they being applied to make sure that exceptions are not too easily granted? Is this a proper role for procedure to play?

3-9. How would you compare the approaches taken by the courts in *Seacoast, Buttrey* and *Chemical Waste Management*? After *Chemical Waste Management,* how much discretion does the agency have in choosing its procedures? Is *Seacoast* still good law?

3-10. We shall examine fully the *Chevron U.S.A. v. NRDC* case in Chapter Eight, § 8.04. For now, can you state what that case requires and how it applied in *Chemical Waste Management*?

3-11. How much discretion does *Chevron* give an agency when it comes to granting or denying formal adjudication under the APA? Does *Chevron,* in effect, require a court to take a "magic words" approach to the question of when an APA hearing is required?

3-12. Consider the court's approach in *West Chicago, Ill. v. U.S. Nuclear Regulatory Commission,* 701 F.2d 632 (7th Cir. 1983), to the statutory issues raised above. How does it compare to those taken in the previous cases?

Our inquiry cannot end with a finding that the NRC acted in conformance with its own regulations, for we must determine whether those regulations as interpreted violate the governing statute. If the AEA requires a formal hearing in the case of a materials license amendment, then the NRC must provide one, despite its interpretation of the regulations.

The City claims that a materials licensing hearing under Section 189(a) of the AEA must be in accordance with Section 5 of the Administrative Procedure Act (APA), 5 U.S.C. § 554. Section 554 does not by its terms dictate the type of hearing to which a party is entitled; rather it triggers the formal hearing provisions of Sections 556 and 557 of the APA if the adjudication in question is required by the agency's governing statute to be "determined on the record after opportunity for an agency hearing. . . ." The city argues that Section 189(a) of the AEA triggers the formal hearing provisions of the APA because it provides that the "Commission shall grant a hearing upon the request of any person whose interest may be affected by the proceeding, and shall admit any such person as a party to such proceeding." . . .

Although Section 554 specifies that the governing statute must satisfy the "on the record" requirement, those three magic words need not appear for a court to determine that formal hearings are required. *See, e.g., Seacoast Anti-Pollution League v. Costle,* 572 F.2d 872, 876 (1st Cir.), *certiorari denied sub nom.* . . . However, even the City agrees that in the absence of these magic words (Br. at 24), Congress must clearly indicate its intent to trigger the formal, on-the-record hearing provisions of the APA. . . . We find no such clear intention in the legislative history of the AEA, and therefore conclude that formal hearings are not statutorily required for amendments to materials licenses.

701 F.2d at 641.

3-13. Once sections 556 and 557 have been triggered, the parties usually are entitled to a formal APA hearing. It does not *always* follow, however, that such a hearing will be held. There are some cases in which such a hearing would be unnecessary. As the Supreme Court has stated in *Weinberger v. Hynson,* 412 U.S. 609, 621 (1973), "we cannot impute to Congress the design of requiring, nor does due process demand, a hearing when it appears conclusively from the applicant's pleadings that the application cannot succeed." Most agencies thus have a summary judgment rule that allows them to make a decision on the merits, without a formal hearing, when there are no material facts in issue. But when a fact is or is not in issue, however, can be difficult to determine. Is a denial of the facts alleged enough to require a hearing, or must there be some additional evidence alleged to establish the basis for such a denial? *Compare Independent Ins. Agents of America v. Board of Governors,* 648 F.2d 571 (8th Cir.), *reh'g denied,* 664 F.2d 177 (1981), *with Connecticut Bankers Ass'n v. Board of Governors,* 627 F.2d 245 (D.C. Cir. 1980).

3-14. Just how much does the APA restrict the decisionmaking process of the agency? Consider the following:

> Courts adopting the *West Chicago* approach, and commentators who would limit the applicability of the APA adjudicative provisions, have often asserted that a broad and uniform application of those provisions would deprive agencies of needed procedural flexibility or impose upon agency adjudicators "time-consuming . . . courtroom drama." The adjudicatory procedures of the APA, it is argued, reflect the penchant of a bygone era for unnecessary and inefficient trial-type decisionmaking, an outmoded generational blind spot in favor of judicial procedures that are simply out of place in much of today's administrative decisionmaking. Giving broad application to the APA's adjudicative provisions will result in the "judicialization" of agency decisionmaking or, to use a more modern complaint, the "ossification" of the adjudicative process. Surely it is better, it is said, to permit agencies to design, on their own, adjudicative procedures that are more precisely tailored to the regulatory program involved, the nature of the issues that will arise in a particular adjudicatory context, or the diverse administrative needs of various agencies.

> The problem with the forgoing arguments is that they are belied by the very text of the APA's adjudicatory provisions. Those provisions simply do not require compliance with one rigid form of adjudicatory hearing; they do not require a formal, trial-type proceeding in every case to which they apply. To call these provisions "formal" or "trial-type" procedures is to ignore the fact that the drafters of the APA wrote into its adjudicative provisions a great deal of procedural flexibility permitting agencies to make adjudicative decisions with far less formality than that traditionally associated with a judicial trial. Even putting aside those situations in which, under the APA, an agency may be able to avoid any adjudicatory procedures at all or is expressly exempt from compliance with the APA's procedures, the amount of procedural discretion afforded to agency decisionmakers under the APA's adjudicative provisions is really quite remarkable. As I pointed out in 1985, and others have noted more recently, the APA's adjudicative provisions do not require that cross examination be provided in all hearings; they do not even require the use of any oral procedures in many cases. Under the actual text of the APA, agencies may exercise a great deal of control over the scope, timing, and complexity of any adjudicatory proceeding, eliminating procedural formalities where the nature of the issues or the needs of the agency so demand. The fear that expanding the APA's adjudicatory provisions to the broad scope they were originally intended to have will lead to the "ossification" of the adjudicatory process is simply misplaced.

Cooley R. Howarth, Jr., *Restoring the Applicability of the APA's Adjudicatory Procedures,* 56 ADMIN. L. REV. 1043 at 1049 (2004).*

---

* Copyright © 2004 American Bar Association. All rights reserved.

§ 3.03   ADJUDICATION & THE ADMINISTRATIVE PROCEDURE ACT   243

Is Howarth correct with respect to the apparent flexibility of the APA? Under what conditions does § 556 require cross-examination? When does that section entitle a party to compel another to submit to a deposition? Why might agencies nonetheless resist the application of the formal adjudication provisions of the APA to their decisionmaking process? *See Citizen's Awareness Network, Inc. v. NRC, infra.*

3-15. Sections 556 and 557 can also be invoked in APA formal rulemaking proceedings. Section 553(c) provides for formal rulemaking procedures "when rules are required by statute to be made on the record after opportunity for an agency hearing." The Supreme Court in *United States v. Florida East Coast Ry.*, 410 U.S. 224 (1973), essentially applied more of a "magic words" approach to the resolution of a dispute over whether the formal rulemaking provisions of the APA had been triggered. Why would such an approach be particularly appropriate in a rulemaking context? *See infra*, Chapter Four, § 4.02.

3-16. One practical reason why an agency might want to avoid the requirements of formal adjudication is that only an administrative law judge can preside over a formal adjudicatory hearing; however, an agency is free to use a non-ALJ presiding officer for all other hearings. An agency has considerable latitude in selecting non-ALJ presiding officers. They need not be — and indeed the majority are not — lawyers; they can be a member of the agency's staff whose duties may or may not exclusively consist of presiding over hearings; and they may in fact be drawn from outside the agency altogether, for example from a pool of retired judges or full-time academics.

Functionally, ALJs do *not* differ from non-ALJ presiding officers with respect to the types of cases that the ALJ hears. For example, while an ALJ conducts Social Security benefit hearings, 20 C.F.R. § 404.929, a non-ALJ presiding officer conducts substantially similar veterans' benefits hearings with the Board of Veterans' Appeals, 38 C.F.R. § 3.100. What *does* differentiate the two is the independence of the ALJ from the agency. But this independence does not come without cost:

> The APA contains a set of provisions relating to the hiring, evaluation, rotation, compensation, and tenure of ALJs. The Office of Personnel Management selects applicants for the register of new ALJs through a process that is complex and mechanical, and which confers a large advantage on applicants who are veterans. The process allows little room for judgment and discretion, and affords agencies virtually no choice in which ALJs to hire. It does not take account of whether a new ALJ has specialized experience in the regulatory or beneficiary scheme administered by the agency. The APA does not permit agencies to evaluate the work of their ALJs nor to discharge ALJs for anything short of major misconduct. Once hired, an ALJ has virtual lifetime tenure without any probationary period. ALJs are also more highly compensated than most non-ALJ POs. This set of provisions guarantees ALJ independence, but it interferes with an agency's ability to manage its adjudicatory function and increases an agency's costs of conducting adjudication. As a result, it impels agencies to avoid using ALJs if they can do so.

Michael Asimow, *The Spreading Umbrella: Extending the APA's Adjudication Provisions to All Evidentiary Hearings Required by Statute,* 56 ADMIN. L. REV. 1003 (2004).*

3-17. It is argued that the bureaucracy faces significant internal pressures to resist the expansion of the types of hearings requiring an ALJ. A result of this has been an explosion both in the number of non-ALJ presiding officers and in the number of hearings that they conduct. According to a 1992 study conducted by Administrative Law Judge John H. Frye III, 2,692 non-ALJ presiding officers conducted 393,800 proceedings in 1989.[1] When Raymond Limon updated this study ten years later, he found that the ranks of non-ALJ presiding officers had increased by 25% to 3,370, of whom only 1,370 were lawyers.[2] During the same time period, however, the ALJ corps had only grown by 6% to 1,351.

3-18. Formal APA adjudication is often described as adjudication that requires the use of an Administrative Law Judge (ALJ). But many agency adjudications that arguably might also benefit from such a procedural approach, do not use ALJs, nor do they trigger sections 554, 556, and 557 of the APA. Professor Asimov distinguishes these proceedings from informal adjudications (*see* Chapter 5, *infra*) and refers to these as "non-ALJ adjudications." See Asimow, *The Spreading Umbrella: Extending the APA's Adjudication Provisions to All Evidentiary Hearings Required by Statute, supra* **Note 3-16**. These proceedings involve disputes over a wide range of issues, from immigration cases, civil penalty proceedings, as well as entitlement benefits disputes involving the Board of Veterans' Appeals and Medicare cases.

These and many other cases with substantial issues at stake are decided by Presiding Officers (POs). Most POs are not lawyers. Professor Asimow argues that "Congress should impose procedural constraints on non-ALJ hearings without necessarily converting them to ALJ hearings." Do you agree? What do you think of the draft resolution below, passed by the ABA in July, 2000?

PROBLEM 3-1

What are the advantages and disadvantages of the following resolution? How would you change it to fit your views?

---

* Copyright © 2004 American Bar Association. All rights reserved.

[1] *See* John H. Frye III, *Survey of Non-ALJ Hearing Programs in the Federal Government,* 44 ADMIN. L. REV. 261 (1992).

[2] *See* Raymond Limon, Office of Administrative Law Judges, *The Federal Administrative Judiciary Then and Now—A Decade of change 1992-2002* (Dec. 23, 2002), p. 4.

Resolution 113

July 2000

RESOLVED, That the American Bar Association urges Congress, when it considers enactment of legislation relating to new or existing programs that involve agency adjudications with an opportunity for hearing, to consider and determine expressly within the relevant legislation whether the hearing should be subject to the requirements of the Administrative Procedure Act (APA) in 5 U.S.C. §§ 554, 556, and 557, including presiding officer protections, ex parte prohibitions, record-based decisionmaking, and other procedural safeguards.

FURTHER RESOLVED, That in determining the appropriateness of requiring a formal APA adjudication, Congress should consider the following factors:

1. Whether the adjudication is likely to involve substantial impact on personal liberties or freedom, orders that carry with them a finding of criminal-like culpability, imposition of sanctions with substantial economic effect on a party or interested person, or determination of discrimination under civil rights or analogous laws.

2. Whether the adjudication would be similar to, or the functional equivalent of, a current type of adjudication in which an administrative law judge presides.

3. Whether the adjudication would be one in which adjudicators ought to be lawyers. It is recognized that some proceedings might require participation by additional adjudicators with other types of specialized expertise.

FURTHER RESOLVED, That in order to preserve the uniformity of process and of qualifications of presiding officers contemplated by the APA, Congress should amend the APA to provide prospectively that, absent a statutory requirement to the contrary in any future legislation that creates the opportunity for a hearing in an adjudication, such a hearing shall be subject to 5 U.S.C. §§ 554, 556, and 557. . . .

CITIZENS AWARENESS NETWORK, INC. v. NUCLEAR REGULATORY COMMISSION

First Circuit Court of Appeals,
391 F.3d 338 (2004)

Before SELYA, LIPEZ and HOWARD, CIRCUIT JUDGES.

SELYA, CIRCUIT JUDGE.

Disenchanted with its existing procedural framework for the conduct of adjudicatory hearings, the Nuclear Regulatory Commission (NRC or Commission) promulgated new rules designed to make its hearing processes more efficient. These new rules greatly reduce the level of formality in reactor licensing proceedings but, at the same time, place certain unaccustomed restrictions upon the parties. The petitioners and petitioner-intervenors are public interest groups. Supported by the Attorneys General of five states (who have filed a helpful amicus brief), they claim that the new rules violate a statutory requirement that all reactor licensing hearings be conducted in accordance with sections 554, 556, and 557 of the Administrative Procedure Act (APA), 5 U.S.C. §§ 554, 556 & 557.[3] . . .

I. BACKGROUND

The NRC is the federal agency charged with regulating the use of nuclear energy, including the licensing of reactors used for power generation. The Atomic Energy Act requires the Commission to hold a hearing "upon the request of any person whose interest may be affected," before granting a new license, a license amendment, or a license renewal.

The NRC's predecessor agency, the Atomic Energy Commission (AEC), originally interpreted this provision as requiring on-the-record hearings in accordance with the APA. These hearings closely resembled federal court trials, complete with a full panoply of discovery devices and direct and cross-examination of witnesses by advocates for the parties. Such hearings proved to be very lengthy; some lasted as long as seven years.

In 1982, the NRC relaxed its approach for certain types of licensing proceedings. Although the results were heartening, the Commission nevertheless retained the full range of trial-like procedures for reactor licensing cases. The passage of time brought further changes: faced with the prospect of hearings on many license renewal applications in the near future — a large number of reactors were initially licensed in the decade from 1960 to 1970 and the standard term for such licenses was forty years — the Commission began to reassess its adjudicatory processes, focusing particularly on the procedures used in reactor licensing cases. The NRC's issuance, in 1998, of a policy on the conduct of adjudicatory proceedings, marked the inception of this process. This policy statement reiterated the NRC's commitment to expeditious adjudication and urged hearing officers to employ a variety of innovative case-management techniques in order to improve hearing efficiency.

While encouraging better utilization of existing procedures, the Commission also began pondering possible procedural revisions. In January of 1999, the NRC's general counsel drafted a legal memorandum concluding that the Atomic Energy Act did not require reactor licensing hearings to be on the record and, accordingly, that the Commission had the option of replacing the existing format with a truncated regime. Later that year, the Commission held a widely attended workshop on hearing procedures. Building on this foundation, the Commission published a notice of proposed rulemaking on April 16, 2001, suggesting a major revision of its hearing procedures. In an accompanying statement, the Commission took the position that section 189 of the Atomic

---

[3] In the pages that follow, we use the modifiers "on the record" and "formal" interchangeably to refer to adjudications conducted in accordance with sections 554, 556, and 557 of the APA.

§ 3.03   ADJUDICATION & THE ADMINISTRATIVE PROCEDURE ACT   247

Energy Act, 42 U.S.C. § 2239, does not require reactor licensing proceedings to be on the record.

On January 14, 2004, the NRC published a final rule, along with a response to the comments that the proposed rule had generated. With minor exceptions, the final rule replicated the proposed rule. The statement of considerations for the final rule reiterated the Commission's view that reactor licensing hearings may be informal.

The new rules took effect on February 13, 2004. Although they apply to all adjudications conducted by the NRC, the petitioners only challenge their application to reactor licensing proceedings. We therefore confine our ensuing discussion to that aspect of the new rules.

Under the old protocol, all reactor licensing hearings were conducted according to the procedures outlined in 10 C.F.R. part 2, subpart G. The subpart G rules resemble those associated with judicial proceedings. They include a complete armamentarium of traditional discovery devices (e.g., requests for document production, interrogatories, and depositions). The parties may make motions for summary disposition (although the hearing officer is not required to entertain them). There is an evidentiary hearing at which testimony is presented through direct and cross-examination of witnesses by the parties.

Under the new rules, reactor licensing hearings are, for the most part, to be conducted according to a less elaborate set of procedures described in 10 C.F.R. pt. 2, subpart L. The new subpart — which differs materially from the old subpart L — limns a streamlined hearing procedure. Unlike subpart G, subpart L does not provide for traditional discovery. Instead, parties in hearings governed by subpart L are required to make certain mandatory disclosures (akin to "open file" discovery) anent expert witnesses, expert witness reports, relevant documents, data compilations, and claims of privilege.

The hearings themselves also differ. Under subpart L, the presumption is that all interrogation of witnesses will be undertaken by the hearing officer, not the litigants. Parties are allowed to submit proposed questions in advance of the hearing, but the presiding officer is under no compulsion to pose them. Parties are not allowed to submit proposed questions during the hearing unless requested to do so by the presiding officer. Cross-examination is not available as of right, although a party may request permission to conduct cross-examination that it deems "necessary to ensure the development of an adequate record for decision." A party seeking leave to conduct cross-examination must submit a cross-examination plan, which will be included in the record of the proceeding regardless of whether the request is allowed.

The petitioners — we use that phrase broadly to include the petitioner-intervenors — took umbrage at these changes and brought these petitions for judicial review. Their primary claim is that the Commission erred in its determination that reactor licensing proceedings do not have to be fully formal adjudications. In their view, the new rules do not comply with the APA's requirements for on-the-record adjudication and, therefore, cannot stand. . . .

III. THE MERITS

. . . .

The mainstay of the petitioners' challenge is the proposition that the new rules exceed the Commission's statutory authority. The petitioners start with the premise that 42 U.S.C. § 2239 requires the NRC to conduct licensing hearings on the record, that is, in strict accordance with the relevant provisions of the APA. In their view, the new rules fail to satisfy that requirement and, therefore, must be pole-axed. In the pages that follow, we examine both the petitioners' premise and their conclusion.

Section 2239 requires the Commission, "upon the request of any person whose interest may be affected" by certain agency actions, to hold "a hearing." It does not explicitly require that the hearing be on the record. We have held, however, that the degree of formality that a hearing must afford does not necessarily turn on the presence or absence of an explicit statutory directive. If, even absent such a directive, the nature of the hearing that Congress intended to grant is clear, then that intention governs. We assume arguendo, favorably to the petitioners, that the *Seacoast* rule still obtains.

The petitioners advance several arguments for holding that Congress, in enacting section 2239, purposed to require on-the-record hearings in reactor licensing cases. In addition to canvassing the legislative history and cataloging the relevant amendments to the statute, they point out that for approximately four decades the NRC and its predecessor agency, the AEC, interpreted the statute as requiring on-the-record hearings in reactor licensing proceedings. In response, the NRC highlights the ambiguity of the statute and attempts to situate the latest round of changes in a larger history of procedural experimentation. The Commission also notes that some courts have interpreted section 2239 to allow informal hearings in licensing proceedings not involving reactors. *See, e.g., City of W. Chicago v. U.S. NRC*, 701 F.2d 632, 645 (7th Cir.1983) (licensing of nuclear materials). Last — but far from least — the Commission urges us to defer to its judgment that informal hearings are a suitable prophylactic for reactor licensing.

For years, the courts of appeals have avoided the question of whether section 2239 requires reactor licensing hearings to be on the record. We too decline to resolve this issue. Because the new rules adopted by the Commission meet the requirements of the APA it does not matter what type of hearing the NRC is required to conduct in reactor licensing cases. . . .

We begin with the question of whether the new rules fall below the APA's minimum requirements by eliminating discovery. The Commission points out, and the petitioners do not seriously contest, that the APA does not explicitly require the provision of any discovery devices in formal adjudications. *See* 5 U.S.C. § 556. Thus, if the APA requires the Commission to provide any discovery to satisfy the standards for formal adjudications, that discovery must be necessary either to effectuate some other procedural right guaranteed by the APA or to ensure an adequate record for judicial review.

The petitioners suggest that discovery is necessary to realize the right of citizen-intervenors to present their case and submit an informed rebuttal. *See* 5 U.S.C. § 556. If discovery is unavailable, this thesis runs, citizen-intervenors

§ 3.03   ADJUDICATION & THE ADMINISTRATIVE PROCEDURE ACT   249

will be unable to gather the evidence needed to support their contentions and, thus, will be shut out of meaningful participation in licensing hearings.

This thesis is composed of more cry than wool. The petitioners argue as if the new rules have eliminated all access to information from opposing parties — but that is a gross distortion. The new rules provide meaningful access to information from adverse parties in the form of a system of mandatory disclosure. Although there might well be less information available to citizen-intervenors under the new rules, the difference is one of degree. There is simply no principled way that we can say that the difference occasioned by replacing traditional discovery methods with mandatory disclosure is such that citizen-intervenors are left with no means of adequately presenting their case.

Nor do we think that full-dress discovery is essential to ensure a satisfactory record for judicial review. The Commission's final decision in any hearing must survive review based on the evidence adduced in the hearing. 5 U.S.C. § 556(e). The applicant bears the burden of proof in any licensing hearing, *id.* § 556(d), and it will have every incentive to proffer sufficient information to allow the agency to reach a reasoned decision. That same quantum of information should be adequate for a reviewing court to determine whether the agency's action is supportable.

To say more on this point would be to paint the lily. There is simply no discovery-linked conflict between the new rules and the APA's on-the-record adjudication requirement. The petitioners' first line of argument is, therefore, a dead end.

Turning to cross-examination, the petitioners' contentions fare no better: the new rules meet the APA's requirements. To explain this conclusion, we first must strip away the rhetorical flourishes in which the petitioners shroud their reasoning.

It is important to understand that, contrary to the petitioners' importunings, the new rules do not extirpate cross-examination. Rather, they restrict its use to situations in which it is "necessary to ensure an adequate record for decision." The legitimacy of this restriction must be weighed in light of the fact that the APA does not provide an absolute right of cross-examination in on-the-record hearings. The APA affords a right only to such cross-examination as may be necessary for a full and fair adjudication of the facts. Equally to the point, "[t]he party seeking to cross-examine bears the burden of showing that cross-examination is in fact necessary."

The Commission represents that, despite the difference in language, it interprets the standard for allowing cross-examination under the new rules to be equivalent to the APA standard. When an agency provides a plausible interpretation of its own procedural rules and there is no record or pattern of contrary conduct a court has no right either to slough off that interpretation or to deem it disingenuous. Given the Commission's stated interpretation, the new rules on cross-examination cannot be termed inconsistent with the dictates of the APA. Nor do we see how cross-examination that is not "necessary to ensure an adequate record for decision" could be necessary to ensure appropriate judicial review.

Because we find that the new rules meet the APA requirements for on-the-record adjudications, we hold that their promulgation does not exceed the Commission's authority. Consequently, the petitioners' ultra vires argument founders. . . .

[The court went on to reject petitioners claims that the rules were arbitrary and capricious as well as their constitutional claims.]

§ 3.04 Party Status and Intervention in an APA Proceeding

Assuming that a formal APA hearing applies, who is and who should be a party to an agency adjudicatory proceeding when sections 554, 556 and 557 are triggered? Who should be allowed to intervene? The APA defines a "party" to include "a person or agency named or admitted as a party in an agency proceeding, and a person or agency admitted by an agency as a party for limited purposes." 5 U.S.C. § 551(3). Is this helpful? As you refine your definition, what theory of the administrative process does it suggest? Are you concerned with legitimizing agency results? Are you concerned that all relevant points of view be presented?

The formal adjudicatory provisions of the APA make no provisions for intervenors. How should an agency determine who can and who cannot intervene? Do you fear that competitors will seek to intervene as parties for non-public interest purposes? Might they want only to delay the proceedings and raise the costs of whatever the applicant involved seeks? Is it possible to distinguish between intervenors with a genuine public interest concern and those without? How does the court seek to resolve these issues below?

OFFICE OF COMMUNICATION OF UNITED CHURCH OF CHRIST v. FEDERAL COMMUNICATIONS COMMISSION

District of Columbia Court of Appeals
359 F.2d 994 (1966)

Before BURGER, MCGOWAN and TAMM, CIRCUIT JUDGES.

BURGER, CIRCUIT JUDGE:

This is an appeal from a decision of the Federal Communications Commission granting to the Intervenor a one-year renewal of its license to operate television station WLBT in Jackson, Mississippi. Appellants filed with the Commission a timely petition to intervene to present evidence and arguments opposing the renewal application. The Commission dismissed Appellants' petition and, without a hearing, took the unusual step of granting a restricted and conditional renewal of the license. Instead of granting the usual three-year renewal, it limited the license to one year from June 1, 1965, and imposed what it characterizes here as "strict conditions" on WLBT's operations in that one-year probationary period.

§ 3.04   ADJUDICATION & THE ADMINISTRATIVE PROCEDURE ACT   251

Because the question whether representatives of the listening public have standing to intervene in a license renewal proceeding is one of first impression, we have given particularly close attention to the background of these issues and to the Commission's reasons for denying standing to Appellants.

Background

The complaints against Intervenor embrace charges of discrimination on racial and religious grounds and of excessive commercials. As the Commission's order indicates, the first complaints go back to 1955 when it was claimed that WLBT had deliberately cut off a network program about race relations problems on which the General Counsel of the NAACP was appearing and had flashed on the viewers' screens a "Sorry, Cable Trouble" sign. In 1957 another complaint was made to the Commission that WLBT had presented a program urging the maintenance of racial segregation and had refused requests for time to present the opposing viewpoint. Since then numerous other complaints have been made.

When WLBT sought a renewal of its license in 1958, the Commission at first deferred action because of complaints of this character but eventually granted the usual three-year renewal . . . .

Shortly after the outbreak of prolonged civil disturbances centering in large part around the University of Mississippi in September 1962, the Commission again received complaints that various Mississippi radio and television stations, including WLBT, had presented programs concerning racial integration in which only one viewpoint was aired. In 1963 the Commission investigated and requested the stations to submit detailed factual reports on their programs dealing with racial issues. On March 3, 1964, while the Commission was considering WLBT's responses, WLBT filed the license renewal application presently under review.

To block license renewal, Appellants filed a petition in the Commission urging denial of WLBT's application and asking to intervene in their own behalf and as representatives of "all other television viewers in the State of Mississippi." The petition stated that the Office of Communication of the United Church of Christ is an instrumentality of the United Church of Christ, a national denomination with substantial membership within WLBT's prime service area. It listed Appellants Henry and Smith as individual residents of Mississippi, and asserted that both owned television sets and that one lived within the prime service area of WLBT; both are described as leaders in Mississippi civic and civil rights groups. Dr. Henry is president of the Mississippi NAACP; both have been politically active. Each has had a number of controversies with WLBT over allotment of time to present views in opposition to those expressed by WLBT editorials and programs. . . .

The petition claimed that WLBT failed to serve the general public because it provided a disproportionate amount of commercials and entertainment and did not give a fair and balanced presentation of controversial issues, especially those concerning Negroes, who comprise almost forty-five per cent of the total population within its prime service area; it also claimed discrimination against local activities of the Catholic Church.

. . . .

The Commission's denial of standing to Appellants was based on the theory that, absent a potential direct, substantial injury or adverse effect from the administrative action under consideration, a petitioner has no standing before the Commission and that the only types of effects sufficient to support standing are economic injury and electrical interference. It asserted its traditional position that members of the listening public do not suffer any injury peculiar to them and that allowing them standing would pose great administrative burdens.

. . . .

The Commission's rigid adherence to a requirement of direct economic injury in the commercial sense operates to give standing to an electronics manufacturer who competes with the owner of a radio-television station only in the sale of appliances, while it denies standing to spokesmen for the listeners, who are most directly concerned with and intimately affected by the performance of a licensee. Since the concept of standing is a practical and functional one designed to insure that only those with a genuine and legitimate interest can participate in a proceeding, we can see no reason to exclude those with such an obvious and acute concern as the listening audience. This much seems essential to insure that the holders of broadcasting licenses be responsive to the needs of the audience, without which the broadcaster could not exist. . . .

The theory that the Commission can always effectively represent the listener interests in a renewal proceeding without the aid and participation of legitimate listener representatives fulfilling the role of private attorneys general is one of those assumptions we collectively try to work with so long as they are reasonably adequate. When it becomes clear, as it does to us now, that it is no longer a valid assumption which stands up under the realities of actual experience, neither we nor the Commission can continue to rely on it. The gradual expansion and evolution of concepts of standing in administrative law attests that experience rather than logic or fixed rules has been accepted as the guide. . . .

We cannot believe that the Congressional mandate of public participation which the Commission says it seeks to fulfill was meant to be limited to writing letters to the Commission, to inspection of records, to the Commission's grace in considering listener claims, or to mere non-participating appearance at hearings. We cannot fail to note that the long history of complaints against WLBT beginning in 1955 had left the Commission virtually unmoved in the subsequent renewal proceedings, and it seems not unlikely that the 1964 renewal application might well have been routinely granted except for the determined and sustained efforts of Appellants at no small expense to themselves. Such beneficial contribution as these Appellants, or some of them, can make must not be left to the grace of the Commission. . . .

We recognize the risks [that] regulatory agencies, the Federal Communications Commission in particular, would ill serve the public interest if the courts imposed such heavy burdens on them as to overtax their capacities. The

§ 3.04 ADJUDICATION & THE ADMINISTRATIVE PROCEDURE ACT   253

competing consideration is that experience demonstrates consumers are generally among the best vindicators of the public interest. In order to safeguard the public interest in broadcasting, therefore, we hold that some "audience participation" must be allowed in license renewal proceedings. We recognize this will create problems for the Commission but it does not necessarily follow that "hosts" of protestors must be granted standing to challenge a renewal application or that the Commission need allow the administrative processes to be obstructed or overwhelmed by captious or purely obstructive protests. The Commission can avoid such results by developing appropriate regulations by statutory rulemaking. Although it denied Appellants standing, it employed *ad hoc* criteria in determining that these Appellants were responsible spokesmen for representative groups having significant roots in the listening community. These criteria can afford a basis for developing formalized standards to regulate and limit public intervention to spokesmen who can be helpful. A petition for such intervention must "contain specific allegations of fact sufficient to show that the petitioner is a party in interest and that a grant of the application would be *prima facie* inconsistent" with the public interest. 74 Stat. 891 (1960), 47 U.S.C. 309(d)(1) (1964).

The responsible and representative groups eligible to intervene cannot here be enumerated or categorized specifically; such community organizations as civic associations, professional societies, unions, churches, and educational institutions or associations might well be helpful to the Commission. These groups are found in every community; they usually concern themselves with a wide range of community problems and tend to be representatives of broad as distinguished from narrow interests, public as distinguished from private or commercial interests.

The Commission should be accorded broad discretion in establishing and applying rules for such public participation, including rules for determining which community representatives are to be allowed to participate and how many are reasonably required to give the Commission the assistance it needs in vindicating the public interest. The usefulness of any particular petitioner for intervention must be judged in relation to other petitioners and the nature of the claims it asserts as basis for standing. Moreover it is no novelty in the administrative process to require consolidation of petitions and briefs to avoid multiplicity of parties and duplication of effort.

The fears of regulatory agencies that their processes will be inundated by expansion of standing criteria are rarely borne out. Always a restraining factor is the expense of participation in the administrative process, an economic reality which will operate to limit the number of those who will seek participation; legal and related expenses of administrative proceedings are such that even those with large economic interests find the costs burdensome. Moreover, the listening public seeking intervention in a license renewal proceeding cannot attract lawyers to represent their cause by the prospect of lucrative contingent fees, as can be done, for example, in rate cases.

We are aware that there may be efforts to exploit the enlargement of intervention, including spurious petitions from private interests not concerned with the quality of broadcast programming, since such private interests may sometimes cloak themselves with a semblance of public interest advocates.

But this problem, as we have noted, can be dealt with by the Commission under its inherent powers and by rulemaking. . . .

[The court went on to reverse the Commission's decision and to remand the case back to the Commission.]

NOTES AND QUESTIONS

3-19. In determining who may be a "party" to this administrative proceeding, does the Court equate standing in a judicial proceeding with standing in a Commission proceeding? Is it necessary that the "case or controversy" limitations of Article III, § 2 of the Constitution apply to the standing of a litigant before an Article I court? *See also Scenic Hudson Preservation Conf. v. FDC,* 354 F.2d 608 (D.C. Cir. 1965). For a more extensive examination of Article III standing, *see* Chapter Nine, *infra*.

3-20. An administrative proceeding can involve anywhere from two to 202 attorneys or more. Administrative law cases involve the government or the agency and a regulated entity, but some of the beneficiaries of the statutory regime may also wish to intervene as parties. Moreover, under many regulatory schemes, other regulated entities may have an interest in the outcome of the case. For example, consider a natural gas rate making hearing that involves an interstate pipeline. The interstate pipeline itself would be a party as would, of course, the agency that is seeking to set rates on that pipeline. But other interstate pipelines might also be interested, since the case might involve issues that would set policy or establish a precedent that would affect them in rate cases that they might bring in the future. In addition, various customers of the interstate pipeline, including interstate and intrastate distribution companies, may be interested in the outcome of the proceeding, since they will be buying gas from that interstate pipeline, and wish to do so at the best rate possible. Those distribution companies will also have customers and these may be direct consumers, some of whom are industrial consumers, some of whom are commercial consumers and some of whom may be residential consumers of natural gas. All of these various interests will wish to intervene and be a part of a proceeding designed to set the interstate rate on the sale of natural gas by an interstate pipeline. Who should intervene and how can one structure these proceedings so as to insure that they do not become totally unwieldy?

How one decides questions like these and how far one is willing to go to allow for the participation of parties whose interests may be at best tangential or simply ideological depends, to no small extent, on one's theory of the administrative process. If the theory is based on an interest group model which posits the public interest as the outcome of a clash of various interests, then there would be a high premium set on insuring that all interests are heard and that the agency have the opportunity to resolve conflicts among these interests and thereby further the public interest. Indeed, legitimacy of the administrative process could be said to turn on how adequately the agency not only resolved these conflicting interests, but how thorough they were in insuring that these various interests were voiced. In addition, this philosophy or approach to the administrative process might imply strongly that interests which were unable to be represented due, for example, to lack of funds, be funded to insure that all such interests are presented.

Why might you want to construe "party" or "intervenor" more broadly in an administrative setting? Consider the following in Stewart, *The Reformation of American Administrative Law:* [*]

> The expansion of the traditional model to afford participation rights in the process of agency decision and judicial review to a wide variety of affected interests must ultimately rest on the premise that such procedural changes will be an effective and workable means of assuring improved agency decisions. Advocates of extended access believe that an enlarged system of formal proceedings can, by securing adequate consideration of the interests of all affected persons, yield outcomes that better serve society as a whole. The credibility of this belief must now be considered.
>
> Although the courts have displayed caution in expanding and reworking administrative law doctrine to ensure the representation of all affected interests, the thrust of decisions over the past decade supports the assessment of the Court of Appeals for the District of Columbia Circuit that: "In recent years, the concept that public participation in decisions which involve the public interest is not only valuable but indispensable has gained increasing support." The principle of interest group representation in agency adjudication has been warmly endorsed by commentators and by the Administrative Conference of the United States. Such participation, it is claimed, will not only improve the quality of agency decisions and make them more responsive to the needs of the various participating interests, but is valuable in itself because it gives citizens a sense of involvement in the process of government, and increases confidence in the fairness of government decisions. Indeed, litigation on behalf of widely-shared "public" interests is explicitly defended as a substitute political process that enables the "citizen to cast a different kind of vote, [which] informs the court that . . . a particular point of view is being ignored or underestimated" by the agency. Its ultimate aim is seen as "a basic reordering of governmental institutions so that access and influence may be had by all."
>
> Not only is the expansion of participation rights applauded, but it is urged that resources be made available to facilitate the representation of otherwise unrepresented interests by private attorneys and by governmental agencies such as a proposed federal consumer advocate agency. Such proposals follow logically from the premise that justice results when all interests are considered.

3-21. Do you agree with this approach? What theory of administrative law does it represent? Are there limits to such an interest group approach? Practical limits? Theoretical limits? Section 555 of the APA provides that, in informal adjudicatory matters: "A party is entitled to appear in person or by

---

[*] 88 Harv. L. Rev. 1667, 1760 (1975). Copyright © 1975 by Harvard Law Review Association. All rights reserved.

or with counsel . . . in an agency proceeding. So far as the orderly conduct of public business permits, an interested person may appear before an agency or its responsible employees. . . ." What are the limits of "orderly conduct of agency proceedings"? Must all intervenors have the same rights or can some be limited in the way they participate?

3-22. In *Envirocare of Utah, Inc. v. NRC*, 194 F.3d 72 (D.C. Cir. 1999), the Court stated:

> Federal agencies may, and sometimes do, permit persons to intervene in administrative proceedings even though these persons would not have standing to challenge the agency's final action in federal court. Agencies, of course, are not constrained by Article III of the Constitution; nor are they governed by judicially-created standing doctrines restricting access to the federal courts.

The court then went on to state the issue in this case as follows: "Is the converse true? May an agency refuse to grant a hearing to persons who would satisfy the criteria for judicial standing and refuse to allow them to intervene in administrative proceedings?" What do you think?

3-23. Can it be argued that despite the interest group model of participation in administrative agency proceedings, agencies are, in fact, captured by the very interests they regulate? What does "capture" mean? Marver Bernstein describes this process as "clientalism," "[t]he repeated identification of the public interest with a particular private interest" caused by "the dependence of an agency on the support and consent of the regulated." M. Bernstein, *Regulating Business By Independent Commission* 270 (Princeton University Press 1955).* Bernstein goes on to note:

> In the period of maturity, . . . [t]he commission becomes more concerned with the general health of the industry and tries to prevent changes which adversely affect it. Cut off from the mainstream of political life, the commission's standards of regulation are determined in the light of the desires of the industry affected. It is unlikely that the commission, in this period, will be able to extend regulation beyond the limits acceptable to the regulated groups.
>
> . . . .
>
> The close of the period of maturity is marked by the commission's surrender to the regulated. Politically isolated, lacking a firm basis of public support, lethargic in attitude and approach, bowed down by precedent and backlogs, unsupported in its demands for more staff and money, the commission finally becomes a captive of the regulated groups.

M. Bernstein, *supra,* at 87–90. James Landis referred to this capture process as "industry orientation":

> It arises primarily from the fact that of necessity contacts with the industry are frequent and generally productive of intelligent ideas. Contacts with the public, however, are rare and generally unproductive of anything except complaint. . . .

---

* Copyright © 1955 Princeton University Press, 1983 renewed PUP. Reprinted by permission of Princeton University Press.

Irrespective of the absence of social contacts and the acceptance of undue hospitality, it is the daily machine-gun-like impact on both agency and its staff of industry representation that makes for industry orientation on the part of many honest and capable agency members as well as agency staffs.

Chairman of Subcomm. on Administrative Practice and Procedure of the Senate Comm. on the Judiciary, 86th Cong., 2d Sess., Report on Regulatory Agencies to the President-Elect 71 (Comm. Print 1960) (J. Landis).

Richard Posner, on the other hand, finds the capture theory unsatisfactory because it lacks any theoretical foundation:

> No reason is suggested for characterizing the interaction between the regulatory agency and the regulated firm by a metaphor of conquest, and surely the regulatory process is better viewed as the outcome of implicit (sometimes explicit) bargaining between the agency and the regulated firms. No reason is suggested as to why the regulated industry should be the only interest group able to influence an agency. Customers of the regulated firm have an obvious interest in the outcome of the regulatory process — why may they not be able to "capture" the agency as effectively as the regulated firms, or more so? No reason is suggested as to why industries are able to capture only existing agencies — never to procure the creation of an agency that will promote their interests — or why an industry strong enough to capture an agency set up to tame it could not prevent the creation of the agency in the first place.

Posner, *Theories of Economic Regulation,* 5 BELL J. ECON. & MGMT. SCI. 335, 342 (1974).**

Posner also contends that the "theory" is contradicted by three bodies of evidence.

> First, not every agency is characterized by a pristine virtue; often there is no occasion for conquest. . . . Second, the theory has no predictive or explanatory power at all when a single agency regulates separate industries having conflicting interests. . . . Third, the capture theory ignores a good deal of evidence that the interests promoted by regulatory agencies are frequently those of customer groups rather than those of the regulated firms themselves.

Id. at 342.

§ 3.05 Evidence

Congress may explicitly provide for the admission of certain kinds of evidence in an agency setting, even though that evidence would be inadmissible in court proceedings. Some courts have reasoned that the agency's chief function is investigation, and therefore it should not be hampered in its inquiry by narrow rules "where a strict correspondence is required between allegation and proof." Implicit in these and other decisions is the belief that agencies, as "triers of fact" in administrative proceedings, are more sophisticated and expert in the subject matter before them. Therefore they do not

---

** Copyright © 1974 by the RAND Corporation. All rights reserved.

require the same protective shield of evidentiary rules intended for jury trials.

Absent express Congressional limitations, the administrative law judge has the power to make reasonable determinations as to the admissibility of materials in proceedings before her. This broad power is derived from the Administrative Procedure Act, which provides in § 556(d) for "the exclusion of irrelevant, immaterial or unduly repetitious evidence." Agencies usually apply this provision in such a way that favors inclusion rather than exclusion of evidence and courts usually defer to the agency's decision to include or exclude the evidence in question.*

[A] Rules of Evidence

Section 556(d) of the APA provides that "[a] party is entitled to present his case or defense by oral or documentary evidence." For a variety of reasons, however, strict rules of evidence do not apply to administrative hearings.

There are, nevertheless, some limits on an agency's ability to either exclude or rely on certain levels of evidence in certain contexts. Consider the following case.

CALHOUN v. BAILAR

Ninth Circuit Court of Appeals
626 F.2d 145 (1980)

KARLTON, DISTRICT JUDGE.

Plaintiff challenges his discharge for falsifying mail volume records on the ground that the administrative findings were not supported by substantial evidence. He appeals from the district court's entry of summary judgment. The issue he posits on appeal is whether or not hearsay statements, subsequently disavowed on direct examination, constitute "substantial" evidence sufficient to support the administrative determination.

. . . .

I

FACTS

For our purposes, the facts may be briefly summarized. Plaintiff was Acting Tour II Superintendent at the Rincon Annex of the United States Post Office in San Francisco. His duties included the supervision of several postal clerks engaged in compiling and reporting information on the volume of mail handled

---

* Reprinted from Alfred C. Aman, Jr. & William Mayton, *Administrative Law*, 222 (2d ed. 2001), with permission of Thompson West.

by various distribution operations at Rincon Annex. He was charged with the falsification of mail volume records, or with directing his subordinates to falsify the records and, after an administrative hearing and appeal, discharged.

The Notice of Removal served upon Appellant relied upon the affidavits of four of his subordinates. Three of the affiants aver that they had either falsified records at Appellant's direction or had observed him directing others to falsify the records.

At the administrative hearing the officer who took the affidavits laid a proper foundation for their admission, testifying that each affiant was warned both orally and in writing of his or her constitutional rights and was given an opportunity to review and revise the statement before swearing to it. The affidavits were received into evidence without objection. No later motion to strike the affidavits was made.

On direct examination each of the affiants attempted to disavow his or her affidavit. Affiant Scroggins completely disavowed the affidavit on direct examination but refused to answer any questions on cross examination, presumably on self-incrimination grounds. Evidence was later admitted that clearly contradicted his statement on direct examination that he had never reweighed mail. Additionally, another witness, Inspector Johns, testified that Scroggins had admitted to him that he had reweighed mail at Appellant's behest.

Affiant Gaffey denied on direct his averment that he had been promised additional overtime or a step increase in salary in return for falsifying the records, but otherwise apparently affirmed his averment that Appellant directed him to falsify records.

Affiant Whitley totally disavowed her affidavit and testified that she was coerced into signing it.

Inspector Johns was the only other major witness. He testified that he had observed widespread falsification during Appellant's tenure as supervisor, and introduced statistical evidence that tended to show falsification in Appellant's unit. Other evidence corroborated Johns' testimony that falsification was occurring, although this testimony, like Johns', did not directly tie the falsification to Appellant.

As noted, Appellant did not challenge the admissibility of the affidavits at any time during the administrative process. At most, he argued the weight that should be given to the affidavits. The hearing examiner found that the affidavits were more credible evidence than the statements made on direct examination, in part because of the witnesses' refusal to answer questions put in cross examination and because portions of the affidavit were corroborated by other evidence. This conclusion was sustained by the Appeals Review Board.

II

DISCUSSION

There is no question that the statements in the affidavits would constitute substantial evidence if they were introduced as direct testimony. The affidavits individually and cumulatively support a finding that Appellant was involved in the falsification of records. Indeed, Appellant concedes that the affidavits themselves would be sufficient to support a finding if they were uncontradicted. Appellant argues, however, that hearsay statements disavowed by a declarant can never supply substantial evidence. We decline to adopt such a rigid rule, both because it is unnecessary to the resolution of this case and because the substantial evidence test is quintessentially a case-by-case analysis requiring review of the whole record. Nevertheless, the case does raise important and difficult questions concerning the procedure for dealing with administrative hearsay evidence.

We begin with a recognition that strict rules of evidence do not apply in the administrative context. Indeed, the Administrative Procedure Act provides that "*Any* oral or documentary evidence may be received, but every agency shall as a matter of policy provide for the exclusion of irrelevant, immaterial, or unduly repetitious evidence. A sanction may not be imposed or rule or order issued except on consideration of the whole record or those parts thereof cited by a party and supported by and in accordance with the reliable, probative, and substantial evidence." 5 U.S.C. § 556(d) (emphasis added).

Perhaps the classic exception to strict rules of evidence in the administrative context concerns hearsay evidence. Not only is there no administrative rule of automatic exclusion for hearsay evidence, but the only limit to the admissibility of hearsay evidence is that it bear satisfactorily indicia of reliability. We have stated the test of admissibility as requiring that the hearsay be probative and its use fundamentally fair.

Thus, it is not the hearsay nature *per se* of the proffered evidence that is significant, it is its probative value, reliability and the fairness of its use that are determinative. *Richardson v. Perales*, 402 U.S. 389 (1971), illustrates the appropriate analysis. In that case the issue was whether physicians' written reports of the medical examinations they had made of a disability claimant could constitute substantial evidence to support a finding of nondisability "when the claimant *objects to the admissibility of those reports and when the only live testimony is presented by his side and is contrary to the reports.*" (Emphasis added). The Court rejected a rigid rule and held that the proffered hearsay evidence could constitute substantial evidence. In doing so, the court explained that there could be no blanket rejection of administrative reliance on hearsay evidence irrespective of reliability and probative value.

Although *Richardson* arose in the context of a Social Security hearing, various courts have followed its reasoning to hold that hearsay, if reliable and credible, could constitute substantial evidence in a variety of administrative settings.

We too reject any *per se* rule that holds that hearsay can never be substantial evidence. To constitute substantial evidence, hearsay declarations, like any other evidence, must meet minimum criteria for admissibility it must have probative value and bear indicia of reliability. Although no bright line test can be established, cases isolate a number of factors that may be helpful in such an analysis. First, as *Richardson* teaches, the independence or possible bias of the declarant must be considered as well as the type of hearsay material submitted. In *Richardson*, the Court laid great stress on the fact that the reports were independent medical reports routinely prepared and submitted in disability cases. Other factors that should be considered are whether the statements are signed and sworn to as opposed to anonymous, oral, or unsworn, whether or not the statements are contradicted by direct testimony, whether or not the declarant is available to testify and, if so, whether or not the party objecting to the hearsay statements subpoenaes the declarant, or whether the declarant is unavailable and no other evidence is available, the credibility of the declarant if a witness, or of the witness testifying to the hearsay, and finally, whether or not the hearsay is corroborated. Although not controlling, the Federal Rules of Evidence 803(24) standards for the admission of hearsay not specifically covered by any exception but bearing "circumstantial guarantees of trustworthiness" may be of assistance.

There remains only the question of the appropriate vehicle for application of these factors. As noted, hearsay evidence, once admitted, may be relied upon by the agency in many circumstances. The test of reliability requires an examination of many factors including credibility. Reviewing courts must take the record as they find it in administrative cases and thus have no opportunity to develop the record. A rule which requires administrative consideration of probative value and reliability in the first instance comports with common sense and the limited review of administrative actions. Such a rule would also comport with the general rule that hearsay admitted without objection is ordinarily given its normal probative effect.

We therefore hold that hearsay evidence admitted without objection or later motion to strike may constitute substantial evidence in like manner as any other evidence. This rule encourages the full development of the record and allows the administrative examiner to determine questions of reliability and probative value in the first instance. If the hearing examiner overrules an objection or a motion to strike, the reviewing court is nonetheless presented with a developed record.

. . . .

. . . [T]he affidavits clearly provide substantial evidence to support the discharge. Although the affidavits are contradicted and partially repudiated by other testimony, we have long held that credibility issues should be resolved by the trier of fact and not be disturbed on appeal, and that where "there is conflicting evidence sufficient to support either outcome, we must affirm the decision actually made." *Rhinehart v. Finch* (9th Cir. 1971) 438 F.2d 920, 921.[5]

Accordingly, the judgment of the district court is affirmed.

---

[5] Obviously in so saying we do not mean to suggest that we would weigh the evidence in the same manner as the administrative examiner did or that we would arrive at the same conclusion. Moreover, we do not suggest that had the objection been raised either the hearing examiner or this court would have arrived at the same conclusion as to whether the affidavits did possess sufficient indicia of reliability so that the decision could properly rest upon them.

NOTES AND QUESTIONS

3-24. We will examine more fully the substantial evidence test and the scope of judicial review its application entails in Chapter 8, § 8.03, *infra*.

3-25. When should hearsay constitute substantial evidence? When should it not? Can uncorroborated hearsay evidence constitute substantial evidence? Should it?

3-26. Specify the differences between administrative adjudication in this case and that before a jury in federal court. Do those differences justify different approaches to the rules of evidence? Why or why not? *See generally*, William H. Kuehnle, *Standards of Evidence in Administrative Proceedings*, 49 N.Y.L. Sch. L. Rev. 829 (2004-2005).

3-27. Can evidence that is suppressed in a criminal proceeding as the fruit of an illegal search and seizure be introduced in an administrative proceeding? In *Boyd v. Constantine*, 613 N.E.2d 511 (N.Y. 1993), a state trooper was involved in a criminal prosecution for the purchase of marijuana. Evidence of his possession of marijuana was disallowed in the criminal case, but an administrative proceeding was brought against him from the police force. The evidence was allowed in the administrative hearing. The Court ruled:

> [W]e conclude that the evidence seized by the Buffalo City police officers should have been admitted in the State Police's administrative proceeding. The Buffalo City Police could not have foreseen, when they searched the vehicle, that defendant would be the subject to an administrative disciplinary proceeding by the Division of State Police. They did not know, prior to the search, that defendant was a State Trooper. Nor were the Buffalo City police officers acting as agents of the Division of State Police. Thus, only negligible deterrence would result from the exclusion of the evidence. On the other hand, the suppression of the evidence would have a significant adverse impact upon the truth-finding process in administrative proceedings concerning police officers involved in drug-related incidents. Stated differently, the benefit to be gained from precluding police officers, who unlawfully possess controlled substances, from making arrests — including arrests for drug-related offences — clearly outweighs any deterrent effect that may arise from applying the exclusionary rule to preclude evidence unlawfully obtained by the Buffalo City police officers and sought to be admitted by the Division of State Police in an administrative disciplinary proceeding.

Id. at 514.

[B] Official Notice

The APA recognizes the official notice doctrine often invoked by courts. Section 556(e) states: "[w]hen an agency decision rests on official notice of a material fact not appearing in the record, a party is entitled, on timely request,

§ 3.05   ADJUDICATION & THE ADMINISTRATIVE PROCEDURE ACT   263

to an opportunity to show the contrary." As the following case shows, official notice can be taken even if the APA does not apply, and though the range of facts eligible for official notice by courts is narrower then the range of facts eligible by an administrative decisionmaker, there are limits. What is the legal basis upon which these limits are justified?

CASTILLO-VILLAGRA v. IMMIGRATION AND NATURALIZATION SERVICE

Ninth Circuit Court of Appeals
972 F.2d 1017 (1992)

Before CHOY, NORRIS and KLEINFELD, CIRCUIT JUDGES.

KLEINFELD, CIRCUIT JUDGE:

This case turns on the breadth of the doctrine of administrative notice. We grant a petition for review of a decision of the Board of Immigration Appeals and reverse, because the Board improperly took notice of the effect of the change of government in Nicaragua on whether petitioners' fear of persecution was well-founded.

Teresa de Jesus Castillo-Villagra and her two adult daughters unsuccessfully sought asylum. They claimed that they had a well-founded fear of persecution by the Sandinistas because of their anti-Sandinista political opinions. While their case was pending, Violeta Chamorro, a democrat, was elected president of Nicaragua, and her democratic coalition, UNO, defeated the Sandinistas in an election. The Board of Immigration Appeals took administrative notice of the election and determined that because the Sandinistas had lost, the threat to petitioners from the Sandinistas had disappeared.

Petitioners were given no notice or opportunity to be heard regarding whether notice should be taken or whether the political changes in Nicaragua obviated their fear of returning. They claim that the Sandinistas retain enough power so that they still need asylum. Despite the election of the new president and parliamentary majority, the Sandinistas retained control of the army and the police, according to the State Department Country Report. The hearings were in December 1987, and February 1988, the Immigration Judge rendered his decision in February 1988, and the briefing on appeal before the BIA was completed in October 1989, all prior to the election, so no one had occasion to develop a record about the possibility that the Sandinistas might someday lose control. The election, with its surprise result in favor of UNO and Chamorro, was in April 1990. The BIA issued its decision in October 1990, without inviting supplementation of the record or briefs, yet based entirely on the election result subsequent to the record and briefs.

We determine that the Board should not have resolved the question of the effect of the change of government on petitioners without giving them notice of its intent to do so and an opportunity to show cause why notice should not be taken, or the record supplemented by further evidence. For these reasons, we reverse.

. . . .

III. ADMINISTRATIVE NOTICE

Petitioners' attorney explained that they had no quarrel with the BIA's taking notice that Violeta Chamorro had won election to the presidency, and that the UNO, a non-Sandinista coalition, had won a majority in parliament. Their claim is that the Sandinistas retain control of the police and the army, and still have sufficient sway to persecute their political adversaries, who include petitioners. The record, both the testimony by petitioners about the Sandinistas' use of street mobs, arrests, Sandinista movement control of ration cards and promotions, and the State Department Country Report, allows for the plausibility of petitioners' claim.

A. APA or INA?

To decide whether administrative notice was appropriate, first we must decide whether the question should be analyzed under the Administrative Procedure Act or the Immigration and Naturalization Act. The petitioners argue that the Administrative Procedure Act ("the APA"), bars administrative notice in the circumstances of this case. The APA provides that no subsequent statute shall be deemed to modify it "except to the extent that it does so expressly." 5 U.S.C. § 559. Section 242(b) of the Immigration and Nationality Act of 1952 ("the INA"), sets out in some detail the procedural framework governing deportation proceedings, and provides that "[t]he procedure so prescribed shall be the sole and exclusive procedure for determining the deportability of an alien under this section." We conclude that the INA displaces the APA on this question, so we do not analyze the administrative notice issue under the APA.

. . . .

B. Proper Scope of Notice.

Notice is a way to establish the existence of facts without evidence. In federal courts, notice may be taken of facts relating to the particular case, though no evidence is introduced, where the fact is "not subject to reasonable dispute," either because it is "generally known within the territorial jurisdiction," or is "capable of accurate and ready determination by resort to sources whose accuracy cannot reasonably be questioned." Thayer saw notice more as a branch of the theory of knowledge, or law in general, than the law of evidence, because "[i]n conducting a process of judicial reasoning, as of other reasoning, not a step can be taken without assuming something which has not been proved. . . ." James B. Thayer, *A Preliminary Treatise on Evidence* 279 (1898). Neither judges nor jurors need check their knowledge and experience of life at the courthouse door.[1]

---

[1] In a case for the sale of intoxicating liquor, a court properly refused a defense request for an instruction requiring the prosecution to prove that gin was intoxicating liquor, because

The appropriate scope of notice is broader in administrative proceedings than in trials, especially jury trials. *Banks v. Schweiker*, 654 F.2d 637 (9th Cir. 1981). Partly this is because the rules of evidence are more liberal and the volume of cases is so much greater in administrative proceedings. Professor Kenneth Culp Davis distinguished between adjudicative facts, which are those concerning the immediate parties, and legislative facts, which help the tribunal determine law and policy and are ordinarily general facts not concerning the immediate parties. Kenneth Culp Davis, *Judicial Notice*, 55 COLUM. L. REV. 945, 952 (1955). Davis' argument that notice of legislative facts may properly be taken more liberally than notice of adjudicative facts generally has been accepted.

While in proceedings in court notice is quite restricted for adjudicative facts, it is broader in administrative proceedings. A case before an administrative agency, unlike one before a court, "is rarely an isolated phenomenon, but is rather merely one unit in a mass of related cases . . . [which] often involve fact questions which have frequently been explored by the same tribunal." Walter Gellhorn, *Official Notice in Administrative Adjudication*, 20 TEX. L. REV. 131, 136 (1941). The tribunal learns from its cases.[2] Moreover, volume and repetition affect peoples' ability to pay attention. Because of the quantity of similar cases before an agency such as the INS, if notice is not taken more broadly in administrative hearings, litigants may have an uphill battle maintaining the attention of the administrative judges. Even if the law allows people to tell officials the exact same and obvious thing hundreds of times, the officials may find it very hard to listen attentively after the first dozen or two repetitions. Hearings may degenerate into an empty form if the adjudicators cannot focus attention upon what is noteworthy about the particular case. The broader notice available in administrative hearings may, if properly used, facilitate more genuine hearings, as opposed to "hearings" in which the finder of fact hears, but cannot, because of the repetition, listen.

But the administrative desirability of notice as a substitute for evidence cannot be allowed to outweigh fairness to individual litigants. Unregulated notice, even of legislative facts, gives finders of fact "a dangerous freedom." Notice of facts without warning may deny "the fair hearing essential to due process," and amount to "condemnation without trial." *Ohio Bell Telephone Co. v. Public Utils. Comm'n*, 301 U.S. 292, 300 (1937).[3]

The facts of which the INS took notice in this case were in part legislative in nature. They included: (1) that Violeta Chamorro had been elected

---

"everybody who knows what gin is, knows not only that it is a liquor, but also that it is intoxicating. . . . No jury can be supposed to be so ignorant as not to know what gin is." *Id.* at 297 n. 1 (quoting *Com. v. Peckham*, 2 Gray 514).

[2] Gellhorn speaks of the facts learned from repetitive litigation, as when an Officer of the Bureau of Marine Inspection and Navigation knows that pier 45 in San Francisco points toward Alcatraz Island, a ship will make a broad sweep to the left to pass under the bridge, and the current is south-westerly at a certain time. If a witness testifies to the contrary, the *officer* knows the testimony is false.

[3] Thayer's formulation cannot be improved upon, "[t]he function is, indeed, a delicate one; if [the doctrine of judicial notice] is too loosely or ignorantly exercised it may annul the principles of evidence and even of substantive law. But the failure to exercise it tends daily to smother trials with technicality, and monstrously lengthens them out." Thayer, *supra*, at 309 (footnote omitted).

president, (2) that her non-Sandinista coalition had gained a majority in parliament, and (3) that the Sandinistas were ousted from power. The facts were also in part adjudicative, that the Castillo-Villagra family had nothing more to fear from the Sandinistas. The first two facts are plainly legislative and not debatable. It would be a waste of time to allow evidence regarding them. The third legislative fact, that the Sandinistas were ousted from power, was debatable, since the Sandinistas retained power over the police and the military. The adjudicative fact required both a debatable assumption about the amount of power retained by the Sandinistas, and an assumption about the particular salience of the Castillo-Villagra family as an irritant to Sandinistas who may retain enough power in Jinotega or the university to persecute them.

The question of proper scope and manner of administrative notice before the INS is one of first impression in the Circuit. We decided upon a somewhat analogous question in *Banks v. Schweiker*, 654 F.2d 637 (9th Cir.1981), although *Banks* is not controlling in this case because it arose in a social security context in which the APA and social security regulations applied. The reasoning in *Banks*, however, is applicable here, and we see no reason to choose a different path for INS cases.

In *Banks* we held that an adjudicator could properly take notice of how social security office personnel ordinarily dealt with inquiries such as Banks had made, as a basis for rejecting Banks' testimony as not credible. We rejected for administrative proceedings the applicability of the principle in Federal Rule of Evidence 201(b), that adjudicative facts may be noticed only if "not subject to reasonable dispute," and rejected in the administrative context the tradition of caution associated with taking notice under that rule. Instead, we adopted "a rule of convenience," that "the ALJ should take notice of adjudicative facts, whenever, 'the ALJ at the hearing knows of information that will be useful in making the decision.'"

The justifications for a rule of convenience apply equally in the INS context. The agency has a large volume of cases. Its officers work in a specialized area with many similar cases, so they grow familiar with conditions abroad from many witnesses and exhibits. The burden of producing evidence may be especially great when it involves changing political conditions in a foreign country. The repetitiveness of such evidence, as large numbers of petitioners from particular countries pass through the system, may interfere with its heuristic power. It is significant for the scope of notice that the asylum seeker has the burden of proof. Where the asylum seeker is given the opportunity to offer evidence rebutting the proposition of which notice is taken, notice does not substitute for evidence which the agency would otherwise have to produce. Instead, it directs the asylum seeker's presentation to the propositions likely to have a practical effect on the outcome.

The problem arises, in this case as in *Banks*, when the petitioner is denied a fair opportunity to rebut the proposition of which notice is taken. An essential concomitant of a rule of convenience is a fair opportunity to respond. "When the rule of convenience is applied to allow wide latitude, however, it is essential that the parties be afforded an opportunity to present information 'which might bear upon the propriety of noticing the fact, or upon the truth

§ 3.05   ADJUDICATION & THE ADMINISTRATIVE PROCEDURE ACT   267

of the matter to be noticed.'" *Banks* at 641. In *Banks*, and in this case, the petitioners were not given a fair opportunity to be heard. They might have been able to show either that the conditions affecting them in Nicaragua were too complex, unsettled and particularized for notice to be appropriate, or that their political enemies retained sufficient power in the country, Jinotega or the university to give rise to a "well-founded fear."

There are three separable issues with regard to notice: (1) whether notice may be taken at all, (2) whether warning must be given before notice is taken, and (3) whether rebuttal evidence must be allowed against the proposition of which notice is taken. The distinctions between legislative and adjudicative facts, and between facts generally known and those known only to some, used in Federal Rule of Evidence 201, are but factors to be weighed in the administrative context.

Because of the multidimensional nature of administrative notice decisions, the only practical solution is to give the agency discretion, subject to review for abuse of discretion, not only for whether to take notice, but also for whether to allow rebuttal evidence and even for whether the parties must be notified that notice will be taken. The Fifth Circuit has determined that INS taking of administrative notice is reviewed for abuse of discretion, . . . and so do we. It is not necessary to warn that administrative notice will be taken of the fact that water runs downhill. Some propositions, however, may require that notice not be taken, or that warning be given, or that rebuttal evidence be allowed. The agency's discretion must be exercised in such a way as to be fair in the circumstances.[5]

The agency would not have to accord any opportunity to the applicants to offer evidence to rebut the propositions that Chamorro won the election and that UNO won a majority in parliament, since those facts are legislative, indisputable, and general. The agency should have warned that it would consider these facts even though they were not in existence at the time of the hearing and appellate briefs, so that the parties could have moved for leave to supplement their briefs, supplement the evidence, withdraw their applications for asylum, or seek other relief. The agency should also have warned, prior to final decision, that it intended to take notice that the Sandinistas were out of power, and that any well-founded fear of persecution the applicants might have had before the election could no longer be well-founded, and then given the parties an opportunity to show cause why notice should not be taken of these propositions. Depending on the showing made, fairness might or might not have required that the parties be allowed to present evidence on these propositions.

---

[5] In evaluating whether discretion was abused a court may find a useful a number of factors formulated by Professor Davis. These include whether the facts at issue are: (1) narrow and specific or broad and general; (2) central or peripheral; (3) readily accepted or controversial; (4) purely factual or mixed with judgment, policy or political preference; (5) readily provable or provable only with difficulty or not at all; or, (6) facts about the parties or facts or unrelated to them. Kenneth Culp Davis, *Facts in Lawmaking*, 80 COLUM. L. REV. 931, 932 (1980) (also see Davis, *Judicial Notice*, 55 COLUM. L. REV. at 977). These factors, as well as any others as may be appropriate, provide useful guidance to a court conducting an inquiry regarding an agency's abuse of discretion.

It may be that, were the petitioners given an opportunity to respond to the INS view of the effect of the change in government, they could make no case for a well-founded fear. Maria's application asks for "the opportunity to stay in this country until the situation changes in our own." Aliens from different parts of the country or with different histories might have different and particularized situations, with respect to fear of persecution in post-election Nicaragua. But the agency should not have assumed away petitioners' case.

. . . .

We recognize that other circuits have resolved this question somewhat differently. *Kaczmarczyk v. INS*, 933 F.2d 588 (7th Cir. 1991), holds that, for a Polish Solidarity worker, the INS could properly take notice that Solidarity had joined the ruling coalition so its supporters were no longer being persecuted. The court took notice that, by the time the appeal was decided, the Communist Party had been excluded from the government. This is consistent with our decision, that the INS could properly take notice that the Sandinistas had lost the presidency and their parliamentary majority. The Seventh Circuit reaches the same conclusion, that due process requires that the applicant be allowed an opportunity to rebut, that we do:

We believe the due process clause of the fifth amendment requires that petitioners be allowed an opportunity to rebut officially noticed facts, particularly when, as in this case, those facts are crucial to — indeed dispositive of — the outcome of the administrative proceeding.

. . . .

We note, finally, that *not* to allow petitioners an opportunity to rebut noticed facts would sanction the creation of an unregulated back door through which unrebuttable, non-record evidence could be introduced against asylum petitioners outside of the statutorily-mandated hearing context.

. . . .

In the case at bar, the applicants had a plausible claim that they might still have a well-founded fear of persecution despite the Chamorro election. The record they developed before the election allowed for the conclusion that Nicaragua had been dominated by the Sandinista party, and that Sandinista power flowed from the party, not just from the government. It may be that the party's permeation of society enables it to persecute opponents, even with the presidency and some departments of government in other hands. Perhaps the Nicaraguan government is not so strong and hierarchical as to render impotent any political movement which does not control the presidency. In some forms of political organization, a party may be more powerful than the formal government:

> What strikes the observer of the totalitarian state is certainly not its monolithic structure. On the contrary, all serious students of the subject agree at least on the co-existence (or the conflict) of a dual authority, the party and the state. . . . It has also been frequently observed that the relationship between the two sources of authority, between state and party, is one of ostensible and real authority, so that the government machine is usually pictured as the powerless facade which hides and protects the real power of the party.

Hannah Arendt, *The Origins of Totalitarianism* 395 (1958).

We take notice, for the limited purpose of determining whether the petitioners' claim is sufficiently plausible so that they should be allowed to present evidence, of the State Department country report on Nicaragua for 1990. This report says that the military and police remained under Sandinista control in 1990 despite the election, including the renamed General Directorate of State Security "which was responsible for numerous and significant human rights violations." The report notes continuing "politically motivated killings, some involving members of the security forces, police abuse of detainees," violence and killings by Sandinista supporters, and other political persecution similar to what Maria testified about before the election. For example, "[t]hroughout the year, Sandinista mobs (turbas), sometimes joined by the police or army, frequently used forced entry into private homes as a means to intimidate their political opponents. Prominent UNO supporters typically were singled out for these attacks, in which the turbas smashed windows, damaged automobiles and other property, and shouted death threats."

Of course we suggest no determination as to whether Nicaragua was the kind of regime Hannah Arendt describes above, before or after the election. The point is, the propositions that the Sandinistas retain sufficient power to persecute petitioners, and that the petitioners have a well-founded fear of such persecution should they return to the town of Jinotega or the university in Managua, were seriously debatable, despite the election. Petitioners were never allowed to be heard on these propositions. Is their fear that they will be "disappeared" well-founded, despite the Chamorro election? Will the Sandinistas, because of their control of the police and military, still be in a position to carry out their threat of 20 years imprisonment if the sisters are caught demonstrating against them again? Will their house be stoned by party-orchestrated gangs because of their political opinions? Maybe petitioners' alleged fear of Sandinista persecution was ended by the election. Or maybe one swallow does not make a summer. Aristotle, *Nicomachean Ethics*, book 1, chapter 7. Neither we nor, without opportunity for a hearing, the BIA, can properly say whether applicants have a well-founded fear of persecution by the Sandinistas if they return to Nicaragua.

. . . .

We vacate the orders of deportation and remand for proceedings at which the asylum applicants may be heard on the appropriateness of notice and introduce evidence regarding the facts of which notice is taken.

REVERSED AND REMANDED.

NOTES AND QUESTIONS

3-28. What is the doctrine of official notice? When can an agency take official notice of certain facts? What can an agency officially notice? What must an agency do to take official notice and still be fair to the parties involved?

3-29. What do you expect to happen on remand of this case? What case can the claimant make?

3-30. Why does the Court conclude that the doctrine of official notice is broader for an agency than for a court? *See* Gellhorn, *Rules of Evidence and Official Notice in Formal Administrative Hearings,* 1971 DUKE L.J. 1.

3-31. How does official notice of evidence differ from the evaluation of evidence?

[C] Burden of Proof

DIRECTOR, OFFICE OF WORKERS' COMPENSATION PROGRAMS, DEPARTMENT OF LABOR v. GREENWICH COLLIERIES.

United States Supreme Court
512 U.S. 267 (1994)

JUSTICE O'CONNOR delivered the opinion of the Court.

In adjudicating benefits claims under the Black Lung Benefits Act (BLBA), 83 Stat. 792, as amended, 30 U.S.C. § 901 *et seq.* (1988 ed. and Supp. IV), and the Longshore and Harbor Workers' Compensation Act (LHWCA), 44 Stat. 1424, as amended, 33 U.S.C. § 901 *et seq.*, the Department of Labor applies what it calls the "true doubt" rule. This rule essentially shifts the burden of persuasion to the party opposing the benefits claim — when the evidence is evenly balanced, the benefits claimant wins. This litigation presents the question whether the rule is consistent with § 7(c) of the Administrative Procedure Act (APA), which states that "[e]xcept as otherwise provided by statute, the proponent of a rule or order has the burden of proof." 5 U.S.C. § 556(d).

I

We review two separate decisions of the Court of Appeals for the Third Circuit. In one, Andrew Ondecko applied for disability benefits under the BLBA after working as a coal miner for 31 years. The Administrative Law Judge (ALJ) determined that Ondecko had pneumoconiosis (or black lung disease), that he was totally disabled by the disease, and that the disease resulted from coal mine employment. In resolving the first two issues, the ALJ relied on the true doubt rule. In resolving the third, she relied on the rebuttable presumption that a miner with pneumoconiosis who worked in the mines for at least 10 years developed the disease because of his employment. The Department's Benefits Review Board affirmed, concluding that the (ALJ) had considered all the evidence, had found each side's evidence to be equally probative, and had properly resolved the dispute in Ondecko's favor under the true doubt rule. The Court of Appeals vacated the Board's decision, holding that the true doubt rule is inconsistent with the Department's own regulations under the BLBA, § 718.403, as well as with *Mullins Coal Co. of Va. v. Director, Office of Workers' Compensation Programs,* 484 U.S. 135 (1987).

In the other case, Michael Santoro suffered a work-related back and neck injury while employed by respondent Maher Terminals. Within a few months Santoro was diagnosed with nerve cancer, and he died shortly thereafter. His widow filed a claim under the LHWCA alleging that the work injury had rendered her husband disabled and caused his death. After reviewing the evidence for both sides, the ALJ found it equally probative and, relying on the true doubt rule, awarded benefits to the claimant. The Board affirmed, finding no error in the ALJ's analysis or his application of the true doubt rule. The Court of Appeals reversed, holding that the true doubt rule is inconsistent with § 7(c) of the APA. In so holding, the court expressly disagreed with *Freeman United Coal Mining Co. v. Office of Workers' Compensation Programs*, 988 F.2d 706 (CA7 1993). We granted certiorari to resolve the conflict.

II

[The Court held that § 7(c) of the APA, 5 U.S.C. § 556(d), applies to adjudications under the LHWCA and the BLBA.]

III

We turn now to the meaning of "burden of proof" as used in § 7(c). Respondents contend that the Court of Appeals was correct in reading "burden of proof" to include the burden of *persuasion*. The Department disagrees, contending that "burden of proof" imposes only the burden of *production* (i.e., the burden of going forward with evidence). The cases turn on this dispute, for if respondents are correct, the true doubt rule must fall: because the true doubt rule places the burden of persuasion on the party opposing the benefits award, it would violate § 7(c)'s requirement that the burden of persuasion rest with the party seeking the award.

A

Because the term "burden of proof" is nowhere defined in the APA, our task is to construe it in accord with its ordinary or natural meaning. It is easier to state this task than to accomplish it, for the meaning of words may change over time, and many words have several meanings even at a fixed point in time. Here we must seek to ascertain the ordinary meaning of "burden of proof" in 1946, the year the APA was enacted.

For many years the term "burden of proof" was ambiguous because the term was used to describe two distinct concepts. Burden of proof was frequently used to refer to what we now call the burden of persuasion — the notion that if the evidence is evenly balanced, the party that bears the burden of persuasion must lose. But it was also used to refer to what we now call the burden of production — a party's obligation to come forward with evidence to support its claim. *See* J. Thayer, *Evidence at the Common Law* 355-384 (1898) (detailing various uses of the term "burden of proof" among 19th-century English and American courts).

The Supreme Judicial Court of Massachusetts was the leading proponent of the view that burden of proof should be limited to burden of persuasion.

In what became an oft-cited case, Chief Justice Lemuel Shaw attempted to distinguish the burden of proof from the burden of producing evidence. *Powers v. Russell*, 30 Mass. 69 (1833). According to the Massachusetts court, "the party whose case requires the proof of [a] fact, has all along the burden of proof." . . . Though the burden of proving the fact remains where it started, once the party with this burden establishes a prima facie case, the burden to "produce evidence" shifts. The only time the burden of proof — as opposed to the burden to produce evidence — might shift is in the case of affirmative defenses. In the century after *Powers*, the Supreme Judicial Court of Massachusetts continued to carefully distinguish between the burden of proof and the burden of production.

Despite the efforts of the Massachusetts court, the dual use of the term continued throughout the late 19th and early 20th centuries. *See* 4 J. Wigmore, *Evidence* §§ 2486-2487, pp. 3524-3529 (1905). . . . The ambiguity confounded the treatise writers, who despaired over the "lamentable ambiguity of phrase and confusion of terminology under which our law has so long suffered." Wigmore, *supra*, at 3521-3522. The writers praised the "clear-thinking" efforts of courts like the Supreme Judicial Court of Massachusetts, and agreed that the legal profession should endeavor to clarify one of its most basic terms. . . .

This Court tried to eliminate the ambiguity in the term "burden of proof" when it adopted the Massachusetts approach. *Hill v. Smith*, 260 U.S. 592 (1923). Justice Holmes wrote for a unanimous Court that "it will not be necessary to repeat the distinction, familiar in Massachusetts since the time of Chief Justice Shaw, and elaborated in the opinion below, between the burden of proof and the necessity of producing evidence to meet that already produced. The distinction is now very generally accepted, although often blurred by careless speech." *Id*.

In the two decades after *Hill*, our opinions consistently distinguished between burden of proof, which we defined as burden of persuasion, and an alternative concept, which we increasingly referred to as the burden of production or the burden of going forward with the evidence. During this period the Courts of Appeals also limited the meaning of burden of proof to burden of persuasion, and explicitly distinguished this concept from the burden of production.

The emerging consensus on a definition of burden of proof was reflected in the evidence treatises of the 1930's and 1940's. "The burden of proof is the obligation which rests on one of the parties to an action to persuade the trier of the facts, generally the jury, of the truth of a proposition which he has affirmatively asserted by the pleadings." W. Richardson, *Evidence* 143 (6th ed. 1944); *see also* 1 B. Jones, *Law of Evidence in Civil Cases* 310 (4th ed. 1938) ("The modern authorities are substantially agreed that, in its strict primary sense, 'burden of proof' signifies the duty or obligation of establishing, in the mind of the trier of facts, conviction on the ultimate issue"). . . .

We interpret Congress' use of the term "burden of proof" in light of this history, and presume Congress intended the phrase to have the meaning generally accepted in the legal community at the time of enactment. These principles lead us to conclude that the drafters of the APA used the term

§ 3.05   ADJUDICATION & THE ADMINISTRATIVE PROCEDURE ACT   273

"burden of proof" to mean the burden of persuasion. As we have explained, though the term had once been ambiguous, that ambiguity had largely been eliminated by the early 20th century. After *Hill*, courts and commentators almost unanimously agreed that the definition was settled. And Congress indicated that it shared this settled understanding, when in the Communications Act of 1934 it explicitly distinguished between the burden of proof and the burden of production. Accordingly, we conclude that as of 1946 the ordinary meaning of burden of proof was burden of persuasion, and we understand the APA's unadorned reference to "burden of proof" to refer to the burden of persuasion.

B

We recognize that we have previously asserted the contrary conclusion as to the meaning of burden of proof in § 7(c) of the APA. In *NLRB v. Transportation Management Corp.*, 462 U.S. 393 (1983), we reviewed the National Labor Relations Board's (NLRB's) conclusion that the employer had discharged the employee because of the employee's protected union activity. In such cases the NLRB employed a burden shifting formula typical in dual motive cases: The employee had the burden of persuading the NLRB that antiunion animus contributed to the employer's firing decision; the burden then shifted to the employer to establish as an affirmative defense that it would have fired the employee for permissible reasons even if the employee had not been involved in union activity. . . . The employer claimed that the NLRB's burden shifting formula was inconsistent with the National Labor Relations Act (NLRA), but we upheld it as a reasonable construction of the NLRA.

The employer in *Transportation Management* argued that the NLRB's approach violated § 7(c)'s burden of proof provision, which the employer read as imposing the burden of persuasion on the employee. In a footnote, we summarily rejected this argument, concluding that "[§ 7(c)] . . . determines only the burden of going forward, not the burden of persuasion. . . ." 462 U.S., at 404, n. 7. In light of our discussion in Part II-A above, we do not think our cursory conclusion in the *Transportation Management* footnote withstands scrutiny. The central issue in *Transportation Management* was whether the NLRB's burden shifting approach was consistent with the NLRA. The parties and the amici in *Transportation Management* treated the APA argument as an afterthought, devoting only one or two sentences to the question. None of the briefs in the case attempted to explain the ordinary meaning of the term. *Transportation Management*'s cursory answer to an ancillary and largely unbriefed question does not warrant the same level of deference we typically give our precedents.

Moreover, *Transportation Management* reached its conclusion without referring to *Steadman v. SEC*, 450 U.S. 91 (1981), our principal decision interpreting the meaning of § 7(c). In *Steadman* we considered what *standard* of proof § 7(c) required, and we held that the proponent of a rule or order under § 7(c) had to meet its burden by a preponderance of the evidence, not by clear and convincing evidence. Though we did not explicitly state that § 7(c) imposes the burden of persuasion on the party seeking the rule or order, our reasoning strongly implied that this must be so. We assumed that burden of proof meant burden of persuasion when we said that we had to decide "the degree of proof which must be adduced by the proponent of a rule or order *to carry its burden of persuasion* in an administrative proceeding." *Id.*, at 95. More important, our holding that the party with the burden of proof must prove its case by a preponderance only makes sense if the burden of proof means the burden of persuasion. A standard of proof, such as preponderance of the evidence, can apply only to a burden of persuasion, not to a burden of production.

We do not slight the importance of adhering to precedent, particularly in a case involving statutory interpretation. But here our precedents are in tension, and we think our approach in *Steadman* makes more sense than does the *Transportation Management* footnote. And although we reject *Transportation Management*'s reading of § 7(c), the holding in that case remains intact. The NLRB's approach in *Transportation Management* is consistent with § 7(c) because the NLRB first required the employee to persuade it that antiunion sentiment contributed to the employer's decision. Only then did the NLRB place the burden of persuasion on the employer as to its affirmative defense.

C (Legislative history)

In addition to the *Transportation Management* footnote, the Department relies on the Senate and House Judiciary Committee Reports on the APA to support its claim that burden of proof means only burden of production. We find this legislative history unavailing. The Senate Judiciary Committee Report on the APA states as follows:

> "That the proponent of a rule or order has the burden of proof means not only that the party initiating the proceeding has the general burden of coming forward with a prima facie case but that other parties, who are proponents of some different result, also for that purpose have a burden to maintain. Similarly the requirement that no sanction be imposed or rule or order be issued except upon evidence of the kind specified means that the proponents of a denial of relief must sustain such denial by that kind of evidence. For example, credible and credited evidence submitted by the applicant for a license may not be ignored except upon the requisite kind and quality of contrary evidence. No agency is authorized to stand mute and arbitrarily disbelieve credible evidence. Except as applicants for a license or other privilege may be required to come forward with a prima facie showing, no agency is entitled to presume that the conduct of any person or status of any enterprise is unlawful or improper." S. Rep. No. 752, 79th Cong., 1st Sess., 22 (1945).

The House Judiciary Committee Report contains identical language, along with the following:

> "In other words, this section means that every proponent of a rule or order or the denial thereof has the burden of coming forward with sufficient evidence therefor; and in determining applications for licenses or other relief any fact, conduct, or status so shown by credible and credited evidence must be accepted as true except as the contrary has been shown or such evidence has been rebutted or impeached by duly credited evidence or by facts

officially noticed and stated." H.R. Rep. No. 1980, 79th Cong., 2d Sess., 36 (1946), U.S. Code Cong. Serv. 1946, 1195.

The Department argues that this legislative history indicates congressional intent to impose a burden of production on the proponent. But even if that is so, it does not mean that § 7(c) is concerned *only* with imposing a burden of production. That Congress intended to impose a burden of production does not mean that Congress did not also intend to impose a burden of persuasion.

Moreover, these passages are subject to a natural interpretation compatible with congressional intent to impose a burden of persuasion on the party seeking an order. The primary purpose of these passages is not to define or allocate the burden of proof. The quoted passages are primarily concerned with the burden placed on the *opponent* in administrative hearings ("other parties . . . have a burden to maintain"), particularly where the opponent is the Government. The Committee appeared concerned with those cases in which the "proponent" seeks a license or other privilege from the Government, and in such cases did not want to allow the agency "to stand mute and arbitrarily disbelieve credible evidence." The Reports make clear that once the licensee establishes a prima facie case, the burden shifts to the Government to rebut it. This is perfectly compatible with a rule placing the burden of persuasion on the applicant, because when the party with the burden of persuasion establishes a prima facie case supported by "credible and credited evidence," it must either be rebutted or accepted as true.

The legislative history the Department relies on is imprecise and only marginally relevant. Congress chose to use the term "burden of proof" in the text of the statute, and given the substantial evidence that the ordinary meaning of burden of proof was burden of persuasion, this legislative history cannot carry the day.

D

In part due to Congress' recognition that claims such as those involved here would be difficult to prove, claimants in adjudications under these statutes benefit from certain statutory presumptions easing their burden. . . . Similarly, the Department's solicitude for benefits claimants is reflected in the regulations adopting additional presumptions. *See* 20 CFR §§ 718.301-718.306 (1993). But with the true doubt rule the Department attempts to go one step further. In so doing, it runs afoul of the APA, a statute designed "to introduce greater uniformity of procedure and standardization of administrative practice among the diverse agencies whose customs had departed widely from each other." *Wong Yang Sung v. McGrath*, 339 U.S. 33, 41 (1950). That concern is directly implicated here, for under the Department's reading each agency would be free to decide who shall bear the burden of persuasion. Accordingly, the Department cannot allocate the burden of persuasion in a manner that conflicts with the APA.

IV

Under the Department's true doubt rule, when the evidence is evenly balanced the claimant wins. Under § 7(c), however, when the evidence is evenly balanced, the benefits claimant must lose. Accordingly, we hold that the true doubt rule violates § 7(c) of the APA.

. . . .

Affirmed.

JUSTICE SOUTER, with whom JUSTICE BLACKMUN and JUSTICE STEVENS join, dissenting.

. . . .

The majority's holding that "burden of proof" in the first sentence of this provision means "burden of persuasion" surely carries the force of the preferred meaning of the term in today's general usage, as the Court's opinion demonstrates. But we are concerned here not with the commonly preferred meaning of the term today, but with its meaning as understood and intended by Congress in enacting § 7(c) of the APA in 1946. That is not a matter about which preference has been constant, or Congress silent, or even a subject of first impression for this Court.

. . . .

Although the Court works hard to show that the phrase had acquired a settled meaning in the alternative sense by the time the APA was passed in 1946, there is good evidence that the courts were still using the term either way . . . [and] commentators did not think the ambiguity of the phrase had disappeared before passage of the APA, and, at the time, some even thought it unsettled whether burden of persuasion or of going forward with the evidence was the primary meaning of the phrase. . . .

Although standard usage had not made a choice of meanings by 1946, Congress did make one, and the meaning it chose for the phrase as used in § 7(c) was "burden of production." . . . Because Congress stated that "burden of proof means" a "burden of coming forward," and further explained that the burden could be shouldered by both proponents and opponents of a rule or order, the strong probability is that Congress meant to use "burden of proof" to mean burden of coming forward and not burden of persuasion, for a burden of persuasion cannot simultaneously rest on both parties. The commentators agree. "The legislative history suggests that the term 'burden of proof' was intended to denote the 'burden of going forward.'" 1 C. Koch, *Administrative Law and Practice* § 6.42, p. 486 (1985). . . .

NOTES AND QUESTIONS

3-32. What were the issues confronting the Court in *Greenwich Collieries*? How does the court distinguish among the burden of proof, the burden of persuasion, and the burden of production? Why does it conclude that the true doubt rule violated the APA?

3-33. How would you describe the interpretive approach used by the court when interpreting the APA? What impact is it likely to have on the long-term flexibility of the APA? For a criticism of this approach, *see* Peter Strauss, *Changing Times: The APA at Fifty*, 63 U. CHI. L. REV. 1389, 1392-93 (1996). *But see*, Stephen F. Williams, *The Era of "Risk-Risk" and the Problem of Keeping the APA Up to Date*, 63 U. CHI. L. REV. 1375, 1385-87 (1996).

3-34. How significant to the outcome of an administrative proceeding is determining who has the burden of proof? How hard or easy, for example, is it to prove that a particular product either is safe or unsafe or that a certain action is either environmentally harmful or not?

3-35. Formal adjudication pursuant to sections 554, 556 and 557 also requires findings of fact and reasons. Specifically, section 557(c)(A) provides that "all decisions, including initial, recommended, and tentative decisions . . . shall include a statement of findings and conclusions, and the reasons or basis therefor, on all the material issues of fact, law or discretion presented on the record. . . ." What is the purpose of providing findings and reasons in an administrative case? What does it mean to say that this enhances the fairness of the proceeding? Why does that necessarily follow?

§ 3.06 The Administrative Structure of Formal Adjudication — Combination of Functions and the Constitution

Thus far we have examined the hearing processes that come into play when the APA's formal adjudicatory provisions are involved. These pre-hearing and hearing processes take place within an administrative structure also established by the APA and, to some extent, the Constitution as well. Just as there are some differences in the hearing processes that occur within an agency as compared to a court, there also are some major structural differences with which the APA must deal. These flow from the fact that agency adjudication often occurs within agencies that combine rulemaking, enforcement and adjudicatory functions. This gives rise to problems of independence and bias that are particularly apparent in the administrative process. We shall now examine some of the legal — statutory and constitutional — issues that arise. We begin with the Constitution.

WITHROW v. LARKIN

United States Supreme Court
421 U.S. 35 (1975)

MR. JUSTICE WHITE delivered the opinion of the Court.

The statutes of the State of Wisconsin forbid the practice of medicine without a license from an Examining Board composed of practicing physicians. The statutes also define and forbid various acts of professional misconduct, proscribe fee splitting, and make illegal the practice of medicine under any name other than the name under which a license has issued if the public would be misled, such practice would constitute unfair competition with another physician, or other detriment to the profession would result. To enforce these provisions, the Examining Board is empowered under Wis. Stat. Ann.

§§ 448.17 and 448.18 (1974) to warn and reprimand, temporarily to suspend the license, and "to institute criminal action or action to revoke license when it finds probable cause therefor under criminal or revocation statute. . . ." When an investigative proceeding before the Examining Board was commenced against him, appellee brought this suit against appellants, the individual members of the Board, seeking an injunction against the enforcement of the statutes. The District Court issued a preliminary injunction, the appellants appealed, and we noted probable jurisdiction . . . .

I

Appellee, a resident of Michigan and licensed to practice medicine there, obtained a Wisconsin license in August 1971 under a reciprocity agreement between Michigan and Wisconsin governing medical licensing. His practice in Wisconsin consisted of performing abortions at an office in Milwaukee. On June 20, 1973, the Board sent to appellee a notice that it would hold an investigative hearing on July 12, 1973, under Wis. Stat. Ann. § 448.17 to determine whether he had engaged in certain proscribed acts. The hearing would be closed to the public, although appellee and his attorney could attend. They would not, however, be permitted to cross-examine witnesses. Based upon the evidence presented at the hearing, the Board would decide "whether to warn or reprimand if it finds such practice and whether to institute criminal action or action to revoke license if probable cause therefor exists under criminal or revocation statutes." . . .

On September 18, 1973, the Board sent to appellee a notice that a "contested hearing" would be held on October 4, 1973, to determine whether appellee had engaged in certain prohibited acts and that based upon the evidence adduced at the hearing the Board would determine whether his license would be suspended temporarily under Wis. Stat. § 448.18(7). Appellee moved for a restraining order against the contested hearing. The District Court granted the motion on October 1, 1973. . . .

The Board complied and did not go forward with the contested hearing. Instead, it noticed and held a final investigative session on October 4, 1973, at which appellee's attorney, but not appellee, appeared. The Board thereupon issued "Findings of Fact," "Conclusions of Law," and a "Decision" in which the Board found that appellee had engaged in specified conduct proscribed by the statute. The operative portion of its "Decision" was the following:

"Within the meaning of sec. 448.17, Stats., it is hereby determined that there is probable cause to believe that licensee has violated the criminal provisions of ch. 448, Stats., and that there is probable cause for an action to revoke the license of the licensee for engaging in professional conduct.

"Therefore, it is the decision of this Board that the Secretary verify this document and file it as a verified complaint with the District Attorney of Milwaukee County in accordance with sec. 448.18(2), Stats., for the purpose of initiating an action to revoke the license of Duane R. Larkin, M.D., to practice medicine and surgery in the State of Wisconsin and initiating appropriate actions for violation of the criminal laws relating to the practice of medicine." . . .

On November 19, 1973, the three-judge District Court found (with an opinion following on December 21, 1973) that § 448.18(7) was unconstitutional as a violation of due process guarantees and enjoined the Board from enforcing it. . . .

III

The District Court framed the constitutional issue, which it addressed as being whether "for the board temporarily to suspend Dr. Larkin's license at its own contested hearing on charges evolving from its own investigation would constitute a denial to him of his rights to procedural due process."[13]

. . .

Concededly, a "fair trial in a fair tribunal is a basic requirement of due process.". . . This applies to administrative agencies which adjudicate as well as to courts. . . . Not only is a biased decisionmaker constitutionally unacceptable but "our system of law has always endeavored to prevent even the probability of unfairness.". . . In pursuit of this end, various situations have been identified in which experience teaches that the probability of actual bias on the part of the judge or decisionmaker is too high to be constitutionally tolerable. Among these cases are those in which the adjudicator has a pecuniary interest in the outcome and in which he has been the target of personal abuse or criticism from the party before him.

The contention that the combination of investigative and adjudicative functions necessarily creates an unconstitutional risk of bias in administrative adjudication has a much more difficult burden of persuasion to carry. It must overcome a presumption of honesty and integrity in those serving as adjudicators; and it must convince that, under a realistic appraisal of psychological tendencies and human weakness, conferring investigative and adjudicative powers on the same individuals poses such a risk of actual bias or prejudgment that the practice must be forbidden if the guarantee of due process is to be adequately implemented.

Very similar claims have been squarely rejected in prior decisions of this Court. In *FTC v. Cement Institute*, 333 U.S. 683 (1948), the Federal Trade Commission had instituted proceedings concerning the respondents' multiple basing-point delivered-price system. It was demanded that the Commission members disqualify themselves because long before the Commission had filed its complaint it had investigated the parties and reported to Congress and to the President, and its members had testified before congressional committees concerning the legality of such a pricing system. At least some of the members had disclosed their opinion that the system was illegal. The issue of bias was brought here and confronted "on the assumption that such an opinion had been formed by the entire membership of the Commission as a result of its prior official investigations." . . . The court rejected the claim saying:

---

[13] After the District Court made its decision, the Board altered its procedures. It now assigns each new case to one of the members for investigation, and the remainder of the Board has no contact with the investigative process. . . . That change, designed to accommodate the Board's procedures to the District Court's decision does not affect this case.

[T]he fact that the Commission had entertained such views as the result of its prior *ex parte* investigations did not necessarily mean that the minds of its members were irrevocably closed on the subject of the respondents' basing point practices. Here, in contrast to the Commission's investigations, members of the cement industry were legally authorized participants in the hearings. They produced evidence — volumes of it. They were free to point out to the Commission by testimony, by cross-examination of witnesses, and by arguments, conditions of the trade practices under attack which they thought kept these practices within the range of legally permissible business activities. . . .

In specific response to a due process argument, the court asserted:

No decision of this Court would require us to hold that it would be a violation of procedural due process for a judge to sit in a case after he had expressed an opinion as to whether certain types of conduct were prohibited by law. In fact, judges frequently try the same case more than once and decide identical issues each time, although these issues involve questions both of law and fact. Certainly, the Federal Trade Commission cannot possibly be under stronger constitutional compulsions in this respect than a court. . . .

More recently we have sustained against due process objection a system in which a Social Security examiner has responsibility for developing the facts and making a decision as to disability claims, and observed that the challenge to this combination of functions "assumes too much and would bring down too many procedures designed, and working well, for a governmental structure of great and growing complexity." *Richardson v. Perales,* 402 U.S. 389, 410 (1971).

That is not to say that there is nothing to the argument that those who have investigated should not then adjudicate. The issue is substantial, it is not new, and legislators and others concerned with the operations of administrative agencies have given much attention to whether and to what extent distinctive administrative functions should be performed by the same persons. No single answer has been reached. Indeed, the growth, variety, and complexity of the administrative processes have made any one solution highly unlikely. Within the Federal Government itself, Congress has addressed the issue in several different ways, providing for varying degrees of separation from complete separation of functions to virtually none at all. For the generality of agencies, Congress has been content with § 5 of the Administrative Procedure Act, 5 U.S.C. § 554(d), which provides that no employee engaged in investigating or prosecuting may also participate or advise in the adjudicating function, but which also expressly exempts from this prohibition "the agency or a member or members of the body comprising the agency."

It is not surprising, therefore, to find that "[t]he case law, both federal and state, generally rejects the idea that the combination [of] judging [and] investigating functions is a denial of due process. . . ." 2 K. Davis, *Administrative Law Treatise* § 13.02, p. 175 (1958). Similarly, our cases, although they reflect the substance of the problem, offer no support for the bald proposition applied in this case by the District Court that agency members who participate in an investigation are disqualified from adjudicating. The incredible variety of administrative mechanisms in this country will not yield to any single organizing principle.

Appellee relies heavily on *In re Murchison, supra*, in which a state judge, empowered under state law to sit as a "one-man grand jury" and to compel witnesses to testify before him in secret about possible crimes, charged two such witnesses with criminal contempt, one for perjury and the other for refusing to answer certain questions, and then himself tried and convicted them. This Court found the procedure to be a denial of due process of law not only because the judge in effect became part of the prosecution and assumed an adversary position, but also because as a judge, passing on guilt or innocence, he very likely relied on "his own personal knowledge and impression of what had occurred in the grand jury room," an impression that "could not be tested by adequate cross-examination." . . .

Plainly enough, *Murchison* has not been understood to stand for the broad rule that the members of an administrative agency may not investigate the facts, institute proceedings, and then make the necessary adjudications. The court did not purport to question the *Cement Institute* case, *supra,* or the Administrative Procedure Act and did not lay down any general principle that a judge before whom an alleged contempt is committed may not bring and preside over the ensuing contempt proceedings. The accepted rule is to the contrary. . . .

Nor is there anything in this case that comes within the strictures of *Murchison*.[20] When the Board instituted its investigative procedures, it stated only that it would investigate whether proscribed conduct had occurred. Later in noticing the adversary hearing, it asserted only that it would determine if violations had been committed which would warrant suspension of appellee's license. Without doubt, the Board then anticipated that the proceeding would eventuate in an adjudication of the issue; but there was no more evidence of bias or the risk of bias or prejudgment than inhered in the very fact that the Board had investigated and would now adjudicate. Of course, we should be alert to the possibilities of bias that may lurk in the way particular procedures actually work in practice. The processes utilized by the Board, however, do not in themselves contain an unacceptable risk of bias. The investigative proceeding had been closed to the public, but appellee and his counsel were permitted to be present throughout; counsel actually attended the hearings and knew the facts presented to the Board. No specific foundation has been presented for suspecting that the Board had been prejudiced by its investigation or would be disabled from hearing and deciding on the basis of the evidence to be presented at the contested hearing. The mere exposure to evidence presented in nonadversary investigative procedures is insufficient in itself to impugn the fairness of the board members at a later adversary hearing. Without a showing to the contrary, state administrators "are assumed to be men

---

[20] It is asserted by appellants, . . . and not denied by appellee that an agency employee performed the actual investigation and gathering of evidence in this case and that an assistant attorney general then presented the evidence to the Board at the investigative hearings. While not essential to our decision upholding the constitutionality of the Board's sequence of functions, these facts, if true, show that the Board had organized itself internally to minimize the risks arising from combining investigation and adjudication, including the possibility of Board members relying at later suspension hearings upon evidence not then fully subject to effective confrontation.

of conscience and intellectual discipline, capable of judging a particular controversy fairly on the basis of its own circumstances." *United States v. Morgan,* 313 U.S. 409, 421 (1941).

We are of the view, therefore, that the District Court was in error when it entered the restraining order against the Board's contested hearing and when it granted the preliminary injunction based on the untenable view that it would be unconstitutional for the Board to suspend appellee's license "at its own contested hearing on charges evolving from its own investigation. . . ." The contested hearing should have been permitted to proceed.

IV

Nor do we think the situation substantially different because the Board, when it was prevented from going forward with the contested hearing, proceeded to make and issue formal findings of fact and conclusions of law asserting that there was probable cause to believe that appellee had engaged in various acts prohibited by the Wisconsin statutes. These findings and conclusions were verified and filed with the district attorney for the purpose of initiating revocation and criminal proceedings. Although the District Court did not emphasize this aspect of the case before it, appellee stresses it in attempting to show prejudice and prejudgment. We are not persuaded.

Judges repeatedly issue arrest warrants on the basis that there is probable cause to believe that a crime has been committed and that the person named in the warrant has committed it. Judges also preside at preliminary hearings where they must decide whether the evidence is sufficient to hold a defendant for trial. Neither of these pretrial involvements has been thought to raise any constitutional barrier against the judge's presiding over the criminal trial and, if the trial is without a jury, against making the necessary determination of guilt or innocence. Nor has it been thought that a judge is disqualified from presiding over injunction proceedings because he has initially assessed the facts in issuing or denying a temporary restraining order or a preliminary injunction. It is also very typical for the members of administrative agencies to receive the results of investigations, to approve the filing of charges or formal complaints instituting enforcement proceedings, and then to participate in the ensuing hearings. This mode of procedure does not violate the Administrative Procedure Act, and it does not violate due process of law. We should also remember that it is not contrary to due process to allow judges and administrators who have had their initial decisions reversed on appeal to confront and decide the same questions a second time around. . . .

Here, the Board stayed within the accepted bounds of due process. Having investigated, it issued findings and conclusions asserting the commission of certain acts and ultimately concluding that there was probable cause to believe that appellee had violated the statutes.

The risk of bias or prejudgment in this sequence of functions has not been considered to be intolerably high or to raise a sufficiently great possibility that the adjudicators would be so psychologically wedded to their complaints that they would consciously or unconsciously avoid the appearance of having erred or changed position. Indeed, just as there is no logical inconsistency between a finding of probable cause and an acquittal in a criminal proceeding, there is no incompatibility between the agency filing a complaint based on probable cause and a subsequent decision, when all the evidence is in, that there has been no violation of the statute. Here, if the Board now proceeded after an adversary hearing to determine that appellee's license to practice should not be temporarily suspended, it would not implicitly be admitting error in its prior finding of probable cause. Its position most probably would merely reflect the benefit of a more complete view of the evidence afforded by an adversary hearing.

The initial charge or determination of probable cause and the ultimate adjudication have different bases and purposes. The fact that the same agency makes them in tandem and that they relate to the same issues does not result in a procedural due process violation. Clearly, if the initial view of the facts based on the evidence derived from nonadversarial processes as a practical or legal matter foreclosed fair and effective consideration at a subsequent adversary hearing leading to ultimate decision, a substantial due process question would be raised. But in our view, that is not this case.

That the combination of investigative and adjudicative functions does not, without more, constitute a due process violation, does not, of course, preclude a court from determining from the special facts and circumstances present in the case before it that the risk of unfairness is intolerably high. Findings of that kind made by judges with special insights into local realities are entitled to respect, but injunctions resting on such factors should be accompanied by at least the minimum findings required by Rules 52(a) and 65(d).

The judgment of the District Court is reversed and the case is remanded to that court for further proceedings consistent with this opinion.

So ordered.

NOTES AND QUESTIONS

3-36. Why did Dr. Larkin believe that his due process rights could not be upheld by the Examining Board?

3-37. How does Justice White respond on behalf of the Court? Do you agree with his comparison of administrative processes to the criminal process? If the Examining Board could not render this decision, who would decide this case? What must the plaintiff prove in this case in order to prevail?

3-38. Can you distinguish between *structural* bias and *individual* bias? When does the Constitution condemn individual bias? Does it ever condemn structural bias? Does the APA require more structural protection than the Constitution?

PROBLEM 3-2

One of the major concerns about privatization of governmental services is that a corporation will put the interests of shareholders ahead of the interests of the public who uses the service. To what extent, if any, can the government structure the contract that outsources the public responsibilities to private providers so as to reduce such potential conflicts of interest?

For example, imagine that the state wants to privatize welfare eligibility determinations, that is, decisions about which citizens who apply for welfare meet the income requirements and are considered eligible for the program. What economic incentives (wrongful denial of benefits or wrongful awarding of benefits) do the following contract arrangements create for a private corporation that wishes to maximize profit from the contract?

1. The government pays the corporation a flat fee per year, no matter how many applicants actually apply for welfare.

2. The government pays the corporation a set amount for each applicant that the corporation processes.

3. The government pays the corporation a flat fee either per year or per application, but the corporation receives a bonus if fewer applications are approved (after all appeals have been exhausted) than projected.

4. The government pays the corporation a flat fee either per year or per application, the corporation receives a bonus if fewer applications are approved (after all appeals have been exhausted) than projected, but the corporation's payment is reduced a set amount for each denial of benefits that is reversed on appeal.

At the end of the contract period, how should the government evaluate the corporation's performance to decide whether the government should renew the contract? The number of applications denied? The number of applications approved? The number of complaints filed? The number of appeals filed? Something else?

PROBLEM 3-3

State X is concerned about the increasing pressure that its food stamp program is placing on its budget. The state estimates that at least 5% of new recipients of food stamps each year should not, in fact, receive the benefit because they do not meet the state's financial guidelines. Nevertheless, the state concludes that governmental waste and inefficiency allows these applicants who should not receive benefits to receive them.

In order to reduce the number of "undeserving" applicants who are accepted into the program, the state decided to privatize the administration of the program. The state solicited bids for a three-year contract to administer the program, which can be renewed for an additional three years. Of the four companies that submitted bids for the contract, the state selected Outsource, Inc.

Suppose that under the terms of the contract, Outsource receives $25 for each application that it processes and an additional $50 for each application that it determines fails to meet the state's financial guidelines. If you work for Outsource as a person called upon to decide whether an applicant meets the financial guidelines to receive benefits what pressures do you face? How will you resolve conflicts in the evidence about the applicant's financial status?

Suppose instead that under the contract, Outsource only receives $25 for each application that it processes, with no additional money should it deny the application. Once again, you work for Outsource to decide whether an applicant meets the financial requirements to receive benefits. What pressures do you face? Do these pressures change as it comes closer to the time that the state has to decide whether to extend Outsource's contract? In other words, what will Outsource say when it makes the sales pitch to the state as to why the state should let Outsource continue to operate the contract rather than awarding the contract to a competitor?

PROBLEM 3-4

Assume State X has privatized the management of its prisons. The private company that runs the prisons is also in charge of the disciplinary hearings within the prison that, from time to time, are necessary when prisoners misbehave. The consequences of a decision to incarcerate a prisoner in solitary confinement include not only the punishment of being in "the hole," but a loss of good time credits on a prisoner's record; that is, it is likely that he will be in jail longer because of these violations. Does this create any conflicts of interest issues for the private adjudicators? Do these conflicts rise to a constitutional level?

WEISS v. UNITED STATES.

Supreme Court of the United States
510 U.S. 163 (1994)

. . . .

CHIEF JUSTICE REHNQUIST delivered the opinion of the Court.

We must decide in these cases whether the current method of appointing military judges violates the Appointments Clause of the Constitution, and whether the lack of a fixed term of office for military judges violates the Fifth Amendment's Due Process Clause. We conclude that neither constitutional provision is violated.

Petitioner Weiss, a United States Marine, pleaded guilty at a special court-martial to one count of larceny, in violation of Article 121 of the Uniform Code of Military Justice (UCMJ or Code), 10 U.S.C. § 921. He was sentenced to three months of confinement, partial forfeiture of pay, and a bad-conduct discharge. Petitioner Hernandez, also a Marine, pleaded guilty to the possession, importation, and distribution of cocaine, in violation of Article 112a, UCMJ, 10 U.S.C. § 912a, and conspiracy, in violation of Article 81, UCMJ, 10 U.S.C. § 881. He was sentenced to 25 years of confinement, forfeiture of all pay, a reduction in rank, and a dishonorable discharge. The convening authority reduced Hernandez' sentence to 20 years of confinement.

The Navy-Marine Corps Court of Military Review, in separate appeals, affirmed petitioners' convictions. The Court of Military Appeals granted plenary review in petitioner Weiss' case to address his contention that the judges in his case had no authority to convict him because their appointments violated the Appointments Clause, and their lack of a fixed term of office violated the Due Process Clause. Relying on its recent decision in *United States v. Graf*, 35 M.J. 450 (1992), in which the court unanimously held that due process does not require military judges to have a fixed term of office, the court rejected Weiss' due process argument. 36 M.J. 224, 235, n. 1 (1992). In a splintered decision, the court also rejected petitioner's Appointments Clause challenge.

. . . .

The Court of Military Appeals accordingly affirmed petitioner Weiss' conviction. Based on its decision in *Weiss*, the court, in an unpublished opinion, also affirmed petitioner Hernandez' conviction. Weiss and Hernandez then jointly petitioned for our review, and we granted certiorari.

It will help in understanding the issues involved to review briefly the contours of the military justice system and the role of military judges within that system. Pursuant to Article I of the Constitution, Congress has established three tiers of military courts. *See* U.S. Const., Art. I, § 8, cl. 14. At the trial level are the courts-martial, of which there are three types: summary, special, and general. The summary court-martial adjudicates only minor offenses, has jurisdiction only over servicemembers, and can be conducted only with their consent. It is presided over by a single commissioned officer who can impose up to one month of confinement and other relatively modest punishments.

The special court-martial usually consists of a military judge and three court-martial members,[1] although the Code allows the members to sit without a judge, or the accused to elect to be tried by the judge alone. A special court-martial has jurisdiction over most offenses under the UCMJ, but it may impose punishment no greater than six months of confinement, three months of hard labor without confinement, a bad-conduct discharge, partial and temporary forfeiture of pay, and a reduction in grade. The general court-martial consists of either a military judge and at least five members, or the judge alone if the accused so requests. A general court-martial has jurisdiction over all offenses under the UCMJ and may impose any lawful sentence, including death.

The military judge, a position that has officially existed only since passage of the Military Justice Act of 1968, acts as presiding officer at a special or general court-martial. The judge rules on all legal questions, and instructs court-martial members regarding the law and procedures to be followed. The members decide guilt or innocence and impose sentence unless, of course, the trial is before the judge alone. No sentence imposed becomes final until it is approved by the officer who convened the court-martial.

Military trial judges must be commissioned officers of the Armed Forces[2] and members of the bar of a federal court or a State's highest court. The judges are selected and certified as qualified by the Judge Advocate General of their branch of the Armed Forces.[3] They do not serve for fixed terms and may perform judicial duties only when assigned to do so by the appropriate Judge Advocate General. While serving as judges, officers may also, with the approval of the Judge Advocate General, perform other tasks unrelated to their judicial duties. There are approximately 74 judges currently certified to preside at general and special courts-martial. An additional 25 are certified to preside only over special courts-martial.

. . . .

I

[The court then considered petitioners' argument regarding the appointment of these judges, concluding that it did not violate the Appointments Clause of the Constitution.]

---

[1] Court-martial members may be officers or enlisted personnel, depending on the military status of the accused; the members' responsibilities are analogous to, but somewhat greater than, those of civilian jurors.

[2] All commissioned officers are appointed by the President, with the advice and consent of the Senate.

[3] The Judge Advocate General for each service is the principal legal officer for that service.

II

Petitioners next contend that the Due Process Clause requires that military judges must have a fixed term of office. Petitioners recognize, as they must, that the Constitution does not require life tenure for Article I judges, including military judges. Nor does the trial by an Article I judge lacking life tenure violate an accused's due process rights. Petitioners thus confine their argument to the assertion that due process requires military judges to serve for some fixed length of time — however short.

Congress, of course, is subject to the requirements of the Due Process Clause when legislating in the area of military affairs, and that Clause provides some measure of protection to defendants in military proceedings. But in determining what process is due, courts "must give particular deference to the determination of Congress, made under its authority to regulate the land and naval forces, U.S. Const., Art. I, § 8." *Middendorf v. Henry*, 425 U.S. 25 (1976). Petitioners urge that we apply the due process analysis established in *Mathews v. Eldridge*, 424 U.S. 319, 334-335 (1976). The Government contends that *Medina v. California*, 505 U.S. 437 (1992), supplies the appropriate analytical framework.

Neither *Mathews* nor *Medina*, however, arose in the military context, and we have recognized in past cases that "the tests and limitations [of due process] may differ because of the military context." *Rostker v. Goldberg*, 453 U.S. 57, 67 (1981). The difference arises from the fact that the Constitution contemplates that Congress has "plenary control over rights, duties, and responsibilities in the framework of the Military Establishment, including regulations, procedures, and remedies related to military discipline." Judicial deference thus "is at its apogee" when reviewing congressional decisionmaking in this area. Our deference extends to rules relating to the rights of servicemembers: "Congress has primary responsibility for the delicate task of balancing the rights of servicemen against the needs of the military. . . . [W]e have adhered to this principle of deference in a variety of contexts where, as here, the constitutional rights of servicemen were implicated."

We therefore believe that the appropriate standard to apply in these cases is found in *Middendorf, supra*, where we also faced a due process challenge to a facet of the military justice system. In determining whether the Due Process Clause requires that servicemembers appearing before a summary court-martial be assisted by counsel, we asked "whether the factors militating in favor of counsel at summary courts-martial are so extraordinarily weighty as to overcome the balance struck by Congress." 425 U.S., at 44. We ask the same question here with respect to fixed terms of office for military judges.

It is elementary that "a fair trial in a fair tribunal is a basic requirement of due process." A necessary component of a fair trial is an impartial judge. *Tumey v. Ohio*, 273 U.S. 510, 532 (1927). Petitioners, however, do not allege that the judges in their cases were or appeared to be biased. Instead, they ask us to assume that a military judge who does not have a fixed term of office lacks the independence necessary to ensure impartiality. Neither history nor current practice, however, supports such an assumption.

A

Although a fixed term of office is a traditional component of the Anglo-American civilian judicial system, it has never been a part of the military justice tradition. The early English military tribunals, which served as the model for our own military justice system, were historically convened and presided over by a military general. No tenured military judge presided.

In the United States, although Congress has on numerous occasions during our history revised the procedures governing courts-martial, it has never required tenured judges to preside over courts-martial or to hear immediate appeals therefrom.[6] Indeed, as already mentioned, Congress did not even create the position of military judge until 1968. Courts-martial thus have been conducted in this country for over 200 years without the presence of a tenured judge, and for over 150 years without the presence of any judge at all.

B

As the Court of Military Appeals observed in *Graf*, 35 M.J., at 462, the historical maintenance of the military justice system without tenured judges "suggests the absence of a fundamental fairness problem." Petitioners in effect urge us to disregard this history, but we are unwilling to do so. We do not mean to say that any practice in military courts which might have been accepted at some time in history automatically satisfies due process of law today. But as Congress has taken affirmative steps to make the system of military justice more like the American system of civilian justice, it has nonetheless chosen not to give tenure to military judges. The question under the Due Process Clause is whether the existence of such tenure is such an extraordinarily weighty factor as to overcome the balance struck by Congress. And the historical fact that military judges have never had tenure is a factor that must be weighed in this calculation.

A fixed term of office, as petitioners recognize, is not an end in itself. It is a means of promoting judicial independence, which in turn helps to ensure judicial impartiality. We believe the applicable provisions of the UCMJ, and corresponding regulations, by insulating military judges from the effects of command influence, sufficiently preserve judicial impartiality so as to satisfy the Due Process Clause.

Article 26 places military judges under the authority of the appropriate Judge Advocate General rather than under the authority of the convening officer. Rather than exacerbating the alleged problems relating to judicial independence, as petitioners suggest, we believe this structure helps protect that independence. Like all military officers, Congress made military judges accountable to a superior officer for the performance of their duties. By placing

---

[6] Congress did create a nine-member commission in 1983 to examine, *inter alia*, the possibility of providing tenure for military judges. Military Justice Act of 1983, Pub.L. 98-209, § 9(b), 97 Stat. 1393, 1404-1405 (1983). The commission published its report a year later, in which it recommended against providing a guaranteed term of office for military trial and appellate judges. *See* D. Schlueter, *Military Criminal Justice: Practice and Procedure* 33-34, and nn. 86, 87 (3d ed. 1992) (listing members of commission and describing report). Congress has taken no further action on the subject.

judges under the control of Judge Advocates General, who have no interest in the outcome of a particular court-martial, we believe Congress has achieved an acceptable balance between independence and accountability.

Article 26 also protects against unlawful command influence by precluding a convening authority or any commanding officer from preparing or reviewing any report concerning the effectiveness, fitness, or efficiency of a military judge relating to his judicial duties. Article 37 prohibits convening authorities from censuring, reprimanding, or admonishing a military judge "with respect to the findings or sentence adjudged by the court, or with respect to any other exercise of its or his functions in the conduct of the proceeding." Any officer who "knowingly and intentionally fails to enforce or comply" with Article 37 "shall be punished as a court-martial may direct." The Code also provides that a military judge, either trial or appellate, must refrain from adjudicating a case in which he has previously participated, and the Code allows the accused to challenge both a court-martial member and a court-martial judge for cause. The Code also allows the accused to learn the identity of the military judge before choosing whether to be tried by the judge alone, or by the judge and court-martial members.

The entire system, finally, is overseen by the Court of Military Appeals, which is composed entirely of civilian judges who serve for fixed terms of 15 years. That court has demonstrated its vigilance in checking any attempts to exert improper influence over military judges. . . .

The absence of tenure as a historical matter in the system of military justice, and the number of safeguards in place to ensure impartiality, lead us to reject petitioners' due process challenge. Petitioners have fallen far short of demonstrating that the factors favoring fixed terms of office are so extraordinarily weighty as to overcome the balance achieved by Congress.

. . . .

Affirmed.

NOTES AND QUESTIONS

3-39. How does this tribunal compare to those established to deal with the detainees in Guantanamo, *supra* at Chapter 2, § 2.07?

3-40. What role does history play in the court's decision? How much weight does the court give to the fact that military judges have never had tenure or a fixed term?

§ 3.07 The Administrative Law Judge and an Unbiased Decisionmaker

The Administrative Procedures Act created the position of Administrative Law Judge (ALJ). Prior to this Act, hearing examiners, as they were then called, usually were "subordinate employees chosen by the agencies, and the power of the agencies to control and influence such personnel made questionable the contention of any agency that its proceedings assured fundamental fairness." They were perceived as "mere tools of the agency concerned" and thus as substantially undermining the faith of the administrative process.

The APA sought to allay these fears by vesting ALJs with an independence from their respective agencies. Tenure and compensation decisions were removed from agency control and vested largely in the Civil Service Commission, now the Office of Personnel Management. In addition, ALJs were exempted from performance ratings required for other civil service employees. They could be removed by the agency which employed them only for cause and after a hearing before the Merit Systems Protection Board.

The APA also followed essentially a judicial model when it came to ensuring that an ALJ was insulated from certain officials within an agency that is otherwise pursuing a variety of non-judicial tasks. Section 554(d) of the Act sets forth the basic guidelines respecting internal separation of functions.*

GROLIER, INC. v. FEDERAL TRADE COMMISSION

Ninth Circuit Court of Appeals
615 F.2d 1213 (1980)

Before WALLACE and ANDERSON, CIRCUIT JUDGES, and SOLOMON, DISTRICT JUDGE.

OPINION

WALLACE, CIRCUIT JUDGE:

On March 13, 1978, the Federal Trade Commission (FTC) entered a final cease and desist order against Grolier, Incorporated and 14 of its wholly-owned subsidiaries (Grolier) designed to correct Grolier's adjudged violations of 15 U.S.C. § 45. By this appeal, pursuant to 15 U.S.C. § 45, Grolier seeks to have that order set aside because of alleged procedural and substantive errors. We set aside the order and remand this case to the FTC for further consideration.

I

Grolier is engaged in the door-to-door and mail order sale of encyclopedias and related reference publications. On March 9, 1972, the FTC issued an administrative complaint charging Grolier with unfair methods of competition and unfair or deceptive acts or practices in connection with its sales activities, pricing representations, promotion techniques, recruitment practices, debt

---

* Reprinted from Alfred C. Aman, Jr. &amp William Mayton, *Administrative Law*, 240-41 (2d ed. 2001), with permission of Thomson West.

collection, and mail order operations. The case was initially assigned to an Administrative Law Judge (ALJ), who, after presiding at hearings throughout 1973 and 1974, retired from federal service before rendering a decision. A second ALJ was then assigned to complete the case, but he promptly recused himself. In February 1975, Theodore P. von Brand, the third ALJ assigned to the case, began hearings and decided to recall many of the witnesses who had previously testified in the proceedings. In January 1976, four months before completion of the hearings, ALJ von Brand informed the parties that he had served as an attorney-advisor to former FTC Commissioner A. Everett MacIntyre from 1963 through January 1971, during which period Grolier was intermittently investigated and charged by the FTC. Records available to Grolier indicated that Commissioner MacIntyre attended at least one meeting between it and representatives of the FTC.

Upon learning of ALJ von Brand's advisory responsibilities during the eight-year period, Grolier requested that the judge disqualify himself from further participation in the proceedings. The judge denied the request, stating that he did not recall working on matters involving Grolier while serving as legal advisor to the Commissioner. Grolier then filed with the FTC a formal motion for disqualification and removal of ALJ von Brand, at the same time requesting the FTC to permit discovery of specified FTC records which would have tended to show the nature and extent of the judge's contact with the Grolier case. The FTC denied both the motion for disqualification and the requested discovery.

After hearing a substantial part of the case *de novo*, ALJ von Brand concluded the hearings in May 1976 and issued his decision and recommended cease and desist order in October 1976. On appeal, the FTC adopted in large part the decision and order of ALJ von Brand and reaffirmed denial of the disqualification motion and request for discovery.

II

Grolier argued before the FTC, and now argues before us, that failure to disqualify ALJ von Brand from the case violated both section 554(d) of the Administrative Procedure Act (APA), 5 U.S.C. § 554(d), and the Due Process guarantee of the Fifth Amendment. Grolier also claims that the FTC erred in denying the requested discovery. Upon considering the § 554(d) claim and the denial of discovery, we remand the case to the FTC for further consideration. Consequently, we do not here reach Grolier's claims of due process violation and of error in the cease and desist order.

[A] Section 554(d)

Most federal administrative agencies combine within one organization a number of responsibilities that our system of government normally seeks to separate. They formulate policy as does the legislature, administer policy as does the executive, and adjudicate controversies as does the judiciary. They investigate infractions of statutes or regulations, prosecute those against whom their investigation has established a *prima facie* case, and judge the case they themselves have presented. W. Gellhorn & C. Byse, *Administrative*

Law, Cases and Comments 1035 (1974). Nowhere is this combination of functions more apparent than in the FTC.

> [T]he Federal Trade Commission receives a charge, ordinarily filed by a consumer or a competitor, that a business concern is engaging in an unfair trade practice. The charge is investigated by the Commission's personnel. If the Commission's investigator digs up enough evidence to show the charge to be substantial, a complaint issues in the Commission's name. An attorney employed by the Commission presents evidence (or "prosecutes") in support of the complaint at a hearing before an administrative law judge named by the Commission. The Commission's designated judge considers whether the Commission's attorney has proved the soundness of the Commission's case against the respondent. And in the end the Commission, aided by its staff, decides whether or not the respondent has committed the unfair trade practice of which the Commission had complained.

Id. at 1034–35.

In an effort to minimize any unfairness caused by this consolidation of responsibilities, the APA mandates an internal separation of the investigatory-prosecutorial functions from adjudicative responsibilities. The relevant portion of APA § 554(d) states:

> An employee or agent engaged in the performance of investigative or prosecuting functions for an agency in a case may not, in that or a factually related case, participate or advise in the decision, recommended decision, or agency review pursuant to section 557 of this title. . . .

To violate section 554(d), then, an agency employee must, in the same or a factually related case, (1) engage in "investigative or prosecuting functions,"[2] and (2) "participate or advise in the decision." Neither Grolier nor the FTC contests the fact that ALJ von Brand's actions meet the latter of these two requirements. The point of their disagreement, and the issue which we must resolve, is whether ALJ von Brand meets the first requirement, *i.e.*, whether his employment as an attorney-advisor to Commissioner MacIntyre constituted "investigative or prosecuting functions" in this or a factually related case.

Grolier contends that attorney-advisors come within the meaning of "investigative or prosecuting functions" because they are chargeable with knowledge of all matters that come before the FTC during their employment. Grolier urges that Congress intended to prevent adjudication by persons previously exposed to *ex parte* information like that developed by the FTC in its investigative and prosecutive activities. In other words, because ALJ von Brand is presumed to have knowledge of every FTC investigation conducted during his eight-year tenure as an attorney-advisor, Grolier would disqualify him from participating in the adjudication of any case investigated during that period, even those with which he had no contact.

---

[2] Despite the statutory language that an employee is precluded from participating in the adjudication of a case only when he is "engaged" in the investigation or prosecution of that case, we conclude that Congress did not intend to limit the separation of functions to those persons contemporaneously performing both. Such a reading would permit an agency employee to become immersed in the investigation of a case, resign from the investigative position, and then be appointed judge to render the decision. Such was not the intention of Congress.

The FTC's argument is equally extreme. It contends that because Congress was principally concerned with preventing adjudication by those who have developed, through investigative or prosecutorial zeal, a "will to win" that is incompatible with objective adjudication, section 554(d) applies only to those employed in the actual investigative and prosecutive branches of the FTC. Since attorney-advisors are employed in neither of those branches, the FTC contends that ALJ von Brand is not disqualified by section 554(d). Under such analysis, even an attorney-advisor who involves himself in a case to the point of losing all objectivity could later, without violating the APA, render judgment in that case simply because he was never employed in certain branches of the FTC organization. Neither Grolier's nor the FTC's position is convincing. To determine the scope of section 554(d), we must examine the legislative history of the APA.

In 1939 President Roosevelt "directed the Attorney General to name a committee of eminent lawyers, jurists, scholars, and administrators to review the entire administrative process in the various departments of the executive Government and to recommend improvements, including the suggestion of any needed legislation." *Wong Yang Sung v. McGrath*, 339 U.S. 33, 38–39, *modified*, 339 U.S. 908 (1950). The report of this committee became the blueprint for the APA and is "still a primary source of information about the federal administrative process." K. Davis, *Administrative Law and Government* 13 (2d ed. 1975). . . . In responding to the much criticized union of the investigative, prosecutive and adjudicative functions within agencies, the committee report suggested the creation of hearing commissioners, now administrative law judges, as a "separate unit in each agency's organization" with "no functions other than those of presiding at hearings . . . and . . . deciding the cases that fall within the agency's jurisdiction." Report of the Attorney General's Committee on Administrative Procedure 50 (1941), S. Doc. No. 8, 77th Cong., 1st Sess. 50 (1941) (footnote omitted). Two reasons crucial to our decision were given for this recommended separation: "the investigators, if allowed to participate (in adjudication), would be likely to interpolate facts and information discovered by them *ex parte* and not adduced at the hearing, where the testimony is sworn and subject to cross-examination and rebuttal;" and "[a] man who has buried himself in one side of an issue is disabled from bringing to its decision that dispassionate judgment which Anglo-American tradition demands of officials who decide questions." . . .

It is evident that Congress intended to address these two concerns by separating investigative-prosecuting functions from adjudicative functions. Section 554(d)(1) expressly forbids ALJ acquisition of *ex parte* information. This provision, along with 5 U.S.C. § 557(d)(1),[4] illustrates Congress' concern

---

[4] "Section 557(d)(1) states in part:

(d)(1) In any agency proceeding which is subject to subsection (a) of this section, except to the extent required for the disposition of *ex parte* matters as authorized by law —

(A) no interested person outside the agency shall make or knowingly cause to be made to any member of the body comprising the agency, administrative law judge, or other employee who is or may reasonably be expected to be involved in the decisional process of the proceeding, an *ex parte* communication relevant to the merits of the proceeding;

(B) no member of the body comprising the agency, administrative law judge, or other employee who is or may reasonably be expected to be involved in the decisional process of the proceeding, shall make or knowingly cause to be made to any interested person outside the agency an *ex parte* communication relevant to the merits of the proceeding. . . .

over possible use in the decisional process of information received outside of the controlled adjudicative setting. Congress' second concern, precluding from adjudicative functions those who have developed a "will to win," is evident in the legislative history of the APA. In explaining its adoption of language substantially the same as that currently contained in section 554(d), the Senate Judiciary Committee specifically adopted the majority recommendation of the Attorney General's Committee, expressing concern over the "man who has buried himself in one side of an issue." Senate Judiciary Committee Print, 79th Cong., 1st Sess. 15 (1945). . . .

Regarding the APA, the Supreme Court has stated that "it would be a disservice to our form of government and to the administrative process itself if the courts should fail, so far as the terms of the Act warrant, to give effect to its remedial purposes where the evils it was aimed at appear." *Wong Yang Sung v. McGrath, supra*, 339 U.S. at 41. We conclude that by forbidding adjudication by persons "engaged in the performance of investigative or prosecuting functions," Congress intended to preclude from decisionmaking in a particular case not only individuals with the title of "investigator" or "prosecutor," but all persons who had, in that or a factually related case, been involved with *ex parte* information, or who had developed, by prior involvement with the case, a "will to win." An attorney-advisor may, therefore, come within the prohibition of section 554(d) if he has had such involvement. The FTC decision to the contrary was error.[5]

The FTC argues, however, that even if section 554(d) has the broad meaning that we conclude it does, ALJ von Brand and all other former attorney-advisors are exempted from the 554(d) prohibition by APA language immunizing "the agency or a member or members of the body comprising the agency." 5 U.S.C. § 554(d)(2)(C). It contends that the necessarily close relationship between attorney-advisors and agency members requires that an advisor be extended privileges coequal with his commission member's responsibilities so that he may freely advise the member on the full range of problems considered by the FTC. This argument would be compelling if made on behalf of an attorney-advisor or other FTC employee who must counsel the member at both the investigative and decisionmaking stages of a case. But ALJ von Brand is no longer an attorney-advisor; his ALJ position does not necessitate involvement in the adjudication of this particular case. The exemption from 554(d) was created only for those positions in which involvement in all phases of a case is dictated "by the very nature of administrative agencies, where the same authority is responsible for both the investigation-prosecution and the hearing and decision of cases." . . . We reject the argument that ALJ von Brand is exempted from the § 554(d) separation of functions.

As mentioned earlier, Grolier contends that ALJ von Brand is chargeable with knowledge of all investigative and prosecutorial activities undertaken by the FTC during his tenure as an attorney-advisor. Therefore, it argues,

---

[5] In concluding that former attorney-advisors are not within the proscription of § 554(d), the FTC focused solely upon the congressional desire to prevent adjudication by those who had developed a "will to win." *In re Grolier, Inc.*, 87 F.T.C. 179, 180 (1976). With such a narrow focus, their conclusion was not unreasonable. It was erroneous, however, because it overlooked the equally important congressional desire to prevent adjudicative interpolation of *ex parte* facts.

actual possession of *ex parte* information in the Grolier case need not be shown; ALJ von Brand is disqualified *per se* by virtue of his former position. The authority cited in support of this argument is not persuasive. Moreover, we can find no court that has adopted a *per se* approach to disqualification under § 554(d). On the contrary, those courts which have considered the question have focused not upon the former position of the challenged adjudicator, but upon his actual involvement, while in that former position, with the case he is now deciding. . . . We conclude, therefore, that under § 554(d), attorney-advisors are "precluded only from participating in the adjudication of cases in which they have actually performed such ('investigative and prosecuting') functions, and in 'factually related' cases." *Au Yi Lau v. I.N.S., supra*, 181 U.S. App. D.C. at 106, 555 F.2d at 1043. For purposes of disqualification, they are not chargeable with involvement in all cases that were before the agency during their advisorship.

In resolving the question of ALJ von Brand's qualification to adjudicate the Grolier case, then, we must look to his activity during the time that he served as attorney-advisor to Commissioner MacIntyre. If he was sufficiently involved with the case to be apprised of *ex parte* information, § 554(d) requires his disqualification. His current inability to recall that information is irrelevant. Once an attorney-advisor is shown to have been "engaged in the performance of investigative or prosecuting functions" through prior acquaintance with *ex parte* information, § 554(d) says he "may not . . . participate or advise in the decision . . ." of the case. It does not condition this disqualification upon recollection of the *ex parte* facts.

Grolier has the burden of showing ALJ von Brand's prior acquaintance with *ex parte* information. . . . Where, as here, the court is presented with no evidence of actual involvement in the Grolier case by then attorney-advisor von Brand, the normal course of action would be to refuse to disqualify him. In this case, however, Grolier attempted to require such evidence by requesting discovery of specified FTC documents. If discovery was wrongly denied, Grolier was improperly hindered in its efforts to meet its burden of proof and failure to do so should not weigh against it. We therefore consider the propriety of the FTC's refusal to permit discovery.

[B] Discovery Request

The FTC's denial of Grolier's request for discovery was the direct result of its erroneous conclusion that attorney-advisors did not perform "investigative or prosecuting functions" within the meaning of 554(d). After making that conclusion it stated: "Because we do not believe that Judge von Brand would be subject to disqualification even if it could be shown that he advised Commissioner MacIntyre on matters pertaining to these respondents, the discovery requests are denied." . . . From the discussion in Part A of this opinion, it is evident that ALJ von Brand's prior involvement in the case is not irrelevant as the FTC supposed; rather, it is the very crux of the disqualification issue.

We conclude, therefore, that the case should be remanded to the FTC for reconsideration of the discovery denial and, in light of the results of that reconsideration, the disqualification motion. We do not say that the FTC must grant discovery; but we do say that a flat refusal to disclose anything at all about ALJ von Brand's prior involvement in the Grolier case is error. The FTC must produce sufficient information to permit it and a reviewing court, to make an accurate 554(d) determination. . . .

ORDER SET ASIDE AND CAUSE REMANDED.

NOTES AND QUESTIONS

3-41. Is it realistic to assume that ALJ von Brand knew *nothing* about the Grolier litigation? How much must he know before disqualification is required? How much must he remember?

3-42. If the parties know of an ALJ's prior involvement in a case, when must they make their objections known? Is it possible to waive one's right to an impartial judge? *See Gibson v. FTC,* 682 F.2d 554 (5th Cir. 1982), *reh'g denied,* 688 F.2d 840 (1982), *cert. denied,* 460 U.S. 1068 (1983).

3-43. The court focuses on the FTC's denial of Grolier's motion for discovery. Discovery generally is neither required by the APA nor the Constitution. Yet, in some situations a fair hearing on an important issue is impossible without it. If the FTC were to again deny Grolier's discovery request, would Grolier have a due process argument to make? What would that argument be? If you were the judge, how would you decide the case?

3-44. Protecting ALJ independence has long been an important goal of the administrative process. ALJs are usually assigned to a particular agency, but their compensation and job tenure depend on the Federal Office of Personnel Management and the Merit Systems Protection Board. Their attachment to a particular agency, however, gives some reformers pause. Consider the following description of the system by Jeffrey Lubbers in *A Unified Corps of ALJs: A Proposal to Test the Idea at the Federal Level,* 65 JUDICATURE 272–73 (1981):*

> The Administrative Procedure Act contains several provisions designed to preserve the independence and impartiality of the ALJ. It limits the role of the employing agency in the selection and appointment process, and it requires that the ALJ (and other agency decisionmakers) conduct business in an impartial manner. Moreover, if a party files a disqualification petition against an ALJ in any case, the agency must determine that issue on the record, as part of the decision in that case. The APA also prescribes that an ALJ may not be responsible to, or subject to supervision by, anyone performing investigative or prosecutorial functions for an agency. This "separation of functions" requirement is designed to prevent the investigative or prosecutorial arm of an agency from controlling a hearing or influencing the ALJ.

---

* Copyright © 1981 by American Judicature Society. All rights reserved.

Finally, to ensure that the ALJ is insulated from improper agency pressure and controls, the APA contains two other provisions to make the ALJ more independent of the employing agency: ALJs are to be assigned to their cases in rotation so far as practicable, and they may not perform duties inconsistent with their role as ALJs.

They also receive their pay as prescribed by the Office of Personnel Management, independently of agency recommendations or ratings, and they are removable only for good cause after a hearing before the Merit Systems Protection Board.

Despite these safeguards, some observers suggest this quasi-independent status of ALJs should be transformed into complete independence. Indeed, Congress has, in several enforcement programs, provided specifically for increased separation of agency prosecuting and adjudicating functions. In 1947, shortly after the passage of the APA, Congress passed the Taft-Hartley Act, which created a strict separation between the NLRB general counsel and the Board, its staff and its ALJs. In other programs, Congress has gone even further.

Thus, in 1975 Congress established as an independent agency the National Transportation Safety Board, (once part of the Department of Transportation) to hear challenges brought by pilots when the FAA issues license denials, suspensions and revocation actions. It also established the wholly adjudicatory Occupational Safety and Health Review Commission in 1970 and Federal Mine Safety and Health Review Commission in 1977 to hear challenges to civil penalty impositions and abatement orders issued by the Department of Labor. The Safety Board and the two Review Commissions each have a separate corps of ALJs which makes initial decisions on such challenges, subject to review by the Board or Commission.

But even as Congress has created these adjudicatory agencies, which act somewhat like agencies and somewhat like courts (leading to some knotty procedural problems and turf battles), it has left unchanged the structure of older enforcement agencies like the FTC, SEC and Postal Service. Meanwhile, it has also created new enforcement agencies like the Consumer Product Safety commission and Commodity Futures Trading Commission, and added new enforcement programs in the Departments of Agriculture, Commerce, Interior and Labor that lack any elements of separation of prosecutory and adjudicatory functions beyond those specified in the APA.

A unified ALJ Corps would remove ALJs from individual agencies and house them under a separate roof. Do you think this is a good idea? Why? What theory of administrative law does your analysis best fit? What assumptions are you making about the administrative process in taking your position?

3-45. For an historical analysis of Administrative Law Judges, *see* David J. Gifford, *Federal Administrative Law Judges: The Relevance of Past Choices to Future Directions*, 49 ADMIN. L. REV. 1 (1997).

PROBLEM 3-5

The city of Santa Ana, California, sought to fire police detention officer Quintero for stealing goods held at the police station. Hugh Halford, the person who prosecuted this case before the Personnel board had, on previous occasions, served as an advisor to the Board.

The attorney for Officer Quintero argued that "it would be only natural for the Board members, who have looked to Halford for advice and guidance, to give more credence to his arguments when deciding this case." The state court agreed with this argument and dismissed the case. Is this the correct result?

§ 3.08 *Ex Parte* Communications

PROFESSIONAL AIR TRAFFIC CONTROLLERS ORG. (PATCO) v. FEDERAL LABOR RELATIONS AUTHORITY

District of Columbia Court of Appeals
685 F.2d 547 (1982)

Before ROBINSON, CHIEF JUDGE, MACKINNON and EDWARDS, CIRCUIT JUDGES.

Opinion for the Court filed by CIRCUIT JUDGE HARRY T. EDWARDS.

Concurring opinions filed by CHIEF JUDGE SPOTTSWOOD W. ROBINSON, III and CIRCUIT JUDGE MacKINNON.

. . . .

HARRY T. EDWARDS, CIRCUIT JUDGE:

Federal employees have long been forbidden from striking against their employer, the federal government, and thereby denying their services to the public at large. The United States Code presently prohibits a person who "participates in a strike . . . against the Government of the United States" from accepting or holding a position in the federal government, 5 U.S.C. § 7311(2) (1976). Newly hired federal employees are required to execute an affidavit attesting that they have not struck and will not strike against the government, 5 U.S.C. § 3333(a) (1976). In addition, since the inception of formal collective bargaining between federal employee unions and the federal government, unions have been required to disavow the strike as an economic weapon. Since 1969, striking has been expressly designated a union unfair labor practice.

In 1978, Congress enacted the Civil Service Reform Act, Title VII of which provides the first statutory basis for collective bargaining between the federal government and employee unions. Title VII in no way reduced the existing legal proscriptions against strikes by federal employees and unions representing employees in the federal service. Rather, the Act added a new provision applicable to federal employee unions that strike against the government.

Under section 7120(f) of Title VII, Congress provided that the Federal Labor Relations Authority ("FLRA" or "Authority") shall "revoke the exclusive recognition status" of a recognized union, or "take any other appropriate disciplinary action" against any labor organization, where it is found that the union has called, participated in or condoned a strike, work stoppage or slowdown against a federal agency in a labor-management dispute. 5 U.S.C. § 7120(f) (Supp. IV 1980).

In this case we review the first application of section 7120(f) by the FLRA. After the Professional Air Traffic Controllers Organization ("PATCO") called a nationwide strike of air traffic controllers against the Federal Aviation Administration ("FAA") in the summer of 1981, the Authority revoked PATCO's status as exclusive bargaining representative for the controllers. For the reasons set forth below, we affirm the decision of the Authority.

I. BACKGROUND

A. *The PATCO Strike*

The Professional Air Traffic Controllers Organization has been the recognized exclusive bargaining representative for air traffic controllers employed by the Federal Aviation Administration since the early 1970s. Faced with the expiration of an existing collective bargaining agreement, PATCO and the FAA began negotiations for a new contract in early 1981. A tentative agreement was reached in June, but was overwhelmingly rejected by the PATCO rank and file. Following this rejection, negotiations began again in late July. PATCO announced a strike deadline of Monday, August 3, 1981.

Failing to reach a satisfactory accord, PATCO struck the FAA on the morning of August 3. Over seventy percent of the nation's federally employed air traffic controllers walked off the job, significantly reducing the number of private and commercial flights in the United States.

In prompt response to the PATCO job actions, the Government obtained restraining orders against the strike, and then civil and criminal contempt citations when the restraining orders were not heeded. The Government also fired some 11,000 striking air traffic controllers who did not return to work by 11:00 a.m. on August 5, 1981. In addition, on August 3, 1981, the FAA filed an unfair labor practice charge against PATCO with the Federal Labor Relations Authority. On that same day, an FLRA Regional Director issued a complaint on the unfair labor practice charge, alleging strike activity prohibited by 5 U.S.C. § 7116(b)(7) (Supp. IV 1980) and seeking revocation of PATCO's certification under the Civil Service Reform Act. The complaint noticed a hearing for one week later, August 10, 1981.

II. *EX PARTE* COMMUNICATIONS DURING THE FLRA PROCEEDINGS

Unfortunately, allegations of improprieties during the FLRA's consideration of this case forced us to delay our review on the merits. Only a day before oral argument, the Department of Justice, which represents the FAA in this

§ 3.08   ADJUDICATION & THE ADMINISTRATIVE PROCEDURE ACT   301

review, informed the court that the Department of Justice Criminal Division and the FBI had investigated allegations of an improper contact between a "well-known labor leader" and FLRA Member Applewhaite during the pendency of the PATCO case. We were understandably concerned about the suggestion that attempts had been made to influence the Authority improperly and about the possible inference that the Authority's decision might have been affected by these attempts.

Because our concerns extended beyond the presence or absence of criminal wrongdoing to the protection of the integrity of the administrative and judicial decisionmaking processes, we were not prepared to rely solely on the decision of the Criminal Division to close its investigation as proof that no improper influence had been exercised. Instead, we invoked a procedure that this court has occasionally employed in like situations in the past. Without assuming that anything improper had in fact occurred or had affected the FLRA Decision in this case, we ordered the FLRA "to hold, with the aid of a specially-appointed administrative law judge, an evidentiary hearing to determine the nature, extent, source and effect of any and all *ex parte* communications and other approaches that may have been made to any member or members of the FLRA while the PATCO case was pending before it." *Professional Air Traffic Controllers Organization v. FLRA*, 672 F.2d 109, 113 (D.C. Cir. 1982) (per curiam) (order directing special evidentiary hearing).

Following our remand on the *ex parte* communications issue, John M. Vittone, an Administrative Law Judge with the Civil Aeronautics Board, was appointed to preside over an evidentiary proceeding. . . .

A. A.L.J. Vittone's Findings

A.L.J. Vittone's inquiry led to the disclosure of a number of communications with FLRA Members that were at least arguably related to the Authority's consideration of the PATCO case. We find the vast majority of these communications unobjectionable. . . . Three occurrences, however, are somewhat more troubling and require our careful review and discussion. We first summarize A.L.J. Vittone's findings regarding them.

   1. The Meeting Between Member Applewhaite and FLRA General Counsel Gordon

On August 10, 1981 (one week after the unfair labor practice complaint against PATCO was filed), H. Stephan Gordon, the FLRA General Counsel, was in [FLRA] Member Applewhaite's office discussing administrative matters unrelated to the PATCO case. During Gordon's discussion with Member Applewhaite, Ms. Ellen Stern, an attorney with the FLRA Solicitor's office, entered Member Applewhaite's office to deliver a copy of a memorandum entitled "Decertification of Labor Organization Participating in the Conduct of a Strike in Violation of Section 7116(b)(7) of the Statute." Ms. Stern had prepared the memo at the request of [FLRA] Member Frazier. With General Counsel Gordon present, Ms. Stern proceeded to discuss her memorandum, which dealt with whether the Civil Service Reform Act makes revocation of a striking union's exclusive recognition status mandatory or discretionary and, assuming it is discretionary, what other disciplinary actions might be taken.

During Ms. Stern's discussion, both Member Applewhaite and General Counsel Gordon asked her general questions (*e.g.*, regarding the availability of other remedies and whether she had researched the relevant legislative history). General Counsel Gordon did not ask Member Applewhaite any questions or express any views on the issues discussed in the memorandum. Nor did Member Applewhaite express any opinion on the correct statutory interpretation. While the conversation at least implicitly focused on the PATCO case, the facts of the case and the appropriate disposition were not discussed. The discussion ended after ten or fifteen minutes.

A.L.J. Vittone concluded that "[t]he conversation had no effect or impact on Member Applewhaite's ultimate decision in the PATCO case." . . .

2. Secretary Lewis' Telephone Calls to Members Frazier and Applewhaite

During the morning of August 13, 1981, Secretary of Transportation Andrew L. Lewis, Jr. telephoned Member Frazier. Secretary Lewis stated that he was not calling about the substance of the PATCO case, but wanted Member Frazier to know that, contrary to some news reports, no meaningful efforts to settle the strike were underway. Secretary Lewis also stated that the Department of Transportation would appreciate expeditious handling of the case. Not wanting to discuss the PATCO case with Secretary Lewis, Member Frazier replied, "I understand your position perfectly, Mr. Secretary." Secretary Lewis then inquired whether Member Applewhaite was in Washington, D.C. at that time. Member Frazier replied that he was, but that Chairman Haughton was out of town. Although Member Frazier offered to convey the Secretary's message to Member Applewhaite, Secretary Lewis stated that he would call personally.

Member Frazier discussed Secretary Lewis' call with FLRA Solicitor Robert Freehling, describing it as relating to status and settlement. Solicitor Freehling advised Member Frazier that the communication did not fall within the *ex parte* prohibitions of the FLRA Rules.

Member Frazier also advised Member Applewhaite of Secretary Lewis' telephone call. In anticipation of a call, Member Applewhaite located the FLRA Rules regarding the time limits for processing an appeal from an A.L.J. decision in an unfair labor practice case. When Secretary Lewis telephoned and stated his concern that the case not be delayed, Member Applewhaite interrupted the Secretary to inform him that if he wished to obtain expedited handling of the case, he would have to comply with the FLRA Rules and file a written motion. Secretary Lewis stated that he was unaware that papers had to be filed and that he would contact his General Counsel immediately. The conversation ended without further discussion.

During the afternoon of August 13, the FAA filed a Motion to Modify Time Limits for Filing Exceptions, requesting that the time limit be reduced from the usual twenty-five days to seven days. On August 14, the FLRA General Counsel filed a similar motion. On August 17, PATCO filed an opposition to these motions and a motion to extend the time for filing exceptions to sixty days. On August 18, 1981, the FLRA Members considered the three pending motions, denied all three, and decided instead to reduce the usual twenty-five day period for filing exceptions to nineteen days.

Upon considering this evidence, Judge Vittone concluded that: (1) the FAA's filing of a motion to expedite may have been in response to Secretary Lewis' conversation with Member Applewhaite, . . . (2) Chairman Haughton was unaware of Secretary Lewis' telephone calls when he considered the motions on August 18, . . . (3) "Secretary Lewis' call had an undetermined effect on Member Applewhaite's and Member Frazier's decision to reduce the time period for filing exceptions," . . . and (4) the telephone calls "had no effect on Member Applewhaite's or Member Frazier's ultimate decision on the merits of the PATCO case." . . .

3. Member Applewhaite's Dinner with Albert Shanker

Since 1974 Albert Shanker has been President of the American Federation of Teachers, a large public-sector labor union, and a member of the Executive Council of the AFL-CIO.[26] Since 1964 Mr. Shanker has been President of the AFT's New York City Local, the United Federation of Teachers. Before joining the FLRA, Member Applewhaite had been associated with the New York Public Employment Relations Board. Through their contacts in New York, Mr. Shanker and Member Applewhaite had become professional and social friends.

The Applewhaite/Shanker Dinner. During the week of September 20, 1981, Mr. Shanker was in Washington, D.C. on business. On September 21, Mr. Shanker made arrangements to have dinner with Member Applewhaite that evening. Although he did not inform Member Applewhaite of his intentions when he made the arrangements, Mr. Shanker candidly admitted that he wanted to have dinner with Member Applewhaite because he felt strongly about the PATCO case and wanted to communicate directly to Member Applewhaite his sentiments, previously expressed in public statements, that PATCO should not be severely punished for its strike. In particular, Mr. Shanker believed that revocation of PATCO's exclusive recognition status would be an excessive punishment. After accepting the invitation, Member Applewhaite informed Member Frazier and Chairman Haughton that he was having dinner with Mr. Shanker.

Member Applewhaite and Mr. Shanker talked for about an hour and a half during their dinner on September 21. Most of the discussion concerned the preceding Saturday's Solidarity Day Rally, an upcoming tuition tax credit referendum in the District of Columbia, and mutual friends from New York. Near the end of the dinner, however, the conversation turned to labor law matters relevant to the PATCO case. The two men discussed various approaches to public employee strikes in New York, Pennsylvania and the federal government. Mr. Shanker expressed his view that the punishment of a striking union should fit the crime and that revocation of certification as a punishment for an illegal strike was tantamount to "killing a union." The record is clear that Mr. Shanker made no threats or promises to Member Applewhaite; likewise, the evidence also indicates that Member Applewhaite never revealed his position regarding the PATCO case.

Near the end of their conversation, Member Applewhaite commented that because the PATCO case was hotly contested, he would be viewed with

---

[26] The AFL-CIO presented oral argument to the FLRA in the PATCO case as *amicus curiae*. Mr. Shanker, however, was unaware of the *amicus* status of the AFL-CIO at all times relevant to our consideration.

disfavor by whichever side he voted against. Member Applewhaite also observed that he was concerned about his prospects for reappointment to the FLRA in July 1982. Mr. Shanker, in turn, responded that Member Applewhaite had no commitments from anyone and urged him to vote without regard to personal considerations. The dinner concluded and the two men departed.

The FLRA Decisional Process. On the afternoon of September 21, before the Applewhaite/Shanker dinner, the FLRA Members had had their first formal conference on the PATCO case, which had been argued to them five days earlier. Members Frazier and Applewhaite both favored revocation of PATCO's exclusive recognition status and took the position that PATCO would no longer be a labor organization within the meaning of the Civil Service Reform Act. Member Frazier favored an indefinite revocation; Member Applewhaite favored a revocation for a fixed period of one to three years. Chairman Haughton agreed that an illegal strike had occurred, but favored suspension, not revocation, of PATCO's collective bargaining status.

After September 21, Member Applewhaite considered other remedies, short of revocation, to deal with the PATCO strike. For over two weeks Member Applewhaite sought to find common ground with Chairman Haughton. Those efforts to agree on an alternative solution failed and, on October 9, Member Applewhaite finally decided to vote with Member Frazier for revocation. (Member Applewhaite apparently was concerned that the FLRA have a majority favoring one remedy, rather than render three opinions favoring three different dispositions.) All three Members drafted their final opinions by October 19. The drafts were exchanged and responses inserted. With some polishing, but no substantive change of positions, the opinions issued on October 22, 1981.

The Members' Responses to the Applewhaite/Shanker Dinner. While these negotiations within the Authority were going on, Member Frazier became concerned that Mr. Shanker might have influenced Member Applewhaite's position in the case. On September 22, Member Frazier visited Member Applewhaite to inquire about his dinner with Mr. Shanker. Member Frazier understood Member Applewhaite to say that Shanker had said that if Member Applewhaite voted against PATCO, then Applewhaite would be unable to get work as an arbitrator when he left the FLRA. Member Frazier also understood Member Applewhaite to say that he was then leaning against voting for revocation. (A.L.J. Vittone found that Shanker had made no such threats during the dinner, and concluded that Member Frazier reached this conclusion based on some miscommunication or misunderstanding.)

On September 22 and again on September 28, Member Frazier advised Member Applewhaite to talk to Solicitor Freehling about his dinner with Mr. Shanker. Member Applewhaite did so on September 28, and they concluded that no promises of benefits or threats had occurred and, therefore, that no crime had been committed. Solicitor Freehling also advised Member Applewhaite of the FLRA Rules on *ex parte* contacts. Member Applewhaite then told Chairman Haughton that he had discussed the dinner meeting with Solicitor Freehling and that there were no problems.

Member Frazier later asked Solicitor Freehling if Member Applewhaite had discussed his dinner with Mr. Shanker. Solicitor Freehling told Member

§ 3.08   ADJUDICATION & THE ADMINISTRATIVE PROCEDURE ACT   305

Frazier that they had talked and that Member Applewhaite had concluded that there were no problems involved. Despite these assurances, Member Frazier contacted his personal attorney. Sometime in early October, Member Frazier's attorney contacted the FBI. The FBI interviewed Member Frazier on October 17 and then other FLRA Members and staff. FBI agents interviewed Member Applewhaite on October 22, the day the FLRA Decision issued. (Member Applewhaite was thus unaware of the FBI investigation until after he reached his final decision in the PATCO case.)

The A.L.J.'s Conclusions. A.L.J. Vittone concluded: "The Shanker-Applewhaite dinner had no effect on the ultimate decision of Mr. Applewhaite in the PATCO case. Member Applewhaite's final decision in the PATCO case was substantially the same as the position he discussed at the September 21 meeting of the members." Later in his recommended findings, A.L.J. Vittone commented:

> It is clear that Mr. Shanker's message to Mr. Applewhaite was that revocation of certification was a drastic remedy out of proportion to the violation. However, as I stated in my findings, I do not believe that the dinner had any effect on the final decision of the FLRA in the PATCO case. At the very most, the effect was transitory in nature, and occurred from September 21 to October 9.

B. The Parties' Positions

Each of the FLRA Members argue[s] that their individual contacts with persons outside of the Authority were not improper. In addition, each of the Members supports A.L.J. Vittone's findings that the various contacts, their own and their colleagues', had no effect on the ultimate decision of the PATCO case. Member Applewhaite alone disputes A.L.J. Vittone's finding that his dinner with Mr. Shanker may have had a transitory effect on his consideration of the case. Mr. Shanker also argues that his dinner with Member Applewhaite was not inappropriate and that it had no effect on the decision. In addition to the individual Members and Mr. Shanker, the FLRA (represented by its Acting Solicitor) and the FAA agree with the finding of no effect on the decision in the case.

PATCO, *amicus* Skirlick, and *amici* McClure, Hough and Tierney are less sanguine about the implications of Judge Vittone's findings. Each of them argue that the disclosed communications were improper and require remedial action. The *amici* contend that, due to the *ex parte* contacts, the Authority had an irrational sense of urgency about the case. This, they argue, prejudiced their ability to participate in the unfair labor practice proceeding and to protect the interests of nonstriking controllers.

C. Applicable Legal Standards

    1. The Statutory Prohibition of *Ex Parte* Contacts and the FLRA Rules

The Civil Service Reform Act requires that FLRA unfair labor practice hearings, to the extent practicable, be conducted in accordance with the provisions of the Administrative Procedure Act. 5 U.S.C. § 7118(a)(6) (Supp.

IV 1980). Since FLRA unfair labor practice hearings are formal adjudications within the meaning of the APA, *see* 5 U.S.C. § 551(7) (1976), section 557(d) governs *ex parte* communications. *Id.* § 557(d).

Section 557(d) was enacted by Congress as part of the Government in the Sunshine Act, Pub. L. No. 94–409, § 4(a), 90 Stat. 1241, 1246 (1976). The section prohibits *ex parte* communications "relevant to the merits of the proceeding" between an "interested person" and an agency decisionmaker, 5 U.S.C. § 557(d)(1)(A), (B) (1976), requires the agency decisionmaker to place any prohibited communications on the public record, *id.* § 557(d)(1)(C), grants the agency the authority to require an infringing party "to show cause why his claim or interest should not be dismissed, denied, disregarded, or otherwise adversely affected on account of (a) violation," *id.* § 557(d)(1)(D), and defines the time period during which the statutory prohibitions are applicable, *id.* § 557(d)(1)(E). The FLRA has adopted rules that, with minor variations, parallel the requirements of section 557(d). . . .

Three features of the prohibition on *ex parte* communications in agency adjudications are particularly relevant to the contacts here at issue. First, by its terms, section 557(d) applies only to *ex parte* communications to or from an "interested person." Congress did not intend, however, that the prohibition on *ex parte* communications would therefore have only a limited application. A House Report explained:

> The term "interested person" is intended to be a wide, inclusive term covering any individual or other person with an interest in the agency proceeding that is greater than the general interest the public as a whole may have. The interest need not be monetary, nor need a person to (sic) be a party to, or intervenor in, the agency proceeding to come under this section. The term includes, but is not limited to, parties, competitors, public officials, and nonprofit or public interest organizations and associations with a special interest in the matter regulated. The term does not include a member of the public at large who makes a casual or general expression of opinion about a pending proceeding.

H.R. Rep. No. 880, Pt. I, 94th Cong., 2d Sess. 19–20 (1976), U.S. Code Cong. & Admin. News 1976, p. 2183, 2201. . . .

Second, the Government in the Sunshine Act defines an "*ex parte* communication" as "an oral or written communication not on the public record to which reasonable prior notice to all parties is not given, but . . . not includ[ing] requests for status reports on any matter or proceeding. . . ." 5 U.S.C. § 551(4) (1976). Requests for status reports are thus allowed under the statute, even when directed to an agency decisionmaker rather than to another agency employee. Nevertheless, the legislative history of the Act cautions:

> A request for a status report or a background discussion may in effect amount to an indirect or subtle effort to influence the substantive outcome of the proceedings. The judgment will have to be made whether a particular communication could affect the agency's decision on the merits. In doubtful cases the agency official should treat the communication as *ex parte* so as to protect the integrity of the decision making process.

S. Rep. No. 354, *supra*, at 37 . . . .

Third, and in direct contrast to status reports, section 557(d) explicitly prohibits communications "relevant to the merits of the proceeding." The congressional reports state that the phrase should "be construed broadly and . . . include more than the phrase 'fact in issue' currently used in [section 554(d)(1) of] the Administrative Procedure Act." S. Rep. No. 354, *supra*, at 36, Sunshine Act Sourcebook at 231 . . . . While the phrase must be interpreted to effectuate the dual purposes of the Government in the Sunshine Act, *i.e.*, of giving notice of improper contacts and of providing all interested parties an opportunity to respond to illegal communications, . . . the scope of this provision is not unlimited. Congress explicitly noted that the statute does not prohibit procedural inquiries, *see id.* at 36, Sunshine Act Sourcebook at 231, or other communications "not relevant to the merits," S. Rep. No. 1178, 94th Cong., 2d Sess. 29 (1976) (Conference Report), Sunshine Act Sourcebook at 811.

In sum, Congress sought to establish common-sense guidelines to govern *ex parte* contacts in administrative hearings, rather than rigidly defined and woodenly applied rules. The disclosure of *ex parte* communications serves two distinct interests. Disclosure is important in its own right to prevent the appearance of impropriety from secret communications in a proceeding that is required to be decided on the record. Disclosure is also important as an instrument of fair decisionmaking; only if a party knows the arguments presented to a decisionmaker can the party respond effectively and ensure that its position is fairly considered. When these interests of openness and opportunity for response are threatened by an *ex parte* communication, the communication must be disclosed. It matters not whether the communication comes from someone other than a formal party or if the communication is clothed in the guise of a procedural inquiry. If, however, the communication is truly not relevant to the merits of an adjudication and, therefore, does not threaten the interests of openness and effective response, disclosure is unnecessary. Congress did not intend to erect meaningless procedural barriers to effective agency action. It is thus with these interests in mind that the statutory prohibition on *ex parte* communications must be applied.

2. Remedies for *Ex Parte* Communications

Section 557(d) contains two possible administrative remedies for improper *ex parte* communications. The first is disclosure of the communication and its content. 5 U.S.C. § 557(d)(1)(C) (1976). The second requires the violating party to "show cause why his claim or interest in the proceeding should not be dismissed, denied, disregarded, or otherwise adversely affected on account of [the] violation." *Id.* § 557(d)(1)(D); *see also id.* § 556(d). Congress did not intend, however, that an agency would require a party to "show cause" after every violation or that an agency would dismiss a party's interest more than rarely. . . . Indeed, the statutory language clearly states that a party's interest in the proceeding may be adversely affected only "to the extent consistent with the interests of justice and the policy of the underlying statutes." 5 U.S.C. § 557(d)(1)(D) (1976).

The Government in the Sunshine Act contains no specific provisions for judicial remedy of improper *ex parte* communications. However, we may infer from approving citations in the House and Senate Reports that Congress did not intend to alter the existing case law regarding *ex parte* communications and the legal effect of such contacts on agency decisions. . . .

Under the case law in this Circuit, improper *ex parte* communications, even when undisclosed during agency proceedings, do not necessarily void an agency decision. Rather, agency proceedings that have been blemished by *ex parte* communications have been held to be voidable. . . . In enforcing this standard, a court must consider whether, as a result of improper *ex parte* communications, the agency's decisionmaking process was irrevocably tainted so as to make the ultimate judgment of the agency unfair, either to an innocent party or to the public interest that the agency was obliged to protect. In making this determination, a number of considerations may be relevant: the gravity of the *ex parte* communications; whether the contacts may have influenced the agency's ultimate decision; whether the party making the improper contacts benefitted from the agency's ultimate decision; whether the contents of the communications were unknown to opposing parties, who therefore had no opportunity to respond; and whether vacation of the agency's decision and remand for new proceedings would serve a useful purpose. Since the principal concerns of the court are the integrity of the process and the fairness of the result, mechanical rules have little place in a judicial decision whether to vacate a voidable agency proceeding. Instead, any such decision must of necessity be an exercise of equitable discretion.

D. Analysis of the Alleged *Ex Parte* Communications with FLRA Members

With the foregoing considerations in mind, we have analyzed A.L.J. Vittone's findings thoroughly and given careful thought to the positions urged by the parties. As we noted earlier, the vast majority of the reported contacts between FLRA Members and persons outside the Authority are not troubling. They relate to inquiries about the expected date of issuance of the FLRA's opinion, information from a third party regarding settlement efforts, statements regarding the running of PATCO's time to respond to Chairman Haughton's conditional dissent, and other communications unrelated to the merits of the case.

After extensive review of the three troubling incidents that we describe in Part II.A. *supra*, we believe that they too provide insufficient reason to vacate the FLRA Decision or to remand this case for further proceedings before the Authority. The special evidentiary hearing before Judge Vittone was ordered by this court not because we assumed that the A.L.J. would find serious wrongs or improprieties, but because the allegations of misconduct were serious enough to require full exploration. Public officials are held to high standards of behavior, and only through a special inquiry could we clear the air of any doubt that the FLRA Decision in this case was not unfairly influenced.

After unavoidable time, effort and expense, both by the parties and by the individual FLRA Members, A.L.J. Vittone formulated his findings. Except as otherwise noted below, we accept them. We conclude that at least one and possibly two of the contacts documented by the A.L.J. probably infringed the statutory prohibitions on *ex parte* communications. The incidents reported by the A.L.J. also included some evident, albeit unintended, indiscretions in a highly charged and widely publicized case. Nevertheless, we agree with A.L.J. Vittone that the *ex parte* contacts here at issue had no effect on the ultimate decision of the FLRA. Moreover, we conclude that the statutory infringements and other indiscretions are not so serious as to require us to vacate the FLRA Decision or to remand the case to the Authority. On the facts of this case, we believe that to vacate and remand would be a gesture of futility. . . .

 3. Member Applewhaite's Dinner with Albert Shanker

Of course, the most troublesome *ex parte* communication in this case occurred during the September 21 dinner meeting between Member Applewhaite and American Federation of Teachers President Albert Shanker — the "well-known labor leader" mentioned in Assistant Attorney General McGrath's affidavit. . . . Because allegations arising from this dinner occasioned our order of an evidentiary hearing, A.L.J. Vittone and the participants in the hearing before him centered much of their attention on this incident. We, too, have carefully focused on the Applewhaite/Shanker dinner in our review of the *ex parte* contacts. We agree — as do all the parties before us — with A.L.J. Vittone's finding that the dinner had no effect on the FLRA Decision in the case. After thorough consideration, we further conclude that the incident does not require a remand to the Authority.

At the outset, we are faced with the question whether Mr. Shanker was an "interested person" to the proceeding under section 557(d) and the FLRA Rules. Mr. Shanker argues that he was not. He suggests that his only connection with the unfair labor practice case was his membership on the Executive Council of the AFL-CIO which, unbeknownst to him, had participated as *amicus curiae* in the oral argument of the PATCO case before the FLRA. This relationship to the proceeding, Mr. Shanker contends, is too tenuous to qualify him as an "interested person" forbidden to make *ex parte* communications to the Authority Members.

As noted above, Congress did not intend such a narrow construction of the term "interested person." . . . The Senate Committee on Government Operations deleted a provision in the original bill that exempted *ex parte* communications involving persons who were neither parties, intervenors nor government officials. . . . The House and Senate Reports agreed that the term covers "any individual or other person with an interest in the agency proceeding that is greater than the general interest the public as a whole may have. The interest need not be monetary, nor need a person be a party to, or intervenor in, the agency proceeding. . . ."

We believe that Mr. Shanker falls within the intended scope of the term "interested person." Mr. Shanker was (and is) the President of a major public-sector labor union. As such, he has a special and well-known interest in the union movement and the developing law of labor relations in the public sector. The PATCO strike, of course, was the subject of extensive media coverage and public comment. Some union leaders undoubtedly felt that the hard line taken against PATCO by the Administration might have an adverse effect on other unions, both in the federal and in state and local government sectors. Mr.

Shanker apparently shared this concern. From August 3, 1981 to September 21, 1981, Mr. Shanker and his union made a series of widely publicized statements in support of PATCO. Mr. Shanker urged repeatedly in public statements that disproportionately severe punishment not be inflicted on PATCO. He spoke frequently on this subject, was interviewed about the PATCO strike on a nationally televised news program, and published a number of columns in the *New York Times* discussing the PATCO situation. Thus, Mr. Shanker's actions, as well as his union office, belie his implicit claim that he had no greater interest in the case than a member of the general public. Regardless of the amicus status of the AFL-CIO, and Mr. Shanker's lack of knowledge thereof, he was an "interested person" within the meaning of 5 U.S.C. § 557(d) (1976).

Even if we were to adopt Mr. Shanker's position that he was not an interested person, we are astonished at his claim that he did nothing wrong. Mr. Shanker frankly concedes that he "desired to have dinner with Member Applewhaite because he felt strongly about the PATCO case and he wished to communicate directly to Member Applewhaite sentiments he had previously expressed in public.". . . While we appreciate Mr. Shanker's forthright admission, we must wonder whether it is a product of candor or a failure to comprehend that his conduct was improper. In case any doubt still lingers, we take the opportunity to make one thing clear: It is simply unacceptable behavior for any person directly to attempt to influence the decision of a judicial officer in a pending case outside of the formal, public proceedings. This is true for the general public, for "interested persons," and for the formal parties to the case. This rule applies to administrative adjudications as well as to cases in Article III courts.

We think it a mockery of justice to even suggest that judges or other decisionmakers may be properly approached on the merits of a case during the pendency of an adjudication. Administrative and judicial adjudications are viable only so long as the integrity of the decisionmaking processes remains inviolate. There would be no way to protect the sanctity of adjudicatory processes if we were to condone direct attempts to influence decisionmakers through *ex parte* contacts.

We do not hold, however, that Member Applewhaite committed an impropriety when he accepted Mr. Shanker's dinner invitation. Member Applewhaite and Mr. Shanker were professional and social friends. We recognize, of course, that a judge "must have neighbors, friends and acquaintances, business and social relations, and be a part of his day and generation.". . . Similarly, Member Applewhaite was not required to renounce his friendships, either personal or professional, when he was appointed to the FLRA. When Mr. Shanker called Member Applewhaite on September 21, Member Applewhaite was unaware of Mr. Shanker's purpose in arranging the dinner. He therefore had no reason to reject the invitation.

The majority of the dinner conversation was unrelated to the PATCO case. Only in the last fifteen minutes of the dinner did the discussion become relevant to the PATCO dispute, apparently when Mr. Shanker raised the topic of local approaches to public employee strikes in New York and Pennsylvania. . . . At this point, and as the conversation turned to the discipline appropriate for a striking union like PATCO, Member Applewhaite should have promptly terminated the discussion. Had Mr. Shanker persisted in discussing his views of the PATCO case, Member Applewhaite should have informed him in no uncertain terms that such behavior was inappropriate. Unfortunately, he did not do so.

This indiscretion, this failure to steer the conversation away from the PATCO case, eventually led to the special evidentiary hearing in this case. The hearing has filled in much of the "factual picture" left incomplete by the McGrath affidavit and the FBI reports. . . . We now know that Mr. Shanker did not in any way threaten Member Applewhaite during their dinner. Mr. Shanker did not tell Member Applewhaite that if he voted to decertify PATCO he would be unable to get cases as an arbitrator if and when he left the FLRA. Mr. Shanker did not say that he was speaking "for top AFL-CIO officials" or that Member Applewhaite would need labor support to secure reappointment. Moreover, Mr. Shanker did not make any promises of any kind to Member Applewhaite, and Member Applewhaite did not reveal how he intended to vote in the PATCO case. . . .

In these circumstances, we do not believe that it is necessary to vacate the FLRA Decision and remand the case. First, while Mr. Shanker's purpose and conduct were improper, and while Member Applewhaite should not have entertained Mr. Shanker's views on the desirability of decertifying a striking union, no threats or promises were made. Though plainly inappropriate, the *ex parte* communication was limited to a ten or fifteen minute discussion, often couched in general terms, of the appropriate discipline for a striking public employee union. This behavior falls short of the "corrupt tampering with the adjudicatory process" found by this court in *WKAT, Inc. v. FCC,* 296 F.2d 375, 383 (D.C. Cir.), *cert. denied,* 368 U.S. 841 (1961).

Second, A.L.J. Vittone found that the Applewhaite/Shanker dinner had no effect on the ultimate decision of Member Applewhaite or of the FLRA as a whole in the PATCO case. None of the parties have disputed this finding. . . .

Third, no party benefitted from the improper contact. The ultimate decision was adverse to PATCO, the party whose interests were most closely aligned with Mr. Shanker's position. . . .

Finally, we cannot say that the parties were unfairly deprived of an opportunity to refute the arguments propounded in the *ex parte* communication. . . .

We in no way condone Mr. Shanker's behavior in this case. Nor do we approve Member Applewhaite's failure to avoid discussion of a case pending before the Authority. Nevertheless, we do not believe that the Applewhaite/Shanker dinner, as detailed in A.L.J. Vittone's findings, irrevocably tainted the Authority's decision-making process or resulted in a decision unfair either to the parties or to the public interest. . . .

NOTES AND QUESTIONS

3-46. When are agency proceedings that have been "blemished by *ex parte* communications" held to be void? What remedies does the APA provide for *ex parte* contacts? What kind of approach does the *PATCO* court take to this issue? Does the appearance of impropriety enter into its calculations? What, ultimately, is determinative in this case?

3-47. Is this approach the court takes in this case in accord with the provisions and intent of the APA?

3-48. How would this case have been decided if these contacts occurred during the course of a trial in federal court? Would there be any differences in the analysis? What would account for these differences?

3-49. For a case holding that the APA's ban on *ex parte* communications in adjudicatory proceedings applied in the context of the endangered species act, see Portland Audubon Society v. Endangered Species, 984 F.2d 1534 (9th Cir. 1993). In that case, the court held that a decision to grant or deny an exemption to the Endangered Species Act was an adjudication "on the record," thus triggering §§ 554, 556 and 557 of the APA.

§ 3.09 Pre-Judgment

CINDERELLA CAREER AND FINISHING SCHOOLS, INC. v. FEDERAL TRADE COMMISSION

District of Columbia Court of Appeals
425 F.2d 583 (1970)

Before TAMM, MACKINNON and ROBB, CIRCUIT JUDGES.

TAMM, CIRCUIT JUDGE:

This is a petition to review orders of the Federal Trade Commission which required petitioners Cinderella Career College and Finishing Schools, Inc. (hereinafter Cinderella), Stephen Corporation (the corporate entity which operates Cinderella), and Vincent Malzac (the sole owner of the stock of Cinderella and Stephen Corporation), to cease and desist from engaging in certain practices which were allegedly unfair and deceptive.

After the Commission filed its complaint under section 5 of the Federal Trade Commission Act, 15 U.S.C. § 45 (1964), which charged Cinderella with making representations and advertising in a manner which was false, misleading and deceptive, a hearing examiner held a lengthy series of hearings which consumed a total of sixteen days; these proceedings are reported in 1,810 pages of transcript. After the Commission had called twenty-nine witnesses and the petitioners twenty-three, and after the FTC had introduced 157 exhibits and petitioners 90, the hearing examiner ruled in a ninety-three

§ 3.09   ADJUDICATION & THE ADMINISTRATIVE PROCEDURE ACT   313

page initial decision that the charges in the complaint should be dismissed. . . .

We are faced with two principal issues on this appeal: whether the action of the Commission in reversing the hearing examiner comports with standards of due process, and whether then Chairman Paul Rand Dixon should have recused himself from participation in the review of the initial decision due to public statements he had previously made which allegedly indicated prejudgment of the case on his part.

[The court held that there were due process violations in the way the Commission decided this case.]

. . . .

II. DISQUALIFICATION OF CHAIRMAN DIXON

An additional ground which requires remand of these proceedings — and which would have required reversal even in the absence of the above-described procedural irregularities — is participation in the proceedings by the then Chairman of the Federal Trade Commission, Paul Rand Dixon.

Notice that the hearing examiner's dismissal of all charges would be appealed was filed by the Commission staff on February 1, 1968. On March 12, 1968, this court's decision was handed down in a prior appeal arising from this same complaint, in which we upheld the Commission's issuance of press releases which called attention to the pending proceedings. Then, on March 15, 1968, while the appeal from the examiner's decision was pending before him, Chairman Dixon made a speech before the Government Relations Workshop of the National Newspaper Association in which he stated:

> What kind of vigor can a reputable newspaper exhibit? The quick answer, of course, pertains to its editorial policy, its willingness to present the news without bias. However, that is only half the coin. How about ethics on the business side of running a paper? What standards are maintained on advertising acceptance? What would be the attitude toward accepting good money for advertising by a merchant who conducts a "going out of business" sale every five months? What about carrying ads that offer college educations in five weeks, fortunes by raising mushrooms in the basement, getting rid of pimples with a magic lotion, or becoming an airline's hostess by attending a charm school? Or, to raise the target a bit, how many newspapers would hesitate to accept an ad promising an unqualified guarantee for a product when the guarantee is subject to many limitations? Without belaboring the point, I'm sure you're aware that advertising acceptance standards could stand more tightening by newspapers. Granted that newspapers are not in the advertising policing business, their advertising managers are savvy enough to smell deception when the odor is strong enough. And it is in the public interest, as well as their own, that their sensory organs become more discriminating. The Federal Trade Commission, even where it has jurisdiction, could not protect the public as quickly.

It requires no superior olfactory powers to recognize that the danger of unfairness through prejudgment is not diminished by a cloak of self-righteousness. We have no concern for or interest in the public statements of government officers, but we are charged with the responsibility of making certain that the image of the administrative process is not transformed from a Rubens to a Modigliani.

We indicated in our earlier opinion in this case that "there is in fact and law authority in the Commission, acting in the public interest, to alert the public to *suspected violations* of the law by *factual press releases* whenever the Commission shall have reason to believe that a respondent is engaged in activities made unlawful by the Act. . . ." *FTC v. Cinderella Career & Finishing Schools, Inc.,* 131 U.S. App. D.C. 331, 337, 404 F.2d 1308, 1314 (1968) (emphasis added). This does not give individual Commissioners license to prejudge cases or to make speeches which give the appearance that the case has been prejudged. Conduct such as this may have the effect of entrenching a Commissioner in a position which he has publicly stated, making it difficult, if not impossible, for him to reach a different conclusion in the event he deems it necessary to do so after consideration of the record. There is a marked difference between the issuance of a press release which states that the Commission has filed a complaint because it has "reason to believe" that there have been violations, and statements by a Commissioner after an appeal has been filed which give the appearance that he has already prejudged the case and that the ultimate determination of the merits will move in predestined grooves. While these two situations — Commission press releases and a Commissioner's pre-decision public statements — are similar in appearance, they are obviously of a different order of merit.

As we noted in our earlier opinion, Congress has specifically vested the administrative agencies both with the "power to act in an accusatory capacity" and with the "responsibility of ultimately determining the merits of the charges so presented." 131 U.S. App. D.C. at 338, 404 F.2d at 1315.

Chairman Dixon, sensitive to theory but insensitive to reality, made the following statement in declining to recuse himself from this case after petitioners requested that he withdraw:

> As . . . I have stated . . . this principle "is not a rigid command of the law, compelling disqualification for trifling causes, but a consideration addressed to the discretion and sound judgment of the administrator himself in determining whether, irrespective of the law's requirements, he should disqualify himself."

To this tenet of self-appraisal we apply Lord Macaulay's evaluation more than 100 years ago of our American government: "It has one drawback — it is all sail and no anchor." We find it hard to believe that former Chairman Dixon is so indifferent to the dictates of the Courts of Appeals that he has chosen once again to put his personal determination of what the law requires ahead of what the courts have time and again told him the law requires. If this is a question of "discretion and judgment," Commissioner Dixon has exercised questionable discretion and very poor judgment indeed, in directing his shafts and squibs at a case awaiting his official action. We can use his own words in telling Commissioner Dixon that he has acted "irrespective of the law's requirements"; we will spell out for him once again, avoiding tired cliche and weary generalization, in no uncertain terms, exactly what those

§ 3.09   ADJUDICATION & THE ADMINISTRATIVE PROCEDURE ACT   315

requirements are, in the fervent hope that this will be the last time we have to travel this wearisome road.

The test for disqualification has been succinctly stated as being whether "a disinterested observer may conclude that [the agency] has in some measure adjudged the facts as well as the law of a particular case in advance of hearing it." *Gilligan, Will & Co. v. SEC*, 267 F.2d 461, 469 (2d Cir.), *cert. denied*, 361 U.S. 896 (1959).

That test was cited with approval by this court in *Texaco, Inc. v. FTC*, 118 U.S. App. D.C. 366, 336 F.2d 754 (1964), vacated and remanded on other grounds, 381 U.S. 739. (1965). In that case Chairman Dixon made a speech before the National Congress of Petroleum Retailers, Inc. while a case against Texaco was pending before the examiner on remand. After restating the test for disqualification, this court said:

> [A] disinterested reader of Chairman Dixon's speech could hardly fail to conclude that he had in some measure decided in advance that Texaco had violated the Act.

118 U.S. App. D.C. at 372, 336 F.2d at 760. We further stated that such an administrative hearing "must be attended, not only with every element of fairness but with the very appearance of complete fairness," citing *Amos Treat & Co. v. SEC*, 113 U.S. App. D.C. 100, 107, 306 F.2d 260, 267 (1962). We therefore concluded that Chairman Dixon's participation in the Texaco case amounted to a denial of due process.

After our decision in *Texaco* the United States Court of Appeals for the Sixth Circuit was required to reverse a decision of the FTC because Chairman Dixon refused to recuse himself from the case even though he had served as Chief Counsel and Staff Director to the Senate Subcommittee which made the initial investigation into the production and sale of the "wonder drug" tetracycline. *American Cyanamid Co. v. FTC*, 363 F.2d 757 (1966). Incredible though it may seem, the court was compelled to note in that case that:

> [T]he Commission is a fact-finding body. As Chairman, Mr. Dixon sat with the other members as triers of the facts and *joined in making the factual determination* upon which the order of the Commission is based. *As counsel for the Senate Subcommittee, he had investigated and developed many of these same facts.*

363 F.2d at 767 (emphasis added). It is appalling to witness such insensitivity to the requirements of due process; it is even more remarkable to find ourselves once again confronted with a situation in which Mr. Dixon, pouncing on the most convenient victim, has determined either to distort the holdings in the cited cases beyond all reasonable interpretation or to ignore them altogether. We are constrained to this harshness of language because of Mr. Dixon's flagrant disregard of prior decisions.

The rationale for remanding the case despite the fact that former Chairman Dixon's vote was not necessary for a majority is well established:

> Litigants are entitled to an impartial tribunal whether it consists of one man or twenty and there is no way which we know of whereby the influence of one upon the others can be quantitatively measured.

Berkshire Employees Ass'n of Berkshire Knitting Mills v. NLRB, 121 F.2d 235, 239 (3d Cir. 1941). This rationale was cited with approval in the *American Cyanamid* opinion; we adopt the position of our sister circuits on this point.

II. CONCLUSION

For the reasons set forth above we vacate the order of the Commission and remand with instructions that the Commissioners consider the record and evidence in reviewing the initial decision, without the participation of Commissioner Dixon.

Vacated and remanded.

NOTES AND QUESTIONS

3-50. What is the rule established in this case? Did the court correctly apply it in this case?

3-51. Is the court reacting to the statements made in this case or to the fact that Chairman Dixon made them?

3-52. How would this case be decided if this were a rulemaking proceeding, rather than an adjudication? *See* Chapter Four, *infra*.

3-53. A federal judge must recuse himself from a case "in which his impartiality might be reasonably questioned." 28 U.S.C. § 455(a) (2005). Would this statute prevent a federal judge from hearing a case involving a friend of the judge, who was being sued in his official governmental capacity? What if, in addition to being friends, the judge and the government official named in the suit went duck hunting together as part of a large group of hunters, but the judge and the official were never alone together during the trip, and never discussed the pending case? *See Cheney v. United States Dist. Court for the Dist. of Columbia,* 124 S. Ct. 1391 (2004) (Scalia, J.) (opinion regarding motion for recusal). Imagine instead that an Administrative Law Judge was hearing the case. Would the APA require the judge to recuse herself? Is the APA standard different from the standard for federal judges? Why or why not? Should the two standards be different?

3-54. For a case involving prejudgment bias arising in the context of a high school student's suspension from the school basketball team, see *Butler v. Oak Creek-Franklin School District,* 172 F. Supp. 2d 1102 (2001).

PROBLEM 3-6

Paul Smith pleaded guilty to two counts of securities violations four years ago. Consequently, he lost his job as a stock broker. Last September, Paul

§ 3.09 ADJUDICATION & THE ADMINISTRATIVE PROCEDURE ACT 317

found a new job in the securities industry with Stock, Corp.; and he sought an SEC license to handle securities. The SEC denied his request to handle securities at Stock, Corp. in December of last year. (*Smith I*).

In January of this year, the SEC initiated a case against Paul based on his criminal convictions for securities violations. Under the applicable law, the SEC had to decide whether the public interest required it to prohibit Paul from taking *any* employment in the securities industry. This November, the SEC decided 5-0, in *Smith II*, that it should permanently bar Paul from employment in the securities industry.

Paul challenges *Smith II* in federal court claiming that the SEC was impermissibly biased against him. In support of his claim, Paul points to a guest lecture that the Chairwoman gave to a securities regulation class at a law school in February of this year, while *Smith II* was still pending. The class had been studying the sanctions that the SEC can impose on employees in the industry, and the professor invited the Chairwoman to share some real world experience with the class. During the Q&A following the lecture, the Chairwoman said the following: "I hope that you all realize how seriously securities violations can be. Just last December, for example, *we permanently barred Paul Smith from any employment in the securities industry for committing securities violations*."

The trial judge asks for your opinion about whether she should vacate *Smith II* on the grounds of prejudgment prejudice. What do you say? Does your answer change if the Chairwoman recused herself from the vote in *Smith II* the day before the vote was taken?

Chapter 4
AGENCY RULEMAKING

§ 4.01 What Is a Rule?

The Administrative Procedure Act, 6 U.S.C. § 551(8) defines a "rule" as —

> the whole or part of an agency statement of general or particular applicability and future effect designed to implement, interpret, or prescribe law or policy or describing the organization, procedure, or practice requirements of an agency and includes the approval or prescription for the future of rates, wages, corporate or financial structures or reorganizations thereof, prices, facilities, appliances, services or allowances therefor or of valuations, costs, or accounting, or practices bearing on any of the foregoing.

An order is defined as "a final disposition whether affirmative, negative, injunctive, or declaratory in form, of an agency in a matter other than rule making but including licensing." 5 U.S.C. § 551(b). Are these definitions helpful in distinguishing a rule from an order? What do you make of the fact that the APA's definition of a rule includes agency statements "of general *or particular* applicability and future effect"? Does "particular applicability" suggest an order rather than a rule? Recall our discussion of Problem 1-1, *supra*.

The Attorney General's Manual on the APA sheds some light on the definition of a rule with its discussion of the APA's distinction between rulemaking processes and adjudicatory processes.

> [T]he entire Act is based upon a dichotomy between rule making and adjudication. Examination of the legislative history of the definitions and of the differences in the required procedures for rule making and for adjudication discloses highly practical concepts of rule making and adjudication. Rule making is agency action which regulates the future conduct of either groups of persons or a single person; it is essentially legislative in nature, not only because it operates in the future but also because it is primarily concerned with policy considerations. The object of the rule making proceeding is the implementation or prescription of law or policy for the future, rather than the evaluation of a respondent's past conduct. Typically, the issues relate not to the evidentiary facts, as to which the veracity and demeanor of witnesses would often be important, but rather to the policy-making conclusions to be drawn from the facts. . . . Conversely, adjudication is concerned with the determination of past and present rights and liabilities. Normally, there is involved a decision as to whether past conduct was unlawful, so that the proceeding is characterized by an accusatory flavor and may result in disciplinary action. Or, it may involve the determination of a person's right to benefits under existing law so that the issues relate to whether he is within the established category of persons entitled

to such benefits. In such proceedings, the issues of fact are often sharply controverted.*

Consider also Professor Schauer's more general discussion of rules. How does his analysis apply to the cases that follow?

Schauer, A BRIEF NOTE ON THE LOGIC OF RULES, WITH SPECIAL REFERENCE TO *BOWEN v. GEORGETOWN*

42 ADMIN. L. REV. 447, 449-54 (1990)**

Commonly, we think that there is an enormous difference between descriptive and prescriptive rules. Just as we recognize the differences between the laws of physics and the laws of New Jersey, and recognize that you can break the law of Texas although you cannot break the law of gravity, so too do we ordinarily draw a distinction with respect to the word *rule*. Inspired primarily by the work of H.L.A. Hart, theorists now take for granted the difference between rules and habits, even though we use the word *rule* for both. We say that "as a rule" we drink coffee in the morning, and there is nothing odd about saying that "as a rule the Alps are snow-covered in May." The common (but peculiar) expression — "That's the exception that proves the rule" — makes reference to such *descriptive* rules, contrasting them to those rules of etiquette, morality, and law that have *prescriptive* force. "Seat belts must be fastened at all times" is a prescriptive rule, seeking to apply pressure to human conduct in a way that an empirical generalization about the frequency of seat belt usage does not, even though the latter might still be couched in terms using the word *rule* — "As a rule people wear seat belts in this city."

. . . .

Rules, prescriptive *and* descriptive, thus speak to types and not to particulars. Unless we mean to describe more instances than one, or unless we mean to prescribe more actions than one, it is simply a mistake to use the word *rule*. Ordinary language thereby highlights a difference between the particular and the general that is as significant for prescriptions as it is for reports of empirical regularity. This difference is reflected in the common terminological difference between a command and an order, or even between a command and a rule, with the term *command* being typically reserved for those prescriptions that are particular rather than general. This difference is also, of course, reflected in legal doctrine. Where the question is whether the constitutional requirements of notice, right to be heard, and other procedural due process mandates are applicable, we have now accepted that the primary question to ask is one that looks to whether the determinations at issue are individualized or not, in other words, whether those determinations are particular or general. And most relevantly for our purposes, the distinction between

---

* Attorney General's Manual on the Administrative Procedure Act 16 (1947).

** Copyright © 1990 by American Bar Association. Reprinted by permission.

rulemaking and adjudication is based on similar premises and embodies a distinction between determinations that are in some important way particular and those that are in the same important way general.

But if rules are defined by virtue of their generality, if there are, by definition, no rules for particulars, then what does it mean, in this context, to say that rules must be general? We are now approaching the crux of our problem.

The distinction between particular and general prescriptions can be reflected in any one of three dimensions. First, a general prescription might refer to one act rather than to a category of acts. If on a particular occasion I am told by my wife to stay out of her workshop this is quite different from a rule pursuant to which the workshop is off-limits. *This* act of entering the workshop is a particular act, but the category of workshop-enterings is general. Rules, ordinarily, become rules by virtue of possessing this type of categorical generality with respect to acts.

Second, prescriptions might be particular in applying only to one person and contrastingly general in applying to categories of persons or even to all people. Insofar as some prescription relates to the behavior of only one person, as with the immediately preceding example, it lacks a dimension of generality we commonly associate with legal rules. Note, for example, the constitutional prohibition on bills of attainder, the traditional albeit now-relaxed constitutional skepticism regarding laws that grant benefits to only one person or entity, and the fact that common usage distinguishes the "laws" or "statute" enacted by congress from "private bills." By contrast, therefore, we typically expect that rules will apply to categories of persons, a distinction that relates with special importance to the adjudication/rulemaking dichotomy.

Third, a prescription could be particular or general along a temporal dimension. Whether applying to a particular act or a category of acts, to one person or to a category of persons, a prescription might apply only *now,* or might extend into the future. The military's distinction between an order and a *standing order* captures this idea, recognizing that there is a difference between orders, even orders applying to a category of acts performed by an entire battery of soldiers — "All soldiers will stop talking" — that have a moderately specific and closed time frame and those orders that extend on into a limited or unlimited future.

As generations of philosophical and legal scholarship have taught us, none of these distinctions is perfect, and with respect to all, the difference between the particular and the general is often more one of degree than of kind. A general category might refer only to one person — all of the women Supreme Court Justices sitting in 1989 — and even a temporally limited prescription takes place along a period of time. The order prohibiting soldiers from talking appears particular even though it covers a period of time longer than an instant. Despite these difficulties, our ability to work with the distinction between the particular and the general, whether in law or without, indicates that, as with many complex or fuzzy distinctions, the distinctions still serve us tolerably well in the normal cases even if there are close cases at the margin. But what is important is the fact that we now see that there are not one but three dimensions along which the distinction between the particular and the general might be drawn and thus three dimensions along which we might distinguish particular decisionmaking from more general rulemaking. Any attempt to distinguish a rule from something else must thus, if careful, address not only the distinction between the general and the particular, but also the fact that distinction might exist in one, two, or three different ways. How many of those ways, and which ones, are then necessary to identify a decision as "general"?

The question I have just asked enables us to see the definition in 5 U.S.C. section 551(4) in a different light. Given that the purpose of that definition is to define a rule, and given that the purpose of the definition of a rule is to enable a distinction to be drawn between rules and more particular forms of decisionmaking, then it would make sense to see that definition as an attempt to address this question — as an attempt to determine which of the three dimensions of generality are necessary for a decision to count as a rule for APA purposes.

When we look at the relevant language [of 5 U.S.C. § 551 . . .], we see that, tellingly, it includes an agency statement "of general or particular applicability." Thus, the definition of a rule in the APA is seemingly designed to *avoid* having the distinction between an order and a rule turn on either of the first two dimensions of particularity and generality discussed above. That is, the definition appears to reject, for these purposes, a distinction drawn either on the basis of the number of parties concerned or on the basis of the number of acts encompassed. This is confirmed by the complementary provision, 5 U.S.C. section 551(6), which defines "order." In that definition we find no mention of any distinction between the general and the particular in terms either of the number of parties or the number of acts encompassed, but we do find the phrase "final disposition." Consequently, the mutually reinforcing sections 551(4) and 551(6) both support a distinction between an order and a rule where nothing turns on a distinction between a particular party and many parties, or between a particular act and many acts, but has everything turn on temporal particularity and generality. As with the military's distinction between an order and a standing order, everything turns on whether the time frame is open or closed. Given the way the sections abjure any distinction between particular and general parties or acts, it could not be otherwise. Without *some* distinction between the particular and the general there is no distinction between a rule and order. Given that there are only three candidates for the particular/general dimension, with two of them being expressly precluded by section 551(4) and implicitly precluded in section 551(6), there is only one left, and it is that one remaining dimension that is called forth and given legal effect by three phrases: "and future effect" in section 551(4), "for the future" in section 551(4), and "final disposition" in section 551(6).

Now that we see all of this, two matters become clear. One, the distinction drawn by sections 551(4) and 551(6) is a distinction between whether a decision speaks forward or not, with some decisions, those involving a "final disposition," not speaking forward, and others, those having "future" and speaking "for the future" being the ones that do speak forward, with the speak forward/speak currently distinction being crucial. Second, and the central corollary of the first, is that *nothing* in the speak forward/speak to the present distinction addresses the question of *when the now/forward distinction is drawn*. In other words, nothing in this way of drawing the distinction, or in the necessity of drawing some particular/general distinction, suggests one answer or another to the question of when "the future" starts. Some decisions will pertain to a certain narrow temporal time frame, and these will be the "orders," and others will pertain to an open-ended time frame, and these are the "rules," but *that* distinction has nothing to do with when that time frame is or starts and nothing to do with the relationship between the time frame and the time of the making of the decision.

To put the same point differently (and perhaps slightly more clearly), we are now able to appreciate that the creation of an open-ended rule and the designation of the starting time for the open-ended period encompassed by that rule are two distinct issues. Once we understand, especially from the conjunction of "general" and "particular" in section 551(4) that "and future effect" and "for the future" can be seen most plausibly as addressing *only* the first of these questions, then we can see that the second question need not be taken either to have been answered or even addressed by the pertinent language.

It thus appears that the question of retroactivity, the question of the permissible starting date for a rule that speaks to the future from the perspective of when that rule takes effect, need not be taken to have been answered by the provisions of section 551(4). . . .

How do Justice Kennedy and, in particular, Justice Scalia deal with the issue of retroactivity in the following case? Why was the rule invalid for the majority? Could Congress have avoided the problem? How? As far as Justice Scalia is concerned, what impact does the language of the APA have on the outcome of the case?

BOWEN v. GEORGETOWN UNIV. HOSPITAL

United States Supreme Court
488 U.S. 204 (1988)

JUSTICE KENNEDY delivered the opinion of the Court.

Under the Medicare program, health care providers are reimbursed by the Government for expenses incurred in providing medical services to Medicare beneficiaries. . . . Congress has authorized the Secretary of Health and Human Services to promulgate regulations setting limits on the levels of Medicare costs that will be reimbursed. The question presented here is whether the Secretary may exercise this rulemaking authority to promulgate cost limits that are retroactive.

I

The Secretary's authority to adopt cost-limit rules is established by § 223(b) of the Social Security Amendments of 1972. . . . This authority was first implemented in 1974 by promulgation of a cost-limit schedule for hospital services; new cost-limit schedules were issued on an annual basis thereafter. On June 30, 1981, the Secretary issued a cost-limit schedule that included technical changes in the methods for calculating cost limits. One of these changes affected the method for calculating the "wage index," a factor used to reflect the salary levels for hospital employees in different parts of the country. Under the prior rule, the wage index for a given geographic area was calculated by using the average salary levels for all hospitals in the area; the 1981 rule provided that wages paid by Federal Government hospitals would be excluded from that computation. . . .

Various hospitals in the District of Columbia area brought suit in United States District Court seeking to have the 1981 schedule invalidated. On April 29, 1983, the District Court struck down the 1981 wage-index rule, concluding that the Secretary had violated the Administrative Procedure Act (APA), 5 U.S.C. § 551 *et seq.*, by failing to provide notice and an opportunity for public comment before issuing the rule. The court did not enjoin enforcement of the rule, however, finding it lacked jurisdiction to do so because the hospitals had not yet exhausted their administrative reimbursement remedies. The court's order stated:

> If the Secretary wishes to put in place a valid prospective wage index, she should begin proper notice and comment proceedings; any wage index currently in place that has been promulgated without notice and comment is invalid as was the 1981 schedule.

The Secretary did not pursue an appeal. Instead, after recognizing the invalidity of the rule, . . . the Secretary settled the hospitals' cost reimbursement reports by applying the pre-1981 wage-index method.

In February 1984, the Secretary published a notice seeking public comment on a proposal to reissue the 1981 wage-index rule, retroactive to July 1, 1981. Because Congress had subsequently amended the Medicare Act to require significantly different cost reimbursement procedures, the readoption of the modified wage-index method was to apply exclusively to a 15-month period commencing July 1, 1981. After considering the comments received, the Secretary reissued the 1981 schedule in final form on November 26, 1984, and proceeded to recoup sums previously paid as a result of the District Court's ruling in DCHA. In effect, the Secretary had promulgated a rule retroactively, and the net result was as if the original rule had never been set aside. Respondents, a group of seven hospitals who had benefitted from the invalidation of the 1981 schedule, were required to return over $2 million in reimbursement payments. After exhausting administrative remedies, they sought judicial review under the applicable provisions of the APA, claiming that the retroactive schedule was invalid under both the APA and the Medicare Act.

The United States District Court for the District of Columbia granted summary judgment for respondents. . . . The court held that retroactive application was not justified under the circumstances of the case.

The Secretary appealed to the United States Court of Appeals for the District of Columbia Circuit, which affirmed . . . [o]n the alternative grounds that the APA, as a general matter, forbids retroactive rulemaking and the Medicare Act, by specific terms, bars retroactive cost-limit rules. We granted certiorari, and we now affirm.

II

It is axiomatic that an administrative agency's power to promulgate legislative regulations is limited to the authority delegated by Congress. In determining the validity of the Secretary's retroactive cost-limit rule, the threshold question is whether the Medicare Act authorizes retroactive rulemaking.

Retroactivity is not favored in the law. Thus, congressional enactments and administrative rules will not be construed to have retroactive effect unless their language requires this result. . . . By the same principle, a statutory grant of legislative rulemaking authority will not, as a general matter, be understood to encompass the power to promulgate retroactive rules unless that power is conveyed by Congress in express terms. . . . Even where some substantial justification for retroactive rulemaking is presented, courts should be reluctant to find such authority absent an express statutory grant.

The Secretary contends that the Medicare Act provides the necessary authority to promulgate retroactive cost-limit rules in the unusual circumstances of this case. He rests on alternative grounds: first, the specific grant of authority to promulgate regulations to "provide for the making of suitable retroactive corrective adjustments," 42 U.S.C. § 1395x(v)(1)(A)(ii); and second, the general grant of authority to promulgate cost limit rules. We consider these alternatives in turn.

A

The authority to promulgate cost reimbursement regulations is set forth in § 1395x(v)(1)(A). That subparagraph also provides that:

> "Such regulations shall . . . (ii) provide for the making of suitable retroactive corrective adjustments where, for a provider of services for any fiscal period, the aggregate reimbursement produced by the methods of determining costs proves to be either inadequate or excessive."

This provision on its face permits some form of retroactive action. We cannot accept the Secretary's argument, however, that it provides authority for the retroactive promulgation of cost-limit rules. To the contrary, we agree with the Court of Appeals that clause (ii) directs the Secretary to establish a procedure for making case-by-case adjustments to reimbursement payments where the regulations prescribing computation methods do not reach the correct result in individual cases. The structure and language of the statute require the conclusion that the retroactivity provision applies only to case-by-case adjudication, not to rulemaking. . . .

B

The statutory provisions establishing the Secretary's general rulemaking power contain no express authorization of retroactive rulemaking. Any light that might be shed on this matter by suggestions of legislative intent also indicates that no such authority was contemplated. . . .

The legislative history of the cost-limit provision directly addresses the issue of retroactivity. In discussing the authority granted by § 223(b) of the 1972 amendments, the House and Senate Committee Reports expressed a desire to forbid retroactive cost-limit rules: "The proposed new authority to set limits on costs . . . would be exercised on a prospective, rather than retrospective, basis so that the provider would know in advance the limits to Government recognition of incurred costs and have the opportunity to act to avoid having costs that are not reimbursable."

The Secretary's past administrative practice is consistent with this interpretation of the statute. . . .

The Secretary nonetheless suggests that, whatever the limits on his power to promulgate retroactive regulations in the normal course of events, judicial invalidation of a prospective rule is a unique occurrence that creates a heightened need, and thus a justification, for retroactive curative rulemaking. The Secretary warns that congressional intent and important administrative goals may be frustrated unless an invalidated rule can be cured of its defect and made applicable to past time periods. The argument is further advanced that the countervailing reliance interests are less compelling than in the usual case of retroactive rulemaking, because the original, invalidated rule provided at least some notice to the individuals and entities subject to its provisions.

Whatever weight the Secretary's contentions might have in other contexts, they need not be addressed here. The case before us is resolved by the particular statutory scheme in question. Our interpretation of the Medicare Act compels the conclusion that the Secretary has no authority to promulgate retroactive cost-limit rules.

The 1984 reinstatement of the 1981 cost-limit rule is invalid. The judgment of the Court of Appeals is affirmed.

JUSTICE SCALIA, concurring.

I agree with the Court that general principles of administrative law suggest that § 223(b) of the Medicare Act, does not permit retroactive application of the Secretary of Health and Human Service's 1984 cost-limit rule. I write separately because I find it incomplete to discuss general principles of administrative law without reference to the basic structural legislation which is the embodiment of those principles, The Administrative Procedure Act (APA). . . . I agree with the District of Columbia Circuit that the APA independently confirms the judgment we have reached.

The first part of the APA's definition of "rule" states that a rule

"means the whole or a part of an agency statement of general or particular applicability *and future effect* designed to implement, interpret, or prescribe law or policy or describing the organization, procedure, or practice requirements of an agency. . . ." 5 U.S.C. § 551(4). . . . (emphasis added). . . .

The only plausible reading of the italicized phrase is that rules have legal consequences only for the future. It could not possibly mean that merely some of their legal consequences must be for the future, though they may also have legal consequences for the past, since that description would not enable rules to be distinguished from "orders," *see* 5 U.S.C. § 551(6), and would thus destroy the entire dichotomy upon which the most significant portions of the APA are based. (Adjudication — the process for formulating orders, *see* § 551(7) — has future as well as past legal consequences, since the principles announced in an adjudication cannot be departed from in future adjudications without reason.)

Nor could "future effect" in this definition mean merely "taking effect in the future," that is, having a future effective date even though, once effective, altering the law applied in the past. That reading, urged by the Government, produces a definition of "rule" that is meaningless, since obviously all agency statements have "future effect" in the sense that they do not take effect until after they are made. . . .

In short, there is really no alternative except the obvious meaning, that a rule is a statement that has legal consequences only for the future. If the first part of the definition left any doubt of this, however, it is surely eliminated by the second part (which the Acting Solicitor General's brief regrettably submerges in ellipsis). After the portion set forth above, the definition continues that a rule

> "includes the approval or prescription for the future of rates, wages, corporate or financial structures or reorganizations thereof, prices, facilities, appliances, services or allowances therefor or of valuations, costs, or accounting, or practices bearing on any of the foregoing." 5 U.C.S. § 551(4).

It seems to me clear that the phrase "for the future" — which even more obviously refers to future operation rather than a future effective date — is not meant to add a requirement to those contained in the earlier part of the definition, but rather to repeat, in a more particularized context, the prior requirement "of future effect." And even if one thought otherwise it would not matter for purposes of the present case, since the HEW "cost-limit" rules governing reimbursement are a "prescription" of "practices bearing on" "allowances" for "services."

The position the Government takes in this litigation is out of accord with its own most authoritative interpretation of the APA, the 1947 Attorney General's Manual on the Administrative Procedure Act (AG's Manual), which we have repeatedly given great weight. That document was prepared by the same Office of the Assistant Solicitor General that had advised Congress in the latter stages of enacting the APA, and was originally issued "as a guide to the agencies in adjusting their procedures to the requirements of the Act." AG's Manual 6. Its analysis is plainly out of accord with the Government's position here:

> "Of particular importance is the fact that 'rule' includes agency statements not only of general applicability but also those of particular applicability applying either to a class or to a single person. In either case, they must be of future effect, implementing or prescribing future law. . . .

> "[T]he the entire Act is based upon a dichotomy between rule making and adjudication. . . . Rule making is agency action which regulates the future conduct of either groups of persons or a single person; it is essentially

legislative in nature, not only because it operates in the future but also because it is primarily concerned with policy considerations. . . . Conversely, adjudication is concerned with the determination of past and present rights and liabilities." *Id.*, at 13–14.

These statements cannot conceivably be reconciled with the Government's position here that a rule has future effect merely because it is made effective in the future. Moreover, the clarity of these statements cannot be disregarded on the basis of the single sentence, elsewhere in the Manual, that "[n]othing in the Act precludes the issuance of retroactive rules when otherwise legal and accompanied by the finding required by section 4(c)." What that statement means (apart from the inexplicable reference to section 4(c), 5 U.S.C. § 553(d), which would appear to have no application, no matter which interpretation is adopted), is clarified by the immediately following citation to the portion of the legislative history supporting it, namely, H.R. Rep. No. 1980, 79th Cong. 2d Sess., 49, n. 1 (1946). That Report states that "[t]he phrase 'future effect' does not preclude agencies from considering and, so far as legally authorized, dealing with past transactions in prescribing rules for the future." The Treasury Department might prescribe, for example, that for purposes of assessing future income tax liability, income from certain trusts that has previously been considered nontaxable will be taxable — whether those trusts were established before or after the effective date of the regulation. That is not retroactivity in the sense at issue here, *i.e.*, in the sense of altering the past legal consequences of past actions. Rather, it is what has been characterized as "secondary" retroactivity. . . . A rule with exclusively future effect (taxation of future trust income) can unquestionably affect past transactions (rendering the previously established trusts less desirable in the future), but it does not for that reason cease to be a rule under the APA. Thus, with respect to the present matter, there is no question that the Secretary could have applied her new wage-index formulas to respondents in the future, even though respondents may have been operating under long-term labor and supply contracts negotiated in reliance upon the pre-existing rule. But when the Secretary prescribed such a formula for costs reimbursable while the prior rule was in effect, she changed the law retroactively, a function not performable by rule under the APA.

A rule that has unreasonable secondary retroactivity — for example, altering future regulation in a manner that makes worthless substantial past investment incurred in reliance upon the prior rule — may for that reason be "arbitrary or capricious," *see* 5 U.S.C. § 706, and thus invalid. In reference to such situations, there are to be found in many cases statements to the effect that "[w]here a rule has retroactive effects, it may nonetheless be sustained in spite of such retroactivity if it is reasonable." It is erroneous, however, to extend this "reasonableness" inquiry to purported rules that not merely affect past transactions but change what was the law in the past. Quite simply, a rule is an agency statement "of future effect," not "of future effect and/or reasonable past effect."

Although the APA was enacted over 40 years ago, this Court has never directly confronted whether the statute authorizes retroactive rules. This in itself casts doubt on the Government's position. If so obviously useful an instrument was available to the agencies, one would expect that we would previously have had occasion to review its exercise. . . .

The issue here is not constitutionality, but rather whether there is any good reason to doubt that the APA means what it says. For purposes of resolving that question, it does not at all follow that, since Congress itself possesses the power retroactively to change its laws, it must have meant agencies to possess the power retroactively to change their regulations. Retroactive legislation has always been looked upon with disfavor, . . . and even its constitutionality has been conditioned upon a rationality requirement beyond that applied to other legislation. . . . It is entirely unsurprising, therefore, that even though Congress wields such a power itself, it has been unwilling to confer it upon the agencies. Given the traditional attitude towards retroactive legislation, the regime established by the APA is an entirely reasonable one: Where quasi-legislative action is required, an agency cannot act with retroactive effect without some special congressional authorization. That is what the APA says, and there is no reason to think Congress did not mean it. . . .

INDUSTRIAL SAFETY EQUIPMENT ASS'N INC. v. E.P.A.

District of Columbia Court of Appeals
837 F.2d 1115 (1988)

WALD, CHIEF JUDGE:

This controversy concerns the adequacy of various types of asbestos-protection respirators. The National Institute for Occupational Safety and Health (NIOSH) and the Environmental Protection Agency (EPA) published in April, 1986, a report recommending that "supplied-air" respirators be used for maximum protection against asbestos exposure. Both agencies are authorized by statute to disseminate health information to the public. . . . Occupational Safety and Health Administration (OSHA) and EPA regulations, however, permit industry members to use numerous devices not recommended in the Guide. Plaintiffs-appellants Industrial Safety Equipment Association (ISEA), et al., brought a district court action on June 10, 1986 seeking declaratory and injunctive relief against publication of the Guide. They argued that the Guide violated the Administrative Procedure Act (APA) because it "constitutes or has the effect of new agency regulations," decertifying eleven lawful respirator types, yet it was not promulgated according to proper rulemaking processes. . . . [On appeal, various issues were raised. The Court of Appeals upheld the District Court's decision. Our focus is on its discussion of rules.]

I. BACKGROUND

OSHA and EPA regulations protect employees against the serious health hazard posed by asbestos in the workplace. Both sets of regulations require that asbestos-protection respirators be selected from among those certified by the NIOSH and the Mine Safety and Health Administration (MSHA). Specifically, there are thirteen federally approved respirators, ranging from "air purifying respirators" (filter devices) recommended for use when asbestos concentrations are relatively low, to "powered air purifying respirators," and finally to "supplied-air respirators" (self-contained breathing apparatuses), recommended as concentrations become progressively higher.

In April, 1986, the EPA and the NIOSH published the Guide with the stated purpose of providing "a single source for the best and most current information on worker respiratory protection against asbestos." Both parties to this dispute agree that the Guide is also intended "to provide employers with guidelines for developing effective respiratory protection programs." . . . The largest section of the Guide describes a model program for asbestos abatement operations. The preface explains that the Guide's recommendations not only satisfy existing regulations but also incorporate the most current scientific information about how best to minimize worker exposure. The Guide carefully distinguishes between the thirteen respirators all of which meet federal standards and the two types that the Guide recommends because they provide the maximum amount of worker protection. The most controversial passage in the Guide reads:

> The respirator types numbered 3 through 13 above are not recommended by NIOSH or EPA for use against asbestos. However, various existing regulations allow their use. In fact, the existing respirator certification regulations (30 C.F.R. Part 11) requires NIOSH to certify . . . [these eleven]. However, as a matter of public health policy, NIOSH and EPA do not recommend their use in asbestos environments.

Appellants claim that this disapproval of eleven lawful devices amounts to agency rulemaking, subject to review under the APA, because the action effectively "decertifies" the existing respirators marketed or used by appellants. The EPA counters that because the Guide formally binds no one, it cannot be viewed as rulemaking. Although we do not adopt the EPA's broad assertion that only legally binding publications can ever be reviewable, neither do we accept ISEA's characterization of the Guide as a *de facto* decertification of the respirators. We conclude that the EPA and NIOSH's publication of the Guide does not amount to agency action subject to judicial review.

II. ANALYSIS

A. *The Administrative Procedure Act*

. . . .

ISEA rests reviewability entirely on its characterization of the Guide as an agency rule. To adopt a substantive rule, an agency must comply with the APA's section 553 notice and comment requirements. Because no such rulemaking occurred in the present case, ISEA argues both that the Guide is invalid and that the district court's dismissal should be reversed. The EPA and NIOSH, on the other hand, contend that the Guide is not a substantive rule, that it is unreviewable, and, alternatively, that it did not require notice and comment proceedings. We hold that the facts support the district court's conclusion that the Guide does not qualify as agency action and hence is not reviewable.

The APA defines rule as "the whole or a part of an agency statement of general or particular applicability and future effect designed to implement, interpret, or prescribe law or policy. . . ." 5 U.S.C. § 551(4). Clearly Congress did not intend that the APA definition of a rule be construed so broadly that every agency action would be subject to judicial review. ISEA contends, however, that the "Guide takes the extra step necessary to make a 'report' an unlawful rulemaking; *i.e.,* it transcends the mere reporting of factual matters and attempts to change and implement law and policy within the statutory definition of rulemaking.". . . The facts suggest otherwise, however. The Guide does not change any law or official policy presently in effect. It does not narrow or alter the grounds on which the NIOSH will act to certify any of the thirteen lawful respirator types. Instead of repudiating the minimum protections prescribed in current regulations, the Guide offers a full ranking of all the lawful devices according to their effectiveness at protecting workers. Pointing out unique features of the two most protective respirators, the Guide limits itself to recommending them as "the maximum feasible level of respiratory protection." Clearly, then, there is no effective repeal of the EPA or NIOSH's current legal obligation to approve for use all thirteen respirator devices.

The advisory character of the NIOSH/EPA report is most evident when one examines the Guide. Starting with its conclusion that "no level of exposure [to asbestos] is known to be without risk," the Guide elaborates a model respiratory protection program for asbestos abatement operations. It emphasizes throughout that the model is an ideal, not a regimen presently mandated by law. . . .

Most important, in the section marked "Respiratory Selection," the EPA underscores the distinction between the present legal requirements and the current information that informs the Guide's recommendations. In the subsection entitled "Respirators Allowable Under Existing Regulations for Protection Against Asbestos," where the EPA criticizes existing regulations for not providing maximum protection, there are repeated assurances that the less protective devices still satisfy OSHA and EPA regulations.

Our conclusion that the Guide does not constitute an agency rule is reinforced by the fact that the Guide — a NIOSH/EPA "technical report" — was published neither in the Federal Register nor in the Code of Federal Regulations, which contains only documents "having general applicability and legal effect."

ISEA nonetheless relies on the alleged "substantial impact" of the Guide's criticisms on manufacturers of the disfavored respirators. We note first that this court has rejected the notion that the mere fact that an agency action has "substantial impact" "transform[s] it into a legislative rule." *See American Postal Workers Union v. United States Postal Service,* 707 F.2d 548, 560 (D.C. Cir. 1983) (specifically applied to § 553 notice and comment requirements). Second, publication of the Guide, which favors respirators that offer the maximum protection against asbestos, establishes no rule that the regulated industry must obey. In and of itself the Guide does not deny any rights to the appellants. Rather, any effect it might have on respirator manufacturers is indirect and arises from the reactions and choices of industry customers and workers.[11] Unions may stiffen their bargaining positions on safety precautions. Perhaps sales of several respirator types will decline; perhaps not, if appellants are correct in their view that the Guide's recommendations are unfounded. In any case, these repercussions from the dissemination of information designed to provide the industry with up-to-date safety recommendations do not convert the Guide into a reviewable rule or sanction. The district court correctly dismissed the action insofar as it was brought on APA grounds. . . .

NOTES AND QUESTIONS

4-1. Why is prospectivity so essential an element of a rule? What are the dangers inherent in retroactive rulemaking? Under what circumstances might Congress authorize such retroactivity? *See* William V. Luneberg, *Retroactivity and Administrative Rulemaking*, 1991 DUKE L.J. 106 (arguing that agencies often need the flexibility to adopt retroactive rules).

4-2. Is it possible to engage in retroactive rulemaking in the context of an adjudication? Is retroactivity any less of a problem in that context than it is in *Bowen*? *See SEC v. Chenery*, § 4.03[B], *infra*.

4-3. If you apply Professor Schauer's analysis to the rule in *Bowen*, is Justice Scalia correct in saying that his reading of the APA is the only reading? If not, is it the best reading of the APA? Why or why not?

4-4. Professor Levin argues that Congress should amend the APA so that the definition of a "rule" would focus on generality, rather than on prospectivity. *See* Ronald M. Levin, *The Case for (Finally) Fixing the APA's Definition of "Rule,"* 56 ADMIN. L. REV. 1077 (2004). Indeed, this is the approach of the Model State Administrative Procedure Act, § 1-102(10) (1981) (defining a rule as "the whole or a part of an agency statement of general applicability that implements, interprets, or prescribes (i) law or policy, or (ii) the organization, procedures, or practice requirements of an agency."). He disagrees with Justice Scalia about the practical consequences of prohibiting retroactive "rules." Because all agency actions under the APA that are not rules are orders, 5 U.S.C. § 551(6) (2004), "the consequence of declaring that a retroactive rule is not a 'rule' for APA purposes would be that the rule *could* be issued *without*

---

[11] Again even if we found that the Guide's publication were a reviewable action it would not follow that notice and comment were required. *Cf.* 2 K. Davis, *Administrative Law Treatise* § 7:20 (1979) (caution that miscellaneous informal agency action, such as "supervising, advising, applying pressure, publicizing [even though these activities may have 'substantial impact'] . . . rather clearly has to be generally free from any requirement of notice and comment proceedings"). Day-to-day informality and flexibility is indispensable to the agency function; moreover, agencies should not be deterred from producing information that will benefit the public. *Cf. Ford Motor Credit Co. v. Milhollin,* 444 U.S. 555, 565 (1980) (agency need not follow § 533 procedures in "information letters," though these statements often begin: "The staff's position is. . . .").

the safeguards of notice and comment procedure — surely a bad result, in light of the harsh effects that retroactive liability can have on members of the public." Levin at 8 (emphasis in original).

4-5. What other elements of a rule are you able to glean from the court's discussion in *Industrial Safety Equipment Association*?

4-6. Do you think that the EPA's Guide will have any impact on the industries who make the disfavored respirators? When does the dissemination of information rise to the level of a rule or agency action subject to judicial review? What if the information disseminated was known to be false or was, in fact, misleading? *See Impro Products, Inc. v. Block*, 722 F.2d 845 (D.C. Cir. 1983).

4-7. How important is it to preserve the kind of agency flexibility evidenced in ISEA? Do you agree with the court's observations in footnote 11? If not, what kinds of procedures do you recommend?

4-8. The plaintiffs in *ISEA* argue that the Guide has "substantial impact" on manufacturers of the disfavored respirators. Why, in their view, does this make it a rule? Does the language of § 553 of the APA support their argument?

4-9. Does the application of a rule that has been remanded to an agency for lack of adequate reasoning, but not vacated, violate the ban on retroactivity? *See ICORE, Inc. v. F.C.C.*, 985 F.2d 1075 (D.C. Cir. 1993). In upholding the application of the rule, the court noted that in *ICORE*, "in contrast to *Georgetown University Hospital*, the court considering the rule initially found it inappropriate to set the rule aside. The court's decision on that point represented a careful consideration of the risk of disruption and of the likelihood that the rule was altogether sound at the core. . . . Petitioners offer no reason why a rule so treated, and in fact applied during the entire interim period, should be treated the same as the rule initially 'struck down' in *Georgetown University Hospital*." *Id.* at 1081. Consider the following case and *see* Kristina Daugirdas, *Evaluating Remand Without Vacatur: A New Judicial Remedy for Defective Agency Rulemakings*, 80 N.Y.U. L. REV. 278 (2005).

SUGAR CANE GROWERS COOPERATIVE OF FLORIDA v. VENEMAN

United States Court of Appeals,
District of Columbia Circuit.
289 F.3d 89 (2002)

SILBERMAN, SENIOR CIRCUIT JUDGE:

. . . .

In the United States, sugar production, which the government supports through a variety of programs, is about evenly divided between sugar cane and sugar beet production. This suit involves the Department's choice of a particular method of support. Appellants are self-described small-, medium- and large-sized sugar cane growers, processors, refiners and marketers, who together make up a "significant" portion of the total domestic sugar cane production, which mostly occurs in the Gulf Belt and Hawaii. Sugar beets grow primarily in the North and West, and sugar beet farmers tend to harvest significantly fewer acres per producer than sugar cane farmers. The Department supports sugar production through a program of non-recourse loans; if the market price of sugar drops below the forfeiture price, producers may forfeit their crops to the Department in satisfaction of these loans rather than try to repay in cash, which effectively guarantees a minimum price for harvested and processed sugar. With the low sugar prices over the past several years, the Department has accumulated more than 700,000 tons of sugar, for which it pays approximately $1.35 million per month in storage fees. The presence of that potential supply (or "overhang") may depress somewhat sugar prices and it exacerbates the problem of limited sugar storage, which is particularly troublesome for sugar beet farmers.

The Food Security Act gives the Department authority to implement a payment-in-kind (PIK) program for sugar, which it did for sugar beet farmers in August 2000. For the 2000 PIK program, sugar beet farmers submitted bids to the Department offering to destroy (or "divert") a certain amount of their crops in return for sugar from USDA storage. A farmer's bid is his asking price for that amount of destruction; the price is expressed in terms of a percentage of the three-year average value of the crop yield for the acreage diverted. Thus, a farmer bidding 80 percent would receive eight dollars for every acre destroyed if an average acre of their farm produced ten dollars worth of sugar. In fact, the average bid was approximately 84 percent and resulted in the distribution of about 277,000 tons of government sugar and the diversion of approximately 102,000 acres. Participants were prohibited from participating in future PIK programs if they increased their acreage planted with sugar beets over 2000 levels. The Agency did not proceed by notice and comment, but no party challenged that decision or the program itself.

Appellants claim the 2000 PIK program unfairly provided participants with below-harvest-cost government sugar which gave them a competitive advantage over appellants. And they claim that the program depressed sugar prices. Actually, the price of sugar rose, but it is not clear what caused the increase. According to appellants, although initial forecasts predicted that the diverted acreage would lead to lower sugar crop volume in 2000, subsequent forecasts increased substantially in the months following implementation of the PIK program — to 23.6 tons per acre in December 2000 from 22.8 tons per acre before August 2000. Appellants contend that the yield increase (or "yield slippage") resulted in part from farmers taking their lowest-yielding crops out of production for the PIK program. With the yield slippage, additional beet sugar supplies ended up on the market, and PIK farmers received more sugar through the program than they would have if they had produced sugar on the diverted acres. And the greater supplies of sugar, it is argued, necessarily depressed sugar prices below that which would otherwise have obtained. The government insists that the program had a positive effect on the price of sugar, at least in part because it reduced the government's sugar supply and storage fees, ameliorating the overhang effect and storage scarcity problem.

In January 2001, the Department met with interested persons (including representatives of appellants) and indicated that while it was considering a PIK program for the 2001 sugar crop, it would not do so without notice and comment. The Agency also asked those present about the effectiveness of the 2000 PIK program and their thoughts on the desirability and structure of a potential 2001 program. Appellants claim that they were unable to comment satisfactorily because the data on the 2000 program was not yet available. Before August 2001, Department employees had approximately a dozen contacts with sugar industry representatives regarding the possibility of a 2001 program.

The Department announced by an August 31, 2001 press release, however, that it was implementing a PIK program for the 2001 sugar crop without using APA rulemaking. The Agency followed that announcement a week later with a "Notice of Program Implementation" in the September 7, 2001 Federal Register. For the 2001 PIK program, the Department set a 200,000 ton limit in order to encourage more competitive bidding and made both beet and cane sugar producers eligible. But a statutory restriction limiting payments to $20,000 per producer effectively eliminated appellants' opportunity to participate because of their size. Particularly troubling appellants, the government waived its 2000 PIK program restriction on future eligibility by participants who had increased their crop acreage; it merely included a similar restriction on 2001 participants. In contrast to the 2000 PIK program, in which the government disbursed all of the allotted sugar at the same time, in 2001 the Department indicated that it would stagger disbursement. After announcing the program, the Department received more than 6,000 bids and accepted 4,655 bids, some as high as 87.9931 percent. The final data on bids is not a part of the summary judgment record, nor is the disbursement schedule.

Appellants filed suit shortly after the press release appeared, seeking injunctive and declaratory relief. They argued that the Department did not comply with the APA because it promulgated a rule without notice-and-comment rulemaking; that it violated the Food Security Act of 1985 by not making required findings. . . .

[The court held that the plaintiffs had standing.]

III.

Turning to the merits, we take up first appellants' APA claim. The APA sets forth several steps an agency must take when engaged in rulemaking: it must publish a general notice of proposed rulemaking in the Federal Register; give an opportunity for interested persons to participate in the rulemaking through submission of written data, views, or arguments; and issue publication of a concise general statement of the rule's basis and purpose. 5 U.S.C. § 553(b), (c). The government defends the Department's failure to engage in notice-and-comment rulemaking by asserting the PIK announcement was not really a rule and, even if it were, the failure to engage in rulemaking was a harmless error.

The APA defines a rule very broadly as:

> the whole or a part of an agency statement of general or particular applicability and future effect designed to implement, interpret, or prescribe law or policy or describing the organization, procedure, or practice requirements of an agency and includes the approval or prescription for the future of rates, wages, corporate or financial structures or reorganizations thereof, prices, facilities, appliances, services or allowances therefor or of valuations, costs, or accounting, or practices bearing on any of the foregoing.

5 U.S.C. § 551(4). We have recognized that notwithstanding the breadth of the APA's definition an agency pronouncement that lacks the firmness of a proscribed standard — particularly certain policy statements — is not a rule. But the government does not claim that its package of announcements is a policy statement. Instead, the government argues that because the announcement of the 2001 PIK program was an "isolated agency act" that did not propose to affect subsequent Department acts and had "no future effect on any other party before the agency" it was not a rule. The government would have us see its announcement of the PIK program as analogous to an agency's award of a contract pursuant to an invitation of bids or an agency's decision to approve an application or a proposal — in administrative law terms an informal adjudication (which is the technical term for an executive action).

We have little difficulty — as did the district court — in rejecting this argument. The August 31 press release, the September Questions and Answers and most notably the September 7 Notice of Program Implementation set forth the bid submission procedures which all applicants must follow, the payment limitations of the program, and the sanctions that will be imposed on participants if they plant more in *future* years than in 2001. It is simply absurd to call this anything but a rule "by any other name."

As a variation on the government's second standing argument — that appellants have not demonstrated injury because they cannot show that if the Department had acted pursuant to section 553 the result would have been altered — the government alternatively claims harmless error. We are told that appellants cannot identify any additional arguments they would have made in a notice-and-comment procedure that they did not make to the Department in the several informal sessions. And we are reminded that the Department did make certain changes to the 2001 PIK program in response to appellants' concerns. It is true that we have recognized certain technical APA errors as harmless. For example, in *Sheppard v. Sullivan*, 906 F.2d 756, 761-62 (D.C. Cir. 1990), a challenge to an agency adjudication in a benefits case, we held that a failure to undertake formal notice and comment with respect to a program manual was harmless. But, in so doing, we applied the standard set out in *McLouth Steel Prods. Corp. v. Thomas*, 838 F.2d 1317, 1324 (D.C. Cir. 1988), under which an utter failure to comply with notice and comment cannot be considered harmless if there is any uncertainty at all as to the effect of that failure. . . .

Here the government would have us virtually repeal section 553's requirements: if the government could skip those procedures, engage in informal consultation, and then be protected from judicial review unless a petitioner could show a new argument — not presented informally — section 553 obviously would be eviscerated. The government could avoid the necessity of publishing a notice of a proposed rule and perhaps, most important, would not be obliged to set forth a statement of the basis and purpose of the rule, which needs to take account of the major comments — and often is a major focus of judicial review. . . .

. . . .

There remains the question of remedy. Normally when an agency so clearly violates the APA we would vacate its action — in this case its "non-rule rule" — and simply remand for the agency to start again. Unfortunately, because we denied preliminary relief in this case, the 2001 program was launched and crops were plowed under. The egg has been scrambled and there is no apparent way to restore the status quo ante. Appellants suggested that if we were to vacate, the Federal Court of Claims would have the responsibility of allocating damages. But that seems an invitation to chaos. Moreover, although the government did not — could not have for the first time on appeal — assert a good cause for omitting notice and comment, it is at least possible that the Department could establish good cause because of timing exigencies.

Appellants insist that we have no discretion in the matter; if the Department violated the APA — which it did — its actions must be vacated. But that is simply not the law. Instead, "[t]he decision whether to vacate depends on 'the seriousness of the order's deficiencies (and thus the extent of doubt whether the agency chose correctly) and the disruptive consequences of an interim change that may itself be changed.'" We have previously remanded without vacating when the agency failed to follow notice-and-comment procedures.

Accordingly, we reverse the district court's grant of summary judgment and remand to that court to in turn remand to the Department.

So ordered.

§ 4.02 Formal and Informal Rules and Rulemaking Processes

[A] Overview

Having concluded that a rule is involved does not, of course, end our analysis. There are various kinds of rules that differ primarily in terms of the rulemaking procedures that are required to promulgate them. We shall examine those rules exempt from these procedures *infra*. Here we focus on both informal and formal rules. The Administrative Procedure Act provides explicitly for informal and formal rulemaking processes. The procedures for informal rulemaking are set forth in section 553. That section provides for notice and comment rulemaking; that is to say, before an agency can issue a final, binding informal rule, it must publish a notice of its proposed rule and provide an opportunity for the public to comment on this rule by way of written statements. Only after considering these comments may the agency issue a final rule. Notice and comment procedures thus allow the general public as well as the regulated and the beneficiaries of a rule to call the agencies' attention to potential problems with the proposed rule, and to offer suggestions for their resolution. Section 553(c) also requires that a concise statement of the basis and purpose of this rule accompany its publication in final form.

The APA also provides for formal rulemaking procedures. Section 553(c) triggers the formal adjudicatory procedures of the APA when Congress provides that a rule "be made on the record after opportunity for an agency hearing."

In *United States v. Florida East Coast Railway,* 410 U.S. 224 (1973), the Supreme Court held that section 1(14)(a) of the Interstate Commerce Act did not require that the agency use formal as opposed to informal rulemaking procedures. The Interstate Commerce Act required a decision be made "after hearing"; it did not use the "magic words" of section 553(c) — *i.e.*, a hearing "on the record after opportunity for an agency hearing." Thus, the court concluded that the formal rulemaking provisions of the APA set forth in sections 556 and 557 were not triggered:

> We think this treatment of the term "hearing" in the Administrative Procedure Act affords a sufficient basis for concluding that the requirement of a "hearing" contained in § 1(14)(a), in a situation where the Commission was acting under the 1966 statutory rulemaking authority that Congress had conferred upon it, did not by its own force require the Commission either to hear oral testimony, to permit cross-examination of Commission witnesses, or to hear oral argument. Here, the Commission promulgated a tentative draft of an order, and accorded all interested parties 60 days in which to file statements of position, submissions of evidence, and other relevant observations. The parties had fair notice of exactly what the Commission proposed to do, and were given an opportunity to comment, to object, or to make some other form of written submission. The final order of the Commission indicates that it gave consideration to the statements of the two appellees here. Given the "open-ended" nature of the proceedings, and the Commission's announced willingness to consider proposals for modification after operating experience had been acquired, we think the hearing requirement of § 1(14)(a) of the Act was met.

410 U.S. 241–42. Precisely how does formal rulemaking differ from informal rulemaking? Is cross-examination required in formal rulemaking? *See* § 556(d). In formal rulemaking, is there a record upon which a decision must be based and supported by substantial evidence? *See* § 556(d),(e). Must there be an oral hearing? *See* § 556(b). May there be *ex parte* contracts? *See* § 557(d). Do the APA's separation of functions provisions apply to formal rulemaking proceedings? *See* § 554(d). What kinds of findings must be made? *See* § 557(c). How do these provisions differ from those in section 553?

Quite apart from the informal and formal rulemaking procedures set forth by the APA, a third and more common category of rulemaking procedure has emerged in various agency enabling acts: hybrid rulemaking. Hybrid rulemaking combines aspects of formal rulemaking with informal rulemaking. Hybrid procedures seek to provide more process than the procedural floor set forth by the informal rulemaking provisions of section 553, but less than the full range of formal adjudicatory procedures set forth by sections 556 and 557.

As we shall see, hybrid rulemaking is very much a product of the health, safety and environmental legislation of the 1970's, but it has also resulted from additional procedures required by agencies themselves or, especially in the early 1970's, by the federal courts.

We shall first examine informal rulemaking under section 553 of the APA; then, we shall look at hybrid rulemaking procedures.

[B] Informal Rulemaking Processes — Notice and Comment

CHOCOLATE MFRS. ASS'N OF UNITED STATES v. BLOCK

Fourth Circuit Court of Appeals
755 F.2d 1098 (1985)

Before Russell and Sprouse, Circuit Judges, and Hargrove, United States District Judge for the District of Maryland, sitting by designation.

Sprouse, Circuit Judge:

Chocolate Manufacturers Association (CMA) appeals from the decision of the district court denying it relief from a rule promulgated by the Food and Nutrition Service (FNS) of the United States Department of Agriculture (USDA or Department). CMA protests that part of the rule that prohibits the use of chocolate flavored milk[1] in the federally funded Special Supplemental Food Program for Women, Infants and Children (WIC Program). Holding that the Department's proposed rulemaking did not provide adequate notice that the elimination of flavored milk would be considered in the rulemaking procedure, we reverse.

I

. . . .

The WIC Program was established by Congress in 1972 to assist pregnant, postpartum, and breastfeeding women, infants and young children from families with inadequate income whose physical and mental health is in danger because of inadequate nutrition or health care. Under the program, the Department designs food packages reflecting the different nutritional needs of women, infants, and children and provides cash grants to state or local agencies, which distribute cash or vouchers to qualifying individuals in accordance with Departmental regulations as to the type and quantity of food.

In 1975 Congress revised and extended the WIC Program through fiscal year 1978 and, for the first time, defined the "supplemental foods" which the program was established to provide. The term:

> shall mean those foods containing nutrients known to be lacking in the diets of populations at nutritional risk and, in particular, those foods and food products containing high-quality protein, iron, calcium, vitamin A, and

---

[1] Referred to hereafter as "flavored milk."

vitamin C. . . . The contents of the food package shall be made available in such a manner as to provide flexibility, taking into account medical and nutritional objectives and cultural eating patterns. . . .

Pursuant to this statutory definition, the Department promulgated new regulations specifying the contents of WIC Program food packages. These regulations specified that flavored milk was an acceptable substitute for fluid whole milk in the food packages for women and children, but not infants. This regulation formalized the Department's practice of permitting the substitution of flavored milk, a practice observed in the WIC Program since its inception in 1973 as well as in several of the other food programs administered by the Department.

In 1978 Congress, in extending the WIC Program through fiscal year 1982, redefined the term "supplemental foods" to mean:

> those foods containing nutrients determined by nutritional research to be lacking in the diets of pregnant, breastfeeding, and postpartum women, infants, and children, as prescribed by the Secretary. State agencies may, with the approval of the Secretary, substitute different foods providing the nutritional equivalent of foods prescribed by the Secretary, to allow for different cultural eating patterns. . . .

> The Secretary shall prescribe by regulation supplemental foods to be made available in the program under this section. To the degree possible, the Secretary shall assure that the fat, sugar, and salt content of the prescribed foods is appropriate. . . .

To comply with this statutory redefinition, the Department moved to redraft its regulations specifying the WIC Program food packages. In doing so it relied upon information collected during an extensive investigative effort which had begun in 1977. In June 1977 the Department held public hearings in seven cities and elicited testimony on the structure and administration of the WIC Program. . . . In addition to information gathered at the public hearings, the Department received periodic reports from the National Advisory Council on Maternal, Infant, and Fetal Nutrition, as well as recommendations from a Food Package Advisory Panel convened in October 1978.

Using this information as well as its own research as a basis, the Department in November 1979 published for comment the proposed rule at issue in this case. Along with the proposed rule, the Department published a preamble discussing the general purpose of the rule and acknowledging the congressional directive that the Department design food packages containing the requisite nutritional value and appropriate levels of fat, sugar, and salt. Discussing the issue of sugar at length, it noted, for example, that continued inclusion of high sugar cereals may be "contrary to nutrition education principles and may lead to unsound eating practices." It also noted that high sugar foods are more expensive than foods with lower sugar content, and that allowing them would be "inconsistent with the goal of teaching participants economical food buying patterns."

The rule proposed a maximum sugar content specifically for authorized cereals. The preamble also contained a discussion of the sugar content in juice, but the Department did not propose to reduce the allowable amount of sugar in juice because of technical problems involved in any reduction. Neither the rule nor the preamble discussed sugar in relation to flavoring in milk. Under the proposed rule, the food packages for women and children without special dietary needs included milk that could be "flavored or unflavored."

The notice allowed sixty days for comment and specifically invited comment on the entire scope of the proposed rules: "The public is invited to submit written comments in favor of or in objection to the proposed regulations or to make recommendations for alternatives not considered in the proposed regulations." Over 1,000 comments were received from state and local agencies, congressional offices, interest groups, and WIC Program participants and others. Seventy-eight commenters, mostly local WIC administrators, recommended that the agency delete flavored milk from the list of approved supplemental foods.

In promulgating the final rule, the Department, responding to these public comments, deleted flavored milk from the list, explaining:

> In the previous regulations, women and children were allowed to receive flavored or unflavored milk. No change in this provision was proposed by the Department. However, 78 commenters requested the deletion of flavored milk from the food packages since flavored milk has a higher sugar content than unflavored milk. They indicated that providing flavored milk contradicts nutrition education and the Department's proposal to limit sugar in the food packages. Furthermore, flavored milk is more expensive than unflavored milk. The Department agrees with these concerns. There are significant differences in the sugar content of fluid whole milk and low fat chocolate milk. Fluid whole milk supplies 12.0 grams of carbohydrate per cup compared to 27.3 grams of carbohydrate per cup provided by low fat chocolate milk. If we assume that the major portion of carbohydrate in milk is in the form of simple sugar, fluid whole milk contains 4.9% sugar contrasted with 10.9% sugar in low fat chocolate milk. Therefore, to reinforce nutrition education, for consistency with the Department's philosophy about sugar in the food packages, and to maintain food package costs at economic levels, the Department is deleting flavored milk from the food packages for women and children. Although the deletion of flavored milk was not proposed, the comments and the Department's policy on sugar validate this change.

45 Fed. Reg. 74854, 74865-66 (1980).

After the final rule was issued, CMA petitioned the Department to reopen the rulemaking to allow it to comment, maintaining that it had been misled into believing that the deletion of flavored milk would not be considered. In a letter to CMA dated November 18, 1981, the Department indicated that it would reopen the issue of flavored milk for "further public comments" and would request "rationale both supporting and opposing the disallowance of flavored milk in the WIC Program." It subsequently reversed this position, however, and declined to reopen the rulemaking procedure. On this appeal, CMA contends first that the Department did not provide notice that the disallowance of flavored milk would be considered, and second that the Department gave no reasoned justification for changing its position about the nutritional value of chocolate in the food distributed under its authority. The Department responds to the first contention by arguing that its notice advised the public of its general concern about high sugar content in the proposed food packages and that this should have alerted potentially interested commenters that it would consider eliminating any food with high sugar content. It also argues in effect that the inclusion of flavored milk in the proposed rule carried with it the implication that both inclusion and exclusion would be considered in the rulemaking process. Because we agree with CMA that the Department provided inadequate notice and, therefore, that it must reopen the comment period on the rule, we do not reach the issue of the reasonable justification for its change of position.

II

The requirement of notice and a fair opportunity to be heard is basic to administrative law. . . . Our single chore is to determine if the Department's notice provided interested persons, including CMA, with that opportunity. We must decide whether inclusion of flavored milk in the allowable food packages under the proposed rule should have alerted interested persons that the Department might reverse its position and exclude flavored milk if adverse comments recommended its deletion from the program.

Section 4 of the Administrative Procedure Act (APA) requires that the notice in the Federal Register of a proposed rulemaking contain "either the terms or substance of the proposed rule or a description of the subjects and issues involved." 5 U.S.C. § 553(b)(3) (1982). The purpose of the notice-and-comment procedure is both "to allow the agency to benefit from the experience and input of the parties who file comments . . . and to see to it that the agency maintains a flexible and open-minded attitude towards its own rules." *National Tour Brokers Ass'n v. United States,* 591 F.2d 896, 902 (D.C. Cir. 1978). The notice-and-comment procedure encourages public participation in the administrative process and educates the agency, thereby helping to ensure informed agency decisionmaking. . . .

The Department's published notice here consisted of the proposed rule and a preamble discussing the negative effect of high sugar content in general and specifically in relation to some foods such as cereals and juices, but it did not mention high sugar content in flavored milk. The proposed rule eliminated certain foods with high sugar content but specifically authorized flavored milk as part of the permissible diet. In a discussion characterized by pointed identification of foods with high sugar content, flavored milk was conspicuous by its exclusion. If after comments the agency had adopted without change the proposed rule as its final rule, there could have been no possible objection to the adequacy of notice. The public was fully notified as to what the Department considered to be a healthy and adequate diet for its target group. The final rule, however, dramatically altered the proposed rule, changing for the first time the milk content of the diet by deleting flavored milk. The agency concedes that the elimination of flavored milk by the final rule is a complete reversal from its treatment in the proposed rule, but it explains that the reversal was caused by the comments received from 78 interested parties — primarily professional administrators of the WIC Program.

This presents then not the simple question of whether the notice of a proposed rule adequately informs the public of its intent, but rather the question of how to judge the adequacy of the notice when the proposal it describes is replaced by a final rule which reaches a conclusion exactly opposite to that proposed, on the basis of comments received from parties representing only a single view of a controversy.[13] In reviewing the propriety of such agency action, we are not constrained by the same degree of deference we afford most agency determinations. "Though our review of an agency's final decision is relatively narrow, we must be strict in reviewing an agency's compliance with procedural rules.". . . "The question of adequacy of notice where a proposed rule is changed after comment . . . requires careful consideration on a case-by-case basis."

There is no question that an agency may promulgate a final rule that differs in some particulars from its proposal. Otherwise the agency "can learn from the comments on its proposals only at the peril of starting a new procedural round of commentary." *International Harvester Co. v. Ruckelshaus,* 478 F.2d 615, 632 n. 51 (D.C. Cir. 1973). An agency, however, does not have carte blanche to establish a rule contrary to its original proposal simply because it receives suggestions to alter it during the comment period. An interested party must have been alerted by the notice to the possibility of the changes eventually adopted from the comments. . . . Although an agency, in its notice of proposed rulemaking, need not identify precisely every potential regulatory change, . . . the notice must be sufficiently descriptive to provide interested parties with a fair opportunity to comment and to participate in the rulemaking. . . .

The test devised by the First Circuit for determining adequacy of notice of a change in a proposed rule occurring after comments appears to us to be sound: notice is adequate if the changes in the original plan "are in character with the original scheme," and the final rule is a "logical outgrowth" of the notice and comments already given. . . . Stated differently, if the final rule materially alters the issues involved in the rulemaking or, as stated in *Rowell v. Andrus,* 631 F.2d 699, 702 n. 2 (10th Cir. 1980), if the final rule "substantially departs from the terms or substance of the proposed rule," the notice is inadequate.

There can be no doubt that the final rule in the instant case was the "outgrowth" of the original rule proposed by the agency, but the question of

---

[13] In dissenting from the Supreme Court's denial of certiorari in *Eli Lilly & Co. v. Costle,* 444 U.S. 1096 (1980), Justice Rehnquist noted that the case presented:

an issue of great importance, which cannot help but become greater as time goes on and more and more administrative proceedings are conducted either directly under the Administrative Procedure Act . . . or similar provisions in new Acts of Congress for review of agency action. That question is the degree to which an agency, which publishes a rule for notice and comment under § 4 of the Administrative Procedure Act and very substantially changes the rule in response to the comments it receives, is obliged to publish the revised rule to allow another opportunity for notice and comment. . . .

. . . [W]hen we consider the very significant effects that a "rulemaking" procedure may have upon the parties involved. . . . I think this Court should grant certiorari to examine the question.

444 U.S. at 1096–97.

whether the change in it was in character with the original scheme and whether it was a "logical outgrowth" is not easy to answer. In resolving this difficult issue, we recognize that, although helpful, verbal formulations are not omnipotent talismans, and we agree that in the final analysis each case "must turn on how well the notice that the agency gave serves the policies underlying the notice requirement." *Small Refiner Lead Phase-Down Task Force v. EPA,* 705 F.2d 506, 547 (D.C. Cir. 1983). Under either view, we do not feel that CMA was fairly treated or that the administrative rulemaking process was well served by the drastic alteration of the rule without an opportunity for CMA to be heard.

It is apparent that for many years the Department of Agriculture has permitted the use of chocolate in some form in the food distribution programs that it administers. The only time the Department has proposed to remove chocolate in any form from its programs was in April 1978 when it sought to characterize chocolate as a candy and remove it from the School Lunch Program. That proposal was withdrawn after CMA commented, supporting chocolate as a part of the diet. Chocolate flavored milk has been a permissible part of the WIC Program diet since its inception and there have been no proposals for its removal until the present controversy.

The Department sponsored commendable information-gathering proceedings prior to publishing its proposed rule. Together with its own research, the information gathered in the pre-publication information solicitations formed the basis for the proposed rule. Most of the same information was presented to Congress prior to enactment of the 1978 statute that precipitated the 1979 rulemaking here in controversy. The National Advisory Council on Maternal, Infant, and Fetal Nutrition provided information and advice. Regional council meetings were open to the public and held in diverse areas of the country. Department of Agriculture personnel attended a number of regional, state, and local meetings and gathered opinions concerning possible changes in the food packages. The agency also gathered a food package advisory panel of experts seeking their recommendations. Food packages were designed based on the information and advice gleaned from these sources. In all of these activities setting out and discussing food packages, including the proposed rule and its preamble, the Department never suggested that flavored milk be removed from the WIC Program.

The published preamble to the proposed rule consisted of twelve pages in the Federal Register discussing in detail factors that would be considered in making the final rule. Two pages were devoted to a general discussion of nutrients, including protein, iron, calcium, vitamin A, vitamin C, folic acid, zinc, and fiber, and the dangers of overconsumption of sugar, fat, and salt. The preamble discussed some foods containing these ingredients and foods posing specific problems. It did not discuss flavored milk. . . .

At the time the proposed rulemaking was published, neither CMA nor the public in general could have had any indication from the history of either the WIC Program or any other food distribution programs that flavored milk was not part of the acceptable diet for women and children without special dietary needs. The discussion in the preamble to the proposed rule was very detailed and identified specific foods which the agency was examining for excess sugar.

This specificity, together with total silence concerning any suggestion of eliminating flavored milk, strongly indicated that flavored milk was not at issue. The proposed rule positively and unqualifiedly approved the continued use of flavored milk. Under the specific circumstances of this case, it cannot be said that the ultimate changes in the proposed rule were in character with the original scheme or a logical outgrowth of the notice. We can well accept that, in general, an approval of a practice in a proposed rule may properly alert interested parties that the practice may be disapproved in the final rule in the event of adverse comments. The total effect of the history of the use of flavored milk, the preamble discussion, and the proposed rule, however, could have led interested persons only to conclude that a change in flavored milk would not be considered. Although ultimately their comments may well have been futile, CMA and other interested persons at least should have had the opportunity to make them. We believe that there was insufficient notice that the deletion of flavored milk from the WIC Program would be considered if adverse comments were received, and, therefore, that affected parties did not receive a fair opportunity to contribute to the administrative rulemaking process. That process was ill-served by the misleading or inadequate notice concerning the permissibility of chocolate flavored milk in the WIC Program and "does not serve the policy underlying the notice requirement."

The judgment of the district court is therefore reversed, and the case is remanded to the administrative agency with instructions to reopen the comment period and thereby afford interested parties a fair opportunity to comment on the proposed changes in the rule.

REVERSED AND REMANDED WITH INSTRUCTIONS.

NOTES AND QUESTIONS

4-10. If you were general counsel to an administrative agency, what advice would you give the agency to ensure that the notice it provided in rulemaking proceedings was adequate for purposes of section 553? Would you recommend specific proposals to help focus the thrust of the comments to be received? Are there any dangers with this approach? Would you, in the alternative, recommend more general statements of the rule's purposes? Are there any dangers with this approach?

4-11. When would you recommend that the agency engage in a second round of notice and comments? Consider the following:

The Administrative Conference has recommended that agencies consider providing for two cycles of notice and comment where comments bring new issues to the attention of the agency, as well as rulemakings where from the outset the agency anticipates that the issues will be unusually complex or where the first notice contained only a general description of the subject and the issues. Other circumstances that might support a second cycle include the availability of new studies or experiments while the rulemaking is in progress; supervening legal developments such as statutes, regulations or court decisions that significantly affect the rulemaking; or any other important change in the framework of agency analysis of the rulemaking.

ACUS, *A Guide to Federal Agency Rulemaking,* p. 186 (Administrative Conf. of U.S., 2d ed. 1991).

4-12. What factors militate against a second round of notice and comment? Should courts engage in an inquiry into the futility of a second cycle before ordering an agency to reopen the comment period? What if more than 78 of the initial commenters advocated deleting flavored milk from the list? What if more than 90% recommended such a change in the proposed rule?

UNITED STATES v. NOVA SCOTIA FOOD PRODUCTS CORP.

Second Circuit Court of Appeals
568 F.2d 240 (1970)

Before WATERMAN and GURFEIN, CIRCUIT JUDGES, and BLUMENFELD, DISTRICT JUDGE.

GURFEIN, CIRCUIT JUDGE:

This appeal involving a regulation of the Food and Drug Administration is not here upon a direct review of agency action. It is an appeal from a judgment of the District Court for the Eastern District of New York (Hon. John J. Dooling, Judge) enjoining the appellants, after a hearing, from processing hot smoked whitefish except in accordance with time-temperature-salinity (T-T-S) regulations contained in 21 C.F.R. Part 122 (1977). . . .

The injunction was sought and granted on the ground that smoked whitefish which has been processed in violation of the T-T-S regulation is "adulterated." Food, Drug and Cosmetics Act ("the Act") §§ 302(a) and 301(k). . . .

Appellant Nova Scotia receives frozen or iced whitefish in interstate commerce which it processes by brining, smoking and cooking. The fish are then sold as smoked whitefish.

The regulations cited above require that hot-process smoked fish be heated by a controlled heat process that provides a monitoring system positioned in as many strategic locations in the oven as necessary to assure a continuous temperature through each fish of not less than 180° F. for a minimum of 30 minutes for fish which have been brined to contain 3.5% Water phase salt or at 150° F. for a minimum of 30 minutes if the salinity was at 5% Water phase. Since each fish must meet these requirements, it is necessary to heat an entire batch of fish to even higher temperatures so that the lowest temperature for any fish will meet the minimum requirements.

Government inspection of appellants' plant established without question that the minimum T-T-S requirements were not being met. There is no substantial claim that the plant was processing whitefish under "insanitary conditions" in any other material respect. Appellants, on their part, do not defend on the ground that they were in compliance, but rather that the requirements could not be met if a marketable whitefish was to be produced. They defend upon the grounds that the regulation is invalid (1) because it is beyond the authority delegated by the statute; (2) because the FDA improperly relied upon undisclosed evidence in promulgating the regulation and because it is not supported by the administrative record; and (3) because there was no adequate statement setting forth the basis of the regulation. We reject the contention that the regulation is beyond the authority delegated by the statute, but we find serious inadequacies in the procedure followed in the promulgation of the regulation and hold it to be invalid as applied to the appellants herein.

The hazard which the FDA sought to minimize was the outgrowth and toxin formation of Clostridium botulinum Type E spores of the bacteria which sometimes inhabit fish. There had been an occurrence of several cases of botulism traced to consumption of fish from inland waters in 1960 and 1963 which stimulated considerable bacteriological research. These bacteria can be present in the soil and water of various regions. They can invade fish in their natural habitat and can be further disseminated in the course of evisceration and preparation of the fish for cooking. A failure to destroy such spores through an adequate brining, thermal, and refrigeration process was found to be dangerous to public health.

The Commissioner of Food and Drugs ("Commissioner"), employing informal "notice-and-comment" procedures under 21 U.S.C. § 371(a), issued a proposal for the control of C. botulinum bacteria Type E in fish. For his statutory authority to promulgate the regulations, the Commissioner specifically relied only upon § 342(a)(4) of the Act which provides:

> A food shall be deemed to be adulterated —
>
> (4) if it has been prepared, packed, or held under insanitary conditions whereby it may have become contaminated with filth, or whereby it may have been rendered injurious to health;

Similar guidelines for smoking fish had been suggested by the FDA several years earlier, and were generally made known to people in the industry. At that stage, however, they were merely guidelines without substantive effect as law. Responding to the Commissioner's invitation in the notice of proposed rulemaking, members of the industry, including appellants and the intervenor-appellant, submitted comments on the proposed regulation.

The Commissioner thereafter issued the final regulations in which he adopted certain suggestions made in the comments, including a suggestion by the National Fisheries Institute, Inc. ("the Institute"), the intervenor herein. . . . The original proposal provided that the fish would have to be cooked to a temperature of 180° F. for at least 30 minutes, if the fish have been brined to contain 3.5% water phase salt, with no alternative. In the final regulation, an alternative suggested by the intervenor "that the parameter of 150° F. for 30 minutes and 5% salt in the water phase be established as an alternate procedure to that stated in the proposed regulation for an interim period until specific parameters can be established" was accepted, but as a permanent part of the regulation rather than for an interim period.

The intervenor suggested that "specific parameters" be established. This referred to particular processing parameters for different species of fish on a "species by species" basis. Such "species by species" determination was proposed not only by the intervenor but also by the Bureau of Commercial Fisheries of the Department of the Interior. That Bureau objected to the general application of the T-T-S requirement proposed by the FDA on the ground that application of the regulation to all species of fish being smoked was not commercially feasible, and that the regulation should therefore specify time-temperature-salinity requirements, as developed by research and study, on a species-by-species basis. The Bureau suggested that "wholesomeness considerations could be more practically and adequately realized by reducing processing temperature and using suitable concentrations of nitrite and salt." The Commissioner took cognizance of the suggestion, but decided, nevertheless, to impose the T-T-S requirement on all species of fish (except chub, which were regulated by 21 C.F.R. 172.177 (1977) [dealing with food additives]).

He did acknowledge, however, in his "basis and purpose" statement required by the Administrative Procedure Act ("APA"), 5 U.S.C. § 553(c), that "adequate times, temperatures and salt concentrations have not been demonstrated for each individual species of fish presently smoked." 35 F.R. 17,401 (Nov. 13, 1970). The Commissioner concluded, nevertheless, that "the processing requirements of the proposed regulations are the safest now known to prevent the outgrowth and toxin formation of *C. botulism* Type E." He determined that "the conditions of current good manufacturing practice for this industry should be established without further delay."

The Commissioner did not answer the suggestion by the Bureau of Fisheries that nitrite and salt as additives could safely lower the high temperature otherwise required, a solution which the FDA had accepted in the case of chub. Nor did the Commissioner respond to the claim of Nova Scotia through its trade association, the Association of Smoked Fish Processors, Inc., Technical Center that "[t]he proposed process requirements suggested by the FDA for hot processed smoked fish are neither commercially feasible nor based on sound scientific evidence obtained with the variety of smoked fish products to be included under this regulation."

Nova Scotia, in its own comment, wrote to the Commissioner that "the heating of certain types of fish to high temperatures will completely destroy the product." It suggested, as an alternative, that "specific processing procedures could be established for each species after adequate work and experimention [sic] has been done but not before." We have noted above that the response given by the Commissioner was in general terms. He did not specifically aver that the T-T-S requirements as applied to whitefish were, in fact, commercially feasible.

When, after several inspections and warnings, Nova Scotia failed to comply with the regulation, an action by the United States Attorney for injunctive relief was filed on April 7, 1976, six years later, and resulted in the judgment here on appeal. The District Court denied a stay pending appeal, and no application for a stay was made to this court.

I.

[The court upheld the FDA's statutory authority to issue the rules in question.]

II.

. . . .

B

The key issues were (1) whether, in the light of the rather scant history of botulism in whitefish, that species should have been considered separately rather than included in a general regulation which failed to distinguish species from species; (2) whether the application of the proposed T-T-S requirements to smoked whitefish made the whitefish commercially unsalable; and (3) whether the agency recognized that prospect, but nevertheless decided that the public health needs should prevail even if that meant commercial death for the whitefish industry. The procedural issues were whether, in the light of these key questions, the agency procedure was inadequate because (i) it failed to disclose to interested parties the scientific data and the methodology upon which it relied; and (ii) because it failed utterly to address itself to the pertinent question of commercial feasibility.

1.

The History of Botulism in Whitefish

The history of botulism occurrence in whitefish, as established in the trial record, which we must assume was available to the FDA in 1970, is as follows. Between 1899 and 1964 there were only eight cases of botulism reported as attributable to hot-smoked whitefish. In all eight instances, vacuum-packed whitefish was involved. All of the eight cases occurred in 1960 and 1963. The industry has abandoned vacuum-packing, and there has not been a single case of botulism associated with commercially prepared whitefish since 1963, though 2,750,000 pounds of whitefish are processed annually. Thus, in the seven-year period from 1964 through 1970, 17.25 million pounds of whitefish have been commercially processed in the United States without a single reported case of botulism. The evidence also disclosed that defendant Nova Scotia has been in business some 56 years, and that there has never been a case of botulism illness from the whitefish processed by it.

2.

The Scientific Data

Interested parties were not informed of the scientific data, or at least of a selection of such data deemed important by the agency, so that comments could be addressed to the data. Appellants argue that unless the scientific data relied upon by the agency are spread upon the public records, criticism of the methodology used or the meaning to be inferred from the data is rendered impossible.

We agree with appellants in this case, for although we recognize that an agency may resort to its own expertise outside the record in an informal rulemaking procedure, we do not believe that when the pertinent research material is readily available and the agency has no special expertise on the precise parameters involved, there is any reason to conceal the scientific data relied upon from the interested parties. As Judge Leventhal said in *Portland Cement Ass'n v. Ruckelshaus,* 158 U.S. App. D.C. 308, 326, 486 F.2d 375, 393 (1973): "It is not consonant with the purpose of a rulemaking proceeding to promulgate rules on the basis of inadequate data, or on data that [in] critical degree, *is known only to the agency.*" (Emphasis added.) This is not a case where the agency methodology was based on material supplied by the interested parties themselves. . . . Here all the scientific research was collected by the agency, and none of it was disclosed to interested parties as the material upon which the proposed rule would be fashioned.[15] Nor was an articulate effort made to connect the scientific requirements to available technology that would make commercial survival possible, though the burden of proof was on the agency. This required it to "bear a burden of adducing a reasoned presentation supporting the reliability of its methodology." . . .

If the failure to notify interested persons of the scientific research upon which the agency was relying actually prevented the presentation of relevant comment, the agency may be held not to have considered all "the relevant factors." We can think of no sound reasons for secrecy or reluctance to expose to public view (with an exception for trade secrets or national security) the ingredients of the deliberative process. . . . Indeed, the FDA's own regulations now specifically require that every notice of proposed rulemaking contain "references to all data and information on which the Commissioner relies for the proposal (copies or a full list of which shall be a part of the administrative file on the matter. . . .)." 21 C.F.R. § 10.40(b)(1) (1977). And this is, undoubtedly, the trend.

We think that the scientific data should have been disclosed to focus on the proper interpretation of "insanitary conditions." When the basis for a proposed rule is a scientific decision, the scientific material which is believed to support the rule should be exposed to the view of interested parties for their comment. One cannot ask for comment on a scientific paper without allowing the participants to read the paper. Scientific research is sometimes rejected for diverse inadequacies of methodology; and statistical results are sometimes rebutted because of a lack of adequate gathering technique or of supportable extrapolation. Such is the stuff of scientific debate. To suppress meaningful comment by failure to disclose the basic data relied upon is akin to rejecting comment altogether. For unless there is common ground, the comments are unlikely to be of a quality that might impress a careful agency. The inadequacy of comment in turn leads in the direction of arbitrary decision-making. We

---

[15] We recognize the problem posed by Judge Leventhal in *International Harvester* that a proceeding might never end if such submission required a reply *ad infinitum, ibid.* Here the exposure of the scientific research relied on simply would have required a single round of comment addressed thereto.

do not speak of findings of fact, for such are not technically required in the informal rulemaking procedures. We speak rather of what the agency should make known so as to elicit comments that probe the fundamentals. Informal rulemaking does not lend itself to a rigid pattern. Especially, in the circumstance of our broad reading of statutory authority in support of the agency, we conclude that the failure to disclose to interested persons the scientific data upon which the FDA relied was procedurally erroneous. Moreover, the burden was upon the agency to articulate rationally why the rule should apply to a large and diverse class, with the same T-T-S parameters made applicable to all species.

C

Appellants additionally attack the "concise general statement" required by APA, 5 U.S.C. § 553, as inadequate. We think that, in the circumstances, it was less than adequate. It is not in keeping with the rational process to leave vital questions, raised by comments which are of cogent materiality, completely unanswered. The agencies certainly have a good deal of discretion in expressing the basis of a rule, but the agencies do not have quite the prerogative of obscurantism reserved to legislatures. "Congress did not purport to transfer its legislative power to the unbounded discretion of the regulatory body." . . .

The test of adequacy of the "concise general statement" was expressed by Judge McGowan in the following terms:

> "We do not expect the agency to discuss every item of fact or opinion included in the submissions made to it in informal rulemaking. We do expect that, if the judicial review which Congress has thought it important to provide is to be meaningful, the 'concise general statement of . . . basis and purpose' mandated by Section 4 will enable us to see what major issues of policy were ventilated by the informal proceedings and why the agency reacted to them as it did." *Automotive Parts & Accessories Ass'n v. Boyd,* 132 U.S. App. D.C. 200, 208, 407 F.2d 330, 338 (1968).

The Secretary was squarely faced with the question whether it was necessary to formulate a rule with specific parameters that applied to all species of fish, and particularly whether lower temperatures with the addition of nitrite and salt would not be sufficient. Though this alternative was suggested by an agency of the federal government, its suggestion, though acknowledged, was never answered.

Moreover, the comment that to apply the proposed T-T-S requirements to whitefish would destroy the commercial product was neither discussed nor answered. We think that to sanction silence in the face of such vital questions would be to make the statutory requirement of a "concise general statement" less than an adequate safeguard against arbitrary decision-making. . . .

We cannot, on this appeal, remand to the agency to allow further comments by interested parties, addressed to the scientific data now disclosed at the trial below. We hold in this enforcement proceeding, therefore, that the regulation, as it affects non-vacuum-packed hot-smoked whitefish, was promulgated in an arbitrary manner and is invalid.

When the District Court held the regulation to be valid, it properly exercised its discretion to grant the injunction. In view of our conclusion to the contrary, we must reverse the grant of the injunction and direct that the complaint be dismissed.

NOTES AND QUESTIONS

4-13. What is meaningful public participation? What must an agency do to assure it occurs? How much of the background scientific data must an agency make available?

4-14. Does section 553 of the APA say anything about a rulemaking record? Does the court assume that there must be one? Of what does or should it consist?

4-15. Consider the following history of the evolution of the rulemaking record in the Administrative Conference of the United States document, *A Guide to Federal Agency Rulemaking* (ACUS, 2d ed. 1991), at 204–06:

When the APA was enacted, it was not generally thought that agencies needed to develop factual support for legislative rules. Of course, agencies frequently would have developed factual support for a rule in anticipation of a court challenge, if not simply as a matter of sound agency practice. In fact, the legislative history of section 553 indicates that the Act's drafters expected agencies to use their discretion to develop supporting records if the nature of the particular proceeding required it.

One reason the APA drafters were content to give agencies discretion to develop record support for legislative rules was that when the APA was enacted, the validity of rules generally was determined on judicial review of an agency enforcement action. A record for review was thus developed either in the agency proceeding or *de novo* in the reviewing court.

Another reason for the latitude given agencies to produce factual support for rules was the presumption in favor of the existence of facts supporting a rule. This presumption was established by *Pacific States Box & Basket Co. v. White,* a case where the Supreme Court applied the "rational basis" test used in review of legislation to rulemaking (a "quasi-legislative" process). The effect of this presumption was to place upon a rule challenger the burden of disproving supporting factual premises and rationales for the rule, at least as applied to it. The agency had no burden to show, in the first instance, factual support for the rule.

As we shall see in § 4.02[E], *infra*, especially with the passage of hybrid rulemaking statutes, Congress now often requires a rulemaking record. To what extent can a court read that requirement into either the APA or its more general duty to engage in meaningful judicial review?

PROBLEM 4-1

The current design for the e-rulemaking system (which, admittedly, is only in its infancy) allows an interested party to search for rules open for public comment. The website displays the text of the draft from the Federal Register and provides a box in which to type a comment. Clicking a button marked "Submit Comments" sends the comment about the rulemaking from the regulations.gov website to the agency.

Transposing the notice-and-comment process as is on the Internet so that anyone can post a comment reduces the costs of participation. Unifying disparate agency procedures into a centralized "portal" removes the hurdle of learning agency practices. Automating the comment process makes it simpler for interest groups to participate using bots — small software "robots" — to generate instantly thousands of responses from stored membership lists. Suddenly, anyone or anything can participate from anywhere. And that is precisely the problem.

Without the tools and methods to coordinate participation, quality input will be lost; malicious, irrelevant material will rise to the surface, and information will not reach those who need it. The current plan for e-rulemaking is nothing short of a disaster. Attention and investment are focused on digitizing paper — dragging the agency file cabinet into cyberspace — rather than on the workings of participation, which informs the process. Managing documents is necessary to inform rulemaking but should follow from the dictates of managing people and organizing their ideas. In short, e-rulemaking, as currently proposed, will frustrate the goals of citizen participation and exacerbate the status quo in which the reading of public comments has to be outsourced to third-party consultants.

It is, therefore, imperative for lawyers, policymakers, social scientists and those who understand the goals of citizen participation to demand attention to the technology for participation before "notice-and-comment" becomes "notice-and-spam."

Beth Simone Noveck, *Public Participation in Electronic Rulemaking: Electronic Democracy or Notice-and-Spam?* 30 ADMIN. & REG. L. NEWS 7 (Fall, 2004).*

(1) How might this technology have affected the processes discussed in *Chocolate Mfrs.* and *Nova Scotia*, discussed above?

(2) What problems do you anticipate if the system described above is implemented without any changes? What proposals would you make to get the most out of this technology and thereby improve democracy? Can those who comment interact with one another? Can the comments be sorted out by industry or background? Can this technology help with compliance? Should the agency publish a blog that indicates how best to comply and who appears to be complying? Or could users create their own "compliance weblogs?"

---

* Copyright © 2004 by American Bar Association. Reprinted by permission.

For an excellent discussion of these and other issues, *see* Beth Simone Noveck, *The Electronic Revolution in Rulemaking*, 53 EMORY L.J. 433, at 495–510; Cary Coglianese, *E-Rulemaking: Information Technology and the Regulatory Process*, 56 ADMIN. L. REV. 353, (2004).

[C] Administrative Common Law

In 1976, Judges Leventhal and Bazelon of the Court of Appeals for the District of Columbia engaged in a famous debate. In *Ethyl Corp. v. EPA*, 541 F.2d 1, 66 (D.C. Cir. 1976), Judge Bazelon argued that:

> . . . in cases of great technological complexity, the best way for courts to guard against unreasonable or erroneous administrative decisions is not for the judges themselves to scrutinize the technical merits of each decision. Rather, it is to establish a decision-making process that assures a reasoned decision that can be held up to the scrutiny of the scientific community and the public.

(quoting *International Harvester Co. v. Ruckelshaus,* 478 F.2d 615, 652 (1973) (Bazelon, C.J., concurring).)

Judge Leventhal, on the other hand, contended that:

> Our present system of review assumes judges will acquire whatever technical knowledge is necessary as background for decision of the legal questions. It may be that some judges are not initially equipped for this role, just as they may not be technically equipped initially to decide issues of obviousness and infringement in patent cases. If technical difficulties loom large, Congress may push to establish specialized courts. Thus far, it has proceeded on the assumption that we can both have the important values secured by generalist judges and rely on them to acquire whatever technical background is necessary. . . .
>
> The substantive review of administrative action is modest, but cannot be carried out in a vacuum of understanding. Better no judicial review at all than a charade that gives the imprimatur without the substance of judicial confirmation that the agency is not acting unreasonably. . . .

541 F.2d. at 69.

For some time prior to and after the *Ethyl* case, the D.C. Circuit, particularly when it confronted challenges to agency rules dealing with complex environmental issues, often remanded agency rules back to the agency with instructions to use decisionmaking procedures that went beyond those set forth in section 553 of the APA. In *Portland Cement Association v. Ruckelshaus,* 486 F.2d 375 (D.C. Cir. 1973), *cert. denied,* 423 U.S. 1025 (1975), for example, the court dealt with agency rulemaking and the Clean Air Act. It remanded certain EPA rules back to the agency with instructions that the agency reopen its rulemaking proceedings to give manufacturers an opportunity to comment upon certain evidence involving agency test results. More importantly, the court also required that the agency respond specifically to petitioners' complaints about the methodology the agency used to arrive at the pollution emission standards formulated under the Clean Air Act. As we shall see, many of the procedural innovations of the courts were adopted by Congress when it passed a number of new health and environmental statutes in the 1970's that included hybrid rulemaking provisions. The following case, however, deals with section 553 and the limits of judicial attempts to require more than the procedures set forth in that Act. Is there such a thing as administrative common law? If so, what is it? Should it exist? What role does this decision contemplate a reviewing court will play? Is that role appropriate?

VERMONT YANKEE NUCLEAR POWER CORP. v. NATURAL RESOURCES DEFENSE COUNCIL

United States Supreme Court
435 U.S. 519 (1978)

MR. JUSTICE REHNQUIST delivered the opinion of the Court.

In 1946, Congress enacted the Administrative Procedure Act, which as we have noted elsewhere was not only "a new, basic and comprehensive regulation of procedures in many agencies," *Wong Yang Sung v. McGrath*, 339 U.S. 33 (1950), but was also a legislative enactment which settled "long-continued and hard-fought contentions, and enacts a formula upon which opposing social and political forces have come to rest." . . . Section 4 of the Act, 5 U.S.C. § 553 (1976 ed.), dealing with rulemaking, requires in subsection (b) that "notice of proposed rule making shall be published in the Federal Register . . .," describes the contents of that notice, and goes on to require in subsection (c) that after the notice the agency "shall give interested persons an opportunity to participate in the rule making through submission of written data, views, or arguments with or without opportunity for oral presentation. After consideration of the relevant matter presented, the agency shall incorporate in the rules adopted a concise general statement of their basis and purpose." Interpreting this provision of the Act in *United States v. Allegheny-Ludlum Steel Corp.*, 406 U.S. 742 (1972), and *United States v. Florida East Coast R. Co.*, 410 U.S. 224 (1973), we held that generally speaking this section of the Act established the maximum procedural requirements which Congress was willing to have the courts impose upon agencies in conducting rulemaking procedures.[1] Agencies are free to grant additional procedural rights in the exercise of their discretion, but reviewing courts are generally not free to impose them if the agencies have not chosen to grant them. This is not to say necessarily that there are no circumstances which would ever justify a court in overturning agency action because of a failure to employ procedures beyond those required by the statute. But such circumstances, if they exist, are extremely rare.

---

[1] While there was division in this Court in *United States v. Florida East Coast R. Co.*, with respect to the constitutionality of such an interpretation in a case involving ratemaking, which Mr. Justice Douglas and Mr. Justice Stewart felt was "adjudicatory" within the terms of the Act, the cases in the Court of Appeals for the District of Columbia Circuit which we review here involve rulemaking procedures in their most pristine sense.

Even apart from the Administrative Procedure Act this Court has for more than four decades emphasized that the formulation of procedures was basically to be left within the discretion of the agencies to which Congress had confided the responsibility for substantive judgments. In *FCC v. Schreiber*, 381 U.S. 279, 290 (1965), the court explicated this principle, describing it as "an outgrowth of the congressional determination that administrative agencies and administrators will be familiar with the industries which they regulate and will be in a better position than federal courts or Congress itself to design procedural rules adapted to the peculiarities of the industry and the tasks of the agency involved." . . .

It is in the light of this background of statutory and decisional law that we granted certiorari to review two judgments of the Court of Appeals for the District of Columbia Circuit because of our concern that they had seriously misread or misapplied this statutory and decisional law cautioning reviewing courts against engrafting their own notions of proper procedures upon agencies entrusted with substantive functions by Congress. . . . We conclude that the Court of Appeals has done just that in these cases, and we therefore remand them to it for further proceedings. . . .

I

A

Under the Atomic Energy Act of 1954, as amended, 42 U.S.C. § 2011 *et seq.*, the Atomic Energy Commission[2] was given broad regulatory authority over the development of nuclear energy. Under the terms of the Act, a utility seeking to construct and operate a nuclear power plant must obtain a separate permit or license at both the construction and the operation stage of the project. In order to obtain the construction permit, the utility must file a preliminary safety analysis report, an environmental report, and certain information regarding the antitrust implications of the proposed project. . . . This application then undergoes exhaustive review by the Commission's staff and by the Advisory Committee on Reactor Safeguards (ACRS), a group of distinguished experts in the field of atomic energy. Both groups submit to the Commission their own evaluations, which then become part of the record of the utility's application.[3] . . . The Commission staff also undertakes the review required by the National Environmental Policy Act of 1969 (NEPA), 83 Stat. 852, 42 U.S.C. § 4321 *et seq.*, and prepares a draft environmental impact statement, which, after being circulated for comment . . . is revised and becomes a final environmental impact statement. Thereupon a three-member Atomic Safety and Licensing Board conducts a public adjudicatory hearing, 42 U.S.C. § 2241, and reaches a decision[4] which can be appealed

---

[2] The licensing and regulatory functions of the Atomic Energy Commission (AEC) were transferred to the Nuclear Regulatory Commission (NRC) by the Energy Reorganization Act of 1974, 42 U.S.C. § 5801 *et seq.* (1970 ed., Supp. V). Hereinafter both the AEC and NRC will be referred to as the Commission.

[3] ACRS is required to review each construction permit application for the purpose of informing the Commission of the "hazards of proposed or existing reactor facilities and the adequacy of proposed reactor safety standards." 42 U.S.C. § 2039.

[4] The Licensing Board issues a permit if it concludes that there is reasonable assurance that

to the Atomic Safety and Licensing Appeal Board, and currently, in the Commission's discretion, to the Commission itself. . . . The final agency decision may be appealed to the courts of appeals. . . . The same sort of process occurs when the utility applies for a license to operate the plant, 10 CFR § 50.34(b) (1977), except that a hearing need only be held in contested cases and may be limited to the matters in controversy.[5]

These cases arise from two separate decisions of the Court of Appeals for the District of Columbia Circuit. [Both were written by C.J. Bazelon.] In the first, the court remanded a decision of the Commission to grant a license to petitioner Vermont Yankee Nuclear Power Corp. to operate a nuclear power plant. *Natural Resources Defense Council v. NRC,* 178 U.S. App. D.C. 336, 547 F.2d 633 (1976). In the second, the court remanded a decision of that same agency to grant a permit to petitioner Consumers Power Co. to construct two pressurized water nuclear reactors to generate electricity and steam. *Aeschliman v. NRC,* 178 U.S. App. D.C. 325, 547 F.2d 622 (1976).

B

In December 1967, after the mandatory adjudicatory hearing and necessary review, the Commission granted petitioner Vermont Yankee a permit to build a nuclear power plant in Vernon, Vt. Thereafter, Vermont Yankee applied for an operating license. Respondent Natural Resources Defense Council (NRDC) objected to the granting of a license, however, and therefore a hearing on the application commenced on August 10, 1971. Excluded from consideration at the hearings, over NRDC's objection, was the issue of the environmental effects of operations to reprocess fuel or dispose of wastes resulting from the reprocessing operations.[6] This ruling was affirmed by the Appeal Board in June 1972.

In November 1972, however, the Commission, making specific reference to the Appeal Board's decision with respect to the Vermont Yankee license, instituted rulemaking proceedings "that would specifically deal with the question of consideration of environmental effects associated with the uranium fuel cycle in the individual cost-benefit analyses for light water cooled nuclear power reactors." . . . The notice of proposed rulemaking offered two alternatives, both predicated on a report prepared by the Commission's staff entitled

---

the proposed plant can be constructed and operated without undue risk, 42 U.S.C. § 2241; 10 CFR § 50.35(a) (1977), and that the environmental cost-benefit balance favors the issuance of a permit.

[5] When a license application is contested, the Licensing Board must find reasonable assurance that the plant can be operated without undue risk and will not be inimical to the common defense and security or to the health and safety of the public. *See* 42 U.S.C. § 2232(a); 10 CFR § 50.57(a) (1977). The Licensing Board's decision is subject to review similar to that afforded the Board's decision with respect to a construction permit.

[6] The nuclear fission which takes place in light-water nuclear reactors apparently converts its principal fuel, uranium, into plutonium which is itself highly radioactive but can be used as reactor fuel if separated from the remaining uranium and radioactive waste products. Fuel reprocessing refers to the process necessary to recapture usable plutonium. Waste disposal, at the present stage of technological development, refers to the storage of the very long lived and highly radioactive waste products until they detoxify sufficiently that they no longer present an environmental hazard. There are presently no physical or chemical steps which render this waste less toxic, other than simply the passage of time.

Environmental Survey of the Nuclear Fuel Cycle. The first would have required no quantitative evaluation of the environmental hazards of fuel reprocessing or disposal because the Environmental Survey had found them to be slight. The second would have specified numerical values for the environmental impact of this part of the fuel cycle, which values would then be incorporated into a table, along with the other relevant factors, to determine the overall cost-benefit balance for each operating license. . . .

Much of the controversy in this case revolves around the procedures used in the rulemaking hearing which commenced in February 1973. In a supplemental notice of hearing the Commission indicated that while discovery or cross-examination would not be utilized, the Environmental Survey would be available to the public before the hearing along with the extensive background documents cited therein. All participants would be given a reasonable opportunity to present their position and could be represented by counsel if they so desired. Written and, time permitting, oral statements would be received and incorporated into the record. All persons giving oral statements would be subject to questioning by the Commission. At the conclusion of the hearing, a transcript would be made available to the public and the record would remain open for 30 days to allow the filing of supplemental written statements. . . . More than 40 individuals and organizations representing a wide variety of interests submitted written comments. On January 17, 1973, the Licensing Board held a planning session to schedule the appearance of witnesses and to discuss methods for compiling a record. The hearing was held on February 1 and 2, with participation by a number of groups, including the Commission's staff, the United States Environmental Protection Agency, a manufacturer of reactor equipment, a trade association from the nuclear industry, a group of electric utility companies, and a group called Consolidated National Intervenors which represented 79 groups and individuals including respondent NRDC.

After the hearing, the Commission's staff filed a supplemental document for the purpose of clarifying and revising the Environmental Survey. Then the Licensing Board forwarded its report to the Commission without rendering any decision. The Licensing Board identified as the principal procedural question the propriety of declining to use full formal adjudicatory procedures. The major substantive issue was the technical adequacy of the Environmental Survey.

In April 1974, the Commission issued a rule which adopted the second of the two proposed alternatives described above. The Commission also approved the procedures used at the hearing,[7] and indicated that the record, including

---

[7] The Commission stated:

In our view, the procedures adopted provide a more than adequate basis for formulation of the rule we adopted. All parties were fully heard. Nothing offered was excluded. The record does not indicate that any evidentiary material would have been received under different procedures. Nor did the proponent of the strict "adjudicatory" approach make an offer of proof — or even remotely suggest — what substantive matters it would develop under different procedures. In addition, we note that 11 documents including the Survey were available to the parties several weeks before the hearing, and the Regulatory staff, though not requested to do so, made available various drafts and handwritten notes. Under all of the circumstances, we conclude that adjudicatory type procedures were not warranted here.

the Environmental Survey, provided an "adequate data base for the regulation adopted." . . . Finally, the Commission ruled that to the extent the rule differed from the Appeal Board decisions in *Vermont Yankee* "those decisions have no further precedential significance," . . . but that since "the environmental effects of the uranium fuel cycle have been shown to be relatively insignificant, . . . it is unnecessary to apply the amendment to applicant's environmental reports submitted prior to its effective date or to Final Environmental Statements for which Draft Environmental Statements have been circulated for comment prior to the effective date,". . . .

Respondents appealed from both the Commission's adoption of the rule and its decision to grant Vermont Yankee's license to the Court of Appeals for the District of Columbia Circuit.

C

[The Court then described the *Consumers Power Co.* case.]

D

With respect to the challenge of Vermont Yankee's license, the court first ruled that in the absence of effective rulemaking proceedings,[8] the Commission must deal with the environmental impact of fuel reprocessing and disposal in individual licensing proceedings. 178 U.S. App. D.C., at 344, 547 F.2d, at 641. The court then examined the rulemaking proceedings and, despite the fact that it appeared that the agency employed all the procedures required by 5 U.S.C. § 553 (1976 ed.) and more, the court determined the proceedings to be inadequate and overturned the rule. Accordingly, the Commission's determination with respect to Vermont Yankee's license was also remanded for further proceedings.[9]

---

[8] In the Court of Appeals no one questioned the Commission's authority to deal with fuel cycle issues by informal rulemaking as opposed to adjudication. 178 U.S. App. D.C., at 345–346, 547 F.2d, at 642–643. Neither does anyone seriously question before this Court the Commission's authority in this respect.

[9] After the decision of the Court of Appeals the Commission promulgated a new interim rule pending issuance of a final rule. 42 Fed. Reg. 13803 (1977).

As we read the opinion of the Court of Appeals, its view that reviewing courts may in the absence of special circumstances justifying such a course of action impose additional procedural requirements on agency action raises questions of such significance in this area of the law as to warrant our granting certiorari and deciding the case. Since the vast majority of challenges to administrative agency action are brought to the Court of Appeals for the District of Columbia Circuit, the decision of that court in this case will serve as precedent for many more proceedings for judicial review of agency actions than would the decision of another Court of Appeals. Finally, this decision will continue to play a major role in the instant litigation regardless of the Commission's decision to press ahead with further rulemaking proceedings. . . . [N]ot only is the NRDC relying on the decision of the Court of Appeals as a device to force the agency to provide more procedures, but it is also challenging the interim rules promulgated by the agency in the Court of Appeals, alleging again the inadequacy of the procedures and citing the opinion of the Court of Appeals as binding precedent to that effect.

II

A (Vermont Yankee case)

Petitioner Vermont Yankee first argues that the Commission may grant a license to operate a nuclear reactor without any consideration of waste disposal and fuel reprocessing. We find, however, that this issue is no longer presented by the record in this case. The Commission does not contend that it is not required to consider the environmental impact of the spent fuel processes when licensing nuclear power plants. Indeed, the Commission has publicly stated subsequent to the Court of Appeals' decision in the instant case that consideration of the environmental impact of the back end of the fuel cycle in "the environmental impact statements for individual LWR's [light-water power reactors] would represent a full and candid assessment of costs and benefits consistent with the legal requirements and spirit of NEPA." Even prior to the Court of Appeals' decision the Commission implicitly agreed that it would consider the back end of the fuel cycle in all licensing proceedings: It indicated that it was not necessary to reopen prior licensing proceedings because "the environmental effects of the uranium fuel cycle have been shown to be relatively insignificant," and thus incorporation of those effects into the cost-benefit analysis would not change the results of such licensing proceedings. App. 395. Thus, at this stage of the proceedings the only question presented for review in this regard is whether the Commission may consider the environmental impact of the fuel processes when licensing nuclear reactors. In addition to the weight which normally attaches to the agency's determination of such a question, other reasons support the Commission's conclusion.

Vermont Yankee will produce annually well over 100 pounds of radioactive wastes, some of which will be highly toxic. The Commission itself, in a pamphlet published by its information office, clearly recognizes that these wastes "pose the most severe potential health hazard. . . ." Many of these substances must be isolated for anywhere from 600 to hundreds of thousands of years. It is hard to argue that these wastes do not constitute "adverse environmental effects which cannot be avoided should the proposal be implemented," or that by operating nuclear power plants we are not making "irreversible and irretrievable commitments of resources." As the Court of Appeals recognized, the environmental impact of the radioactive wastes produced by a nuclear power plant is analytically indistinguishable from the environmental effects of "the stack gases produced by a coal-burning power plant." For these reasons we hold that the Commission acted well within its statutory authority when it considered the back end of the fuel cycle in individual licensing proceedings.

B (Invalidation of fuel cycle rule)

We next turn to the invalidation of the fuel cycle rule. But before determining whether the Court of Appeals reached a permissible result, we must determine exactly what result it did reach, and in this case that is no mean feat. . . .

After a thorough examination of the opinion itself, we conclude that while the matter is not entirely free from doubt, the majority of the Court of Appeals struck down the rule because of the perceived inadequacies of the procedures employed in the rulemaking proceedings. The court first determined the intervenors' primary argument to be "that the decision to preclude 'discovery or cross-examination' denied them a meaningful opportunity to participate in the proceedings as guaranteed by due process." . . . The court then went on to frame the issue for decision thus:

> Thus, we are called upon to decide whether the procedures provided by the agency were sufficient to ventilate the issues.

The court conceded that absent extraordinary circumstances it is improper for a reviewing court to prescribe the procedural format an agency must follow, but it likewise clearly thought it entirely appropriate to "scrutinize the record as a whole to insure that genuine opportunities to participate in a meaningful way were provided. . . ." The court also refrained from actually ordering the agency to follow any specific procedures, but there is little doubt in our minds that the ineluctable mandate of the court's decision is that the procedures afforded during the hearings were inadequate. This conclusion is particularly buttressed by the fact that after the court examined the record, particularly the testimony of Dr. Pittman, and declared it insufficient, the court proceeded to discuss at some length the necessity for further procedural devices or a more "sensitive" application of those devices employed during the proceedings. The exploration of the record and the statement regarding its insufficiency might initially lead one to conclude that the court was only examining the sufficiency of the evidence, but the remaining portions of the opinion dispel any doubt that this was certainly not the sole or even the principal basis of the decision. Accordingly, we feel compelled to address the opinion on its own terms, and we conclude that it was wrong.

In prior opinions we have intimated that even in a rulemaking proceeding when an agency is making a "quasi-judicial" determination by which a very small number of persons are "exceptionally affected, in each case upon individual grounds," in some circumstances additional procedures may be required in order to afford the aggrieved individuals due process.[16] *United States v. Florida East Coast R. Co.,* 410 U.S., at 242–245, quoting from *Bi-Metallic Investment Co. v. State Board of Equalization,* 239 U.S. 441, 446 (1915). It might also be true, although we do not think the issue is presented in this case and accordingly do not decide it, that a totally unjustified departure from well-settled agency procedures of long standing might require judicial correction.

But this much is absolutely clear. Absent constitutional constraints or extremely compelling circumstances the "administrative agencies 'should be free to fashion their own rules of procedure and to pursue methods of inquiry capable of permitting them to discharge their multitudinous duties'." *FCC v.*

---

[16] Respondent NRDC does not now argue that additional procedural devices were required under the Constitution. Since this was clearly a rulemaking proceeding in its purest form, we see nothing to support such a view. *See United States v. Florida East Coast R. Co.,* 410 U.S. 224, 244–245 (1973); *Bowles v. Willingham,* 321 U.S. 503 (1944); *Bi-Metallic Investment Co. v. State Board of Equalization,* 239 U.S. 441 (1915).

Schreiber, 381 U.S., at 290, quoting from *FCC v. Pottsville Broadcasting Co.,* 309 U.S., at 143. Indeed, our cases could hardly be more explicit in this regard. . . .

Respondent NRDC argues that § 4 of the Administrative Procedure Act, 5 U.S.C. § 553 (1976 ed.), merely establishes lower procedural bounds and that a court may routinely require more than the minimum when an agency's proposed rule addresses complex or technical factual issues or "Issues of Great Public Import." We have, however, previously shown that our decisions reject this view. We also think the legislative history, even the part which it cites, does not bear out its contention. The Senate Report explains what eventually became § 4 thus:

> "This subsection states . . . the minimum requirements of public rule making procedure short of statutory hearing. Under it agencies might in addition confer with industry advisory committees, consult organizations, hold informal 'hearings,' and the like. Considerations of practicality, necessity, and public interest . . . will naturally govern the agency's determination of the extent to which public proceedings should go. Matters of great import, or those where the public submission of facts will be either useful to the agency or a protection to the public, should naturally be accorded more elaborate public procedures." S. Rep. No. 752, 79th Cong., 1st Sess., 14–15 (1945).

The House Report is in complete accord . . . . And the Attorney General's Manual on the Administrative Procedure Act 31, 35 (1947), a contemporaneous interpretation previously given some deference by this Court because of the role played by the Department of Justice in drafting the legislation, further confirms that view. In short, all of this leaves little doubt that Congress intended that the discretion of the *agencies* and not that of the courts be exercised in determining when extra procedural devices should be employed.

There are compelling reasons for construing § 4 in this manner. In the first place, if courts continually review agency proceedings to determine whether the agency employed procedures which were, in the court's opinion, perfectly tailored to reach what the court perceives to be the "best" or "correct" result, judicial review would be totally unpredictable. And the agencies, operating under this vague injunction to employ the "best" procedures and facing the threat of reversal if they did not, would undoubtedly adopt full adjudicatory procedures in every instance. Not only would this totally disrupt the statutory scheme, through which Congress enacted "a formula upon which opposing social and political forces have come to rest," *Wong Yang Sung v. McGrath,* 339 U.S., at 40, but all the inherent advantages of informal rulemaking would be totally lost.

Secondly, it is obvious that the court in these cases reviewed the agency's choice of procedures on the basis of the record actually produced at the hearing, and not on the basis of the information available to the agency when it made the decision to structure the proceedings in a certain way. This sort of Monday morning quarterbacking not only encourages but almost compels the agency to conduct all rulemaking proceedings with the full panoply of procedural devices normally associated only with adjudicatory hearings.

Finally, and perhaps most importantly, this sort of review fundamentally misconceives the nature of the standard for judicial review of an agency rule. The court below uncritically assumed that additional procedures will automatically result in a more adequate record because it will give interested parties more of an opportunity to participate in and contribute to the proceedings. But informal rulemaking need not be based solely on the transcript of a hearing held before an agency. Indeed, the agency need not even hold a formal hearing. *See* 5 U.S.C. § 553(c) (1976 ed.). Thus, the adequacy of the "record" in this type of proceeding is not correlated directly to the type of procedural devices employed, but rather turns on whether the agency has followed the statutory mandate of the Administrative Procedure Act or other relevant statutes. If the agency is compelled to support the rule which it ultimately adopts with the type of record produced only after a full adjudicatory hearing, it simply will have no choice but to conduct a full adjudicatory hearing prior to promulgating every rule. In sum, this sort of unwarranted judicial examination of perceived procedural shortcomings of a rulemaking proceeding can do nothing but seriously interfere with that process prescribed by Congress.

In short, nothing in the APA, NEPA, the circumstances of this case, the nature of the issues being considered, past agency practice, or the statutory mandate under which the Commission operates permitted the court to review and overturn the rulemaking proceeding on the basis of the procedural devices employed (or not employed) by the Commission so long as the Commission employed at least the statutory minima, a matter about which there is no doubt in this case.

There remains, of course, the question of whether the challenged rule finds sufficient justification in the administrative proceedings that it should be upheld by the reviewing court. Judge Tamm, concurring in the result reached by the majority of the Court of Appeals, thought that it did not. There are also intimations in the majority opinion which suggest that the judges who joined it likewise may have thought the administrative proceedings an insufficient basis upon which to predicate the rule in question. We accordingly remand so that the Court of Appeals may review the rule as the Administrative Procedure Act provides. We have made it abundantly clear before that when there is a contemporaneous explanation of the agency decision, the validity of that action must "stand or fall on the propriety of that finding, judged, of course, by the appropriate standard of review. If that finding is not sustainable on the administrative record made, then the Comptroller's decision must be vacated and the matter remanded to him for further consideration." *Camp v. Pitts*, 411 U.S. 138, 143 (1973). *See also SEC v. Chenery Corp.*, 318 U.S. 80 (1943). The court should engage in this kind of review and not stray beyond the judicial province to explore the procedural format or to impose upon the agency its own notion of which procedures are "best" or most likely to further some vague, undefined public good.

III

. . . .

All this leads us to make one further observation of some relevance to this case. To say that the Court of Appeals' final reason for remanding is insubstantial at best is a gross understatement. Consumers Power first applied in 1969 for a construction permit — not even an operating license, just a construction permit. The proposed plant underwent an incredibly extensive review. The reports filed and reviewed literally fill books. The proceedings took years, and the actual hearings themselves over two weeks. To then nullify that effort seven years later because one report refers to other problems, which problems admittedly have been discussed at length in other reports available to the public, borders on the Kafkaesque. Nuclear energy may some day be a cheap, safe source of power or it may not. But Congress has made a choice to at least try nuclear energy, establishing a reasonable review process in which courts are to play only a limited role. The fundamental policy questions appropriately resolved in Congress and in the state legislatures are not subject to reexamination in the federal courts under the guise of judicial review of agency action. Time may prove wrong the decision to develop nuclear energy, but it is Congress or the States within their appropriate agencies which must eventually make that judgment. In the meantime courts should perform their appointed function. NEPA does set forth significant substantive goals for the Nation, but its mandate to the agencies is essentially procedural. It is to insure a fully informed and well-considered decision, not necessarily a decision the judges of the Court of Appeals or of this Court would have reached had they been members of the decisionmaking unit of the agency. Administrative decisions should be set aside in this context, as in every other, only for substantial procedural or substantive reasons as mandated by statute, *Consolo v. FMC,* 383 U.S. 607, 620 (1966), not simply because the court is unhappy with the result reached. And a single alleged oversight on a peripheral issue, urged by parties who never fully cooperated or indeed raised the issue below, must not be made the basis for overturning a decision properly made after an otherwise exhaustive proceeding.

Reversed and remanded.

Mr. Justice Blackmun and Mr. Justice Powell took no part in the consideration or decision of these cases.

NOTES AND QUESTIONS

4-16. What procedures did the agency provide in this case, over and above those required by § 553? What additional procedures did NRDC demand and why?

4-17. Why did the agency reject those requests? Why did the court remand this case?

4-18. Are there any circumstances under which the court in *Vermont Yankee* would allow the judicial imposition of additional procedures on an agency? Do you agree that the excerpted portions of legislative history of § 4 bear out Justice Rehnquist's conclusion that Congress did not intend the courts to exercise discretion in determining when extra procedural devices should be employed?

4-19. If there is to be judicial review of agency action, presumably it must be "meaningful judicial review." Are additional procedures sometimes necessary to assure meaningful judicial review or should a court simply remand the case to the agency to do whatever is necessary to assure such review?

4-20. Does meaningful judicial review depend upon a rulemaking record? Does section 553 say anything about a record? If a record is implicitly required, does that violate the holding of *Vermont Yankee*? For a discussion of the rulemaking record, *see* Note 4-14, *supra*.

4-21. Was this an appropriate use of informal rulemaking by the agency in the case? When can you substitute rulemaking procedures for adjudicatory procedures?

PROBLEM 4-2

The purpose of this problem is to reconstruct the litigation strategies and theories of parties involved in the *Vermont Yankee* litigation.

(1) As the attorney for Vermont Yankee, what are your primary goals in this litigation? What do you think of the agency's decision to use informal rulemaking procedures to resolve the issue of nuclear waste? What advantages and what disadvantages do you see in this manner of proceeding? What kind of record will you want to develop? Will it withstand judicial review?

(2) As attorney for NRDC, what are your primary goals in this litigation? What are your views on the agency's decision to resolve the nuclear waste issue through informal rulemaking? Why do you wish to resist this procedure? What kind of hearing do you envisage? Why do you want that kind of hearing? Is your primary audience the agency or the court or the public? How important is delay to you? What is the impact of delay? Are there ethical limits to the use of the litigation process to effectuate delay? Do you have reasons, independent of delay, for the procedures you advocate? What are they?

(3) As attorney for the utility company, what are your primary goals? Why did you recommend the use of informal rulemaking procedures? What are you trying to accomplish with these procedures? Are these procedures fair? Why did you augment them? Why did you resist augmenting them further?

(4) As a Justice of the United States Supreme Court, how would you have resolved this case?

[D] Hybrid Rulemaking Procedures

Sections 553, 556 and 557 set forth a procedural spectrum for rulemaking that ranges from the relatively minimal notice and comment procedures of informal rulemaking to the adjudicatory procedures of formal rulemaking. As we have seen above, the *Vermont Yankee* case by and large put an end to hybrid rulemaking under the APA. In the 1970s, however, Congress passed a number of statutes that, to a large extent, supplanted the informal and formal rulemaking provisions of the APA. These statutes required the use of hybrid rulemaking procedures that fall somewhere between informal and formal rulemaking. To a large extent these new procedural provisions and approaches to policymaking coincided with the environmental movement in the United States and the passage of new environmental, health, and safety statutes. Congress, for example, passed the Occupational Safety and Health Act of 1970, the Consumer Product Safety Act of 1972, and the Clean Air Act Amendments of 1977. These statutes, and those like them, along with their procedural provisions, created new issues for courts. Consider the following case. What is the nature of the statute involved? What new provisions does it contain? What problems does this present to the reviewing court? How does the court resolve those problems? Why might traditional formal or informal procedures have been inadequate for the substantive issues with which the agency and then the court must deal?

INDUSTRIAL UNION DEPARTMENT, AFL-CIO v. HODGSON

District of Columbia Court of Appeals
499 F.2d 467 (1974)

Before McGowan, Leventhal and MacKinnon, Circuit Judges.

McGowan, Circuit Judge:

This direct review proceeding presents a classic case of what Judge Friendly has aptly termed "a new form of 'uneasy partnership' between agency and court that results whenever Congress delegates decision making of a legislative character to the one, subject to review by the other." *Associated Industries v. United States Dept. of Labor*, 487 F.2d 342, 354 (2d Cir. 1973). The angularity of this relationship is only sharpened when, as here, Congress — with no apparent awareness of anomaly — has explicitly combined an informal agency procedure with a standard of review traditionally conceived of as suited to formal adjudication or rulemaking. The federal courts, hard pressed as they are by the flood of new tasks imposed upon them by Congress, surely have some claim to be spared additional burdens deriving from the illogic of legislative compromise. At the least, it would have been helpful if there had been some recognition by Congress that the quick answer it gave to a legislative stalemate posed serious problems for a reviewing court, and that there would inevitably have to be some latitude accorded it to surmount those problems consistently with the legislative purposes. The duty remains, in any event, to decide the case before us in accordance with our statutory mandate, however dimly the rationale, if any, underlying it can be perceived.

The petition before us seeks review of standards promulgated by the Secretary of Labor under the Occupational Safety and Health Act of 1970,

29 U.S.C. § 651 *et seq.*, (hereinafter OSHA). The standards in question regulate the atmospheric concentrations of asbestos dust in industrial workplaces. Petitioners are unions whose members are affected by the health hazards of asbestos dust. They challenge the timetable established by the standards for the achievement of permissible levels of concentration, and object to portions of the standards concerning methods of compliance, monitoring intervals and techniques, cautionary labels and notices, and medical examinations and records. We remand two of such issues to the Secretary for further consideration. In all other respects, the petition is denied.

I

A. *The Occupational Safety and Health Act*

Technological progress in industry appears not to have been accompanied uniformly by corresponding reductions in the health hazards of industrial working conditions. More than 2.2 million persons are disabled on the job each year, and in 1967 the Surgeon General estimated that approximately 400,000 new cases of occupational disease would occur in each succeeding year. The Chairman of the Committee on Labor and Public Welfare summarized the problem as follows:

> Not only are occupational diseases which first came to light at the beginning of the Industrial Revolution still undermining the health of workers, but new substances, new processes, and new sources of energy are presenting health problems of ever-increasing complexity.

Foreword, Legislative History of the Occupational Safety and Health Act of 1970 (hereinafter Legis. Hist.).

OSHA, the first comprehensive attempt by Congress to deal with these problems, covers every employer whose business affects interstate commerce. Eschewing any attempt to establish substantive provisions to control all these various employers, the Act erects a general framework to govern the development of regulations, and delegates the task of formulating particular health and safety standards to the Secretary of Labor. Civil and criminal sanctions are provided to enforce compliance.

OSHA specifies the procedure to be followed in the promulgation of standards, and provides for the establishment of a research institute and the appointment of advisory committees to assist the Secretary. The substantive provisions of the Act impose a general obligation upon employers to provide safe working conditions. 29 U.S.C. § 654(a)(1) (1970). The Secretary is required to promulgate standards to control particular health hazards that come to his attention. Certain types of controls, including monitoring, medical examinations, warnings, record keeping, and specific protective measures are specified by the statute itself, but the decision as to when and how they should be required with regard to particular health hazards is left to the Secretary.

B. *Asbestos*

Asbestos is a generic term applicable to a number of fibrous, inorganic, silicate minerals that are incombustible in air. Its commercial value is high, and its uses are many and varied. Asbestos can be woven into cloth, used in powder form, or incorporated into materials of various shapes and consistencies. Almost one million tons of asbestos are used in this country annually; and, for many purposes, it cannot easily be replaced with other substances.

Unfortunately, asbestos is as hazardous to health as it is useful to industry. During its production and use, tiny asbestos fibers are released as a dust in the air, and, over the course of this century, thousands of workers have been killed or disabled by the effects of inhaling these fibers. There are no precise figures concerning the number of workers involved, but it is estimated that three to five million workers are exposed to some extent to asbestos fibers in the building construction and shipyard industries alone. While OSHA was under consideration in Congress, the health hazards of the asbestos industry were among the examples used to stress the need for legislation.

C. *Proceedings before the Secretary*

Within a few months of the effective date of OSHA, petitioners requested the Secretary to establish an emergency standard to control concentrations of asbestos dust. The Secretary promptly issued a temporary standard and set in motion the procedure for establishment of a permanent standard. Notice of the proposed rulemaking was published, and interested persons were invited to submit their views. NIOSH [National Institute for Occupational Safety and Health] submitted its recommendations, as did the Advisory Committee. These were made public, and the Secretary conducted a hearing at which various representatives and experts appeared on behalf of interested parties. On the basis of these recommendations and a formidable record of documents and oral testimony, including highly technical statements by expert witnesses, the Secretary established the standards in question.[9] His statement of reasons covers some four and one-half pages of the Federal Register.[10]

---

[9] A qualified hearing examiner presided over the four days consumed by the public hearing. At the close his only function was to certify the record to the Secretary, which consisted of the written statements and comments on the proposed standards received prior to the hearing in response to the notice of rulemaking, the transcript of the hearing itself, and many exhibits received during the hearing and in a further period allowed after the hearing for this purpose. The Joint Appendix filed in this court contains over 1100 pages, of which over 400 are from the hearing transcript. The testimonial pattern generally was for the witnesses to read long statements, at the close of which they were subject to cross-examination. The questions actually asked tended to be few, sporadic, and perfunctory, and the record resembles nothing so much as that of a typical legislative committee hearing.

[10] The statutory direction is that the Secretary, whenever he promulgates a standard, "shall include a statement of the reasons for such action. . . ." 29 U.S.C. § 655(e). The Secretary has by regulation, 29 C.F.R. § 1911.18(b), as amended, 37 F.R. 8655 (1972), defined this task in these terms:

> Any rule or standard adopted . . . shall incorporate a concise general statement of its basis and purpose. The statement is not required to include specific and detailed findings and conclusions of the kind customarily associated with formal proceedings. However, the statement will show the significant issues which have been faced, and will articulate the rationale for their solution.

Petitioners have not challenged the propriety of this formulation.

Petitioners allege no procedural errors in the promulgation of these standards, but they characterize them as inadequate to protect the health of employees as required by the Act. They attack the Secretary's interpretation of OSHA in certain particulars, as well as the enforcement measures he has selected.

II

OSHA is a self-contained statute in the sense that it does not depend upon reference to the Administrative Procedure Act for specification of the procedures to be followed. It prescribes that the process of promulgating a standard is to be initiated by the publication of a proposed rule. Interested persons are given a period of 30 days thereafter within which to submit written data or comments. Within this period any interested person may submit written objections, and may request a public hearing thereon. In such event, the Secretary shall publish a notice specifying the particular standard involved and stating the time and place of the hearing. Within 60 days after the completion of such hearing, the Secretary shall make his decision. Judicial review by the courts of appeals is provided.

This procedure is characteristic of the informal rulemaking contemplated by Section 4 of the APA, 5 U.S.C. § 553, and it was so understood by the Congress. By regulation, however, the secretary, although describing it as "legislative in type," has provided that the oral hearing called for in the statute shall contain some elements normally associated with the adjudicatory or formal rule-making model. As indicated in the text of the regulations, set forth in the margin,[12] the Secretary apparently concluded that this was necessary because of the necessity of having a record to which the statutorily mandated substantial evidence test could be meaningfully applied by a reviewing court. The only controversy we have in this case as to the procedural requirements of the statute is not with respect to the manner in which the rulemaking was

---

[12] In 29 C.F.R. § 1911.15 ("Nature of Hearing"), the Secretary stated in relevant part:

(a)(2) Section 6(b)(3) provides an opportunity for a hearing on objections to proposed rule making, and section 6(f) provides in connection with the judicial review of standards, that determinations of the Secretary shall be conclusive if supported by substantial evidence in the record as a whole. Although these sections are not read as requiring a rule making proceeding within the meaning of the last sentence of 5 U.S.C. § 553(c) requiring the application of the formal requirements of 5 U.S.C. §§ 556 and 557, they do suggest a Congressional expectation that the rule making would be on the basis of a record to which a substantial evidence test, where pertinent, may be applied in the event an informal hearing is held.

(3) The oral hearing shall be legislative in type. However, fairness may require an opportunity for cross-examination on crucial issues. The presiding officer is empowered to permit cross-examination under such circumstances. . . .

(b) Although any hearing shall be informal and legislative in type, this part is intended to provide more than the bare essentials of informal rule making under 5 U.S.C. § 553. The additional requirements are the following:

"(1) The presiding officer shall be a hearing examiner appointed under 5 U.S.C. § 3105.

"(2) The presiding officer shall provide an opportunity for cross-examination on crucial issues.

"(3) The hearing shall be reported verbatim, and a transcript shall be available to any interested person on such terms as the presiding officer may provide."

done by the Secretary, but as to the reach of the substantial evidence test in the course of judicial review.

The substantial evidence test has customarily been directed to adjudicatory proceedings or formal rulemaking. The hybrid nature of OSHA in this respect can be explained historically, if not logically, as a legislative compromise. The Conference Report reflects that the Senate bill called for informal rulemaking, but the House version specified formal rulemaking and substantial evidence review. The House receded on the procedure for promulgating standards, but the substantial evidence standard of review was adopted.[14]

One question generated by this anomalous combination is whether the determinations in question here are of the kind to which substantial evidence review can appropriately be applied. The Government in its argument suggested that a proper accommodation could be effected by construing the statute to require substantial evidence review of factual determinations, while weighing the inferences of policy drawn from those facts in terms of their freedom from arbitrariness or irrationality. We do not believe this approach would affect the rigorousness of our review to the extent the Government seems to suppose, or that petitioners purport to fear. The analysis may, however, be useful for the purpose of clarifying the diverse nature of the judicial task imposed upon us by a statute like OSHA.

Another problem arising from substantial evidence review of informal proceedings concerns the adequacy of the record to permit meaningful performance of the required review. Although this issue has not been directly raised in argument, it underlies much of the controversy concerning the sufficiency of the evidence to support various specific determinations of the Secretary. Thus some explication of the procedural implications of the prescribed substantial evidence standard of review should help to clarify our resolution of the particular substantive issues presented by this petition.

Faced with the fact that his determinations were commanded by Congress to be reviewed under a substantial evidence standard, the Secretary did voluntarily move his procedures significantly towards the formal model. He directed that (1) a qualified hearing examiner should preside over the oral hearing, (2) cross-examination should be permitted, and (3) a verbatim transcript made. The total record in this case was in part created under the conditions that obtain in a formal proceeding. In substantial remaining part, however, it consists of a melange of written statements, letters, reports, and similar materials received outside the bounds of the oral hearing and untested by anything approaching the adversary process.

Thus, in some degree the record approaches the form of one customarily conceived of as appropriate for substantial evidence review. In other respects, it does not. On a record of this mixed nature, when the facts underlying the Secretary's determinations are susceptible of being found in the usual sense, that must be done, and the reviewing court will weigh them by the substantial evidence standard. But, in a statute like OSHA where the decision making

---

[14] This combination is made even more confusing by a statement in the report that seems to indicate that the Conference Committee thought the substantial evidence standard was less exacting then the standard of rationality ordinarily applicable to the results of informal rulemaking.

vested in the Secretary is legislative in character, there are areas where explicit factual findings are not possible, and the act of decision is essentially a prediction based upon pure legislative judgment, as when a Congressman decides to vote for or against a particular bill.

OSHA sets forth general policy objectives and establishes the basic procedural framework for the promulgation of standards, but the formulation of specific substantive provisions is left largely to the Secretary. The Secretary's task thus contains "elements of both a legislative policy determination and an adjudicative resolution of disputed facts." Although in practice these elements may so intertwine as to be virtually inseparable, they are conceptually distinct and can only be regarded as such by a reviewing court.

From extensive and often conflicting evidence, the Secretary in this case made numerous factual determinations. With respect to some of those questions, the evidence was such that the task consisted primarily of evaluating the data and drawing conclusions from it. The court can review that data in the record and determine whether it reflects substantial support for the Secretary's findings. But some of the questions involved in the promulgation of these standards are on the frontiers of scientific knowledge, and consequently as to them insufficient data is presently available to make a fully informed factual determination. Decision making must in that circumstance depend to a greater extent upon policy judgments and less upon purely factual analysis. Thus, in addition to currently unresolved factual issues, the formulation of standards involves choices that by their nature require basic policy determinations rather than resolution of factual controversies. Judicial review of inherently legislative decisions of this sort is obviously an undertaking of different dimensions.

For example, in this case the evidence indicated that reliable data is not currently available with respect to the precisely predictable health effects of various levels of exposure to asbestos dust; nevertheless, the Secretary was obligated to establish some specific level as the maximum permissible exposure. After considering all the conflicting evidence, the Secretary explained his decision to adopt, over strong employer objection, a relatively low limit in terms of the severe health consequences which could result from overexposure. Inasmuch as the protection of the health of employees is the overriding concern of OSHA, this choice is doubtless sound, but it rests in the final analysis on an essentially legislative policy judgment, rather than a factual determination, concerning the relative risks of underprotection as compared to overprotection.

Regardless of the manner in which the task of judicial review is articulated, policy choices of this sort are not susceptible to the same type of verification or refutation by reference to the record as are some factual questions. Consequently, the court's approach must necessarily be different no matter how the standards of review are labeled. That does not mean that such decisions escape exacting scrutiny, for, as this court has stated in a similar context:

> This exercise need be no less searching and strict in its weighing of whether the agency has performed in accordance with the Congressional purposes, but, because it is addressed to different materials, it inevitably varies from

the adjudicatory model. The paramount objective is to see whether the agency, given an essentially legislative task to perform, has carried it out in a manner calculated to negate the dangers of arbitrariness and irrationality in the formulation of rules for general application in the future.

Automotive Parts & Accessories Ass'n v. Boyd, 132 U.S. App. D.C. 200, 407 F.2d 330, 338 (1968).

We do not understand Congress to have in this instance nullified this approach for all purposes by directing substantial evidence review. As noted above, that provision is important as an indication of how we should approach certain kinds of questions and what kind of record we should demand of the Secretary. But it is surely not to be taken as a direction by Congress that we treat the Secretary's decision making under OSHA as something different from what it is, namely, the exercise of delegated power to make within certain limits decisions that Congress normally makes itself, and by processes, as the courts have long recognized and accepted, peculiar to itself. A due respect for the boundaries between the legislative and the judicial function dictates that we approach our reviewing task with a flexibility informed and shaped by sensitivity to the diverse origins of the determinations that enter into a legislative judgment.

What we are entitled to at all events is a careful identification by the Secretary, when his proposed standards are challenged, of the reasons why he chooses to follow one course rather than another. Where that choice purports to be based on the existence of certain determinable facts, the Secretary must, in form as well as substance, find those facts from evidence in the record. By the same token, when the Secretary is obliged to make policy judgments where no factual certainties exist or where facts alone do not provide the answer, he should so state and go on to identify the considerations he found persuasive.

Judge Friendly concluded his ruminations in *Associated Industries* with an expression of doubt as to "whether judicial review of legislative standards resulting from informal rule-making will ultimately prove to be feasible." That is certainly a serious and substantial question. Whether it can eventually be answered affirmatively must depend in large measure upon the care and good sense with which both the delegatee of what is essentially legislative power and the reviewing court go about their respective duties. In the case of OSHA, the Secretary has wisely acted by regulation to go beyond the minimum requirements of the statute and to expand his capacity to find facts by providing an evidentiary hearing in which cross-examination is available. We think it equally the part of wisdom and restraint on our part to show a comparable flexibility, and to be always mindful that at least some legislative judgments cannot be anchored securely and solely in demonstrable fact. Such a principle, far from being destructive of the Congressional purpose to provide judicial review, seems to us within the Congressional contemplation as essential to its preservation. . . .

NOTES AND QUESTIONS

4-22. How do the rulemaking procedures set forth in the statute under review in this case differ from formal and informal rulemaking under the APA? Why do you suppose that Congress chose to write such a statute?

4-23. How does the Secretary interpret the statute in this case and what procedures does he set forth to carry out its goals? Do you think that these procedures increase public participation? Are they likely to help lead to better decisions? Are they likely to increase the time it will take for an agency to promulgate a final rule? Why?

4-24. More recently, Congress has passed numerous statutes requiring various risk assessment and cost-benefit procedures. These also have complicated rulemaking procedural provisions that go well beyond the basic § 553 notice and comment procedures of the APA. *See, e.g.*, section 307(d) of the Clean Air Act, 42 U.S.C. § 7607(d), and sections 4(b)(5) and 19 of TSCA, 15 U.S.C. §§ 2603(b)(5), 2618. Compare the 1996 Safe Drinking Water Act Amendments, 42 U.S.C. § 300g-i, and the Food Quality Protection Act, 21 U.S.C. § 346a, passed within three days of each other but with very different approaches to risk assessment and toxic substances.

The procedural complexity of these and other statutes dealing with rules, coupled with, as we shall see, Executive oversight at the OMB and, from time to time, Congressional oversight as well, see Chapters 6 and 7, *infra*, and various doctrines of judicial review, see Chapter 8, *infra*, contributes to what some commentators have called rule ossification. Consider the following

> Although no detailed empirical studies exist on the comparative burdensomeness of informal rulemaking and alternative regulatory vehicles, it is difficult to disagree with the conclusion that it is much harder for an agency to promulgate a rule now than it was twenty years ago. Agency explanations for rules are far more lengthy and intricate than they were in the 1960s and early 1970s. The "concise general statement of basis and purpose" for the original primary and secondary ambient air quality standards promulgated under the Clean Air Act Amendments of 1970 consisted of a single page in the Federal Register when they were promulgated in 1971. The preamble to the 1987 revision of a single primary standard consumed 36 pages in the Federal Register and was supported by a 100-plus-page staff paper, a lengthy Regulatory Impact Analysis that cost the agency millions of dollars, and a multi-volume criteria document.
>
> The agencies also take much longer to write the lengthy preambles and technical support documents and to address public comments on proposed rules. The Occupational Safety and Health Administration (OSHA) in 1972 spent about six months from inception to publication of the final rule on its first occupational health standard for asbestos. Two of its next three health standards, a generic rule for fourteen carcinogens and a standard for vinyl chloride, took about one year, and nine months, respectively. The

next three standards, for cotton dust, acrylonitrile, and arsenic, each took over three-and-one-half years. These last three standards were promulgated during the relatively activist Carter Administration when OSHA was anxious to write new rules to protect workers. Today, OSHA health standards rarely take less than five years to promulgate.

. . . .

Once an agency has endured the considerable expense and turmoil of writing a rule, it has every incentive to leave well enough alone. Once the legal and political dust has settled, an agency is inclined to let sleeping dogs lie. Even when forced by statute to revisit existing rules, an agency is very reluctant to change them. For example, EPA has a statutory obligation to reexamine its national ambient air quality standards every five years, but it has rarely completed the process without the additional incentive of a court order. And when it does promulgate a revised standard, it tends to set the standard at or near existing levels, in part because of the difficulty of justifying any departures from the status quo. Similarly, although OSHA devoted most of its standard-setting efforts at the outset of the Reagan Administration to reexamining several rules, the final results did not differ in any significant regard from the existing regulations. Thus, an agency's general reluctance to revisit old rules may disserve both regulatees and regulatory beneficiaries.

Frustrated agencies are beginning to explore techniques for avoiding notice-and-comment rulemaking altogether, such as establishing rules in adjudications. [. . . .] To the extent that agencies establish rules in adjudications in order to avoid informal rulemaking, regulatees are not put on notice of the standards of conduct that such agencies are applying to them. As a result, both regulatees and regulatory beneficiaries are deprived of the open opportunity that informal rulemaking provides to influence the agencies' thinking.

Perhaps more troublesome to the goals of open government is the increasing tendency of agencies to engage in "nonrule rulemaking" through relatively less formal devices such as policy statements, interpretative rules, manuals, and other informal devices. Although informal guidance documents and technical manuals are a necessary part of a complex administrative regime, they are promulgated without the benefit of comments by an interested public.

Thomas O. McGarity, *Some Thoughts on "Deossifying" the Rulemaking Process*, 41 DUKE L.J. 1385, 1387–93 (1992).*

See also Peter L. Strauss, *From Expertise to Politics: The Transformation of American Rulemaking,* 31 WAKE FOREST L. REV. 745 (1996); David A. Codevilla, Robert A. Anthony, *Pro-ossification: A Harder Look at Agency Policy Statements*, 31 WAKE FOREST L. REV. 667 (1996); Richard J. Pierce, *Seven Ways to Deossify Agency Rulemaking*, 47 ADMIN. L. REV. 59 (1995); Paul R. Verkuil, *Comment: Rulemaking Ossification — A Modest Proposal*, 47 ADMIN. L. REV. 453 (1995); Mark Seidenfeld, *Demystifying Deossification: Rethinking*

---

* Copyright © 1992 by Thomas O. McGarity. All rights reserved.

Recent Proposals to Modify Judicial Review of Notice and Comment Rulemaking, 75 TEX. L. REV. 483 (1997); William S. Jordan III, *Ossification Revisited: Does Arbitrary and Capricious Review Significantly Interfere with Agency Ability to Achieve Regulatory Goals Through Informal Rulemaking?* 94 Nw. U. L. REV. 393 (2000).

We shall examine some of these informal devices, *i.e.* various exemptions from rulemaking, in the next section. To understand more fully some of the incentives to avoid notice and comment, consider *Appalachian Power Company v. EPA*, 208 F.3d 1015, 1020 (D.C. Cir. 2000):

> The phenomenon we see in this case is familiar. Congress passes a broadly worded statute. The agency follows with regulations containing broad language, open-ended phrases, ambiguous standards and the like. Then as years pass, the agency issues circulars or guidance or memoranda, explaining, interpreting, defining and often expanding the commands in the regulations. One guidance document may yield another and then another and so on. Several words in a regulation may spawn hundreds of pages of text as the agency offers more and more detail regarding what its regulations demand of regulated entities. Law is made, without notice and comment, without public participation, and without publication in the Federal Register or the Code of Federal Regulations. With the advent of the Internet, the agency does not need these official publications to ensure widespread circulation; it can inform those affected simply by posting its new guidance or memoranda or policy statement on its web site. An agency operating in this way gains a large advantage. "It can issue or amend its real rules, i.e., its interpretative rules and policy statements, quickly and inexpensively without following any statutorily prescribed procedures." Richard J. Pierce, Jr., *Seven Ways to Deossify Agency Rulemaking*, 47 ADMIN. L. REV. 59, 85 (1995). The agency may also think there is another advantage — immunizing its lawmaking from judicial review.

4-25. *Hodgson* deals with a number of issues that go to the scope of judicial review. We shall return to those issues, in detail, in Chapter Eight, § 8.06, *infra*. For now, however, it is useful to consider what effect the combination of rulemaking and adjudicatory procedure have on the way courts review the ultimate product of these procedures. Specifically, should such statutes lead to closer judicial review? *See generally* Antonin Scalia and Frank Goodman, *Procedural Aspects of the Consumer Product Safety Act*, 2 U.C.L.A. L. REV. 899 (1973) (arguing that there ought to be no difference in the degree of judicial scrutiny). How should *ex parte* contacts in the context of hybrid rulemaking be treated? Consider the following case.

UNITED STATES STEELWORKERS OF AMERICA v. MARSHALL

District of Columbia Court of Appeals
647 F.2d 1189 (1980)

Before WRIGHT, CHIEF JUDGE, and ROBINSON and MACKINNON, CIRCUIT JUDGES.

Opinion for the court filed by CHIEF JUDGE J. SKELLY WRIGHT.

Dissenting opinion filed by CIRCUIT JUDGE MACKINNON.

J. SKELLY WRIGHT, CHIEF JUDGE:

In November 1978 the Occupational Safety and Health Administration (OSHA), exercising its authority and responsibility under Section 6 of the Occupational Safety and Health Act, 29 U.S.C. § 655 (1976), issued new rules designed to protect American workers from exposure to airborne lead in the workplace. In these consolidated appeals petitioners representing both labor union and industry interests challenge virtually every aspect of the new lead standard and the massive rulemaking from which it emerged. The unions claim that OSHA has failed to carry out its statutory duty to ensure that "no employee will suffer material impairment of health. . . ." *Id.* § 655(b)(5). The industry parties charge OSHA with almost every procedural sin of which an agency can be guilty in informal rulemaking, attack some of the most important substantive provisions of the standard as exceeding OSHA's statutory authority, and assert that the agency has failed to present substantial evidence to support the factual bases of the standard. Though the numerous challenges to the standard and the size and complexity of the rulemaking require of us a lengthy analysis of the issues, we affirm most of the new occupational lead standard, remanding to the agency for reconsideration only the question of the feasibility of the standard for a number of the affected industries.

. . . .

III. PROCEDURAL CLAIMS

OSHA was occasionally careless or inefficient in its procedures throughout this rulemaking, and we readily concede that procedural purists will never place the lead standard in the Pantheon of administrative proceedings. Moreover, we concede that most of LIA's [Lead Industry Association] procedural claims raise difficult legal issues, and indeed force us to consider a number of important questions of informal rulemaking procedure that have not been fully resolved by this circuit in recent years. Nevertheless, we enter this area under two important restraints. First, as a legal matter, we generally have no power to impose extra-statutory procedural requirements on the agency unless it has violated the Constitution or flagrantly disregarded minimal principles of procedural fairness. *Vermont Yankee Nuclear Power Corp.*

v. Natural Resources Defense Council, Inc., 435 U.S. 519 (1978). Second, as both a legal and a practical matter, we must recognize the procedural flexibility inherent in informal rulemaking, as well as the difficulty an agency faces in managing hundreds of comments and witnesses and developing coherent standard out of tens of thousands of pages of record evidence.

The OSH Act requires the agency to follow procedures more stringent than the minimal ones established in the Administrative Procedure Act, 5 U.S.C. § 553 (1976). Thus the agency must give interested parties the opportunity to request a public hearing on objections to a proposed rule, and must publish notice of the time and place for such hearing in the Federal Register. 29 U.S.C. § 655(b)(3) (1976). Moreover, the agency has added to these statutory procedures by rule. Thus OSHA itself requires a hearing examiner at oral hearings, who must provide an opportunity for cross-examination on important issues and offer interested persons verbatim transcripts of the hearing.

Nevertheless, Congress' decision to impose the substantial evidence test on OSHA does not alter the essentially informal character of OSHA rulemaking. *Industrial Union Dept., AFL-CIO v. Hodgson*, 499 F.2d 467, 472–473 (D.C. Cir. 1974). Just recently, we emphasized that the presence of procedures beyond those mandated by Section 553 of the APA neither converts the essentially legislative process of informal rulemaking into something akin to adjudication, nor empowers courts to turn rulemaking into courtroom trials. *Ass'n of Nat'l Advertisers, Inc. v. FTC*, 627 F.2d 1151 (D.C. Cir. 1979). Thus, as we examine the procedural claims in the lead proceeding, we must avoid imposing procedural constraints beyond those in APA Section 553, the OSH Act, and the Due Process Clause, and we remain bound by judicial construction of the demands of APA Section 553 as our source for the general principles of informal rulemaking.

Acting under these constraints, we ultimately find nothing illegal in OSHA's procedural conduct.

A. Bias of the Decisionmaker

LIA urges us to vacate the entire lead standard because, in its view, the official who ultimately set the standard, Assistant Secretary of Labor Eula Bingham, had prejudged the essential issues in the rulemaking proceeding. For proof of this allegedly fatal bias, LIA points to a speech Bingham delivered on November 3, 1978 to a United Steelworkers of America conference on occupational exposure to lead.

Bingham's speech began innocuously, if dramatically ("Brothers and Sisters"), by noting her concern for workers and by recognizing how much OSHA depended on their unique perspective when it gathered information in setting safety standards. But after asserting that she and Secretary of Labor Marshall were "determined" to have a lead standard, Bingham proceeded to suggest her predisposition on important issues. As to the medical removal protection provision (MRP):

> I think that there may be some apprehension because Assistant Secretaries in the past have not always understood, or have not known how to spell the words medical removal protection, or rate retention . . . . Well, I learned to spell those words a long time ago on the coke Oven Advisory

Committee, and if you want to know how I feel about it, you need only to look up my comments during those Committee hearings. As far as I'm concerned, it is impossible to have a Lead Standard without it. . . .

As to the dangers of lead:

. . . I can tell you about a plant within 300 miles of the city where workers are told to go to the hospital from work and receive therapy that would drag out poison and precious metals. And then they're sent back to be poisoned again. I bet I could go down to the hospitals of this city and find a worker that is undergoing kidney dialysis, and I'll bet you a dinner that some of those workers have been in lead plants.

As to economic feasibility:

I have told some people that I have never aspired to be an economist, but I tell you I can smell a phony issue when I see one. And to say that safety and health regulation are inflationary is phony. . . .

. . . I don't understand a society such as ours [sic] which is not willing to pay a dollar more for a battery to insure that workers do not have to pay for that battery with their lives.

The speech went on to urge workers "to control their own destiny" by educating themselves about the lead problem, and ended by calling for political support in the imminent congressional elections for candidates sympathetic to OSHA's goals.

Were it our task to assess the wisdom and propriety of an administrator's public conduct, we might well admonish Dr. Bingham for this speech. She served her agency poorly by making statements so susceptible to an inference of bias, especially statements to a group so passionately involved in the proceedings. But our task is rather to measure her conduct against the legal standards for determining whether an official is so biased as to be incapable of finding facts and setting policy on the basis of the objective record before her. Moreover, we must bear in mind that this particular speech, though delivered five days before the Secretary of Labor signed the final standard and ten days before he released it, came 30 days after Bingham had effectively made her own decision on the standard and ten days after she had approved the final language.

An administrative official is presumed to be objective and "capable of judging a particular controversy fairly on the basis of its own circumstances." *United States v. Morgan*, 313 U.S. 409, 421 (1941). Whether the official is engaged in adjudication or rulemaking, mere proof that she has taken a public position, or has expressed strong views, or holds an underlying philosophy with respect to an issue in dispute cannot overcome that presumption. . . . Nor is that presumption overcome when the official's alleged predisposition derives from her participation in earlier proceedings on the same issue. *FTC v. Cement Institute*, 33 U.S. 683, 702–703 (1948). To disqualify administrators because of opinions they expressed or developed in earlier proceedings would mean that "experience acquired from their work . . . would be a handicap instead of an advantage."

When Congress creates an agency with an express mission — in OSHA's case, to protect workers' health and safety — the agency officials will almost inevitably form views on the best means of carrying out that mission. The subjective partiality of an official of such an agency does not invalidate a proceeding that the agency conducts in good faith.

This court has indeed required disqualification of an agency adjudicator when his public statements about pending cases revealed he "has in some measure adjudged the facts as well as the law of a particular case in advance of hearing it." *Cinderella Career & Finishing Schools, Inc. v. FTC,* 425 F.2d 583, 591 (D.C. Cir. 1970), *quoting Gilligan Will & Co. v. SEC,* 267 F.2d 461, 469 (2d Cir.), *cert. denied,* 361 U.S. 896 (1959). . . . And, although these cases involved adjudication, we could perhaps logically apply them to hybrid rulemaking proceedings like the present one in which the factual predicates of final rules are subject to review under the substantial evidence test.

So applied, however, these cases would lead us to vacate the lead standard only if Dr. Bingham had demonstrably made up her mind about important and specific factual questions and was impervious to contrary evidence. This test would be hard enough for petitioners to meet. But in *Ass'n of Nat'l Advertisers, Inc. v. FTC, supra,* handed down after oral argument in the present case, we raised an even higher barrier to claims of bias in rulemaking proceedings. We stressed there the difference between the essentially "legislative" factfinding of a rulemaker and the trial-type factfinding of an adjudicator, and thus held that the *Cinderella* test was inappropriate. We concluded that an agency official must be disqualified from rulemaking "only when there has been a clear and convincing showing that [she] has an unalterably closed mind on matters critical to the disposition of the proceeding." 627 F.2d at 1195.

The relevant statute in *Ass'n of Nat'l Advertisers, Inc. v. FTC, supra,* Section 18 of the Federal Trade Commission Act, 15 U.S.C. § 57a (1976), like the OSH Act, creates procedures more formal than the minimal ones required for informal rulemaking by 6 U.S.C. § 553 (1976). We held, however, that even in such hybrid rulemaking the findings of fact so intertwine with the policies that emerge from them that we could not, as we could in *Cinderella,* "cleave law from fact" in deciding whether the official had prejudged factual issues. 627 F.2d at 1168.[14]

Dr. Bingham's general expression of solidarity with the Steelworkers was legally harmless. Her call for support for congressional candidates sympathetic to her agency's mission did not bear on any specific issues in the case, and is probably the sort of political activity we simply must accept from a political appointee. Thus her bias, if any, shows up in her remarks about MRP, the dangers of lead poisoning, and the inflationary effect of the lead standard.

Had she made these remarks before the rulemaking began or while OSHA was receiving public comments, we might still have had to strain precedent

---

[14] FTC Chairman Pertschuk had made public statements expressing his strong belief in the harm advertising caused small children and in the need for stringent rules to curb that harm. Our decision stated that in presenting legal and policy arguments for the rules Pertschuk "not unnaturally employed the factual assumptions that underlie the rationale for Commission action," but that his use of such assumptions "did not necessarily bind him to them forever." *Ass'n of Nat'l Advertisers, Inc. v. FTC,* 627 F.2d 1151, 1172 (D.C. Cir. 1979). We also noted that the very requirement that an agency issue a formal notice of proposed rulemaking assumes that the agency head will make tentative conclusions of fact to help focus the rulemaking comments. 627 F.2d at 1173.

to find grounds for disqualification. Her remarks on MRP do not bear on any specific factual issues, but rather reveal a general predisposition on a matter of policy, of the sort held legally harmless in *FTC v. Cement Institute, supra,* and *Ass'n of Nat'l Advertisers, Inc. v. FTC, supra.* Her remarks about endangered workers do bear on a factual question, but only very generally; they reveal no prejudgment on the precise and complex factual issues in the case, such as the exact blood-lead level at which disease develops. Finally, although the speech does allude specifically to the cost of the standard to the battery industry, Dr. Bingham's expression of disbelief in the inflationary effect of the standard is really part of a general rhetorical flourish about the danger of undervaluing worker health.

In any event, the fact remains that Dr. Bingham delivered the speech *after* she decided on the standard and *after* the record had been closed. We can thus infer bias only if we construe her remarks retroactively. There may be cases warranting such judicial mindreading, but they would have to involve far more explicit and detailed statements by the allegedly biased person. The only language of predisposition in Bingham's speech that we can plausibly read retroactively is that on MRP,[15] and her statement on that subject falls within the category of views derived from administrative experience to which the Supreme Court referred in *FTC v. Cement Institute, supra,* 333 U.S. at 70. Thus, Bingham's speech simply does not reveal prejudgment with sufficient specificity to prove bias under the *Cinderella* standard, and, all the more so, does not constitute the "clear and convincing" evidence demanded by *Ass'n of Nat'l Advertisers, Inc. v. FTC, supra.* Judicial review of rulemaking, unlike the ABA Canon of Ethics, does not attack the mere appearance of impropriety. Bingham's speech, however unfortunate, does not prove the proceedings unfair.

B. *Improper Staff Role and Separation of Functions*

LIA aims its next procedural attack at OSHA staff attorneys who, LIA argues, acted essentially as advocates for a stringent lead standard by consulting with and persuading the Assistant Secretary as she drew her conclusions from the record. LIA would have us conclude that the agency decisionmaker engaged in *ex parte,* off-the-record contacts with one of the adverse sides in the rulemaking, thereby rendering the proceedings unfair. Grounding its contention somewhat equivocally on due process, the procedural principles inherent in hybrid rulemaking, and OSHA's own regulations providing for cross-examination, LIA asks us to invalidate the entire proceeding.

---

[15] Bingham had been chairperson of the advisory committee empaneled by the Secretary to aid him in setting a standard for coke ovens. In that role she voted for a medical removal provision, but the Secretary decided not to include the provision in the coke oven standard. Since that time Bingham has overseen the issuance of at least one OSHA standard — for arsenic — that contains no MRP provision. *See* 43 Fed. Reg. 19584 (1978). Though LIA notes that the record on the arsenic standard had been closed before Bingham assumed her new job, that standard does at least show that Bingham's views did not force OSHA into an unyielding posture. Similarly, though the cotton dust standard issued under Bingham's direction does provide for retaining wages for removed workers, . . . that provision, triggered by a worker's inability to wear a respirator, differs noticeably from the lead MRP, . . . which depends on the measured blood-lead level in a worker's body.

The key agency employee in question was Richard Gross, a lawyer in the Office of the Solicitor at OSHA, who served as a so-called "standard's attorney" throughout the rulemaking. . . . The standard's attorney was at the center of activity throughout the rulemaking. He worked with the regular OSHA staff in reviewing preliminary research and drafting the proposed standard, all the while offering informal legal advice. He helped organize the public hearings and, having immersed himself in the scientific literature and in the submitted public comments, he communicated regularly with the prospective expert witnesses. In these communications he briefed the witnesses on the issues they were to address in their testimony, explained the positions of the agency, the industry, and the unions on key questions, discussed the likely criticism of the experts' testimony, and asked the experts for any new information that supported or contradicted the OSHA proposal.[18] During the hearing itself he conducted all initial questioning of OSHA witnesses and cross-examined all other witnesses. After the hearings he assisted the Assistant Secretary by reviewing the evidence in the record, preparing summaries, analyses, and recommendations, and helping draft the Preamble to the final standard.

In a proceeding to create a general rule it makes little sense to speak of an agency employee advocating for one "side" over another. However contentious the proceeding, the concept of advocacy does not apply easily where the agency is not determining the specific rights of a specific party, and where the proposed rule undergoes detailed change in its journey toward a final rule. Indeed, as OSHA notes, the true adversaries here may well have been the industry and the unions, since the final standard, while in no sense a mathematical compromise, did fall between the old standard, to which the industry had resigned itself, and the extremely stringent one the unions urged. . . . Thus, the standard's attorney may have been an advocate for *some* new lead standard, and probably even a stringent one, but not necessarily for one specific standard supported by one specific party.

Nevertheless, the adversary tone and format of the proceedings are obvious. At the very least, the standard's attorney was committed to the general principles of the proposed standard, and so inevitably represented those principles "against" the industry parties so obviously adverse to them. Moreover, by conducting the "direct examination" of OSHA witnesses and the cross-examination of all others, the standard's attorney certainly created the public impression of conventional legal advocacy. Thus OSHA's portrayal of his role, while logical, is a bit disingenuous. The Assistant Secretary might

---

[18] The letters of Gross' colleague, Donald Kuchenbecker, to two of the expert medical witnesses best reveal the work of the standard's attorney. The letters are exhaustively detailed and generally quite neutral in briefing the witnesses on the important medical issues and urging them to supply all new relevant evidence, including any at odds with a stringent lead standard. Nevertheless, Kuchenbecker did make some imprudent remarks. He told Dr. Piomelli that it "would not be helpful to OSHA" if the latter were to state that there was no correlation between air-lead and blood-lead measurements, and told both Dr. Piomelli and Dr. Seppalainen that OSHA wanted to avoid the "ticklish issue" of how to accommodate female workers of child-bearing age if feasibility limits required OSHA to set a standard that threatened such women but not other workers.

In context, these remarks do not overcome the generally objective import of the letters; moreover, Kuchenbecker himself did not advise the Assistant Secretary on the final standard, and we are loath to project his attitude onto Gross.

well have been able to assess the record more objectively — if less efficiently — had the standard's attorney not been constantly at her side. Therefore, although we have some doubt about calling the standard's attorney an "advocate" in the context of such rulemaking,[19] we will *assume* he played that role so we can measure his conduct against the legal constraints on the agency.

We note at the outset that nothing in the Administrative Procedure Act bars a staff advocate from advising the decisionmaker in setting a final rule. The APA deals with *ex parte* contacts in two provisions. 5 U.S.C. § 554(d) (1976), which applies solely to adjudications, prohibits any off-the-record communication between an agency decisionmaker and any other person about a fact in issue, and in particular bars any prosecuting or investigating employee of the agency from participating in final decisions. Since an OSHA proceeding to set a safety and health standard is obviously rulemaking, and not adjudication, *Industrial Union Dept., AFL-CIO v. Hodgson, supra*, 499 F.2d at 472-473; *see* 5 U.S.C. § 551(4) (1976), that provision cannot apply here.[21] 5 U.S.C. § 557(d) (1976), which applied to formal rulemaking as well as adjudication, prohibits *ex parte* communications relevant to the merits of a proceeding between the agency and *interested parties outside the agency*. Even were we to ignore our own determination and Congress' that the OSH Act creates essentially informal rulemaking, this provision cannot apply to *ex parte* contacts wholly among agency employees.

Moreover, in establishing the special hybrid procedures in the OSH Act, Congress never intended to impose the separation-of-functions requirement it imposes in adjudications. The legislative history shows that Congress

---

[19] We also have some doubt as to the wisdom of singling out a staff *lawyer* in this case, when other, nonlegal, staff people probably participated with great vigor both in developing the agency position during the hearings and in advising the Assistant Secretary in drafting the final standard. In the major case in this court to address the issue of staff influence, *Hercules, Inc. v. EPA*, 598 F.2d 91 (D.C. Cir. 1978), the agency decisionmaker admitted she had consulted with a wide range of staff employees after the record was closed. Nevertheless, in expressing concern about the propriety of staff influence there, we focused solely on the conduct of the staff attorneys, even though they were the only staff people consulted with whom the decisionmaker did *not* discuss factual or policy questions. Drawing a generic distinction between lawyers and nonlawyers in an informal rulemaking may be dubious practice. But we need not decide the matter here, because we hold that the standard's attorney's conduct did not impair the proceedings even if that conduct was generically different from his colleagues'.

[21] The Attorney General's Manual on the Administrative Procedure Act (1947), which is helpful in construing the APA because the Justice Department helped to draft the statute, *Vermont Yankee Nuclear Power Corp. v. Natural Resources Defense Council, Inc.*, 435 U.S. at 546 & n. 19 notes:

> Not only were the draftsmen and proponents of the bill aware of this realistic distinction between rule making and adjudication, but they shaped the entire Act around it . . . the Act leaves the hearing officer entirely free to consult with any other member of the agency's staff. In fact, the intermediate decision may be made by the agency itself or by a responsible officer other than the hearing officer. This reflects the fact that the purpose of the rule making proceeding is to determine policy. Policy is not made in Federal agencies by individual hearing examiners; rather it is formulated by the agency heads relying heavily upon the expert staffs which have been hired for that purpose. And so the Act recognizes that in rule making the intermediate decisions will be more useful to the parties in advising them of the real issues in the case if such decisions reflect the views of the agency heads or of their responsible officers who assist them in determining policy. . . .

Attorney General's Manual at 15.

consistently turned back efforts to impose such formal procedures on OSHA standard-setting. Adding to informal rulemaking the special requirement of a substantial evidence test does not change the essential character of the rulemaking, *Ass'n of Nat'l Advertisers, Inc. v. FTC, supra,* 627 F.2d at 1161, especially under a statute like the OSH Act which does not even require a hearing before the agency sets a standard, *see* 29 U.S.C. § 655(b)(3) (1976).[24]

Thus we can discern no statutory basis in either the APA or the OSH Act for a separation-of-functions requirement in OSHA rulemaking. And under the Supreme Court's decision in *Vermont Yankee Nuclear Power Corp. v. Natural Resources Defense Council, Inc., supra* that is virtually the end of the inquiry. Unless we find that the standard's attorney here violated the due process rights of the petitioners, 435 U.S. at 543, or that this is one of those "extremely compelling circumstances" in which courts remain free to impose nonconstitutional extra-statutory procedures on agencies, *id.*, we must reject LIA's challenge here.

In recent cases we have in fact gone beyond the strict terms of the APA and the substantive agency statute to impose a ban on *ex parte* contacts. In *Home Box Office, Inc. v. FCC,* 567 F.2d 9, 51–59 (D.C. Cir.) *(per curiam),* we held that off-the-record communications between members of the agency and interested outside parties violated the due process rights of parties not privy to the communications. In *United States Lines, Inc. v. FMC,* 584 F.2d 519, 536–543 (D.C. Cir. 1978), decided after *Vermont Yankee,* we reaffirmed the principle of *Home Box Office,* finding the ban on *ex parte* contacts there inherent in the statutory requirements of a hearing and judicial review under the arbitrary and capricious standard. *See Nat'l Small Shipments Traffic Conference, Inc. v. ICC,* 590 F.2d 345, 351 (D.C. Cir. 1978). But neither of these cases involved improper influence of staff on agency decisionmakers, nor does the reasoning of either case lead us to apply the ban on *ex parte* contacts to agency staff.

In *Home Box Office,* of course, we expressed our general concern that whenever the record fails to disclose important communications that may have influenced the agency decisionmaker, the court cannot fully exercise its power of review. *Home Box Office, Inc. v. FCC, supra,* 567 F.2d at 54. But we spoke there in the context of massive evidence that industry parties financially interested in the rulemaking secretly lobbied with FCC staff and commissioners. We stated:

> [T]he evidence is certainly consistent with often-voiced claims of undue industry influence over Commission proceedings, and we are particularly concerned that the final shaping of the rules we are reviewing here may have been by compromise among the contending industry forces, rather than by exercise of the independent discretion in the public interest the Communications Act vests in individual commissioners. . . .

---

[24] As Judge Leventhal put it in *American Airlines, Inc. v. CAB,* 359 F.2d 624, 629 (D.C. Cir.):

[R]ule making is a vital part of the administrative process, particularly adapted to and needful for sound evolution of policy . . ., [and] is not to be shackled, in the absence of clear and specific Congressional requirement, by importation of formalities developed for the adjudicatory process and basically unsuited for policy rule making. . . .

Of course, the mere fact that this particular proceeding became highly adversarial cannot transform informal rulemaking into something else. . . .

Id. at 53. Influence from within an agency poses no such threat. Moreover, in summarizing our guidance for the agencies in *Home Box Office* we identified the type of communication we were restricting specifically as that between the agency and "any interested private party, or an attorney or agent for any party[.]" *Id.* at 57. In *United States Lines,* where the agency abruptly reversed its decision on the antitrust exemption of a shipping agreement after it heard *ex parte* legal arguments from private parties, we stated that "adversarial comment is particularly critical where, as here, *ex parte* communications are made by a party interested in securing the Commission approval necessary for the legality of its contracts[.]" *United States Lines, Inc. v. FMC, supra,* 584 F.2d at 542.

Neither the constitutional[28] nor the implicit statutory principles that decided these cases apply with any force to the type of staff influence LIA challenges here. Moreover, an OSHA rulemaking proceeding is of a character wholly distinct from that of a proceeding which resolves "conflicting private claims to a valuable privilege," *Sangamon Valley Television Corp. v. United States,* 269 F.2d 221, 224 (D.C. Cir. 1959), *quoted in Home Box Office, Inc. v. FCC, supra,* 567 F.2d at 55, and from a "quasi-adjudicatory" proceeding in which we found the potential for bias as great as that in a case of competing claims, *United States Lines, Inc. v. FMC, supra,* 584 F.2d at 539, 542. . . .

Rulemaking is essentially an institutional, not an individual, process, and it is not vulnerable to communication within an agency in the same sense as it is to communication from without. In an enormously complex proceeding like an OSHA standard setting, it may simply be unrealistic to expect an official facing a massive, almost inchoate, record to isolate herself from the people with whom she worked in generating the record. *See Braniff Airways, Inc. v. CAB,* 379 F.2d 453, 561 (D.C. Cir. 1967). In any event we rest our decision not on our own theory of agency management, but on the state of the law.

C. *Improper Use of Consultants*

LIA makes two attacks on OSHA's reliance on out-of-house consultants in developing the lead standard.

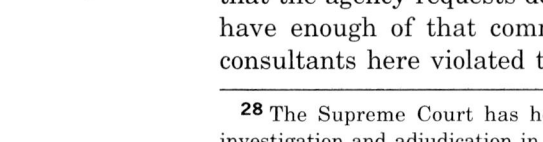

The first attack goes to the *general* use of consultants and the effect thereof on the Assistant Secretary's exercise of her duty to determine the final standard. LIA contends that the Assistant Secretary hired so many consultants and relied on them so heavily for so many tasks that she essentially abdicated her responsibility for setting the lead standard to outsiders. OSHA itself admits it lacked sufficient staff expertise to deal with all the important issues without outside help, thus perhaps earning LIA's ironic observation that the agency requests deference to its expertise while pleading it does not have enough of that commodity. But the question is whether the use of consultants here violated the law. . . .

---

[28] The Supreme Court has held that due process does not require separation between investigation and adjudication in an agency proceeding. *Withrow v. Larkin,* 421 U.S. 35, 47–52 (1974). As a *general* rule, due process probably imposes no constraints on informal rulemaking beyond those imposed by statute. . . . Thus we are very wary of extending the due process reasoning of *Home Box Office.*

LIA asserts that no case has considered and upheld the legality of such reliance. But neither can LIA locate a case or statute forbidding such a practice, and once again we are restrained by *Vermont Yankee Nuclear Power Corp. v. Natural Resources Defense Council, Inc., supra,* in imposing procedural rules on the agencies. . . .

LIA's second attack goes to *specific* uses of consultants, and alleges damage to the state of the rulemaking record, rather than to the Assistant Secretary's fulfillment of her personal responsibility. After closing the record, OSHA sought help from outside consultants in reviewing the record and preparing the Preamble. Two consultants were primary. The agency asked David Burton and DBA to help review the record to determine the feasibility of a permissible air-lead standard of 50 ug/m3, as opposed to the 100 ug/m3 standard the agency had proposed in the original notice of rulemaking, and on which most of the public commentary had focused. And OSHA asked Nicholas Ashford and CPA to analyze, in light of the record, the possibility of marking a correlation between air-lead levels and blood-lead levels. Both these consultants had previously aided OSHA by supplying on-the-record reports and testifying as expert witnesses at the public hearings. Both fulfilled the new requests by submitting written reports, of 117 and 192 pages respectively, neither of which the agency has released or placed in the rulemaking record. LIA contends that the reports are illegal *ex parte* communications which, like the communications with the staff advocates described earlier, constitute "secret briefs" and off-the-record evidence which LIA was deprived of a chance to rebut and the court a chance to review.

We note first that, as in the case of the staff-influence charge discussed earlier, LIA has not identified any hard data or new legal arguments which are contained only in the allegedly improper *ex parte* communications and on which OSHA demonstrably relied in setting the standard. Thus LIA has not shown that OSHA has materially prejudiced parties who were not privy to the communications. Rather, LIA asks us to infer that there must have been such *ex parte* evidence or legal argument, its request essentially relying on three factors: (1) the consultants were not agency employees; (2) they had previously testified as expert witnesses and prepared on-the-record reports; and (3) the documents we have before us, which describe the agreements and expectations between OSHA and the consultants and the content of the undisclosed reports, imply that actual new evidence was requested and supplied. We find the first two factors legally irrelevant, or at least insufficient to prove impropriety. As for the third, as we demonstrate below, we simply reject LIA's construction of the documents.

Were we to construe these factors otherwise, we might face the difficult task of resolving the scope of the *ex parte* contacts doctrine as generated by *Home Box Office, Inc. v. FCC, supra,* and developed by *United States Lines, Inc. v. FMC, supra:* Does the doctrine apply to a rulemaking proceeding leading to a truly general regulation, as opposed to a proceeding resolving "conflicting private claims to a valuable privilege" like that in *Home Box Office* or quasi-adjudication like *United States Lines*?[33] But we need not address that question here, because the documents show that the communications between the agency and the consultants were simply part of the deliberative process of drawing conclusions from the public record. The consultants acted after the record was closed as the functional equivalent of agency staff, so the question of the legal propriety of OSHA's reliance on DBA and CPA is foreclosed by our earlier conclusion that neither the APA nor the *Home Box Office* doctrine imposes a separation-of-functions requirement on the agencies. Thus, even though we readily assume that OSHA used the consultants' reports — and even incorporated parts of them verbatim in the Preamble — LIA has suffered no legal prejudice from such use. . . .

NOTES AND QUESTIONS

4-26. How do you characterize an Administrator of an agency during the course of a rulemaking proceeding? Is she essentially a legislator? If so, of what relevance are speeches given by legislators before, during or after a bill was passed? Would you be surprised if legislators dealt with and were influenced by their staff or constituents? Why should an Administrator be treated differently? How differently? Like a judge?

4-27. What standard does this case establish for bias in a rulemaking proceeding? What kind of proof would be necessary to meet this standard?

4-28. This case deals with *ex parte* contacts with agency staff and consultants. How does it distinguish these contacts from those in *Home Box Office*?

4-29. Assume that, as in *Home Box Office*, the agency was engaged in informal rulemaking under § 553 of the APA. Assume further that there are *ex parte* contacts with the Commissioners by members of the industry directly involved in a rulemaking proceeding. Does not *Vermont Yankee* ban judicial relief in this context? Why or why not? See Sidney Shapiro, *Two Cheers for HBO: The Problem of the Nonpublic Record*, 54 ADMIN. L. REV. 853 (2002).

4-30. Assume that the *ex parte* contacts that occur during the course of a rulemaking proceeding (either hybrid, informal or formal) are by members of the Executive Branch — the President, his staff or members of the Office of Management and Budget. Are such contacts allowed in the course of a rulemaking proceeding? Consider Judge Wald's arguments below, dealing with the procedural requirements of the Clean Air Act in *Sierra Club v. Costle*, 657 F.2d 298, 404–08 (D.C. Cir. 1981). Do you agree?

---

[33] LIA contends that because the lead standard threatened enormous costs for the industries and a windfall to employees through the medical removal provision, the rulemaking remains subject to the *ex parte* contact doctrine even under the narrower formulations in Judge MacKinnon's special concurring opinion in *Home Box Office, Inc. v. FCC, supra* note 20, 567 F.2d at 61, and in *Action for Children's Television, Inc. v. FCC, supra* note 29, 564 F.2d at 477. But virtually any important new regulation will be expensive for some parties and economically beneficial to others, and we do not think the limiting principles suggested in these cases can sensibly apply to a general rulemaking where distinct parties are not seeking or competing for specific legal privileges of great monetary value.

> Oral face-to-face discussions are not prohibited anywhere, anytime, in the Act. The absence of such prohibition may have arisen from the nature of the informal rulemaking procedures Congress had in mind. Where agency action resembles judicial action, where it involves formal rulemaking adjudication, or quasi-adjudication among "conflicting private claims to a valuable privilege," the insulation of the decisionmaker from *ex parte* contacts is justified by basic notions of due process to the parties involved. But where agency action involves informal rulemaking of a policymaking sort, the concept of *ex parte* contacts is of more questionable utility.
>
> Under our system of government, the very legitimacy of general policymaking performed by unelected administrators depends in no small part upon the openness, accessibility, and amenability of these officials to the needs and ideas of the public from whom their ultimate authority derives, and upon whom their commands must fall. As judges we are insulated from these pressures because of the nature of the judicial process in which we participate; but we must refrain from the easy temptation to look askance to [sic] all face-to-face lobbying efforts, regardless of the forum in which they occur, merely because we see them as inappropriate in the judicial context. Furthermore, the importance to effective regulation of continuing contact with a regulated industry, other affected groups, and the public cannot be underestimated. Informal contacts may enable the agency to win needed support for its program, reduce future enforcement requirements by helping those regulated to anticipate and shape their plans for the future, and spur the provision of information which the agency needs.

Judge Wald went on to emphasize the important policy role played by the President and why certain kinds of communications during the policy making process are important.

> The authority of the President to control and supervise executive policymaking is derived from the Constitution; the desirability of such control is demonstrable from the practical realities of administrative rulemaking. Regulations such as those involved here demand a careful weighing of cost, environmental, and energy considerations. They also have broad implications for national economic policy. Our form of government simply could not function effectively or rationally if key executive policymakers were isolated from each other and from the Chief Executive. Single mission agencies do not always have the answers to complex regulatory problems. An overworked administrator exposed on a 24-hour basis to a dedicated but zealous staff needs to know the arguments and ideas of policymakers in other agencies as well as in the White House.

4-31. What about *ex parte* communications from Congress? *Sierra Club v. Costle* arose in part from a challenge to an EPA rule issued pursuant to the Clean Air Act on the grounds that there had been off-the-record meetings between the EPA and a Senator. The court noted:

> The meetings did underscore [the Senator's] deep concerns for EPA, but there is no evidence he attempted actively to use "extraneous" pressures to further his position. Americans rightly expect their elected representatives to voice their grievances and preferences concerning the administration of our laws. We believe it entirely proper for Congressional

representatives vigorously to represent the interests of their constituents before administrative agencies engaged in informal general policy rulemaking, so long as individual congressmen do not frustrate the intent of Congress as a whole as expressed in statute, nor undermine applicable rules of procedure. . . .

Sierra Club v. Costle, 657 F.2d at 409.

4-32. We shall return to other important aspects of the rulemaking process when we examine judicial review of agency rules. In particular, the requirement of section 553 of a concise statement of basis and purpose in the issuance of a final rule has resulted in the judicial doctrine of reasoned decisionmaking. *See* Chapter Eight, *infra.* In addition, the Executive Branch also imposes its own procedural controls on the rulemaking process, principally through the application of executive order 12,866. We shall examine this in detail in Chapter Seven, *infra.* Finally, statutes such as the Regulatory Flexibility Act and the Paperwork Reduction Act also affect rulemaking. We shall discuss these acts in Chapter Seven, *infra.*

[E] Exceptions to Section 553 Rulemaking Procedures

AMERICAN HOSPITAL ASSOC. v. BOWEN

District of Columbia Court of Appeals
834 F.2d 1037 (1987)

Before WALD, CHIEF JUDGE, MIKVA and SILBERMAN, CIRCUIT JUDGES.

Opinion for the court filed by CHIEF JUDGE WALD. . . .

WALD, CHIEF JUDGE:

We face here the issue of whether the Department of Health and Human Services ("HHS"), in implementing the system of "peer review" of Medicare outlays called for by Congress in its 1982 amendments to the Medicare Act, erred in not first undertaking the notice and comment rulemaking generally prescribed by the Administrative Procedure Act ("APA"), 5 U.S.C. § 553. Because we conclude that the directives issued and contracts entered into by HHS constitute mere procedural rules or general statements of policy that do not substantially alter the rights or interests of regulated hospitals, we hold that HHS has satisfied the requirements of § 553 of the APA, and therefore reverse the judgment of the district court.

I. THE FACTUAL SETTING OF THIS CASE

Since 1965, the Medicare program has provided for the reimbursement by the federal government of those medical expenses incurred by persons over 65 and of persons suffering from certain disabilities. Typically, this reimbursement has been paid directly to the hospitals and doctors who provide health care to Medicare recipients.

In 1982, Congress amended the Medicare Act to provide for a new method of reviewing the quality and appropriateness of the health care provided by these medical providers to Medicare beneficiaries. It did so by passing the Peer Review Improvement Act of 1982, . . . which called for HHS to contract with "peer review organizations," or PROs, private organizations of doctors that would monitor "some or all of the professional activities" of the provider of Medicare services in their areas. A primary goal of Congress was to put into place a review system that would crack down on excessive reimbursements to hospitals for treatments of Medicare patients.

In passing the 1982 amendments, Congress painted with a broad brush, leaving HHS to fill in many important details of the workings of peer review. The amendments require HHS to designate geographic areas generally corresponding to each state, to be served by individual peer review organizations. HHS must then enter into an agreement, initially for a two-year term, with a PRO in each area. Entities seeking to qualify as PROs must contain a sufficient number of physicians practicing in the PRO area to carry out the requisite review functions.

The agency has broad discretion in negotiating each of these contracts. As the district court observed, HHS may negotiate different agreements with each PRO, and it may make agreements without regard to any federal law regarding contracts which it determines to be inconsistent with the PRO program. A typical provision on which PRO contracts differ is the type of activities that an individual PRO is expected to review. On this contractual term, as on others, the goal of HHS' flexibility is to encourage PROs to be responsive to distinctive community needs and practices, apparently a shortcoming in the system of review preceding the PRO system. The PRO contract must, however, specify the types of cases it will review, and it must include negotiated objectives against which the PRO will be judged. Typically, PROs have been compensated according to fixed-price contracts, under which they receive a pre-determined amount of money for all services performed under the two-year contract.

Under the 1982 amendments, hospitals, in turn, must enter into contracts with the HHS-designated PRO in their area in order to participate in the Medicare program and thus be eligible for reimbursements. The hospital must agree, as part of its contract with the PRO, to allow the PRO to review the validity of diagnostic information provided by the hospital, to review the completeness, adequacy and quality of care provided, to review the appropriateness of hospital admissions, and to review the appropriateness of care provided for which the hospital or health care provider seeks extra Medicare payments. Congress required hospitals to enter into such agreements by November 15, 1984. Deficit Reduction Act of 1984, Pub. L. No. 98–369, § 2347(b).

The principal function of a PRO, once having been designated by HHS and having entered into agreements with hospitals in its jurisdiction, is to review for conformance with the substantive standards of the Medicare Act the professional activities of physicians, hospitals, and other providers of health care. The standard of review is whether the services and items provided by the doctor or hospital "are or were reasonable and medically necessary," and thus whether these activities satisfy the standards for federal government reimbursement under Medicare. The PRO's determination on whether Medicare should pay for the services in question is generally conclusive. When the PRO program first began, these reimbursements were retrospective ones, based upon the "reasonable cost" of providing medical services to Medicare beneficiaries. Since 1983, when Congress further modified the Medicare system by passing the Social Security Amendments of 1983, Medicare expenses have been paid prospectively to providers according to a predetermined rate based on which "diagnosis related group," or DRG, a patient is deemed to fall into.

Beyond those relatively skeletal requirements, Congress left much of the specifics of the hospital-PRO relationship to the inventiveness of HHS, empowering it to promulgate regulations governing PROs in order to implement the peer review program. The legislative history of the peer review amendments suggests that this was no oversight: Congress apparently expected HHS to design and put into place the numerous procedures necessary to administer the PRO program.

The initial flurry of regulations promulgated by HHS filled in a variety of these details regarding PRO procedures. Many of these procedures were aimed at harmonizing the PRO concept with the new system of reimbursing Medicare providers prospectively. The procedures detailed in these regulations included basic PRO review functions, reporting hospitals' misrepresentations, DRG validation, review of hospital determinations of noncoverage, and payment for coverage exceeding the standard amount allotted for each diagnostic group.

The parties to this case agree that these regulations were promulgated in conformance with the Administrative Procedure Act, 5 U.S.C. § 553, and thus they are not under challenge here.

In addition to these regulations, HHS issued a series of directives and transmittals governing the PRO program that are the subject of this lawsuit. . . . These transmittals contain a wide variety of instructions, guidelines and procedures covering aspects of the PRO program. HHS also shaped the PRO program when it issued the Request for Proposals ("RFP"), a document soliciting proposed contracts from entities seeking to become PROs. The RFP, among other things, told would-be PROs what review procedures their proposals must address, and what provisions their bids must contain. The contracts entered into between HHS and the PROs contain the provisions required by the RFP.

HHS concedes that neither the transmittals, the RFP, nor the contracts ultimately entered into were issued pursuant to the notice and comment procedures generally required by § 553 of the APA.

The plaintiff in this action is the American Hospital Association ("AHA"), an Illinois nonstock corporation that represents 6,000 member hospitals serving approximately 30 million patients a year, more than 9 million of them Medicare beneficiaries. The facts of its dispute with HHS leading to this lawsuit are essentially as recounted by the district court. *See American Hospital Association,* 640 F. Supp. at 458.

On October 10, 1984, complaining of . . . "the small and incomplete selection of regulations" HHS had published implementing the PRO program and the large number of procedures set forth in documents not published as regulations, AHA filed with HHS a petition for rulemaking, pursuant to 5 U.S.C. § 553(e). In it, AHA requested HHS to promulgate a complete set of regulations governing all aspects of the PRO program. . . . AHA sent another letter on January 8, 1985, requesting a date for HHS' response. No response to this letter was ever received.

On January 29, 1985, AHA brought suit against HHS in the District Court for the District of Columbia. Its complaint argued that HHS had circumvented the notice and comment requirements of § 553 of the APA, and asked that the court declare the transmittals and directives, as well as the RFP's and the contracts entered into by HHS and the PROs, invalid for failure to comply with § 553. It also asked the court to order HHS to promulgate all regulations implementing the PRO program in accordance with notice and comment procedures. . . .

The district court, on cross-motions for summary judgment and on HHS' motion to dismiss, held that virtually all of HHS' communications . . . were invalid for failure to comply with the APA's notice and comment requirements. The court's May 30, 1986 order also invalidated the RFP's and the contracts entered into thereunder as violative of § 553. . . .

II. DISCUSSION

A. *The Analytic Framework of APA § 553*

Section 553 of the Administrative Procedure Act requires agencies to afford notice of a proposed rulemaking and an opportunity for public comment prior to a rule's promulgation, amendment, modification, or repeal. Congress, however, crafted several exceptions to these notice and comment requirements, determining that they should not apply

> (A) to interpretative rules, general statements of policy, or rules of agency organization, practice or procedure; or

> (B) when the agency for good cause finds (and incorporates the finding and a brief statement of reasons therefor in the rules issued) that notice and public procedure thereon are impracticable, unnecessary, or contrary to the public interest.

Section 553(b). The issue in this case is whether the various pronouncements made by HHS in the course of its implementation of the peer review program fall within the first class of exceptions: those for interpretive rules, procedural rules, or general statements of policy. We begin our analysis by noting that Congress intended the exceptions to § 553's notice and comment requirements to be narrow ones. The purposes of according notice and comment opportunities were twofold: "to reintroduce public participation and fairness to affected parties after governmental authority has been delegated to unrepresentative agencies," *Batterton v. Marshall*, 648 F.2d 694, 703 (D.C. Cir. 1980), and to "assure[] that the agency will have before it the facts and information relevant to a particular administrative problem, as well as suggestions for alternative solutions." *Guardian Federal Savings & Loan Insurance Corp.*, 589 F.2d 658, 662 (D.C. Cir. 1978). In light of the obvious importance of these policy goals of maximum participation and full information, we have consistently declined to allow the exceptions itemized in § 553 to swallow the APA's well-intentioned directive. . . .

The reading of the § 553 exemptions that seems most consonant with Congress' purposes in adopting the APA is to construe them as an attempt to preserve agency flexibility in dealing with limited situations where substantive rights are not at stake. The exceptions have a common theme in that they "accommodate situations where the policies promoted by public participation in rulemaking are outweighed by the countervailing considerations of effectiveness, efficiency, expedition and reduction in expense." *Guardian Federal Savings & Loan Association,* 589 F.2d at 662. Agency actions or statements falling within the three exemptions:

> are not determinative of issues or rights addressed. They express the agency's intended course of action, its tentative view of the meaning of a particular statutory term, or internal house-keeping measures organizing agency activities. They do not, however, foreclose alternate courses of action or conclusively affect rights of private parties. Although an agency empowered to enact legislative rules may choose to issue non-legislative statements, an agency without legislative rulemaking authority may issue only non-binding statements. Unlike legislative rules, non-binding policy statements carry no more weight on judicial review than their inherent persuasiveness commands.

Batterton, 648 F.2d at 702 (footnotes omitted).

The function of § 553's first exemption, that for "interpretive rules," is to allow agencies to explain ambiguous terms in legislative enactments without having to undertake cumbersome proceedings. As we explained long ago in *Gibson Wine Co. v. Snyder,* 194 F.2d 329, 331 (D.C. Cir. 1952), "'regulations,' 'substantive rules,' or 'legislative rules' are those which create law, usually implementary to an existing law; whereas interpretive rules are statements as to what [an] administrative officer thinks the statute or regulation means."

While the spectrum between a clearly interpretive rule and a clearly substantive one is a hazy continuum, our cases, deploying different verbal tests, have generally sought to distinguish cases in which an agency is merely explicating Congress' desires from those cases in which the agency is adding substantive content of its own. Substantive rules are ones which "grant rights, impose obligations, or produce other significant effects on private interests," or which "effect a change in existing law or policy." Interpretive rules, by contrast, "are those which merely clarify or explain existing law or regulations," are "essentially hortatory and instructional," and "do not have the full force and effect of a substantive rule but [are] in the form of an explanation of particular terms." Determining whether a given agency action is interpretive or legislative is an extraordinarily case-specific endeavor. As in the area of federal preemption jurisprudence, analogizing to prior cases is often of limited utility in light of the exceptional degree to which decisions in this doctrinal area turn on their precise facts. Nevertheless, recent cases shed some light on the scope of the § 553 interpretive rules exemption. In *Cabais v. Egger,* 690 F.2d 234 (D.C. Cir. 1982), we upheld as interpretive of the Federal

Unemployment Tax Act directives from the Secretary of Agriculture recommending to state agencies that they pass legislation conforming their unemployment income plans to a federal scheme as they were required to do under a federal statute. *Cabais* thus stands for the important proposition that where an agency activity merely reminds parties of existing duties, it is interpretive, not legislative. . . . By contrast, the classic example of an agency rule held not to be interpretive — and thus requiring notice and comment as a prerequisite to validity — was the use by a parole board of guidelines establishing specific factors for determining parole eligibility that were "calculated to have a substantial effect on ultimate parole decisions." See *Pickus v. United States Board of Parole,* 507 F.2d 1107, 1112–13 (D.C. Cir. 1974).

The function of the second § 553 exemption, for "general policy statements," is to allow agencies to announce their "tentative intentions for the future," see *Pacific Gas & Electric Co. v. FPC,* 506 F.2d 33, 38 (D.C. Cir. 1974), without binding themselves. We have previously contrasted "a properly adopted substantive rule" with a "general statement of policy," observing that while a substantive rule "establishes a standard of conduct which has the force of law" in subsequent proceedings,

> [a] general statement of policy, on the other hand, does not establish a "binding norm." It is not finally determinative of the issues or rights to which it is addressed. The agency cannot apply or rely upon a general statement of policy as law because a general statement of policy only announces what the agency seeks to establish as policy.

The perimeters of the exemption for general statements of policy, like those for interpretive pronouncements, are fuzzy. Nevertheless, our prior cases, in seeking to discern the line between these two types of agency pronouncements, have provided considerable guidance. One useful formulation is the two-criteria test set forth by Judge McGowan in *American Bus Association v. United States*:

> First, courts have said that, unless a pronouncement acts prospectively, it is a binding norm. Thus . . . a statement of policy may not have a present effect: "a 'general statement of policy' is one that does not impose any rights and obligations" . . . .
>
> The second criterion is whether a purported policy statement genuinely leaves the agency and its decisionmakers free to exercise discretion.

627 F.2d 525, 529 (D.C. Cir. 1980) (citations and footnote omitted). In applying these two criteria, we have observed that an agency's characterization of its own action, while not decisive, is a factor that we do consider.

Cases interpreting the § 553 exemption for general statements of policy, like those applying the interpretive rule exemption, also tend to turn on the distinctive facts of the case and thus are not susceptible to easy generalization. We offer here several telling examples of cases upholding agency pronouncements as constituting mere statements of policy, not subject to notice and comment requirements. In *TRAC,* we held that an FCC order eliminating six broadcast regulatory policies that had not been established in rulemaking was a nonbinding general statement of policy, because the Commission had conceded both that it was not bound by its statement of repeal, and that under certain circumstances it might still consider the application of the supposedly defunct regulations. Likewise, in *Pacific Gas,* we held that a Federal Power Commission order setting forth the Commission's view of the proper priority schedule to be followed in curtailing supplies of natural gas to certain customers in the hypothetical event of a natural gas shortage was nonbinding and hence a mere policy statement. Finally, in *Brock v. Cathedral Bluffs Shale Oil Co.,* 796 F.2d 533 (D.C. Cir. 1986), we upheld as a mere general statement of policy the Secretary of Labor's "guidelines" on when to cite independent contractors for violating safety standards, placing heavy emphasis on the agency's frequent assertions in the past that the Secretary retained discretion to supersede these guidelines in particular cases. By contrast, we found no such retained discretion in *Batterton,* where we held that the Department of Labor's statistical methodology for calculating unemployment statistics triggering an emergency job program was binding and hence not a mere general statement, or in *Community Nutrition,* where we held that the Food and Drug Administration's determination of "action levels" that told food producers the allowable limits of certain contaminants in food was also a binding norm requiring the agency to undertake notice and comment procedures.

The distinctive purpose of § 553's third exemption, for "rules of agency organization, procedure or practice," is to ensure "that agencies retain latitude in organizing their internal operations."

> A useful articulation of the exemption's critical feature is that it covers agency actions that do not themselves alter the rights or interests of parties, although it may alter the manner in which parties present themselves or their viewpoints to the agency.

> Over time, our circuit in applying the § 553 exemption for procedural rules has gradually shifted focus from asking whether a given procedure has a "substantial impact" on parties, *see Pickus,* 507 F.2d at 1112–13, to inquiring more broadly whether the agency action also encodes a substantive value judgment or puts a stamp of approval or disapproval on a given type of behavior. The gradual move away from looking solely into the substantiality of the impact reflects a candid recognition that even unambiguously procedural measures affect parties to some degree.

> While the range of cases applying this exemption may appear idiosyncratic, a few recent decisions of this and other circuits illustrate the scope and limits of the procedural exemption. In *Neighborhood TV Co., Inc. v. FCC,* 742 F.2d 629 (D.C. Cir. 1984), we held that a FCC decision to freeze applications for television licenses on some frequencies affected an applicant's interest "only incidentally," *id.* at 637, and thus was procedural. In *Guardian Federal Savings & Loan Association,* we held that a directive specifying that requisite audits be performed by nonagency accountants was exempt as a procedural measure. And in *United States Department of Labor v. Kast Metals Corp.,* 744 F.2d 1145 (5th Cir. 1984), a case to which we shall return in greater depth later, the Fifth Circuit held that the agency's rules governing the selection of employers for workplace safety investigations was a procedural rule. By contrast, we have struck down as nonprocedural an agency rule foreclosing home health agencies from the right to deal with the Secretary of HHS in

order to gain reimbursement for Medicare, *see National Association of Home Health Agencies,* and, as noted earlier, we have held that a parole board's selection of parole eligibility guidelines had the intent and effect of changing substantive outcomes. . . .

PRO Manual IM85–2, promulgated by HHS in March, 1985, is a 70–page document that defines procedures governing many of the review functions of PROs. In our view, the district court correctly held IM85–2 to replicate the earlier PSRO Transmittal No. 107, the document initially challenged by AHA, and therefore we, like the district court, confine our analysis to the later document. . . .

The opinion of the district court, invalidating IM85–2, rejected the argument by appellants below that the transmittal falls within § 553's exemption for interpretive rules. The court observed, for instance, that "[t]hese requirements and others like them throughout the document are not mere statements of what HHS thinks the statutes and regulations require. These are precise obligations which, while consistent with broad statutory directives, are not interpretations of any explicit statutory provisions." 640 F. Supp. at 463. The district court opinion also notes that "the procedures in the document are unmistakably absent from the statutes and regulations, and it is apparent that the document is HHS' fundamental source for implementing PRO review functions. It does not merely interpret or elucidate HHS's official position." 640 F. Supp. at 462. Here, as elsewhere in its opinion, the district court's heavy focus on why the interpretive rule exemption did not apply apparently reflects the overwhelming emphasis placed on that prong of § 553 by HHS in its arguments below, although the agency did technically preserve its objections on the grounds that the other two § 553 exemptions applied.

While we share the view of the district court that the commands of IM85-2 are not valid as interpretive rules, we find this conclusion beside the point. The requirements set forth in the transmittal are classic procedural rules, exempt under that distinctive prong of § 553. The bulk of the regulations in the transmittal set forth an enforcement plan for HHS's agents in monitoring the quality of and necessity for various operations. They essentially establish a frequency and focus of PRO review, urging its enforcement agents to concentrate their limited resources on particular areas where HHS evidently believes PRO attention will prove most fruitful. . . .

We venture the guess that, had HHS established identical terms governing the frequency and focus of review by directly issuing orders to its own officers, the agency's enforcement plan would then appear more unambiguously as a valid use of its enforcement authority. But it is substance, not form, to which § 553 looks: the fact that the agency reached the identical result by operating through a private intermediary under contract with the agency hardly dictates a different result under § 553.

The manual imposes no new burdens on hospitals that warrant notice and comment review. This is not a case in which HHS has urged its reviewing agents to utilize a different standard of review in specified medical areas; rather, it asks only that they examine a greater share of operations in given medical areas. Were HHS to have inserted a new standard of review governing PRO scrutiny of a given procedure, or to have inserted a presumption of invalidity when reviewing certain operations, its measures would surely require notice and comment, as well as close scrutiny to insure that it was consistent with the agency's statutory mandate. *See, e.g., Pickus.* But that is not this case.

At worst, Manual IM85–2 burdens hospitals by (1) making it more likely that their transgressions from Medicare's standards will not go unnoticed and (2) imposing on them the incidental inconveniences of complying with an enforcement scheme. The former concern is patently illegitimate: Congress' very purpose in instituting peer review was to crack down on reimbursements for medical activity not covered by Medicare. As for the second burden, case law clearly establishes that such derivative burdens hardly dictate notice and comment review. Accordingly, we hold that PRO Manual IM85–2 is a procedural rule exempt from § 553's notice and comment requirements. . . .

HOCTOR v. UNITED STATES DEPARTMENT OF AGRICULTURE

United States Court of Appeals, Seventh Circuit
82 F.3d 165 (1996)

Before POSNER, CHIEF JUDGE, and DIANE P. WOOD and EVANS, CIRCUIT JUDGES.

POSNER, CHIEF JUDGE.

A rule promulgated by an agency that is subject to the Administrative Procedure Act is invalid unless the agency first issues a public notice of proposed rulemaking, describing the substance of the proposed rule, and gives the public an opportunity to submit written comments; and if after receiving the comments it decides to promulgate the rule it must set forth the basis and purpose of the rule in a public statement. 5 U.S.C. §§ 553(b), (c). These procedural requirements do not apply, however, to "interpretative rules, general statements of policy, or rules of agency organization, procedure, or practice." 5 U.S.C. § 553(b)(A). Distinguishing between a "legislative" rule, to which the notice and comment provisions of the Act apply, and an interpretive rule, to which these provisions do not apply, is often very difficult — and often very important to regulated firms, the public, and the agency. Notice and comment rulemaking is time-consuming, facilitates the marshaling of opposition to a proposed rule, and may result in the creation of a very long record that may in turn provide a basis for a judicial challenge to the rule if the agency decides to promulgate it. There are no formalities attendant upon the promulgation of an interpretive rule, but this is tolerable because such a rule is "only" an interpretation. Every governmental agency that enforces a less than crystalline statute must interpret the statute, and it does the public a favor if it announces the interpretation in advance of enforcement, whether the announcement takes the form of a rule or of a policy statement, which the Administrative Procedure Act assimilates to an interpretive rule.

It would be no favor to the public to discourage the announcement of agencies' interpretations by burdening the interpretive process with cumbersome formalities.

The question presented by this appeal from an order of the Department of Agriculture is whether a rule for the secure containment of animals, a rule promulgated by the Department under the Animal Welfare Act, 7 U.S.C. §§ 2131 et seq., without compliance with the notice and comment requirements of the Administrative Procedure Act, is nevertheless valid because it is merely an interpretive rule. Enacted in 1966, the Animal Welfare Act, as its title implies, is primarily designed to assure the humane treatment of animals. The Act requires the licensing of dealers (with obvious exceptions, for example retail pet stores) and exhibitors, and authorizes the Department to impose sanctions on licensees who violate either the statute itself or the rules promulgated by the Department under the authority of 7 U.S.C. § 2151, which authorizes the Secretary of Agriculture "to promulgate such rules, regulations, and orders as he may deem necessary in order to effectuate the purposes of [the Act]." The Act provides guidance to the exercise of this rulemaking authority by requiring the Department to formulate standards "to govern the humane handling, care, treatment, and transportation of animals by dealers," and these standards must include minimum requirements "for handling, housing, feeding, watering, sanitation," etc. 7 U.S.C. § 2143(a).

The Department has employed the notice and comment procedure to promulgate a regulation, the validity of which is not questioned, that is entitled "structural strength" and that provides that "the facility [housing the animals] must be constructed of such material and of such strength as appropriate for the animals involved. The indoor and outdoor housing facilities shall be structurally sound and shall be maintained in good repair to protect the animals from injury and to contain the animals." 9 C.F.R. § 3.125(a).

Enter the petitioner, Patrick Hoctor, who in 1982 began dealing in exotic animals on his farm outside of Terre Haute. In a 25-acre compound he raised a variety of animals including "Big Cats" — a typical inventory included three lions, two tigers, seven ligers (a liger is a cross between a male lion and a female tiger, and is thus to be distinguished from a tigon), six cougars, and two snow leopards. The animals were in pens ("primary enclosures" in the jargon of the administration of the Animal Welfare Act). The area in which the pens were located was surrounded by a fence ("containment fence"). In addition, Hoctor erected a fence around the entire compound ("perimeter fence"). At the suggestion of a veterinarian employed by the Agriculture Department who was assigned to inspect the facility when Hoctor started his animal dealership in 1982, Hoctor made the perimeter fence six feet high.

The following year the Department issued an internal memorandum addressed to its force of inspectors in which it said that all "dangerous animals," defined as including, among members of the cat family, lions, tigers, and leopards, must be inside a perimeter fence at least eight feet high. This provision is the so-called interpretive rule, interpreting the housing regulation quoted above. An agency has, of course, the power, indeed the inescapable duty, to interpret its own legislative rules, such as the housing standard, just as it has the power and duty to interpret a statute that it enforces. *Stinson v. United States*, 508 U.S. 36, 42-46 (1993).

On several occasions beginning in 1990, Hoctor was cited by a Department of Agriculture inspector for violating 9 C.F.R. § 3.125(a), the housing standard, by failing to have an eight-foot perimeter fence. Eventually the Department sanctioned Hoctor for this and other alleged violations, and he has sought judicial review limited, however, to the perimeter fence. He is a small dealer and it would cost him many thousands of dollars to replace his six-foot-high fence with an eight-foot-high fence. Indeed, we were told at argument that pending the resolution of his dispute over the fence he has discontinued dealing in Big Cats. The parties agree that unless the rule requiring a perimeter fence at least eight feet high is a valid interpretive rule, the sanction for violating it was improper.

We may assume, though we need not decide, that the Department of Agriculture has the statutory authority to require dealers in dangerous animals to enclose their compounds with eight-foot-high fences. The fence is a backup fail-safe device, since the animals are kept in pens, cages, or other enclosures within the compound, in an area that is itself fenced, rather than being free to roam throughout the compound. Since animals sometimes break out or are carelessly let out of their pens, a fail-safe device seems highly appropriate, to say the least. Two lions once got out of their pen on Hoctor's property, and he had to shoot them. Yet, when he did so, they were still within the containment fence. The Department's regulations do not require a containment fence, and it is unclear to us why, if that fence was adequate — and we are given no reason to suppose it was not — Hoctor should have had to put up an additional fence, let alone one eight-feet high. But we lay any doubts on this score to one side. And we may also assume that the containment of dangerous animals is a proper concern of the Department in the enforcement of the Animal Welfare Act, even though the purpose of the Act is to protect animals from people rather than people from animals. Even Big Cats are not safe outside their compounds, and with a lawyer's ingenuity the Department's able counsel reminded us at argument that if one of those Cats mauled or threatened a human being, the Cat might get into serious trouble and thus it is necessary to protect human beings from Big Cats *in order to protect the Cats from human beings*, which is the important thing under the Act. In fact Hoctor had shot the two lions because they were dangerously close to one of his employees. Since tort liability for injury caused by a wild animal is strict, *Burns v. Gleason*, 819 F.2d 555 (5th Cir. 1987); *Behrens v. Bertram Mills Circus Ltd.*, [1957] 2 Q.B. 1; W. Page Keeton et al., *Prosser and Keeton on the Law of Torts* § 76, p. 542 (5th ed. 1984), the common law, at least, is solicitous for the protection of the citizens of Terre Haute against escapees from Hoctor's menagerie even if the Animal Welfare Act is not. The internal memorandum also justifies the eight-foot requirement as a means of protecting the animals from animal predators, though one might have supposed the Big Cats able to protect themselves against the native Indiana fauna.

Another issue that we need not resolve besides the issue of the statutory authority for the challenged rule is whether the Department might have cited Hoctor for having a perimeter fence that was *in fact*, considering the number and type of his animals, the topography of the compound, the design and structure of the protective enclosures and the containment fence, the proximity of highways or inhabited areas, and the design of the perimeter fence itself, too low to be safe, as distinct from merely being lower than eight feet. No regulation is targeted on the problem of containment other than 9 C.F.R. § 3.125, which seems to be concerned with the strength of enclosures rather than their height. But maybe there is some implicit statutory duty of containment that Hoctor might have been thought to have violated even if there were no rule requiring an eight-foot-high perimeter fence.

We need not decide. The only ground on which the Department defends sanctioning Hoctor for not having a high enough fence is that requiring an eight-foot-high perimeter fence for dangerous animals is an interpretation of the Department's own structural-strength regulation, and "provided an agency's interpretation of its own regulations does not violate the Constitution or a federal statute, it must be given 'controlling weight unless it is plainly erroneous or inconsistent with the regulation.'" *Stinson v. United States, supra,* 508 U.S. at 44-46. The "provided" clause does not announce a demanding standard of judicial review, although the absence of any reference in the housing regulation to fences or height must give us pause. The regulation appears only to require that pens and other animal housing be sturdy enough in design and construction, and sufficiently well maintained, to prevent the animals from breaking through the enclosure — not that any enclosure, whether a pen or a perimeter fence, be high enough to prevent the animals from escaping by jumping over the enclosure. The Department's counsel made the wonderful lawyer's argument that the eight-foot rule is consistent with the regulation because a fence lower than eight feet has zero structural strength between its height (here six feet) and the eight-foot required minimum. The two feet by which Hoctor's fence fell short could not have contained a groundhog, let alone a liger, since it was empty space.

Our doubts about the scope of the regulation that the eight-foot rule is said to be "interpreting" might seem irrelevant, since even if a rule requiring an eight-foot perimeter fence could not be based on the regulation, it could be based on the statute itself, which in requiring the Department to establish minimum standards for the housing of animals presumably authorizes it to promulgate standards for secure containment. But if the eight-foot rule were deemed one of those minimum standards that the Department is required by statute to create, it could not possibly be thought an *interpretive* rule. For what would it be interpreting? When Congress authorizes an agency to create standards, it is delegating legislative authority, rather than itself setting forth a standard which the agency might then particularize through interpretation. Put differently, when a statute does not impose a duty on the persons subject to it but instead authorizes (or requires — it makes no difference) an agency to impose a duty, the formulation of that duty becomes a legislative task entrusted to the agency. Provided that a rule promulgated pursuant to such a delegation is intended to bind, and not merely to be a tentative statement of the agency's view, which would make it just a policy statement, and not a rule at all, the rule would be the clearest possible example of a legislative rule, as to which the notice and comment procedure not followed here is mandatory, as distinct from an interpretive rule; for there would be nothing to interpret. *American Mining Congress v. Mine Safety & Health Administration*, 995 F.2d 1106, 1109 (D.C. Cir. 1993); Robert A. Anthony, "*'Interpretive' Rules, 'Legislative' Rules and 'Spurious' Rules: Lifting the Smog*," 8 ADMIN. L.J. of AM. UNIV. 1 (1994). That is why the Department *must* argue that its eight-foot rule is an interpretation of the structural-strength regulation — itself a standard, and therefore interpretable, in order to avoid reversal.

Even if, despite the doubts that we expressed earlier, the eight-foot rule is consistent with, even in some sense authorized by, the structural-strength regulation, it would not necessarily follow that it is an interpretive rule. It is that only if it can be derived from the regulation by a process reasonably described as interpretation. *Metropolitan School District v. Davila*, 969 F.2d 485, 490 (7th Cir. 1992). Supposing that the regulation imposes a general duty of secure containment, the question is, then, Can a requirement that the duty be implemented by erecting an eight-foot-high perimeter fence be thought an interpretation of that general duty?

"Interpretation" in the narrow sense is the ascertainment of meaning. It is obvious that eight feet is not part of the meaning of secure containment. But "interpretation" is often used in a much broader sense. A process of "interpretation" has transformed the Constitution into a body of law undreamt of by the framers. To skeptics the *Miranda* rule is as remote from the text of the Fifth Amendment as the eight-foot rule is from the text of 9 C.F.R. § 3.125(a). But our task in this case is not to plumb the mysteries of legal theory; it is merely to give effect to a distinction that the Administrative Procedure Act makes, and we can do this by referring to the purpose of the distinction. The purpose is to separate the cases in which notice and comment rulemaking is required from the cases in which it is not required. As we noted at the outset, unless a statute or regulation is of crystalline transparency, the agency enforcing it cannot avoid interpreting it, and the agency would be stymied in its enforcement duties if every time it brought a case on a new theory it had to pause for a bout, possibly lasting several years, of notice and comment rulemaking. Besides being unavoidably continuous, statutory interpretation normally proceeds without the aid of elaborate factual inquiries. When it is an executive or administrative agency that is doing the interpreting it brings to the task a greater knowledge of the regulated activity than the judicial or legislative branches have, and this knowledge is to some extent a substitute for formal fact-gathering.

At the other extreme from what might be called normal or routine interpretation is the making of reasonable but arbitrary (not in the "arbitrary or capricious" sense) rules that are consistent with the statute or regulation under which the rules are promulgated but not derived from it, because they represent an arbitrary choice among methods of implementation. A rule that turns on a number is likely to be arbitrary in this sense. There is no way to reason to an eight-foot perimeter-fence rule as opposed to a seven-and-a-half foot fence or a nine-foot fence or a ten-foot fence. None of these candidates for a rule is uniquely appropriate to, and in that sense derivable from, the duty of secure containment. This point becomes even clearer if we note that the eight-foot rule actually has another component — the fence must be at least three feet from any animal's pen. Why three feet? Why not four? Or two?

The reason courts refuse to create statutes of limitations is precisely the difficulty of reasoning to a number by the methods of reasoning used by courts. *Hemmings v. Barian*, 822 F.2d 688, 689 (7th Cir. 1987). One cannot extract from the concept of a tort that a tort suit should be barred unless brought within one, or two, or three, or five years. The choice is arbitrary and courts are uncomfortable with making arbitrary choices. They see this as a legislative function. Legislators have the democratic legitimacy to make choices among value judgments, choices based on hunch or guesswork or even the toss of a coin, and other arbitrary choices. When agencies base rules on arbitrary choices they are legislating, and so these rules are legislative or substantive and require notice and comment rulemaking, a procedure that is analogous to the procedure employed by legislatures in making statutes. The notice of proposed rulemaking corresponds to the bill and the reception of written comments to the hearing on the bill.

The common sense of requiring notice and comment rulemaking for legislative rules is well illustrated by the facts of this case. There is no process of cloistered, appellate-court type reasoning by which the Department of Agriculture could have excogitated the eight-foot rule from the structural-strength regulation. The rule is arbitrary in the sense that it could well be different without significant impairment of any regulatory purpose. But this does not make the rule a matter of indifference to the people subject to it. There are thousands of animal dealers, and some unknown fraction of these face the prospect of having to tear down their existing fences and build new, higher ones at great cost. The concerns of these dealers are legitimate and since, as we are stressing, the rule could well be otherwise, the agency was obliged to listen to them before settling on a final rule and to provide some justification for that rule, though not so tight or logical a justification as a court would be expected to offer for a new judge-made rule. Notice and comment is the procedure by which the persons affected by legislative rules are enabled to communicate their concerns in a comprehensive and systematic fashion to the legislating agency. The Department's lawyer speculated that if the notice and comment route had been followed in this case the Department would have received thousands of comments. The greater the public interest in a rule, the greater reason to allow the public to participate in its formation.

We are not saying that an interpretive rule can never have a numerical component. *See, e.g., American Mining Congress v. Mine Safety & Health Administration, supra*, 995 F.2d at 1108, 1113; *St. Mary's Hospital v. Blue Cross & Blue Shield Ass'n.*, 788 F.2d 888, 889-91 (2d Cir. 1986). There is merely an empirical relation between interpretation and generality on the one hand, and legislation and specificity on the other. Especially in scientific and other technical areas, where quantitative criteria are common, a rule that translates a general norm into a number may be justifiable as interpretation. The mine safety agency in the *American Mining* case could refer to established medical criteria, expressed in terms of numerical evaluations of x-rays, for diagnosing black-lung disease. 995 F.2d at 1112-13. Even in a nontechnical area the use of a number as a rule of thumb to guide the application of a general norm will often be legitimately interpretive. Had the Department of Agriculture said in the internal memorandum that it could not imagine a case in which a perimeter fence for dangerous animals that was lower than eight feet would provide secure containment, and would therefore presume, subject to rebuttal, that a lower fence was insecure, it would have been on stronger ground. For it would have been tying the rule to the animating standard, that of secure containment, rather than making it stand free of the standard, self-contained, unbending, arbitrary. To switch metaphors, the "flatter" a rule is, the harder it is to conceive of it as merely spelling out what is in some sense latent in a statute or regulation, and the eight-foot rule in its present form is as flat as they come. At argument the Department's lawyer tried to loosen up the rule, implying that the Department might have bent it if Hoctor proposed to dig a moat or to electrify his six-foot fence. But an agency's lawyer is not authorized to amend its rules in order to make them more palatable to the reviewing court.

The Department's position might seem further undermined by the fact that it has used the notice and comment procedure to promulgate rules prescribing perimeter fences for dogs and monkeys. 9 C.F.R. §§ 3.6(c)(2)(ii), 3.77(f). Why it proceeded differently for dangerous animals is unexplained. But we attach no weight to the Department's inconsistency, not only because it would be unwise to penalize the Department for having at least partially complied with the requirements of the Administrative Procedure Act, but also because there is nothing in the Act to forbid an agency to use the notice and comment procedure in cases in which it is not required to do so. We are mindful that the court in *United States v. Picciotto*, 875 F.2d 345, 348 (D.C. Cir. 1989), thought that the fact that an agency had used notice and comment rulemaking in a setting similar to the case before the court was evidence that the agency "intended" to promulgate a legislative rule in that case, only without bothering with notice and comment. The inference is strained, and in any event we think the agency's "intent," though a frequently cited factor, is rather a makeweight. What the agency intends is to promulgate a rule. It is for the courts to say whether it is the kind of rule that is valid only if promulgated after notice and comment. It is that kind of rule if, as in the present case, it cannot be derived by interpretation. The order under review, based as it was on a rule that is invalid because not promulgated in accordance with the required procedure, is therefore

VACATED.

NOTES AND QUESTIONS

4-33. What are the purposes of the various exemptions to 553 rulemaking set forth in section 553(b)(A) and (B)?

4-34. How does the court differentiate between interpretive and substantive rules? Between procedural and substantive rules? Between rules and policy statements? Are you satisfied with its approach?

4-35. What would you think of an approach that focused primarily on the effects of certain rules — *i.e.,* if they had "a substantial impact" on certain citizens, notice and comment rulemaking would be required? Would such an approach be consistent with *Vermont Yankee*?

4-36. There are exemptions to § 553 other than those discussed in *Bowen*. Under § 553(b)(B), notice and comment are not required when the agency for good cause finds the application of those procedures to be "impracticable, unnecessary or contrary to the public interest." What do you think the purpose of this exemption might be? Can you think of cases where comments are not likely to be useful? Or cases where the agency must act quickly? What if the need to act quickly derives from statutorily or judicially imposed deadlines to issue rules? What if it derives from the need to prevent danger to the public? Should this exemption be applied narrowly or broadly? *See generally*, *Action on Smoking and Health v. CAB*, 713 F.2d 795 (D.C. Cir. 1983) (applying § 553(b)(B) narrowly); *Asbestos Information Assoc. v. OSHA*, 727 F.2d 415 (5th Cir. 1984); Jordan, *The Administrative Procedure Act's "Good Cause" Exemption*, 36 ADMIN. L. REV. 113 (1984).

4-37. There are other exemptions as well. *See* § 553(a)(2) (agency management and personnel) and § 553(a)(1) (military and foreign affairs). How should regulations created to carry out international trade agreements be treated under the APA? Would they fall under § 553(a)(1)'s exemption, as being involved with "a military or foreign affairs function of the United States"? *See American Association of Exporters and Importers v. U.S.*, 751 F.2d 1239, 1249 (Fed. Cir. 1985) (court held that President was exempt from § 553 so as "to allow more cautious and sensitive consideration of those matters which so affect relations with the Governments that, for example, public rulemaking provisions, would provoke definitely undesirable international consequences").

4-38. Section 553(a)(2) of the APA provides for what are called "proprietary exemptions." Specifically, it excludes from 553 procedures all rules relating to "public property, loans, grants, benefits and contracts." Why should such an exemption be included in the APA? Would rules dealing with the Department of Defense's procurement contracts be exempt from the APA? What about rules governing grants from the National Endowment for the Humanities? This exemption has received a good deal of criticism. *See* ACUS Recommendations, No. 69-8, "Elimination of Certain Exemptions from the APA Rulemaking Requirements," 1 C.F.R. § 305.69-8 (1988).

4-39. *See Housing Authority of Omaha v. United States Housing Authority*, 468 F.2d 1, 9 (8th Cir. 1972).

The exemptions of matters under Section 553(a)(2) relating to "public benefits," could conceivably include virtually every activity of government. However, since an expansive reading of the exemption clause could easily carve the heart out of the notice provisions of Section 553, it is fairly obvious that Congress did not intend for the exemptions to be interpreted that broadly. The legislative history tends to support this logic. The Senate Judiciary Committee reported on its version (S.7) of the Administrative Procedure Act as follows: "It should be noted . . . that the exceptions apply only 'to the extent' that the excepted subjects are directly involved." S.Rep. 752, 79th Cong., 1st Sess. 13 (1945). Not only were exempted regulations limited to those where the excepted subjects were directly involved, but also the excepted subjects appeared to be limited in their scope to those where the government had a "proprietary" or other unique interest. The specific exemption for "public contracts" seems to have developed from a concern to avoid having the notice section applied to minimum wage determinations of the Department of Labor in connection with public contracts. S.Doc. 248, 79th Cong., 2d Sess. 17-18 (1946). In 1946 the Department of Labor was authorized to issue public contracts under the Davis-Bacon Act and the Walsh-Healey Act. In *Perkins v. Lukens Steel Co.*, 310 U.S. 113, 129 (1940), the court held that the government must be free from vexatious restraints which interfere with the manner in which it may dispatch its own internal affairs. To insure that the notice provisions of the APA would not be used in a similar manner to restrain the government's administration of public contracts, Congress included the exemption. *See* Reich, *Administrative Procedure Act: Analysis of its Requirement as to Rule-Making*, 33 A.B.A.J. 315, 317 (1947).

4-40. What would happen if § 553(a)(2) did not automatically exclude the contracting process from having to go through notice and comment? Would an agency have to use notice and comment for every contract — including those, for example, involving the purchase of small quantities of office supplies like paper clips or involving the way a company promises to operate a private prison? APA § 553(b)(3)(B) permits an agency to dispense with notice and comment proceedings "when the agency for good cause finds (and incorporates the finding and a brief statement of reasons therefor in the rules issued) that notice and public procedure thereon are impracticable, unnecessary, or contrary to the public interest." What kinds of contracts would or would not undergo notice and comment? *See generally* Arthur E. Bonfield, *Public Participation in Federal Rulemaking Relating to Public Property, Loans, Grants, Benefits, or Contracts*, 118 U. PA. L. REV. 540 (1970).

4-41. How should contracts that outsource or privatize basic agency responsibilities be handled? Should they be subject to notice and comment? What role should the APA play?

The APA by its own terms applies only to agencies. Section 551(1) defines agency as "each authority of the Government of the United States . . . ." What happens when a governmental responsibility is contracted out or delegated to a wholly private entity? For example, it has become common to contract out the management of prisons at both the federal and state level to private management companies. It is possible that our state action doctrine might trigger due process protections, but such a decision is contingent specifically on finding governmental involvement in these actions. It may be that this will be the case, especially when prisons are involved, but the extension of the APA to such activities should not be restricted only to prisons, but to all private entities to whom governmental responsibilities have been delegated. Current approaches to welfare are involving the private sector in new ways with private firms, in some cases, deciding welfare eligibility. Various proposals to reform social security now seek to utilize the market and private entities in what is, for that program, a new approach.

Triggering the APA need not require the "full panoply" of extensive and costly adjudicatory procedures that were devised in an earlier era for rate-making cases or the application of command and control regulation. A separate procedural provision designed for private actors could be crafted, one which not only emphasizes flexibility, but also public involvement and the basic public law protections of notice, participation, transparency, and some form of accountability. . . .

Alfred C. Aman, Jr., *Proposals for Reforming the Administrative Procedure Act: Globalization, Democracy and the Furtherance of a Global Public Interest*, 6 IND. J. GLOBAL LEGAL STUD. 397, 415-16 (1999).*

4-42. In *Hoctor*, why couldn't the eight-foot requirement promulgated in the Agriculture Department's internal memorandum provide the basis for Hoctor's citation in this case? Was there anything that could show that a six-foot-high fence was not secure enough? Can a regulation requiring secure containment be interpreted to require a specific height with a specific distance from pens?

4-43. Professor William Funk agues that the court makes this harder than it should be:

> *Hoctor* reflects a common mistake courts make, holding that a rule the agency claims is a nonlegislative rule is really an invalid legislative rule, *because only a legislative rule could achieve the effect the agency sought in the particular proceeding*, rather than holding that the nonlegislative rule cannot have the effect the agency seeks to give it *precisely because it is a nonlegislative rule*. In *Hoctor*, had the agency engaged in notice-and-comment rulemaking to establish an 8-foot high with 3-foot separation from pens requirement in order to ensure secure containment, and if there was an adequate basis in the rulemaking record to demonstrate that such a rule was not arbitrary and capricious, such a rule would have established a legal requirement, the violation of which would have been sanctionable. This fact, however, does not make the manual provision, adopted without notice and comment, an invalid legislative rule; it means that the manual provision simply cannot provide the legal basis for assessing a violation of the secure containment regulation.

William F. Funk, *When is a "Rule" a Regulation? Marking a Clear Line Between Nonlegislative Rules and Legislative Rules*, 54 ADMIN. L. REV. 659 (2002).**

PROBLEM 4-3

In 1987, Congress amended the Federal Aviation Act relating to civil penalties. These amendments were meant to strengthen the enforcement powers of the Federal Aviation Administration (FAA). To this end, Congress raised to $10,000 the maximum penalty for a single violation of the FAA's aviation standards and it established a "demonstration program" authorizing the FAA

---

* Copyright © 1999 by Trustees of Indiana University. Reprinted with the permission of the Indiana University Press, all rights reserved.

** Copyright © 2002 American Bar Association. Reprinted with permission.

to prosecute and adjudicate administrative penalty actions involving less than $50,000. Under the terms of the demonstration program, the FAA was granted the authority to assess administrative penalties for a two-year period and then report to Congress on its effectiveness.

To carry out these amendments, the FAA promulgated certain Penalty Rules. These rules established a schedule of civil penalties, including fines of up to $10,000 for violations of safety standards promulgated pursuant to the Federal Aviation Act. The Penalty Rules also established a comprehensive adjudicatory scheme providing for formal notice, settlement procedures, discovery, an ALJ adversarial hearing and an administrative appeal.

The FAA, however, chose *not* to promulgate these rules pursuant to the notice and comment provisions of the APA. It did respond to comments made after it issued these rules, but there was no opportunity to do so before they took effect.

Many commercial and non-commercial aviators were quite concerned with what they perceived to be the rules' procedural bias in favor of the FAA. They challenged these rules in court, arguing that it was legally wrong for the FAA to by-pass the informal rulemaking procedures of the APA.

(a) Assume you are counsel for the FAA. What is the legal basis for your claim that section 533 procedures were not required?

(b) Assume you are counsel for the Air Transport Association of America, a group representing commercial aviation interests. What counter-arguments would you make?

(c) Assume you are clerking for the judge asked to write the opinion resolving this dispute. She asks you for a memorandum setting forth the law on this issue. How do you resolve this case?

(d) After you have thought this through, see *Air Transport Association of America v. DOT,* 900 F.2d 369 (D.C. Cir. 1990).

PROBLEM 4-4

The Food and Drug Administration (FDA) has jurisdiction to prevent the sale of food containing "[a]ny poisonous or deleterious substance where such substance is required in the production thereof or cannot be avoided by good manufacturing practice." 21 U.S.C.S. § 346 (2004). If the substance is required for production of the food or is an unavoidable contaminant, then the FDA has the jurisdiction to pass regulations limiting the amount of the substance present in food. *Id.*

Last week, one of the broadcast networks aired a news story about one scientist's recent discovery of a new kind of mold that grows on corn. The scientist tentatively hypothesizes that the by-products the mold produces as it grows can cause illness in humans if ingested in moderate amounts. On the broadcast, the network also excerpted interviews with two other scientists who doubt that the by-products can cause illness in humans.

a) If the FDA wishes to regulate this by-product, must it engage in notice and comment rulemaking to determine whether the by-product is in fact harmful to humans? Or, can the FDA simply issue an "interpretative rule" today announcing that the agency will interpret "poisonous or deleterious substance" to include the mold by-product?

b) Assume now that the FDA uses notice and comment rulemaking to establish a regulation setting the maximum permissible level of the by-product in foods that use corn as 20 parts per billion. Assume further that a new FDA commissioner has just taken office — one of a different party than the one in power when the original regulation was promulgated. The new commissioner thinks that 20 parts per billion is an unrealistically low threshold for processed food. Can the FDA issue a "statement of policy" today announcing that it will not initiate enforcement actions against food processors unless its field inspectors discover that the mold by-product is present at a level greater than 35 parts per billion? Or, must the FDA engage in notice and comment rulemaking to amend the regulation?

c) Assume now that the FDA issued the "statement of policy" discussed in the previous subsection, and that it did not use notice and comment procedures. Assume further that the "statement of policy" generated a great deal of negative publicity for the agency (and, by implication, for the president). In response, the commissioner picks up the phone and directs the head of the enforcement division to bring an enforcement proceeding against the next food producer who distributes a product in which the mold by-product is present at levels between 20 parts and 30 parts per billion. Can that food producer, whose product contains the mold by-product at level of 21 parts per billion, use the agency's "statement of policy" to defend itself in the enforcement proceeding?

d) Does the wording of the "statement of policy" at issue in the previous two subsections affect your answer? Why or why not?

§ 4.03 Choosing Rulemaking or Adjudication

[A] Introduction

Thus far, we have examined the adjudicatory and rulemaking procedures mandated by the Constitution, the APA, agency enabling acts, and an agency's own regulations. The questions we now pose are these: (1) when should an agency use rulemaking as opposed to adjudicatory procedures and (2) who should make this choice?

[B] The Power to Choose

SEC v. CHENERY CORP.

United States Supreme Court
332 U.S. 194 (1947)

MR. JUSTICE MURPHY delivered the opinion of the Court.

This case is here for the second time. In *S.E.C. v. Chenery Corporation,* 318 U.S. 80, we held that an order of the Securities and Exchange Commission could not be sustained on the grounds upon which that agency acted. We therefore directed that the case be remanded to the Commission for such further proceedings as might be appropriate. On remand, the Commission reexamined the problem, recast its rationale and reached the same result. The issue now is whether the Commission's action is proper in light of the principles established in our prior decision.

When the case was first here, we emphasized a simple but fundamental rule of administrative law. That rule is to the effect that a reviewing court, in dealing with a determination or judgment which an administrative agency alone is authorized to make, must judge the propriety of such action solely by the grounds invoked by the agency. If those grounds are inadequate or improper, the court is powerless to affirm the administrative action by substituting what it considers to be a more adequate or proper basis. To do so would propel the court into the domain which Congress has set aside exclusively for the administrative agency.

We also emphasized in our prior decision an important corollary of the foregoing rule. If the administrative action is to be tested by the basis upon which it purports to rest, that basis must be set forth with such clarity as to be understandable. It will not do for a court to be compelled to guess at the theory underlying the agency's action; nor can a court be expected to chisel that which must be precise from what the agency has left vague and indecisive. In other words, "We must know what a decision means before the duty becomes ours to say whether it is right or wrong." . . .

Applying this rule and its corollary, the court was unable to sustain the Commission's original action. The Commission had been dealing with the reorganization of the Federal Water Service Corporation (Federal), a holding company registered under the Public Utility Holding Company Act of 1935, 49 Stat. 803. During the period when successive reorganization plans proposed by the management were before the Commission, the officers, directors and controlling stockholders of Federal purchased a substantial amount of Federal's preferred stock on the over-the-counter market. Under the fourth reorganization plan, this preferred stock was to be converted into common stock of a new corporation; on the basis of the purchases of preferred stock, the management would have received more than 10% of this new common stock. It was frankly admitted that the management's purpose in buying the preferred stock was to protect its interest in the new company. It was also plain that there was no fraud or lack of disclosure in making these purchases.

§ 4.03   AGENCY RULEMAKING   409

But the Commission would not approve the fourth plan so long as the preferred stock purchased by the management was to be treated on a parity with the other preferred stock. It felt that the officers and directors of a holding company in the process of reorganization under the Act were fiduciaries and were under a duty not to trade in the securities of that company during the reorganization period. 8 S.E.C. 893, 915–921. And so the plan was amended to provide that the preferred stock acquired by the management, unlike that held by others, was not to be converted into the new common stock; instead, it was to be surrendered at cost plus dividends accumulated since the purchase dates. As amended, the plan was approved by the Commission over the management's objections. 10 S.E.C. 200.

The court interpreted the Commission's order approving this amended plan as grounded solely upon judicial authority. The Commission appeared to have treated the preferred stock acquired by the management in accordance with what it thought were standards theretofore recognized by courts. If it intended to create new standards growing out of its experience in effectuating the legislative policy, it failed to express itself with sufficient clarity and precision to be so understood. Hence the order was judged by the only standards clearly invoked by the Commission. On that basis, the order could not stand. The opinion pointed out that courts do not impose upon officers and directors of a corporation any fiduciary duty to its stockholders which precludes them merely because they are officers and directors, from buying and selling the corporation's stock. Nor was it felt that the cases upon which the Commission relied established any principles of law or equity which in themselves would be sufficient to justify this order.

The opinion further noted that neither Congress nor the Commission had promulgated any general rule proscribing such action as the purchase of preferred stock by Federal's management. And the only judge-made rule of equity which might have justified the Commission's order related to fraud or mismanagement of the reorganization by the officers and directors, matters which were admittedly absent in this situation.

After the case was remanded to the Commission, Federal Water and Gas Corp. (Federal Water), the surviving corporation under the reorganization plan, made an application for approval of an amendment to the plan to provide for the issuance of new common stock of the reorganized company. This stock was to be distributed to the members of Federal's management on the basis of the shares of the old preferred stock which they had acquired during the period of reorganization, thereby placing them in the same position as the public holders of the old preferred stock. The intervening members of Federal's management joined in this request. The Commission denied the application in an order issued on February 7, 1945. That order was reversed by the Court of Appeals, which felt that our prior decision precluded such action by the Commission.

The latest order of the Commission definitely avoids the fatal error of relying on judicial precedents which do not sustain it. This time, after a thorough reexamination of the problem in light of the purposes and standards of the Holding Company Act, the Commission has concluded that the proposed transaction is inconsistent with the standards of §§ 7 and 11 of the Act. It has drawn heavily upon its accumulated experience in dealing with utility reorganizations. And it has expressed its reasons with a clarity and thoroughness that admit of no doubt as to the underlying basis of its order.

The argument is pressed upon us, however, that the Commission was foreclosed from taking such a step following our prior decision. It is said that, in the absence of findings of conscious wrongdoing on the part of Federal's management, the Commission could not determine by an order in this particular case that it was inconsistent with the statutory standards to permit Federal's management to realize a profit through the reorganization purchases. All that it could do was to enter an order allowing an amendment to the plan so that the proposed transaction could be consummated. Under this view, the Commission would be free only to promulgate a general rule outlawing such profits in future utility reorganizations; but such a rule would have to be prospective in nature and have no retroactive effect upon the instant situation.

We reject this contention, for it grows out of a misapprehension of our prior decision and of the Commission's statutory duties. We held no more and no less than that the Commission's first order was insupportable for the reasons supplied by that agency. But when the case left this Court, the problem whether Federal's management should be treated equally with other preferred stockholders still lacked a final and complete answer. It was clear that the Commission could not give a negative answer by resort to prior judicial declarations. And it was also clear that the Commission was not bound by settled judicial precedents in a situation of this nature. 318 U.S. at 89. Still unsettled, however, was the answer the Commission might give were it to bring to bear on the facts the proper administrative and statutory considerations, a function which belongs exclusively to the Commission in the first instance. The administrative process had taken an erroneous rather than a final turn. Hence we carefully refrained from expressing any views as to the propriety of an order rooted in the proper and relevant considerations. . . .

When the case was directed to be remanded to the Commission for such further proceedings as might be appropriate, it was with the thought that the Commission would give full effect to its duties in harmony with the views we had expressed. . . . This obviously meant something more than the entry of a perfunctory order giving parity treatment to the management holdings of preferred stock. The fact that the Commission had committed a legal error in its first disposition of the case certainly gave Federal's management no vested right to receive the benefits of such an order. . . . After the remand was made, therefore, the Commission was bound to deal with the problem afresh, performing the function delegated to it by Congress. . . .

The absence of a general rule or regulation governing management trading during reorganization did not affect the Commission's duties in relation to the particular proposal before it. The Commission was asked to grant or deny effectiveness to a proposed amendment to Federal's reorganization plan whereby the management would be accorded parity treatment on its holdings. It could do that only in the form of an order, entered after a due consideration of the particular facts in light of the relevant and proper standards. That was true regardless of whether those standards previously had been spelled out in a general rule or regulation. Indeed, if the Commission rightly felt that the proposed amendment was inconsistent with those standards, an order giving effect to the amendment merely because there was no general rule or regulation covering the matter would be unjustified.

It is true that our prior decision explicitly recognized the possibility that the Commission might have promulgated a general rule dealing with this problem under its statutory rule-making powers, in which case the issue for our consideration would have been entirely different from that which did confront us. 318 U.S. 92–93. But we did not mean to imply thereby that the failure of the Commission to anticipate this problem and to promulgate a general rule withdrew all power from that agency to perform its statutory duty in this case. To hold that the Commission had no alternative in this proceeding but to approve the proposed transaction, while formulating any general rules it might desire for use in future cases of this nature, would be to stultify the administrative process. That we refuse to do.

Since the Commission, unlike a court, does have the ability to make new law prospectively through the exercise of its rule-making powers, it has less reason to rely upon *ad hoc* adjudication to formulate new standards of conduct within the framework of the Holding Company Act. The function of filling in the interstices of the Act should be performed, as much as possible, through this quasi-legislative promulgation of rules to be applied in the future. But any rigid requirement to that effect would make the administrative process inflexible and incapable of dealing with many of the specialized problems which arise. . . . Not every principle essential to the effective administration of a statute can or should be cast immediately into the mold of a general rule. Some principles must await their own development, while others must be adjusted to meet particular, unforeseeable situations. In performing its important functions in these respects, therefore, an administrative agency must be equipped to act either by general rule or by individual order. To insist upon one form of action to the exclusion of the other is to exalt form over necessity.

In other words, problems may arise in a case which the administrative agency could not reasonably foresee, problems which must be solved despite the absence of a relevant general rule. Or the agency may not have had sufficient experience with a particular problem to warrant rigidifying its tentative judgment into a hard and fast rule. Or the problem may be so specialized and varying in nature as to be impossible to capture within the boundaries of a general rule. In those situations, the agency must retain power to deal with the problems on a case-to-case basis if the administrative process is to be effective. There is thus a very definite place for the case-by-case evolution of statutory standards. And the choice made between proceeding by general rule or by individual, *ad hoc* litigation is one that lies primarily in the informed discretion of the administrative agency. . . .

Hence we refuse to say that the Commission, which had not previously been confronted with the problem of management trading during reorganization, was forbidden from utilizing this particular proceeding for announcing and applying a new standard of conduct. . . . That such action might have a retroactive effect was not necessarily fatal to its validity. Every case of first impression has a retroactive effect, whether the new principle is announced by a court or by an administrative agency. But such retroactivity must be balanced against the mischief of producing a result which is contrary to a statutory design or to legal and equitable principles. If that mischief is greater than the ill effect of the retroactive application of a new standard, it is not the type of retroactivity which is condemned by law. . . .

And so in this case, the fact that the Commission's order might retroactively prevent Federal's management from securing the profits and control which were the objects of the preferred stock purchases may well be outweighed by the dangers inherent in such purchases from the statutory standpoint. If that is true, the argument of retroactivity becomes nothing more than a claim that the Commission lacks power to enforce the standards of the Act in this proceeding. Such a claim deserves rejection.

The problem in this case thus resolves itself into a determination of whether the Commission's action in denying effectiveness to the proposed amendment to the Federal reorganization plan can be justified on the basis upon which it clearly rests. As we have noted, the Commission avoided placing its sole reliance on inapplicable judicial precedents. Rather it has derived its conclusions from the particular facts in the case, its general experience in reorganization matters and its informed view of statutory requirements. It is those matters which are the guide for our review.

The Commission concluded that it could not find that the reorganization plan, if amended as proposed, would be "fair and equitable to the persons affected (thereby)" within the meaning of § 11(e) of the Act, under which the reorganization was taking place. Its view was that the amended plan would involve the issuance of securities on terms "detrimental to the public interest or the interest of investors" contrary to §§ 7(d)(6) and 7(e), and would result in an "unfair or inequitable distribution of voting power" among the Federal security holders within the meaning of § 7(e). It was led to this result "not by proof that the interveners (Federal's management) committed acts of conscious wrongdoing but by the character of the conflicting interests created by the interveners' program of stock purchases carried out while plans for reorganization were under consideration."

The Commission noted that Federal's management controlled a large multistate utility system and that its influence permeated down to the lowest tier of operating companies. The financial, operational and accounting policies of the parent and its subsidiaries were therefore under the management's strict control. The broad range of business judgments vested in Federal's management multiplied opportunities for affecting the market price of Federal's outstanding securities and made the exercise of judgment on any matter a subject of greatest significance to investors. Added to these normal managerial powers, the Commission pointed out that a holding company management obtains special powers in the course of a voluntary reorganization under § 11(e) of the Holding Company Act. The management represents the stockholders in such a reorganization, initiates the proceeding, draws up and files the plan, and can file amendments thereto at any time. These additional powers may introduce conflicts between the management's normal interests and its responsibilities to the various classes of stockholders which it represents in the reorganization. Moreover, because of its representative status, the management has special opportunities to obtain advance information of the attitude of the Commission. Drawing upon its experience, the Commission indicated that all these normal and special powers of the holding company management during the course of a § 11(e) reorganization placed in the management's command "a formidable battery of devices that would enable it, if it should choose to use them selfishly, to affect in material degree the ultimate allocation of new securities among the various existing classes, to influence the market for its own gain and to manipulate or obstruct the reorganization required by the mandate of the statute." In that setting, the Commission felt that a management program of stock purchase would give rise to the temptation and the opportunity to shape the reorganization proceeding so as to encourage public selling on the market at low prices. No management could engage in such a program without raising serious questions as to whether its personal interests had not opposed its duties "to exercise disinterested judgment in matters pertaining to subsidiaries' accounting, budgetary and dividend policies, to present publicly an unprejudiced financial picture of the enterprise, and to effectuate a fair and feasible plan expeditiously."

The Commission further felt that its answer should be the same even where proof of intentional wrongdoing on the management's part is lacking. Assuming a conflict of interests, the Commission thought that the absence of actual misconduct is immaterial; injury to the public investors and to the corporation may result just as readily. "Questionable transactions may be explained away, and an abuse of investors and the administrative process may be perpetrated without evil intent, yet the injury will remain." Moreover, the Commission was of the view that the delays and the difficulties involved in probing the mental processes and personal integrity of corporate officials do not warrant any distinction on the basis of evil intent, the plain fact being "that an absence of unfairness or detriment in cases of this sort would be practically impossible to establish by proof."

. . . .

The scope of our review of an administrative order wherein a new principle is announced and applied is no different from that which pertains to ordinary administrative action. The wisdom of the principle adopted is none of our concern. . . . Our duty is at an end when it becomes evident that the Commission's action is based upon substantial evidence and is consistent with the authority granted by Congress. . . .

. . . .

The Commission's conclusion here rests squarely in that area where administrative judgments are entitled to the greatest amount of weight by appellate courts. It is the product of administrative experience, appreciation of the complexities of the problem, realization of the statutory policies, and responsible treatment of the uncontested facts. It is the type of judgment which administrative agencies are best equipped to make and which justifies the use of the administrative process. Whether we agree or disagree with the result reached, it is an allowable judgment which we cannot disturb.

Reversed.

MR. JUSTICE BURTON concurs in the result.

The CHIEF JUSTICE and MR. JUSTICE DOUGLAS took no part in the consideration or decision of this case.

MR. JUSTICE JACKSON, dissenting.

The court by this present decision sustains the identical administrative order which only recently it held invalid. *S.E.C. v. Chenery Corp.,* 318 U.S. 80. As the court correctly notes, the Commission has only "recast its rationale and reached the same result." (Par. 1.). There being no change in the order, no additional evidence in the record and no amendment of relevant legislation, it is clear that there has been a shift in attitude between that of the controlling membership of the court when the case was first here and that of those who have the power of decision on this second review.

I feel constrained to disagree with the reasoning offered to rationalize this shift. It makes judicial review of administrative orders a hopeless formality for the litigant, even where granted to him by Congress. It reduces the judicial process in such cases to a mere feint. While the opinion does not have the adherence of a majority of the full Court, if its pronouncements should become governing principles they would, in practice, put most administrative orders over and above the law.

I.

The essential facts are few and are not in dispute. This corporation filed with the Securities and exchange Commission a voluntary plan of reorganization. While the reorganization proceedings were pending sixteen officers and directors bought on the open market about 7½% of the corporation's preferred stock. Both the Commission and the Court admit that these purchases were not forbidden by any law, judicial precedent, regulation or rule of the Commission. Nevertheless, the Commission has ordered these individuals to surrender their shares to the corporation at cost plus 4% interest, and the court now approves that order.

It is helpful, before considering whether this order is authorized by law, to reflect on what it is and what it is not. It is not conceivably a discharge of the Commission's duty to determine whether a proposed plan of reorganization would be "fair and equitable." It has nothing to do with the corporate structure, or the classes and amounts of stock, or voting rights or dividend preferences. It does not remotely affect the impersonal financial or legal factors of the plan. It is a personal deprivation denying particular persons the right to continue to own their stock and to exercise its privileges. Other persons who bought at the same time and price in the open market would be allowed to keep and convert their stock. Thus, the order is in no sense an exercise of the function of control over the terms and relations of the corporate securities.

Neither is the order one merely to regulate the future use of property. It literally takes valuable property away from its lawful owners for the benefit of other private parties without full compensation and the court expressly approves the taking. It says that the stock owned by these persons is denied conversion along with similar stock owned by others; "instead, it was to be surrendered at cost plus dividends accumulated since the purchase dates." It should be noted that this formula was subsequently altered to read "cost plus 4% interest." That this basis was less than its value is recognized, for the court says "That stock had been purchased in the market at prices that were depressed in relation to what the management anticipated would be, and what in fact was, the earning and asset value of its reorganization equivalent." Admittedly, the value above cost, and interest on it, simply is taken from the owners without compensation. No such power has ever been confirmed in any administrative body.

It should also be noted that neither the court nor the Commission purports to adjudge a forfeiture of this property as a consequence of sharp dealing or breach of trust. The court says, "The Commission admitted that the good faith and personal integrity of this management were not in question. . . ." And again, "It was frankly admitted that the management's purpose in buying the preferred stock was to protect its interest in the new company. It was also plain that there was no fraud or lack of disclosure in making these purchases."

II.

The reversal of the position of this Court is due to a fundamental change in prevailing philosophy. The basic assumption of the earlier opinion as therein stated was, *"But before transactions otherwise legal can be outlawed or denied their usual business consequences, they must fall under the ban of some standards of conduct prescribed by an agency of government authorized to prescribe such standards. . . ." S.E.C. v. Chenery Corp.,* 318 U.S. 80, stated thus: *"The absence of a general rule or regulation governing management trading during reorganization did not affect the Commission's duties in relation to the particular proposal before it."* This puts in juxtaposition the two conflicting philosophies which produce opposite results in the same case and on the same facts. The difference between the first and the latest decision of the court is thus simply the difference between holding that administrative orders must have a basis in law and a holding that absence of a legal basis is no ground on which courts may annul them.

As there admittedly is no law or regulation to support this order, we peruse the court's opinion diligently to find on what grounds it is now held that the Court of Appeals, on pain of being reversed for error, was required to stamp this order with its approval. We find but one. That is the principle of judicial deference to administrative experience. That argument is five times stressed in as many different contexts, and I quote just enough to identify the instances: "The Commission," it says, "has drawn heavily upon its accumulated experience in dealing with utility reorganizations." "Rather it has derived its conclusions from the particular facts in the case, its general experience in reorganization matters and its informed view of statutory requirements." "Drawing upon its experience, the Commission indicated. . . .", etc. ". . . the Commission has made a thorough examination of the problem, utilizing statutory standards and its own accumulated experience with reorganization matters." And finally, of the order the court says, "It is the product of administrative experience," etc.

What are we to make of this reiterated deference to "administrative experience" when in another context the court says, "Hence, we refuse to say that the Commission, *which had not previously been confronted with the problem of management trading during reorganization,* was forbidden from utilizing this particular proceeding for announcing and applying *a new standard of conduct*"? (Emphasis supplied.)

The court's reasoning adds up to this: The Commission must be sustained because of its accumulated experience in solving a problem with which it had never before been confronted!

Of course, thus to uphold the Commission by professing to find that it has enunciated a "new standard of conduct" brings the court squarely against the invalidity of retroactive law-making. But the court does not falter. "That such action might have a retroactive effect was not necessarily fatal to its validity." "But such retroactivity must be balanced against the mischief of producing a result which is contrary to a statutory design or to legal and equitable principles." Of course, if what these parties did really was condemned by "statutory design" or "legal and equitable principles," it could be stopped without resort to a new rule and there would be no retroactivity to condone. But if it had been the court's view that some law already prohibited the purchases, it would hardly have been necessary three sentences earlier to hold that the Commission was not prohibited "from utilizing this particular proceedings for announcing and applying a *new standard of conduct.*" (Emphasis supplied.)

I give up. Now I realize fully what Mark Twain meant when he said, "The more you explain it, the more I don't understand it."

III.

. . . .

I suggest that administrative experience is of weight in judicial review only to this point — it is a persuasive reason for deference to the Commission in the exercise of its discretionary powers under and within the law. It cannot be invoked to support action outside of the law. And what action is, and what is not, within the law must be determined by courts, when authorized to review, no matter how much deference is due to the agency's fact finding. . . .

The truth is that in this decision the court approves the commission's assertion of power to govern the matter *without* law, power to force surrender of stock so purchased whenever it will, and power also to overlook such acquisitions if it so chooses. The reasons which will lead it to take one course as against the other remain locked in its own breast, and it has not and apparently does not intend to commit them to any rule or regulation. This administrative authoritarianism, this power to decide without law, is what the court seems to approve in so many words: "The absence of a general rule or regulation governing management trading during reorganization did not affect the Commission's duties. . . ." This seems to me to undervalue and to belittle the place of law, even in the system of administrative justice. It calls to mind Mr. Justice Cardozo's statement that "Law as a guide to conduct is reduced to the level of mere futility if it is unknown and unknowable."

. . . .

Mr. Justice Frankfurter joins in this opinion.

NATIONAL LABOR RELATIONS BOARD v. BELL AEROSPACE COMPANY

United States Supreme Court
416 U.S. 267 (1974)

MR. JUSTICE POWELL delivered the opinion of the court.

This case presents two questions: first, whether the National Labor Relations Board properly determined that all "managerial employees," except those whose participation in a labor organization would create a conflict of interest with their job responsibilities, are covered by the National Labor Relations Act; and second, whether the Board must proceed by rulemaking rather than by adjudication in determining whether certain buyers are "managerial employees." We answer both questions in the negative.

I

[The court held, as to question one, that the NLRB "is not now free" to reinterpret the NLRA to exclude only those managerial employees susceptible to conflicts of interest if unionized.]

. . . .

II

In view of our conclusion, the case must be remanded to permit the Board to apply the proper legal standard in determining the status of these buyers. *SEC v. Chenery Corp.* [*Chenery I*], 318 U.S. 80, 85 (1943). We express no opinion as to whether these buyers fall within the category of "managerial employees."

III

The Court of Appeals also held that, although the Board was not precluded from determining that buyers or some types of buyers were not "managerial employees," it could do so only by invoking its rulemaking procedures under § 6 of the Act, 29 U.S.C. § 156. We disagree.

At the outset, the precise nature of the present issue must be noted. The question is not whether the Board should have resorted to rulemaking, or in fact improperly promulgated a "rule," when in the context of the prior representation proceeding it held that the Act covers all "managerial employees" except those meeting the new "conflict of interest in labor relations" touchstone. Our conclusion that the Board applied the wrong legal standard makes consideration of that issue unnecessary. Rather, the present question is whether on remand the Board must invoke its rulemaking procedures if it determines, in light of our opinion, that these buyers are not "managerial employees" under the Act. The Court of Appeals thought that rulemaking was required because any Board finding that the company's buyers are not "managerial" would be contrary to its prior decisions and would presumably be in the nature of a general rule designed "to fit all cases at all times."

A similar issue was presented to this Court in its second decision in *SEC v. Chenery Corp.*, 332 U.S. 194 (1947) (*Chenery II*).[23] . . .

The Court concluded that "the choice made between proceeding by general rule or by individual, *ad hoc* litigation is one that lies primarily in the informed discretion of the administrative agency." *Id.*, at 203.

And in *NLRB v. Wyman-Gordon Co.*, 394 U.S. 759 (1969), the court upheld a Board order enforcing an election list requirement first promulgated in an earlier adjudicative proceeding in *Excelsior Underwear Inc.*, 156 N.L.R.B. 1236 (1966). The plurality opinion of MR. JUSTICE FORTAS, joined by THE CHIEF JUSTICE, MR. JUSTICE STEWART, and MR. JUSTICE WHITE, recognized that "[a]djudicated cases may and do . . . serve as vehicles for the formulation of agency policies, which are applied and announced therein," and that such cases "generally provide a guide to action that the agency may be expected to take in future cases." . . . The concurring opinion of MR. JUSTICE BLACK, joined by MR. JUSTICE BRENNAN and MR. JUSTICE MARSHALL, also noted that the Board had both adjudicative and rule-making powers and that the choice between the two was "within its informed discretion." . . .

The views expressed in *Chenery II* and *Wyman-Gordon* make plain that the Board is not precluded from announcing new principles in an adjudicative proceeding and that the choice between rulemaking and adjudication lies in the first instance within the Board's discretion. Although there may be situations where the Board's reliance on adjudication would amount to an abuse of discretion or a violation of the Act, nothing in the present case would justify such a conclusion. Indeed, there is ample indication that adjudication is especially appropriate in the instant context. As the Court of Appeals noted, "[t]here must be tens of thousands of manufacturing, wholesale and retail units which employ buyers, and hundreds of thousands of the latter." Moreover, duties of buyers vary widely depending on the company or industry. It is doubtful whether any generalized standard could be framed which would have more than marginal utility. The Board thus has reason to proceed with caution, developing its standards in a case-by-case manner with attention to the specific character of the buyers' authority and duties in each company. The Board's judgment that adjudication best serves this purpose is entitled to great weight.

The possible reliance of industry on the Board's past decisions with respect to buyers does not require a different result. It has not been shown that the adverse consequences ensuing from such reliance are so substantial that the Board should be precluded from reconsidering the issue in an adjudicative proceeding. Furthermore, this is not a case in which some new liability is sought to be imposed on individuals for past actions which were taken in good-faith reliance on Board pronouncements, nor are fines or damages involved here. In any event, concern about such consequences is largely speculative,

---

[23] *Chenery II* did not involve § 4 of the APA, 5 U.S.C. § 553, but is nevertheless analogous.

for the Board has not yet finally determined whether these buyers are "managerial."

It is true, of course, that rulemaking would provide the Board with a forum for soliciting the informed views of those affected in industry and labor before embarking on a new course. But surely the Board has discretion to decide that the adjudicative procedures in this case may also produce the relevant information necessary to mature and fair consideration of the issues. Those most immediately affected, the buyers and the company in the particular case, are accorded a full opportunity to be heard before the Board makes its determination. The judgment of the Court of Appeals is therefore affirmed in part and reversed in part, and the cause remanded to that court with directions to remand to the Board for further proceedings in conformity with this opinion.

It is so ordered.

MR. JUSTICE WHITE, with whom MR. JUSTICE BRENNAN, MR. JUSTICE STEWART, and MR. JUSTICE MARSHALL join, dissenting in part.

I concur in Part III of the court's opinion insofar as it holds that the Board was not required to resort to rulemaking in deciding this case, but I dissent from its holding in Part II that managerial employees as a class are not "employees" within the meaning of the National Labor Relations Act. . . .

The Board's decisions in this area have not established a cohesive and precise pattern of rulings. It is often difficult to tell whether an individual decision is based on the propriety of excluding certain employees from a particular bargaining unit or whether the worker under consideration is thought to be outside the scope of the Act. But this Court has consistently said that it will accept the Board's determination of whether a particular individual is an "employee" under the Act if that determination "has 'warrant in the record' and a reasonable basis in law," *NLRB v. Hearst Publications, Inc.*, 322 U.S. 111, 131 (1944). . . . There is no reason here to hamstring the Board and deny a broad category of employees those protections of the Act which neither the statutory language nor its legislative history requires, simply because the Board at one time interpreted the Act — erroneously it seems to me — to exclude all managerial as well as supervisory employees.

I respectfully dissent.

NOTES AND QUESTIONS

4-44. In *Chenery II,* why does the court conclude that the agency and not the Court must make the decision in this case? Is there any question concerning the legal authority of the Commission to do so?

4-45. How does this case look from the viewpoint of the Chenery brothers? Did they knowingly engage in illegal activity? Did they have any reason to suspect that what they were doing was wrong? Is there any indication that they personally benefitted from the reorganization in this case?

4-46. If the SEC had used a rule rather than an order to promulgate its policy, how would the outcome of this case differ, as far as the Chenery brothers were concerned?

4-47. In *Bell Aerospace,* what criteria does the Court set forth to guide the agency in its choice of procedures? What would you have to show if you wanted a court to overturn the agency's choice of procedure? Why give the agency so much discretion in this regard? For a case that would require an agency to use its rulemaking powers, see *Ford Motor Co. v. FTC,* 673 F.2d 1008 (9th Cir. 1981).

4-48. Can a court uphold an agency decision that relies on a rule in an adjudicative decision when it subsequently becomes clear that the rule was procedurally invalid? *See Independent U.S. Tanker Owners Comm. v. Lewis,* 690 F.2d 908 (D.C. Cir. 1982).

4-49. What are the advantages of rulemaking and adjudication? Consider the following from the Administrative Conference of the United States, *A Guide to Federal Agency Rulemaking*:

Rulemaking and adjudication both can be used to establish standards of conduct for those who are regulated. Both types of decisionmaking can be used to create the necessary predicate for penalizing violators of those standards. They both require the assembly of sufficient factual information to support wise policy judgments. Nevertheless, there are various advantages associated with each procedure.

1. *Advantages of Rulemaking*

. . . .

(1) A rule formulated after rulemaking, with its wider notice and broader opportunities for participation, is fairer to the class of persons who would be affected by a new "rule" than a rule announced in an adjudication. Such broader participation also makes rulemaking more efficient as an information-gathering technique for the agency.

(2) Rulemaking is superior to adjudication as a means of making new law because rulemaking is "normally prospective while adjudication normally involves prescribing consequences for past conduct or present status."

(3) The articulation of a generally applicable rule provides greater clarity to those affected as well as greater uniformity in enforcement.

(4) Rulemaking is more efficient from the agency's point of view because its procedures offer more flexibility, at least when the choice is between the notice-and-comment requirements of section 553 of the APA and the formal adjudicatory procedures of sections 554, 556 and 557. Two of the most significant elements of this flexibility are the agency's broad control over the procedure for the presentation of information and argument and the agency's freedom to resort to its staff expertise without the inhibitions of separation-of-functions requirements.

(5) Since the agency is better able to control the scope and the pace of a rulemaking proceeding, use of rulemaking to formulate policy gives the

agency better control of its agenda and enables it to define and to focus on the policy issues without the distractions of individual adjudicative issues.

(6) Rulemaking is also more efficient for the agency because it can result in the adoption of a general principle which can thereafter be applied without reexamination, thereby eliminating case-by-case adjudications.

Another major advantage of policymaking through rules is their broader binding effect. Valid legislative rules are binding and enforceable on the public: that is, they have the force and effect of law. Decisions and orders in an adjudication, on the other hand, are typically binding only on the parties involved, and the rule stated in the proceeding would only have precedential effect in subsequent adjudications. . . .

2. *Advantages of Adjudication*

. . . .

(1) Rulemaking's increasing procedural complexity can be avoided. New statutes and executive orders have imposed many new requirements on the rulemaking process. Whatever their benefits in other respects, clearance provisions (OMB review, paperwork reduction provisions), impact statements (regulatory impact analyses, regulatory flexibility analyses) and statutes requiring more cumbersome hybrid procedures tend to make rulemaking by some agencies a more difficult and protracted venture. If an area is equally susceptible to regulation by adjudication or rulemaking — where, for example, there are a small number of firms engaged in the regulated activity — policymaking through adjudication may be more efficient.

(2) Modifications can be made more easily. Specific rules may become obsolete more quickly than more general statutory standards. However, modifications or repeal of rules for policy or technical reasons may be difficult or protracted because a new rulemaking has to be conducted. This may be especially difficult for agencies governed by "hybrid" rulemaking statutes, or for rules defined as "major rules" under Executive Order 12291. [*See* Chap. 7, § 7.05, *infra.*]

(3) Conflict can be minimized. At least one commentator has explained the NLRB's previously steadfast reluctance to abandon the making of policy through adjudication as based on a desire to avoid political conflicts with congressional oversight committees and other overseers. The premise is that the slow case-by-case accretion of policy is less dramatic or visible, easier to modify, and yet also more impregnable to political attack.

(4) Adjudicatory decisions can be situation-specific, thus potentially avoiding overinclusiveness or underinclusiveness. Rules may unintentionally be overinclusive, reaching unanticipated fact situations, thereby deterring socially desirable behavior or imposing unnecessary costs on society. On the other hand, a rulemaking intended to create a predicate for regulatory sanctions may lead to rules whose terms miss some of the conduct sought to be affected. Subsequent enforcement adjudications may be more easily rebuffed as a result. Related to this problem is one of targeting resources. Enforcement against egregious violators of the statutory standards is thought by some to be more cost-effective, less cumbersome, and more

politically palatable than attempting to promulgate an industry-wide standard. . . .

"There is thus clearly an interplay between rulemaking and adjudication. Rules issued after public participation in notice-and-comment proceedings establish general principles that will be binding on the public and applied to individual parties in adjudicatory proceedings. Rulemaking may not ordinarily be used as a substitute for individualized adjudication without implicating due process considerations; however, rules issued after informal proceedings may limit the issues to be adjudicated in subsequent proceedings and reduce the agency burden in establishing statutory violations. Ultimately, however, it is up to the agency to determine which method of policymaking it wishes to use in a particular context."

For a recent case analyzing retroactivity in the context of black lung disease, see *National Mining Association v. Department of Labor*, 292 F.3d 849 (D.C. Cir. 2002). For an excellent discussion of agency choices involving rulemaking and adjudication, see M. Elizabeth Magill, *Agency Choice of Policymaking Form*, 71 U. CHI. L. REV. 1383, 1403–42 (2004).

[C] The Need For and Agency Use of Rules

HECKLER, SECRETARY OF HEALTH AND HUMAN SERVICES v. CAMPBELL

United States Supreme Court
461 U.S. 458 (1981)

JUSTICE POWELL delivered the opinion of the court.

The issue is whether the Secretary of Health and Human Services may rely on published medical-vocational guidelines to determine a claimant's right to Social Security disability benefits.

I

The Social Security Act defines "disability" in terms of the effect a physical or mental impairment has on a person's ability to function in the workplace. It provides disability benefits only to persons who are unable "to engage in any substantial gainful activity by reason of any medically determinable physical or mental impairment." . . . And it specifies that a person must "not only [be] unable to do his previous work but [must be unable], considering his age, education, and work experience, [to] engage in any other kind of substantial gainful work which exists in the national economy, regardless of whether such work exists in the immediate area in which he lives, or whether a specific job vacancy exists for him, or whether he would be hired if he applied for work." . . .

In 1978, the Secretary of Health and Human Services promulgated regulations implementing this definition. . . . The regulations recognize that certain impairments are so severe that they prevent a person from pursuing any gainful work. A claimant who establishes that he suffers from one of these impairments will be considered disabled without further inquiry. If a claimant suffers from a less severe impairment, the Secretary must determine whether the claimant retains the ability to perform either his former work or some less demanding employment. If a claimant can pursue his former occupation, he is not entitled to disability benefits. If he cannot, the Secretary must determine whether the claimant retains the capacity to pursue less demanding work.

The regulations divide this last inquiry into two stages. First, the Secretary must assess each claimant's present job qualifications. The regulations direct the Secretary to consider the factors Congress has identified as relevant: physical ability, age, education and work experience. . . . Second, she must consider whether jobs exist in the national economy that a person having the claimant's qualifications could perform. . . . Prior to 1978, the Secretary relied on vocational experts to establish the existence of suitable jobs in the national economy. After a claimant's limitations and abilities had been determined at a hearing, a vocational expert ordinarily would testify whether work existed that the claimant could perform. Although this testimony often was based on standardized guides, . . . vocational experts frequently were criticized for their inconsistent treatment of similarly situated claimants. . . . To improve both the uniformity and efficiency[2] of this determination, the Secretary promulgated medical-vocational guidelines as part of the 1978 regulations. . . .

These guidelines relieve the Secretary of the need to rely on vocational experts by establishing through rulemaking the types and numbers of jobs that exist in the national economy. They consist of a matrix of the four factors identified by Congress — physical ability, age, education, and work experience[3] — and set forth rules that identify whether jobs requiring specific combinations of these factors exist in significant numbers in the national economy.[4] Where a claimant's qualifications correspond to the job requirements identified by a rule,[5] the guidelines direct a conclusion as to whether work exists

---

[2] The Social Security hearing system is "probably the largest adjudicating agency in the western world." J. Mashaw *et al.*, *Social Security Hearings and Appeals*, p. xi (1978). Approximately 2.3 million claims for disability benefits were filed in fiscal year 1981. Department of Health and Human Services, Social Security Annual Report to the Congress for Fiscal Year 1981, pp. 32, 35 (1982). More than a quarter of a million of these claims require a hearing before an Administrative Law Judge. *Id.*, at 38. The need for efficiency is self-evident.

[3] Each of these four factors is divided into defined categories. A person's ability to perform physical tasks, for example, is categorized according to the physical exertion requirements necessary to perform varying classes of jobs — *i.e.*, whether a claimant can perform sedentary, light, medium, heavy, or very heavy work. . . . Each of these work categories is defined in terms of the physical demands it places on a worker, such as the weight of objects he must lift and whether extensive movement or use of arm and leg controls is required.

[4] For example, Rule 202.10 provides that a significant number of jobs exist for a person who can perform light work, is closely approaching advanced age, has a limited education but who is literate and can communicate in English, and whose previous work has been unskilled.

[5] The regulations recognize that the rules only describe "major functional and vocational patterns." If an individual's capabilities are not described accurately by a rule, the regulations make clear that the individual's particular limitations must be considered. Additionally, the regulations declare that the Administrative Law Judge will not apply the age categories "mechanically in a borderline situation," and recognize that some claimants may possess limitations that are not factored into the guidelines. Thus, the regulations provide that the rules will be applied only when they describe a claimant's abilities and limitations accurately.

that the claimant could perform. If such work exists, the claimant is not considered disabled.

II

In 1979, Carmen Campbell applied for disability benefits because a back condition and hypertension prevented her from continuing her work as a hotel maid. After her application was denied, she requested a hearing *de novo* before an Administrative Law Judge.[6] He determined that her back problem was not severe enough to find her disabled without further inquiry, and accordingly considered whether she retained the ability to perform either her past work or some less strenuous job. . . . He concluded that even though Campbell's back condition prevented her from returning to her work as a maid, she retained the physical capacity to do light work. In accordance with the regulations, he found that Campbell was 52-years old, that her previous employment consisted of unskilled jobs and that she had a limited education. . . . He noted that Campbell, who had been born in Panama, experienced difficulty in speaking and writing English. She was able, however, to understand and read English fairly well. . . . Relying on the medical-vocational guidelines, the Administrative Law Judge found that a significant number of jobs existed that a person of Campbell's qualifications could perform. Accordingly, he concluded that she was not disabled.[7] . . .

This determination was upheld by both the Social Security Appeals Council, . . . and the District Court for the Eastern District of New York. . . . The Court of Appeals for the Second Circuit reversed. It accepted the Administrative Law Judge's determination that Campbell retained the ability to do light work. And it did not suggest that he had classified Campbell's age, education, or work experience incorrectly. . . . The court found that the medical-vocational guidelines did not provide the specific evidence that it previously had required. It explained that in the absence of such a showing, "the claimant is deprived of any real chance to present evidence showing that she cannot in fact perform the types of jobs that are administratively noticed by the guidelines." . . .

We granted certiorari to resolve a conflict among the Courts of Appeals. . . . We now reverse.

---

[6] The Social Security Act provides each claimant with a right to a *de novo* hearing.

[7] The Administrative Law Judge did not accept Campbell's claim that her hypertension constituted an impairment. He found that this claim was not documented by the record and noted that her current medication appeared sufficient to keep her blood pressure under control. Campbell later reapplied for disability benefits and was found disabled as of January 1, 1981. The Secretary's subsequent decision does not moot this case since Campbell is claiming entitlement to benefits prior to January 1, 1981.

III

. . . .

A

The Court of Appeals held that "[i]n failing to show suitable available alternative jobs for Ms. Campbell, the Secretary's finding of 'not disabled' is not supported by substantial evidence." It thus rejected the proposition that "the guidelines provide adequate evidence of a claimant's ability to perform a specific alternative occupation," and remanded for the Secretary to put into evidence "particular types of jobs suitable to the capabilities of Ms. Campbell." The court's requirement that additional evidence be introduced on this issue prevents the Secretary from putting the guidelines to their intended use and implicitly calls their validity into question. Accordingly, we think the decision below requires us to consider whether the Secretary may rely on medical-vocational guidelines in appropriate cases.

The Social Security Act directs the Secretary to "adopt reasonable and proper rules and regulations to regulate and provide for the nature and extent of the proofs and evidence and the method of taking and furnishing the same" in disability cases. 42 U.S.C. § 405(a). . . .

We do not think that the Secretary's reliance on medical-vocational guidelines is inconsistent with the Social Security Act. It is true that the statutory scheme contemplates that disability hearings will be individualized determinations based on evidence adduced at a hearing. . . . But this does not bar the Secretary from relying on rulemaking to resolve certain classes of issues. The court has recognized that even where an agency's enabling statute expressly requires it to hold a hearing, the agency may rely on its rulemaking authority to determine issues that do not require case-by-case consideration. See *FPC v. Texaco, Inc.*, 377 U.S. 33, 41-44 (1964); *United States v. Storer Broadcasting Co.*, 351 U.S. 192, 205 (1956). A contrary holding would require the agency continually to relitigate issues that may be established fairly and efficiently in a single rulemaking proceeding. . . .

As noted above, in determining whether a claimant can perform less strenuous work, the Secretary must make two determinations. She must assess each claimant's individual abilities and then determine whether jobs exist that a person having the claimant's qualifications could perform. The first inquiry involves a determination of historic facts, and the regulations properly require the Secretary to make these findings on the basis of evidence adduced at a hearing. We note that the regulations afford claimants ample opportunity both to present evidence relating to their own abilities and to offer evidence that the guidelines do not apply to them.[11] The second inquiry

---

[11] Both *FPC v. Texaco, Inc.*, 377 U.S. 33, 40 (1964), and *United States v. Storer Broadcasting Co.*, 351 U.S. 192, 205 (1956), were careful to note that the statutory scheme at issue allowed an individual applicant to show that the rule promulgated should not be applied to him. The regulations here provide a claimant with equal or greater protection since they state that an Administrative Law Judge will not apply the rules contained in the guidelines when they fail to describe a claimant's particular limitations. . . .

requires the Secretary to determine an issue that is not unique to each claimant — the types and numbers of jobs that exist in the national economy. This type of general factual issue may be resolved as fairly through rulemaking as by introducing the testimony of vocational experts at each disability hearing.

As the Secretary has argued, the use of published guidelines brings with it a uniformity that previously had been perceived as lacking. To require the Secretary to relitigate the existence of jobs in the national economy at each hearing would hinder needlessly an already overburdened agency. We conclude that the Secretary's use of medical-vocational guidelines does not conflict with the statute, nor can we say on the record before us that they are arbitrary and capricious.

B

We now consider Campbell's argument that the Court of Appeals properly required the Secretary to specify alternative available jobs. Campbell contends that such a showing informs claimants of the type of issues to be established at the hearing and is required by both the Secretary's regulation, . . . and the Due Process Clause.

The Court of Appeals did not find that the Secretary failed to give sufficient notice in violation of the Due Process Clause or any statutory provision designed to implement it. . . . Nor did it find that the Secretary violated any duty imposed by regulation. . . . Rather the court's reference to notice and an opportunity to respond appears to be based on a principle of administrative law — that when an agency takes official or administrative notice of facts, a litigant must be given an adequate opportunity to respond. *See* 5 U.S.C. § 556(3). . . .

This principle is inapplicable, however, when the agency has promulgated valid regulations. Its purpose is to provide a procedural safeguard: to ensure the accuracy of the facts of which an agency takes notice. But when the accuracy of those facts already has been tested fairly during rulemaking, the rulemaking proceeding itself provides sufficient procedural protection. . . .

IV

The Court of Appeals' decision would require the Secretary to introduce evidence of specific available jobs that respondent could perform. It would limit severely her ability to rely on the medical-vocational guidelines. We think the Secretary reasonably could choose to rely on these guidelines in appropriate cases rather than on the testimony of a vocational expert in each case. Accordingly, the judgment of the Court of Appeals is

Reversed.

JUSTICE BRENNAN, concurring.

I join the court's opinion. It merits comment, however, that the hearing respondent received, . . . if it is in any way indicative of standard practice, reflects poorly on the Administrative Law Judge's adherence to what Chief Judge Godbold has called his "duty of inquiry":

> "[T]here is a 'basic obligation' on the ALJ in these nonadversarial proceedings to develop a full and fair record, which obligation rises to a 'special duty . . . to scrupulously and conscientiously explore for all relevant facts' where an unrepresented claimant has not waived counsel. This duty of inquiry on the ALJ would include, in a case decided under the grids, a duty to inquire into possible nonexertional impairments and into exertional limitations that prevent a full range of work." *Broz v. Schweiker,* 677 F.2d 1351, 1364 (CA11 1982).

. . . The Administrative Law Judge's "duty to inquire" takes on special urgency where, as here, the claimant has little education and limited fluency in English, and, given that the claimant already has a right to a hearing, the additional cost of pursuing relevant issues at the hearing is minimal.

In order to find that respondent was not disabled, the Secretary had to determine that she had the physical capacity to do "light work," . . . a determination that required a finding that she was capable of frequent lifting or carrying of objects weighing up to 10 pounds and sometimes lifting up to 20 pounds. . . . The hearing record included one disinterested doctor's report of a medical examination of respondent that concluded with the unexplained statement "Patient may return to light-duty work," and a subsequent report by a second disinterested doctor stating that respondent could lift and carry only "up to 10 pounds." . . . In finding that respondent could perform "light work," the Administrative Law Judge rejected the second doctor's report as "without basis." . . . Yet he failed entirely to adduce evidence relevant to this issue at respondent's hearing. At several points during the hearing, respondent stated that she could not lift things, but the Administrative Law Judge did not question her on the subject at all,[12] nor did he make any inquiry whether by "light-duty work" the first doctor meant the same thing as the Secretary's term "light work."

The Administrative Law Judge further failed to inquire whether factors besides strength, age, or education, combined with her other impairments, rendered respondent disabled. . . . Apparently such factors could have been dispositive of the case before us: The Secretary has since determined that respondent is in fact disabled, . . . based on consideration of severe emotional complications not explored at all by the Administrative Law Judge in the hearing that led to her petition for review in this case.[13]

---

[12] The following colloquy appears on the record:

"**Q.** Can you bend?

"**A.** I cannot bend. The doctor warned me not to lift weights.

"**Q.** Uh-huh.

"**A.** And —

"**Q.** I notice you have stood up several times since you've been in here."

At no point did the Administrative Law Judge so much as ask respondent how she did her shopping, or any other question that might have elicited information on the crucial question of how much she could regularly lift.

[13] . . . The decision appears to have rested on evidence similar to the evidence in the record at the hearing in this case, except that the Administrative Law Judge took note that respondent was "an obese, sad individual, who had marked difficulties in sitting, standing, and walking," and he found that her back disorder was "complicated by a severe emotional overlay." . . .

This issue was not presented to the Court of Appeals, nor passed upon by it. . . . In terms of ensuring fair and accurate determinations of disability claims, the obligation that the Court of Appeals would have placed on Administrative Law Judges was a poor substitute for good-faith performance of the "duty of inquiry" they already have. The federal courts have been successful in enforcing this duty in the past, . . . and I respectfully suggest that the Secretary insist upon its faithful performance in future cases.

[JUSTICE MARSHALL also filed an opinion concurring in part and dissenting in part.]

ALLISON v. BLOCK

Eighth Circuit Court of Appeals
723 F.2d 631 (1981)

Before LAY, CHIEF JUDGE, and HEANEY and ARNOLD, CIRCUIT JUDGES.

HEANEY, CIRCUIT JUDGE.

In 1978, Congress enacted 7 U.S.C. § 1981a (1982), an amendment to the Consolidated Farm and Rural Development Act of 1961 (CFRDA). . . . Two years thereafter, Roger and Shirley Allison defaulted on farm loans granted to them by the Farmers Home Administration (FmHA) of the United States Department of Agriculture (USDA) under the CFRDA. The Allisons brought suit in the United States District Court for the Western District of Missouri seeking consideration of their eligibility for a section 1981a deferral on the foreclosure of their farm by the Secretary of Agriculture (Secretary). The district court enjoined foreclosure on the Allisons' farm until the Secretary complied with the letter and spirit of section 1981a. . . .

I.

BACKGROUND

The Allisons own and operate a farm in Howard County, Missouri. On December 20, 1977, they obtained FmHA financing under the CFRDA in the amount of $103,800, secured by a deed of trust on their realty. Because of adverse weather conditions in 1977 and low grain and livestock prices in 1978 they failed to turn a profit on the operation of the farm during those years. On December 22, 1978, Roger Allison applied for an FmHA economic emergency loan. The FmHA Howard County Committee denied the application. On appeal, the State Director of the FmHA approved a $29,000 operating loan but denied refinancing assistance. On June 26, 1979, the Assistant Administrator of the FmHA reversed the State Director's decision insofar as it denied Allison's reorganization loan request, holding that the denial "was unreasonable because [he] met the eligibility requirements. . . . [and] the proposed

Farm and Home Plan submitted by Allison on April 9, 1979, showed reasonable repayment ability." . . . On August 24, 1979, the Allisons received a $190,000 reorganization loan, secured by a deed of trust on their farm. On April 28, 1980, they received a $29,750 operating loan, secured by a deed of trust and liens on their equipment, livestock, supplies, and inventory.

Adverse weather and economic conditions continued to hamper the Allisons' farming operations. In 1979, a dry planting season followed by an early frost reduced their crop yield significantly. In 1980, a severe drought contributed to an eighty-seven percent reduction in corn yield and a sixty-eight percent reduction in bean yield. Following these losses, the Allisons became delinquent on their FmHA loan payments.

On November 6, 1980, an FmHA County Supervisor advised Roger Allison to sell the Allisons' breeding stock and equipment in order to make payments on their loans. Allison complied and, in the spring of 1981, the FmHA applied the proceeds of these sales to reduce the delinquency on the Allisons' April 28, 1980, operating loan.

On May 14, 1981, the FmHA accelerated the Allisons' indebtedness, as to both principal and interest, for failure to make timely payments and failure to pay real estate taxes. It notified them that their loans, which were classified as emergency (EM) and economic emergency (EE) loans, would be foreclosed unless the total indebtedness was paid by June 15, 1981. The Allisons appealed the acceleration notice to the FmHA District Director and Assistant Administrator; both upheld the decision. The Allisons then brought their final administrative appeal before the Administrator of the FmHA (Administrator). Pending this appeal, Roger Allison read in a farming magazine about possible loan deferral relief under federal statute and requested such relief from the Administrator. On August 10, 1982, the Program Assistant to the Administrator denied the Allisons' appeal, rejecting the alternatives of consolidation rescheduling, reamortization, or deferral because the Allisons "did not have the potential to generate sufficient farm income to repay family living and farm operating expenses plus debt service even if a deferral had been granted." . . .

On October 27, 1982, the Allisons filed the present action requesting declaratory and injunctive relief from the acceleration of their loans and foreclosure on their property. They alleged that the Secretary's failure to promulgate adequate procedural and substantive regulations creating a program for loan deferrals under 7 U.S.C. § 1981a (1982) violated that statute, amounted to a denial of equal protection and due process, and constituted an abuse of administrative discretion. . . .

II.

STATUTORY REQUIREMENTS

On appeal, the Secretary asserts that the district court erred in requiring special procedures or standards to be followed by virtue of section 1981a with regard to FmHA loan servicing and foreclosure activities.[1] The gist of his

---

[1] The district court found it unnecessary to reach the constitutional claims raised by the Allisons because of the statutory violation. We also decline to meet the constitutional issues.

argument is that section 1981a merely created an additional power to be wielded at the discretion of the agency, or placed in the secretary's "back pocket" for safekeeping. We reject this argument and affirm the district court. The full text of section 1981a is as follows:

> In addition to any other authority that the Secretary may have to defer principal and interest and forego foreclosure, the Secretary may permit, at the request of the borrower, the deferral of principal and interest on any outstanding loan made, insured, or held by the Secretary under this Chapter, or under the provisions of any other law administered by the Farmers Home Administration, and may forego foreclosure of any such loan, for such period as the Secretary deems necessary upon a showing by the borrower that due to circumstances beyond the borrower's control, the borrower is temporarily unable to continue making payments of such principal and interest when due without unduly impairing the standard of living of the borrower. The Secretary may permit interest that accrues during the deferral period on any loan deferred under this section to bear no interest during or after such period: *Provided,* that if the security instrument securing such loan is foreclosed such interest as is included in the purchase price at such foreclosure shall become part of the principal and draw interest from the date of foreclosure at the rate prescribed by law.
> 7 U.S.C. § 1981a (1982).

The Secretary would have us hold that this statute requires no adjudicatory or regulatory administrative action because it creates no administrative procedural requirements nor any substantive right to relief from loan acceleration of foreclosure. We refuse to so hold. In our view, section 1981a creates a right to have certain uniform procedures established and requires the Secretary to develop substantive standards applicable to deferral applications.

A. Procedural Requirements

Section 1981a expressly conditions the Secretary's authority to grant relief to CFRDA borrowers upon two actions by the borrower: (1) a request for such relief; and (2) a showing that, because of circumstances beyond the borrower's control, he or she is temporarily unable to continue payments of principal and interest without unduly impairing his or her standard of living. Following such a request and showing, the Secretary "may permit" deferral of payments of principal and interest and "may forego" foreclosure.

We agree with several federal district courts which have held that . . . Congress intended the Secretary to give notice of the availability of section 1981a relief to all CFRDA borrowers subject to loan acceleration of foreclosure and to establish a uniform procedure under which borrowers can make the requisite request and *prima facie* showing. . . . The requirement of a request by the borrower prior to consideration for section 1981a relief presupposes that the borrower has knowledge of the availability of such relief. Notice to the borrower is therefore indispensable. In like manner, the requirement of a showing of *prima facie* eligibility is necessarily premised upon the expectation that some procedure will be provided under which the borrower may make the requisite showing. Thus, the rudimentary elements of adequate notice and an opportunity to be heard are embodied in the language of section 1981a. . . .

Furthermore, the legislative history underlying the statute supports the conclusion that the Secretary is required to give notice to defaulting CFRDA borrowers and to create a procedure for asserting section 1981a claims. . . .

Against this backdrop of statutory language and legislative history, we cannot accept the Secretary's assertion that Congress left the implementation of section 1981a a matter of unfettered administrative discretion. . . .

We therefore affirm the injunction against foreclosure of the Allisons' farm until the Secretary has complied with his responsibilities to provide adequate notice and procedures under which the Allisons may make the requisite *prima facie* showing and otherwise demonstrate their eligibility for a section 1981a deferral. Because the Allisons already have notice of the existence of section 1981a, the Secretary may fulfill the notice requirement of the statute in this case by giving the Allisons personal notice of the proper procedures once established.

B. Substantive Standards

The district court found that the Secretary abused his discretion in dealing with the Allisons "by failing to fully consider the applicability of 7 U.S.C § 1981a's loan deferral relief." . . . As we read the court's opinion, the statute itself, and its legislative history, this conclusion encompasses more than the procedural formalities which we have just discussed. Good faith consideration of the section 1981a deferral alternative by the Secretary requires the existence of some substantive standards which, if met, entitle the borrower to relief. Because any other construction would render the statute mere procedural "window-dressing," a result abhorrent to the language and purpose of the 1978 agricultural credit legislation and absurd as a matter of policy, we hold that section 1981a also requires the development of substantive standards at the agency level to guide the Secretary's discretion in making individual deferral decisions. . . .

We cannot accept the Secretary's implicit assertion that the discretion to decide individual cases includes the authority to decide, without formal rulemaking, that — regardless of a borrower's request and *prima facie* showing, and the particular facts of the case — no CFRDA borrower is eligible for section 1981a deferral relief. . . .

Section 1981a expressly creates *prima facie* substantive standards of eligibility for deferral relief — "that due to circumstances beyond the borrower's control, the borrower is temporarily unable to continue making payments of . . . principal and interest when due without unduly impairing the standard of living of the borrower." Besides contemplating the existence of a procedure under which the borrower may make the *prima facie* showing, these preliminary substantive standards limit the number of borrowers eligible for section 1981a relief, indicating Congress's expectation that at lease some of those borrowers would in fact merit such relief. Indeed, the title to section 1981a, as presented to Congress and codified as enacted, refers to a "moratorium and policy on foreclosures." . . . Congress surely would not consider an empty procedural shell, with no substantive measure of relief, to be a policy at all.

Furthermore, the legislative history behind section 1981a exhibits Congress's intent that the Secretary respect the substantive standards explicitly set forth, and establish whatever other standards consistent with and necessary to the statute, in administering the emergency loan deferral program. The congressional debates all revolve around the structure and content of the "program" authorized by section 1981a, a strange term if the Secretary could merely make a decision unsupported by administrative investigation or public comment that no borrower deserves the relief which Congress authorized. . . .

We do not decide in what manner the Secretary must develop the substantive standards applicable to section 1981a deferral requests. The District of Columbia Circuit noted under similar circumstances:

> If regulations of general applicability were formulated, it would of course be possible to explain individual decisions by reference to the appropriate regulation. It may well be, however, that standards . . . can best be developed piecemeal, as the Secretary evaluates [particular cases]. Even so, he has an obligation to articulate the criteria that he develops in making each individual decision. We cannot assume, in the absence of adequate explanation, that proper standards are implicit in every exercise of administrative discretion.

Environmental Defense Fund, Inc. v. Ruckelshaus, 439 F.2d 584, 596 (D.C. Cir. 1971). Although we believe that formal rulemaking would better insure a uniform set of substantive standards to govern section 1981a requests, we recognize that the Secretary may decide to develop the criteria through adjudicative processes which give some precedential effect to prior FmHA loan deferral decisions. . . . The fact remains at present, however, that the Secretary has chosen neither a process of reasoned decisionmaking to safeguard against an abuse of section 1981a discretion nor the publication of uniform regulations to be used as substantive standards to guide the exercise of that discretion. . . . We cannot accept this complete abdication of the Secretary's responsibilities under section 1981a.

For purposes of the present appeal, we affirm the injunction against foreclosure on the Allisons' farm not only pending proper notice of the procedures developed to process section 1981a requests, as previously discussed, but also pending publication of uniform substantive regulations or a reasoned decision on their particular request consistent with section 1981a requests nationwide.[3] We emphasize that, should the Secretary decide to develop substantive criteria through case-by-case adjudication, he cannot achieve this goal by considering each case in isolation. The Supreme Court succinctly stated, "No matter how rational or consistent with congressional intent a particular decision might be, the determination of eligibility cannot be made on an *ad hoc* basis by the dispenser of the funds." . . . Thus, even if the Secretary does not publish formal findings of fact and conclusions of law in each case, he must clearly articulate the reasons for each section 1981a decision in a manner susceptible to judicial review for an abuse of discretion. . . .

---

[3] To the extent that the Secretary argues that the FmHA in fact made a reasoned decision to deny deferral relief to the Allisons, we affirm the district court's holding that the reasons given for that denial were "conclusory, unsupported,and contradictory," and the decision was thus an abuse of discretion. . . .

III.

CONCLUSION

We realize that the plight of many farmers throughout the nation is so bleak that the forbearance of creditors will not save their operations. We are also aware, however, that the agricultural industry is especially vulnerable to the changing winds of time, nature, fate, and the economy; farmers of skill, perseverance, and dedication are no less vulnerable. Congress in 1978 clearly expressed its intent to assist farmers blown astray by these winds by granting those who could show that their inability to meet their financial obligations was temporary more time to repay their debts to the government. It commissioned the Secretary to implement this intent not as a private banker, but as a public broker. We view the Secretary's conscious disregard of section 1981a as contrary to that commission, and therefore affirm the injunction on foreclosure of the Allisons' farm until the intent of Congress becomes the action of the Secretary.

NOTES AND QUESTIONS

4-50. Do the guidelines used in *Heckler* increase or decrease the fairness of the agency's procedures, when viewed through the eyes of the applicants? Are these provisions too rigid? Should some provision of administrative equity be allowed to operate? Would that undercut the goal of the guidelines?

4-51. Does the nature of the decisions that must be made in *Heckler* require the kind of grid set forth in this case? How much discretion is there in the application of these rules to individual cases?

4-52. Why does the agency's subsequent reversal in 1981 of the ALJ's decisions in 1979 say about the arbitrary nature of these proceedings? On what basis do you suppose the second ALJ determined that Ms. Campbell was "sad"? How many jobs constitute a sufficient number? What if all those jobs are concentrated in a distant area of the country?

4-53. What is the effect of requiring rules in *Allison v. Block*? Do they increase the fairness of the process? Why can't the agency in that case rely fully on its discretion to foreclose loans like those in this proceeding? Must public agencies operate differently from banks? Why?

4-54. Does the use of such permissive language as "may permit" in section 1981a suggest a greater degree of discretion? How might Congress have supplied more explicit direction to the Secretary? Why might they have elected not to do so?

4-55. Would APA section 553(a)(2) exempt the Secretary from using informal rulemaking in this case? Is that why the court makes reference to "formal rulemaking" in Part II B? What kind of rulemaking proceedings would you recommend, if you were the Secretary's general counsel? Why?

Chapter 5
INFORMAL AGENCY ACTION AND ALTERNATIVES TO DISPUTE RESOLUTION

§ 5.01 Introduction

Formal adjudicatory and rulemaking procedures apply to a very small percentage of the decisions made by administrative agencies. More than ninety percent of administrative agency decisions are made informally and are not subject to either the adjudicatory or rulemaking requirements of the APA.[1] This is as it should be. Informal agency processes have been aptly described as "the lifeblood of the administrative process."[2] They include all sorts of decisions, such as personnel decisions, in-house organizational decisions, individual license applications, inspections, tests and a variety of other agency activities necessary for the agency to administer what are often high-volume case loads and to function smoothly on a day-to-day basis. Informal agency decisions, in short, comprise the everyday business of an administrative agency's substantive agenda.

To judicialize all of these various activities undoubtedly would result in stagnation and inability on the part of agencies to function effectively. Yet, it would be wrong to assume that all of these activities are trivial. Many informal agency actions can have profound public impact and individual effects. An important concern of this chapter is to consider what kinds of informal agency actions should be subject to some procedural protection. How should those actions be defined? How much procedural protection should be afforded? Who should make these procedural determinations and when should there be judicial review?

The APA does not deal explicitly with informal adjudication, though it does speak directly to informal agency decisionmaking. Section 555(e) applies to an agency denial "in whole or in part of a written application, petition, or other request of an interested person made in connection with any agency proceedings." Except in affirming a prior denial or when the denial is self-explanatory, the notice of denial shall be accompanied by "a brief statement of the grounds for denial." Most informal agency actions lie outside the purview of this APA provision. As the following cases make clear, however, this does not mean that such informal actions always escape judicial review.

Consider the following case. Was judicial review justified? We will examine the standards of judicial review courts use in Chapter 8, *infra*. Our focus with this case is on the type of decision the agency made. What was the precise agency action that gave rise to this case? How would you characterize this

---

[1] *See* Freidman, *Summary Action By Administrative Agencies*, 40 U. CHI. L. REV. 1 (1972).

[2] *Final Report of the Attorney General's Committee on Administrative Procedure*, S. Doc. No. 8, 77th Cong., 1st. Sess. 35 (1941).

action? Was it an order? How does the Court characterize it? Given the Court's characterization, what follows legally? Why?

§ 5.02 Informal Agency Adjudication

CITIZENS TO PRESERVE OVERTON PARK v. VOLPE

United States Supreme Court
401 U.S. 402 (1971)

Opinion of the Court by MR. JUSTICE MARSHALL, announced by MR. JUSTICE STEWART.

The growing public concern about the quality of our natural environment has prompted Congress in recent years to enact legislation designed to curb the accelerating destruction of our country's natural beauty. We are concerned in this case with § 4(f) of the Department of Transportation Act of 1966, as amended,[2] and § 18(a) of the Federal-Aid Highway Act of 1968, 82 Stat. 823, 23 U.S.C. § 138. . . . These statutes prohibit the Secretary of Transportation from authorizing the use of federal funds to finance the construction of highways through public parks if a "feasible and prudent" alternative route exists. If no such route is available, the statutes allow him to approve construction through parks only if there has been "all possible planning to minimize harm" to the park.

Petitioners, private citizens as well as local and national conservation organizations, contend that the Secretary has violated these statutes by authorizing the expenditure of federal funds for the construction of a six-lane interstate highway through a public park in Memphis, Tennessee. Their claim was rejected by the District Court, which granted the Secretary's motion for summary judgment, and the Court of Appeals for the Sixth Circuit affirmed. After oral argument, this Court granted a stay that halted construction and, treating the application for the stay as a petition for certiorari, granted review. 400 U.S. 939 [(1970)]. We now reverse the judgment below and remand for further proceedings in the District Court.

Overton Park is a 342-acre city park located near the center of Memphis. The park contains a zoo, a nine-hole municipal golf course, an outdoor theater, nature trails, a bridle path, an art academy, picnic areas, and 170 acres of

---

[2] "It is hereby declared to be the national policy that special effort should be made to preserve the natural beauty of the countryside and public park and recreation lands, wildlife and waterfowl refuges, and historic sites. The Secretary of Transportation shall cooperate and consult with the Secretaries of the Interior, Housing and Urban Development, and Agriculture, and with the States in developing transportation plans and programs that include measures to maintain or enhance the natural beauty of the lands traversed. After August 23, 1968, the Secretary shall not approve any program or project which requires the use of any publicly owned land from a public park, recreation area, or wildlife and waterfowl refuge of national, State, or local significance as determined by the Federal, State, or local officials having jurisdiction thereof, or any land from an historic site of national, State, or local significance as so determined by such officials unless (1) there is no feasible and prudent alternative to the use of such land, and (2) such program includes all possible planning to minimize harm to such park, recreational area, wildlife and waterfowl refuge, or historic site resulting from such use."

forest. The proposed highway, which is to be a six-lane, high-speed, expressway, will sever the zoo from the rest of the park. Although the roadway will be depressed below ground level except where it crosses a small creek, 26 acres of the park will be destroyed. . . .

Although the route through the park was approved by the Bureau of Public Roads in 1956 and by the Federal Highway Administrator in 1966, the enactment of § 4(f) of the Department of Transportation Act prevented distribution of federal funds for the section of the highway designated to go through Overton Park until the Secretary of Transportation determined whether the requirements of § 4(f) had been met. Federal funding for the rest of the project was, however, available; and the state acquired a right-of-way on both sides of the park.[14] In April 1968, the Secretary announced that he concurred in the judgment of local officials that I-40 should be built through the park. And in September 1969 the State acquired the right-of-way inside Overton Park from the city.[15] Final approval for the project — the route as well as the design — was not announced until November 1969, after Congress had reiterated in § 138 of the Federal-Aid Highway Act that highway construction through public parks was to be restricted. Neither announcement approving the route and design of I-40 was accompanied by a statement of the Secretary's factual findings. He did not indicate why he believed there were no feasible and prudent alternative routes or why design changes could not be made to reduce the harm to the park.

Petitioners contend that the Secretary's action is invalid without such formal findings and that the Secretary did not make an independent determination but merely relied on the judgment of the Memphis City Council. . . .

Respondents argue that it was unnecessary for the Secretary to make formal findings, and that he did, in fact, exercise his own independent judgment which was supported by the facts. In the District Court, respondents introduced affidavits, prepared specifically for this litigation, which indicated that the Secretary had made the decision and that the decision was supportable. These affidavits were contradicted by affidavits introduced by petitioners. . . .

The District Court and the Court of Appeals found that formal findings by the Secretary were not necessary and refused to order the deposition of the former Federal Highway Administrator because those courts believed that probing of the mental processes of an administrative decisionmaker was prohibited. And, believing that the Secretary's authority was wide and reviewing courts' authority narrow in the approval of highway routes, the lower courts held that the affidavits contained no basis for a determination that the Secretary had exceeded his authority.

We agree that formal findings were not required. But we do not believe that in this case judicial review based solely on litigation affidavits was adequate.

---

[14] The Secretary approved these acquisitions in 1967 shortly after the effective date of § 4(f).

[15] The State paid the City $2,000,000 for the 26-acre right-of-way and $206,000 to the Memphis Park Commission to replace park facilities that were to be destroyed by the highway. The city of Memphis has used $1,000,000 of these funds to pay for a new 160-acre park and it is anticipated that additional parkland will be acquired with the remaining money.

A threshold question — whether petitioners are entitled to any judicial review — is easily answered. Section 701 of the Administrative Procedure Act — provides that the action of "each authority of the Government of the United States," which includes the Department of Transportation, is subject to judicial review except where "agency action is committed to agency discretion by law." In this case, there is no indication that Congress sought to prohibit judicial review and there is most certainly no "showing of 'clear and convincing evidence' of a . . . legislative intent" to restrict access to judicial review. *Abbott Laboratories v. Gardner,* 387 U.S. 136, 141 (1967). . . .

Similarly, the Secretary's decision here does not fall within the exception for action "committed to agency discretion." This is a very narrow exception. Berger, *Administrative Arbitrariness and Judicial Review,* 65 COLUM. L. REV. 55 (1965). The legislative history of the Administrative Procedure Act indicates that it is applicable in those rare instances where "statutes are drawn in such broad terms that in a given case there is no law to apply." S. Rep. No. 752, 79th Cong., 1st Sess., 26 (1945).

Section 4(f) of the Department of Transportation Act and § 138 of the Federal-Aid Highway Act are clear and specific directives. Both the Department of Transportation Act and the Federal-Aid Highway Act provide that the Secretary "shall not approve any program or project" that requires the use of any public parkland "unless (1) there is no feasible and prudent alternative to the use of such land, and (2) such program includes all possible planning to minimize harm to such park. . . ." This language is a plain and explicit bar to the use of federal funds for construction of highways through parks — only the most unusual situations are exempted.

Despite the clarity of the statutory language, respondents argue that the Secretary has wide discretion. They recognize that the requirement that there be no "feasible" alternative route admits of little administrative discretion. For this exemption to apply the Secretary must find that as a matter of sound engineering it would not be feasible to build the highway along any other route. Respondents argue, however, that the requirement that there be no other "prudent" route requires the Secretary to engage in a wide-ranging balancing of competing interests. They contend that the Secretary should weigh the detriment resulting from the destruction of parkland against the cost of other routes, safety considerations, and other factors, and determine on the basis of the importance that he attaches to these other factors whether, on balance, alternative feasible routes would be "prudent."

But no such wide-ranging endeavor was intended. It is obvious that in most cases considerations of cost, directness of route, and community disruption will indicate that parkland should be used for highway construction whenever possible. Although it may be necessary to transfer funds from one jurisdiction to another, there will always be a smaller outlay required from the public purse when parkland is used since the public already owns the land and there will be no need to pay for right-of-way. And since people do not live or work in parks, if a highway is built on parkland no one will have to leave his home or give up his business. Such factors are common to substantially all highway construction. Thus, if Congress intended these factors to be on an equal footing with preservation of parkland there would have been no need for the statutes.

Congress clearly did not intend that cost and disruption of the community were to be ignored by the Secretary.[28] But the very existence of the statutes[29] indicates that protection of parkland was to be given paramount importance. The few green havens that are public parks were not to be lost unless there were truly unusual factors present in a particular case or the cost or community disruption resulting from alternative routes reached extraordinary magnitudes. If the statutes are to have any meaning, the Secretary cannot approve the destruction of parkland unless he finds that alternative routes present unique problems.

Plainly, there is "law to apply" and thus the exemption for action "committed to agency discretion" is inapplicable. But the existence of judicial review is only the start: the standard for review must also be determined. . . . [The Court then considered the applicability of various standards of review.]

Petitioners argue that the Secretary's approval of the construction of I-40 through Overton Park is subject to [either substantial evidence or *de novo* review]. . . . Neither of these standards is, however, applicable.

Review under the substantial-evidence test is authorized only when the agency action is taken pursuant to a rulemaking provision of the Administrative Procedure Act itself, 5 U.S.C. § 553 . . . or when the agency action is based on a public adjudicatory hearing. See 5 U.S.C. §§ 556, 557. . . . The Secretary's decision to allow the expenditure of federal funds to build [the highway] through Overton Park was plainly not an exercise of a rulemaking function. . . . And the only hearing that is required by either the Administrative Procedure Act or the statutes regulating the distribution of federal funds for highway construction is a public hearing conducted by local officials for the purpose of informing the community about the proposed project and eliciting community views on the design and route. 23 U.S.C. § 128. . . . The hearing is nonadjudicatory, quasi-legislative in nature. It is not designed to produce a record that is to be the basis of agency action — the basic requirement for substantial-evidence review. . . .

Petitioners' alternative argument also fails. *De novo* review of whether the Secretary's decision was "unwarranted by the facts" is authorized by § 706(2)(F) in only two circumstances. First, such *de novo* review is authorized when the action is adjudicatory in nature and the agency factfinding procedures are inadequate. And, there may be independent judicial factfinding when issues that were not before the agency are raised in a proceeding to enforce nonadjudicatory agency action. . . . Neither situation exists here.

---

[28] The legislative history indicates that the Secretary is not to limit his consideration to information supplied by state and local officials but is to go beyond this information and reach his own independent decision. 114 Cong. Rec. 24036-24037.

[29] The legislative history of both § 4(f) of the Department of Transportation Act, . . . and § 138 of the Federal Aid Highway Act . . . is ambiguous. The legislative committee reports tend to support respondents' view that the statutes are merely general directives to the Secretary requiring him to consider the importance of parkland as well as cost, community disruption, and other factors. See, e.g., S. Rep. No. 1340, 90th Cong., 2d Sess., 19; H.R. Rep. No. 1537, 90th Cong., 2d Sess., 12. Statements by proponents of the statutes as well as the Senate committee report on § 4(f) indicate, however, that the Secretary was to have limited authority. See, e.g., 114 Cong. Rec. 24033-24037; S. Rep. No. 1569, 89th Cong., 2d Sess., 22. See also H.R. Conf. Rep. No. 2236, 89th Cong., 2d Sess., 25. Because of this ambiguity it is clear that we must look primarily to the statutes themselves to find the legislative intent.

Even though there is no *de novo* review in this case and the Secretary's approval of the route of I-40 does not have ultimately to meet the substantial-evidence test, the generally applicable standards of § 706 require the reviewing court to engage in a substantial inquiry. Certainly, the Secretary's decision is entitled to a presumption of regularity. . . . But that presumption is not to shield his action from a thorough, probing, in-depth review.

The court is first required to decide whether the Secretary acted within the scope of his authority. . . . This determination naturally begins with a delineation of the scope of the Secretary's authority and discretion. L. Jaffe, *Judicial Control of Administrative Action* 359 (1965). As has been shown, Congress has specified only a small range of choices that the Secretary can make. Also involved in this initial inquiry is a determination of whether on the facts the Secretary's decision can reasonably be said to be within that range. The reviewing court must consider whether the Secretary properly construed his authority to approve the use of parkland as limited to situations where there are no feasible alternative routes or where feasible alternative routes involve uniquely difficult problems. And the reviewing court must be able to find that the Secretary could have reasonably believed that in this case there are no feasible alternatives or that alternatives do involve unique problems.

Scrutiny of the facts does not end, however, with the determination that the Secretary has acted within the scope of his statutory authority. Section 706(2)(A) requires a finding that the actual choice made was not "arbitrary, capricious, an abuse of discretion or otherwise not in accordance with law." . . . To make this finding the court must consider whether the decision was based on a consideration of the relevant factors and whether there has been a clear error of judgment. . . . Although this inquiry into the facts is to be searching and careful, the ultimate standard of review is a narrow one. The court is not empowered to substitute its judgment for that of the agency.

The final inquiry is whether the Secretary's action followed the necessary procedural requirements. Here the only procedural error alleged is the failure of the Secretary to make formal findings and state his reason for allowing the highway to be built through the park.

Undoubtedly, review of the Secretary's action is hampered by his failure to make such findings, but the absence of formal findings does not necessarily require that the case be remanded to the Secretary. Neither the Department of Transportation Act nor the Federal-Aid Highway Act requires such formal findings. Moreover, the Administrative Procedure Act requirements that there be formal findings in certain rulemaking and adjudicatory proceedings do not apply to the Secretary's action here. . . . And although formal findings may be required in some cases in the absence of statutory directives when the nature of the agency action is ambiguous, those situations are rare. . . . Plainly, there is no ambiguity here; the Secretary has approved the construction of I-40 through Overton Park and has approved a specific design for the project.

. . . .

. . . Moreover, there is an administrative record that allows the full, prompt review of the Secretary's action that is sought without additional delay which would result from having a remand to the Secretary.

§ 5.02   INFORMAL AGENCY ACTION   441

That administrative record is not, however, before us. The lower courts based their review on the litigation affidavits that were presented. These affidavits were merely *"post hoc"* rationalizations, *Burlington Truck Lines v. United States,* 371 U.S. 156, 168-169 (1962), which have traditionally been found to be an inadequate basis for review. *Burlington Truck Lines v. United States, supra*; *SEC v. Chenery Corp.,* 318 U.S. 80, 87 (1943). And they clearly do not constitute the "whole record" compiled by the agency: the basis for review required by § 706 of the Administrative Procedure Act. . . .

Thus it is necessary to remand this case to the District Court for plenary review of the Secretary's decision. That review is to be based on the full administrative record that was before the Secretary at the time he made his decision. But since the bare record may not disclose the factors that were considered or the Secretary's construction of the evidence it may be necessary for the District Court to require some explanation in order to determine if the Secretary acted within the scope of his authority and if the Secretary's action was justifiable under the applicable standard.

The court may require the administrative officials who participated in the decision to give testimony explaining their action. Of course, such inquiry into the mental processes of administrative decisionmakers is usually to be avoided. *United States v. Morgan,* 313 U.S. 409, 422 (1941). And where there are administrative findings that were made at the same time as the decision, as was the case in *Morgan,* there must be a strong showing of bad faith or improper behavior before such inquiry may be made. But here there are no such formal findings and it may be that the only way there can be effective judicial review is by examining the decisionmakers themselves. . . .

The District Court is not, however, required to make such an inquiry. It may be that the Secretary can prepare formal findings including the information required by DOT Order 5610.1 that will provide an adequate explanation for his action. Such an explanation will, to some extent, be a *"post hoc* rationalization"* and thus must be viewed critically. If the District Court decides that additional explanation is necessary, that court should consider which method will prove the most expeditious so that full review may be had as soon as possible.

Reversed and remanded.

MR. JUSTICE DOUGLAS took no part in the consideration or decision of this case. [MR. JUSTICE BLACK, with whom MR. JUSTICE BRENNAN concurred, dissented stating "I do not agree that the whole matter should be remanded to the District Court. I think the case should be sent back to the Secretary of Transportation." MR. JUSTICE BLACKMUN concurred with the majority, but filed a separate opinion.]

CAMP v. PITTS

United States Supreme Court
411 U.S. 138 (1973)

PER CURIAM.

In its present posture this case presents a narrow, but substantial, question with respect to the proper procedure to be followed when a reviewing court determines that an administrative agency's stated justification for informal action does not provide an adequate basis for judicial review.

In 1967, respondents submitted an application to the Comptroller of the Currency for a certificate authorizing them to organize a new bank in Hartsville, South Carolina. . . . On the basis of information received from a national bank examiner and from various interested parties, the Comptroller denied the application and notified respondents of his decision through a brief letter, which stated in part: "[W]e have concluded that the factors in support of the establishment of a new National Bank in this area are not favorable." No formal hearings were required by the controlling statute or guaranteed by the applicable regulations, although the latter provided for hearings when requested and when granted at the discretion of the Comptroller. Respondents did not request a formal hearing but asked for reconsideration. That request was granted and a supplemental field examination quest was granted and a supplemental field examination was conducted, whereupon the Comptroller again denied the application, this time stating in a letter that "we were unable to reach a favorable conclusion as to the need factor," and explaining that conclusion to some extent.[2] Respondents then brought an action in federal district court seeking review of the Comptroller's decision. The entire administrative record was placed before the court, and, upon an examination of that record and of the two letters of explanation, the court granted summary judgment against respondents, holding that *de novo* review was not warranted in the circumstances and finding that "although the Comptroller may have erred, there is substantial basis for his determination, and . . . it was neither capricious nor arbitrary." 329 F. Supp. 1302, 1308. On appeal, the Court of Appeals did not reach the merits. Rather, it held the Comptroller's ruling was "unacceptable" because "its basis" was not stated with sufficient clarity to permit judicial review. . . . For the present, the Comptroller does not challenge this aspect of the court's decision. He does, however, seek review here of the procedures that the Court of Appeals specifically ordered to be followed in the District Court on remand. The court held that the case should be remanded "for a trial *de novo* before the District Court" because "the Comptroller has twice inadequately and inarticulately resolved the [respondents'] presentation." The court further specified that in the District Court, respondents "will open the trial with proof of their application and compliance with the statutory inquiries, and proffer of any other relevant evidence." Then, "[t]estimony may . . . be adduced by the Comptroller or intervenors manifesting opposition, if any, to the new bank." On the basis of the record thus made, the District Court was instructed to make its own findings of fact and conclusions of law in order to determine "whether the [respondents] have

---

[2] The letter reads in part:

On each application we endeavor to develop the need and convenience factors in conjunction with all other banking factors and in this case we were unable to reach a favorable conclusion as to the need factor. The record reflects that this market area is now served by the People's Bank with deposits of $7.2MM, the Bank of Hartsville with deposits of $12.8MM, the First Federal Savings and Loan Association with deposits of $8.2MM and the Sonoco Employees Credit Union with deposits of $6.5MM. The aforementioned are as of December 31, 1968.

shown by a preponderance of evidence that the Comptroller's ruling is capricious or an abuse of discretion." 463 F.2d, at 634.

We agree with the Comptroller that the trial procedures thus outlined by the Court of Appeals for the remand in this case are unwarranted under present law.

Unquestionably, the Comptroller's action is subject to judicial review under the Administrative Procedure Act (APA), 5 U.S.C. § 701. . . . But is also clear that neither the National Bank Act nor the APA requires the Comptroller to hold a hearing or to make formal findings on the hearing record when passing on applications for new banking authorities. . . .

The appropriate standard for review was, accordingly, whether the Comptroller's adjudication was "arbitrary, capricious, an abuse of discretion, or otherwise not in accordance with law," as specified in 5 U.S.C. § 706(2)(A). In applying that standard, the focal point for judicial review should be the administrative record already in existence, not some new record made initially in the reviewing court. . . .

If, as the Court of Appeals held and as the Comptroller does not now contest, there was such failure to explain administrative action as to frustrate effective judicial review, the remedy was not to hold a *de novo* hearing but, as contemplated by *Overton Park,* to obtain from the agency, either through affidavits or testimony, such additional explanation of the reasons for the agency decision as may prove necessary. We add a caveat, however. Unlike *Overton Park,* in the present case there was contemporaneous explanation of the agency decision. The explanation may have been curt, but it surely indicated the determinative reason for the final action taken: the finding that a new bank was an uneconomic venture in light of the banking needs and the banking services already available in the surrounding community. The validity of the Comptroller's action must, therefore, stand or fall on the propriety of that finding, judged, of course, by the appropriate standard of review. If that finding is not sustainable on the administrative record made, then the Comptroller's decision must be vacated and the matter remanded to him for further consideration. . . . It is in this context that the Court of Appeals should determine whether and to what extent, in the light of the administrative record, further explanation is necessary to a proper assessment of the agency's decision.

The petition for certiorari is granted, the judgment of the Court of Appeals is vacated, and the case is remanded for further proceedings consistent with this opinion.

It is so ordered.

NOTES AND QUESTIONS

5-1. What was the nature of the agency action involved in *Overton Park*? Do you agree with the Court's characterization of that action?

5-2. How do you think the decision in *Overton Park* was really made? Assume that the Secretary of Transportation is busily making a series of important phone calls, preparing a speech he is to give next week and worrying about hiring a new staff assistant when one of his staffers puts her head in his office and says: "Chief, what are we going to do about those highway funds for Memphis?" The Secretary responds: "I'm not sure, but I am getting a lot of pressure to go ahead. The Memphis City Council is for it. What do you think?" The staff assistant replies: "I think it's a good route — cheap, no houses are destroyed, no neighborhoods are split in two and as far as the park is concerned, I understand that the City plans to use the money it receives for it to create new parks throughout the city." Just then the phone rings. It's the White House. As he picks up, the Secretary says: "I don't have any more time to deal with this. Sounds O.K. Let it roll."

Is this kind of decision susceptible to judicial review? Should it be? Would it be unduly restrictive of the decisionmaking process if a court concluded that, under such circumstances, memoranda should be prepared contemporaneously with a decision of this kind setting out the legal justifications for the agency's actions?

5-3. Suppose that the staffer in the decisionmaking scenario described above testifies concerning her statements about the city's plans to use the money it receives for the park to create new parks throughout the city. Would that satisfy Section 4(f)'s requirement that the Secretary consider alternatives? What does Section 4(f) require the Secretary to do and how do we know he has done it? Can we assume that he will uphold the law that applies to him? Is there a presumption to this effect? Should there be?

5-4. Did the Court assume that there was an agency record already in existence in this case? Why? What did the Court think it consisted of? Why does the Court refuse to accept litigation affidavits prepared at the time of trial? What kind of record is it looking for and why?

5-5. The late Professor Nathan Nathanson has written that, in *Overton*, "what starts out by definition to be neither a decision on the administrative record nor an administrative hearing on the record becomes in substance both." Nathanson, *Probing the Mind of the Administrator: Hearing Variations and Standards of Judicial Review Under the Administrative Procedure Act and Other Federal Statutes,* 75 COLUM. L. REV. 721, 768 (1975). Do you agree? On remand, *Overton Park* resulted in a 25-day trial. The District Court ultimately reversed the Secretary's decision and remanded the case to him for another decision in accordance with law. The Secretary ultimately decided against funding the highway. This was clearly a victory for the petitioners in this case, but was it an appropriate role for the Court to play? Is this the kind of informal decision that should be judicialized? Is it too political to be judicialized? Is it too important not to be?

5-6. Knowing what you now know about the litigation to which this case gave rise, what would you, as the staffer for Secretary Volpe, have suggested when he first made this decision? What procedural advice would you have given him? Does *Camp v. Pitts* set forth any helpful procedural guidelines?

5-7. How should an administrative record be developed in a case such as *Overton Park* and *Camp v. Pitts*? What are the costs involved in creating an administrative record by "probing the mental processes of the administrative decisionmakers" involved?

5-8. Why should an agency give reasons for its informal actions? *See Roelfs v. Secretary of Air Force*, 628 F.2d 594 (D.C. Cir. 1980).

PENSION BENEFIT GUARANTY CORPORATION v. LTV CORP.

United States Supreme Court
496 U.S. 633 (1990)

JUSTICE BLACKMUN delivered the opinion of the Court.

In this case we must determine whether the decision of the Pension Benefit Guaranty Corporation (PBGC) to restore certain pension plans under § 4047 of the Employee Retirement Income Security Act of 1974 (ERISA) was, as the Court of Appeals concluded, arbitrary and capricious or contrary to law, within the meaning of the Administrative Procedure Act (APA), 5 U.S.C. § 706.

I

Petitioner PBGC is a wholly owned United States Government corporation . . . modeled after the Federal Deposit Insurance Corporation. . . . The Board of Directors of the PBGC consists of the Secretaries of the Treasury, Labor, and Commerce. . . . The PBGC administers and enforces Title IV of ERISA. Title IV includes a mandatory Government insurance program that protects the pension benefits of over 30 million private-sector American workers who participate in plans covered by the Title. . . .

When a plan covered under Title IV terminates with insufficient assets to satisfy its pension obligations to the employees, the PBGC becomes trustee of the plan, taking over the plan's assets and liabilities. The PBGC then uses the plan's assets to cover what it can of the benefit obligations. . . . The PBGC then must add its own funds to ensure payment of most of the remaining "nonforfeitable" benefits, *i.e.*, those benefits to which participants have earned entitlement under the plan terms as of the date of termination. . . . ERISA does place limits on the benefits PBGC may guarantee upon plan termination, however, even if an employee is entitled to greater benefits under the terms of the plan. . . . In addition, benefit increases resulting from plan amendments adopted within five years of the termination are not paid in full. Finally, active plan participants (current employees) cease to earn additional benefits under the plan upon its termination and lose entitlement to most benefits not yet fully earned as of the date of plan termination. . . .

The cost of the PBGC insurance is borne primarily by employers that maintain ongoing pension plans. Sections 4006 and 4007 of ERISA require these employers to pay annual premiums. . . . The insurance program is also financed by statutory liability imposed on employers who terminate underfunded pension plans. Upon termination, the employer becomes liable to the PBGC for the benefits that the PBGC will pay out. Because the PBGC historically has recovered only a small portion of that liability, Congress repeatedly has been forced to increase the annual premiums. Even with these increases, the PBGC in its most recent annual report noted liabilities of $4 billion and assets of only $2.4 billion, leaving a deficit of over $1.5 billion.

As noted above, plan termination is the insurable event under Title IV. Plans may be terminated "voluntarily" by an employer or "involuntarily" by the PBGC. An employer may terminate a plan voluntarily in one of two ways. It may proceed with a "standard termination" only if it has sufficient assets to pay all benefit commitments. A standard termination thus does not implicate PBGC insurance responsibilities. If an employer wishes to terminate a plan whose assets are insufficient to pay all benefits, the employer must demonstrate that it is in financial "distress" . . . . Neither a standard nor a distress termination by the employer, however, is permitted if termination would violate the terms of an existing collective-bargaining agreement. . . .

The PBGC, though, may terminate a plan "involuntarily," notwithstanding the existence of a collective-bargaining agreement. . . . Section 4042 of ERISA provides that the PBGC may terminate a plan whenever it determines that:

(1) the plan has not met the minimum funding standard required under section 412 of title 26, or has been notified by the Secretary of the Treasury that a notice of deficiency under section 6212 of title 26 has been mailed with respect to the tax imposed under section 4791(a) of title 26,

(2) the plan will be unable to pay benefits when due,

(3) the reportable event described in section 1343(b)(7) of this title has occurred, or

(4) the possible long-run loss of the [PBGC] with respect to the plan may reasonably be expected to increase unreasonably if the plan is not terminated. 29 U.S.C. § 1342(a).

Termination can be undone by PBGC. Section 4047 of ERISA, 29 U.S.C. § 1347, provides:

In the case of a plan which has been terminated under section 1341 or 1342 of this title the [PBGC] is authorized in any such case in which [it] determines such action to be appropriate and consistent with its duties under this subchapter, to take such action as may be necessary to restore the plan to its pretermination status, including, but not limited to, the transfer to the employer or a plan administrator of control or part or all of the remaining assets and liabilities of the plan.

When a plan is restored, full benefits are reinstated, and the employer, rather than the PBGC, again is responsible for the plan's unfunded liabilities.

II

This case arose after respondent The LTV Corporation (LTV Corp.) and many of its subsidiaries, including LTV Steel Company Inc. (LTV Steel) (collectively LTV), in July 1986 filed petitions for reorganization under Chapter 11 of the Bankruptcy Code. At that time, LTV Steel was the sponsor of three defined benefit pension plans (Plans) covered by Title IV of ERISA. Two of the Plans were the products of collective-bargaining negotiations with the United Steelworkers of America (Steelworkers). The third was for non-union salaried employees. Chronically underfunded, the Plans, by late 1986, had unfunded liabilities for promised benefits of almost $2.3 billion. Approximately $2.1 billion of this amount was covered by PBGC insurance.

It is undisputed that one of LTV Corp's principal goals in filing the Chapter 11 petitions was the restructuring of LTV Steel's pension obligations, a goal which could be accomplished if the Plans were terminated and responsibility for the unfunded liabilities was placed on the PBGC. LTV Steel then could negotiate with its employees for new pension arrangements. LTV, however, could not voluntarily terminate the Plans because two of them had been negotiated in collective bargaining. LTV therefore sought to have the PBGC terminate the Plans.

To that end, LTV advised the PBGC in 1986 that it could not continue to provide complete funding for the Plans. PBGC estimated that, without continued funding, the Plans' $2.1 billion underfunding could increase by as much as $65 million by December 1987 and another $63 million by December 1988, unless the Plans were terminated. Moreover, extensive plant shutdowns were anticipated. These shutdowns, if they occurred before the Plans were terminated, would have required the payment of significant "shutdown benefits." The PBGC estimated that such benefits could increase the Plans' liabilities by as much as $300 million to $700 million, of which up to $500 million would be covered by PBGC insurance. Confronted with this information, the PBGC, invoking § 4042(a)(4) of ERISA . . . determined that the Plans should be terminated in order to protect the insurance program from the unreasonable risk of large losses, and commenced termination proceedings in the District Court. With LTV's consent, the Plans were terminated effective January 13, 1987.

In early August 1987, the PBGC determined that the financial factors on which it had relied in terminating the Plans had changed significantly. Of particular significance to the PBGC was its belief that the steel industry, including LTV Steel, was experiencing a dramatic turnaround. As a result, the PBGC concluded it no longer faced the imminent risk, central to its original termination decision, of large unfunded liabilities stemming from plant shutdowns. . . .

The Director issued a notice of restoration on September 22, 1987, indicating the PBGC's intent to restore the terminated Plans. The PBGC notice explained that the restoration decision was based on (1) LTV's establishment of "a retirement program that results in an abuse of the pension plan termination insurance system established by Title IV of ERISA," and (2) LTV's "improved financial circumstances." . . . Restoration meant that the Plans were ongoing, and that LTV again would be responsible for administering and funding them.

LTV refused to comply with the restoration decision. This prompted the PBGC to initiate an enforcement action in the District Court. The court vacated the PBGC's restoration decision, . . .

The Court of Appeals for the Second Circuit affirmed, holding that the PBGC's restoration decision was . . . arbitrary and capricious because the PBGC's decisionmaking process of informal adjudication lacked adequate procedural safeguards. . . .

Because of the significant administrative law questions raised by this case, and the importance of the PBGC's insurance program, we granted certiorari.

III

[The Court found that PBGC's actions were justified on the merits.]

. . . .

Finally, we consider the Court of Appeals' ruling that the agency procedures were inadequate in this particular case. Relying upon a passage in *Bowman Transportation, Inc. v. Arkansas-Best Freight System, Inc.,* 419 U.S. 281, 288, n. 4 (1974), the court held that the PBGC's decision was arbitrary and capricious because the "PBGC neither apprised LTV of the material on which it was to base its decision, gave LTV an adequate opportunity to offer contrary evidence, proceeded in accordance with ascertainable standards" . . . nor provided [LTV] a statement showing its reasoning in applying those standards. . . . The court suggested that on remand the agency was required to do each of these things.

The PBGC argues that this holding conflicts with *Vermont Yankee Nuclear Power Corp. v. Natural Resources Defense Council, Inc.,* 435 U.S. 519 (1978), where, the PBGC contends, this Court made clear that when the Due Process Clause is not implicated and an agency's governing statute contains no specific procedural mandates, the AOA establishes the maximum procedural requirements a reviewing court may impose on agencies. Although *Vermont Yankee* concerned additional procedures imposed by the Court of Appeals for the District of Columbia Circuit on the Atomic Energy Commission when the agency was engaging in informal rulemaking, the PBGC argues that the informal adjudication process by which the restoration decision was made should be governed by the same principles.

Respondents counter by arguing that courts, under some circumstances, do require agencies to undertake additional procedures. As support for this proposition, they rely on *Citizens to Preserve Overton Park, Inc. v. Volpe,* 401 U.S. 402 (1971). In *Overton Park,* the Court concluded that the Secretary of Transportation's "*post hoc* rationalizations" regarding a decision to authorize the construction of a highway did not provide "an [a]dequate basis for [judicial] review" for purposes of § 706 of the APA. . . . Accordingly, the Court directed the District Court on remand to consider evidence that shed light on the Secretary's reasoning at the time he made the decision. Of particular relevance for present purposes, the Court in *Overton Park* intimated that one recourse for the District Court might be a remand to the agency for a fuller explanation of the agency's reasoning at the time of the agency action. . . . Subsequent cases have made clear that remanding to the agency in fact is the preferred course. *See Florida Power & Light Co. v. Lorion,* 470 U.S. 729, 744 (1985) ("[I]f the reviewing court simply cannot evaluate the challenged agency action on the basis of the record before it, the proper course, except in rare circumstances, is to remand to the agency for additional investigation or explanation"). Respondents contend that the instant case is controlled by *Overton Park* rather than *Vermont Yankee,* and that the Court of Appeals' ruling was thus correct.

We believe that respondents' argument is wide of the mark. We begin by noting that although one initially might feel that there is some tension between *Vermont Yankee* and *Overton Park,* the two cases are not necessarily inconsistent. *Vermont Yankee* stands for the general proposition that courts are not free to impose upon agencies specific procedural requirements that have no basis in the APA. . . . At most, *Overton Park* suggests that § 706(2)(A), which directs a court to ensure that an agency action is not arbitrary and capricious or otherwise contrary to law, imposes a general "procedural" requirement of sorts by mandating that an agency take whatever steps it needs to provide an explanation that will enable the court to evaluate the agency's rationale at the time of decision.

Here, unlike in *Overton Park,* the Court of Appeals did not suggest that the administrative record was inadequate to enable the court to fulfill its duties under § 706. Rather, to support its ruling, the court focused on "fundamental fairness" to LTV. . . . With the possible exception of the absence of "ascertainable standards" — by which we are not exactly sure what the Court of Appeals meant — the procedural inadequacies cited by the court all relate to LTV's role in the PBGC's decisionmaking process. But the court did not point to any provision in ERISA or the APA which gives LTV the procedural rights the court identified. Thus, the court's holding runs afoul of *Vermont Yankee* and finds no support in *Overton Park.*

Nor is *Arkansas-Best,* the case on which the Court of Appeals relied, to the contrary. The statement relied upon (which was dictum) said: "A party is entitled, of course, to know the issues on which decision will turn and to be apprised of the factual material on which the agency relies for decision so that he may rebut it." 419 U.S., at 288, n. 4. That statement was entirely correct in the context of *Arkansas-Best,* which involved a formal adjudication by the Interstate Commerce Commission pursuant to the trial-type procedures set forth in §§ 5, 7 and 8 of the APA, 5 U.S.C. §§ 554, 556–557, which include requirements that parties be given notice of "the matters of fact and law asserted," § 554(b)(3), an opportunity for "the submission and consideration of facts [and] arguments," § 554(c)(1), and an opportunity to submit "proposed findings and conclusions" or "exceptions," § 557(c)(1), (2). The determination in this case, however, was lawfully made by informal adjudication, the minimal requirements for which are set forth in the APA, 5 U.S.C. § 555, and do not include such elements. A failure to provide them where the Due Process Clause itself does not require them (which has not been asserted here) is therefore not unlawful.

IV

We conclude that the PBGC's failure to consider all potentially relevant areas of law did not render its restoration decision arbitrary and capricious.

We also conclude that the PBGC's anti-follow-on policy, an asserted basis for the restoration decision, is not contrary to clear congressional intent and is based on a permissible construction of § 4047. Finally, we find the procedures employed by the PBGC to be consistent with the APA. Accordingly, the judgment of the Court of Appeals is reversed, and the case is remanded for further proceedings consistent with this opinion.

It is so ordered.

[JUSTICE WHITE, with whom JUSTICE O'CONNOR joined, concurred in part and dissented in part. JUSTICE STEVENS dissented. Their opinions are omitted.]

NOTES AND QUESTIONS

5-9. What is the nature of the decision made by the Pension Benefit Guaranty Corporation (PBGC)? What are the procedural requirements for such a decision? What is the legal basis for those procedural requirements?

5-10. To what extent does *LTV* modify or affect the holding in *Overton Park*? How would you distinguish these two cases? Of what effect is the Court's decision in *LTV* not to require the PBGC to consider factors from statutes other than ERISA?

5-11. What is the nature of the administrative record in this case? How does it compare to that in *Overton Park*? What impact do these differences have on the outcome of *LTV*?

5-12. How does the Court in *LTV* reconcile the decisions in *Vermont Yankee* and *Overton Park*? We shall examine *Vermont Yankee* in detail in Chapter Six, § 6.02[C] *infra*. See also *State Farm Mutual,* Chapter Nine, § 9.06.

5-13. The Court in *LTV* states that "the determination in this case . . . was lawfully made by informal adjudication, the minimal requirements for which are set forth in the APA, 5 U.S.C. § 555 . . . ." Professor Krotoszynski has argued that that would surprise the framers of the APA who thought they had intentionally omitted informal adjudications from the scope of the statute.

Section 555, entitled, "Ancillary Matters," does not seem addressed to informal adjudications per se. Moreover, the Attorney General's Manual confirms this understanding: "Section 6 [5 U.S.C. § 555] defines various procedural rights of private parties which may be incidental to rule making, adjudication, or the exercise of any other agency authority." Thus, it would be accurate to say that section 555 applies to informal adjudications (unless Congress expressly exempts a particular proceeding or the proceeding falls within a matter otherwise exempt from the APA's provisions), but it would be something of an overstatement to suggest that the APA itself addresses, in a direct fashion, informal adjudications.

If the APA exempted, by simply not addressing, informal adjudication from judicial review, one might quibble with the decision, but it would not be a cause to suggest amendment of the APA itself. But, the APA's failure to address informal adjudication does not, in fact, leave such matters outside the scope of judicial review. Instead, plaintiffs must bring challenges to adverse agency actions in informal adjudications under the rubric of either an organic statute or, as is more commonly the case, as a constitutional claim.

Procedural due process, substantive due process, and equal protection all provide a potential basis for challenging an arbitrary agency action in the context of an informal adjudication. One might well ask whether leaving such claims to constitutional common law adjudication makes more sense than amending the APA itself to address such agency action more directly.

In my view, it would be better to provide for statutory review of informal adjudications, at least in some situations. This would lead to more consistent treatment of would-be plaintiffs with functionally identical claims. It also would help to pretermit pesky circuit splits in areas of constitutional law that may charitably be described as "morasses."

Accordingly . . . my proposal for amending the APA would be to adopt a new subsection in 5 U.S.C. § 554 that addresses directly and sets forth minimal procedural safeguards in the context of informal agency adjudications.

Do you agree? What would this provision include?

See Ronald J. Krotoszynski, Jr., *Taming the Tail that Wags the Dog: Ex Post and Ex Ante Constraints on Informal Adjudication*, 56 ADMIN. L. REV. 1057.*

§ 5.03 Administrative Equity

Informal agency actions can take an almost infinite variety of forms and occur within a wide range of contexts. It is impossible to categorize all of them, but there are some kinds of agency actions that take place in many or most agencies. Many agencies, for example, regularly consider requests from individuals or particular, regulated entities for exceptions or waivers to general rules. Similarly, most agencies receive requests for clarification of their rules or interpretations of their meaning in light of certain factual contexts. We refer to these kinds of requests and the agency processes by which they are decided as a form of administrative equity. The resolution of requests like these can be very revealing as to the basic values and norms of the underlying regulatory structure. Like the intersection of nature and culture, requests for exceptions, for example, often highlight the intersection of the market and regulation. Consider the following excerpt:

---

* Copyright © 2004 by American Bar Association. Reprinted by permission.

Alfred C. Aman, Jr., ADMINISTRATIVE EQUITY: AN ANALYSIS OF EXCEPTIONS TO ADMINISTRATIVE RULES

1982 DUKE L.J. 277, 280-283 (1982) *

Administrative equity serves as a bridge between collectively determined rules and the reality of the particular case. It refers to the substantive principles and norms that may justify individual exceptions to rules of general applicability. Administrative equity is thus primarily concerned with the impact of a regulatory scheme on those required to bear the regulatory costs. An entity whose pollution exceeds the maximum level allowed under a certain regulation may, for example, seek a temporary exemption from compliance while the necessary pollution-control equipment is installed. Similarly, an oil producer bound by maximum pricing regulations may seek an exception to these rules when the regulated price is so low that it is no longer profitable to operate certain wells. The principles used by regulators to grant or deny such requests constitute administrative equity. These principles allow the administrator "to rectify the shortcoming . . . of the lawgiver due to the generality of his statement." . . .

The development of administrative jurisdiction over cases challenging the applicability of general rules to particular situations is analogous to the development of jurisdiction in the English Court of Chancery over two types of cases described by Professor Maitland. One type involved petitions that sought justice in individual cases from or against the "king":

> Many of these petitions . . . seek for justice not merely from the king but against the king. If anybody is to be called the wrong doer, it is the king himself. For example, he is in possession of land which has been seized by his officers as an escheat while really the late tenant has left an heir. Now the king can not be sued by action — no writ will go against him; the heir if he wants justice must petition for it humbly.
>
> Such matters as these are referred to the Chancellor.

In the administrative context, the king appears in the form of a secretary, commissioner, or administrator. The "injustices" perpetrated by the king usually involve the imposition of excessive or unnecessary regulatory costs arising from allegedly over-broad rules. In theory, petitions challenging administrative rules of general applicability lie against the administrative king; however, when the challenge is that the rule as applied to a particular entity is unreasonable, the likelihood of prevailing on the merits is slight. The "king" cannot be effectively sued in cases in which the complaint is that the general should not apply to the particular.

Seeking individual exceptions to administrative rules is similar to the development of Chancery jurisdiction over a second type of case described by Professor Maitland. In these cases, the Chancellor intervened because the petitioner could not obtain an effective remedy at common law: "Very often the petitioner requires some relief at the expense of some other person. He complains that for some reason or another he can not get a remedy in

---

* Copyright © 1982 by Alfred C. Aman, Jr. All rights reserved.

the ordinary course of justice and yet he is entitled to a remedy." Although in the administrative setting such claims are brought against the "king" rather than against another individual, often the relief granted is "at the expense of some other person." If, for example, one firm is allowed to sell its oil at a price higher than its competitors' prices, or is allowed additional time to install pollution control devices, relief is in effect at the expense of those to whom the general rules continue to apply — the petitioner's competitors. Moreover, just as the inadequacy of the common law courts to provide necessary remedies contributed to the rise of the English Court of Chancery, the inadequacy of judicial remedies for administrative equitable claims gives rise to a similar institutional need in modern times.

The inability of judicial review of administrative action to provide individualized relief is attributable to established constitutional and administrative law doctrines. Legislatures enjoy enormous discretion when devising regulatory statutes, particularly in the area of economic regulation. When a litigant asserts that an economic regulation is unconstitutional, the test applied is whether there is a rational basis for the legislature's action. The use of a rational-basis test almost ensures that the statute will be upheld. Thus, attacks on the overall reasonableness of an economic regulatory statute almost never succeed. There is usually no basis for constitutional attack when economic legislation is classified in a plausible way, despite its unequal impact on some or its unreasonableness as applied to a particular party. In extreme cases, a constitutional claim of taking might lie, but the likelihood of success in such cases is remote. Generally, courts look to the overall scope and purpose of the statute, not to its individual impact.

Similarly, the substantive validity of rules promulgated by an agency traditionally has been subject to a two-pronged test that presumes the validity of the rule. The first question is whether the rule is within the agency's authority, as set forth in its enabling act. If it is, the rule is upheld unless it is "arbitrary and capricious and an abuse of discretion." A corollary of the arbitrary-and-capricious standard is the maxim that "courts will not substitute their judgment for that of the administrator." As a result, substantive attacks on the statute authorizing the regulation or on the rules promulgated pursuant to that statute usually have little chance of success. Though the king can be sued, it is often fruitless to try to invalidate a statute or a rule on the ground that it affects one or a few of those who are otherwise validly regulated in an arguably unreasonable manner.

There are, of course, other ways to challenge the validity of a rule as applied. The interested party can engage in prohibited conduct, be prosecuted, and then raise his peculiar circumstances as a defense. The kinds of claims the accused may wish to make, however, are not likely to constitute a valid substantive defense to an enforcement action, but will be more in the nature of a plea for mercy at the sentencing stage. This plea for mercy is cold comfort for those who believe that economic survival compels them to disregard or "aggressively interpret" the law involved.

Pre-enforcement judicial review offers a solution to the obey-or-be-prosecuted dilemma and an alternative to agency exception relief as well. Courts have limited this type of review, however, by requiring that litigants exhaust administrative remedies before seeking pre-enforcement review. Even when pre-enforcement judicial review is available, the scope of the issues that may be raised usually is limited to issues of law.

Finally, there is a disguised way of challenging the applicability of a rule to a particular situation. One may raise procedural issues that apply to rulemaking in general, but that are really the result of substantive concerns. Such procedural challenges are often made to delay the application of a rule as much as to create an opportunity for a more favorable substantive result. To the extent that administrative equitable processes eliminate the need for some of these claims, the regulatory process benefits.

In short, courts generally have not been receptive to legal arguments that seek to invalidate a rule, particularly when the claim is that the rule in question appears unreasonable when applied to one or a few of those it regulates. Such claims seldom rise to constitutional dimensions and rarely enable a court to conclude that the agency acted in an arbitrary or capricious manner. If such a "petitioner wants justice, he must petition for it humbly. Such matters as these are referred to the Chancellor." Just as equitable remedies were needed because common law remedies were often unavailable or too inflexible, administrative equity of a substantive nature is necessary because individualized judicial remedies are usually not available, pre-enforcement judicial review is often too limited, and prosecution is too high a price to pay for noncompliance, particularly when it is unclear what may be pleaded as a defense. Many regulatory systems provide an explicit means of seeking equitable relief.

In light of this above discussion, consider the following case. How much process should the petitioner have in a proceeding such as this?

CHEMICAL MANUFACTURERS ASSOCIATION v. NATURAL RESOURCES DEFENSE COUNCIL, INC.

United States Supreme Court
470 U.S. 116 (1985)

JUSTICE WHITE delivered the opinion of the Court.

These cases present the question whether the Environmental Protection Agency (EPA) may issue certain variances from toxic pollutant effluent limitations promulgated under the Clean Water Act. . . .

I

As part of a consolidated lawsuit, respondent Natural Resources Defense Council (NRDC) sought a declaration that § 301(l) of the Clean Water Act, 33 U.S.C. § 1311(l), prohibited EPA from issuing "fundamentally different factor" (FDF) variances for pollutants listed as toxic under the Act. Petitioners EPA and Chemical Manufacturers Association (CMA) argued otherwise. . . .

The 1977 amendments to the Clean Water Act reflected Congress' increased concern with the dangers of toxic pollutants. The Act, as then amended, allows specific statutory modifications of effluent limitations for economic and water-quality reasons in §§ 301(c) and (g). Section 301(1), however, added by the 1977 amendments, provides:

> The Administrator may not modify any requirement of this section as it applies to any specific pollutant which is on the toxic pollutant list under section 307(a)(1) of this Act. 91 Stat. 1590.

In the aftermath of the 1977 amendments, EPA continued its practice of occasionally granting FDF variances for BPT requirements. The Agency also promulgated regulations explicitly allowing FDF variances for pretreatment standards and BAT requirements. Under these regulations, EPA granted FDF variances, but infrequently.

As part of its consolidated lawsuit, respondent NRDC here challenged pretreatment standards for indirect dischargers and sought a declaration that § 301(l) barred any FDF variance with respect to toxic pollutants. In an earlier case, the Fourth Circuit had rejected a similar argument, finding that § 301(l) was ambiguous on the issue of whether it applied to FDF variances and therefore deferring to the administrative agency's interpretation that such variances were permitted. Contrariwise, the Third Circuit here ruled in favor of NRDC, and against petitioners EPA and CMA, holding that § 301(l) forbids the issuance of FDF variances for toxic pollutants. We granted certiorari to resolve this conflict between the Courts of Appeals and to decide this important question of environmental law. We reverse.

II

Section 301(l) states that EPA may not "modify" any requirement of § 301 insofar as toxic materials are concerned. EPA insists that § 301(l) prohibits only those modifications expressly permitted by other provisions of § 301, namely, those that § 301(c) and § 301(g) would allow on economic or water-quality grounds. Section 301(l), it is urged, does not address the very different issue of FDF variances. This view of the agency charged with administering the statute is entitled to considerable deference; and to sustain it, we need not find that it is the only permissible construction that EPA might have adopted but only that EPA's understanding of this very "complex statute" is a sufficiently rational one to preclude a court from substituting its judgment for that of EPA. . . . Of course, if Congress has clearly expressed an intent contrary to that of the Agency, our duty is to enforce the will of Congress. . . .

A

NRDC insists that the language of § 301(l) is itself enough to require affirmance of the Court of Appeals, since on its face it forbids any modifications of the effluent limitations that EPA must promulgate for toxic pollutants. If the word "modify" in § 301(l) is read in its broadest sense, that is, to encompass any change or alteration in the standards, NRDC is correct. But it makes little sense to construe the section to forbid EPA to amend its own standards, even to correct an error or to impose stricter requirements.

Furthermore, reading § 301(l) in this manner would forbid what § 307(b)(2) expressly directs: EPA is there required to "revise" its pretreatment standards "from time to time, as control technology, processes, operating methods, or other alternatives change." As NRDC does and must concede, . . . § 301(l) cannot be read to forbid every change in the toxic waste standards. The word "modify" thus has no plain meaning as used in § 301(l), and is the proper subject of construction by EPA and the courts. NRDC would construe it to forbid the kind of alteration involved in an FDF variance, while the Agency would confine the section to prohibiting the partial modifications that § 301(c) would otherwise permit. Since EPA asserts that the FDF variance is more like a revision permitted by § 307 than it is like a § 301(c) or (g) modification, and since, as will become evident, we think there is a reasonable basis for such a position, we conclude that the statutory language does not foreclose the Agency's view of the statute. We should defer to that view unless the legislative history or the purpose and structure of the statute clearly reveal a contrary intent on the part of Congress. NRDC submits that the legislative materials evince such a contrary intent. We disagree.

B

[The Court then examined the legislative history involved, finding a lack of "unambiguous congressional intention to forbid all FDF waivers with respect to toxic materials."]

. . . .

C

Neither are we convinced that FDF variances threaten to frustrate the goals and operation of the statutory scheme set up by Congress. The nature of FDF variances has been spelled out both by this Court and by the Agency itself. The regulation explains that its purpose is to remedy categories which were not accurately drawn because information was either not available to or not considered by the Administrator in setting the original categories and limitations. . . . An FDF variance does not excuse compliance with a correct requirement, but instead represents an acknowledgment that not all relevant factors were taken sufficiently into account in framing that requirement originally, and that those relevant factors, properly considered, would have justified — indeed, required — the creation of a subcategory for the discharger in question. As we have recognized, the FDF variance is a laudable corrective mechanism, "an acknowledgment that the uniform . . . limitation was set without reference to the full range of current practices, to which the Administrator was to refer." It is, essentially, not an exception to the standard-setting process, but rather a more fine-tuned application of it.

EPA and CMA point out that the availability of FDF variances makes bearable the enormous burden faced by EPA in promulgating categories of sources and setting effluent limitations. Acting under stringent timetables, EPA must collect and analyze large amounts of technical information concerning complex industrial categories. Understandably, EPA may not be apprised of and will fail to consider unique factors applicable to atypical plants during the categorical rulemaking process, and it is thus important that EPA's nationally binding categorical pretreatment standards for indirect dischargers be tempered with the flexibility that the FDF variance mechanism offers, a mechanism repugnant to neither the goals nor the operation of the Act.

III

Viewed in its entirety, neither the language nor the legislative history of the Act demonstrates a clear congressional intent to forbid EPA's sensible variance mechanism for tailoring the categories it promulgates. In the absence of a congressional directive to the contrary, we accept EPA's conclusion that § 301(l) does not prohibit FDF variances. . . .

Here we are not dealing with an agency's change of position with the advent of a different administration, but rather with EPA's consistent interpretation since the 1970's. NRDC argues that its construction of the statute is better supported by policy considerations. But we do not sit to judge the relative wisdom of competing statutory interpretations. Here EPA's construction, fairly understood, is not inconsistent with the language, goals, or operation of the Act. Nor does the administration of EPA's regulation undermine the will of Congress.

The judgment of the Court of Appeals is reversed.

It is so ordered.

JUSTICE MARSHALL, with whom JUSTICE BLACKMUN and JUSTICE STEVENS join, and with whom JUSTICE O'CONNOR joins as to Parts I, II, and III, dissenting.

In these cases, the Environmental Protection Agency (EPA) maintains that it may issue, on a case-by-case basis, individualized variances from the national standards that limit the discharge of toxic water pollutants. EPA asserts this power in the face of a provision of the Clean Water Act that expressly withdraws from the agency the authority to "modify" the national standards for such pollutants. The Court today defers to EPA's interpretation of the Clean Water Act even though that interpretation is inconsistent with the clear intent of Congress, as evidenced by the statutory language, history, structure, and purpose. I had not read our cases to permit judicial deference to an agency's construction of a statute when that construction is inconsistent with the clear intent of Congress.

[In Parts I, II, and III, the dissent argues that both "the plain meaning of the statute and the legislative history show a clear congressional intent to ban all 'modifications.' "]

IV

. . . .

B

. . . FDF variances are not an alternative way of complying with the statutory command to set rules of general applicability. They do not implement the Clean Water Act's technology-based requirements; instead, like §§ 301(c) and (g) modifications, they are case-by-case departures from such requirements. In fact, in the past, EPA itself has referred to FDF variances as "exception[s] to [a] general rule of applicability." . . .

FDF variances not only take the same form as §§ 301(c) and (g) modifications, but they also serve closely analogous functions. . . . [T]he purpose of exceptions is to soften the harshness of general rules. . . . A § 301(c) modification, for example, relieves a firm of its obligation to meet an applicable rule when compliance with that rule would place the firm in a serious hardship. . . . FDF variances also temper — albeit in a slightly different way — the effects of the nationwide, categorical standards. They relieve a firm of its obligation to comply with a rule that would impose on that firm a disproportionate share of the regulatory burden.[21] . . . In fact, EPA itself has characterized FDF variances as "'safety valves' in regulatory schemes of general applicability." . . . Thus, FDF variances are exceptions that provide the type of flexibility that § 301(l) sought to ban.

The Court accepts EPA's present characterization that FDF variances are a hybrid: "more like" a revision permitted by § 307 than like a §§ 301(c) and (g) modification. . . . But a requirement that, by definition, applies to only one discharger cannot be considered "more like" a rule of general applicability than like an exception to such a rule. Clearly, it *is* an exception.

The Court's error is to overlook the distinction between general rules and exceptions. Instead, it focuses on the differences between the grounds for exceptions provided by §§ 301(c) and (g) on the one hand, and by the FDF provisions on the other. Thus, the Court makes its cuts along an entirely different — and irrelevant — axis. For EPA to prevail, the Court must show that Congress found that exceptions based on economic capability or water-quality factors were especially undesirable. If this were true, then exceptions based on other factors would be less undesirable, and it would make sense to decide the cases on the basis of the extent to which the factors taken into account in granting FDF variances differ from §§ 301(c) and (g) factors. The

---

[21] Commentators have identified two categories of exceptions that are relevant in these cases: hardship exceptions and fairness exceptions. *See e.g.*, Aman, *Administrative Equity: An Analysis of Exceptions to Administrative Rules*, 1982 DUKE L.J. 277, 293-294; Shapiro, *Administrative Discretion: The Next Stage*, 92 YALE L.J. 1487, 1504 (1983); Schuck, *When the Exception Becomes the Rule: Regulatory Equity and the Formulation of Energy Policy Through an Exceptions Process*, 1984 DUKE L.J. 163, 283-289. Under this classification, a § 301(c) modification is a hardship exception and an FDF variance is a fairness exception. A § 301(g) modification is a different type of fairness exception. It seeks to ensure that a firm not be forced to comply with the categorical standards when no environmental benefit would accrue from such compliance. *See* Aman, *supra*, at 311-312.

This classification of exceptions is reflected in several statutes. For example, the Department of Energy Organization Act, 42 U.S.C. § 7194(a); the Natural Gas Policy Act, 15 U.S.C. § 3412(c); and the Energy Policy and Conservation Act, 42 U.S.C. § 6393(a)(4), all provide for exceptions based on "special hardship, inequity, or unfair distribution of burdens." Of course, a "special hardship" exception is analogous to a § 301(c) modification; an "inequity or unfair distribution of burdens" exception is analogous to an FDF variance. Thus, the structure of these statutes supports the proposition that an FDF variance is an exception to a general rule. *Cf. Overstreet v. North Shore Corp.*, 318 U.S. 125, 128 (1943) (determining scope of phrase "engaged in interstate commerce" under the Fair Labor Standards Act by reference to use of that term in the Federal Employers' Liability Act).

Court's position, however, is inconsistent with the clear purpose of § 301(l). As I have shown, there is absolutely no reason to believe that this provision was designed to ban §§ 301(c) and (g) modifications because there was something particularly pernicious about such exceptions. . . . Rather, the congressional concern was that exceptions would weaken the standards for the control of toxic pollutants. This concern defines the relevant criterion: whether something is a general rule or an exception to such a rule. Sections 301(c) and (g) modifications are at one end of the axis not because they are based on economic or water-quality factors, but because they are exceptions to general rules. Section 307(b) revisions are at the other end of the axis not because they are based on factors taken into account in setting the standards, but because they are rules of general applicability. Of course, FDF variances, which are nothing but exceptions to general rules, are at the same end of the axis as §§ 301(c) and (g) modifications.

For the foregoing reasons, it is apparent that § 301(l) prohibits FDF variances from the pretreatment standards for toxic pollutants. I therefore dissent.

[JUSTICE O'CONNOR's one paragraph dissent is omitted.]

NOTES AND QUESTIONS

5-14. What is the statutory basis for allowing exceptions in this case? Why would NRDC oppose this interpretation? Does the Constitution require some sort of exception relief?

5-15. Exceptions or waivers to agency rules are somewhat akin to injunctions. If granted, they, in effect, stay the application of a rule to the particular entity seeking the exception. There are, however, a number of other agency devices that seek to provide clarification or interpretation of an agency's rules. The IRS, for example, issues rulings and interpretations aimed at providing guidance to taxpayers. Such devices are often like advisory opinions. The advice an agency gives can come in many forms. It may be through rulings, interpretations or no-action letters, but it might also be over the telephone. A knowledgeable staff person at an agency may seek to be helpful, but what happens if his advice is followed, and it was wrong? Does the party who followed it have a cause of action? Further, even when a ruling is issued, what precedential effect does it have? Can others rely on it? Can the agency change its mind? Consider the following case.

5-16. For a discussion of the role exceptions and implied waivers can play at the EPA, *see* Dennis D. Hirsch, *Bill and Al's XL-ENT Adventure: An Analysis of the EPA's Legal Authority to Implement the Clinton Administration's Project XL,* 1998 U. ILL. L. REV. 129 (1998).

5-17. For a further discussion of exceptions, waivers and other administrative equity devices, *see* Robert L. Glicksman & Sidney A. Shapiro, *Improving Regulation Through Incremental Adjustment,* 52 U. KAN. L. REV. 1179 (2004); Jonathan R. Bolton, *The Case of the Disappearing Statute: A Legal and Policy*

460 ADMINISTRATIVE LAW § 5.03

Critique of the Use of Section 1115 Waivers to Restructure the Medicaid Program, 37 COLUM. J.L. & SOC. PROBS. 91 (2003); Lars Noah, *Administrative Arm-Twisting in the Shadow of Congressional Delegations of Authority*, 1997 WIS. L. REV. 873 (1997); Jim Rossi, *Waivers, Flexibility, and Reviewability*, 72 CHI.-KENT L. REV. 1359 (1997); Marshall J. Breger, *Regulatory Flexibility and the Administrative State*, 32 TULSA L.J. 325 (1996); Bradford C. Mank, *What Comes After Technology: Using an "Exceptions Process" to Improve Residual Risk Regulation of Hazardous Air Pollutants*, 13 STAN. ENVTL. L.J. 263 (1994); Frederick Schauer, *Exceptions*, 58 U. CHI. L. REV. 871 (1991).

KIXMILLER v. SEC

District of Columbia Court of Appeals
492 F.2d 641 (1974)

Before TAMM, ROBINSON and ROBB, CIRCUIT JUDGES.

PER CURIAM:

Petitioner seeks review in this court of advice informally given a corporation by the staff of the Securities and Exchange Commission. The advice was that the staff, for reasons stated, would not recommend action by the Commission respecting the contemplated exclusion from management's proxy materials of a stockholder's proposals for action at a stockholders' meeting. The Commission has refused either to examine the staff's view of the matter or to express a view of its own; it now asserts that we lack jurisdiction to consider the petition for review and urges dismissal. We grant the motion and dismiss the petition.

I

On November 19, 1971, petitioner, a Class B stockholder of the Washington Post Company, informed the company's general counsel of his intention to submit three proposals relating to general business matters for consideration at the 1972 annual meeting of stockholders. He requested that his propositions and supporting statements, which he set out in a letter to the Company, be incorporated into management's proxy materials as allegedly required by proxy rules adopted by the Commission pursuant to Section 14 of the Securities Exchange Act of 1934.

Rule 14a-8(a) of the proxy rules requires the issuer of proxy materials to include any proposals (not otherwise excludable under provisions of the rules) submitted by "any security holder entitled to vote at a meeting of security holders of the issuer." The company, following the procedure established by the rules, informed the Commission's Division of Corporate Finance of its intention to omit petitioner's proposals from its 1972 proxy statements, and sought confirmation that the Division would not urge action by the

Commission on that account. Petitioner filed memoranda and supporting materials in opposition to the request for a no-action decision.

The Division issued a letter opinion on March 8, 1972, stating that it would not recommend that the Commission take enforcement action, and expressing the ground for that decision.[8] Petitioner then asked the Commission to reexamine the Division's ruling; but was later informed that the Commission "declined to review the staff's position or hold an oral hearing . . . [or] to issue an informal statement on the matter." This petition for review followed.

II

Our authority to directly review Commission action springs solely from Section 25(a) of the Securities Exchange Act of 1934, which confines our jurisdiction to "order[s] issued by the Commission. . . ." We think members of the Commission's staff, like staff personnel of other agencies, "have no authority individually or collectively to make 'orders,'" and that, on the contrary, "[o]nly the Commission makes orders." Here the Commission made no order on the merits of petitioner's claim; rather, it emphatically "declined to review the staff's position." It follows that what petitioner seeks to have reviewed in this court is not an "order issued by the Commission."

Petitioner relies heavily on *Medical Committee for Human Rights v. Securities and Exchange Commission,* wherein we reviewed on the merits the Commission's approval of a no-action ruling by its staff. We think, however, that very different jurisdictional consequences flow from the antithetical roles which the Commission played in *Medical Committee* and here. There, after the staff announced that it would not recommend action respecting a company's omission of a stockholder's proposal from its proxy materials, the Commission examined the staff's no-action determination and accepted it. As our opinion in *Medical Committee* recounted, the Commission, "after reviewing the petitioner's proxy claim," "exercised its discretion to review [the] controversy," and "approved the recommendation of the [staff] that no objection be raised. . . ." In sum, *Medical Committee* involved a no-action ruling by the staff which was sanctioned by the Commission, and that, we held, constituted administrative action subject to judicial review.

In sharp contrast to that decision is the Commission's refusal here to in any way probe or pass on the staff's no-action position. The distinction is between the Commission's reexamination and affirmance of the staff's conclusion on the one hand, and the Commission's declension of any review or adjudication on the other. We recognized the vitality of that distinction when in *Medical Committee* we admonished that the availability of judicial review of a staff no-action decision respecting proxy proposals "depends upon the Commission's initial determination to review the staff decision." That precondition is not met here.

---

[8] The letter stated in part:

It would obviously be inconsistent with [the] purpose [of preventing management's proxy materials from being misleading] to require inclusion of a proposal in the proxy materials if the proponent could not legally present it at the meeting. Since there appears to be some basis for [the company's position] this Division will not recommend enforcement action. . . .

III

We are mindful that administrative inaction may become judicially cognizable, and that yet another question here is whether the Commission erred in flatly refusing to deal with petitioner's claim. But assuming, without deciding, that the refusal is otherwise encompassed by Section 25(a),[24] we are not at liberty to override it.

The Securities Exchange Act of 1934 provides that "the Commission may, in its discretion, make such investigations as it deems necessary," and that "it may in its discretion bring an action" in court. An agency's decision to refrain from an investigation or an enforcement action is generally unreviewable and, as to the agency before us, the specifications of the Act leave no doubt on that score.

The Commission, by regulation, has served notice that its informal procedures are ordinarily to be matters of staff activity, and will involve the Commission only when special circumstances so warrant.[29] We discern nothing arbitrary or abusive in this policy as applied in the case at bar. In *Medical Committee,* "we recognize[d] that there is a legitimate domain of administrative discretion in the proxy area," carved out by the necessity that the Commission "process a formidable number of proxy statements in limited time and with insufficient manpower." "Obviously," we said, "not all proxy proposals can or should be given detailed consideration by the full Commission"; and we hastened to add that "even the boldest advocates of judicial review recognize that the agencies' internal management decisions and allocations of priorities are not a proper subject of inquiry by the courts."

The Commission offers informal advice by its staff on a vast number of proxy solicitations.[34] Sheer volume of this wholesome activity belies Commission review in every such instance. It must be remembered that a dissatisfied stockholder is free to litigate proxy-solicitation questions judicially, with or without prior administrative resort to the staff or the Commission. It is for the Commission to initially draw the line on administrative review of staff decisions in this area, and we cannot say that its regulation has done so unreasonably. And finding no legal fault in the Commission's discretionary exercise here, we are powerless to upset it.

---

[24] "Agency action," as defined in the Administrative Procedure Act, "includes . . . failure to act," 5 U.S.C. § 551(13) (1970), and the Act commands the reviewing court to "compel agency action unlawfully withheld or unreasonably delayed." *Id.* § 706(1) (1970). But § 25(a) of the Securities Exchange Act of 1934, which sets our jurisdiction, "applies in terms only to 'orders,' a narrower concept than that of 'agency action' reviewable in district courts. . . ." *Independent Brokers-Dealers Trade Ass'n v. SEC,* 142 U.S. App. D.C. 384, 395, 442 F.2d 132, 143 (1971).

[29] "The informal procedures of the Commission are largely concerned with the rendering of advice and assistance by the Commission's staff to members of the public dealing with the Commission. . . . In certain instances an informal statement of the views of the Commission may be obtained. The staff, upon request, or on its motion will generally present questions to the Commission which involve matters of substantial importance and where the issues are novel or highly complex, although the granting of a request for an informal statement by the Commission is entirely within its discretion." 17 C.F.R. § 202.1(d) (1973).

[34] We are informed by the Commission that during fiscal year 1973, the staff processed 7,023 proxy statements and 141 information statements to be submitted to stockholders in lieu of proxy soliciting materials, and with respect to substantially all of these statements furnished a staff letter commenting on its apparent adequacy under the proxy rules.

Motion to dismiss granted.

NOTES AND QUESTIONS

5-18. Who provided the advice in this case? What form did this advice take? Who is responsible for the accuracy of this advice?

5-19. Should counsel for the corporation be entitled to rely on this advice? Was there any way to make this advice more definitive or final?

5-20. How do you characterize a no-action letter? Is it like a request for an exception or waiver or is it more like a request for a ruling or a declaratory order? Consider the following taxonomy. Where does the no-action letter in *Kixmiller* fit in?

> Administrative equity takes many forms. For example, the Department of Energy Act confers specific power on the Secretary to make "adjustments" to rules of general applicability. The term "adjustment" includes exceptions, exemptions, modifications, rescissions, and interpretations. Similarly, other agencies provide opportunities for waiver, no-action letters, variances, or rulings. All of these "adjustments" provide, in lieu of enforcement proceedings, mechanisms for giving special meaning to rules of general applicability in particular cases.
>
> Administrative adjustments fall into two broad categories. Some are in the nature of declaratory judgments or advisory opinions. Rulings or interpretations, for example, generally determine whether a particular regulation applies to a certain set of facts and, if so, how. Usually, these determinations are made before any action has been taken and apply only to the petitioner. Similarly, rescissions and modifications apply to particular orders and particular petitioners. The second category of adjustments is similar to an injunction. The petitioner does not seek a clarification of how a rule applies; he seeks an order that the rule does not apply to him at all. In effect, this adjustment enjoins application of the rule to the petitioner.

Aman, *supra*, 1982 DUKE L.J. at 286–87.* *See also* Powell, *Sinners, Supplicants and Samaritans: Agency Advice Giving in Relation to Section 554(e) of the Administrative Procedure Act*, 63 N.C. L. REV. 339, 366 (1985).

5-21. Section 554(e) of the APA states that "the agency, with like effect, as in the case of other orders, and its sound discretion, may issue a declaratory order to terminate a controversy or remove uncertainty." As Lubbers and Morant note, however that "[t]he relative disuse of declaratory orders is curious." Jeffrey S. Lubbers & Blake D. Morant, *A Reexamination of Federal Agency Use of Declaratory Orders*, 56 ADMIN. L. REV. 1097, 1100 (2004). We shall examine *infra* the litigation that arose because there was a disagreement concerning an agency's jurisdiction over a particular problem. For example, after the FDA instituted a rulemaking proceeding designed to potentially

---

* Copyright © 1982 by Alfred C. Aman, Jr. All rights reserved.

regulate tobacco products, the agency received over 700,000 comments. The agency, after reading and considering the comments, promulgated a complex regulatory scheme with a 700-page statement of basis and purpose for its rule. Four and one half years later, the Supreme Court's decision in *FDA v. Brown & Williamson Tobacco Corp.*, *infra*, Chapter 8, § 8.04, invalidated the regulations because the agency lacked the statutory jurisdiction to regulate tobacco products. Could the FDA have avoided this expenditure of time and resources by simply issuing a declaratory order that it had jurisdiction to regulate tobacco products under Section 554(e) of the APA? Lubbers and Morant argue:

> [D]eclaratory orders constitute flexible, procedural tools with significant utility, benefiting both agencies and private parties. Agencies (and regulated parties) should therefore consider using declaratory orders to resolve preliminary matters involving jurisdictional questions. In such cases, the declaratory order can efficiently and expeditiously determine the appropriate venue of pending claims or disputes, thereby reserving resources for subsequent litigation of substantive issues associated with a claim. . . .
>
> An agency may issue a declaratory order on its own initiative or at the request of a petitioner. When issued, declaratory orders are as binding and judicially reviewable "as like orders," but whether to issue one is within the discretion of the agency. In this respect, petitions to issue a declaratory order resemble petitions to initiate a rulemaking under § 553(e) of the APA.
>
> The fact that the declaratory order provision falls within the formal adjudication section of the APA (§ 554) would seemingly require agencies to use formal adjudicatory procedures to issue such an order. In many such proceedings, however, the facts are not in dispute; therefore, the agency can use a summary decision process. Moreover, in recent years, numerous courts have upheld agency declaratory orders issued after more informal "paper hearing" processes that are not significantly different from the notice-and-comment rulemaking process.

Jeffrey S. Lubbers & Blake D. Morant, *A Reexamination of Federal Agency Use of Declaratory Orders*, 56 ADMIN. L. REV. 1097, 1100–02.*

PROBLEM 5-1

Assume that a safety commission has issued a rule mandating that only certain kinds of scaffolding be used when constructing buildings of a particular size. The type of scaffolding required is very sturdy and expensive. The Collapso Company rarely builds buildings of the size the Safety Commission is particularly concerned with and it has developed a light-weight and effective

---

* Copyright © 2004 by American Bar Association. Reprinted by permission.

form of scaffolding that is, in its view, as safe as what the rule requires, but half the price. The Company wishes to seek a variance, pursuant to a statutory provision that provides that "the conditions, practices, means, methods, operations or processes used . . . by an employer will provide employment and places of employment to his employees which are as safe and healthful as these which would prevail if he complied with the standard." How would you characterize the kind of variance they are seeking? What are their arguments? Should it be granted?

PROBLEM 5-2

The Lindgren Company manufactures cement and in the process emits pollutants that violate recently passed environmental regulations. The Company sought a variance under a statute that would grant one "only in those extraordinary situations in which the cost of compliance is wholly disproportionate to the benefits; doubts are to be resolved in favor of denial."

(a) Assume that the Company seeks a permanent variance and produces evidence that shows that it is not technologically possible for it to reduce its pollution and continue to manufacture its product. Failure to grant the variance would mean the Company would have to close. The owners would, of course, lose most of their investment and one hundred fifty jobs would be lost. On the other hand, various members of the community and particularly the neighborhood in which the Lindgren Company was located testified that the pollution was manifestly causing problems:

> "It tracks in on my carpet. It is all over the window sills. It is the type of dirt that you cannot clean unless you get a cleaner on a cloth. . . ." "I washed out a white blouse and hung it out on the line . . . and when I went out to get it, it was completely covered. . . ." "I could not sit out in my back lawn when this smoke would come across. . . . You would be sitting there, and all of a sudden you would look down, and you are covered with soot. . . ."

Assume you are a member of the Pollution Control Board that hears this request. What is your decision and why?

(b) Assume that the technology to reduce pollution exists and Lindgren's argument is that it needs a variance for seven months while it switches over to this new technology. If it were to close during that seven month period, it would not have the resources to reopen and change technologies. What would your decision be and why?

PROBLEM 5-3

Assume that the Lindgren Corporation produces its products and emits a certain pollutant called X into the atmosphere. When it combines with another pollutant, Y, the combination is responsible for a kind of acid that is terribly damaging to lakes, rivers, fish and wildlife. Only pollutant X is regulated, not pollutant Y.

Assume further that the Carefree Company has a technology in place that produces the same products as Lindgren but releases only pollutant Y. Since it is unregulated, it can now produce much more efficiently and undersell Lindgren by quite a bit. Lindgren fears it may be going out of business and seeks exception relief under the standard set forth above. What are its arguments? Should it prevail? Is this the proper kind of case for exception relief? What other relief should it seek?

§ 5.04 Conditions and Commitments

In addition to exceptions, waivers, no-action letters, rulings and the like, another common form of informal agency action involves the use of conditions or voluntary commitments. When an applicant applies to an agency for a license or permission to undertake certain kinds of regulated activity, an agency will often authorize the activity on the condition that the applicant undertake certain actions that, in effect, assure the agency that its regulatory goals will be fully carried out. Sometimes these assurances are made voluntarily in the form of voluntary commitments; sometimes, they may appear in a commission order authorizing the activity requested, as a condition of the permission being granted.

The Federal Reserve Board administers the Bank Holding Company Act (BHCA) and, in that capacity, makes extensive use of conditioning powers. Bank holding companies (BHCs) must have the Board's permission if they are to expand their banking interests or acquire certain non-banking interests. They submit their applications to the Federal Reserve where they are first reviewed by certain staff members who work for the Board. There is, at this stage, a good deal of conversation about the particular application and whether or not it is likely to succeed when it is presented to the Board. Certainly, the recommendation of the staff person involved to grant or deny the application can be crucial. Given the numbers of applications and the varied responsibilities of the Federal Reserve Board members, they are not likely to have the time nor the interest to examine each application in any detail.

The staff person in charge often has legitimate concerns about some of the applications. A BHC, for example, may wish to acquire another bank, but in so doing, the combination of banks that will results may have an anticompetitive effect. The staff person may, therefore, be willing to allow the acquisition of one bank if the BHC agrees to divest itself of its holdings in another bank.

Thus, the staff person may say that the Board would be willing to grant your application on the condition that you divest your shares in Bank X. Similarly, the staff person may suggest that a voluntary commitment on the part of the acquiring BHC to divest itself of the shares of another bank would ensure smooth sailing for the BHC's application. Consider the following excerpt, which sets forth three phases of the regulatory process at the Federal Reserve Board and analyzes the informal regulatory negotiation that is involved. The three phases referred to below are: (1) the informational phase; (2) the bargaining phase; and (3) the adversarial phase.

Aman, BARGAINING FOR JUSTICE: AN EXAMINATION OF THE USE AND LIMITS OF CONDITIONS BY THE FEDERAL RESERVE BOARD

74 Iowa L. Rev. 837, 879-83 (1989) *

A. Three Models — An Overview

The Board's action at the preliminary stage of an application usually prevents the need for a formal or informal hearing. The Board routinely may approve an uncontroversial application. If an application is controversial, however, the Board may indicate to the applicant that problems exist with the initial submission. An applicant may withdraw the application at this preliminary stage, particularly if it appears that it is going to be denied. An applicant may revise and amend the application to respond to the staff's concerns. This phase of the administrative process is based less on a judgmental model and more on an informational model and, ultimately, on a bargaining or negotiation model of the administrative process.

An applicant may not have supplied the data and information necessary for the Board to act. The application is thus deniable because it is incomplete. At this preliminary stage of the proceeding, the agency staff simply is requesting information that the Board needs to consider the merits of the applicant's proposal and to reach the next, more judgmental part of the process. In its purest form, this phase of the process involves no disputes over facts or law. Of course, conflicts can arise during the informational phase. Disputes over the relevancy of the information sought and provided can reflect the applicant's and staff's differing theories of the case. At this point, the ninety-one-day rule comes into play. New requests for information toll the ninety-one-day period and thus extend the time period in which the agency must make its decision. Controversial cases — cases in which the theory of the case held by staff differs significantly from that of the applicant — can take more than ninety-one days to be resolved. Theoretically, the informational phase of the process should be distinct from the judgmental phases. In most instances, this is the case. It is possible, however, for an application

---

* Copyright © 1989. Reprinted by permission.

to founder at this stage because of a disagreement over the relevancy or availability of requested information.

Once an application is informationally complete, the agency begins to consider its merits. The merits include not only *what* the applicant seeks to accomplish, but *who* the applicant is. The staff must consider not only the competitive effects of a proposed acquisition and the degree to which the nonbank that the applicant wishes to acquire is related to banking, but also the financial status of the applicant: can it successfully do what it seeks permission to accomplish? In addition, the Board must consider the long term policy implications of granting or denying the application. At least three decisionmaking factors interact when the Board reaches the merits of an application: (1) the legal requirements of the Act; (2) the factual context of a particular application; and (3) the policy implications of allowing the applicant to pursue the course of action it proposes.

Once it reacts to the merits of the case, the Board adheres to a bargaining or negotiation model of agency decisionmaking. From a purely theoretical viewpoint, this model of dispute settlement differs from the adversarial model inherent in the adjudicatory hearings. . . . Though perhaps oversimplified, especially as applied to the administrative process, Professor Gulliver's description helpfully captures some of the key differences between these two, pure models:

[t]he picture of negotiation is one of two sets of people, the disputing parties or their representatives, facing each other across a table or from opposite sides of an open space. They exchange information and opinion, engage in argument and discussion, and sooner or later propose offers and counter offers relating to the issues in dispute between them, seeking an outcome acceptable to both sides. The comparable picture of adjudication is that of two [or more] parties . . . who, separated from one another, face an adjudicator who sits in front of, apart from, and often raised above them. They address him, offering information, opinion, and arguments. Each seeks to refute the other's presentation and to persuade the adjudicator to favor his own case. Eventually the adjudicator pronounces his decision on the issues, often sorting out and summing up the information given to him and explaining his judgment.

Clearly, the crucial difference between the two models is the absence of the third-party decision maker who is present not only at the formal adjudications carried on at the Federal Reserve Board on rare occasions, but also at the more informal Board hearings. Given that final Board orders are subject to judicial review, that neutral third party theoretically may enter the process at a later point in the proceedings.

In reality, however, most Board proceedings, particularly at the early stages of the application process, more accurately fit within the negotiation or bargaining model. A decision made during the early stages of the process appears to be, and often is, a joint decision. The applicant, of course, wishes to have its application granted. The staff may wish to do so, but may be troubled by certain aspects of the proposal. They may suggest changes or condition approval upon commitments the applicant is willing to make. Each party can obtain only what in the end the other is prepared to allow. If staff and petitioner have a different view of the legal significance of the facts presented in a particular application, informal discussions and bargaining may enable one side to move closer to the other's point of view. Regulatory conditions and voluntary commitments often play a significant role in this phase of the process. Particularly from the applicants' point of view, conditions and voluntary commitments are the very currency of the negotiating process.

From the agency's viewpoint, a condition is a well established regulatory device that enables it to tailor its decision to the peculiarities of the applicant, further a policy goal it wishes to achieve, or both. It allows the agency to grant the benefit that the applicant seeks, and to obtain some assurances in exchange. Conditions can be fact-specific and peculiar to the individual applicant or represent a general policy that may or may not be implicated by the facts of the case. Because conditions usually appear in final agency orders, they are presumably supported by the administrative record, and their legality can be tested at the adversarial stage of the agency's proceedings and through judicial review.

Not all conditions necessarily require support by the record, nor are they always susceptible to judicial review. This is particularly true when conditions take the form of voluntary commitments. Such commitments often are not a part of the Fed's final order, nor are they eligible for judicial review. Voluntary commitments usually are found in letters of transmittal between the Fed and the applicant, and confidentiality may require that they not be included in the final order. If they are truly voluntary, they also may represent so fact-specific an agreement between the Board and the applicant that they have little general relevance and no real precedential effect. Such commitments often are the result of the bargaining phase of the regulatory process and represent requirements that were voluntarily accepted by the applicant to meet the Fed's applicant-specific regulatory concerns. In some cases, the Fed does not seek the commitments that are volunteered by applicants who hope to expedite the decisionmaking process and eliminate doubt concerning the appropriateness of their proposal. As we shall see below, however, "voluntariness" is a complicated concept. In some contexts, a commitment may result from an applicant's sense that its application would be denied unless it "voluntarily" agreed to a condition that it thought was unwise, unnecessary, or even *ultra vires*.

Not all issues arising under sections 3 and 4 of the Bank Holding Act are resolved informally. The Fed occasionally uses full-blown formal hearings, as well as more informal adjudicatory hearings before the Board. These formal or informal hearings are based on an adversarial model of administrative law. They assume that there are disputes over facts, law, or policy, and that there is a need for a neutral third party to resolve them. Such decisions are subject to judicial review.

It is impossible to segregate the three phases of the administrative process. The informational, bargaining, and adjudicatory phases of dispute settlement, particularly as applied to the application process, overlap and intersect in many ways. We have already discussed how the informational needs of the agency can implicate the judgmental aspects of the bargaining process. Similarly, the Fed's bargaining stage has adjudicatory overtones, particularly when what is in contention is not the significance of the facts, but the significance of broad questions of law and policy. Because the administrative staff inherently has greater bargaining power than the applicant, the staff takes on the qualities of an adjudicator as well as a negotiator. By resolving the legal questions themselves, the staff effectively can decide the case, particularly if time and circumstances preclude resort to the more adversarial phase of the process.

This is often the case. Most merger or acquisition opportunities require very prompt action, putting pressure on both the Board and the applicants to settle contentious matters quickly. Conditions and commitments expedite agreement, making appeals to the Board to resolve issues of fact, law, or policy unlikely. Applicants rarely resort to the courts or to the formal adjudicatory hearings provided under sections 3 and 4 because the deal struck in the negotiation will seldom survive litigation.

Board members tend to treat voluntary commitments as waivers of an applicant's arguments on the legal and policy issues inherent in their applications. Thus, they have a way of becoming a *fait accompli,* making Board involvement in the policy implications of voluntary commitments unlikely and judicial review impossible. There is no need to build a record for purposes of judicial review if the commitment is a voluntary one; the applicant cannot agree to a commitment and then renege on the deal by going to court. Negotiated commitments, therefore, in effect often are as final as formally adjudicated orders.

Theoretically, the bargaining stage of the process should be different than the adjudicatory or adversarial phase. No third party determines the outcome of the bargaining phase. The only outcome is the one to which both disputants agree, even though their reasons for acceptance are likely to be very different. The Fed's legal monopoly on the regulatory benefits that applicants seek in section 3 and section 4 cases, however, can significantly diminish the relative bargaining strength of the applicant and, in certain regulatory contexts, improperly convert the bargaining phase of the regulatory process into an adjudicatory one.

Of course, the nature of regulation properly militates against equality of bargaining positions between the regulated and the regulator. No one expects them to be equal. For example, Congress gave the Fed power to coerce the kind of behavior that the law requires from banks and bank holding companies. Nevertheless, our focus is on the bargaining process and the use of this process as a regulatory tool. It is important to understand both the advantages and the limitations of the informal bargaining process if the regulation is to occur within that context. An applicant's ability and opportunity to bargain are extremely important to the success of the application processes Congress established in the BHCA. Of vital importance is the decisionmaking flexibility that this process provides. In most cases, flexibility is preferable to the all-or-nothing consequences of either granting the application as requested, or denying it outright. The nature of an individually oriented application process allows an agency to tailor its regulatory powers to the case at hand.

Definite risks, however, attach to this kind of negotiated regulation. Not all negotiated outcomes are proper, particularly when the bargaining involves disputed issues of law and unarticulated or unclear Board policies. While most cases may be handled in a routine fashion, and are susceptible to negotiated decisions, difficult cases can raise serious questions concerning the substance of commitments and the extent to which they are voluntarily accepted. The process by which these commitments are made arguably should be more, rather than less formal. Certain kinds of regulatory outcomes are best achieved through the use of adjudicatory and rulemaking proceedings, rather than informal bargaining processes. . . .

FIRST BANCORPORATION v. BOARD OF GOVERNORS OF THE FEDERAL RESERVE SYSTEM

Tenth Circuit Court of Appeals
728 F.2d 434 (1984)

Before SETH, CHIEF JUDGE, SEYMOUR, CIRCUIT JUDGE, and CHILSON, DISTRICT JUDGE.

SETH, CHIEF JUDGE.

The petitioner, First Bancorporation, seeks a review of two decisions of the Board of Governors of the Federal Reserve System. By these orders the Board conditionally authorized the petitioner to acquire the Beehive Financial Corporation and directed the petitioner to comply with similar conditions with respect to a previously acquired subsidiary, the Foothill Thrift & Loan Company. Both Beehive and Foothill are industrial loan companies subject to Utah law.

The petitioner is a bank holding company organized under the laws of Utah. The Bank Holding Company Act provides that a bank holding company may not acquire a nonbank unless the company to be acquired is "so closely related to banking . . . as to be a proper incident thereto." 12 U.S.C. § 1843(c)(8). The Board's Regulation Y provides that industrial loan companies are among those activities that are proper incidents to banking. 12 C.F.R. § 225.4(a)(2).

In 1979, the petitioner applied to the Board to operate an industrial loan company, Foothill Thrift & Loan. The Board unconditionally approved the application. In 1981, Foothill began offering negotiable order of withdrawal (NOW) accounts. NOW accounts are interest-bearing accounts from which the account holder may withdraw funds by a negotiable order. Foothill's NOW accounts are offered pursuant to a Utah regulation requiring that Foothill, as an industrial loan company, must reserve the right to require thirty days' notice from the account holder before making a withdrawal. . . .

In August 1981, the petitioner applied to the Board to acquire Beehive Financial Corporation, another Utah industrial loan company. The petitioner intended to offer NOW accounts through Beehive.

The Board conditionally approved the petitioner's acquisition of Beehive subject to two conditions. The Board's initial condition was that Beehive not offer both NOW accounts and make commercial loans. The Board's theory in imposing that condition was that if Beehive were to do both, it would be a bank rather than an industrial loan company under the Act, and would thus not be eligible for acquisition as a nonbank entity under section 4 of the Act. The Board's second condition was that if Beehive should elect to forego commercial lending and offer NOW accounts, it had to agree to subject the NOW accounts to Board regulations as to reserves and interest limitations.

Along with its letter to petitioner conditionally approving the Beehive acquisition, the Board ordered that the petitioner's industrial loan company, Foothill, should now also conform to the conditions announced as to Beehive. The Board forwarded copies of the Beehive order to other bank holding companies suggesting that the Board had adopted the Beehive decision as its policy.

The petitioner sought review of both the Beehive and Foothill orders in this court. Beehive has subsequently been acquired by an unrelated company since the filing of the petition for review; however, there remains a controversy as to the Board's Foothill order.

The Board as mentioned, directed Foothill to choose between offering NOW accounts and making commercial loans. Foothill provided both services. The Board argues that unless Foothill elected to perform only one such function it will be considered a "bank" under the Act.

The petitioner contends that Foothill cannot be considered a bank under the Act because it does not meet the Act's definition of a bank. Section 2(c) of the Act defines a bank as an institution "which (1) accepts deposits that the depositor has a *legal right* to withdraw on demand, and (2) engages in the business of making commercial loans." 12 U.S.C. § 1841(c) (emphasis added). The petitioner argues that its NOW accounts are not deposits that the depositor has a *legal right* to withdraw on demand. Utah law, it asserts, requires that an industrial loan company must reserve the legal right to require thirty days' notice before it makes payment. There being no legal right to withdraw on demand the petitioner asserts that Foothill cannot be considered a bank.

The Board determined that NOW accounts were demand deposits within the meaning of the Act. It concluded that by accepting such deposits and by offering commercial loans, Foothill was a bank under the Act.

We need look no further than the Act's definition of a "bank" to resolve this dispute. As the Supreme Court has announced, "There is, of course, no more persuasive evidence of the purpose of a statute than the words by which the legislature undertook to give expression to its wishes." *United States v. American Trucking Associations,* 310 U.S. 534, 60 S. Ct. 1069, 84 L. Ed. 1345 [(1940)]. As mentioned, section 2(c) of the Act defines "bank" as an institution which makes commercial loans and "accepts deposits that the depositor has a *legal right* to withdraw on demand." 12 U.S.C. § 1841(c) (emphasis added). Utah law specifically proscribes industrial loan companies from accepting demand deposits, requiring instead that the companies reserve the legal right to demand notice prior to withdrawal. There is therefore no legal right of withdrawal on demand. . . .

. . . .

The Board further ordered that if Foothill should continue to offer NOW accounts, it should subject those accounts to the interest-rate ceilings and reserve requirements prescribed by the board in Regulations D and Q. 12 C.F.R. §§ 204, 217. The Board purports to assert this authority under the public benefits provision of section 4(c)(8), 12 U.S.C. § 1843(c)(8). Section 4(c)(8) is one of the exceptions to the general rule that a bank holding company may not own or control a nonbank. It provides that if the Board determines that the entity to be acquired is a proper incident of banking and that the proposed activity "can reasonably be expected to produce benefits to the public" then the acquisition shall be approved. In determining whether public benefits will accrue, the Board is to weigh the benefits "such as greater convenience, increased competition, or gains in efficiency" against "possible adverse effects, such as undue concentration of resources, decreased or unfair competition, conflicts of interest or unsound banking practices."

The Board has adopted a commonly accepted two-step process for reviewing section 4(c)(8) applications. . . . First, the Board determines whether the type of activity proposed is closely related and incidental to banking. This is accomplished by reference to the Board's Regulation Y which lists permissible banking-related activities. 12 C.F.R. § 225. Regulation Y was promulgated under the Board's rulemaking authority. Second, the Board determines on a case by case basis whether the public benefits of the specific activity proposed in the application outweigh the potential adverse effects. . . .

The Board argues that we must give deference to its § 4(c)(8) determinations and affirm the Board's factual findings if they are supported by substantial evidence. 12 U.S.C. § 1848.

The discretionary balancing that comprises the second part of the review is not at issue here. The petitioner asserts that the Foothill order is a rule of general applicability subject to the rulemaking provisions of § 553 of the Administrative Procedure Act, and is not, as the Board claims, merely an adjudication of the activity's merits.

The distinction between legislative and adjudicative facts is often subtle or blurred. Administrative agencies are not "precluded from announcing new principles in an adjudicative proceeding and . . . the choice between rulemaking and adjudication lies in the first instance within the [agency's] discretion." *N.L.R.B. v. Bell Aerospace Co.,* 416 U.S. 267, 294 [(1974)]. . . . However, like all grants of discretion, "there may be situations where the [agency's] reliance on adjudication would amount to an abuse of discretion. . . ." *N.L.R.B. v. Bell Aerospace Co.,* 416 U.S., at 294.

It is not useful here to delve too deeply into the theoretical distinctions separating administrative and legislative facts. Rather, it is preferable to see how the board has utilized the Beehive and Foothill orders *post hoc*. On at least three occasions, the board has instructed other bank holding companies that its policy towards NOW accounts was determined in its Beehive order. . . . The Board's order was thus merely a vehicle by which a general policy would be changed. *See* 5 U.S.C. § 551(4).

That the Board's order is an attempt to construct policy by adjudication is evident. The Board examined no specific facts as to the potential adverse effects of unregulated Foothill NOW accounts. The Board instead made broad conclusions that "unless the NOW accounts offered by Beehive Thrift are subject to interest rate limitations and reserve requirements . . . [it] is likely . . . [that] the important public policy objectives of the Depository Institutions Deregulation and Monetary Control Act . . . [will be undermined]." Rec. Vol. I, at 259. This is a broad policy announcement. The Board made no conclusions at all with respect to Foothill. Thus, the Board's order contains no adjudicative facts having any particularized relevance to the petitioner. We must conclude that the Board abused its discretion by improperly attempting to propose legislative policy by an adjudicative order. . . .

. . . .

The orders and decisions of the Board here reviewed are set aside.

It is so ordered.

NOTES AND QUESTIONS

5-22. What was wrong with the conditions the Board prescribed? Can the Board condition an order by requiring an activity it has no direct substantive power to require? If it has the substantive power, can it use the condition to create a general policy applicable to all applicants?

5-23. From a procedural point of view, what is wrong with a condition that is then treated as a precedent and, in effect, a rule? Should a condition ever be so general? Why or why not?

5-24. What kind of conditions were involved in this case? How do they compare, as regulatory tools, to exceptions and the other forms of administrative equity examined earlier? Consider the following:

Alfred C. Aman, Jr. and William Mayton, ADMINISTRATIVE LAW

267-69 (Thompson West 2d ed. 2001) *

Requests for exceptions, waivers and other adjustments are initiated by the regulated. Such requests may result in clarification of existing law or, in the case of exceptions and waivers, exemption from certain rules altogether. They usually turn on the peculiar circumstances of the Petitioner involved. Agencies also can take the peculiar facts of an applicant into account by tailoring their regulatory powers to that entity. Indeed, somewhat akin to exceptions are

---

* Reprinted by permission of Thompson West.

conditional orders or an applicant's advance voluntary consent to certain agency actions. While exceptions and waivers often result in less regulation for the regulated entities who seek them, conditions and commitments usually represent a form of more specific, individual regulatory requirements. In both instances, regulation is being shaped largely by the individual needs of the particular regulated entity with which the agency deals. . . .

The various substantive contexts in which an agency issues a conditional order or agrees to grant certain authority in light of an applicant's voluntary commitment to carry out or abstain from carrying out certain activities raise a number of issues. In general, these include questions of law, policy and fact. Working at this level of generality, at least five types of agency conditions or commitments are possible. A perfect condition is one that is based on clear law, clear agency policy and is narrowly tailored to the facts of a particular applicant before the agency. This kind of condition allows the agency to tailor its regulatory demands to fit the precise situation of the applicant before it. Such a condition, being so narrow and fact-specific, is unlikely to have any precedential value. It allows the applicant to obtain approval of its proposed action in a manner that ensures the agency's regulatory duties and goals are fully carried out. The informal give and take between agency staff and private counsel constitute the only procedure available in most cases involving this kind of informal agency action.

A second kind of condition can be called a policy condition; such a condition is fact-specific and within the agency's legal authority, but it may implicate policies not yet fully articulated by the agency. Such conditions can raise procedural issues similar to those involved in determining whether an agency should use adjudication or rulemaking when formulating policy. But policy making at so early a stage in the agency's proceedings, however, raises its own difficulties. The bargaining process usually consists of a discussion between a staff member of the agency and private counsel. By voluntarily agreeing to a condition, the applicant knows that it can expedite its petition, but such a condition or voluntary commitment often is treated as essentially a *fait accompli* by the agency that reviews the order. Policy made in this manner, especially significant policy, does not begin to receive the kind of public scrutiny applied to the results of rulemaking proceedings. When the case proceeds to consideration by the full commission or board, there may not have been a full policy review. Given the voluntary nature of the commitment it is not likely that courts will review this aspect of the order. Thus, the policy involved receives even less outside scrutiny than if it had been developed in an adjudication. This kind of *ad hoc* approach to policy making is thus relatively invisible and not necessarily consistent or well thought out. Conditions with significant policy implications are thus not appropriate for the very informal processes of negotiation that occur in such contexts.

An even more controversial third kind of condition is one in which the parties agree to take or forego certain actions over which the agency's actual regulatory authority is uncertain. An applicant eager to close a deal or avoid protracted litigation may be willing to agree to such a condition, thus allowing the agency to extend its regulatory jurisdiction informally and in a manner also effectively immune from judicial review. A fourth type of agency condition is one that does not relate to the specific facts in the petition of the applicant. Such a condition is wholly prospective in nature and designed to prevent future action that may or may not be contemplated by the applicant. This kind of regulation may avoid future litigation, but it can be particularly coercive when demanded of an applicant whose own factual situation does not necessarily raise or justify the restriction. Finally, a fifth type of condition or commitment is the null condition, one that is clearly beyond the authority of the Commission to impose, and thus not grounded in any known or articulated policy, and not even fact-specific to the applicant involved. . . .

PROBLEM 5-4

Assume that you are General Counsel of the Federal Reserve Board. You are aware of the need to condition Board orders, and you realize that this kind of regulatory flexibility is crucial if the law involved is to be applied properly in the individual cases before the Board. Yet, you also know that over time these conditions and commitments create a significant body of law. What procedures do you think should be employed to be sure that this law is known to the public generally? What if these conditions and commitments, over time, add up to a change in Board policy? What procedures might you recommend?

§ 5.05 Alternative Dispute Resolution Techniques

[A] Overview

Historically, one of the primary purposes of the administrative process and administrative adjudication was to provide an alternative means of dispute resolution to costly, lengthy judicial proceedings.* Some commentators now contend, however, that the administrative process itself has become an unduly burdensome, costly and time-consuming way to resolve disputes. Congress has responded with the passage of two bills aimed at encouraging Alternative Dispute Resolution (ADR) techniques in the administrative process: the Administrative Dispute Resolution Act and the Negotiated Rulemaking Act of 1990. This section shall examine some of the legal issues emerging from the increased use of such ADR approaches as settlement, mediation, arbitration and negotiation in the administrative process. For an overview of ADR and the administrative process, consider the following:

> Administrative agencies and the procedures they employ arose, in part, as an alternative dispute resolution mechanism. They were a reaction to the formality, cost and delay experienced by parties who had to litigate their regulatory disputes in federal and state courts. Some critics now contend that the administrative process itself has become unduly formal, costly and

---

* See Harter, *Points on a Continuum: Dispute Resolution Procedures and the Administrative Process,* 1 ADMIN. L.J. 143, 144 (1987).

time-consuming. Moreover, many administrative agencies must deal with an enormous caseload. Some of these cases involve disputes that are inherently more amenable to alternative dispute resolution (ADR) methods. Arbitration, for example, may be more efficient than administrative adjudication for resolving monetary disputes between private parties, especially if these disputes do not involve significant policy or legal issues. Proponents of ADR also argue that the primary value of these techniques is that they increase the satisfaction of the participants involved. For the most part, participants are more directly involved in the decisionmaking process itself and that process is usually cheaper and faster. For reasons such as these, alternative dispute resolution techniques are now consistently proposed as an important reform of the administrative decisionmaking process. They include processes that have long been a part of the administrative process, such as settlement and negotiation. But they also include less commonly used techniques such as arbitration, mediation and mini-trials.

No one can deny the importance of flexibility, informality and an appropriate fit of procedure to substance. Nor can efficiency values be ignored, particularly in programs with enormous caseloads. But critics of ADR maintain that the application of these techniques to the administrative process does not always result in more expeditious dispute resolution. More fundamentally, ADR skeptics maintain that ADR can be viewed as a procedural analogue to substantive decontrol. Carried too far, some techniques can, in effect, privatize administrative procedures raising not only philosophical and policy issues, but important constitutional and statutory questions as well.

Alfred C. Aman, Jr. & William Mayton, *Administrative Law* 273-276 (2d ed. 2001).*

[B] Settlement

A settlement is a consensus-based solution to a dispute in which the parties themselves render a decision by means of a negotiated agreement. As a dispute resolution technique, settlement has long been a part of the Administrative Process. The APA, for example, speaks to settlement in section 554(c), requiring agencies to give "all interested parties opportunity for . . . offers of settlement . . . when time, the nature of the proceeding, and the public interest permit." Presiding administrative law judges often act as settlement judges and some agency regulations provide explicitly for different ALJs to act as settlement judges. Both the recently enacted Administrative Dispute Resolution Act and the APA contemplate that agencies shall entertain settlement requests, but neither requires that they be accepted. Nor do these laws mandate any particular settlement procedures. Agencies differ in this regard. To get some sense of what settlement is and the kinds of issues that arise at some agencies, we will look first at settlement at the Federal Energy Regulatory Commission (FERC).

---

* Reprinted by permission of Thompson West.

UNITED MUNICIPAL DISTRIBUTORS GROUP v. FERC

District of Columbia Court of Appeals
732 F.2d 202 (1984)

Before SCALIA and STARR, CIRCUIT JUDGES, and GESELL, UNITED STATES DISTRICT JUDGE for the District of Columbia.

Opinion for the Court filed by CIRCUIT JUDGE STARR.

STARR, CIRCUIT JUDGE:

. . . .

I.

On June 30, 1981, United [Gas Pipe Line Company], a large gas pipeline company, filed an application for an increase in its rates pursuant to section 4 of the NGA [Natural Gas Act], 15 U.S.C. § 717c. FERC accepted the rates for filing and suspended their effectiveness for the maximum period of five months, until January 1, 1982, after which they became effective subject to refund. . . . The Commission permitted some twenty parties, including United's direct and indirect customers and several state utility commissions, to intervene. Following settlement negotiations among United, the various intervenors, and the Commission staff, United filed a settlement agreement with the Commission on October 1, 1982. The Commission staff submitted comments in support of the settlement. Only UMDG [United Municipal Distributors Group] filed comments in opposition. . . . UMDG argued that the settlement should be conditioned upon the inclusion of a reservation clause, which would permit resolution of an issue known as the "consolidated tax" or "stand-alone" issue following the completion of judicial review of another FERC proceeding involving this specific issue.[1]

The presiding administrative law judge (ALJ) certified the settlement proposal to the Commission. . . . In doing so, the ALJ concluded

---

[1] The consolidated tax issue concerns how regulated entities, such as United, compute their tax allowances for purposes of ratemaking under 15 U.S.C. § 717c. United and its corporate affiliates elected to file consolidated tax returns under 26 U.S.C. §§ 1501-05 (1982) rather than separate returns. One of the results of filing a consolidated return is that the "losses of an affiliate [corporation] can be set off against the taxable income of other affiliates in the group." *City of Charlottesville v. FERC*, 661 F.2d 945, 946 n. 6 (D.C. Cir. 1981). The Commission in the orders reviewed by this court in the *City of Charlottesville* decision approved the computation of the tax allowance for purposes of ratemaking on a "stand-alone" basis — as if the company actually paid taxes on a stand-alone basis, independent of its affiliates. *Id.* at 946. Thus, the tax-reducing effect that results when the company files a consolidated return with its corporate affiliates is not reflected in the computation of the tax allowance for the ratemaking.

In *City of Charlottesville,* this court held that, although the Commission has statutory authority to follow the stand-alone policy, the rate orders at issue in that case were not supported by substantial evidence. *Id.* at 954. This court therefore remanded the case to FERC. FERC has, subsequent to the orders in this case, reaffirmed its stand-alone policy.

that there are no material facts in dispute, that there is substantial evidence in the record upon which the Commission may base a reasoned decision on the merits of all contested issues, [and] that a formal evidentiary hearing would serve no useful public purpose. . . .

The Commission, by order issued February 3, 1983, approved the settlement "in its entirety as to all of United's customers except UMDG". . . . FERC found that, by attempting to reserve the consolidated tax issue, UMDG had rejected the "entire settlement package." The Commission therefore remanded for a full hearing under section 4 of the NGA on the rates to be charged UMDG by United. The Commission denied UMDG's petition for rehearing, stating:

> When a party contests a proposed settlement the Commission may act on the settlement as an on the merits resolution of the issues raised based upon substantial evidence. That is not what the Commission did in this instance. We approved the uncontested settlement between United and the majority of its customers and remanded the question of rates for the one contesting party ([U]MDG) for a hearing. We did not attempt to decide the issue of just and reasonable rates for [U]MDG, but, rather, provided it the full due process opportunity to present its case to the Commission. . . .
>
> We believe our order reflects a prudent policy. That policy is one of preserving a settlement for the vast majority of the contented parties, allowing them to have the benefit of their bargain. The one contesting party will have the full due process right of a hearing. We thus encourage the settlement process while affording any party dissatisfied with a proposed settlement an opportunity to process his case. . . .

. . . This court granted a stay of that portion of the FERC order remanding UMDG's part of the case to the ALJ for a rate hearing, stating that "the granting of this stay, while it maintains the status quo, is not a vindication of petitioner's claims; we express no view on the merits of this case."

II.

[The court then held that FERC's orders were subject to judicial review.]

. . . .

B. *The Validity of The Commission's Approval of the Settlement.*

1. *Statutes, Regulations, and Judicial Precedent Governing Settlements.*

UMDG vigorously argues that the statutes, regulations, and judicial decisions governing settlements of rate cases under section 4 of the NGA do not authorize the procedure used by FERC in this instance.[7] UMDG also argues that the Commission's action contravenes regulations and judicial precedent governing FERC's settlement authority. We find neither argument persuasive.

---

[7] The Commission's authority to settle informally ratemaking proceedings stems from its statutory authority to conduct ratemaking proceedings under section 4(e) of the NGA, 15 U.S.C. § 717c(e) (1982) and from section 554(c)(1) of the Administrative Procedure Act ("APA"), which provides for "the submission and consideration of facts, arguments, [and] offers of settlement . . . when . . . the public interest permits." 5 U.S.C. § 554(c) (1982).

The Commission rule governing contested settlements provides:

(h) *Contested Offers of Settlement*

(1)(i) If the Commission determines that any offer of settlement is contested in whole or in part, by any party, the Commission may decide the merits of the contested settlement issues, if the record contains substantial evidence upon which to base a reasoned decision or the Commission determines there is no genuine issue of material fact.

(ii) If the Commission finds that the record lacks substantial evidence or that the issue cannot be severed from the offer of settlement the Commission will:

(A) Establish procedures for the purpose of receiving additional evidence before a presiding officer upon which a decision on the contested issues may be reasonably based; or

(B) *Take other action which the Commission deems appropriate.*

(iii) If contested issues are severable, the uncontested portions may be severed and decided in accordance with paragraph (g) of this section.[8]

Rule 602(h), 18 C.F.R. § 385.602(h) (1982) (emphasis added).

Under the Commission's regulations, an *uncontested* offer of settlement may be approved if the Commission finds that the settlement is fair and reasonable and in the public interest. A *contested* offer of settlement may be approved as a decision on the merits under Rule 602(h) if supported by substantial evidence as required by section 4 of the NGA, 15 U.S.C. § 717c(e). Rule 602(h) also allows the Commission to approve a contested settlement if no genuine issues of material fact exist as to the contested issues. This procedure permits the resolution of issues without lengthy and costly hearings on every issue and "is in effect a 'summary judgment' granted on 'motion' by the litigants when there is no issue of fact." . . . Finally, the regulations permit the Commission to sever uncontested portions of a settlement and to approve those portions while setting the contested portions of the case for a hearing.

In deciding to approve the settlement as to all parties except UMDG, the Commission decided not to sever the consolidated tax issue under Rule 602(h)(1)(iii), for the simple reason that it considered the tax aspect of the settlement to be part of an "inseparable package."[9] Instead, the Commission approved the settlement as to all other parties as if it were an uncontested settlement under Rule 602(g)[10] . . . .

---

[8] Paragraph (g) governs uncontested offers of settlement and provides that the presiding administrative law judge may certify uncontested offers of settlement to the Commission and that "[a]n uncontested offer of settlement may be approved by the Commission upon a finding that the settlement appears to be fair and reasonable and in the public interest." Rule 602(g), 18 C.F.R. § 385.602(g) (1982). The Commission's regulations thus permit it to approve uncontested offers of settlement without a determination on the merits that the rates approved are "just and reasonable." The Commission's approval of an uncontested settlement has no precedential value as settled practice. . . .

[9] The Commission did, however, approve a provision of the settlement severing an issue known as the "liquid and liquefiable hydrocarbon issue" and reserved that issue for a full hearing.

[10] The Commission thus did not determine that the consolidated tax issue raised no genuine issue of material fact, contrary to the ALJ's determination. *See* Administrative Law Judge's Certification of Settlement Proposal, *United Gas Pipe Line Co.*, 21 FERC (CCH) ¶ 63,041 (Nov. 12, 1982).

The governing regulations plainly do not forbid the Commission's action in this case. To the contrary, the regulations confer upon the Commission broad authority to "[t]ake other action which the Commission deems appropriate" when the Commission determines that "the issue cannot be severed from the offer of settlement."

In addition to the plain language of the rule, FERC's interpretation is clearly entitled to deference under well established principles of law. We therefore reject UMDG's contention that, under the regulations governing contested settlements, FERC's choices are limited to the three alternatives of approving the settlement as a binding, on-the-merits resolution of issues raised based upon substantial evidence; disapproving the settlement in full; or severing the contested issue and approving the remaining uncontested portions. The regulations, by their terms, do not preclude the action taken by FERC here. . . .

UMDG argues, finally, that the Commission's action contravenes the proscription against unduly discriminatory rates set forth in section 4 of the NGA, 15 U.S.C. § 717c(b) (1982). That provision prohibits natural gas companies subject to the Commission's jurisdiction from

(1) mak[ing] or grant[ing] any undue preference or advantage to any person or subject[ing] any person to any undue prejudice or disadvantage, or

(2) maintain[ing] any unreasonable difference in rates, charges, service, facilities or in any other respect, either as between localities or as between classes of service.

According to UMDG, the result of FERC's approval of the instant settlement is that United will charge UMDG's members different rates from those charged other United customers receiving the same service. This difference in rates, under UMDG's theory of the case, is unduly discriminatory. UMDG further contends that the Commission's policy permits "rate discrimination" based upon the financial resources of the party or parties who seek to reserve statutory rights in a particular settlement and opines that natural gas pipelines could use FERC's misguided approach to adopt a "divide and conquer" strategy in defeating objections to proposed rate increases.[18]

This court recently rejected this very argument in the context of a proceeding under section 205(b) of the FPA, 16 U.S.C. § 824d(b) (1982), which contains language identical in all pertinent respects to that in section 4 of the NGA. In *Cities of Bethany, et al. v. FERC*, 727 F.2d 1131 (D.C. Cir. 1984), this court held that a rate disparity among customers of the same public utility that was solely the result of a settlement among some of the parties was not unlawfully discriminatory. . . . In so concluding, the court observed that the mere fact of a rate disparity does not establish unlawful discrimination and that rate differences "may be justified and rendered lawful by facts — cost of service or otherwise.". . . Thus, the court observed that fixed rate contracts

---

[18] This argument assumes that the remand for a hearing on the rates will necessarily result in a full trial with the attendant costs of such a hearing — an expense UMDG argues it cannot bear. UMDG overstates its case in making this assumption. It is not at all obvious that UMDG will have to litigate each and every issue in this case fully, since United and UMDG may enter into stipulations regarding various issues.

between the parties may justify a rate disparity. . . . The court recognized, however, that settlements between a utility and a customer may not be completely analogous to a fixed-rate contract because settlement agreements may extend only for a specified term of years. The court nonetheless concluded that a settlement agreement reached in good faith and not involving improper conduct, and which does not unduly burden a customer group, may justify a rate disparity, since settlements would be severely discouraged if rate disparities arising out of settlements were considered unlawfully discriminatory. . . . The court concluded that the criteria were met and therefore upheld the settlement at issue there.

The same reasoning applies to the settlement at issue here. UMDG has advanced no argument that the instant settlement reflects a "sweetheart deal" or that improper means were used to reach it. We therefore conclude that FERC's approval of the settlement does not violate section 4 of the NGA.

For the foregoing reasons, the Commission's orders are affirmed.

Affirmed.

NOTES AND QUESTIONS

5-25. How does settlement of an administrative agency case differ from settlement of a private case? Are there likely to be more parties? Are the issues likely to be more complex?

5-26. What kinds of cases are most likely to "settle out" in the administrative setting? Cases with factual issues in dispute? Legal issues? Policy issues? Should cases that involve important policy questions be resolved through settlement procedures? For a discussion of such issues in the context of public law litigation in federal court, see Fiss, *Against Settlement,* 93 YALE L. REV. 1073 (1984).

5-27. What do you think of the way the court in *United Municipal Distributors Group* deals with the parties that refuse to settle? Are there any dangers with this approach? Are you persuaded by the court's statement in footnote 18, or do you think the likelihood of one party trying a case of this magnitude is not very great?

5-28. Who should hear settlement offers during the litigation — the presiding ALJ or a different ALJ, brought in specially for settlement purposes? As a litigant, which approach would you prefer?

5-29. The court's approach in *United Municipal Distributors Group* was reaffirmed by the D.C. Circuit in *Arctic Slope Regional Corp. v. FERC,* 832 F.2d 158 (D.C. Cir. 1987), *cert. denied,* 488 U.S. 868 (1988). For a discussion of FERC settlement procedures, see Walker, *Settlement Practice at the FERC: Boom or Bane,* 7 ENERGY L.J. 343 (1986).

5-30. The Environmental Protection Agency has made extensive use of settlement techniques. *See generally* Anderson, *Negotiation and Informal*

Agency Action: The Case of Superfund, 1985 DUKE L.J. 261; Leue, *Private Party Settlements in the Superfund Amendment and Reauthorization Act of 1986 (SARA)*, 8 STAN. ENVTL. L.J. 131 (1989).

5-31. It is important to note that Congress has sought to encourage the use of various ADR techniques by federal administrative agencies with the passage of the Administrative Dispute Resolution Act in 1990. Pub. L. 101-552, 104 Stat. 2736 (1990). This Act amends the APA to enable and, indeed, encourage parties to federal administrative proceedings to resolve their disputes in various ways, including mediation and arbitration. Agency use of ADR remains completely discretionary, but the Act sets forth guidelines to help determine the cases to which ADR techniques are particularly appropriate. *See* Alfred C. Aman, Jr. & William Mayton, *Administrative Law Treatise*, pp. 277-79 (Thompson West 2d ed. 2001).

5-32. It has been suggested that settlement arguments can be used to alter the substantive content of rules. Declaratory orders, for example, can be used by an agency to settle ambiguity in a rule and prevent litigation. As Jeffrey M. Gaba has noted:

> Settlement agreements can . . . be used to specify the substantive content — even the precise language — of regulations. Substantive agreements arise in the course of lawsuits seeking judicial review of a putative final regulation. In resolving the lawsuit, the parties may negotiate a substantive modification of the regulation that will satisfy their objectives.

Jeffrey M. Gaba, *Informal Rulemaking By Settlement Agreement*, 73 GEO. L.J. 1241, 1245 (1985);* *see also*, Jim Rossi, *Bargaining in the Shadow of Administrative Procedure: The Public Interest in Rulemaking Settlement*, 51 DUKE L.J. 1015, 1056 (2001).

[C] Arbitration

Arbitration is adjudication by private adjudicators. It is a common means of resolving private disputes, but it has increasingly been used in the administrative process. Under the Federal Insecticide, Fungicide and Rodenticide Act (FIFRA), for example, arbitration is used to resolve disputes that arise concerning the price paid by pesticide manufacturers for data submitted to the EPA by other manufacturers. Using private adjudicators for disputes arising in public programs such as FIFRA can, as we shall see, raise important statutory and constitutional issues.

---

* Copyright © 1985 by Georgetown Law Journal. All rights reserved.

THOMAS v. UNION CARBIDE AGR. PRODUCTS CO.

United States Supreme Court
473 U.S. 568 (1985)

JUSTICE O'CONNOR delivered the opinion of the Court.

. . . .

I

. . . .

A

As a precondition for registration of a pesticide, manufacturers must submit research data to the Environmental Protection Agency (EPA) concerning the product's health, safety, and environmental effects. The 1972 Act established data-sharing provisions intended to streamline pesticide registration procedures, increase competition, and avoid unnecessary duplication of data-generation costs. . . . Some evidence suggests that before 1972 data submitted by one registrant had "as a matter of practice but without statutory authority, been considered by the Administrator to support the registration of the same or a similar product by another registrant." . . . Such registrations were colloquially known as "me too" or "follow-on" registrations. Section 3(c)(1)(D) of the 1972 Act provided statutory authority for the use of previously submitted data as well as a scheme for sharing the costs of data generation.

In effect, the provision instituted a mandatory data-licensing scheme. The amount of compensation was to be negotiated by the parties, or, in the event negotiations failed, was to be determined by the EPA, subject to judicial review upon instigation of the original data submitter. The scope of the 1972 data-consideration provision, however, was limited, for any data designated as "trade secrets or commercial or financial information" . . . could not be considered at all by EPA to support another registration unless the original submitter consented. *Ruckelshaus v. Monsanto Co.* [467 U.S. 986], at 992-993 [(1984)].

Congress enacted the original data-compensation provision in 1972 because it believed "recognizing a limited proprietary interest" in data submitted to support pesticide registrations would provide an added incentive beyond statutory patent protection for research and development of new pesticides. . . . The data submitters, however, contended that basic health, safety, and environmental data essential to registration of a competing pesticide qualified for protection as a trade secret. With EPA bogged down in cataloging data and the pesticide industry embroiled in litigation over what types of data could legitimately be designated "trade secrets," new pesticide registrations "ground to a virtual halt." . . .

The 1978 amendments were a response to the "logjam of litigation that resulted from controversies over data compensation and trade secret protection." *Id.* Congress viewed data-sharing as essential to the registration scheme, *id.*, at 7, but concluded EPA must be relieved of the task of valuation because disputes regarding the compensation scheme had "for all practical purposes, tied up their registration process" and "[EPA] lacked the expertise necessary to establish the proper amount of compensation." . . . Legislators and the Agency agreed that "[d]etermining the amount and terms of such compensation are matters that do not require active government involvement [and] compensation payable should be determined to the fullest extent practicable, within the private sector." . . .

Against this background, Congress in 1978 amended § 3(c)(1)(D) and § 10(b) to clarify that the trade secret exemption from the data-consideration provision did not extend to health, safety, and environmental data. In addition, the 1978 amendments granted data submitters a 10-year period of exclusive use for data submitted after September 30, 1978, during which time the data may not be cited without the original submitter's permission. . . .

Regarding compensation for use of data not protected by the 10-year exclusive use provision, the amendment substituted for the EPA Administrator's determination of the appropriate compensation a system of negotiation and binding arbitration to resolve compensation disputes among registrants. Section 3(c)(1)(D)(ii) authorizes EPA to consider data already in its files in support of a new registration, permit, or new use, but "only if the applicant has made an offer to compensate the original data submitter." If the applicant and data submitter fail to agree, either may invoke binding arbitration. The arbitrator's decision is subject to judicial review only for "fraud, misrepresentation, or other misconduct." . . . The statute contains its own sanctions. Should an applicant or data submitter fail to comply with the scheme, the Administrator is required to cancel the new registration or to consider the data without compensation to the original submitter. The Administrator may also issue orders regarding sale or use of existing pesticide stocks. . . .

The concept of retaining statutory compensation but substituting binding arbitration for valuation of data by EPA emerged as a compromise. This approach was developed by representatives of the major chemical manufacturers, who sought to retain the controversial compensation provision, in discussions with industry groups representing follow-on registrants, whose attempts to register pesticides had been roadblocked by litigation since 1972. . . .

B

Appellees are 13 large firms engaged in the development and marketing of chemicals used to manufacture pesticides. Each has in the past submitted data to EPA in support of registrations of various pesticides. When the 1978 amendments went into effect, these firms were engaged in litigation in the Southern District of New York challenging the constitutionality under Article I and the Fifth Amendment of the provisions authorizing data-sharing and disclosure of data to the public. In response to this Court's decision in *Northern Pipeline Construction Co. v. Marathon Pipe Line Co.*, 458 U.S. 50 (1982), appellees amended their complaint to allege that the statutory mechanism of binding arbitration for determining the amount of compensation due them violates Article III of the Constitution. Article III, § 1, provides that "[t]he judicial Power of the United States, shall be vested" in courts whose judges enjoy tenure "during good Behaviour" and compensation that "shall not be diminished during their Continuance in Office." Appellees allege Congress in FIFRA transgressed this limitation by allocating to arbitrators the functions of judicial officers and severely limiting review by an Article III court.

. . . .

II

. . . .

III

Appellees contend that Article III bars Congress from requiring arbitration of disputes among registrants concerning compensation under FIFRA without also affording substantial review by tenured judges of the arbitrator's decision. Article III, § 1, establishes a broad policy that federal judicial power shall be vested in courts whose judges enjoy life tenure and fixed compensation. These requirements protect the role of the independent judiciary within the constitutional scheme of tripartite government and assure impartial adjudication in federal courts. . . .

An absolute construction of Article III is not possible in this area of "frequently arcane distinctions and confusing precedents." *Northern Pipeline Construction Co. v. Marathon Pipe Line Co.,* 458 U.S., at 90 (opinion concurring in judgment). "[N]either this Court nor Congress has read the Constitution as requiring every federal question arising under the federal law . . . to be tried in an Art. III court before a judge enjoying life tenure and protection against salary reduction." *Palmore v. United States,* 411 U.S. 389, 407 (1973). Instead, the Court has long recognized that Congress is not barred from acting pursuant to its powers under Article I to vest decisionmaking authority in tribunals that lack the attributes of Article III courts. . . . Many matters that involve the application of legal standards to facts and affect private interests are routinely decided by agency action with limited or no review by Article III courts. . . .

The Court's most recent pronouncement on the meaning of Article III is *Northern Pipeline.* A divided Court was unable to agree on the precise scope and nature of Article III's limitations. The Court's holding in that case establishes only that Congress may not vest in a non-Article III court the power to adjudicate, render final judgment, and issue binding orders in a traditional contract action arising under state law, without consent of the litigants, and subject only to ordinary appellate review. 458 U.S., at 84 (plurality opinion); *id.,* at 90-92 (opinion concurring in judgment); *id.,* at 92 (BURGER, C.J., dissenting).

A

Appellees contend that their claims to compensation under FIFRA are a matter of state law, and thus are encompassed by the holding of *Northern Pipeline*. We disagree. Any right to compensation from follow-on registrants under § 3(c)(1)(D)(ii) for EPA's use of data results from FIFRA and does not depend on or replace a right to such compensation under state law. . . . As a matter of state law, property rights in a trade secret are extinguished when a company discloses its trade secret to persons not obligated to protect the confidentiality of the information. . . . Therefore registrants who submit data with notice of the scheme established by the 1978 amendments, and its qualified protection of trade secrets as defined in § 10, can claim no property interest under state law in data subject to § 3(c)(1)(D)(ii). . . . Nor do individuals who submitted data prior to 1978 have a right to compensation under FIFRA that depends on state law. To be sure, such users might have a claim that the new scheme results in a taking of property interests protected by state law. . . . Compensation for any uncompensated taking is available under the Tucker Act. For purposes of compensation under FIFRA's regulatory scheme, however, it is the "mandatory licensing provision" that creates the relationship between the data submitter and the follow-on registrant, and federal law supplies the rule of decision. . . .

Alternatively, appellees contend that FIFRA confers a "private right" to compensation, requiring either Article III adjudication or review by an Article III court sufficient to retain "the essential attributes of the judicial power." . . . This "private right" argument rests on the distinction between public and private rights drawn by the plurality in *Northern Pipeline*. The *Northern Pipeline* plurality construed the Court's prior opinions to permit only three clearly defined exceptions to the rule of Article III adjudication: military tribunals, territorial courts, and decisions involving "public" as opposed to "private" rights. Drawing upon language in *Crowell v. Benson* [285 U.S. 22 (1932)], . . . the plurality defined "public rights" as "matters arising between the Government and persons subject to its authority in connection with the performance of the constitutional functions of the executive or legislative departments." . . . It identified "private rights" as "the liability of one individual to another under the law as defined." . . .

This theory that the public rights/private rights dichotomy of *Crowell* and *Murray's Lessee v. Hoboken Land & Improvement Co.*, 18 How. 272 (1856), provides a bright-line test for determining the requirements of Article III did not command a majority of the Court in *Northern Pipeline*. Insofar as appellees interpret that case and *Crowell* as establishing that the right to an Article III forum is absolute unless the Federal Government is a party of record, we cannot agree. . . . Nor did a majority of the Court endorse the implication of the private right/public right dichotomy that Article III has no force simply because a dispute is between the Government and an individual. . . .

B

Chief Justice Hughes, writing for the Court in *Crowell,* expressly rejected a formalistic or abstract Article III inquiry, stating:

"In deciding whether the Congress, in enacting the statute under review, has exceeded the limits of its authority to prescribe procedure . . ., *regard must be had, as in other cases where constitutional limits are invoked, not to mere matters of form but to the substance of what is required.*" 285 U.S., at 53 (emphasis added).

Crowell held that Congress could replace a seaman's traditional negligence action in admiralty with a statutory scheme of strict liability. In response to practical concerns, Congress rejected adjudication in Article III courts and instead provided that claims for compensation would be determined in an administrative proceeding by a deputy commissioner appointed by the United States Employees' Compensation Commission. . . . "[T]he findings of the deputy commissioner, supported by evidence and within the scope of his authority," were final with respect to injuries to employees within the purview of the statute. . . . Although such findings clearly concern obligations among private parties, this fact did not make the scheme invalid under Article III. Instead, after finding that the administrative proceedings satisfied due process, . . . *Crowell* concluded that the judicial review afforded by the statute, including review of matters of law, "provides for the appropriate exercise of the judicial function in this class of cases." . . .

The enduring lesson of *Crowell* is that practical attention to substance rather than doctrinaire reliance on formal categories should inform application of Article III. . . . The extent of judicial review afforded by the legislation reviewed in *Crowell* does not constitute a minimal requirement of Article III without regard to the origin of the right at issue or the concerns guiding the selection by Congress of a particular method for resolving disputes. In assessing the degree of judicial involvement required by Article III in this case, we note that the statute considered in *Crowell* is different from FIFRA in significant respects. Most importantly, the statute in *Crowell* displaced a traditional cause of action and affected a pre-existing relationship based on a common-law contract for hire. Thus it clearly fell within the range of matters reserved to Article III courts under the holding of *Northern Pipeline*. . . .

If the identity of the parties alone determined the requirements of Article III, under appellees' theory the constitutionality of many quasi-adjudicative activities carried on by administrative agencies involving claims between individuals would be thrown into doubt. . . .

The Court has treated as a matter of "public right" an essentially adversary proceeding to invoke tariff protections against a competitor, as well as an administrative proceeding to determine the rights of landlords and tenants. . . . These proceedings surely determine liabilities of individuals. Such schemes would be beyond the power of Congress under appellees' interpretation of *Crowell*. In essence, the public rights doctrine reflects simply a pragmatic understanding that when Congress selects a quasi-judicial method of resolving matters that "could be conclusively determined by the Executive and Legislative Branches," the danger of encroaching on the judicial powers is reduced. *Northern Pipeline Construction Co. v. Marathon Pipe Line Co.*, 458 U.S., at 68, 102 S. Ct., at 2870 (plurality opinion), citing *Crowell v. Benson*, 285 U.S., at 50.

C

Looking beyond form to the substance of what FIFRA accomplishes, we note several aspects of FIFRA that persuade us the arbitration scheme adopted by Congress does not contravene Article III. First, the right created by FIFRA is not a purely "private" right, but bears many of the characteristics of a "public" right. Use of a registrant's data to support a follow-on registration serves a public purpose as an integral part of a program safeguarding the public health. Congress has the power, under Article I, to authorize an agency administering a complex regulatory scheme to allocate costs and benefits among voluntary participants in the program without providing an Article III adjudication. It also has the power to condition issuance of registrations or licenses on compliance with agency procedures. Article III is not so inflexible that it bars Congress from shifting the task of data valuation from the agency to the interested parties. . . .

The 1978 amendments represent a pragmatic solution to the difficult problem of spreading the costs of generating adequate information regarding the safety, health, and environmental impact of a potentially dangerous product. Congress, without implicating Article III, could have authorized EPA to charge follow-on registrants fees to cover the cost of data and could have directly subsidized FIFRA data submitters for their contributions of needed data. . . . Instead, it selected a framework that collapses these two steps into one, and permits the parties to fix the amount of compensation, with binding arbitration to resolve intractable disputes. Removing the task of valuation from agency personnel to civilian arbitrators, selected by agreement of the parties or appointed on a case-by-case basis by an independent federal agency, surely does not diminish the likelihood of impartial decisionmaking, free from political influence. . . .

The near disaster of the FIFRA 1972 amendments and the danger to public health of further delay in pesticide registration led Congress to select arbitration as the appropriate method of dispute resolution. Given the nature of the right at issue and the concerns motivating the Legislature, we do not think this system threatens the independent role of the Judiciary in our constitutional scheme. "To hold otherwise would be to defeat the obvious purpose of the legislation to furnish a prompt, continuous, expert and inexpensive method for dealing with a class of questions of fact which are peculiarly suited to examination and determination by an administrative agency specially assigned to that task." . . .

We note as well that the FIFRA arbitration scheme incorporates its own system of internal sanctions and relies only tangentially, if at all, on the Judicial Branch for enforcement. . . . The danger of Congress or the Executive encroaching on the Article III judicial powers is at a minimum when no unwilling defendant is subjected to judicial enforcement power as a result of the agency "adjudication." . . .

We need not decide in this case whether a private party could initiate an action in court to enforce a FIFRA arbitration. . . . FIFRA contains no provision explicitly authorizing a party to invoke judicial process to compel arbitration or enforce an award. . . .

Finally, we note that FIFRA limits but does not preclude review of the arbitration proceeding by an Article III court. We conclude that, in the circumstances, the review afforded preserves the "appropriate exercise of the judicial function." . . . FIFRA at a minimum allows private parties to secure Article III review of the arbitrator's "findings and determination" for fraud, misconduct, or misrepresentation. § 3(c)(1)(D)(ii). This provision protects against arbitrators who abuse or exceed their powers or willfully misconstrue their mandate under the governing law. . . . Moreover, review of constitutional error is preserved, . . . and FIFRA, therefore, does not obstruct whatever judicial review might be required by due process. . . . We need not identify the extent to which due process may require review of determinations by the arbitrator because the parties stipulated below to abandon any due process claims. . . . For purposes of our analysis, it is sufficient to note that FIFRA does provide for limited Article III review, including whatever review is independently required by due process considerations.

IV

. . . .

[The Court also rejected arguments based on Article I.]

V

. . . .

[JUSTICE BRENNAN, with whom JUSTICE MARSHALL and JUSTICE BLACKMUN join, wrote a concurring opinion. JUSTICE STEVENS wrote a separate concurring opinion.]

NOTES AND QUESTIONS

5-33. Why does the Court conclude that Article III is not violated in this case? How important is the fact that the parties involved in this case actually consented to arbitration?

5-34. How much judicial review of an arbitrator's judgments exists? To what extent would more extensive judicial review undercut the goals of arbitration? Why?

5-35. Is this case consistent in its approach to the constitutional issues involved with the majority's approach in *Schor v. Commodity Futures Trading Committee, infra* Chapter Six, § 6.11.

5-36. Does arbitration raise any Article II concerns? How are arbitrators appointed? *See* Chapter Seven, § 7.03, *infra*. What about Article I? Does arbitration involve the delegation of administrative power to private decisionmakers?

DEVINE v. PASTORE

District of Columbia Court of Appeals
732 F.2d 213 (1984)

Before BORK and SCALIA, CIRCUIT JUDGES, and WILLIAMS, SENIOR DISTRICT JUDGE.

Opinion for the Court filed by CIRCUIT JUDGE SCALIA.

SCALIA, CIRCUIT JUDGE:

Petitioner, Director of the Office of Personnel Management, seeks review of an order of arbitrator Joseph M. Pastore, Jr., mitigating the penalty of removal imposed by the Customs Service against James Estrella, a Customs Inspector, for the theft of merchandise entrusted to him. Because we find that the arbitrator erred in making his own assessment of an appropriate penalty rather than merely determining whether the penalty imposed by the agency was arbitrary or capricious; and may also have committed the error of considering the disciplinary factors set forth in the collective bargaining agreement controlling, to the exclusion of other factors permitted by federal personnel law; we grant the petition for review and remand the case to the arbitrator.

I

James Estrella was a Customs Inspector assigned to the Maersk Terminal Wharf, Port Newark, New Jersey. He had been a Customs Inspector for four of his nearly thirty years of government employment. Customs Inspectors are responsible for the administration and enforcement of the laws governing the import and export of merchandise; they operate independently, under only limited general supervision. On August 29, 1980, security officers for Maersk Lines observed Estrella remove from the cargo area a shirt worth approximately $14 at retail and place it in his car. Following an investigation, and Estrella's response to the charges, the Customs Service issued an order removing Estrella from his position, effective April 9, 1981.

The national collective bargaining agreement negotiated between the United States Customs Service and the National Treasury Employees Union ("NTEU"), Estrella's collective bargaining representative, contains a grievance procedure and a procedure of submitting unresolved grievances to arbitration. It also contains provisions relating to the discipline of employees and the factors management should weigh in determining an appropriate penalty. Estrella filed a grievance relating to his dismissal on April 20, 1981. When this could not be resolved informally, the NTEU invoked arbitration on his behalf. The parties selected Joseph M. Pastore, Jr., to serve as arbitrator.

Both the Customs Service and the NTEU introduced evidence concerning whether Estrella had taken the shirt, and argument concerning whether the penalty of removal was appropriate. Both parties[1] agreed that the appropriateness of the penalty should be judged by the following question which was derived from the contract's discipline terms:

> Was the removal of the grievant in violation of the *contractual requirements for removal* only for such cases as will promote the efficiency of the Service; discipline to be progressive in nature; and like penalties for like offenses and, if so, what shall the remedy be?

In re Arbitration between the National Treasury Employees Union and the United States Customs Service, Initial Opinion and Award at 5 (Jan. 26, 1982) (Pastore, Arb.) (emphasis added).

The arbitrator found on January 26, 1982, that Estrella had placed the shirt in his car for his own use, and that although Estrella's actions "did tend to impair the efficiency of the Service," his removal was not consistent with the contractual policies of progressive discipline and like penalties for like offenses. *Id.* at 25. The arbitrator also found the action inconsistent with his own interpretation of the agency's Table of Offenses and Discipline. Accordingly, he mitigated Estrella's discipline to a thirty-one day suspension.

On March 5, 1982, the Office of Personnel Management ("OPM") intervened to request the arbitrator to reconsider. OPM argued, as it has in this court, that the arbitrator erred in failing to apply the "arbitrary, capricious, or clearly erroneous" standard in reviewing the agency's decision. The arbitrator denied OPM's reconsideration request on May 20, 1982. The opinion on reconsideration again reviewed the evidence supporting the penalty and reaffirmed that the removal sanction was not justified under the contractual tests. . . .

II

Section 7121 of the civil service law, 5 U.S.C. § 7121(f) (1982), authorizes the Director of the Office of Personnel Management to seek judicial review of the decisions of arbitrators in the same manner as he is empowered by § 7703 to seek review of decisions of the Merit Systems Protection Board (MSPB), *id.* at § 7703. The Director may petition for review of those orders having a "substantial impact" on the operation of the civil service system. The granting of such a petition is at the discretion of the court. *Id.* at § 7703(d). Our consideration of this case persuades us that the resolution of the issues it presents can have a substantial impact on civil service law, and the case is therefore appropriate for review. . . .

III

The Civil Service Reform Act of 1978, Pub. L. No. 95–454, 92 Stat. 1111 (codified as amended in scattered sections of 5 U.S.C. (1982)), established alternative procedures for review of agency actions removing employees. An employee has the option of pursuing the Act's appellate procedures by taking his appeal to the MSPB, or he may pursue the negotiated grievance procedures

---

[1] The parties to the arbitration were the NTEU and the Customs Service. The Office of Personnel Management did not intervene until after the arbitrator issued his Initial Opinion and Award.

contained in the employee's collective bargaining agreement. 5 U.S.C. § 7121(e)(1) (1982). Estrella initiated the latter procedure by filing a grievance. Grievance procedures, typically culminating in arbitration, and MSPB review differ in many respects. Arbitration is recognized as "faster, cheaper, less formal, more responsive to industrial needs, and more conducive to the preservation of ongoing employment relations." *Devine v. White, supra,* 697 F.2d at 435. While undoubtedly hoping to encourage employee selection of the grievance-arbitration process, Congress did not wish that choice to be made on the basis of a predictable difference in substantive outcome. To the contrary, it envisioned a system that would, as between arbitration and MSPB procedures, "promote consistency . . . and . . . avoid forum shopping." . . . This court has previously noted that substantial disuniformity between the review powers of arbitrators and of the MSPB would frustrate congressional intent. *See Local 2578, American Federation of Government Employees v. General Services Administration,* 711 F.2d 261, 265 (D.C. Cir. 1983).

One of the areas in which uniformity is required is the standard of review applied by the decisionmaker. The statute itself, 5 U.S.C. § 7121(e)(2), is explicit on the point, stating that in those matters appealable to the MSPB "an arbitrator shall be governed by section 7701(c)(1) of this title, as applicable" — the section setting forth the MSPB's standards of review. In *Local 2578, supra,* in holding that an arbitrator erred by reducing to review an agency's choice of penalties, we said: "The inequity of an arbitrator having less authority than the MSPB to deal with the same adverse action is self-evident; an aggrieved employee would be likely to choose the forum providing the greatest independent review of an adverse decision." 711 F.2d at 265. *Local 2578* involved an arbitrator who had declined to review the appropriateness of a penalty entirely. But its reasoning applies as well to the standard of review, and supports the conclusion not only that the arbitrator's authority can be no less than the MSPB's but also that it can be no greater. In fact, this corollary has even more substantial support, since it is demanded not only by the congressional intent to prevent outcome-related forum shopping, but also by that provision of the Civil Service Reform Act which prohibits any collective bargaining agreement to "affect the authority of any management official of any agency . . . to suspend, remove, reduce in grade or pay, or take other disciplinary action against . . . employees." 5 U.S.C. § 7106(a)(A). That provision would be violated if an agreement could, by providing for arbitration, alter the test that must be met to support such agency action, making it more rigorous than that which the law (and the MSPB) would provide.

It is clear that in the present case the arbitrator applied a different (and more intensive) standard of review than would have been applied by the MSPB. In responding to OPM's motion for reconsideration he said:

> The question presented to the Arbitrator was *not,* as OPM contends, whether the adverse action of discharge was within the spectrum of available penalties which might be imposed by the Service nor was the question presented to the Arbitrator, directly, one of testing to determine whether the adverse action imposed upon the grievant was "arbitrary and capricious." Rather, the parties freely solicited the opinion and judgment of the Arbitrator only with respect to the *contractual test* of whether the

> removal of James Estrella met each of the three conditions of (1) efficiency impairment; (2) like penalty for like offenses; and, (3) progressive discipline as cited in Article 30 of the Agreement.

Opinion on Reconsideration at 6 (emphasis in original). He noted that he had been asked by the parties to "determine whether certain provisions of Article 30 of the Agreement were violated by the Service and 'if so, what shall the remedy be?'" and that his obligation was "morally, to attempt to decide in a manner which is just to the individuals involved while at the same time maintaining productive union-management peace and harmony." *Id.* at 15. This differs from MSPB review in that it constitutes a direct application of the arbitrator's own judgment regarding the appropriate penalty, rather than according what the Board has described as "appropriate deference to the primary discretion which has been entrusted to agency management, not to the Board," *Douglas v. Veterans Administration,* 5 MSPB 313, 328 (1981).

> The Board's role in this process is not to insist that the balance be struck precisely where the Board would choose to strike it if the Board were in the agency's shoes in the first instance; such an approach would fail to accord proper deference to the agency's primary discretion in managing its workforce. . . . Only if the Board finds that the agency failed to weigh the relevant factors, or that the agency's judgment clearly exceeded the limits of reasonableness, is it appropriate for the Board then to specify how the agency's decision should be corrected to bring the penalty within the parameters of reasonableness.

Id. at 332-33. We have approved this standard of review in *Parsons v. United States Department of the Air Force,* 707 F.2d 1406, 1409 (D.C. Cir. 1983).

The arbitrator's review may also have differed from that which would correctly be applied by the MSPB in that he considered the relevant factors to be those set forth in the NTEU-Customs Service collective bargaining agreement. But if a collective bargaining agreement were able to fix the factors governing discipline, it would "affect the authority of [a] management official of [an] agency . . . to . . . take . . . disciplinary action," 5 U.S.C. § 7106(a)(2)(A) — which, as we have said above, the law prohibits. Thus, if the disciplinary factors recited in the NTEU-Customs Service agreement were different from the factors permitted and required by federal personnel law, we would be confronted with the issue whether a provision not properly includable in a collective bargaining agreement must nonetheless be given effect unless challenged directly pursuant to the procedures set forth in the Federal Service Labor–Management Relations title of the Civil Service Reform Act, 5 U.S.C. §§ 7116(a)(5), 7117(c) (1982). We find it unnecessary to reach that issue, however, since the present agreement can be interpreted in a fashion that renders it unquestionably lawful. Although it does not recite all the factors relevant under federal personnel law, those factors it does recite are consistent with them, and the remaining factors can reasonably be considered subsumed within the contract's residual phrase "any other factors or circumstances bearing upon the incidents or acts involved." . . . But although the language of the agreement may be given this breadth, there is nothing to indicate that the arbitrator interpreted it that way. To the extent the arbitrator considered himself, by reason of being bound to the specific factors enumerated in the agreement, unable to take account of all the factors permissible under federal personnel law, he would have been misinterpreting the agreement and thus misapplying the law.

IV

Since the arbitrator applied an erroneous standard of review, we must set aside his determination. OPM has urged us to resolve this matter finally here, on the ground that the agency could not, as a matter of law, be reversed in the circumstances of this case. We decline to do so, if only because the circumstances may not have been fully developed in the record if the parties (both of whom were applying the contractual test) believed that test to exclude any of the factors relevant under federal personnel law. We think it preferable to remand this proceeding to the arbitrator for reconsideration of the issue of level of discipline under the proper standard and taking into account all appropriate factors, with the ability to receive any further evidence that such reconsideration may render desirable.

The factors relevant under federal personnel law are set forth at some length in *Douglas v. Veterans Administration, supra*, 5 MSPB at 329-32. . . . The standard which must be met, in the application of those factors, has been variously described by the board as whether the disciplinary action is "clearly excessive"; "arbitrary, capricious, or unreasonable"; "too harsh and unreasonable under the circumstances"; "unduly harsh, arbitrary, and unreasonable"; "an abuse of agency discretion, or . . . [reflecting] an inherent disproportion between the offense and the personnel action, or disparity in treatment"; "unreasonable"; "clearly excessive in proportion to the sustained charges"; "violat[ive of] the principle of like penalties for like offenses, or . . . otherwise unreasonable under all the relevant circumstances"; and "within tolerable limits of reasonableness." . . .

We further note that if the arbitrator finds the agency action insupportable on this basis, his subsequent task is not to select that discipline which in his independent view is appropriate, but merely to reduce the agency's to a level that is "within the parameters of reasonableness," *Douglas v. Veterans Administration, supra*, 5 MSPB at 333 — that is, to reduce it only so much as is necessary to bring it to a level that can be sustained.

Petition granted.

NOTES AND QUESTIONS

5-37. Why is it so vital that the arbitrator apply the same standards as the Merit Systems Protection Board ("MSPB")? How did Congress intend to mesh traditional administrative adjudication with arbitration?

5-38. Why did the court remand this case to the arbitrator?

5-39. What are the advantages of arbitration over administrative adjudication in this case from society's point of view? From the litigators' points of view?

[D] Other ADR Approaches and Their Critics

Mediation and mini-trials are also increasingly common at the administrative level. Consider the following:

Harter, POINTS ON A CONTINUUM: DISPUTE RESOLUTION PROCEDURES AND THE ADMINISTRATIVE PROCESS*

1 ADMIN. L.J. AM. U. 143, 147-50 (1987)

D. *Minitrial*

In a minitrial, the lawyers for each party are given a relatively short period — ranging from several hours to several days — to make their best case, generally following the exchange of important documents and other factual materials. The parties will sometimes call witnesses, but generally only arguments based on previously presented evidence and the legal conclusions that flow from the issues are presented. The attorneys make these presentations to representatives of the parties (executives) who have the authority to settle the controversy and usually, but not always, a neutral third party. When the arguments are concluded the representatives then meet to negotiate an agreement.

The process is designed so that the executives may view their own case in perspective, evaluating its strengths and weaknesses against those of the other party. The neutral may be called upon to render an opinion as to how a court or jury would decide the controversy. The parties may also ask the neutral for more limited advice. The neutral is, therefore, more an agent of reality than an arbitrator. As such, his or her report would potentially change the bargaining position of the parties, thus providing an incentive to settle before the report is issued. The report may also convince a party that its case is not as strong as originally believed and hence that a settlement may be the advisable route. The function of the minitrial is to convert what could be a complex, protracted legal battle into a business decision to be made by the executives of the parties.

E. *Mediation*

Mediation is, simply, a negotiation involving a mediator. A mediator is a neutral third party who assists the parties in negotiating an agreement. The mediator has no independent authority and does not render a decision; the parties make the decision themselves.

---

* Copyright © 1987 by Administrative Law Journal of American University. Reprinted with permission. All rights reserved.

The mediator, however, may be quite active in the negotiation process. He will usually help the parties frame the issues, and analyze their actual needs, as well as the needs of the other side. Another important role played by the mediator is to deflate unreasonably ambitious assertions and desires. He or she will likely offer suggestions for possible solutions for settling the issues and draft materials for the consideration of the negotiators. Some of these suggestions may, of course, come from the parties themselves, but they will be communicated in such a manner as to avoid locking a party into an idea that does not work. The mediator may also need to communicate to the parties what is likely to happen if an agreement is not reached. In the current vernacular, the mediator will help the parties define their "best alternative to a negotiated agreement" (BATNA).

The mediator may meet privately with the parties and shuttle back and forth between them. Private meetings are frequently helpful in developing a negotiation framework and sufficiently defining the issues so that the parties can address them directly in a meeting. Without prior definition, the parties may find the risk of direct discussion too great. Moreover, the shuttling can save valuable time by reducing the need for more direct, face-to-face meetings, which are always difficult to schedule among senior representatives. The mediator can also deflect attention from the negotiators by being the spokesperson to those not engaged in the discussions. More importantly, the mediator also serves as the proponent of the process itself and can help keep discussions on track and moving.

The increased use of ADR in general, however, both in agencies and in courts, is not without its critics. To what extent does the following critique of ADR in general apply to the administrative process in particular?

Edwards, ALTERNATIVE DISPUTE RESOLUTION: PANACEA OR ANATHEMA?

*99 HARV. L. REV. 668, 676-82 (1986)** *

If we can assume that it is possible to finance and administer truly efficient *systems* of dispute resolution, then there would appear to be no significant objections to the use of even wholly independent ADR mechanisms to resolve private disputes that do not implicate important public values. For instance, settling minor grievances between neighbors according to local mores or resolving simple contract disputes by commercial norms may lead to the disposition of more disputes and the greater satisfaction of the participants. In strictly private disputes, ADR mechanisms such as arbitration often are superior to adjudication. Disputes can be resolved by neutrals with substantive expertise, preferably chosen by the parties, and the substance of disputes

---

* Copyright © 1986 by Harvard Law Review Association. All rights reserved.

can be examined without issue-obscuring procedural rules. Tens of thousands of cases are resolved this way each year by labor and commercial arbitration, and even more private disputes undoubtedly could be better resolved through ADR than by adjudication.

However, if ADR is extended to resolve difficult issues of constitutional or public law-making use of nonlegal values to resolve important social issues or allowing those the law seeks to regulate to delimit public rights and duties — there is real reason for concern. An oft-forgotten virtue of adjudication is that it ensures the proper resolution and application of public values. In our rush to embrace alternatives to litigation, we must be careful not to endanger what law has accomplished or to destroy this important function of formal adjudication. As Professor Fiss notes:

> Adjudication uses public resources, and employees not strangers chosen by the parties but public officials chosen by a process in which the public participates. These officials, like members of the legislative and executive branches, possess a power that has been defined and conferred by public law, not by private agreement. Their job is not to maximize the ends of private parties, not simply to secure the peace, but to explicate and give force to the values embodied in authoritative texts such as the constitution and statutes: to interpret those values and to bring reality in accord with them.

The concern here is that ADR will replace the rule of law with nonlegal values. J. Anthony Lucas' masterful study of Boston during the busing crisis highlights the critical point that often our nation's most basic values — such as equal justice under the law — conflict with local nonlegal mores. This was true in Boston during the school desegregation battle, and it was true in the South during the civil rights battles of the sixties. This conflict, however, between national public values reflected in rules of law and nonlegal values that might be embraced in alternative dispute resolution, exists in even more mundane public issues.

For example, many environmental disputes are now settled by negotiation and mediation instead of adjudication. Indeed, as my colleague Judge Wald recently observed, there is little hope that Superfund legislation can solve our nations's toxic waste problem unless the vast bulk of toxic waste disputes are resolved through negotiation, rather than litigation. Yet, as necessary as environmental negotiation may be, it is still troubling. When Congress or a government agency has enacted strict environmental protection standards, negotiations that compromise these strict standards with weaker standards result in the application of values that are simply inconsistent with the rule of law. Furthermore, environmental mediation and negotiation present the danger that environmental standards will be set by private groups without the democratic checks of governmental institutions. Professor Schoenbroad recently has written of an impressive environmental mediation involving the settlement of disputes concerning the Hudson River. According to Schoenbroad, in that case private parties bypassed federal and state agencies, reached an accommodation on environmental issues, and then presented the settlement to governmental regulators. The alternative to approval of the settlement was continued litigation, which was already in its seventeenth year, with no end in sight.

The resulting agreement may have been laudable in bringing an end to protracted litigation. But surely the mere resolution of a dispute is not proof that the public interest has been served. This is not to say that private settlements can never produce results that are consistent with the public interest; rather, it is to say that private settlements are troubling when we have no assurance that the legislative — or agency — mandated standards have been followed, and when we have no satisfactory explanation as to why there may have been a variance from the rule of law.

In the Hudson River example, we should be concerned if private negotiators settled the environmental dispute without any meaningful input or participation from government regulators, or if the private parties negotiated a settlement at variance with the environmental standard that had been established by government agencies. If, however, government agencies promulgated the governing environmental standards pursuant to legislatively established rulemaking procedures (which, of course, involve public participation), and if the private parties negotiated a settlement in accordance with these agency standards and subject to agency approval, then the ADR process may be seen to have worked well in conjunction with the rule of law. Indeed, the environmental negotiators may have facilitated the implementation of the rule of law by doing what agency regulators had been unable to achieve for seventeen years. . . .

Even with these concerns, however, there are a number of promising areas in which we might employ ADR in lieu of traditional litigation. Once a body of law is well developed, arbitration and other ADR mechanisms can be structured in such a way that public rights and duties would not be defined and delimited by private groups. The recent experience of labor arbitrators in the federal sector, who are required to police compliance with laws, rules, and regulations, suggests that the interpretation and application of law may not lie outside the competence of arbitrators. So long as we restrict arbitrators to the application of clearly defined rules of law, and strictly confine the articulation of public laws to our courts, ADR can be an effective means of reducing mushrooming caseloads. Employment discrimination cases offer a promising example. Many employment discrimination cases are highly fact-bound and can be resolved by applying established principles of law. Others, however, present novel questions that should be resolved by a court. If the more routine cases could be certified to an effective alternative dispute resolution system that would have the authority to make some final determinations, the courts could devote greater attention to novel legal questions, and the overall efficiency of an anti-discrimination law might be enhanced.

In other areas, we could capitalize on the substantive expertise and standards developed by well-established ADR mechanisms. For example, the experience and standards developed through decades of labor arbitration and mediation could prove particularly useful in settling disputes between non-unionized employees and their employees in cases of "unjust dismissal." Labor arbitrators have developed fine-tuned standards for just-cause terminations, which they could easily transfer to the nonunion workplace, thus providing similar protection to nonunion employees. Similarly, the expertise developed over the years by commercial arbitrators could be used to settle other business disputes, which now often require years of litigation. We should also encourage more private parties to accept binding arbitration voluntarily. Recently, the SEC and the securities industry developed a system of securities arbitration used in thousands of securities law cases. If this system is fair to investors and to broker-dealers, perhaps we should permit investors to commit themselves by contract to binding arbitration.

Additionally, the qualities of labor arbitration that make it so successful in the context of collective bargaining are readily transferable to other fields of law. The presence of a skilled neutral with substantive expertise, the avoidance of issue-obscuring procedural rules, the arbitrator's freedom to exercise common sense, the selection of arbitrators by the parties, and the tradition of limited judicial review of arbitral decisions — factors that make arbitration superior to litigation in labor cases — would make arbitration superior to litigation in other contexts as well. Although the labor context has the benefit of a collective bargaining agreement providing rules not subject to arbitrary change by one party, the experience with federal employees demonstrates that arbitration can achieve substantial benefits even when it is limited to the interpretation of rules imposed unilaterally. Perhaps arbitration could prove useful in moderating disagreements between citizens, in resolving grievances of citizens against social service agencies, and in resolving complaints of prisoners over conditions of confinement. . . .

ADR can thus play a vital role in constructing a judicial system that is both more manageable and more responsive to the needs of our citizens. It is essential — as the foregoing examples illustrate — that this role of ADR be strictly limited to prevent the resolution of important constitutional and public law issues by ADR mechanisms that are independent of our courts. Fortunately, few ADR programs have attempted to remove public law issues from the courts. Although this may merely reflect the relative youth of the ADR movement, it may also manifest an awareness of the danger of public law resolution in nonjudicial fora.

ADR has a long history in the United States and it is becoming a major alternative to judicial processes. For a chronological account of ADR and how ADR has developed over time, *see Past, Present & Future: Building on 70 Years of Innovation — The AAA Looks to the 21st Century*, 51-SEP DISP RESOL. J. 109 (1997). *See also* Thomas J. Stipanowich, *ADR and the "Vanishing Trial": The Growth and Impact of "Alternative Dispute Resolution,"* 1 J. EMPIRICAL LEGAL STUD. 843, 872–74 (2004). He notes that the ADR cases reported by the AAA have increased from 63,171 to 230,258 in just ten years. Of course, the American Arbitration Association has a strong interest in promoting ADR, but it is not alone in promoting alternatives to litigation. The Clinton administration, under the guidance of Vice President Gore, also took ADR very seriously as a way to reduce the cost of rulemaking. By 1994, the National Performance Review's emphasis on negotiated rulemaking and ADR had prompted twenty-four federal agencies to review contract disputes with a

[E] Negotiated Rulemaking

In Chapter Five, we have, thus far, considered various ADR techniques and their applicability to the administrative process. ADR is not, however, limited only to adjudicatory contexts. Given the increasingly adversarial atmosphere that surrounds agency rulemaking, not to speak of the procedural complexities introduced by hybrid rulemaking and the almost inevitable judicial appeals that follow, negotiated approaches to policymaking are becoming increasingly common. Congress passed the Negotiated Rulemaking Act of 1990 in an attempt to encourage the involvement of affected parties in the initial stages of the policymaking process prior to publication of a notice of proposed rulemaking. *See* Pub. L. 101-648, 104 Stat. 4969.*

The Negotiated Rulemaking Act was renewed in 1996. *See* Pub. L. No. 104-320 (110 Stat. 3870). Negotiated Rulemaking has become increasingly popular in certain agencies. On topics as divergent as lawnmower emissions, Laura A. Stefani, *Reducing CO and HC Emissions from Small Nonroad Spark-ignition Engines: How Manufacturers Must Comply with New CAA Regulations*, 3 ENVTL. LAW 531 (1997), safe drinking water, William E. Cox, *Evolution of the Safe Drinking Water Act: A Search for Effective Quality Assurance Strategy and Workable Concepts of Federalism,* 21 WM. & MARY ENVTL. L. & POL'Y REV. 69 (1997), and clean air, Margaret L. Claiborne, *Regulation by Consensus: The Expanded Use of Regulatory Negotiation Under the Clean Air Act,* 11-Fall NAT. RESOURCES & ENV'T 44 (1996), the Environmental Protection Agency has made extensive use of negotiated rulemaking prior to the notice-and-comment stage. The Education Department is *required* to use negotiated rulemaking, at least in part, in § 1431 of the Elementary and Secondary Education Act of 1965. *See also,* J. Gregory Smith, *Alternative Dispute Resolution and the Wetlands Manual Debate: Could Negotiated Rulemaking Have Avoided the Impasse?* 9 OHIO ST. J. on DISP. RESOL. 415, 432 (1994). Not everyone is thrilled with all aspects of negotiated rulemaking, however. One attorney at the National Resources Defense Council commented that it took a full 30 days of work, rather than the usual three days required to comment on a traditionally-proposed rule, to provide the necessary negotiated rulemaking input for woodburning stove regulations (testimony on § 1504 before the Committee on Governmental Affairs, United States Senate, May 13, 1988). For an empirical assessment of the effectiveness, or lack thereof, of the Negotiated Rulemaking Act, see Cary Coglianese, *Assessing Consensus: The Promise and Performance of Negotiated Rulemaking,* 46 DUKE L.J. 1255 (1997) (concluding that the procedure has not been superior to informal rulemaking).

Does the court's interpretation of the Negotiated Rulemaking Act below ensure that this Act will be as effective as Congress had hoped?

---

* For a more extensive description and discussion of this Act, *see* A. Aman & W. Mayton, *supra, Administrative Law Treatise,* 298–305 (2d Ed., 2001).

USA GROUP LOAN SERVICES, INCORPORATED, USA v. RILEY

United States Court of Appeals, Seventh Circuit
82 F.3d 708 (1996)

Before POSNER, CHIEF JUDGE, and DIANE P. WOOD and EVANS, CIRCUIT JUDGES.

POSNER, CHIEF JUDGE.

The federal government has an enormous program, administered by the Department of Education, of subsidizing student loans. The loans are made by banks but are guaranteed by state and private agencies that have reinsurance contracts with the Department, making it the indirect guarantor of the loans and thus inducing banks to make what would otherwise be risky loans. The proceeds of the loans are used to pay tuition and other expenses; so the colleges and other schools whose students are receiving these loans are also involved in the federal program. Like so many government programs, the student loan program places heavy administrative burdens on the entities involved in it — the lenders, the guarantors, and the institutions.  A whole industry of "servicers" has arisen to relieve these entities of some of the administrative burdens. As agents of the educational institutions, the servicers maintain records of the institution's student loans. As agents of the banks, they collect the loans from the students as the loans come due and dun the students when they are slow in paying. As agents of the guarantors, the servicers keep track of defaults and make sure that the banks comply with the various conditions for triggering the guarantees. In any of these roles a servicer who makes a mistake can end up costing the federal government money. If the servicer remits loan moneys to a school for the tuition of a student not eligible for a loan, or fails to pursue a defaulting student, or honors an invalid claim by a bank for reimbursement from a guarantor, federal money is disbursed in violation of the regulations governing the student loan program.

Mistakes and outright fraud by servicers, some resulting in large losses of federal money, led Congress in 1992 to amend Title IV of the Higher Education Act to authorize the Secretary of Education to "prescribe . . . regulations applicable to third party servicers (including regulations concerning financial responsibility standards for, and the assessment of liabilities for program violations against, such servicers) to establish minimum standards with respect to sound management and accountability." . . . The Secretary has done this, see 34 C.F.R. Parts 668, 682 (1994); Dept. of Education, *Student Assistance General Provisions*, 59 Fed. Reg. 22348 (Apr. 29, 1994), esp. pp. 22405, 22408–10, and the servicers have brought this suit to invalidate portions of the regulations on substantive and procedural grounds. The district court rejected the challenge, and the servicers appeal.

. . . .

§ 5.05   INFORMAL AGENCY ACTION   503

The remaining arguments are procedural and the main one is that the Secretary adopted the challenged regulation in violation of the conditions of "negotiated rulemaking," a novelty in the administrative process. The 1992 amendment to the Higher Education Act, under which the regulation was promulgated, required that the Secretary submit any draft regulation to a process of negotiated rulemaking, to be conducted in accordance with recommendations made by the Administrative Conference of the United States and codified in 1 C.F.R. §§ 305.82-4 and 305.85-5 and with "any successor recommendation, regulation, or law." 20 U.S.C. § 1098a(b). A "successor law" to the Administrative Conference's recommendations had in fact been enacted in 1990. It is the Negotiated Rulemaking Act, 5 U.S.C. §§ 561 *et seq.* . . . The Act and the Administrative Conference's recommendations authorize the agency, in advance of the notice and comment rulemaking proceeding, to submit draft regulations to the industry or other groups that are likely to be significantly affected by the regulations and to negotiate with them over the form and substance of the regulations. The hope is that these negotiations will produce a better draft as the basis for the notice and comment proceeding. The 1992 amendment to the Higher Education Act made negotiated rulemaking mandatory in proceedings implementing the amendment, as we have seen.

The servicers argue that the Department negotiated in bad faith with them. Neither the 1992 amendment nor the Negotiated Rulemaking Act specifies a remedy for such a case, and the latter act strongly implies there is none. . . . But even if a regulation could be invalidated because the agency had failed to negotiate in good faith, this would not carry the day for the servicers.

During the negotiations, an official of the Department of Education promised the servicers that the Department would abide by any consensus reached by them unless there were compelling reasons to depart. The propriety of such a promise may be questioned. It sounds like an abdication of regulatory authority to the regulated, the full burgeoning of the interest-group state, and the final confirmation of the "capture" theory of administrative regulation. At all events, although the servicers reached a firm consensus that they should not be liable for their mistakes the Department refused to abide by its official's promise. What is more, the draft regulations that the Department submitted to the negotiating process capped the servicers' liability at the amount of the fees they received from their customers, yet when it came time to propose a regulation as the basis for the notice and comment rulemaking the Department abandoned the cap. The breach of the promise to abide by consensus in the absence of compelling reasons not here suggested, and the unexplained withdrawal of the Department's proposal to cap the servicers' liability, form the basis for the claim that the Department negotiated in bad faith.

We have doubts about the propriety of the official's promise to abide by a consensus of the regulated industry, but we have no doubt that the Negotiated Rulemaking Act did not make the promise enforceable. *Natural Resources Defense Council, Inc. v. EPA*, 859 F.2d 156, 194 (D.C. Cir. 1988) (*per curiam*). The practical effect of enforcing it would be to make the Act extinguish notice and comment rulemaking in all cases in which it was preceded by negotiated rulemaking; the comments would be irrelevant if the agency were already bound by promises that it had made to the industry. There is no textual or other clue that the Act meant to do this. Unlike collective bargaining negotiations, to which the servicers compare negotiated rulemaking, the Act does not envisage that the negotiations will end in a binding contract. The Act simply creates a consultative process in advance of the more formal arms' length procedure of notice and comment rulemaking. See 5 U.S.C. § 566(f).

The complaint about the Secretary's refusal to adhere to the proposal to cap the servicers' liability misconceives the nature of negotiation. The Secretary proposed the cap in an effort to be accommodating and deflect the industry's wrath. The industry, in retrospect improvidently, rejected the proposal, holding out for no liability. So, naturally, the Secretary withdrew the proposal. A rule that a rejected offer places a ceiling on the offeror's demands would destroy negotiation. Neither party would dare make an offer, as the other party would be certain to reject it in order to limit the future demands that his opponent could make. This concern lies behind the principle that settlement offers are not admissible in litigation if the settlement effort breaks down. Fed. R. Evid. 408. By the same token, the negotiating position of the parties in negotiated rulemaking ought not be admissible in a challenge to the rule eventually promulgated when the negotiation failed.

The servicers argue that they should be allowed to conduct discovery to uncover the full perfidy of the Department's conduct in the negotiations. Discovery is rarely proper in the judicial review of administrative action. The court is supposed to make its decision on the basis of the administrative record, not create its own record. There are exceptions, summarized in *Animal Defense Council v. Hodel*, 840 F.2d 1432, 1436 (9th Cir. 1988), amended, 867 F.2d 1244 (1989), and the main one has some potential applicability here: discovery is proper when it is necessary to create a record without which the challenge to the agency's action cannot be evaluated. *E.g., Citizens to Preserve Overton Park, Inc. v. Volpe*, 401 U.S. 402, (1971). . . . Negotiated rulemaking does not usually produce a comprehensive administrative record, such as notice and comment rulemaking, or a cease and desist order proceeding, or a licensing proceeding would do, any more than a settlement conference will usually produce a full record. Some discovery was conducted in the district court in order to present a picture of what went on at the negotiations between the servicers and the Department. The servicers argue that if only they could get access to the notes of certain participants in the negotiating sessions they could demonstrate additional instances of bad faith on the part of the Department.

Their conception of "bad faith" reflects, as we have noted, a misconception of the negotiation process. It is not bad faith to withdraw an offer after the other side has rejected it. If as we doubt the Negotiated Rulemaking Act creates a remedy as well as a right, we suppose that a refusal to negotiate that *really* was in bad faith, because the agency was determined to stonewall, might invalidate the rule eventually adopted by the agency. But we do not think that the Act was intended to open the door wide to discovery in judicial proceedings challenging regulations issued after the notice and comment proceeding that followed the negotiations. If as in this case the public record discloses no evidence of bad faith on the part of the agency, that should be the end of the inquiry. *Cf. Citizens to Preserve Overton Park, Inc. v. Volpe.* . . .

A contrary conclusion would stretch out such judicial proceedings unconscionably. The Act's purpose — to reduce judicial challenges to regulations by encouraging the parties to narrow their differences in advance of the formal rulemaking proceeding — would be poorly served if the negotiations became a source and focus of litigation.

AFFIRMED.

NOTES AND QUESTIONS

5-40. Why would the agency make the promise it did in this case? What concerned the court if, in fact, this promise had been enforceable?

5-41. What are the purposes of this Act? Consider, first, some of the theoretical advantages of adopting such an approach as set forth in Philip Harter, *Negotiating Regulations: A Cure for Malaise* *

> Negotiating has many advantages over the adversarial process. The parties participate directly and immediately in the decision. They share in its development and concur with it, rather than "participate" by submitting information that the decisionmaker considers in reaching the decision. Frequently, those who participate in the negotiation are closer to the ultimate decisionmaking authority of the interest they represent than traditional intermediaries that represent the interest in an adversarial proceeding. Thus, participants in negotiations can make substantive decisions, rather than acting as experts in the decisionmaking process. In addition, negotiation can be a less expensive means of decisionmaking because it reduces the need to engage in defensive research in anticipation of arguments made by adversaries.
>
> Undoubtedly the prime benefit of direct negotiations is that it enables the participants to focus squarely on their respective interests. They need not advocate and maintain extreme positions before a decisionmaker. Therefore, the parties can develop a feel for the true issues that lie within the advocated extremes and attempt to accommodate fully the competing interests. . . .
>
> Negotiation enables the parties to rank their concerns and to make trades to maximize their respective interests. In a traditional proceeding an agency may be unable to anticipate the intensity with which the respective parties may view the various provisions of a proposed rule. The agency may focus on an aspect of a rule that is critical to one party, but not of particular interest to other parties. An agency simply would have to guess how to reconcile such an issue because it would not know how to rank the parties' concerns. An interested party, however, could easily decide to accommodate another party in return for concession on a critical point. An example of

---

* 71 GEO. L.J. 1, 28–29 (1982) Copyright © 1982 Georgetown Law Journal Association. Reprinted by permission.

such a trade off process would be when a beneficiary of a proposed regulation argues that the standard should be stringent with early compliance by the regulated company. A company that must comply with the regulation might counter that the standard should be more lenient with a long lead time for compliance. An agency faced with this situation might decide to require a lax standard in response to the company's claims of excessive burdens and require a short deadline in response to the need for immediate protection. Everyone involved, however, may be more content with precisely the opposite result. A rule allowing a longer time to implement a more stringent standard might benefit both parties because the shorter time for implementation might cause disruptions that would offset any savings resulting from the reduced level of regulation.

Rulemaking by negotiation can reduce the time and cost of developing regulations by emphasizing practical and empirical concerns rather than theoretical predictions. In developing a regulation under the current system, an agency must prove a factual case, at least preliminarily, and anticipate the factual information that will be submitted in the record. Because the agency lacks direct access to empirical data, the information used is often of a theoretical nature derived from models. In negotiations, the parties in interest decide together what information is necessary to make a reasonably informed decision. Therefore, the data used in negotiations may not have to be as theoretical or as extensive as it is in an adversary process. For example, one agency proposed a regulation based on highly technical, theoretical data. The parties argued that the theoretical data was unnecessary because it simply did not reflect the practical experiences of the parties and of another agency. The agency determined the validity of the assertion and modified its regulation accordingly. The lesson of this example is that the data can emphasize practical and empirical concerns rather than theoretical predictions. In turn, this emphasis on practical experience can reduce the time and cost of developing regulations by reducing the need for developing extensive theoretical data.

Negotiation also can enable the participants to focus on the details of a regulation. In the adversary process, the big points must be hit and hit hard, while the subtleties and details frequently are overlooked. Or, even if the details are not overlooked, the decisionmaker may not appreciate their consequences. In negotiations, however, interested parties can directly address all aspects of a problem in attempting to formulate workable solutions.

Overarching all the other benefits of negotiations is the added legitimacy a rule would acquire if all parties viewed the rule as reasonable and endorsed it without a fight. Affected parties would participate in the development of a rule by sharing in the decisions, ranking their own concerns and needs, and trading them with other parties. Regardless of whether the horse under design turns out to be a five-legged camel or a Kentucky Derby winner, the resulting rule would have a validity beyond those developed under the current procedures. Moreover, nothing indicates that the results would be of any lesser quality than those developed currently. Surely the Code of Federal Regulations stable has as many camels as derby winners.

While attempts to limit the complexity and cost of policymaking are laudable, indeed, consider some of the problems suggested below with the concept of regulatory negotiation:

Negotiated rulemaking is not without its critics. . . .

Regulatory negotiation proved more popular in alternative dispute resolution circles than among administrative law scholars, who attacked it first on theoretical and later on empirical grounds. For some, the mere idea of negotiating rules with stakeholders seemed anathema to the traditional concept of the agency as a faithful agent of Congress. Regulatory negotiation invites agency abdication of responsibility, they argued, by shifting the decision-making burden to stakeholders who owe no duty to the public or to Congress. The process thus embodies what many administrative law theorists viscerally fear: the last step from a system of arm's-length interest representation — which preserves the agency's hierarchical authority — to one of direct interest group bargaining. At a time when public choice theory and its unsentimental account of the legislative and administrative process was on the ascendance in law schools, regulatory negotiation seemed to portend its darkest implications.

Critics argued, moreover, that even if a consensus-based approach to rulemaking might meet democratic standards of legitimacy under some circumstances, surely regulatory negotiation would not succeed in practice. First, the process is insufficiently inclusive because only a limited number of parties can participate without negotiations becoming unwieldy. Moreover, the power to convene a negotiating group carries with it the power to manipulate outcomes. Alone, or in collusion with powerful groups, the agency might rig outcomes in advance through the selection of some stakeholders and the exclusion of others.

In addition, critics anticipated that a consensus approach would favor more powerful, well-financed interests with access to money, information, and technical expertise. Trade associations and large firms in particular would enjoy significant advantages over smaller parties or parties with fewer resources, such as state governments, environmental or labor groups, or small businesses. This advantage, critics believed, would translate into influence over the outcomes. Moreover, even if agencies could balance negotiating committees with representatives from all sides, no single interest could adequately represent the average voter or consumer and, for this reason alone, the process would fall short of American standards of democratic legitimacy. Indeed, critics suspected that regulatory negotiation would be more likely than conventional rulemaking to undermine the public interest and lead to outcomes of dubious legality. For some or all of these reasons, critics viewed regulatory negotiation as, at best, a minor reform for use in limited and tightly controlled circumstances, or, at worst, fundamentally undemocratic. . . .

Defenders of reg neg retorted that negotiated rules were far from secret deals. The Negotiated Rulemaking Act of 1990 ("NRA") requires federal agencies to provide notice of regulatory negotiations in the

Federal Register, to formally charter reg neg committees, and to observe the transparency and accountability requirements of the Federal Advisory Committee Act. Any individual or organization that might be "significantly affected" by a proposed rule can apply for membership in a reg neg committee, and even if the agency rejects their application, they remain free to attend as spectators. Most significantly, the NRA requires that the agency submit negotiated rules to traditional notice and comment.

In addition, many public choice scholars argue that agencies have no incentive to shirk their accountability to congressional principals, who control agency budgets, appoint top personnel, and oversee agency authority. Agencies thus have no incentive to be less responsive to congressional preferences in negotiated rulemaking than in conventional rulemaking.

Proponents of reg neg argued that, in view of these safeguards, agencies are equally accountable for negotiated and conventional rules. Moreover, external checks on agency decision making remain undisturbed by reg neg. Providing they meet traditional standing hurdles, any party may seek judicial review of a negotiated rule, and upon review the rule is entitled to no greater deference for having been negotiated. Indeed, Congress specifically declined to provide for a lower standard of review in the NRA.

Finally, in an attempt to show that reg neg was not a dramatic departure from traditional rulemaking, proponents pointed out that informal negotiation with stakeholders has always been an essential part of the rulemaking process. Negotiated rulemaking merely formalizes negotiation and utilizes it earlier in the rulemaking process, when it is likely to be most useful. In this view, agencies actually conform to congressional intent by using processes like reg neg; consultation with the entities that might be harmed by legislation is precisely what Congress intends when it delegates decision-making authority to the agency.

Jody Freeman & Laura I. Langbein, *Regulatory Negotiation and the Legitimacy Benefit*, 9 N.Y.U. ENVT'L L.J. 60, 71-5 (2000).*

5-42. Consider the following from Professors Shapiro and Glicksman:

Whereas agencies typically have only a few notice and comment proceedings in a year to adopt new rules at the front-end of the process, they are likely to have considerably more adjustment proceedings during a similar time frame. In light of their limited resources, environmental and other citizens groups may find it more difficult to participate fully in adjustment proceedings than to participate in the development of new rules at the front-end of the process. By comparison, regulated entities will be participants in every such process because they will have requested the change.

---

* Copyright © 2000 by New York University Environmental Law Journal. All rights reserved.

Whereas rulemaking proceedings occur in Washington, D.C., where most national environmental and other citizen organizations are located, adjustment proceedings also occur in regional offices far from Washington. In light of the limited resources of environmental and other pubic interest groups, those groups may not be able to participate in dozens of back-end proceedings involving requests for regulatory adjustments. Moreover, although regional or local groups may be in a better position to participate in adjudications in a regional office, some of these groups lack the scientific and technical resources to participate effectively in adjustment proceedings to the extent that such decisions turn on this information. Indeed, even the national organizations may not be able to afford to marshal the scientific and technical resources to participate in dozens of adjustment proceedings.

Sidney A. Shapiro & Robert L. Glicksman, *The APA and the Back-End of Regulation: Procedures for Informal Adjudication*, 56 ADMIN. L. REV. 1159.[*]

If environmental groups and other public interest groups concentrate their resources in Washington, D.C. so as to be able to vigorously lobby Congress for tough laws and to be a vocal participant in agency rulemaking decisions, does their inability to effectively participate in case-by-case adjustments of the rule or statute cancel out their influence in the formulation of the rule or statute? In other words, can Congressmen and the President (the person to whom most agency heads ultimately answer) campaign on their "pro-environment" rules when speaking to groups concerned about the environment while still being able to campaign on "flexibility" to pro-industry groups?

---

[*] Copyright © 2004 by American Bar Association. Reprinted by permission.

PART TWO

LEGISLATIVE, EXECUTIVE AND JUDICIAL CONTROL OF AGENCY DISCRETION: OUTSIDE THE WALLS OF THE AGENCY

LEGISLATIVE, EXECUTIVE AND JUDICIAL CONTROL OF AGENCY DISCRETION: OUTSIDE THE WALLS OF THE AGENCY

Part I of this book has examined the statutory and constitutional issues that arise when agencies exercise their adjudicatory, rulemaking and informal powers. The processes that agencies use to exercise these powers, of necessity, limit an agency's discretion. But the three branches of government — the Legislative, Executive, and Judiciary — also may seek to control or at least influence agency discretion more directly. There are a variety of political controls that the legislative and executive branches of government can employ. These, as we shall see, can range from executive use of the appointment power to legislative control over agency budgets. Moreover, judicial review of both the substance and the processes of agency decisionmaking represents another important source of outside control over agency discretion.

Chapters Six and Seven will explore various legislative and executive devices to influence agency discretion and the kinds of legal issues such control can create. Since our focus is primarily on these legal issues, it will be case-oriented. It is important, however, to underscore the fact that many legislative and executive approaches to agency control are political in nature and often not susceptible to judicial review. Chapters Eight and Nine will undertake an in-depth examination of judicial review of agency discretion. They will focus, in particular, on section 706 of the APA. Finally, Chapter Ten will conclude with various other forms of agency control. In particular, it examines the agency's duty to provide information to the public under the Freedom of Information Act as well as agency obligations under statutes such as the Privacy Act, the Federal Advisory Committee Act and the Government in the Sunshine Act.

Chapter 6
Legislative Control of Agency Discretion

§ 6.01 Introduction

A great deal of the power that agencies exercise is not readily susceptible to judicial review. For example, agencies usually set their own regulatory priorities, emphasizing some aspects of their power, while minimizing others. As new administrations come to power, with new regulatory agendas and new perceptions of the regulatory and deregulatory issues of the day, agency appointees often seek to allocate their budgetary resources differently and to exercise their powers in new ways. As we have seen in Chapter 5, agencies can also engage in a variety of informal agency actions from informal adjudication to a kind of regulation by "raised eyebrow." The well-timed press release or website update can have a profound regulatory impact. Agencies do, indeed, play an important policymaking role and are part of the political process as a whole.

Though much of their power is not susceptible to direct judicial review, agencies may be held politically accountable in various ways to the two democratically elected branches of the government — the Legislative and the Executive. This chapter will focus on the various ways by which the legislature seeks to hold agencies accountable and influence the exercise of their discretion. Chapter 7 will then examine various ways in which the Executive branch similarly attempts to play a significant, supervisory role.

§ 6.02 Legislative Influence Over Agency Discretion: Constitutional Limitations

Congress can exercise a great deal of control over administrative agencies by the way it drafts the statutes that create them in the first place. Congress can delegate authority to an agency in an open-ended or a more specific manner. The more specific the delegation, the less discretion the agency has in exercising its powers. Congress also sets forth the procedures an agency must use. It can trigger the APA or include more specific procedural requirements in the agency's own enabling act. In addition, the structure of the agency that Congress chooses to establish can also affect the kind of discretion an agency may exercise. Executive, cabinet level agencies such as the Department of Labor can be much more directly accountable to the President and the executive branch than an independent regulatory commission such as the Federal Energy Regulatory Commission or the Securities and Exchange Commission.

Congress also can exercise a variety of oversight functions once an agency has been created and is carrying out its statutory duties. Along with the executive branch, the Senate is involved in the appointments process. Agency heads and other "officers of the United States" are appointed by the President with the advice and consent of the Senate. The Senate can, if it chooses, reject some of the President's appointments. (We shall examine the appointments clause in § 7.03, *infra*.) More significantly, Congress has the power of the purse and agencies must submit their budgets for Congressional approval on an annual basis. In addition, Congress may also compel an agency to report to it regularly by holding committee or sub-committee hearings and by requiring the agency to file formal reports on a regular basis. These reports and hearings can also encourage a great deal of informal contact between agency and congressional staffs that provide yet another, though more informal, means of Congressional oversight and feedback.

Agencies are very much a part of the political process and their heads, for the most part, are likely to be politically astute and sensitive to the predilections of the legislative and executive branches. There are, however, some legal limits on the amount of legislative influence and, more importantly, on the circumstances under which that influence can be exercised. Consider the following case.

PILLSBURY CO. v. FTC

Fifth Circuit Court of Appeals
354 F.2d 952 (1966)

TUTTLE, CHIEF JUDGE.

[The Federal Trade Commission found that Pillsbury had violated § 7 of the Clayton Act. Consequently, it ordered Pillsbury to divest two of its holdings, the Ballard & Ballard Co. and the Duff's Baking Mix Division of American Home Products Corp. Pillsbury petitioned the Court to review and set aside the FTC order.

[After considering several matters on appeal, the Court focused on a procedural due process challenge: whether Congress improperly interfered in the FTC's decisional processes while the *Pillsbury* case was being decided.]

. . . The alleged interference, we hasten to add, was not alleged improper influence behind closed doors but was rather interference in the nature of questions and statements made by members of two Senate and House subcommittees having responsibility for legislation dealing with antitrust matters, all clearly spread upon the record.

Briefly stated, the criticism of the conduct of the members of the House and Senate arises in this manner: Following the filing of the complaint against Pillsbury on June 16, 1952, the Government undertook to make out its case in chief. On April 22, 1953, the hearing examiner granted Pillsbury's motion to dismiss, taking the position that the record lacked figures showing the sales volume of the various Pillsbury products after the challenged acquisitions had taken place and that there were no "authentic or reliable" figures showing the sales and production of competing companies in the industry. On appeal, the Commission reversed by an order dated December 21, 1953. Thereafter, the Pillsbury Company undertook to introduce its evidence, and evidence for both parties continued to be received for the next several years.

During the months of May and June, 1955, hearings were held before the subcommittee on antitrust and monopoly of the Committee of the Judiciary of the United States Senate, and before the antitrust subcommittee of the Committee on Judiciary of the House of Representatives. At these hearings, Mr. Howrey, the then Chairman of the Commission, and several of the members of his staff, appeared including Mr. Kintner, the then General Counsel and later Chairman of the Commission, who wrote the final opinion from which this appeal is prosecuted.

It is to be noted that these hearings were held after the Commission had issued its interlocutory order, but long before the examiner made his Initial Decision on the merits, and, of course, before the Commission made its final Decision in 1960.

In this interlocutory opinion of the Commission, reversing the dismissal of the *Pillsbury* case by the examiner, the Commission rejected an argument made by the Government (counsel supporting the complaint) to the effect that where a showing that a company in the field having a substantial share of the business of the industry acquires the assets of competitors so that the resulting merged entity would meet the "substantiality" test of *Standard Oil Co. of California v. United States,* 337 U.S. 293 (1949), no further proof need be introduced in support of the complaint. This is what will be hereafter spoken of as the "*per se*" doctrine. The Commission in its order reversing the order of dismissal rejected this contention and expressly held that the *per se* doctrine did not apply under § 7, as amended.

The posture of the case at the time of Mr. Howrey's appearance before the Senate Committee, therefore, was that the Commission had found sufficient evidence to make a *prima facie* case of acquisition of competitors by a company having a substantial share of the business in the specified fields of industry, and a *prima facie* case of other conditions in the industry to make out an affirmative case of a "substantial lessening of competition." The Commission had, thus, given Pillsbury an opportunity to introduce countervailing evidence. Some had already been introduced and the prospects were that this would continue for a considerable period of time.

When Chairman Howrey appeared before the Senate subcommittee on June 1, 1955, he met a barrage of questioning by the members of the committee challenging his view of the requirements of § 7 and the application of the *per se* doctrine announced by the Supreme Court in the Standard Stations case, *Standard Oil Co. of California v. United States,* 337 U.S. 293 (1949), in a Clayton Act 3 case, to § 7 proceedings. A number of the members of the committee challenged the correctness of his and the Commission's position in holding that a mere showing of a substantial increase in the share of the market after merger would not be sufficient to satisfy the requirement of § 7 of a showing that "the effect of such acquisition may be substantially to lessen competition."

Much of the questioning criticized by the petitioner here is in the nature of questions and comments by members of the committee in which they forcefully expressed their own opinions that the *per se* doctrine should apply and that it was the intent of Congress that it should apply.

The thrust of the comments and questions was that there was no need to carry on the long and complicated inquiry into all of the surrounding matters reflecting on the conditions in the industry if the Commission should determine that there was a substantial acquisition by a substantial number of the industry; that monopolies ought to be stopped quickly, and that Congress did not intend the Commission to apply the "rule of reason" in § 7 proceedings.

The questions were so probing that Mr. Howrey, the chairman of the Commission, announced to chairman Kefauver of the subcommittee that he would have to disqualify himself from further participation in the *Pillsbury* case. . . .

On Wednesday, June 1, 1955, FTC chairman Edward F. Howrey appeared before the Senate subcommittee on Antitrust and Monopoly. This was, as already stated, after the remand of the Pillsbury proceedings to the hearing examiner by the Commission in 1953, and the Pillsbury matter was still pending before the hearing examiner at the time of this Senate hearing. In the afternoon session, chairman Howrey was accompanied by Robert P. Secrest, Earl W. Kintner, and Joseph E. Sheehy. . . . [O]f the four Commissioners who actually participated in the final 1960 Pillsbury decision, two (Commissioners Secrest and Kintner) were substantially exposed to whatever "interference" was embodied in the hearings and one (Commissioner Kern) was at least indirectly "affected" by reason of his FTC status in 1955 as Secrest's assistant.

[The court then quoted extensively from the questioning of chairman Howrey by the members of the Senate subcommittee.]

. . . We conclude that the proceedings just outlined constituted an improper intrusion into the adjudicatory processes of the Commission and were of such a damaging character as to have required at least some of the members in addition to the chairman to disqualify themselves. We think it illuminating to quote Chairman Howrey's statement relative to his decision to disqualify himself, which he read into the record at the House subcommittee hearing. He said:

> . . . I wrote the opinion (in the *Pillsbury* case). It is still a pending adjudication; and because of some of the penetrating questions over on the Senate side, I felt compelled to withdraw from the case because I did not think I could be judicial any more when I had been such an advocate of its views in answering questions.

In view of the inordinate lapse of time in this proceeding, brought to undo what was done by mergers completed in 1951, we are naturally loathe to frustrate the proceedings at this late date. However, common justice to a litigant requires that we invalidate the order entered by a quasi-judicial tribunal that was importuned by members of the United States Senate, however innocent they intended their conduct to be, to arrive at the ultimate conclusion which they did reach.

§ 6.02   LEGISLATIVE CONTROL   519

As early as 1776 it was clear that ours was destined to be a government of laws and not of men. In their complaint against the abuses of the British crown, the framers of the Declaration of Independence included the statement that: "He has made Judges dependent on his Will alone, for the tenure of their offices, and the amount and payment of their salaries." Although our Founding Fathers attempted to lay this question to rest on the federal level through Article III, Section 1 of the United States Constitution, the emergence of administrative tribunals as the "fourth branch" of our federal government has revived the problem. Consequently, the federal judicial function, to the extent that it is exercised by administrative bodies, has not been able to make a clean break with the implicit influence inherent in Congressional control over tenure and salary.

But, as we all know, the problem is not as simple as this, since the arsenal of tools with which an administrative agency implements its broad statutory mandates also includes legislative rule-making power. It is this latter power which sets regulatory agencies apart from courts of law and results in their functions being labelled "quasi-judicial" and "quasi-legislative."

We are sensible of the fact that, pursuant to its quasi-legislative function, it frequently becomes necessary for a commission to set forth policy statements or interpretative rules (to be distinguished from strict "legislative" rules, *see generally* 1 Davis, *Administrative Law* § 5.03-.04 (1958)) in order to inform interested parties of its official position on various matters. This is as it should be.

At times similar statements of official position are elicited in Congressional hearings. In this context, the agencies are sometimes called to task for failing to adhere to the "intent of Congress" in supplying meaning to the often broad statutory standards from which the agencies derive their authority, *e.g.*, "substantially to lessen competition" to or "to tend to create a monopoly." There are those who "take a rather dim view of (such) committee pronouncements as to what agency policy should be, save when this is incident to proposals for amendatory legislation." Friendly, *The Federal Administrative Agencies* 169 (Harvard University Press 1962). Although such investigatory methods raise serious policy questions as to the *de facto* "independence" of the federal regulatory agencies, it seems doubtful that they raise any constitutional issues. However, when such an investigation focuses directly and substantially upon the mental decisional processes of a Commission *in a case which is pending before it,* Congress is no longer intervening in the agency's legislative function, but rather, in its *judicial* function. At this latter point, we become concerned with the right of private litigants to a fair trial and, equally important, with their right to the appearance of impartiality, which cannot be maintained unless those who exercise the judicial function are free from powerful external influences. . . .

To subject an administrator to a searching examination as to how and why he reached his decision in a case still pending before him, and to criticize him for reaching the "wrong" decision, as the Senate subcommittee did in this case, sacrifices the appearance of impartiality — the *sine qua non* of American judicial justice — in favor of some short-run notions regarding the Congressional intent underlying an amendment to a statute, unfettered administration of which was committed by Congress to the Federal Trade Commission (*See* 15 U.S.C.A. § 21).

It may be argued that such officials as members of the Federal Trade Commission are sufficiently aware of the realities of governmental, not to say "political," life as to be able to withstand such questioning as we have outlined here. However, this court is not so "sophisticated" that it can shrug off such a procedural due process claim merely because the officials involved should be able to discount what is said and to disregard the force of the intrusion into the adjudicatory process. We conclude that we can preserve the rights of the litigants in a case such as this without having any adverse effect upon the legitimate exercise of the investigative power of Congress. What we do is to preserve the integrity of the judicial aspect of the administrative process.

. . .

We are fully aware of the reluctance expressed by the Supreme Court to disqualify the members of the Federal Trade Commission for bias or prejudice (a somewhat different basis than that urged here) in *Federal Trade Commission v. Cement Institute,* 333 U.S. 683 (1948). There the Court seems to have placed its decision largely on the grounds of necessity. The Court said, "This complaint could not have been acted upon by the Commission or by any other government agency," since "Congress has provided for no such contingency (as disqualification). It has not directed that the Commission disqualify itself under any circumstances. . . ." The quoted language would be equally applicable here if the alternative to affirming the order were a judgment prohibiting consideration and decision by the Commission for all time. Such is not the case.

Bearing in mind the generally accepted principle enunciated by the Supreme Court in *United States v. Morgan,* 313 U.S. 409 (1941), that the questioning of a judge as to his judicial processes "would be destructive of judicial responsibility," we seek to find a solution that guarantees a fair tribunal and that does not frustrate the purposes of the law.

Although we conclude that the course of the questioning before the Senate subcommittee in June 1955 deprived the petitioner of the kind of hearing contemplated by the Supreme Court in its opinion in *Offutt v. United States,* 348 U.S. 11 (1956), we are convinced that the Commission is not permanently disqualified to decide this case. We are convinced that the passage of time, coupled with the changes in personnel on the Commission, sufficiently insulate the present members from any outward effect from what occurred in 1955. . . .

We conclude that the order appealed from must be vacated and the case remanded to the Commission. The Commission as now constituted can then determine what steps should then appropriately be taken in view of both the lapse of time and the present state of the case law applying § 7.

The Order is vacated and the case is remanded to the Commission.

NOTES AND QUESTIONS

6-1. In *Pillsbury Co. v. FTC,* what test does the Court use for deciding when congressional oversight violates the procedural due process rights of the litigants? How should this case be applied to the hybrid rulemaking proceedings we examined in Chapter Four? What if Congress sought to question administrators in the midst of a hybrid rulemaking proceeding about the findings of fact they were making during the course of their investigation?

§ 6.03 Article I of the Constitution

The Constitution divides or separates power among three co-equal branches of government. Article I, Section 1 of the Constitution vests "all legislative Powers herein granted . . . in a Congress of the United States, which shall consist of a Senate and House of Representatives. . . ." Article I, Section 8 specifies that "Congress shall have Power . . . to make all Laws which shall be *necessary and proper* for carrying into Execution the foregoing Powers and all other Powers vested by this Constitution in the Government of the United States, or in any Department or Office thereof." Thus, the constitutional mandate that "*all* legislative power" be vested in Congress is qualified by the "necessary and proper" clause. What are the Constitutional limits on the ability of Congress to control agency discretion?

In Chapter Four, we explored the various and extensive procedural checks on agencies as they exercise their rulemaking authority. It should also be clear, however, that the substantive breadth and scope of that rulemaking authority can be, and often is, substantial. At what point are we willing to say that the legislative power exercised by an administrative agency could or should only have been exercised by the Congress of the United States? How much specific guidance must the Congress provide when it delegates its legislative authority to an administrative agency?

Such questions have long been raised in the courts. Chief Justice Marshall put it this way in *Wayman v. Southard,* 23 U.S. (10 Wheat.) 1, 15–16 (1825):

> Congress may certainly delegate to others, powers which the legislature may rightfully exercise itself. . . . The line has not exactly been drawn which separates those important subjects, which must be entirely regulated by the legislature itself, from those of less interest, in which a general provision must be made and power given to those who are to act under such general provisions to fill up the details.

In over a century and a half since *Wayman* was decided, the line is no less clear. There is, however, an argument to be made for judicial restraint in assessing the validity of congressional delegations. Consider Justice Scalia's comments in his dissent in *Mistretta v. U.S.,* 488 U.S. 361, at 416 (1989):

Since Congress is no less endowed with common sense than we are, and better equipped to inform itself of the "necessities" of government; and since the factors bearing upon those necessities are both multifarious and . . . highly political . . . it is small wonder that we have almost never felt qualified to second-guess Congress regarding the permissible degree of policy judgment that can be left to those executing or applying the law.

There have, however, been a few cases in which the Supreme Court directly has struck down Acts of Congress because of the way the legislature delegated its authority to an administrative agency — *Panama Refining Co. v. Ryan*, 293 U.S. 388 (1934), *A.L.A. Schechter Poultry Corp. v. United States*, 295 U.S. 495 (1935), and *Carter v. Carter Coal Co.*, 298 U.S. 238 (1936). As you consider one of these cases below, the *Schechter Poultry* case, articulate the nondelegation doctrine espoused by the Court. Having done that, consider whether it was correctly applied in *Schechter*.

IMMIGRATION AND NATURALIZATION SERVICE v. CHADHA

United States Supreme Court
462 U.S. 919 (1983)

CHIEF JUSTICE BURGER delivered the opinion of the Court.

. . . .

I

Chadha is an East Indian who was born in Kenya and holds a British passport. He was lawfully admitted to the United States in 1966 on a nonimmigrant student visa. His visa expired on June 30, 1972. On October 11, 1973, the District Director of the Immigration and Naturalization Service ordered Chadha to show cause why he should not be deported for having "remained in the United States for a longer time than permitted." Pursuant to § 242(b) of the Immigration and Nationality Act (Act), 8 U.S.C. § 1252(b), a deportation hearing was held before an immigration judge on January 11, 1974. Chadha conceded that he was deportable for overstaying his visa and the hearing was adjourned to enable him to file an application for suspension of deportation under § 244(a)(1) of the Act, 8 U.S.C. § 1254(a)(1). Section 244(a)(1) provides:

As hereinafter prescribed in this section, the Attorney General may, in his discretion, suspend deportation and adjust the status to that of an alien lawfully admitted for permanent residence, in the case of an alien who applies to the Attorney General for suspension of deportation and —

(1) is deportable under any law of the United States except the provisions specified in paragraph (2) of this subsection; has been physically present in the United States for a continuous period of not less than seven years immediately preceding the date of such application, and proves that during all of such period he was and is a person of good moral character; and is a person whose deportation would, in the opinion of the Attorney General, result in extreme hardship to the alien or to his spouse, parent, or child, who is a citizen of the United States or an alien lawfully admitted for permanent residence.[1]

After Chadha submitted his application for suspension of deportation, the deportation hearing was resumed on February 7, 1974. On the basis of evidence adduced at the hearing, affidavits submitted with the application, and the results of a character investigation conducted by the INS, the immigration judge, on June 25, 1974, ordered that Chadha's deportation be suspended. The immigration judge found that Chadha met the requirements of § 244(a)(1): he had resided continuously in the United States for over seven years, was of good moral character, and would suffer "extreme hardship" if deported.

Pursuant to § 244(c)(1) of the Act, 8 U.S.C. § 1254(c)(1), the immigration judge suspended Chadha's deportation and a report of the suspension was transmitted to Congress. Section 244(c)(1) provides:

Upon application by any alien who is found by the Attorney General to meet the requirements of subsection (a) of this section the Attorney General may in his discretion suspend deportation of such alien. If the deportation of any alien is suspended under the provisions of this subsection, a complete and detailed statement of the facts and pertinent provisions of law in the case shall be reported to the Congress with the reasons for such suspension. Such reports shall be submitted on the first day of each calendar month in which Congress is in session.

Once the Attorney General's recommendation for suspension of Chadha's deportation was conveyed to Congress, Congress had the power under § 244(c)(2) of the Act, 8 U.S.C. § 1254(c)(2), to veto the Attorney General's determination that Chadha should not be deported. Section 244(c)(2) provides:

(2) In the case of an alien specified in paragraph (1) of subsection (a) of this subsection —

if during the session of the Congress at which a case is reported, or prior to the close of the session of the Congress next following the session at which a case is reported, either the Senate or the House of Representatives passes a resolution stating in substance that it does not favor the suspension of such deportation, the Attorney General shall thereupon deport such alien or authorize the alien's voluntary departure at his own expense under the order of deportation in the manner provided by law. If, within the time above specified, neither the Senate nor the House of Representatives shall pass

---

[1] Congress delegated the major responsibilities for enforcement of the Immigration and Nationality Act to the Attorney General. 8 U.S.C. § 1103(a). The Attorney General discharges his responsibilities through the Immigration and Naturalization Service, a division of the Department of Justice. *Ibid.*

such a resolution, the Attorney General shall cancel deportation proceedings.

The June 25, 1974 order of the immigration judge suspending Chadha's deportation remained outstanding as a valid order for a year and a half. For reasons not disclosed by the record, Congress did not exercise the veto authority reserved to it under § 244(c)(2) until the first session of the 94th Congress. This was the final session in which Congress, pursuant to § 244(c)(2), could act to veto the Attorney General's determination that Chadha should not be deported. The session ended on December 19, 1975. 121 Cong. Rec. 42014, 42277 (1975). Absent Congressional action, Chadha's deportation proceedings would have been canceled after this date and his status adjusted to that of a permanent resident alien. . . .

On December 12, 1975, Representative Eilberg, Chairman of the Judiciary Subcommittee on Immigration, Citizenship, and International Law, introduced a resolution opposing "the granting of permanent residence in the United States to [six] aliens," including Chadha. . . . The resolution was referred to the House Committee on the Judiciary. On December 16, 1975, the resolution was discharged from further consideration by the House Committee on the Judiciary and submitted to the House of Representatives for a vote. . . . The resolution had not been printed and was not made available to other Members of the House prior to or at the time it was voted on. So far as the record before us shows, the House consideration of the resolution was based on Representative Eilberg's statement from the floor that:

> [i]t was the feeling of the committee, after reviewing 340 cases, that the aliens contained in the resolution [Chadha and five others] did not meet these statutory requirements, particularly as it relates to hardship; and it is the opinion of the committee that their deportation should not be suspended.

The resolution was passed without debate or recorded vote. Since the House action was pursuant to § 244(c)(2), the resolution was not treated as an Article I legislative act; it was not submitted to the Senate or presented to the President for his action.

After the House veto of the Attorney General's decision to allow Chadha to remain in the United States, the immigration judge reopened the deportation proceedings to implement the House order deporting Chadha. Chadha moved to terminate the proceedings on the ground that § 244(c)(2) is unconstitutional. The immigration judge held that he had no authority to rule on the constitutional validity of § 244(c)(2). On November 8, 1976, Chadha was ordered deported pursuant to the House action.

Chadha appealed the deportation order to the Board of Immigration Appeals again contending that § 244(c)(2) is unconstitutional. The Board held that it had "no power to declare unconstitutional an act of Congress" and Chadha's appeal was dismissed.

. . . Chadha filed a petition for review of the deportation order in the United States Court of Appeals for the Ninth Circuit. The Immigration and Naturalization Service agreed with Chadha's position before the Court of Appeals and joined him in arguing that § 244(c)(2) is unconstitutional. In light of the importance of the question, the Court of Appeals invited both the Senate and the House of Representatives to file briefs *amici curiae.*

After full briefing and oral argument, the Court of Appeals held that the House was without constitutional authority to order Chadha's deportation; accordingly it directed the Attorney General "to cease and desist from taking any steps to deport this alien based upon the resolution enacted by the House of Representatives." 634 F.2d 408, 436 (1980). The essence of its holding was that § 244(c)(2) violates the constitutional doctrine of separation of powers.

We granted certiorari, and we now affirm.

. . . .

III

A

We turn now to the question whether action of one House of Congress under § 244(c)(2) violates strictures of the Constitution. We begin, of course, with the presumption that the challenged statute is valid. Its wisdom is not the concern of the courts; if a challenged action does not violate the Constitution, it must be sustained. . . .

By the same token, the fact that a given law or procedure is efficient, convenient, and useful in facilitating functions of government, standing alone, will not save it if it is contrary to the Constitution. Convenience and efficiency are not the primary objectives — or the hallmarks — of democratic government and our inquiry is sharpened rather than blunted by the fact that Congressional veto provisions are appearing with increasing frequency in statutes which delegate authority to executive and independent agencies:

> "Since 1932, when the first veto provision was enacted into law, 295 congressional veto-type procedures have been inserted in 196 different statutes as follows: from 1932 to 1939, five statutes were affected; from 1940-49, nineteen statutes; between 1950-59, thirty-four statutes; and from 1960-69, forty-nine. From the year 1970 through 1975, at least one hundred sixty-three such provisions were included in eighty-nine laws." Abourezk, *The Congressional Veto: A Contemporary Response to Executive Encroachment on Legislative Prerogatives,* 52 IND. L. REV. [sic] 323, 324 (1977). . . .

Explicit and unambiguous provisions of the Constitution prescribe and define the respective functions of the Congress and of the Executive in the legislative process. Since the precise terms of those familiar provisions are critical to the resolution of this case, we set them out verbatim. Art. I provides:

> "All legislative Powers herein granted shall be vested in a Congress of the United States, which shall consist of a Senate *and* House of Representatives." Art. I, § 1. (Emphasis added).

> "Every Bill which shall have passed the House of Representatives *and* the Senate, *shall,* before it becomes a Law, be presented to the President of the United States; . . ." Art. I, § 7, cl. 2. (Emphasis added).

> "*Every* Order, Resolution, or Vote to which the Concurrence of the Senate and House of Representatives may be necessary (except on a question of

Adjournment) *shall be* presented to the President of the United States; and before the Same shall take Effect, *shall be* approved by him, or being disapproved by him, *shall be* repassed by two thirds of the Senate and House of Representatives, according to the Rules and Limitations prescribed in the Case of a Bill." Art. I, § 7, cl. 3. (Emphasis added).

These provisions of Art. I are integral parts of the constitutional design for the separation of powers. We have recently noted that "[t]he principle of separation of powers was not simply an abstract generalization in the minds of the Framers: it was woven into the documents that they drafted in Philadelphia in the summer of 1787." *Buckley v. Valeo,* 424 U.S., at 124. . . . The very structure of the articles delegating and separating powers under Arts. I, II, and III exemplify the concept of separation of powers and we now turn to Art. I.

B

The Presentment Clauses

. . . The decision to provide the President with a limited and qualified power to nullify proposed legislation by veto was based on the profound conviction of the Framers that the powers conferred on Congress were the powers to be most carefully circumscribed. It is beyond doubt that lawmaking was a power to be shared by both Houses and the President. In *The Federalist* No. 73 (H. Lodge ed. 1888), Hamilton focused on the President's role in making laws:

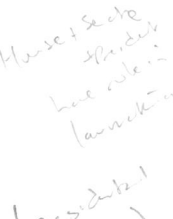

"If even no propensity had ever discovered itself in the legislative body to invade the rights of the Executive, the rules of just reasoning and theoretic propriety would of themselves teach us that the one ought not to be left to the mercy of the other, but ought to possess a constitutional and effectual power of self-defense." *Id.,* at 457–458.

See also *The Federalist* No. 51. . . .

The President's role in the lawmaking process also reflects the Framers' careful efforts to check whatever propensity a particular Congress might have to enact oppressive, improvident, or ill-considered measures. . . .

C

Bicameralism

The bicameral requirement of Art. I, §§ 1, 7 was of scarcely less concern to the Framers than was the Presidential veto and indeed the two concepts are interdependent. By providing that no law could take effect without the concurrence of the prescribed majority of the Members of both Houses, the Framers reemphasized their belief, already remarked upon in connection with the Presentment Clauses, that legislation should not be enacted unless it has been carefully and fully considered by the Nation's elected officials. In the Constitutional Convention debates on the need for a bicameral legislature, James Wilson, later to become a Justice of this Court, commented:

"Despotism comes on mankind in different shapes. Sometimes in an Executive, sometimes in a military, one. Is there danger of a Legislative despotism? Theory & practice both proclaim it. If the Legislative authority be not restrained, there can be neither liberty nor stability; and it can only be restrained by dividing it within itself, into distinct and independent branches. In a single house there is no check, but the inadequate one, of the virtue & good sense of those who compose it." 1 M. Farrand, [*The Records of the Federal Convention of 1787*] 254. . . .

These observations are consistent with what many of the Framers expressed, none more cogently than Madison in pointing up the need to divide and disperse power in order to protect liberty:

"In republican government, the legislative authority necessarily predominates. The remedy for this inconvenience is to divide the legislature into different branches; and to render them, by different modes of election and different principles of action, as little connected with each other as the nature of their common functions and their common dependence on the society will admit." *The Federalist* No. 51, p. 324. (H. Lodge ed. 1888) (sometimes attributed to "Hamilton or Madison" but now generally attributed to Madison).

See also The Federalist No. 62.

. . . .

IV

The Constitution sought to divide the delegated powers of the new federal government into three defined categories, legislative, executive and judicial, to assure, as nearly as possible, that each Branch of government would confine itself to its assigned responsibility. The hydraulic pressure inherent within each of the separate Branches to exceed the outer limits of its power, even to accomplish desirable objectives, must be resisted.

Although not "hermetically" sealed from one another, *Buckley v. Valeo,* 424 U.S., at 121, the powers delegated to the three Branches are functionally identifiable. When any Branch acts, it is presumptively exercising the power the Constitution has delegated to it. *See J.W. Hampton & Co. v. United States,* 276 U.S. 394, 406 (1928). When the Executive acts, it presumptively acts in an executive or administrative capacity as defined in Art. II. And when, as here, one House of Congress purports to act, it is presumptively acting within its assigned sphere.

Beginning with this presumption, we must nevertheless establish that the challenged action under § 244(c)(2) is of the kind to which the procedural requirements of Art. I, § 7 apply. . . . Whether actions taken by either House are, in law and fact, an exercise of legislative power depends not on their form but upon "whether they contain matter which is properly to be regarded as legislative in its character and effect." S. Rep. 1335, 54th Cong., 2d Sess., 8 (1897).

Examination of the action taken here by one House pursuant to § 244(c)(2) reveals that it was essentially legislative in purpose and effect. In purporting to exercise power defined in Art. I, § 8, cl. 4 to "establish an uniform Rule of Naturalization," the House took action that had the purpose and effect of altering the legal rights, duties and relations of persons, including the Attorney General, Executive Branch officials and Chadha, all outside the legislative branch. Section 244(c)(2) purports to authorize one House of Congress to require the Attorney General to deport an individual alien whose deportation otherwise would be canceled under § 244. The one-House veto operated in this case to overrule the Attorney General and mandate Chadha's deportation; absent the House action, Chadha would remain in the United States. Congress has *acted* and its action has altered Chadha's status.

The legislative character of the one-House veto in this case is confirmed by the character of the congressional action it supplants. Neither the House of Representatives nor the Senate contends that, absent the veto provision in § 244(c)(2), either of them, or both of them acting together, could effectively require the Attorney General to deport an alien once the Attorney General, in the exercise of legislatively delegated authority,[16] had determined the alien should remain in the United States. Without the challenged provision in § 244(c)(2), this could have been achieved, if at all, only by legislation requiring deportation. . . . Amendment and repeal of statutes, no less than enactment, must conform with Art. I.

---

[16] Congress protests that affirming the Court of Appeals in this case will sanction "lawmaking by the Attorney General. . . . Why is the Attorney General exempt from submitting his proposed changes in the law to the full bicameral process?" Brief of the United States House of Representatives 40. To be sure, some administrative agency action — rule making, for example — may resemble "lawmaking." *See* 5 U.S.C. § 551(4), which defines an agency's "rule" as "the whole or part of an agency statement of general or particular applicability and future effect designed to implement, interpret, or prescribe law or policy. . . ." This Court has referred to agency activity as being "quasi-legislative" in character. *Humphrey's Executor v. United States,* 295 U.S. 602, 628 (1935). Clearly, however, "[i]n the framework of our Constitution, the President's power to see that the laws are faithfully executed refutes the idea that he is to be a lawmaker." *Youngstown Sheet & Tube Co. v. Sawyer,* 343 U.S. 579, 587 (1952). *See Buckley v. Valeo,* 424 U.S. at 123 (1976). When the Attorney General performs his duties pursuant to § 244, he does not exercise "legislative" power. *See Ernst & Ernst v. Hochfelder,* 425 U.S. 185, 213–214 (1976). The bicameral process is not necessary as a check on the Executive's administration of the laws because his administrative activity cannot reach beyond the limits of the statute that created it — a statute duly enacted pursuant to Art. I, §§ 1, 7. The constitutionality of the Attorney General's execution of the authority delegated to him by § 244 involves only a question of delegation doctrine. The courts, when a case or controversy arises, can always "ascertain whether the will of Congress has been obeyed," *Yakus v. United States,* 321 U.S. 414, 425 (1944), and can enforce adherence to statutory standards. *See Youngstown Sheet & Tube Co. v. Sawyer,* 424 U.S. at 585; *Ethyl Corp. v. EPA,* 176 U.S. App. D.C. 373, 440, 541 F.2d 1, 68 (en banc) (separate statement of Leventhal, J.), *cert. denied,* 426 U.S. 941 (1976); L. Jaffe, *Judicial Control of Administrative Action* 320 (1965). It is clear, therefore, that the Attorney General acts in his presumptively Art. II capacity when he administers the Immigration and Nationality Act. Executive action under legislatively delegated authority that might resemble "legislative" action in some respects is not subject to the approval of both Houses of Congress and the President for the reason that the Constitution does not so require. That kind of Executive action is always subject to check by the terms of the legislation that authorized it; and if that authority is exceeded it is open to judicial review as well as the power of Congress to modify or revoke the authority entirely. A one-House veto is clearly legislative in both character and effect and is not so checked; the need for the check provided by Art. I, §§ 1, 7 is therefore clear. Congress' authority to delegate portions of its power to administrative agencies provides no support for the argument that Congress can constitutionally control administration of the laws by way of a Congressional veto.

The nature of the decision implemented by the one-House veto in this case further manifests its legislative character. After long experience with the clumsy, time-consuming private bill procedure, Congress made a deliberate choice to delegate to the Executive Branch, and specifically to the Attorney General, the authority to allow deportable aliens to remain in this country in certain specified circumstances. It is not disputed that this choice to delegate authority is precisely the kind of decision that can be implemented only in accordance with the procedures set out in Art. I. Disagreement with the Attorney General's decision on Chadha's deportation — that is, Congress' decision to deport Chadha — no less than Congress' original choice to delegate to the Attorney General the authority to make that decision, involves determinations of policy that Congress can implement in only one way; [sic] bicameral passage followed by presentment to the President. Congress must abide by its delegation of authority until that delegation is legislatively altered or revoked.[19]

. . . .

. . . The bicameral requirement, the Presentment Clauses, the President's veto, and Congress' power to override a veto were intended to erect enduring checks on each Branch and to protect the people from the improvident exercise of power by mandating certain prescribed steps. To preserve those checks, and maintain the separation of powers, the carefully defined limits on the power of each Branch must not be eroded. To accomplish what has been attempted by one House of Congress in this case requires action in conformity with the express procedures of the Constitution's prescription for legislative action: passage by a majority of both Houses and presentment to the President.[23]

The veto authorized by § 244(c)(2) doubtless has been in many respects a convenient shortcut; the "sharing" with the Executive by Congress of its

---

[19] This does not mean that Congress is required to capitulate to "the accretion of policy control by forces outside its chambers." Javits and Klein, *Congressional Oversight and the Legislative Veto: A Constitutional Analysis*, 52 N.Y.U. L. REV. 455, 462 (1977). The Constitution provides Congress with abundant means to oversee and control its administrative creatures. Beyond the obvious fact that Congress ultimately controls administrative agencies in the legislation that creates them, other means of control, such as durational limits on authorizations and formal reporting requirements, lie well within Congress' constitutional power. *See id.*, at 460–461; Kaiser, *Congressional Action to Overturn Agency Rules: Alternatives to the "Legislative Veto"*, 32 AD. L. REV. 667 (1980). . . .

[23] . . . JUSTICE WHITE suggests that the Attorney General's action under § 244(c)(1) suspending deportation is equivalent to a proposal for legislation and that because Congressional approval is indicated "by failure to veto, the one-House veto satisfies the requirement of bicameral approval." *See infra*, p. 594. However, as the Court of Appeals noted, that approach "would analogize the effect of the one house disapproval to the failure of one house to vote affirmatively on a private bill." 634 F.2d, at 435. Even if it were clear that Congress entertained such an arcane theory when it enacted § 244(c)(2), which JUSTICE WHITE does not suggest, this would amount to nothing less than an amending of Art. I. The legislative steps outlined in Art. I are not empty formalities; they were designed to assure that both Houses of Congress and the President participate in the exercise of lawmaking authority. This does not mean that legislation must always be preceded by debate; on the contrary, we have said that it is not necessary for a legislative body to "articulate its reasons for enacting a statute." *United States Railroad Retirement Board v. Fritz*, 449 U.S. 166, 179 (1980). But the steps required by Art. I, §§ 1, 7 make certain that there is an opportunity for deliberation and debate. To allow Congress to evade the strictures of the Constitution and in effect enact Executive proposals into law by mere silence cannot be squared with Art. I.

authority over aliens in this manner is, on its face, an appealing compromise. In purely practical terms, it is obviously easier for action to be taken by one House without submission to the President; but it is crystal clear from the records of the Convention, contemporaneous writings and debates, that the Framers ranked other values higher than efficiency. The records of the Convention and debates in the States preceding ratification underscore the common desire to define and limit the exercise of the newly created federal powers affecting the states and the people. There is unmistakable expression of a determination that legislation by the national Congress be a step-by-step, deliberate and deliberative process.

The choices we discern as having been made in the Constitutional Convention impose burdens on governmental processes that often seem clumsy, inefficient, even unworkable, but those hard choices were consciously made by men who had lived under a form of government that permitted arbitrary governmental acts to go unchecked. There is no support in the Constitution or decisions of this Court for the proposition that the cumbersomeness and delays often encountered in complying with explicit Constitutional standards may be avoided, either by the Congress or by the President. . . . With all the obvious flaws of delay, untidiness, and potential for abuse, we have not yet found a better way to preserve freedom than by making the exercise of power subject to the carefully crafted restraints spelled out in the Constitution.

V

We hold that the Congressional veto provision in § 244(c)(2) is severable from the Act and that it is unconstitutional. Accordingly, the judgment of the Court of Appeals is

Affirmed.

JUSTICE POWELL, concurring in the judgment.

The Court's decision, based on the Presentment Clauses, Art. I, § 7, cls. 2 and 3, apparently will invalidate every use of the legislative veto. The breadth of this holding gives one pause. Congress has included the veto in literally hundreds of statutes, dating back to the 1930s. Congress clearly views this procedure as essential to controlling the delegation of power to administrative agencies.[1] One reasonably may disagree with Congress' assessment of the veto's utility, but the respect due its judgment as a coordinate branch of Government cautions that our holding should be no more extensive than necessary to decide these cases. In my view, the case may be decided on a narrower ground. When Congress finds that a particular person does not satisfy the statutory criteria for permanent residence in this country it has assumed a judicial function in violation of the principle of separation of powers. Accordingly, I concur only in the judgment. . . .

---

[1] As JUSTICE WHITE's dissenting opinion explains, the legislative veto has been included in a wide variety of statutes, ranging from bills for executive reorganization to the War Powers Resolution. *See infra,* pp. 587–588. Whether the veto complies with the Presentment Clauses may well turn on the particular context in which it is exercised, and I would be hesitant to conclude that every veto is unconstitutional on the basis of the unusual example presented by this litigation.

II

. . . .

On its face, the House's action appears clearly adjudicatory.[7] The House did not enact a general rule; rather it made its own determination that six specific persons did not comply with certain statutory criteria. It thus undertook the type of decision that traditionally has been left to other branches. Even if the House did not make a *de novo* determination, but simply reviewed the Immigration and Naturalization Service's findings, it still assumed a function ordinarily entrusted to the federal courts.[8] . . . Where, as here, Congress has exercised a power "that cannot possibly be regarded as merely in aid of the legislative function of Congress," *Buckley v. Valeo*, 424 U.S., at 138, the decisions of this Court have held that Congress impermissibly assumed a function that the Constitution entrusted to another branch. . . .

The impropriety of the House's assumption of this function is confirmed by the fact that its action raises the very danger the Framers sought to avoid — the exercise of unchecked power. In deciding whether Chadha deserves to be deported, Congress is not subject to any internal constraints that prevent it from arbitrarily depriving him of the right to remain in this country. Unlike the judiciary or an administrative agency, Congress is not bound by established substantive rules. Nor is it subject to the procedural safeguards, such as the right to counsel and a hearing before an impartial tribunal, that are present when a court or an agency[10] adjudicates individual rights. The only effective constraint on Congress' power is political, but Congress is most accountable politically when it prescribes rules of general applicability. When

---

[7] The Court concludes that Congress' action was legislative in character because each branch "presumptively act[s] within its assigned sphere." The Court's presumption provides a useful starting point, but does not conclude the inquiry. Nor does the fact that the House's action alters an individual's legal status indicate, as the Court reasons, *see supra,* p. 581, that the action is legislative rather than adjudicative in nature. In determining whether one branch unconstitutionally has assumed a power central to another branch, the traditional characterization of the assumed power as legislative, executive, or judicial may provide some guidance. *See Springer v. Philippine Islands,* 277 U.S. 189, 203 (1928). But reasonable minds may disagree over the character of an act and the more helpful inquiry, in my view, is whether the act in question raises the dangers the Framers sought to avoid.

[8] The Court reasons in response to this argument that the one-house veto exercised in this case was not judicial in nature because the decision of the Immigration and Naturalization Service did not present a justiciable issue that could have been reviewed by a court on appeal. . . . The Court notes that since the administrative agency decided the case in favor of Chadha, there was no aggrieved party who could appeal. Reliance by the Court on this fact misses the point. Even if review of the particular decision to suspend deportation is not committed to the courts, the House of Representatives assumed a function that generally is entrusted to an impartial tribunal. In my view, the legislative branch in effect acted as an appellate court by overruling the Service's application of established law to Chadha. And unlike a court or an administrative agency, it did not provide Chadha with the right to counsel or a hearing before acting. Although the parallel is not entirely complete, the effect on Chadha's personal rights would not have been different in principle had he been acquitted of a federal crime and thereafter found by one House of Congress to have been guilty.

[10] We have recognized that independent regulatory agencies and departments of the Executive Branch often exercise authority that is "judicial in nature." *Buckley v. Valeo,* 424 U.S. 1, 140–141 (1976). This function, however, forms part of the agencies' execution of public law and is subject to the procedural safeguards, including judicial review, provided by the administrative Procedure Act, *see* 5 U.S.C. § 551 *et seq.* . . .

it decides rights of specific persons, those rights are subject to "the tyranny of a shifting majority."

CHIEF JUSTICE MRSHALL observed: "It is the peculiar province of the legislature to prescribe general rules for the government of society; the application of those rules would seem to be the duty of other departments." *Fletcher v. Peck,* 10 U.S. 87, 136 (1810). In my view, when Congress undertook to apply its rules to Chadha, it exceeded the scope of its constitutionally prescribed authority. I would not reach the broader question whether legislative vetoes are invalid under the Presentment Clauses.

JUSTICE WHITE, dissenting.

Today the Court not only invalidates § 244(c)(2) of the Immigration and Nationality Act, but also sounds the death knell for nearly 200 other statutory provisions in which Congress has reserved a "legislative veto." For this reason, the Court's decision is of surpassing importance. And it is for this reason that the Court would have been well-advised to decide the case, if possible, on the narrower grounds of separation of powers, leaving for full consideration the constitutionality of other congressional review statutes operating on such varied matters as war powers and agency rulemaking, some of which concern the independent regulatory agencies.

The prominence of the legislative veto mechanism in our contemporary political system and its importance to Congress can hardly be overstated. It has become a central means by which Congress secures the accountability of executive and independent agencies. Without the legislative veto, Congress is faced with a Hobson's choice: either to refrain from delegating the necessary authority, leaving itself with a hopeless task of writing laws with the requisite specificity to cover endless special circumstances across the entire policy landscape, or in the alternative, to abdicate its law-making function to the executive branch and independent agencies. To choose the former leaves major national problems unresolved; to opt for the latter risks unaccountable policymaking by those not elected to fill that role. Accordingly, over the past five decades, the legislative veto has been placed in nearly 200 statutes. The device is known in every field of governmental concern: reorganization, budgets, foreign affairs, war powers, and regulation of trade, safety, energy, the environment and the economy.

I

The legislative veto developed initially in response to the problems of reorganizing the sprawling Government structure created in response to the Depression. The Reorganization Acts established the chief model for the legislative veto. When President Hoover requested authority to reorganize the Government in 1929, he coupled his request that the "Congress be willing to delegate its authority over the problem (subject to defined principles) to the Executive" with a proposal for legislative review. . . . Congress followed President Hoover's suggestion and authorized reorganization subject to legislative review. . . . Although the reorganization authority reenacted in 1933 did not contain a legislative veto provision, the provision returned during the Roosevelt Administration and has since been renewed numerous times.

Over the years, the provision was used extensively. Presidents submitted 115 reorganization plans to Congress of which 23 were disapproved by Congress pursuant to legislative veto provisions. . . .

Shortly after adoption of the Reorganization Act of 1939, . . . Congress and the President applied the legislative veto procedure to resolve the delegation problem for national security and foreign affairs. World War II occasioned the need to transfer greater authority to the President in these areas. The legislative veto offered the means by which Congress could confer additional authority while preserving its own constitutional role. During World War II, Congress enacted over thirty statutes conferring powers on the Executive with legislative veto provisions. President Roosevelt accepted the veto as the necessary price for obtaining exceptional authority.

Over the quarter century following World War II, Presidents continued to accept legislative vetoes by one or both Houses as constitutional, while regularly denouncing provisions by which Congressional committees reviewed Executive activity.[5] The legislative veto balanced delegations of statutory authority in new areas of governmental involvement: the space program, international agreements on nuclear energy, tariff arrangements, and adjustment of federal pay rates.

During the 1970's the legislative veto was important in resolving a series of major constitutional disputes between the President and Congress over claims of the President to broad impoundment, war, and national emergency powers. The key provision of the War Powers Resolution, 50 U.S.C. § 1544(c), authorizes the termination by concurrent resolution of the use of armed forces in hostilities. A similar measure resolved the problem posed by Presidential claims of inherent power to impound appropriations. Congressional Budget and Impoundment Control Act of 1974, 31 U.S.C. § 1403. In conference, a compromise was achieved under which permanent impoundments, termed "rescissions," would require approval through enactment of legislation. In contrast, temporary impoundments, or "deferrals," would become effective unless disapproved by one House. This compromise provided the President with flexibility, while preserving ultimate Congressional control over the budget.[7] Although the War Powers Resolution was enacted over President Nixon's veto, the Impoundment Control Act was enacted with the President's approval. . . .

In the energy field, the legislative veto served to balance broad delegations in legislation emerging from the energy crisis of the 1970's. In the educational field, it was found that fragmented and narrow grant programs "inevitably lead to Executive-Legislative confrontations" because they ineptly limited the Commissioner of Education's authority. . . . In the trade regulation area, the veto preserved Congressional authority over the Federal Trade Commission's

---

[5] Presidential objections to the veto, until the veto by President Nixon of the War Powers Resolution, principally concerned bills authorizing committee vetoes. As the Senate Subcommittee on Separation of Powers found in 1969, "an accommodation was reached years ago on legislative vetoes exercised by the entire Congress or by one House, [while] disputes have continued to arise over the committee form of the veto." S. Rep. No. 91–549, p. 14 (1969). . . .

[7] The Impoundment Control Act's provision for legislative review has been used extensively. Presidents have submitted hundreds of proposed budget deferrals, of which 65 have been disapproved by resolutions of the House or Senate with no protest by the Executive. . . .

broad mandate to make rules to prevent businesses from engaging in "unfair or deceptive acts or practices in commerce."

Even this brief review suffices to demonstrate that the legislative veto is more than "efficient, convenient, and useful." . . . It is an important if not indispensable political invention that allows the President and Congress to resolve major constitutional and policy differences, assures the accountability of independent regulatory agencies, and preserves Congress' control over lawmaking. Perhaps there are other means of accommodation and accountability, but the increasing reliance of Congress upon the legislative veto suggests that the alternatives to which Congress must now turn are not entirely satisfactory.[10]

The history of the legislative veto also makes clear that it has not been a sword with which Congress has struck out to aggrandize itself at the expense of the other branches — the concerns of Madison and Hamilton. Rather, the veto has been a means of defense, a reservation of ultimate authority necessary if Congress is to fulfill its designated role under Article I as the nation's lawmaker. While the President has often objected to particular legislative vetoes, generally those left in the hands of congressional committees, the Executive has more often agreed to legislative review as the price for a broad delegation of authority. To be sure, the President may have preferred unrestricted power, but that could be precisely why Congress thought it essential to retain a check on the exercise of delegated authority.

---

[10] While Congress could write certain statutes with greater specificity, it is unlikely that this is a realistic or even desirable substitute for the legislative veto. "Political volatility and the controversy of many issues would prevent Congress from reaching agreement on many major problems if specificity were required in their enactments." Fuchs, *Administrative Agencies and the Energy Problem,* 47 Ind. L.J. 606, 608 (1972); Stewart, *Reformation of American Administrative Law,* 88 HARV. L. REV. 1667, 1695–1696 (1975). For example, in the deportation context, the solution is not for Congress to create more refined categorizations of the deportable aliens whose status should be subject to change. In 1979, the Immigration and Naturalization Service proposed regulations setting forth factors to be considered in the exercise of discretion under numerous provisions of the Act, but not including § 244, to ensure "fair and uniform" adjudication "under appropriate discretionary criteria." 44 Fed. Reg. 36187 (1979). The proposed rule was canceled in 1981, because "[t]here is an inherent failure in any attempt to list those factors which should be considered in the exercise of discretion. It is impossible to list or foresee all of the adverse or favorable factors which may be present in a given set of circumstances." 46 Fed. Reg. 9119 (1981).

Oversight hearings and congressional investigations have their purpose, but unless Congress is to be rendered a think tank or debating society, they are no substitute for the exercise of actual authority. The "laying" procedure approved in *Sibbach v. Wilson,* 312 U.S. 1, 15, (1941), while satisfactory for certain measures, has its own shortcomings. Because a new law must be passed to restrain administrative action, Congress must delegate authority without the certain ability of being able to check its exercise.

Finally, the passage of corrective legislation after agency regulations take effect or Executive Branch officials have acted entail the drawbacks endemic to a retroactive response. "*Post hoc* substantive revision of legislation, the only available corrective mechanism in the absence of post-enactment review could have serious prejudicial consequences; if Congress retroactively tampered with a price control system after prices have been set, the economy could be damaged and private interests seriously impaired; if Congress rescinded the sale of arms to a foreign country, our relations with that Country would be severely strained; and if Congress reshuffled the bureaucracy after a President's reorganization proposal had taken effect, the results could be chaotic." Javits and Klein, *Congressional Oversight and the Legislative Veto: A Constitutional Analysis,* 52 N.Y.U. L. REV. 455, 464 (1977) (footnote omitted).

II

For all these reasons, the apparent sweep of the Court's decision today is regrettable. The Court's Article I analysis appears to invalidate all legislative vetoes irrespective of form or subject. Because the legislative veto is commonly found as a check upon rulemaking by administrative agencies and upon broad-based policy decisions of the Executive Branch, it is particularly unfortunate that the Court reaches its decision in a case involving the exercise of a veto over deportation decisions regarding particular individuals. Courts should always be wary of striking statutes as unconstitutional; to strike an entire class of statutes based on consideration of a somewhat atypical and more-readily indictable exemplar of the class is irresponsible. . . .

III

. . . .

If Congress may delegate lawmaking power to independent and executive agencies, it is most difficult to understand Article I as forbidding Congress from also reserving a check on legislative power for itself. Absent the veto, the agencies receiving delegations of legislative or quasi-legislative power may issue regulations having the force of law without bicameral approval and without the President's signature. It is thus not apparent why the reservation of a veto over the exercise of that legislative power must be subject to a more exacting test. In both cases, it is enough that the initial statutory authorizations comply with the Article I requirements.

. . . .

C

The Court also takes no account of perhaps the most relevant consideration: However resolutions of disapproval under § 244(c)(2) are formally characterized, in reality, a departure from the status quo occurs only upon the concurrence of opinion among the House, Senate, and President. Reservations of legislative authority to be exercised by Congress should be upheld if the exercise of such reserved authority is consistent with the distribution of and limits upon legislative power that Article I provides.

1

. . . .

The history of the Immigration Act makes clear that § 244(c)(2) did not alter the division of actual authority between Congress and the Executive. At all times, whether through private bills, or through affirmative concurrent resolutions, or through the present one-House veto, a permanent change in a deportable alien's status could be accomplished only with the agreement of the Attorney General, the House, and the Senate.

2

The central concern of the presentation and bicameralism requirements of Article I is that when a departure from the legal status quo is undertaken, it is done with the approval of the President and both Houses of Congress — or, in the event of a presidential veto, a two-thirds majority in both Houses. This interest is fully satisfied by the operation of § 244(c)(2). The President's approval is found in the Attorney General's action in recommending to Congress that the deportation order for a given alien be suspended. The House and the Senate indicate their approval of the Executive's action by not passing a resolution of disapproval within the statutory period. Thus, a change in the legal status quo — the deportability of the alien — is consummated only with the approval of each of the three relevant actors. The disagreement of any one of the three maintains the alien's pre-existing status: the Executive may choose not to recommend suspension; the House and Senate may each veto the recommendation. The effect on the rights and obligations of the affected individuals and upon the legislative system is precisely the same as if a private bill were introduced but failed to receive the necessary approval. "The President and the two Houses enjoy exactly the same say in what the law is to be as would have been true for each without the presence of the one-House veto, and nothing in the law is changed absent the concurrence of the President and a majority in each House."

. . . .

Thus understood, § 244(c)(2) fully effectuates the purposes of the bicameralism and presentation requirements. . . .

V

I regret that I am in disagreement with my colleagues on the fundamental questions that this case presents. But even more I regret the destructive scope of the Court's holding. It reflects a profoundly different conception of the Constitution than that held by the Courts which sanctioned the modern administrative state. Today's decision strikes down in one fell swoop provisions in more laws enacted by Congress than the Court has cumulatively invalidated in its history. I fear it will now be more difficult "to insur[e] that the fundamental policy decisions in our society will be made not by an appointed official but by the body immediately responsible to the people," *Arizona v. California,* 373 U.S. 546, 626 (1963) (HARLAN, J., dissenting in part). I must dissent.

[The dissenting opinion of JUSTICE REHNQUIST is omitted.]

NOTES AND QUESTIONS

6-2. Is a one-house or a two-house veto tantamount to the amendment of a statute? If so, why? If not, why not?

6-3. Chief Justice Burger reasons that "the House took action that had the purpose and effect of altering the legal rights, duties, and relations of persons . . . all outside the legislative branch." He concludes that this was, therefore, legislative. Do you agree with this reasoning? Do not actions taken by the executive and the judiciary do the same thing? Does this make their actions legislative as well? *See* Strauss, *Was There a Baby in the Bathwater? A Comment on the Supreme Court's Legislative Veto Decision,* 1983 Duke L.J. 812–17 (1983).

6-4. How does Justice Powell conceive of this case? Is the problem for him, in this case, more akin to that of criminal procedure? Was the matter being vetoed a rule or an adjudication? What kind of separation-of-powers approach does Justice Powell suggest?

6-5. What about Justice White? Why is he willing to uphold these veto provisions? How would you characterize his constitutional approach to the separation of powers issues that he identifies?

6-6. Consider the following description of various types of separation-of-powers analyses. How would you characterize the opinions in *Chadha* in light of the approaches identified by Professor Strauss, below? *See* Strauss, *The Place of Agencies in Government: Separation of Power and the Fourth Branch:*[*]

> Three differing approaches have been used in the effort to understand issues such as these. The first, "separation of powers," supposes that what government does can be characterized in terms of the kind of act performed — legislating, enforcing, and determining the particular application of law — and that for the safety of the citizenry from tyrannous government these three functions must be kept in distinct places. Congress legislates, and it only legislates; the President sees to the faithful execution of those laws and, in the domestic context at least, that is all he does; the courts decide specific cases of law-application, and that is their sole function. These three powers of government are kept radically separate, because if the same body exercised all three of them, or even two, it might no longer be possible to keep it within the constraints of law.
>
> "Separation of functions" suggests a somewhat different idea, grounded more in considerations of individual fairness in particular proceedings than in the need for structural protection against tyrannical government generally. It admits that for agencies (as distinct from the constitutionally named heads of government) the same body often does exercise all three of the characteristic governmental powers, albeit in a web of other controls — judicial review and legislative and executive oversight. As these controls are thought to give reasonable assurance against systemic lawlessness, the separation-of-functions inquiry asks to what extent constitutional due process for the particular individual(s) who may be involved with an agency in a given proceeding requires special measures to assure the objectivity or impartiality of that proceeding. The powers are not kept separate, at least in general, but certain procedural protections — for example, the requirement of an on-the-record hearing before an "impartial" trier — may be afforded.
>
> "Checks and balances" is the third idea, one that to a degree bridges the gap between these two domains. Like separation of powers, it seeks to protect the citizens from the emergence of tyrannical government by

---

[*] This article originally appeared at 84 COLUM. L. REV. 573, 577–78 (1984). Copyright © 1984 by Columbia Law Review. All rights reserved.

establishing multiple heads of authority in government, which are then pitted one against another in a continuous struggle; the intent of that struggle is to deny to any one (or two) of them the capacity ever to consolidate all governmental authority in itself, while permitting the whole effectively to carry forward the work of government. Unlike separation of powers, however, the checks-and-balances idea does not suppose a radical division of government into three parts, with particular functions neatly parceled out among them. Rather, the focus is on relationships and interconnections, on maintaining the conditions in which the intended struggle at the apex may continue. From this perspective, as from the perspective of separation of functions, it is not important how powers below the apex are treated; the important question is whether the relationship of each of the three named actors of the Constitution to the exercise of those powers is such as to promise a continuation of their effective independence and interdependence.

6-7. Given the demise of the legislative veto, alternatives to the veto now take on greater significance. Some statutes are passed with so-called sunset clauses — that is, provisions that require the agency to terminate its duties after a term of years, unless Congress re-authorizes their authority. Congress may also try to rely on joint resolutions either to approve or disapprove of agency action; or Congress can pass so-called report-and-wait statutes — *i.e.* statutes that require an agency to wait a period of time before its rules take effect so that Congress can pass new legislation if it so desires? How do these compare to the legislative veto struck down in *Chadha* in terms of the legislature's ability to control agency discretion?

6-8. The Congressional Review Act, Public Law No. 104-121, was enacted in 1996. The Congressional Review Act allows Congress to review all new federal rules issued by government agencies, and to overrule them with the passing of a joint resolution. The Congressional Review Act gives Congress a 60 session day window to review and reject proposed agency rules.

Under the Act, agencies are required to submit reports for all proposed rules to the General Accounting Office (GAO) and to each house of Congress. The report must contain "(i) a copy of the rule; (ii) a concise general statement relating to the rule, including whether is a major rule; and (iii) the proposed effective date of the rule." The Comptroller General has 15 days from the rule's publication in the Federal Register or receipt of the agency's report by Congress, to provide a report to Congress on each major rule proposed.

If Congress disapproves of a proposed rule, it must enact a joint resolution of disapproval pursuant to § 802. The process is expedited, and after a limited period on the Congressional floor, a resolution of disapproval will be issued or the rule will be accepted. In effect, the review serves as a Congressional veto of proposed agency rules. Additionally, as joint resolutions are presented to the President, if the President supports a rule that Congress does not, the resolution of disapproval must pass with a two-thirds vote in each house.

Since its enactment, the Congressional Review Act has only been used to repeal an agency rule once. In March of 2001, the U.S. Senate and House of Representatives voted to repeal the Occupational Safety and Health Administration (OSHA) "Ergonomics Program Standard." After the resolution passed both houses of Congress, President George W. Bush signed into law a repeal of the Ergonomics Standard.

Is the Congressional Review Act reconcilable with the rule-making scheme created by the APA? What sort of impact does the Congressional Review Act have on traditional formal or notice-and-comment rule-making? Does it have an impact? *See* Peter A. Pfohl, *Congressional Review of Agency Rulemaking: The 104th Congress and the Salvage Timber Directive*, 14 J. L. & POLITICS 1 (1998). *See also*, Morton Rosenberg, *Whatever Happened to Congressional Review of Agency Rulemaking?: A Brief Overview, Assessment and Proposal for Reform*, 51 ADMIN. L. REV. 1051 (1999).

6-9. There are, of course, a number of purely political controls that the legislature may exercise over agencies. The appropriations process is one of the most effective ways for Congress to review an agency's performance and express its pleasure or dissatisfaction. Cutting or threatening to cut an agency's budget usually has a very direct effect on an agency. Once funds are appropriated, Congress can still play a direct supervisory role through oversight hearings. Many federal statutes specifically provide for periodic oversight hearings. Moreover, specific congressional committees or subcommittees may also call for hearings at any time to pursue certain aspects of an agency's policy. There also exist less formal ways for Congress to intervene. One way is intervention by individual legislators, inquiring into the status of particular issues and cases pending in an agency or lodging complaints with the agency when they disagree with its decisions. *See generally*, A. Aman and W. Mayton, *Administrative Law*, 620–23 (West Pub. Co. 2d ed., 2001).

6-10. Of course, there are also various statutes by which Congress attempts to control agency discretion. Congress has passed a number of statutes that govern factors the agency must evaluate, specify information it must provide, and procedures it must use so that parties other than the issuing agency can review their regulations. These include, for example, the National Environmental Policy Act of 1969 (NEPA), the Regulatory Flexibility Act of 1980, and the Paperwork Reduction Act of 1980. Such acts attempt to establish certain procedures designed to limit the adverse impact an agency might have on the environment or on various regulated entities, particularly small businesses. In addition, other statutes such as the Freedom of Information Act and the Government in the Sunshine Act attempt to ensure a flow of information to the public and a modicum of open governmental decisionmaking to encourage agencies to operate appropriately. Other statutes, such as the Civil Service Reform Act and the 1978 Ethics in Government Act try to guard the integrity of agency decisionmakers. Still other statutes seek to monitor the processes by which agencies make rules with so-called "hammer" provisions, mandating that rules be issued by a specified date. *See, e.g.*, 42 U.S.C.A. § 6924(d)(1)(2) (EPA required to act within certain time period). The Unfunded Mandate Reform Act limits the ability of regulatory agencies to place burdens on state, local and tribal governments.

§ 6.04 The Delegation Doctrine

A.L.A. SCHECHTER POULTRY CORP. v. UNITED STATES

United States Supreme Court
295 U.S. 495 (1935)

Mr. Chief Justice Hughes delivered the opinion of the Court.

Petitioners in No. 854 were convicted in the District Court of the United States for the Eastern District of New York on eighteen counts of an indictment charging violations of what is known as the "Live Poultry Code," and on an additional count for conspiracy to commit such violations. By demurrer to the indictment and appropriate motions on the trial, the defendants contended (1) that the code had been adopted pursuant to an unconstitutional delegation by Congress of legislative power. . . .

The "Live Poultry Code" was promulgated under § 3 of the National Industrial Recovery Act. That section . . . authorizes the President to approve "codes of fair competition." Such a code may be approved for a trade or industry, upon application by one or more trade or industrial associations or groups, if the President finds (1) that such associations or groups "impose no inequitable restrictions on admission to membership therein and are truly representative," and (2) that such codes are not designed "to promote monopolies or to eliminate or oppress small enterprises and will not operate to discriminate against them, and will tend to effectuate the policy" of Title I of the Act. Such codes "shall not permit monopolies or monopolistic practices." As a condition of his approval, the President may "impose such conditions (including requirements for the making of reports and the keeping of accounts) for the protection of consumers, competitors, employees, and others, and in furtherance of the public interest, and may provide such exceptions to and exemptions from the provisions of such code as the President in his discretion deems necessary to effectuate the policy herein declared." Where such a code has not been approved, the President may prescribe one, either on his own motion or on complaint. Violation of any provision of a code (so approved or prescribed) "in any transaction in or affecting interstate or foreign commerce" is made a misdemeanor punishable by a fine of not more than $500 for each offense, and each day the violation continues is to be deemed a separate offense. . . .

We recently had occasion to review the pertinent decisions and the general principles which govern the determination of this question. *Panama Refining Company v. Ryan*. . . . The Congress is not permitted to abdicate or to transfer to others the essential legislative functions with which it is thus vested. We have repeatedly recognized the necessity of adapting legislation to complex conditions involving a host of details with which the national Legislature cannot deal directly. We pointed out in the *Panama Refining Company* case that the Constitution has never been regarded as denying to Congress the necessary resources of flexibility and practicality, which will enable it to perform its function in laying down policies and establishing standards, while leaving to selected instrumentalities the making of subordinate rules within prescribed limits and the determination of facts to which the policy as declared by the Legislature is to apply. But we said that the constant recognition of the necessity and validity of such provisions, and the wide range of administrative authority which has been developed by means of them, cannot be allowed to obscure the limitations of the authority to delegate, if our constitutional system is to be maintained.

Accordingly, we look to the statute to see whether Congress has overstepped these limitations — whether Congress in authorizing "codes of fair competition" has itself established the standards of legal obligation, thus performing its essential legislative function, or, by the failure to enact such standards, has attempted to transfer that function to others.

The aspect in which the question is now presented is distinct from that which was before us in the case of the *Panama Refining Company*. There the subject of the statutory prohibition was defined. National Industrial Recovery Act, § 9(c). That subject was the transportation in interstate and foreign commerce of petroleum and petroleum products which are produced or withdrawn from storage in excess of the amount permitted by state authority. The question was with respect to the range of discretion given to the President in prohibiting that transportation. . . . As to the "codes of fair competition," under section 3 of the act, the question is more fundamental. It is whether there is any adequate definition of the subject to which the codes are to be addressed.

What is meant by "fair competition" as the term is used in the act? Does it refer to a category established in the law, and is the authority to make codes limited accordingly? Or is it used as a convenient designation for whatever set of laws the formulators of a code for a particular trade or industry may propose and the President may approve (subject to certain restrictions), or the President may himself prescribe, as being wise and beneficent provisions for the government of the trade or industry in order to accomplish the broad purposes of rehabilitation, correction, and expansion which are stated in the first section of Title I?

The Act does not define "fair competition." "Unfair competition," as known to the common law, is a limited concept. . . . But it is evident that in its widest range, "unfair competition," as it has been understood in the law, does not reach the objectives of the codes which are authorized by the National Industrial Recovery Act. The codes may, indeed, cover conduct which existing law condemns, but they are not limited to conduct of that sort. The Government does not contend that the act contemplates such a limitation. It would be opposed both to the declared purposes of the act and to its administrative construction.

The Federal Trade Commission Act (§ 5) introduced the expression "unfair methods of competition," which were declared to be unlawful. That was an expression new in the law. Debate apparently convinced the sponsors of the legislation that the words "unfair competition," in the light of their meaning at common law, were too narrow. We have said that the substituted phrase has a broader meaning, that it does not admit of precise definition; its scope being left to judicial determination as controversies arise. . . . To make this possible, Congress set up a special procedure. A commission, a quasi-judicial body, was created. Provision was made for formal complaint, for notice and hearing, for appropriate findings of fact supported by adequate evidence, and for judicial review to give assurance that the action of the commission is taken within its statutory authority. In providing for codes, the National Industrial Recovery Act dispenses with this administrative procedure and with any administrative procedure of an analogous character. But the difference between the code plan of the Recovery Act and the scheme of the Federal Trade Commission Act lies not only in procedure but in subject-matter. We cannot regard the "fair competition" of the codes as antithetical to the "unfair methods of competition" of the Federal Trade Commission Act. The "fair competition" of the codes has a much broader range and a new significance. The Recovery Act provides that it shall not be construed to impair the powers of the Federal Trade Commission, but, when a code is approved, its provisions are to be the "standards of fair competition" for the trade or industry concerned, and any violation of such standards in any transaction in or affecting interstate or foreign commerce is to be deemed "an unfair method of competition" within the meaning of the Federal Trade Commission Act. . . .

The Government urges that the codes will "consist of rules of competition deemed fair for each industry by representative members of that industry — by the persons most vitally concerned and most familiar with its problems." Instances are cited in which Congress has availed itself of such assistance; as, *e.g.,* in the exercise of its authority over the public domain, with respect to the recognition of local customs or rules of miners as to mining claims, or, in matters of a more or less technical nature, as in designating the standard height of drawbars. But would it be seriously contended that Congress could delegate its legislative authority to trade or industrial associations or groups so as to empower them to enact the laws they deem to be wise and beneficent for the rehabilitation and expansion of their trade or industries? Could trade or industrial associations or groups be constituted legislative bodies for that purpose because such associations or groups are familiar with the problems of their enterprises? And could an effort of that sort be made valid by such a preface of generalities as to permissible aims as we find in section 1 of Title I? The answer is obvious. Such a delegation of legislative power is unknown to our law, and is utterly inconsistent with the constitutional prerogatives and duties of Congress.

The question, then, turns upon the authority which § 3 of the Recovery Act vests in the President to approve or prescribe. If the codes have standing as penal statutes, this must be due to the effect of the executive action. But Congress cannot delegate legislative power to the President to exercise an unfettered discretion to make whatever laws he thinks may be needed or advisable for the rehabilitation and expansion of trade or industry.

Accordingly we turn to the Recovery Act to ascertain what limits have been set to the exercise of the President's discretion. *First,* the President, as a condition of approval, is required to find that the trade or industrial associations or groups which propose a code "impose no inequitable restrictions on admission to membership" and are "truly representative." That condition, however, relates only to the status of the initiators of the new laws and not to the permissible scope of such laws. *Second,* the President is required to find that the code is not "designed to promote monopolies or to eliminate or oppress small enterprises and will not operate to discriminate against them." And to this is added a proviso that the code "shall not permit monopolies or monopolistic practices." But these restrictions leave virtually untouched the field of policy envisaged by section 1, and, in that wide field of legislative possibilities, the proponents of a code, refraining from monopolistic designs, may roam at will, and the President may approve or disapprove their proposals as he may see fit. That is the precise effect of the further finding that the President is to make — that the code "will tend to effectuate the policy of this title." While this is called a finding, it is really but a statement of an opinion as to the general effect upon the promotion of trade or industry of a scheme of laws. These are the only findings which Congress has made essential in order to put into operation a legislative code having the aims described in the "Declaration of Policy."

Nor is the breadth of the President's discretion left to the necessary implications of this limited requirement as to his findings. As already noted, the President in approving a code may impose his own conditions, adding to or taking from what is proposed, as "in his discretion" he thinks necessary "to effectuate the policy" declared by the Act. Of course, he has no less liberty when he prescribes a code on his own motion or on complaint, and he is free to prescribe one if a code has not been approved. The Act provides for the creation by the President of administrative agencies to assist him, but the action or reports of such agencies, or of his other assistants — their recommendations and findings in relation to the making of codes — have no sanction beyond the will of the President, who may accept, modify, or reject them as he pleases. Such recommendations or findings in no way limit the authority which § 3 undertakes to vest in the President with no other conditions than those there specified. And this authority relates to a host of different trades and industries, thus extending the President's discretion to all the varieties of laws which he may deem to be beneficial in dealing with the vast array of commercial and industrial activities throughout the country.

Such a sweeping delegation of legislative power finds no support in the decisions upon which the government especially relies. By the Interstate Commerce Act, Congress has itself provided a code of laws regulating the activities of the common carriers subject to the act, in order to assure the performance of their services upon just and reasonable terms, with adequate facilities and without unjust discrimination. Congress from time to time has elaborated its requirements, as needs have been disclosed. To facilitate the application of the standards prescribed by the act, Congress has provided an expert body. That administrative agency, in dealing with particular cases, is required to act upon notice and hearing, and its orders must be supported by findings of fact which in turn are sustained by evidence.

. . . When the [Interstate Commerce] Commission is authorized to issue, for the construction, extension, or abandonment of lines, a certificate of "public convenience and necessity," or to permit the acquisition by one carrier of the control of another, if that is found to be "in the public interest," we have pointed out that these provisions are not left without standards to guide determination. The authority conferred has direct relation to the standards prescribed for the service of common carriers, and can be exercised only upon findings, based upon evidence, with respect to particular conditions of transportation.

Similarly, we have held that the Radio Act of 1927 established standards to govern radio communications, and, in view of the limited number of available broadcasting frequencies, Congress authorized allocation and licenses. The Federal Radio Commission was created as the licensing authority, in order to secure a reasonable equality of opportunity in radio transmission and reception. The authority of the Commission to grant licenses "as public convenience, interest or necessity requires" was limited by the nature of radio communications, and by the scope, character, and quality of the services to be rendered and the relative advantages to be derived through distribution of facilities. These standards established by Congress were to be enforced upon hearing and evidence by an administrative body acting under statutory restrictions adapted to the particular activity. . . .

To summarize and conclude upon this point: Section 3 of the Recovery Act is without precedent. It supplies no standards for any trade, industry, or activity. It does not undertake to prescribe rules of conduct to be applied to particular states of fact determined by appropriate administrative procedure. Instead of prescribing rules of conduct, it authorizes the making of codes to prescribe them. For that legislative undertaking, § 3 sets up no standards, aside from the statement of the general aims of rehabilitation, correction, and expansion described in section 1. In view of the scope of that broad declaration and of the nature of the few restrictions that are imposed, the discretion of the President in approving or prescribing codes, and thus enacting laws for the government of trade and industry throughout the country, is virtually unfettered. We think that the code-making authority thus conferred is an unconstitutional delegation of legislative power. . . .

MR. JUSTICE CARDOZO (concurring).

The delegated power of legislation which has found expression in this code is not canalized within banks that keep it from overflowing. It is unconfined and vagrant, if I may borrow my own words in an earlier opinion. *Panama Refining Co. v. Ryan,* 293 U.S. 388, 440.

This court has held that delegation may be unlawful, though the act to be performed is definite and single, if the necessity, time, and occasion of performance have been left in the end to the discretion of the delegate. *Panama Refining Co. v. Ryan, supra.* I thought that ruling went too far. I pointed out in an opinion that there had been "no grant to the Executive of any roving commission to inquire into evils and then, upon discovering them, do anything he pleases." 293 U.S. at page 435. Choice, though within limits, had been given him "as to the occasion, but none whatever as to the means." Here, in the case before us, is an attempted delegation not confined to any single act nor to any class or group of acts identified or described by reference to a standard. Here in effect is a roving commission to inquire into evils and upon discovery correct them.

I have said that there is no standard, definite or even approximate, to which legislation must conform. Let me make my meaning more precise. If codes of fair competition are codes eliminating "unfair" methods of competition ascertained upon inquiry to prevail in one industry or another, there is no unlawful delegation of legislative functions when the President is directed to inquire into such practices and denounce them when discovered. For many years a like power has been committed to the Federal Trade Commission with the approval of this court in a long series of decisions. . . . Delegation in such circumstances is born of the necessities of the occasion. The industries of the country are too many and diverse to make it possible for Congress, in respect of matters such as these, to legislate directly with adequate appreciation of varying conditions. Nor is the substance of the power changed because the President may act at the instance of trade or industrial associations having special knowledge of the facts. Their function is strictly advisory; it is the *imprimatur* of the President that begets the quality of law. When the task that is set before one is that of cleaning house, it is prudent as well as usual to take counsel of the dwellers.

But there is another conception of codes of fair competition, their significance and function, which leads to very different consequences, though it is one that is struggling now for recognition and acceptance. By this other conception a code is not to be restricted to the elimination of business practices that would be characterized by general acceptance as oppressive or unfair. It is to include whatever ordinances may be desirable or helpful for the well-being or prosperity of the industry affected. In that view, the function of its adoption is not merely negative, but positive; the planning of improvements as well as the extirpation of abuses. What is fair, as thus conceived, is not something to be contrasted with what is unfair or fraudulent or tricky. The extension becomes as wide as the field of industrial regulation. If that conception shall prevail, anything that Congress may do within the limits of the commerce clause for the betterment of business may be done by the President upon the recommendation of a trade association by calling it a code. This is delegation running riot. No such plenitude of power is susceptible of transfer. The statute, however, aims at nothing less, as one can learn both from its terms and from the administrative practice under it. Nothing less is aimed at by the code now submitted to our scrutiny. . . .

NOTES AND QUESTIONS

6-11. State the delegation doctrine as formulated by the Court in *Schechter*. What is the Constitutional basis of this doctrine? What must Congress do to meet the requirements this doctrine imposes?

6-12. What is a standard? How precise must it be? Can it be inferred from the overall purposes of a statute as set forth directly in its declarations of policy as well as indirectly in all of a statute's provisions?

6-13. Knowing what you now know about the outcome of this case, how would you have drafted section 3 of the National Recovery Act in *Schechter* to survive judicial review? How would you draft section 9(c) struck down in *Panama*? Do you think Congress was irresponsible in its failure to be more precise? Compare the degree of Congressional responsibility evident in these cases with that of *Industrial Union Department, AFL-CIO v. American Petroleum Institute, infra,* § 6.06.

6-14. What, in the Court's opinion in *Schechter,* is the fatal flaw in section 3 of the National Industrial Recovery Act? Is it the lack of standards or the lack of procedure? Who wrote the codes of fair competition? Were there any public procedures to which they were exposed? In *Schechter,* is there a delegation of Congressional power to an administrative agency or to private trade associations? Even if there were adequate standards in this case, would the delegation of legislative power to private entities withstand constitutional scrutiny?

6-15. Why does Cardozo concur in *Schechter*? How does this case differ, as far as he is concerned, from *Panama Refining Co. v. Ryan*?

6-16. Is it significant that *Schecter* and *Panama Refining* came up in the context of the New Deal? Was the Court primarily concerned with how the legislature delegated its legislative power or was it primarily concerned with the tremendous change in the role the federal government now sought to play in the national economy?

6-17. What is the philosophical basis of the non-delegation doctrine? Consider the following in Paul Craig, *Public Law and Democracy in the United Kingdom and the United States of America* 117 (Oxford Press 1990):[*]

> A pluralist conception of democracy, with its emphasis upon group bargain, places stress upon process considerations. It favours delegation of power as a method of more finely accommodating such bargains between competing groups. It also fosters interest representation with the object of ensuring that those affected by agency decisions will be able to participate in their formulation. What is of interest, in the light of the preceding discussion, is the extent to which the courts have not only fostered such process rights, but have also felt the need for more substantive forms of judicial control. The infirmities of pluralism may indicate that, while process rights are a necessary element of administrative law, they are not sufficient; that more substantive judicial control is necessary in order to guard against the danger of overpowering faction. . . . In the complex modern world a tension is created. On the one hand, it may be felt that certain activities require control of regulation. On the other, the inner thrust of pluralism indicates that authority should emerge from individual bargains for it to prove acceptable. Broad delegations of power to administrative agencies before which interested parties compete and bargain become the mechanism whereby this tension is eased.

---

[*] Copyright © 1990. Reprinted by permission of Oxford University Press.

§ 6.05 The Delegation Doctrine Since *Panama* and *Schechter*

One could say that the federal delegation doctrine peaked in 1934–35. *Panama* and *Schechter* are the only two federal Supreme Court cases explicitly to declare an Act of Congress unconstitutional on delegation doctrine grounds. Yet, nearly sixty years of being used primarily in dissents does not mean that these cases were or are irrelevant today. They have not been overruled. They remain, as one administrative law wag has put it, "pulsating amoebas" in the law. More important, there is a great deal of statutory interpretation that takes place in the shadow of the delegation doctrine. A basic canon of statutory construction is that constitutional issues should, whenever possible, be avoided. Courts often narrow broad delegations of legislative power to avoid having to decide whether Congress unconstitutionally delegated its powers to an agency.

In *Kent v. Dulles* 357 U.S. 116 (1958), for example, the Court dealt with the Passport Act of 1926. That Act codified the authority of the Secretary of State to "grant and issue passports . . . under such rules as the President shall designate and prescribe." In 1952 the Secretary issued an Executive Order prohibiting the issuance of passports to members or supporters of the Communist Party, or to persons believed to be going abroad to advance the cause of Communism. To obtain a passport, you had to execute an affidavit that answered questions dealing with one's present or past affiliations with the Communist Party. Kent made an application for a passport, but he refused to execute such an affidavit. His application was denied because of this, but also because he was thought to be a Communist.

Justice Douglas wrote for the majority, noting that what was at stake in this case was the constitutional right to travel. "If that 'liberty' is to be regulated, it must be pursuant to the lawmaking functions of the Congress. And if that power is delegated, the standards must be adequate to pass scrutiny by the accepted tests. . . . Where such activities . . . are involved, we will construe narrowly all delegated powers that curtail or dilute them. . . . We hesitate to find in this broad generalized power an authority to trench so heavily on the rights of the citizen."

In the more recent case of *Industrial Union Department, AFL-CIO v. American Petroleum Institute,* 448 U.S. 607 (1980), *infra* at § 7.04, Justice Stevens' approach to the statute in question was very much influenced by the delegation doctrine. Rather than run afoul of that doctrine, he sought to save the statute, as we shall see, by giving its delegation clause a narrow interpretation.

Yet, it would be an overstatement to contend that the delegation doctrine of *Panama* and *Schechter* ever really became a major factor in judicial review of most congressional statutes. As courts became more reconciled with an active federal governmental role in our economy during and after the New Deal, deference to legislative decisions to intervene in the economy in the immediate post-New Deal era grew considerably. Along with the Supreme Court's willingness to read the Commerce and Taking Clauses of the Constitution very broadly as well as, essentially, to ignore the Tenth Amendment and the Contracts Clause, courts increasingly took a very liberal view towards the delegation doctrine. *Panama* and *Schechter* rarely appeared, except in the odd dissent here and there. This, in fact, prompted Justice Marshall to remark in *Federal Power Commission v. New England Power Co.,* 415 U.S. 345, 352 (1974) that "lawyers who try to win cases by arguing that congressional delegations are unconstitutional almost invariably do more harm than good to their clients' interests."

An excellent example of the usual judicial approach to delegation arguments was that of Judge Leventhal of the D.C. Circuit Court of Appeals in *Amalgamated Meat Cutters & Butcher Workmen v. Connally,* 337 F. Supp. 737 (1971). This case dealt with the Economic Stabilization Act of 1970. That Act gave the President broad authority to issue orders and regulations to stabilize prices, rents, wages and salaries. It was attacked as an undue delegation of legislative power. Judge Leventhal, writing for majority, noted:

> We may usefully begin with the modest observation that the Constitution does not forbid every delegation of "legislative" power. This was recognized explicitly at least as long ago as *Norwegian Nitrogen Products Co. v. United States,* 288 U.S. 294, 305 . . . (1933), where Justice Cardozo stated that the tariff provision under consideration involved "in substance a delegation, though a permissible one, of the legislative process."

> There may thus be added to the outworn doctrines interred in the cause of wisdom the conception developed in *Field v. Clark,* 143 U.S. 649, 692–93, . . . which centers the validity of a delegation by Congress to the President on whether he "was the mere agent of the lawmaking department to ascertain and declare the event upon which its expressed will was to take effect." That officials may lawfully be given far greater authority than the power to recognize a triggering condition was recognized within twenty years in the famous *Grimaud,* case where a unanimous Court "admitted that it is difficult to define the line which separates legislative power to make laws, from administrative authority to make regulations." There is no analytical difference, no difference in kind, between the legislative function — of prescribing rules for the future — that is exercised by the legislature or by the agency implementing the authority conferred by the legislature. The problem is one of limits.

> An agency assigned to a task has its freedom of action circumscribed not only by the constitutional limitations that bind Congress but by the parameters described by the legislature as hedges defining areas open to the agency. The question is the extent to which the Constitution limits a legislature that may think it proper

and needful to give the agency broad flexibility to cope with the conditions it encounters. . . .

The legislative power granted to Congress by the Constitution includes the power to avail itself of "the necessary resources of flexibility and practicality . . . to perform its function." The spaciousness of the legislative authority is underscored by the following quotations from the *Yakus* opinion voicing the elements of the applicable principles: "The Constitution as a continuously operative charter of the government does not demand the impossible or the impracticable." Congress is free to delegate legislative authority provided it has exercised "the essentials of the legislative function" — of determining the basic legislative policy and formulating a rule of conduct — held satisfied by "the rule, with penal sanctions, that prices shall not be greater than those fixed by maximum price regulations which conform to standards and will tend to further the policy which Congress has established." The key question is not answered by noting that the authority delegated is broad, or broader than Congress might have selected if it had chosen to operate within a narrower range. The issue is whether the legislative description of the task assigned "sufficiently marks the field within which the Administrator is to act so that it may be known whether he has kept within it in compliance with the legislative will."

The *Yakus* ruling of Chief Justice Stone carries forward the doctrine earlier articulated by Chief Justice Taft in *Hampton* that there is no forbidden delegation of legislative power "if Congress shall lay down by legislative act an intelligible principle" to which the official or agency must conform.

Concepts of control and accountability define the constitutional requirement. The principle permitting a delegation of legislative power, if there has been sufficient demarcation of the field to permit a judgment whether the agency has kept within the legislative will, establishes a principle of accountability under which compatibility with the legislative design may be ascertained not only by Congress but by the courts and the public. That principle was conjoined in *Yakus* with a recognition that the burden is on the party who assails a legislature's choice of means for effecting its purpose, a burden that is met "[o]nly if we could say that there is an absence of standards for the guidance of the Administrator's action, so that it would be impossible in a proper proceeding to ascertain whether the will of Congress has been obeyed."

These doctrines have been applied to sustain legislation that delegated broad authority indeed in order to assure requisite flexibility to the officials or agencies designated to discharge the tasks assigned by Congress. . . . But perhaps the broadest delegation yet sustained and the one closest to the case before us came in *Yakus*, for the ultimate standard in the 1942 statute was only that the maximum prices be "generally fair and equitable." . . .

Under these governing concepts we cannot say that in the Act before us there is such an absence of standards that it would be impossible to ascertain whether the will of Congress has been obeyed. . . .

§ 6.06 Delegation Doctrine Revival?

INDUSTRIAL UNION DEPARTMENT, AFL-CIO v. AMERICAN PETROLEUM INSTITUTE

United States Supreme Court
448 U.S. 607 (1980)

MR. JUSTICE STEVENS announced the judgment of the Court and delivered an opinion, in which THE CHIEF JUSTICE and MR. JUSTICE STEWART joined and in Parts I, II, III-A, III-B, III-C and III-E of which MR. JUSTICE POWELL joined.

The Occupational Safety and Health Act of 1970 (Act), 84 Stat. 1590, 29 U.S.C. § 651 *et seq.*, was enacted for the purpose of ensuring safe and healthful working conditions for every working man and woman in the Nation. This litigation concerns a standard promulgated by the Secretary of Labor to regulate occupational exposure to benzene, a substance which has been shown to cause cancer at high exposure levels. The principal question is whether such a showing is a sufficient basis for a standard that places the most stringent limitation on exposure to benzene that is technologically and economically possible.

The Act delegates broad authority to the Secretary to promulgate different kinds of standards. The basic definition of an "occupational safety and health standard" is found in § 3(8), which provides:

The term "occupational safety and health standard" means a standard which requires conditions, or the adoption or use of one or more practices, means, methods, operations, or processes, reasonably necessary or appropriate to provide safe or healthful employment and places of employment.

Where toxic materials or harmful physical agents are concerned, a standard must also comply with § 6(b)(5), which provides:

The Secretary, in promulgating standards dealing with toxic materials or harmful physical agents under this subsection, shall set the standard which most adequately assures, to the extent feasible, on the basis of the best available evidence, that no employee will suffer material impairment of health or functional capacity even if such employee has regular exposure to the hazard dealt with by such standard for the period of his working life. Development of standards under this subsection shall be based upon research, demonstrations, experiments, and such other information as may be appropriate. In addition to the attainment of the highest degree of health and safety protection for the employee, other considerations shall be the latest available scientific data in the field, the feasibility of the standards, and experience gained under this and other health and safety laws.

Wherever the toxic material to be regulated is a carcinogen, the Secretary has taken the position that no safe exposure level can be determined and that § 6(b)(5) requires him to set an exposure limit at the lowest technologically feasible level that will not impair the viability of the industries regulated. In this case, after having determined that there is a causal connection between benzene and leukemia (a cancer of the white blood cells), the Secretary set an exposure limit on airborne concentrations of benzene of one part benzene per million parts of air (1 ppm), regulated dermal and eye contact with solutions containing benzene, and imposed complex monitoring and medical testing requirements on employers whose workplaces contain 0.5 ppm or more of benzene. . . .

I

Benzene is a familiar and important commodity. It is a colorless, aromatic liquid that evaporates rapidly under ordinary atmospheric conditions. Approximately 11 billion pounds of benzene were produced in the United States in 1976. Ninety-four percent of that total was produced by the petroleum and petrochemical industries, with the remainder produced by the steel industry as a byproduct of coking operations. Benzene is used in manufacturing a variety of products including motor fuels (which may contain as much as 2% benzene), solvents, detergents, pesticides, and other organic chemicals.

The entire population of the United States is exposed to small quantities of benzene, ranging from a few parts per billion to 0.5 ppm, in the ambient air. Over one million workers are subject to additional low-level exposures as a consequence of their employment. The majority of these employees work in gasoline service stations, benzene production (petroleum refineries and coking operations), chemical processing, benzene transportation, rubber manufacturing, and laboratory operations.

Benzene is a toxic substance. Although it could conceivably cause harm to a person who swallowed or touched it, the principal risk of harm comes from inhalation of benzene vapors. When these vapors are inhaled, the benzene diffuses through the lungs and is quickly absorbed into the blood. Exposure to high concentrations produces an almost immediate effect on the central nervous system. Inhalation of concentrations of 20,000 ppm can be fatal within minutes; exposures in the range of 250 to 500 ppm can cause vertigo, nausea, and other symptoms of mild poisoning. 43 Fed. Reg. 5921 (1978). Persistent exposures at levels above 25–40 ppm may lead to blood deficiencies and diseases of the blood-forming organs, including aplastic anemia, which is generally fatal.

Industrial health experts have long been aware that exposure to benzene may lead to various types of nonmalignant diseases. By 1948 the evidence connecting high levels of benzene to serious blood disorders had become so strong that the Commonwealth of Massachusetts imposed a 35 ppm limitation on workplaces within its jurisdiction. In 1969 the American National Standards Institute (ANSI) adopted a national consensus standard of 10 ppm averaged over an 8-hour period with a ceiling concentration of 25 ppm for 10-minute periods or a maximum peak concentration of 50 ppm. In 1971, after the Occupational Safety and Health Act was passed, the Secretary adopted this consensus standard as the federal standard. . . .

[Subsequently, OSHA began notice and comment procedures to adopt a new standard.]

In its published statement giving notice of the proposed permanent standard, OSHA did not ask for comments as to whether or not benzene presented a significant health risk at exposures of 10 ppm or less. Rather, it asked for comments as to whether 1 ppm was the minimum feasible exposure limit. As OSHA's Deputy Director of Health Standards, Grover Wrenn, testified at the hearing, this formulation of the issue to be considered by the Agency was consistent with OSHA's general policy with respect to carcinogens. Whenever a carcinogen is involved, OSHA will presume that no safe level of exposure exists in the absence of clear proof establishing such a level and will accordingly set the exposure limit at the lowest level feasible. The proposed 1 ppm exposure limit in this case thus was established not on the basis of a proven hazard at 10 ppm, but rather on the basis of "OSHA's best judgment at the time of the proposal of the feasibility of compliance with the proposed standard by the [a]ffected industries." . . .

Public hearings were held on the proposed standard, commencing on July 19, 1977. The final standard was issued on February 10, 1978. 29 CFR § 1910.1028 (1979). In its final form, the benzene standard is designed to protect workers from whatever hazards are associated with low-level benzene exposures by requiring employers to monitor workplaces to determine the level of exposure, to provide medical examinations when the level rises above 0.5 ppm, and to institute whatever engineering or other controls are necessary to keep exposures at or below 1 ppm. . . .

As presently formulated, the benzene standard is an expensive way of providing some additional protection for a relatively small number of employees. According to OSHA's figures, the standard will require capital investments in engineering controls of approximately $266 million, first-year operating costs (for monitoring, medical testing, employee training, and respirators) of $187 million to $205 million and recurring annual costs of approximately $34 million. 43 Fed. Reg. 5934 (1978). The figures outlined in OSHA's explanation of the costs of compliance to various industries indicate that only 35,000 employees would gain any benefit from the regulation in terms of a reduction in their exposure to benzene. Over two-thirds of these workers (24,450) are employed in the rubber-manufacturing industry. Compliance costs in that industry are estimated to be rather low, with no capital costs and initial operating expenses estimated at only $34 million ($1,390 per employee); recurring annual costs would also be rather low, totalling less than

$1 million. By contrast, the segment of the petroleum refining industry that produces benzene would be required to incur $24 million in capital costs and $600,000 in first-year operating expenses to provide additional protection for 300 workers ($82,000 per employee), while the petrochemical industry would be required to incur $20.9 million in capital costs and $1 million in initial operating expenses for the benefit of 552 employees ($39,675 per employee).

Although OSHA did not quantify the benefits to each category of worker in terms of decreased exposure to benzene, it appears from the economic impact study done at OSHA's direction that those benefits may be relatively small. Thus, although the current exposure limit is 10 ppm, the actual exposures outlined in that study are often considerably lower. For example, for the period 1970–1975 the petrochemical industry reported that, out of a total of 496 employees exposed to benzene, only 53 were exposed to levels between 1 and 5 ppm and only 7 (all at the same plant) were exposed to between 5 and 10 ppm. . . .

II

The critical issue at this point in the litigation is whether the Court of Appeals was correct in refusing to enforce the 1 ppm exposure limit on the ground that it was not supported by appropriate findings. . . .

In the end OSHA's rationale for lowering the permissible exposure limit to 1 ppm was based, not on any finding that leukemia has ever been caused by exposure to 10 ppm of benzene and that it will *not* be caused by exposure to 1 ppm, but rather on a series of assumptions indicating that some leukemias might result from exposure to 10 ppm and that the number of cases might be reduced by reducing the exposure level to 1 ppm. In reaching that result, the Agency first unequivocally concluded that benzene is a human carcinogen. Second, it concluded that industry had failed to prove that there is a safe threshold level of exposure to benzene below which no excess leukemia cases would occur. In reaching this conclusion OSHA rejected industry contentions that certain epidemiological studies indicating no excess risk of leukemia among workers exposed at levels below 10 ppm were sufficient to establish that the threshold level of safe exposure was at or above 10 ppm. It also rejected an industry witness' testimony that a dose-response curve could be constructed on the basis of the reported epidemiological studies and that his curve indicated that reducing the permissible exposure limit from 10 to 1 ppm would prevent at most one leukemia and one other cancer death every six years.

Third, the Agency applied its standard policy with respect to carcinogens, concluding that, in the absence of definitive proof of a safe level, it must be assumed that any level above zero presents some increased risk of cancer. As the federal parties point out in their brief, there are a number of scientists and public health specialists who subscribe to this view, theorizing that a susceptible person may contract cancer from the absorption of even one molecule of a carcinogen like benzene.

Fourth, the Agency reiterated its view of the Act, stating that it was required by § 6(b)(5) to set the standard either at the level that has been demonstrated to be safe or at the lowest level feasible, whichever is higher. If no safe level is established, as in this case, the Secretary's interpretation of the statute automatically leads to the selection of an exposure limit that is the lowest feasible. Because of benzene's importance to the economy, no one has ever suggested that it would be feasible to eliminate its use entirely, or to try to limit exposures to the small amounts that are omnipresent. Rather, the Agency selected 1 ppm as a workable exposure level, . . . and then determined that compliance with that level was technologically feasible and that "the economic impact of . . . [compliance] will not be such as to threaten the financial welfare of the affected firms or the general economy." It therefore held that 1 ppm was the minimum feasible exposure level within the meaning of § 6(b)(5) of the Act.

Finally, although the Agency did not refer in its discussion of the pertinent legal authority to any duty to identify the anticipated benefits of the new standard, it did conclude that some benefits were likely to result from reducing the exposure limit from 10 ppm to 1 ppm. . . . In light of the Agency's disavowal of any ability to determine the numbers of employees likely to be adversely affected by exposures of 10 ppm, the Court of Appeals held this finding to be unsupported by the record. It is noteworthy that at no point in its lengthy explanation did the Agency quote or even cite § 3(8) of the Act. It made no finding that any of the provisions of the new standard were "reasonably necessary or appropriate to provide safe or healthful employment and places of employment." Nor did it allude to the possibility that any such finding might have been appropriate.

III

Our resolution of the issues in these cases turns, to a large extent, on the meaning of and the relationship between § 3(8), which defines a health and safety standard as a standard that is "reasonably necessary and appropriate to provide safe or healthful employment," and § 6(b)(5), which directs the Secretary in promulgating a health and safety standard for toxic materials to "set the standard which most adequately assures, to the extent feasible, on the basis of the best available evidence, that no employee will suffer material impairment of health or functional capacity. . . ."

In the Government's view, § 3(8)'s definition of the term "standard" has no legal significance or at best merely requires that a standard not be totally irrational. It takes the position that § 6(b)(5) is controlling and that it requires OSHA to promulgate a standard that either gives an absolute assurance of safety for each and every worker or reduces exposures to the lowest level feasible. The Government interprets "feasible" as meaning technologically achievable at a cost that would not impair the viability of the industries subject to the regulation. The respondent industry representatives, on the other hand, argue that the Court of Appeals was correct in holding that the "reasonably necessary and appropriate" language of § 3(8), along with the feasibility requirement of § 6(b)(5), requires the Agency to quantify both the costs and the benefits of a proposed rule and to conclude that they are roughly commensurate.

In our view, it is not necessary to decide whether either the Government or industry is entirely correct. For we think it is clear that § 3(8) does apply to all permanent standards promulgated under the Act and that it requires the Secretary, before issuing any standard, to determine that it is reasonably necessary and appropriate to remedy a significant risk of material health impairment. Only after the Secretary has made the threshold determination that such a risk exists with respect to a toxic substance, would it be necessary to decide whether § 6(b)(5) requires him to select the most protective standard he can consistent with economic and technological feasibility, or whether, as respondents argue, the benefits of the regulation must be commensurate with the costs of its implementation. Because the Secretary did not make the required threshold finding in these cases, we have no occasion to determine whether costs must be weighed against benefits in an appropriate case.

A

Under the Government's view, § 3(8), if it has any substantive content at all, merely requires OSHA to issue standards that are reasonably calculated to produce a safer or more healthy work environment. Apart from this minimal requirement of rationality, the Government argues that § 3(8) imposes no limits on the Agency's power, and thus would not prevent it from requiring employers to do whatever would be "reasonably necessary" to eliminate all risks of any harm from their workplaces. With respect to toxic substances and harmful physical agents, the Government takes an even more extreme position. Relying on § 6(b)(5)'s direction to set a standard "which most adequately assures . . . that no employee will suffer material impairment of health or functional capacity," the Government contends that the Secretary is required to impose standards that either guarantee workplaces that are free from any risk of material health impairment, however small, or that come as close as possible to doing so without ruining entire industries.

If the purpose of the statute were to eliminate completely and with absolute certainty any risk of serious harm, we would agree that it would be proper for the Secretary to interpret §§ 3(8) and 6(b)(5) in this fashion. But we think it is clear that the statute was not designed to require employers to provide absolutely risk-free workplaces whenever it is technologically feasible to do so, so long as the cost is not great enough to destroy an entire industry. Rather, both the language and structure of the Act, as well as its legislative history, indicate that it was intended to require the elimination, as far as feasible, of significant risks of harm.

B

By empowering the Secretary to promulgate standards that are "reasonably necessary or appropriate to provide safe or healthful employment and places of employment," the Act implies that, before promulgating any standard, the Secretary must make a finding that the workplaces in question are not safe. But "safe" is not the equivalent of "risk-free." There are many activities that we engage in every day — such as driving a car or even breathing city air — that entail some risk of accident or material health impairment;

nevertheless, few people would consider these activities "unsafe." Similarly, a workplace can hardly be considered "unsafe" unless it threatens the workers with a significant risk of harm.

Therefore, before he can promulgate any permanent health or safety standard, the Secretary is required to make a threshold finding that a place of employment is unsafe — in the sense that significant risks are present and can be eliminated or lessened by a change in practices. This requirement applies to permanent standards promulgated pursuant to § 6(b)(5), as well as to other types of permanent standards. For there is no reason why § 3(8)'s definition of a standard should not be deemed incorporated by reference into § 6(b)(5). The standards promulgated pursuant to § 6(b)(5) are just one species of the genus of standards governed by the basic requirement. That section repeatedly uses the term "standard" without suggesting any exception from, or qualification of, the general definition; on the contrary, its directs the Secretary to select "the standard" — that is to say, one of various possible alternatives that satisfy the basic definition in § 3(8) — that is most protective. . . .

This interpretation of §§ 3(8) and 6(b)(5) is supported by the other provisions of the Act. . . .

In the absence of a clear mandate in the Act, it is unreasonable to assume that Congress intended to give the Secretary the unprecedented power over American industry that would result from the Government's view of §§ 3(8) and 6(b)(5), coupled with OSHA's cancer policy. Expert testimony that a substance is probably a human carcinogen — either because it has caused cancer in animals or because individuals have contracted cancer following extremely high exposures — would justify the conclusion that the substance poses some risk of serious harm no matter how minute the exposure and no matter how many experts testified that they regarded the risk as insignificant. That conclusion would in turn justify pervasive regulation limited only by the constraint of feasibility. In light of the fact that there are literally thousands of substances used in the workplace that have been identified as carcinogens or suspect carcinogens, the Government's theory would give OSHA power to impose enormous costs that might produce little, if any, discernible benefit.

If the Government was correct in arguing that neither § 3(8) nor § 6(b)(5) requires that the risk from a toxic substance be quantified sufficiently to enable the Secretary to characterize it as significant in an understandable way, the statute would make such a "sweeping delegation of legislative power" that it might be unconstitutional under the Court's reasoning in *A.L.A. Schechter Poultry Corp. v. United States,* 295 U.S. 495, 539 and *Panama Refining Co. v. Ryan,* 293 U.S. 388. A construction of the statute that avoids this kind of open-ended grant should certainly be favored.

C

The legislative history also supports the conclusion that Congress was concerned, not with absolute safety, but with the elimination of significant harm. The examples of industrial hazards referred to in the Committee hearings and debates all involved situations in which the risk was unquestionably significant. For example, the Senate Committee on Labor and Public

Welfare noted that byssinosis, a disabling lung disease caused by breathing cotton dust, affected as many as 30% of the workers in carding or spinning rooms in some American cotton mills and that as many as 100,000 active or retired workers were then suffering from the disease. It also noted that statistics indicated that 20,000 out of 50,000 workers who had performed insulation work were likely to die of asbestosis, lung cancer, or mesothelioma as a result of breathing asbestos fibers. . . . Moreover, Congress specifically amended § 6(b)(5) to make it perfectly clear that it does not require the Secretary to promulgate standards that would assure an absolutely risk-free workplace. . . .

OSHA's concessions to practicality in beginning with a 1 ppm exposure limit and using an action level concept implicitly adopt an interpretation of the statute as not requiring regulation of insignificant risks. It is entirely consistent with this interpretation to hold that the Act also requires the Agency to limit its endeavors in the standard-setting area to eliminating significant risks of harm.

Finally, with respect to the legislative history, it is important to note that Congress repeatedly expressed its concern about allowing the Secretary to have too much power over American industry. Thus, Congress refused to give the Secretary the power to shut down plants unilaterally because of an imminent danger, . . . and narrowly circumscribed the Secretary's power to issue temporary emergency standards. This effort by Congress to limit the Secretary's power is not consistent with a view that the mere possibility that some employee somewhere in the country may confront some risk of cancer is a sufficient basis for the exercise of the Secretary's power to require the expenditure of hundreds of millions of dollars to minimize that risk.

D

Given the conclusion that the Act empowers the Secretary to promulgate health and safety standards only where a significant risk of harm exists, the critical issue becomes how to define and allocate the burden of proving the significance of the risk in a case such as this, where scientific knowledge is imperfect and the precise quantification of risks is therefore impossible. The Agency's position is that there is substantial evidence in the record to support its conclusion that there is no absolutely safe level for a carcinogen and that, therefore, the burden is properly on industry to prove, apparently beyond a shadow of a doubt, that there is a safe level for benzene exposure. The Agency argues that, because of the uncertainties in this area, any other approach would render it helpless, forcing it to wait for the leukemia deaths that it believes are likely to occur before taking any regulatory action.

We disagree. As we read the statute, the burden was on the Agency to show, on the basis of substantial evidence, that it is at least more likely than not that long-term exposure to 10 ppm of benzene presents a significant risk of material health impairment. . . .

E

. . . .

In this case the record makes it perfectly clear that the Secretary relied squarely on a special policy for carcinogens that imposed the burden on industry of proving the existence of a safe level of exposure, thereby avoiding the Secretary's threshold responsibility of establishing the need for more stringent standards. In so interpreting his statutory authority, the Secretary exceeded his power. . . .

The judgment of the Court of Appeals remanding the petition for review to the Secretary for further proceedings is affirmed.

MR. CHIEF JUSTICE BURGER, concurring.

These cases press upon the Court difficult unanswered questions on the frontiers of science and medicine. The statute and the legislative history give ambiguous signals as to how the Secretary is directed to operate in this area. The opinion by MR. JUSTICE STEVENS takes on a difficult task to decode the message of the statute as to guidelines for administrative action. . . . When the administrative record reveals only scant or minimal risk of material health impairment, responsible administration calls for avoidance of extravagant, comprehensive regulation. Perfect safety is a chimera; regulation must not strangle human activity in the search for the impossible.

MR. JUSTICE POWELL, concurring in part and concurring in the judgment.

I join Parts I, II, III-A III-B, III-C, and III-E of the plurality opinion.[1] The Occupational Safety and Health Administration relied in large part on its "carcinogen policy" — which had not been adopted formally — in promulgating the benzene exposure and dermal contact regulation at issue of these cases. For the reasons stated by the plurality, I agree that §§ 6(b)(5) and 3(8) of the Occupational Safety and Health Act of 1970, 29 U.S.C. §§ 655(b)(5) and 652(8), must be read together. They require OSHA to make a threshold finding that proposed occupational health standards are reasonably necessary to provide safe workplaces. . . .

Although I regard the question as close, I do not disagree with the plurality's view that OSHA has failed, on this record, to carry its burden of proof on the threshold issues summarized above. But even if one assumes that OSHA properly met this burden, I conclude that the statute also requires the agency to determine that the economic effects of its standard bear a reasonable relationship to the expected benefits. An occupational health standard is neither "reasonably necessary" nor "feasible," as required by statute, if it calls for expenditures wholly disproportionate to the expected health and safety benefits. . . .

I therefore would not lightly assume that Congress intended OSHA to require reduction of health risks found to be significant *whenever* it also finds that the affected industry can bear the costs. . . . Perhaps more significantly,

---

[1] . . . I . . . express no view on the question whether a different interpretation of the statute would violate the nondelegation doctrine of *A.L.A. Schechter Poultry Corp. v. United States,* 295 U.S. 495 (1935), and *Panama Refining Co. v. Ryan,* 293 U.S. 388 (1935).

however, OSHA's interpretation of § 6(b)(5) would force it to regulate in a manner inconsistent with the important health and safety purposes of the legislation we construe today. Thousands of toxic substances present risks that fairly could be characterized as "significant." . . . Even if OSHA succeeded in selecting the gravest risks for earliest regulation, a standard-setting process that ignored economic considerations would result in a serious misallocation of resources and a lower effective level of safety than could be achieved under standards set with reference to the comparative benefits available at a lower cost.[7] I would not attribute such an irrational intention to Congress. . . .

MR. JUSTICE REHNQUIST, concurring in the judgment.

. . . According to the Secretary, who is one of the petitioners herein, § 6(b)(5) imposes upon him an absolute duty, in regulating harmful substances like benzene for which no safe level is known, to set the standard for permissible exposure at the lowest level that "can be achieved at bearable cost with available technology." . . . While the Secretary does not attempt to refine the concept of "bearable cost," he apparently believes that a proposed standard is economically feasible so long as its impact "will not be such as to threaten the financial welfare of the affected firms or the general economy."

Respondents reply, and the lower court agreed, that § 6(b)(5) must be read in light of another provision in the same Act, § 3(8), which defines an "occupational health and safety standard" as

> . . . a standard which requires conditions, or the adoption or use of one or more practices, means, methods, operations, or processes, reasonably necessary or appropriate to provide safe or healthful employment and places of employment.

According to respondents, § 6(b)(5), as tempered by § 3(8), requires the Secretary to demonstrate that any particular health standard is justifiable on the basis of a rough balancing of costs and benefits.

In considering these alternative interpretations, my colleagues manifest a good deal of uncertainty, and ultimately divide over whether the Secretary produced sufficient evidence that the proposed standard for benzene will result in any appreciable benefits at all. This uncertainty, I would suggest, is eminently justified, since I believe that this litigation presents the Court with what has to be one of the most difficult issues that could confront a decisionmaker: whether the statistical possibility of future deaths should ever be disregarded in light of the economic costs of preventing those deaths. I would also suggest that the widely varying positions advanced in the briefs of the parties and in the opinions of MR. JUSTICE STEVENS, THE CHIEF JUSTICE, MR. JUSTICE POWELL, and MR. JUSTICE MARSHALL demonstrate, perhaps better than any other fact, that Congress, the governmental body best suited and most obligated to make the choice confronting us in this litigation, has improperly delegated that choice to the Secretary of Labor and, derivatively, to this Court.

---

[7] For example, OSHA's reading of § 6(b)(5) could force the depletion of an industry's resources in an effort to reduce a single risk by some speculative amount, even though other significant risks remain unregulated.

I

In his Second Treatise of Civil Government, published in 1690, John Locke wrote that "[t]he power of the legislative, being derived from the people by a positive voluntary grant and institution, can be no other than what that positive grant conveyed, which being only to make laws, and not to make legislators, the legislative can have no power to transfer their authority of making laws and place it in other hands." Two hundred years later, this Court expressly recognized the existence of and the necessity for limits on Congress' ability to delegate its authority to representatives of the Executive Branch: "That Congress cannot delegate legislative power to the president is a principle universally recognized as vital to the integrity and maintenance of the system of government ordained by the Constitution." *Field v. Clark,* 143 U.S. 649, 692 (1892).

The rule against delegation of legislative power is not, however, so cardinal a principle as to allow for no exception. The Framers of the Constitution were practical statesmen, who saw that the doctrine of separation of powers was a two-sided coin. James Madison, in Federalist Paper No. 48, for example, recognized that while the division of authority among the various branches of government was a useful principle, "the degree of separation which the maxim requires, as essential to a free government, can never in practice be duly maintained." *The Federalist No. 48,* p. 308 (H. Lodge ed. 1888).

This Court also has recognized that a hermetic sealing-off of the three branches of government from one another could easily frustrate the establishment of a National Government capable of effectively exercising the substantive powers granted to the various branches by the Constitution. MR. CHIEF JUSTICE TAFT, writing for the Court in *J. W. Hampton & Co. v. United States,* 276 U.S. 394 (1928), noted the practicalities of the balance that has to be struck:

> "[T]he rule is that in the actual administration of the government Congress or the Legislature should exercise the legislative power, the President or the state executive, the Governor, the executive power, and the courts or the judiciary the judicial power, and in carrying out that constitutional division into three branches it is a breach of the national fundamental law if Congress gives up its legislative power and transfers it to the President, or to the Judicial branch, or if by law it attempts to invest itself or its members with either executive power or judicial power. This is not to say that the three branches are not coordinate parts of one government and that each in the field of its duties may not invoke the action of the two other branches in so far as the action invoked shall not be an assumption of the constitutional field of action of another branch. In determining what it may do in seeking assistance from another branch, the extent and character of that assistance must be fixed according to common sense and the inherent necessities of the governmental co-ordination."

During the third and fourth decades of this century, this Court within a relatively short period of time struck down several Acts of Congress on the grounds that they exceeded the authority of Congress under the Commerce Clause or under the nondelegation principle of separation of powers, and at the same time struck down state statutes because they violated "substantive" due process or interfered with interstate commerce. *See generally* R. Jackson, *The Struggle for Judicial Supremacy* 48–123 (1949). When many of these decisions were later overruled, the principle that Congress could not simply transfer its legislative authority to the Executive fell under a cloud. Yet in my opinion decisions such as *Panama Refining Co. v. Ryan,* 293 U.S. 388 (1935), suffer from none of the excesses of judicial policymaking that plagued some of the other decisions of that era. The many later decisions that have upheld congressional delegations of authority to the Executive Branch have done so largely on the theory that Congress may wish to exercise its authority in a particular field, but because the field is sufficiently technical, the ground to be covered sufficiently large, and the Members of Congress themselves not necessarily expert in the area in which they choose to legislate, the most that may be asked under the separation-of-powers doctrine is that Congress lay down the general policy and standards that animate the law, leaving the agency to refine those standards, "fill in the blanks," or apply the standards to particular cases. These decisions, to my mind, simply illustrate the above-quoted principle stated more than 50 years ago by Mr. Chief Justice Taft that delegations of legislative authority must be judged "according to common sense and the inherent necessities of the governmental co-ordination."

Viewing the legislation at issue here in light of these principles, I believe that it fails to pass muster. Read literally, the relevant portion of § 6(b)(5) is completely precatory, admonishing the Secretary to adopt the most protective standard if he can, but excusing him from that duty if he cannot. In the case of a hazardous substance for which a "safe" level is either unknown or impractical, the language of § 6(b)(5) gives the Secretary absolutely no indication where on the continuum of relative safety he should draw his line. Especially in light of the importance of the interests at stake, I have no doubt that the provision at issue, standing alone, would violate the doctrine against uncanalized delegations of legislative power. For me the remaining question, then, is whether additional standards are ascertainable from the legislative history or statutory context of § 6(b)(5) or, if not, whether such a standardless delegation was justifiable in light of the "inherent necessities" of the situation.

II

One of the primary sources looked to by this Court in adding gloss to an otherwise broad grant of legislative authority is the legislative history of the statute in question&hellip .

. . . [T]he legislative history contains nothing to indicate that the language "to the extent feasible" does anything other than render what had been a clear, if somewhat unrealistic, standard largely, if not entirely, precatory. There is certainly nothing to indicate that these words, as used in § 6(b)(5), are limited to technological and economic feasibility. When Congress has wanted to limit the concept of feasibility in this fashion, it has said so, as is evidenced in a statute enacted the same week as the provision at issue here. I also question whether the Secretary wants to assume the duties such an interpretation would impose upon him. In these cases, for example, the Secretary actually declined to adopt a standard lower than 1 ppm for some industries, not because it was economically or technologically infeasible, but rather because "different levels for different industries would result in serious administrative difficulties." . . . If § 6(b)(5) authorizes the Secretary to reject a more protective standard in the interest of administrative feasibility, I have little doubt that he could reject such standards for any reason whatsoever, including even political feasibility.

IV

As formulated and enforced by this Court, the nondelegation doctrine serves three important functions. First, and most abstractly, it ensures to the extent consistent with orderly governmental administration that important choices of social policy are made by Congress, the branch of our Government most responsive to the popular will. Second, the doctrine guarantees that, to the extent Congress finds it necessary to delegate authority, it provides the recipient of that authority with an "intelligible principle" to guide the exercise of the delegated discretion. *Panama Refining Co. v. Ryan*, 293 U.S., at 430. Third, and derivative of the second, the doctrine ensures that courts charged with reviewing the exercise of delegated legislative discretion will be able to test that exercise against ascertainable standards. . . .

I believe the legislation at issue here fails on all three counts. The decision whether the law of diminishing returns should have any place in the regulation of toxic substances is quintessentially one of legislative policy. For Congress to pass that decision on to the Secretary in the manner it did violates, in my mind, John Locke's caveat — reflected in the cases cited earlier in this opinion — that legislatures are to make laws, not legislators. Nor, as I think the prior discussion amply demonstrates, do the provisions at issue or their legislative history provide the Secretary with any guidance that might lead him to his somewhat tentative conclusion that he must eliminate exposure to benzene as far as technologically and economically possible. Finally, I would suggest that the standard of "feasibility" renders meaningful judicial review impossible.

We ought not to shy away from our judicial duty to invalidate unconstitutional delegations of legislative authority solely out of concern that we should thereby reinvigorate discredited constitutional doctrines of the pre-New Deal era. If the nondelegation doctrine has fallen into the same desuetude as have substantive due process and restrictive interpretations of the Commerce Clause, it is, as one writer has phrased it, "a case of death by association." J. Ely, *Democracy and Distrust, A Theory of Judicial Review* 133 (1980). . . .

If we are ever to reshoulder the burden of ensuring that Congress itself make the critical policy decisions, these are surely the cases in which to do it. It is difficult to imagine a more obvious example of Congress simply avoiding a choice which was both fundamental for purposes of the statute and yet politically so divisive that the necessary decision or compromise was difficult, if not impossible, to hammer out in the legislative forge. Far from detracting from the substantive authority of Congress, a declaration that the first sentence of § 6(b)(5) of the Occupational Safety and Health Act constitutes an invalid delegation to the Secretary of Labor would preserve the authority of Congress. If Congress wishes to legislate in an area which it has not previously sought to enter, it will in today's political world undoubtedly run into opposition no matter how the legislation is formulated. But that is the very essence of legislative authority under our system. It is the hard choices, and not the filling in of the blanks, which must be made by the elected representatives of the people. When fundamental policy decisions underlying important legislation about to be enacted are to be made, the buck stops with Congress and the President insofar as he exercises his constitutional role in the legislative process.

I would invalidate the first sentence of § 6(b)(5) of the occupational Safety and Health Act of 1970 as it applies to any toxic substance or harmful physical agent for which a safe level, that is, a level at which "no employee will suffer material impairment of health or functional capacity even if such employee has regular exposure to [that hazard] for the period of his working life," is, according to the Secretary, unknown or otherwise "infeasible." Absent further congressional action, the Secretary would then have to choose, when acting pursuant to § 6(b)(5), between setting a safe standard or setting no standard at all. Accordingly, for the reasons stated above, I concur in the judgment of the Court affirming the judgment of the Court of Appeals.

MR. JUSTICE MARSHALL, with whom MR. JUSTICE BRENNAN, MR. JUSTICE WHITE, and MR. JUSTICE BLACKMUN join, dissenting. [That opinion has been omitted.]

NOTES AND QUESTIONS

6-18. What role did the delegation doctrine play in Justice Stevens' approach to the statutory questions involved in this case?

6-19. What approach does Chief Justice Burger take to these issues? Justice Powell?

6-20. How does Justice Rehnquist's approach differ from the above approaches to the statutory issues involved in this case? What specific and fundamental policy issue does Justice Rehnquist believe Congress failed to decide? Do you agree? Should Congress have decided that question? Could it have? Why did it fail to do so?

6-21. How does the regulation in this case differ from the regulation in *Panama, Schechter,* and *Meatcutters,* and from the regulation in *Curtiss-Wright* (cited in Part III of Justice Rehnquist's concurrence)? Do these differences make it easier or harder for Congress to be more specific in its legislation? *See generally,* Aman, *Administrative Law in a Global Era* 103–07 (Cornell University Press, 1992).

PROBLEM 6-1

Consider the following dialogue:

Congressperson Concerned: I am really worried about the long-term effects of exposure to certain chemicals on human beings. We know that there seems very definitely to be a correlation between certain diseases and exposure to some chemicals. I mean, what if we are in the process of poisoning ourselves to death?

Congressperson Action: Let's pass a statute that regulates this problem. The use of some chemicals should be flatly prohibited; others should be tested before they go on the market and then closely monitored if they are allowed to be used. Let's write a law that does that.

Congressperson Skeptical: What precisely is the problem that concerns you and how is this legislation going to help? Are you talking about trying to prevent serious diseases, like cancer, or do you also want to cover nonmalignant maladies? Do we know what chemicals cause cancer, how long it takes for the cancer to develop, how much exposure is necessary? How can we write a statute dealing with such unclear issues that have so long a time frame when we know so little about all of this? We need more study, don't we?

Congressperson Action: How can we stand still in the face of this kind of uncertainty? To do nothing is to do something. It is to opt for the status quo, at best, and that may mean that we are exposing ourselves and our children to chemicals that are doing serious harm to us right now. In ten years, what good is it to say, "I told you so?" We need to at least *start* regulating these chemicals. At a bare minimum, we need to tell the regulators to begin to educate themselves and us about the dangers — both current and potential — of some of these chemicals and to put together a plan of action.

Congressperson Skeptical: You mean, you want them to write the legislation for us?

Congressperson Action: No. We tell them what to worry about; how to worry about it; and some standard to adhere to. We do that all the time in a variety of areas of law.

Congressperson Efficiency: What kind of standard do you have in mind? You sound like you want more certainty or protection here than may really be possible. Do you have any idea what the impact of various safety standards may be on our industries and on our economy?

Congressperson Action: Well, we don't have to take an absolutist approach to safety. Let's just say we want to do what's reasonable. Our administrators should begin to take reasonable steps to begin to protect us from the possibilities of serious disease that science may tell us exists.

Congressperson Skeptical: What does that mean? Anything the administrators have a mind to do? Who decides what's reasonable? Who decides how much cost to impose on our industries? Why, it's like giving these unelected officials the power to tax American chemical industries!

Congressperson Action: No, not necessarily. Reasonable means sensible. The costs that are incurred are external costs that producers should bear. To the extent they are then passed on to consumers, that means price then reflects the true cost to society of using these various pesticides, cleaners, and the like. We can write a law that says: "Don't go too far, but don't stand still either."

Congressperson Compromise: Look, if we don't do something and someone discovers that these chemicals are the cause of terrible diseases, we're going to look awfully bad. Let's let the agency go ahead in a reasonable way. I'm not worried that they'll go too far, because I want to see a great deal of procedure written into this Act, too. Let's make sure the Agency's rulemaking processes give industry every opportunity to respond to their proposals and talk some sense into them. Then let's make sure there is judicial review too. By the time the agency can get a rule through, it should be pretty sensible. So, we should put something in about how reasonable we want everyone to be and then let's provide the procedural framework for everyone to fight it out. We have a pluralistic society. Let's make sure every group gets its say. The political process will work its magic. Extreme solutions are unlikely.

Congressperson Cynical: I like it. We can be for and against regulation at the same time. If the agency goes too far or not far enough, we can blame them for being irresponsible. If they are effective and deal with the problem, we can claim the credit! And, at worst, I know my industrial constituents might be able to tie them up in so many procedural knots that nothing too serious can really happen.

Congressperson Locke: My dear friends, what of your oath of office? I have only one question for you: How much is a human life worth? We must decide that question forthrightly and directly. Otherwise, we are abdicating our responsibilities to unelected officials. We are delegating policymaking to individuals who are not really accountable to the electorate.

Congressperson Action: Can we really answer that question? Are we writing a contract between two persons or are we trying to establish a complicated regulatory structure that begins to deal with important but terribly complex issues? I think we have to leave some room for agency experimentation and we must act in the face of uncertainty. As far as the cost of a human life is concerned, we just have to do our best to balance all these factors — life, cost, uncertainty, scientific advances, danger — both real and potential. An agency can do this because the balance among these factors constantly changes. You can't use a formula. You must ultimately rely on the good faith discretion of human beings — yes, human bureaucrats! That is *not* a contradiction in terms.

Congressperson Efficiency: Yes, but at what price? Isn't our job to put some cost parameters on all of this?

Congressperson Action: That's covered by my reasonableness requirement. Let's just do it! No need to keep talking and talking.

Congressperson Deliberative: I think it is very important that we *not* just act without careful deliberation here. First of all, we need to be deliberative and articulate the public interest behind this legislation. We need to hold hearings to learn more about the substantive problems that concern us. In so doing, we must protect against becoming the conduits of private interest pressure groups. We must transcend the self-serving arguments of many of our constituents and discount the obviously private-regarding points of view they will press upon us. But we must hear them out to determine what *we* believe the public interest to be. The fact is that there is a public interest to articulate here. Science tells us there may very well be serious future health problems caused by some chemicals. *We* need to identify these public interests and then legislate in a way that serves *those* interests, not the private interests of the individual groups that make up our constituencies. We are not human consensatrons, just aggregating all private preferences and then voting accordingly. We are thinking, independent representatives. We need more information to be sure we do the *right* thing as opposed to the politically expedient thing.

Call the Roll: Whom do you wish represented you? If you were a member of Congress and participated in the debate, what would you add? How much and what kind of political bargaining do you want to occur in the legislative process?

PROBLEM 6-2

Assume that a state statute authorizes a state public service commission to set electricity rates that are "just and reasonable and not unduly discriminatory." An electric utility company files for a $300 million dollar rate increase. It seeks to spread the revenue responsibility for that increase by dividing that amount equally among the three classes of the utility's consumers — the industrial class, the residential class and the commercial class.

Customers are grouped into classes based on the utility's cost of serving them. Industrial customers usually consume large amounts of electricity; they take the electricity at higher voltages, so there is less need for transformers to step the voltage down. Moreover, they tend to have high load factors — that is the demand they place on the utility for electricity is very steady.

Contrast the industrial consumer with a residential consumer. As a class, residentials consume a great deal of electricity, but individuals consume very little compared to large industrials. This means that there must be electricity poles and individual wires going into a variety of homes. Moreover, each home will have its own meter and that meter must be read. The costs to the utility serving residential consumers are thus greater than those a serving an industrial user. Also, residential consumers may put a high demand for electricity on the utility at any given time during the day, but the demand is not steady. A student may come home from a long day at the library, turn on the airconditioning, the lights, and the T.V. The utility must be able to meet this demand, but the load factor of the residentials is often low. They make a high demand, but it is not steady.

The commercial class of electricity users are drug stores, shopping malls and they fall somewhere between the cost of serving industrials and residentials.

Now, assume that the Legal Aid Society represents some low income consumers whose fixed incomes can barely afford the kind of increase the utility proposes. They have tried to get the legislature to issue energy stamps — *i.e.*, subsidies for the poor to apply towards increased energy costs. Legal Aid now seeks to argue that the State Commission should create a separate rate — a lifeline rate. Those consumers who use less than 300 kilowatt hours of electricity per billing period, as they believe many of their poor clients do, should receive those hours at a substantial discount. The shortfall in revenue that this creates is to be made up by putting an additional charge on the industrial class of consumers.

Assume, first of all, that you represent the Legal Aid Society. Does the Commission have the authority to enact your rate? On what theory? How do you define "rate"? What statutory arguments do you anticipate will be made in opposition to your proposal?

Assume you represent an industrial consumer of electricity that opposes this rate. What legal arguments will you make? What kind of evidentiary record would you like to develop to aid your cause?

MISTRETTA v. UNITED STATES

United States Supreme Court
488 U.S. 361 (1988)

[Mistretta pleaded guilty to an indictment for drug dealing and was sentenced in accord with guidelines promulgated by the United States Sentencing Commission. He challenged the Commission's authority, in part because he contended that its authority was the result of an unconstitutional delegation of power.]

JUSTICE BLACKMUN delivered the opinion of the Court.

. . . .

C
The Sentencing Commission

The Commission is established "as an independent commission in the judicial branch of the United States." It has seven voting members (one of whom is the Chairman) appointed by the President "by and with the advice and consent of the Senate." "At least three of the members shall be Federal judges selected after considering a list of six judges recommended to the President by the Judicial Conference of the United States." No more than four members of the Commission shall be members of the same political party. The

Attorney General, or his designee, is an *ex officio* non-voting member. The Chairman and other members of the Commission are subject to removal by the President "only for neglect of duty or malfeasance in office or for other good cause shown." Except for initial staggering of terms, a voting member serves for six years and may not serve more than two full terms.

D
The Responsibilities of the Commission

In addition to the duty the Commission has to promulgate determinative-sentence guidelines, it is under an obligation periodically to "review and revise" the guidelines. It is to "consult with authorities on, and individual and institutional representatives of, various aspects of the Federal criminal justice system." It must report to Congress "any amendments of the guidelines." It is to make recommendations to Congress whether the grades or maximum penalties should be modified. It must submit to Congress at least annually an analysis of the operation of the guidelines. It is to issue "general policy statements" regarding their application. And it has the power to "establish general policies . . . as are necessary to carry out the purposes" of the legislation; to "monitor the performance of probation officers" with respect to the guidelines; to "devise and conduct periodic training programs of instruction in sentencing techniques for judicial and probation personnel" and others; and to "perform such other functions as are required to permit Federal courts to meet their responsibilities" as to sentencing. . . .

III
Delegation of Power

Petitioner argues that in delegating the power to promulgate sentencing guidelines for every federal criminal offense to an independent Sentencing Commission, Congress has granted the Commission excessive legislative discretion in violation of the constitutionally based nondelegation doctrine. We do not agree.

The nondelegation doctrine is rooted in the principle of separation of powers that underlies our tripartite system of Government. The Constitution provides that "[a]ll legislative Powers herein granted shall be vested in a Congress of the United States," U.S. Const., Art. I, § 1, and we long have insisted that "the integrity and maintenance of the system of government ordained by the Constitution" mandate that Congress generally cannot delegate its legislative power to another Branch. *Field v. Clark,* 143 U.S. 649, 692 (1892). We also have recognized, however, that the separation-of-powers principle, and the nondelegation doctrine in particular, do not prevent Congress from obtaining the assistance of its coordinate Branches. In a passage now enshrined in our jurisprudence, Chief Justice Taft, writing for the Court, explained our approach to such cooperative ventures: "In determining what [Congress] may do in seeking assistance from another branch, the extent and character of that assistance must be fixed according to common sense and the inherent necessities of the government co-ordination." *J.W. Hampton, Jr., & Co. v. United States,* 276 U.S. 394, 406 (1928). So long as Congress "shall lay down by legislative act an intelligible principle to which the person or body authorized to [exercise the delegated authority] is directed to conform, such legislative action is not a forbidden delegation of legislative power." *Id.,* at 409.

Applying this "intelligible principle" test to congressional delegations, our jurisprudence has been driven by a practical understanding that in our increasingly complex society, replete with ever changing and more technical problems, Congress simply cannot do its job absent an ability to delegate power under broad general directives. . . . Accordingly, this Court has deemed it "constitutionally sufficient if Congress clearly delineates the general policy, the public agency which is to apply it, and the boundaries of this delegated authority."

Until 1935, this Court never struck down a challenged statute on delegation grounds. . . . After invalidating in 1935 two statutes as excessive delegations, see *A.L.A. Schechter Poultry Corp. v. United States,* 295 U.S. 495, and *Panama Refining Co. v. Ryan, supra,* we have upheld, again without deviation, Congress' ability to delegate power under broad standards.[7]

In light of our approval of these broad delegations, we harbor no doubt that Congress' delegation of authority to the Sentencing Commission is sufficiently specific and detailed to meet constitutional requirements. Congress charged the Commission with three goals: to "assure the meeting of the purposes of sentencing as set forth" in the Act; to "provide certainty and fairness in meeting the purposes of sentencing, avoiding unwarranted sentencing disparities among defendants with similar records . . . while maintaining sufficient flexibility to permit individualized sentences," where appropriate; and to "reflect, to the extent practicable, advancement in knowledge of human behavior as it relates to the criminal justice process." . . . Congress further specified four "purposes" of sentencing that the Commission must pursue in carrying out its mandate: "to reflect the seriousness of the offense, to promote respect for the law, and to provide just punishment for the offense"; "to afford adequate deterrence to criminal conduct"; "to protect the public from further crimes of the defendant"; and "to provide the defendant with needed . . . correctional treatment." . . .

In addition, Congress prescribed the specific tool — the guidelines system — for the Commission to use in regulating sentencing. More particularly, Congress directed the Commission to develop a system of "sentencing ranges" applicable "for each category of offense involving each category of defendant."[8]

---

[7] In *Schechter* and *Panama Refining* the Court concluded that Congress had failed to articulate any policy or standard that would serve to confine the discretion of the authorities to whom Congress had delegated power. No delegation of the kind at issue in those cases is present here. The Act does not make crimes of acts never before criminalized, see *Fahey v. Mallonee,* 332 U.S. 245, 249 (1947) (analyzing *Panama Refining*), or delegate regulatory power to private individuals, see *Yakus v. United States,* 321 U.S. 414, 424 (1944) (analyzing *Schechter*). In recent years, our application of the nondelegation doctrine principally has been limited to the interpretation of statutory texts, and, more particularly, to giving narrow constructions to statutory delegations that might otherwise be thought to be unconstitutional. See *e.g., Industrial Union Dept. v. American Petroleum Institute,* 448 U.S. 607, 646 (1980); *National Cable Television Ass'n v. United States,* 415 U.S. 336, 342 (1974).

[8] Congress mandated that the guidelines include:

"(A) a determination whether to impose a sentence to probation, a fine, or a term of imprisonment;

Congress instructed the Commission that these sentencing ranges must be consistent with pertinent provisions of Title 18 of the United States Code and could not include sentences in excess of the statutory maxima. Congress also required that for sentences of imprisonment, "the maximum of the range established for such a term shall not exceed the minimum of that range by more than the greater of 25 percent or 6 months, except that, if the minimum term of the range is 30 years or more, the maximum may be life imprisonment." Moreover, Congress directed the Commission to use current average sentences "as a starting point" for its structuring of the sentencing ranges.

To guide the Commission in its formulation of offense categories, Congress directed it to consider seven factors: the grade of the offense; the aggravating and mitigating circumstances of the crime; the nature and degree of the harm caused by the crime; the community view of the gravity of the offense; the public concern generated by the crime; the deterrent effect that a particular sentence may have on others; and the current incidence of the offense.[9] Congress set forth 11 factors for the Commission to consider in establishing categories of defendants. These include the offender's age, education, vocational skills, mental and emotional condition, physical condition (including drug dependence), previous employment record, family ties and responsibilities, community ties, role in the offense, criminal history, and degree of dependence upon crime for a livelihood. Congress also prohibited the Commission from considering the "race, sex, national origin, creed, and socioeconomic status of offenders," and instructed that the guidelines should reflect the "general inappropriateness" of considering certain other factors, such as current unemployment, that might serve as proxies for forbidden factors.

In addition to these overarching constraints, Congress provided even more detailed guidance to the Commission about categories of offenses and offender characteristics. Congress directed that guidelines require a term of confinement at or near the statutory maximum for certain crimes of violence and for drug offenses, particularly when committed by recidivists. Congress further directed that the Commission assure a substantial term of imprisonment for an offense constituting a third felony conviction, for a career felon, for one convicted of a managerial role in a racketeering enterprise, for a crime of violence by an offender on release from a prior felony conviction, and for

---

"(B) a determination as to the appropriate amount of a fine or the appropriate length of a term of probation or a term of imprisonment;

"(C) a determination whether a sentence to a term of imprisonment should include a requirement that the defendant be placed on a term of supervised release after imprisonment, and, if so, the appropriate length of such a term; and

"(D) a determination whether multiple sentences to terms of imprisonment should be ordered to run concurrently or consecutively." 28 U.S.C. § 994(a)(1).

[9] The Senate Report on the legislation elaborated on the purpose to be served by each factor. The Report noted, for example, that the reference to the community view of the gravity of an offense was "not intended to mean that a sentence might be enhanced because of public outcry about a single offense," but "to suggest that changed community norms concerning certain particular criminal behavior might be justification for increasing or decreasing the recommended penalties for the offense." Report at 170. The Report, moreover, gave specific examples of areas in which prevailing sentences might be too lenient, including the treatment of major white-collar criminals. *Id.* at 177.

an offense involving a substantial quantity of narcotics. Congress also instructed "that the guidelines reflect . . . the general appropriateness of imposing a term of imprisonment" for a crime of violence that resulted in serious bodily injury. On the other hand, Congress directed that guidelines reflect the general inappropriateness of imposing a sentence of imprisonment "in cases in which the defendant is a first offender who has not been convicted of a crime of violence or an otherwise serious offense." Congress also enumerated various aggravating and mitigating circumstances, such as, respectively, multiple offenses or substantial assistance to the Government, to be reflected in the guidelines. In other words, although Congress granted the Commission substantial discretion in formulating guidelines, in actuality it legislated a full hierarchy of punishment — from near maximum imprisonment, to substantial imprisonment, to some imprisonment, to alternatives — and stipulated the most important offense and offender characteristics to place defendants within these categories.

We cannot dispute petitioner's contention that the Commission enjoys significant discretion in formulating guidelines. The Commission does have discretionary authority to determine the relative severity of federal crimes and to assess the relative weight of the offender characteristics that Congress listed for the Commission to consider. . . . The Commission also has significant discretion to determine which crimes have been punished too leniently, and which too severely. Congress has called upon the Commission to exercise its judgment about which types of crimes and which types of criminals are to be considered similar for the purposes of sentencing.

But our cases do not at all suggest that delegations of this type may not carry with them the need to exercise judgment on matters of policy. . . .

Developing proportionate penalties for hundreds of different crimes by a virtually limitless array of offenders is precisely the sort of intricate, labor-intensive task for which delegation to an expert body is especially appropriate. Although Congress has delegated significant discretion to the Commission to draw judgments from its analysis of existing sentencing practice and alternative sentencing models, "Congress is not confined to that method of executing its policy which involves the least possible delegation of discretion to administrative officers." *Yakus v. United States,* 321 U.S., at 425–426. We have no doubt that in the hands of the Commission "the criteria which Congress has supplied are wholly adequate for carrying out the general policy and purpose" of the Act. . . .

JUSTICE SCALIA, dissenting.

While the products of the Sentencing Commission's labors have been given the modest name "Guidelines," . . . they have the force and effect of laws, prescribing the sentences criminal defendants are to receive. A judge who disregards them will be reversed. I dissent from today's decision because I can find no place within our constitutional system for an agency created by Congress to exercise no governmental power other than the making of laws.

I

. . . .

It should be apparent from the above that the decisions made by the Commission are far from technical, but are heavily laden (or ought to be) with value judgments and policy assessments. . . .

Petitioner's most fundamental and far-reaching challenge to the Commission is that Congress' commitment of such broad policy responsibility to any institution is an unconstitutional delegation of legislative power. It is difficult to imagine a principle more essential to democratic government than that upon which the doctrine of unconstitutional delegation is founded: Except in a few areas constitutionally committed to the Executive Branch, the basic policy decisions governing society are to be made by the Legislature. Our Members of Congress could not, even if they wished, vote all power to the President and adjourn *sine die.*

But while the doctrine of unconstitutional delegation is unquestionably a fundamental element of our constitutional system, it is not an element readily enforceable by the courts. Once it is conceded, as it must be, that no statute can be entirely precise, and that some judgments, even some judgments involving policy considerations, must be left to the officers executing the law and to the judges applying it, the debate over unconstitutional delegation becomes a debate not over a point of principle but over a question of degree. As Chief Justice Taft expressed the point for the Court in the landmark case of *J.W. Hampton, Jr., & Co. v. United States,* 276 U.S. 394, 406 (1928), the limits of delegation "must be fixed according to common sense and the inherent necessities of the governmental co-ordination." Since Congress is no less endowed with common sense than we are, and better equipped to inform itself of the "necessities" of government; and since the factors bearing upon those necessities are both multifarious and (in the nonpartisan sense) highly political — including, for example, whether the Nation is at war, . . . or whether for other reasons "emergency is instinct in the situation," . . . it is a small wonder that we have almost never felt qualified to second-guess Congress regarding the permissible degree of policy judgment that can be left to those executing or applying the law. As the Court points out, we have invoked the doctrine of unconstitutional delegation to invalidate a law only twice in our history, over half a century ago. *See Panama Refining Co. v. Ryan,* 293 U.S. 388 (1935); *A.L.A. Schechter Poultry Corp. v. United States,* 295 U.S. 495 (1935). What legislated standard, one must wonder, can possibly be too vague to survive judicial scrutiny, when we have repeatedly upheld, in various contexts, a "public interest" standard? . . .

In short, I fully agree with the Court's rejection of petitioner's contention that the doctrine of unconstitutional delegation of legislative authority has been violated because of the lack of intelligible, congressionally prescribed standards to guide the Commission.

II

Precisely because the scope of delegation is largely uncontrollable by the courts, we must be particularly rigorous in preserving the Constitution's structural restrictions that deter excessive delegation. The major one, it seems to me, is that the power to make law cannot be exercised by anyone other than Congress, except in conjunction with the lawful exercise of executive or judicial power.

The whole theory of lawful congressional "delegation" is not that Congress is sometimes too busy or too divided and can therefore assign its responsibility of making law to someone else; but rather that a certain degree of discretion, and thus of lawmaking, inheres in most executive or judicial action, and it is up to Congress, by the relative specificity or generality of its statutory commands, to determine — up to a point — how small or how large that degree shall be. Thus, the courts could be given the power to say precisely what constitutes a "restraint of trade," . . . or to adopt rules of procedure, . . . or to prescribe by rule the manner in which their officers shall execute their judgments, . . . because that "lawmaking" was ancillary to their exercise of judicial powers. And the Executive could be given the power to adopt policies and rules specifying in detail what radio and television licenses will be in the "public interest, convenience or necessity," because that we ancillary to the exercise of its executive powers in granting and policing licenses and making a "fair and equitable allocation" of the electromagnetic spectrum. . . . Or to take examples closer to the case before us: Trial judges could be given the power to determine what factors justify a greater or lesser sentence within the statutorily prescribed limits because that was ancillary to their exercise of the judicial power of pronouncing sentence upon individual defendants. And the President, through the Parole Commission subject to his appointment and removal, could be given the power to issue Guidelines specifying when parole would be available, because that was ancillary to the President's exercise of the executive power to hold and release federal prisoners. . . .

The focus of controversy, in the long line of our so-called excessive delegation cases, has been whether the degree of generality contained in the authorization for exercise of executive or judicial powers in a particular field is so unacceptably high as to amount to a delegation of legislative powers. I say "so-called excessive delegation" because although that convenient terminology is often used, what is really at issue is whether there has been any delegation of legislative power, which occurs (rarely) when Congress authorizes the exercise of executive or judicial power without adequate standards. Strictly speaking, there is no acceptable delegation of legislative power. As John Locke put it almost 300 years ago, "[t]he power of the legislative being derived from the people by a positive voluntary grant and institution, can be no other, than what the positive grant conveyed, which being only to make laws, and not to make legislators, the legislative can have no power to transfer their authority of making laws, and place it in other hands." J. Locke, *Second Treatise of Government* 87 (R. Cox ed. 1982). Or, as we have less epigrammatically said: "That Congress cannot delegate legislative power to the President is a principle universally recognized as vital to the integrity and maintenance of the system of government ordained by the Constitution." *Field v. Clark, supra,* at 692. In the present case, however, a pure delegation of legislative power is precisely what we have before us. It is irrelevant whether the standards are adequate, because they are not standards related to the exercise of executive or judicial powers; they are, plainly and simply, standards for further legislation.

The lawmaking function of the Sentencing Commission is completely divorced from any responsibility for execution of the law or adjudication of private rights under the law. It is divorced from responsibility for execution of the law not only because the Commission is not said to be "located in the Executive Branch" (as I shall discuss presently, I doubt whether Congress can "locate" an entity within one Branch or another for constitutional purposes by merely saying so); but, more importantly, because the Commission neither exercises any executive power on its own, nor is subject to the control of the President who does. The only functions it performs, apart from prescribing the law, . . . conducting the investigations useful and necessary for prescribing the law, . . . and clarifying the intended application of the law that it prescribes, . . . are data collection and intragovernmental advice giving and education. . . . These latter activities — similar to functions performed by congressional agencies and even congressional staff — neither determine nor affect private rights, and do not constitute an exercise of governmental power. . . . And the Commission's lawmaking is completely divorced from the exercise of judicial powers since, not being a court, it has no judicial powers itself, nor is it subject to the control of any other body with judicial powers. The power to make law at issue here, in other words, is not ancillary but quite naked. The situation is no different in principle from what would exist if Congress gave the same power of writing sentencing laws to a congressional agency such as the General Accounting Office, or to members of its staff.

The delegation of lawmaking authority to the Commission is, in short, unsupported by any legitimating theory to explain why it is not a delegation of legislative power. To disregard structural legitimacy is wrong in itself — but since structure has purpose, the disregard also has adverse practical consequences. In this case, as suggested earlier, the consequence is to facilitate and encourage judicially uncontrollable delegation. . . .

By reason of today's decision, I anticipate that Congress will find delegation of its lawmaking powers much more attractive in the future. If rulemaking can be entirely unrelated to the exercise of judicial or executive powers, I foresee all manner of "expert" bodies, insulated from the political process, to which Congress will delegate various portions of its lawmaking responsibility. How tempting to create an expert Medical Commission (mostly M.D.'s, with perhaps a few Ph.D.'s in moral philosophy) to dispose of such thorny, "no-win" political issues as the withholding of life-support systems in federally funded hospitals, or the use of fetal tissue for research. This is an undemocratic precedent that we set — not because of the scope of the delegated power, but because its recipient is not one of the three Branches of Government. The only governmental power the Commission possesses is the power to make law; and it is not the Congress. . . .

NOTES AND QUESTIONS

6-22. What does the majority's approach to the issues in *Mistretta* indicate as far as revival of the non-delegation doctrine is concerned?

6-23. Does Justice Scalia agree with the majority's approach? On what does he base his dissent?

6-24. How would you describe Justice Scalia's approach to these issues? If adopted, would this be an appropriate role for courts to play when it comes to reviewing legislation?

6-25. Consider the excerpt from Professor Strauss in § 6.03, note **6-6**, how would you characterize the separation-of-powers approach proposed by Justice Scalia?

WHITMAN v. AMERICAN TRUCKING ASSOCIATIONS, INC.

Supreme Court of the United States
531 U.S. 457 (2001)

JUSTICE SCALIA delivered the opinion of the Court.

These cases present the following questions: (1) Whether § 109(b)(1) of the Clean Air Act (CAA) delegates legislative power to the Administrator of the Environmental Protection Agency (EPA). (2) Whether the Administrator may consider the costs of implementation in setting national ambient air quality standards (NAAQS) under § 109(b)(1). . . .

I

Section 109(a) of the CAA, as added, 84 Stat. 1679, and amended, 42 U.S.C. § 7409(a), requires the Administrator of the EPA to promulgate NAAQS for each air pollutant for which "air quality criteria" have been issued under § 108, 42 U.S.C. § 7408. Once a NAAQS has been promulgated, the Administrator must review the standard (and the criteria on which it is based) "at five-year intervals" and make "such revisions . . . as may be appropriate." CAA § 109(d)(1), 42 U.S.C. § 7409(d)(1). These cases arose when, on July 18, 1997, the Administrator revised the NAAQS for particulate matter and ozone. . . . American Trucking Associations, Inc., and its co-respondents in No. 99-1257 — which include, in addition to other private companies, the States of Michigan, Ohio, and West Virginia — challenged the new standards in the Court of Appeals for the District of Columbia Circuit, pursuant to 42 U.S.C. § 7607(b)(1).

. . . .

II

In *Lead Industries Assn., Inc. v. EPA* the District of Columbia Circuit held that "economic considerations [may] play no part in the promulgation of ambient air quality standards under Section 109" of the CAA. In the present cases, the court adhered to that holding, as it had done on many other occasions. Respondents argue that these decisions are incorrect. We disagree; and since the first step in assessing whether a statute delegates legislative power is to determine what authority the statute confers, we address that issue of interpretation first and reach respondents' constitutional arguments in Part III, *infra*.

Section 109(b)(1) instructs the EPA to set primary ambient air quality standards "the attainment and maintenance of which . . . are requisite to protect the public health" with "an adequate margin of safety." 42 U.S.C. § 7409(b)(1). Were it not for the hundreds of pages of briefing respondents have submitted on the issue, one would have thought it fairly clear that this text does not permit the EPA to consider costs in setting the standards. The language, as one scholar has noted, "is absolute." D. Currie, *Air Pollution: Federal Law and Analysis* 4–15 (1981). The EPA, "based on" the information about health effects contained in the technical "criteria" documents compiled under § 108(a)(2), 42 U.S.C. § 7408(a)(2), is to identify the maximum airborne concentration of a pollutant that the public health can tolerate, decrease the concentration to provide an "adequate" margin of safety, and set the standard at that level. Nowhere are the costs of achieving such a standard made part of that initial calculation.

Against this most natural of readings, respondents make a lengthy, spirited, but ultimately unsuccessful attack. They begin with the object of § 109(b)(1)'s focus, the "public health." When the term first appeared in federal clean air legislation — in the Act of July 14, 1955 (1955 Act), 69 Stat. 322, which expressed "recognition of the dangers to the public health" from air pollution — its ordinary meaning was "[t]he health of the community." *Webster's New International Dictionary* 2005 (2d ed.1950). Respondents argue, however, that § 109(b)(1), as added by the Clean Air Amendments of 1970, 84 Stat. 1676, meant to use the term's secondary meaning: "[t]he ways and means of conserving the health of the members of a community, as by preventive medicine, organized care of the sick, etc." *Ibid*. Words that can have more than one meaning are given content, however, by their surroundings, and in the context of § 109(b)(1) this second definition makes no sense. Congress could not have meant to instruct the Administrator to set NAAQS at a level "requisite to protect" "the art and science dealing with the protection and improvement of community health." *Webster's Third New International Dictionary* 1836 (1981). We therefore revert to the primary definition of the term: the health of the public.

Even so, respondents argue, many more factors than air pollution affect public health. In particular, the economic cost of implementing a very stringent standard might produce health losses sufficient to offset the health gains achieved in cleaning the air — for example, by closing down whole industries and thereby impoverishing the workers and consumers dependent upon those industries. That is unquestionably true, and Congress was unquestionably aware of it. Thus, Congress had commissioned in the Air Quality Act of 1967 (1967 Act) "a detailed estimate of the cost of carrying out the provisions of this Act; a comprehensive study of the cost of program implementation by affected units of government; and a comprehensive study of the economic impact of air quality standards on the Nation's industries, communities, and other contributing sources of pollution." § 2, 81 Stat. 505. The 1970 Congress, armed with the results of this study, . . . not only anticipated that compliance costs could injure the public health, but provided for that precise exigency. Section 110(f)(1) of the CAA permitted the Administrator to waive the compliance deadline for stationary sources if, *inter alia*, sufficient control measures were simply unavailable and "the continued operation of such sources is essential . . . to *the public health or welfare*." Other provisions explicitly permitted or required economic costs to be taken into account in implementing the air quality standards. Section 111(b)(1)(B), for example, commanded the Administrator to set "standards of performance" for certain new sources of emissions that as specified in § 111(a)(1) were to "reflec[t] the degree of emission limitation achievable through the application of the best system of emission reduction which (taking into account the cost of achieving such reduction) the Administrator determines has been adequately demonstrated." Section 202(a)(2) prescribed that emissions standards for automobiles could take effect only "after such period as the Administrator finds necessary to permit the development and application of the requisite technology, giving appropriate consideration to the cost of compliance within such period." 84 Stat. 1690. Subsequent amendments to the CAA have added many more provisions directing, in explicit language, that the Administrator consider costs in performing various duties. *See, e.g.*, 42 U.S.C. § 7545(k)(1) (reformulate gasoline to "require the greatest reduction in emissions . . . taking into consideration the cost of achieving such emissions reductions"); § 7547(a)(3) (emission reduction for nonroad vehicles to be set "giving appropriate consideration to the cost" of the standards). We have therefore refused to find implicit in ambiguous sections of the CAA an authorization to consider costs that has elsewhere, and so often, been expressly granted.

Accordingly, to prevail in their present challenge, respondents must show a textual commitment of authority to the EPA to consider costs in setting NAAQS under § 109(b)(1). And because § 109(b)(1) and the NAAQS for which it provides are the engine that drives nearly all of Title I of the CAA, 42 U.S.C. §§ 7401-7515, that textual commitment must be a clear one. Congress, we have held, does not alter the fundamental details of a regulatory scheme in vague terms or ancillary provisions — it does not, one might say, hide elephants in mouseholes. Respondents' textual arguments ultimately founder upon this principle.

. . . .

It should be clear from what we have said that the canon requiring texts to be so construed as to avoid serious constitutional problems has no application here. No matter how severe the constitutional doubt, courts may choose only between reasonably available interpretations of a text. The text of § 109(b), interpreted in its statutory and historical context and with appreciation for its importance to the CAA as a whole, unambiguously bars cost considerations from the NAAQS-setting process, and thus ends the matter for us as well as the EPA. We therefore affirm the judgment of the Court of Appeals on this point.

III

Section 109(b)(1) of the CAA instructs the EPA to set "ambient air quality standards the attainment and maintenance of which in the judgment of the Administrator, based on [the] criteria [documents of § 108] and allowing an adequate margin of safety, are requisite to protect the public health." 42 U.S.C. § 7409(b)(1). The Court of Appeals held that this section as interpreted by the Administrator did not provide an "intelligible principle" to guide the EPA's exercise of authority in setting NAAQS. "[The] EPA," it said, "lack[ed] any determinate criteria for drawing lines. It has failed to state intelligibly how much is too much." The court hence found that the EPA's interpretation (but not the statute itself) violated the nondelegation doctrine. We disagree.

In a delegation challenge, the constitutional question is whether the statute has delegated legislative power to the agency. Article I, § 1, of the Constitution vests "[a]ll legislative Powers herein granted . . . in a Congress of the United States." This text permits no delegation of those powers and so we repeatedly have said that when Congress confers decisionmaking authority upon agencies Congress must "lay down by legislative act an intelligible principle to which the person or body authorized to [act] is directed to conform." *J.W. Hampton, Jr., & Co. v. United States*, 276 U.S. 394, 409 (1928). We have never suggested that an agency can cure an unlawful delegation of legislative power by adopting in its discretion a limiting construction of the statute. . . . The idea that an agency can cure an unconstitutionally standardless delegation of power by declining to exercise some of that power seems to us internally contradictory. The very choice of which portion of the power to exercise — that is to say, the prescription of the standard that Congress had omitted — would *itself* be an exercise of the forbidden legislative authority. Whether the statute delegates legislative power is a question for the courts, and an agency's voluntary self-denial has no bearing upon the answer.

We agree with the Solicitor General that the text of § 109(b)(1) of the CAA at a minimum requires that "[f]or a discrete set of pollutants and based on published air quality criteria that reflect the latest scientific knowledge, [the] EPA must establish uniform national standards at a level that is requisite to protect public health from the adverse effects of the pollutant in the ambient air." Tr. of Oral Arg. in No. 99-1257, p. 5. Requisite, in turn, "mean[s] sufficient, but not more than necessary." *Id.*, at 7. These limits on the EPA's discretion are strikingly similar to the ones we approved in *Touby v. United States*, 500 U.S. 160 (1991), which permitted the Attorney General to designate a drug as a controlled substance for purposes of criminal drug enforcement if doing so was "'necessary to avoid an imminent hazard to the public safety.'" *Id.*, at 163. They also resemble the Occupational Safety and Health Act of 1970 provision requiring the agency to "'set the standard which most adequately assures, to the extent feasible, on the basis of the best available evidence, that no employee will suffer any impairment of health'" — which the Court upheld in *Industrial Union Dept., AFL-CIO v. American Petroleum Institute*, 448 U.S. 607, 646 (1980), and which even then — JUSTICE REHNQUIST, who alone in that case thought the statute violated the nondelegation doctrine would have upheld if, like the statute here, it did not permit economic costs to be considered.

The scope of discretion § 109(b)(1) allows is in fact well within the outer limits of our nondelegation precedents. In the history of the Court we have found the requisite "intelligible principle" lacking in only two statutes, one of which provided literally no guidance for the exercise of discretion, and the other of which conferred authority to regulate the entire economy on the basis of no more precise a standard than stimulating the economy by assuring "fair competition." See *Panama Refining Co. v. Ryan*, 293 U.S. 388 (1935); *A.L.A. Schechter Poultry Corp. v. United States*, 295 U.S. 495 (1935). We have, on the other hand, upheld the validity of § 11(b)(2) of the Public Utility Holding Company Act of 1935, 49 Stat. 821, which gave the Securities and Exchange Commission authority to modify the structure of holding company systems so as to ensure that they are not "unduly or unnecessarily complicate[d]" and do not "unfairly or inequitably distribute voting power among security holders." *American Power & Light Co. v. SEC*, 329 U.S. 90, 104 (1946). We have approved the wartime conferral of agency power to fix the prices of commodities at a level that " 'will be generally fair and equitable and will effectuate the [in some respects conflicting] purposes of th[e] Act.' " *Yakus v. United States*, 321 U.S. 414, 420, 423–426 (1944). And we have found an "intelligible principle" in various statutes authorizing regulation in the "public interest." *See, e.g.*, *National Broadcasting Co. v. United States*, 319 U.S. 190, 225–226 (1943) (Federal Communications Commission's power to regulate airwaves); *New York Central Securities Corp. v. United States*, 287 U.S. 12, 24–25 (1932) (Interstate Commerce Commission's power to approve railroad consolidations). In short, we have "almost never felt qualified to second-guess Congress regarding the permissible degree of policy judgment that can be left to those executing or applying the law." *Mistretta v. United States*, 488 U.S. 361, 416 (1989) (SCALIA, J., dissenting).

It is true enough that the degree of agency discretion that is acceptable varies according to the scope of the power congressionally conferred. While Congress need not provide any direction to the EPA regarding the manner in which it is to define "country elevators," which are to be exempt from new-stationary-source regulations governing grain elevators, see 42 U.S.C. § 7411(i), it must provide substantial guidance on setting air standards that affect the entire national economy. But even in sweeping regulatory schemes we have never demanded, as the Court of Appeals did here, that statutes provide a "determinate criterion" for saying "how much [of the regulated harm] is too much." 175 F.3d, at 1034. . . . It is therefore not conclusive for delegation purposes that, as respondents argue, ozone and particulate matter are "nonthreshold" pollutants that inflict a continuum of adverse health effects at any airborne concentration greater than zero, and hence require the EPA to make judgments of degree. "[A] certain degree of discretion, and thus of lawmaking, inheres in most executive or judicial action." *Mistretta v. United States*, *supra*, at 417 (SCALIA, J., dissenting) (emphasis deleted); see 488 U.S., at 378–379 (majority opinion). Section 109(b)(1) of the CAA, which to repeat we interpret as requiring the EPA to set air quality standards at the level that is "requisite" — that is, not lower or higher than is necessary — to protect the public health with an adequate margin of safety, fits comfortably within the scope of discretion permitted by our precedent.

We therefore reverse the judgment of the Court of Appeals remanding for reinterpretation that would avoid a supposed delegation of legislative power. It will remain for the Court of Appeals — on the remand that we direct for other reasons — to dispose of any other preserved challenge to the NAAQS under the judicial-review provisions contained in 42 U.S.C. § 7607(d)(9).

IV

The final two issues on which we granted certiorari concern the EPA's authority to implement the revised ozone NAAQS in areas whose ozone levels currently exceed the maximum level permitted by that standard. . . .

[The Court held that the EPA's implementation policy for revised ozone NAAQS in "nonattainment" areas was final agency action subject to judicial review; the issue was ripe for review, and the 1990 amendments to the 1990 CAA amendments regarding ozone were ambiguous, requiring deference to EPA's interpretations. The EPA, however, could not enforce its revised ozone NAAQS in such a way as to render the ozone specific CAA amendment nugatory].

JUSTICE THOMAS, concurring.

I agree with the majority that § 109's directive to the agency is no less an "intelligible principle" than a host of other directives that we have approved. I also agree that the Court of Appeals' remand to the agency to make its own corrective interpretation does not accord with our understanding of the delegation issue. I write separately, however, to express my concern that there may nevertheless be a genuine constitutional problem with § 109, a problem which the parties did not address.

The parties to these cases who briefed the constitutional issue wrangled over constitutional doctrine with barely a nod to the text of the Constitution. Although this Court since 1928 has treated the "intelligible principle" requirement as the only constitutional limit on congressional grants of power to administrative agencies, see *J.W. Hampton, Jr., & Co. v. United States*, 276 U.S. 394, 409 (1928), the Constitution does not speak of "intelligible principles." Rather, it speaks in much simpler terms: "*All* legislative Powers herein granted shall be vested in a Congress." U.S. Const., Art. 1, § 1 (emphasis added). I am not convinced that the intelligible principle doctrine serves to prevent all cessions of legislative power. I believe that there are cases in which the principle is intelligible and yet the significance of the delegated decision is simply too great for the decision to be called anything other than "legislative."

As it is, none of the parties to these cases has examined the text of the Constitution or asked us to reconsider our precedents on cessions of legislative power. On a future day, however, I would be willing to address the question whether our delegation jurisprudence has strayed too far from our Founders' understanding of separation of powers.

JUSTICE STEVENS, with whom JUSTICE SOUTER joins, concurring in part and concurring in the judgment.

Section 109(b)(1) delegates to the Administrator of the Environmental Protection Agency (EPA) the authority to promulgate national ambient air quality standards (NAAQS). In Part III of its opinion, the Court convincingly explains why the Court of Appeals erred when it concluded that § 109 effected "an unconstitutional delegation of legislative power." *American Trucking Assns., Inc. v. EPA*, 175 F.3d 1027, 1033 (C.A.D.C.1999) (*per curiam*). I wholeheartedly endorse the Court's result and endorse its explanation of its reasons, albeit with the following caveat.

The Court has two choices. We could choose to articulate our ultimate disposition of this issue by frankly acknowledging that the power delegated to the EPA is "legislative" but nevertheless conclude that the delegation is constitutional because adequately limited by the terms of the authorizing statute. Alternatively, we could pretend, as the Court does, that the authority delegated to the EPA is somehow not "legislative power." Despite the fact that there is language in our opinions that supports the Court's articulation of our holding, I am persuaded that it would be both wiser and more faithful to what we have actually done in delegation cases to admit that agency rulemaking authority is "legislative power."

The proper characterization of governmental power should generally depend on the nature of the power, not on the identity of the person exercising it. If the NAAQS that the EPA promulgated had been prescribed by Congress, everyone would agree that those rules would be the product of an exercise of "legislative power." The same characterization is appropriate when an agency exercises rulemaking authority pursuant to a permissible delegation from Congress.

My view is not only more faithful to normal English usage, but is also fully consistent with the text of the Constitution. In Article I, the Framers vested "All legislative Powers" in the Congress, Art. I, § 1, just as in Article II they vested the "executive Power" in the President, Art. II, § 1. Those provisions do not purport to limit the authority of either recipient of power to delegate authority to others. Surely the authority granted to members of the Cabinet and federal law enforcement agents is properly characterized as "Executive" even though not exercised by the President. *Cf. Morrison v. Olson*, 487 U.S. 654, 705–706 (1988) (SCALIA, J., dissenting) (arguing that the independent counsel exercised "executive power" unconstrained by the President).

It seems clear that an executive agency's exercise of rulemaking authority pursuant to a valid delegation from Congress is "legislative." As long as the delegation provides a sufficiently intelligible principle, there is nothing inherently unconstitutional about it. Accordingly, while I join Parts I, II, and IV of the Court's opinion, and agree with almost everything said in Part III, I would hold that when Congress enacted § 109, it effected a constitutional delegation of legislative power to the EPA.

JUSTICE BREYER, concurring in part and concurring in the judgment.

I join Parts I, III, and IV of the Court's opinion. I also agree with the Court's determination in Part II that the Clean Air Act does not permit the Environmental Protection Agency to consider the economic costs of implementation when setting national ambient air quality standards under § 109(b)(1) of the Act. But I would not rest this conclusion solely upon § 109's language or upon a presumption, such as the Court's presumption that any authority the Act grants the EPA to consider costs must flow from a "textual commitment" that is "clear." In order better to achieve regulatory goals — for example, to allocate resources so that they save more lives or produce a cleaner environment — regulators must often take account of all of a proposed regulation's adverse effects, at least where those adverse effects clearly threaten serious and disproportionate public harm. Hence, I believe that, other things being equal, we should read silences or ambiguities in the language of regulatory statutes as permitting, not forbidding, this type of rational regulation.

In these cases, however, other things are not equal. Here, legislative history, along with the statute's structure, indicates that § 109's language reflects a congressional decision not to delegate to the agency the legal authority to consider economic costs of compliance.

. . . .

Although I rely more heavily than does the Court upon legislative history and alternative sources of statutory flexibility, I reach the same ultimate conclusion. Section 109 does not delegate to the EPA authority to base the national ambient air quality standards, in whole or in part, upon the economic costs of compliance.

NOTES AND QUESTIONS

6-26. Does the majority opinion essentially end the delegation revival for the foreseeable future?

6-27. How do Justice Scalia's and Justice Breyer's approaches to these issues differ? Which do you find more persuasive? Why?

6-27. How would you characterize Justice Thomas' approach to these issues? Is his perspective likely to take on more importance in the future? What kinds of congressional power cannot be delegated? The power to tax? The power to declare war? The power to impeach?

6-28. What about privatization? How far can Congress go in authorizing private entities to carry out heretofore public functions? Does the nature of the function matter? Should it be easier, constitutionally speaking, to privatize snow removal than military responsibilities involving combat? What about the outsourcing of military operations involving lethal force? Are some functions inherently governmental? What makes a function "inherently governmental"?

6-29. Does the non-delegation doctrine, in any way, prevent the delegation of what were previously governmental functions and responsibilities to the private sector?

§ 6.07 Delegation and Privatization

The trend toward privatization in the U.S. is "virtually a national obsession," as Gillian Metzger notes in *Privatization as Delegation*, 103 COLUM. L. REV. 1367, 1437–39 (2003):*

> Private delegation doctrine takes over where state action leaves off. Rather than asking whether ostensibly private actors should be considered public for constitutional purposes, it accepts their private status and asks instead whether the Constitution prohibits governments from delegating certain powers to private actors. . . .
>
> The story of constitutional law's treatment of privatization is not complete without discussion of private delegation doctrine, although the most salient characteristic of current private delegation doctrine is its dormant status. A variety of private delegations came before the Supreme Court in the period from the end of the nineteenth century to the beginning of the twentieth. The New Deal gave sharp focus to the private delegation doctrine, as reliance on private regulation and corporatism represented cornerstones of President Roosevelt's early efforts to revive the national economy. At first, the Supreme Court responded with hostility to the incorporation of private actors into public regulation. In *Carter v. Carter Coal Co.*, the Court invalidated legislation making wage and hour agreements entered into by a majority of miners and large coal producers in a particular region binding on all miners and producers in that area. According to the Court, "in the very nature of things, one person may not be entrusted with the power to regulate the business of another," and allowing a majority of private participants in an industry to do so therefore constituted "clearly arbitrary" interference with the minority's personal liberty and property in violation of due process. But the Court soon effectively reversed course. In *Currin v. Wallace*, it sustained a regulatory scheme under which the Secretary of Agriculture was authorized to impose uniform tobacco standards binding on all tobacco sales in an area if two-thirds of the growers voted in favor of such regulation. Similarly, in *Sunshine Anthracite Coal Co. v. Adkins*, the Court upheld a later incarnation of the Bituminous Coal Act which allowed local coal producers sitting on local coal boards to set rules governing the sale of coal, with these rules being subject to approval, disapproval, or modification by the government's Bituminous Coal Commission.
>
> In neither *Currin* nor *Sunshine* did the Court overrule *Carter*. Instead, it held that, unlike *Carter*, these cases did not involve delegation of legislative power to private actors: in *Currin*, because public officials determined the substantive content of the regulations and private individuals were limited to deciding only whether these regulations would go into effect; and in *Sunshine*, because the statute required public officials to review and place an official imprimatur upon the privately devised regulations. The Court's distinguishing of *Carter* has empirical support; rather than wholesale delegation of regulatory power to unsupervised private actors, later New Deal measures embodied private involvement in public regulatory structures. In subsequent decisions, the Court has continued to

---

* Copyright © 2003 by Columbia Law Review. All rights reserved.

emphasize the presence of government review of private decisionmaking in upholding private delegations. Moreover, several lower courts have suggested that private delegations may violate due process, at least absent government supervision, and the Court itself has occasionally echoed *Carter*'s concern about the potential for abuse associated with private delegations.

Yet while *Carter*'s constitutional prohibition on private delegations thus remains alive in theory, it is all but dead in practice. Almost all private delegations are upheld. Courts are satisfied by formal provision for government ratification, however perfunctory. The private delegations that have been sustained often involve substantial direct control over third parties; even seemingly limited delegations that simply grant private entities the power to trigger government action, such as the ability to force an administrative hearing or commence a civil penalty action, can be quite significant. Interestingly, many decisions examining private delegations at the federal level use essentially the same framework as is applied to "public" delegations — that is, legislative grants of power to the executive branch — thereby suggesting that the Court sees such private delegations as presenting nothing beyond ordinary separation of powers issues.

Issues involving privatization and delegation, however, should not be viewed as unconnected to other kinds of delegation and regulation issues in general. Consider the global context of privatization and its relationship to other forms of deregulation and disaggregated public power.

Aman, PRIVATIZATION, DEMOCRACY AND HUMAN RIGHTS: DEMOCRACY DEFICITS IN THE U. S. AND THE NEED TO EXTEND THE PROVINCE OF ADMINISTRATIVE LAW

Privatization and Human Rights in the Age of Globalization (Koen De Feyter & Felipe Gómez Isa, eds. 2005) [*]

Global competition and the drive for lower taxes and lower regulatory costs that it encourages accounts, in part, for the growth of what we might call a 'non-state public sector,' one that evades the administrative law protections normally applied to a state entity, while bringing to bear the efficiencies of the market to the task at hand. Such approaches implicitly assume a zero sum public/private game — that is, as some matters are moved from the public to the private sphere, nothing fundamental changes in what we think of as public or as private. Markets are markets and the government is the government. If anything, government can only be improved by the demands of the

---

[*] Copyright © 2005 by intersentia. All rights reserved.

market, but the two spheres remain relatively autonomous. Changes in technology or regulatory technique may favor one mode of regulation over another. Such change may be innovative, but it need not be seen as transformative in nature if all that changes is the relative degree of how much we now choose to make public and how much we now leave to the private sphere.

But this is not the case. It is not just the recourse to the market that makes such change significant, but the change itself, located in the underlying relationship of states to markets. It is the fundamental realignment in the way states and markets interrelate and at times, even merge, blurring and erasing the boundary between the two, that requires us to examine these delegations to the market at the domestic level as part of a larger picture. Several other forms of delegation of state power are involved, including. (1) various 'de facto delegations' to the market that result from inadequate funding of the regulatory regime in place; (2) delegations to private transnational entities, whose regulation would most likely require a multi-lateral approach, as well as (3) delegations to the international branch of government such as delegations to international organisations such as the WTO; and (4) the devolution of federal responsibilities to states or, in effect, delegations to sub-national or regional entities. The cumulative effect of all of these various delegations, especially privatisation, amounts to a new situation that requires that we see administrative law in a new light. The newly enlarging private sphere is not the result of simply a shift of preference for the private over the public, or the international over the national, but a new way of organising public responsibilities and politics. Indeed, the cumulative impact of these delegations, (including the privatisation of social services, the deregulation of various industries as well as the increased reliance on such public policy tools as school vouchers, tax credits, and faith based initiatives) in effect, privatise the public square, disaggregating the public and fusing concepts of citizenship with consumerism.

Such changes do not argue for a return to the past. Rather, they constitute new regulatory and procedural questions that require new solutions. Some of the new questions are: how best can non-state actors be involved in decision making processes; how can we maximise the flow of information involving these decisions, and how can we mitigate conflict of interest concerns that arise from the fusion of public and private that typify many markets and market approaches to policy issues — issues ranging from private prisons to welfare eligibility. Fundamental issues of democracy are now at stake.

PROBLEM 6-3

Various state senators have come to you seeking advice on how to draft legislation that will allow the state to privatize the state's prisons. Specifically, the state knows that, due to overcrowding in its current prisons, it will need to build several new prisons; however, if this is done in the usual way — as public prisons — the state will have to raise taxes for the capital investment necessary to build them. The legislators believe a private firm could build and manage these prisons more efficiently, thereby avoiding an increase in state taxes. Still, the legislators have a number of concerns and questions for you. In formulating your answers, keep in mind that they are very concerned about getting the maximum savings for the state that privatization can provide.

(1) How should the contract be negotiated? Should the public be notified of its terms? When should this occur?

(2) Who should monitor the way the contract is being carried out? The State Board of Prisons? Should there be a new, independent commission established to do this monitoring?

(3) Can the private prison management firm determine the rules governing the conduct of inmates?

(4) Can the state allow the private prison company to decide when an inmate has violated the rules of conduct for the prison if a violation will reduce the "good time" credit the prisoner will receive (thus lengthening the time actually served)?

(5) Who should decide whether a particular inmate is suitable for a minimum security prison? What about deciding that a prisoner is suitable for furlough or work release?

(6) Who needs to keep track of the release date for each prisoner?

(7) Can this prison operate a business staffed with prisoners — for example, furniture making?

(8) Who should decide what educational and recreational program this prison should provide? Must they be the same as the programs at the publicly run prisons?

(9) Assuming that the state enters into a detailed contract with a private company (with great specificity, including the kind and quality of food to be served) who should be entitled to sue to enforce those contractual provisions — the state, the public, and/or the prisoners themselves?

For a discussion of various state privatization statutes and approaches to privatizing prisons, see Alfred C. Aman, Jr., *The Democracy Deficit: Taming Globalization Through Law Reform*, Chapter 4 (NYU Press, 2004).

§ 6.08 The Delegation of Judicial Power: Article III

Chapter Two examined the constitutional constraints imposed on agency adjudication by the Fifth and Fourteenth Amendments to the Constitution. There are other constitutional constraints as well, such as those that affect the power of Congress to authorize agency adjudication in the first instance. Article III of the Constitution states that the "judicial power of the United

States shall be vested in one Supreme Court and in such inferior Courts as the Congress may from time to time ordain and establish."

What if Congress chooses to create not only Article III courts whose judges are insulated by life tenure, but Article I courts whose judges have no such protection? Can Congress establish administrative adjudicatory bodies and delegate what might otherwise be Article III judicial power to these bodies? The answer to this question evokes important constitutional separation of powers concerns as well as a rich history of the political battles that have long surrounded administrative adjudication. As Professor Paul Verkuil has written,

> *Londoner,* and subsequent decisions introduced the modern era of administrative law. First, acknowledging the legitimacy of the administrative tribunal, they then addressed the question of what procedures the tribunal must follow. This inquiry was to create a profound clash over the role of the adversary system in determining administrative procedure.[*]

Keeping certain kinds of cases in court rather than allowing them to be heard by an administrative tribunal became a major goal of those who generally distrusted agency adjudication and often were also devoted to maintaining a *laissez-faire* economy. As Verkuil points out,

> this connection between adversary procedures and *laissez-faire* had much to do with the bar's initial resistance to administrative solutions. The events surrounding Roscoe Pound's controversial address to the ABA in 1906 emphasized this phenomenon. Pound shocked the lawyers at that time by speaking derisively of the cherished adversary system as the sporting theory of justice and documenting its inefficiencies and intricacies. He also advocated a removal of certain matters from the courts to administrative tribunals where they could be subjected to disposition in more efficient inquisitorial fashion.[**]

It is instructive to experience Pound first hand. What was his approach to the separation of powers issues raised by administrative agencies?

Pound, ADMINISTRATION OF JUSTICE IN THE MODERN CITY

26 Harv. L. Rev. 302, 322-24 (1912-13)[***]

Finally, there is the problem of freeing administration from the rigid limitations imposed in the eighteenth century, and by imitation in all our constitutions down to the end of the nineteenth century, through fear of executive tyranny. In the eighteenth century, separation of powers and a

---

[*] Verkuil, *The Emerging Concept of Administrative Procedure*. This article originally appeared at 78 Colum. L. Rev. 258, 264 (1978). Copyright © 1978 by Columbia Law Review. All rights reserved.

[**] *Id.* at 265.

[***] Copyright © 1913 by the Harvard Law Review Association. All rights reserved.

system of checks and balances were regarded as essential to liberty; as absolute and fundamental principles of law and of politics. Accordingly the framers of our constitutions, state and federal, sought to make them the basis of our government. But the attempt to make an exact analytical scheme of the powers of government according to the threefold division has broken down. For sovereignty is a unit. The so-called three powers are not three distinct things: they are three general types of manifestation of one power. In the development of sovereignty, these three types have been differentiated gradually as a result of experience that certain things, which demand special competency or special training or special attention, are done better by those who devote thereto their whole time or their whole attention for the time being. The principle involved, therefore, is no more than the principle involved in all specialization. If the officers of a court may best gather and study statistics of judicial administration to the end that such administration be improved, if to that end they may best conduct laboratories for criminological research, there is nothing in the nature of a court to prevent. Whether such things shall be done by a ministry of justice or by attachés of a tribunal is a question of mere expediency. But above this, to secure social interests in the modern city we must greatly enlarge the scope of administration. For reasons already suggested, the Anglo-American started out to leave to the courts what in other lands was committed to administration and inspection and executive supervision. He was averse to inspection and supervision in advance of action, preferring to show the individual his duty by a general law, to leave him free to act according to his judgment, and to prosecute him and impose the predetermined penalty in case his free action infringed the law. This attempt to confine administrative action to the inevitable minimum, which originally was fundamental in our polity, resulted in the nineteenth century in a multitude of rules which hindered as against few which helped. Regulation of public utilities, factory inspection, food inspection, tenement-house inspection, and building laws are compelling us to turn more and more from the criminal law to administrative prevention. Yet such prevention still usually requires judicial action to make it effective. On the other hand, in the reaction from the extravagant judicial control of the last century there is danger that we withdraw these matters wholly from the domain of law. To work out an adequate system of administrative law is not the least of the tasks of the immediate future.

Working out the system of administrative law Pound envisioned required some constitutional ingenuity.* To what extent did the Constitution allow for non-Article III courts to adjudicate disputes that might otherwise arise in federal court? Consider the following case.

---

* For an analysis and history of the doctrinal changes leading up to *Crowell v. Benson*, see Young, *Public Rights and Federal Judicial Power: From* Murray's Lessee *through* Crowell *to* Schor, 35 BUFF. L. REV. 765 (1986).

§ 6.09 *Crowell v. Benson*

Alfred C. Aman, Jr. & William T. Mayton, ADMINISTRATIVE LAW
122-23 (Thomson West, 2d ed. 2001)

The grand assault on assigning judicial power to agencies rather than courts constituted under Article III came in *Crowell v. Benson*. This New Deal case involved a major social initiative, a workman's compensation scheme established by Congress and implemented by an agency, the United States Employees Compensation Commission. By statute, Congress had made maritime employers liable to their employees for their on-the-job injuries "irrespective of fault" and according to a fixed schedule of damages. The responsibility for administering this scheme was placed in the Employees Compensation Commission. Clearly, the Commission performed a judicial function as it determined "the circumstances, nature, extent and consequences of the injuries sustained by the employee" and awarded compensation according to a table of damages for those injuries.

This allocation of power was challenged by an employer, on the grounds that in it Congress had assigned the Commission a judicial function that the Constitution reserved to federal courts. In its analysis of this argument, the Court noted that all compensation orders of the Commission were appealable to an appropriate federal district court, and that in significant respect, this right of appeal reserved judicial power to an Article III court. Commission orders were subject to review according to a division between issues of law and fact. The form of review was *de novo* as to matters of law and, in effect, "substantial evidence" for factual matters. Respecting issues of law, the Commission's judicial power was clearly valid. A reviewing court had full power, under the *de novo* standard of review prescribed by Congress, to itself determine matters of law and to reverse contrary agency decisions. "Interpretation of the laws," the Court explained, is "the proper and peculiar responsibility of the courts." Under the facts of *Crowell*, this responsibility had been fully reserved for Article III courts.

The Commission's power to make factual determinations was, however, considerably insulated from judicial review. These important determinations, so long as they were not "without evidence or 'contrary to the indisputable character of the evidence,'" bound the courts. Consequently, in factual matters the agency had been allocated a significant judicial power, and the question was whether this allocation of power was consistent with Article III.

An answer was arrived at by way of analogy. The Commission's "findings of fact" the Court explained, "were closely analogous to the findings of the amount of damages that are made, according to familiar practice, by commissioners or assessors; and the reservation of full authority to the court to deal with matters of law provides for the appropriate exercise of the judicial function in this class of cases." Considering this "familiar practice" of delegating fact-finding to referees, the Court concluded, "there is no requirement that in order to maintain the essential attributes of judicial power, all determinations of fact in constitutional courts shall be made by judges." This "agencies as adjuncts to the courts" explanation is not, however, altogether persuasive. The adjuncts the Court spoke of, referees and trustees and so forth, work for the courts for specific purposes. Agencies have much more power and their own purposes.

But overall, the result in *Crowell* — that the essential attributes of judicial power are retained in Article III courts so long as those courts may fully correct agency determinations on matters of law and overturn unreasonable findings as to matters of fact — seems reasonable, certainly in the circumstances of that case. The Commission's authority had been limited to a narrow area (on-the-job injuries in the maritime industry) where agency expertise and routine might usefully supplant the general processes of federal courts. In this context, the Court was "unable to find any constitutional obstacle to the action of the Congress in availing itself of a method shown by experience to be essential in order to apply its standards to the thousands of cases involved, thus relieving the court of a most serious burden while preserving their complete authority to insure the proper application of the law." . . .

While the result in *Crowell* is reasonable, a rationale used by the Supreme Court en route to that result is not. This rationale turned on a distinction, between public rights and private rights, a distinction apparently offered as a means of determining when judicial power is appropriately allocated to agencies. While this public and private distinction might have been taken as a best-forgotten dictum, it has not at all been disremembered. It is how the courts, today, often speak of Article III and agencies. . . .*

§ 6.10 Administrative Adjudication and Jury Trials

ATLAS ROOFING, INC. v. OCCUPATIONAL SAFETY AND HEALTH REVIEW COMM'N

United States Supreme Court
430 U.S. 442 (1977)

MR. JUSTICE WHITE delivered the opinion of the Court.

The issue in these cases is whether, consistent with the Seventh Amendment, Congress may create a new cause of action in the Government for civil penalties enforceable in an administrative agency where there is no jury trial.

I

After extensive investigation, Congress concluded, in 1970, that work-related deaths and injuries had become a "drastic" national problem.[1] Finding

---

* Alfred C. Aman, Jr. & William T. Mayton, 2d ed., 2001, with permission of Thomson West.

[1] The Senate Report stated:

"The problem of assuring safe and healthful workplaces for our working men and women ranks in importance with any that engages the national attention today. . . . 14,500 persons are killed annually as a result of industrial accidents; accordingly, during the past four years more Americans have been killed where they work than in the Vietnam War. By the lowest the existing state statutory remedies as well as state common-law actions for negligence and wrongful death to be inadequate to protect the employee population from death and injury due to unsafe working conditions, Congress enacted the Occupational Safety and Health Act of 1970 (OSHA or Act), 84 Stat. 1590, 29 U.S.C. § 651, *et seq.* The Act created a new statutory duty to avoid maintaining unsafe or unhealthy working conditions, and empowers the Secretary of Labor to promulgate health and safety standards. Two new remedies were provided permitting the Federal Government, proceeding before an administrative agency, (1) to obtain abatement orders requiring employers to correct unsafe working conditions and (2) to impose civil penalties on any employer maintaining any unsafe working condition. Each remedy exists whether or not an employee is actually injured or killed as a result of the condition, and existing state statutory and common-law remedies for actual injury and death remain unaffected.

Under the Act, inspectors, representing the Secretary of Labor, are authorized to conduct reasonable safety and health inspections. . . . If a violation is discovered, the inspector, on behalf of the Secretary, issues a citation to the employer fixing a reasonable time for its abatement and, in his discretion, proposing a civil penalty. §§ 658, 659. Such proposed penalties may range from nothing for *de minimis* and nonserious violations, to not more than $1,000 for serious violations, to a maximum of $10,000 for willful or repeated violations. . . .

If the employer wishes to contest the penalty or the abatement order, he may do so by notifying the Secretary of Labor within 15 days, in which event the abatement order is automatically stayed. . . . An evidentiary hearing is then held before an administrative law judge of the Occupational Safety and Health Review Commission. The Commission consists of three members, appointed for six-year terms, each of whom is qualified "by reason of training, education or experience" to adjudicate contested citations and assess penalties. . . . At this hearing the burden is on the Secretary to establish the elements of the alleged violation and the propriety of his proposed abatement order and proposed penalty; and the judge is empowered to affirm, modify, or vacate any or all of these items, giving due consideration in his penalty assessment to "the size of the business of the employer . . ., the gravity of the violation, the good faith of the employer, and the history of previous violations." . . . The judge's decision becomes the Commission's final and appealable order unless within 30 days a Commissioner directs that it be reviewed by the full Commission. . . .

---

count, 2.2 million persons are disabled on the job each year, resulting in the loss of 250 million man days of work, many times more than are lost through strikes.

"In addition to the individual human tragedies involved, the economic impact of industrial deaths and disability is staggering. Over $1.5 billion is wasted in lost wages, and the annual loss to the Gross National Product is estimated to be over $8 billion. Vast resources that could be available for productive use are siphoned off to pay workmen's compensation benefits and medical expenses.

"This 'grim current scene' . . . represents a worsening trend, for the fact is that the number of disabling injuries per million man hours worked is today 20% higher than in 1958." S. Rep. No. 91–1282, p. 2 (1970), Leg. Hist. 142. . . .

If review is granted, the Commission's subsequent order directing abatement and the payment of any assessed penalty becomes final unless the employer timely petitions for judicial review in the appropriate court of appeals. . . . The Secretary similarly may seek review of Commission orders, . . . but, in either case, "[t]he findings of the Commission with respect to questions of fact, if supported by substantial evidence on the record considered as a whole, shall be conclusive." . . . If the employer fails to pay the assessed penalty, the Secretary may commence a collection action in a federal district court in which neither the fact of the violation nor the propriety of the penalty assessed may be retried. § 666(k). Thus, the penalty may be collected without the employer's ever being entitled to a jury determination of the facts constituting the violation.

II

Petitioners were separately cited by the Secretary and ordered immediately to abate pertinent hazards after inspections of their respective worksites conducted in 1972 revealed conditions that assertedly violated a mandatory occupational safety standard promulgated by the Secretary under § 5(a)(2) of the Act. . . . In each case an employee's death had resulted. Petitioner Irey was cited for a willful violation of 29 CFR § 1926.652(b) and Table P-1 (1976) — a safety standard promulgated by the Secretary under the Act requiring the sides of trenches in "unstable or soft material" to be "shored, . . . sloped, or otherwise supported by means of sufficient strength to protect the employees working within them." The Secretary proposed a penalty of $7,500 for this violation and ordered the hazard abated immediately.

Petitioner Atlas was cited for a serious violation of 29 CFR(b)(1) and (f)(5)(ii)(1976), which require that roof opening covers be "so installed as to prevent accidental displacement." The Secretary proposed a penalty of $600 for this violation and ordered the hazard abated immediately.

Petitioners timely contested these citations and were afforded hearings before Administrative Law Judges of the Commission. The judges, and later the Commission, affirmed the findings of violations and accompanying abatement requirements and assessed petitioner Irey a reduced civil penalty of $5,000 and petitioner Atlas the civil penalty of $600 which the Secretary had proposed. Petitioners respectively thereupon sought judicial review in the Courts of Appeals for the Third and Fifth Circuits, challenging both the Commission's factual findings that violations had occurred and the constitutionality of the Act's enforcement procedures.

A panel of the Court of Appeals for the Third Circuit affirmed the Commission's orders in the *Irey* case over petitioner's and a dissenter's contention that the failure to afford the employer a jury trial on the question whether he had violated OSHA was in violation of the Seventh Amendment to the United States Constitution which provides for jury trial in most civil suits at common law. 519 F.2d 1200. On rehearing en banc, the Court of Appeals for the Third Circuit, over four dissents, adhered to the original panel's decision. *Id.*, at 1215. It concluded that this Court's rulings to date "leave no doubt that the Seventh Amendment is not applicable, at least in the context of a case such as this one, and that Congress is free to provide an administrative enforcement scheme without the intervention of a jury at any stage." *Id.*, at 1218.

The Court of Appeals for the Fifth Circuit also affirmed the Commission's order in the *Atlas* case over a similar claim that the enforcement scheme violated the Seventh Amendment. . . . We granted the petitions for writs of certiorari limited to the important question whether the Seventh Amendment prevents Congress from assigning to an administrative agency, under these circumstances the task of adjudicating violations of OSHA.[5] . . .

III

The Seventh Amendment provides that "[i]n Suits at common law, where the value in controversy shall exceed twenty dollars, the right of trial by jury shall be preserved. . . ." The phrase "Suits at common law" has been construed to refer to cases tried prior to the adoption of the Seventh Amendment in courts of law in which jury trial was customary as distinguished from courts of equity or admiralty in which jury trial was not. . . . Petitioners claim that a suit in a federal court by the Government for civil penalties for violation of a statute is a suit for a money judgment which is classically a suit at common law . . . and that the defendant therefore has a Seventh Amendment right to a jury determination of all issues of fact in such a case. . . . Petitioners then claim that to permit Congress to assign the function of adjudicating the Government's rights to civil penalties for violation of the statute to a different forum — an administrative agency in which no jury is available — would be to permit Congress to deprive a defendant of his Seventh Amendment jury right. We disagree. At least in cases in which "public rights" are being litigated — *e.g.*, cases in which the Government sues in its sovereign capacity to enforce public rights created by statutes within the power of Congress to enact the Seventh Amendment does not prohibit Congress from assigning the factfinding function and initial adjudication to an administrative forum with which the jury would be incompatible.[7]

Congress has often created new statutory obligations, provided for civil penalties for their violation, and committed exclusively to an administrative agency the function of deciding whether a violation has in fact occurred. These statutory schemes have been sustained by this Court, albeit often without express reference to the Seventh Amendment. Thus taxes may constitutionally be assessed and collected together with penalties, with the relevant facts in some instances being adjudicated only by an administrative agency. . . . Neither of these cases expressly discussed the question whether the taxation

---

[5] Each petitioner also argued below that the enforcement scheme violates the constitutional requirements that juries decide fact issues in criminal cases arguing that the fines involved are "penal" in nature. Each petitioner asked this Court in its petition for a writ of certiorari to review the unfavorable rulings of the courts below on this issue. . . .

[7] These cases do not involve purely "private rights." In cases which do involve only "private rights," this Court has accepted factfinding by an administrative agency, without intervention by a jury, only as an adjunct to an Art. III court, analogizing the agency to a jury or a special master and permitting it in admiralty cases to perform the function of the special master. *Crowell v. Benson*, 285 U.S. 22, 51-65 (1932). The Court there said: "On the common-law side of the federal courts, the aid of juries is not only deemed appropriate but is required by the Constitution itself." *Id.*, at 51.

scheme violated the Seventh Amendment. However, in *Helvering v. Mitchell*, 303 U.S. 391 (1938), the Court said, in rejecting a claim under the Sixth Amendment that the assessment and adjudication of tax penalties could not be made without a jury, that "the determination of the facts upon which liability is based may be by an administrative agency instead of a jury," *id.*, at 402. Similarly, Congress has entrusted to an administrative agency the task of adjudicating violations of the customs and immigration laws and assessing penalties based thereon.

In *Block v. Hirsh*, 256 U.S. 135 (1921), the Court sustained Congress' power to pass a statute, applicable to the District of Columbia, temporarily suspending landlords' legal remedy of ejectment and relegating them to an administrative factfinding forum charged with determining fair rents at which tenants could hold over despite the expiration of their leases. In that case the Court squarely rejected a challenge to the statute based on the Seventh Amendment, stating:

> "The statute is objected to on the further ground that landlords and tenants are deprived by it of a trial by jury on the right to possession of the land. *If the power of the Commission established by the statute to regulate the relation is established, as we think it is, by what we have said, this objection amounts to little. To regulate the relation and to decide the facts affecting it are hardly separable.*" *Id.*, at 158. (Emphasis added.)

In *Crowell v. Benson*, 285 U.S. 22 (1932), apparently referring to the above-cited line of authority, the Court stated:

> "[T]he distinction is at once apparent between cases of private right and those which arise *between the Government and persons subject to its authority in connection with the performance of the constitutional functions of the executive or legislative departments.* . . . [T]he Congress, in exercising the powers confided to it may establish 'legislative' courts . . . to serve as special tribunals 'to examine and determine various matters, arising between the government and others, which from their nature do not require judicial determination and yet are susceptible of it.' But *'the mode of determining matters of this class is completely within congressional control.* Congress may reserve to itself the power to decide, *may delegate that power to executive officers,* or may commit it to judicial tribunals. . . .' Familiar illustrations of *administrative agencies created for the determination of such matters are found in connection with the exercise of the congressional power as to interstate* and foreign *commerce,* taxation, immigration, the public lands, public health, the facilities of the post office, pensions, and payments to veterans." *Id.*, at 50-51. (Emphasis added.)

[The Court went on to analyze several more recent cases.]

In sum, the cases discussed above stand clearly for the proposition that when Congress creates new statutory "public rights," it may assign their adjudication to an administrative agency with which a jury trial would be incompatible, without violating the Seventh Amendment's injunction that jury trial is to be "preserved" in "suits at common law."[13] Congress is not required by the Seventh Amendment to choke the already crowded federal courts with new types of litigation or prevented from committing some new types of litigation to administrative agencies with special competence in the relevant field. This is the case even if the Seventh Amendment would have required a jury where the adjudication of those rights is assigned to a federal court of law instead of an administrative agency. . . .

Third is the assertion that the right to jury trial was never intended to depend on the identity of the forum to which Congress has chosen to submit a dispute; otherwise, it is said, Congress could utterly destroy the right to a jury trial by always providing for administrative rather than judicial resolution of the vast range of cases that now arise in the courts. The argument is well put, but it overstates the holdings of our prior cases and is in any event unpersuasive. Our prior cases support administrative factfinding in only those situations involving "public rights," *e.g.,* where the Government is involved in its sovereign capacity under an otherwise valid statute creating enforceable public rights. Wholly private tort, contract, and property cases, as well as a vast range of other cases as well are not at all implicated.

More to the point, it is apparent from the history of jury trial in civil matters that factfinding, which is the essential function of the jury in civil cases, *Colgrove v. Battin,* 413 U.S. 149, 157 (1973), was never the exclusive province of the jury under either the English or American legal systems at the time of the adoption of the Seventh Amendment; and the question whether a fact would be found by a jury turned to a considerable degree on the nature of the forum in which a litigant found himself. Critical factfinding was performed without juries in suits in equity, and there were no juries in admiralty, *Parsons v. Bedford,* 3 Pet. 433, 7 L. Ed. 732 (1830); nor were there juries in the military justice system. The jury was the factfinding mode in most suits in the common–law courts, but it was not exclusively so: Condemnation was a suit at common law but constitutionally could be tried without a jury. . . . The question whether a particular case was to be tried in a court of equity without a jury or a court of law with a jury did not depend on whether the suit involved factfinding or on the nature of the facts to be found. Factfinding could be a critical matter either at law or in equity. Rather, as a general rule, the decision turned on whether courts of law supplied a cause of action and an adequate remedy to the litigant. If it [sic] did, then the case would be tried in a court of law before a jury. Otherwise the case would be tried to a court of equity sitting without a jury. Thus, suits for damages for breach of contract, for example, were suits at common law with the issues of the making of the contract and its breach to be decided by a jury; but specific performance was a remedy unavailable in a court of law and where such relief was sought the case would be tried in a court of equity with the facts as to making and breach to be ascertained by the court.

---

[13] We note that the decision of the administrative tribunal in these cases on the law is subject to review in the federal courts of appeals, and on the facts is subject to review by such courts of appeals under a substantial-evidence test. Thus, these cases do not present the question whether Congress may commit the adjudication of public rights and the imposition of fines for their violation to an administrative agency without any sort of intervention by a court at any stage of the proceedings.

The Seventh Amendment was declaratory of the existing law, for it required only that jury trial in suits at common law was to be "preserved." It thus did not purport to require a jury trial where none was required before. Moreover, it did not seek to change the factfinding mode in equity or admiralty or to freeze equity jurisdiction as it existed in 1789, preventing it from developing new remedies where those available in courts of law were inadequate. . . .

The point is that the Seventh Amendment was never intended to establish the jury as the exclusive mechanism for factfinding in civil cases. It took the existing legal order as it found it, and there is little or no basis for concluding that the Amendment should now be interpreted to provide an impenetrable barrier to administrative factfinding under otherwise valid federal regulatory statutes. We cannot conclude that the Amendment rendered Congress powerless when it concluded that remedies available in courts of law were inadequate to cope with a problem within Congress' power to regulate — to create new public rights and remedies by statute and commit their enforcement, if it chose, to a tribunal other than a court of law — such as an administrative agency in which facts are not found by juries. . . .

Thus, history and our cases support the proposition that the right to a jury trial turns not solely on the nature of the issue to be resolved but also on the forum in which it is to be resolved.[16] Congress found the common law and other existing remedies for work injuries resulting from unsafe working conditions to be inadequate to protect the Nation's working men and women. It created a new cause of action, and remedies therefor, unknown to the common law, and placed their enforcement in a tribunal supplying speedy and expert resolutions of the issues involved. The Seventh Amendment is no bar to the creation of new rights or to their enforcement outside the regular courts of law.

The judgments below are affirmed.

It is so ordered.

MR. JUSTICE BLACKMUN took no part in the decision of these cases.

NOTES AND QUESTIONS

6-30. Why does the Court reject the government's Seventh Amendment argument? What test does it formulate to determine when a jury trial is appropriate in cases like this?

6-31. Why does this case involve a public, as opposed to a private, right? How are these rights defined?

---

[16] Petitioners claim that permitting Congress to control the jury-right question by picking the forum is to delegate to it, rather than this Court, the final power to decide Seventh Amendment issues. The claim is incorrect. The Seventh Amendment prevents Congress from depriving a litigant of a jury trial in a "legal" action before a tribunal customarily utilizing a jury as its factfinding arm, *Pernell v. Southall Realty,* 416 U.S. 363 (1974), and this Court has the final decision on the question whether a jury is required.

6-32. Is Justice White's opinion based on any principles that you can articulate? What is the basis of the opinion? Is expediency the underlying basis of this opinion, or can you construct a more principled approach? How would Roscoe Pound have ruled in this case? (*See* excerpt, p. 587, *supra*). For critical commentary on this case, *see* Kirst, *Administrative Penalties and the Civil Jury: The Supreme Court's Assault on the 7th Amendment,* 126 U. PA. L. REV. 1281 (1978); Luneberg & Nordenberg, *Specially Qualified Juries and Expert Nonjury Tribunals: Alternatives for Coping with the Complexities of Modern Civil Litigation,* 67 VA. L. REV. 887, 950–1007 (1981). *See generally,* Curie, *OSHA,* 1976 AM. B. FOUND. RES. J. 1107, 1153–56 (1976). For more on the applicability of the Seventh Amendment to legislative courts, see Ellen E. Sward, *Legislative Courts, Article III, and the Seventh Amendment,* 77 N.C. L. REV. 1037 (1999).

PROBLEM 6-4

Assume that OSHA has the power to exact fines of up to $1,000,000 per violation of its regulations. Assume further that, after a hearing on the record, one persistent, willful violator of OSHA safety regulations is assessed a fine of $10,000,000 and that you represent that company. Does this client have a jury trial argument to make after *Atlas*? What is that argument? When does or when should the Sixth Amendment apply? To what extent should the Sixth Amendment also be a constitutional limitation on agency adjudication?

§ 6.11 The Return of *Crowell v. Benson*

For years, the distinction employed in *Crowell* between public and private rights was, if not abandoned, at least used infrequently. Similarly, distinctions between the constitutional and jurisdictional facts were largely only of academic interest and were abandoned by the courts. As we shall see in other parts of this book, in the late 1970's and throughout much of the 1980's, a number of important separation-of-powers issues began to reappear on the Supreme Court's agenda. In addition to cases like *Atlas,* the "ghost" of *Crowell v. Benson* was being "cited" in cases raising Article III concerns in various contexts.

Consider the following case. Why was Justice Brennan so concerned about the role of bankruptcy judges? Do bankruptcy judges threaten to undermine the integrity of the federal courts? What was Congress trying to do when it created these judgeships? Was it improperly interfering with federal court jurisdiction?

NORTHERN PIPELINE CONSTRUCTION CO. v. MARATHON PIPE LINE CO.

United States Supreme Court
458 U.S. 50 (1982)

[This case involved the constitutionality of the Bankruptcy Act of 1978. Bankruptcy judges were Article I judges authorized to conduct trials of state contract and tort cases brought by the estates of bankrupt persons against third parties, even if diversity of citizenship existed. A plurality of the Court, in an opinion by Justice Brennan clearly found these powers far too extensive for an Article I Court. In the excerpted opinion below, Justice Brennan, writing for Justices Marshall, Blackmun, and Stevens, attempted to restate or, perhaps redefine, the kinds of cases in which Article I courts could replace Article III courts.]

. . . It is undisputed that the bankruptcy judges whose offices were created by the Bankruptcy Act of 1978 do not enjoy the protections constitutionally afforded to Art. III judges. The bankruptcy judges do not serve for life subject to their continued "good Behaviour." Rather, they are appointed for 14-year terms, and can be removed by the judicial council of the circuit in which they serve on grounds of "incompetency, misconduct, neglect of duty, or physical or mental disability." Second, the salaries of the bankruptcy judges are not immune from diminution by Congress. . . . In short, there is no doubt that the bankruptcy judges created by the Act are not Art. III judges. That Congress chose to vest such broad jurisdiction in non-Art. III bankruptcy courts, after giving substantial consideration to the constitutionality of the Act, is of course reason to respect the congressional conclusion. . . . But at the same time,

> "[d]eciding whether a matter has in any measure been committed by the Constitution to another branch of government, or whether the action of that branch exceeds whatever authority has been committed, is itself a delicate exercise in constitutional interpretation, and is a responsibility of this Court as ultimate interpreter of the Constitution." *Baker v. Carr,* 369 U.S. 186, 211 (1962).

With these principles in mind, we turn to the question presented for decision: whether the Bankruptcy Act of 1978 violates the command of Art. III that the judicial power of the United States must be vested in courts whose judges enjoy the protections and safeguards specified in that Article.

Appellants suggest two grounds for upholding the Act's conferral of broad adjudicative powers upon judges unprotected by Art. III. First, it is urged that "pursuant to its enumerated Article I powers, Congress may establish legislative courts that have jurisdiction to decide cases to which the Article III judicial power of the United States extends." Brief for United States 9. Referring to our precedents upholding the validity of "legislative courts," appellants suggest that "the plenary grants of power in Article I permit Congress to establish non-Article III tribunals in specialized areas having particularized needs and warranting distinctive treatment," such as the area of bankruptcy law. . . . Second, appellants contend that even if the Constitution does require that this bankruptcy-related action be adjudicated in an Art. III court, the Act in fact satisfies that requirement. "Bankruptcy jurisdiction was vested in the district court" of the judicial district in which the bankruptcy court is located, "and the exercise of that jurisdiction by the adjunct bankruptcy court was made subject to appeal as of right to an Article III court." . . . Analogizing the role of the bankruptcy court to that of a special master, appellants urge us to conclude that this "adjunct" system established by Congress satisfies the requirements of Art. III. We consider these arguments in turn.

III

Congress did not constitute the bankruptcy courts as legislative courts. Appellants contend, however, that the bankruptcy courts could have been so constituted, and that as a result the "adjunct" system in fact chosen by Congress does not impermissibly encroach upon the judicial power. In advancing this argument, appellants rely upon cases in which we have identified certain matters that "congress may or may not bring within the cognizance of [Art. III courts], as it may deem proper." *Murray's Lessee v. Hoboken Land & Improvement Co.*, 18 How. 272, 284 (1856). But when properly understood, these precedents represent no broad departure from the constitutional command that the judicial power of the United States must be vested in Art. III courts. Rather, they reduce to three narrow situations not subject to that command, each recognizing a circumstance in which the grant of power to the Legislative and Executive Branches was historically and constitutionally so exceptional that the congressional assertion of a power to create legislative courts was consistent with, rather than threatening to, the constitutional mandate of separation of powers. These precedents simply acknowledge that the literal command of Art. III, assigning the judicial power of the United States to courts insulated from Legislative or Executive interference, must be interpreted in light of the historical context in which the Constitution was written, and of the structural imperatives of the Constitution as a whole. . . . [The Court then discussed and distinguished precedents dealing with non-Article III territorial Courts, and cases involving courts martial].

Finally, appellants rely on a third group of cases, in which this Court has upheld the constitutionality of legislative courts and administrative agencies created by Congress to adjudicate cases involving "public rights."[18] The "public rights" doctrine was first set forth in *Murray's Lessee v. Hoboken Land & Improvement Co.,* 18 How. 272 (1856):

---

[18] Congress' power to create legislative courts to adjudicate public rights carries with it the lesser power to create administrative agencies for the same purpose, and to provide for review of those agency decisions in Art. III courts. *See, e.g., Atlas Roofing Co. v. Occupational Safety and Health Review Comm'n,* 430 U.S. 442, 450 (1977).

"[W]e do not consider congress can either withdraw from judicial cognizance any matter which, from its nature, is the subject of a suit at the common law, or in equity, or admiralty; nor, on the other hand, can it bring under the judicial power a matter which, from its nature, is not a subject for judicial determination. At the same time there are matters, *involving public rights,* which may be presented in such form that the judicial power is capable of acting on them, and which are susceptible of judicial determination, but which congress may or may not bring within the cognizance of the courts of the United States, as it may deem proper." *Id.*, at 284 (emphasis added).

This doctrine may be explained in part by reference to the traditional principle of sovereign immunity, which recognizes that the Government may attach conditions to its consent to be sued. . . . But the public-rights doctrine also draws upon the principle of separation of powers, and a historical understanding that certain prerogatives were reserved to the political Branches of Government. The doctrine extends only to matters arising "between the Government and persons subject to its authority in connection with the performance of the constitutional functions of the executive or legislative departments," *Crowell v. Benson,* 285 U.S. 22, 50 (1932), and only to matters that historically could have been determined exclusively by those departments. . . . The understanding of these cases is that the Framers expected that Congress would be free to commit such matters completely to nonjudicial executive determination, and that as a result there can be no constitutional objection to Congress' employing the less drastic expedient of committing their determination to a legislative court or an administrative agency. *Crowell v. Benson, supra,* at 50.

The public-rights doctrine is grounded in a historically recognized distinction between matters that could be conclusively determined by the Executive and Legislative Branches and matters that are "inherently . . . judicial." *Ex parte Bakelite Corp., supra,* at 458. . . . For example, the Court in *Murray's Lessee* looked to the law of England and the States at the time the Constitution was adopted, in order to determine whether the issue presented was customarily cognizable in the courts. . . . Concluding that the matter had not traditionally been one for judicial determination, the Court perceived no bar to Congress' establishment of summary procedures, outside of Art. III courts, to collect a debt due to the Government from one of its customs agents. On the same premise, the court in *Ex parte Bakelite Corp., supra,* held that the Court of Customs Appeals had been properly constituted by Congress as a legislative court. . . .

The distinction between public rights and private rights has not been definitively explained in our precedents.[22] Nor is it necessary to do so in the present cases, for it suffices to observe that a matter of public rights must

---

[22] *Crowell v. Benson,* 285 U.S. 22 (1932), attempted to catalog some of the matters that fall within the public-rights doctrine:

"Familiar illustrations of administrative agencies created for the determination of such matters are found in connection with the exercise of the congressional power as to interstate and foreign commerce, taxation, immigration, the public lands, public health, the facilities of the post office, pensions and payments to veterans." *Id.,* at 51 (footnote omitted).

§ 6.11　　　　　　　　　LEGISLATIVE CONTROL　　　　　　　　　601

at a minimum arise "between the government and others." . . . In contrast, "the liability of one individual to another under the law as defined," *Crowell v. Benson, supra,* at 51, is a matter of private rights. Our precedents clearly establish that only controversies in the former category may be removed from Art. III courts and delegated to legislative courts or administrative agencies for their determination. *See Atlas Roofing Co. v. Occupational Safety and Health Review Comm'n,* 430 U.S. 442, 450, n. 7 (1977); *Crowell v. Benson, supra,* at 50-51. . . . Private-rights disputes, on the other hand, lie at the core of the historically recognized judicial power.

In sum, this Court has identified three situations in which Art. III does not bar the creation of legislative courts. In each of these situations, the Court has recognized certain exceptional powers bestowed upon Congress by the Constitution or by historical consensus. Only in the face of such an exceptional grant of power has the Court declined to hold the authority of Congress subject to the general prescriptions of Art. III.

We discern no such exceptional grant of power applicable in the cases before us. The courts created by the Bankruptcy Act of 1978 do not lie exclusively outside the States of the Federal Union, like those in the District of Columbia and the Territories. Nor do the bankruptcy courts bear any resemblance to courts-martial, which are founded upon the Constitution's grant of plenary authority over the Nation's military forces to the Legislative and Executive Branches. Finally, the substantive legal rights at issue in the present action cannot be deemed "public rights." Appellants argue that a discharge in bankruptcy is indeed a "public right," similar to such congressionally created benefits as "radio station licenses, pilot licenses, or certificates for common carriers" granted by administrative agencies. . . . But the restructuring of debtor-creditor relations, which is at the core of the federal bankruptcy power, must be distinguished from the adjudication of state-created private rights, such as the right to recover contract damages that is at issue in this case. The former may well be a "public right," but the latter obviously is not. Appellant Northern's right to recover contract damages to augment its estate is "one of private right, that is, of the liability of one individual to another under the law as defined." *Crowell v. Benson,* 285 U.S., at 51. . . .

IV

Appellants advance a second argument for upholding the constitutionality of the Act: that "viewed within the entire judicial framework set up by Congress," the bankruptcy court is merely an "adjunct" to the district court, and that the delegation of certain adjudicative functions to the bankruptcy court is accordingly consistent with the principle that the judicial power of the United States must be vested in Art. III courts. . . .

We hold that the Bankruptcy Act of 1978 carries the possibility of . . . an unwarranted encroachment. Many of the rights subject to adjudication by the Act's bankruptcy courts, . . . are not of Congress' creation. Indeed, the cases before us, which center upon appellant Northern's claim for damages for breach of contract and misrepresentation, involve a right created by state law, a right independent of and antecedent to the reorganization petition that conferred jurisdiction upon the Bankruptcy Court. Accordingly, Congress' authority to control the manner in which that right is adjudicated, through assignment of historically judicial functions to a non-Art. III "adjunct," plainly must be deemed at a minimum. Yet it is equally plain that Congress has vested the "adjunct" bankruptcy judges with powers over Northern's state-created right that far exceed the powers that it has vested in administrative agencies that adjudicate only rights of Congress' own creation.

Unlike the administrative scheme that we reviewed in *Crowell,* the Act vests all "essential attributes" of the judicial power of the United States in the "adjunct" bankruptcy court. First, the agency in *Crowell* made only specialized, narrowly confined factual determinations regarding a particularized area of law. In contrast, the subject-matter jurisdiction of the bankruptcy courts encompasses not only traditional matters of bankruptcy, but also "all civil proceedings arising under title 11 or arising in or related to cases under title 11." . . . Second, while the agency in *Crowell* engaged in statutorily channeled factfinding functions, the bankruptcy courts exercise "all of the jurisdiction" conferred by the Act on the district courts, § 1471(c). Third, the agency in *Crowell* possessed only a limited power to issue compensation orders pursuant to specialized procedures, and its orders could be enforced only by order of the district court. By contrast, the bankruptcy courts exercise all ordinary powers of district courts, including the power to preside over jury trials, . . . the power to issue declaratory judgments, § 2201, the power to issue writs of habeas corpus, § 2256, and the power to issue any order, process, or judgment appropriate for the enforcement of the provisions of Title 11, 11 U.S.C. § 105(a) (1976 ed., Supp. IV). Fourth, while orders issued by the agency in *Crowell* were to be set aside if "not supported by the evidence," the judgments of the bankruptcy courts are apparently subject to review only under the more deferential "clearly erroneous" standard. . . . Finally, the agency in *Crowell* was required by law to seek enforcement of its compensation orders in the district court. In contrast, the bankruptcy courts issue final judgments, which are binding and enforceable even in the absence of an appeal. . . .

We conclude that 28 U.S.C. § 1471 (1976 ed., Supp. IV), as added by § 241(a) of the Bankruptcy Act of 1978, has impermissibly removed most, if not all, of "the essential attributes of the judicial power" from the Art. III district court, and has vested those attributes in a non-Art. III adjunct. Such a grant of jurisdiction cannot be sustained as an exercise of Congress' power to create adjuncts to Art. III courts. . . .

JUSTICE REHNQUIST, with whom JUSTICE O'CONNOR joins, concurring in the judgment.

Were I to agree with the plurality that the question presented by these cases is "whether the assignment by Congress to bankruptcy judges of the jurisdiction granted in 28 U.S.C. § 1471 (1976 ed., Supp. IV) by § 241(a) of the Bankruptcy Act of 1978 violates Art. III of the Constitution," *ante,* at 52, I would with considerable reluctance embark on the duty of deciding this broad question. But appellee Marathon Pipe Line Co. has not been subjected to the full range of authority granted bankruptcy courts by § 1471. It was named as a defendant in a suit brought by appellant Northern Pipeline Construction Co. in a United States Bankruptcy Court. The suit sought damages for, *inter alia,* breaches of contract and warranty. Marathon moved to dismiss the action on the grounds that the Bankruptcy Act of 1978, which authorized the suit, violated Art. III of the Constitution insofar as it established bankruptcy judges whose tenure and salary protection do not conform to the requirements of Art. III.

With the cases in this posture, Marathon has simply been named defendant in a lawsuit about a contract, a lawsuit initiated by appellant Northern after having previously filed a petition for reorganization under the Bankruptcy Act. Marathon may object to proceeding further with this lawsuit on the grounds that if it is to be resolved by an agency of the United States, it may be resolved only by an agency which exercises "[t]he judicial power of the United States" described by Art. III of the Constitution. But resolution of any objections it may make on this ground to the exercise of a different authority conferred on bankruptcy courts by the 1978 Act . . . should await the exercise of such authority. . . .

The cases dealing with the authority of Congress to create courts other than by use of its power under Art. III do not admit of easy synthesis. In the interval of nearly 150 years between *American Insurance Co. v. Canter,* 1 Pet. 511, 7 L. Ed. 242 (1828), and *Palmore v. United States,* 411 U.S. 389 (1973), the Court addressed the question infrequently. I need not decide whether these cases in fact support a general proposition and three tidy exceptions, as the plurality believes, or whether instead they are but landmarks on a judicial "darkling plain" where ignorant armies have clashed by night, as JUSTICE WHITE apparently believes them to be. None of the cases has gone so far as to sanction the type of adjudication to which Marathon will be subjected against its will under the provisions of the 1978 Act. To whatever extent different powers granted under that Act might be sustained under the "public rights" doctrine of *Murray's Lessee v. Hoboken Land & Improvement Co.,* 18 How. 272 (1856), and succeeding cases, I am satisfied that the adjudication of Northern's lawsuit cannot be so sustained. . . .

CHIEF JUSTICE BURGER, dissenting [opinion omitted].

JUSTICE WHITE, with whom THE CHIEF JUSTICE and JUSTICE POWELL join, dissenting.

Article III, § 1, of the Constitution is straightforward and uncomplicated on its face:

> The judicial Power of the United States, shall be vested in one supreme Court, and in such inferior Courts as the Congress may from time to time ordain and establish. The Judges, both of the supreme and inferior Courts, shall hold their Offices during good Behavior, and shall at stated Times, receive for their Services, a Compensation, which shall not be diminished during their Continuance in Office.

Any reader could easily take this provision to mean that although Congress was free to establish such lower courts as it saw fit, any court that it did establish would be an "inferior" court exercising "judicial Power of the United States" and so must be manned by judges possessing both life tenure and a guaranteed minimal income. This would be an eminently sensible reading and one that, as the plurality shows, is well founded in both the documentary sources and the political doctrine of separation of powers that stands behind much of our constitutional structure. . . .

If this simple reading were correct and we were free to disregard 150 years of history, these would be easy cases and the plurality opinion could end with its observation that "[i]t is undisputed that the bankruptcy judges whose offices were created by the Bankruptcy Act of 1978 do not enjoy the protections constitutionally afforded to Art. III judges." . . . The fact that the plurality must go on to deal with what has been characterized as one of the most confusing and controversial areas of constitutional law itself indicates the gross oversimplification implicit in the plurality's claim that "our Constitution unambiguously enunciates a fundamental principle — that the 'judicial Power of the United States' must be reposed in an independent Judiciary [and] provides clear institutional protections for that independence." . . . While this is fine rhetoric, analytically it serves only to put a distracting and superficial gloss on a difficult question.

That question is what limits Art. III places on Congress' ability to create adjudicative institutions designed to carry out federal policy established pursuant to the substantive authority given Congress elsewhere in the Constitution. Whether fortunate or unfortunate, at this point in the history of constitutional law that question can no longer be answered by looking only to the constitutional text. This Court's cases construing that text must also be considered. In its attempt to pigeonhole these cases, the plurality does violence to their meaning and creates an artificial structure that itself lacks coherence. . . .

[After analyzing the majority's opinion and reading the cases differently, the dissent, quoting from *Palmore v. United States*, 411 U.S. 389 (1973), sets forth the following approach to these issues:]

"[T]he requirements of Art. III, which are applicable where laws of national applicability and affairs of national concern are at stake, must in proper circumstances give way to accommodate plenary grants of power to Congress to legislate with respect to specialized areas having particularized needs and warranting distinctive treatment." 411 U.S., at 407-408.

I do not suggest that the Court should simply look to the strength of the legislative interest and ask itself if that interest is more compelling than the values furthered by Art. III. The inquiry should, rather, focus equally on those Art. III values and ask whether and to what extent the legislative scheme accommodates them or, conversely, substantially undermines them. The burden on Art. III values should then be measured against the values Congress hopes to serve through the use of Art. I courts.

To be more concrete: *Crowell, supra,* suggests that the presence of appellate review by an Art. III court will go a long way toward insuring a proper separation of powers. Appellate review of the decisions of legislative courts, like appellate review of state-court decisions, provides a firm check on the ability of the political institutions of government to ignore or transgress constitutional limits on their own authority. Obviously, therefore, a scheme of Art. I courts that provides for appellate review by Art. III courts should be substantially less controversial than a legislative attempt entirely to avoid judicial review in a constitutional court.

Similarly, as long as the proposed Art. I courts are designed to deal with issues likely to be of little interest to the political branches, there is less reason to fear that such courts represent a dangerous accumulation of power in one of the political branches of government. Chief Justice Vinson suggested as much when he stated that the Court should guard against any congressional attempt "to transfer jurisdiction . . . for the purpose of emasculating" constitutional courts. *National Insurance Co. v. Tidewater Co.,* 337 U.S., at 644.

V

. . . .

Finally, I have no doubt that the ends that Congress sought to accomplish by creating a system of non-Art. III bankruptcy courts were at least as compelling as the ends found to be satisfactory in *Palmore v. United States,* 411 U.S. 389 (1973), or the ends that have traditionally justified the creation of legislative courts. The stresses placed upon the old bankruptcy system by the tremendous increase in bankruptcy cases were well documented and were clearly a matter to which Congress could respond. I do not believe it is possible to challenge Congress' further determination that it was necessary to create a specialized court to deal with bankruptcy matters. This was the nearly uniform conclusion of all those that testified before Congress on the question of reform of the bankruptcy system, as well as the conclusion of the Commission on Bankruptcy Laws established by Congress in 1970 to explore possible improvements in the system.

The real question is not whether Congress was justified in establishing a specialized bankruptcy court, but rather whether it was justified in failing to create a specialized, Art. III bankruptcy court. My own view is that the very fact of extreme specialization may be enough, and certainly has been enough in the past, to justify the creation of a legislative court. Congress may legitimately consider the effect on the federal judiciary of the addition of several hundred specialized judges: We are, on the whole, a body of generalists. The addition of several hundred specialists may substantially change, whether for good or bad, the character of the federal bench. Moreover, Congress may have desired to maintain some flexibility in its possible future responses to the general problem of bankruptcy. There is no question that the existence of several hundred bankruptcy judges with life tenure would have severely limited Congress' future options. Furthermore, the number of bankruptcies may fluctuate, producing a substantially reduced need for bankruptcy judges. Congress may have thought that, in that event, a bankruptcy specialist should not as a general matter serve as a judge in the countless nonspecialized cases that come before the federal district courts. It would then face the prospect of large numbers of idle federal judges. Finally, Congress may have believed that the change from bankruptcy referees to Art. I judges was far less dramatic, and so less disruptive of the existing bankruptcy and constitutional court systems, than would be a change to Art. III judges.

For all of these reasons, I would defer to the congressional judgment. Accordingly, I dissent.

NOTES AND QUESTIONS

6-33. One of the important aspects of this plurality opinion is that it resurrected parts of *Crowell v. Benson* long thought to be irrelevant, or at least not likely to be controlling in future cases. Indeed, during the fifty years "[f]rom *Crowell* to *Northern Pipeline,* the Supreme Court allowed Congress increasing flexibility in circumventing Article III's tenure requirements. With only a few minor exceptions, the Court decided cases and wrote its opinions in a way that did little to indicate a willingness to resist the more alarming possibilities raised by *Crowell*'s broad statements." Young, *Public Rights and Federal Judicial Power: From* Murray's Lessee *through* Crowell *to* Schor, 35 BUFF. L. REV. 765, 841 (1986). The plurality opinion certainly serves notice that there are Article III limitations on the delegation of judicial power to Article I courts. What are the limitations articulated in this case?

6-34. Focusing on the plurality's reasoning, particularly with regard to the public rights exception to Article III, what constitutes a public right? Is the plurality itself sure on this point? Is the concurring opinion in accord with the plurality's rather tidy arrangement of cases into three categories, including a public rights category?

6-35. If a case does not fall into any of the plurality's three categories, is it constitutionally possible to create an Article I court? Are any further exceptions possible?

6-36. What is the difference between an Article I court and adjudicatory bodies that are merely adjuncts to Article III courts? Was the administrative court in *Crowell* merely an adjunct? What are the elements of an adjunct court?

6-37. What are the Article III limits on congressional establishment of so-called adjunct courts? Put another way, when does an Article I adjudicatory body cease being an adjunct and become a court? If the body deals with public rights, can the adjunct be more powerful than if it deals only with private rights? How important is judicial review by an Article III court of the decisions made by Article I adjuncts? Is judicial review alone important? Is the standard of review used by the Court also significant? *See generally,* Redish, *Legislative Courts, Administrative Agencies and the* Northern Pipeline *Decision,* 1983 DUKE L.J. 197.

6-38. *Compare* the dissent's approach to the constitutional issues in this case with that of the plurality. Is Justice White's approach consistent with the way he approached the constitutional issues in *Atlas Roofing*? Does he believe that there really has been a major shift in the balance of power among the branches of government in this case?

6-39. *Northern Pipeline* raised a number of issues, not the least of which was the constitutionality of agency adjudication that, at least practically speaking, was long thought to have been settled. The bright lines the plurality tried to draw between public rights cases and private rights cases suggested an approach to the separation of powers issues implicit in these cases that was formalistic and had great potential for future litigation that could profoundly affect the ability of some administrative agencies to exist, much less act. As we shall see later in the course, a strict or formalistic constitutional approach to separation of powers issues was not limited only to Article III and the judiciary. This approach also was evident in the way the Court decided the constitutionality of legislative vetoes in *INS v. Chadha, infra* at Chapter Eight, § 8.01 and the constitutional limits of the appointment and removal powers of the President. *See Bowsher v. Synar, infra* at Chapter Seven, § 7.04. At this point in the course, it is, therefore, not only important to analyze the results the Court reached in *Northern Pipeline,* but also the constitutional approach that the Court employed. There are various approaches or methodologies to separation-of-powers issues that will, as you shall see, provide an analytical framework for understanding and critiquing the Court's decisions in related areas of constitutional and administrative law. What approaches can you discern in *Northern Pipeline*?

6-40. The approach to separation-of-powers issues adopted by the plurality in *Northern Pipeline* was significantly modified in the subsequent case of *Thomas v. Union Carbide Agricultural Products Co.,* 473 U.S. 568 (1985). Though the decision in *Thomas* was unanimous, the majority was composed of the dissenters in *Northern Pipeline,* plus the two concurring Justices, Rehnquist and O'Connor. The Justices that made up the plurality in *Northern Pipeline* filed their own concurring opinions, Justice Brennan writing for Justices Marshall and Blackmun, and Justice Stevens concurring on his own.

The case was a complicated one, involving the Federal Insecticide, Fungicide and Rodenticide Act (FIFRA). The Act requires that pesticides be registered with the Environmental Protection Agency (EPA) before they are sold. Before the EPA will allow registration, however, the manufacturer must make available certain data concerning the product's health, safety and environmental effects. This data often is of value to competitors and has trade secret status until it is made public.

FIFRA, thus, does not allow a second manufacturer to register a pesticide if it has used the data submitted by another unless there has been an offer to compensate the original registrant. Even if there has been such an offer, it might not have been accepted. The Act thus provides for binding arbitration of this dispute. If the parties cannot agree on an arbitrator, one will be appointed, whose decision is final "except for fraud, misrepresentation or other misconduct by one of the parties to the arbitration or the arbitrator. . . ." 7 U.S.C. § 136a(c)(1)(D)(ii) (1982).

In *Thomas,* the first submitter of the data would not accept a subsequent user's offer nor the outcome of the arbitration. It challenged the entire arbitration scheme as being violative of Article III. Specifically, Union Carbide argued that FIFRA, in effect, substituted a new federal right for a state-created property right and then required adjudication of this new right by a non-Article III judge (or arbitrator) whose decision could only be reviewed for "fraud, misconduct or other misconduct. . . ."

Justice O'Connor described the issue as whether "Article III of the Constitution prohibits Congress from selecting binding arbitration with only limited judicial review as the mechanism for resolving disputes among participants in FIFRA's pesticide registration scheme." The Court concluded it does not. Of particular significance for our purposes is the approach the Court took to the Article III questions presented. It largely eschewed the bright line the plurality in *Northern Pipeline* drew between public and private rights. Yet, Justice O'Connor did define the right involved in *Thomas*, as a public one: "the right created by FIFRA is not [a] purely 'private' right, but bears many of the characteristics of a 'public' right. Use of a registrant's data . . . serves a public purpose." 473 U.S. at 589. This definition of a public right was so broad as to undercut considerably the approach in *Northern*. Of even greater significance, however, was the more functional, flexible approach to separation-of-powers questions the majority took in this case. This approach is very much the one that the majority adopted in *Commodity Futures Trading Commission v. Schor*, 478 U.S. 833 (1986), the case we shall now examine in full.

COMMODITY FUTURES TRADING COMMISSION v. SCHOR

United States Supreme Court
478 U.S. 833 (1986)

JUSTICE O'CONNOR delivered the opinion of the Court.

The question presented is whether the Commodity Exchange Act (CEA or Act), 7 U.S.C. § 1 *et seq.*, empowers the Commodity Futures Trading Commission (CFTC or Commission) to entertain state law counterclaims in reparation proceedings and, if so, whether that grant of authority violates Article III of the Constitution.

I

The CEA broadly prohibits fraudulent and manipulative conduct in connection with commodity futures transactions. In 1974, Congress "overhaul[ed]" the Act in order to institute a more "comprehensive regulatory structure to oversee the volatile and esoteric futures trading complex." H.R. Rep. No. 93-975, p. 1 (1974). *See* Pub. L. 93-463, 88 Stat. 1389. Congress also determined that the broad regulatory powers of the CEA were most appropriately vested in an agency which would be relatively immune from the "political winds that sweep Washington." H.R. Rep. No. 93-975, pp. 44, 70. It therefore created an independent agency, the CFTC, and entrusted to it sweeping authority to implement the CEA.

Among the duties assigned to the CFTC was the administration of a reparations procedure through which disgruntled customers of professional commodity brokers could seek redress for the brokers' violations of the Act or CFTC regulations. Thus, § 14 of the CEA, 7 U.S.C.A. § 18 (Supp. 1986), provides that any person injured by such violations may apply to the Commission for an order directing the offender to pay reparations to the complainant and may enforce that order in federal district court. Congress intended this administrative procedure to be an "inexpensive and expeditious" alternative to existing fora available to aggrieved customers, namely, the courts and arbitration. S. Rep. No. 95–850, p. 11 (1978). . . .

In conformance with the congressional goal of promoting efficient dispute resolution, the CFTC promulgated a regulation in 1976 which allows it to adjudicate counterclaims "aris[ing] out of the transaction or occurrence or series of transactions or occurrences set forth in the complaint." . . . This permissive counterclaim rule leaves the respondent in a reparations proceeding free to seek relief against the reparations complainant in other fora.

The instant dispute arose in February 1980, when respondents Schor and Mortgage Services of America invoked the CFTC's reparations jurisdiction by filing complaints against petitioner ContiCommodity Services, Inc. (Conti), a commodity futures broker, and Richard L. Sandor, a Conti employee. Schor had an account with Conti which contained a debit balance because Schor's net futures trading losses and expenses, such as commissions, exceeded the funds deposited in the account. Schor alleged that this debit balance was the result of Conti's numerous violations of the CEA. . . .

Before receiving notice that Schor had commenced the reparations proceeding, Conti had filed a diversity action in Federal District Court to recover the debit balance. . . . Schor counterclaimed in this action, reiterating his charges that the debit balance was due to Conti's violations of the CEA. Schor also moved on two separate occasions to dismiss or stay the district court action, arguing that the continuation of the federal action would be a waste of judicial resources and an undue burden on the litigants in view of the fact that "[t]he reparations proceedings . . . will fully . . . resolve and adjudicate all the rights of the parties to this action with respect to the transactions which are the subject matter of this action." . . .

Although the District Court declined to stay or dismiss the suit, Conti voluntarily dismissed the federal court action and presented its debit balance claim by way of a counterclaim in the CFTC reparations proceeding. Conti denied violating the CEA and instead insisted that the debit balance resulted from Schor's trading, and was therefore a simple debt owed by Schor. . . .

After discovery, briefing and a hearing, the Administrative Law Judge (ALJ) in Schor's reparations proceeding ruled in Conti's favor on both Schor's claims and Conti's counterclaims. After this ruling, Schor for the first time challenged the CFTC's statutory authority to adjudicate Conti's counterclaim. The ALJ rejected Schor's challenge, stating himself "bound by agency regulations and published agency policies." The Commission declined to review the decision and allowed it to become final, at which point Schor filed a petition for review with the Court of Appeals for the District of Columbia Circuit. Prior to oral argument, the Court of Appeals, *sua sponte,* raised the question of whether CFTC could constitutionally adjudicate Conti's counterclaims in light of *Northern Pipeline Construction Co. v. Marathon Pipe Line Co.,* 458 U.S. 50 (1982) . . . in which this Court held that "Congress may not vest in a non-Article III court the power to adjudicate, render final judgment, and issue binding orders in a traditional contract action arising under state law, without consent of the litigants, and subject only to ordinary appellate review." *Thomas v. Union Carbide Agricultural Products Co.,* 473 U.S. 568, 584.

After briefing and argument, the Court of Appeals upheld the CFTC's decision on Schor's claim in most respects, but ordered the dismissal of Conti's counterclaims on the ground that "the CFTC lacks authority (subject matter competence) to adjudicate" common law counterclaims. 239 U.S. App. D.C., at 161, 740 F.2d, at 1264. In support of this latter ruling, the Court of Appeals reasoned that the CFTC's exercise of jurisdiction over Conti's common law counterclaim gave rise to "[s]erious constitutional problems" under *Northern Pipeline*. . . . The Court of Appeals therefore concluded that, under well-established principles of statutory construction, the relevant inquiry was whether the CEA was " 'fairly susceptible' of [an alternative] construction," such that Article III objections, and thus unnecessary constitutional adjudication, could be avoided. . . .

. . . This Court granted the CFTC's petition for certiorari, vacated the court of appeals' judgment, and remanded the case for further consideration in light of *Thomas, supra,* at 582–593, 473 U.S. 568 (1985). We had there ruled that the arbitration scheme established under the Federal Insecticide, Fungicide, and Rodenticide Act (FIFRA), . . . does not contravene Article III and, more generally, held that "Congress, acting for a valid legislative purpose pursuant to its constitutional powers under Article I, may create a seemingly 'private' right that is so closely integrated into a public regulatory scheme as to be a matter appropriate for agency resolution with limited involvement by the Article III judiciary." 473 U.S., at 593.

On remand, the Court of Appeals reinstated its prior judgment. It reaffirmed its earlier view that *Northern Pipeline* drew into serious question the Commission's authority to decide debit-balance counterclaims in reparations proceedings; concluded that nothing in *Thomas* altered that view; and again held that, in light of the constitutional problems posed by the CFTC's adjudication of common law counterclaims, the CEA should be construed to authorize the CFTC to adjudicate only counterclaims arising from violations of the Act or CFTC regulations. . . .

We again granted certiorari, 474 U.S. 1018 (1985), and now reverse.

II

[The Court concluded that it was "squarely faced with the question of whether the CFTC's assumption of jurisdiction over common law counterclaims violates Article III of the Constitution."]

III

Article III, § 1 directs that the "judicial Power of the United States shall be vested in one supreme Court and in such inferior Courts as the Congress may from time to time ordain and establish," and provides that these federal courts shall be staffed by judges who hold office during good behavior, and whose compensation shall not be diminished during tenure in office. Schor claims that these provisions prohibit Congress from authorizing the initial

§ 6.11　　　　　　　　　LEGISLATIVE CONTROL　　　　　　　　　　611

adjudication of common law counterclaims by the CFTC, an administrative agency whose adjudicatory officers do not enjoy the tenure and salary protections embodied in Article III.

Although our precedents in this area do not admit of easy synthesis, they do establish that the resolution of claims such as Schor's cannot turn on conclusory reference to the language of Article III. *See, e.g., Thomas,* 473 U.S., at 583. Rather, the constitutionality of a given congressional delegation of adjudicative functions to a non-Article III body must be assessed by reference to the purposes underlying the requirements of Article III. *See, e.g., id.,* at 590, *Northern Pipeline,* 458 U.S., at 64. This inquiry, in turn, is guided by the principle that "practical attention to substance rather than doctrinaire reliance on formal categories should inform application of Article III." *Thomas, supra,* at 587. *See also Crowell v. Benson,* 285 U.S., at 53.

A

Article III, § 1 serves both to protect "the role of the independent judiciary within the constitutional scheme of tripartite government," *Thomas, supra,* at 583, and to safeguard litigants' "right to have claims decided before judges who are free from potential domination by other branches of government." *United States v. Will,* 449 U.S. 200, 218 (1980). . . . Although our cases have provided us with little occasion to discuss the nature or significance of this latter safeguard, our prior discussions of Article III, § 1's guarantee of an independent and impartial adjudication by the federal judiciary of matters within the judicial power of the United States intimated that this guarantee serves to protect primarily personal, rather than structural, interests. . . .

Our precedents also demonstrate, however, that Article III does not confer on litigants an absolute right to the plenary consideration of every nature of claim by an Article III court. . . . Moreover, as a personal right, Article III's guarantee of an impartial and independent federal adjudication is subject to waiver, just as are other personal constitutional rights that dictate the procedures by which civil and criminal matters must be tried. . . .

In the instant case, Schor indisputably waived any right he may have possessed to the full trial of Conti's counterclaim before an Article III court. Schor expressly demanded that Conti proceed on its counterclaim in the reparations proceeding rather than before the District Court, and was content to have the entire dispute settled in the forum he had selected until the ALJ ruled against him on all counts; it was only after the ALJ rendered a decision to which he objected that Schor raised any challenge to the CFTC's consideration of Conti's counterclaim.

Even were there no evidence of an express waiver here, Schor's election to forgo his right to proceed in state or federal court on his claim and his decision to seek relief instead in a CFTC reparations proceeding constituted an effective waiver. Three years before Schor instituted his reparations action, a private right of action under the CEA was explicitly recognized in the circuit in which Schor and Conti filed suit in District Court. . . . Moreover, at the time Schor decided to seek relief before the CFTC rather than in the federal courts, the CFTC's regulations made clear that it was empowered to adjudicate all counterclaims "aris[ing] out of the same transaction or occurrence or series of transactions or occurrences set forth in the complaint." . . . Thus, Schor had the option of having the common law counterclaim against him adjudicated in a federal Article III court, but, with full knowledge that the CFTC would exercise jurisdiction over that claim, chose to avail himself of the quicker and less expensive procedure Congress had provided him. In such circumstances, it is clear that Schor effectively agreed to an adjudication by the CFTC of the entire controversy by seeking relief in this alternative forum. . . .

B

As noted above, our precedents establish that Article III, § 1 not only preserves to litigants their interest in an impartial and independent federal adjudication of claims within the judicial power of the United States, but also serves as "an inseparable element of the constitutional system of checks and balances." *Northern Pipeline, supra* at 53. . . . Article III, § 1 safeguards the role of the Judicial Branch in our tripartite system by barring congressional attempts "to transfer jurisdiction [to non-Article III tribunals] for the purpose of emasculating" constitutional courts, . . . and thereby preventing "the encroachment or aggrandizement of one branch at the expense of the other." *Buckley v. Valeo,* 424 U.S. 1, 122 (1976) (*per curiam*). To the extent that this structural principle is implicated in a given case, the parties cannot by consent cure the constitutional difficulty for the same reason that the parties by consent cannot confer on federal courts subject matter jurisdiction beyond the limitations imposed by Article III, § 2. . . . When these Article III limitations are at issue, notions of consent and waiver cannot be dispositive because the limitations serve institutional interests that the parties cannot be expected to protect.

In determining the extent to which a given congressional decision to authorize the adjudication of Article III business in a non-Article III tribunal impermissibly threatens the institutional integrity of the Judicial Branch, the Court has declined to adopt formalistic and unbending rules. *Thomas,* 473 U.S., at 587. Although such rules might lend a greater degree of coherence to this area of the law, they might also unduly constrict Congress' ability to take needed and innovative action pursuant to its Article I powers. Thus, in reviewing Article III challenges, we have weighed a number of factors, none of which has been deemed determinative, with an eye to the practical effect that the congressional action will have on the constitutionally assigned role of the federal judiciary. . . . Among the factors upon which we have focused are the extent to which the "essential attributes of judicial power" are reserved to Article III courts, and, conversely, the extent to which the non-Article III forum exercises the range of jurisdiction and powers normally vested only in Article III courts, the origins and importance of the right to be adjudicated, and the concerns that drove Congress to depart from the requirements of Article III. . . .

An examination of the relative allocation of powers between the CFTC and Article III courts in light of the considerations given prominence in our precedents demonstrates that the congressional scheme does not impermissibly intrude on the province of the judiciary. The CFTC's adjudicatory powers depart from the traditional agency model in just one respect: the CFTC's jurisdiction over common law counterclaims. While wholesale importation of concepts of pendent or ancillary jurisdiction into the agency context may create greater constitutional difficulties, we decline to endorse an absolute prohibition on such jurisdiction out of fear of where some hypothetical "slippery slope" may deposit us. Indeed, the CFTC's exercise of this type of jurisdiction is not without precedent. Thus, in *RFC v. Bankers Trust Co.,* 318 U.S. 163, 168-171 (1943), we saw no constitutional difficulty in the initial adjudication of a state law claim by a federal agency, subject to judicial review, when that claim was ancillary to a federal law dispute. Similarly, in *Katchen v. Landy,* 382 U.S. 323 (1966), this Court upheld a bankruptcy referee's power to hear and decide state law counterclaims against a creditor who filed a claim in bankruptcy when those counterclaims arose out of the same transaction. We reasoned that, as a practical matter, requiring the trustee to commence a plenary action to recover on its counterclaim would be a "meaningless gesture." . . .

In the instant case, we are likewise persuaded that there is little practical reason to find that this single deviation from the agency model is fatal to the congressional scheme. Aside from its authorization of counterclaim jurisdiction, the CEA leaves far more of the "essential attributes of judicial power" to Article III courts than did that portion of the Bankruptcy Act found unconstitutional in *Northern Pipeline.* The CEA scheme in fact hews closely to the agency model approved by the Court in *Crowell v. Benson,* 285 U.S. 22 (1932).

The CFTC, like the agency in *Crowell,* deals only with a "particularized area of law," *Northern Pipeline, supra,* at 85, whereas the jurisdiction of the bankruptcy courts found unconstitutional in *Northern Pipeline* extended to broadly "all civil proceedings arising under title 11 or arising in or *related to* cases under title 11." 28 U.S.C. § 1471(b) (quoted in *Northern Pipeline,* 458 U.S., at 85) (emphasis added). CFTC orders, like those of the agency in *Crowell,* but unlike those of the bankruptcy courts under the 1978 Act, are enforceable only by order of the District Court. . . . CFTC orders are also reviewed under the same "weight of the evidence" standard sustained in *Crowell,* rather than the more deferential standard found lacking in *Northern Pipeline.* . . . The legal rulings of the CFTC, like the legal determinations of the agency in *Crowell,* are subject to *de novo* review. Finally, the CFTC, unlike the bankruptcy courts under the 1978 Act, does not exercise "all ordinary powers of district courts," and thus may not, for instance, preside over jury trials or issue writs of habeas corpus. . . .

Of course, the nature of the claim has significance in our Article III analysis quite apart from the method prescribed for its adjudication. The counterclaim asserted in this case is a "private" right for which state law provides the rule of decision. It is therefore a claim of the kind assumed to be at the "core" of matters normally reserved to Article III courts. . . . Yet this conclusion does not end our inquiry; just as this Court has rejected any attempt to make determinative for Article III purposes the distinction between public rights and private rights, *Thomas, supra,* at 585-586, there is no reason inherent in separation of powers principles to accord the state law character of a claim talismanic power in Article III inquiries. . . .

We have explained that "the public rights doctrine reflects simply a pragmatic understanding that when Congress selects a quasi–judicial method of resolving matters that 'could be conclusively determined by the Executive and Legislative Branches,' the danger of encroaching on the judicial powers" is less than when private rights, which are normally within the purview of the judiciary, are relegated as an initial matter to administrative adjudication. *Thomas, supra,* 473 U.S., at 589 (quoting *Northern Pipeline, supra,* at 68). Similarly, the state law character of a claim is significant for purposes of determining the effect that an initial adjudication of those claims by a non-Article III tribunal will have on the separation of powers for the simple reason that private, common law rights were historically the types of matters subject to resolution by Article III courts. . . . The risk that Congress may improperly have encroached on the federal judiciary is obviously magnified when Congress "withdraw[s] from judicial cognizance any matter which, from its nature, is the subject of a suit at the common law, or in equity, or admiralty" and which therefore has traditionally been tried in Article III courts, and allocates the decision of those matters to a non-Article III forum of its own creation. *Murray's Lessee v. The Hoboken Land and Improvement Co.,* 18 How. 272, 284 (1856). Accordingly, where private, common law rights are at stake, our examination of the congressional attempt to control the manner in which those rights are adjudicated has been searching. . . . In this litigation, however, "[l]ooking beyond form to the substance of what" Congress has done, we are persuaded that the congressional authorization of limited CFTC jurisdiction over a narrow class of common law claims as an incident to the CFTC's primary, and unchallenged, adjudicative function does not create a substantial threat to the separation of powers. . . .

It is clear that Congress has not attempted to "withdraw from judicial cognizance" the determination of Conti's right to the sum represented by the debit balance in Schor's account. Congress gave the CFTC the authority to adjudicate such matters, but the decision to invoke this forum is left entirely to the parties and the power of the federal judiciary to take jurisdiction of these matters is unaffected. In such circumstances, separation of powers concerns are diminished, for it seems self-evident that just as Congress may encourage parties to settle a dispute out of court or resort to arbitration without impermissible incursions on the separation of powers, Congress may make available a quasi-judicial mechanism through which willing parties may, at their option, elect to resolve their differences. This is not to say, of course, that if Congress created a phalanx of non-Article III tribunals equipped to handle the entire business of the Article III courts without any Article III supervision or control and without evidence of valid and specific legislative necessities, the fact that the parties had the election to proceed in their forum of choice would necessarily save the scheme from constitutional attack. . . . But this case obviously bears no resemblance to such a scenario, given the degree of judicial control saved to the federal courts, . . . as well as the congressional purpose behind the jurisdictional delegation, the demonstrated need for the delegation, and the limited nature of the delegation.

When Congress authorized the CFTC to adjudicate counterclaims, its primary focus was on making effective a specific and limited federal regulatory scheme, not on allocating jurisdiction among federal tribunals. Congress intended to create an inexpensive and expeditious alternative forum through which customers could enforce the provisions of the CEA against professional brokers. Its decision to endow the CFTC with jurisdiction over such reparations claims is readily understandable given the perception that the CFTC was relatively immune from political pressures, . . . and the obvious expertise that the Commission possesses in applying the CEA and its own regulations. This reparations scheme itself is of unquestioned constitutional validity. . . . It was only to ensure the effectiveness of this scheme that Congress authorized the CFTC to assert jurisdiction over common law counterclaims. Indeed, as was explained above, absent the CFTC's exercise of that authority, the purposes of the reparations procedure would have been confounded.

It also bears emphasis that the CFTC's assertion of counterclaim jurisdiction is limited to that which is necessary to make the reparations procedure workable. *See* 7 U.S.C. § 12a(5). The CFTC adjudication of common law counterclaims is incidental to, and completely dependent upon, adjudication of reparations claims created by federal law, and in actual fact is limited to claims arising out of the same transaction or occurrence as the reparations claim.

In such circumstances, the magnitude of any intrusion on the Judicial Branch can only be termed *de minimis.* Conversely, were we to hold that the Legislative Branch may not permit such limited cognizance of common law counterclaims at the election of the parties, it is clear that we would "defeat the obvious purpose of the legislation to furnish a prompt, continuous, expert and inexpensive method for dealing with a class of questions of fact which are peculiarly suited to examination and determination by an administrative agency specially assigned to that task." *Crowell v. Benson, supra* at 46. *See also Thomas, supra* at 583-584. We do not think Article III compels this degree of prophylaxis.

Nor does our decision in *Bowsher v. Synar,* [this case was decided on the same day. It is set forth in Chapter Seven, § 7.04, *infra*] . . . require a contrary result. Unlike *Bowsher,* this case raises no question of the aggrandizement of congressional power at the expense of a coordinate branch. Instead, the separation of powers question presented in this case is whether Congress impermissibly undermined, without appreciable expansion of its own power, the role of the Judicial Branch. In any case, we have, consistent with *Bowsher,* looked to a number of factors in evaluating the extent to which the congressional scheme endangers separation of powers principles under the circumstances presented, but have found no genuine threat to those principles to be present in this case.

In so doing, we have also been faithful to our Article III precedents, which counsel that bright line rules cannot effectively be employed to yield broad principles applicable in all Article III inquiries. . . . Rather, due regard must be given in each case to the unique aspects of the congressional plan at issue and its practical consequences in light of the larger concerns that underlie Article III. We conclude that the limited jurisdiction that the CFTC asserts over state law claims as a necessary incident to the adjudication of federal claims willingly submitted by the parties for initial agency adjudication does not contravene separation of powers principles or Article III. . . .

The judgment of the Court of Appeals for the District of Columbia Circuit is reversed and the case remanded for further proceedings consistent with this opinion.

It is so ordered.

JUSTICE BRENNAN, with whom JUSTICE MARSHALL joins, dissenting.

Article III, § 1, of the Constitution provides that "[t]he judicial Power of the United States, shall be vested in one supreme Court, and in such inferior Courts as the Congress may from time to time ordain and establish." It further specifies that the federal judicial power must be exercised by judges who "shall hold their Offices during good Behavior, and [who] shall, at stated Times, receive for their Services a Compensation, which shall not be diminished during their Continuance in Office."

On its face, Article III, § 1, seems to prohibit the vesting of any judicial functions in either the Legislative or the Executive Branches. The Court has, however, recognized three narrow exceptions to the otherwise absolute mandate of Article III: territorial courts, . . . courts martial, and courts that adjudicate certain disputes concerning public rights. . . . Unlike the Court, I would limit the judicial authority of non-Article III federal tribunals to these few, long-established exceptions and would countenance no further erosion of Article III's mandate. . . .

NOTES AND QUESTIONS

6-41. The Court notes that the personal right of the commodity broker's customer in *Schor* to an Article III court had been waived. How would this case have been decided if there had been no such waiver?

6-42. Compare the majority's approach in *Schor* to that of the plurality in *Northern Pipeline*. What differences do you detect? What accounts for these differences?

6-43. Could you reach the same result in *Schor* by using the analysis and rhetoric of the plurality opinion in *Northern Pipeline*? Is the Commission in *Schor* not an adjunct of an Article III court? Does the majority in *Schor* use this approach?

6-44. What factors does the majority in *Schor* wish to consider to determine whether there has been an infringement on the powers of Article III courts?

6-45. Does the majority in *Schor* engage in a balancing approach? What goes into the balance? How does this square with Justice White's dissent in *Northern Pipeline*?

6-46. Does the balancing approach the Court applies in *Schor* sufficiently protect Article III courts? Consider the following summary in Young, *Public Rights and Federal Judicial Power: From* Murray's Lessee *through* Crowell *to* Schor, 35 BUFF. L. REV. 35 BUFF. L. REV. at 863–65 (1986):*

---

* Copyright © 1986 Buffalo Law Review. All rights reserved.

As the history of the public-rights exception . . . up to the time of *Crowell,* should make clear, the public rights category has not been a stable one. The standard nineteenth century public-rights case was a contest between a department of government and an individual concerning entitlement to a privilege. When regulation of private business became acceptable to some degree, the category of public-rights adjudication was extended, *de facto,* beyond cases involving privileges, to cover public law-enforcement suits brought by the government. Starting with actions against the railroads in 1887, extended to some suits against ordinary business corporations in 1914, and applied to many nominally private-rights actions in 1932, federal non-article III adjudication spread with a new view of the public interest.

In 1927, John Dickinson noted that the choice of recognition of a private right or a public action, or both, is largely a question of means for the legislature. Even early in this century, on occasion, private rights of action against private parties were conferred legislatively, largely for public purposes. Conversely, some suits by the government were old common-law actions in public-law garb. This has been even more true during recent years. Indeed, today it is often, though not always, fruitless to attempt to distinguish between federal rights of action created or recognized primarily for private, individual benefit, and those created as incentives for private policing of public values. As a result, any attempted public/private distinction, particularly a nominal one focusing on the nature of the parties to an adjudication, seems to provide no useful foundation for an exception to article III's requirements.

The Court has finally come to some recognition of these facts in *Thomas* and in *Schor.* The focus now is off arbitrary distinctions between the public and the private and between article I courts and adjuncts. The focus is now properly on balancing the need for non-article III adjudication against the threat it poses to a variety of private interests and rights, and to the tenured judiciary. The Court currently emphasizes the interplay of (1) the source, importance, and sensitivity of the rights to be adjudicated, (2) the practical need for non-article III adjudication, (3) the portion of the judicial power spectrum preempted by non-article III institutions, and (4) the degree of review available in the article III courts.

Given the long history of exceptions to article III, this look directly at the problem is for the good. Looking backwards nearly 200 years, it is, however, natural to wonder whether the changes were not so dramatic as to warrant a constitutional amendment. At some point, it becomes clear that a constitutional "symbol" has been so changed that it bears no resemblance to its former self. Perhaps even for so-called loose constructionists, this marks the limit of acceptable informal constitutional amendment by the courts. Our vantage point obscures the difficulty in recognizing when this point approaches: the dramatic change in article III, with a few exceptions, has been the product of a great many small adjustments. I understand and respect the sentiments of those who would wipe out 200 years of exceptions as illegitimate and of those who would seek the legitimating effect of a constitutional amendment. Neither approach seems realistic today.

Without abandoning 200 years of case law, the Court's current approach seems the best alternative for preserving a meaningful article III. The current Supreme Court continues to take the position that non-article III adjudication seems easiest to justify where congressionally created rights are at issue. Given the vast powers of the federal government to tax and to regulate, such cases may be of greater importance and sensitivity than actions resembling common-law damage suits. Still, the *Schor* Court's criteria may allow it to deal deftly with this constitutional-prudential problem by invalidating the more threatening forms of non-article III adjudication.

Do you agree? Is the balancing approach the Court now uses so open-ended they can do whatever they wish? *See Morrison v. Olson, infra,* SCALIA, J., dissenting.

6-47. Do you have any theories concerning why these issues would return to the fore over fifty years after *Crowell* was decided? Did the Court handle them any better this time around?

6-48. Consider the following argument about the relationship between Article I "tribunals" and Article III courts:

Although the Constitution speaks of "courts" both in Article III and elsewhere, it contains but a single reference to "tribunals," one appearing in the Inferior Tribunals Clause of Article I. Most observers have treated the words as synonyms, assuming that when Congress exercises the power to create inferior tribunals under Article I, the tribunals in question must meet the requirements of Article III and employ judges with salary and tenure protections. Distinguishing Article III courts from Article I tribunals, however, creates new possibilities. In particular, Article III can then be read to vest the judicial power in inferior federal "courts" but not in some inferior "tribunals" created under Article I. This interpretation suggests that Congress enjoys a degree of flexibility in creating Article I tribunals. On such a reading, the Inferior Tribunals Clause may empower Congress to create inferior "tribunals" with judges who lack Article III protections. While these tribunals must remain inferior to the Supreme Court and the judicial department, Article I does not require that they employ life-tenured judges and Article III does not formally invest these tribunals with the judicial power of the United States.

Such an "inferior tribunals" approach has a number of virtues. First, it suggests a textual solution to the nettlesome problem of incorporating Article I tribunals into the framework of Article III courts. This approach explains how the Court can insist on a strict adherence to the Article III requirement of life-tenured judges for lower federal courts, all of which exercise the judicial power of the United States, yet still recognize that the strict requirements of Article III do not apply to certain tribunals that Congress creates pursuant to Article I. Complementing this textual predicate for Congress's power to create tribunals, the Article I requirement of "inferiority" offers an important justification for the widely accepted notion that the legality of such tribunals depends in part on the availability of judicial review in Article III courts.

. . . .

Finally, the inferior tribunals thesis provides an account of the scope and limits of congressional power to create tribunals outside of Article III. In contrast to the consensus in the literature, which portrays their creation as an act of simple expediency, institutional history reveals that Congress often created Article I tribunals as forums to hear disputes that, for one reason or another, were thought to lie beyond the judicial power of the United States. Article III permits federal courts to exercise power only in circumstances in which the judicial department is to have the last word, free from revision at the hands of the political departments. Such a requirement of judicial finality was thought to preclude Article III courts from hearing "public rights" claims for money against the federal government, at least when Congress retained legislative discretion over payment, and proceedings in the nature of courts-martial, which were subject to review that occurred inside the executive branch. Similarly, Article III courts exercising the limited judicial power of the United States were not thought appropriate to hear disputes over the local common law of contract, property, and probate that filled the dockets of the territorial courts.

The perceived inability of the Article III judiciary to hear disputes in the first instance did not mean that Congress could place the work of Article I tribunals entirely beyond the reach of the constitutional courts. To the contrary, Article III courts frequently oversaw the work of Article I tribunals. Article III courts policed the jurisdictional boundaries of courts-martial, either by considering petitions for writs of habeas corpus by those claiming to have been wrongly detained for trial before such tribunals, or by hearing common law suits for trespass against those who convened such tribunals unlawfully. . . .

This portrait of Article I tribunals as acting outside of the judicial power while remaining subject to the oversight and control of Article III courts finds a reflection in modern cases and helps to solve a number of problems in the literature. Perhaps most importantly, it makes clear that the recognition of exceptions to Article III does not imply that Congress can create tribunals and place them entirely beyond the supervisory authority of the federal courts. It thus avoids the problem — sometimes implicit in discussions of exceptionalism — that Congress might frustrate the judiciary's role entirely through reliance upon one or more exceptions. The most pressing modern variant of this argument arises from President George W. Bush's decision to create military tribunals for the adjudication of criminal claims against individuals designated as enemy combatants. Although the government has argued for an exceedingly restricted judicial role in overseeing the operation of such tribunals, the inferior tribunals account rejects this contention. At least when such tribunals operate within the jurisdiction of the United States, they must remain inferior to the Supreme Court and subject to judicial review as to certain claims of federal right.

James E. Pfander, *Article I Tribunals, Article III Courts, and the Judicial Power of the United States*, 118 HARV. L. REV. 643, 650-53 (2004).*

---

* Copyright © 2004 Harvard Law Review Association. All rights reserved.

Chapter 7
EXECUTIVE CONTROL OF AGENCY DISCRETION

§ 7.01 Introduction

The Constitutional basis for executive control of the bureaucracy is found in Article II of the Constitution, which vests executive power in the President. As Professor Corwin noted long ago, however, "executive power" is a "term of uncertain content."[1] Article II refers specifically to some issues that directly affect administrative agencies. Article II, § 2, cl. 1, for example, requires "the Opinion, in writing" of certain heads of departments at the President's request; Article II, § 2, cl. 2 gives the President the power to appoint "officers of the United States" with the "advice and consent of the Senate." More important, Article II, § 3 requires that the President "take care that the laws be faithfully executed." As Professor Strauss has noted, "these provisions suggest a supervisory, perhaps even a caretaker presidential role."[2]

For a variety of reasons, both the need for and the reality of executive control of the bureaucracy has been steadily increasing. The federal bureaucracy itself has grown considerably since the New Deal. As Professor Lowi has noted, "Congress enacted more regulatory programs in the five years between 1969 and 1974 than during any other comparable period in our history, including the first five years of the New Deal."[3] He describes a "binge" in new programs, embraced by Republicans as well as Democrats, who enacted regulatory policies "broader in scope and more unconditional in delegated discretion than any other programs in American history."[4] Illustrative of this expansion was the 300% increase in the number of pages in the Federal Register over this period, growing from 20,000 pages in 1970 to 60,000 pages by 1976.[5]

As Presidents have sought to assert greater executive control, particularly in deregulatory contexts, tensions have arisen between the Congress and the President that highlight some important institutional differences between the Congress and the Presidency. Consider the following:

---

[1] E. Corwin, *The President: Office and Power* 3 (1957).

[2] Strauss, *The Place of Agencies in Government: Separation of Powers and the Fourth Branch*, 84 COLUM. L. REV. 573, 598 (1984).

[3] Lowi, *Two Roads to Serfdom: Liberalism, Conservatism, and Administrative Power*, 36 AM. U. L. REV. 295, 298 (1987).

[4] *Id.*

[5] *See, e.g.,* Theodore Lowi, *The End of Liberalism: The Second Republic of the United States* 113 (2d. ed. 1979) (citing William Lilley & James C. Miller, *The New Social Regulation*, THE PUBLIC INTEREST (Spring 1977, at 49).

Aman, ADMINISTRATIVE LAW IN A GLOBAL ERA

121-25 (Cornell Univ. Press 1992)*

Perhaps the most significant trend in administrative law, particularly since the beginnings of the Environmental Era, is the steady increase in presidential power over the administrative process. Gone are the days when an effective President merely managed legislative policymaking and carried out traditional executive functions such as foreign affairs. As the bureaucracy has grown, particularly with the addition of the legislative programs and new bureaucracies established in the 1970s, it has become unwieldy and has produced a great quantity of new law. As we have seen, effective executive coordination of these various law-making centers, many of which are executive in character, requires greater executive influence over policy initiation and implementation as well as greater executive control over the legal output of the bureaucracy. This is particularly true for strong Presidents who seek to effect sweeping policy changes through comprehensive administrative reforms. Too much executive influence, however, can transform the administrative presidency into a modified form of parliamentary government. The executive does not control the legislative process, but it does control the administrative process. To the extent Congress fails to constrain the executive or participate more directly in the creation of a regulatory framework for a new era, the executive's increasing domination of the law-making power of the administrative process begins to suggest the control of a prime minister rather than the supervisory role of a president.

The significant increase in the scope of executive management of the law-making processes of agencies, both executive and independent, coincides with the increasing failure of Congress to act authoritatively or consistently regarding comprehensive regulatory reforms, particularly when those reforms have global consequences. By nature, Congress' outlook is more domestic and regional, if not parochial, than that of the President. From an institutional point of view, the President is the official one can expect to have not only a national, but also an international, perspective. His responsibility for foreign affairs and for our nation's role in the interdependent global economy, at least hypothetically, obliges him to take a more global outlook. It is more difficult to capture a decision maker with such a broad and varied constituency. To the extent comprehensive regulatory reforms that recognize global realities are possible, they are more likely to be generated more consistently at the presidential level.

Nevertheless, Congress is theoretically the body that can create new regulatory histories and new beginnings by passing new laws or repealing old ones. It can, if it chooses, wipe clean the statutory slate, leaving only the market in its place. The fact that Congress rarely takes such radical action is due, in part, to what political scientists have described as the "science of muddling through." Congress often acts as if it collectively has a predominantly common-law cast of mind and usually effects change incrementally. Moreover, an institution created to represent local and regional interests may

---

* Copyright © 1992. Reprinted by permission of Cornell University Press. All rights reserved.

have a particularly difficult time coping with issues that have a significant global component. Indeed, some of the institutional changes in Congress arguably have exacerbated these gradualist tendencies, transforming Congress' penchant for moderation into inaction, making Congress too easily manipulated by groups whose main goal is to maintain the status quo.

The increased emphasis on re-election in Congress, and the excessive careerism and parochialism that this preoccupation can spawn, coupled with the breakdown of party hierarchy and discipline, make decisive, innovative congressional action increasingly rare. Institutional changes in Congress's own in-house structure and procedures can also mitigate against decisive change. As one commentator has noted, "the organization of Congress meets remarkably well the needs of its members." Interest group politics accord a disproportionate amount of power to those seeking to preserve the status quo and enable elected officials to pursue an increasingly narrow conception of their job.

Perhaps even more important, the rise of political action committees (PACs) and the role that money plays on Capital Hill make Congress too responsive to short-term political demands. This does not necessarily result in rapid or radical change. Rather, it increases the ability of one interest group to stymie the goals of another, particularly when comprehensive change is demanded. Change that requires some clear commitment to an overriding vision is likely to provoke a variety of powerful, wealthy groups, both for and against the change.

The Global Era will accelerate these forces of fragmentation in Congress by raising a series of new issues and concerns that ultimately will require major, comprehensive legislative change, the kind of change most difficult for Congress to accomplish. More fundamentally, however, the Global Era highlights the institutional limits of Congress. Congress is an institution created to focus largely on local and regional concerns. As an institution, Congress often has conceptualized global regulatory concerns in protectionist terms. Thus, the ability of Congress as an institution to take a truly global perspective on future issues is and will likely remain a major institutional and political challenge.

Along with the application of market approaches to regulation in this Global Era is an increase in the use of market approaches to explain congressional behavior. Public choice theories tend to see individual congressmen as subject to various political vectors capable of moving them in directions directly proportional to the strength of the political force represented. These theories almost always assume passive venality on the part of legislators. Whatever their empirical merits, these theories illustrate quite clearly a perspective on legislative politics as removed from, if not antithetical to, principled deliberation in the public interest. Congress is increasingly a collection of local enterprises in which legislators act as independent contractors, rather than as representatives of an organic body with a definitive national purpose. In the absence of an almost overwhelmingly strong political force for change, Congress seems increasingly content to live with a stalemate rather than risk comprehensive change, especially before the politics of new situations are fully sorted out. Unfortunately, stasis can often be worse than inappropriate reforms.

Increased executive control over agency policymaking in the 1970s and 1980s has occurred largely at the expense of congressional control. To some extent, however, Congress has apparently approved of this shift, both affirmatively and passively. Congress has affirmatively created many agencies that are more executive in nature than the independent agencies of the New Deal. One would expect the President to exercise control over these entities. But the executive control that has resulted is not limited to increased coordination and clarity of purpose. The executive has introduced substantive changes as well, particularly in the context of deregulation. Many of the substantive, deregulatory policies of the executive have been implemented by agencies, and Congress has neither affirmed these new directions nor disapproved of them. The New Deal and Environmental Eras . . . [were] marked by the passage of specific congressional programs, inspired or at least backed by the President. Congress passed the laws that courts ultimately interpreted and extended in the New Deal Era and in the Environmental Era that followed. While agency deregulation under these acts can be interpreted as similar to the regulatory extensions that agencies adopted in previous eras, it is important to emphasize that the most distinctive feature of the politics of efficiency is that no specific legislative program marks this new era. With the exception of congressional deregulation of the Civil Aeronautics Board and a few other deregulatory statutes, deregulation is essentially a program carried out by the executive branch through executive orders, appointments of efficiency-minded individuals, vigorous executive control over decisions not to enforce certain existing rules and regulations, and agency attempts to rescind some rules and replace them with more cost-effective or market-oriented approaches.

With few exceptions, Congress has neither repealed nor amended the statutes now used to effect these changes. Its primary contribution to deregulation has been indirect, in the form of budgetary legislation and tax reductions. These statutes have pressured agencies to scale down their programs, goals, and statutory mandates. But such statutes differ markedly from those of the New Deal and Environmental Eras. Their impact on substantive law is indirect. They do not provide the legal guidance to courts that statutory interpretation usually requires. They are more like presidential speeches, hortatory rather than prescriptive. They are all part of the atmosphere or mood of the times — a mood that agencies have tried to read, and, occasionally force, into their own statutory mandates.

The rise of the administrative presidency is, in short, spurred by the management needs of an unwieldy bureaucracy and the new substantive demands of a global era. But management evolves into legislation when the market becomes an end in and of itself. If the same processes of change used in the Environmental and New Deal Eras are to be used to define the contours of the Global Era, Congress must play a much more direct and substantive role. There are constitutional and statutory limits to the extent of change possible if only an administrative strategy is employed. Congress and the President must define the global scope of our regulatory structure. Both branches must help to shape the contours of a new global relevant body of law.

We shall now examine some of the primary sources of executive control, including the power to appoint and the power to remove certain officers of the United States. We shall begin, however, with an attempt by Congress to give the executive branch greater control over government spending in the form of a line item veto.

§ 7.02 Controlling Spending: The Line Item Veto

CLINTON v. CITY OF NEW YORK

Supreme Court of the United States
524 U.S. 417 (1998)

STEVENS, J., delivered the opinion of the Court, in which REHNQUIST, C.J., and KENNEDY, SOUTER, THOMAS, and GINSBURG, JJ., joined. KENNEDY, J., filed a concurring opinion. SCALIA, J., filed an opinion concurring in part and dissenting in part, in which O'CONNOR, J., joined, and in which BREYER, J., joined as to Part III. BREYER, J., filed a dissenting opinion, in which O'CONNOR and SCALIA, JJ., joined as to Part III.

JUSTICE STEVENS delivered the opinion of the Court.

The Line Item Veto Act (Act) was enacted in April 1996 and became effective on January 1, 1997. The following day, six Members of Congress who had voted against the Act brought suit in the District Court for the District of Columbia challenging its constitutionality. On April 10, 1997, the District Court entered an order holding that the Act is unconstitutional. *Byrd v. Raines*, 956 F.Supp. 25 (D.D.C.1997). In obedience to the statutory direction to allow a direct, expedited appeal to this Court, we promptly noted probable jurisdiction and expedited review. We determined, however, that the Members of Congress did not have standing to sue because they had not "alleged a sufficiently concrete injury to have established Article III standing," *Raines v. Byrd*, 521 U.S. 811, 830 (1997); thus, "[i]n . . . light of [the] overriding and time-honored concern about keeping the Judiciary's power within its proper constitutional sphere," *id.*, at 820, we remanded the case to the District Court with instructions to dismiss the complaint for lack of jurisdiction.

Less than two months after our decision in that case, the President exercised his authority to cancel one provision in the Balanced Budget Act of 1997 . . . and two provisions in the Taxpayer Relief Act of 1997. . . . Appellees, claiming that they had been injured by two of those cancellations, filed these cases in the District Court. That Court again held the statute invalid, and we again expedited our review. We now hold that these appellees have standing to challenge the constitutionality of the Act and, reaching the merits, we agree that the cancellation procedures set forth in the Act violate the Presentment Clause, Art. I, § 7, cl. 2, of the Constitution.

I

We begin by reviewing the canceled items that are at issue in these cases.

Section 4722(c) of the Balanced Budget Act

Title XIX of the Social Security Act, 79 Stat. 343, as amended, authorizes the Federal Government to transfer huge sums of money to the States to help finance medical care for the indigent. In 1991, Congress directed that those federal subsidies be reduced by the amount of certain taxes levied by the States on health care providers. In 1994, the Department of Health and Human Services (HHS) notified the State of New York that 15 of its taxes were covered by the 1991 Act, and that as of June 30, 1994, the statute therefore required New York to return $955 million to the United States. The notice advised the State that it could apply for a waiver on certain statutory grounds. New York did request a waiver for those tax programs, as well as for a number of others, but HHS has not formally acted on any of those waiver requests. New York has estimated that the amount at issue for the period from October 1992 through March 1997 is as high as $2.6 billion.

Because HHS had not taken any action on the waiver requests, New York turned to Congress for relief. On August 5, 1997, Congress enacted a law that resolved the issue in New York's favor. Section 4722(c) of the Balanced Budget Act of 1997 identifies the disputed taxes and provides that they "are deemed to be permissible health care related taxes and in compliance with the requirements" of the relevant provisions of the 1991 statute.

On August 11, 1997, the President sent identical notices to the Senate and to the House of Representatives canceling "one item of new direct spending," specifying § 4722(c) as that item, and stating that he had determined that "this cancellation will reduce the Federal budget deficit." He explained that § 4722(c) would have permitted New York "to continue relying upon impermissible provider taxes to finance its Medicaid program" and that "[t]his preferential treatment would have increased Medicaid costs, would have treated New York differently from all other States, and would have established a costly precedent for other States to request comparable treatment."

Section 968 of the Taxpayer Relief Act of 1977

A person who realizes a profit from the sale of securities is generally subject to a capital gains tax. Under existing law, however, an ordinary business corporation can acquire a corporation, including a food processing or refining company, in a merger or stock-for-stock transaction in which no gain is recognized to the seller; the seller's tax payment, therefore, is deferred. If, however, the purchaser is a farmers' cooperative, the parties cannot structure such a transaction because the stock of the cooperative may be held only by its members; thus, a seller dealing with a farmers' cooperative cannot obtain the benefits of tax deferral.

In § 968 of the Taxpayer Relief Act of 1997, Congress amended § 1042 of the Internal Revenue Code to permit owners of certain food refiners and processors to defer the recognition of gain if they sell their stock to eligible farmers' cooperatives. The purpose of the amendment, as repeatedly explained by its sponsors, was "to facilitate the transfer of refiners and processors to farmers' cooperatives." The amendment to § 1042 was one of the 79 "limited tax benefits" authorized by the Taxpayer Relief Act of 1997 and specifically identified in Title XVII of that Act as "subject to [the] line item veto."

On the same date that he canceled the "item of new direct spending" involving New York's health care programs, the President also canceled this limited tax benefit. In his explanation of that action, the President endorsed the objective of encouraging "value-added farming through the purchase by farmers' cooperatives of refiners or processors of agricultural goods," but concluded that the provision lacked safeguards and also "failed to target its benefits to small-and-medium-size cooperatives."

II

Appellees filed two separate actions against the President and other federal officials challenging these two cancellations. The plaintiffs in the first case are the City of New York, two hospital associations, one hospital, and two unions representing health care employees. The plaintiffs in the second are a farmers' cooperative consisting of about 30 potato growers in Idaho and an individual farmer who is a member and officer of the cooperative. The District Court consolidated the two cases and determined that at least one of the plaintiffs in each had standing under Article III of the Constitution.

. . . .

On the merits, the District Court held that the cancellations did not conform to the constitutionally mandated procedures for the enactment or repeal of laws in two respects. First, the laws that resulted after the cancellations "were different from those consented to by both Houses of Congress." Moreover, the President violated Article I "when he unilaterally canceled provisions of duly enacted statutes." As a separate basis for its decision, the District Court also held that the Act "impermissibly disrupts the balance of powers among the three branches of government."

. . . .

IV

The Line Item Veto Act gives the President the power to "cancel in whole" three types of provisions that have been signed into law: "(1) any dollar amount of discretionary budget authority; (2) any item of new direct spending; or (3) any limited tax benefit." It is undisputed that the New York case involves an "item of new direct spending" and that the Snake River case involves a "limited tax benefit" as those terms are defined in the Act. It is also undisputed that each of those provisions had been signed into law pursuant to Article I, § 7, of the Constitution before it was canceled.

The Act requires the President to adhere to precise procedures whenever he exercises his cancellation authority. In identifying items for cancellation he must consider the legislative history, the purposes, and other relevant information about the items. He must determine, with respect to each cancellation, that it will "(i) reduce the Federal budget deficit; (ii) not impair any essential Government functions; and (iii) not harm the national interest." Moreover, he must transmit a special message to Congress notifying it of each cancellation within five calendar days (excluding Sundays) after the enactment of the canceled provision. It is undisputed that the President meticulously followed these procedures in these cases.

A cancellation takes effect upon receipt by Congress of the special message from the President. If, however, a "disapproval bill" pertaining to a special message is enacted into law, the cancellations set forth in that message become "null and void." The Act sets forth a detailed expedited procedure for the consideration of a "disapproval bill," but no such bill was passed for either of the cancellations involved in these cases. A majority vote of both Houses is sufficient to enact a disapproval bill. The Act does not grant the President the authority to cancel a disapproval bill, but he does, of course, retain his constitutional authority to veto such a bill.

The effect of a cancellation is plainly stated in § 691e, which defines the principal terms used in the Act. With respect to both an item of new direct spending and a limited tax benefit, the cancellation prevents the item "from having legal force or effect." Thus, under the plain text of the statute, the two actions of the President that are challenged in these cases prevented one section of the Balanced Budget Act of 1997 and one section of the Taxpayer Relief Act of 1997 "from having legal force or effect." The remaining provisions of those statutes, with the exception of the second canceled item in the latter, continue to have the same force and effect as they had when signed into law.

In both legal and practical effect, the President has amended two Acts of Congress by repealing a portion of each. "[R]epeal of statutes, no less than enactment, must conform with Art. I." *INS v. Chadha*, 462 U.S. 919, 954 (1983). . . . Although the Constitution expressly authorizes the President to play a role in the process of enacting statutes, it is silent on the subject of unilateral Presidential action that either repeals or amends parts of duly enacted statutes. . . .

V

The Government advances two related arguments to support its position that despite the unambiguous provisions of the Act, cancellations do not amend or repeal properly enacted statutes in violation of the Presentment Clause. First, relying primarily on *Field v. Clark*, 143 U.S. 649 (1892), the Government contends that the cancellations were merely exercises of discretionary authority granted to the President by the Balanced Budget Act and the Taxpayer Relief Act read in light of the previously enacted Line Item Veto Act. Second, the Government submits that the substance of the authority to cancel tax and spending items "is, in practical effect, no more and no less than the power to 'decline to spend' specified sums of money, or to 'decline to implement' specified tax measures." Neither argument is persuasive.

In *Field v. Clark*, the Court upheld the constitutionality of the Tariff Act of 1890. That statute contained a "free list" of almost 300 specific articles that were exempted from import duties "unless otherwise specially provided for in this act." Section 3 was a special provision that directed the President to suspend that exemption for sugar, molasses, coffee, tea, and hides "whenever, and so often" as he should be satisfied that any country producing and exporting those products imposed duties on the agricultural products of the United States that he deemed to be "reciprocally unequal and unreasonable. . . ." The section then specified the duties to be imposed on those products during any such suspension. The Court provided this explanation for its conclusion that § 3 had not delegated legislative power to the President:

> "Nothing involving the expediency or the just operation of such legislation was left to the determination of the President. . . . [W]hen he ascertained the fact that duties and exactions, reciprocally unequal and unreasonable, were imposed upon the agricultural or other products of the United States by a country producing and exporting sugar, molasses, coffee, tea or hides, it became his duty to issue a proclamation declaring the suspension, as to that country, which Congress had determined should occur. He had no discretion in the premises except in respect to the duration of the suspension so ordered. But that related only to the enforcement of the policy established by Congress. As the suspension was absolutely required when the President ascertained the existence of a particular fact, it cannot be said that in ascertaining that fact and in issuing his proclamation, in obedience to the legislative will, he exercised the function of making laws. . . . It was a part of the law itself as it left the hands of Congress that the provisions, full and complete in themselves, permitting the free introduction of sugars, molasses, coffee, tea and hides, from particular countries, should be suspended, in a given contingency, and that in case of such suspensions certain duties should be imposed."

This passage identifies three critical differences between the power to suspend the exemption from import duties and the power to cancel portions of a duly enacted statute. First, the exercise of the suspension power was contingent upon a condition that did not exist when the Tariff Act was passed: the imposition of "reciprocally unequal and unreasonable" import duties by other countries. In contrast, the exercise of the cancellation power within five days after the enactment of the Balanced Budget and Tax Reform Acts necessarily was based on the same conditions that Congress evaluated when it passed those statutes. Second, under the Tariff Act, when the President determined that the contingency had arisen, he had a duty to suspend; in contrast, while it is true that the President was required by the Act to make three determinations before he canceled a provision, those determinations did not qualify his discretion to cancel or not to cancel. Finally, whenever the President suspended an exemption under the Tariff Act, he was executing the policy that Congress had embodied in the statute. In contrast, whenever the President cancels an item of new direct spending or a limited tax benefit he is rejecting the policy judgment made by Congress and relying on his own policy judgment. . . .

Neither are we persuaded by the Government's contention that the President's authority to cancel new direct spending and tax benefit items is no greater than his traditional authority to decline to spend appropriated funds.

The Government has reviewed in some detail the series of statutes in which Congress has given the Executive broad discretion over the expenditure of appropriated funds. For example, the First Congress appropriated "sum[s] not exceeding" specified amounts to be spent on various Government operations. In those statutes, as in later years, the President was given wide discretion with respect to both the amounts to be spent and how the money would be allocated among different functions. It is argued that the Line Item Veto Act merely confers comparable discretionary authority over the expenditure of appropriated funds. The critical difference between this statute and all of its predecessors, however, is that unlike any of them, this Act gives the President the unilateral power to change the text of duly enacted statutes. None of the Act's predecessors could even arguably have been construed to authorize such a change. . . .

VI

. . . .

. . . The Balanced Budget Act of 1997 is a 500-page document that became "Public Law 105-33" after three procedural steps were taken: (1) a bill containing its exact text was approved by a majority of the Members of the House of Representatives; (2) the Senate approved precisely the same text; and (3) that text was signed into law by the President. The Constitution explicitly requires that each of those three steps be taken before a bill may "become a law." Art. I, § 7. If one paragraph of that text had been omitted at any one of those three stages, Public Law 105-33 would not have been validly enacted. If the Line Item Veto Act were valid, it would authorize the President to create a different law — one whose text was not voted on by either House of Congress or presented to the President for signature. Something that might be known as "Public Law 105-33 as modified by the President" may or may not be desirable, but it is surely not a document that may "become a law" pursuant to the procedures designed by the Framers of Article I, § 7, of the Constitution.

If there is to be a new procedure in which the President will play a different role in determining the final text of what may "become a law," such change must come not by legislation but through the amendment procedures set forth in Article V of the Constitution.

The judgment of the District Court is affirmed.

It is so ordered.

JUSTICE KENNEDY, concurring.

A Nation cannot plunder its own treasury without putting its Constitution and its survival in peril. The statute before us, then, is of first importance, for it seems undeniable the Act will tend to restrain persistent excessive spending. Nevertheless, for the reasons given by JUSTICE STEVENS in the opinion for the Court, the statute must be found invalid. Failure of political will does not justify unconstitutional remedies.

I write to respond to my colleague JUSTICE BREYER, who observes that the statute does not threaten the liberties of individual citizens, a point on which

I disagree. The argument is related to his earlier suggestion that our role is lessened here because the two political branches are adjusting their own powers between themselves. To say the political branches have a somewhat free hand to reallocate their own authority would seem to require acceptance of two premises: first, that the public good demands it, and second, that liberty is not at risk. The former premise is inadmissible. The Constitution's structure requires a stability which transcends the convenience of the moment. The latter premise, too, is flawed. Liberty is always at stake when one or more of the branches seek to transgress the separation of powers. . . .

In recent years, perhaps, we have come to think of liberty as defined by that word in the Fifth and Fourteenth Amendments and as illuminated by the other provisions of the Bill of Rights. The conception of liberty embraced by the Framers was not so confined. They used the principles of separation of powers and federalism to secure liberty in the fundamental political sense of the term, quite in addition to the idea of freedom from intrusive governmental acts. The idea and the promise were that when the people delegate some degree of control to a remote central authority, one branch of government ought not possess the power to shape their destiny without a sufficient check from the other two. In this vision, liberty demands limits on the ability of any one branch to influence basic political decisions. . . .

The principal object of the statute, it is true, was not to enhance the President's power to reward one group and punish another, to help one set of taxpayers and hurt another, to favor one State and ignore another. Yet these are its undeniable effects. The law establishes a new mechanism which gives the President the sole ability to hurt a group that is a visible target, in order to disfavor the group or to extract further concessions from Congress. The law is the functional equivalent of a line item veto and enhances the President's powers beyond what the Framers would have endorsed.

It is no answer, of course, to say that Congress surrendered its authority by its own hand; nor does it suffice to point out that a new statute, signed by the President or enacted over his veto, could restore to Congress the power it now seeks to relinquish. That a congressional cession of power is voluntary does not make it innocuous. The Constitution is a compact enduring for more than our time, and one Congress cannot yield up its own powers, much less those of other Congresses to follow. Abdication of responsibility is not part of the constitutional design.

. . . .

JUSTICE SCALIA, with whom JUSTICE O'CONNOR joins, and with whom JUSTICE BREYER joins as to Part III, concurring in part and dissenting in part.

. . . .

III

. . . .

Article I, § 7, of the Constitution obviously prevents the President from canceling a law that Congress has not authorized him to cancel. Such action cannot possibly be considered part of his execution of the law, and if it is legislative action, as the Court observes, "'repeal of statutes, no less than enactment, must conform with Art. I.'" *Ante*, at 2103, quoting from *INS v. Chadha*, 462 U.S. 919, 954 (1983). But that is not this case. It was certainly arguable, as an original matter, that Art. I, § 7, also prevents the President from canceling a law which itself *authorizes* the President to cancel it. But as the Court acknowledges, that argument has long since been made and rejected. In 1809, Congress passed a law authorizing the President to cancel trade restrictions against Great Britain and France if either revoked edicts directed at the United States. Joseph Story regarded the conferral of that authority as entirely unremarkable in *The Orono*, 18 F. Cas. 830, No. 10,585, (CCD Mass. 1812). The Tariff Act of 1890 authorized the President to "suspend, by proclamation to that effect" certain of its provisions if he determined that other countries were imposing "reciprocally unequal and unreasonable" duties. This Court upheld the constitutionality of that Act in *Field v. Clark*. . . .

As much as the Court goes on about Art. I, § 7, therefore, that provision does not demand the result the Court reaches. It no more categorically prohibits the Executive *reduction* of congressional dispositions in the course of implementing statutes that authorize such reduction, than it categorically prohibits the Executive *augmentation* of congressional dispositions in the course of implementing statutes that authorize such augmentation — generally known as substantive rulemaking. There are, to be sure, limits upon the former just as there are limits upon the latter — and I am prepared to acknowledge that the limits upon the former may be much more severe. Those limits are established, however, not by some categorical prohibition of Art. I, § 7, which our cases conclusively disprove, but by what has come to be known as the doctrine of unconstitutional delegation of legislative authority: When authorized Executive reduction or augmentation is allowed to go too far, it usurps the nondelegable function of Congress and violates the separation of powers.

It is this doctrine, and not the Presentment Clause, that was discussed in the *Field* opinion, and it is this doctrine, and not the Presentment Clause, that is the issue presented by the statute before us here. . . .

Insofar as the degree of political, "lawmaking" power conferred upon the Executive is concerned, there is not a dime's worth of difference between Congress's authorizing the President to *cancel* a spending item, and Congress's authorizing money to be spent on a particular item at the President's discretion. And the latter has been done since the founding of the Nation. From 1789-1791, the First Congress made lump-sum appropriations for the entire Government — "sum[s] not exceeding" specified amounts for broad purposes. From a very early date Congress also made permissive individual appropriations, leaving the decision whether to spend the money to the President's unfettered discretion. In 1803, it appropriated $50,000 for the President to build "not exceeding fifteen gun boats, to be armed, manned and fitted out, and employed for such purposes as in his opinion the public service may require," President Jefferson reported that "[t]he sum of fifty thousand dollars appropriated by Congress for providing gun boats remains unexpended. The favorable and peaceable turn of affairs on the Mississippi rendered an immediate execution of that law unnecessary." Examples of appropriations committed to the discretion of the President abound in our history. . . . The constitutionality of such appropriations has never seriously been questioned. . . .

The short of the matter is this: Had the Line Item Veto Act authorized the President to "decline to spend" any item of spending contained in the Balanced Budget Act of 1997, there is not the slightest doubt that authorization would have been constitutional. What the Line Item Veto Act does instead — authorizing the President to "cancel" an item of spending — is technically different. But the technical difference does *not* relate to the technicalities of the Presentment Clause, which have been fully complied with; and the doctrine of unconstitutional delegation, which *is* at issue here, is preeminently *not* a doctrine of technicalities. The title of the Line Item Veto Act, which was perhaps designed to simplify for public comprehension, or perhaps merely to comply with the terms of a campaign pledge, has succeeded in faking out the Supreme Court. The President's action it authorizes in fact is not a line-item veto and thus does not offend Art. I, § 7; and insofar as the substance of that action is concerned, it is no different from what Congress has permitted the President to do since the formation of the Union. . . .

JUSTICE BREYER, with whom JUSTICE O'CONNOR and JUSTICE SCALIA join as to Part III, dissenting.

I

I agree with the Court that the parties have standing, but I do not agree with its ultimate conclusion. In my view the Line Item Veto Act (Act) does not violate any specific textual constitutional command, nor does it violate any implicit separation-of-powers principle. Consequently, I believe that the Act is constitutional.

II

I approach the constitutional question before us with three general considerations in mind. *First*, the Act represents a legislative effort to provide the President with the power to give effect to some, but not to all, of the expenditure and revenue-diminishing provisions contained in a single massive appropriations bill. And this objective is constitutionally proper.

When our Nation was founded, Congress could easily have provided the President with this kind of power. In that time period, our population was less than 4 million, federal employees numbered fewer than 5,000, annual federal budget outlays totaled approximately $4 million, and the entire operative text of Congress' first general appropriations law read as follows:

> "Be it enacted . . . [t]hat there be appropriated for the service of the present year, to be paid out of the monies which arise, either from the requisitions heretofore made upon the several states, or from the duties on import and tonnage, the following sums, viz. A sum not exceeding two hundred and sixteen thousand dollars for defraying the expenses of the civil list, under the late and present government; a sum not exceeding one

hundred and thirty-seven thousand dollars for defraying the expenses of the department of war; a sum not exceeding one hundred and ninety thousand dollars for discharging the warrants issued by the late board of treasury, and remaining unsatisfied; and a sum not exceeding ninety-six thousand dollars for paying the pensions to invalids." Act of Sept. 29, 1789, ch. 23, § 1, 1 Stat. 95.

At that time, a Congress, wishing to give a President the power to select among appropriations, could simply have embodied each appropriation in a separate bill, each bill subject to a separate Presidential veto.

Today, however, our population is about 250 million, the Federal Government employs more than 4 million people, the annual federal budget is $1.5 trillion, and a typical budget appropriations bill may have a dozen titles, hundreds of sections, and spread across more than 500 pages of the Statutes at Large. Congress cannot divide such a bill into thousands, or tens of thousands, of separate appropriations bills, each one of which the President would have to sign, or to veto, separately. Thus, the question is whether the Constitution permits Congress to choose a particular novel *means* to achieve this same, constitutionally legitimate, *end*. . . .

[T]he fact that the Act may closely resemble a different, literally unconstitutional, arrangement is beside the point. To drive exactly 65 miles per hour on an interstate highway closely resembles an act that violates the speed limit. But it does not violate that limit, for small differences matter when the question is one of literal violation of law. No more does this Act literally violate the Constitution's words. . . .

III

The Court believes that the Act violates the literal text of the Constitution. A simple syllogism captures its basic reasoning:

Major Premise: The Constitution sets forth an exclusive method for enacting, repealing, or amending laws.

Minor Premise: The Act authorizes the President to "repea[l] or amen[d]" laws in a different way, namely by announcing a cancellation of a portion of a previously enacted law.

Conclusion: The Act is inconsistent with the Constitution.

I find this syllogism unconvincing, however, because its Minor Premise is faulty. When the President "canceled" the two appropriation measures now before us, he did not repeal any law nor did he amend any law. He simply *followed* the law, leaving the statutes, as they are literally written, intact.

To understand why one cannot say, *literally speaking*, that the President has repealed or amended any law, imagine how the provisions of law before us might have been, but were not, written. Imagine that the canceled New York health care tax provision at issue here had instead said the following:

"Section One. Taxes . . . that were collected by the State of New York from a health care provider before June 1, 1997, and for which a waiver of the provisions [requiring payment] have been sought . . . are deemed to be permissible health care related taxes . . . *provided however that the President may prevent the just-mentioned provision from having legal force or effect if he determines x, y, and z.* (Assume x, y and z to be the same determinations required by the Line Item Veto Act)."

Whatever a person might say, or think, about the constitutionality of this imaginary law, there is one thing the English language would prevent one from saying. One could not say that a President who "prevent[s]" the deeming language from "having legal force or effect," has either *repealed* or *amended* this particular hypothetical statute. Rather, the President has *followed* that law to the letter. He has exercised the power it explicitly delegates to him. He has executed the law, not repealed it. . . .

[T]he delegated power to nullify statutory language was *itself* created and defined by Congress, and included in the statute books on an equal footing with (indeed, as a component part of) the sections that are potentially subject to nullification. As a Pennsylvania court put the matter more than a century ago: "The legislature cannot delegate its power to make a law; but it can make a law to delegate a power." *Locke's Appeal*, 72 Pa. 491, 498 (1873).

. . . .

IV

Because I disagree with the Court's holding of literal violation, I must consider whether the Act nonetheless violates separation-of-powers principles — principles that arise out of the Constitution's vesting of the "executive Power" in "a President," U.S. Const., Art. II, § 1, and "[a]ll legislative Powers" in "a Congress," Art. I, § 1. There are three relevant separation-of-powers questions here: (1) Has Congress given the President the wrong kind of power, *i.e.*, "non-Executive" power? (2) Has Congress given the President the power to "encroach" upon Congress' own constitutionally reserved territory? (3) Has Congress given the President too much power, violating the doctrine of "nondelegation"? These three limitations help assure "adequate control by the citizen's Representatives in Congress," upon which JUSTICE KENNEDY properly insists. And with respect to *this* Act, the answer to all these questions is "no."

A

Viewed conceptually, the power the Act conveys is the right kind of power. It is "executive." As explained above, an exercise of that power "executes" the Act. Conceptually speaking, it closely resembles the kind of delegated authority — to spend or not to spend appropriations, to change or not to change tariff rates — that Congress has frequently granted the President, any differences being differences in degree, not kind.

The fact that one could also characterize this kind of power as "legislative," say, if Congress itself (by amending the appropriations bill) prevented a provision from taking effect, is beside the point. This Court has frequently found that the exercise of a particular power, such as the power to make rules of broad applicability, *American Trucking Assns., Inc. v. United States*, 344 U.S. 298, 310-313 (1953), or to adjudicate claims, *Crowell v. Benson*, 285 U.S., at 50-51, 54; *Wiener v. United States*, 357 U.S. 349, 354-356 (1958), can fall within the constitutional purview of more than one branch of Government. . . .

The Court has upheld congressional delegation of rulemaking power and adjudicatory power to federal agencies, *American Trucking Assns. v. United States*, guideline-writing power to a Sentencing Commission, *Mistretta v. United States*, 488 U.S. 361, at 412 (1989), and prosecutor-appointment power to judges, *Morrison v. Olson*, 487 U.S. 654, 696-697 (1988). It is far easier *conceptually* to reconcile the power at issue here with the relevant constitutional description ("executive") than in many of these cases. . . .

[O]ne cannot say that the Act "encroaches" upon Congress' power, when Congress retained the power to insert, by simple majority, into any future appropriations bill, into any section of any such bill, or into any phrase of any section, a provision that says the Act will not apply. Congress also retained the power to "disapprov[e]," and thereby reinstate, any of the President's cancellations. And it is Congress that drafts and enacts the appropriations statutes that are subject to the Act in the first place — and thereby defines the outer limits of the President's cancellation authority. Thus *this* Act is not the sort of delegation "without . . . sufficient check" that concerns JUSTICE KENNEDY. Indeed, the President acts only in response to, and on the terms set by, the Congress. . . .

Nor can one say the Act's grant of power "aggrandizes" the Presidential office. The grant is limited to the context of the budget. It is limited to the power to spend, or not to spend, particular appropriated items, and the power to permit, or not to permit, specific limited exemptions from generally applicable tax law from taking effect. These powers, as I will explain in detail, resemble those the President has exercised in the past on other occasions. The delegation of those powers to the President may strengthen the Presidency, but any such change in Executive Branch authority seems minute when compared with the changes worked by delegations of other kinds of authority that the Court in the past has upheld.

C

The "nondelegation" doctrine represents an added constitutional check upon Congress' authority to delegate power to the Executive Branch. And it raises a more serious constitutional obstacle here. . . .

The Act before us seeks to create . . . [an intelligible] principle in three ways. The first is procedural. The Act tells the President that, in "identifying dollar amounts [or] . . . items . . . for cancellation" (which I take to refer to his selection of the amounts or items he will "prevent from having legal force or effect"), he is to "consider," among other things,

> "the legislative history, construction, and purposes of the law which contains [those amounts or items, and] . . . any specific sources of information referenced in such law or . . . the best available information. . . ."

The second is purposive. The clear purpose behind the Act, confirmed by its legislative history, is to promote "greater fiscal accountability" and to "eliminate wasteful federal spending and . . . special tax breaks."

The third is substantive. The President must determine that, to "prevent" the item or amount "from having legal force or effect" will "reduce the Federal budget deficit; . . . not impair any essential Government functions; and . . . not harm the national interest."

The resulting standards are broad. But this Court has upheld standards that are equally broad, or broader. . . .

Indeed, the Court has only twice in its history found that a congressional delegation of power violated the "nondelegation" doctrine. One such case, *Panama Refining Co. v. Ryan*, 293 U.S. 388 (1935), was in a sense a special case, for it was discovered in the midst of the case that the particular exercise of the power at issue, the promulgation of a Petroleum Code under the National Industrial Recovery Act, did not contain any legally operative sentence. The other case, *A.L.A. Schechter Poultry Corp. v. United States*, 295 U.S. 495 (1935), involved a delegation through the National Industrial Recovery Act, 48 Stat. 195, that contained not simply a broad standard ("fair competition"), but also the conferral of power on private parties to promulgate rules applying that standard to virtually all of American industry. As Justice Cardozo put it, the legislation exemplified "delegation running riot," which created a "roving commission to inquire into evils and upon discovery correct them." *Id.*, at 553, 551 (concurring opinion).

The case before us does not involve any such "roving commission," nor does it involve delegation to private parties, nor does it bring all of American industry within its scope. It is limited to one area of Government, the budget, and it seeks to give the President the power, in one portion of that budget, to tailor spending and special tax relief to what he concludes are the demands of fiscal responsibility. Nor is the standard that governs his judgment, though broad, any broader than the standard that currently governs the award of television licenses, namely, "public convenience, interest, *or* necessity." (emphasis added). To the contrary, (a) the broadly phrased limitations in the Act, together with (b) its evident deficit reduction purpose, and (c) a procedure that guarantees Presidential awareness of the reasons for including a particular provision in a budget bill, taken together, guide the President's exercise of his discretionary powers.

. . . .

V

In sum, I recognize that the Act before us is novel. In a sense, it skirts a constitutional edge. But that edge has to do with means, not ends. The means chosen do not amount literally to the enactment, repeal, or amendment of a law. Nor, for that matter, do they amount literally to the "line item veto" that the Act's title announces. Those means do not violate any basic separation-of-powers principle. They do not improperly shift the constitutionally foreseen balance of power from Congress to the President. Nor, since they comply with separation-of-powers principles, do they threaten the liberties of individual citizens. They represent an experiment that may, or may not, help representative government work better. The Constitution, in my view, authorizes Congress and the President to try novel methods in this way. Consequently, with respect, I dissent.

NOTES AND QUESTIONS

7-1. Is this case, in effect, the mirror image of *Chadha, supra* § 6.02?

7-2. How does one deal with "midnight substantive riders" inserted into massive appropriation bills and, in most cases, known only to the author of the rider? Can the President, politically speaking, really veto the entire piece of legislation? Would that be wise to do?

§ 7.03 The Power to Appoint

BUCKLEY v. VALEO

United States Supreme Court
424 U.S. 1 (1976)

[This case involved a number of issues, including a challenge to the constitutionality of the way the commissioners of the Federal Election Commission were appointed. That commission was composed of six voting members, two appointed by the President, two appointed by the President *pro tempore* of the Senate, and two appointed by the Speaker of the House of Representatives. All six were subject to confirmation by a majority of both Houses of Congress. The Court issued a per curiam opinion.]

Appellants urge that since Congress has given the Commission wide-ranging rule-making and enforcement powers with respect to the substantive provisions of the Act, Congress is precluded under the principle of separation of powers from vesting in itself the authority to appoint those who will exercise such authority. Their argument is based on the language of Art. II, § 2, cl. 2, of the Constitution, which provides in pertinent part as follows:

"[The President] shall nominate, and by and with the Advice and Consent of the Senate, shall appoint . . . all other Officers of the United States, whose Appointments are not herein otherwise provided for, and which shall be established by Law: but the Congress may by Law vest the Appointment of such inferior Officers, as they think proper, in the President alone, in the Courts of Law, or in the Heads of Departments."

Appellants' argument is that this provision is the exclusive method by which those charged with executing the laws of the United States may be chosen. Congress, they assert, cannot have it both ways. If the Legislature wishes the Commission to exercise all of the conferred powers, then its members are in fact "Officers of the United States" and must be appointed under the Appointments Clause. But if Congress insists upon retaining the power to appoint, then the members of the Commission may not discharge those many functions of the Commission which can be performed only by "Officers of the United States," as that term must be construed within the doctrine of separation of powers.

Appellee Commission and amici in support of the Commission urge that the Framers of the Constitution, while mindful of the need for checks and balances among the three branches of the National Government, had no intention of denying to the Legislative Branch authority to appoint its own officers. Congress, either under the Appointments Clause or under its grants of substantive legislative authority and the Necessary and Proper Clause in Art. I, is in their view empowered to provide for the appointment to the Commission in the manner which it did because the Commission is performing "appropriate legislative functions."

The majority of the Court of Appeals recognized the importance of the doctrine of separation of powers which is at the heart of our Constitution, and . . . that the Legislative Branch may not exercise executive authority by retaining the power to appoint those who will execute its laws. But it . . . concluded that Congress had sufficient authority under the Necessary and Proper Clause of Art. I of the Constitution not only to establish the Commission but to appoint the commission's members. . . .

1. Separation of Powers

We do not think appellants' arguments based upon Art. II, § 2, cl. 2, of the Constitution may be so easily dismissed as did the majority of the Court of Appeals. Our inquiry of necessity touches upon the fundamental principles of the Government established by the Framers of the Constitution, and all litigants and all of the courts which have addressed themselves to the matter start on common ground in the recognition of the intent of the Framers that the powers of the three great branches of the national Government be largely separate from one another.

James Madison, writing in the *Federalist* No. 47, defended the work of the Framers against the charge that these three governmental powers were not *entirely* separate from one another in the proposed Constitution. He asserted that while there was some admixture, the Constitution was nonetheless true to Montesquieu's well known maxim that the legislative, executive, and judicial departments ought to be separate and distinct:

> The reasons on which Montesquieu grounds his maxim are a further demonstration of his meaning. "When the legislative and executive powers are united in the same person or body," says he, "there can be no liberty, because apprehensions may arise lest *the same* monarch or senate should *enact* tyrannical laws to *execute* them in a tyrannical manner." Again: "Were the power of judging joined with the legislative, the life and liberty of the subject would be exposed to arbitrary control, for *the judge* would then be *the legislator*. Were it joined to the executive power, *the judge* might behave with all the violence of *an oppressor*." Some of these reasons are more fully explained in other passages; but briefly stated as they are here, they sufficiently establish the meaning which we have put on this celebrated maxim of this celebrated author.

Yet it is also clear from the provisions of the Constitution itself, and from the Federalist Papers, that the Constitution by no means contemplates total separation of each of these three essential branches of Government. The President is a participant in the lawmaking process by virtue of his authority to veto bills enacted by Congress. The Senate is a participant in the appointive process by virtue of its authority to refuse to confirm persons nominated to office by the President. The men who met in Philadelphia in the summer of 1787 were practical statesmen, experienced in politics, who viewed the principle of separation of powers as a vital check against tyranny. But they likewise saw that a hermetic sealing off of the three branches of Government from one another would preclude the establishment of a Nation capable of governing itself effectively.

Mr. Chief Justice Taft, writing for the Court in *Hampton & Co. v. United States,* 276 U.S. 394 (1928), after stating the general principle of separation of powers found in the United States Constitution, went on to observe:

> [T]he rule is that in the actual administration of the government Congress or the Legislature should exercise the legislative power, the President or the State executive, the Governor, the executive power, and the Courts or the judiciary the judicial power, and in carrying out that constitutional division into three branches it is a breach of the National fundamental law if Congress gives up its legislative power and transfers it to the President, or to the Judicial branch, or if by law it attempts to invest itself or its members with either executive power or judicial power. This is not to say that the three branches are not co-ordinate parts of one government and that each in the field of its duties may not invoke the action of the two other branches in so far as the action invoked shall not be an assumption of the constitutional field of action of another branch. In determining what it may do in seeking assistance from another branch, the extent and character of that assistance must be fixed according to common sense and the inherent necessities of the governmental co-ordination. *Id.,* at 406, 72 L. Ed. 624, 48 S. Ct. 348.

More recently, Mr. Justice Jackson, concurring in the opinion and the judgment of the Court in *Youngstown Sheet & Tube Co. v. Sawyer,* 343 U.S. 579, 635, (1952), succinctly characterized this understanding:

> While the Constitution diffuses power the better to secure liberty, it also contemplates that practice will integrate the dispersed powers into a workable government. It enjoins upon its branches separateness but interdependence, autonomy but reciprocity.

The Framers regarded the checks and balances that they had built into the tripartite Federal Government as a self-executing safeguard against the encroachment or aggrandizement of one branch at the expense of the other. As Madison put it in *Federalist* No. 51:

> This policy of supplying, by opposite and rival interests, the defect of better motives, might be traced through the whole system of human affairs, private as well as public. We see it particularly displayed in all the subordinate distributions of power, where the constant aim is to divide and arrange the several offices in such a manner as that each may be a check on the other — that the private interest of every individual may be a sentinel over the public rights. These inventions of prudence cannot be less requisite in the distribution of the supreme powers of the State.

This Court has not hesitated to enforce the principle of separation of powers embodied in the Constitution when its application has proved necessary for the decisions of cases or controversies properly before it. The Court has held that executive or administrative duties of a nonjudicial nature may not be imposed on judges holding office under Art. III of the Constitution. *United States v. Ferreira,* 13 How. 40, 14 L. Ed. 42 (1852); *Hayburn's Case,* 2 Dall. 409, 1 L. Ed. 436 (1792). The Court has held that the President may not execute and exercise legislative authority belonging only to Congress. *Youngstown Sheet & Tube Co. v. Sawyer, supra.* In the course of its opinion in that case, the Court said:

> In the framework of our Constitution, the President's power to see that the laws are faithfully executed refutes the idea that he is to be lawmaker. The Constitution limits his functions in the lawmaking process to the recommending of laws he thinks wise and the vetoing of laws he thinks bad. And the Constitution is neither silent nor equivocal about who shall make laws which the President is to execute. The first section of the first article says that "All legislative Powers herein granted shall be vested in a Congress of the United States. . . ."

More closely in point to the facts of the present case is this Court's decision in *Springer v. Philippine Islands,* 277 U.S. 189, 72 L. Ed. 845, 48 S. Ct. 480 (1928), where the Court held that the legislature of the Philippine Islands could not provide for legislative appointment to executive agencies.

2. The Appointments Clause

The principle of separation of powers was not simply an abstract generalization in the minds of the Framers: it was woven into the document that they drafted in Philadelphia in the summer of 1787. Article I, § 1, declares: "All legislative Powers herein granted shall be vested in a Congress of the United States." Article II, § 1, vests the executive power "in a President of the United States of America," and Art. III, § 1, declares that "The judicial Power of the United States, shall be vested in one supreme Court, and in such inferior Courts as the Congress may from time to time ordain and establish." The further concern of the Framers of the Constitution with maintenance of the separation of powers is found in the so-called "Ineligibility" and "Incompatibility" Clauses contained in Art. I, § 6:

> No Senator or Representative shall, during the Time for which he was elected, be appointed to any civil Office under the Authority of the United States, which shall have been created, or the Emoluments whereof shall have been increased during such time; and no Person holding any Office under the United States, shall be a Member of either House during his Continuance in Office.

It is in the context of these cognate provisions of the document that we must examine the language of Art. II, § 2, cl 2, which appellants contend provides the only authorization for appointment of those to whom substantial executive or administrative authority is given by statute. . . .

The Appointments Clause could, of course, be read as merely dealing with etiquette or protocol in describing "Officers of the United States," but the drafters had a less frivolous purpose in mind. This conclusion is supported by language from *United States v. Germaine,* 99 U.S. 508, 509–510, 25 L. Ed. 482 (1879):

The Constitution for purposes of appointment very clearly divides all its officers into two classes. The primary class requires a nomination by the President and confirmation by the Senate. But foreseeing that when offices became numerous, and sudden removals necessary, this mode might be inconvenient, it was provided that, in regard to officers inferior to those specially mentioned, Congress might by law vest their appointment in the President alone, in the courts of law, or in the heads of departments. *That all persons who can be said to hold an office under the government about to be established under the Constitution were intended to be included within one or the other of these modes of appointment there can be but little doubt.* (Emphasis supplied.)

We think that the term "Officers of the United States" as used in Art. II, defined to include "all persons who can be said to hold an office under the government" in *United States v. Germaine, supra,* is a term intended to have substantive meaning. We think its fair import is that any appointee exercising significant authority pursuant to the laws of the United States is an Officer of the United States, and must, therefore, be appointed in the manner prescribed by § 2, cl 2, of that Article.

If "all persons who can be said to hold an office under the government about to be established under the Constitution were intended to be included within one or the other of these modes of appointment," *United States v. Germaine, supra,* it is difficult to see how the members of the Commission may escape inclusion. If a Postmaster first class, *Myers v. United States,* 272 U.S. 52 (1926), and the clerk of a district court, *Ex parte Hennen,* 13 Pet 230, 10 L. Ed. 138 (1839), are inferior officers of the United States within the meaning of the Appointments Clause, as they are, surely the Commissioners before us are at the very least such "inferior Officers" within the meaning of that Clause.[162]

Although two members of the Commission are initially selected by the President, his nominations are subject to confirmation not merely by the Senate, but by the House of Representatives as well. The remaining four voting members of the Commission are appointed by the President *pro tempore* of the Senate and by the Speaker of the House. While the second part of the Clause authorizes Congress to vest the appointment of the officers described in that part in "the Courts of Law, or in the Heads of Departments," neither the Speaker of the House nor the President *pro tempore* of the Senate comes within this language.

The phrase "Heads of Departments," used as it is in conjunction with the phrase "Courts of Law," suggests that the Departments referred to are themselves in the executive Branch or at least have some connection with that branch. While the Clause expressly authorizes Congress to vest the appointment of certain officers in the "Courts of Law," the absence of similar language

---

[162] "Officers of the United States" do not include all employees of the United States, but there is no claim made that the Commissioners are employees of the United States rather than officers. Employees are lesser functionaries subordinate to officers of the United States, *see Auffmordt v. Hedden,* 137 U.S. 310, 327 (1890); *United States v. Germaine, supra,* whereas the Commissioners, appointed for a statutory term, are not subject to the control or direction of any other executive, judicial, or legislative authority.

§ 7.03 EXECUTIVE CONTROL OF AGENCY DISCRETION 643

to include Congress must mean that neither Congress nor its officers were included within the language "Heads of Departments" in this part of cl 2.

Thus with respect to four of the six voting members of the Commission, neither the President, the head of any department, nor the Judiciary has any voice in their selections. . . .

Appellee Commission and *amici* contend somewhat obliquely that because the Framers had no intention of relegating Congress to a position below that of the coequal Judicial and Executive Branches of the National Government, the Appointments Clause must somehow be read to include Congress or its officers as among those in whom the appointment power may be vested. But the debates of the Constitutional Convention, and the Federalist Papers, are replete with expressions of fear that the Legislative Branch of the National Government will aggrandize itself at the expense of the other two branches. The debates during the Convention, and the evolution of the draft version of the Constitution, seem to us to lend considerable support to our reading of the language of the Appointments Clause itself.

An interim version of the draft Constitution had vested in the Senate the authority to appoint Ambassadors, public Ministers, and Judges of the Supreme Court, and the language of Art. II as finally adopted is a distinct change in this regard. We believe that it was a deliberate change made by the Framers with the intent to deny Congress any authority itself to appoint those who were "Officers of the United States." . . . [The Court then set forth some of the debates on the floor of the Convention to prove its point.]

Appellee Commission and *amici* urge that because of what they conceive to be the extraordinary authority reposed in Congress to regulate elections, this case stands on a different footing than if Congress had exercised its legislative authority in another field. There is, of course, no doubt that Congress has express authority to regulate congressional elections, by virtue of the power conferred in Art. I, § 4.[174] This Court has also held that it has very broad authority to prevent corruption in national Presidential elections. . . . But Congress has plenary authority in all areas in which it has substantive legislative jurisdiction, *McCulloch v. Maryland,* 4 Wheat 316 (1819), so long as the exercise of that authority does not offend some other constitutional restriction. We see no reason to believe that the authority of Congress over federal election practices is of such a wholly different nature from the other grants of authority to Congress that it may be employed in such a manner as to offend well-established constitutional restrictions stemming from the separation of powers.

The position that because Congress has been given explicit and plenary authority to regulate a field of activity, it must therefore have the power to appoint those who are to administer the regulatory statute is both novel and contrary to the language of the Appointments Clause. Unless their selection is elsewhere provided for, all officers of the United States are to be appointed in accordance with the Clause. Principal officers are selected by the President

---

[174] "The Times, Places and Manner of holding Elections for Senators and Representatives, shall be prescribed in each State by the Legislature thereof; but the Congress may at any time by Law make or alter such Regulations, except as to the Places of choosing Senators."

with the advice and consent of the Senate. Inferior officers Congress may allow to be appointed by the President alone, by the heads of departments, or by the Judiciary. No class or type of officer is excluded because of its special functions. The President appoints judicial as well as executive officers. Neither has it been disputed — and apparently it is not now disputed — that the Clause controls the appointment of the members of a typical administrative agency even though its functions, as this Court recognized in *Humphrey's Executor v. United States,* 295 U.S. 602, 624 (1935), may be "predominantly quasi-judicial and quasi-legislative" rather than executive. The Court in that case carefully emphasized that although the members of such agencies were to be independent of the Executive in their day-to-day operations, the Executive was not excluded from selecting them. . . .

Appellee Commission and *amici* finally contend, and the majority of the Court of Appeals agreed with them, that whatever shortcomings the provision for the appointment of members of the Commission might have under Art. II, Congress had ample authority under the Necessary and Proper Clause of Art. I to effectuate this result. We do not agree. The proper inquiry when considering the Necessary and Proper Clause is not the authority of Congress to create an office or a commission, which is broad indeed, but rather its authority to provide that its own officers may make appointments to such office or commission.

So framed, the claim that Congress may provide for this manner of appointment under the Necessary and Proper Clause of Art. I stands on no better footing than the claim that it may provide for such manner of appointment because of its substantive authority to regulate federal elections. Congress could not, merely because it concluded that such a measure was "necessary and proper" to the discharge of its substantive legislative authority, pass a bill of attainder or *ex post facto* law contrary to the prohibitions contained in § 9 of Art. I. No more may it vest in itself, or in its officers, the authority to appoint officers of the United States when the Appointments Clause by clear implication prohibits it from doing so. . . .

3. The Commission's Powers

Thus, on the assumption that all of the powers granted in the statute may be exercised by an agency whose members have been appointed in accordance with the Appointments Clause, the ultimate question is which, if any, of those powers may be exercised by the present voting Commissioners, none of whom was appointed as provided by that Clause. Our previous description of the statutory provisions, . . . disclosed that the Commission's powers fall generally into three categories: functions relating to the flow of necessary information — receipt, dissemination, and investigation; functions with respect to the Commission's task of fleshing out the statute — rulemaking and advisory opinions; and functions necessary to ensure compliance with the statute and rules — informal procedures, administrative determinations and hearings, and civil suits.

Insofar as the powers confided in the Commission are essentially of an investigative and informative nature, falling in the same general category as those powers which Congress might delegate to one of its own committees, there can be no question that the Commission as presently constituted may exercise them. . . .

But when we go beyond this type of authority to the more substantial powers exercised by the Commission, we reach a different result. The Commissions' enforcement power, exemplified by its discretionary power to seek judicial relief, is authority that cannot possibly be regarded as merely in aid of the legislative functions of Congress. A lawsuit is the ultimate remedy for a breach of the law, and it is to the President, and not to the Congress, that the Constitution entrusts the responsibility to "take Care that the Laws be faithfully executed." Art. II, § 3. . . .

We hold that these provisions of the Act, vesting in the Commission primary responsibility for conducting civil litigation in the courts of the United States for vindicating public rights, violate Art. II, § 2, cl 2, of the Constitution. Such functions may be discharged only by persons who are "Officers of the United States" within the language of that section.

All aspects of the Act are brought within the Commission's broad administrative powers: rulemaking, advisory opinions, and determinations of eligibility for funds and even for federal elective office itself. These functions, exercised free from day-to-day supervision of either Congress or the Executive Branch, are more legislative and judicial in nature than are the Commission's enforcement powers, and are of kinds usually performed by independent regulatory agencies or by some department in the Executive Branch under the direction of an Act of Congress. Congress viewed these broad powers as essential to effective and impartial administration of the entire substantive framework of the Act. Yet each of these functions also represents the performance of a significant governmental duty exercised pursuant to a public law. While the President may not insist that such functions be delegated to an appointee of his removable at will, *Humphrey's Executor v. United States,* 295 U.S. 602 (1935), none of them operates merely in aid of congressional authority to legislate or is sufficiently removed from the administration and enforcement of public law to allow it to be performed by the present Commission. These administrative functions may therefore be exercised only by persons who are "Officers of the United States." . . .

MORRISON v. OLSON

United States Supreme Court
487 U.S. 654 (1987)

Chief Justice Rehnquist delivered the opinion of the Court.

This case presents us with a challenge to the independent counsel provisions of the Ethics in Government Act of 1978, 28 U.S.C. §§ 79, 691 *et seq.* We hold today that these provisions of the Act do not violate the Appointments Clause of the Constitution, Art. II, § 2, cl. 2, or the limitations of Article III, nor do they impermissibly interfere with the President's authority under Article II in violation of the constitutional principle of separation of powers.

I

Briefly stated, Title VI of the Ethics in Government Act (Title VI or the Act), . . . allows for the appointment of an "independent counsel" to investigate and, if appropriate, prosecute certain high ranking Government officials for violations of federal criminal laws.[2] The Act requires the Attorney General, upon receipt of information that he determines is "sufficient to constitute grounds to investigate whether any person [covered by the Act] may have violated any Federal criminal law," to conduct a preliminary investigation of the matter. When the Attorney General has completed this investigation, or 90 days has elapsed, he is required to report to a special court (the Special Division) created by the Act "for the purpose of appointing independent counsel."[3] If the Attorney General determines that "there are no reasonable grounds to believe that further investigation is warranted," then he must notify the Special Division of this result. In such a case, "the division of the court shall have no power to appoint an independent counsel." If, however, the Attorney General has determined that there are "reasonable grounds to believe that further investigation or prosecution is warranted," then he "shall apply to the division of the court for the appointment of an independent counsel."[4] The Attorney General's application to the court "shall contain sufficient information to assist the [court] in selecting an independent counsel and in defining that independent counsel's prosecutorial jurisdiction." Upon receiving this application, the Special Division "shall appoint an appropriate

---

[2] Under 28 U.S.C. § 59(a) (1982 ed., Supp. V), the statute applies to violations of "any Federal criminal law other than a violation classified as a Class B or C misdemeanor or an infraction." See also § 591(c) ("any Federal criminal law other than a violation classified as a Class B or C misdemeanor or an infraction"). Section 691(b) sets forth the individuals who may be the target of an investigation by the Attorney General, including the President and Vice President, Cabinet level officials, certain high ranking officials in the Executive Office of the President and the Justice Department, the Director and Deputy Director of Central Intelligence, the Commissioner of Internal Revenue, and certain officials involved in the President's national political campaign. Pursuant to § 591(c), the Attorney General may also conduct a preliminary investigation of persons not named in § 591(b) if an investigation by the Attorney General or other Department of Justice official "may result in a personal, financial, or political conflict of interest."

[3] The Special Division is a division of the United States Court of Appeals for the District of Columbia Circuit. . . . The court consists of three circuit court judges or justices appointed by the Chief Justice of the United States. One of the judges must be a judge of the United States Court of Appeals for the District of Columbia Circuit, and no two of the judges may be named to the Special Division from a particular court. The judges are appointed for 2-year terms, with any vacancy being filled only for the remainder of the 2-year period.

[4] The Act also requires the Attorney General to apply for the appointment of an independent counsel if 90 days elapse from the receipt of the information triggering the preliminary investigation without a determination by the Attorney General that there are no reasonable grounds to believe that further investigation or prosecution is warranted. § 592(c)(1). Pursuant to § 592(f), the Attorney General's decision to apply to the Special Division for the appointment of an independent counsel is not reviewable "in any court."

independent counsel and shall define that independent counsel's prosecutorial jurisdiction."⁵

With respect to all matters within the independent counsel's jurisdiction, the Act grants the counsel "full power and independent authority to exercise all investigative and prosecutorial functions and powers of the Department of Justice, the Attorney General, and any other officer or employee of the Department of Justice."⁶ . . . Under § 594(a)(9), the counsel's powers include "initiating and conducting prosecutions in any court of competent jurisdiction, framing and signing indictments, filing information, and handling all aspects of any case, in the name of the United States." The counsel may appoint employees, § 594(e). The Act also states that an independent counsel "shall, except where not possible, comply with the written or other established policies of the Department of Justice respecting enforcement of the criminal laws." . . .

The Appointments Clause of Article II reads as follows:

"[The President] shall nominate, and by and with the Advice and Consent of the senate, shall appoint Ambassadors, other public Ministers and Consuls, Judges of the Supreme Court, and all other Officers of the United States, whose Appointments are not herein otherwise provided for, and which shall be established by Law: but the Congress may by Law vest the Appointment of such inferior Officers, as they think proper, in the President alone, in the Courts of Law, or in the Heads of Departments." U.S. Const., Art. II, § 2, cl. 2.

The parties do not dispute that "[t]he Constitution for purposes of appointment . . . divides all its officers into two classes." *United States v. Germaine,* 99 U.S. 508, 509 (1879). As we stated in *Buckley v. Valeo,* 424 U.S. 1, 139 (1976): "Principal officers are selected by the President with the advice and consent of the Senate. Inferior officers Congress may allow to appointed by the President alone, by the heads of departments, or by the Judiciary." The initial question is accordingly, whether appellant is an "inferior" or a "principal" officer. If she is the latter, as the Court of Appeals concluded, then the Act is in violation of the Appointments Clause.

The line between "inferior" and "principal" officers is one that is far from clear, and the Framers provided little guidance into where it should be drawn. We need not attempt here to decide exactly where the line falls between the two types of officers, because in our view appellant clearly falls on the "inferior officer" side of that line. Several factors lead to this conclusion.

First, appellant is subject to removal by a higher Executive Branch official. Although appellant may not be "subordinate" to the Attorney General (and

---

⁵ Upon request of the Attorney General, in lieu of appointing an independent counsel the Special Division may "expand the prosecutorial jurisdiction of an independent counsel." § 593(c). Section 593 also authorizes the Special Division to fill vacancies arising because of the death, resignation, or removal of an independent counsel. § 593(e). The court, in addition, is empowered to grant limited extensions of time for the Attorney General's preliminary investigation, § 592(a)(3), and to award attorney's fees to unindicted individuals who were the subject of an investigation by an independent counsel, § 593(f) (as amended by Pub. L. 101–191, 101 Stat. 1293).

⁶ The Attorney General, however, retains "direction or control as to those matters that specifically require the Attorney General's personal action under section 2516 of title 18." § 594(a).

the President) insofar as she possesses a degree of independent discretion to exercise the powers delegated to her under the Act, the fact that she can be removed by the Attorney General indicates that she is to some degree "inferior" in rank and authority. Second, appellant is empowered by the Act to perform only certain, limited duties. An independent counsel's role is restricted primarily to investigation and, if appropriate, prosecution for certain federal crimes. Admittedly, the Act delegates to appellant "full power and independent authority to exercise all investigative and prosecutorial functions and powers of the Department of Justice," § 594(a), but this grant of authority does not include any authority to formulate policy for the Government or the Executive Branch, nor does it give appellant any administrative duties outside of those necessary to operate her office. The Act specifically provides that in policy matters appellant is to comply to the extent possible with the policies of the Department. § 594(f).

Third, appellant's office is limited in jurisdiction. Not only is the Act itself restricted in applicability to certain federal officials suspected of certain serious federal crimes, but an independent counsel can only act within the scope of the jurisdiction that has been granted by the Special Division pursuant to a request by the Attorney General. Finally, appellant's office is limited in tenure. There is concededly no time limit on the appointment of a particular counsel. Nonetheless, the office of independent counsel is "temporary" in the sense that an independent counsel is appointed essentially to accomplish a single task, and when that task is over the office is terminated, either by the counsel herself or by action of the Special Division. Unlike other prosecutors, appellant has not ongoing responsibilities that extend beyond the accomplishment of the mission that she was appointed for and authorized by the Special Division to undertake. In our view, these factors relating to the "ideas of tenure, duration . . . and duties" of the independent counsel, *Germaine, supra*, at 511, are sufficient to establish that appellant is an "inferior" officer in the constitutional sense. . . .

This does not, however, end our inquiry under the Appointments Clause. Appellees argue that even if appellant is an "inferior" officer, the Clause does not empower Congress to place the power to appoint such an officer outside the Executive Branch. They contend that the clause does not contemplate congressional authorization of "interbranch appointments," in which an officer of one branch is appointed by officers of another branch. The relevant language of the Appointments Clause is worth repeating. It reads: ". . . but the Congress may by Law vest the Appointment of such inferior Officers, as they think proper, in the President alone, in the courts of Law, or in the Heads of Departments." On its face, the language of this "excepting clause" admits of no limitation on interbranch appointments. Indeed, the inclusion of "as they think proper" seems clearly to give Congress significant discretion to determine whether it is "proper" to vest the appointment of, for example, executive officials in the "courts of Law." . . .

We do not mean to say that Congress' power to provide for interbranch appointments of "inferior officers" is unlimited. In addition to separation of powers concerns, which would arise if such provisions for appointment had the potential to impair the constitutional functions assigned to one of the branches, *Siebold* itself suggested that Congress' decision to vest the appointment power in the courts would be improper if there was some "incongruity" between the functions normally performed by the courts and the performance of their duty to appoint. 100 U.S., at 398 ("[T]he duty to appoint inferior officers, when required thereto by law, is a constitutional duty of the courts; and in the present case there is no such incongruity in the duty required as to excuse the courts from its performance, or to render their acts void"). In this case, however, we do not think it impermissible for Congress to vest the power to appoint independent counsel in a specially created federal court. . . .

JUSTICE SCALIA, dissenting.

. . . [T]he Court does not attempt to "decide exactly" what establishes the line between principal and "inferior" officers, but is confident that, whatever the line may be, appellant "clearly falls on the 'inferior officer' side" of it. The Court gives three reasons: *First*, she "is subject to removal by a higher Executive Branch official," namely, the Attorney General. *Second*, she is "empowered by the Act to perform only certain, limited duties." *Third*, her office is "limited in jurisdiction" and "limited in tenure."

The first of these lends no support to the view that appellant is an inferior officer. Appellant is removable only for "good cause" or physical or mental incapacity. By contrast, most (if not all) *principal officers* in the Executive Branch may be removed by the President *at will*. I fail to see how the fact that appellant is more difficult to remove than most principal officers helps to establish that she is an inferior officer. . . .

The second reason offered by the Court — that appellant performs only certain, limited duties — may be relevant to whether she is an inferior officer, but it mischaracterizes the extent of her powers. As the Court states: "Admittedly, the Act delegates to appellant [the] '*full power and independent authority to exercise all investigative and prosecutorial functions and powers of the Department of Justice.*'" . . . Once all of this is "admitted," it seems to me impossible to maintain that appellant's authority is so "limited" as to render her an inferior officer. . . .

The final set of reasons given by the Court for why the independent counsel clearly is an inferior officer emphasizes the limited nature of her jurisdiction and tenure. Taking the latter first, I find nothing unusually limited about the independent counsel's tenure. To the contrary, unlike most high-ranking Executive Branch officials, she continues to serve until she (or the Special Division) decides that her work is substantially completed. This particular independent prosecutor has already served more than two years, which is at least as long as many Cabinet officials. As to the scope of her jurisdiction, there can be no doubt that is small (though far from unimportant). But within it she exercises more than the full power of the Attorney General. The Ambassador to Luxembourg is not anything less than a principal officer, simply because Luxembourg is small. And the federal judge who sits in a small district is not for that reason "inferior in rank and authority." . . .

More fundamentally, however, it is not clear from the Court's opinion why the factors it discusses — even if applied correctly to the facts of this case — are determinative of the question of inferior officer status. The apparent source of these factors is a statement in *United States v. Germaine*, 99 U.S. 508, 511 (1879), that "the term [officer] embraces the ideas of tenure, duration, emolument, and duties." Besides the fact that this was dictum, it was dictum in a case where the distinguishing characteristics of inferior officers versus superior officers were in no way relevant, but rather only the distinguishing characteristics of an "officer of the United States" (to which the criminal statute at issue applied) as opposed to a mere *employee*. Rather than erect a theory of who is an inferior officer on the foundation of such an irrelevancy, I think it preferable to look to the text of the Constitution and the division of power that it establishes. These demonstrate, I think, that the independent counsel is not an inferior officer because she is not *subordinate* to any officer in the Executive Branch (indeed, not even to the President). . . . At the only other point in the Constitution at which the word "inferior" appears, it plainly connotes a relationship of subordination. Article III vests the judicial power of the United States in "one supreme Court, and in such *inferior* Courts as the Congress may from time to time ordain and establish.' U.S. Const., Art. III, § 1 (emphasis added). In Federalist No. 81, Hamilton pauses to describe the "inferior" courts authorized by Article III as inferior in the sense that they are "subordinate" to the Supreme Court. . . .

To be sure, it is not a *sufficient* condition for "inferior" officer status that one be subordinate to a principal officer. Even an officer who is subordinate to a department head can be a principal officer. . . . But it is surely a *necessary* condition for inferior officer status that the officer be subordinate to another officer. . .

NOTES AND QUESTIONS

7-3. How does the Court in *Buckley* approach the issue of whether the Commissioners were, in fact, "Officers of the United States"? How does it decide this issue? Does it offer any guidance as to how to differentiate between "Officers of the United States" and "inferior officers"? Does this distinction matter for the outcome of this case?

7-4. What are the practical consequences of striking down the Act? How does this ruling bear on contemporary efforts at election reform?

7-5. Recall Professor Strauss' three constitutional approaches to separation-of-powers issues set forth above in note 6-6. How would you characterize the approach taken by the Court in *Buckley*?

7-6. How does the Court resolve the appointments clause issue in *Morrison*? What criteria does it use? Do you agree with the application of these criteria? What if the person being prosecuted were the Attorney General or the President of the United States? Would the independent counsel still be an "inferior officer"?

7-7. What are the constitutional limits to interbranch appointments? Could Congress place the appointments of various under secretaries of defense in the judicial branch? Why or why not?

7-8. Kenneth Starr's investigation of President William Jefferson Clinton evoked widespread, severe, and ultimately fatal criticism of the position of the Independent Counsel, a role that was created by the Ethics in Government Act in 1978 and abolished in 1999. Legal scholars, columnists, and members of Congress accused Starr of being unaccountable, politically motivated, and unscrupulous, and denounced the position of Independent Counsel as a failure. After several hearings that included testimony from academics, practicing attorneys, former independent counsels, and Starr himself, Congress allowed the statute to expire on its scheduled sunset date of June 30, 1999.

. . . .

Criticisms of Starr fell into two categories: (1) attacks on the broad powers granted by the Independent Counsel statute, and (2) objections to specific acts of alleged misconduct by Starr. The first category consisted of critiques of the Independent Counsel's lack of accountability, unlimited budget, and abuse of discretion. The second category focused on practices, policies, and specific acts undertaken by Starr and his team of prosecutors that many members of the public found shocking, distasteful, or unfair. Such practices included, most famously, the sequestering and interrogation of the President's paramour, Monica Lewinsky, the compelled appearance of Ms. Lewinsky's mother before a federal grand jury, and the arguably vindictive prosecution of a number of individuals who failed to cooperate with Starr's investigation.

Angela J. Davis, *The American Prosecutor: Independence, Power, and the Threat of Tyranny*, 86 IOWA L. REV. 393, 395–397 (2001).* *See also* Fedwa Malti-Douglas, *The Starr Report Disrobed* (2000).

7-9. The Supreme Court has also construed the phrases "Courts of Law" and "Heads of Departments." In *Freytag v. Commissioner of Internal Revenue*, 501 U.S. 868 (1991), the Court dealt with the appointment of special trial judges by the Chief Judge of the U.S. Tax Court. The Court unanimously agreed that the trial judges were "inferior officers" under Article II. The Court split, 5-4, on how best to categorize the Tax Court. Could an Article I court be considered to be a "Court of Law" or must it be a "Department"? Justice Blackmun, writing for the majority, concluded that the Tax Court exercised judicial powers similar to an Article III Court and, thus, could be considered a "Court of Law" for appointment purposes. In dissent, Justice Scalia argued that "Courts of Law" meant only Article III Courts. The Tax Court, in his view, could only be categorized as a department for purposes of the Appointments Clause.

In reaching its conclusion, the majority emphasized the importance of limiting the range of appointment powers. Specifically, the Court noted at 111 S. Ct. 2641–42:

> The "manipulation of official appointments" had long been one of the American revolutionary generation's greatest grievances against executive power . . . because "the power of appointment to offices" was deemed "the most insidious and powerful weapon of eighteenth century despotism." . . .

---

* Angela J. Davis, *The American Prosecutor: Independence, Power, and the Threat of Tyranny*eit;, 86 IOWA L. REV. 393, 395-397 (2001) (reprinted with permission)

Those who framed our Constitution addressed these concerns by carefully husbanding the appointment power to limit its diffusion. Although the debate on the Appointments Clause was brief, the sparse record indicates the Framers' determination to limit the distribution of the power of appointment. The Constitutional Convention rejected Madison's complaint that the Appointments Clause did "not go far enough if it be necessary at all": Madison argued that "Superior Officers below Heads of Departments ought in some cases to have the appointment of the lesser offices." 2 *Records of the Federal Convention of 1787*, pp. 627–628 (M. Farrand rev. 1966). The Framers understood, however, that by limiting the appointment power, they could ensure that those who wielded it were accountable to political force and the will of the people. Thus, the Clause bespeaks a principle of limitation by dividing the power to appoint the principal federal officers — Ambassadors, Ministers, Heads of Departments, and Judges — between the Executive and Legislative Branches. . . . Even with respect to "inferior officers," the Clause allows Congress only limited authority to devolve appointment power on the President, his Heads of Departments, and the Courts of Law.

7-10. In *Weiss v. United States*, the Supreme Court held that the President can appoint commissioned military officers as military judges without first needing to seek the advice and consent of the Senate, 510 U.S. 164 (1994). The Court rejected the argument that the position of military judge is so different from other positions a commissioned officer can be assigned to that the Appointments Clause requires Senate action. Of course, Congress could require separate appointments; but it need not do so.

§ 7.04 The Power to Remove

HUMPHREY'S EXECUTOR v. UNITED STATES

United States Supreme Court
295 U.S. 602 (1935)

Mr. Justice Sutherland delivered the opinion of the Court.

Plaintiff brought suit in the Court of Claims against the United States to recover a sum of money alleged to be due the deceased for salary as a Federal Trade Commissioner from October 8, 1933, when the President undertook to remove him from office, to the time of his death on February 14, 1934. The court below has certified to this court two questions . . . in respect of the power of the President to make the removal. The material facts which give rise to the questions are as follows:

§ 7.04   EXECUTIVE CONTROL OF AGENCY DISCRETION   653

William E. Humphrey, the decedent, on December 10, 1931, was nominated by President Hoover to succeed himself as a member of the Federal Trade Commission and was confirmed by the United States Senate. He was duly commissioned for a term of seven years expiring September 25, 1938; and, after taking the required oath of office, entered upon his duties. On July 25, 1933, President Roosevelt addressed a letter to the commissioner asking for his resignation, on the ground "that the aims and purposes of the administration with respect to the work of the Commission can be carried out most effectively with personnel of my own selection," but disclaiming any reflection upon the commissioner personally or upon his services. The commissioner replied, asking time to consult his friends. After some further correspondence upon the subject, the President, on August 31, 1933, wrote the commissioner expressing the hope that the resignation would be forthcoming and saying:

> "You will, I know, realize that I do not feel that your mind and my mind go along together on either the policies or the administering of the Federal Trade Commission, and, frankly, I think it is best for the people of this country that I should have a full confidence."

The commissioner declined to sign, and on October 7, 1933, the President wrote him:

> "Effective as of this date, you are hereby removed from the office of Commissioner of the Federal Trade Commission."

Humphrey never acquiesced in this action, but continued thereafter to insist that he was still a member of the commission, entitled to perform its duties and receive the compensation provided by law at the rate of $10,000 per annum. . . .

. . . The question first to be considered is whether, by the provisions of § 1 of the Federal Trade Commission Act already quoted, the President's power is limited to removal for the specific causes enumerated therein. . . .

. . . But if the intention of Congress that no removal should be made during the specified term except for one or more of the enumerated causes were not clear upon the face of the statute, as we think it is, it would be made clear by a consideration of the character of the commission and the legislative history which accompanied and preceded the passage of the act.

The commission is to be nonpartisan; and it must, from the very nature of its duties, act with entire impartiality. It is charged with the enforcement of no policy except the policy of the law. Its duties are neither political nor executive, but predominantly quasi-judicial and quasi-legislative. Like the Interstate Commerce Commission, its members are called upon to exercise the trained judgment of a body of experts "appointed by law and informed by experience." . . .

The legislative reports in both houses of Congress clearly reflect the view that a fixed term was necessary to the effective and fair administration of the law. In the report to the Senate (No. 597, Sixty-third Cong., 2d Sess., pp. 10–11), the Senate Committee on Interstate Commerce, in support of the bill which afterwards became the act in question, after referring to the provision fixing the term of office at seven years, so arranged that the membership would not be subject to complete change at any one time, said:

"The work of this commission will be of a most exacting and difficult character, demanding persons who have experience in the problems to be met — that is, a proper knowledge of both the public requirements and the practical affairs of industry. It is manifestly desirable that the terms of the commissioners shall be long enough to give them an opportunity to acquire the expertness in dealing with these special questions concerning industry that comes from experience. . . ."

Thus, the language of the act, the legislative reports and the general purposes of the legislation as reflected by the debates, all combine to demonstrate the Congressional intent to create a body of experts who shall gain experience by length of service — a body which shall be independent of Executive authority, *except in its selection,* and free to exercise its judgment without the leave or hindrance of any other official or any department of the government. To the accomplishment of these purposes it is clear that Congress was of the opinion that length and certainty of tenure would vitally contribute. And to hold that, nevertheless, the members of the commission continue in office at the mere will of the President, might be to thwart, in large measure, the very ends which Congress sought to realize by definitely fixing the term of office.

We conclude that the intent of the act is to limit the executive power of removal to the causes enumerated, the existence of none of which is claimed here; and we pass to the second question.

. . . To support its contention that the removal provision of § 1, as we have just construed it, is an unconstitutional interference with the executive power of the President, the government's chief reliance is *Myers v. United States,* 272 U.S. 52 [1926]. That case has been so recently decided, and the prevailing and dissenting opinions so fully review the general subject of the power of executive removal, that further discussion would add little of value to the wealth of material there collected. These opinions examine at length the historical, legislative and judicial data bearing upon the question. . . . Nevertheless, the narrow point actually decided was only that the President had power to remove a postmaster of the first class, without the advice and consent of the Senate, as required by act of Congress. . . .

. . . .

The office of a postmaster is so essentially unlike the office now involved that the decision in the *Myers* case cannot be accepted as controlling our decision here. A postmaster is an executive officer restricted in the performance of executive functions. He is charged with no duty at all related to either the legislative or judicial power. The actual decision in the *Myers* case finds support in the theory that such an officer is merely one of the units in the executive department and hence inherently subject to the exclusive and illimitable power of removal by the chief executive, whose subordinate and aid he is. Putting aside *dicta,* which may be followed if sufficiently persuasive but which are not controlling, the necessary reach of the decision goes far enough to include all purely executive officers. It goes no farther; — much less does it include an officer who occupies no place in the executive department and who exercises no part of the executive power vested by the Constitution in the President.

The Federal Trade Commission is an administrative body created by Congress to carry into effect legislative policies embodied in the statute, in accordance with the legislative standard therein prescribed, and to perform other specified duties as a legislative or as a judicial aid. Such a body cannot in any proper sense be characterized as an arm or an eye of the executive. Its duties are performed without executive leave and, in the contemplation of the statute, must be free from executive control. In administering the provisions of the statute in respect of "unfair methods of competition" — that is to say in filling in and administering the details embodied by the general standard — the commission acts in part quasi-legislatively and in part quasi-judicially. In making investigations and reports thereon for the information of Congress under § 6, in aid of the legislative power, it acts as a legislative agency. Under § 7, which authorizes the commission to act as a master in chancery under rules prescribed by the court, it acts as an agency of the judiciary. To the extent that it exercises any executive function — as distinguished from executive power in the constitutional sense — it does so in the discharge and effectuation of its quasi-legislative or quasi-judicial powers, or as an agency of the legislative or judicial department of the government.[1]

. . . The authority of Congress, in creating quasi-legislative or quasi-judicial agencies, to require them to act in discharge of their duties independently of executive control, cannot well be doubted; and that authority includes, as an appropriate incident, power to fix the period during which they shall continue in office, and to forbid their removal except for cause in the meantime. For it is quite evident that one who holds his office only during the pleasure of another, cannot be depended upon to maintain an attitude of independence against the latter's will.

. . . .

The result of what we now have said is this: Whether the power of the President to remove an officer shall prevail over the authority of Congress to condition the power by fixing a definite term and precluding a removal except for cause, will depend upon the character of the office; the *Myers* decision, affirming the power of the President alone to make the removal, is confined to purely executive officers; and as to officers of the kind here under consideration, we hold that no removal can be made during the prescribed term for which the officer is appointed, except for one or more of the causes named in the applicable statute.

To the extent that, between the decision in the *Myers* case, which sustains the unrestrictable power of the President to remove purely executive officers, and our present decision that such power does not extend to an office such as that here involved, there shall remain a field of doubt, we leave such cases as may fall within it for future consideration and determination as they may arise.

---

[1] The provision of § 6(d) of the act which authorizes the President to direct an investigation and report of the commission in relation to alleged violations of the anti-trust acts, is so obviously collateral to the main design of the act as not to detract from the force of this general statement as to the character of that body.

[A brief concurring opinion of MR. JUSTICE MCREYNOLDS, referring to his *Myers* dissent, is omitted.]

NOTES AND QUESTIONS

7-11. Prior to *Humphrey,* as the Court notes, the leading case on removal was *Myers v. U.S.,* 272 U.S. 52 (1926). That case involved President Wilson's removal of a postmaster general. As Chief Justice Taft explained in *Myers*:

> [T]here may be duties of a quasi-judicial character imposed on executive officers and members of executive tribunals whose decisions after hearing affect interests of individuals, the discharge of which the President can not in a particular case properly influence or control. But even in such a case he may consider the decision after its rendition as a reason for removing the officer, on the ground that the discretion regularly entrusted to that officer by statute has not been on the whole intelligently or wisely exercised. Otherwise he does not discharge his own constitutional duty of seeing that the laws be faithfully executed.

Given the Court's approach in *Myers,* how would you have advised President Roosevelt if he asked whether he had the power to remove Humphrey?

7-12. Are you comfortable with the way the *Humphrey* court distinguishes *Myers*? What is a purely executive office? Can you distinguish between an executive power as opposed to an executive function? Does the Court in *Humphrey* provide any guidance?

7-13. Many years after *Humphrey* was decided, Justice Jackson wrote in his book, *The Struggle for Judicial Supremacy,*[*] page 106, that:

> What the Court had before declared to be a constitutional duty of the President had become in Mr. Roosevelt a constitutional offense. Small wonder that the decision became a political instrument. Those who saw executive dictatorship just round the corner had their fears confirmed: the President could be restrained only by the Court. Those who thought the ghost of dictatorship wore judicial robes had their fears, too, confirmed: the Court was applying to President Roosevelt rules different from those it had applied to his predecessors.

In retrospect, do you think that the Court's approach to these separation of powers issues justified the fears of those who foresaw a dramatic expansion of the administrative state? Did this approach make it easier or harder to uphold the constitutionality of agencies engaged in policymaking, enforcement and adjudication?

7-14. What do you think of the Court's conception of an independent agency? Compare this to the lower court's opinion in *Bowsher v. Synar,* a case dealing with the constitutionality of the Balanced Budget and Emergency Deficit Control Act of 1985, 626 F. Supp. 1374, 1398 (1986):

---

[*] Copyright © 1941. Vintage Books.

It is not as obvious today as it seemed in the 1930s that there can be such things as genuinely "independent" regulatory agencies, bodies of impartial experts whose independence from the President does not entail correspondingly greater dependence upon the committees of Congress to which they are then immediately accountable; or indeed, that the decisions of such agencies so clearly involve scientific judgment rather than political choice that it is even theoretically desirable to insulate them from the democratic process.

Along with such doubts about the policy justifications for independent agencies, the district court also expressed serious concern about the overall constitutionality of the so-called "headless fourth branch."

It has . . . always been difficult to reconcile *Humphrey's Executor*'s "headless fourth branch" with a constitutional text and tradition establishing three branches of government. . . .

Id. The lower court emphasized that doctrinal changes had occurred since *Humphrey's Executor* had been decided, citing *INS v. Chadha* as an example of the Supreme Court's acknowledgment of such changes:

[S]ome of the language of the majority opinion in *Chadha* does not lie comfortably beside the central revelation of *Humphrey's Executor* that an officer such as a Federal Trade Commissioner "occupies no place in the executive department," and that an agency which exercises only "quasi-legislative or quasi-judicial powers" is "an agency of the legislative or judicial departments of the government."

Id. at 1399. Did the Supreme Court agree? Consider the following case.

BOWSHER v. SYNAR

United States Supreme Court
478 U.S. 714 (1986)

CHIEF JUSTICE BURGER delivered the opinion of the Court.

The question presented by these appeals is whether the assignment by Congress to the Comptroller General of the United States of certain functions under the Balanced Budget and Emergency Deficit Control Act of 1985 violates the doctrine of separation of powers.

I

A

On December 12, 1985, the President signed into law the Balanced Budget and Emergency Deficit Control Act of 1985, . . . popularly known as the "Gramm-Rudman-Hollings Act." The purpose of the Act is to eliminate the federal budget deficit. To that end, the Act sets a "maximum deficit amount" for federal spending for each of fiscal years 1986 through 1991. The size of that maximum deficit amount progressively reduces to zero in fiscal year 1991. If in any fiscal year the federal budget deficit exceeds the maximum deficit amount by more than a specified sum, the Act requires across-the-board cuts in federal spending to reach the targeted deficit level, with half of the cuts made to defense programs and the other half made to non-defense programs. The Act exempts certain priority programs from these cuts. § 255.

These "automatic" reductions are accomplished through a rather complicated procedure, spelled out in § 251, the so-called "reporting provisions" of the Act. Each year, the Directors of the Office of Management and Budget (OMB) and the Congressional Budget Office (CBO) independently estimate the amount of the federal budget deficit for the upcoming fiscal year. If that deficit exceeds the maximum targeted deficit amount for that fiscal year by more than a specified amount, the Directors of OMB and CBO independently calculate, on a program-by-program basis, the budget reductions necessary to ensure that the deficit does not exceed the maximum deficit amount. The Act then requires the Directors to report jointly their deficit estimates and budget reduction calculations to the Comptroller General.

The Comptroller General, after reviewing the Directors' reports, then reports his conclusions to the President. § 251(b). The President in turn must issue a "sequestration" order mandating the spending reductions specified by the Comptroller General. § 252. There follows a period during which Congress may by legislation reduce spending to obviate, in whole or in part, the need for the sequestration order. If such reductions are not enacted, the sequestration order becomes effective and the spending reductions included in that order are made.

Anticipating constitutional challenge to these procedures, the Act also contains a "fallback" deficit reduction process to take effect "[i]n the event that any of the reporting procedures described in section 251 are invalidated." § 274(f). Under these provisions, the report prepared by the Directors of OMB and the CBO is submitted directly to a specially-created Temporary Joint Committee on Deficit Reduction, which must report in five days to both Houses a joint resolution setting forth the content of the Directors' report. Congress then must vote on the resolution under special rules, which render amendments out of order. If the resolution is passed and signed by the President, it then serves as the basis for a Presidential sequestration order.

B

Within hours of the President's signing of the Act,[1] Congressman Synar, who had voted against the Act, filed a complaint seeking declaratory relief that the Act was unconstitutional. Eleven other Members later joined Congressman Synar's suit. A virtually identical lawsuit was also filed by the National Treasury Employees Union. The Union alleged that its members had

---

[1] In his signing statement, the President expressed his view that the Act was constitutionally defective because of the Comptroller General's ability to exercise supervisory authority over the President. [*Ed.* Why did the President then sign the bill? Did he have a duty to veto the legislation?] *Statement on Signing H.R. Res. 372 Into Law,* 21 Weekly Comp. of Pres. Doc. 1491 (1985).

been injured as a result of the Act's automatic spending reduction provisions, which have suspended certain cost-of-living benefit increases to the Union's members.

A three-judge District Court . . . invalidated the reporting provisions. *Synar v. United States,* 626 F. Supp. 1374 (D.C. 1986) (Scalia, Johnson, and Gasch, JJ.). . . .

Although the District Court concluded that the Act survived a delegation doctrine challenge, it held that the role of the Comptroller General in the deficit reduction process violated the constitutionally imposed separation of powers. . . .

Appeals were taken directly to this Court pursuant to § 274(b) of the Act. We noted probable jurisdiction and expedited consideration of the appeals. 475 U.S. 1009. . . . We affirm. . . .

III

. . . .

The Constitution does not contemplate an active role for Congress in the supervision of officers charged with the execution of the laws it enacts. The President appoints "Officers of the United States" with the "Advice and Consent of the Senate. . . ." Article II, § 2. Once the appointment has been made and confirmed, however, the Constitution explicitly provides for removal of Officers of the United States by Congress only upon impeachment by the House of Representatives and conviction by the Senate. An impeachment by the House and trial by the Senate can rest only on "Treason, Bribery or other high Crimes and Misdemeanors." Article II, § 4. A direct congressional role in the removal of officers charged with the execution of the laws beyond this limited one is inconsistent with separation of powers.

. . . .

This Court first directly addressed this issue in *Myers v. United States,* 272 U.S. 52, 47 S. Ct. 21 (1926). At issue in *Myers* was a statute providing that certain postmasters could be removed only "by and with the advice and consent of the Senate." The President removed one such Postmaster without Senate approval, and a lawsuit ensued. Chief Justice Taft, writing for the Court, declared the statute unconstitutional on the ground that for Congress to "draw to itself, or to either branch of it, the power to remove or the right to participate in the exercise of that power . . . would be . . . to infringe the constitutional principle of the separation of governmental powers." *Id.,* at 161.

A decade later, in *Humphrey's Executor v. United States,* 295 U.S. 602 (1935), relied upon heavily by appellants, a Federal Trade Commissioner who had been removed by the President sought backpay. *Humphrey's Executor* involved an issue not presented either in the *Myers* case or in this case — *i.e.,* the power of Congress to limit the President's powers of removal of a Federal Trade Commissioner. 295 U.S., at 630.[4] The relevant statute

---

[4] Appellants therefore are wide of the mark in arguing that an affirmance in this case requires casting doubt on the status of "independent" agencies because no issues involving such agencies are presented here. The statutes establishing independent agencies typically specify either that

permitted removal "by the President," but only "for inefficiency, neglect of duty, or malfeasance in office." Justice Sutherland, speaking for the Court, upheld the statute, holding that "illimitable power of removal is not possessed by the President [with respect to Federal Trade Commissioners]." 295 U.S., at 628–629. The Court distinguished *Myers,* reaffirming its holding that congressional participation in the removal of executive officers is unconstitutional. . . .

. . . To permit the execution of the laws to be vested in an officer answerable only to Congress would, in practical terms, reserve in Congress control over the execution of the laws. . . . The structure of the Constitution does not permit Congress to execute the laws; it follows that Congress cannot grant to an officer under its control what it does not possess. . . . With these principles in mind, we turn to consideration of whether the Comptroller General is controlled by Congress.

IV

Appellants urge that the Comptroller General performs his duties independently and is not subservient to Congress. We agree with the District Court that this contention does not bear close scrutiny.

The critical factor lies in the provisions of the statute defining the Comptroller General's office relating to removability.[5] Although the Comptroller General is nominated by the President from a list of three individuals recommended by the Speaker of the House of Representatives and the President *pro tempore* of the Senate, see 31 U.S.C. § 703(a)(2), and confirmed by the Senate, he is removable only at the initiative of Congress. He may be removed not only by impeachment but also by joint resolution of Congress "at any time" resting on any one of the following bases:

"(i) permanent disability;
"(ii) inefficiency;
"(iii) neglect of duty;
"(iv) malfeasance; or
"(v) a felony or conduct involving moral turpitude."

31 U.S.C. § 703(e)(1)B.[7]

---

the agency members are removable by the President for specified causes, *see, e.g.,* 15 U.S.C. § 41 (members of the Federal Trade Commission may be removed by the President "for inefficiency, neglect of duty, or malfeasance in office"), or else do not specify a removal procedure, *see, e.g.,* 2 U.S.C. § 437c (Federal Election Commission). This case involves nothing like these statutes, but rather a statute that provides for direct congressional involvement over the decision to remove the Comptroller General. Appellants have referred us to no independent agency whose members are removable by the Congress for certain causes short of impeachable offenses, as is the Comptroller General. . . .

[5] We reject appellants' argument that consideration of the effect of a removal provision is not "ripe" until that provision is actually used. As the District Court concluded, "it is the Comptroller General's presumed desire to avoid removal by pleasing Congress, which creates the here-and-now subservience to another branch that raises separation-of-powers problems." *Synar v. United States,* 626 F. Supp. 1374, 1392 (D.C. 1986). The Impeachment Clause of the Constitution can hardly be thought to be undermined because of nonuse.

[7] Although the President could veto such a joint resolution, the veto could be overridden by a two-thirds vote of both Houses of Congress. Thus, the Comptroller General could be removed in the face of Presidential opposition. Like the District Court, 626 F. Supp., at 1393, n. 21, we therefore read the removal provision as authorizing removal by Congress alone.

This provision was included, as one Congressman explained in urging passage of the Act, because Congress "felt that [the Comptroller General] should be brought under the sole control of Congress, so that Congress at the moment when it found he was inefficient and was not carrying on the duties of his office as he should and as the Congress expected, could remove him without the long, tedious process of a trial by impeachment." 61 Cong. Rec. 1081 (1921).

The removal provision was an important part of the legislative scheme. . . . Representative Sisson observed that the removal provisions would give "[t]he Congress of the United States . . . absolute control of the man's destiny in office." 61 Cong. Rec. 987 (1921). The ultimate design was to "give the legislative branch of the Government control of the audit, not through the power of appointment, but through the power of removal." 58 Cong. Rec. 7211 (1919) (Rep. Temple).

JUSTICE WHITE contends: "The statute does not permit anyone to remove the Comptroller at will; removal is permitted only for specified cause, with the existence of cause to be determined by Congress following a hearing. Any removal under the statute would presumably be subject to post-termination judicial review to ensure that a hearing had in fact been held and that the finding of cause for removal was not arbitrary." . . . The statute permits removal for "inefficiency," "neglect of duty," or "malfeasance." These terms are very broad and, as interpreted by Congress, could sustain removal of a Comptroller General for any number of actual or perceived transgressions of the legislative will. The Constitutional Convention chose to permit impeachment of executive officers only for "Treason, Bribery, or other high Crimes and Misdemeanors." It rejected language that would have permitted impeachment for "maladministration," with Madison arguing that "[s]o vague a term will be equivalent to a tenure during pleasure of the Senate." 2 M. Farrand, p. 550 (1911). . . .

This much said, we must also add that the dissent is simply in error to suggest that the political realities reveal that the Comptroller General is free from influence by Congress. . . . The Comptroller General heads the General Accounting Office (GAO), "an instrumentality of the United States Government independent of the executive departments," . . . which was created by Congress in 1921 as part of the Budget and Accounting Act of 1921. . . . Congress created the office because it believed that it "needed an officer, responsible to it alone, to check upon the application of public funds in accordance with appropriations." . . .

. . . .

Over the years, the Comptrollers General have also viewed themselves as part of the Legislative Branch. . . .

Against this background, we see no escape from the conclusion that, because Congress has retained removal authority over the Comptroller General, he may not be entrusted with executive powers. The remaining question is whether the Comptroller General has been assigned such powers in the Balanced Budget and Emergency Deficit Control Act of 1985.

V

[The Court reviewed the Comptroller General's responsibilities under the Act, particularly his duty to prepare a "report" that contains "detailed estimates of projected federal revenues and expenditures. The report must also specify the reductions, if any, necessary to reduce the deficit to the target for the appropriate fiscal year. The reductions must be set forth on a program-by-program basis." The Court concluded that the Comptroller General's functions clearly involved "execution of the law in constitutional terms."]

. . . Congress of course initially determined the content of the Balanced Budget and Emergency Deficit Control Act; and undoubtedly the content of the Act determines the nature of the executive duty. However, as *Chadha* makes clear, once Congress makes its choice in enacting legislation, its participation ends. Congress can thereafter control the execution of its enactment only indirectly — by passing new legislation. . . . By placing the responsibility for execution of the Balanced Budget and Emergency Deficit Control Act in the hands of an officer who is subject to removal only by itself, Congress in effect has retained control over the execution of the Act and has intruded into the executive function. The Constitution does not permit such intrusion.

VI

We now turn to the final issue of remedy. . . . The language of the Balanced Budget and Emergency Deficit Control Act itself settles the issue. In § 274(f), Congress has explicitly provided "fallback" provisions in the Act that take effect "[i]n the event . . . *any* of the reporting procedures described in section 251 are invalidated." § 274(f)(1) (emphasis added). The fallback provisions are "'fully operative as a law,'" *Buckley v. Valeo,* 424 U.S., at 108. . . . Assuming that appellants are correct in urging that this matter must be resolved on the basis of congressional intent, the intent appears to have been for § 274(f) to be given effect in this situation. . . .

VII

. . . .

Our judgment is stayed for a period not to exceed 60 days to permit Congress to implement the fallback provisions.

It is so ordered.

Justice Stevens, with whom Justice Marshall joins, concurring in the judgment.

. . . It is not the dormant, carefully circumscribed congressional removal power that represents the primary constitutional evil. . . . Rather, I am convinced that the Comptroller General must be characterized as an agent of Congress because of his longstanding statutory responsibilities; that the powers assigned to him under the Gramm-Rudman-Hollings Act require him to make policy that will bind the Nation; and that, when Congress, or a component or an agent of Congress, seeks to make policy that will bind the

Nation, it must follow the procedures mandated by Article I of the Constitution — through passage by both Houses and presentment to the President. In short, Congress may not exercise its fundamental power to formulate national policy by delegating that power to one of its two Houses, to a legislative committee, or to an individual agent of the Congress such as the Speaker of the House of Representatives, the Sergeant at Arms of the Senate, or the Director of the Congressional Budget Office. *INS v. Chadha,* 462 U.S. 919 (1983). That principle, I believe, is applicable to the Comptroller General.

I

. . . .

The notion that the removal power at issue here automatically creates some kind of "here-and-now subservience" of the Comptroller General to Congress is belied by history. There is no evidence that Congress has ever removed, or threatened to remove, the Comptroller General for reasons of policy. Moreover, the President has long possessed a comparable power to remove members of the Federal Trade Commission, yet it is universally accepted that they are independent of, rather than subservient to, the President in performing their official duties. Thus, the statute that the Court construed in *Humphrey's Executor v. United States,* 295 U.S. 602 (1935), provided:

> "Any commissioner may be removed by the President for inefficiency, neglect of duty, or malfeasance in office." 38 Stat. 718.

In upholding the congressional limitations on the President's power of removal, the Court stressed the independence of the Commission from the President.[2] There was no suggestion that the retained Presidential removal powers — similar to those at issue here — created a subservience to the President.[3]

[T]he *Humphrey's Executor* analysis at least demonstrates that it is entirely proper for Congress to specify the qualifications for an office that it has created, and that the prescription of what might be termed "dereliction-of-

---

[2] *See Humphrey's Executor,* 295 U.S., at 625–626 (describing congressional intention to create "a body which shall be independent of executive authority, *except in its selection,* and free to exercise its judgment without the leave or hindrance of any other official or any department of the government") (emphasis in original).

[3] The manner in which President Roosevelt exercised his removal power further underscores the propriety of presuming that Congress, and the President, will not use statutorily prescribed removal causes as pretexts for other removal reasons. President Roosevelt never claimed that his removal of Humphrey was for one of the statutorily prescribed reasons — inefficiency, neglect of duty, or malfeasance in office. The President's removal letter merely stated:

> " 'Effective as of this date you are hereby removed from the office of Commissioner of the Federal Trade Commission.' " *See id.*, at 619. Previously, the President had written to Commissioner Humphrey stating:

> " 'You will, I know, realize that I do not feel that your mind and my mind go along together on either the policies or the administering of the Federal Trade Commission, and, frankly, I think it is best for the people of this country that I should have a full confidence.' " *Ibid.*

duty" removal standards does not itself impair the independence of the official subject to such standards.[4]

The fact that Congress retained for itself the power to remove the Comptroller General thus is not necessarily an adequate reason for concluding that his role in the Gramm-Rudman-Hollings budget reduction process is unconstitutional. It is, however, a fact that lends support to my ultimate conclusion that, in exercising his functions under this Act, he serves as an agent of the Congress.

. . . .

III

Everyone agrees that the powers assigned to the Comptroller General by § 251(b) and § 251(c)(2) of the Gramm-Rudman-Hollings Act are extremely important. They require him to exercise sophisticated economic judgment concerning anticipated trends in the Nation's economy, projected levels of unemployment, interest rates, and the special problems that may be confronted by the many components of a vast federal bureaucracy. His duties are anything but ministerial — he is not merely a clerk wearing a "green eye shade" as he undertakes these tasks. Rather, he is vested with the kind of responsibilities that Congress has elected to discharge itself under the fallback provision that will become effective if and when § 251(b) and § 251(c)(2) are held invalid. Unless we make the naive assumption that the economic destiny of the Nation could be safely entrusted to a mindless bank of computers, the powers that this Act vests in the Comptroller General must be recognized as having transcendent importance.[12]

The Court concludes that the Gramm-Rudman-Hollings Act impermissibly assigns the Comptroller General "executive powers." . . . JUSTICE WHITE's dissent agrees that "the powers exercised by the Comptroller under the Act may be characterized as 'executive' in that they involve the interpretation and carrying out of the Act's mandate." . . . This conclusion is not only far from

---

[4] Indeed, even in *Myers v. United States*, 272 U.S. 52 (1926), in its challenge to the provision requiring Senate approval of the removal of a postmaster, the Federal Government assumed that Congress had power to limit the terms of removal to reasons that relate to the office. Solicitor General Beck recognized "that the power of removal may be subject to such general laws as do not destroy the exercise by the President of his power of removal, and which leaves to him the exercise of the power subject to such general laws as may fairly measure the standard of public service." . . . At oral argument, the Solicitor General explained his position:

"Mr. Beck . . . Suppose the Congress creates an office and says that it shall only be filled by a man learned in the law; and suppose it further provides that, if a man ceases to be a member of the bar, he shall be removed. I am not prepared to say that such a law can not be reconciled with the Constitution. What I do say is that, when the condition imposed upon the creation of the office has no reasonable relation to the office; when it is not a legislative standard to be applied by the President, and is not the declaration of qualifications, but is the creation of an appointing power other than the President, then Congress has crossed the dead line, for it has usurped the prerogative of the President." 272 U.S., at 96–97.

[12] The element of judgment that the Comptroller General must exercise is evident by the congressional recognition that there may be "differences between the contents of [his] report and the report of the Directors" of the Congressional Budget Office and the Office of Management and Budget. § 251(b)(2).

obvious but also rests on the unstated and unsound premise that there is a definite line that distinguishes executive power from legislative power.

. . . .

One reason that the exercise of legislative, executive, and judicial powers cannot be categorically distributed among three mutually exclusive branches of Government is that governmental power cannot always be readily characterized with only one of those three labels. On the contrary, as our cases demonstrate, a particular function, like a chameleon, will often take on the aspect of the office to which it is assigned. For this reason, "[w]hen any Branch acts, it is presumptively exercising the power the Constitution has delegated to it." *INS v. Chadha,* 462 U.S., at 951.[13]

. . . .

The powers delegated to the Comptroller General by § 251 of the Act before us today have a similar chameleon-like quality. The District Court persuasively explained why they may be appropriately characterized as executive powers. But, when that delegation is held invalid, the "fallback provision" provides that the report that would otherwise be issued by the Comptroller General shall be issued by Congress itself. In the event that the resolution is enacted, the congressional report will have the same legal consequences as if it had been issued by the Comptroller General. In that event, moreover, surely no one would suggest that Congress had acted in any capacity other than "legislative." Since the District Court expressly recognized the validity of what it described as the " 'fallback' deficit reduction process," *Synar v. United States,* 626 F. Supp. 1374, 1377 (D.C. 1986), it obviously did not doubt the constitutionality of the performance by Congress of the functions delegated to the Comptroller General.

. . . .

Thus, I do not agree that the Comptroller General's responsibilities under the Gramm-Rudman-Hollings Act must be termed "executive powers," or even that our inquiry is much advanced by using that term. For, whatever the label given the functions to be performed by the Comptroller General under § 251 — or by the Congress under § 274 — the District Court had no difficulty in concluding that Congress could delegate the performance of those functions to another branch of the Government. If the delegation to a stranger is permissible, why may not Congress delegate the same responsibilities to one of its own agents? That is the central question before us today.

---

[13] "Perhaps as a matter of political science we could say that Congress should only concern itself with broad principles of policy and leave their application in particular cases to the executive branch. But no such rule can be found in the Constitution itself or in legislative practice. It is fruitless, therefore, to try to draw any sharp and logical line between legislative and executive functions. Characteristically, the draftsmen of 1787 did not even attempt doctrinaire definitions, but placed their reliance in the mechanics of the Constitution. One of their principal devices was to vest the legislative powers in the two Houses of Congress and to make the President a part of the legislative process by requiring that all bills passed by the two Houses be submitted to him for his approval or disapproval, his disapproval or veto to be overridden only by a two-thirds vote of each House. It is in such checks upon powers, rather than in the classifications of powers, that our governmental system finds equilibrium." Ginnane, *The Control of Federal Administration by Congressional Resolutions and Committees,* 66 HARV. L. REV. 569, 571 (1953) (footnote omitted).

IV

. . . .

The Gramm-Rudman-Hollings Act assigns to the Comptroller General the duty to make policy decisions that have the force of law. . . . Article I of the Constitution specifies the procedures that Congress must follow when it makes policy that binds the Nation: its legislation must be approved by both Houses of Congress and presented to the President. . . . If Congress were free to delegate its policymaking authority to one of its components, or to one of its agents, it would be able to evade "the carefully crafted restraints spelled out in the Constitution." [*Chadha*] at 959. That danger — congressional action that evades constitutional restraints — is not present when Congress delegates lawmaking power to the executive or to an independent agency.

. . . .

In my opinion, Congress itself could not exercise the Gramm-Rudman-Hollings functions through a concurrent resolution. The fact that the fallback provision in § 274 requires a joint resolution rather than a concurrent resolution indicates that Congress endorsed this view. I think it equally clear that Congress may not simply delegate those functions to an agent such as the Congressional Budget Office. Since I am persuaded that the Comptroller General is also fairly deemed to be an agent of Congress, he too cannot exercise such functions. . . .

I concur in the judgment.

JUSTICE WHITE, dissenting.

The Court, acting in the name of separation of powers, takes upon itself to strike down the Gramm-Rudman-Hollings Act, one of the most novel and far-reaching legislative responses to a national crisis since the New Deal. The basis of the Court's action is a solitary provision of another statute that was passed over 60 years ago and has lain dormant since that time. I cannot concur in the Court's action. Like the Court, I will not purport to speak to the wisdom of the policies incorporated in the legislation the Court invalidates; that is a matter for the Congress and the Executive, *both* of which expressed their assent to the statute barely half a year ago. I will, however, address the wisdom of the Court's willingness to interpose its distressingly formalistic view of separation of powers as a bar to the attainment of governmental objectives through the means chosen by the Congress and the President in the legislative process established by the Constitution. . . . Today's result is even more misguided. As I will explain, the Court's decision rests on a feature of the legislative scheme that is of minimal practical significance and that presents no substantial threat to the basic scheme of separation of powers. In attaching dispositive significance to what should be regarded as a triviality, the Court neglects what has in the past been recognized as a fundamental principle governing consideration of disputes over separation of powers:

> "The actual art of governing under our Constitution does not and cannot conform to judicial definitions of the power of any of its branches based on isolated clauses or even single Articles torn from context. While the Constitution diffuses power the better to secure liberty, it also contemplates

I

Before examining the merits of the Court's argument, I wish to emphasize what it is that the Court quite pointedly and correctly does *not* hold: namely, that "executive" powers of the sort granted the Comptroller by the Act may only be exercised by officers removable at will by the President. The Court's apparent unwillingness to accept this argument, which has been tendered in this Court by the Solicitor General,[2] is fully consistent with the Court's longstanding recognition that it is within the power of Congress under the "Necessary and Proper" Clause, Art. I, § 8, to vest authority that falls within the Court's definition of executive power in officers who are not subject to removal at will by the President and are therefore not under the President's direct control. *See, e.g., Humphrey's Executor v. United States,* 295 U.S. 602 (1935); *Wiener v. United States,* 357 U.S. 349 (1958).[3] In an earlier day, in which simpler notions of the role of government in society prevailed, it was perhaps plausible to insist that all "executive" officers be subject to an unqualified Presidential removal power, *see Myers v. United States,* 272 U.S. 52 (1926); but with the advent and triumph of the administrative state and the accompanying multiplication of the tasks undertaken by the Federal Government, the Court has been virtually compelled to recognize that Congress may reasonably deem it "necessary and proper" to vest some among the broad new array of governmental functions in officers who are free from the partisanship that may be expected of agents wholly dependent upon the President.

The Court's recognition of the legitimacy of legislation vesting "executive" authority in officers independent of the President does not imply derogation of the President's own constitutional authority — indeed, duty — to "take Care that the Laws be faithfully executed," Art. II, § 3, for any such duty is necessarily limited to a great extent by the content of the laws enacted by the Congress. As Justice Holmes put it: "The duty of the President to see that

---

[2] The Solicitor General appeared on behalf of the "United States," or, more properly, the Executive Departments, which intervened to attack the constitutionality of the statute that the Chief Executive had earlier endorsed and signed into law.

[3] Although the Court in *Humphrey's Executor* characterized the powers of the Federal Trade Commissioner whose tenure was at issue as "quasi-legislative" and "quasi-judicial," it is clear that the FTC's power to enforce and give content to the Federal Trade Commission Act's proscription of "unfair" acts and practices and methods of competition is in fact "executive" in the same sense as is the Comptroller's authority under Gramm-Rudman-Hollings — that is, it involves the implementation (or the interpretation and application) of an Act of Congress. Thus, although the Court in *Humphrey's Executor* found the use of the labels "quasi-legislative" and "quasi-judicial" helpful in "distinguishing" its then-recent decision in *Myers v. United States,* 272 U.S. 52 (1926), these terms are hardly of any use in limiting the holding of the case; as Justice Jackson pointed out, "[t]he mere retreat to the qualifying 'quasi' is implicit with confession that all recognized classifications have broken down, and 'quasi' is a smooth cover which we draw over our confusion as we might use a counterpane to conceal a disordered bed." *FTC v. Ruberoid Co.,* 343 U.S. 470, 487–488 (1952).

the laws be executed is a duty that does not go beyond the laws or require him to achieve more than Congress sees fit to leave within his power." *Myers v. United States, supra* at 177. Justice Holmes perhaps overstated his case, for there are undoubtedly executive functions that, regardless of the enactments of Congress, must be performed by officers subject to removal at will by the President. Whether a particular function falls within this class or within the far larger class that may be relegated to independent officers "will depend upon the character of the office." *Humphrey's Executor, supra* at 631. In determining whether a limitation on the President's power to remove an officer performing executive functions constitutes a violation of the constitutional scheme of separation of powers, a court must "focu[s] on the extent to which [such a limitation] prevents the Executive Branch from accomplishing its constitutionally assigned functions." *Nixon v. Administrator of General Services*, 433 U.S. 425, 443 (1977). "Only where the potential for disruption is present must we then determine whether that impact is satisfied by an overriding need to promote objectives within the constitutional authority of Congress." *Ibid.* This inquiry is, to be sure, not one that will beget easy answers; it provides nothing approaching a bright-line rule or set of rules. Such an inquiry, however, is necessitated by the recognition that "formalistic and unbending rules" in the area of separation of powers may "unduly constrict Congress' ability to take needed and innovative action pursuant to its Article I powers." *Commodity Futures Trading Comm'n v. Schor* [478 U.S. 833, 851 (1985)].

It is evident (and nothing in the Court's opinion is to the contrary) that the powers exercised by the Comptroller General under the Gramm-Rudman-Hollings Act are not such that vesting them in an officer not subject to removal at will by the President would in itself improperly interfere with Presidential powers. . . . Rather, the result of such a delegation, from the standpoint of the President, is no different from the result of more traditional forms of appropriation: under either system, the level of funds available to the Executive Branch to carry out its duties is not within the President's discretionary control. To be sure, if the budget-cutting mechanism required the responsible officer to exercise a great deal of policymaking discretion, one might argue that having created such broad discretion Congress had some obligation based upon Art. II to vest it in the Chief Executive or his agents. In Gramm-Rudman-Hollings, however, Congress has done no such thing; instead, it has created a precise and articulated set of criteria designed to minimize the degree of policy choice exercised by the officer executing the statute and to ensure that the relative spending priorities established by Congress in the appropriations it passes into law remain unaltered. Given that the exercise of policy choice by the officer executing the statute would be inimical to Congress' goal in enacting "automatic" budget-cutting measures, it is eminently reasonable and proper for Congress to vest the budget-cutting authority in an officer who is to the greatest degree possible nonpartisan and independent of the President and his political agenda and who therefore may be relied upon not to allow his calculations to be colored by political considerations. Such a delegation deprives the President of no authority that is rightfully his.

II

... [T]he question remains whether, as the Court concludes, the fact that the officer to whom Congress has delegated the authority to implement the Act is removable by a joint resolution of Congress should require invalidation of the Act. The Court's decision, . . . is based on a syllogism: the Act vests the Comptroller with "executive power;" such power may not be exercised by Congress or its agents; the Comptroller is an agent of Congress because he is removable by Congress; therefore the Act is invalid. . . .

The statute does not permit anyone to remove the Comptroller at will; removal is permitted only for specified cause, with the existence of cause to be determined by Congress following a hearing. Any removal under the statute would presumably be subject to post-termination judicial review to ensure that a hearing had in fact been held and that the finding of cause for removal was not arbitrary.[8] . . . These procedural and substantive limitations on the removal power militate strongly against the characterization of the Comptroller as a mere agent of Congress by virtue of the removal authority. . . .

More importantly, the substantial role played by the President in the process of removal through joint resolution reduces to utter insignificance the possibility that the threat of removal will induce subservience to the Congress. . . . The requirement of Presidential approval obviates the possibility that the Comptroller will perceive himself as so completely at the mercy of Congress that he will function as its tool.[9] If the Comptroller's conduct in office is not so unsatisfactory to the President as to convince the latter that removal is required under the statutory standard, Congress will have no independent power to coerce the Comptroller unless it can muster a two-thirds majority in both Houses — a feat of bipartisanship more difficult than that required to impeach and convict. The incremental *in terrorem* effect of the possibility of congressional removal in the face of a Presidential veto is therefore exceedingly unlikely to have any discernible impact on the extent of congressional influence over the Comptroller.

. . . .

The majority's contrary conclusion rests on the rigid dogma that, outside of the impeachment process, any "direct congressional role in the removal of officers charged with the execution of the laws . . . is inconsistent with separation of powers." Reliance on such an unyielding principle to strike down a statute posing no real danger of aggrandizement of congressional power is extremely misguided and insensitive to our constitutional role. . . . [T]he role of this Court should be limited to determining whether the Act so alters the

---

[8] *Cf. Humphrey's Executor v. United States,* 295 U.S. 602 (1935), in which the Court entertained a challenge to Presidential removal under a statute that similarly limited removals to specified cause.

[9] The Court cites statements made by supporters of the Budget and Accounting Act indicating their belief that the Act's removal provisions would render the Comptroller subservient to Congress by giving Congress "'absolute control of the man's destiny in office.'" . . . The Court's scholarship, however, is faulty: at the time all of these statements were made — including Representative Sisson's statement of May 3, 1921 — the proposed legislation provided for removal by concurrent resolution, with no Presidential role. *See* 61 Cong. Rec. 983, 989–992, 1079–1085 (1921).

balance of authority among the branches of government as to pose a genuine threat to the basic division between the lawmaking power and the power to execute the law. Because I see no such threat, I cannot join the Court in striking down the Act.

I dissent.

JUSTICE BLACKMUN, dissenting.

. . . .

Appellees have not sought invalidation of the 1921 provision that authorizes Congress to remove the Comptroller General by joint resolution; indeed, it is far from clear they would have standing to request such a judgment. The only relief sought in this case is nullification of the automatic budget-reduction provisions of the Deficit Control Act, and that relief should not be awarded even if the Court is correct that those provisions are constitutionally incompatible with Congress' authority to remove the Comptroller General by joint resolution. Any incompatibility, I feel, should be cured by refusing to allow congressional removal — if it ever is attempted — and not by striking down the central provisions of the Deficit Control Act.

. . . .

I do not claim that the 1921 removal provision is a piece of statutory deadwood utterly without contemporary significance. But it comes close. Rarely if ever invoked even for symbolic purposes, the removal provision certainly pales in importance beside the legislative scheme the Court strikes down today — an extraordinarily far-reaching response to a deficit problem of unprecedented proportions. Because I believe that the constitutional defect found by the Court cannot justify the remedy it has imposed, I respectfully dissent.

NOTES AND QUESTIONS

7-15. Can you characterize the constitutional methodology used in the various Justices' opinions in this case? Why does the majority feel compelled to take, in effect, what amounts to a constitutional hard look at this statute? How does this approach compare to that of Justice Stevens? Justice White? Justice Blackmun? How does it compare to the various opinions in *INS v. Chadha, supra,* § 6.03, or in *CFTC v. Schor, supra,* § 6.11?

7-16. How does the majority deal with the constitutionality of independent commissions? If you were general counsel to the Federal Trade Commission and the chairperson of the Commission asked for your opinion as to the constitutionality of that commission, what would you say? Would you be confident of victory should the issue arise directly in the Supreme Court?

7-17. Assume that you were involved in the litigation leading to the Supreme Court's decision in *Morrison v. Olson.* Based on *Chadha* and *Bowsher,* what outcome would you have predicted at the outset of this case? If you suspected the Court might invalidate the Ethics in Government Act

§ 7.04　　EXECUTIVE CONTROL OF AGENCY DISCRETION　　671

because of its removal provisions, would you be very confident of the outcome of a direct challenge to the constitutionality of the Federal Trade Commission? Does footnote 4 in *Bowsher* give you much solace?

7-18. Is there a difference between Chief Justice Burger's and Justice White's concerns about undue political pressure? Which branch of government — executive or legislative — would be more likely to exert "political" pressure on the Comptroller General?

7-19. Is a special prosecutor a purely executive officer? Does a special prosecutor exercise a core executive function or power? If so, why does the majority in *Morrison v. Olson* uphold the statute? As you read the following case, can you reconcile its approach and outcome with the majority opinions in *Chadha* and *Bowsher*?

MORRISON v. OLSON

United States Supreme Court
487 U.S. 654 (1987)

[The part of this case dealing with the Court's approach to the appointments clause issues presented is reprinted in § 7.03]

. . . .

Two statutory provisions govern the length of an independent counsel's tenure in office. The first defines the procedure for removing an independent counsel. Section 596(a)(1) [of the Ethics in Government Act of 1978 (28 U.S.C. §§ 49, 591 *et seq.*)] provides:

> An independent counsel appointed under this chapter may be removed from office, other than by impeachment and conviction, only by the personal action of the Attorney General and only for good cause, physical disability, mental incapacity, or any other condition that substantially impairs the performance of such independent counsel's duties.

If an independent counsel is removed pursuant to this section, the Attorney General is required to submit a report to both the Special Division* and the Judiciary Committees of the Senate and the House "specifying the facts found and the ultimate grounds for such removal." § 596(a)(2). Under the current version of the Act, an independent counsel can obtain judicial review of the Attorney General's action by filing a civil action in the United States District Court for the District of Columbia. Members of the Special Division "may not hear or determine any such civil action or any appeal of a decision in any such

---

* [*Ed. note*: The Special Division is "a special court created by the Act for the purpose of appointing independent counsels." 487 U.S. 661 (quoting 28 U.S.C. § 49). For a more particularized description of the make-up of the Special Division, *see* footnote 3 of the majority opinion.]

civil action." The reviewing court is authorized to grant reinstatement or "other appropriate relief." § 596(a)(3).[8]

The other provision governing the tenure of the independent counsel defines the procedures for "terminating" the counsel's office. Under § 596(b)(1), the office of an independent counsel terminates when he or she notifies the Attorney General that he or she has completed or substantially completed any investigations or prosecutions undertaken pursuant to the Act. . . .

V

. . . .

We now turn to consider whether the Act is invalid under the constitutional principle of separation of powers. Two related issues must be addressed: The first is whether the provision of the Act restricting the Attorney General's power to remove the independent counsel to only those instances in which he can show "good cause," taken by itself, impermissibly interferes with the President's exercise of his constitutionally appointed functions. The second is whether, taken as a whole, the Act violates the separation of powers by reducing the President's ability to control the prosecutorial powers wielded by the independent counsel.

A

Two Terms ago we had occasion to consider whether it was consistent with he separation of powers for Congress to pass a statute that authorized a Government official who is removable only by Congress to participate in what we found to be "executive powers." *Bowsher v. Synar*, 478 U.S. 714, 730 (1986). We held in *Bowsher* that "Congress cannot reserve for itself the power of removal of an officer charged with the execution of the laws except by impeachment." A primary antecedent for this ruling was our 1926 decision in *Myers v. United States*, 272 U.S. 52. *Myers* had considered the propriety of a federal statute by which certain postmasters of the United States could be removed by the President only "by and with the advice and consent of the Senate." There too, Congress' attempt to involve itself in the removal of an executive official was found to be sufficient grounds to render the statute invalid. As we observed in *Bowsher*, the essence of the decision in *Myers* was the judgment that the Constitution prevents Congress from "draw[ing] to itself . . . the power to remove or the right to participate in the exercise of that power. To do this would be to go beyond the words and implications of the [Appointments Clause] and to infringe the constitutional principle of the separation of governmental powers." . . .

Unlike both *Bowsher* and *Myers*, this case does not involve an attempt by Congress itself to gain a role in the removal of executive officials other than its established powers of impeachment and conviction. The Act instead puts

---

[8] Under the Act as originally enacted, an independent counsel who was removed could obtain judicial review of the Attorney General's decision in a civil action commenced before the Special Division. If the removal was "based on error of law or fact," the court could order "reinstatement or other appropriate relief." 28 U.S.C. § 596(a)(3).

the removal power squarely in the hands of the Executive Branch; an independent counsel may be removed from office, "only by the personal action of the Attorney General, and only for good cause." § 596(a)(1).[23] There is no requirement of congressional approval of the Attorney General's removal decision, though the decision is subject to judicial review. § 596(a)(3). In our view, the removal provisions of the Act make this case more analogous to *Humphrey's Executor v. United States,* 295 U.S. 602 (1935), and *Wiener v. United States,* 357 U.S. 349 (1958), than to *Myers* or *Bowsher.*

In *Humphrey's Executor,* the issue was whether a statute restricting the President's power to remove the Commissioners of the Federal Trade Commission (FTC) only for "inefficiency, neglect of duty, or malfeasance in office" was consistent with the Constitution. 295 U.S., at 619. We stated that whether Congress can "condition the [President's power of removal] by fixing a definite term and precluding a removal except for cause, will depend upon the character of the office." Contrary to the implication of some dicta in *Myers,* the President's power to remove Government officials simply was not "all-inclusive in respect of civil officers with the exception of the judiciary provided for by the Constitution." 295 U.S., at 629. At least in regard to "quasi-legislative" and "quasi-judicial" agencies such as the FTC,[25] "[t]he authority of Congress, in creating [such] agencies, to require them to act in discharge of their duties independently of executive control . . . includes, as an appropriate incident, power to fix the period during which they shall continue in office, and to forbid their removal except for cause in the meantime." In *Humphrey's Executor,* we found it "plain" that the Constitution did not give the President "illimitable power of removal" over the officers of independent agencies. Were the President to have the power to remove FTC commissioners at will, the "coercive influence" of the removal power would "threate[n] the independence of [the] commission." . . .

Appellees contend that *Humphrey's Executor* . . . [is] distinguishable from this case because they did not involve officials who performed a "core executive function." They argue that our decision in *Humphrey's Executor* rests on a distinction between "purely executive" officials and officials who exercise "quasi-legislative" and "quasi-judicial" powers. In their view, when a "purely executive" official is involved, the governing precedent is *Myers,* not *Humphrey's Executor.* . . . And, under *Myers,* the President must have absolute discretion to discharge "purely" executive officials at will. . . .

We undoubtedly did rely on the terms "quasi-legislative" and "quasi-judicial" to distinguish the officials involved in *Humphrey's Executor* . . . from those in *Myers,* but our present considered view is that the determination of whether

---

[23] As noted, an independent counsel may also be removed through impeachment and conviction. In addition, the Attorney General may remove a counsel for "physical disability, mental incapacity, or any other condition that substantially impairs the performance" of his duties. § 596(a)(1).

[25] . . . We described the FTC as "an administrative body created by Congress to carry into effect legislative policies embodied in the statute in accordance with the legislative standard therein prescribed, and to perform other specified duties as a legislative or as a judicial aid." Such an agency was not "an arm or an eye of the executive," and the commissioners were intended to perform their duties "without executive leave and . . . free from executive control." *Id.,* at 628. As we put it at the time, the powers of the FTC were not "purely" executive, but were "quasi-legislative or quasi-judicial." *Ibid.*

the Constitution allows Congress to impose a "good cause"-type restriction on the President's power to remove an official cannot be made to turn on whether or not that official is classified as "purely executive." The analysis contained in our removal cases is designed not to define rigid categories of those officials who may or may not be removed at will by the President,[28] but to ensure that Congress does not interfere with the President's exercise of the "executive power" and his constitutionally appointed duty to "take care that the laws be faithfully executed" under Article II. *Myers* was undoubtedly correct in its holding, and in its broader suggestion that there are some "purely executive" officials who must be removable by the President at will if he is to be able to accomplish his constitutional role. . . .

Considering for the moment the "good cause" removal provision in isolation from the other parts of the Act at issue in this case, we cannot say that the imposition of a "good cause" standard for removal by itself unduly trammels on executive authority. There is no real dispute that the functions performed by the independent counsel are "executive" in the sense that they are law enforcement functions that typically have been undertaken by officials within the Executive Branch. As we noted above, however, the independent counsel is an inferior officer under the Appointments Clause, with limited jurisdiction and tenure and lacking policymaking or significant administrative authority. Although the counsel exercises no small amount of discretion and judgment in deciding how to carry out his or her duties under the Act, we simply do not see how the President's need to control the exercise of that discretion is so central to the functioning of the Executive Branch as to require as a matter of constitutional law that the counsel be terminable at will by the President.[31]

Nor do we think that the "good cause" removal provision at issue here impermissibly burdens the President's power to control or supervise the independent counsel, as an executive official, in the execution of his or her

---

[28] The difficulty of defining such categories of "executive" or "quasi-legislative" officials is illustrated by a comparison of our decisions in cases such as *Humphrey's Executor, Buckley v. Valeo,* 424 U.S. 1, 140–141 (1976), and *Bowsher, supra,* at 732–734. In *Buckley,* we indicated that the functions of the Federal Election Commission are "administrative," and "more legislative and judicial in nature," and are "of kinds usually performed by independent regulatory agencies or by some department in the Executive Branch under the direction of an Act of Congress." 424 U.S., at 140–141. In *Bowsher,* we found that the functions of the Comptroller General were "executive" in nature, in that he was required to "exercise judgment concerning facts that affect the application of the Act," and he must "interpret the provisions of the Act to determine precisely what budgetary calculations are required." 478 U.S., at 733. *Compare* this with the description of the FTC's powers in *Humphrey's Executor,* which we stated "occupie[d] no place in the executive department": "The [FTC] is an administrative body created by Congress to carry into effect legislative policies embodied in the statute in accordance with the legislative standard therein prescribed, and to perform other specified duties as a legislative or as a judicial aid." 295 U.S., at 628. As JUSTICE WHITE noted in his dissent in *Bowsher,* it is hard to dispute that the powers of the FTC at the time of *Humphrey's Executor* would at the present time be considered "executive," at least to some degree. *See* 478 U.S., at 761, n. 3.

[31] We note by way of comparison that various federal agencies whose officers are covered by "good cause" removal restrictions exercise civil enforcement powers that are analogous to the prosecutorial powers wielded by an independent counsel. *See, e.g.,* 15 U.S.C. § 45(m) (giving the FTC the authority to bring civil actions to recover civil penalties for the violations of rules respecting unfair competition); 15 U.S.C. §§ 2061, 2071, 2076(b)(7)(A) (giving the Consumer Product Safety Commission the authority to obtain injunctions and apply for seizure of hazardous products).

duties under the Act. This is not a case in which the power to remove an executive official has been completely stripped from the President, thus providing no means for the President to ensure the "faithful execution" of the laws. Rather, because the independent counsel may be terminated for "good cause," the Executive, through the Attorney General, retains ample authority to assure that the counsel is competently performing his or her statutory responsibilities in a manner that comports with the provisions of the Act . . . .

B

The final question to be addressed is whether the Act, taken as a whole, violates the principle of separation of powers by unduly interfering with the role of the Executive Branch. Time and again we have reaffirmed the importance in our constitutional scheme of the separation of governmental powers into the three coordinate branches. . . . As we stated in *Buckley v. Valeo*, 424 U.S. 1 (1976), the system of separated powers and checks and balances established in the Constitution was regarded by the Framers as "a self-executing safeguard against the encroachment or aggrandizement of one branch at the expense of the other." . . . We have not hesitated to invalidate provisions of law which violate this principle. . . . On the other hand, we have never held that the Constitution requires that the three branches of Government "operate with absolute independence." *United States v. Nixon*, 418 U.S., at 707. . . .

We observe first that this case does not involve an attempt by Congress to increase its own powers at the expense of the Executive Branch. *Commodity Futures Trading Comm'n v. Schor*, 478 U.S., at 856. Unlike some of our previous cases, most recently *Bowsher v. Synar*, this case simply does not pose a "dange[r] of congressional usurpation of Executive Branch functions." . . . Indeed, with the exception of the power of impeachment — which applies to all officers of the United States — Congress retained for itself no powers of control or supervision over an independent counsel. The Act does empower certain Members of Congress to request the Attorney General to apply for the appointment of an independent counsel, but the Attorney General has no duty to comply with the request, although he must respond within a certain time limit. § 529(g). Other than that, Congress' role under the Act is limited to receiving reports or other information and oversight of the independent counsel's activities, § 595(a), functions that we have recognized generally as being incidental to the legislative function of Congress. . . .

Similarly, we do not think that the Act works any *judicial* usurpation of properly executive functions. As should be apparent from our discussion of the Appointments Clause above, the power to appoint inferior officers such as independent counsel is not in itself an "executive" function in the constitutional sense, at least when Congress has exercised its power to vest the appointment of an inferior officer in the "courts of Law." . . .

Finally, we do not think that the Act "impermissibly undermine[s]" the powers of the Executive Branch, . . . or "disrupts the proper balance between the coordinate branches [by] prevent[ing] the Executive Branch from accomplishing its constitutionally assigned functions." . . . It is undeniable that the

Act reduces the amount of control or supervision that the Attorney General and, through him, the President exercises over the investigation and prosecution of a certain class of alleged criminal activity. The Attorney General is not allowed to appoint the individual of his choice; he does not determine the counsel's jurisdiction; and his power to remove a counsel is limited. Nonetheless, the Act does give the Attorney General several means of supervising or controlling the prosecutorial powers that may be wielded by an independent counsel. Most importantly, the Attorney General retains the power to remove the counsel for "good cause," a power that we have already concluded provides the Executive with substantial ability to ensure that the laws are "faithfully executed" by an independent counsel. No independent counsel may be appointed without a specific request by the Attorney General, and the Attorney General's decision not to request appointment if he finds "no reasonable grounds to believe that further investigation is warranted" is committed to his unreviewable discretion. The Act thus gives the Executive a degree of control over the power to initiate an investigation by the independent counsel. In addition, the jurisdiction of the independent counsel is defined with reference to the facts submitted by the Attorney General, and once a counsel is appointed, the Act requires that the counsel abide by Justice Department policy unless it is not "possible" to do so. Notwithstanding the fact that the counsel is to some degree "independent" and free from executive supervision to a greater extent than other federal prosecutors, in our view these features of the Act give the Executive Branch sufficient control over the independent counsel to ensure that the President is able to perform his constitutionally assigned duties.

VI

In sum, we conclude today that it does not violate the Appointments Clause for Congress to vest the appointment of independent counsel in the Special Division; that the powers exercised by the Special Division under the Act do not violate Article III; and that the Act does not violate the separation of powers principle by impermissibly interfering with the functions of the Executive Branch. The decision of the Court of Appeals is therefore

Reversed.

JUSTICE KENNEDY took no part in the consideration or decision of this case.

JUSTICE SCALIA, dissenting.

. . . .

The principle of separation of powers is expressed in our Constitution in the first section of each of the first three Articles. Article I, § 1 provides that "[a]ll legislative Powers herein granted shall be vested in a Congress of the United States, which shall consist of a Senate and House of Representatives." Article III, § 1, provides that "[t]he judicial Power of the United States, shall be vested in one supreme Court, and in such inferior Courts as the Congress may from time to time ordain and establish." And the provision at issue here, Art. II, § 1, cl. 1, provides that "[t]he executive Power shall be vested in a President of the United States of America." . . .

That is what this suit is about. Power. The allocation of power among Congress, the President and the courts in such fashion as to preserve the equilibrium the Constitution sought to establish — so that "a gradual concentration of the several powers in the same department," *Federalist* No. 51, p. 321 (J. Madison), can effectively be resisted. Frequently an issue of this sort will come before the Court clad, so to speak, in sheep's clothing: the potential of the asserted principle to effect important change in the equilibrium of power is not immediately evident, and must be discerned by a careful and perceptive analysis. But this wolf comes as a wolf.. . . .

II

. . . .

To repeat, Article II, § 1, cl. 1, of the Constitution provides:

"The executive Power shall be vested in a President of the United States."

As I described at the outset of this opinion, this does not mean *some* of the executive power, but *all of the executive power*. It seems to me, therefore, that the decision of the Court of Appeals invalidating the present statute must be upheld on fundamental separation-of-powers principles if the following two questions are answered affirmatively: (1) Is the conduct of a criminal prosecution (and of an investigation to decide whether to prosecute) the exercise of purely executive power? (2) Does the statute deprive the President of the United States of exclusive control over the exercise of that power? Surprising to say, the Court appears to concede an affirmative answer to both questions, but seeks to avoid the inevitable conclusion that since the statute vests some purely executive power in a person who is not the President of the United States it is void.

The Court concedes that "[t]here is no real dispute that the functions performed by the independent counsel are 'executive'," though it qualifies that concession by adding "in the sense that they are law enforcement functions that typically have been undertaken by officials within the Executive Branch." . . . The qualifier adds nothing but atmosphere. In what *other* sense can one identify "the executive Power" that is supposed to be vested in the President (unless it includes everything the Executive Branch is given to do) *except* by reference to what has always and everywhere — if conducted by government at all — been conducted never by the legislature, never by the courts, and always by the executive. There is no possible doubt that the independent counsel's functions fit this description. She is vested with the "full power and independent authority to exercise all *investigative and prosecutorial* functions and powers of the Department of Justice [and] the Attorney General." 28 U.S.C. § 594(a) (1982 ed., Supp. V) (emphasis added). Governmental investigation and prosecution of crimes is a quintessentially executive function. . . .

As for the second question, whether the statute before us deprives the President of exclusive control over that quintessentially executive activity: The Court does not, and could not possibly, assert that it does not. That is indeed the whole object of the statute. Instead, the Court points out that the President, through his Attorney General, has at least *some* control. That concession is alone enough to invalidate the statute, but I cannot refrain from pointing out that the Court greatly exaggerates the extent of that "some" Presidential control. "Most importan[t]" among these controls, the Court asserts, is the Attorney General's "power to remove the counsel for 'good cause.'" . . . This is somewhat like referring to shackles as an effective means of locomotion. As we recognized in *Humphrey's Executor v. United States,* 295 U.S. 602 (1935) — indeed, what *Humphrey's Executor* was all about — limiting removal power to "good cause" is an impediment to, not an effective grant of, Presidential control. . . . What we in *Humphrey's Executor* found to be a means of eliminating Presidential control, the Court today considers the "most importan[t]" means of assuring Presidential control. Congress, of course, operated under no such illusion when it enacted this statute, describing the "good cause" limitation as "protecting the independent counsel's ability to act independently of the President's direct control" since it permits removal only for "misconduct." . . .

The utter incompatibility of the Court's approach with our constitutional traditions can be made more clear, perhaps, by applying it to the powers of the other two branches. Is it conceivable that if Congress passed a statute depriving itself of less than full and entire control over some insignificant area of legislation, we would inquire whether the matter was "*so central* to the functioning of the Legislative Branch" as really to require complete control, or whether the statute gives Congress "*sufficient* control over the surrogate legislator to ensure that Congress is able to perform its constitutionally assigned duties"? Of course we would have none of that. Once we determined that a purely legislative power was at issue we would require it to be exercised, wholly and entirely, by Congress. . . .

The Court has, nonetheless, replaced the clear constitutional prescription that the executive power belongs to the President with a "balancing test." What are the standards to determine how the balance is to be struck, that is, how much removal of Presidential power is too much? Many countries of the world get along with an executive that is much weaker than ours — in fact, entirely dependent upon the continued support of the legislature. Once we depart from the text of the Constitution, just where short of that do we stop? The most amazing feature of the Court's opinion is that it does not even purport to give an answer. It simply *announces,* with no analysis, that the ability to control the decision whether to investigate and prosecute the President's closest advisors, and indeed the President himself, is not "so central to the functioning of the Executive Branch" as to be constitutionally required to be within the President's control. Apparently that is so because we say it is so. Having abandoned as the basis for our decisionmaking the text of Article II that "the executive Power" must be vested in the President, the Court does not even attempt to craft a *substitute* criterion — a "justiciable standard," . . . however remote from the Constitution — that today governs, and in the future will govern, the decision of such questions. Evidently, the governing standard is to be what might be called the unfettered wisdom of a majority of this Court, revealed to an obedient people on a case-by-case basis. This is not only not the government of laws that the Constitution established; it is not a government of laws at all. . . .

. . . .

NOTES AND QUESTIONS

7-20. How would you characterize the majority's constitutional approach in *Morrison*? With what other Supreme Court opinions does it resonate? Justice White's dissent in *Chadha*? His dissent in *Bowsher*?

7-21. Can this case be explained as one involving a conflict of interest on the part of the Attorney General, thus necessitating greater judicial deference to the political bargain struck by the executive and legislative branches of government in order to preserve the independence of judicial investigation/oversight of the Executive Branch?

7-22. Or does Justice Rehnquist see issues such as these as essentially political questions? Is that the end result of the approach taken in this case? If so, does he indicate where he might draw the line between an acceptable political resolution and a constitutional violation?

7-23. What accounts for the Court's apparent change of approach and direction in this case? What factors does it identify as central to the balance it wishes to strike?

7-24. How would you characterize Justice Scalia's approach? What theory of the executive branch underlies his analysis? Is this theory correct? What are the implications of his approach? For example, consider the executive orders discussed in the next section. Would executive orders that begin to look a good deal like legislation violate the approach set forth by Justice Scalia? Along with his theory of the executive, is there also a very broad conception of what executive power, in fact, is?

7-25. *U.S. v. Mistretta, supra,* Chapter Seven, § 7.04, presented a number of separation of powers issues in addition to delegation questions. The Court had the opportunity, once again, to resurrect a more vigorous approach to separation of powers issues. Once again, however, it essentially deferred to the legislative bargain struck by Congress and the executive when they passed the U.S. Sentencing Commission Act.

In a passage now commonplace in our cases, Justice Jackson summarized the pragmatic, flexible view of differentiated governmental power to which we are heir:

> "While the Constitution diffuses power the better to secure liberty, it also contemplates that practice will integrate the dispersed powers into a workable government. It enjoins upon its branches separateness but interdependence, autonomy but reciprocity." *Youngstown Sheet & Tube Co. v. Sawyer,* 343 U.S. 579, 635 (1952) (concurring opinion).

In adopting this flexible understanding of separation of powers, we simply have recognized Madison's teaching that the greatest security against tyranny — the accumulation of excessive authority in a single Branch — lies not in a hermetic division among the Branches, but in a carefully crafted system of checked and balanced power within each Branch. . . .

488 U.S. at 381. Justice Scalia, however, dissented:

> Today's decision follows the regrettable tendency of our recent separation-of-powers jurisprudence . . . to treat the Constitution as though it were no more than a generalized prescription that the functions of the Branches should not be commingled too much — how much is too much to be determined, case-by-case, by this Court. The Constitution is not that. Rather, as its name suggests, it is a prescribed structure, a framework, for the conduct of government. In designing that structure, the Framers *themselves* considered how much commingling was, in the generality of things, acceptable, and set forth their conclusions in the document. That is the meaning of the statements concerning acceptable commingling made by Madison in defense of the proposed Constitution, and now routinely used as an excuse for disregarding it. When he said, as the Court correctly quotes, that separation of powers "d[oes] not mean that these [three] departments ought to have no *partial agency* in, or no *controul* [sic] over the acts of each other," . . . his point was that the commingling specifically provided for in the structure that he and his colleagues had designed — the presidential veto over legislation, the Senate's confirmation of executive and judicial officers, the Senate's ratification of treaties, the Congress' power to impeach and remove executive and judicial officers — did not violate a proper understanding of separation of powers. He would be aghast, I think, to hear those words used as justification for ignoring that carefully designed structure so long as, in the changing view of the Supreme Court from time to time, "too much commingling" does not occur. Consideration of the degree of commingling that a particular disposition produces may be appropriate at the margins, where the outline of the framework itself is not clear; but it seems to me far from a marginal question whether our constitutional structure allows for a body which is not the Congress, and yet exercises no governmental powers except the making of rules that have the effect of laws.
>
> I think the Court errs, in other words, not so much because it mistakes the degree of commingling, but because it fails to recognize that this case is not about commingling, but about the creation of a new Branch altogether, a sort of junior-varsity Congress. It may well be that in some circumstances such a Branch would be desirable; perhaps the agency before us here will prove to be so. But there are many desirable dispositions that do not accord with the constitutional structure we live under. And in the long run the improvisation of a constitutional structure on the basis of currently perceived utility will be disastrous.

488 U.S. at 426-27 (emphasis in original).

§ 7.05 Executive Oversight: Executive Orders and the Office of Management and Budget

The executive branch exercises considerable direct control over the day-to-day activities of federal administrative agencies, especially executive agencies, through the issuance of executive orders. The power of the executive branch to issue such orders is not unlimited. As the Court noted in *Youngstown Sheet and Tube v. Sawyer,* 343 U.S. 579 (1952), the President's power to issue such orders "must stem either from an act of Congress or from the Constitution itself." 343 U.S. at 585. Courts have generally been willing to interpret these powers very broadly. If the President has the Constitutional duty to ensure that the laws are faithfully executed, it follows that, at the very least, he or she has the power to issue instructions to her officers to ensure that these tasks are carried out.

Executive orders, however, can sometimes take on a significance and character that go beyond the details of the law they seek to enforce and resemble closely new legislation. As the bureaucracy has grown, the lawmaking potential and reality of that bureaucracy has become more and more significant. Executive orders and the Office of Management and Budget, in particular, have become crucial in the President's attempts to coordinate, supervise and control the policy making functions of executive agencies and, at least on a voluntary basis, independent commissions as well. Consider the following.

Alfred C. Aman, Jr. & William T. Mayton, ADMINISTRATIVE LAW *

570–72 (Thompson West 2d ed. 2001)

One of the most important executive agencies used to carry out the directives of Presidential executive orders is the Office of Management and Budget (OMB). Given the importance of that office for executive influence over policy making, we shall examine it and some of the executive orders it administers in some detail. . . .

The Office of Management and Budget had its beginnings in the Budget and Accounting Act of 1921. That Act created the Bureau of the Budget, thereby facilitating the President's ability to formulate a national budget. The Bureau of the Budget was viewed as a technical advisor, bipartisan and neutral in nature. Its functions grew in importance, but as late as 1970, it continued to maintain its image as essentially a neutral, technical advisory office

In 1970, however, President Nixon renamed the Bureau of the Budget the Office of Management and Budget (OMB), expanded its powers and changed some of its tasks and goals. In particular, the Office began to play the role of coordinator, attempting to ensure that various administrative policies and priorities were consistent with one another. In addition, there was growing concern in the executive branch that, left on their own, agencies would spend too much money. To counteract these tendencies, centralized budget reviews and priorities were advocated. These changes in direction transformed OMB into a more effective presidential device for controlling the policymaking direction of the bureaucracy, particularly executive agencies.

---

* Reprinted from *Administrative Law,* Alfred C. Aman, Jr. & William T. Mayton, 2d ed., 2001, with permission of Thomson West.

President Nixon was the first President to use OMB to review agency actions pursuant to a Presidential executive order. President Nixon's OMB instituted so-called "Quality-of-Life" reviews. Under its provisions, the EPA was required to circulate proposed regulations among other agencies and to respond to their comments. In 1974, President Ford issued Executive Order 11,821, amended by E.O. 11,949. These orders required agencies to prepare so-called "inflation impact statements" for all major regulations, defined as those having an impact in excess of $100 million.

Congress reacted to the changes in OMB's power and role by imposing new controls. In 1976, Congress passed legislation making the appointments of OMB Director and Deputy Director subject to Senate Confirmation. Also, OMB lost its final veto authority over independent regulatory agencies' information-gathering programs. As a result, the General Accounting Office's power increased, giving it greater program evaluation functions and increased oversight responsibilities concerning potential Presidential impoundments of funds. Congress also created a central budget evaluator of its own, the Congressional Budget Office, thereby ending OMB's monopoly on the processing of agency budget requests. Finally, Congress severely reduced the President's authority to impound agency funds and consequently shape policy. Congress, however, failed to divorce completely the presidency from the administrative process, and OMB retained substantial policy-making responsibilities.

President Carter further expanded OMB power in his attempt to control the bureaucracy by issuance of Executive Order 12,044. Among other things, this order required that agencies set forth their rulemaking agenda in semiannual regulatory calendars, that they re-evaluate old rules, and that they conduct regulatory analysis of proposed rules having an impact of $100 million of more per year. President Carter later created a Regulatory Council to screen proposed rules and guard against duplication and established a Regulatory Analysis Review Group (RARG), composed of representatives of 36 executive and independent agencies. The primary responsibility of this group was to review carefully the regulatory analysis of fifteen to twenty of the most important rules proposed by certain agencies. . . .

The efforts to influence the bureaucracy by Presidents Nixon, Ford and Carter provided the foundation for the more extensive controls imposed by President Reagan under Executive Order 12,291. Similar to the orders that preceded it, Order 12,291 required that agencies justify their major rules with a regulatory Impact Analysis (RIA).

Steven Croley, WHITE HOUSE REVIEW OF AGENCY RULEMAKING: AN EMPIRICAL INVESTIGATION

*70 U. CHI. L. REV. 821 (2003)**

. . . .

In early 1981, President Ronald Reagan issued his famous Executive Order number 12291. Among other things, Executive Order 12291 required agencies to submit to the Director of the Office of Management and Budget ("OMB") a "Regulatory Impact Analysis" for all of their "major" rules. Executive Order 12291 defined "major" rule as any rule likely to: (1) have an annual effect on the economy of $100 million or more; (2) impose a major increase in costs or prices for consumers, industries, government agencies, or geographic regions; or (3) have a significant adverse effect on competition, employment, investment, productivity, or innovation. For such rules, agencies' regulatory impact analyses had to provide an assessment of the costs and benefits, a calculation of a rule's net benefits, and a description of alternative courses of action that might achieve the same regulatory goal together with an explanation of the reasons why those alternatives, if cheaper, could not legally be adopted. Executive Order 12291 further required agencies to submit regulatory impact analyses twice, once accompanying a given "proposed" form and, following the notice-and-comment period, once again for the pending "final" version of the same rule. Such analyses would allow the White House, through the Director of OMB acting under the direction of the "Presidential Task Force on Regulatory Relief," to approve or seek changes in all major rules. Finally, Executive Order 12291 also required agencies to publish their regulatory agendas for each year, and to initiate reviews of all of their rules currently in effect.

In early 1985, President Reagan, following his reelection, issued Executive Order number 12498, expressly "intended to complement the existing regulatory planning and review procedures" outlined in Executive Order 12291. Executive Order 12498 further solidified the Reagan White House's control, or assertion of control, over rulemaking agencies. Executive Order 12498 required agencies to submit to the Director of OMB a statement of their regulatory policies, goals, and objectives for each year. The order also required agencies to ensure that such plans were consistent with the goals of the agency "and of the Administration," including "the Administration's regulatory principles." Together, Executive Orders 12291 and 12498 went far, at least by design, to make the Reagan White House a central part of the process of agency rulemaking. Agencies now had to obtain OMB clearance for their major rulemaking initiatives not once but twice during a rule's development, and furthermore had to provide advance notice to the White House of regulatory initiatives in the form of annual reports of their regulatory intentions.

---

* Copyright © 2003 University of Chicago. All rights reserved.

Wherever the White House believed an agency's regulatory impact analysis did not justify its rule, the White House could require the agency to change if not abandon its rule. Little wonder that the orders have often been characterized as one of the most significant developments in administrative law of the 1980s.

. . . .

During the first year of his first term, President Clinton revoked Executive Orders 12291 and 12498, a move widely anticipated given their infamy among enemies of cost-benefit analysis and friends of regulation. Yet, surprisingly to some, Clinton replaced the Reagan orders with his own, Executive Order number 12866, which resembled the Reagan orders in many crucial ways. Like Executive Order 12291, Clinton's executive order required an assessment of the expected costs and benefits of agencies' major rules. And like Executive Order 12498, the Clinton order required agencies to submit their regulatory plans and agenda, in addition to pending major rules, to OMB — or more specifically, to OMB's Office of Information and Regulatory Affairs ("OIRA"), identified by Executive Order 12866 as OMB's "repository of expertise concerning regulatory issues." Thus the Clinton order embodied both the substantive and procedural aspects of the Reagan orders — imposing cost-benefit criteria for major rules and designating OMB as the central overseer and clearinghouse for agency rulemaking. Executive Order 12866 also contemplated a central role for the vice president in overseeing agency decisionmaking, much as previous vice presidents had in the Reagan and Bush administrations, though now within a formally established framework.

. . . .

While important similarities outnumbered important differences, Executive Order 12866 did depart from the Reagan orders in several noteworthy respects. For example, intending to "assure greater openness and accountability in the regulatory review process," the Clinton order limited receipt of oral communications "initiated by persons not employed by the executive branch of the Federal Government" regarding a rule under review to the Administrator of OIRA. The order furthermore required OIRA publicly to disclose information about communications between OIRA personnel and any person who is not employed by the executive branch, and to maintain a publicly available communications log containing the status of all regulatory actions, a notation of all written communications between OIRA personnel and outside parties, and the dates and names of individuals participating in all substantive oral communications, including meetings and telephone conversations, between OIRA personnel and outside parties. Executive Order 12866 also made clear that enhancing public health and safety, protecting the environment, and reducing discrimination were to be counted on the benefit side of the ledger when calculating a rule's costs and benefits. In short, Executive Order 12866 sought to preserve the basic methodology and institutional structure of the Reagan orders but to avoid the criticisms they met, particularly with respect to openness and the inclusion of intangible benefits in the cost-benefit calculus. Most fundamentally, however, the Clinton order embraced both the general principles of cost-benefit analysis, instructing agencies to select regulatory approaches that "maximize net benefits," just as

§ 7.05   EXECUTIVE CONTROL OF AGENCY DISCRETION   685

Executive Order 12291 did, and the centrality of the White House itself to the rule-planning and rulemaking process, just as Executive Order 12498 did.

Immediately following the issuance of Executive Order 12866, the Director of OMB sent a memorandum to all "heads of executive departments and agencies, and independent regulatory agencies," stating that OIRA would have "primary responsibility" under the order for a number of "specific regulatory review and planning functions." The Director's memorandum also explained that the Administrator of OIRA had prepared a detailed memorandum, dated the same day and attached to his own, providing specific guidance on how Executive Order 12866 should be implemented. The OMB Director urged agency heads to give the Administrator's memorandum immediate attention. Among other things, the Administrator's implementing memorandum made clear that one of the purposes of Executive Order 12866 was "greater selectivity in the regulations reviewed by OIRA." Accordingly, the Administrator directed agencies to focus on the distinction between "economically significant" and otherwise "significant" rules, and to provide OIRA with more detailed information concerning the former. The Administrator also explained that OIRA would place in its public reading room a list of all meetings and telephone conversations between OIRA and the public or Congress during which the substance of a rule under OIRA review was discussed. In addition, the Administrator explained that parties outside of the executive branch of government should communicate their concerns to the rulemaking agency before meeting with OIRA, and that OIRA would invite "policy-level officials" from the issuing agency to all such meetings.

. . . .

[W]hile OMB is not an expert in any substantive regulatory field, it has become an expert in the field of regulation itself. Accordingly, OIRA has developed a special institutional capacity for distinguishing between, on the one hand, regulation likely to advance sound regulatory policy, and on the other, regulation that — however well intentioned — may lead to unintended and undesirable consequences. In addition to mere coordination, in other words, White House review provides a "quality check" on pending rules. On this view, OIRA's small size and technocratic orientation are important virtues. Centralized expertise offers a needed antidote to the topsy-turvy world of congressional and bureaucratic regulatory politics.

Defenders of greater White House control further argue that the president is uniquely situated to advance national interests, as opposed to the factional interests that are often promoted by Congress, and that consequently find expression in agency decisions. According to this argument, presidential control over agencies is desirable, even necessary, because it promotes evenhandedness in regulatory decisionmaking. Because the president's constituency is a national one, the president can best aggregate and balance competing interests in the course of developing sound regulatory policy. Greater presidential control is desirable not merely because it avoids inconsistencies, redundancies, and unintended consequences in agency rulemaking, but more importantly because it helps to ensure that all relevant interests are identified and counted. According to one variation of this view, OIRA's specialized institutional focus might also promote reasoned deliberation about regulatory alternatives more effectively than other, more cumbersome, regulatory institutions. Either way, presidential oversight tends to promote the general welfare.

Another version of the argument in favor of a strong president, the unitary executive thesis, insists that presidential control over agencies is necessary not just to promote a national orientation in agency rulemaking, but also to preserve the political and constitutional legitimacy of the regulatory state. In the absence of presidential control, there are insufficient checks on agency decisionmakers. Agencies might advance their own visions of good regulatory policy, but, electorally unaccountable, those visions lack political legitimacy. No less importantly, because the Constitution contemplates that the executive power of the United States resides in the president, agencies not closely overseen by and answerable to the president lack constitutional moorings. Activist White House oversight thus is not only desirable but necessary to preserve the constitutional legitimacy of the regulatory state.

But critics see trouble with activist White House oversight. For one, they see greater presidential control over agencies as unrealistic. While the White House may exert control over particular agency decisions from time to time, scarcity of presidential resources limits the extent to which the president can effectively monitor — much less influence — most agency decisions. Inevitably, substantial agency autonomy is a fact of regulatory life. Presidential control, therefore, will tend to be ad hoc and politically motivated, not based entirely on a deep understanding of the relevant regulatory issues.

The argument continues that to the extent White House control is possible, it is undesirable. This is true because greater White House centralization upsets a balance between law and politics already struck by the legislature and reinforced by the courts. By this account, activist presidential oversight is meddlesome, for Congress delegates regulatory power to agencies, not to the president, and while the president is charged with executing the law, that constitutional charge does not justify presidential reshaping of agencies' regulatory initiatives. With respect to agency rulemaking in particular, critics of greater presidential control have argued that the president should not "behave[] as if rulemakings were his rulemakings." In addition, where the president and an agency disagree in a particular case, the president should not simply rely on his removal power to insist that the agency yield. Instead, the agency, Congress's delegatee, should carry the day. Where agencies go astray by failing to follow congressional intent, courts or, if necessary, Congress itself can correct for agency waywardness. Where, on the other hand, Congress has left room for agency discretion, that discretion should not be replaced by presidential prerogative.

The strongest form of this argument goes farther, alleging that greater White House control not only improperly reallocates regulatory power away from Congress and agencies, but more ominously provides the White House with a means to deliver regulatory benefits to politically important constituencies at the expense of the general welfare. According to this view, the president is accountable not to national interests, but to influential interests with much more at stake. Thus, interest groups that did not get everything they wanted in the legislative and administrative arenas find in the White House review process yet another forum to advance their goals. By appealing to the White House to scrutinize what are for them undesirable regulatory decisions, powerful interest groups might see their regulatory preferences realized after all, thus upsetting whatever compromises were reached in the legislative and administrative processes.

What is worse, because the review process is opaque, the White House is able to provide regulatory favoritism to its important constituencies without attracting much notice, which provides opportunity for the White House to benefit those constituencies even where doing so is undesirable from the perspective of sound public policy. In other words, the absence of transparency associated with White House control means the president can reap political benefits without incurring the political costs that would come with well-publicized regulatory favoritism. On this view, the president not only has no special claim to represent national interests, but also is motivated and well positioned to advance his own. . . .

Consider Executive Order 12,866 (excerpted below). Does it raise any separation of powers concerns? How does it explicitly avoid the problem of being a form of "executive legislation"? How would you assess the overall constitutionality of this order in light of the precedents above — namely *Chadha*, *Buckley*, *Bowsher* and *Morrison*? For an analysis of this order and a comparison of it with earlier Reagan/Bush orders, see *Colloquium, The Fifth Annual Robert C. Byrd Conference on the Administrative Process: The First Year of Clinton/Gore: Reinventing Government or Redefining Reagan/Bush Initiatives?*, 8 ADMIN. L.J. AM. U. 23 (1994); Ellen Siegler, *Executive Order 12,866: An Analysis of the New Executive Order on Regulatory Planning and Review*, 24 ENVT'L L. REP. 10,070 (1994). For a discussion of the similarities between Reagan/Bush and Clinton/Gore regulatory initiatives and some of the reasons for those similarities, see, Alfred C. Aman, Jr., *A Global Perspective on Current Regulatory Reforms: Rejection, Relocation, or Reinvention?*, 2 IND. J. GLOBAL LEGAL STUD. 429 (1993).

EXECUTIVE ORDER 12866

58 FR 51735 (September 30, 1993)

. . . .

Section 1. *Statement of Regulatory Philosophy and Principles.*

(a) *The Regulatory Philosophy*. Federal agencies should promulgate only such regulations as are required by law, are necessary to interpret the law, or are made necessary by compelling public need, such as material failures of private markets to protect or improve the health and safety of the public, the environment, or the well-being of the American people. In deciding whether and how to regulate, agencies should assess all costs and benefits of available regulatory alternatives, including the alternative of not regulating. Costs and benefits shall be understood to include both quantifiable measures (to the fullest extent that these can be usefully estimated) and qualitative measures of costs and benefits that are difficult to quantify, but nevertheless essential to consider. Further, in choosing among alternative regulatory approaches, agencies should select those approaches that maximize net benefits (including potential economic, environmental, public health and safety, and other advantages; distributive impacts; and equity), unless a statute requires another regulatory approach.

(b) *The Principles of Regulation.* To ensure that the agencies' regulatory programs are consistent with the philosophy set forth above, agencies should adhere to the following principles, to the extent permitted by law and where applicable:

(1) Each agency shall identify the problem that it intends to address (including, where applicable, the failures of private markets or public institutions that warrant new agency action) as well as assess the significance of that problem.

(2) Each agency shall examine whether existing regulations (or other law) have created, or contributed to, the problem that a new regulation is intended to correct and whether those regulations (or other law) should be modified to achieve the intended goal of regulation more effectively.

(3) Each agency shall identify and assess available alternatives to direct regulation, including providing economic incentives to encourage the desired behavior, such as user fees or marketable permits, or providing information upon which choices can be made by the public.

(4) In setting regulatory priorities, each agency shall consider, to the extent reasonable, the degree and nature of the risks posed by various substances or activities within its jurisdiction.

(5) When an agency determines that a regulation is the best available method of achieving the regulatory objective, it shall design its regulations in the most cost-effective manner to achieve the regulatory objective. In doing so, each agency shall consider incentives for innovation, consistency, predictability, the costs of enforcement and compliance (to the government, regulated entities, and the public), flexibility, distributive impacts, and equity.

(6) Each agency shall assess both the costs and the benefits of the intended regulation and, recognizing that some costs and benefits are difficult to quantify, propose or adopt a regulation only upon a reasoned determination that the benefits of the intended regulation justify its costs.

(7) Each agency shall base its decisions on the best reasonably obtainable scientific, technical, economic, and other information concerning the need for, and consequences of, the intended regulation.

(8) Each agency shall identify and assess alternative forms of regulation and shall, to the extent feasible, specify performance objectives, rather than specifying the behavior or manner of compliance that regulated entities must adopt.

(9) Wherever feasible, agencies shall seek views of appropriate State, local, and tribal officials before imposing regulatory requirements that might significantly or uniquely affect those governmental entities. Each agency shall assess the effects of Federal regulations on State, local, and tribal governments, including specifically the availability of resources to carry out those mandates, and seek to minimize those burdens that uniquely or significantly affect such governmental entities, consistent with achieving regulatory objectives. In addition, as appropriate, agencies shall seek to harmonize Federal regulatory actions with related State, local, and tribal regulatory and other governmental functions.

(10) Each agency shall avoid regulations that are inconsistent, incompatible, or duplicative with its other regulations or those of other Federal agencies.

(11) Each agency shall tailor its regulations to impose the least burden on society, including individuals, businesses of differing sizes, and other entities (including small communities and governmental entities), consistent with obtaining the regulatory objectives, taking into account, among other things, and to the extent practicable, the costs of cumulative regulations.

(12) Each agency shall draft its regulations to be simple and easy to understand, with the goal of minimizing the potential for uncertainty and litigation arising from such uncertainty.

Sec. 2. *Organization.* An efficient regulatory planning and review process is vital to ensure that the Federal Government's regulatory system best serves the American people.

(a) *The Agencies.* Because Federal agencies are the repositories of significant substantive expertise and experience, they are responsible for developing regulations and assuring that the regulations are consistent with applicable law, the President's priorities, and the principles set forth in this Executive order.

(b) *The Office of Management and Budget.* Coordinated review of agency rulemaking is necessary to ensure that regulations are consistent with applicable law, the President's priorities, and the principles set forth in this Executive order, and that decisions made by one agency do not conflict with the policies or actions taken or planned by another agency. The Office of Management and Budget (OMB) shall carry out that review function. Within OMB, the Office of Information and Regulatory Affairs (OIRA) is the repository of expertise concerning regulatory issues, including methodologies and procedures that affect more than one agency, this Executive order, and the President's regulatory policies. To the extent permitted by law, OMB shall provide guidance to agencies and assist the President, the Vice President, and other regulatory policy advisors to the President in regulatory planning and shall be the entity that reviews individual regulations, as provided by this Executive order.

(c) *The Vice President.* The Vice President is the principal advisor to the President on, and shall coordinate the development and presentation of recommendations concerning, regulatory policy, planning, and review, as set forth in this Executive order. In fulfilling their responsibilities under this Executive order, the President and the Vice President shall be assisted by the regulatory policy advisors within the Executive Office of the President and by such agency officials and personnel as the President and the Vice President may, from time to time, consult.

Sec. 3. *Definitions*. For purposes of this Executive order: (a) "Advisors" refers to such regulatory policy advisors to the President as the President and Vice President may from time to time consult, including, among others: (1) the Director of OMB; (2) the Chair (or another member) of the Council of Economic Advisers; (3) the Assistant to the President for Economic Policy; (4) the Assistant to the President for Domestic Policy; (5) the Assistant to the President for National Security Affairs; (6) the Assistant to the President for Science and Technology; (7) the Assistant to the President for Intergovernmental Affairs; (8) the Assistant to the President and Staff Secretary; (9) the Assistant to the President and Chief of Staff to the Vice President; (10) the Assistant to the President and Counsel to the President; (11) the Deputy Assistant to the President and Director of the White House Office on Environmental Policy; and (12) the Administrator of OIRA, who also shall coordinate communications relating to this Executive order among the agencies, OMB, the other Advisors, and the Office of the Vice President.

(b) "Agency," unless otherwise indicated, means any authority of the United States that is an "agency" under 44 U.S.C. 3502(1), other than those considered to be independent regulatory agencies, as defined in 44 U.S.C. 3502(10).

(c) "Director" means the Director of OMB.

(d) "Regulation" or "rule" means an agency statement of general applicability and future effect, which the agency intends to have the force and effect of law, that is designed to implement, interpret, or prescribe law or policy or to describe the procedure or practice requirements of an agency. It does not, however, include:

(1) Regulations or rules issued in accordance with the formal rulemaking provisions of 5 U.S.C. 556, 557;

(2) Regulations or rules that pertain to a military or foreign affairs function of the United States, other than procurement regulations and regulations involving the import or export of non-defense articles and services;

(3) Regulations or rules that are limited to agency organization, management, or personnel matters; or

(4) Any other category of regulations exempted by the Administrator of OIRA.

(e) "Regulatory action" means any substantive action by an agency (normally published in the *Federal Register*) that promulgates or is expected to lead to the promulgation of a final rule or regulation, including notices of inquiry, advance notices of proposed rulemaking, and notices of proposed rulemaking.

(f) "Significant regulatory action" means any regulatory action that is likely to result in a rule that may:

(1) Have an annual effect on the economy of $100 million or more or adversely affect in a material way the economy, a sector of the economy,

productivity, competition, jobs, the environment, public health or safety, or State, local, or tribal governments or communities;

(2) Create a serious inconsistency or otherwise interfere with an action taken or planned by another agency;

(3) Materially alter the budgetary impact of entitlements, grants, user fees, or loan programs or the rights and obligations of recipients thereof; or

(4) Raise novel legal or policy issues arising out of legal mandates, the President's priorities, or the principles set forth in this Executive order.

Sec. 4. *Planning Mechanism.* In order to have an effective regulatory program, to provide for coordination of regulations, to maximize consultation and the resolution of potential conflicts at an early stage, to involve the public and its State, local, and tribal officials in regulatory planning, and to ensure that new or revised regulations promote the President's priorities and the principles set forth in this Executive order, these procedures shall be followed, to the extent permitted by law:

(a) *Agencies' Policy Meeting.* Early in each year's planning cycle, the Vice President shall convene a meeting of the Advisors and the heads of agencies to seek a common understanding of priorities and to coordinate regulatory efforts to be accomplished in the upcoming year.

(b) *Unified Regulatory Agenda.* For purposes of this subsection, the term "agency" or "agencies" shall also include those considered to be independent regulatory agencies, as defined in 44 U.S.C. 3502(10). Each agency shall prepare an agenda of all regulations under development or review, at a time and in a manner specified by the Administrator of OIRA. The description of each regulatory action shall contain, at a minimum, a regulation identifier number, a brief summary of the action, the legal authority for the action, any legal deadline for the action, and the name and telephone number of a knowledgeable agency official. Agencies may incorporate the information required under 5 U.S.C. 602 and 41 U.S.C. 402 into these agendas.

(c) *The Regulatory Plan.* For purposes of this subsection, the term "agency" or "agencies" shall also include those considered to be independent regulatory agencies, as defined in 44 U.S.C. 3502(10).

(1) As part of the Unified Regulatory Agenda, beginning in 1994, each agency shall prepare a Regulatory Plan (Plan) of the most important significant regulatory actions that the agency reasonably expects to issue in proposed or final form in that fiscal year or thereafter. The Plan shall be approved personally by the agency head and shall contain at a minimum:

(A) A statement of the agency's regulatory objectives and priorities and how they relate to the President's priorities;

(B) A summary of each planned significant regulatory action including, to the extent possible, alternatives to be considered and preliminary estimates of the anticipated costs and benefits;

(C) A summary of the legal basis for each such action, including whether any aspect of the action is required by statute or court order;

(D) A statement of the need for each such action and, if applicable, how the action will reduce risks to public health, safety, or the environment, as well as how the magnitude of the risk addressed by the action relates to other risks within the jurisdiction of the agency;

(E) The agency's schedule for action, including a statement of any applicable statutory or judicial deadlines; and

(F) The name, address, and telephone number of a person the public may contact for additional information about the planned regulatory action.

(2) Each agency shall forward its Plan to OIRA by June 1st of each year.

(3) Within 10 calendar days after OIRA has received an agency's Plan, OIRA shall circulate it to other affected agencies, the Advisors, and the Vice President.

(4) An agency head who believes that a planned regulatory action of another agency may conflict with its own policy or action taken or planned shall promptly notify, in writing, the Administrator of OIRA, who shall forward that communication to the issuing agency, the Advisors, and the Vice President.

(5) If the Administrator of OIRA believes that a planned regulatory action of an agency may be inconsistent with the President's priorities or the principles set forth in this Executive order or may be in conflict with any policy or action taken or planned by another agency, the Administrator of OIRA shall promptly notify, in writing, the affected agencies, the Advisors, and the Vice President.

(6) The Vice President, with the Advisors' assistance, may consult with the heads of agencies with respect to their Plans and, in appropriate instances, request further consideration or inter-agency coordination.

(7) The Plans developed by the issuing agency shall be published annually in the October publication of the Unified Regulatory Agenda. This publication shall be made available to the Congress; State, local, and tribal governments; and the public. Any views on any aspect of any agency Plan, including whether any planned regulatory action might conflict with any other planned or existing regulation, impose any unintended consequences on the public, or confer any unclaimed benefits on the public, should be directed to the issuing agency, with a copy to OIRA. . . .

WILLIAM J. CLINTON

THE WHITE HOUSE,
September 30, 1993.

§ 7.06 The Limits of Executive Control and the Role of OMB

ENVIRONMENTAL DEFENSE FUND v. THOMAS

District of Columbia District Court
627 F. Supp. 566 (1986)

FLANNERY, DISTRICT JUDGE.

. . . .

I. Background

In November of 1984, Congress enacted the Hazardous and Solid Waste Amendments of 1984 ("1984 Amendments"), Pub. L. 98–616 (Nov. 8, 1984), which amended the Resource Conservation and Recovery Act ("RCRA"), 42 U.S.C. § 6924. RCRA is a comprehensive statute designed to regulate the management of hazardous and solid wastes. One of the new amendments, Section 3004(w) of RCRA, 42 U.S.C. § 6924(w), provides that "[n]ot later than March 1, 1985, the (Environmental Protection Agency or "EPA") Administrator shall promulgate final permitting standards under this section for underground tanks that cannot be entered for inspection."

This deadline was not met. Plaintiffs contend that EPA's ability to promulgate the regulations was further prevented by the unlawful interference of the Office of Management and Budget ("OMB"). Plaintiffs, Environmental Defense Fund Inc. ("EDF") and two individuals brought suit in this court on May 30, 1985. Plaintiffs seek an order that EPA must promulgate the regulations by April 25, 1986. Plaintiffs also seek injunctive relief against OMB to prevent similar interference in the future.

Defendants EPA and OMB want until June 30, 1986 to promulgate the regulations. Further, they contend that this court has no jurisdiction to grant injunctive relief against OMB of this kind. . . .

II. Jurisdiction

Both parties agree that RCRA gives this court jurisdiction to order the Administrator of EPA to perform nondiscretionary duties and allows this court to set a date by which EPA must promulgate the hazardous waste tank regulations. 42 U.S.C. § 6972(a)(2). The only real dispute is by which deadline EPA can reasonably be ordered to promulgate final standards.

Jurisdiction to grant injunctive relief against OMB is the more controversial aspect of this suit. At the crux of this disagreement is the lawfulness of OMB's activity pursuant to the Congressional deadline and pursuant to Executive Order 12291, 46 Fed. Reg. 13193 (Feb. 17, 1981), 3 C.F.R. 127 (1982) ("EO 12291"). *

EO 12291 directs executive agencies to submit all proposed and final rules to OMB for pre-publication review to determine if they are consistent with certain criteria (*e.g.,* the regulations must be based on adequate information,

---

* Editor's Note: Executive Order 12291 preceded Executive Order 12866 *supra* § 7.05.

the potential benefits must outweigh the potential costs, the net benefits to society must be maximized, and the alternative involving the least net cost to society must be chosen). Also, the order states that "major rules" are submitted to OMB for review 60 days before publication of proposed rules and 30 days prior to publication of final rules. All other rules are submitted to OMB for review 10 days before publication of proposed rules and 10 days prior to publication of final rules. OMB is deemed to have concluded its review after expiration of these time periods unless it notifies the agency that it has extended its review pursuant to Section 3(f). This extension may be indefinite.

OMB's authority is qualified by the rule. Section 8(a)(2) of EO 12291 exempts regulations "for which consideration or reconsideration under the terms of this Order would conflict with deadlines imposed by statute or by judicial order." Further, "[n]othing in this subsection shall be construed as displacing the agencies' responsibilities delegated by law." Sec. 3(f)(3). The executive order also limits OMB's authority by authorizing OMB to exercise its review only "to the extent permitted by law."

Plaintiffs contend that OMB's interference with the promulgation of the EPA regulations unlawfully delayed their promulgation, in violation of both the RCRA amendments and the Administrative Procedure Act ("APA"), 5 U.S.C. § 706. Plaintiffs argue that under 28 U.S.C. § 1331 and § 1361, this court may exercise inherent equitable powers to grant injunctive relief preventing further OMB interference.

Defendants respond that ordering OMB to refrain from reviewing any proposed regulations under RCRA whenever such review would delay promulgation of the regulation beyond a statutory deadline is an unjustifiable and inappropriate use of this court's power. As defendants see it, neither the RCRA nor the APA gives this court jurisdiction over OMB in this matter. Further, there is no jurisdiction to enforce any constraints found within the Executive Order itself.

There is no doubt that this court has jurisdiction over both plaintiffs' RCRA and APA claims against the Administrator of EPA. 42 U.S.C. § 6972(a)(2) and 5 U.S.C. § 702. In compelling EPA to perform non-discretionary duties, however, it is also appropriate to fashion equitable relief to ensure that such duties are performed without the interference of other officials acting outside the scope of their authority in contravention of federal law. Though injunctive relief is not appropriate in these circumstances, as discussed below, there can be no doubt that an executive agency or agencies can be enjoined by this court from failing to execute laws enacted by Congress.

III. Discussion

While the merits of relief against EPA and relief against OMB can be discussed separately, first a discussion of what exactly caused the delay in promulgating the regulations is in order. From the documents released by OMB and EPA under seal, an interesting picture of OMB involvement in the promulgation process emerges.

Congress set March 1, 1985, as the deadline for promulgating the regulations. OMB commenced its review of the proposed permitting standards on March 4, 1985. Since these were not "major rules" under the meaning of EO

§ 7.06   EXECUTIVE CONTROL OF AGENCY DISCRETION   695

12291, EPA anticipated that OMB would complete its review within 10 days. On March 15, 1985, EPA staff briefed OMB staff on the proposed regulations. OMB refused to clear the regulations and on March 25, 1985, notified EPA that it was extending its review of the proposed regulations. OMB apparently wanted EPA to gather additional information prior to promulgating the regulations even though it would delay the process. By April 10, 1985, EPA had still not received any formal comments from OMB.

By April 12, 1985, it was clear that OMB had serious differences with EPA over what regulations to propose. At a meeting of April 16, 1985 between OMB and EPA staff members, OMB sought significant changes in the proposed regulations in four areas. The idea, apparently, was to shift the goal of the regulations away from EPA's philosophy of containing all leaks of waste disposals to OMB's philosophy of preventing only leaks of waste that can be demonstrated by risk analysis to threaten harm to human health.

Internal disagreement within OMB further delayed OMB's consideration of the regulations. Some OMB staff members apparently felt that OMB should not be dictating substantive policy decisions to EPA while others felt the precedent being set an important one for OMB review of other RCRA regulations.

After this suit was filed on May 30, 1985, OMB continued to seek specific changes in EPA's proposed regulations as well as changes not previously discussed. After various negotiations regarding the substance of the regulations, OMB completed its review and cleared the proposed regulations on June 12, 1985. The EPA Administrator signed them June 14, 1985 and the proposed regulations were published in the Federal Register on June 26, 1985, 50 Fed. Reg. 26444, after OMB approved some last-minute stylistic changes made by EPA staff.

A. The Final Date for Promulgating the Regulations

. . . .

Promulgation of regulations 16 months after a Congressional deadline is highly irresponsible. Congress was aware of the complexity of these hazardous waste regulations and yet decided that quick promulgation was of paramount importance. Now that the damage is done, however, this court must fashion an equitable remedy that best achieves the Congressional purpose. This court has previously felt bound to accept a proposed schedule by EPA where EPA demonstrates through affidavit that it is "proceeding in good faith," rather than mandate flat guidelines of its own. After reviewing the proposed schedule set forth by EPA in this case, it appears that the June 30, 1986 deadline is reasonable. This date is only two months later than the date sought by plaintiffs. Therefore, it is ordered that the regulations be promulgated by that time. Failure to do so would be capricious and would merit stronger equitable treatment.

B. OMB's Interference with the Promulgation Process

From the discussion above, it seems clear that OMB did contribute to the delay in the promulgation of the regulations by insisting on certain substantive changes. The released documents show that EPA was ready to announce proposed regulations in the Federal Register as early as March 31, 1985, but due to OMB it did not happen until three months later.

A certain degree of deference must be given to the authority of the President to control and supervise executive policymaking. . . . Yet, the use of EO 12291 to create delays and to impose substantive changes raises some constitutional concerns. Congress enacts environmental legislation after years of study and deliberation, and then delegates to the expert judgment of the EPA Administrator the authority to issue regulations carrying out the aims of the law. Under EO 12291, if used improperly, OMB could withhold approval until the acceptance of certain content in the promulgation of any new EPA regulation, thereby encroaching upon the independence and expertise of EPA. Further, unsuccessful executive lobbying on Capitol Hill can still be pursued administratively by delaying the enactment of regulations beyond the date of a statutory deadline. This is incompatible with the will of Congress and cannot be sustained as a valid exercise of the President's Article II powers.

Such concerns were noted by Congress when EO 12291 was passed. In order to ensure the legality of the operation of EO 12291, James C. Miller III, now the director but then the administrator of OMB's Office of Information and Regulatory Affairs ("OIRA"), appeared before a congressional committee and stressed the importance of construing narrowly the authority granted to OMB. Mr. Miller testified:

> President Reagan's Executive order imposes on the agencies only "to the extent permitted by law" and only to the extent that its terms would not "conflict with deadlines imposed by statute or by judicial order." The limited application of (EO 12291) is a crucial point, one that insures [its] legality and the legality of actions pursuant to (it). . . . If a statute or a court order establishes a date for a rulemaking action, the Executive Order 12291 cannot delay that action.

Testimony of James C. Miller III, in *Role of OMB in Regulation: Hearing Before the Subcomm. on Oversight and Investigation of House Comm. on Energy & Commerce,* 97th Cong., 1st Sess 46 (1981). The Justice Department has also emphasized that EO 12291 must be construed narrowly to survive legal challenge.

> [I]t is clear that the President's exercise of supervisory powers must conform to legislation enacted by Congress. In issuing directives to govern the Executive Branch, the President may not, as a general proposition, require or permit agencies to transgress boundaries set by Congress.

U.S. Department of Justice, Office of Legal Counsel Opinion on EO 12291, February 13, 1981.

This court has previously found that in certain egregious situations, statutory delay caused by OMB review is in contravention to applicable law under Section 8(a)(2) of EO 12291 and therefore that no further OMB review could occur. . . . In the case at bar, enjoining OMB from interacting at all with EPA simply because OMB might cause delay past the new judicial deadline is premature and an unwarranted intrusion into discretionary executive consultations.

§ 7.06 EXECUTIVE CONTROL OF AGENCY DISCRETION 697

There is, however, some credence in plaintiffs' fear that the regulations due June 30, 1986, may still be delayed by OMB. While defendants claim that OMB review of the final regulations in May of 1986 will be concurrent with EPA senior level review, such concurrent review of the proposed regulations in the spring of 1985 resulted in considerable delay. Concurrent review does not eliminate delay, since any changes sought by OMB must then be reviewed by senior level EPA officials. This court declares therefore that further review by OMB which creates any delay in meeting the June 30, 1986 deadline is unreasonable and unacceptable. EPA is obligated to promulgate the regulations by that date and may not use the excuse of OMB review to refrain from doing so.

Plaintiffs also protest that OMB routinely reviews other EPA regulations subject to statutory deadlines even if such review will delay promulgation beyond the deadline. Unless this court declares that OMB has no authority to delay promulgation of all EPA regulations beyond statutory deadlines, OMB will continue to do so both for the Section 3004(w) standards and for other RCRA regulations subject to statutory deadlines in the 1984 amendments. Through answers to interrogatories, plaintiffs show that EPA submitted 169 regulations to OMB which were subject to statutory or judicial deadlines, and on 86 occasions OMB extended its review beyond the time periods outlined in EO 12291. OMB's propensity to extend review has become so great that EPA keeps a running record of the number of its rulemaking actions under extended review by OMB and the resulting delays. The average delay per regulation is 91 days; total delays were more than 311 weeks. Apparently Section 8(a)(2) of EO 12291 is simply ignored.

Congress clearly is concerned with OMB's use of EO 12291 with regard to the deadlines set within the 1984 Amendments. The House Committee report that accompanied the 1984 Amendments states:

> The Committee is extremely concerned that EPA has not been able to comply with past statutory mandates and timetables, not just for RCRA, but for virtually all its programs. . . . The Administrator's ability to meet this deadline (for publishing a schedule for land disposal ban decisions) as with all other deadlines in this bill, shall not be impaired in any way whatsoever by Executive Order 12291.

Hazardous Waste Control and Enforcement Act of 1983, Report of House Comm. on Energy and Commerce, 98th Cong., 1st Sess., May 17, 1983, at 34, 35, 1984 U.S. Code Cong. & Admin. News 5576, 5593–94.

The Hazardous and Solid Waste Amendments of 1984 added at least 44 new deadlines to RCRA, 29 of which must be satisfied within the next 20 months.

This court declares that OMB has no authority to use its regulatory review under EO 12291 to delay promulgation of EPA regulations arising from the 1984 Amendments of the RCRA beyond the date of a statutory deadline. Thus, if a deadline already has expired, OMB has no authority to delay regulations subject to the deadline in order to review them under the executive order. If the deadline is about to expire, OMB may review the regulations only until the time at which OMB review will result in the deadline being missed. From its tracking system, EPA can determine when further delay due to OMB review will result in a deadline being missed.

While this may be an intrusion into the degree of flexibility the executive agencies have in taking their time about promulgating these regulations, this is simply a judicial recognition of law as passed by Congress and of the method for dealing with deadlines laid down by the President himself. Such a recognition is not new. . . . Indeed, OMB itself admits that it cannot prevent an agency from complying with statutory requirements. Yet declaratory relief is necessary to ensure compliance with the clearly expressed will of Congress. This is not an inappropriate interference with the interaction of executive agencies; all such interaction may continue absent a "conflict with deadlines imposed by statute or by judicial order." Sec. 8, EO 12291.

Executive order, No. 12,612, promulgated by the Reagan Administration, mandated that agencies take into account, "to the extent permitted by law, certain principles of federalism." Though the following case does not rely on this order *per se,* it involved the Secretary of Labor's attempt to use federalism principles as a means of delaying further the issuance of certain rules. Is this appropriate executive influence? Consider the D.C. Circuit's response:

FARMWORKER JUSTICE FUND, INC. v. BROCK

District of Columbia Court of Appeals
811 F.2d 613 (1987)

WALD, CHIEF JUDGE:

This appeal culminates a 14-year struggle to compel the Secretary of Labor under the Occupational and Health Safety Act (OSH Act) to issue a field sanitation standard providing access to drinking water and toilets for several million American agricultural workers. The rulemaking record demonstrates beyond dispute that lack of drinking water and toilets causes the spread of contagion, bladder disease, and heat-prostration among farmworkers. Yet resistance to issuing the standard, a counterpart of which is already in place for every other OSHA-covered type of employment, has been intractable. An arsenal of administrative law doctrines has provided the justification for ricocheting the case between the agency and the courts for over a decade: a decade in which field workers have gone without benefit of drinking water or the most rudimentary sanitary facilities. With our decision today ordering the field sanitation rule to issue, we hope to bring to an end this disgraceful chapter of legal neglect.

. . . .

I. History

[The court recounted the 14-year history of this case. It went on to note that:]

In his new Notice of Proposed Rulemaking, however, the Secretary for the first time raised a question about the need for a federal standard at all: "in light of the existence of state field sanitation standards covering a substantial portion of such workers[,] and in light of the fact of voluntary provision of these items [drinking water, toilet and handwashing facilities] by agricultural employers[,] there is a serious question whether the evidence establishes the need for a federal field sanitation standard." 49 Fed. Reg. at 7591. The Secretary directed OSHA to conduct public hearings addressing this issue. . . .

In January 1985, one month before the 31-month deadline set forth in the settlement agreement [approved in 1982 by the District Court] was due to run out, the Secretary filed a request with the District Court for an extension of time, claiming that the new rulemaking proceeding could not be completed until April 16, 1985, at the earliest.

On March 6, 1985, without ruling on the extension issue, the District Court transferred the case to this court under the authority of *International Union, United Automobile, Aerospace & Agricultural Implement Workers of America, UAW v. Donovan,* 756 F.2d 162 (D.C. 1985). Then, on March 29, 1985, this court decided the issue: "Respondents have met their burden of demonstrating that the proposed deviation from the time frame set out in the settlement agreement is in good faith." . . . We added, however, this note of caution: "we will look with extreme displeasure on any variance from the schedule and will not hesitate to set a date certain for completion of the administrative proceeding if they unreasonably delay." . . .

On April 16, 1985, the Secretary issued a "[f]inal [d]etermination . . . that a federal field sanitation standard will not be issued at this time." 50 Fed. Reg. 15,086, 15,087. The Secretary cited two reasons for this decision, which it characterized as "Priorities" and "Federalism." As to "Priorities," the Secretary stated:

> [A] federal field sanitation standard, if promulgated, would, in accordance with well-settled OSHA policy, be given a very low priority in enforcement relative to most other health standards already in effect and in development (e.g., asbestos, lead, various chemical carcinogens). It would not be appropriate to divert resources from the enforcement of other OSHA health standards already in effect and protecting workers from more life-threatening chemical exposures.

50 Fed. Reg. at 15,088.

As to "Federalism," the Secretary stated: "'Federalism' involves a concept designed to restore an appropriate balance of responsibility between state and federal government and is appropriately applied in those instances where states are already taking charge of their police power responsibilities." 50 Fed. Reg. at 15,090. Thus, the Secretary "believe[d] it more appropriate that the states, which increasingly are moving to regulate this problem, be allowed to do so in accordance with each state's specific concerns for public health and particular conditions in agriculture." *Id.* at 15,088.

Eight days after this "final" decision, the newly appointed Secretary of Labor, William E. Brock, stated during his confirmation hearings that he would reconsider this no-standard decision. . . . On October 21, 1985, Secretary Brock in fact did revoke the April 16 decision, but he did not promulgate a field sanitation standard in its stead. Rather, he announced he would delay promulgation of a national standard for an additional two years in order to give state governments an opportunity to develop and implement their own adequate field sanitation standards. At the end of the first 18 months of this two-year period,

> OSHA will evaluate the states' response. If the Agency determines that the states have acted to adequately protect farmworkers, no further federal action would be required. However, if OSHA determines that the states' response is inadequate, then within 6 months after that determination OSHA will issue its own field sanitation standard.

50 Fed. Reg. 42,660, 42,662.

The Secretary justified this decision as follows:

> . . . the *clear evidence* in the record to date of *unacceptable risks* to the health of farmworkers arising from the *currently inadequate provision* of sanitary facilities and drinking water at their worksites means that the decision not to issue a federal standard must now be set aside. While not rejecting the policy reasons set forth in the April 16 determination, the Secretary now finds that a different balance must be struck in order to give proper weight to the health risks posed. Thus, based on his review of the record, the Secretary has reached a determination that *further regulation is required* to deal with farmworkers' health problems. However, he continues to believe that state action responsive to this need would be preferable to, and more effective than federal action. He therefore has decided to afford the states an opportunity to take adequate action to protect farmworkers, and he is offering assistance to the states for this task. In the event that the states fail within the specified time to take advantage of this opportunity, the Secretary is committed to promulgating a federal standard to provide such protection. Because the Secretary believes that further regulation, preferably on a state level, is needed to protect farmers adequately and because the April 16 determination not to issue a federal standard did not adequately take into account the health risks posed, that decision is hereby superseded.

Id. at 42,660 (emphasis added [by the court]).

Now, 14 years after the original petition was filed with the Secretary, petitioners' challenge to this latest decision by the Secretary not to issue the standard is before us.

II.

. . . .

III. The Merits of the October 21 Decision

The Secretary's October 21 decision presents a novel question for judicial review: can the Secretary after completion of rulemaking proceedings, decide not to promulgate a proposed occupational safety or health standard he finds to be necessary to fulfill the purposes of the OSH Act solely in the hope that state governments will provide equivalent protection within the next two years? In this case, the new Secretary announced he was reversing his predecessor's decision not to issue a regulation because of his own assessment that there was "clear evidence" in the record of "unacceptable risks to the health of farmworkers arising from the currently inadequate provision of sanitary facilities and drinking water." 50 Fed. Reg. at 42,660. In reconsidering his predecessor's April 16 decision not to issue a field sanitation standard at all, the Secretary emphasized that he had "thoroughly reviewed [not only] the evidence in the record. . . . [but] the policy reasons behind that [earlier] determination, [including] the severe limitations on OSHA's resources [and] OSHA's other priorities." *Id.* At the end of that review, the Secretary "reached a determination that further regulation is required to deal with farmworkers' health problems," and explicitly "commit[ed] OSHA to the issuance of a federal field sanitation standard within 24 months in the event the states do not take the necessary action within the next 18 months." *Id.* Thus, it is critical to keep in mind that in reviewing the Secretary's October 21 decision, the court is not evaluating the Secretary's fundamental administrative decision about how best to allocate his agency's resources or to order its priorities. The Secretary has already made that decision in favor of federal regulation of farmworkers' sanitation needs, based on current conditions. Rather, the court is reviewing only the second part of the Secretary's decision that, once the need for a particular occupational health standard has been shown in a rulemaking proceeding, the Secretary may nonetheless refuse to promulgate it, because of a desire or hope that the states will fill the regulatory gap. . . .

A. *The Impermissibility of the Secretary's First Two Justifications*

We first consider the import of the Secretary's frequent assertions that "state regulation of field sanitation is *preferable* to federal regulation," terminology repeated at three separate points in his October 21 decision. . . . This language is open to several different but not necessarily mutually exclusive interpretations.

1. *The Secretary's belief about "appropriate" federal-state relations*

The October 21 decision appears to argue that in our American system of government, state regulation in aid of social needs or welfare is usually "preferable" to federal regulation for two reasons: citizens feel more in touch or at home with their state or local governments than with the federal bureaucracy in Washington and state governments are generally more competent to regulate than their federal counterpart. Indeed, in the October 21 decision, the Secretary emphasized that "[s]tates without field sanitation standards can draw on their closer relationship with their constituents, both growers and farmworkers, and their long experience with analogous public health problems to promulgate and enforce appropriate standards," and continued that "[s]anitation, like many other public health issues, has traditionally been a primary concern of state and local officials." . . . These remarks suggest that the October 21 decision was motivated, in part, by the Secretary's concept about the proper roles of the federal and state governments in our system. The earlier April 16 decision was even more explicit in this respect: "'Federalism' involves a concept designed to restore an appropriate balance of responsibility between state & federal government. . . ." . . . Because in October the Secretary stated that he "continues to believe that state action . . . would be preferable to . . . federal action," we must assume that the October decision was based, at least to some degree, upon his particular view of "appropriate" federal-state relations. . . .

To the extent, then, that the October decision rests on such a preference, the Secretary acted beyond the scope of his discretion. Although the Secretary might prefer that state governments regulate "public health issues" because they have "traditionally been a primary concern of state and local officials," Congress, in adopting the OSH Act, decided that the federal government would take the lead in regulating the field of occupational health. However much the Secretary might wish to "restore" what he considers to be "an appropriate balance of responsibility between state and federal governments," he is bound to enforce what Congress already determined to be the "appropriate balance of responsibility between state and federal governments" in the field of occupational health and safety. . . . In short, the Secretary may not withhold or delay issuance of a standard within his jurisdiction because he holds a different vision of the federal government's role in this field than the role envisioned by Congress and enacted into law in the OSH statute.

. . . .

Thus, we conclude that the Secretary is foreclosed from withholding or delaying occupational health and safety standards within his jurisdiction because he believes that state governments have a "closer relationship with their constituents" than the federal government, or because the states have considerable experience in confronting "public health problems." These grounds are not only sufficiently broad in nature to apply to any occupational health standard within the Secretary's jurisdiction, but they conflict with clearly articulated premises of the OSH Act. In short, the Secretary may not abdicate the responsibility which Congress entrusted to him, because he differs with the allocation of federal-state responsibility encapsulated in the Act. Insofar as the Secretary's statement that "state regulation of field sanitation is preferable to federal regulation" reflects a reliance on his particular vision of "federalism" as a reason for not issuing the farmworker standard now, we hold that this basis for the October 21 decision exceeded the scope of the Secretary's discretion under the OSH Act.

. . . .

CONCLUSION

In *Public Citizen v. Steed*, 733 F.2d 93, 98, 105 (D.C. Cir. 1984), "[i]n the context of a thirteen year gap twixt law and enforcement," we observed that "it is hard to imagine a more sorry performance of a congressional mandate than that carried out by NHTSA and its predecessors." Unfortunately, truth is often stranger than fantasy. In this case, for 14 years farmworkers have been unsuccessfully petitioning the Department of Labor to provide sanitation standards equivalent to those which the federal government under the OSH Act has guaranteed to *all other workers* in its jurisdiction. The Secretary's justification for the latest decision to delay reflected a combination of (1) his particular vision of "federalism," a vision categorically rejected by Congress when it originally passed the OSH Act, . . . and (3) an unsupported and unrealistic hope that state governments would suddenly move, en masse, to fill the need. Thus, the Secretary has exceeded the scope of his authority and acted contrary to law in relying on (1) . . . and delayed agency action unreasonably in relying on (3). Because 5 U.S.C. § 706(1) directs "[t]he reviewing court" to "compel agency action unlawfully withheld or unreasonably delayed," we now order the Secretary to issue the federal field sanitation standard, which he has admitted is necessary for the health and safety of farmworkers, within 30 days from the issuance of this mandate.

It is so ordered.

[The concurring opinion of SENIOR DISTRICT JUDGE WILL, and the concurring and dissenting opinion of CIRCUIT JUDGE WILLIAMS have been omitted.]

This decision was vacated on May 7, 1987, after the court received a letter from respondents dated April 28, 1987, "advising the Court of the issuance of field sanitation standards by the Secretary of Labor. . . ." 817 F.2d 890 (D.C. Cir. 1987).

NOTES AND QUESTIONS

7-26. What triggers judicial review in *Thomas*? In *Brock*? How does the Court deal with the delays in these two cases? Why do you think these delays occurred? Were the agencies, with OMB, trying to come up with the most effective and efficient regulations they could or were they trying to deregulate? If they are deregulating, is deregulation through OMB review appropriate? Under what circumstances?

7-27. Quite apart from the use of executive orders to try indirectly to encourage deregulation, what do you see as the primary advantages and disadvantages of OMB review? What effect is such review likely to have on the APA's assurances of public participation? Are these "ex parte" contacts? What about delay? Are there any separation of powers problems on the face of order 12,866? Are there such problems in their application? Can these orders constitutionally be applied to independent commissions?

On the other hand, why is the Office of the President a particularly good place to centralize and coordinate disparate agency tasks? What are the explicit and inherent constitutional duties and powers in Article II with regard to the bureaucracy? Why should such powers be concentrated in an office with a national constituency? What is the significance of the electoral accountability of the President?

7-28. During his tenure in office, President Clinton,

[F]requent[ly] [ordered the] issuance of formal and published memoranda to executive branch agency heads instructing them to take specified action within the scope of the discretionary power delegated to them by Congress. These directives, issued prior to OMB review (in the case of rules) or independent of this review (in the case of other administrative action, not subject to the OMB process), enabled Clinton and his White House staff to instigate, rather than merely check, administrative action. The memoranda became, ever increasingly over the course of eight years, Clinton's primary means, self-consciously undertaken, both of setting an administrative agenda that reflected and advanced his policy and political preferences and of ensuring the execution of this program.

Elena Kagan, *Presidential Administration*, 114 HARV. L. REV. 2245, 2290 (2001).*

While President Clinton was not the first to issue theses kinds of directives relating to substantive regulatory policy — President Reagan issued nine and President George H.W. Bush issued four — Clinton issued 107 of these directives, more than any of his predecessors. *Id.* at 2294–95.

§ 7.07 Executive and Congressional Participation In Agency Rulemaking Proceedings

Thus far, we have focused on the role of the executive in a phase of the rulemaking process that precedes the public phase of rulemaking procedures. To what extent can and should the executive engage in *ex parte* contacts with interested parties after the public phase of a rulemaking has begun? After it has concluded? Consider this excerpt from the following case:

SIERRA CLUB v. COSTLE

District of Columbia Court of Appeals
657 F.2d 298 (1981)

[This case involved a variety of substantive and procedural attacks on certain new source performance standards for coal-fired power plants promulgated by the Environmental Protection Agency pursuant to the Clean Air Act. Included in Part V (E) of the 100 page opinion was an attack on *ex parte* contacts made by Congress and the Executive during the rulemaking process. Judge Wald wrote for the Court.]

2. Meetings Held With Individuals Outside EPA

The statute does not explicitly treat the issue of post-comment period meetings with individuals outside EPA. Oral face-to-face discussions are not prohibited anywhere, anytime, in the Act. The absence of such prohibition may have arisen from the nature of the informal rulemaking procedures Congress had in mind. Where agency action resembles judicial action, where it involves formal rulemaking, adjudication, or quasi-adjudication among "conflicting private claims to a valuable privilege," the insulation of the decisionmaker from *ex parte* contacts is justified by basic notions of due process to the parties

---

* Copyright © 2001 Harvard Law Review Association. All rights reserved.

involved. But where agency action involves informal rulemaking of a policy-making sort, the concept of *ex parte* contacts is of more questionable utility.[501]

Under our system of government,(footnote omitted) the very legitimacy of general policymaking performed by unelected administrators depends in no small part upon the openness, accessibility, and amenability of these officials to the needs and ideas of the public from whom their ultimate authority derives, and upon whom their commands must fall. As judges we are insulated from these pressures because of the nature of the judicial process in which we participate; but we must refrain from the easy temptation to look askance at all face-to-face lobbying efforts, regardless of the forum in which they occur, merely because we see them as inappropriate in the judicial context.[503] Furthermore, the importance to effective regulation of continuing contact with a regulated industry, other affected groups, and the public cannot be [over]estimated. Informal contacts may enable the agency to win needed support for its program, reduce future enforcement requirements by helping those regulated to anticipate and shape their plans for the future, and spur the provision of information which the agency needs. The possibility of course exists that in permitting *ex parte* communications with rulemakers we create the danger of "one administrative record for the public and this court and another for the Commission." Under the Clean Air Act procedures, however, "[t]he promulgated rule may not be based (in part or whole) on any information or data which has not been placed in the docket. . . ." Thus EPA must justify its rulemaking solely on the basis of the record it compiles and makes public.

Regardless of this court's views on the need to restrict all post-comment contacts in the informal rulemaking context, however, it is clear to us that

---

[501] *See generally* Verkuil, [*Jawboning Administrative Agencies: Ex Parte Contacts by the White House*, 80 COLUM. L. REV. 943, 975–76 (1980)]:

> It should not be forgotten that informal rulemaking involves "interested persons," rather than "parties" in the usual adjudicative sense of the term. The concept of "*ex parte*" implies a different decisional structure from that involving mere "interested persons." One can only have a contact without "parties" present in a proceeding where parties are involved, namely, adjudication or formal rulemaking.

See also Verkuil, *The Emerging Concept of Administrative Procedure*, 78 COLUM. L. REV. 258, 290 (1978); Nathanson, *Report to the Select Committee on Ex Parte Communications in Informal Rulemaking Proceedings*, 30 ADMIN. L. REV. 377, 396–97 (1978):

> In the ordinary rulemaking proceedings the parties are not identified in advance. Neither are conflicting interests established in advance among those subject to the proposed regulations. . . . In such a situation the very concept of *ex parte* communications is strikingly out of place; there are no parties to begin with, and it is not known what parties will develop and what their conflicting interests will be.

[503] *See* Remarks of Carl McGowan (Chief Judge, U.S. Court of Appeals, D.C. Circuit), Ass'n of Amer. Law Schools, Section on Admin. Law (San Antonio, Texas, Jan. 4, 1981):

> I think it likely that ambivalence will continue to pervade the *ex parte* contact problem until we face up to the question of whether legislation by informal rulemaking under delegated authority is, in terms of process, to be assimilated to lawmaking by the Congress itself, or to the adversary trial carried on in the sanitized and insulated atmosphere of the courthouse. Anyone with experience of both knows that a courtroom differs markedly in style and tone from a legislative chamber. The customs, the traditions, the mores, if you please, of the processes of persuasion, are emphatically not the same. What is acceptable in the one is alien to the other.

See generally Ex Parte Communication During Informal Rulemaking, 14 COLUM. J.L. & SOC. PROB. 269, 275 (1979).

Congress has decided not to do so in the statute which controls this case. As we have previously noted:

> Where Congress wanted to prohibit *ex parte* contacts it clearly did so. Thus APA § 5(c) forbids *ex parte* contacts when an "adjudication" is underway, but even that prohibition does not apply to "the agency or a member or members of the body comprising the agency." 5 U.S.C. § 554(d)(C) (1970). . . . If Congress wanted to forbid or limit *ex parte* contact in every case of informal rulemaking, it certainly had a perfect opportunity of doing so when it enacted the Government in the Sunshine Act, Pub. L. No. 94–409, 90 Stat. 1241 (Sept. 13, 1976). . . . *That it did not extend the ex parte contact provisions of the amended section 557 to section 553* — even though such an extension was urged upon it during the hearing — is a sound indication that Congress still does not favor a *per se* prohibition or even a "logging" requirement in all such proceedings.

Lacking a statutory basis for its position, EDF would have us extend our decision in *Home Box Office, Inc. v. FCC* to cover all meetings with individuals outside EPA during the post-comment period. Later decisions of this court, however, have declined to apply *Home Box Office* to informal rulemaking of the general policymaking sort involved here, and there is no precedent for applying it to the procedures found in the Clean Air Act Amendments of 1977.

It still can be argued, however, that if oral communications are to be freely permitted after the close of the comment period, then at least some adequate summary of them must be made in order to preserve the integrity of the rulemaking docket, which under the statute must be the sole repository of material upon which EPA intends to rely. The statute does not require the docketing of all post-comment period conversations and meetings, but we believe that a fair inference can be drawn that in some instances such docketing may be needed in order to give practical effect to section 307(d)(4)(B)(i), which provides that all *documents* "of central relevance to the rulemaking" shall be placed in the docket as soon as possible after their availability. This is so because unless *oral* communications of central relevance to the rulemaking are also docketed in some fashion or other, information central to the justification of the rule could be obtained without ever appearing on the docket, simply by communicating it by voice rather than by pen, thereby frustrating the command of section 307 that the final rule not be "based (in part or whole) on any information or data which has not been placed in the docket. . . ."

EDF is understandably wary of a rule which permits the agency to decide for itself when oral communications are of such central relevance that a docket entry for them is required. Yet the statute itself vests EPA with discretion to decide whether "documents" are of central relevance and therefore must be placed in the docket; surely EPA can be given no less discretion in docketing oral communications, concerning which the statute has no explicit requirements whatsoever. Furthermore, this court has already recognized that the relative significance of various communications to the outcome of the rule is a factor in determining whether their disclosure is required. A judicially imposed blanket requirement that all post-comment period oral communications be docketed would, on the other hand, contravene our limited powers of review, would stifle desirable experimentation in the area by Congress and the agencies, and is unnecessary for achieving the goal of an established, procedure-defined docket, *viz.*, to enable reviewing courts to fully evaluate the stated justification given by the agency for its final rule.

Turning to the particular oral communications in this case, we find that only two of the nine contested meetings were undocketed by EPA. The agency has maintained that, as to the May 1 meeting where Senate staff people were briefed on EPA's analysis concerning the impact of alternative emissions ceilings upon coal reserves, its failure to place a summary of the briefing in the docket was an oversight. We find no evidence that this oversight was anything but an honest inadvertence; furthermore, a briefing of this sort by EPA which simply provides background information about an upcoming rule is not the type of oral communication which would require a docket entry under the statute.

The other undocketed meeting occurred at the White House and involved the President and his White House staff. Because this meeting involves considerations unique to intra-executive meetings, it is discussed in the section immediately *infra*.

(a) Intra Executive Branch Meetings

We have already held that a blanket prohibition against meetings during the post-comment period with individuals outside EPA is unwarranted, and this perforce applies to meetings with White House officials. We have not yet addressed, however, the issue whether such oral communications with White House staff, or the President himself, must be docketed on the rulemaking record, and we now turn to that issue. The facts, as noted earlier, present us with a single undocketed meeting held on April 30, 1979, at 10:00 a.m., attended by the President, White House staff, other high ranking members of the Executive Branch, as well as EPA officials, and which concerned the issues and options presented by the rulemaking.

We note initially that section 307 makes specific provision for including in the rulemaking docket the "written comments" of other executive agencies along with accompanying documents on any proposed draft rules circulated in advance of the rulemaking proceeding. Drafts of the final rule submitted to an executive review process prior to promulgation, as well as all "written comments," "documents," and "written responses" resulting from such interagency review process, are also to be put in the docket prior to promulgation. This specific requirement does not mention informal meetings or conversations concerning the rule which are not part of the initial or final review processes, nor does it refer to oral comments of any sort. Yet it is hard to believe Congress was unaware that intra-executive meetings and oral comments would occur throughout the rulemaking process. We assume, therefore, that unless expressly forbidden by Congress, such intra-executive contacts may take place, both during and after the public comment period; the only real issue is whether they must be noted and summarized in the docket.

The court recognizes the basic need of the President and his White House staff to monitor the consistency of executive agency regulations with Administration policy. He and his White House advisers surely must be briefed fully and frequently about rules in the making, and their contributions to policy-making considered. The executive power under our Constitution, after all, is not shared — it rests exclusively with the President. The idea of a "plural executive," or a President with a council of state, was considered and rejected by the Constitutional Convention. Instead the Founders chose to risk the potential for tyranny inherent in placing power in one person, in order to gain the advantages of accountability fixed on a single source. To ensure the President's control and supervision over the Executive Branch, the Constitution — and its judicial gloss — vests him with the powers of appointment and removal, the power to demand written opinions from executive officers, and the right to invoke executive privilege to protect consultative privacy. In the particular case of EPA, Presidential authority is clear since it has never been considered an "independent agency," but always part of the Executive Branch.

The authority of the President to control and supervise executive policymaking is derived from the Constitution; the desirability of such control is demonstrable from the practical realities of administrative rulemaking. Regulations such as those involved here demand a careful weighing of cost, environmental, and energy considerations. They also have broad implications for national economic policy. Our form of government simply could not function effectively or rationally if key executive policymakers were isolated from each other and from the Chief Executive. Single mission agencies do not always have the answers to complex regulatory problems. An overworked administrator exposed on a 24-hour basis to a dedicated but zealous staff needs to know the arguments and ideas of policymakers in other agencies as well as in the White House.

We recognize, however, that there may be instances where the docketing of conversations between the President or his staff and other Executive Branch officers or rulemakers may be necessary to ensure due process. This may be true, for example, where such conversations directly concern the outcome of adjudications or quasi-adjudicatory proceedings; there is no inherent executive power to control the rights of individuals in such settings. Docketing may also be necessary in some circumstances where a statute like this one *specifically requires* that essential "information or data" upon which a rule is based be docketed. But in the absence of any further Congressional requirements, we hold that it was not unlawful in this case for EPA not to docket a face-to-face policy session involving the President and EPA officials during the post-comment period, since EPA makes no effort to base the rule on any "information or data" arising from that meeting. Where the President himself is directly involved in oral communications with Executive Branch officials, Article II considerations — combined with the strictures of *Vermont Yankee* — require that courts tread with extraordinary caution in mandating disclosure beyond that already required by statute.

The purposes of full-record review which underlie the need for disclosing *ex parte* conversations in some settings do not require that courts know the details of every White House contact, including a Presidential one, in this informal rulemaking setting. After all, any rule issued here with or without White House assistance must have the requisite *factual support* in the rulemaking record, and under this particular statute the Administrator may not base the rule in whole or in part on any *"information or data"* which is not in the record, no matter what the source. The courts will monitor all this, but they need not be omniscient to perform their role effectively. Of course, it is always possible that undisclosed Presidential prodding may direct an outcome that *is* factually based on the record, but different from the outcome that would have obtained in the absence of Presidential involvement. In such a case, it would be true that the political process did affect the outcome in a way the courts could not police. But we do not believe that Congress intended that the courts convert informal rulemaking into a rarified technocratic process, unaffected by political considerations or the presence of Presidential power. In sum, we find that the existence of intra-Executive Branch meetings during the post-comment period, and the failure to docket one such meeting involving the President, violated neither the procedures mandated by the Clean Air Act nor due process.

(b) Meetings Involving Alleged Congressional Pressure

Finally, EDF challenges the rulemaking on the basis of alleged Congressional pressure, citing principally two meetings with Senator Byrd. EDF asserts that under the controlling case law the political interference demonstrated in this case represents a separate and independent ground for invalidating this rulemaking. But among the cases EDF cites in support of its position, only *D.C. Federation of Civil Associations v. Volpe*[534] seems relevant to the facts here.

In *D.C. Federation* the Secretary of Transportation, pursuant to applicable federal statutes, made certain safety and environmental findings in designating a proposed bridge as part of the interstate highway system. Civic associations sought to have these determinations set aside for their failure to meet certain statutory standards, and because of possible tainting by reason of improper Congressional influence. Such influence chiefly included public statements by the Chairman of the House Subcommittee on the District of Columbia, Representative Natcher, indicating in no uncertain terms that money earmarked for the construction of the District of Columbia's subway system would be withheld unless the Secretary approved the bridge. While a majority of this court could not decide whether Representative Natcher's extraneous pressure had in fact influenced the Secretary's decision, a majority did agree on the controlling principle of law: "that the decision [of the Secretary] would be invalid if based in whole or in part on the pressures emanating from Representative Natcher." In remanding to the Secretary for new determinations concerning the bridge, however, the court went out of its way to "emphasize that we have not found — nor, for that matter, have we sought — any suggestions of impropriety or illegality in the actions of Representative Natcher and others who strongly advocate the bridge." The court remanded simply so that the Secretary could make this decision strictly and solely on the basis of considerations made relevant by Congress in the applicable statute.

D.C. Federation thus requires that two conditions be met before an administrative rulemaking may be overturned simply on the grounds of Congressional pressure. First, the content of the pressure upon the Secretary is designed to force him to decide upon factors not made relevant by Congress in the

---

[534] 459 F.2d 1231 (D.C. Cir. 1971), *cert. denied*, 405 U.S. 1030, 92 S. Ct. 1290, 31 L. Ed. 2d 489 (1972).

applicable statute. Representative Natcher's threats were of precisely that character, since deciding to approve the bridge in order to free the "hostage" mass transit appropriation was not among the decisionmaking factors Congress had in mind when it enacted the highway approval provisions of Title 23 of the United States Code. Second, the Secretary's determination must be affected by those extraneous considerations.

In the case before us, there is no persuasive evidence that either criterion is satisfied. Senator Byrd requested a meeting in order to express "strongly" his already well-known views that the SO_2 standards' impact on coal reserves was a matter of concern to him. EPA initiated a second responsive meeting to report its reaction to the reserve data submitted by the NCA. In neither meeting is there any allegation that EPA made any commitments to Senator Byrd. The meetings did underscore Senator Byrd's deep concerns for EPA, but there is no evidence he attempted actively to use "extraneous" pressures to further his position. Americans rightly expect their elected representatives to voice their grievances and preferences concerning the administration of our laws. We believe it entirely proper for Congressional representatives vigorously to represent the interests of their constituents before administrative agencies engaged in informal, general policy rulemaking, so long as individual Congressmen do not frustrate the intent of Congress as a whole as expressed in statute, nor undermine applicable rules of procedure. Where Congressmen keep their comments focused on the substance of the proposed rule — and we have no substantial evidence to cause us to believe Senator Byrd did not do so here[539] — administrative agencies are expected to balance Congressional pressure with the pressures emanating from all other sources. To hold otherwise would deprive the agencies of legitimate sources of information and call into question the validity of nearly every controversial rulemaking.

. . . .

NOTES AND QUESTIONS

7-29. How do the executive contacts in this case differ from those when OMB reviews an agency rule under Executive Order 12,866? Do these differences require a different result in this case? Why or why not?

7-30. To what extent does the fact that an agency's decision must be justified by the record protect against undue influence by the executive or the

---

[539] The only hint we are provided that extraneous "threats" were made comes from a newspaper article which states, in part,

> The ceiling decision came after two weeks of what one Senate source called "hard-ball arm-twisting" by Byrd and other coal state Senators. Byrd summoned Costle and White House adviser Stuart Eizenstat *strongly hinting* that the Administration needs his support on strategic arms limitation treaty (SALT) and the windfall profits tax, according to Senate and Administration sources.

The Washington Post, May 5, 1979, at A–1 (emphasis supplied [by the court]). We do not believe that a single newspaper account of strong "hint[s]" represents substantial evidence of extraneous pressure significant enough to warrant a finding of unlawful congressional interference.

Congress? Are rulemaking records likely to be very precise? Are all comments equal or are some comments "more equal"?

7-31. What, if anything, is lost by docketing executive and congressional comments of this sort? Does it risk overjudicializing the proceeding?

7-32. The Court notes that the outcome of such contacts in an adjudicatory proceeding would be different. If an administrator in a rulemaking proceeding is not to be treated as a judge, does it follow that he or she should be treated like a legislator? Were they in this case? Is there some middle ground for conceptualizing the role of an administrator in a rulemaking proceeding that falls somewhere between a judge and a legislator? Reread Chief Judge McGowan's observations in footnote 503 of *Costle* regarding disparate persuasive processes. Why might these differences be important and what do they tell us about the unique roles of each actor?

7-33. What role does Judge Wald envisage for the executive in cases such as these and does that role accord with the expertise of the agency? When is agency expertise supplanted by executive and congressional politics? What rule should or can courts play when this occurs?

7-34. In *Portland Audubon Society v. Endangered Species*, 984 F.2d 1534 (9th Cir. 1993), the court distinguished the adjudicatory context in which the *ex parte* contacts arose in this case from those in *Sierra Club v. Costle*. The court stated that "[*Costle*] was based explicitly on the fact that the proceeding involved was *informal* rulemaking to which the APA restrictions on *ex parte* communications are not applicable. In fact, while the *Costle* court recognized that political pressure from the President may not be inappropriate in informal rulemaking proceedings, it acknowledged that the contrary is true in formal adjudications." *Id.* at 1545–46 (emphasis in original).

7-35. Consider a typical statute granting rulemaking authority to an agency. For example, 43 U.S.C. § 363 (2004) provides: "The *Secretary of the Interior* is hereby authorized to perform any and all acts and make such rules and regulations as may be necessary for the purposes of carrying out the provisions of this Act [43 U.S.C. § 361-363] into full force and effect." (emphasis added) Consider also that while the president nominates department or agency heads, the Senate must approve the person nominated to the post. Assume that the Secretary of the Interior feels that a particular rule is "necessary for the purposes of carrying [out] the provisions" of our statute above, and the senators who confirmed the secretary believed that she supported this proposed rule. Assume also that the head of OIRA is concerned that the rule will be too costly. Finally, assume that the president tells the Secretary, "I don't know what your staff was thinking when they proposed this rule, and I certainly don't think it is a 'necessary' rule. Actually, I think that the rule should explicitly permit the activity that this rule is trying to prohibit."

Should the secretary adopt the rule? Why or why not? Can the president even have this kind of conversation with the secretary about a proposed rule? If the president can have this conversation, must the contents of the conversation by disclosed in the administrative record? Does you answer depend on whether the secretary adopts the rule that the president did not like or whether the secretary adopts the rule that the president proposed? Suppose that instead of the president, it was the president's chief of staff who had the conversation with the secretary — any change in your answer?

§ 7.08 OMB and the Data Quality Act

In 2001, Congress passed the Data Quality Act (DQA),* requiring agencies to issue guidelines designed to ensure the quality, objectivity, utility and integrity of the information that they disseminate. It requires that they establish an administrative process that allows affected persons to seek and obtain corrections of that information and they are to report annually to OMB concerning the complaints they receive in this regard and how they have been dealt with. Congress directs OMB to provide policy and procedural guidance to agencies conceiving these guidelines.

The Act was enacted as a two-paragraph provision buried in a huge Appropriations Bill. It states, in full:

> (a) IN GENERAL. — The Director of the Office of Management and Budget shall, by not later than September 30, 2001, and with public and Federal agency involvement, issue guidelines under sections 3504(d)(1) and 3516 of title 44, United States Code, that provide policy and procedural guidance to Federal agencies for ensuring and maximizing the quality, objectivity, utility, and integrity of information (including statistical information) disseminated by Federal agencies in fulfillment of the purposes and provisions of chapter 35 of title 44, United States Code, commonly referred to as the Paperwork Reduction Act.
>
> (b) CONTENT OF GUIDELINES. — The guidelines under subsection (a) shall—
>
> > (1) apply to the sharing by Federal agencies of, and access to, information disseminated by Federal agencies; and
> >
> > (2) require that each Federal agency to which the guidelines apply—
> >
> > > (A) issue guidelines ensuring and maximizing the quality, objectivity, utility, and integrity of information (including statistical information) disseminated by the agency, by not later than 1 year after the date of issuance of the guidelines under subsection (a);
> > >
> > > (B) establish administrative mechanisms allowing affected persons to seek and obtain correction of information maintained and disseminated by the agency that does not comply with the guidelines issued under subsection (a); and
> > >
> > > (C) report periodically to the Director— (i) the number and nature of complaints received by the agency regarding the accuracy of information disseminated by the

---

* Consolidated Appropriations Act 2001, Pub. L. No. 106-554, § 515, 114 Stat. 2763 (2001).

agency; and (ii) how such complaints were handled by the agency.

Because it was a rider to an appropriations bill, there is no legislative history of any kind to shed light on what, for example, Congress meant by "dissemination." This is a crucial term, since only information that is "disseminated" is subject to the guidelines of "quality, objectivity, utility and integrity." As James T. O'Reilly has noted in, *The 411 on 515: How OIRA's Expanded Information Roles in 2002 Will Impact Rulemaking and Agency Publicity Actions*, 54 ADMIN. L. REV. 835, 846-47 (2002):[*]

> How will the information dissemination roles of 515 fit with the rulemaking analysis roles under Executive Orders, that are the more familiar task of OIRA? The 515 norms relate to quality of data being relied upon; the data sets are already disclosed at some point during the rulemaking, but section 515 insists that the agencies check the data for quality and (much more importantly) allow complaints to be made for correction of the data. The analysis roles deal with quality of the decisional factors and how the factors are balanced. An agency that shows that it cares more attentively about its data quality will presumably do a better job with the entire rulemaking process.
>
> The quality of technical support data has an impact on credibility and challenges to quality have an impact on the public's acceptance of the agency rules. The statistics on which the agency relies to support an economic regulatory control would be subject to challenge by a person who complains that the data is inaccurate. In anticipation of future environmental rulemaking or pronouncements of policy, the Environmental Protection Agency can expect trade groups representing industrial firms to file hundreds of section 515 complaints beginning in late 2002, when its correction rules must become effective.
>
> The impact of section 515 will be to allow businesses, organizations, nonprofits, states, and other groups to check the statistics the agency is using and to compel the agency to explain the errors in that data before the rulemaking is completed. Beyond statistics, which are part, but not all, of the covered information, section 515 will allow complaints about a lack of "objectivity," which may mean the selection of decisional criteria other than the criteria that an "objective" peer norm would have selected. But, section 515 has several potential applications. The complaint may arrive before, during, or after an agency uses that data in press releases, rules, adjudication of penalties, or other agency actions. It is foreseeable that the defense sequence for lawyers defending post-2002 civil penalty cases will routinely involve discovery, Freedom of Information Act requests, section 515 complaints, and a request for stay pending outcome of the agency's response to the section 515 critique.

What do you think the impact of this Act will or should be? Consider the following summary of a report filed by OMB, in *Developments in*

---

[*] Copyright © 2002 American Bar Association. All rights reserved.

Administrative Law and Regulatory Practice 163–64 (ABA, Jeffrey Lubbers, ed. 2003-2004):*

Perhaps in an effort to get a grasp on the true nature of the law they had passed, Congress included in a Conference Report in a 2004 Appropriations Act a request to OMB to provide a report on the progress (or lack thereof) made under the DQA. OMB filed the Report on April 30, 2004. It is available on the OMB website.**

The Report stressed: "The Bush Administration is committed to vigorous implementation of the [DQA]. We believe it provides an excellent opportunity to enhance both the competence and accountability of government."

The highlights of the Report are OMB's list of findings that refute common criticisms made against the DQA. Or as OMB referred to the issues in this section, "Perceptions and Realities." The first "misperception" characterized by OMB, for instance, is that agencies would be "inundated" with DQA correction requests. OMB found that there had only been 35 correction requests so far that were directly attributable to the DQA, with most of these going to the EPA, HHS, and DOI.

The second "misperception" according to OMB was that the correction process would be used overwhelmingly by industry (as distinguished from environmental and other public interest groups). OMB responded that it was "pleased to report" the process had been used by "virtually all segments of society," and singled out the Sierra Club, the John Muir Society, and Senators Boxer and Jeffords among others.

Not surprisingly, the OMB Report drew a rebuke from critics on the pro-regulatory side of the fence. For a detailed, point-by point refutation, see "the Reality of Data Quality Act's First Year: A Correction of OMB's Report to Congress." For instance, the critics claim OMB's estimate of the number of correction requests is far too low, and claim that even though OMB is correct that Sierra Club and public interest groups have filed DQA correction requests, the great majority of correction requests have come from industry groups. . . .

How does the peer review process differ from rulemaking processes? How will implementation of this Act likely affect the problems of rule ossification referred to in Chapter 4? What is the relationship of this Act to judicial review? Are agency decisions over what is and is not influential information reviewable? Do they represent formal agency action? Who has standing to bring these cases? If they are reviewable, what impact will this review have on agency rulemaking? *See* Chapters 8 and 9, *infra*. Finally, what is the relationship of this Act to the Federal Advisory Committee Act (FACA), *infra*, Chapter 10, § 10.03?

§ 7.09 OMB and Privatization

Under the Federal Activities Inventory Reform Act, Pub. L. 105–270, 112 Stat. 2382 (1998), most agencies must classify each service that they provide

---

* Copyright © 2004 by American Bar Association. Reprinted by permission.
** www.whitehouse.gov/omb/inforeg/infopoltech.html#iq.

as an "inherently governmental function" or as "commercial" in nature. The agency must compete against the private sector to be able to continue to perform those commercial activities. If the private sector can perform the same activities for less money, the activities must generally be contracted out; conversely, agencies can continue to perform commercial activities that they can perform more cheaply than the private sector could.

According to the Act,

> The term [inherently governmental function] includes activities that require either the exercise of discretion in applying Federal Government authority or the making of value judgments in making decisions for the Federal Government, including judgments relating to monetary transactions and entitlements. An inherently governmental function involves, among other things, the interpretation and execution of the laws of the United States so as—
>
> (i) to bind the United States to take or not to take some action by contract, policy, regulation, authorization, order, or otherwise;
>
> (ii) to determine, protect, and advance United States economic, political, territorial, property, or other interests by military or diplomatic action, civil or criminal judicial proceedings, contract management, or otherwise;
>
> (iii) to significantly affect the life, liberty, or property of private persons;
>
> (iv) to commission, appoint, direct, or control officers or employees of the United States; or
>
> (v) to exert ultimate control over the acquisition, use, or disposition of the property, real or personal, tangible or intangible, of the United States, including the collection, control, or disbursement of appropriated and other Federal funds.

Id. at § 5(B). OMB Circular A-76, which implements the Act, takes the position that an activity requiring an exercise of discretion is not automatically an inherently governmental function.

> Rather, the use of discretion [is] deemed inherently governmental if it commits the government to a course of action when two or more alternative courses of action exist and decision making is not already limited or guided by existing policies, procedures, directions, orders, and other guidance that (1) identify specified ranges of acceptable decisions or conduct and (2) subject the discretionary authority to final approval or regular oversight by agency officials.

OMB Circular A-76 at App. B(2).

Before an agency can classify a service as inherently governmental, the agency must justify in writing to the OMB the reasons for this proposed classification. (But no such written justification is required if an agency proposes to classify a service as commercial.) The agency then publishes its classification of services in the Federal Register. Any interested party, as defined in the act, can obtain an appeal within the agency as to the decision to classify a service either as inherently governmental or as commercial. "Interested party" includes the agency employees and their unions as well as those private parties that either want to compete for the service or have an interest that would be harmed if the agency de-privatized the service. Federal Activities Inventory Reform Act, § 3(b), PUB. L. 105-270, 112 Stat. 2382 (1998). But while public employees (or their private counterparts) can appeal outside the agency, under public contract law, if they are not awarded the contract at all, the public employees cannot appeal outside the agency the decision about whether to privatize at all. The same is not true for private parties: They can appeal on the grounds that they did not win the contract because the agency incorrectly characterized the service as an inherently governmental function. *See* Paul R. Verkuil, *Public Law Limitations on Privatization of Government Functions*, Cardozo Legal Studies Research Paper No. 104 (March 1, 2005) available at: http://papers.ssrn.com/sol3/papers.cfm?abstract_id=681517.

When it comes to such outsourcing of governmental functions, it usually is assumed that competition in the private sector will result in more efficiency in providing certain services. But consider the following:

> Today, we associate the utility of contractors with the notion that the private sector brings market forces to bear on government activities. This is true where commercial markets exist for government purchases — *e.g.*, the purchase of computer equipment, food, maintenance services. Where Government is the primary, or predominant, purchaser of the services or goods, however, the picture is less clear. . . .
>
> In the classic market, the failure of individual competitors is not cause for public concern. If, however, the Government desires the benefits of a competitive market, it may need to subsidize continued competition. Where only a handful of contractors dominate (e.g., Boeing and/or Lockheed Martin), a tension exists between the principle of rewarding or penalizing performance and the need to assure continued availability of alternative providers. In this context, the failure, suspension, or debarment of a major contractor may prove unacceptable.
>
> In short, the invocation of competition as key to the benefits of contracting may not square with the realities of the "government market," particularly where the item purchased is not a commercial staple. By statute, competition is the preferred means of contracting. In federal procurement practice, competition is limited by (1) socioeconomic preferences, which limit opportunities to members of a designated class (e.g., small businesses); (2) provision for solicitation from a limited number of sources; (3) bundling of work into larger or more diversified contracts; (4) effective delegation of contracting determinations to contractors themselves, under the award of large contracts with provision for substantial subcontracting; and (5) the limited number of providers of key public goods and services. These limitations on the market all have their justifications, but they are limitations nonetheless.

Dan Guttman, *Governance By Contract: Constitutional Visions; Time for Reflection and Choice*, 33 PUB. CONT. L.J. 321 343–44 (2004).*

Quite apart from cost and competitive considerations, are there other reasons to contract out governmental functions? Are there reasons to contract

---

* Copyright © 2004 by American Bar Association. Reprinted by permission.

out inherently governmental functions as well? Are such contracts ever justified? *See* The Aviation and Transportation Security Act, Pub. L. No. 107-71 § 110(2)(a), 115 Stat. 597 (2001) (airport security was explicitly exempted from OMB Circular A-76).

Chapter 8
JUDICIAL CONTROL OF AGENCY DISCRETION

§ 8.01 Overview

Chapters Six and Seven focused primarily on constitutional and policy issues that arise from various forms of legislative and executive control of agency discretion. The primary purpose of this chapter is to examine the role that courts play when they seek to control agency discretion. Specifically, this chapter will examine the standards of judicial review set forth in section 706 of the APA. One of our primary goals will be to understand more fully what these standards means in actual practice.

Section 706(2)(E), for example, requires that agency findings of fact in formal adjudicatory proceedings be supported by "substantial evidence" in the record. That verbal formulation — "substantial evidence" — constitutes the standard of judicial review to be applied to findings of fact in an adjudicatory case. How that standard is applied, and the likely outcome of the individual cases to which it is applied, gives us some sense of the scope or intensity of judicial review the standard implies. In short, we are interested not only in determining what standards of judicial review courts will apply in various factual policy and legal contexts, but also in the scope or intensity of judicial review that then results.

This determination inevitably leads to broader issues such as what the purposes of judicial review of agency action should be and the theory or theories of the administrative process that underlie these purposes. We have already engaged in some of this analysis. Earlier chapters of this book have examined the statutory and constitutional constraints that apply to agency adjudicatory, rulemaking and informal agency actions. We know, for example, that administrative agencies are created by Congress to carry out certain statutorily defined duties. One major purpose of judicial review, therefore, is to assure that agencies exercise their powers in accordance with the substantive goals and limits proscribed by Congress. If an agency could freely act in an *ultra vires* manner, its decisions would undercut completely the separation-of-powers principles we have already examined. Article I, § 1 places legislative power in the Congress, not the agency. Thus, section 706(2)(C) of the APA gives courts the power to set aside agency action found to be "in excess of statutory jurisdiction, authority, or limitations, or short of statutory right."

Similarly, an agency cannot engage in activities which, though authorized by statute, are unconstitutional. As we have also noted throughout this book, courts have, on occasion, been called upon to strike down statutes as unconstitutional when Congress itself has gone too far. This power is reflected in section 706(2)(B) of the APA which authorizes a court to hold unlawful or to set aside agency action found to be "contrary to constitutional right, power, privilege, or immunity."

The need to examine *what* agencies can and cannot do substantively is tied to the separation-of-powers principles examined in Chapters Six and Seven. If agencies could interpret their statutes in such a way as to give them powers the legislature or the Constitution does not authorize, they would clearly violate separation-of-powers principles, no matter what approach they took to such issues. The APA, however, also authorizes courts to examine *how* agencies exercise their substantive powers — that is, what procedures they employ. If an agency were free to make any findings of fact it so desired, engage in *ex parte* contacts just before it made its adjudicatory decisions, or give no reasons whatsoever for changes in policy it undertakes, separation-of-powers concerns would also be implicated. Without these procedural constraints, an agency might freely exercise power outside its statutory powers or beyond the Constitution itself. More important, the procedures an agency uses when it exercises its substantive powers inevitably involve values that go to the heart of agency legitimacy itself. These values include fairness, openness, public participation, accurate decision-making and the need for agencies to wield their power in such a way as to make the unelected agency officials involved accountable to the legislative, executive, and judicial branches of government. Thus, section 706(2)(A) of the APA provides that agency rules not be "arbitrary, capricious or an abuse of discretion," and section 706(2)(D) provides that courts set aside agency action that is "without observance of procedure required by law."

Agencies thus exercise a great deal of discretion not only in *what* they decide, but in *how* they decide the issues before them. In considering the scope of judicial review of agency findings of fact, or interpretations of law or the creation of new agency policies, a number of institutional questions are raised that involve the respective decisionmaking roles that courts should play. Sorting out these roles and determining the extent to which a court should or should not defer to an agency in various contexts can raise important theoretical as well as statutory and constitutional issues. If, for example, you believe that agency decisionmakers might be captured by the very interests they were created to regulate, you might be more willing to give courts greater scope when reviewing agency decisions, especially, for example, those that seem to spread the costs of the decision widely throughout the public, while concentrating the benefits gained on only a few. If you believe that Congress itself is subject to capture or that legislative histories are primarily the product of self-interested lobbying groups and not necessarily the reflection of the public interest, this too can affect the way you believe courts should or should not use legislative history in reviewing an agency interpretation of law. Should courts attempt to articulate the public interest perspective inherent in such legislative histories or is that impossible? Are statutes the product of groups competing in a legislative marketplace for special privileges or are they the result of pluralistic bargaining aimed at achieving a result in the public interest, broadly conceived? Your theory of the legislative process will affect your analysis of the court's role in reviewing statutes.

Finally, as we assess and attempt to formulate certain basic principles of judicial review of agency action and the legislation on which it is based, we cannot disregard the overall social and political context in which courts operate. This context is usually reflected in the enabling statutes that govern agency action, the make up and characteristics of the agencies themselves, and the nature of their regulatory tasks. Agencies have a way of remaining a part of the legal landscape long after both the substance and the perception of the problems they were created to solve have changed considerably. What role should courts play in the evolution, growth and, on occasion, the decline of administrative agency power?

In short, underlying your analysis of the doctrinal issues we shall now examine are implicit theories of the administrative and the legislative processes. Try to articulate the theory or theories you think are implicit in the various approaches taken by courts and litigants in the cases that follow. What is your theory of the administrative process? What is your theory of the legislative process?

§ 8.02 Judicial Review of Questions of Fact

A fact, as one wag has put it, is a "peculiar reordering of reality expressed in terms of a theoretic interest." For our purposes, the significance of a fact in a particular legal proceeding often depends upon the legal theory through which you view the case. The need to distinguish legal theories from raw or basic facts can, as we shall see, sometimes lead to some judicial confusion concerning the standard a court uses when reviewing the "facts" of the case before it. Consider the following case.

O'LEARY v. BROWN-PACIFIC-MAXON

United States Supreme Court
340 U.S. 504 (1951)

MR. JUSTICE FRANKFURTER delivered the opinion of the Court.

In this case we are called upon to review an award of compensation under the Longshoremen's and Harbor Workers' Compensation Act. . . . The award was made on a claim arising from the accidental death of an employee of Brown-Pacific-Maxon, Inc., a government contractor operating on the island of Guam. Brown-Pacific maintained for its employees a recreation center near the shoreline, along which ran a channel so dangerous for swimmers that its use was forbidden and signs to that effect erected. John Valak, the employee, spent the afternoon at the center, and was waiting for his employer's bus to take him from the area when he saw or heard two men, standing on the reefs beyond the channel, signaling for help. Followed by nearly twenty others, he plunged in to effect a rescue. In attempting to swim the channel to reach the two men he was drowned.

A claim was filed by his dependent mother, based on the Longshoremen's Act and on an Act of August 16, 1941, extending the compensation provisions to certain employment in overseas possessions. . . . In due course of the statutory procedure, the Deputy Commissioner found as a "fact" that "at the time of his drowning and death the deceased was using the recreational facilities sponsored and made available by the employer for the use of its employees and such participation by the deceased was an incident of his employment, and that his drowning and death arose out of and in the course of said employment. . . ." Accordingly, he awarded a death benefit of $9.38 per week. Brown-Pacific and its insurance carrier thereupon petitioned the District Court under § 21 of the Act to set aside the award. That court denied the petition on the ground that "there is substantial evidence . . . to sustain the compensation order." On appeal, the Court of Appeals for the Ninth Circuit reversed. It concluded that "The lethal currents were not a part of the recreational facilities supplied by the employer and the swimming in them for the rescue of the unknown man was not recreation. It was an act entirely disconnected from any use for which the recreational camp was provided and not in the course of Valak's employment." 182 F.2d 772, 773. We granted certiorari, 340 U.S. 849, because the case brought into question judicial review of awards under the Longshoremen's Act in light of the Administrative Procedure Act.

The Longshoremen's and Harbor Workers' Act authorizes payment of compensation for "accidental injury or death arising out of and in the course of employment." . . . As we read its opinion the Court of Appeals entertained the view that this standard precluded an award for injuries incurred in an attempt to rescue persons not known to be in the employer's service, undertaken in forbidden waters outside the employer's premises. We think this is too restricted an interpretation of the Act. Workmen's compensation is not confined by common-law conceptions of scope of employment. . . . The test of recovery is not a causal relation between the nature of employment of the injured person and the accident. . . . Nor is it necessary that the employee be engaged at the time of the injury in activity of benefit to his employer. All that is required is that the "obligations or conditions" of employment create the "zone of special danger" out of which the injury arose. A reasonable rescue attempt, like pursuit in aid of an officer making an arrest, may be "one of the risks of the employment, an incident of the service, foreseeable, if not foreseen, and so covered by the statute." . . . This is not to say that there are not cases "where an employee, even with the laudable purpose of helping another, might go so far from his employment and become so thoroughly disconnected from the service of his employer that it would be entirely unreasonable to say that injuries suffered by him arose out of and in the course of his employment." *Waters v. Taylor Co.*, 218 N.Y. at 252, 112 N.E. at 728. We hold only that rescue attempts such as that before us are not necessarily excluded from the coverage of the Act as the kind of conduct that employees engage in as frolics of their own.

The Deputy Commissioner treated the question whether the particular rescue attempt described by the evidence was one of the class covered by the Act as a question of "fact." Doing so only serves to illustrate once more the variety of ascertainments covered by the blanket term "fact." Here of course it does not connote a simple, external, physical event as to which there is conflicting testimony. The conclusion concerns a combination of happenings and the inferences drawn from them. In part at least, the inferences presuppose applicable standards for assessing the simple, external facts. Yet the standards are not so severable from the experience of industry nor of such a nature as to be peculiarly appropriate for independent judicial ascertainment as "questions of law."

Both sides conceded that the scope of judicial review of such findings of fact is governed by the Administrative Procedure Act. . . . The standard, therefore, is that discussed in *Universal Camera Corp. v. Labor Board,* 340 U.S. 474. It is sufficiently described by saying that the findings are to be accepted unless they are unsupported by substantial evidence on the record considered as a whole. The District Court recognized this standard.

When this Court determines that a Court of Appeals has applied an incorrect principle of law, wise judicial administration normally counsels remand of the cause to the Court of Appeals with instructions to reconsider the record. *Compare Universal Camera Corp. v. Labor Board.* In this instance, however, we have a slim record and the relevant standard is not difficult to apply; and we think the litigation had better terminate now. Accordingly we have ourselves examined the record to assess the sufficiency of the evidence.

We are satisfied that the record supports the Deputy Commissioner's finding. The pertinent evidence was presented by the written statements of four persons and the testimony of one witness. It is, on the whole, consistent and credible. From it the Deputy Commissioner could rationally infer that Valak acted reasonably in attempting the rescue, and that his death may fairly be attributable to the risks of the employment. We do not mean that the evidence compelled this inference; we do not suggest that had the Deputy Commissioner decided against the claimant, a court would have been justified in disturbing his conclusion. We hold only that on this record the decision of the District Court that the award should not be set aside should be sustained.

Reversed.

Mr. Justice Minton, with whom Mr. Justice Jackson and Mr. Justice Burton join, dissented.

Liability accrues in the instant case only if the death arose out of and in the course of the employment. This is a statutory provision common to all Workmen's Compensation Acts. There must be more than death and the relationship of employee and employer. There must be some connection between the death and the employment. Not in any common-law sense of causal connection but in the common-sense, everyday, realistic view. The Deputy Commissioner knew that, so he found as a *fact* that "at the time of his drowning and death the deceased was using the recreational facilities sponsored and made available by the employer for the use of its employees and such participation by the deceased was an incident of his employment. . . ." This finding is false and has no scintilla of evidence or inference to support it.

I am unable to understand how this Court can say this is a fact based upon evidence. It is undisputed upon this record that the deceased, at the time he met his death, was outside the recreational area in the performance of a voluntary act of attempted rescue of someone unknown to the record. There can be no inference of liability here unless liability follows from the mere relationship of employer and employee. The attempt to rescue was an isolated, voluntary act of bravery of the deceased in no manner arising out of or in the course of his employment. The only relation his employment had with the attempted rescue and the following death was that his employment put him on the Island of Guam. . . .

NOTES AND QUESTIONS

8-1. As far as the majority of the Court is concerned, what was the question of fact involved in this case? What was the question of fact for the dissent? How are they defining "fact"?

8-2. How would you characterize the questions concerning what the decedent was doing at the time he attempted the rescue? How did he die? Did he die by drowning? Are these issues of fact? What makes them relevant to the outcome of this case?

8-3. How should one characterize the application to such facts of a legal standard such as "in the course of employment"? Is that another kind of fact? Is it a question of law or is it a question of mixed fact and law? Should not these two questions — whatever label is affixed to them — be separated for analytical purposes?

8-4. Does Professor Jaffe's formulation of what a fact is provide any help?

"A 'Finding of fact' is the assertion that a phenomenon has happened or will be happening, independent of or anterior to any assertion as to its legal effect."

L. Jaffe, *Judicial Control of Administrative Action* 548 (1965). Professor Jaffe was well aware that Courts seldom divided questions of fact from the application of law to facts as clearly as they should. As he also noted, "the device of characterizing a question as one of fact or as 'mixed' permits the court to pretend that it *must* affirm the administrative action if it is supported by 'evidence' or is 'reasonable.'" Jaffe, at 547.

8-5. What do you think of the Court's approach to these issues in *Saginaw Broadcasting v. FCC,* 96 F.2d 554, 559–60 (D.C. Cir. 1938).

In discussing the necessary content of findings of fact, it will be helpful to spell out the process which a commission properly follows in reaching a decision. The process necessarily includes at least four parts: (1) evidence must be taken and weighed, both as to its accuracy and credibility; (2) from attentive consideration of this evidence a determination of facts of a basic or underlying nature must be reached; (3) from these basic facts the ultimate facts, usually in the language of the statute, are to be inferred, or not, as the case may be; (4) from this finding the decision will follow by the application of the statutory criterion. For example, before the Communications Commission may grant a construction permit it must, under the statute, be convinced that the public interest, convenience, or necessity will be served. An affirmative or negative finding on this topic would be a finding of ultimate fact. This ultimate fact, however, will be reached by inference from basic facts, such as, for example, the probable existence or non-existence of electrical interference, in view of the number of other stations operating in the area, their power, wave length, and the like. These basic facts will themselves appear or fail to appear, as the case may be, from the evidence introduced when attentively considered. Thus, upon the issue of electrical interference evidence may be introduced concerning power and wave length of a proposed station and of existing stations, and expert opinion based upon this evidence may be offered as to the likelihood of interference; and expert opinion based on evidence of field measurements of signal strength of existing stations may also be offered. This testimony may conflict. It is the Commission's duty to find from such evidence the basic facts as to the operation of the proposed and present stations in respect of power, wave length, and the like, and whether or not electrical interference will result from the operations of the proposed station, and then to find as an ultimate fact whether public interest, convenience, or necessity will be served by granting or not granting the application.

8-6. What standard of review should apply to the application of a statutory standard to a set of agreed-upon facts? What kind of question is that? Consider the following in R. Levin, *Identifying Questions of Law in Administrative Law*:[*]

> The law-fact distinction has a venerable pedigree. It had entered the vocabulary of administrative law by the nineteenth century and was well recognized by at least the 1930s. In retrospect, one can easily understand why this distinction took hold. It bore a comforting resemblance to the familiar guidelines by which the functions of judge and jury are divided: law issues are within the judge's province, fact issues are within the jury's, and the former are much more freely reviewable on appeal than the latter.
>
> Many of the writers who propound this dualism have recognized, however, that a large fraction of the issues that courts review for rationality cannot be regarded as "factual" in an analytical sense, that is, as issues involving mere descriptions by the agency of past, present, or future reality. Courts frequently allow an agency wide leeway not only in making pure factual findings from the evidence, but also in applying legal standards to them. Illustrative of these questions of "law application" — also called "mixed questions of law and fact" — would be an agency's decision whether a public utility's rates are "just and reasonable," or whether an allegedly work-related injury was received within the scope of the worker's employment. In situations of this kind, the agency is creating norms of conduct, and thus is making law in a realistic sense; yet its doing so does not seem to trigger the "independent judgment" review standard supposedly associated with questions of law. . . .
>
> In summary, even though commentators still refer to the law-fact distinction as the proper starting point for scope-of-review theory, that dichotomy

---

[*] 74 GEO. L.J. 23–26 (1985). Copyright © 1985 by Georgetown Law Journal. All rights reserved.

has proved unwieldy and misleading. The traditional view defines "question of fact" overbroadly; the Jaffe view defines "question of law" overbroadly. We would do better to abandon this obsolete framework and recognize a middle category, which we may call "questions of discretion." A question of law, then, for scope of review purposes, should be defined as an issue that requires the making of normative judgments, unlike a question of fact, *and* that is open to independent reconsideration by a reviewing court, unlike a question of discretion. "Questions of discretion," on the other hand, are those normative issues which call for an inquiry into the "rationality" of an agency's determination — a less intrusive inquiry than one in which the court independently decides whether the agency's determination was "correct." . . .

Does this approach help?

§ 8.03 Judicial Review of Findings of Fact — The Substantial Evidence Standard

In formal adjudicatory proceedings pursuant to sections 554, 556 and 557 of the APA, such findings of fact must be supported in the record by "substantial evidence." What constitutes "substantial evidence"? What is the scope of judicial review when this standard is applied?

UNIVERSAL CAMERA CORP. v. NLRB

United States Supreme Court
340 U.S. 474 (1951)

Mr. Justice Frankfurter delivered the opinion of the Court.

The essential issue raised by this case and its companion, *National Labor Relations Board v. Pittsburgh Steamship Co.*, is the effect of the Administrative Procedure Act and the legislation colloquially known as the Taft-Hartley Act on the duty of Courts of Appeals when called upon to review orders of the National Labor Relations Board. . . .

I.

Want of certainty in judicial review of Labor Board decisions partly reflects the intractability of any formula to furnish definiteness of content for all the impalpable factors involved in judicial review. But in part doubts as to the nature of the reviewing power and uncertainties in its application derive from history, and to that extent an elucidation of this history may clear them away.

The Wagner Act provided: "The findings of the Board as to the facts, if supported by evidence, shall be conclusive." . . . This Court read "evidence" to mean "substantial evidence," . . . and we said that "[s]ubstantial evidence is more than a mere scintilla. It means such relevant evidence as a reasonable mind might accept as adequate to support a conclusion." *Consolidated Edison Co. v. National Labor Relations Board,* 305 U.S. 197, 229. Accordingly, it "must do more than create a suspicion of the existence of the fact to be established. . . . It must be enough to justify, if the trial were to a jury, a refusal to direct a verdict when the conclusion sought to be drawn from it is one of fact for the jury." *National Labor Relations Board v. Columbian Enameling & Stamping Co.,* 306 U.S. 292, 300.

The very smoothness of the "substantial evidence" formula as the standard for reviewing the evidentiary validity of the Board's findings established its currency. But the inevitably variant applications of the standard to conflicting evidence soon brought contrariety of views and in due course bred criticism. Even though the whole record may have been canvassed in order to determine whether the evidentiary foundation of a determination by the Board was "substantial," the phrasing of this Court's process of review readily lent itself to the notion that it was enough that the evidence supporting the Board's result was "substantial" when considered by itself. It is fair to say that by imperceptible steps regard for the fact-finding function of the Board led to the assumption that the requirements of the Wagner Act were met when the reviewing court could find in the record evidence which, when viewed in isolation, substantiated the Board's findings. . . . This is not to say that every member of this Court was consciously guided by this view or that the Court ever explicitly avowed this practice as doctrine. What matters is that the belief justifiably arose that the Court had so construed the obligation to review.

Criticism of so contracted a reviewing power reinforced dissatisfaction felt in various quarters with the Board's administration of the Wagner Act in the years preceding the war. The scheme of the Act was attacked as an inherently unfair fusion of the functions of prosecutor and judge. Accusations of partisan bias were not wanting. The "irresponsible admission and weighing of hearsay, opinion, and emotional speculation in place of factual evidence" was said to be a "serious menace." No doubt some, perhaps even much, of the criticism was baseless and some surely was reckless. What is here relevant, however, is the climate of opinion thereby generated and its effect on Congress. Protests against "shocking injustices" and intimations of judicial "abdication"[8] with which some courts granted enforcement of the Board's orders stimulated pressures for legislative relief from alleged administrative excesses.

The strength of these pressures was reflected in the passage in 1940 of the Walter-Logan Bill. It was vetoed by President Roosevelt, partly because it

---

[8] In *National Labor Relations Board v. Standard Oil Co.,* 138 F.2d 885, 887, Judge Learned Hand said, "We understand the law to be that the decision of the Board upon that issue is for all practical purposes not open to us at all; certainly not after we have once decided that there was 'substantial' evidence that the 'disestablished' union was immediately preceded by a period during which there was a 'dominated' union. . . .

"[W]e recognize how momentous may be such an abdication of any power of review. . . ."

imposed unduly rigid limitations on the administrative process, and partly because of the investigation into the actual operation of the administrative process then being conducted by an experienced committee appointed by the Attorney General. It is worth noting that despite its aim to tighten control over administrative determinations of fact, the Walter-Logan Bill contented itself with the conventional formula that an agency's decision could be set aside if "the findings of fact are not supported by substantial evidence."

The final report of the Attorney General's Committee was submitted in January, 1941. The majority concluded that "[d]issatisfaction with the existing standards as to the scope of judicial review derives largely from dissatisfaction with the fact-finding procedures now employed by the administrative bodies." Departure from the "substantial evidence" test, it thought, would either create unnecessary uncertainty or transfer to courts the responsibility for ascertaining and assaying matters the significance of which lies outside judicial competence. Accordingly, it recommended against legislation embodying a general scheme of judicial review.

Three members of the Committee registered a dissent. Their view was that the "present system or lack of system of judicial review" led to inconsistency and uncertainty. They reported that under a "prevalent" interpretation of the "substantial evidence" rule "if what is called 'substantial evidence' is found anywhere in the record to support conclusions of fact, the courts are said to be obliged to sustain the decision without reference to how heavily the countervailing evidence may preponderate — unless indeed the stage of arbitrary decision is reached. Under this interpretation, the courts need to read only one side of the case and, if they find any evidence there, the administrative action is to be sustained and the record to the contrary is to be ignored." Their view led them to recommend that Congress enact principles of review applicable to all agencies not excepted by unique characteristics. One of these principles was expressed by the formula that judicial review could extend to "findings, inferences, or conclusions of fact unsupported, upon the whole record, by substantial evidence." So far as the history of this movement for enlarged review reveals, the phrase "upon the whole record" makes its first appearance in this recommendation of the minority of the Attorney General's Committee. This evidence of the close relationship between the phrase and the criticism out of which it arose is important, for the substance of this formula for judicial review found its way into the statute books when Congress with unquestioning — we might even say uncritical — unanimity enacted the Administrative Procedure Act.

One is tempted to say "uncritical" because the legislative history of that Act hardly speaks with that clarity of purpose which Congress supposedly furnishes courts in order to enable them to enforce its true will. On the one hand, the sponsors of the legislation indicated that they were reaffirming the prevailing "substantial evidence" test. But with equal clarity they expressed disapproval of the manner in which the courts were applying their own standard. The committee reports of both houses refer to the practice of agencies to rely upon "suspicion, surmise, implications, or plainly incredible evidence," and indicate that courts are to exact higher standards "in the exercise of their independent judgment" and on consideration of "the whole record."

Similar dissatisfaction with too restricted application of the "substantial evidence" test is reflected in the legislative history of the Taft-Hartley Act. The bill as reported to the House provided that the "findings of the Board as to the facts shall be conclusive unless it is made to appear to the satisfaction of the court either (1) that the findings of fact are against the manifest weight of the evidence, or (2) that the findings of fact are not supported by substantial evidence." The bill left the House with this provision. Early committee prints in the Senate provided for review by "weight of the evidence" or "clearly erroneous" standards. But, as the Senate Committee Report relates, "it was finally decided to conform the statute to the corresponding section of the Administrative Procedure Act where the substantial evidence test prevails. In order to clarify any ambiguity in that statute, however, the committee inserted the words 'questions of fact, if supported by substantial evidence on the record considered as a whole. . . .'"[21]

This phraseology was adopted by the Senate. The House conferees agreed. . . .

It is fair to say that in all this Congress expressed a mood. And it expressed its mood not merely by oratory but by legislation. As legislation that mood must be respected, even though it can only serve as a standard for judgment and not as a body of rigid rules assuring sameness of applications. Enforcement of such broad standards implies subtlety of mind and solidity of judgment. But it is not for us to question that Congress may assume such qualities in the federal judiciary.

From the legislative story we have summarized, two concrete conclusions do emerge. One is the identity of aim of the Administrative Procedure Act and the Taft-Hartley Act regarding the proof with which the Labor Board must support a decision. The other is that now Congress has left no room for doubt as to the kind of scrutiny which a Court of Appeals must give the record before the Board to satisfy itself that the Board's order rests on adequate proof. . . .

Whether or not it was ever permissible for courts to determine the substantiality of evidence supporting a Labor Board decision merely on the basis of evidence which in and of itself justified it, without taking into account contradictory evidence or evidence from which conflicting inferences could be drawn, the new legislation definitively precludes such a theory of review and bars its practice. The substantiality of evidence must take into account whatever in the record fairly detracts from its weight. This is clearly the significance of the requirement in both statutes that courts consider the whole record. Committee reports and the adoption in the Administrative Procedure Act of the minority views of the Attorney General's Committee demonstrate that to enjoin such a duty on the reviewing court was one of the important purposes of the movement which eventuated in that enactment.

---

[21] . . . Senator Taft gave this explanation to the Senate of the meaning of the section: "In the first place, the evidence must be substantial; in the second place, it must still look substantial when viewed in the light of the entire record. That does not go so far as saying that a decision can be reversed on the weight of the evidence. It does not go quite so far as the power given to a circuit court of appeals to review a district-court decision, but it goes a great deal further than the present law, and gives the court greater opportunity to reverse an obviously unjust decision on the part of the National Labor Relations Board."

To be sure, the requirement for canvassing "the whole record" in order to ascertain substantiality does not furnish a calculus of value by which a reviewing court can assess the evidence. Nor was it intended to negative the function of the Labor Board as one of those agencies presumably equipped or informed by experience to deal with a specialized field of knowledge, whose findings within that field carry the authority of an expertness which courts do not possess and therefore must respect. Nor does it mean that even as to matters not requiring expertise a court may displace the Board's choice between two fairly conflicting views, even though the court would justifiably have made a different choice had the matter been before it *de novo*. Congress has merely made it clear that a reviewing court is not barred from setting aside a Board decision when it cannot conscientiously find that the evidence supporting that decision is substantial, when viewed in the light that the record in its entirety furnishes, including the body of evidence opposed to the Board's view.

There remains, then, the question whether enactment of these two statutes has altered the scope of review other than to require that substantiality be determined in the light of all that the record relevantly presents. A formula for judicial review of administrative action may afford grounds for certitude but cannot assure certainty of application. Some scope for judicial discretion in applying the formula can be avoided only by falsifying the actual process of judging or by using the formula as an instrument of futile casuistry. It cannot be too often repeated that judges are not automata. The ultimate reliance for the fair operation of any standard is a judiciary of high competence and character and the constant play of an informed professional critique upon its work.

Since the precise way in which courts interfere with agency findings cannot be imprisoned within any form of words, new formulas attempting to rephrase the old are not likely to be more helpful than the old. There are no talismanic words that can avoid the process of judgment. The difficulty is that we cannot escape, in relation to this problem, the use of undefined defining terms.

Whatever changes were made by the Administrative Procedure and Taft-Hartley Acts are clearly within this area where precise definition is impossible. Retention of the familiar "substantial evidence" terminology indicates that no drastic reversal of attitude was intended.

But a standard leaving an unavoidable margin for individual judgment does not leave the judicial judgment at large even though the phrasing of the standard does not wholly fence it in. The legislative history of these Acts demonstrates a purpose to impose on courts a responsibility which has not always been recognized. Of course it is a statute and not a committee report which we are interpreting. But the fair interpretation of a statute is often "the art of proliferating a purpose," . . . revealed more by the demonstrable forces that produced it than by its precise phrasing.

The adoption in these statutes of the judicially-constructed "substantial evidence" test was a response to pressures for stricter and more uniform practice, not a reflection of approval of all existing practices. To find the change so elusive that it cannot be precisely defined does not mean it may be ignored. . . .

We conclude, therefore, that the Administrative Procedure Act and the Taft-Hartley Act direct that courts must now assume more responsibility for the reasonableness and fairness of Labor Board decisions than some courts have shown in the past. Reviewing courts must be influenced by a feeling that they are not to abdicate the conventional judicial function. Congress has imposed on them responsibility for assuring that the Board keeps within reasonable grounds. That responsibility is not less real because it is limited to enforcing the requirement that evidence appear substantial when viewed, on the record as a whole, by courts invested with the authority and enjoying the prestige of the Courts of Appeals. The Board's findings are entitled to respect; but they must nonetheless be set aside when the record before a Court of Appeals clearly precludes the Board's decision from being justified by a fair estimate of the worth of the testimony of witnesses or its informed judgment on matters within its special competence or both.

From this it follows that enactment of these statutes does not require every Court of Appeals to alter its practice. Some — perhaps a majority — have always applied the attitude reflected in this legislation. To explore whether a particular court should or should not alter its practice would only divert attention from the application of the standard now prescribed to a futile inquiry into the nature of the test formerly used by a particular court.

Our power to review the correctness of application of the present standard ought seldom to be called into action. Whether on the record as a whole there is substantial evidence to support agency findings is a question which Congress has placed in the keeping of the Courts of Appeals. This Court will intervene only in what ought to be the rare instance when the standard appears to have been misapprehended or grossly misapplied.

II.

. . . .

The decision of the Court of Appeals is assailed on two grounds. It is said (1) that the court erred in holding that it was barred from taking into account the report of the examiner on questions of fact insofar as that report was rejected by the Board, and (2) that the Board's order was not supported by substantial evidence on the record considered as a whole, even apart from the validity of the court's refusal to consider the rejected portions of the examiner's report.

The latter contention is easily met. It is true that two of the earlier decisions of the court below were among those disapproved by Congress. But this disapproval, we have seen, may well have been caused by unintended intimations of judicial phrasing. And in any event, it is clear from the court's opinion in this case that it in fact did consider the "record as a whole," and did not deem itself merely the judicial echo of the Board's conclusion. The testimony of the company's witnesses was inconsistent, and there was clear evidence that the complaining employee had been discharged by an officer who was at one time influenced against him because of his appearance at the Board hearing. On such a record we could not say that it would be error to grant enforcement.

The first contention, however, raises serious questions to which we now turn.

III.

The Court of Appeals deemed itself bound by the Board's rejection of the examiner's findings because the court considered these findings not "as unassailable as a master's." They are not. Section 10(c) of the Labor Management Relations Act provides that "If upon the preponderance of the testimony taken the Board shall be of the opinion that any person named in the complaint has engaged in or is engaging in any such unfair labor practice, then the Board shall state its findings of fact. . . ." The responsibility for decision thus placed on the Board is wholly inconsistent with the notion that it has power to reverse an examiner's findings only when they are "clearly erroneous." Such a limitation would make so drastic a departure from prior administrative practice that explicitness would be required.

The Court of Appeals concluded from this premise "that, although the Board would be wrong in totally disregarding his findings, it is practically impossible for a court, upon review of those findings which the Board itself substitutes, to consider the Board's reversal as a factor in the court's own decision. This we say, because we cannot find any middle ground between doing that and treating such a reversal as error, whenever it would be such, if done by a judge to a master in equity." Much as we respect the logical acumen of the Chief Judge of the Court of Appeals, we do not find ourselves pinioned between the horns of his dilemma.

We are aware that to give the examiner's findings less finality than a master's, and yet entitle them to consideration in striking the account, is to introduce another and an unruly factor into the judgmatical process of review. But we ought not to fashion an exclusionary rule merely to reduce the number of imponderables to be considered by reviewing courts.

The Taft-Hartley Act provides that "The findings of the Board with respect to questions of fact if supported by substantial evidence on the record considered as a whole shall be conclusive." Surely an examiner's report is as much a part of the record as the complaint or the testimony. According to the Administrative Procedure Act, "All decisions (including initial, recommended, or tentative decisions) shall become a part of the record. . . ." We found that this Act's provision for judicial review has the same meaning as that in the Taft-Hartley Act. The similarity of the two statutes in language and purpose also requires that the definition of "record" found in the Administrative Procedure Act be construed to be applicable as well to the term "record" as used in the Taft-Hartley Act.

It is therefore difficult to escape the conclusion that the plain language of the statutes directs a reviewing court to determine the substantiality of evidence on the record including the examiner's report. The conclusion is confirmed by the indications in the legislative history that enhancement of the status and function of the trial examiner was one of the important purposes of the movement for administrative reform.

This aim was set forth by the Attorney General's Committee on Administrative Procedure:

> In general, the relationship upon appeal between the hearing commissioner and the agency ought to a considerable extent to be that of trial court to appellate court. Conclusions, interpretations, law, and policy should, of course, be open to full review. On the other hand, on matters which the hearing commissioner, having heard the evidence and seen the witnesses, is best qualified to decide, the agency should be reluctant to disturb his findings unless error is clearly shown.

Apparently it was the Committee's opinion that these recommendations should not be obligatory. For the bill which accompanied the Final Report required only that hearing officers make an initial decision which would become final in the absence of further agency action, and that agencies which differed on the facts from their examiners give reasons and record citations supporting their conclusion. This proposal was further moderated by the Administrative Procedure Act. It permits agencies to use examiners to record testimony but not to evaluate it, and contains the rather obscure provision that an agency which reviews an examiner's report has "all the powers which it would have in making the initial decision."

But this refusal to make mandatory the recommendations of the Attorney General's Committee should not be construed as a repudiation of them. Nothing in the statutes suggests that the Labor Board should not be influenced by the examiner's opportunity to observe the witnesses he hears and sees and the Board does not. Nothing suggests that reviewing courts should not give to the examiner's report such probative force as it intrinsically commands. To the contrary, § 11 of the Administrative Procedure Act contains detailed provisions designed to maintain high standards of independence and competence in examiners. . . .

We do not require that the examiner's findings be given more weight than in reason and in the light of judicial experience they deserve. The "substantial evidence" standard is not modified in any way when the Board and its examiner disagree. We intend only to recognize that evidence supporting a conclusion may be less substantial when an impartial, experienced examiner who has observed the witnesses and lived with the case has drawn conclusions different from the Board's than when he has reached the same conclusion. The findings of the examiner are to be considered along with the consistency and inherent probability of testimony. The significance of his report, of course, depends largely on the importance of credibility in the particular case. To give it this significance does not seem to us materially more difficult than to heed the other factors which in sum determine whether evidence is "substantial."

. . .

We therefore remand the cause to the Court of Appeals. On reconsideration of the record it should accord the findings of the trial examiner the relevance that they reasonably command in answering the comprehensive question whether the evidence supporting the Board's order is substantial. But the court need not limit its reexamination of the case to the effect of that report on its decision. We leave it free to grant or deny enforcement as it thinks the principles expressed in this opinion dictate.

Judgment vacated and cause remanded.

Mr. Justice Black and Mr. Justice Douglas concur with parts I and II of this opinion but as to part III agree with the opinion of the court below.

NOTES AND QUESTIONS

8-7. There are three major issues in this case. The first concerns the application of the substantial evidence test to the whole record or only to portions of the record. How does the Court decide this question? What is the significance of the Court's ruling in this regard? Does it lessen or increase the power of the reviewing court?

8-8. The second issue is whether the APA's codification of the substantial evidence standard altered the test as applied in other contexts? What does the Court rule in this regard and what is the significance of that ruling?

8-9. The third issue is what does the "substantial evidence" standard really mean? How much evidence is enough? Is the Court very helpful in this regard? What is the underlying rationale of such a standard? Given that rationale, would you expect that standard to be a very rigorous one? Why or why not?

8-10. Might you expect other factors to affect a court's judgment of what is and what is not substantial? What about what is at stake in the proceeding? Should you require more evidence if there is a life-or-death issue involved? *See, e.g., NLRB v. Walton Mfg. Co.,* 369 U.S. 404 (1962) (court rejects use of a differential approach based on what is at stake).

8-11. What should be the result when there is a disagreement between the Commission and the ALJ regarding the findings of fact at the trial level? To which decision should a reviewing court pay attention? How important is the fact that the trial judge was able, personally, to observe the demeanor of the testifying witness? Consider Judge Duniway's comments in partial dissent in *Penasquitos Village Inc. v. NLRB,* 565 F.2d 1074 (9th Cir. 1977):

> I am convinced, both from experience as a trial lawyer and from experience as an appellate judge, that much that is thought and said about the trier of fact as a lie detector is myth or folklore. Every trial lawyer knows, and most trial judges will admit, that it is not unusual for an accomplished liar to fool a jury (or, even, heaven forbid, a trial judge) into believing him because his demeanor is so convincing. The expression of his countenance may be open and frank; he may sit squarely in the chair, with no squirming; he may show no nervousness; his answers to questions may be clear, concise and audible, and given without hesitation; his coloration may be normal — neither pale nor flushed. In short, he may appear to be the trial lawyer's ideal witness. He may also be a consummate liar. In such a case, the fact finder may fit Iago's description of Othello:
>
>> The Moor is of a free and open nature, That thinks men honest that but seem to be so;

And will as tenderly be led by the nose as asses are.
(*Othello*, Act 1, Sc. 3, 1. 405–8)

On the other hand, another fact finder seeing and hearing the same witness may conclude that he is just too good a testifier, that he is an expert actor, and that he is also a liar.

Conversely, many trial lawyers, and some trial judges, will admit that the demeanor of a perfectly honest but unsophisticated or timid witness may be — or can be made by an astute cross-examiner to be — such that he will be thought by the jury or the judge to be a liar. He may be unable to face the cross-examiner, the jury, or the judge; he may slouch and squirm in the chair; he may be obviously tense and nervous; his answers to questions may be indirect, rambling, and inaudible; he may hesitate before answering; he may alternately turn pale and blush. In short, he may, to the trier of fact, be a liar, but in fact be entirely truthful. Again, however, another fact finder, seeing and hearing the same witness, may attribute his demeanor to the natural timidity of the average not very well educated and non-public sort of person when dragged to court against his will and forced to testify and face a hostile cross-examiner, and conclude that the witness is telling the truth.

While there are innumerable cases that state and restate the importance of a witness's demeanor to the trier of fact, there are very few that deal with the proper effect of this or that aspect of demeanor. Those that I can find tend to confirm my view that myth and folklore are involved.

See also Ruth Wodak-Engel, *Determination of Guilt, in* M. O'Barr, *Language and Power* (1984).

8-12. Section 706(2)(F) allows *de novo* judicial review "to the extent that the facts are subject to trial *de novo* by the reviewing court." *Citizens to Preserve Overton Park v. Volpe,* 701 U.S. 402 (1971), which we have examined *supra,* Chapter 5, interpreted this section narrowly, applying it only in two circumstances: (1) when the action is adjudicatory in nature and the fact finding procedures are inadequate, or (2) when issues not originally before the agency are raised in subsequent proceedings to enforce non-adjudicatory agency action. Statutes themselves can require *de novo* review, *see, e.g., Agosto v. INS,* 476 U.S. 748 (1978), noting that a *de novo* trial of the issue of citizenship in deportation cases is assured. Also, *de novo* factfinding is often used when constitutional issues are involved, or when so-called constitutional or jurisdictional facts are involved. *See, e.g., Porter v. Califano,* 592 F.2d 770 (5th Cir. 1979). As the court noted in that case, which involved the First Amendment: "Judicial deference to agency fact-finding and decision-making is generally premised on the existence of agency expertise in a particular specialized or technical area. But, in general, courts, not agencies, are expert on the First Amendment." *Id.* at 780, n. 16.

8-13. The "substantial evidence" standard also has been incorporated in many hybrid rulemaking provisions. *See Industrial Union Dept., AFL-CIO v. Hodgson,* 499 F.2d 467 (D.C. Cir. 1974), Chapter Six, § 6.02[E], *supra.* Generally, rules that are not supported by substantial evidence are viewed as "arbitrary, capricious and an abuse of discretion." These two standards of judicial review usually converge. *See, e.g., Association of Data Processing Service Orgs. v. Board of Governors of the Fed. Res. Sys.,* 745 F.2d 677 (D.C. Cir. 1984) ("it is impossible to conceive of a 'nonarbitrary factual' judgment supported only by evidence that is not substantial in the APA sense"). *See generally,* Note, *Convergency of the Substantial Evidence and Arbitrary and Capricious Standards of Review During Informal Rulemaking,* 54 GEO. WASH. L. REV. 541 (1986). We shall examine the arbitrary and capricious standard of review in section 8.06, *infra.*

§ 8.04 Questions of Law

Section 706 of the APA authorizes a reviewing court to "decide all relevant questions of law, interpret constitutional and statutory provisions, and determine the meaning or applicability of the terms of an agency action."[1] As we have seen, a court may "hold unlawful and set aside agency action"[2] that it finds unconstitutional,[3] in excess of an agency's statutory powers,[4] made contrary to required procedures or "otherwise not in accordance with law."[5] By its very terms, the APA thus refers to at least three different types of questions of law — those that involve constitutional questions, those that involve statutory issues and those that involve legal issues that arise from the procedures used by an agency.

There are also more subtle distinctions among the various types of questions of law courts decide. Some involve the jurisdictional power of an agency to act. *See, e.g., Phillips Petroleum Co. v. Wisconsin,* 347 U.S. 672 (1954). Others involve the application of a statutory term to a set of facts and are often complicated by the fact that courts are reviewing an agency decision that seems to merge the agency's legal interpretation of a statutory term with its own fact finding functions. Is this the case with *NLRB v. Hearst Publications,* below?

Still other legal issues involve the agency's interpretation of its own regulations.[6] Some of those regulations may be in the form of legislative or interpretative rules,[7] or the consideration of the constitutional effects of

---

[1] 5 U.S.C. § 706.

[2] 5 U.S.C. § 706(2).

[3] 5 U.S.C. § 706(2)(B).

[4] 5 U.S.C. § 706(2)(c).

[5] 5 U.S.C. § 706(2)(A).

[6] *See, e.g., Ford Motor Credit Co. v. Milhollin,* 444 U.S. 555 (1980) (involving, in part, application by the Federal Reserve Board of its own Regulation Z).

[7] Traditionally courts have been more deferential to agency interpretations embodied in legislative rules as opposed to interpretative rules. *See infra,* § 8.05. *Compare Chrysler Corp v. Brown,* 441 U.S. 281, 295 (1979) (legislative or substantive rules), *with Skidmore v. Swift and Co.,* 323 U.S. 134 (1944) (interpretative rules); *but see Chevron U.S.A. v. NRDC,* 467 U.S. 837 (1984) (the court's deferential approach fails to distinguish explicitly between the kinds of rules involved).

certain agency action.⁸ All these legal contexts present various questions of law, and courts often treat these various kinds of legal questions differently, deferring to the agency in some cases and engaging in essentially *de novo* review in others.

To further complicate matters, these various legal issues arise in a variety of factual contexts. Some cases may involve agency decisions that have, quite literally, life and death effects on the litigants involved.⁹ Others arise in the context of highly technical statutory regimes that require expert bureaucratic solutions if day to day agency life is to proceed apace;¹⁰ still others may implicate important separation of powers concerns.¹¹ As you examine the courts' approaches to these various levels of questions of law, can you devise a theory of judicial review that explains the results reached?

We shall begin with *NLRB v. Hearst*. How many questions of law can you identify in this case? What is the scope of the Court's review regarding each of these questions of law?

NATIONAL LABOR RELATIONS BOARD v. HEARST PUBLICATIONS, INC.

United States Supreme Court
322 U.S. 111 (1944)

Mr. Justice Rutledge delivered the opinion of the Court.

These cases arise from the refusal of respondents, publishers of four Los Angeles daily newspapers, to bargain collectively with a union representing newsboys who distribute their papers on the streets of that city. Respondents' contention that they were not required to bargain because the newsboys are not their "employees" within the meaning of that term in the National Labor Relations Act,¹ presents the important question which we granted certiorari to resolve.

---

⁸ *See, e.g., Porter v. Califano*, 592 F.2d 770 (9th Cir. 1979) (free speech issues); *Bill Johnson's Restaurant, Inc. v. NLRB*, 461 U.S. 731, 743–44 (1983) (a baseless lawsuit filed by an employer against an employee for exercising his rights under § 7 of the NLRA is not immunized by the First Amendment right to petition and may be enjoined by the NLRB); *Fla. Gulf Coast Bldg. & Const. Trailer v. NLRB*, 796 F.2d 1328, 1346 (11th Cir. 1986) (peaceful and orderly distribution of handbills is a form of speech protected by the First Amendment and may not be enjoined by the NLRB as a violation of § 8(b)(4)(ii)(B) of the NLRA).

⁹ *See, e.g., Industrial Union Dept. v. American Petroleum Inst.*, 448 U.S. 607 (1980) (involving benzene regulations) *supra*, Chapter Seven, § 7.04.

¹⁰ *See, e.g., Sierra Club v. Costle*, 657 F.2d 298, 314 (D.C. Cir. 1981) *supra*, Chapter Eight, section 8.7; (in reviewing regulation promulgated by the Environmental Protection Agency the court found the volume and technical complexity of the material necessary for its review "daunting.")

¹¹ *See, e.g., Chevron U.S.A. v. NRDC*, 467 U.S. 837 (1984), *infra*, in § 8.04.

¹ Section 2(3) of the Act provides that "The term 'employee' shall include any employee, and shall not be limited to the employees of a particular employer, unless the Act explicitly states

The proceedings before the National Labor Relations Board were begun with the filing of four petitions for investigation and certification by Los Angeles Newsboys Local Industrial Union No. 75. Hearings were held in a consolidated proceeding after which the Board made findings of fact and concluded that the regular full-time newsboys selling each paper were employees within the Act and that questions affecting commerce concerning the representation of employees had arisen. It designated appropriate units and ordered elections. . . . At these the union was selected as their representative by majorities of the eligible newsboys. After the union was appropriately certified, . . . the respondents refused to bargain with it. Thereupon proceedings under § 10 . . . were instituted, a hearing was held and respondents were found to have violated §§ 8(1) and 8(5) of the Act. . . . They were ordered to cease and desist from such violations and to bargain collectively with the union upon request.

Upon respondents' petitions for review and the Board's petitions for enforcement, the Circuit Court of Appeals, one judge dissenting, set aside the Board's orders. Rejecting the Board's analysis, the court independently examined the question whether the newsboys are employees within the Act, decided that the statute imports common-law standards to determine that question, and held the newsboys are not employees.

The papers are distributed to the ultimate consumer through a variety of channels, including independent dealers and newsstands often attached to drug, grocery or confectionery stores, carriers who make home deliveries, and newsboys who sell on the streets of the city and its suburbs. Only the last of these are involved in this case.

The newsboys work under varying terms and conditions. They may be "bootjackers," selling to the general public at places other than established corners, or they may sell at fixed "spots." They may sell only casually or part-time, or full-time; and they may be employed regularly and continuously or only temporarily. The units which the Board determined to be appropriate are composed of those who sell full-time at established spots. Those vendors, misnamed boys, are generally mature men, dependent upon the proceeds of their sales for their sustenance, and frequently supporters of families. Working thus as news vendors on a regular basis, often for a number of years, they form a stable group with relatively little turnover, in contrast to schoolboys and others who sell as bootjackers, temporary and casual distributors. . . .

In addition to effectively fixing the compensation, respondents in a variety of ways prescribe, if not the minutiae of daily activities, at least the broad terms and conditions of work. This is accomplished largely through the supervisory efforts of the district managers, who serve as the nexus between the publishers and the newsboys. The district managers assign "spots" or corners to which the newsboys are expected to confine their selling activities. Transfers from one "spot" to another may be ordered by the district manager for reasons of discipline or efficiency or other cause. Transportation to the spots

---

otherwise, and shall include any individual whose work has ceased as a consequence of, or in connection with, any current labor dispute or because of any unfair labor practice, and who has not obtained any other regular and substantially equivalent employment, but shall not include any individual employed as an agricultural laborer, or in the domestic service of any family or person at his home, or any individual employed by his parent or spouse."

from the newspaper building is offered by each of respondents. Hours of work on the spots are determined not simply by the impersonal pressures of the market, but to a real extent by explicit instructions from the district managers. Adherence to the prescribed hours is observed closely by the district managers or other supervisory agents of the publishers. Sanctions, varying in severity from reprimand to dismissal, are visited on the tardy and the delinquent. . . . In this pattern of employment the Board found that the newsboys are an integral part of the publishers' distribution system and circulation organization. And the record discloses that the newsboys and checkmen feel they are employees of the papers; and respondents' supervisory employees, if not respondents themselves, regard them as such.

In addition to questioning the sufficiency of the evidence to sustain these findings, respondents point to a number of other attributes characterizing their relationship with the newsboys and urge that on the entire record the latter cannot be considered their employees. They base this conclusion on the argument that by common-law standards the extent of their control and direction of the newsboys' working activities creates no more than an "independent contractor" relationship and that common-law standards determine the "employee" relationship under the Act. . . .

I.

The principal question is whether the newsboys are "employees." Because Congress did not explicitly define the term, respondents say its meaning must be determined by reference to common-law standards. In their view "common-law standards" are those the courts have applied in distinguishing between "employees" and "independent contractors" when working out various problems unrelated to the Wagner Act's purposes and provisions.

The argument assumes that there is some simple, uniform and easily applicable test which the courts have used, in dealing with such problems, to determine whether persons doing work for others fall in one class or the other. Unfortunately this is not true. Only by a long and tortuous history was the simple formulation worked out which has been stated most frequently as "the test" for deciding whether one who hires another is responsible in tort for his wrongdoing. But this formula has been by no means exclusively controlling in the solution of other problems. And its simplicity has been illusory because it is more largely simplicity of formulation than of application. Few problems in the law have given greater variety of application and conflict in results than the cases arising in the borderland between what is clearly an employer-employee relationship and what is clearly one of independent entrepreneurial dealing. This is true within the limited field of determining vicarious liability in tort. It becomes more so when the field is expanded to include all of the possible applications of the distinction.

It is hardly necessary to stress particular instances of these variations or to emphasize that they have arisen principally, first, in the struggle of the courts to work out common-law liabilities where the legislature has given no guides for judgment, more recently also under statutes which have posed the same problem for solution in the light of the enactment's particular terms and purposes. It is enough to point out that, with reference to an identical problem, results may be contrary over a very considerable region of doubt in applying the distinction, depending upon the state or jurisdiction where the determination is made; and that within a single jurisdiction a person who, for instance, is held to be an "independent contractor" for the purpose of imposing vicarious liability in tort may be an "employee" for the purposes of particular legislation, such as unemployment compensation. . . . In short, the assumed simplicity and uniformity, resulting from application of "common-law standards," does not exist.

Mere reference to these possible variations as characterizing the application of the Wagner Act in the treatment of persons identically situated in the facts surrounding their employment and in the influences tending to disrupt it, would be enough to require pause before accepting a thesis which would introduce them into its administration. This would be true, even if the statute itself had indicated less clearly than it does the intent they should not apply.

Two possible consequences could follow. One would be to refer the decision of who are employees to local state law. The alternative would be to make it turn on a sort of pervading general essence distilled from state law. Congress obviously did not intend the former result. It would introduce variations into the statute's operation as wide as the differences the forty-eight states and other local jurisdictions make in applying the distinction for wholly different purposes. Persons who might be "employees" in one state would be "independent contractors" in another. They would be within or without the statute's protection depending not on whether their situation falls factually within the ambit Congress had in mind, but upon the accidents of the location of their work and the attitude of the particular local jurisdiction in casting doubtful cases one way or the other. Persons working across state lines might fall in one class or the other, possibly both, depending on whether the Board and the courts would be required to give effect to the law of one state or of the adjoining one, or to that of each in relation to the portion of the work done within its borders.

Both the terms and the purposes of the statute, as well as the legislative history, show that Congress had in mind no such patchwork plan for securing freedom of employees' organization and of collective bargaining. The Wagner Act is federal legislation, administered by a national agency, intended to solve a national problem on a national scale. . . .

II.

Whether, given the intended national uniformity, the term "employee" includes such workers as these newsboys must be answered primarily from the history, terms and purposes of the legislation. The word "is not treated by Congress as a word of art having a definite meaning. . . ." Rather "it takes color from its surroundings . . . [in] the statute where it appears," *United States v. American Trucking Associations, Inc.*, 310 U.S. 534, 545, and derives meaning from the context of that statute, which "must be read in the light of the mischief to be corrected and the end to be attained." *South Chicago Coal & Dock Co. v. Bassett*, 309 U.S. 251, 259. . . .

Congress, on the one hand, was not thinking solely of the immediate technical relation of employer and employee. It had in mind at least some other persons than those standing in the proximate legal relation of employee to the particular employer involved in the labor dispute. It cannot be taken, however, that the purpose was to include all other persons who may perform service for another or was to ignore entirely legal classifications made for other purposes. Congress had in mind a wider field than the narrow technical legal relation of "master and servant," as the common law had worked this out in all its variations, and at the same time a narrower one than the entire area of rendering service to others. The question comes down therefore to how much was included of the intermediate region between what is clearly and unequivocally "employment," by any appropriate test, and what is as clearly entrepreneurial enterprise and not employment.

It will not do, for deciding this question as one of uniform national application, to import wholesale the traditional common-law conceptions or some distilled essence of their local variations as exclusively controlling limitations upon the scope of the statute's effectiveness. To do this would be merely to select some of the local, hairline variations for nation-wide application and thus to reject others for coverage under the Act. That result hardly would be consistent with the statute's broad terms and purposes.

Congress was not seeking to solve the nationally harassing problems with which the statute deals by solutions only partially effective. It rather sought to find a broad solution, one that would bring industrial peace by substituting, so far as its power could reach, the rights of workers to self-organization and collective bargaining for the industrial strife which prevails where these rights are not effectively established. Yet only partial solutions would be provided if large segments of workers about whose technical legal position such local differences exist should be wholly excluded from coverage by reason of such differences. Yet that result could not be avoided, if choice must be made among them and controlled by them in deciding who are "employees" within the Act's meaning. Enmeshed in such distinctions, the administration of the statute soon might become encumbered by the same sort of technical legal refinement as has characterized the long evolution of the employee-independent contractor dichotomy in the courts for other purposes. The consequences would be ultimately to defeat, in part at least, the achievement of the statute's objectives. Congress no more intended to import this mass of technicality as a controlling "standard" for uniform national application than to refer decision of the question outright to the local law.

The Act, as its first section states, was designed to avert the "substantial obstructions to the free flow of commerce" which result from "strikes and other forms of industrial strife or unrest" by eliminating the causes of that unrest. It is premised on explicit findings that strikes and industrial strife themselves result in large measure from the refusal of employers to bargain collectively and the inability of individual workers to bargain successfully for improvements in their "wages, hours or other working conditions" with employers who are "organized in the corporate or other forms of ownership association." Hence the avowed and interrelated purposes of the Act are to encourage collective bargaining and to remedy the individual worker's inequality of bargaining power by "protecting the exercise . . . of full freedom of association, self-organization, and designation of representatives of their own choosing, for the purpose of negotiating the terms and conditions of their employment or other mutual aid or protection." 49 Stat. 449, 450.

The mischief at which the Act is aimed and the remedies it offers are not confined exclusively to "employees" within the traditional legal distinctions separating them from "independent contractors." Myriad forms of service relationship, with infinite and subtle variations in the terms of employment, blanket the nation's economy. Some are within this Act, others beyond its coverage. Large numbers will fall clearly on one side or on the other, by whatever test may be applied. But intermediate there will be many, the incidents of whose employment partake in part of the one group, in part of the other, in varying proportions of weight. And consequently the legal pendulum, for purposes of applying the statute, may swing one way or the other, depending upon the weight of this balance and its relation to the special purpose at hand.

Unless the common-law tests are to be imported and made exclusively controlling, without regard to the statute's purposes, it cannot be irrelevant that the particular workers in these cases are subject, as a matter of economic fact, to the evils the statute was designed to eradicate and that the remedies it affords are appropriate for preventing them or curing their harmful effects in this special situation. Interruption of commerce through strikes and unrest may stem as well from labor disputes between some who, for other purposes, are technically "independent contractors" and their employers as from disputes between persons who, for those purposes, are "employees" and their employers. . . . Inequality of bargaining power in controversies over wages, hours and working conditions may as well characterize the status of the one group as of the other. The former, when acting alone, may be as "helpless in dealing with an employer," as "dependent . . . on his daily wage" and as "unable to leave the employ and to resist arbitrary and unfair treatment" as the latter. For each, "union . . . [may be] essential to give . . . opportunity to deal on equality with their employer." And for each, collective bargaining may be appropriate and effective for the "friendly adjustment of industrial disputes arising out of differences as to wages, hours, or other working conditions." In short, when the particular situation of employment combines these characteristics, so that the economic facts of the relation make it more nearly one of employment than of independent business enterprise with respect to the ends sought to be accomplished by the legislation, those characteristics may outweigh technical legal classification for purposes unrelated to the statute's objectives and bring the relation within its protections. . . .

Hence "technical concepts pertinent to an employer's legal responsibility to third persons for the acts of his servants" have been rejected in various applications of this Act both here . . . and in other federal courts. . . . *Labor Board v. Condenser Corp.*, 128 F.2d 67 (C.C.A.). . . . There is no good reason for invoking them to restrict the scope of the term "employee" sought to be done in this case. That term, like other provisions, must be understood with reference to the purpose of the Act and the facts involved in the economic relationship. . . .

It is not necessary in this case to make a completely definitive limitation around the term "employee." That task has been assigned primarily to the agency created by Congress to administer the Act. Determination of "where all the conditions of the relation require protection" involves inquiries for the Board charged with this duty. Everyday experience in the administration of the statute gives it familiarity with the circumstances and backgrounds of employment relationships in various industries, with the abilities and needs of the workers for self organization and collective action, and with the adaptability of collective bargaining for the peaceful settlement of their disputes with their employers. The experience thus acquired must be brought frequently to bear on the question who is an employee under the Act. Resolving that question, like determining whether unfair labor practices have been committed, "belongs to the usual administrative routine" of the Board. *Gray v. Powell,* 314 U.S. 402, 411. . . .

In making that body's determinations as to the facts in these matters conclusive, if supported by evidence, Congress entrusted to it primarily the decision whether the evidence establishes the material facts. Hence in reviewing the Board's ultimate conclusions, it is not the court's function to substitute its own inferences of fact for the Board's, when the latter have support in the record. . . . Undoubtedly questions of statutory interpretation, especially when arising in the first instance in judicial proceedings, are for the courts to resolve, giving appropriate weight to the judgment of those whose special duty is to administer the questioned statute. *Norwegian Nitrogen Products Co. v. United States,* 288 U.S. 294. . . . But where the question is one of specific application of a broad statutory term in a proceeding in which the agency administering the statute must determine it initially, the reviewing court's function is limited. Like the commissioner's determination under the Longshoremen's & Harbor Workers' Act, that a man is not a "member of a crew" . . . or that he was injured "in the course of employment" . . . and the Federal Communications Commission's determination that one company is under the "control" of another . . . the Board's determination that specified persons are "employees" under this Act is to be accepted if it has "warrant in the record" and a reasonable basis in law.

In this case the Board found that the designated newsboys work continuously and regularly, rely upon their earnings for the support of themselves and their families, and have their total wages influenced in large measure by the publishers, who dictate their buying and selling prices, fix their markets and control their supply of papers. Their hours of work and their efforts on the job are supervised and to some extent prescribed by the publishers or their agents. Much of their sales equipment and advertising materials is furnished by the publishers with the intention that it be used for the publisher's benefit. Stating that "the primary consideration in the determination of the applicability of the statutory definition is whether effectuation of the declared policy and purposes of the Act comprehend securing to the individual the rights guaranteed and protection afforded by the Act," the Board concluded that the newsboys are employees. The record sustains the Board's findings and there is ample basis in the law for its conclusion. . . .

Mr. Justice Reed concurs in the result. . . .

Mr. Justice Roberts [dissenting]:

. . . .

I think it plain that newsboys are not "employees" of the respondents within the meaning and intent of the National Labor Relations Act. When Congress, in § 2(3), said "The term 'employee' shall include any employee, . . ." it stated as clearly as language could do it that the provisions of the Act were to extend to those who, as a result of decades of tradition which had become part of the common understanding of our people, bear the named relationship. Clearly also Congress did not delegate to the National Labor Relations Board the function of defining the relationship of employment so as to promote what the Board understood to be the underlying purpose of the statute. The question who is an employee, so as to make the statute applicable to him, is a question of the meaning of the Act and, therefore, is a judicial and not an administrative question. . . .

NOTES AND QUESTIONS

8-14. *Hearst* is often cited to support limited judicial review of an agency's application of a statutory term to a set of facts. What issues does the Court decide *before* it applies the statutory term "employee" to the facts in this case? What is the scope of review as to each of these issues?

8-15. Contrast *Hearst* with *Packard Motor Car Co. v. NLRB*, 330 U.S. 485 (1947). In that case, the Board also had to construe the meaning of the term "employee." In concluding that foremen were covered by the National Labor Relations Act and thus, "a unit appropriate for the purposes of collective bargaining," the Court reviewed the agency's decision much less deferentially: "While we do not say that a determination of a unit of representation cannot be so unreasonable and arbitrary as to exceed the Board's power, we are clear that the decision in question does not do so." 330 U.S. at 491–92. Can you reconcile these two cases? When it comes to law formulation as opposed to law application, is it fair to say that both *Hearst* and *Packard* envision an active judicial review role?

8-16. Do the *Hearst* and *Packard* opinions square with the following statement from the 1941 Report of the Attorney General's Committee on Administrative Procedure, 81–88?

To state the matter very broadly judicial review is generally limited to the inquiry whether the administrative agency acted within the scope of its authority. The wisdom, reasonableness, or expediency of the action in the circumstances are said to be matters of administrative judgment to be determined exclusively by the agency. But the narrow inquiry into the agency's authority to act as it did covers a wide field. The question whether Congress had the constitutional course, always in the background. Short

§ 8.04 JUDICIAL CONTROL 745

of the constitutional issues are the questions of interpretation of the statutes conferring the authority. . . .

Whether the factors upon which the administrative decision was based are such as the agency is permitted to consider and whether the factors which it rejected are such as it is permitted to reject, and what weight is required to be attached to various factors are all questions which the courts can review as questions of law.

8-17. To what extent can a court defer to an agency's determination of what these factors are and the weight they are to receive? To what extent *must* a court defer? Consider the following case. How does it square with *Hearst* and *Packard*?

CHEVRON v. NRDC

United States Supreme Court
467 U.S. 837 (1984)

JUSTICE STEVENS delivered the opinion of the Court.

In the Clean Air Act Amendments of 1977, Pub. L. 95–95, 91 Stat. 685, Congress enacted certain requirements applicable to States that had not achieved the national air quality standards established by the Environmental Protection Agency (EPA) pursuant to earlier legislation. The amended Clean Air Act required these "nonattainment" States to establish a permit program regulating "new or modified major stationary sources" of air pollution. Generally, a permit may not be issued for a new or modified major stationary source unless several stringent conditions are met.[1] The EPA regulation promulgated to implement this permit requirement allows a State to adopt a plantwide definition of the term "stationary source."[2] Under this definition, an existing plant that contains several pollution-emitting devices may install or modify one piece of equipment without meeting the permit conditions if the alteration will not increase the total emissions from the plant. The question presented by these cases is whether EPA's decision to allow States to treat all of the pollution-emitting devices within the same industrial grouping as though they were encased within a single "bubble" is based on a reasonable construction of the statutory term "stationary source."

---

[1] Section 172(b)(6), 42 U.S.C. § 7502(b)(6), provides: "The plan provisions required by subsection (a) shall — . . .

"(6) require permits for the construction and operation of new or modified major stationary sources in accordance with section 173 (relating to permit requirements)." 91 Stat. 747.

[2] "(i) 'Stationary source' means any building, structure, facility, or installation which emits or may emit any air pollutant subject to regulation under the Act.

"(ii) 'Building, structure, facility, or installation' means all of the pollutant-emitting activities which belong to the same industrial grouping, are located on one or more contiguous or adjacent properties, and are under the control of the same person (or persons under common control) except the activities of any vessel." . . .

I

The EPA regulations containing the plantwide definition of the term stationary source were promulgated on October 14, 1981. . . . Respondents filed a timely petition for review in the United States Court of Appeals for the District of Columbia Circuit pursuant to 42 U.S.C. § 7607(b)(1). The Court of Appeals set aside the regulations.

The court observed that the relevant part of the amended Clean Air Act "does not explicitly define what Congress envisioned as a 'stationary source,' to which the permit program . . . should apply," and further stated that the precise issue was not "squarely addressed in the legislative history." *Id.*, at 273, 685 F.2d, at 723. In light of its conclusion that the legislative history bearing on the question was "at best contradictory," it reasoned that "the purposes of the nonattainment program should guide our decision here." 685 F.2d, at 726, n. 39.[5] Based on two of its precedents concerning the applicability of the bubble concept to certain Clean Air Act programs, the court stated that the bubble concept was "mandatory" in programs designed merely to maintain existing air quality, but held that it was "inappropriate" in programs enacted to improve air quality. 685 F.2d, at 726. Since the purpose of the permit program — its *"raison d'etre,"* in the court's view — was to improve air quality, the court held that the bubble concept was inapplicable in these cases under its prior precedents. It therefore set aside the regulations embodying the bubble concept as contrary to law. We granted certiorari to review that judgment, 461 U.S. 956 (1983), and we now reverse.

The basic legal error of the Court of Appeals was to adopt a static judicial definition of the term "stationary source" when it had decided that Congress itself had not commanded that definition. . . .

II

When a court reviews an agency's construction of the statute which it administers, it is confronted with two questions. First, always, is the question whether Congress has directly spoken to the precise question at issue. If the intent of Congress is clear, that is the end of the matter; for the court, as well as the agency, must give effect to the unambiguously expressed intent of Congress.[9] If, however, the court determines Congress has not directly addressed the precise question at issue, the court does not simply impose its own construction on the statute, as would be necessary in the absence of an administrative interpretation. Rather, if the statute is silent or ambiguous

---

[5] The court remarked in this regard:

"We regret, of course, that Congress did not advert specifically to the bubble concept's application to various Clean Air Act programs, and note that a further clarifying statutory directive would facilitate the work of the agency and of the court in their endeavors to serve the legislators' will." 685 F.2d, at 726, n. 39.

[9] The judiciary is the final authority on issues of statutory construction and must reject administrative constructions which are contrary to clear congressional intent. *See, e.g., FEC v. Democratic Senatorial Campaign Committee*, 454 U.S. 27, 32 (1981). . . . If a court, employing traditional tools of statutory construction, ascertains that Congress had an intention on the precise question at issue, that intention is the law and must be given effect.

with respect to the specific issue, the question for the court is whether the agency's answer is based on a permissible construction of the statute.[11]

"The power of an administrative agency to administer a congressionally created . . . program necessarily requires the formulation of policy and the making of rules to fill any gap left, implicitly or explicitly, by Congress." *Morton v. Ruiz,* 415 U.S. 199, 231 (1974). If Congress has explicitly left a gap for the agency to fill, there is an express delegation of authority to the agency to elucidate a specific provision of the statute by regulation. Such legislative regulations are given controlling weight unless they are arbitrary, capricious, or manifestly contrary to the statute. Sometimes the legislative delegation to an agency on a particular question is implicit rather than explicit. In such a case, a court may not substitute its own construction of a statutory provision for a reasonable interpretation made by the administrator of an agency. . . .

In light of these well-settled principles it is clear that the Court of Appeals misconceived the nature of its role in reviewing the regulations at issue. Once it determined, after its own examination of the legislation, that Congress did not actually have an intent regarding the applicability of the bubble concept to the permit program, the question before it was not whether in its view the concept is "inappropriate" in the general context of a program designed to improve air quality, but whether the Administrator's view that it is appropriate in the context of this particular program is a reasonable one. Based on the examination of the legislation and its history which follows, we agree with the Court of Appeals that Congress did not have a specific intention on the applicability of the bubble concept in these cases, and conclude that the EPA's use of that concept here is a reasonable policy choice for the agency to make.

[The Court then reviewed the legislative history of the Act.]

IV

The Clean Air Act Amendments of 1977 are a lengthy, detailed, technical, complex, and comprehensive response to a major social issue. A small portion of the statute . . . expressly deals with nonattainment areas. The focal point of this controversy is one phrase in that portion of the Amendments. . . .

The 1977 Amendments contain no specific reference to the "bubble concept." Nor do they contain a specific definition of the term "stationary source," though they did not disturb the definition of "stationary source" contained in § 111(a)(3), applicable by the terms of the Act to the NSPS program. Section 302(j), however, defines the term "major stationary source" as follows:

> (j) Except as otherwise expressly provided, the terms "major stationary source" and "major emitting facility" mean any stationary facility or source of air pollutants which directly emits, or has the potential to emit, one hundred tons per year or more of any air pollutant (including any major emitting facility or source of fugitive emissions of any such pollutant, as determined by rule by the Administrator).

---

[11] The court need not conclude that the agency construction was the only one it permissibly could have adopted to uphold the construction, or even the reading the court would have reached if the question initially had arisen in a judicial proceeding. . . .

V

The legislative history of the portion of the 1977 Amendments dealing with nonattainment areas does not contain any specific comment on the "bubble concept" or the question whether a plantwide definition of a stationary source is permissible under the permit program. . . .

VI

As previously noted, prior to the 1977 Amendments, the EPA had adhered to a plantwide definition of the term "source" under a NSPS program. After adoption of the 1977 Amendments, proposals for a plantwide definition were considered in at least three formal proceedings. . . .

In August 1980, however, the EPA adopted a regulation that, in essence, applied the basic reasoning of the Court of Appeals in this case. The EPA took particular note of the two then-recent Court of Appeals decisions, which had created the bright-line rule that the "bubble concept" should be employed in a program designed to maintain air quality but not in one designed to enhance air quality. Relying heavily on those cases, EPA adopted a dual definition of "source" for nonattainment areas that required a permit whenever a change in either the entire plant, or one of its components, would result in a significant increase in emissions even if the increase was completely offset by reductions elsewhere in the plant. The EPA expressed the opinion that this interpretation was "more consistent with congressional intent" than the plantwide definition because it "would bring in more sources or modifications for review," but its primary legal analysis was predicated on the two Court of Appeals decisions.

In 1981 a new administration took office and initiated a "Government-wide re-examination of regulatory burdens and complexities." In the context of that review, the EPA reevaluated the various arguments that had been advanced in connection with the proper definition of the term "source" and concluded that the term should be given the same definition in both nonattainment areas and PSD areas.

In explaining its conclusion, the EPA first noted that the definitional issue was not squarely addressed in either the statute or its legislative history and therefore that the issue involved an agency "judgment as how to best carry out the Act." It then set forth several reasons for concluding that the plantwide definition was more appropriate. It pointed out that the dual definition "can act as a disincentive to new investment and modernization by discouraging modifications to existing facilities" and "can actually retard progress in air pollution control by discouraging replacement of older, dirtier processes or pieces of equipment with new, cleaner ones." Moreover, the new definition "would simplify EPA's rules by using the same definition of 'source' for PSD, nonattainment new source review and the construction moratorium. This reduces confusion and inconsistency." *Id.* Finally, the agency explained that additional requirements that remained in place would accomplish the fundamental purposes of achieving attainment with NAAQS's as expeditiously as possible. These conclusions were expressed in a proposed rulemaking in August 1981 that was formally promulgated in October.

VII

In this Court respondents expressly reject the basic rationale of the Court of Appeals' decision. That court viewed the statutory definition of the term "source" as sufficiently flexible to cover either a plantwide definition, a narrower definition covering each unit within a plant, or a dual definition that could apply to both the entire "bubble" and its components. It interpreted the policies of the statute, however, to mandate the plantwide definition in programs designed to maintain clean air and to forbid it in programs designed to improve air quality. Respondents place a fundamentally different construction on the statute. They contend that the text of the Act requires the EPA to use a dual definition — if either a component of a plant, or the plant as a whole, emits over 100 tons of pollutant, it is a major stationary source. They thus contend that the EPA rules adopted in 1980, insofar as they apply to the maintenance of the quality of clean air, as well as the 1981 rules which apply to nonattainment areas, violate the statute. . . .

Based on our examination of the legislative history, we agree with the Court of Appeals that it is unilluminating. The general remarks pointed to by respondents "were obviously not made with this narrow issue in mind and they cannot be said to demonstrate a Congressional desire. . . ." *Jewell Ridge Coal Corp. v. Mine Workers*, 325 U.S. 161, 168–169 (1945). Respondents' argument based on the legislative history relies heavily on Senator Muskie's observation that a new source is subject to the LAER requirement. But the full statement is ambiguous and like the text of § 173 itself, this comment does not tell us what a new source is, much less that it is to have an inflexible definition. We find that the legislative history as a whole is silent on the precise issue before us. It is, however, consistent with the view that the EPA should have broad discretion in implementing the policies of the 1977 Amendments.

More importantly, that history plainly identifies the policy concerns that motivated the enactment; the plantwide definition is fully consistent with one of those concerns — the allowance of reasonable economic growth — and, whether or not we believe it most effectively implements the other, we must recognize that the EPA has advanced a reasonable explanation for its conclusion that the regulations serve the environmental objectives as well. Indeed, its reasoning is supported by the public record developed in the rulemaking process, as well as by certain private studies.[37]

Our review of the EPA's varying interpretations of the word "source" — both before and after the 1977 Amendments — convince us that the agency primarily responsible for administering this important legislation has consistently interpreted it flexibly — not in a sterile textual vacuum, but in the context of implementing policy decisions in a technical and complex arena.

---

[37] "Economists have proposed that economic incentives be substituted for the cumbersome administrative-legal framework. The objective is to make the profit and cost incentives that work so well in the marketplace work for pollution control. . . . [The 'bubble' or 'netting' concept] is a first attempt in this direction. By giving a plant manager flexibility to find the places and processes within a plant that control emissions most cheaply, pollution control can be achieved more quickly and cheaply." L. Lave & G. Omenn, *Cleaning the Air: Reforming the Clean Air Act* 28 (1981) (footnote omitted).

The fact that the agency has from time to time changed its interpretation of the term "source" does not, as respondents argue, lead us to conclude that no deference should be accorded the agency's interpretation of the statute. An initial agency interpretation is not instantly carved in stone. On the contrary, the agency, to engage in informed rulemaking, must consider varying interpretations and the wisdom of its policy on a continuing basis. Moreover, the fact that the agency has adopted different definitions in different contexts adds force to the argument that the definition itself is flexible, particularly since Congress has never indicated any disapproval of a flexible reading of the statute.

Significantly, it was not the agency in 1980, but rather the Court of Appeals that read the statute inflexibly to command a plantwide definition for programs designed to maintain clean air and to forbid such a definition for programs designed to improve air quality. The distinction the court drew may well be a sensible one, but our labored review of the problem has surely disclosed that it is not a distinction that Congress ever articulated itself, or one that the EPA found in the statute before the courts began to review the legislative work product. We conclude that it was the Court of Appeals, rather than Congress or any of the decisionmakers who are authorized by Congress to administer this legislation, that was primarily responsible for the 1980 position taken by the agency.

Policy

The arguments over policy that are advanced in the parties' briefs create the impression that respondents are now waging in a judicial forum a specific policy battle which they ultimately lost in the agency and in the 32 jurisdictions opting for the "bubble concept," but one which was never waged in the Congress. Such policy arguments are more properly addressed to legislators or administrators, not to judges.

In these cases the Administrator's interpretation represents a reasonable accommodation of manifestly competing interests and is entitled to deference: the regulatory scheme is technical and complex, the agency considered the matter in a detailed and reasoned fashion, and the decision involves reconciling conflicting policies. Congress intended to accommodate both interests, but did not do so itself on the level of specificity presented by these cases. Perhaps that body consciously desired the Administrator to strike the balance at this level, thinking that those with great expertise and charged with responsibility for administering the provision would be in a better position to do so; perhaps it simply did not consider the question at this level; and perhaps Congress was unable to forge a coalition on either side of the question, and those on each side decided to take their chances with the scheme devised by the agency. For judicial purposes, it matters not which of these things occurred.

Judges are not experts in the field, and are not part of either political branch of the Government. Courts must, in some cases, reconcile competing political interests, but not on the basis of the judges' personal policy preferences. In contrast, an agency to which Congress has delegated policymaking responsibilities may, within the limits of that delegation, properly rely upon the incumbent administration's views of wise policy to inform its judgments. While agencies are not directly accountable to the people, the Chief Executive is, and it is entirely appropriate for this political branch of the Government to make such policy choices — resolving the competing interests which Congress itself either inadvertently did not resolve, or intentionally left to be resolved by the agency charged with the administration of the statute in light of everyday realities. When a challenge to an agency construction of a statutory provision, fairly conceptualized, really centers on the wisdom of the agency's policy, rather than whether it is a reasonable choice within a gap left open by Congress, the challenge must fail. In such a case, federal judges — who have no constituency — have a duty to respect legitimate policy choices made by those who do. The responsibilities for assessing the wisdom of such policy choices and resolving the struggle between competing views of the public interest are not judicial ones: "Our Constitution vests such responsibilities in the political branches." *TVA v. Hill,* 437 U.S. 153, 195 (1978).

We hold that the EPA's definition of the term "source" is a permissible construction of the statute which seeks to accommodate progress in reducing air pollution with economic growth. . . .

The judgment of the Court of Appeals is reversed.

It is so ordered.

JUSTICE MARSHALL and JUSTICE REHNQUIST took no part in the consideration or decision of these cases.

JUSTICE O'CONNOR took no part in the decision of these cases.

NOTES AND QUESTIONS

8-18. What is a question of law for purposes of *de novo* judicial review under *Hearst*? What kind of question of law results in *de novo* judicial review under *Chevron*? Are these cases reconcilable? Does *Chevron* refine or limit the applicability of *Hearst*?

8-19. State the two-pronged approach of *Chevron*. How does one define "the precise question at issue"? How does one know if Congress was, in fact, "clear" on that issue?

8-20. In *Young v. Community Nutrition Center,* 476 U.S. 974 (1986), the Court dealt with a dispute over section 346 of the Federal Drug and Cosmetic Act. That Act states that "the Secretary shall promulgate regulations limiting the quantity [of any harmful, but unavoidable, added substance] thereon to such extent as he finds necessary for the protection of public health. Respondents argued that this section mandated the promulgation of tolerance levels for unavoidable, unsafe substances in food. The FDA, however, contended that the word "shall" is modified by the phrase "to such extent as he finds necessary for the protection of public health." A majority of the Supreme Court, speaking through Justice O'Connor, concluded that the phrase "to the extent . . . necessary" was "ambiguous" and deferred to the agency's interpretation, despite a good deal of legislative history to the contrary. The Court stated:

As enemies of the dangling participle well know, the English language does not always force a writer to specify which of two possible objects is the one to which a modifying phrase relates. A Congress more precise or more prescient than the one that enacted § 346 might, if it wished petitioner's position to prevail, have placed "to such extent as he finds necessary for the protection of public health" as an appositive phrase immediately after "shall" rather than as a free-floating phrase after "the quantity therein or thereon." A Congress equally fastidious and foresighted, but intending respondents' position to prevail, might have substituted the phrase "to the quantity" for the phrase "to such extent as." But the Congress that actually enacted § 346 took neither tack.

Should facial statutory ambiguity alone be enough to defer so completely to an agency's interpretation of the law? See Justice Stevens' dissenting opinion in *Young,* 476 U.S. at 984.

8-21. Assume that Congress' intent is vague or non-existent as to the question presented in *Chevron.* Should a court assume that Congress has, in fact, delegated the power in question to the agency? Do you agree with the Court in *Chevron* that silence, in effect, means delegation? Why? How far can a Court go in reviewing whether or not such a legislative delegation has, in fact, occurred? *See* Robert Anthony, 7 YALE J. REG. 1, 31–35 (1990).

8-22. If Congress is clear as to the precise question in issue, how far can a court then go in reviewing the agency's legal interpretation? Why?

8-23. If Congress is vague or silent as to a particular statutory term, to what extent and when can a reviewing court rely on legislative history to determine what Congress might have meant?

8-24. What are the traditional tools of statutory construction? Why is the Court so reluctant to rely on legislative history in interpreting vague statutory terms? How is legislative history made? What theory of the legislative process informs your view on this?

8-25. Does judicial reliance on legislative history increase or decrease judicial power? Why? Is this a good or a bad result? Why? Consider the following analysis.

Patricia Wald, *The Sizzling Sleeper: The Use of Legislative History in Construing Statutes in the 1988-89 Term of the U.S. Supreme Court,* 39 AM. UNIV. L. REV. 277, 300–03 (1990).*

What difference does it make if judges look at legislative history or not? What if the Scalia forces do triumph in their insistence on restricting the use of extra-statutory materials for guidance in interpreting statutes? Would not life be easier for everyone, including the judges, if they just read the laws themselves instead of rifling through what one commentator has called the "ashcans of the legislative process"? Unfortunately, the choice is not so simple; there are several fascinating sidebars to this seemingly arcane debate about how to construe statutes, and the result of the debate has important implications for the balance of power in the ongoing tug-of-war among the three branches in our constitutional system. The textualists'

---

* Copyright © 1990 by American University Law Review. All rights reserved.

rationale for what they are trying to do has been presented; the remainder of this Article details some of the reasons why I do not favor their approach. . . .

One needs a sense of context in order to get meaning out of words, in statutes as in life. I am not a literary theorist. I ordinarily do not dabble in semiotics. I am not a deconstructionist. Rather, I am a judge. Every day I am called upon to decide cases on the basis of what statutes mean and what they require of citizens or the government itself. When a statute comes before me to be interpreted, I want first and foremost to get the interpretation right. By that, I mean simply this: *I want to advance rather than impede or frustrate the will of Congress.* To that extent, at least, I am a conservative judge — Congress makes the laws, I try to enforce them as Congress meant them to be enforced. To do this, however, I very often find it not only helpful but *necessary* to consult the legislative history of statutes. Only very occasionally in my experience do litigants come before the federal appellate judicial system with claims that are clearly foreclosed by the plain language of the governing statute. Disputes that are resolved by plain statutory language usually settle long before they make their way into the federal appellate courts.

As a general matter, interpreting statutes is more difficult than one might think from reading judicial opinions. Once a decision is reached, we often mask much of the angst that is involved in getting there. Although judges' opinions often refer to "plain" statutory language, the truth is that statutes are increasingly complex and technical, and a judge may not always be certain as to the meaning of the small print. As we conscientiously embark on our duty to ascertain what the words mean in the context of the statute's aims and purposes, we are almost inevitably drawn to the historical record of what the men and women who proposed and sponsored the legislation intended to enact. We feel better when their words confirm our reading of the text; we worry more when it contradicts the text. This does not mean, as the textualist Justices accuse, that we "transform" every "snippet of analysis" in congressional reports into "the law of the land" or "elevate to the level of statutory text a phrase taken from the legislative history." It does mean, however, that we think again when we face a contradiction between text and history, and we should. That, in a nutshell, explains why we still resort to legislative history even when we label the meaning of a statutory provision "plain" or "clear." Justice Frankfurter wisely acknowledged this view of statutory interpretation almost fifty years ago: "[t]he notion that because the words of a statute are plain, its meaning is also plain, is merely pernicious oversimplification."

Of course, I am aware of the critical scholarship demonstrating that language is inherently indeterminate and will always depend upon both the writer's and the reader's context to give it any meaning. (A Congress of such divergent interests as exists in our nation today has raised this indeterminacy to an art form.) This scholarship reaffirms what we judges already know — that people frequently do not say precisely what they mean, or that even when they do, what they have said will inevitably leave some room for interpretation. In our daily lives, we all act or communicate on the assumption that intent must be culled not only from actual words, but from the situation in which those words were spoken. For example, what were the speeches trying to do? What were the speakers worried about? Were they aware of all facts? Why, then, should judges be asked to ignore all that information when we construe statutes of the most complex sort? Can judges not be trusted to give less weight to an isolated remark of a disgruntled legislator in a floor debate than to the words in the text itself?

The textualists may be doing a disservice to the courts and ultimately to the public by perpetuating the myth that our statutory construction tasks can be disposed of mechanistically in most cases and that the sheer logical force of a statute's language or internal structure can dictate our hard choices of interpretation. That is rarely the case. More typically, the job of statutory construction requires an open and creative mind — one that can draw upon a variety of different sources, text, statutory context, other relevant statutes, and legislative history to extrapolate the most appropriate *meaning* from what are basically only *words*. Judge Learned Hand once wrote that though

> the words used, even in their literal sense, are the primary, and ordinarily the most reliable, source of interpreting the meaning of any writing, . . . [nevertheless] it is one of the surest indexes of a mature and developed jurisprudence not to make a fortress out of the dictionary; but to remember that statutes always have some purpose or object to accomplish, whose sympathetic and imaginative discovery is the surest guide to their meaning.

Such judicious resort to legislative history is an indispensable part of the faithful execution of our interpretive duties as judges, and the notion that legislative history is a kind of Papal Index for judges, I find both illogical and offensive.

Compare Judge Wald's analysis with that of Justice Scalia, *Judicial Deference to Administrative Interpretations of Law,* 1989 DUKE L. REV. 511, 514, 516–17, 520–21 (1989).*

What, then, is the theoretical justification for allowing reasonable administrative interpretations to govern? The cases, old and new, that accept administrative interpretations, often refer to the "expertise" of the agencies in question, their intense familiarity with the history and purposes of the legislation at issue, their practical knowledge of what will best effectuate those purposes. In other words, they are more likely than the courts to reach the correct result. That is, if true, a good practical reason for accepting the agency's views, but hardly a valid theoretical justification for doing so. If I had been sitting on the Supreme Court when Learned Hand was still alive, it would similarly have been, as a practical matter, desirable for me to accept his views in all of his cases under review, on the basis that he is a lot wiser than I, and more likely to get it right. But that would hardly have been theoretically valid. Even if Hand would have been *de facto* superior, I would have been *ex officio* so. So also with judicial acceptance of the agencies' views. If it is, as we have always believed, the constitutional duty of the

---

* Copyright © 1989 by Justice Antonin Scalia. All rights reserved.

courts to say what the law is, we must search for something beyond relative competence as a basis for ignoring that principle when agency action is at issue. . . .

In my view, the theoretical justification for *Chevron* is no different from the theoretical justification for those pre-*Chevron* cases that sometimes deferred to agency legal determinations. As the D.C. Circuit, quoting the First Circuit, expressed it: "The extent to which courts should defer to agency interpretations of law is ultimately a function of Congress' intent on the subject as revealed in the particular statutory scheme at issue." An ambiguity in a statute committed to agency implementation can be attributed to either of two congressional desires: (1) Congress intended a particular result, but was not clear about it; or (2) Congress had no particular intent on the subject, but meant to leave its resolution to the agency. When the former is the case, what we have is genuinely a question of law, properly to be resolved by the courts. When the latter is the case, what we have is the conferral of discretion upon the agency, and the only question of law presented to the courts is whether the agency has acted within the scope of its discretion — *i.e.,* whether its resolution of the ambiguity is reasonable. As I read the history of developments in this field, the pre-*Chevron* decisions sought to choose between (1) and (2) on a statute-by-statute basis. Hence the relevance of such frequently mentioned factors as the degree of the agency's expertise, the complexity of the question at issue, and the existence of rulemaking authority within the agency. All these factors make an intent to corner discretion upon the agency more likely. *Chevron,* however, if it is to be believed, replaced this statute-by-statute evaluation (which was assuredly a font of uncertainty and litigation) with an across-the-board presumption that, in the case of ambiguity, agency discretion is meant.

It is beyond the scope of these remarks to defend that presumption (I was not on the Court, after all, when *Chevron* was decided). Surely, however, it is a more rational presumption today than it would have been thirty years ago — which explains the change in the law. Broad delegation to the Executive is the hallmark of the modern administrative state; agency rulemaking powers are the rule rather than, as they once were, the exception; and as the sheer number of modern departments and agencies suggests, we are awash in agency "expertise." If the *Chevron* rule is not a 100% accurate estimation of modern congressional intent, the prior case-by-case evaluation was not so either . . . and was becoming less and less so, as the sheer volume of modern dockets made it less and less possible for the Supreme Court to police diverse application of an ineffable rule. And to tell the truth, the quest for the "genuine" legislative intent is probably a wild-goose chase anyway. In the vast majority of cases I expect that Congress *neither* (1) intended a single result, nor (2) meant to confer discretion upon the agency, but rather (3) didn't think about the matter at all. If I am correct in that, then any rule adopted in this field represents merely a fictional, presumed intent, and operates principally as a background rule of law against which Congress can legislate. . . .

There is one final point I wish to discuss: What does it take to satisfy the first step of *Chevron* — that is, when is a statute ambiguous? *Chevron* becomes virtually meaningless, it seems to me, if ambiguity exists only when the arguments for and against the various possible interpretations are in absolute equipoise. If nature knows of such equipoise in legal arguments, the courts at least do not. The judicial task, every day, consists of finding the *right* answer, no matter how closely balanced the question may *seem* to be. In appellate opinions, there is no such thing as a tie. If the judicial mentality that is developed by such a system were set to answering the question, "When are the arguments for and against a particular statutory interpretation in equipoise?," I am certain that the response would be "almost never." If *Chevron* is to have any meaning, then, congressional intent must be regarded as "ambiguous" not just when no interpretation is even marginally better than any other, but rather when two or more reasonable, though not necessarily equally valid, interpretations exist. This is indeed intimated by the opinion in *Chevron* — which suggests that the opposite of "ambiguity" is not "resolvability" but rather "clarity." Here, of course, is the chink in *Chevron*'s armor — the ambiguity that prevents it from being an absolutely clear guide to future judicial decisions (though still a better one than what it supplanted). How clear is clear? It is here, if *Chevron* is not abandoned, that the future battles over acceptance of agency interpretations of law will be fought. Some indications of that can already be found in Supreme Court opinions.

I cannot resist the temptation to tie this lecture into an impenetrable whole, by observing that where one stands on this last point — how clear is clear — may have much to do with where one stands on the earlier points of what *Chevron* means and whether *Chevron* is desirable. In my experience, there is a fairly close correlation between the degree to which a person is (for want of a better word) a "strict constructionist" of statutes, and the degree to which that person favors *Chevron* and is willing to give it broad scope. The reason is obvious. One who finds *more* often (as I do) that the meaning of a statute is apparent from its text and from its relationship with other laws, thereby finds *less* often that the triggering requirement for *Chevron* deference exists. It is thus relatively rare that *Chevron* will require me to accept an interpretation which, though reasonable, I would not personally adopt. Contrariwise, one who abhors a "plain meaning" rule, and is willing to permit the apparent meaning of a statute to be impeached by the legislative history, will more frequently find agency-liberating ambiguity, and will discern a much broader range of "reasonable" interpretation that the agency may adopt and to which the courts must pay deference. The frequency with which *Chevron* will require *that* judge to accept an interpretation he thinks wrong is infinitely greater. . . .

IMMIGRATION AND NATURALIZATION SERVICE v. CARDOZA-FONSECA

United States Supreme Court
480 U.S. 421 (1986)

JUSTICE STEVENS delivered the opinion of the Court.

Since 1980, the Immigration and Nationality Act has provided two methods through which an otherwise deportable alien who claims that he will be persecuted if deported can seek relief. Section 243(h) of the Act, requires the Attorney General to withhold deportation of an alien who demonstrates that his "life or freedom would be threatened" on account of one of the listed factors if he is deported. In *INS v. Stevic,* 467 U.S. 407 (1984), we held that to qualify for this entitlement to withholding of deportation, an alien must demonstrate that "it is more likely than not that the alien would be subject to persecution" in the country to which he would be returned. The Refugee Act of 1980, also established a second type of broader relief. Section 208(a) of the Act authorizes the Attorney General, in his discretion, to grant asylum to an alien who is unable or unwilling to return to his home country "because of persecution or a well-founded fear of persecution on account of race, religion, nationality, membership in a particular social group, or political opinion."

In *Stevic,* we rejected an alien's contention that the § 208(a) "well-founded fear" standard governs applications for withholding of deportation under § 243(h). Similarly, today we reject the Government's contention that the § 243(h) standard, which requires an alien to show that he is more likely than not to be subject to persecution, governs applications for asylum under § 208(a). Congress used different, broader language to define the term "refugee" as used in § 208(a) than it used to describe the class of aliens who have a right to withholding of deportation under § 243(h). The Act's establishment of a broad class of refugees who are eligible for a discretionary grant of asylum, and a narrower class of aliens who are given a statutory right not to be deported to the country where they are in danger, mirrors the provisions of the United Nations Protocol Relating to the Status of Refugees, which provided the motivation for the enactment of the Refugee Act of 1980. In addition, the legislative history of the 1980 Act makes it perfectly clear that Congress did not intend the class of aliens who qualify as refugees to be coextensive with the class who qualify for § 243(h) relief.

I

Respondent is a 38-year-old Nicaraguan citizen who entered the United States in 1979 as a visitor. After she remained in the United States longer than permitted, and failed to take advantage of the Immigration and Naturalization Service's (INS) offer of voluntary departure, the INS commenced deportation proceedings against her. Respondent conceded that she was in the country illegally, but requested withholding of deportation pursuant to § 243(h) and asylum as a refugee pursuant to § 208(a).

To support her request under § 243(h), respondent attempted to show that if she were returned to Nicaragua her "life or freedom would be threatened" on account of her political views; to support her request under § 208(a), she attempted to show that she had a "well-founded fear of persecution" upon her return. The evidence supporting both claims related primarily to the activities of respondent's brother who had been tortured and imprisoned because of his political activities in Nicaragua. Both respondent and her brother testified that they believed the Sandinistas knew that the two of them had fled Nicaragua together and that even though she had not been active politically herself, she would be interrogated about her brother's whereabouts and activities. Respondent also testified that because of her brother's status, her own political opposition to the Sandinistas would be brought to that government's attention. Based on these facts, respondent claimed that she would be tortured if forced to return.

The Immigration Judge applied the same standard in evaluating respondent's claim for withholding of deportation under § 243(h) as he did in evaluating her application for asylum under § 208(a). He found that she had not established "a clear probability of persecution" and therefore was not entitled to either form of relief. On appeal, the Board of Immigration Appeals (BIA) agreed that the respondent had "failed to establish that she would suffer persecution within the meaning of section 208(a) or 243(h) of the Immigration and Nationality Act."

In the Court of Appeals for the Ninth Circuit, respondent did not challenge the BIA's decision that she was not entitled to withholding of deportation under § 243(h), but argued that she was eligible for consideration for asylum under § 208(a), and contended that the Immigration Judge and BIA erred in applying the "more likely than not" standard of proof from § 243(h) to her § 208(a) asylum claim. Instead, she asserted, they should have applied the "well-founded fear" standard, which she considered to be more generous. The court agreed. Relying on both the text and the structure of the Act, the court held that the "well-founded fear" standard which governs asylum proceedings is different, and in fact more generous, than the "clear probability" standard which governs withholding of deportation proceedings. Agreeing with the Court of Appeals for the Seventh Circuit, the court interpreted the standard to require asylum applicants to present " 'specific facts' through objective evidence to prove either past persecution or 'good reason' to fear future persecution." The court remanded respondent's asylum claim to the BIA to evaluate under the proper legal standard. We granted certiorari to resolve a circuit conflict on this important question. 475 U.S. 1009 (1986).

The Refugee Act of 1980 established a new statutory procedure for granting asylum to refugees. The 1980 Act added a new § 208(a) to the Immigration and Naturalization Act of 1952, reading as follows:

> The Attorney General shall establish a procedure for an alien physically present in the United States or at a land border or port of entry, irrespective of such alien's status, to apply for asylum, and the alien may be granted asylum in the discretion of the Attorney General if the Attorney General

determines that such alien is a refugee within the meaning of section 1101(a)(42)(A) of this title.

94 Stat. 105, 8 U.S.C. § 1158(a).

Under this section, eligibility for asylum depends entirely on the Attorney General's determination that an alien is a "refugee," as that term is defined in § 101(a)(42), which was also added to the Act in 1980. That section provides:

> The term "refugee" means (A) any person who is outside any country of such person's nationality or, in the case of a person having no nationality, is outside any country in which such person last habitually resided, and who is unable or unwilling to return to, and is unable or unwilling to avail himself or herself of the protection of, that country because of persecution or a well-founded fear of persecution on account of race, religion, nationality, membership in a particular social group, or political opinion. . . .

Thus, the "persecution or well-founded fear of persecution" standard governs the Attorney General's determination whether an alien is eligible for asylum. . . .

The Government argues, however, that even though the "well-founded fear" standard is applicable, there is no difference between it and the "would be threatened" test of § 243(h). It asks us to hold that the only way an applicant can demonstrate a "well-founded fear of persecution" is to prove a "clear probability of persecution." The statutory language does not lend itself to this reading.

To begin with, the language Congress used to describe the two standards conveys very different meanings. The "would be threatened" language of § 243(h) has no subjective component, but instead requires the alien to establish by objective evidence that it is more likely than not that he or she will be subject to persecution upon deportation. In contrast, the reference to "fear" in the § 208(a) standard obviously makes the eligibility determination turn to some extent on the subjective mental state of the alien. "The linguistic difference between the words 'well-founded fear' and 'clear probability' may be as striking as that between a subjective and an objective frame of reference. . . . We simply cannot conclude that the standards are identical." *Guevara-Flores v. INS*, 786 F.2d 1242, 1250 (CA5 1986) . . . .

III

The message conveyed by the plain language of the Act is confirmed by an examination of its history.[12]

[The Court concludes that the legislative history is consistent with the plain meaning of the statute.]

---

[12] As we have explained, the plain language of this statute appears to settle the question before us. Therefore, we look to the legislative history to determine only whether there is "clearly expressed legislative intention" contrary to that language, which would require us to question the strong presumption that Congress expresses its intent through the language it chooses. . . . In this case, far from causing us to question the conclusion that flows from the statutory language, the legislative history adds compelling support to our holding that Congress never intended to restrict eligibility for asylum to aliens who can satisfy § 243(h)'s strict, objective standard.

IV

. . . .

The INS's second principal argument in support of the proposition that the "well-founded fear" and "clear probability" standard are equivalent is that the BIA so construes the two standards. The INS argues that the BIA's construction of the Refugee Act of 1980 is entitled to substantial deference, even if we conclude that the Court of Appeals' reading of the statutes is more in keeping with Congress' intent. This argument is unpersuasive.

The question whether Congress intended the two standards to be identical is a pure question of statutory construction for the courts to decide. Employing traditional tools of statutory construction, we have concluded that Congress did not intend the two standards to be identical. In *Chevron U.S.A., Inc. v. Natural Resources Defense Council, Inc.*, 467 U.S. 837 (1984), we explained:

> The judiciary is the final authority on issues of statutory construction and must reject administrative constructions which are contrary to clear congressional intent. [Citing cases.] If a court, employing traditional tools of statutory construction, ascertains that Congress had an intention on the precise question at issue, that intention is the law and must be given effect.

Id., at 843, n. 9 (citations omitted).

The narrow legal question whether the two standards are the same is, of course, quite different from the question of interpretation that arises in each case in which the agency is required to apply either or both standards to a particular set of facts. There is obviously some ambiguity in a term like "well-founded fear" which can only be given concrete meaning through a process of case-by-case adjudication. In that process of filling "'any gap left, implicitly or explicitly, by Congress,'" the courts must respect the interpretation of the agency to which Congress has delegated the responsibility for administering the statutory program. See *Chevron, supra*, at 843, quoting *Morton v. Ruiz*, 415 U.S. 199, 231 (1974). But our task today is much narrower, and is well within the province of the Judiciary. We do not attempt to set forth a detailed description of how the "well-founded fear" test should be applied. Instead, we merely hold that the Immigration Judge and the BIA were incorrect in holding that the two standards are identical.

Our analysis of the plain language of the Act, . . . and its legislative history, lead inexorably to the conclusion that to show a "well-founded fear of persecution," an alien need not prove that it is more likely than not that he or she will be persecuted in his or her home country. We find these ordinary canons of statutory construction compelling, even without regard to the longstanding principle of construing any lingering ambiguities in deportation statutes in favor of the alien.

Deportation is always a harsh measure; it is all the more replete with danger when the alien makes a claim that he or she will be subject to death or persecution if forced to return to his or her home country. In enacting the Refugee Act of 1980 Congress sought to "give the United States sufficient flexibility to respond to situations involving political or religious dissidents and detainees throughout the world." Our holding today increases that flexibility by rejecting the Government's contention that the Attorney General may not even consider granting asylum to one who fails to satisfy the strict § 243(h) standard. Whether or not a "refugee" is eventually granted asylum is a matter which Congress has left for the Attorney General to decide. But it is clear that Congress did not intend to restrict eligibility for that relief to those who could prove that it is more likely than not that they will be persecuted if deported.

The judgment of the Court of Appeals is

Affirmed.

JUSTICE BLACKMUN's concurring opinion is omitted.

JUSTICE SCALIA, concurring in the judgment.

I agree with the Court that the plain meaning of "well-founded fear" and the structure of the Immigration and Naturalization Act (Act) clearly demonstrate that the "well-founded fear" standard and the "clear probability" standard are not equivalent. I concur in the judgment rather than join the Court's opinion, however, for two reasons. First, despite having reached the above conclusion, the Court undertakes an exhaustive investigation of the legislative history of the Act. . . . It attempts to justify this inquiry by relying upon the doctrine that if the legislative history of an enactment reveals a "'clearly expressed legislative intention' contrary to [the enactment's] language," the Court is required to "question the strong presumption that Congress expresses its intent through the language it chooses." . . . Although it is true that the Court in recent times has expressed approval of this doctrine, that is to my mind an ill-advised deviation from the venerable principle that if the language of a statute is clear, that language must be given effect — at least in the absence of a patent absurdity. . . . Judges interpret laws rather than reconstruct legislators' intentions. Where the language of those laws is clear, we are not free to replace it with an unenacted legislative intent. . . .

I am far more troubled, however, by the Court's discussion of the question whether the INS's interpretation of "well-founded fear" is entitled to deference. Since the Court quite rightly concludes that the INS's interpretation is clearly inconsistent with the plain meaning of that phrase and the structure of the Act, . . . there is simply no need and thus no justification for a discussion of whether the interpretation is entitled to deference. *See Chevron U.S.A., Inc. v. Natural Resources Defense Council, Inc.,* 467 U.S. 837, 842–843 (1984) ("If the intent of Congress is clear, that is the end of the matter; for the court, as well as the agency, must give effect to the unambiguously expressed intent of Congress") (footnote omitted). Even more unjustifiable, however, is the Court's use of this superfluous discussion as the occasion to express controversial, and I believe erroneous, views on the meaning of this Court's decision in *Chevron. Chevron* stated that where there is no "unambiguously expressed intent of Congress," . . . "a court may not substitute its own construction of a statutory provision for a reasonable interpretation made by the administrator of an agency." . . . This Court has consistently interpreted *Chevron* — which has been an extremely important and frequently cited opinion, not only in this Court but in the Courts of Appeals — as holding that courts must give effect to a reasonable agency interpretation of a statute unless that interpretation is inconsistent with a clearly expressed congressional intent. . . . The Court's discussion is flatly inconsistent with this well-established interpretation. The Court first implies that courts may substitute their interpretation of a statute for that of an agency whenever, "[e]mploying traditional tools of statutory construction," they are able to reach a conclusion as to the proper interpretation of the statute. But this approach would make deference a doctrine of desperation, authorizing courts to defer only if they would otherwise be unable to construe the enactment at issue. This is not an interpretation but an evisceration of *Chevron.*

The Court also implies that courts may substitute their interpretation of a statute for that of an agency whenever they face "a pure question of statutory construction for the courts to decide," rather than a "question of interpretation [in which] the agency is required to apply [a legal standard] to a particular set of facts." . . . No support is adduced for this proposition, which is contradicted by the case the Court purports to be interpreting, since in *Chevron* the Court deferred to the Environmental Protection Agency's abstract interpretation of the phrase "stationary source."

In my view, the Court badly misinterprets *Chevron.* More fundamentally, however, I neither share nor understand the Court's eagerness to refashion important principles of administrative law in a case in which such questions are completely unnecessary to the decision and have not been fully briefed by the parties.

I concur in the judgment.

JUSTICE POWELL's dissenting opinion, with whom THE CHIEF JUSTICE and JUSTICE WHITE join, is omitted.

NOTES AND QUESTIONS

8-26. In many of the Supreme Court cases subsequent to *Cardoza-Fonseca* which address similar issues, the Court frequently split over what might be called the *Chevron* question — *i.e.,* whether or not the intent of Congress on the precise question in issue is clear. *Compare Dole v. United Steelworkers of America,* 494 U.S. 26 (1990) (adhering more to the *Cardoza-Fonseca* interpretation of *Chevron*), *with Sullivan v. Everhardt,* 494 U.S. 83 (1990) (invoking a purer *Chevron* analysis).

A number of questions persist after *Chevron* and its progeny. One concerns the place of legislative history in the *Chevron* approach. To what extent may it be used and, perhaps more importantly, *when* may a court resort to the use of legislative history? A second question concerns the vitality and meaning of the apparent addendum that *Cardoza-Fonseca* makes to *Chevron.* When is an issue a "pure question of statutory construction" rather than a mixed question of law and fact? A third question is whether an implicit delegation should always be inferred when agencies interpret ambiguous statutory terms. A fourth issue is the extent to which *Chevron* represents a break with earlier doctrine as set forth in *Hearst* and its progeny or whether it is simply an extension of those traditional principles.

These and other questions raised by *Chevron* have spawned an extensive literature. For those largely critical of *Chevron, see, e.g.,* Cynthia Farina, *Statutory Interpretation and the Balance of Power in the Administrative State,* 89 COLUM. L. REV. 452 (1989); Alfred Aman, *Administrative Law In a Global Era: Progress, Deregulatory Change and the Rise of the Administrative Presidency,* 73 CORNELL L. REV. 1101, 1223–36 (1988); Cass Sunstein, *Constitutionalism After the New Deal,* 101 HARV. L. REV. 421 (1988); Abner Mikva, *How Should Courts Treat Administrative Agencies?,* 36 AM. U. L. REV. 1, 8 (1986); Sidney Shapiro & Robert Glicksman, *Congress, the Supreme Court, and the Quiet Revolution in Administrative Law,* 1988 DUKE L.J. 819, 871; *but see* Antonin Scalia, *Judicial Deference to Administrative Interpretations of Law,* 1989 DUKE L.J. 511; Richard Pierce, Chevron *and Its Aftermath: Judicial Review of Agency Interpretation of Statutory Provisions,* 41 VAND. L. REV. 301 (1988); Kenneth Starr, *Judicial Review in the Post-*Chevron *Era,* 3 YALE J. REG. 283 (1986). *See also* Robert Anthony, *Which Agency Interpretations Should Bind Citizens and Courts?,* 7 YALE J. REG. 1 (1990).

8-27. This literature continues to grow, *see, e.g.,* Richard J. Pierce, Jr., *The Supreme Court's New Hypertextualism: An Invitation to Cacophony and Incoherence in the Administrative State,* 95 COLUM. L. REV. 749, 750 (1995) (arguing that "[The Supreme Court's] post-*Chevron* jurisprudence is so confused that it is difficult to determine what remains of the original, highly deferential test. This inconsistency in applying the test is largely attributable to post-*Chevron* changes in the choice of 'traditional tools of statutory construction,' a phrase the *Chevron* Court used in a footnote to describe the manner in which courts should apply the first part of the test. As the Court has changed the mix of 'tools' it uses and the ways in which it uses those tools, it has gradually ceased to apply step two of the *Chevron* test to uphold an agency construction of ambiguous statutory language, because it rarely acknowledges the existence of ambiguity.") There appears to be more consistency at the appellate level. For an empirical study of all Court of Appeals decisions from 1995-1996 that cited *Chevron*, see Orin S. Kerr, *Shedding Light on* Chevron: *An Empirical Study of the* Chevron *Doctrine in the U.S. Courts of Appeals,* 15 YALE J. REG. 1 (1998) (agency interpretations upheld 73% of the time. Of those overturned, 53% failed step one of the *Chevron* test and 18% failed step two, *i.e.,* their application of the statutory term was upheld to be unreasonable). *See also,* Patricia M. Wald, *Judicial Review in Midpassage: The Uneasy Partnership between Courts and Agencies Plays on,* 32 TULSA L.J. 221 (1996); Thomas W. Merrill, *Textualism and the Future of the* Chevron *Doctrine,* 72 WASH. U. L.Q. 351 (1994).

8-28. As one of your authors has noted elsewhere:

The *Chevron* doctrine has continued to evolve as Supreme Court Justices and judges differ in their views on when and how to apply the *Chevron* doctrine as well as the proper deference to be accorded agency decisions once it has been determined that the *Chevron* approach should be used. These differences have been exacerbated, especially at the Supreme Court level, by the emergence of an approach to statutory construction that some commentators have labeled textualism. A textualist approach to interpretation is not necessarily devoid of context, but the context involved usually is limited to the face of the statute under consideration. As Judge Wald has written, "[t]extualism is a mode of statutory interpretation that relies on text and dictionaries to determine the meaning of statutory provisions and eschews reference to legislative history." As one commentator has noted, a judge using this interpretive methodology seeks to determine "what an ordinary reader of a statute would have understood the words to mean at the time of enactment, not what the intentions of the enacting legislators were." As a result, legislative history is essentially eliminated as a tool of statutory construction, particularly when the court is engaged in step one of the *Chevron* analysis — determining whether Congress spoke to the precise questions at issue.*

8-29. Is it possible for *Chevron* deference ultimately to frustrate the ability of a majority in Congress to legislate? Consider *Rust v. Sullivan*, below.

8-30. How would you describe the approach taken by the Court in *Rust v. Sullivan*, below? Is it more in accord with *Chevron* or *Fonseca*? At what point does the Court resort to legislative history? Why does it reject it? Why might there be ambiguity regarding such issues, both on the face of the statute and in the legislative history?

RUST v. SULLIVAN

United States Supreme Court
500 U.S. 173 (1991)

CHIEF JUSTICE REHNQUIST delivered the opinion of the Court.

[Title X of the Public Health Services Act was enacted in 1970 and has provided federal grant support of family planning clinics. The Act stipulated that none of the grant money "shall be used in programs where abortion is a method of family planning." The first regulations issued under the statute in 1971 required that a Title X project "not provide abortions," but later regulations permitted non-directive counseling of pregnant women as to their options including abortions. In 1998, the Department of Health and Human Services promulgated new regulations that required grant recipients to refrain from giving advice about abortion. If a patient asked, the grantees were instructed to say "the project does not consider abortion an appropriate method of family planning."]

---

* Reprinted from *Administrative Law*, Alfred C. Aman, Jr. & William T. Mayton, 2d ed., 2001, with permission of Thomson West.

. . . .

We need not dwell on the plain language of the statute because we agree with every court to have addressed the issue that the language is ambiguous. The language of s[ection] 1008 — that "[n]one of the funds appropriated under this subchapter shall be used in programs where abortion is a method of family planning" — does not speak directly to the issues of counseling, referral, advocacy, or program integrity. If a statute is "silent or ambiguous with respect to the specific issue, the question for the court is whether the agency's answer is based on a permissible construction of the statute." *Chevron*, 467 U.S., at 842-843. . . .

The Secretary's construction of Title X may not be disturbed as an abuse of discretion if it reflects a plausible construction of the plain language of the statute and does not otherwise conflict with Congress' expressed intent. In determining whether a construction is permissible, "[t]he court need not conclude that the agency construction was the only one it could permissibly have adopted . . . or even the reading the court would have reached if the question initially had arisen in a judicial proceeding." Rather, substantial deference is accorded to the interpretation of the authorizing statute by the agency authorized with administering it.

The broad language of Title X plainly allows the Secretary's construction of the statute. By its own terms, s[ection] 1008 prohibits the use of Title X funds "in programs where abortion is a method of family planning." Title X does not define the term "method of family planning," nor does it enumerate what types of medical and counseling services are entitled to Title X funding. Based on the broad directives provided by Congress in Title X in general and s[ection] 1008 in particular, we are unable to say that the Secretary's construction of the prohibition in s[ection] 1008 to require a ban on counseling, referral, and advocacy within the Title X project, is impermissible. . . .

Petitioners, however, point to language in the statement of purpose in the House Report preceding the passage of Title X stressing the importance of supplying both a full range of family planning information and of developing a comprehensive and coordinated program. Petitioners also rely on the Senate Report, which states:

> "The committee does not view family planning as merely a euphemism for birth control. It is properly a part of comprehensive health care and should consist of much more than the dispensation of contraceptive devices. . . . [A] successful family planning program must contain . . . [m]edical services, including consultation, examination, prescription, and continuing supervision, supplies, instruction, and referral to other medical services as needed."

S. Rep. No. 91–1004, p. 10 (1970). These directly conflicting statements of legislative intent demonstrate amply the inadequacies of the "traditional tools of statutory construction," *Immigration and Naturalization Service v. Cardoza-Fonseca*, 480 U.S., [421] at 446–447, in resolving the issue before us.

When we find, as we do here, that the legislative history is ambiguous and unenlightening on the matters with respect to which the regulations deal, we customarily defer to the expertise of the agency. Petitioners argue, however, that the regulations are entitled to little or no deference because they "reverse a longstanding agency policy that permitted nondirective counseling and referral for abortion," and thus represent a sharp break from the Secretary's prior construction of the statute. Petitioners argue that the agency's prior consistent interpretation of Section 1008 to permit nondirective counseling and to encourage coordination with local and state family planning services is entitled to substantial weight.

This Court has rejected the argument that an agency's interpretation "is not entitled to deference because it represents a sharp break with prior interpretations" of the statute in question. *Chevron*, 467 U.S., at 862. In *Chevron*, we held that a revised interpretation deserves deference because "[a]n initial agency interpretation is not instantly carved in stone" and "the agency, to engage in informed rulemaking, must consider varying interpretations and the wisdom of its policy on a continuing basis." *Id.*, at 863–864. . . . An agency is not required to "establish rules of conduct to last forever," *Motor Vehicle Mfrs. Ass'n of United States v. State Farm Mutual Automobile Ins. Co.*, 463 U.S. 29, 42, . . . but rather "must be given ample latitude to adapt [its] rules and policies to the demands of changing circumstances." *Motor Vehicle Mfrs.*, 463 U.S., at 42.

We find that the Secretary amply justified his change of interpretation with a "reasoned analysis." The Secretary explained that the regulations are a result of his determination, in the wake of the critical reports of the General Accounting Office (GAO) and the Office of the Inspector General (OIG), that prior policy failed to implement properly the statute and that it was necessary to provide "clear and operational guidance to grantees to preserve the distinction between Title X programs and abortion as a method of family planning." He also determined that the new regulations are more in keeping with the original intent of the statute, are justified by client experience under the prior policy, and are supported by a shift in attitude against the "elimination of unborn children by abortion." We believe that these justifications are sufficient to support the Secretary's revised approach. Having concluded that the plain language and legislative history are ambiguous as to Congress' intent in enacting Title X, we must defer to the Secretary's permissible construction of the statute. . . .

III & IV

[The Court went on to reject Petitioners' First and Fifth Amendment claims.]

. . . .

Affirmed.

JUSTICE BLACKMUN, with whom JUSTICE MARSHALL joins, with whom JUSTICE STEVENS joins as to Parts II and III, and with whom JUSTICE O'CONNOR joins as to Part I, dissenting.

[This opinion focused on constitutional law issues.]

JUSTICE STEVENS, dissenting.

In my opinion, the Court has not paid sufficient attention to the language of the controlling statute or to the consistent interpretation accorded the statute by the responsible cabinet officers during four different Presidencies and 18 years. The relevant text of the "Family Planning Services and Population Research Act of 1970" has remained unchanged since its enactment. The preamble to the Act states that it was passed:

> "To promote public health and welfare by expanding, improving, and better coordinating the family planning services and population research activities of the Federal Government, and for other purposes."

The declaration of congressional purposes emphasizes the importance of educating the public about family planning services. Thus, s[ection] 2 of the Act states, in part, that the purpose of the Act is:

> "(1) to assist in making comprehensive voluntary family planning services readily available to all persons desiring such services; . . .
>
> "(5) to develop and make readily available information (including educational materials) on family planning and population growth to all persons desiring such information."

In contrast to the statutory emphasis on making relevant information readily available to the public, the statute contains no suggestion that Congress intended to authorize the suppression or censorship of any information by any Government employee or by any grant recipient. Section 6 of the Act authorizes the provision of federal funds to support the establishment and operation of voluntary family planning projects. The section also empowers the Secretary to promulgate regulations imposing conditions on grant recipients to ensure that "such grants will be effectively utilized for the purposes for which made." S[ection] 300a–4(b). Not a word in the statute, however, authorizes the Secretary to impose any restrictions on the dissemination of truthful information or professional advice by grant recipients.

The word "prohibition" is used only once in the Act. Section 6, which adds to the Public Health Service Act the new Title X, covering the subject of population research and voluntary planning programs, includes the following provision:

PROHIBITION OF ABORTION

> SEC. 1008. None of the funds appropriated under this title shall be used in programs where abortion is a method of family planning.

Read in the context of the entire statute, this prohibition is plainly directed at conduct, rather than the dissemination of information or advice, by potential grant recipients. . . .

The entirely new approach adopted by the Secretary in 1988 was not, in my view, authorized by the statute. The new regulations did not merely reflect a change in a policy determination that the Secretary had been authorized by Congress to make. *Cf. Chevron U.S.A. Inc. v. Natural Resources Defense Counsel, Inc.*, 467 U.S. 837, 865.

Rather, they represented an assumption of policymaking responsibility that Congress had not delegated to the Secretary. *See id.*, at 842–843 ("If the intent of Congress is clear, that is the end of the matter; for the court, as well as the agency, must give effect to the unambiguously expressed intent of Congress"). In a society that abhors censorship and in which policymakers have traditionally placed the highest value on the freedom to communicate, it is unrealistic to conclude that statutory authority to regulate conduct implicitly authorized the Executive to regulate speech.

Because I am convinced that the 1970 Act did not authorize the Secretary to censor the speech of grant recipients or their employees, I would hold the challenged regulations invalid and reverse the judgment of the Court of Appeals. . . .

JUSTICE O'CONNOR, dissenting.

"[W]here an otherwise acceptable construction of a statute would raise serious constitutional problems, the Court will construe the statute to avoid such problems unless such construction is plainly contrary to the intent of Congress." *Edward J. DeBartolo Corp. v. Florida Gulf Coast Building & Construction Trades Council,* 485 U.S. 568, 575, (1988). . . .

This Court acts at the limits of its power when it invalidates a law on constitutional grounds. In recognition of our place in the constitutional scheme, we must act with "great gravity and delicacy" when telling a coordinate branch that its actions are absolutely prohibited absent constitutional amendment. In this case, we need only tell the Secretary that his regulations are not a reasonable interpretation of the statute; we need not tell Congress that it cannot pass such legislation. If we rule solely on statutory grounds, Congress retains the power to force the constitutional question by legislating more explicitly. It may instead choose to do nothing. That decision should be left to Congress; we should not tell Congress what it cannot do before it has chosen to do it. It is enough in this case to conclude that neither the language nor the history of s[ection] 1008 compels the Secretary's interpretation, and that the interpretation raises serious First Amendment concerns. On this basis alone, I would reverse the judgment of the Court of Appeals and invalidate the challenged regulations.

NOTES AND QUESTIONS

8-31. Justice O'Connor's approach would require action by both houses of Congress and the President to reinstate the prohibitions in these regulations. How does this differ from Justice Rehnquist's approach?

8-32. Can Congress correct this interpretation if it concludes that it is not what they intended to occur? How easy or hard do you think this will be?

8-33. Does not the executive branch have the power to veto such a law? Should Congress have been more specific the first time it passed this legislation? Could it have been? In 1992 Congress passed a bill requiring Title X projects to provide their clients with counseling, but it was vetoed by President

Bush. When President Clinton took office, he suspended the 1988 rules and the rules in existence prior to that time were reinstated on an interim basis.

FOOD AND DRUG ADMINISTRATION v. BROWN & WILLIAMSON TOBACCO CORPORATION

Supreme Court of the United States
529 U.S. 120 (2000)

JUSTICE O'CONNOR delivered the opinion of the Court.

This case involves one of the most troubling public health problems facing our Nation today: the thousands of premature deaths that occur each year because of tobacco use. In 1996, the Food and Drug Administration (FDA), after having expressly disavowed any such authority since its inception, asserted jurisdiction to regulate tobacco products. The FDA concluded that nicotine is a "drug" within the meaning of the Food, Drug, and Cosmetic Act (FDCA or Act), and that cigarettes and smokeless tobacco are "combination products" that deliver nicotine to the body. Pursuant to this authority, it promulgated regulations intended to reduce tobacco consumption among children and adolescents. The agency believed that, because most tobacco consumers begin their use before reaching the age of 18, curbing tobacco use by minors could substantially reduce the prevalence of addiction in future generations and thus the incidence of tobacco-related death and disease.

Regardless of how serious the problem an administrative agency seeks to address, however, it may not exercise its authority "in a manner that is inconsistent with the administrative structure that Congress enacted into law." And although agencies are generally entitled to deference in the interpretation of statutes that they administer, a reviewing "court, as well as the agency, must give effect to the unambiguously expressed intent of Congress." *Chevron U.S.A. Inc. v. Natural Resources Defense Council, Inc.*, 467 U.S. 837, 842–843 (1984). In this case, we believe that Congress has clearly precluded the FDA from asserting jurisdiction to regulate tobacco products. Such authority is inconsistent with the intent that Congress has expressed in the FDCA's overall regulatory scheme and in the tobacco-specific legislation that it has enacted subsequent to the FDCA. In light of this clear intent, the FDA's assertion of jurisdiction is impermissible.

I

The FDCA grants the FDA, as the designee of the Secretary of Health and Human Services (HHS), the authority to regulate, among other items, "drugs" and "devices." The Act defines "drug" to include "articles (other than food) intended to affect the structure or any function of the body." 21 U.S.C. § 321(g)(1)(C). It defines "device," in part, as "an instrument, apparatus, implement, machine, contrivance, . . . or other similar or related article, including any component, part, or accessory, which is . . . intended to affect the structure or any function of the body." § 321(h). The Act also grants the FDA the authority to regulate so-called "combination products," which "constitute a combination of a drug, device, or biological product." § 353(g)(1). The FDA has construed this provision as giving it the discretion to regulate combination products as drugs, as devices, or as both.

On August 11, 1995, the FDA published a proposed rule concerning the sale of cigarettes and smokeless tobacco to children and adolescents. The rule, which included several restrictions on the sale, distribution, and advertisement of tobacco products, was designed to reduce the availability and attractiveness of tobacco products to young people. A public comment period followed, during which the FDA received over 700,000 submissions, more than "at any other time in its history on any other subject."

On August 28, 1996, the FDA issued a final rule entitled "Regulations Restricting the Sale and Distribution of Cigarettes and Smokeless Tobacco to Protect Children and Adolescents." The FDA determined that nicotine is a "drug" and that cigarettes and smokeless tobacco are "drug delivery devices," and therefore it had jurisdiction under the FDCA to regulate tobacco products as customarily marketed — that is, without manufacturer claims of therapeutic benefit. First, the FDA found that tobacco products " 'affect the structure or any function of the body' " because nicotine "has significant pharmacological effects." Specifically, nicotine "exerts psychoactive, or mood-altering, effects on the brain" that cause and sustain addiction, have both tranquilizing and stimulating effects, and control weight. Second, the FDA determined that these effects were "intended" under the FDCA because they "are so widely known and foreseeable that [they] may be deemed to have been intended by the manufacturers," consumers use tobacco products "predominantly or nearly exclusively" to obtain these effects, and the statements, research, and actions of manufacturers revealed that they "have 'designed' cigarettes to provide pharmacologically active doses of nicotine to consumers." Finally, the agency concluded that cigarettes and smokeless tobacco are "combination products" because, in addition to containing nicotine, they include device components that deliver a controlled amount of nicotine to the

Having resolved the jurisdictional question, the FDA next explained the policy justifications for its regulations, detailing the deleterious health effects associated with tobacco use. It found that tobacco consumption was "the single leading cause of preventable death in the United States." According to the FDA, "[m]ore than 400,000 people die each year from tobacco-related illnesses, such as cancer, respiratory illnesses, and heart disease." The agency also determined that the only way to reduce the amount of tobacco-related illness and mortality was to reduce the level of addiction, a goal that could be accomplished only by preventing children and adolescents from starting to use tobacco. . . .

Based on these findings, the FDA promulgated regulations concerning tobacco products' promotion, labeling, and accessibility to children and adolescents. The access regulations prohibit the sale of cigarettes or smokeless tobacco to persons younger than 18; require retailers to verify through photo identification the age of all purchasers younger than 27; prohibit the sale of cigarettes in quantities smaller than 20; prohibit the distribution of free samples; and prohibit sales through self-service displays and vending machines except in adult-only locations. The promotion regulations require that any print advertising appear in a black-and-white, text-only format unless the publication in which it appears is read almost exclusively by adults; prohibit outdoor advertising within 1,000 feet of any public playground or school; prohibit the distribution of any promotional items, such as T-shirts or hats, bearing the manufacturer's brand name; and prohibit a manufacturer from sponsoring any athletic, musical, artistic, or other social or cultural event using its brand name. The labeling regulation requires that the statement, "A Nicotine-Delivery Device for Persons 18 or Older," appear on all tobacco product packages.

The FDA promulgated these regulations pursuant to its authority to regulate "restricted devices." *See* 21 U.S.C. § 360j(e). The FDA construed § 353(g)(1) as giving it the discretion to regulate "combination products" using the Act's drug authorities, device authorities, or both, depending on "how the public health goals of the act can be best accomplished." Given the greater flexibility in the FDCA for the regulation of devices, the FDA determined that "the device authorities provide the most appropriate basis for regulating cigarettes and smokeless tobacco." Under 21 U.S.C. § 360j(e), the agency may "require that a device be restricted to sale, distribution, or use . . . upon such other conditions as [the FDA] may prescribe in such regulation, if, because of its potentiality for harmful effect or the collateral measures necessary to its use, [the FDA] determines that there cannot otherwise be reasonable assurance of its safety and effectiveness." The FDA reasoned that its regulations fell within the authority granted by § 360j(e) because they related to the sale or distribution of tobacco products and were necessary for providing a reasonable assurance of safety.

Respondents, a group of tobacco manufacturers, retailers, and advertisers, filed suit in United States District Court for the Middle District of North Carolina challenging the regulations. They moved for summary judgment on the grounds that the FDA lacked jurisdiction to regulate tobacco products as customarily marketed, the regulations exceeded the FDA's authority under 21 U.S.C. § 360j(e), and the advertising restrictions violated the First Amendment. The District Court granted respondents' motion in part and denied it in part. The court held that the FDCA authorizes the FDA to regulate tobacco products as customarily marketed and that the FDA's access and labeling regulations are permissible, but it also found that the agency's advertising and promotion restrictions exceed its authority under § 360j(e). . . .

The Court of Appeals for the Fourth Circuit reversed, holding that Congress has not granted the FDA jurisdiction to regulate tobacco products. . . .

We granted the federal parties' petition for certiorari to determine whether the FDA has authority under the FDCA to regulate tobacco products as customarily marketed.

II

The FDA's assertion of jurisdiction to regulate tobacco products is founded on its conclusions that nicotine is a "drug" and that cigarettes and smokeless tobacco are "drug delivery devices." . . . [T]he FDA's claim to jurisdiction contravenes the clear intent of Congress.

A threshold issue is the appropriate framework for analyzing the FDA's assertion of authority to regulate tobacco products. Because this case involves an administrative agency's construction of a statute that it administers, our analysis is governed by *Chevron U.S.A. Inc. v. Natural Resources Defense Council, Inc.*, 467 U.S. 837 (1984). Under *Chevron*, a reviewing court must first ask "whether Congress has directly spoken to the precise question at issue." If Congress has done so, the inquiry is at an end; the court "must give effect to the unambiguously expressed intent of Congress." But if Congress has not specifically addressed the question, a reviewing court must respect the agency's construction of the statute so long as it is permissible. Such deference is justified because "[t]he responsibilities for assessing the wisdom of such policy choices and resolving the struggle between competing views of the public interest are not judicial ones," *Chevron*, *supra*, at 866, and because of the agency's greater familiarity with the ever-changing facts and circumstances surrounding the subjects regulated.

In determining whether Congress has specifically addressed the question at issue, a reviewing court should not confine itself to examining a particular statutory provision in isolation. The meaning — or ambiguity — of certain words or phrases may only become evident when placed in context. It is a "fundamental canon of statutory construction that the words of a statute must be read in their context and with a view to their place in the overall statutory scheme." A court must therefore interpret the statute "as a symmetrical and coherent regulatory scheme," and "fit, if possible, all parts into an harmonious whole." Similarly, the meaning of one statute may be affected by other Acts, particularly where Congress has spoken subsequently and more specifically to the topic at hand. In addition, we must be guided to a degree by common sense as to the manner in which Congress is likely to delegate a policy decision of such economic and political magnitude to an administrative agency.

With these principles in mind, we find that Congress has directly spoken to the issue here and precluded the FDA's jurisdiction to regulate tobacco products.

A

Viewing the FDCA as a whole, it is evident that one of the Act's core objectives is to ensure that any product regulated by the FDA is "safe" and "effective" for its intended use. . . . Thus, the Act generally requires the FDA to prevent the marketing of any drug or device where the "potential for inflicting death or physical injury is not offset by the possibility of therapeutic benefit." *United States v. Rutherford*, 442 U.S. 544, 556 (1979).

In its rulemaking proceeding, the FDA quite exhaustively documented that "tobacco products are unsafe," "dangerous," and "cause great pain and suffering from illness." It found that the consumption of tobacco products presents "extraordinary health risks," and that "tobacco use is the single leading cause of preventable death in the United States." It stated that "[m]ore than 400,000 people die each year from tobacco-related illnesses, such as cancer, respiratory illnesses, and heart disease, often suffering long and painful deaths," and that "[t]obacco alone kills more people each year in the United States than acquired immunodeficiency syndrome (AIDS), car accidents, alcohol, homicides, illegal drugs, suicides, and fires, combined." Indeed, the FDA characterized smoking as "a pediatric disease," because "one out of every three young people who become regular smokers . . . will die prematurely as a result."

These findings logically imply that, if tobacco products were "devices" under the FDCA, the FDA would be required to remove them from the market. Consider, first, the FDCA's provisions concerning the misbranding of drugs or devices. The Act prohibits "[t]he introduction or delivery for introduction into interstate commerce of any food, drug, device, or cosmetic that is adulterated or misbranded." In light of the FDA's findings, two distinct FDCA provisions would render cigarettes and smokeless tobacco misbranded devices. First, § 352(j) deems a drug or device misbranded "[i]f it is dangerous to health when used in the dosage or manner, or with the frequency or duration prescribed, recommended, or suggested in the labeling thereof." The FDA's findings make clear that tobacco products are "dangerous to health" when used in the manner prescribed. Second, a drug or device is misbranded under the Act "[u]nless its labeling bears . . . adequate directions for use . . . in such manner and form, as are necessary for the protection of users," except where such directions are "not necessary for the protection of the public health." § 352(f)(1). Given the FDA's conclusions concerning the health consequences of tobacco use, there are no directions that could adequately protect consumers. That is, there are no directions that could make tobacco products safe for obtaining their intended effects. Thus, were tobacco products within the FDA's jurisdiction, the Act would deem them misbranded devices that could not be introduced into interstate commerce. Contrary to the dissent's contention, the Act admits no remedial discretion once it is evident that the device is misbranded.

Second, the FDCA requires the FDA to place all devices that it regulates into one of three classifications. The agency relies on a device's classification in determining the degree of control and regulation necessary to ensure that there is "a reasonable assurance of safety and effectiveness." The FDA has yet to classify tobacco products. Instead, the regulations at issue here represent so-called "general controls," which the Act entitles the agency to impose in advance of classification. Although the FDCA prescribes no deadline for device classification, the FDA has stated that it will classify tobacco products "in a future rulemaking" as required by the Act. Given the FDA's findings regarding the health consequences of tobacco use, the agency would have to place cigarettes and smokeless tobacco in Class III because, even after the application of the Act's available controls, they would "presen[t] a potential unreasonable risk of illness or injury." As Class III devices, tobacco products would be subject to the FDCA's premarket approval process. Under these provisions, the FDA would be prohibited from approving an application for premarket approval without "a showing of reasonable assurance that such device is safe under the conditions of use prescribed, recommended, or suggested in the proposed labeling thereof." In view of the FDA's conclusions regarding the health effects of tobacco use, the agency would have no basis for finding any such reasonable assurance of safety. Thus, once the FDA fulfilled its statutory obligation to classify tobacco products, it could not allow them to be marketed.

The FDCA's misbranding and device classification provisions therefore make evident that were the FDA to regulate cigarettes and smokeless tobacco, the Act would require the agency to ban them. In fact, based on these provisions, the FDA itself has previously taken the position that if tobacco products were within its jurisdiction, "they would have to be removed from the market because it would be impossible to prove they were safe for their intended us[e]." Public Health Cigarette Amendments of 1971: Hearings before the Commerce Subcommittee on S. 1454, 92d Cong., 2d Sess., 239 (1972) (hereinafter 1972 Hearings) (statement of FDA Comm'r Charles Edwards). *See also* Cigarette Labeling and Advertising: Hearings before the House Committee on Interstate and Foreign Commerce, 88th Cong., 2d Sess., 18 (1964) (hereinafter 1964 Hearings) (statement of Dept. of Health, Education, and Welfare (HEW) Secretary Anthony Celebrezze that proposed amendments to the FDCA that would have given the FDA jurisdiction over "smoking product[s]" "might well completely outlaw at least cigarettes").

Congress, however, has foreclosed the removal of tobacco products from the market. A provision of the United States Code currently in force states that "[t]he marketing of tobacco constitutes one of the greatest basic industries of the United States with ramifying activities which directly affect interstate and foreign commerce at every point, and stable conditions therein are necessary to the general welfare." 7 U.S.C. § 1311(a). More importantly, Congress has directly addressed the problem of tobacco and health through legislation on six occasions since 1965. *See* Federal Cigarette Labeling and Advertising Act (FCLAA), Pub.L. 89-92, 79 Stat. 282; Public Health Cigarette Smoking Act of 1969, Pub.L. 91-222, 84 Stat. 87; Alcohol and Drug Abuse Amendments of 1983, Pub.L. 98-24, 97 Stat. 175; Comprehensive Smoking Education Act, Pub.L. 98-474, 98 Stat. 2200; Comprehensive Smokeless Tobacco Health Education Act of 1986, Pub.L. 99-252, 100 Stat. 30; Alcohol, Drug Abuse, and Mental Health Administration Reorganization Act, Pub.L. 102-321, § 202, 106 Stat. 394. When Congress enacted these statutes, the adverse health consequences of tobacco use were well known, as were nicotine's pharmacological effects. Nonetheless, Congress stopped well short of ordering a ban. Instead, it has generally regulated the labeling and advertisement of tobacco products, expressly providing that it is the policy of Congress that "commerce and the national economy may be . . . protected to the maximum extent consistent with" consumers "be[ing] adequately informed about any adverse health effects." 15 U.S.C. § 1331. Congress' decisions to regulate labeling and advertising and to adopt the express policy of protecting "commerce and the national economy . . . to the maximum extent" reveal its intent that tobacco products remain on the market. Indeed, the collective premise of these statutes is that cigarettes and smokeless tobacco will continue to be sold in the United States. A ban of tobacco products by the FDA would therefore plainly contradict congressional policy.

The FDA apparently recognized this dilemma and concluded, somewhat ironically, that tobacco products are actually "safe" within the meaning of the FDCA. In promulgating its regulations, the agency conceded that "tobacco products are unsafe, as that term is conventionally understood." Nonetheless, the FDA reasoned that, in determining whether a device is safe under the Act, it must consider "not only the risks presented by a product but also any of the countervailing effects of use of that product, including the consequences of not permitting the product to be marketed." Applying this standard, the FDA found that, because of the high level of addiction among tobacco users, a ban would likely be "dangerous." In particular, current tobacco users could suffer from extreme withdrawal, the health care system and available pharmaceuticals might not be able to meet the treatment demands of those suffering from withdrawal, and a black market offering cigarettes even more dangerous than those currently sold legally would likely develop. The FDA therefore concluded that, "while taking cigarettes and smokeless tobacco off the market could prevent some people from becoming addicted and reduce death and disease for others, the record does not establish that such a ban is the appropriate public health response under the act."

It may well be, as the FDA asserts, that "these factors must be considered when developing a regulatory scheme that achieves the best public health result for these products." But the FDA's judgment that leaving tobacco products on the market "is more effective in achieving public health goals than a ban," is no substitute for the specific safety determinations required by the FDCA's various operative provisions. Several provisions in the Act require the FDA to determine that the *product itself* is safe as used by consumers. That is, the product's probable therapeutic benefits must outweigh its risk of harm. In contrast, the FDA's conception of safety would allow the agency, with respect to each provision of the FDCA that requires the agency to determine a product's "safety" or "dangerousness," to compare the aggregate health effects of alternative administrative actions. This is a qualitatively different inquiry. Thus, although the FDA has concluded that a ban would be "dangerous," it has *not* concluded that tobacco products are "safe" as that term is used throughout the Act.

. . . .

Consequently, the analogy made by the FDA and the dissent to highly toxic drugs used in the treatment of various cancers is unpersuasive. Although "dangerous" in some sense, these drugs are safe within the meaning of the Act because, for certain patients, the therapeutic benefits outweigh the risk of harm. Accordingly, such drugs cannot properly be described as "dangerous to health" under 21 U.S.C. § 352(j). The same is not true for tobacco products. As the FDA has documented in great detail, cigarettes and smokeless tobacco are an unsafe means to obtaining *any* pharmacological effect.

. . . The FDA, consistent with the FDCA, may clearly regulate many "dangerous" products without banning them. Indeed, virtually every drug or device poses dangers under certain conditions. What the FDA may not do is conclude that a drug or device cannot be used safely for any therapeutic purpose and yet, at the same time, allow that product to remain on the market. Such regulation is incompatible with the FDCA's core objective of ensuring that every drug or device is safe and effective.

Considering the FDCA as a whole, it is clear that Congress intended to exclude tobacco products from the FDA's jurisdiction. A fundamental precept of the FDCA is that any product regulated by the FDA — but not banned — must be safe for its intended use. Various provisions of the Act make clear that this refers to the safety of using the product to obtain its intended effects, not the public health ramifications of alternative administrative actions by the FDA. That is, the FDA must determine that there is a reasonable assurance that the product's therapeutic benefits outweigh the risk of harm to the consumer. According to this standard, the FDA has concluded that, although tobacco products might be effective in delivering certain pharmacological effects, they are "unsafe" and "dangerous" when used for these purposes. Consequently, if tobacco products were within the FDA's jurisdiction, the Act would require the FDA to remove them from the market entirely. But a ban would contradict Congress' clear intent as expressed in its more recent, tobacco-specific legislation. The inescapable conclusion is that there is no room for tobacco products within the FDCA's regulatory scheme. If they cannot be used safely for any therapeutic purpose, and yet they cannot be banned, they simply do not fit.

B

In determining whether Congress has spoken directly to the FDA's authority to regulate tobacco, we must also consider in greater detail the tobacco-specific legislation that Congress has enacted over the past 35 years. At the time a statute is enacted, it may have a range of plausible meanings. Over time, however, subsequent acts can shape or focus those meanings. The "classic judicial task of reconciling many laws enacted over time, and getting them to 'make sense' in combination, necessarily assumes that the implications of a statute may be altered by the implications of a later statute." This is particularly so where the scope of the earlier statute is broad but the subsequent statutes more specifically address the topic at hand. . . .

Congress has enacted six separate pieces of legislation since 1965 addressing the problem of tobacco use and human health. . . . In adopting each statute, Congress has acted against the backdrop of the FDA's consistent and repeated statements that it lacked authority under the FDCA to regulate tobacco absent claims of therapeutic benefit by the manufacturer. In fact, on several occasions over this period, and after the health consequences of tobacco use and nicotine's pharmacological effects had become well known, Congress considered and rejected bills that would have granted the FDA such jurisdiction. Under these circumstances, it is evident that Congress' tobacco-specific statutes have effectively ratified the FDA's long-held position that it lacks jurisdiction under the FDCA to regulate tobacco products. Congress has created a distinct regulatory scheme to address the problem of tobacco and health, and that scheme, as presently constructed, precludes any role for the FDA. . . .

Although the dissent takes issue with our discussion of the FDA's change in position, our conclusion does not rely on the fact that the FDA's assertion of jurisdiction represents a sharp break with its prior interpretation of the FDCA. Certainly, an agency's initial interpretation of a statute that it is charged with administering is not "carved in stone." *Chevron*, 467 U.S., at 863. As we recognized in *Motor Vehicle Mfrs. Assn. of United States, Inc. v. State*

Farm Mut. Automobile Ins. Co., 463 U.S. 29 (1983), agencies "must be given ample latitude to 'adapt their rules and policies to the demands of changing circumstances.'" The consistency of the FDA's prior position is significant in this case for a different reason: It provides important context to Congress' enactment of its tobacco-specific legislation. When the FDA repeatedly informed Congress that the FDCA does not grant it the authority to regulate tobacco products, its statements were consistent with the agency's unwavering position since its inception, and with the position that its predecessor agency had first taken in 1914. Although not crucial, the consistency of the FDA's prior position bolsters the conclusion that when Congress created a distinct regulatory scheme addressing the subject of tobacco and health, it understood that the FDA is without jurisdiction to regulate tobacco products and ratified that position.

The dissent also argues that the proper inference to be drawn from Congress' tobacco-specific legislation is "critically ambivalent." We disagree. In that series of statutes, Congress crafted a specific legislative response to the problem of tobacco and health, and it did so with the understanding, based on repeated assertions by the FDA, that the agency has no authority under the FDCA to regulate tobacco products. Moreover, Congress expressly preempted any other regulation of the labeling of tobacco products concerning their health consequences, even though the oversight of labeling is central to the FDCA's regulatory scheme. And in addressing the subject, Congress consistently evidenced its intent to preclude any federal agency from exercising significant policymaking authority in the area. Under these circumstances, we believe the appropriate inference that Congress intended to ratify the FDA's prior position that it lacks jurisdiction — is unmistakable. . . .

C

Finally, our inquiry into whether Congress has directly spoken to the precise question at issue is shaped, at least in some measure, by the nature of the question presented. Deference under *Chevron* to an agency's construction of a statute that it administers is premised on the theory that a statute's ambiguity constitutes an implicit delegation from Congress to the agency to fill in the statutory gaps. See *Chevron, supra*, at 844. In extraordinary cases, however, there may be reason to hesitate before concluding that Congress has intended such an implicit delegation. *Cf.* Breyer, *Judicial Review of Questions of Law and Policy*, 38 ADMIN. L. REV. 363, 370 (1986) ("A court may also ask whether the legal question is an important one. Congress is more likely to have focused upon, and answered, major questions, while leaving interstitial matters to answer themselves in the course of the statute's daily administration").

This is hardly an ordinary case. Contrary to its representations to Congress since 1914, the FDA has now asserted jurisdiction to regulate an industry constituting a significant portion of the American economy. In fact, the FDA contends that, were it to determine that tobacco products provide no "reasonable assurance of safety," it would have the authority to ban cigarettes and smokeless tobacco entirely. Owing to its unique place in American history and society, tobacco has its own unique political history. Congress, for better or for worse, has created a distinct regulatory scheme for tobacco products, squarely rejected proposals to give the FDA jurisdiction over tobacco, and repeatedly acted to preclude any agency from exercising significant policymaking authority in the area. Given this history and the breadth of the authority that the FDA has asserted, we are obliged to defer not to the agency's expansive construction of the statute, but to Congress' consistent judgment to deny the FDA this power.

. . . .

By no means do we question the seriousness of the problem that the FDA has sought to address. The agency has amply demonstrated that tobacco use, particularly among children and adolescents, poses perhaps the single most significant threat to public health in the United States. Nonetheless, no matter how "important, conspicuous, and controversial" the issue, and regardless of how likely the public is to hold the Executive Branch politically accountable, *post*, at 1331, an administrative agency's power to regulate in the public interest must always be grounded in a valid grant of authority from Congress. And " '[i]n our anxiety to effectuate the congressional purpose of protecting the public, we must take care not to extend the scope of the statute beyond the point where Congress indicated it would stop.' " Reading the FDCA as a whole, as well as in conjunction with Congress' subsequent tobacco-specific legislation, it is plain that Congress has not given the FDA the authority that it seeks to exercise here. . . .

JUSTICE BREYER, with whom JUSTICE STEVENS, JUSTICE SOUTER, and JUSTICE GINSBURG join, dissenting.

The Food and Drug Administration (FDA) has the authority to regulate "articles (other than food) intended to affect the structure or any function of the body . . . ." Federal Food, Drug, and Cosmetic Act (FDCA), 21 U.S.C. § 321(g)(1)(C). Unlike the majority, I believe that tobacco products fit within this statutory language.

In its own interpretation, the majority nowhere denies the following two salient points. First, tobacco products (including cigarettes) fall within the scope of this statutory definition, read literally. . . .

Second, the statute's basic purpose — the protection of public health — supports the inclusion of cigarettes within its scope. . . .

Despite the FDCA's literal language and general purpose (both of which support the FDA's finding that cigarettes come within its statutory authority), the majority nonetheless reads the statute as *excluding* tobacco products for two basic reasons:

(1) the FDCA does not "fit" the case of tobacco because the statute requires the FDA to prohibit dangerous drugs or devices (like cigarettes) outright, and the agency concedes that simply banning the sale of cigarettes is not a proper remedy, and

(2) Congress has enacted other statutes, which, when viewed in light of the FDA's long history of denying tobacco-related jurisdiction and considered together with Congress' failure explicitly to grant the agency tobacco-specific authority, demonstrate that Congress did not intend for the FDA to exercise jurisdiction over tobacco.

In my view, neither of these propositions is valid. Rather, the FDCA does not significantly limit the FDA's remedial alternatives. And the later statutes do not tell the FDA it cannot exercise jurisdiction, but simply leave FDA jurisdictional law where Congress found it.

. . . [I] believe that the most important indicia of statutory meaning — language and purpose — along with the FDCA's legislative history (described briefly in Part I) are sufficient to establish that the FDA has authority to regulate tobacco. The statute-specific arguments against jurisdiction that the tobacco companies and the majority rely upon (discussed in Part II) are based on erroneous assumptions and, thus, do not defeat the jurisdiction-supporting thrust of the FDCA's language and purpose. The inferences that the majority draws from later legislative history are not persuasive, since (as I point out in Part III) one can just as easily infer from the later laws that Congress did not intend to affect the FDA's tobacco-related authority at all. And the fact that the FDA changed its mind about the scope of its own jurisdiction is legally insignificant because (as Part IV establishes) the agency's reasons for changing course are fully justified. Finally, as I explain in Part V, the degree of accountability that likely will attach to the FDA's action in this case should alleviate any concern that Congress, rather than an administrative agency, ought to make this important regulatory decision. . . .

C

The majority nonetheless reaches the "inescapable conclusion" that the language and structure of the FDCA as a whole "simply do not fit" the kind of public health problem that tobacco creates. That is because, in the majority's view, the FDCA requires the FDA to ban outright "dangerous" drugs or devices (such as cigarettes); yet, the FDA concedes that an immediate and total cigarette-sale ban is inappropriate.

This argument is curious because it leads with similarly "inescapable" force to precisely the opposite conclusion, namely, that the FDA *does* have jurisdiction but that it must ban cigarettes. More importantly, the argument fails to take into account the fact that a statute interpreted as requiring the FDA to pick a more dangerous over a less dangerous remedy would be a perverse statute, *causing*, rather than preventing, unnecessary harm whenever a total ban is likely the more dangerous response. And one can at least imagine such circumstances.

Suppose, for example, that a commonly used, mildly addictive sleeping pill (or, say, a kind of popular contact lens), plainly within the FDA's jurisdiction, turned out to pose serious health risks for certain consumers. Suppose further that many of those addicted consumers would ignore an immediate total ban, turning to a potentially more dangerous black-market substitute, while a less draconian remedy (say, adequate notice) would wean them gradually away to a safer product. Would the FDCA still *force* the FDA to impose the more dangerous remedy? For the following reasons, I think not.

First, the statute's language does not restrict the FDA's remedial powers in this way. The FDCA permits the FDA to regulate a "combination product" — *i.e.*, a "device" (such as a cigarette) that contains a "drug" (such as nicotine)

— under its "device" provisions. 21 U.S.C. § 353(g)(1). And the FDCA's "device" provisions explicitly grant the FDA wide remedial discretion. . . . The Court points to other statutory subsections which it believes require the FDA to ban a drug or device entirely, even where an outright ban risks more harm than other regulatory responses. But the cited provisions do no such thing. It is true, as the majority contends, that "the FDCA requires the FDA to place all devices" in "one of three classifications" and that Class III devices require "premarket approval." But it is not the case that the FDA *must* place cigarettes in Class III because tobacco itself "presents a potential unreasonable risk of illness or injury." 21 U.S.C. § 360c(a)(1)(C). In fact, Class III applies *only* where *regulation* cannot otherwise "provide reasonable assurance of . . . safety." §§ 360c(a)(1)(A), (B) (placing a device in Class I or Class II when regulation can provide that assurance). Thus, the statute plainly allows the FDA to consider the relative, overall "safety" of a device in light of its regulatory alternatives, and where the FDA has chosen the least dangerous path, *i.e.*, the safest path, then it can — and does — provide a "reasonable assurance" of "safety" within the meaning of the statute. A good football helmet provides a reasonable assurance of safety for the player even if the sport itself is still dangerous. And the safest regulatory choice by definition offers a "reasonable" assurance of safety in a world where the other alternatives are yet more dangerous. . . .

Noting that the FDCA requires banning a "misbranded" drug, the majority also points to 21 U.S.C. § 352(j), which deems a drug or device "misbranded" if "it is dangerous to health when used" as "prescribed, recommended, or suggested in the labeling." In addition, the majority mentions § 352(f)(1), which calls a drug or device "misbranded" unless "its labeling bears . . . adequate directions for use" as "are necessary for the protection of users." But this "misbranding" language is not determinative, for it permits the FDA to conclude that a drug or device is *not* "dangerous to health" and that it *does* have "adequate" directions *when regulated so as to render it as harmless as possible.* And surely the agency can determine that a substance is comparatively "safe" (*not* "dangerous") whenever it would be *less* dangerous to make the product available (subject to regulatory requirements) than suddenly to withdraw it from the market. Any other interpretation risks substantial harm of the sort that my sleeping pill example illustrates. *See supra*, at 1322 and this page. And nothing in the statute prevents the agency from adopting a view of "safety" that would avoid such harm. Indeed, the FDA already seems to have taken this position when permitting distribution of toxic drugs, such as poisons used for chemotherapy, that are dangerous for the user but are not deemed "dangerous to health" in the relevant sense. . . .

The statute's language, then, permits the agency to choose remedies consistent with its basic purpose — the overall protection of public health.

The second reason the FDCA does not require the FDA to select the more dangerous remedy is that, despite the majority's assertions to the contrary, the statute does not distinguish among the kinds of health effects that the agency may take into account when assessing safety. The Court insists that the statute only permits the agency to take into account the health risks and benefits of the "*product itself*" as used by individual consumers, *ante*, at 1304, and, thus, that the FDA is prohibited from considering that a ban on smoking would lead many smokers to suffer severe withdrawal symptoms or to buy possibly stronger, more dangerous, black market cigarettes — considerations that the majority calls "the aggregate health effects of alternative administrative actions." But the FDCA expressly *permits* the FDA to take account of comparative safety in precisely this manner. . . .

I concede that, as a matter of logic, one could consider the FDA's "safety" evaluation to be different from its choice of remedies. But to read the statute to forbid the agency from taking account of the realities of consumer behavior either in assessing safety or in choosing a remedy could increase the risks of harm — doubling the risk of death to each "individual user" in my example above. Why would Congress insist that the FDA ignore such realities, even if the consequent harm would occur only unusually, say, where the FDA evaluates a product (a sleeping pill; a cigarette; a contact lens) that is already on the market, potentially habit forming, or popular? I can find no satisfactory answer to this question. And that, I imagine, is why the statute itself says nothing about any of the distinctions that the Court has tried to draw. . . .

In my view, where linguistically permissible, we should interpret the FDCA in light of Congress' overall desire to protect health. That purpose requires a flexible interpretation that both permits the FDA to take into account the realities of human behavior and allows it, in appropriate cases, to choose from its arsenal of statutory remedies. A statute so interpreted easily "fit[s]" this, and other, drug — and device-related health problems.

III

In the majority's view, laws enacted since 1965 require us to deny jurisdiction, whatever the FDCA might mean in their absence. But why? Do those laws contain language barring FDA jurisdiction? The majority must concede that they do not. Do they contain provisions that are inconsistent with the FDA's exercise of jurisdiction? With one exception, . . . the majority points to no such provision. Do they somehow repeal the principles of law . . . that otherwise would lead to the conclusion that the FDA has jurisdiction in this area? The companies themselves deny making any such claim. Perhaps the later laws "shape" and "focus" what the 1938 Congress meant a generation earlier. *Ante*, at 1306. But this Court has warned against using the views of a later Congress to construe a statute enacted many years before. And, while the majority suggests that the subsequent history "control[s] our construction" of the FDCA, this Court expressly has held that such subsequent views are not "controlling." . . .

Regardless, the later statutes do not support the majority's conclusion. That is because, whatever individual Members of Congress after 1964 may have assumed about the FDA's jurisdiction, the laws they enacted did not embody any such "no jurisdiction" assumption. And one cannot automatically *infer* an antijurisdiction intent, as the majority does, for the later statutes are both (and similarly) consistent with quite a different congressional desire, namely, the intent to proceed without interfering with whatever authority the FDA otherwise may have possessed. . . .

IV

I now turn to the final historical fact that the majority views as a factor in its interpretation of the subsequent legislative history: the FDA's former denials of its tobacco-related authority.

Until the early 1990's, the FDA expressly maintained that the 1938 statute did not give it the power that it now seeks to assert. It then changed its mind. The majority agrees with me that the FDA's change of positions does not make a significant legal difference. Nevertheless, it labels those denials "important context" for drawing an inference about Congress' intent. In my view, the FDA's change of policy, like the subsequent statutes themselves, does nothing to advance the majority's position. . . .

What changed? For one thing, the FDA obtained evidence sufficient to prove the necessary "intent" despite the absence of specific "claims." This evidence, which first became available in the early 1990's, permitted the agency to demonstrate that the tobacco companies *knew* nicotine achieved appetite-suppressing, mood-stabilizing, and habituating effects through chemical (not psychological) means, even at a time when the companies were publicly denying such knowledge.

Moreover, scientific evidence of adverse health effects mounted, until, in the late 1980's, a consensus on the seriousness of the matter became firm. . . .

Finally, administration policy changed. Earlier administrations may have hesitated to assert jurisdiction for the reasons prior Commissioners expressed. Commissioners of the current administration simply took a different regulatory attitude.

Nothing in the law prevents the FDA from changing its policy for such reasons. By the mid-1990's, the evidence needed to prove objective intent — even without an express claim — had been found. The emerging scientific consensus about tobacco's adverse, chemically induced, health effects may have convinced the agency that it should spend its resources on this important regulatory effort. As for the change of administrations, I agree with then — JUSTICE REHNQUIST's statement in a different case, where he wrote:

> "The agency's changed view . . . seems to be related to the election of a new President of a different political party. It is readily apparent that the responsible members of one administration may consider public resistance and uncertainties to be more important than do their counterparts in a previous administration. A change in administration brought about by the people casting their votes is a perfectly reasonable basis for an executive agency's reappraisal of the costs and benefits of its programs and regulations. As long as the agency remains within the bounds established by Congress, it is entitled to assess administrative records and evaluate priorities in light of the philosophy of the administration." *Motor Vehicle Mfrs. Assn. of United States, Inc. v. State Farm Mut. Automobile Ins. Co.*, 463 U.S. 29, 59 (1983) (concurring in part and dissenting in part).

V

One might nonetheless claim that, even if my interpretation of the FDCA and later statutes gets the words right, it lacks a sense of their "music." *See*

Helvering v. Gregory, 69 F.2d 809, 810-811 (C.A.2 1934) (L. Hand, J.) ("[T]he meaning of a [statute] may be more than that of the separate words, as a melody is more than the notes . . ."). Such a claim might rest on either of two grounds.

First, one might claim that, despite the FDA's legal right to change its mind, its original statements played a critical part in the enactment of the later statutes and now should play a critical part in their interpretation. But the FDA's traditional view was largely premised on a perceived inability to prove the necessary statutory "intent" requirement. *See, e.g.*, FDA Enforcement Letter 240 ("The statutory basis for the exclusion of tobacco products from FDA's jurisdiction is the fact that tobacco marketed for chewing or smoking without accompanying therapeutic claims, does not meet the definitions . . . for food, drug, device or cosmetic"). The statement, "we cannot assert jurisdiction over substance X unless it is treated as a food," would not bar jurisdiction if the agency later establishes that substance X is, and is intended to be, eaten. The FDA's denials of tobacco-related authority sufficiently resemble this kind of statement that they should not make the critical interpretive difference.

Second, one might claim that courts, when interpreting statutes, should assume in close cases that a decision with "enormous social consequences," should be made by democratically elected Members of Congress rather than by unelected agency administrators. . . . If there is such a background canon of interpretation, however, I do not believe it controls the outcome here.

Insofar as the decision to regulate tobacco reflects the policy of an administration, it is a decision for which that administration, and those politically elected officials who support it, must (and will) take responsibility. And the very importance of the decision taken here, as well as its attendant publicity, means that the public is likely to be aware of it and to hold those officials politically accountable. Presidents, just like Members of Congress, are elected by the public. Indeed, the President and Vice President are the *only* public officials whom the entire Nation elects. I do not believe that an administrative agency decision of this magnitude — one that is important, conspicuous, and controversial — can escape the kind of public scrutiny that is essential in any democracy. And such a review will take place whether it is the Congress or the Executive Branch that makes the relevant decision. . . .

The upshot is that the Court today holds that a regulatory statute aimed at unsafe drugs and devices does not authorize regulation of a drug (nicotine) and a device (a cigarette) that the Court itself finds unsafe. Far more than most, this particular drug and device risks the life-threatening harms that administrative regulation seeks to rectify. The majority's conclusion is counterintuitive. And, for the reasons set forth, I believe that the law does not require it.

Consequently, I dissent.

NOTES AND QUESTIONS

8-34. How clear is clear? What is the precise question at issue? How closely must Congress address that issue? What tools of statutory construction does the Court employ to determine whether the FDA has jurisdiction to regulate tobacco?

8-35. What impact would the dissent's position have on the FDA's jurisdiction? Is the power to regulate tobacco too controversial to be achieved by agency interpretation alone? What is the significance of the majority's appeal to prior legislative action outside of the statute being considered in this proceeding? Is it legitimate, given the "spirit" of *Chevron*?

§ 8.05 Degrees of Deference

Chevron suggests an approach to deference that is all-inclusive. Yet, before *Chevron* was issued there were a variety of deference doctrines established by the courts, many of which had to do with *the form* in which agencies exercised their power. Consider the following case. Are there reasons other than those stated in *Chevron* for Courts to defer or intervene? What might some of those other reasons be? As we shall see, *infra*, *Skidmore* remains good law in the post-*Chevron* era.

SKIDMORE v. SWIFT

United States Supreme Court
323 U.S. 134 (1944)

Mr. Justice Jackson delivered the opinion of the Court.

Seven employees of the Swift and Company packing plant at Fort Worth, Texas, brought an action under the Fair Labor Standards Act to recover overtime, liquidated damages, and attorneys' fees, totalling approximately $77,000. . . .

It is not denied that the daytime employment of these persons was working time within the Act. . . .

Under their oral agreement of employment, however, petitioners undertook to stay in the fire hall on the Company premises, or within hailing distance, three and a half to four nights a week. This involved no task except to answer alarms, either because of fire or because the sprinkler was set off for some other reason. No fires occurred during the period in issue, the alarms were rare, and the time required for their answer rarely exceeded an hour. For each alarm answered the employees were paid in addition to their fixed compensation an agreed amount, fifty cents at first, and later sixty-four cents. The Company provided a brick fire hall equipped with steam heat and air-conditioned rooms. It provided sleeping quarters, a pool table, a domino table, and a radio. The men used their time in sleep or amusement as they saw fit, except that they were required to stay in or close by the fire hall and be ready to respond to alarms. It is stipulated that "they agreed to remain in the fire hall and stay in it or within hailing distance, subject to call, in event of fire or other casualty, but were not required to perform any specific tasks during these periods of time, except in answering alarms." The trial court found the evidentiary facts as stipulated; it made no findings of fact as such as to whether under the arrangement of the parties and the circumstances of this case, which in some respects differ from those of the *Armour* case, the fire-hall duty or any part thereof constituted working time. It said, however, as a "conclusion of law" that "the time plaintiffs spent in the fire hall subject to call to answer fire alarms does not constitute hours worked, for which overtime compensation is due them under the Fair Labor Standards Act, as interpreted by the Administrator and the Courts," and in its opinion observed, "of course we know pursuing such pleasurable occupations or performing such personal chores, does not constitute work." The Circuit Court of Appeals affirmed.

For reasons set forth in the *Armour* case decided herewith we hold that no principle of law found either in the statute or in Court decisions precludes waiting time from also being working time. We have not attempted to, and we cannot, lay down a legal formula to resolve cases so varied in their facts as are the many situations in which employment involves waiting time. Whether in a concrete case such time falls within or without the Act is a question of fact to be resolved by appropriate findings of the trial court. *Walling v. Jacksonville Paper Co.,* 317 U.S. 564, 572. This involves scrutiny and construction of the agreements between the particular parties, appraisal of their practical construction of the working agreement by conduct, consideration of the nature of the service, and its relation to the waiting time, and all of the surrounding circumstances. Facts may show that the employee was engaged to wait, or they may show that he waited to be engaged. His compensation may cover both waiting and task, or only performance of the task itself. Living quarters may in some situations be furnished as a facility of the task and in another as a part of its compensation. The law does not impose an arrangement upon the parties. It imposes upon the courts the task of finding what the arrangement was. . . .

Congress did not utilize the services of an administrative agency to find facts and to determine in the first instance whether particular cases fall within or without the Act. Instead, it put this responsibility on the courts. *Kirschbaum Co. v. Walling,* 316 U.S. 517, 523. But it did create the office of Administrator, impose upon him a variety of duties, endow him with powers to inform himself of conditions in industries and employments subject to the Act, and put on him the duties of bringing injunction actions to restrain violations. Pursuit of his duties has accumulated a considerable experience in the problems of ascertaining working time in employments involving periods of inactivity and a knowledge of the customs prevailing in reference to their solution. From these he is obliged to reach conclusions as to conduct without the law, so that he should seek injunctions to stop it, and that within the law, so that he has no call to interfere. He has set forth his views of the application of the Act under different circumstances in an interpretative bulletin and in informal rulings. They provide a practical guide to employers and employees as to how the office representing the public interest in its enforcement will seek to apply it. Wage and Hour Division, Interpretative Bulletin No. 13. . . .

There is no statutory provision as to what, if any, deference courts should pay to the Administrator's conclusions. And, while we have given them notice, we have had no occasion to try to prescribe their influence. The rulings of this Administrator are not reached as a result of hearing adversary proceedings in which he finds facts from evidence and reaches conclusions of law from findings of fact. They are not, of course, conclusive, even in the cases with which they directly deal, much less in those to which they apply only by analogy. They do not constitute an interpretation of the Act or a standard for judging factual situations which binds a district court's processes, as an authoritative pronouncement of a higher court might do. But the Administrator's policies are made in pursuance of official duty, based upon more specialized experience and broader investigations and information than is likely to come to a judge in a particular case. They do determine the policy which will guide applications for enforcement by injunction on behalf of the Government. Good administration of the Act and good judicial administration alike require that the standards of public enforcement and those for determining private rights shall be at variance only where justified by very good reasons. The fact that the Administrator's policies and standards are not reached by trial in adversary form does not mean that they are not entitled to respect. This Court has long given considerable and in some cases decisive weight to Treasury Decisions and to interpretative regulations of the Treasury and of other bodies that were not of adversary origin.

We consider that the rulings, interpretations and opinions of the Administrator under this Act, while not controlling upon the courts by reason of their authority, do constitute a body of experience and informed judgment to which courts and litigants may properly resort for guidance. The weight of such a judgment in a particular case will depend upon the thoroughness evident in its consideration, the validity of its reasoning, its consistency with earlier and later pronouncements, and all those factors which give it power to persuade, if lacking power to control.

The courts in the *Armour* case weighed the evidence in the particular case in the light of the Administrator's rulings and reached a result consistent therewith. The evidence in this case in some respects, such as the understanding as to separate compensation for answering alarms, is different. Each case must stand on its own facts. But in this case, although the District Court referred to the Administrator's Bulletin, its evaluation and inquiry were apparently restricted by its notion that waiting time may not be work, an understanding of the law which we hold to be erroneous. Accordingly, the judgment is reversed and the cause remanded for further proceedings consistent herewith.

Reversed.

NOTES AND QUESTIONS

8-36. Is this case consistent with *Chevron*? Why doesn't the Court feel compelled to defer to the agency in this case?

8-37. Does the Court nevertheless defer? Why? What guidelines does the Court suggest for deciding when to defer and when not to defer to agency interpretations such as these?

8-38. How significant is the format that the agency chooses to use when it makes or interprets the law? Consider the following:

UNITED STATES v. MEAD CORPORATION

Supreme Court of the United States
533 U.S. 218 (2001)

SOUTER, J., delivered the opinion of the Court, in which REHNQUIST, C.J., and STEVENS, O'CONNOR, KENNEDY, THOMAS, GINSBURG, and BREYER, JJ., joined. SCALIA, J., filed a dissenting opinion.

JUSTICE SOUTER delivered the opinion of the Court.

The question is whether a tariff classification ruling by the United States Customs Service deserves judicial deference. The Federal Circuit rejected Customs's invocation of *Chevron U.S.A. Inc. v. Natural Resources Defense Council, Inc.*, 467 U.S. 837 (1984), in support of such a ruling, to which it gave no deference. We agree that a tariff classification has no claim to judicial deference under *Chevron*, there being no indication that Congress intended such a ruling to carry the force of law, but we hold that under *Skidmore v. Swift & Co.*, 323 U.S. 134 (1944), the ruling is eligible to claim respect according to its persuasiveness.

I

A

Imports are taxed under the Harmonized Tariff Schedule of the United States (HTSUS), 19 U.S.C. § 1202. Title 19 U.S.C. § 1500(b) provides that Customs "shall, under rules and regulations prescribed by the Secretary [of the Treasury,] . . . fix the final classification and rate of duty applicable to . . . merchandise" under the HTSUS. Section 1502(a) provides that "[t]he Secretary of the Treasury shall establish and promulgate such rules and regulations not inconsistent with the law (including regulations establishing procedures for the issuance of binding rulings prior to the entry of the merchandise concerned), and may disseminate such information as may be necessary to secure a just, impartial, and uniform appraisement of imported merchandise and the classification and assessment of duties thereon at the various ports of entry."[1]

The Secretary provides for tariff rulings before the entry of goods by regulations authorizing "ruling letters" setting tariff classifications for particular imports. 19 CFR § 177.8 (2000). A ruling letter

"represents the official position of the Customs Service with respect to the particular transaction or issue described therein and is binding on all Customs Service personnel in accordance with the provisions of this section until modified or revoked. In the absence of a change of practice or other modification or revocation which affects the principle of the ruling set forth in the ruling letter, that principle may be cited as authority in the disposition of transactions involving the same circumstances." § 177.9(a).

After the transaction that gives it birth, a ruling letter is to "be applied only with respect to transactions involving articles identical to the sample submitted with the ruling request or to articles whose description is identical to the description set forth in the ruling letter." § 177.9(b)(2). As a general matter, such a letter is "subject to modification or revocation without notice to any person, except the person to whom the letter was addressed," § 177.9(c), and the regulations consequently provide that "no other person should rely on the ruling letter or assume that the principles of that ruling will be applied in connection with any transaction other than the one described in the letter," *ibid.* Since ruling letters respond to transactions of the moment, they are not subject to notice and comment before being issued, may be published but need only be made "available for public inspection," 19 U.S.C. § 1625(a), and, at the time this action arose, could be modified without notice and comment under most circumstances, 19 CFR § 177.10(c) (2000). . . .

Any of the 46 port-of-entry Customs offices may issue ruling letters, and so may the Customs Headquarters Office. . . . Most ruling letters contain little or no reasoning, but simply describe goods and state the appropriate category and tariff. A few letters, like the Headquarters ruling at issue here, set out a rationale in some detail.

B

Respondent, the Mead Corporation, imports "day planners," three-ring binders with pages having room for notes of daily schedules and phone numbers and addresses, together with a calendar and suchlike. The tariff

---

[1] The statutory term "ruling" is defined by regulation as "a written statement . . . that interprets and applies the provisions of the Customs and related laws to a specific set of facts." 19 CFR § 177.1(d)(1) (2000).

schedule on point falls under the HTSUS heading for "[r]egisters, account books, notebooks, order books, receipt books, letter pads, memorandum pads, diaries and similar articles," HTSUS subheading 4820.10, which comprises two subcategories. Items in the first, "[d]iaries, notebooks and address books, bound; memorandum pads, letter pads and similar articles," were subject to a tariff of 4.0% at the time in controversy. Objects in the second, covering "[o]ther" items, were free of duty.

Between 1989 and 1993, Customs repeatedly treated day planners under the "other" HTSUS subheading. In January 1993, however, Customs changed its position, and issued a Headquarters ruling letter classifying Mead's day planners as "Diaries . . ., bound" subject to tariff under subheading 4820.10.20. That letter was short on explanation, but after Mead's protest, Customs Headquarters issued a new letter, carefully reasoned but never published, reaching the same conclusion. This letter considered two definitions of "diary" from the Oxford English Dictionary, the first covering a daily journal of the past day's events, the second a book including " 'printed dates for daily memoranda and jottings; also . . . calendars . . . .' " Customs concluded that "diary" was not confined to the first, in part because the broader definition reflects commercial usage and hence the "commercial identity of these items in the marketplace." As for the definition of "bound," Customs concluded that HTSUS was not referring to "bookbinding," but to a less exact sort of fastening described in the Harmonized Commodity Description and Coding System Explanatory Notes to Heading 4820, which spoke of binding by " 'reinforcements or fittings of metal, plastics, etc.' "

Customs rejected Mead's further protest of the second Headquarters ruling letter, and Mead filed suit in the Court of International Trade (CIT). The CIT granted the Government's motion for summary judgment, adopting Customs's reasoning without saying anything about deference. 17 F.Supp.2d 1004 (1998).

Mead then went to the United States Court of Appeals for the Federal Circuit. . . .

The Federal Circuit . . . reversed the CIT and held that Customs classification rulings should not get *Chevron* deference . . . . Rulings are not preceded by notice and comment as under the Administrative Procedure Act (APA), 5 U.S.C. § 553, they "do not carry the force of law and are not, like regulations, intended to clarify the rights and obligations of importers beyond the specific case under review." 185 F.3d, at 1307. The appeals court thought classification rulings had a weaker *Chevron* claim even than Internal Revenue Service interpretive rulings, to which that court gives no deference; unlike rulings by the IRS, Customs rulings issue from many locations and need not be published. 185 F.3d, at 1307–1308.

The Court of Appeals accordingly gave no deference at all to the ruling classifying the Mead day planners and rejected the agency's reasoning as to both "diary" and "bound." It thought that planners were not diaries because they had no space for "relatively extensive notations about events, observations, feelings, or thoughts" in the past. And it concluded that diaries "bound" in subheading 4810.10.20 presupposed "unbound" diaries, such that treating ring-fastened diaries as "bound" would leave the "unbound diary" an empty category.

We granted certiorari in order to consider the limits of *Chevron* deference owed to administrative practice in applying a statute. We hold that administrative implementation of a particular statutory provision qualifies for *Chevron* deference when it appears that Congress delegated authority to the agency generally to make rules carrying the force of law, and that the agency interpretation claiming deference was promulgated in the exercise of that authority. Delegation of such authority may be shown in a variety of ways, as by an agency's power to engage in adjudication or notice-and-comment rulemaking, or by some other indication of a comparable congressional intent. The Customs ruling at issue here fails to qualify, although the possibility that it deserves some deference under *Skidmore* leads us to vacate and remand.

II

A

When Congress has "explicitly left a gap for an agency to fill, there is an express delegation of authority to the agency to elucidate a specific provision of the statute by regulation," *Chevron*, 467 U.S., at 843–44, and any ensuing regulation is binding in the courts unless procedurally defective, arbitrary or capricious in substance, or manifestly contrary to the statute. APA, 5 U.S.C. §§ 706(2)(A), (D). But whether or not they enjoy any express delegation of authority on a particular question, agencies charged with applying a statute necessarily make all sorts of interpretive choices, and while not all of those choices bind judges to follow them, they certainly may influence courts facing questions the agencies have already answered. "[T]he well-reasoned views of the agencies implementing a statute 'constitute a body of experience and informed judgment to which courts and litigants may properly resort for guidance,'" *Bragdon v. Abbott*, 524 U.S. 624, 642 (quoting *Skidmore*, 323 U.S., at 139–140), and "[w]e have long recognized that considerable weight should be accorded to an executive department's construction of a statutory scheme it is entrusted to administer . . . ." *Chevron, supra*, at 844. The fair measure of deference to an agency administering its own statute has been understood to vary with circumstances, and courts have looked to the degree of the agency's care, its consistency, formality, and relative expertness, and to the persuasiveness of the agency's position, see *Skidmore, supra*, at 139–140. The approach has produced a spectrum of judicial responses, from great respect at one end, to near indifference at the other. Justice Jackson summed things up in *Skidmore v. Swift & Co.*:

> "The weight [accorded to an administrative] judgment in a particular case will depend upon the thoroughness evident in its consideration, the validity of its reasoning, its consistency with earlier and later pronouncements, and all those factors which give it power to persuade, if lacking power to control." 323 U.S., at 140.

Since 1984, we have identified a category of interpretive choices distinguished by an additional reason for judicial deference. This Court in *Chevron* recognized that Congress not only engages in express delegation of specific interpretive authority, but that "[s]ometimes the legislative delegation to an agency on a particular question is implicit." 467 U.S., at 844. Congress, that is, may not have expressly delegated authority or responsibility to implement a particular provision or fill a particular gap. Yet it can still be apparent from the agency's generally conferred authority and other statutory circumstances that Congress would expect the agency to be able to speak with the force of law when it addresses ambiguity in the statute or fills a space in the enacted law, even one about which "Congress did not actually have an intent" as to a particular result. *Id.*, at 845. When circumstances implying such an expectation exist, a reviewing court has no business rejecting an agency's exercise of its generally conferred authority to resolve a particular statutory ambiguity simply because the agency's chosen resolution seems unwise, but is obliged to accept the agency's position if Congress has not previously spoken to the point at issue and the agency's interpretation is reasonable, 5 U.S.C. § 706(2) (a reviewing court shall set aside agency action, findings, and conclusions found to be "arbitrary, capricious, an abuse of discretion, or otherwise not in accordance with law").

We have recognized a very good indicator of delegation meriting *Chevron* treatment in express congressional authorizations to engage in the process of rulemaking or adjudication that produces regulations or rulings for which deference is claimed. It is fair to assume generally that Congress contemplates administrative action with the effect of law when it provides for a relatively formal administrative procedure tending to foster the fairness and deliberation that should underlie a pronouncement of such force.[11] Thus, the overwhelming number of our cases applying *Chevron* deference have reviewed the fruits of notice-and-comment rulemaking or formal adjudication. That said, and as significant as notice-and-comment is in pointing to *Chevron* authority, the want of that procedure here does not decide the case, for we have sometimes found reasons for *Chevron* deference even when no such administrative formality was required and none was afforded. . . . The fact that the tariff classification here was not a product of such formal process does not alone, therefore, bar the application of *Chevron*.

There are, nonetheless, ample reasons to deny *Chevron* deference here. The authorization for classification rulings, and Customs's practice in making them, present a case far removed not only from notice-and-comment process, but from any other circumstances reasonably suggesting that Congress ever thought of classification rulings as deserving the deference claimed for them here.

B

No matter which angle we choose for viewing the Customs ruling letter in this case, it fails to qualify under *Chevron*. On the face of the statute, to begin with, the terms of the congressional delegation give no indication that Congress meant to delegate authority to Customs to issue classification rulings with the force of law. We are not, of course, here making any global

---

[11] *See* Merrill & Hickman, Chevron's Domain, 89 GEO. L.J. 833, 872 (2001) ("[I]f *Chevron* rests on a presumption about congressional intent, then *Chevron* should apply only where Congress would want Chevron to apply. In delineating the types of delegations of agency authority that trigger Chevron deference, it is therefore important to determine whether a plausible case can be made that Congress would want such a delegation to mean that agencies enjoy primary interpretational authority").

statement about Customs's authority, for it is true that the general rulemaking power conferred on Customs, *see* 19 U.S.C. § 1624, authorizes some regulation with the force of law, or "legal norms". . . . It is true as well that Congress had classification rulings in mind when it explicitly authorized, in a parenthetical, the issuance of "regulations establishing procedures for the issuance of binding rulings prior to the entry of the merchandise concerned," 19 U.S.C. § 1502(a). The reference to binding classifications does not, however, bespeak the legislative type of activity that would naturally bind more than the parties to the ruling, once the goods classified are admitted into this country. And though the statute's direction to disseminate "information" necessary to "secure" uniformity, *ibid.*, seems to assume that a ruling may be precedent in later transactions, precedential value alone does not add up to *Chevron* entitlement; interpretive rules may sometimes function as precedents, *see* Strauss, *The Rulemaking Continuum*, 41 DUKE L.J. 1463, 1472–1473 (1992), and they enjoy no *Chevron* status as a class. In any event, any precedential claim of a classification ruling is counterbalanced by the provision for independent review of Customs classifications by the CIT, *see* 28 U.S.C. §§ 2638-2640. . . .

It is difficult, in fact, to see in the agency practice itself any indication that Customs ever set out with a lawmaking pretense in mind when it undertook to make classifications like these. Customs does not generally engage in notice-and-comment practice when issuing them, and their treatment by the agency makes it clear that a letter's binding character as a ruling stops short of third parties; Customs has regarded a classification as conclusive only as between itself and the importer to whom it was issued, 19 CFR § 177.9(c) (2000), and even then only until Customs has given advance notice of intended change, §§ 177.9(a), (c). Other importers are in fact warned against assuming any right of detrimental reliance. § 177.9(c).

Indeed, to claim that classifications have legal force is to ignore the reality that 46 different Customs offices issue 10,000 to 15,000 of them each year. Any suggestion that rulings intended to have the force of law are being churned out at a rate of 10,000 a year at an agency's 46 scattered offices is simply self-refuting. Although the circumstances are less startling here, with a Headquarters letter in issue, none of the relevant statutes recognizes this category of rulings as separate or different from others; there is thus no indication that a more potent delegation might have been understood as going to Headquarters even when Headquarters provides developed reasoning, as it did in this instance.

. . . .

In sum, classification rulings are best treated like "interpretations contained in policy statements, agency manuals, and enforcement guidelines." *Christensen*, 529 U.S., at 587. They are beyond the *Chevron* pale.

C

To agree with the Court of Appeals that Customs ruling letters do not fall within *Chevron* is not, however, to place them outside the pale of any deference whatever. *Chevron* did nothing to eliminate *Skidmore*'s holding that an

§ 8.05 JUDICIAL CONTROL 793

agency's interpretation may merit some deference whatever its form, given the "specialized experience and broader investigations and information" available to the agency, 323 U.S., at 139, and given the value of uniformity in its administrative and judicial understandings of what a national law requires. . . .

There is room at least to raise a *Skidmore* claim here, where the regulatory scheme is highly detailed, and Customs can bring the benefit of specialized experience to bear on the subtle questions in this case: whether the daily planner with room for brief daily entries falls under "diaries," when diaries are grouped with "notebooks and address books, bound; memorandum pads, letter pads and similar articles," HTSUS subheading 4820.10.20; and whether a planner with a ring binding should qualify as "bound," when a binding may be typified by a book, but also may have "reinforcements or fittings of metal, plastics, etc.," Harmonized Commodity Description and Coding System Explanatory Notes to Heading 4820, p. 687. A classification ruling in this situation may therefore at least seek a respect proportional to its "power to persuade," *Skidmore, supra,* at 140; *see also Christensen,* 529 U.S., at 587. Such a ruling may surely claim the merit of its writer's thoroughness, logic, and expertness, its fit with prior interpretations, and any other sources of weight.

D

Underlying the position we take here, like the position expressed by JUSTICE SCALIA in dissent, is a choice about the best way to deal with an inescapable feature of the body of congressional legislation authorizing administrative action. That feature is the great variety of ways in which the laws invest the Government's administrative arms with discretion, and with procedures for exercising it, in giving meaning to Acts of Congress. Implementation of a statute may occur in formal adjudication or the choice to defend against judicial challenge; it may occur in a central board or office or in dozens of enforcement agencies dotted across the country; its institutional lawmaking may be confined to the resolution of minute detail or extend to legislative rulemaking on matters intentionally left by Congress to be worked out at the agency level.

Although we all accept the position that the Judiciary should defer to at least some of this multifarious administrative action, we have to decide how to take account of the great range of its variety. If the primary objective is to simplify the judicial process of giving or withholding deference, then the diversity of statutes authorizing discretionary administrative action must be declared irrelevant or minimized. If, on the other hand, it is simply implausible that Congress intended such a broad range of statutory authority to produce only two varieties of administrative action, demanding either *Chevron* deference or none at all, then the breadth of the spectrum of possible agency action must be taken into account. JUSTICE SCALIA's first priority over the years has been to limit and simplify. The Court's choice has been to tailor deference to variety. This acceptance of the range of statutory variation has led the Court to recognize more than one variety of judicial deference, just as the Court has recognized a variety of indicators that Congress would expect *Chevron* deference.[18]

Our respective choices are repeated today. JUSTICE SCALIA would pose the question of deference as an either-or choice. On his view that *Chevron* rendered *Skidmore* anachronistic, when courts owe any deference it is *Chevron* deference that they owe. Whether courts do owe deference in a given case turns, for him, on whether the agency action (if reasonable) is "authoritative." The character of the authoritative derives, in turn, not from breadth of delegation or the agency's procedure in implementing it, but is defined as the "official" position of an agency, and may ultimately be a function of administrative persistence alone.

The Court, on the other hand, said nothing in *Chevron* to eliminate *Skidmore*'s recognition of various justifications for deference depending on statutory circumstances and agency action; *Chevron* was simply a case recognizing that even without express authority to fill a specific statutory gap, circumstances pointing to implicit congressional delegation present a particularly insistent call for deference. Indeed, in holding here that *Chevron* left *Skidmore* intact and applicable where statutory circumstances indicate no intent to delegate general authority to make rules with force of law, or where such authority was not invoked, we hold nothing more than we said last Term in response to the particular statutory circumstances in *Christensen*, to which JUSTICE SCALIA then took exception, just as he does again today.

We think, in sum, that JUSTICE SCALIA's efforts to simplify ultimately run afoul of Congress's indications that different statutes present different reasons for considering respect for the exercise of administrative authority or deference to it. Without being at odds with congressional intent much of the time, we believe that judicial responses to administrative action must continue to differentiate between *Chevron* and *Skidmore*, and that continued recognition of *Skidmore* is necessary for just the reasons Justice Jackson gave when that case was decided.[19]

. . . .

Since the *Skidmore* assessment called for here ought to be made in the first instance by the Court of Appeals for the Federal Circuit or the CIT, we go no further than to vacate the judgment and remand the case for further proceedings consistent with this opinion.

---

[18] It is, of course, true that the limit of *Chevron* deference is not marked by a hard-edged rule. But *Chevron* itself is a good example showing when *Chevron* deference is warranted, while this is a good case showing when it is not. Judges in other, perhaps harder, cases will make reasoned choices between the two examples, the way courts have always done.

[19] Surely Justice Jackson's practical criteria, along with *Chevron*'s concern with congressional understanding, provide more reliable guideposts than conclusory references to the "authoritative" or "official." Even if those terms provided a true criterion, there would have to be something wrong with a standard that accorded the status of substantive law to every one of 10,000 "official" customs classifications rulings turned out each year from over 46 offices placed around the country at the Nation's entryways. . . .

It is so ordered.

JUSTICE SCALIA, dissenting.

Today's opinion makes an avulsive change in judicial review of federal administrative action. Whereas previously a reasonable agency application of an ambiguous statutory provision had to be sustained so long as it represented the agency's authoritative interpretation, henceforth such an application can be set aside unless "it appears that Congress delegated authority to the agency generally to make rules carrying the force of law," as by giving an agency "power to engage in adjudication or notice-and-comment rulemaking, or . . . some other [procedure] indicati[ng] comparable congressional intent," and "the agency interpretation claiming deference was promulgated in the exercise of that authority."[1] What was previously a general presumption of authority in agencies to resolve ambiguity in the statutes they have been authorized to enforce has been changed to a presumption of no such authority, which must be overcome by affirmative legislative intent to the contrary. And whereas previously, when agency authority to resolve ambiguity did not exist the court was free to give the statute what it considered the best interpretation, henceforth the court must supposedly give the agency view some indeterminate amount of so-called *Skidmore* deference. We will be sorting out the consequences of the *Mead* doctrine, which has today replaced the *Chevron* doctrine, for years to come. I would adhere to our established jurisprudence, defer to the reasonable interpretation the Customs Service has given to the statute it is charged with enforcing, and reverse the judgment of the Court of Appeals.

I

. . . .

The Court's new doctrine is neither sound in principle nor sustainable in practice.

A

As to principle: The doctrine of *Chevron* — that all *authoritative* agency interpretations of statutes they are charged with administering deserve deference — was rooted in a legal presumption of congressional intent, important to the division of powers between the Second and Third Branches. When, *Chevron* said, Congress leaves an ambiguity in a statute that is to be administered by an executive agency, it is presumed that Congress meant to give the agency discretion, within the limits of reasonable interpretation, as to how the ambiguity is to be resolved. By committing enforcement of the statute to an agency rather than the courts, Congress committed its initial and primary interpretation to that branch as well.

. . . .

The basis in principle for today's new doctrine can be described as follows: The background rule is that ambiguity in legislative instructions to agencies

---

[1] It is not entirely clear whether the formulation newly minted by the Court today extends to both formal and informal adjudication, or simply the former.

is to be resolved not by the agencies but by the judges. Specific congressional intent to depart from this rule must be found — and while there is no single touchstone for such intent it can generally be found when Congress has authorized the agency to act through (what the Court says is) relatively formal procedures such as informal rulemaking and formal (and informal?) adjudication, and when the agency in fact employs such procedures. The Court's background rule is contradicted by the origins of judicial review of administrative action. But in addition, the Court's principal criterion of congressional intent to supplant its background rule seems to me quite implausible. There is no necessary connection between the formality of procedure and the power of the entity administering the procedure to resolve authoritatively questions of law. The most formal of the procedures the Court refers to — formal adjudication — is modeled after the process used in trial courts, which of course are not generally accorded deference on questions of law. The purpose of such a procedure is to produce a closed record for determination and review of the facts — which implies nothing about the power of the agency subjected to the procedure to resolve authoritatively questions of law.

As for informal rulemaking: While formal adjudication procedures are *prescribed* (either by statute or by the Constitution), informal rulemaking is more typically *authorized* but not required. Agencies with such authority are free to give guidance through rulemaking, but they may proceed to administer their statute case-by-case, "making law" as they implement their program (not necessarily through formal adjudication). See *NLRB v. Bell Aerospace Co.*, 416 U.S. 267, 290–295 (1974); *SEC v. Chenery Corp.*, 332 U.S. 194, 202–203 (1947). Is it likely — or indeed even plausible — that Congress meant, when such an agency chooses rulemaking, to accord the administrators of that agency, *and their successors*, the flexibility of interpreting the ambiguous statute now one way, and later another; but, when such an agency chooses case-by-case administration, to eliminate all future agency discretion by having that same ambiguity resolved authoritatively (and forever) by the courts? Surely that makes no sense. It is also the case that certain significant categories of rules — those involving grant and benefit programs, for example, are exempt from the requirements of informal rulemaking. See 5 U.S.C. § 553(a)(2). Under the Court's novel theory, when an agency takes advantage of that exemption its rules will be deprived of *Chevron* deference, i.e., authoritative effect. Was this either the plausible intent of the APA rulemaking exemption, or the plausible intent of the Congress that established the grant or benefit program?

Some decisions that are neither informal rulemaking nor formal adjudication are required to be made personally by a Cabinet Secretary, without any prescribed procedures. Is it conceivable that decisions specifically committed to these high-level officers are meant to be accorded no deference, while decisions by an administrative law judge left in place without further discretionary agency review, see 5 U.S.C. § 557(b), are authoritative? This seems to me quite absurd, and not at all in accord with any plausible actual intent of Congress.

B

As for the practical effects of the new rule:

1

The principal effect will be protracted confusion. As noted above, the one test for *Chevron* deference that the Court enunciates is wonderfully imprecise: whether "Congress delegated authority to the agency generally to make rules carrying the force of law, . . . as by . . . adjudication[,] notice-and-comment rulemaking, or . . . some other [procedure] indicati[ng] comparable congressional intent." But even this description does not do justice to the utter flabbiness of the Court's criterion, since, in order to maintain the fiction that the new test is really just the old one, applied consistently throughout our case law, the Court must make a virtually open-ended exception to its already imprecise guidance: In the present case, it tells us, the absence of notice-and-comment rulemaking (and "[who knows?] [of] some other [procedure] indicati[ng] comparable congressional intent") is not enough to decide the question of *Chevron* deference, "for we have sometimes found reasons for *Chevron* deference even when no such administrative formality was required and none was afforded." *Ante*, at 2171, 2173. The opinion then goes on to consider a grab bag of other factors — including the factor that used to be the sole criterion for *Chevron* deference: whether the interpretation represented the *authoritative* position of the agency, see *ante*, at 2173–2175. It is hard to know what the lower courts are to make of today's guidance.

2

Another practical effect of today's opinion will be an artificially induced increase in informal rulemaking. Buy stock in the GPO. Since informal rulemaking and formal adjudication are the only more-or-less safe harbors from the storm that the Court has unleashed; and since formal adjudication is not an option but must be mandated by statute or constitutional command; informal rulemaking — which the Court was once careful to make voluntary unless required by statute, see *Bell Aerospace*, *supra*, and *Chenery*, *supra* — will now become a virtual necessity. As I have described, the Court's safe harbor requires not merely that the agency have been given rulemaking authority, but also that the agency have *employed* rulemaking as the means of resolving the statutory ambiguity. (It is hard to understand why that should be so. Surely the mere *conferral* of rulemaking authority demonstrates — if one accepts the Court's logic — a congressional intent to allow the agency to resolve ambiguities. And given that intent, what difference does it make that the agency chooses instead to use another perfectly permissible means for that purpose?) Moreover, the majority's approach will have a perverse effect on the rules that do emerge, given the principle (which the Court leaves untouched today) that judges must defer to reasonable agency interpretations of their own regulations. Agencies will now have high incentive to rush out barebones, ambiguous rules construing statutory ambiguities, which they can then in turn further clarify through informal rulings entitled to judicial respect.

3

Worst of all, the majority's approach will lead to the ossification of large portions of our statutory law. Where *Chevron* applies, statutory ambiguities remain ambiguities subject to the agency's ongoing clarification. They create a space, so to speak, for the exercise of continuing agency discretion. As *Chevron* itself held, the Environmental Protection Agency can interpret "stationary source" to mean a single smokestack, can later replace that interpretation with the "bubble concept" embracing an entire plant, and if that proves undesirable can return again to the original interpretation. 467 U.S., at 853–859, 865–866, 104 S.Ct. 2778. For the indeterminately large number of statutes taken out of *Chevron* by today's decision, however, ambiguity (and hence flexibility) will cease with the first judicial resolution. *Skidmore* deference gives the agency's current position some vague and uncertain amount of respect, but it does not, like *Chevron*, leave the matter within the control of the Executive Branch for the future. Once the court has spoken, it becomes *unlawful* for the agency to take a contradictory position; the statute now says what the court has prescribed. It will be bad enough when this ossification occurs as a result of judicial determination (under today's new principles) that there is no affirmative indication of congressional intent to "delegate"; but it will be positively bizarre when it occurs simply because of an agency's failure to act by rulemaking (rather than informal adjudication) before the issue is presented to the courts.

. . . .

4

And finally, the majority's approach compounds the confusion it creates by breathing new life into the anachronism of *Skidmore*, which sets forth a sliding scale of deference owed an agency's interpretation of a statute that is dependent "upon the thoroughness evident in [the agency's] consideration, the validity of its reasoning, its consistency with earlier and later pronouncements, and all those factors which give it power to persuade, if lacking power to control"; in this way, the appropriate measure of deference will be accorded the "body of experience and informed judgment" that such interpretations often embody, 323 U.S., at 140. Justice Jackson's eloquence notwithstanding, the rule of *Skidmore* deference is an empty truism and a trifling statement of the obvious: A judge should take into account the well-considered views of expert observers.

It was possible to live with the indeterminacy of *Skidmore* deference in earlier times. But in an era when federal statutory law administered by federal agencies is pervasive, and when the ambiguities (intended or unintended) that those statutes contain are innumerable, totality-of-the-circumstances *Skidmore* deference is a recipe for uncertainty, unpredictability, and endless litigation. To condemn a vast body of agency action to that regime (all except rulemaking, formal (and informal?) adjudication, and whatever else might now and then be included within today's intentionally vague formulation of affirmative congressional intent to "delegate") is irresponsible.

II

The Court's pretense that today's opinion is nothing more than application of our prior case law does not withstand analysis. It is, to be sure, impossible

III

To decide the present case, I would adhere to the original formulation of *Chevron*. "'The power of an administrative agency to administer a congressionally created . . . program necessarily requires the formulation of policy and the making of rules to fill any gap left, implicitly or explicitly, by Congress,'" 467 U.S., at 843, (quoting *Morton v. Ruiz*, 415 U.S. 199, 231, (1974)). We accordingly presume — and our precedents have made clear to Congress that we presume — that, absent some clear textual indication to the contrary, "Congress, when it left ambiguity in a statute meant for implementation by an agency, understood that the ambiguity would be resolved, first and foremost, by the agency, and desired the agency (rather than the courts) to possess whatever degree of discretion the ambiguity allows," *Smiley*, 517 U.S., at 740–741, (citing *Chevron, supra*, at 843–44). *Chevron* sets forth an across-the-board presumption, which operates as a background rule of law against which Congress legislates: Ambiguity means Congress intended agency discretion. Any resolution of the ambiguity by the administering agency that is authoritative — that represents the official position of the agency — must be accepted by the courts if it is reaso

Nothing in the statute at issue here displays an intent to modify the background presumption on which *Chevron* deference is based. . . .

There is no doubt that the Customs Service's interpretation represents the authoritative view of the agency. Although the actual ruling letter was signed by only the Director of the Commercial Rulings Branch of Customs Headquarters' Office of Regulations and Rulings, the Solicitor General of the United States has filed a brief, cosigned by the General Counsel of the Department of the Treasury, that represents the position set forth in the ruling letter to be the official position of the Customs Service.[6] No one contends that it is

---

[6] The Court's parting shot, that "there would have to be something wrong with a standard that accorded the status of substantive law to every one of 10,000 'official' customs classifications rulings turned out each year from over 46 offices placed around the country at the Nation's entryways," *ante*, at 2177, n. 19, misses the mark. I do not disagree. The "authoritativeness" of an agency interpretation does not turn upon whether it has been enunciated by someone who is actually employed by the agency. It must represent the judgment of central agency management, approved at the highest levels. I would find that condition to have been satisfied when, a ruling having been attacked in court, the general counsel of the agency has determined that it should be defended. If one thinks that that does not impart sufficient authoritativeness, then surely the line has been crossed when, as here, the General Counsel of the agency and the Solicitor General of the United States have assured this Court that the position represents the agency's authoritative view. (Contrary to the Court's suggestion, there would be nothing bizarre about the fact that this latter approach would entitle the ruling to deference here, though it would not have been entitled to deference in the lower courts.) Affirmation of the official agency position before this court — if that is thought necessary — is no different from the agency's issuing a new rule after the Court of Appeals determination. It establishes a new legal basis for the decision, which this Court must take into account (or remand for that purpose), even though the Court of Appeals could not. . . . And, most important of all, it is a line that focuses attention on the right question: not whether Congress "affirmatively intended" to delegate interpretive authority (if it entrusted

merely a "post hoc rationalizatio[n]" or an "agency litigating positio[n] wholly unsupported by regulations, rulings, or administrative practice," *Bowen v. Georgetown Univ. Hospital*, 488 U.S. 204, 212 (1988).

. . . .

IV

Finally, and least importantly, even were I to accept the Court's revised version of *Chevron* as a correct statement of the law, I would still accord deference to the tariff classification ruling at issue in this case.

. . . .

For the reasons stated, I respectfully dissent from the Court's judgment. I would uphold the Customs Service's construction of Subheading 4820.10.20 of the Harmonized Tariff Schedule of the United States, 19 U.S.C. § 1202, and would reverse the contrary decision of the Court of Appeals. I dissent even more vigorously from the reasoning that produces the Court's judgment, and that makes today's decision one of the most significant opinions ever rendered by the Court dealing with the judicial review of administrative action. Its consequences will be enormous, and almost uniformly bad.

NOTES AND QUESTIONS

8-39. *Christenson v. Harris County*, 529 U.S. 576 (2000), was the precursor of *Mead*. Just one year earlier the Court divided 5-4 on whether *Skidmore* deference or *Chevron* deference applied to the Department of Labor's opinion letter applying the Fair Labor Standards Act. Writing for the majority, Justice Thomas applied *Skidmore* deference to the agency's interpretation and found it unpersuasive:

> Here . . . we confront an interpretation contained in an opinion letter, not one arrived at after, for example, a formal adjudication or notice-and-comment rulemaking. Interpretations such as those in opinion letters — like interpretations contained in policy statements, agency manuals, and enforcement guidelines, all of which lack the force of law — do not warrant *Chevron*-style deference. Instead, interpretations contained in formats such as opinion letters are "entitled to respect" under our decision in *Skidmore v. Swift & Co.*, 323 U.S. 134, 140 (1944), but only to the extent that those interpretations have the "power to persuade," *ibid.* As explained above, we find unpersuasive the agency's interpretation of the statute at issue in this case.

8-40. Professor Weaver argues we now have a dual deference standard — *Chevron*'s actual deference standard, and *Skidmore*'s weight of deference

---

administration of the statute to an agency, it did, because that is how our system works); but whether it is truly the agency's considered view, or just the opinions of some underlings, that are at issue.

approach depending upon the persuasiveness of the agency's argument. Is it likely these different doctrines will be applied rigorously and consistently by the courts? *See* Russell L. Weaver, *The Emperor Has No Clothes:* Christensen, Mead *and Dual Deference Standards*, 54 ADMIN. L. REV. 173 (2002).

8-41. Consider the Supreme Court's approach to these issues in *Alaska Department of Environmental Conservation v. Environmental Protection Agency*, 540 U.S. 461 (2004). In this case, the majority concluded that an EPA interpretation of "longstanding duration," while entitled to "particular deference," was not entitled to "*Chevron* deference." This is because the interpretation appeared in an internal guidance memorandum that lacked the force of law. The majority, thus, applied *Skidmore*, not *Chevron*, but in so doing it upheld the EPA on the grounds that it had "rationally construed the Act's text. . . ." 540 U.S. at 485. Is this essentially the same as *Chevron* deference? Consider the dissent's take on this approach:

> Actions . . . speak louder than words, and the majority ends up giving EPA the very *Chevron* deference — and more — it says should be denied. . . . In applying *Chevron de facto* under these circumstances, however, the majority undermines the well-established distinction our precedents draw between *Chevron* and less deferential forms of judicial review. (540 U.S. at 517–18, Kennedy, J., dissenting).

8-42. What is the relationship of *Chevron* and *Skidmore* deference to *stare decisis*? If a court applies *Skidmore* and, in effect, provides its own independent judicial interpretation of the statutory term in question, does that bind future agency interpretations of the statute? Does this mean that, unlike *Chevron* deference, the application of *Skidmore* deference means that the agency's flexibility and ability to change as conditions change is severely limited? For a discussion of this issue suggesting that the Supreme Court does not necessarily see *Skidmore* deference as quite so confining, *see Yates v. Hendon*, 541 U.S. 1 (2004). *See also Central Laborers' Pension Fund v. Heinz*, 124 S. Ct. 2230 (2004), where Justice Breyer, in concurrence with three other Justices strongly suggests that an agency can trump a judicial interpretation of a statute with the issuance of a regulation it deems necessary. 124 S. Ct. at 2239. *See generally* Richard W. Murphy, *A "New" Counter-*Marbury*: Reconciling* Skidmore *Deference and Agency Interpretive Freedom*, 56 ADMIN. L. REV. 1 (2004); Kenneth A. Bamberger, *Provisional Precedent: Protecting Flexibility in Administrative Policymaking*, 77 N.Y.U. L. REV. 1272 (2002); Richard L. Pierce, Jr., *Reconciling* Chevron *and* Stare Decisis, 85 GEO. L.J. 2225 (1997).

8-43. What do you think of the Court's reliance on Congressional intent in *Mead* to justify the type of deference given an agency interpretation? Is Congress likely to be focused on whether they intended certain agency interpretations to have the force of law and others, not?

8-44. To what extent does the formality of procedural format dictate the deference approach used? *Compare Pharmaceutical Research and Manufacturers of America v. Thompson*, 362 F.3d 817 (D.C. Cir. 2004) (*Chevron* deference provided an agency interpretation despite the fact that interpretation was not the product of a formal administrative process), *with Natural Resources Defense Council v. Abraham*, 355 F.3d 179 (2d Cir. 2004) (*Chevron* deference not provided even though the agency statutory interpretation involved was part of notice and comment rulemaking).

8-45. Is it more fruitful to focus on the "who" as opposed to the "how"?

We contend that the deference question should turn on a different feature of agency process, traditionally ignored in administrative law doctrine and scholarship — that is, the position in the agency hierarchy of the person assuming responsibility for the administrative decision. More briefly said, the Court should refocus its inquiry from the "how" to the "who" of administrative decision making. If the congressional delegatee of the relevant statutory grant of authority takes personal responsibility for the decision, then the agency should command obeisance, within the broad bounds of reasonableness, in resolving statutory ambiguity; if she does not, then the judiciary should render the ultimate interpretive decision. This agency nondelegation principle serves values familiar from the congressional brand of the doctrine, as well as from *Chevron* itself: by offering an incentive to certain actors to take responsibility for interpretive choice, the principle advances both accountability and discipline in decision making. At the same time, the nondelegation principle, as applied in the administrative context to determine the appropriate deference regime, escapes the well-known difficulties of the congressional nondelegation doctrine: the administrative principle will neither lead to excessive centralization nor prove incapable of judicial enforcement. Critical to this analysis is a more general phenomenon often disregarded in discussions of administrative law, yet highly significant for the creation of doctrine: the interplay of political with judicial constraints in shaping agency behavior.

David J. Barron & Elena Kagan, Chevron's *Nondelegation Doctrine*, 2001 SUP. CT. REV. 201, 204–05 (2001).* *See also* Adrian Vermeule, *Introduction: Mead in the Trenches*, 71 GEO. WASH. L. REV. 347 (2003); Thomas W. Merrill & Kathryn Tongue Watts, *Agency Rules with the Force of Law: The Original Convention*, 116 HARV. L. REV. 467 (2002); *Administrative Law Discussion Forum*, 54 ADMIN. L. REV. 1 (2002).

8-46. What, in the end, do you think *Mead* does to *Chevron*? Does it, ultimately, widen the scope of judicial review? Under what circumstances does *Skidmore* trump *Chevron*?

PROBLEM 8-1

Is it time to amend the APA? What do you think of William Anderson's proposal below? *See* William Anderson, *Against* Chevron: *A Modest Proposal*, 56 ADMIN. L. REV. 957 (2004).**

---

* Copyright © 2001 by University of Chicago. All rights reserved.

** *Against* Chevron: *A Modest Proposal*, by William Anderson, published in Administrative Law Review, Volume 56, No.4, Fall 2004. Copyright © 2004 by American Bar Association. Reprinted by permission.

II. The Proposal

What is proposed is the following amendment to § 706 of the APA. Italicized words are additions to the existing language and strikethroughs indicate deletions.

A. Proposed Amendment

Section 706. Scope of Review.

(1) To the extent necessary to decide and when presented, the reviewing court,

(2) Shall decide all relevant questions of law *and* interpret constitutional and

(3) Statutory provisions, *except that in carrying out any of the law-interpreting*

(4) *Functions required by this section the court may defer to a contemporaneous*

(5) *Agency legal interpretation to the extent that the interpretation (a) is*

(6) *Authoritative, (b) significantly reflects relevant agency technical, political or other resources,*

(7) *(c) was formulated through a careful process, including providing*

(8) *Those specially affected with an appropriate opportunity to participate in its*

(9) *Formulation and (d) does not require the special weight of a judicial*

(10) *Pronouncement* ~~and determine the meaning and applicability of the terms of an agency action.~~ The reviewing court shall —

§ 8.06 The Scope of Judicial Review of Agency Rules

[A] The Arbitrary and Capricious Standard of Review and the Rational Basis Test

When courts review the substance of agency rules, under the APA, they apply the standard of review set forth in section 706(2)(A) — namely, whether the rule in question is "arbitrary, capricious an abuse of discretion, or otherwise not in accordance with law." This standard is by no means self-defining, but reviewing courts, particularly during what might be called the "New Deal Era of Administrative Law" — the 1930s through the 1960s — treated this standard as essentially a reasonableness standard. Section 553(c) of the APA requires that each rule be accompanied by a "concise statement of its basis and purpose." Usually, when engaging in APA review, courts were content with a decision that provided a reason, not necessarily the reason the Court might have preferred, or a good reason or, indeed, the best reason that might be provided. The approach taken in *Pacific States Box and Basket Co. v. White,* 296 U.S. 176 (1935), a pre-APA case, very much typified APA review of rules: "[w]here the regulation is within the scope of authority legally delegated, the presumption of the existence of facts justifying its specific exercise attaches." *Id.* at 186.

Beginning around 1970, however, during what we can call the Environmental Era of regulation, courts began to examine agency rules more carefully. The Supreme Court case that epitomized this closer scrutiny was *Citizens to Preserve Overton Park v. Volpe,* 401 U.S. 402 (1971). The case is set forth in Chapter Five. You should now revisit that case to understand fully the scope of judicial review questions that it raises. You will recall that *Overton Park* dealt with informal agency action, not rulemaking. Because it involved the application of the "arbitrary and capricious" standard of judicial review to agency action, however, it had a significant impact on the way lower courts tended to approach scope of judicial review issues involving agency rules.

In reversing the Department of Transportation's decision to fund a six-lane interstate highway through Overton Park in Memphis, Tennessee, the Supreme Court held the Secretary's decision could be reviewed for arbitrariness. Specifically, the Court stated that it "must consider whether the decision was based on a consideration of the relevant factors and whether there had been a clear error of judgment." 401 U.S. at 416. The Court, however, also used a good deal of other language to describe what it was doing. At one point, it stated that even though the "inquiry into the facts is to be searching and careful, the ultimate standard of review is a narrow one." 401 U.S. at 416. At another point in the opinion, the Court stated it must "engage in a substantial inquiry." The Secretary's decision was "entitled to a presumption of regularity," but "that presumption is not to shield his action from a thorough, probing, in-depth review." There is, in effect, language in this opinion to satisfy various scopes of judicial review, from narrow to searching.

One way to read *Overton Park* is to say that the language calling for close judicial scrutiny applies to the questions of law involved in that case and the language emphasizing a narrow scope of review refers to the arbitrariness standard of review. Lower courts, however, often read this case to justify close review of agency rules as well as questions of law. Thus, along with a rational basis approach to the review of agency rules, a hard look doctrine also began to develop.

As we saw earlier in Chapter Four, § 4.02[C], judicial attempts to develop administrative common law often emphasized the importance of procedural approaches that went well beyond the informal rulemaking procedures required by section 553 of the APA. These requirements resulted in a procedural form of the hard look approach. Courts not only asked agencies to take a hard look at what they had done but to do so with additional procedures to ensure that the issues were fully aired. The Supreme Court tried to put an end to this kind of administrative common law, you will recall, in

Vermont Yankee Nuclear Power Corp. v. NRDC, 435 U.S. 519 (1978). Section 553(c), however, also requires that agencies provide a concise statement of the basis and purpose of their rules. This requirement forms the statutory basis for requiring reasoned decisionmaking and, arguably, imposing a judicial standard of review more demanding than a simple rational basis test. Rather than just providing a reason for its actions, agencies are sometimes asked, often implicitly, to give a persuasive reason for their decision. This more demanding approach is often bolstered by the procedural requirements of environmental, health and safety statutes that require hybrid rulemaking procedures and provide for substantial evidence review of certain aspects of agency *policy* determinations. (Recall the *Hodgson* case we studied in Chapter Four, § 4.02[D]).

The upshot is that the arbitrary and capricious standard of review can generate a range of judicial responses to the review of agency rules, from a very deferential rational basis test to almost a form of strict scrutiny. The the following excerpt deals more fully with some of the judicial history leading up to the creation of what is often called the hard look review doctrine or, simply, reasoned decisionmaking. After considering this excerpt, read *Motor Vehicle Manufacturers Association v. State Farm Mutual* very carefully. You should be able to discern several different judicial approaches to the scope of review issues in that case. What should a court do if an agency gives no reason for its actions? What if it gives *a* reason, but not a very convincing one?

[B] The Hard Look Doctrine

A. Aman, ADMINISTRATIVE LAW IN A GLOBAL ERA

33–35 (Cornell Univ. Press 1992)*

Though the hard-look doctrine came into its own during the environmental era, it began much earlier when the New Deal minimal-rationality approach was still very much in vogue. Expressing his disagreement with the Second Circuit's penchant for almost always deferring to agency decisions, Judge Jerome Frank inadvertently set forth the underlying basis of the hard-look doctrine — the use of reason to secure and enhance an agency's legitimacy. Commenting on the Interstate Commerce Commission's use of discretion in determining the accuracy of a railroad's property valuations, he advocated rejection of what he called the doctrine of "woosh-woosh:"

> If, however, the Commission is sustained in this case, and, accordingly, behaves similarly in future cases, then its conduct will indeed be a mystery. Its so-called valuations will then be acceptable, no matter how contrived. In that event, it would be desirable to abandon the word "valuation" — since that word misleadingly connotes some moderately rational judgment — and to substitute some neutral term, devoid of misleading associations, such as "aluation," or, perhaps

---
* Copyright © 1992. Cornell University Press. All rights reserved.

better still, "woosh-woosh." The pertinent doctrine would then be this: "When the I.C.C. has ceremonially woosh-wooshed, judicial scrutiny is barred."

Judge Frank, however, was quick to observe that his desire to overturn this administrative decision was not based on any antiagency bias. Indeed, he was a friend of administrative agencies, but "[t]o condone the Commission's conduct here is to give aid and comfort to the enemies of the administrative process, by sanctioning administrative irresponsibility; the friends of that process should be the first to denounce its abuses. If the courts declare themselves powerless to remedy those abuses, judicial review will become a sham."

A similar desire to protect the administrative process and to emphasize the distinctive role of agencies was the basis for the Supreme Court's decision in *SEC v. Chenery Corp.*, 332 U.S. 194 (1947). In that case the Court refused to give its reasons for a particular result until the agency first set forth its views. Indeed, the Court noted that "a reviewing court, in dealing with a determination or judgment which an administrative agency alone is authorized to make, must judge the propriety of such action solely by the grounds invoked by the agency."

Because notions of expertise were founded upon faith in the reasoning behind agency decisions, the ability of an agency to engage in this process was an important source of its legitimacy and a demonstration that it was, indeed, a responsible agent of Congress. This procedural aspect to the role of reason in agency decision making was at the center of the hard-look doctrine first set forth in *Greater Boston Television Corp. v. FCC,* 403 U.S. 923 (1971).

The underlying premise of this purely procedural version of the hard-look doctrine was that the process of agency reasoning produced good results, which not only enhanced the legitimacy of the agency itself, but also increased the likelihood of wise policies that furthered statutory goals. This emphasis on the agency's need to display a reasoned approach to its tasks, particularly when significant changes in policy were contemplated, had strong overtones of an evolutionary common-law methodology.

Like changes in common law, changes in agency law were expected to occur gradually, to fit into preexisting legal frameworks, and to represent a form of regulatory progress. Change was more likely to occur in this way if it was in fact the product of reasoned analysis and not merely the result of a new set of political forces. The hard-look doctrine thus assumed a high degree of rationality and, along with it, a highly developed doctrine of administrative *stare decisis.* In its most procedural form, it did not seek to have courts substitute their own substantive views for those of the agencies, but rather to have the courts determine whether the agencies had engaged in the process of reasoning in order to ensure that a reasonable approach, if not necessarily the best approach, would, in fact, be taken. Thus, courts could test substantive rationality by requiring that agencies explain the links between the congressionally expressed belief in progress and the reasonableness of the regulation being reviewed. The courts required that reasonableness be articulated, not assumed. The more substantive the courts' demands for articulation became, however, the more power courts had to alter or stop completely the changes proposed by agencies. This kind of exacting review is the essence of the judicial approach and it is a court's primary tool for organizing and ordering reality.

In the 1980s, a third era of Administrative Law became apparent — a Global Era marked by a distinct desire on the part of many agencies to deregulate when possible and, in any event, carry out their regulatory tasks as efficiently as possible. Agency rules were once again at the center of litigation, but now it was often the rescission of rules that was being challenged, rather than the promulgation of new rules. When should the courts defer to such agency policy decisions and when should they invoke a version of the hard-look doctrine?

Consider the following case. How many judicial approaches to the interpretation of the "arbitrary and capricious" standard can you discern? What theory of the administrative process do you think underlies these different approaches? Which approach would you adopt? Why?

MOTOR VEHICLE MFRS. ASSN. v. STATE FARM MUTUAL

United States Supreme Court
453 U.S. 29 (1983)

JUSTICE WHITE delivered the opinion of the Court.

The development of the automobile gave Americans unprecedented freedom to travel, but exacted a high price for enhanced mobility. Since 1929, motor vehicles have been the leading cause of accidental deaths and injuries in the United States. In 1982, 46,300 Americans died in motor vehicle accidents and hundreds of thousands more were maimed and injured. While a consensus exists that the current loss of life on our highways is unacceptably high, improving safety does not admit to easy solution. In 1966, Congress decided that at least part of the answer lies in improving the design and safety features of the vehicle itself. But much of the technology for building safer cars was undeveloped or untested. Before changes in automobile design could be mandated, the effectiveness of these changes had to be studied, their costs examined, and public acceptance considered. This task called for considerable expertise and Congress responded by enacting the National Traffic and Motor Vehicle Safety Act of 1966 (Act), 15 U.S.C. § 1381 *et seq.* (1976 ed. and Supp. V). The Act, created for the purpose of "reduc[ing] traffic accidents and deaths and injuries to persons resulting from traffic accidents," directs the Secretary of Transportation or his delegate to issue motor vehicle safety standards that "shall be practicable, shall meet the need for motor vehicle safety, and shall be stated in objective terms." In issuing these standards, the Secretary is directed to consider "relevant available motor vehicle safety data," whether the proposed standard "is reasonable, practicable and appropriate" for the particular type of motor vehicle, and the "extent to which such standards will contribute to carrying out the purposes" of the Act.

The Act also authorizes judicial review under the provisions of the Administrative Procedure Act (APA), 5 U.S.C. § 706, of all "orders establishing, amending, or revoking a Federal motor vehicle safety standard," 15 U.S.C. § 1392(b). Under this authority, we review today whether NHTSA acted arbitrarily and capriciously in revoking the requirement in Motor Vehicle Safety Standard 208 that new motor vehicles produced after September 1982 be equipped with passive restraints to protect the safety of the occupants of the vehicle in the event of a collision. Briefly summarized, we hold that the agency failed to present an adequate basis and explanation for rescinding the passive restraint requirement and that the agency must either consider the matter further or adhere to or amend Standard 208 along lines which its analysis supports.

I

The regulation whose rescission is at issue bears a complex and convoluted history. Over the course of approximately 60 rulemaking notices, the requirement has been imposed, amended, rescinded, reimposed, and now rescinded again.

As originally issued by the Department of Transportation in 1967, Standard 208 simply required the installation of seatbelts in all automobiles. 32 Fed. Reg. 2415. It soon became apparent that the level of seatbelt use was too low to reduce traffic injuries to an acceptable level. The Department therefore began consideration of "passive occupant restraint systems" — devices that do not depend for their effectiveness upon any action taken by the occupant except that necessary to operate the vehicle. Two types of automatic crash protection emerged: automatic seatbelts and airbags. The automatic seatbelt is a traditional safety belt, which when fastened to the interior of the door remains attached without impeding entry or exit from the vehicle, and deploys automatically without any action on the part of the passenger. The airbag is an inflatable device concealed in the dashboard and steering column. It automatically inflates when a sensor indicates that deceleration forces from an accident have exceeded a preset minimum, then rapidly deflates to dissipate those forces. The lifesaving potential of these devices was immediately recognized, and in 1977, after substantial on-the-road experience with both devices, it was estimated by NHTSA that passive restraints could prevent approximately 12,000 deaths and over 100,000 serious injuries annually.

In 1969, the Department formally proposed a standard requiring the installation of passive restraints, 34 Fed. Reg. 11148, thereby commencing a lengthy series of proceedings. In 1970, the agency revised Standard 208 to include passive protection requirements, and in 1972, the agency amended the Standard to require full passive protection for all front seat occupants of vehicles manufactured after August 15, 1975. In the interim, vehicles built between August 1973 and August 1975 were to carry either passive restraints or lap and shoulder belts coupled with an "ignition interlock" that would prevent starting the vehicle if the belts were not connected. On review, the agency's decision to require passive restraints was found to be supported by "substantial evidence" and upheld. *Chrysler Corp. v. Department of Transportation,* 472 F.2d 659 (CA6 1972).

In preparing for the upcoming model year, most car makers chose the "ignition interlock" option, a decision which was highly unpopular, and led Congress to amend the Act to prohibit a motor vehicle safety standard from requiring or permitting compliance by means of an ignition interlock or a continuous buzzer designed to indicate that safety belts were not in use. Motor Vehicle and Schoolbus Safety Amendments of 1974, Pub. L. 93–492, § 109, 88 Stat. 1482, 15 U.S.C. § 1410b(b). The 1974 Amendments also provided that any safety standard that could be satisfied by a system other than seatbelts would have to be submitted to Congress where it could be vetoed by concurrent resolution of both Houses.

The effective date for mandatory passive restraint systems was extended for a year until August 31, 1976. 40 Fed. Reg. 16217 (1975); *id.,* at 33977. But in June 1976, Secretary of Transportation William T. Coleman, Jr., initiated a new rulemaking on the issue, 41 Fed. Reg. 24070. After hearing testimony and reviewing written comments, Coleman extended the optional alternatives indefinitely and suspended the passive restraint requirement. Although he found passive restraints technologically and economically feasible, the Secretary based his decision on the expectation that there would be widespread public resistance to the new systems. He instead proposed a demonstration project involving up to 500,000 cars installed with passive restraints, in order to smooth the way for public acceptance of mandatory passive restraints at a later date.

Coleman's successor as Secretary of Transportation disagreed. Within months of assuming office, Secretary Brock Adams decided that the demonstration project was unnecessary. He issued a new mandatory passive restraint regulation, known as Modified Standard 208. 42 Fed. Reg. 34289 (1977); 49 CFR § 571.208 (1978). The Modified Standard mandated the phasing in of passive restraints beginning with large cars in model year 1982 and extending to all cars by model year 1984. The two principal systems that would satisfy the Standard were airbags and passive belts; the choice of which system in install was left to the manufacturers. In *Pacific Legal Foundation v. Department of Transportation,* 593 F.2d 1338, *cert. denied,* 444 U.S. 830 (1979), the Court of Appeals upheld Modified Standard 208 as a rational, nonarbitrary regulation consistent with the agency's mandate under the Act. The Standard also survived scrutiny by Congress, which did not exercise its authority under the legislative veto provision of the 1974 Amendments.

Over the next several years, the automobile industry geared up to comply with Modified Standard 208. . . .

In February 1981, however, Secretary of Transportation Andrew Lewis reopened the rulemaking due to changed economic circumstances and, in particular, the difficulties of the automobile industry. Two months later, the agency ordered a one-year delay in the application of the Standard to large cars, extending the deadline to September 1982, and at the same time, proposed the possible rescission of the entire Standard. After receiving written comments and holding public hearings, NHTSA issued a final rule (Notice 25) that rescinded the passive restraint requirement contained in Modified Standard 208.

II

In a statement explaining the rescission, NHTSA maintained that it was no longer able to find, as it had in 1977, that the automatic restraint requirement would produce significant safety benefits. . . . This judgment reflected not a change of opinion on the effectiveness of the technology, but a change in plans by the automobile industry. In 1977, the agency had assumed that airbags would be installed in 60% of all new cars and automatic seatbelts in 40%. By 1981 it became apparent that automobile manufacturers planned to install the automatic seatbelts in approximately 99% of the new cars. For this reason, the lifesaving potential of airbags would not be realized. Moreover, it now appeared that the overwhelming majority of passive belts planned to be installed by manufacturers could be detached easily and left that way permanently. Passive belts, once detached, then required "the same type of affirmative action that is the stumbling block to obtaining high usage levels of manual belts." For this reason, the agency concluded that there was no longer a basis for reliably predicting that the Standard would lead to any significant increased usage of restraints at all.

In view of the possibly minimal safety benefits, the automatic restraint requirement no longer was reasonable or practicable in the agency's view. The requirement would require approximately $1 billion to implement and the agency did not believe it would be reasonable to impose such substantial costs on manufacturers and consumers without more adequate assurance that sufficient safety benefits would accrue. In addition, NHTSA concluded that automatic restraints might have an adverse effect on the public's attitude toward safety. Given the high expense and limited benefits of detachable belts, NHTSA feared that many consumers would regard the Standard as an instance of ineffective regulation, adversely affecting the public's view of safety regulation and, in particular, "poisoning . . . popular sentiment toward efforts to improve occupant restraint systems in the future."

State Farm Mutual Automobile Insurance Co. and the National Association of Independent Insurers filed petitions for review of NHTSA's rescission of the passive restraint Standard. The United States Court of Appeals for the District of Columbia Circuit held that the agency's rescission of the passive restraint requirement was arbitrary and capricious. 680 F.2d 206 (1982). While observing that rescission is not unrelated to an agency's refusal to take action in the first instance, the court concluded that, in this case, NHTSA's discretion to rescind the passive restraint requirement had been restricted by various forms of congressional "reaction" to the passive restraint issue. It then proceeded to find that the rescission of Standard 208 was arbitrary and capricious for three reasons. First, the court found insufficient as a basis for rescission NHTSA's conclusion that it could not reliably predict an increase in belt usage under the Standard. The court held that there was insufficient evidence in the record to sustain NHTSA's position on this issue, and that, "only a well justified refusal to seek more evidence could render rescission non-arbitrary." Second, a majority of the panel concluded that NHTSA inadequately considered the possibility of requiring manufacturers to install nondetachable rather than detachable passive belts. Third, the majority found that the agency acted arbitrarily and capriciously by failing to give any consideration whatever to requiring compliance with Modified Standard 208 by the installation of airbags. . . .

III

Unlike the Court of Appeals, we do not find the appropriate scope of judicial review to be the "most troublesome question" in these cases. Both the Act and the 1974 Amendments concerning occupant crash protection standards indicate that motor vehicle safety standards are to be promulgated under the informal rulemaking procedures of the Administrative Procedure Act. 5 U.S.C. § 553. The agency's action in promulgating such standards therefore may be set aside if found to be "arbitrary, capricious, an abuse of discretion, or otherwise not in accordance with law." 5 U.S.C. § 706(2)(A); *Citizens to Preserve Overton Part v. Volpe*, 401 U.S. 402, 414 (1971). . . . We believe that the rescission or modification of an occupant-protection standard is subject to the same test. Section 103(b) of the Act, states that the procedural and judicial review provisions of the Administrative Procedure Act "shall apply to all orders establishing, amending, or revoking a Federal motor vehicle safety standard," and suggests no difference in the scope of judicial review depending upon the nature of the agency's action.

Petitioner Motor Vehicle Manufacturers Association (MVMA) disagrees, contending that the rescission of an agency rule should be judged by the same standard a court would use to judge an agency's refusal to promulgate a rule in the first place — a standard petitioner believes considerably narrower than the traditional arbitrary-and-capricious test. We reject this view. The Act expressly equates orders "revoking" and "establishing" safety standards; neither that Act nor the APA suggests that revocations are to be treated as refusals to promulgate standards. Petitioner's view would render meaningless Congress' authorization for judicial review of orders revoking safety rules. Moreover, the revocation of an extant regulation is substantially different than a failure to act. Revocation constitutes a reversal of the agency's former views as to the proper course. A "settled course of behavior embodies the agency's informed judgment that, by pursuing that course, it will carry out the policies committed to it by Congress. There is, then, at least a presumption that those policies will be carried out best if the settled rule is adhered to." *Atchison, T. & S.F.R. Co. v. Wichita Bd. of Trade*, 412 U.S. 800, 807–808 (1973). Accordingly, an agency changing its course by rescinding a rule is obligated to supply a reasoned analysis for the change beyond that which may be required when the agency does not act in the first instance.

In so holding, we fully recognize that "[r]egulatory agencies do not establish rules of conduct to last forever," *American Trucking Assns., Inc. v. Atchison, T. & S.F.R. Co.*, 387 U.S. 397, 416 (1967), and that an agency must be given ample latitude to "adapt their rules and policies to the demands of changing circumstances." *Permian Basin Area Rate Cases*, 390 U.S. 747, 784 (1968). But the forces of change do not always or necessarily point in the direction of deregulation. In the abstract, there is no more reason to presume that changing circumstances require the rescission of prior action, instead of a revision in or even the extension of current regulation. If Congress established a presumption from which judicial review should start, that presumption — contrary to petitioners' views — is not *against* safety regulation, but *against* changes in current policy that are not justified by the rulemaking record. While the removal of a regulation may not entail the monetary expenditures and other costs of enacting a new standard, and, accordingly, it may be easier for an agency to justify a deregulatory action, the direction in which an agency chooses to move does not alter the standard of judicial review established by law.

The Department of Transportation accepts the applicability of the "arbitrary and capricious" standard. It argues that under this standard, a reviewing court may not set aside an agency rule that is rational, based on consideration of the relevant factors, and within the scope of the authority delegated to the agency by the statute. We do not disagree with this formulation.[9] The scope of review under the "arbitrary and capricious" standard is narrow and a court is not to substitute its judgment for that of the agency. Nevertheless, the agency must examine the relevant data and articulate a satisfactory explanation for its action including a "rational connection between the facts found and the choice made." *Burlington Truck Lines, Inc. v. United States,* 371 U.S. 156, 168 (1962). In reviewing that explanation, we must "consider whether the decision was based on a consideration of the relevant factors and whether there has been a clear error of judgment." *Bowman Transportation, Inc. v. Arkansas-Best Freight System, Inc., supra,* at 285; *Citizens to Preserve Overton Park v. Volpe, supra,* at 416. Normally, an agency rule would be arbitrary and capricious if the agency has relied on factors which Congress has not intended it to consider, entirely failed to consider an important aspect of the problem, offered an explanation for its decision that runs counter to the evidence before the agency, or is so implausible that it could not be ascribed to a difference in view or the product of agency expertise. The reviewing court should not attempt itself to make up for such deficiencies; we may not supply a reasoned basis for the agency's action that the agency itself has not given. *SEC v. Chenery Corp.,* 332 U.S. 194, 196 (1947). We will, however, "uphold a decision of less than ideal clarity if the agency's path may reasonably be discerned." *Bowman Transportation, Inc. v. Arkansas-Best Freight System, Inc.* . . . . See also *Camp v. Pitts,* 411 U.S. 138, 142–143 (1973) (*per curiam*). For purposes of these cases, it is also relevant that Congress required a record of the rulemaking proceedings to be compiled and submitted to a reviewing court, 15 U.S.C. § 1394, and intended that agency findings under the Act would be supported by "substantial evidence on the record considered as a whole." . . .

---

[9] The Department of Transportation suggests that the arbitrary-and-capricious standard requires no more than the minimum rationality a statute must bear in order to withstand analysis under the Due Process Clause. We do not view as equivalent the presumption of constitutionality afforded legislation drafted by Congress and the presumption of regularity afforded an agency in fulfilling its statutory mandate.

V

The ultimate question before us is whether NHTSA's rescission of the passive restraint requirement of Standard 208 was arbitrary and capricious. We conclude, as did the Court of Appeals, that it was. We also conclude, but for somewhat different reasons, that further consideration of the issue by the agency is therefore required. We deal separately with the rescission as it applies to airbags and as it applies to seatbelts.

A

The first and most obvious reason for finding the rescission arbitrary and capricious is that NHTSA apparently gave no consideration whatever to modifying the Standard to require that airbag technology be utilized. Standard 208 sought to achieve automatic crash protection by requiring automobile manufacturers to install either of two passive restraint devices: airbags or automatic seatbelts. There was no suggestion in the long rulemaking process that led to Standard 208 that if only one of these options were feasible, no passive restraint standard should be promulgated. Indeed, the agency's original proposed Standard contemplated the installation of inflatable restraints in all cars. Automatic belts were added as a means of complying with the Standard because they were believed to be as effective as airbags in achieving the goal of occupant crash protection. . . . At that time, the passive belt approved by the agency could not be detached. Only later, at a manufacturer's behest, did the agency approve of the detachability feature — and only after assurances that the feature would not compromise the safety benefits of the restraint. Although it was then foreseen that 60% of the new cars would contain airbags and 40% would have automatic seatbelts, the ratio between the two was not significant as long as the passive belt would also assure greater passenger safety.

The agency has now determined that the detachable automatic belts will not attain anticipated safety benefits because so many individuals will detach the mechanism. Even if this conclusion were acceptable in its entirety, . . . standing alone it would not justify any more than an amendment of Standard 208 to disallow compliance by means of the one technology which will not provide effective passenger protection. It does not cast doubt on the need for a passive restraint standard or upon the efficacy of airbag technology. In its most recent rulemaking, the agency again acknowledged the lifesaving potential of the airbag:

> The agency has no basis at this time for changing its earlier conclusions in 1976 and 1977 that basic air bag technology is sound and has been sufficiently demonstrated to be effective in those vehicles in current use. . . .

Given the effectiveness ascribed to airbag technology by the agency, the mandate of the Act to achieve traffic safety would suggest that the logical response to the faults of detachable seatbelts would be to require the installation of airbags. At the very least this alternative way of achieving the objectives of the Act should have been addressed and adequate reasons given for its abandonment. But the agency not only did not require compliance through airbags, it also did not even consider the possibility in its 1981 rulemaking. Not one sentence of its rulemaking statement discusses the airbags-only option. Because, as the Court of Appeals stated, "NHTSA's . . . analysis of airbags was nonexistent," 680 F.2d, at 236, what we said in *Burlington Truck Lines, Inc. v. United States,* 371 U.S., at 167, is apropos here:

> There are no findings and no analysis here to justify the choice made, no indication of the basis on which the [agency] exercised its expert discretion. We are not prepared to and the Administrative Procedure Act will not permit us to accept such . . . practice. . . . Expert discretion is the lifeblood of the administrative process, but "unless we make the requirements for administrative action strict and demanding, *expertise,* the strength of modern government, can become a monster which rules with no practical limits on its discretion." *New York v. United States,* 342 U.S. 882, 884 (dissenting opinion)

(footnote omitted).

We have frequently reiterated that an agency must cogently explain why it has exercised its discretion in a given manner, . . . and we reaffirm this principle again today.

The automobile industry has opted for the passive belt over the airbag, but surely it is not enough that the regulated industry has eschewed a given safety device. For nearly a decade, the automobile industry waged the regulatory equivalent of war against the airbag and lost — the inflatable restraint was proved sufficiently effective. Now the automobile industry has decided to employ a seatbelt system which will not meet the safety objectives of Standard 208. This hardly constitutes cause to revoke the Standard itself. Indeed, the Act was necessary because the industry was not sufficiently responsive to safety concerns. The Act intended that safety standards not depend on current technology and could be "technology-forcing" in the sense of inducing the development of superior safety design. If, under the statute, the agency should not defer to the industry's failure to develop safer cars, which it surely should not do, *a fortiori* it may not revoke a safety standard which can be satisfied by current technology simply because the industry has opted for an ineffective seatbelt design.

Although the agency did not address the mandatory airbag option and the Court of Appeals noted that "airbags seem to have none of the problems that NHTSA identified in passive seatbelts," 680 F.2d, at 237, petitioners recite a number of difficulties that they believe would be posed by a mandatory airbag standard. These range from questions concerning the installation of airbags in small cars to that of adverse public reaction. But these are not the agency's reasons for rejecting a mandatory airbag standard. Not having discussed the possibility, the agency submitted no reasons at all. The short — and sufficient — answer to petitioners' submission is that the courts may not accept appellate counsel's *post hoc* rationalizations for agency action. *Burlington Truck Lines, Inc. v. United States,* 371 U.S., at 168. It is well established that an agency's action must be upheld, if at all, on the basis articulated by the agency itself. *SEC v. Chenery Corp.,* 332 U.S., at 196. . . .

Petitioners also invoke our decision in *Vermont Yankee Nuclear Power Corp. v. Natural Resources Defense Council, Inc.,* 435 U.S. 519 (1978), as though it were a talisman under which any agency decision is by definition unimpeachable. Specifically, it is submitted that to require an agency to consider an airbags-only alternative is, in essence, to dictate to the agency the procedures it is to follow. Petitioners both misread *Vermont Yankee* and misconstrue the nature of the remand that is in order. In *Vermont Yankee,* we held that a court may not impose additional procedural requirements upon an agency. We do not require today any specific procedures which NHTSA must follow. Nor do we broadly require an agency to consider all policy alternatives in reaching a decision. It is true that rulemaking "cannot be found wanting simply because the agency failed to include every alternative device and thought conceivable by the mind of man . . . regardless of how uncommon or unknown that alternative may have been. . . ." *Id.*, at 551. But the airbag is more than a policy alternative to the passive restraint Standard; it is a technological alternative within the ambit of the existing Standard. We hold only that given the judgment made in 1977 that airbags are an effective and cost-beneficial life-saving technology, the mandatory passive restraint rule may not be abandoned without any consideration whatsoever of an airbags-only requirement.

B

Although the issue is closer, we also find that the agency was too quick to dismiss the safety benefits of automatic seatbelts. NHTSA's critical finding was that, in light of the industry's plans to install readily detachable passive belts, it could not reliably predict "even a 5 percentage point increase as the minimum level of expected usage increase." 46 Fed. Reg. 53423 (1981). The Court of Appeals rejected this finding because there is "not one iota" of evidence that Modified Standard 208 will fail to increase nationwide seatbelt use by at least 13 percentage points, the level of increased usage necessary for the Standard to justify its cost. Given the lack of probative evidence, the court held that "only a well justified refusal to seek more evidence could render rescission non-arbitrary." 680 F.2d, at 232.

Petitioners object to this conclusion. In their view, "substantial uncertainty" that a regulation will accomplish its intended purpose is sufficient reason, without more, to rescind a regulation. We agree with petitioners that just as an agency reasonably may decline to issue a safety standard if it is uncertain about its efficacy, an agency may also revoke a standard on the basis of serious uncertainties if supported by the record and reasonably explained. Rescission of the passive restraint requirement would not be arbitrary and capricious simply because there was no evidence in direct support of the agency's conclusion. It is not infrequent that the available data do not settle a regulatory issue, and the agency must then exercise its judgment in moving from the facts and probabilities on the record to a policy conclusion. Recognizing that policymaking in a complex society must account for uncertainty, however, does not imply that it is sufficient for an agency to merely recite the terms "substantial uncertainty" as a justification for its actions. As previously noted, the agency must explain the evidence which is available, and must offer a "rational connection between the facts found and the choice made." *Burlington Truck Lines, Inc. v. United States, supra,* at 168. Generally, one aspect of that explanation would be a justification for rescinding the regulation before engaging in a search for further evidence.

In these cases, the agency's explanation for rescission of the passive restraint requirement is *not* sufficient to enable us to conclude that the rescission was the product of reasoned decisionmaking. To reach this conclusion, we do not upset the agency's view of the facts, but we do appreciate the limitations of this record in supporting the agency's decision. We start with the accepted ground that if used, seatbelts unquestionably would save many thousands of lives and would prevent tens of thousands of crippling injuries. . . . [T]he safety benefits of wearing seatbelts are not in doubt, and it is not challenged that were those benefits to accrue, the monetary costs of implementing the Standard would be easily justified. We move next to the fact that there is no direct evidence in support of the agency's finding that detachable automatic belts cannot be predicted to yield a substantial increase in usage. The empirical evidence on the record, consisting of surveys of drivers of automobiles equipped with passive belts, reveals more than a doubling of the usage rate experienced with manual belts. Much of the agency's rulemaking statement — and much of the controversy in these cases — centers on the conclusions that should be drawn from these studies. The agency maintained that the doubling of seatbelt usage in these studies could not be extrapolated to an across-the-board mandatory standard because the passive seatbelts were guarded by ignition interlocks and purchasers of the tested cars are somewhat atypical. Respondents insist these studies demonstrate that Modified Standard 208 will substantially increase seatbelt usage. We believe that it is within the agency's discretion to pass upon the generalizability of these field studies. This is precisely the type of issue which rests within the expertise of NHTSA, and upon which a reviewing court must be most hesitant to intrude.

But accepting the agency's view of the field tests on passive restraints indicates only that there is no reliable real-world experience that usage rates will substantially increase. To be sure, NHTSA opines that "it cannot reliably predict even a 5 percentage point increase as the minimum level of expected increased usage." But this and other statements that passive belts will not yield substantial increases in seatbelt usage apparently take no account of the critical difference between detachable automatic belts and current manual belts. A detached passive belt does require an affirmative act to reconnect it, but — unlike a manual seatbelt — the passive belt, once reattached, will continue to function automatically unless again disconnected. Thus, inertia — a factor which the agency's own studies have found significant in explaining the current low usage rates for seatbelts[18] — works in *favor* of, not *against*, use of the protective device. Since 20% to 50% of motorists currently wear

---

[18] NHTSA commissioned a number of surveys of public attitudes in an effort to better understand why people were not using manual belts and to determine how they would react to passive restraints. The surveys reveal that while 20% to 40% of the public is opposed to wearing manual belts, the larger proportion of the population does not wear belts because they forgot or found manual belts inconvenient or bothersome. RIA, at IV–25, App. 81. In another survey, 38% of the surveyed group responded that they would welcome automatic belts, and 25% would "tolerate" them. *See* RIA, at IV–37, App. 93. NHTSA did not comment upon these attitude surveys in its explanation accompanying the rescission of the passive restraint requirement.

seatbelts on some occasions,[19] there would seem to be grounds to believe that seatbelt use by occasional users will be substantially increased by the detachable passive belts. Whether this is in fact the case is a matter for the agency to decide, but it must bring its expertise to bear on the question.

The agency is correct to look at the costs as well as the benefits of Standard 208. The agency's conclusion that the incremental costs of the requirements were no longer reasonable was predicated on its prediction that the safety benefits of the regulation might be minimal. Specifically, the agency's fears that the public may resent paying more for the automatic belt systems is expressly dependent on the assumption that detachable automatic belts will not produce more than "negligible safety benefits." When the agency reexamines its findings as to the likely increase in seatbelt usage, it must also reconsider its judgment of the reasonableness of the monetary and other costs associated with the Standard. In reaching its judgment, NHTSA should bear in mind that Congress intended safety to be the pre-eminent factor under the Act:

> The Committee intends that safety shall be the overriding consideration in the issuance of standards under this bill. The Committee recognizes . . . that the Secretary will necessarily consider reasonableness of cost, feasibility and adequate leadtime.

S. Rep. No. 1301, 89th Cong., 2d Sess., 6 (1966).

> In establishing standards the Secretary must conform to the requirement that the standard be practicable. This would require consideration of all relevant factors, including technological ability to achieve the goal of a particular standard as well as consideration of economic factors.

> Motor vehicle safety is the paramount purpose of this bill and each standard must be related thereto.

H.R. Rep. No. 1776, 89th Cong., 2d Sess., 16 (1966).

The agency also failed to articulate a basis for not requiring nondetachable belts under Standard 208. It is argued that the concern of the agency with the easy detachability of the currently favored design would be readily solved by a continuous passive belt, which allows the occupant to "spool out" the belt and create the necessary slack for easy extrication from the vehicle. The agency did not separately consider the continuous belt option, but treated it together with the ignition interlock device in a category it titled "Option of Adopting Use-Compelling Features." The agency was concerned that use-compelling devices would "complicate the extrication of [an] occupant from his or her car." "[T]o require that passive belts contain use-compelling features," the agency observed, "could be counterproductive [given] . . . widespread, latent and irrational fear in many members of the public that they could be trapped by the seat belt after a crash." In addition, based on the experience with the ignition interlock, the agency feared that use-compelling features might trigger adverse public reaction.

---

[19] Four surveys of manual belt usage were conducted for NHTSA between 1978 and 1980, leading the agency to report that 40% to 50% of the people use their belts at least some of the time.

By failing to analyze the continuous seatbelts option in its own right, the agency has failed to offer the rational connection between facts and judgment required to pass muster under the arbitrary-and-capricious standard. We agree with the Court of Appeals that NHTSA did not suggest that the emergency release mechanisms used in nondetachable belts are any less effective for emergency egress than the buckle release system used in detachable belts. In 1978, when General Motors obtained the agency's approval to install a continuous passive belt, it assured the agency that nondetachable belts with spool releases were as safe as detachable belts with buckle releases. 43 Fed. Reg. 21912, 21913–21914 (1978). NHTSA was satisfied that this belt design assured easy extricability: "[t]he agency does not believe that the use of [such] release mechanisms will cause serious occupant egress problems. . . ." *Id.*, at 52493, 52494. While the agency is entitled to change its view on the acceptability of continuous passive belts, it is obligated to explain its reasons for doing so.

The agency also failed to offer any explanation why a continuous passive belt would engender the same adverse public reaction as the ignition interlock, and, as the Court of Appeals concluded, "every indication in the record points the other way." 680 F.2d, at 234. We see no basis for equating the two devices: the continuous belt, unlike the ignition interlock, does not interfere with the operation of the vehicle. More importantly, it is the agency's responsibility, not this Court's, to explain its decision.

VI

"An agency's view of what is in the public interest may change, either with or without a change in circumstances. But an agency changing its course must supply a reasoned analysis. . . ." *Greater Boston Television Corp. v. FCC*, 143 U.S. App. D.C. 383, 394, 444 F.2d 841, 852 (1970) (footnote omitted), *cert. denied*, 403 U.S. 923 (1971). We do not accept all of the reasoning of the Court of Appeals but we do conclude that the agency has failed to supply the requisite "reasoned analysis" in this case. Accordingly, we vacate the judgment of the Court of Appeals and remand the cases to that court with directions to remand the matter to the NHTSA for further consideration consistent with this opinion.

So ordered.

JUSTICE REHNQUIST, with whom THE CHIEF JUSTICE, JUSTICE POWELL, and JUSTICE O'CONNOR join, concurring in part and dissenting in part.

I join Parts I, II, III, IV, and V–A of the Court's opinion. In particular, I agree that, since the airbag and continuous spool automatic seatbelt were explicitly approved in the Standard the agency was rescinding, the agency should explain why it declined to leave those requirements intact. In this case, the agency gave no explanation at all. Of course, if the agency can provide a rational explanation, it may adhere to its decision to rescind the entire Standard.

I do not believe, however, that NHTSA's view of detachable automatic seatbelts was arbitrary and capricious. The agency adequately explained its decision to rescind the Standard insofar as it was satisfied by detachable belts.

The statute that requires the Secretary of Transportation to issue motor vehicle safety standards also requires that "[e]ach such . . . standard shall be practicable [and] shall meet the need for motor vehicle safety." The Court rejects the agency's explanation for its conclusion that there is substantial uncertainty whether requiring installation of detachable automatic belts would substantially increase seatbelt usage. The agency chose not to rely on a study showing a substantial increase in seatbelt usage in cars equipped with automatic seatbelts *and* an ignition interlock to prevent the car from being operated when the belts were not in place *and* which were voluntarily purchased with this equipment by consumers. It is reasonable for the agency to decide that this study does not support any conclusion concerning the effect of automatic seatbelts that are installed in all cars whether the consumer wants them or not and are not linked to an ignition interlock system.

The Court rejects this explanation because "there would seem to be grounds to believe that seatbelt use by occasional users will be substantially increased by the detachable passive belts," and the agency did not adequately explain its rejection of these grounds. It seems to me that the agency's explanation, while by no means a model, is adequate. The agency acknowledged that there would probably be some increase in belt usage, but concluded that the increase would be small and not worth the cost of mandatory detachable automatic belts. The agency's obligation is to articulate a " 'rational connection between the facts found and the choice made.' " *Ante*, at 42, 52, quoting *Burlington Truck Lines, Inc. v. United States,* 371 U.S. 156, 168 (1962). I believe it has met this standard.

The agency explicitly stated that it will increase its educational efforts in an attempt to promote public understanding, acceptance, and use of passenger restraint systems. It also stated that it will "initiate efforts with automobile manufacturers to ensure that the public will have [automatic crash protection] technology available. If this does not succeed, the agency will consider regulatory action to assure that the last decade's enormous advances in crash protection technology will not be lost."

The agency's changed view of the standard seems to be related to the election of a new President of a different political party. It is readily apparent that the responsible members of one administration may consider public resistance and uncertainties to be more important than do their counterparts in a previous administration. A change in administration brought about by the people casting their votes is a perfectly reasonable basis for an executive agency's reappraisal of the costs and benefits of its programs and regulations. As long as the agency remains within the bounds established by Congress,* it is entitled to assess administrative records and evaluate priorities in light of the philosophy of the administration.

---

* Of course, a new administration may not refuse to enforce laws of which it does not approve, or to ignore statutory standards in carrying out its regulatory functions. But in this case, as the Court correctly concludes, . . . Congress has not required the agency to require passive restraints.

NOTES AND QUESTIONS

8-47. The majority makes reference to the approach to these issues taken by the D.C. Circuit below. How does the majority opinion differ from the approach taken by the court below?

8-48. There are at least two factual issues here: (1) airbag v. no airbag and detachable seat belts v. automatic seat belts. Did the agency give any reason at all for rejecting the airbag alternative? Did it give a reason for concluding that automatic seatbelts would not work? Did it give a good enough reason to satisfy a majority of the Court?

8-49. What was the basis of the disagreement between the dissent and the majority? Why did the dissent, nevertheless, conclude that the agency's decision must be remanded?

8-50. What theories of the administrative process seem to underlie the approaches of the lower court, the Supreme Court majority and the dissent? Does the fact that deregulation is involved in this case make a difference in outcome? What is the likely impact of these different approaches on the deregulatory initiatives of this or other agencies?

8-51. Is this case consistent in its tone and approach to agency action with *Chevron*? Can these two cases be reconciled? What philosophies of the administrative process underlie these different approaches?

BALTIMORE GAS & ELECTRIC CO. v. NRDC

United States Supreme Court
462 U.S. 87 (1983)

JUSTICE O'CONNOR delivered the opinion of the Court.

Section 102(2)(C) of the National Environmental Policy Act of 1969, requires federal agencies to consider the environmental impact of any major federal action. As part of its generic rulemaking proceedings to evaluate the environmental effects of the nuclear fuel cycle for nuclear powerplants, the Nuclear Regulatory Commission (Commission) decided that licensing boards should assume, for purposes of NEPA, that the permanent storage of certain nuclear wastes would have no significant environmental impact and thus should not affect the decision whether to license a particular nuclear powerplant. We conclude that the Commission complied with NEPA and that its decision is not arbitrary or capricious within the meaning of § 10(e) of the Administrative Procedure Act (APA), 5 U.S.C. § 706.

I

The environmental impact of operating a light-water nuclear power-plant includes the effects of offsite activities necessary to provide fuel for the plant ("front end" activities), and of offsite activities necessary to dispose of the highly toxic and long-lived nuclear wastes generated by the plant ("back end" activities). The dispute in these cases concerns the Commission's adoption of a series of generic rules to evaluate the environmental effects of a nuclear power-plant's fuel cycle. At the heart of each rule is Table S–3, a numerical compilation of the estimated resources used and effluents released by fuel cycle activities supporting a year's operation of a typical light-water reactor. The three versions of Table S–3 contained similar numerical values, although the supporting documentation has been amplified during the course of the proceedings.

The Commission first adopted Table S–3 in 1974, after extensive informal rulemaking proceedings. 39 Fed. Reg. 14188 *et seq.* (1974). This "original" rule, as it later came to be described, declared that in environmental reports and impact statements for individual licensing proceedings the environmental costs of the fuel cycle "shall be as set forth" in Table S–3 and that "[n]o further discussion of such environmental effects shall be required." The original Table S–3 contained no numerical entry for the long-term environmental effects of storing solidified transuranic and high-level wastes, because the Commission staff believed that technology would be developed to isolate the wastes from the environment. The Commission and the parties have later termed this assumption of complete repository integrity as the "zero-release" assumption: the reasonableness of this assumption is at the core of the present controversy.

. . .

II.

We are acutely aware that the extent to which this Nation should rely on nuclear power as a source of energy is an important and sensitive issue. Much of the debate focuses on whether development of nuclear generation facilities should proceed in the face of uncertainties about their long-term effects on the environment. Resolution of these fundamental policy questions lies, however, with Congress and the agencies to which Congress has delegated authority, as well as with state legislatures and, ultimately, the populace as a whole. Congress has assigned the courts only the limited, albeit important, task of reviewing agency action to determine whether the agency conformed with controlling statutes. As we emphasized in our earlier encounter with these very proceedings, "[a]dministrative decisions should be set aside in this context, as in every other, only for substantial procedural or substantive reasons as mandated by statute . . ., not simply because the court is unhappy with the result reached." *Vermont Yankee*, 435 U.S., at 558. . . .

The controlling statute at issue here is the NEPA. NEPA has twin aims. First, it "places upon an agency the obligation to consider every significant aspect of the environmental impact of a proposed action." Second, it ensures that the agency will inform the public that it has indeed considered environmental concerns in its decisionmaking process. Congress in enacting NEPA, however, did not require agencies to elevate environmental concerns over other appropriate considerations. Rather, it required only that the agency take a "hard look" at the environmental consequences before taking major action. The role of the courts is simply to ensure that the agency has adequately considered and disclosed the environmental impact of its actions and that its decision is not arbitrary or capricious. *See generally Citizens to Preserve Overton Park, Inc. v. Volpe,* 401 U.S. 402, 415–417 (1971).

In its Table S–3 rule here, the Commission has determined that the probabilities favor the zero-release assumption, because the Nation is likely to develop methods to store the wastes with no leakage to the environment. The NRDC did not challenge and the Court of Appeals did not decide the reasonableness of this determination, and no party seriously challenges it here. The Commission recognized, however, that the geological, chemical, physical, and other data it relied on in making this prediction were based, in part, on assumptions which involve substantial uncertainties. Again, no one suggests that the uncertainties are trivial or the potential effects insignificant if time proves the zero-release assumption to have been seriously wrong. After confronting the issue, though, the Commission has determined that the uncertainties concerning the development of nuclear waste storage facilities are not sufficient to affect the outcome of any individual licensing decision.

It is clear that the Commission, in making this determination, has made the careful consideration and disclosure required by NEPA. The sheer volume of proceedings before the Commission is impressive. Of far greater importance, the Commission's Statement of Consideration announcing the final Table S–3 rule shows that it has digested this mass of material and disclosed all substantial risks. . . .

Congress did not enact NEPA, of course, so that an agency would contemplate the environmental impact of an action as an abstract exercise. Rather, Congress intended that the "hard look" be incorporated as part of the agency's process of deciding whether to pursue a particular federal action. It was on this ground that the Court of Appeals faulted the Commission's action, for failing to allow the uncertainties potentially to "tip the balance" in a particular licensing decision. As a general proposition, we can agree with the Court of Appeals' determination that an agency must allow all significant environmental risks to be factored into the decision whether to undertake a proposed action. We think, however, that the Court of Appeals erred in concluding the Commission had not complied with this standard.

As *Vermont Yankee* made clear, NEPA does not require agencies to adopt any particular internal decisionmaking structure. Here, the agency has chosen to evaluate generically the environmental impact of the fuel cycle and inform individual licensing boards, through the Table S–3 rule, of its evaluation. The generic method chosen by the agency is clearly an appropriate method of conducting the hard look required by NEPA. . . . The Commission's decision to affix a zero value to the environmental impact of long-term storage would violate NEPA, however, only if the Commission acted arbitrarily and capriciously in deciding generically that the uncertainty was insufficient to affect any individual licensing decision. In assessing whether the Commission's decision is arbitrary and capricious, it is crucial to place the zero-release assumption in context. Three factors are particularly important. First is the Commission's repeated emphasis that the zero-risk assumption — and, indeed, all the Table S–3 rule was made for a limited purpose. . . .

Second, the Commission emphasized that the zero-release assumption is but a single figure in an entire Table, which the Commission expressly designed as a risk-averse estimate of the environmental impact of the fuel cycle. It noted that Table S–3 assumed that the fuel storage canisters and the fuel rod cladding would be corroded before a repository is closed and that all volatile materials in the fuel would escape to the environment. Given that assumption, and the improbability that materials would escape after sealing, the Commission determined that the overall Table represented a conservative (i.e., inflated) statement of environmental impacts. It is not unreasonable for the Commission to counteract the uncertainties in postsealing releases by balancing them with an overestimate of presealing releases. A reviewing court should not magnify a single line item beyond its significance as only part of a larger Table.

Third, a reviewing court must remember that the Commission is making predictions, within its area of special expertise, at the frontiers of science. When examining this kind of scientific determination, as opposed to simple findings of fact, a reviewing court must generally be at its most deferential.

With these three guides in mind, we find the Commission's zero-release assumption to be within the bounds of reasoned decisionmaking required by the APA. . . .

In sum, we think that the zero-release assumption — a policy judgment concerning one line in a conservative Table designed for the limited purpose of individual licensing decisions — is within the bounds of reasoned decisionmaking. It is not our task to determine what decision we, as Commissioners, would have reached. Our only task is to determine whether the Commission has considered the relevant factors and articulated a rational connection between the facts found and the choice made. Under this standard, we think the Commission's zero-release assumption, within the context of Table S–3 as a whole, was not arbitrary and capricious. . . .

For the foregoing reasons, the judgment of the Court of Appeals for the District of Columbia Circuit is reversed.

JUSTICE POWELL took no part in the consideration or decision of these cases.

NOTES AND QUESTIONS

8-52. How would you characterize Justice O'Connor's approach to the review of the issues in this case? Does she take a rational basis approach — *i.e.*, that *any* agency reason is enough? Is it "rational basis with a bite" — *i.e.*, that a pretty good reason is enough? Is it a form of the hard look approach?

8-53. What does Justice O'Connor mean when she says that the agency must take a hard look at the issues? What standard of review does a court use to determine if the agency has done this? Does this differ from an approach in which the court itself takes a hard look? How?

8-54. Whatever standard of review is involved, what kind of rulemaking record is necessary for a court to engage in meaningful judicial review? Does section 553 mandate a record? Based on section 553 what, as a minimum, should be in this record? Can the Court require more or is that a violation of the teachings of *Vermont Yankee*?

8-55. *See* ACUS, *A Guide to Federal Agency Rulemaking,* Part III, Chapter 5, at pages 8–10, which notes:

> Several factors account for the difficulties the courts confront in examining rulemaking records. Rulemaking is essentially a legislative process, encompassing value and policy judgments as well as factual material. Even the "facts" on which the agency relies are accumulated expertise and experience of the agency and others, which are difficult if not impossible to package in the record of the proceeding. . . .
>
> A major issue regarding judicial review of rulemaking is whether the record on review should consist only of materials that were before the agency when it made its final decision or whether the agency may augment the record with additional facts or arguments before the reviewing court. . . .
>
> Regardless of whether or not a statute requires the judicial review be limited to the administrative record that was before the agency when it made its decision, the rulemaking staff should anticipate court rejection of "post-hoc rationalizations" for rules, and close judicial scrutiny of reliance on data attained after the public stage of rulemaking. . . .

See also Pedersen, *Formal Records and Informal Rulemaking,* 85 YALE L.J. 38 (1975).

8-56. Reasoned or adequate decisionmaking remains alive and well in the lower courts. *See, e.g., Bluewater Network v. EPA*, 370 F.3d 1 (D.C. Cir. 2004); *El Rio Santa Cruz Neighborhood Health Center, Inc. v. U.S. Department of Health and Human Services*, 396 F.3d 1265 (D.C. Cir. 2005); *Prometheus Radio Project v. FCC*, 373 F.3d 372 (3d Cir. 2004).

Chapter 9
THE AVAILABILITY AND TIMING OF JUDICIAL REVIEW

§ 9.01 Introduction

Logically prior to questions involving the scope of judicial review are issues concerning whether or not courts should be involved in the first place. Consider the following overview in Aman and Mayton, *Administrative Law*, 339-40:*

> Whether and when the courts will review an agency action, or failure to act, are reasonably complicated matters. These matter, the availability and timing of judicial review, are about divisions of labor between courts and agencies. These divisions turn on the comparative abilities of agencies and courts and on such practical matters as allocating work between agencies and court so as to avoid redundant work. Also, the availability and timing of review implicates constitutional concerns about the role of the courts in a government of separated powers. According to the Supreme Court:
>
>> Judicial adherence to the doctrine of the separation of powers preserves the courts for the decision of issues, between litigants, capable of effective determination. . . . When the courts act continually within these constitutionally imposed boundaries . . . their ability to perform their function as a balance for the peoples' protection against abuse of power by other branches of government remains unimpaired.[1]
>
> While both are similarly grounded in separated powers and a sensible division of work between courts and agencies, the availability and the timing of review are, nonetheless, separately identified. Questions about the *availability* of judicial review are expressed as matters of jurisdiction, standing, and sovereign immunity. Availability of review also includes questions highlighted by the Administrative Procedure Act, of the extent to which Congress has "precluded" review or has so "committed" a matter to agency discretion that it is beyond review. *Timing* of review is identified by reference to the pendency and maturity of agency actions. In this relation, timing involves doctrines of ripeness and exhaustion of administrative remedies. It also involves the doctrine of primary jurisdiction, whether an action is best initiated in an agency or a court.[2]

---

* Reprinted from *Administrative Law*, Alfred C. Aman, Jr. & William T. Mayton, 2d ed., 2001, with permission of Thomson West.

[1] *United Public Workers v. Mitchell*, 330 U.S. 75, 90–91, 67 S.Ct. 556, 564–65, 91 L.Ed. 754 (1947).

[2] These questions of availability and timing of review generally relate to court actions initiated by a private individual. At times, these questions and the impediments they present can be substantially avoided should a person act more passively and defensively, to await an "enforcement action." By an enforcement action, the agency proceeds against the individual in court, to gain the assistance of the court, in forcing the individual to do whatever it is that the agency wants of him.

We will discuss the timing and the availability of judicial review according to the foregoing categories, or doctrines, of ripeness, exhaustion, *et al.* But as you consider these doctrines, you should do so with a particular caution in mind. This is that in practice these doctrines are not all that neat and separate; often, they converge and overlap,[3] as we will from time to time point out. Generally speaking, though, the confusion that may be entailed by the occasional convergences of ripeness, exhaustion, *et al.* can be dissipated by remembering that these doctrines, while emphasizing somewhat different factors, share the common goal of managing a sensible allocation of work between courts and agencies. . . .

§ 9.02 APA Exclusions from Judicial Review

We have already had some exposure to the limitations expressed in sections 701(a)(1) and (a)(2) of the APA. As you will recall, the Supreme Court in *Citizens to Protect Overton Park v. Volpe*, 401 U.S. 402, Chapter Five, § 5.02, interpreted the presumption of reviewability embodied in the APA. Section 701 provides for judicial review except where "statutes preclude judicial review" or "where agency action" is "committed to agency discretion by law." The Court in *Overton Park* held that with regard to the statute before it, there was no "showing of clear and convincing evidence of a . . . legislative intent to restrict access to judicial review." 401 U.S. at 410.

Agencies can also exercise their discretion by not acting. They may refuse to issue new rules that they theoretically have the power to enact; they may decide not to enforce their own regulations in certain contexts or they may decide not to investigate certain possible violations of their rules or issues that may require new regulations.

These kinds of agency discretionary decisions usually go very much to the heart of just how an agency is to be run on a day-to-day basis. Agencies' resources, of course, are not infinite. When can and when should a court review this kind of agency discretion? Under what circumstances can we conclude that such actions are "committed to agency discretion by law"? Consider the following cases.

---

[3] The illustration of these convergences that has gained some fame is the D.C. Circuit's opinion in *Ticor Title Ins. Co. v. FTC*, 814 F.2d 731 (1987), where each of the three judges determined the reviewability of an agency action according to the three separate doctrines of ripeness, exhaustion, and finality. *See* § 9.04, Note 9–37, *infra.*

HECKLER v. CHANEY

United States Supreme Court
470 U.S. 831 (1985)

Justice Rehnquist delivered the opinion of the Court.

This case presents the question of the extent to which a decision of an administrative agency to exercise its "discretion" not to undertake certain enforcement actions is subject to judicial review under the Administrative Procedure Act, 5 U.S.C. § 501 *et seq.* (APA). Respondents are several prison inmates convicted of capital offenses and sentenced to death by lethal injection of drugs. They petitioned the Food and Drug Administration (FDA), alleging that under the circumstances the use of these drugs for capital punishment violated the Federal Food, Drug, and Cosmetic Act, 21 U.S.C. § 301 *et seq.* (FDCA), and requesting that the FDA take various enforcement actions to prevent these violations. The FDA refused their request. We review here a decision of the Court of Appeals for the District of Columbia Circuit, which held the FDA's refusal to take enforcement actions both reviewable and an abuse of discretion, and remanded the case with directions that the agency be required "to fulfill its statutory function." 718 F.2d 1174, 1191 (1983).

I

Respondents have been sentenced to death by lethal injection of drugs under the laws of the States of Oklahoma and Texas. Those States, and several others, have recently adopted this method for carrying out the capital sentence. Respondents first petitioned the FDA, claiming that the drugs used by the States for this purpose, although approved by the FDA for the medical purposes stated on their labels, were not approved for use in human executions. They alleged that the drugs had not been tested for the purpose for which they were to be used, and that, given that the drugs would likely be administered by untrained personnel, it was also likely that the drugs would not induce the quick and painless death intended. They urged that use of these drugs for human execution was the "unapproved use of an approved drug" and constituted a violation of the Act's prohibitions against "misbranding." They also suggested that the FDCA's requirements for approval of "new drugs" applied, since these drugs were now being used for a new purpose. Accordingly, respondents claimed that the FDA was required to approve the drugs as "safe and effective" for human execution before they could be distributed in interstate commerce. *See* 21 U.S.C. § 355. They therefore requested the FDA to take various investigatory and enforcement actions to prevent these perceived violations; they requested the FDA to affix warnings to the labels of all the drugs stating that they were unapproved and unsafe for human execution, to send statements to the drug manufacturers and prison administrators stating that the drugs should not be so used, and to adopt procedures for seizing the drugs from state prisons and to recommend the prosecution of all those in the chain of distribution who knowingly distribute or purchase the drugs with intent to use them for human execution.

The FDA Commissioner responded, refusing to take the requested actions. The Commissioner first detailed his disagreement with respondents' understanding of the scope of FDA jurisdiction over the unapproved use of approved drugs for human execution, concluding that FDA jurisdiction in the area was generally unclear but in any event should not be exercised to interfere with this particular aspect of state criminal justice systems. . . .

For us, this case turns on the important question of the extent to which determinations by the FDA *not to exercise* its enforcement authority over the use of drugs in interstate commerce may be judicially reviewed. That decision in turn involves the construction of two separate but necessarily interrelated statutes, the APA and the FDCA.

The APA's comprehensive provisions for judicial review of "agency actions," are contained in 5 U.S.C. §§ 701–706. Any person "adversely affected or aggrieved" by agency action, *see* § 702, including a "failure to act," is entitled to "judicial review thereof," as long as the action is a "final agency action for which there is no other adequate remedy in a court," *see* § 704. The standards to be applied on review are governed by the provisions of § 706. But before any review at all may be had, a party must first clear the hurdle of § 701(a). That section provides that the chapter on judicial review "applies, according to the provisions thereof, except to the extent that — (1) statutes preclude judicial review; or (2) agency action is committed to agency discretion by law." Petitioner urges that the decision of the FDA to refuse enforcement is an action "committed to agency discretion by law" under § 701(a)(2).

This Court has not had occasion to interpret this second exception in § 701(a) in any great detail. On its face, the section does not obviously lend itself to any particular construction; indeed, one might wonder what difference exists between § (a)(1) and § (a)(2). The former section seems easy in application; it requires construction of the substantive statute involved to determine whether Congress intended to preclude judicial review of certain decisions. That is the approach taken with respect to § (a)(1) in cases such as *Southern R. Co. v. Seaboard Allied Milling Corp.*, 442 U.S. 444 (1979), and *Dunlop v. Bachowski*, 421 U.S., at 567. But one could read the language "committed to agency discretion *by law*" in § (a)(2) to require a similar inquiry. In addition, commentators have pointed out that construction of § (a)(2) is further complicated by the tension between a literal reading of § (a)(2), which exempts from judicial review those decisions committed to agency "discretion," and the primary scope of review prescribed by § 706(2)(A) — whether the agency's action was "arbitrary, capricious, or an *abuse of discretion*." How is it, they ask, that an action committed to agency discretion can be unreviewable and yet courts still can review agency actions for abuse of that discretion? The APA's legislative history provides little help on this score. Mindful, however, of the common-sense principle of statutory construction that sections of a statute generally should be read "to give effect, if possible, to every clause . . .," *see United States v. Menasche*, 348 U.S. 528, 538–539 (1955), we think there is a proper construction of § (a)(2) which satisfies each of these concerns.

This Court first discussed § (a)(2) in *Citizens to Preserve Overton Park v. Volpe*, 401 U.S. 402 (1971). That case dealt with the Secretary of Transportation's approval of the building of an interstate highway through a park in Memphis, Tennessee. The relevant federal statute provided that the Secretary "shall not approve" any program or project using public parkland unless the Secretary first determined that no feasible alternatives were available. Interested citizens challenged the Secretary's approval under the APA, arguing that he had not satisfied the substantive statute's requirements. This Court first addressed the "threshold question" of whether the agency's action was at all reviewable. After setting out the language of § 701(a), the Court stated:

> In this case, there is no indication that Congress sought to prohibit judicial review and there is most certainly no "showing of 'clear and convincing evidence'" of a . . . legislative intent" to restrict access to judicial review. *Abbott Laboratories v. Gardner*, 387 U.S. 136, 141 (1967).

Similarly, the Secretary's decision here does not fall within the exception for action "committed to agency discretion." This is a very narrow exception. . . . The legislative history of the Administrative Procedure Act indicates that it is applicable in those rare instances where "statutes are drawn in such broad terms that in a given case there is no law to apply." S. Rep. No. 752, 79th Cong., 1st Sess., 26 (1945).

The above quote answers several of the questions raised by the language of § 701(a), although it raises others. First, it clearly separates the exception provided by § (a)(1) from the § (a)(2) exception. The former applies when Congress has expressed an intent to preclude judicial review. The latter applies in different circumstances; even where Congress has not affirmatively precluded review, review is not to be had if the statute is drawn so that a court would have no meaningful standard against which to judge the agency's exercise of discretion. In such a case, the statute ("law") can be taken to have "committed" the decisionmaking to the agency's judgment absolutely. This construction avoids conflict with the "abuse of discretion" standard of review in § 706 — if no judicially manageable standards are available for judging how and when an agency should exercise its discretion, then it is impossible to evaluate agency action for "abuse of discretion." In addition, this construction satisfies the principle of statutory construction mentioned earlier, by identifying a separate class of cases to which § 701(a)(2) applies.

To this point our analysis does not differ significantly from that of the Court of Appeals. That court purported to apply the "no law to apply" standard of *Overton Park*. We disagree, however, with that court's insistence that the "narrow construction" of § (a)(2) required application of a presumption of reviewability even to an agency's decision not to undertake certain enforcement actions. Here we think the Court of Appeals broke with tradition, case law, and sound reasoning.

Overton Park did not involve an agency's refusal to take requested enforcement action. It involved an affirmative act of approval under a statute that set clear guidelines for determining when such approval should be given. Refusals to take enforcement steps generally involve precisely the opposite situation, and in that situation we think the presumption is that judicial review is not available. This Court has recognized on several occasions over many years that an agency's decision not to prosecute or enforce, whether through civil or criminal process, is a decision generally committed to an agency's absolute discretion. . . . This recognition of the existence of discretion is attributable in no small part to the general unsuitability for judicial review of agency decisions to refuse enforcement.

The reasons for this general unsuitability are many. First, an agency decision not to enforce often involves a complicated balancing of a number of factors which are peculiarly within its expertise. Thus, the agency must not only assess whether a violation has occurred, but whether agency resources are best spent on this violation or another, whether the agency is likely to succeed if it acts, whether the particular enforcement action requested best fits the agency's overall policies, and, indeed, whether the agency has enough resources to undertake the action at all. An agency generally cannot act against each technical violation of the statute it is charged with enforcing. The agency is far better equipped than the courts to deal with the many variables involved in the proper ordering of its priorities. Similar concerns animate the principles of administrative law that courts generally will defer to an agency's construction of the statute it is charged with implementing, and to the procedures it adopts for implementing that statute.

In addition to these administrative concerns, we note that when an agency refuses to act it generally does not exercise its coercive power over an individual's liberty or property rights, and thus does not infringe upon areas that courts often are called upon to protect. Similarly, when an agency does act to enforce, that action itself provides a focus for judicial review, inasmuch as the agency must have exercised its power in some manner. The action at least can be reviewed to determine whether the agency exceeded its statutory powers. *See, e.g., FTC v. Klesner,* 280 U.S. 19 (1929). Finally, we recognize that an agency's refusal to institute proceedings shares to some extent the characteristics of the decision of a prosecutor in the Executive Branch not to indict — a decision which has long been regarded as the special province of the Executive Branch, inasmuch as it is the Executive who is charged by the Constitution to "take Care that the Laws be faithfully executed." U.S. Const., Art. II, § 3.

We of course only list the above concerns to facilitate understanding of our conclusion that an agency's decision not to take enforcement action should be presumed immune from judicial review under § 701(a)(2). For good reasons, such a decision has traditionally been "committed to agency discretion," and we believe that the Congress enacting the APA did not intend to alter that tradition. . . . In so stating, we emphasize that the decision is only presumptively unreviewable; the presumption may be rebutted where the substantive statute has provided guidelines for the agency to follow in exercising its enforcement powers.[4] Thus, in establishing this presumption

---

[4] We do not have in this case a refusal by the agency to institute proceedings based solely on the belief that it lacks jurisdiction. Nor do we have a situation where it could justifiably be found that the agency has "consciously and expressly adopted a general policy" that is so extreme as to amount to an abdication of its statutory responsibilities. *See, e.g., Adams v. Richardson,* 156 U.S. App. D.C. 267, 480 F.2d 1159 (1973) (en banc). Although we express no opinion on whether such decisions would be unreviewable under § 701(a)(2), we note that in those situations the statute conferring authority on the agency might indicate that such decisions were not "committed to agency discretion."

§ 9.02   THE AVAILABILITY AND TIMING OF JUDICIAL REVIEW   831

in the APA, Congress did not set agencies free to disregard legislative direction in the statutory scheme that the agency administers. Congress may limit an agency's exercise of enforcement power if it wishes, either by setting substantive priorities, or by otherwise circumscribing an agency's power to discriminate among issues or cases it will pursue. How to determine when Congress has done so is the question left open by *Overton Park.*

Dunlop v. Bachowski, 421 U.S. 560 (1975), relied upon heavily by respondents and the majority in the Court of Appeals, presents an example of statutory language which supplied sufficient standards to rebut the presumption of unreviewability. Dunlop involved a suit by a union employee, under the Labor-Management Reporting and Disclosure Act, 29 U.S.C. § 481 *et seq.* (LMRDA), asking the Secretary of Labor to investigate and file suit to set aside a union election. Section 482 provided that, upon filing of a complaint by a union member, "[t]he Secretary shall investigate such complaint and, if he finds probable cause to believe that a violation . . . has occurred . . . he shall . . . bring a civil action. . . ." After investigating the plaintiff's claims the Secretary of Labor declined to file suit, and the plaintiff sought judicial review under the APA. This Court held that review was available. It rejected the Secretary's argument that the statute precluded judicial review, and in a footnote it stated its agreement with the conclusion of the Court of Appeals that the decision was not "an unreviewable exercise of prosecutorial discretion." 421 U.S. at 567, n. 7. Our textual references to the "strong presumption" of reviewability in *Dunlop* were addressed only to the § (a)(1) exception; we were content to rely on the Court of Appeals' opinion to hold that the § (a)(2) exception did not apply. The Court of Appeals, in turn, had found the "principle of absolute prosecutorial discretion" inapplicable, because the language of the LMRDA indicated that the Secretary was required to file suit if certain "clearly defined" factors were present. The decision therefore was not "beyond the judicial capacity to supervise." *Bachowski v. Brennan*, 502 F.2d 79, 87–88 (CA3 1974) (quoting Davis § 28.16, at 984 (1970 Supp.)).

Dunlop is thus consistent with a general presumption of unreviewability of decisions not to enforce. The statute being administered quite clearly withdrew discretion from the agency and provided guidelines for exercise of its enforcement power. Our decision that review was available was not based on "pragmatic considerations," such as those cited by the Court of Appeals, *see* 231 U.S. App. D.C. at 147, 718 F.2d at 1185, that amount to an assessment of whether the interests at stake are important enough to justify intervention in the agencies' decisionmaking. The danger that agencies may not carry out their delegated powers with sufficient vigor does not necessarily lead to the conclusion that courts are the most appropriate body to police this aspect of their performance. That decision is in the first instance for Congress, and we therefore turn to the FDCA to determine whether in this case Congress has provided us with "law to apply." If it has indicated an intent to circumscribe agency enforcement discretion, and has provided meaningful standards for defining the limits of that discretion, there is "law to apply" under § 701(a)(2), and courts may require that the agency follow that law; if it has not, then an agency refusal to institute proceedings is a decision "committed to agency discretion by law" within the meaning of that section. . . .

III

[The Court concluded the FDCA did not circumscribe agency enforcement decisions.]

IV

We therefore conclude that the presumption that agency decisions not to institute proceedings are unreviewable under 5 U.S.C. § 701(a)(2) is not overcome by the enforcement provisions of the FDCA. The FDA's decision not to take the enforcement actions requested by respondents is therefore not subject to judicial review under the APA. The general exception to reviewability provided by § 701(a)(2) for action "committed to agency discretion" remains a narrow one, *see Citizens to Preserve Overton Park v. Volpe,* 401 U.S. 402 (1971), but within that exception are included agency refusals to institute investigative or enforcement proceedings, unless Congress has indicated otherwise. In so holding, we essentially leave to Congress, and not to the courts, the decision as to whether an agency's refusal to institute proceedings should be judicially reviewable. No colorable claim is made in this case that the agency's refusal to institute proceedings violated any constitutional rights of respondents, and we do not address the issue that would be raised in such a case. . . . The fact that the drugs involved in this case are ultimately to be used in imposing the death penalty must not lead this Court or other courts to import profound differences of opinion over the meaning of the Eighth Amendment to the United States Constitution into the domain of administrative law.

The judgment of the Court of Appeals is

Reversed.

JUSTICE BRENNAN, concurring.

Today the Court holds that individual decisions of the Food and Drug Administration not to take enforcement action in response to citizen requests are presumptively not reviewable under the Administrative Procedure Act, 5 U.S.C. §§ 701–706. I concur in this decision. This general presumption is based on the view that, in the normal course of events, Congress intends to allow broad discretion for its administrative agencies to make particular enforcement decisions, and there often may not exist readily discernible "law to apply" for courts to conduct judicial review of nonenforcement decisions. *See Citizens to Preserve Overton Park v. Volpe,* 401 U.S. 402, 410 (1971). I also agree that, despite this general presumption, "Congress did not set agencies free to disregard legislative direction in the statutory scheme that the agency administers." Thus the Court properly does not decide today that nonenforcement decisions are unreviewable in cases where (1) an agency flatly claims that it has no statutory jurisdiction to reach certain conduct, (2) an agency engages in a pattern of nonenforcement of clear statutory language, as in *Adams v. Richardson,* 156 U.S. App. D.C. 267, 480 F.2d 1159 (1973) (*en banc*), (3) an agency has refused to enforce a regulation lawfully promulgated and still in effect, or (4) a nonenforcement decision violates constitutional rights. It is possible to imagine other nonenforcement decisions made for entirely illegitimate reasons, for example, nonenforcement in return for a bribe, judicial review of which would not be foreclosed by the nonreviewability presumption. It may be presumed that Congress does not intend administrative agencies, agents of Congress' own creation, to ignore clear jurisdictional, regulatory, statutory, or constitutional commands, and in some circumstances including those listed above the statutes or regulations at issue may well provide "law to apply" under 5 U.S.C. § 701(a)(2). Individual, isolated nonenforcement decisions, however, must be made by hundreds of agencies each day. It is entirely permissible to presume that Congress has not intended courts to review such mundane matters, absent either some indication of congressional intent to the contrary or proof of circumstances such as those set out above.

On this understanding of the scope of today's decision, I join the Court's opinion.

JUSTICE MARSHALL, concurring in the judgment.

Easy cases at times produce bad law, for in the rush to reach a clearly ordained result, courts may offer up principles, doctrines, and statements that calmer reflection, and a fuller understanding of their implications in concrete settings, would eschew. In my view, the "presumption of unreviewability" announced today is a product of that lack of discipline that easy cases make all too easy. The majority, eager to reverse what it goes out of its way to label as an "implausible result," not only does reverse, as I agree it should, but along the way creates out of whole cloth the notion that agency decisions not to take "enforcement action" are unreviewable unless Congress has rather specifically indicated otherwise. Because this "presumption of unreviewability" is fundamentally at odds with rule-of-law principles firmly embedded in our jurisprudence, because it seeks to truncate an emerging line of judicial authority subjecting enforcement discretion to rational and principled constraint, and because, in the end, the presumption may well be indecipherable, one can only hope that it will come to be understood as a relic of a particular factual setting in which the full implications of such a presumption were neither confronted nor understood. . . . .

NOTES AND QUESTIONS

9-1. Why is there a presumption against judicial review of an agency enforcement decision?

9-2. What form of other agency inaction does, can or should the presumption of unreviewability apply? Should it apply to a petition to re-open an enforcement investigation? *See Center for Auto Safety v. Dole,* 846 F.2d. 1532 (D.C. Cir. 1988). What about claims of unreasonable delay by an agency? *See Cutler v. Hoyes,* 818 F.2d. 879 (D.C. Cir. 1987). In today's complex administrative state, can you always differentiate affirmative decisions to act and refusals to act?

9-3. What constitute meaningful standards sufficient to rebut the presumption of unreviewability? Why was *Dunlop v. Bachowski,* 421 U.S. 560 (1975) decided differently?

9-4. What standard of judicial review applies when a Court concludes that the presumption of unreviewability has been rebutted? *See, e.g., Shelly v. Buck,* 793 F.2d 1368 (D.C. Civ. 1986). In that case, the court decided to review an agency decision not to enforce § 402 of the LMRDA, noting the standard of its review was "quite deferential." What if an agency refuses to issue a rule in response to a petition for rulemaking. Is that reviewable? If so, what standard should apply? What scope of review would you expect? Why? *See, WWHT, Inc. v. FCC,* 656 F.2d 807, 818 (D.C. Cir. 1981).

WEBSTER v. DOE

United States Supreme Court
486 U.S. 592 (1988)

CHIEF JUSTICE REHNQUIST delivered the opinion of the Court.

Section 102(c) of the National Security Act of 1947, 61 Stat. 498, as amended, provides that:

> [T]he Director of Central Intelligence may, in his discretion, terminate the employment of any officer or employee of the Agency whenever he shall deem such termination necessary or advisable in the interests of the United States. . . .

In this case we decide whether, and to what extent, the termination decisions of the Director under § 102(c) are judicially reviewable.

I

Respondent John Doe was first employed by the Central Intelligence Agency (CIA or Agency) in 1973 as a clerk-typist. He received periodic fitness reports that consistently rated him as an excellent or outstanding employee. By 1977, respondent had been promoted to a position as a covert electronics technician.

In January 1982, respondent voluntarily informed a CIA security officer that he was a homosexual. Almost immediately, the Agency placed respondent on paid administrative leave pending an investigation of his sexual orientation and conduct. On February 12 and again on February 17, respondent was extensively questioned by a polygraph officer concerning his homosexuality and possible security violations. Respondent denied having sexual relations with any foreign nationals and maintained that he had not disclosed classified information to any of his sexual partners. After these interviews, the officer told respondent that the polygraph tests indicated that he had truthfully answered all questions. The polygraph officer then prepared a five-page summary of his interviews with respondent, to which respondent was allowed to attach a two-page addendum.

On April 14, 1982, a CIA security agent informed respondent that the Agency's Office of Security had determined that respondent's homosexuality posed a threat to security, but declined to explain the nature of the danger. Respondent was then asked to resign. When he refused to do so, the Office of Security recommended to the CIA Director (petitioner's predecessor) that respondent be dismissed. After reviewing respondent's records and the evaluations of his subordinates, the Director "deemed it necessary and advisable in the interests of the United States to terminate [respondent's] employment with this Agency pursuant to section 102(c) of the National Security Act. . . ." Respondent was also advised that, while the CIA would give him a positive recommendation in any future job search, if he applied for a job requiring a security clearance the Agency would inform the prospective employer that it had concluded that respondent's homosexuality presented a security threat.

Respondent then filed an action against petitioner in United States District Court for the District of Columbia. . . .

The District Court denied petitioner's motion to dismiss, and granted respondent's motion for partial summary judgment. The court determined that the APA provided judicial review of petitioner's termination decisions made under § 102(c) of the NSA, and found that respondent had been unlawfully discharged because the CIA had not followed the procedures described in its own regulations. The District Court declined, however, to address respondent's constitutional claims. Respondent was ordered reinstated to administrative leave status, and the Agency was instructed to reconsider his case using procedures that would supply him with the reasons supporting any termination decision and provide him with an opportunity to respond.

A divided panel of the Court of Appeals for the District of Columbia Circuit vacated the District Court's judgment and remanded the case for further proceedings. The Court of Appeals first decided that judicial review under the APA of the Agency's decision to terminate respondent was not precluded by §§ 701(a)(1) or (a)(2). Turning to the merits, the Court of Appeals found that, while an agency must normally follow its own regulations, the CIA regulations cited by respondent do not limit the Director's discretion in making termination decisions. Moreover, the regulations themselves state that, with respect to terminations pursuant to § 102(c), the Director need not follow standard discharge procedures, but may direct that an employee "be separated immediately and without regard to any suggested procedural steps." The majority thus concluded that the CIA regulations provide no independent source of procedural or substantive protection.

The Court of Appeals went on to hold that respondent must demonstrate that the Director's action was an arbitrary and capricious exercise of his power to discharge employees under § 102(c). Because the record below was unclear on certain points critical to respondent's claim for relief, the Court of Appeals remanded the case to District Court for a determination of the reason for the Director's termination of respondent. We granted certiorari to decide the question whether the Director's decision to discharge a CIA employee under § 102(c) of the NSA is judicially reviewable under the APA.

II

. . . .

In *Citizens to Preserve Overton Park v. Volpe,* 401 U.S. 402 (1971), this Court explained the distinction between §§ 701(a)(1) and (a)(2). Subsection (a)(1) is concerned with whether Congress expressed an intent to prohibit judicial review; subsection (a)(2) applies "in those rare instances where statutes are drawn in such broad terms that in a given case there is 'no law to apply.'" 401 U.S. at 410.

We further explained what it means for an action to be "committed to agency discretion by law" in *Heckler v. Chaney,* 470 U.S. 821 (1985). *Heckler* required the Court to determine whether the Food and Drug Administration's decision not to undertake an enforcement proceeding against the use of certain drugs in administering the death penalty was subject to judicial review. We noted that, under § 701(a)(2), even when Congress has not affirmatively precluded judicial oversight, "review is not to be had if the statute is drawn so that a court would have no meaningful standard against which to judge the agency's exercise of discretion." 470 U.S. at 830. . . .

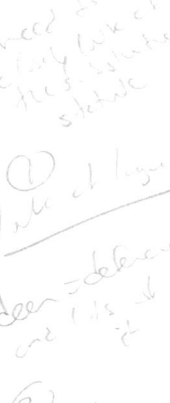

Both *Overton Park* and *Heckler* emphasized that § 701(a)(2) requires careful examination of the statute on which the claim of agency illegality is based (the Federal-Aid Highway Act of 1968 in *Overton Park* and the Federal Food, Drug, and Cosmetic Act in *Heckler*). In the present case, respondent's claims against the CIA arise from the Director's asserted violation of § 102(c) of the National Security Act. As an initial matter, it should be noted that § 102(c) allows termination of an Agency employee whenever the Director "shall *deem* such termination necessary or advisable in the interests of the United States" (emphasis added), not simply when the dismissal is necessary or advisable to those interests. This standard fairly exudes deference to the Director, and appears to us to foreclose the application of any meaningful judicial standard of review. . . .

So too does the overall structure of the NSA. Passed shortly after the close of the Second World War, the NSA created the CIA and gave its Director the responsibility "for protecting intelligence sources and methods from unauthorized disclosure." Section 102(c) is an integral part of that statute, because the Agency's efficacy, and the Nation's security, depend in large measure on the reliability and trustworthiness of the Agency's employees. As we recognized in *Snepp v. United States,* 444 U.S. 507 (1980), employment with the CIA entails a high degree of trust that is perhaps unmatched in government service.

We thus find that the language and structure of § 102(c) indicate that Congress meant to commit individual employee discharges to the Director's discretion, and that § 701(a)(2) accordingly precludes judicial review of these decisions under the APA. We reverse the Court of Appeals to the extent that it found such terminations reviewable by the courts.

III

In addition to his claim that the Director failed to abide by the statutory dictates of § 102(c), respondent also alleged a number of constitutional violations in his amended complaint. . . .

§ 9.02   THE AVAILABILITY AND TIMING OF JUDICIAL REVIEW   837

We share the confusion of the Court of Appeals as to the precise nature of respondent's constitutional claims. It is difficult, if not impossible, to ascertain from the amended complaint whether respondent contends that his termination, based on his homosexuality, is constitutionally impermissible, or whether he asserts that a more pervasive discrimination policy exists in the CIA's employment practices regarding all homosexuals. This ambiguity in the amended complaint is no doubt attributable in part to the inconsistent explanations respondent received from the Agency itself regarding his termination. . . .

Our review of § 102(c) convinces us that it cannot bear the preclusive weight petitioner would have it support. . . . Subsections (a)(1) and (a)(2) of § 701, however, remove from judicial review only those determinations specifically identified by Congress or "committed to agency discretion by law." Nothing in § 102(c) persuades us that Congress meant to preclude consideration of colorable constitutional claims arising out of the actions of the Director pursuant to that section; we believe that a constitutional claim based on an individual discharge may be reviewed by the District Court. We agree with the Court of Appeals that there must be further proceedings in the District Court on this issue. . . .

The judgment of the Court of Appeals is affirmed in part, reversed in part, and the case is remanded for further proceedings consistent with this opinion.

It is so ordered.

JUSTICE KENNEDY took no part in the consideration or decision of this case.

JUSTICE O'CONNOR, concurring in part and dissenting in part.

I agree that the Administrative Procedure Act (APA) does not authorize judicial review of the employment decisions referred to in § 102(c) of the National Security Act. Because § 102(c) does not provide a meaningful standard for judicial review, such decisions are clearly "committed to agency discretion by law" within the meaning of § 701(a)(2) of the APA. I do not understand the Court to say that the exception in § 701(a)(2) is necessarily or fully defined by reference to statutes "drawn in such broad terms that in a given case there is no law to apply." See *Citizens to Preserve Overton Park v. Volpe,* 401 U.S. 402, 410 (1971). Accordingly, I join Parts I and II of the Court's opinion.

I disagree, however, with the Court's conclusion that a constitutional claim challenging the validity of an employment decision covered by § 102(c) may nonetheless be brought in a Federal District Court. Whatever may be the exact scope of Congress' power to close the lower federal courts to constitutional claims in other contexts, I have no doubt about its authority to do so here. . . .

JUSTICE SCALIA, dissenting.

I agree with the Court's apparent holding in Part II of its opinion, . . . that the Director's decision to terminate a CIA employee is "committed to agency discretion by law" within the meaning of 5 U.S.C. § 701(a)(2). But because I do not see how a decision can, either practically or legally, be both unreviewable and yet reviewable for constitutional defect, I regard Part III of the opinion as essentially undoing Part II. I therefore respectfully dissent from the judgment of the Court.

I

Before proceeding to address Part III of the Court's opinion, which I think to be in error, I must discuss one significant element of the analysis in Part II. Though I subscribe to most of that analysis, I disagree with the Court's description of what is required to come within the second paragraph of § 701(a), which provides that judicial review is unavailable "to the extent that . . . agency action is committed to agency discretion by law." The Court's discussion, . . . suggests that the Court of Appeals below was correct in holding that this provision is triggered only when there is "no law to apply." Our precedents amply show that "commit[ment] to agency discretion by law" includes, but is not limited to, situations in which there is "no law to apply." . . .

II

. . . The first response to the Court's grave doubt about the constitutionality of denying all judicial review to a "colorable constitutional claim" is that the denial of all judicial review is not at issue here, but merely the denial of review in United States District Courts. As to that, the law is, and has long been, clear. Article III, § 2 of the Constitution extends the judicial power to "all Cases . . . arising under this Constitution." But Article III, § 1 provides that the judicial power shall be vested "in one supreme Court, *and in such inferior Courts as the Congress may from time to time ordain and establish*" (emphasis added). We long ago held that the power not to create any lower federal courts at all includes the power to invest them with less than all of the judicial power. . . .

Thus, if there is any truth to the proposition that judicial cognizance of constitutional claims cannot be eliminated, it is, at most, that they cannot be eliminated from state courts, and from this Court's appellate jurisdiction over cases from state courts (or cases from federal courts, should there be any) involving such claims. Narrowly viewed, therefore, there is no shadow of a constitutional doubt that we are free to hold that the present suit, whether based on constitutional grounds or not, will not lie. . . .

III

I turn, then, to whether that executive action is, within the meaning of § 701(a)(2), "committed to agency discretion by law." My discussion of this point can be brief, because the answer is compellingly obvious. Section 102(c) of the National Security Act of 1947, 61 Stat. 498, states:

> *Notwithstanding* . . . the provisions of any other law, the Director of Central Intelligence, may, in his discretion, terminate the employment of any officer or employee of the Agency whenever he shall deem such termination necessary or advisable in the interests of the United States. . . .

Further, as the Court declares, § 102(c) is an "integral part" of the National Security Act, which throughout exhibits "extraordinary deference to the Director." Given this statutory text, and given (as discussed above) that the area to which the text pertains is one of predominant executive authority and of traditional judicial abstention, it is difficult to conceive of a statutory scheme that more clearly reflects that "commit[ment] to agency discretion by law" to which § 701(a)(2) refers.

It is baffling to observe that the Court seems to agree with the foregoing assessment, holding that "the language and structure of § 102(c) indicate that Congress meant to commit individual employee discharges to the Director's discretion." Nevertheless, without explanation the Court reaches the conclusion that "a constitutional claim based on an individual discharge may be reviewed by the District Court." It seems to me the Court is attempting the impossible feat of having its cake and eating it too. The opinion states that "[a] discharged employee . . . cannot complain that his termination was not 'necessary or advisable in the interests of the United States,' since that assessment is the Director's alone." But two sentences later it says that "[n]othing in § 102(c) persuades us that Congress meant to preclude consideration of colorable constitutional claims arising out of the actions of the Director pursuant to that section." Which are we to believe? If the former, the case should be at an end. If the § 102(c) assessment is really "the Director's alone," the only conceivable basis for review of respondent's dismissal (which is what this case is about) would be that the dismissal was not really the result of a § 102(c) assessment by the Director. But respondent has never contended that, nor could he. Not only was his counsel formally advised, by letter of May 11, 1982, that "the Director has deemed it necessary and advisable in the interests of the United States to terminate your client's employment with this Agency pursuant to section 102(c)," but the petitioner filed with the court an affidavit by the Director, dated September 17, 1982, stating that "[a]fter careful consideration of the matter, I determined that the termination of Mr. Doe's employment was necessary and advisable in the interests of the United States and, exercising my discretion under the authority granted by section 102(c) . . . I terminated Mr. Doe's employment." Even if the basis for the Director's assessment was the respondent's homosexuality, and even if the connection between that and the interests of the United States is an irrational and hence an unconstitutional one, if that assessment is really "the Director's alone" there is nothing more to litigate about. I cannot imagine what the Court expects the "further proceedings in the District Court" which it commands, to consist of, unless perhaps an academic seminar on the relationship of homosexuality to security risk. For even were the District Court persuaded that no such relationship exists, "that assessment is the Director's alone." . . .

The harm done by today's decision is that, contrary to what Congress knows is preferable, it brings a significant decision-making process of our intelligence services into a forum where it does not belong. Neither the Constitution, nor our laws, nor common sense gives an individual a right to come into court to litigate the reasons for his dismissal as an intelligence agent. It is of course not just *valid* constitutional claims that today's decision makes the basis for judicial review of the Director's action, but all *colorable* constitutional claims, whether meritorious or not. And in determining whether what is colorable

840 ADMINISTRATIVE LAW § 9.02

is in fact meritorious, a court will necessarily have to review the entire decision. . . .

Today's result, however, will have ramifications far beyond creation of the world's only secret intelligence agency that must litigate the dismissal of its agents. If constitutional claims can be raised in this highly sensitive context, it is hard to imagine where they cannot. The assumption that there are any executive decisions that cannot be hauled into the courts may no longer be valid. Also obsolete may be the assumption that we are capable of preserving a sensible common law of judicial review.

I respectfully dissent.

LINCOLN v. VIGIL

Supreme Court of the United States
508 U.S. 182 (1993)

JUSTICE SOUTER delivered the opinion of the Court.

For several years in the late 1970's and early 1980's, the Indian Health Service provided diagnostic and treatment services, referred to collectively as the Indian Children's Program (Program), to handicapped Indian children in the Southwest. In 1985, the Service decided to reallocate the Program's resources to a nationwide effort to assist such children. We hold that the Service's decision to discontinue the Program was "committed to agency discretion by law" and therefore not subject to judicial review under the Administrative Procedure Act, 5 U.S.C. § 701(a)(2). . . .

I

The Indian Health Service, an agency within the Public Health Service of the Department of Health and Human Services, provides health care for some 1.5 million American Indian and Alaska Native people. The Service receives yearly lump-sum appropriations from Congress and expends the funds under authority of the Snyder Act, 42 Stat. 208, as amended, 25 U.S.C. § 13, and the Indian Health Care Improvement Act, 90 Stat. 1400, as amended, 25 U.S.C. § 1601 *et seq.* So far as it concerns us here, the Snyder Act authorizes the Service to "expend such moneys as Congress may from time to time appropriate, for the benefit, care, and assistance of the Indians," for the "relief of distress and conservation of health." 25 U.S.C. § 13. The Improvement Act authorizes expenditures for, *inter alia*, Indian mental-health care, and specifically for "therapeutic and residential treatment centers." § 1621(a)(4)(D).

The Service employs roughly 12,000 people and operates more than 500 health-care facilities in the continental United States and Alaska. . . . This case concerns a collection of related services, commonly known as the Indian Children's Program, that the Service provided from 1978 to 1985. In the words of the Court of Appeals, a "clou[d] [of] bureaucratic haze" obscures the history of the Program, *Vigil v. Rhoades*, 953 F.2d 1225, 1226 (CA10 1992), which seems to have grown out of a plan "to establish therapeutic and residential treatment centers for disturbed Indian children." H.R. Rep. No. 94-1026, pt. 1, p. 80 (1976) (prepared in conjunction with enactment of the Improvement Act). These centers were to be established under a "major cooperative care agreement" between the Service and the Bureau of Indian Affairs, and would have provided such children "with intensive care in a residential setting."

Congress never expressly appropriated funds for these centers. In 1978, however, the Service allocated approximately $292,000 from its fiscal year 1978 appropriation to its office in Albuquerque, New Mexico, for the planning and development of a pilot project for handicapped Indian children, which became known as the Indian Children's Program. The pilot project apparently convinced the Service that a building was needed, and, in 1979, the Service requested $3.5 million from Congress to construct a diagnostic and treatment center for handicapped Indian children. Hearings on Department of the Interior and Related Agencies Appropriations for 1980 before a Subcommittee of the House Committee on Appropriations, 96th Cong., 1st Sess., pt. 8, p. 250 (1979) (hereinafter House Hearings (Fiscal Year 1980)). The appropriation for fiscal year 1980 did not expressly provide the requested funds, however, and legislative reports indicated only that Congress had increased the Service's funding by $300,000 for nationwide expansion and development of the Program in coordination with the Bureau.

Plans for a national program to be managed jointly by the Service and the Bureau were never fulfilled, however, and the Program continued simply as an offering of the Service's Albuquerque office, from which the Program's staff of 11 to 16 employees would make monthly visits to Indian communities in New Mexico and southern Colorado and on the Navajo and Hopi Reservations. . . . Congress never authorized or appropriated moneys expressly for the Program, and the Service continued to pay for its regional activities out of annual lump-sum appropriations from 1980 to 1985, during which period the Service repeatedly apprised Congress of the Program's continuing operation. . . .

Nevertheless, the Service had not abandoned the proposal for a nationwide treatment program, and in June 1985 it notified those who referred patients to the Program that it was "re-evaluating [the Program's] purpose . . . as a national mental health program for Indian children and adolescents." In August 1985, the Service determined that Program staff hitherto assigned to provide direct clinical services should be reassigned as consultants to other nationwide Service programs, and discontinued the direct clinical services to Indian children in the Southwest. The Service announced its decision in a memorandum, dated August 21, 1985, addressed to Service offices and Program referral sources:

"As you are probably aware, the Indian Children's Program has been involved in planning activities focusing on a national program effort. This process has included the termination of all direct clinical services to children in the Albuquerque, Navajo and Hopi reservation service areas. During the months of August and September, . . . staff will [see] children followed by the program in an effort to update programs, identify alternative resources and facilitate obtaining alternative services. In communities where there are no identified resources, meetings with community service providers will be scheduled to facilitate the networking between agencies to secure or advocate for appropriate services."

. . . .

Respondents, handicapped Indian children eligible to receive services through the Program, subsequently brought this action for declaratory and injunctive relief against petitioners, the Director of the Service and others (collectively, the Service), in the United States District Court for the District of New Mexico. Respondents alleged, inter alia, that the Service's decision to discontinue direct clinical services violated the federal trust responsibility to Indians, the Snyder Act, the Improvement Act, the Administrative Procedure Act, various agency regulations, and the Fifth Amendment's Due Process Clause.

The District Court granted summary judgment for respondents. . . .

The Court of Appeals affirmed. Like the District Court, it rejected the Service's argument that the decision to discontinue the Program was committed to agency discretion under the APA. Although the court concededly could identify no statute or regulation even mentioning the Program, it believed that the repeated references to it in the legislative history of the annual appropriations Acts, "in combination with the special relationship between the Indian people and the federal government," provided a basis for judicial review. . . .

II

First is the question whether it was error for the Court of Appeals to hold the substance of the Service's decision to terminate the Program reviewable under the APA. The APA provides that "[a] person suffering legal wrong because of agency action, or adversely affected or aggrieved by agency action within the meaning of a relevant statute, is entitled to judicial review thereof," 5 U.S.C. § 702, and we have read the APA as embodying a "basic presumption of judicial review," *Abbott Laboratories v. Gardner*, 387 U.S. 136, 140 (1967). This is "just" a presumption, however, and under § 701(a)(2) agency action is not subject to judicial review "to the extent that" such action "is committed to agency discretion by law." As we explained in *Heckler v. Chaney*, 470 U.S. 821, 830 (1985), § 701(a)(2) makes it clear that "review is not to be had" in those rare circumstances where the relevant statute "is drawn so that a court would have no meaningful standard against which to judge the agency's exercise of discretion." *See also Webster v. Doe*, 486 U.S. 592, 599–600 (1988); *Citizens to Preserve Overton Park, Inc. v. Volpe*, 401 U.S. 402, 410 (1971). "In such a case, the statute ('law') can be taken to have 'committed' the decisionmaking to the agency's judgment absolutely." *Heckler, supra,* at 830.

Over the years, we have read § 701(a)(2) to preclude judicial review of certain categories of administrative decisions that courts traditionally have regarded as "committed to agency discretion." *See Franklin v. Massachusetts*, 505 U.S. 788, 817, (1992) (STEVENS, J., concurring in part and concurring in judgment); *Webster, supra,* at 609 (SCALIA, J., dissenting). In *Heckler* itself, we held an agency's decision not to institute enforcement proceedings to be presumptively unreviewable under § 701(a)(2). 470 U.S., at 831. An agency's "decision not to enforce often involves a complicated balancing of a number of factors which are peculiarly within its expertise," and for this and other good reasons, we concluded, "such a decision has traditionally been 'committed to agency discretion.'" Similarly, in *ICC v. Locomotive Engineers*, 482 U.S. 270, 282 (1987), we held that § 701(a)(2) precludes judicial review of another type of administrative decision traditionally left to agency discretion, an agency's refusal to grant reconsideration of an action because of material error. In so holding, we emphasized "the impossibility of devising an adequate standard of review for such agency action." Finally, in *Webster, supra*, at 599–601, we held that § 701(a)(2) precludes judicial review of a decision by the Director of Central Intelligence to terminate an employee in the interests of national security, an area of executive action "in which courts have long been hesitant to intrude." *Franklin, supra*, 505 U.S. at 819 (STEVENS, J., concurring in part and concurring in judgment).

The allocation of funds from a lump-sum appropriation is another administrative decision traditionally regarded as committed to agency discretion. After all, the very point of a lump-sum appropriation is to give an agency the capacity to adapt to changing circumstances and meet its statutory responsibilities in what it sees as the most effective or desirable way. . . . For this reason, a fundamental principle of appropriations law is that where "Congress merely appropriates lump-sum amounts without statutorily restricting what can be done with those funds, a clear inference arises that it does not intend to impose legally binding restrictions, and indicia in committee reports and other legislative history as to how the funds should or are expected to be spent do not establish any legal requirements on" the agency. *LTV Aerospace Corp.*, 55 Comp.Gen. 307, 319 (1975). . . . Put another way, a lump-sum appropriation reflects a congressional recognition that an agency must be allowed "flexibility to shift . . . funds within a particular . . . appropriation account so that" the agency "can make necessary adjustments for 'unforeseen developments'" and "'changing requirements,'" *LTV Aerospace Corp., supra*, at 318.

Like the decision against instituting enforcement proceedings, then, an agency's allocation of funds from a lump-sum appropriation requires "a complicated balancing of a number of factors which are peculiarly within its expertise": whether its "resources are best spent" on one program or another; whether it "is likely to succeed" in fulfilling its statutory mandate; whether a particular program "best fits the agency's overall policies"; and, "indeed, whether the agency has enough resources" to fund a program "at all." *Heckler*, 470 U.S., at 831. As in *Heckler*, so here, the "agency is far better equipped than the courts to deal with the many variables involved in the proper ordering of its priorities." *Id.*, at 831–832. Of course, an agency is not free simply to disregard statutory responsibilities: Congress may always circumscribe agency discretion to allocate resources by putting restrictions in the operative statutes (though not, as we have seen, just in the legislative history). *See id.*, at 833. And, of course, we hardly need to note that an agency's decision to ignore congressional expectations may expose it to grave political consequences. But as long as the agency allocates funds from a lump-sum appropriation to meet permissible statutory objectives, § 701(a)(2) gives the courts no leave to intrude. "[T]o [that] extent," the decision to allocate funds "is committed to agency discretion by law." § 701(a)(2).

The Service's decision to discontinue the Program is accordingly unreviewable under § 701(a)(2). As the Court of Appeals recognized, the appropriations Acts for the relevant period do not so much as mention the Program, and both the Snyder Act and the Improvement Act likewise speak about Indian health only in general terms. It is true that the Service repeatedly apprised Congress of the Program's continued operation, but, as we have explained, these representations do not translate through the medium of legislative history into legally binding obligations. The reallocation of agency resources to assist handicapped Indian children nationwide clearly falls within the Service's statutory mandate to provide health care to Indian people, and respondents, indeed, do not seriously contend otherwise. The decision to terminate the Program was committed to the Service's discretion.

The Court of Appeals saw a separate limitation on the Service's discretion in the special trust relationship existing between Indian people and the Federal Government. 953 F.2d, at 1230–1231. We have often spoken of this relationship, *see*, e.g., *Cherokee Nation v. Georgia*, 30 U.S. (5 Pet.) 1, 17 (1831) (Marshall, C.J.) (Indians' "relation to the United States resembles that of a ward to his guardian"), and the law is "well established that the Government in its dealings with Indian tribal property acts in a fiduciary capacity," *United States v. Cherokee Nation of Okla.*, 480 U.S. 700, 707 (1987). Whatever the contours of that relationship, though, it could not limit the Service's discretion to reorder its priorities from serving a subgroup of beneficiaries to serving the broader class of all Indians nationwide. . . .

One final note: although respondents claimed in the District Court that the Service's termination of the Program violated their rights under the Fifth Amendment's Due Process Clause, that court expressly declined to address respondents' constitutional arguments, as did the Court of Appeals. Thus, while the APA contemplates, in the absence of a clear expression of contrary congressional intent, that judicial review will be available for colorable constitutional claims, *see Webster*, 486 U.S., at 603–604, the record at this stage does not allow mature consideration of constitutional issues, which we leave for the Court of Appeals on remand.

. . . .

IV

The judgment of the Court of Appeals is reversed, and the case is remanded for further proceedings consistent with this opinion.

It is so ordered.

NOTES AND QUESTIONS

9-5. Why does the majority in *Webster v. Doe* conclude that section 102(c) of the National Security Act precludes judicial review? Is the statute clear? What test does the majority employ?

9-6. Are Justices O'Connor and Scalia correct in assuming that a matter may still be precluded from judicial review, even if there is "law to apply"?

9-7. What is the basis of Justice Scalia's dissent? Can you separate the constitutional questions from the statutory issues? Can Congress preclude all of these issues from judicial review? Do we know whether Congress intended to preclude the constitutional issues from review as well?

9-8. The Supreme Court has entertained these issues in other cases as well. *See, e.g., Block v. Community Nutrition Institute*, 467 U.S. 340 (1984), where the Court held that the presumption favoring judicial review could be overcome when a contrary congressional intent was "fairly discernible in the statutory scheme." 467 U.S. at 351. The Court seemed to back away from the "clear and convincing" language used in *Overton Park* and derived from *Abbott Laboratories v. Gardner*, 387 U.S. 136 (1967). In *Bowen v. Michigan Academy of Family Physicians*, 476 U.S. 667 (1986), however, the Court stated, in holding certain regulations of the HHS reviewable, that: "we ordinarily presume that Congress intends the executive to obey its statutory commands" and that Congress, therefore, "expects the courts to grant relief when an executive agency violates such commands." 476 U.S. at 681. How would you characterize the Court's attitude toward preclusion in *Webster*? Is it influenced by the fact that national security is involved? How would you characterize Justice Scalia's views?

9-9. In *Lincoln v. Vigil*, what functional characteristics of an agency decision to allocate lump-sum funds exempt it from judicial review? Are such resource decisions intrinsically managerial? Why?

9-10. Aside from "law to apply" what other criteria do these courts use to conclude an agency decision is unreviewable?

§ 9.03 Who Has Standing to Seek Judicial Review?

The following sections examine the questions of (1) *who* can bring certain kinds of law suits, (2) *when* those law suits can or must be filed, (3) and *where* those law suits should be filed. The doctrine of standing governs the "who" question; the doctrines of mootness, ripeness and exhaustion of remedies deal with the "when" question; and the doctrine of primary jurisdiction as well as various statutes deal with such issues as whether an action is to be heard before an agency or a court, and if it is a court, whether it is a district or an appellate court and, finally, the venue of that court.

Our treatment of these issues will necessarily be brief. Issues such as these usually are covered in depth in courses on Federal Courts and Constitutional Law. Our primary goal in this last portion of the chapter is to provide the basic legal framework within which these important questions are raised and to suggest an administrative law perspective on their resolution.

ASSOCIATION OF DATA PROCESSING SERVICE ORGANIZATIONS v. CAMP

United States Supreme Court
397 U.S. 150 (1970)

MR. JUSTICE DOUGLAS delivered the opinion of the Court.

Petitioners sell data processing services to businesses generally. In this suit they seek to challenge a ruling by respondent Comptroller of the Currency that, as an incident to their banking services, national banks, including respondent American National Bank & Trust Company, may make data processing services available to other banks and to bank customers. The District Court dismissed the complaint for lack of standing of petitioners to bring the suit. The Court of Appeals affirmed. The case is here on a petition for writ of certiorari which we granted.

Generalizations about standing to sue are largely worthless as such. One generalization is, however, necessary and that is that the question of standing in the federal courts is to be considered in the framework of Article III which restricts judicial power to "cases" and "controversies." As we recently stated in *Flast v. Cohen,* 392 U.S. 83, 101, "[I]n terms of Article III limitations on federal court jurisdiction, the question of standing is related only to whether the dispute sought to be adjudicated will be presented in an adversary context and in a form historically viewed as capable of judicial resolution." *Flast* was a *taxpayer's* suit. The present is a *competitor's* suit. And while the two have the same Article III starting point, they do not necessarily track one another.

The first question is whether the plaintiff alleges that the challenged action has caused him injury in fact, economic or otherwise. There can be no doubt but that petitioners have satisfied this test. The petitioners not only allege that competition by national banks in the business of providing data processing services might entail some future loss of profits for the petitioners, they also allege that respondent American National Bank & Trust Company was performing or preparing to perform such services for two customers for whom petitioner Data Systems, Inc., had previously agreed or negotiated to perform such services. The petitioners' suit was brought not only against the American

§ 9.03 THE AVAILABILITY AND TIMING OF JUDICIAL REVIEW 847

National Bank & Trust Company, but also against the Comptroller of the Currency. The Comptroller was alleged to have caused petitioners injury in fact by his 1966 ruling which stated:

> Incidental to its banking services, a national bank may make available its data processing equipment or perform data processing services on such equipment for other banks and bank customers.

The Court of Appeals viewed the matter differently, stating:

> [A] plaintiff may challenge alleged illegal competition when as complainant it pursues (1) a legal interest by reason of public charter or contract, . . . (2) a legal interest by reason of statutory protection, . . . or (3) a "public interest" in which Congress has recognized the need for review of administrative action and plaintiff is significantly involved to have standing to represent the public. . . .

Those tests were based on prior decisions of this Court, such as *Tennessee Electric Power Co. v. TVA,* 306 U.S. 118, where private power companies sought to enjoin TVA from operating, claiming that the statutory plan under which it was created was unconstitutional. The Court denied the competitors' standing, holding that they did not have that status "unless the right invaded is a legal right, — one of property, one arising out of contract, one protected against tortious invasion, or one founded on a statute which confers a privilege."

The "legal interest" test goes to the merits. The question of standing is different. It concerns, apart from the "case" or "controversy" test, the question whether the interest sought to be protected by the complainant is arguably within the zone of interests to be protected or regulated by the statute or constitutional guarantee in question. Thus the Administrative Procedure Act grants standing to a person "aggrieved by agency action within the meaning of a relevant statute." That interest, at times, may reflect "aesthetic, conservational, and recreational" as well as economic values. *Scenic Hudson Preservation Conference v. FPC,* 354 F.2d 608, 616; *Office of Communication of United Church of Christ v. FCC,* 359 F.2d 994, 1000-1006. A person or a family may have a spiritual stake in First Amendment values sufficient to give standing to raise issues concerning the Establishment Clause and the Free Exercise Clause. *Abington School District v. Schempp,* 374 U.S. 203. We mention these noneconomic values to emphasize that standing may stem from them as well as from the economic injury on which petitioners rely here. Certainly he who is "likely to be financially" injured, *FCC v. Sanders Bros. Radio Station,* 309 U.S. 470, at 477, may be a reliable private attorney general to litigate the issues of the public interest in the present case.

Apart from Article III jurisdictional questions, problems of standing, as resolved by this Court for its own governance, have involved a "rule of self-restraint." *Barrows v. Jackson,* 346 U.S. 249, 255. Congress can, of course, resolve the question one way or another, save as the requirements of Article III dictate otherwise. *Muskrat v. United States,* 219 U.S. 346.

Where statutes are concerned, the trend is toward enlargement of the class of people who may protest administrative action. The whole drive for enlarging the category of aggrieved "persons" is symptomatic of that trend. In a closely analogous case we held that an existing entrepreneur had standing to challenge the legality of the entrance of a newcomer into the business, because the established business was allegedly protected by a valid city ordinance that protected it from unlawful competition. *Chicago v. Atchison, T. & S.F.R. Co.,* 357 U.S. 77, 83–84. In that tradition was *Hardin v. Kentucky Utilities Co.,* 390 U.S. 1, which involved a section of the TVA Act designed primarily to protect, through area limitations, private utilities against TVA competition. We held that no explicit statutory provision was necessary to confer standing, since the private utility bringing suit was within the class of persons that the statutory provision was designed to protect.

It is argued that the *Chicago* case and the *Hardin* case are relevant here because of § 4 of the Bank Service Corporation Act of 1962, 76 Stat. 1132, 12 U.S.C. § 1864, which provides:

> No bank service corporation may engage in any activity other than the performance of bank services for banks.

The Court of Appeals for the First Circuit held in *Arnold Tours, Inc. v. Camp,* 408 F.2d 1147, 1153, that by reason of § 4 a data processing company has standing to contest the legality of a national bank performing data processing services for other banks and bank customers:

> Section 4 had a broader purpose than regulating only the service corporations. It was also a response to the fears expressed by a few senators, that without such a prohibition, the bill would have enabled "banks to engage in a nonbanking activity," S. Rep. No. 2105, [87th Cong., 2d Sess., 7–12] (Supplemental views of Senators Proxmire, Douglas, and Neuberger), and thus constitute "a serious exception to the accepted public policy which strictly limits banks to banking." (Supplemental views of Senators Muskie and Clark). We think Congress has provided the sufficient statutory aid to standing even though the competition may not be the precise kind Congress legislated against.

We do not put the issue in those words, for they implicate the merits. We do think, however, that § 4 arguably brings a competitor within the zone of interests protected by it.

That leaves the remaining question, whether judicial review of the Comptroller's action has been precluded. We do not think it has been. There is great contrariety among administrative agencies created by Congress as respects "the extent to which, and the procedures by which, different measures of control afford judicial review of administrative action." *Stark v. Wickard,* 321 U.S. 288, 312 (Frankfurter, J., dissenting). The answer, of course, depends on the particular enactment under which review is sought. It turns on "the existence of courts and the intent of Congress as deduced from the statutes and precedents."

The Administrative Procedure Act provides that the provisions of the Act authorizing judicial review apply "except to the extent that — (1) statutes preclude judicial review; or (2) agency action is committed to agency discretion by law." . . .

We read § 701(a) as sympathetic to the issue presented in this case. As stated in the House Report:

The statutes of Congress are not merely advisory when they relate to administrative agencies, any more than in other cases. To preclude judicial review under this bill a statute, if not specific in withholding such review, must upon its face give clear and convincing evidence of an intent to withhold it. The mere failure to provide specially by statute for judicial review is certainly no evidence of intent to withhold review.

There is no presumption against judicial review and in favor of administrative absolutism (*see Abbott Laboratories v. Gardner,* 387 U.S. 136, 140), unless that purpose is fairly discernible in the statutory scheme. *Cf. Switchmen's Union v. National Mediation Board,* 320 U.S. 297.

We find no evidence that Congress in either the Bank Service Corporation Act or the National Bank Act sought to preclude judicial review of administrative rulings by the Comptroller as to the legitimate scope of activities available to national banks under those statutes. Both Acts are clearly "relevant" statutes within the meaning of § 702. The Acts do not in terms protect a specified group. But their general policy is apparent; and those whose interests are directly affected by a broad or narrow interpretation of the Acts are easily identifiable. It is clear that petitioners, as competitors of national banks which are engaging in data processing services, are within that class of "aggrieved" persons who, under § 702, are entitled to judicial review of "agency action."

Whether anything in the Bank Service Corporation Act or the National Bank Act gives petitioners a "legal interest" that protects them against violations of those Acts, and whether the actions of respondents did in fact violate either of those Acts, are questions which go to the merits and remain to be decided below.

We hold that petitioners have standing to sue and that the case should be remanded for a hearing on the merits.

Reversed and remanded.

NOTES AND QUESTIONS

9-11. Prior to *Data Processing*, the so-called legal right/legal interest test was in effect. A plaintiff complaining of governmental action had to show that the official had invaded an interest protected by common law or created as an individual right by statute. As Jerome Frank wrote for the Second Circuit in *Associated Industries of New York State v. Ickes,* 134 F.2d 694, 700, *vacated as moot,* 320 U.S. 707 (1943):

> In a suit in a federal court by a citizen against a government officer, complaining of alleged past or threatened future unlawful conduct by the defendant, there is no justiciable "controversy," without which, under Article III, Sec. 2 of the Constitution, the court has no jurisdiction, unless the citizen shows that such conduct or threatened conduct invades or will invade a private substantive legally protected interest of the plaintiff citizen; such

invaded interest must be either of a "recognized" character, at "common law" or a substantive private legally protected interest created by statute. In other words, unless the citizen first shows that, if the defendant were a private person having no official status, the particular defendant's conduct or threatened conduct would give rise to a cause of action against him by that particular citizen, the court cannot consider whether the defendant officer's conduct is or is not authorized by statute; for the statute comes into the case, if at all, only by way of a defense or of justification for acts of the defendant. . . .

In *Associated Industries v. Ickes,* what is the basis of petitioners' standing? Why should standing be restricted only to common law rights? How does such an approach compare to the right/privilege distinction discussed in Chapter 2?

9-12. In 1946, with the passage of the APA, Congress provided in 5 U.S.C. § 702 that "a person suffering legal wrong because of agency action, or adversely affected or aggrieved by agency action within the meaning of a relevant statute, is entitled to judicial review thereof." Under § 702, would the purported beneficiaries of a regulatory statute have standing to bring suit under it? What does "adversely affected in fact" mean?

9-13. How does the Court in *Data Processing* define "injury in fact"? Of what importance to the court is the existence of a "legal" interest? What is and what is not "within the zone of interests" protected by the statutory or constitutional concerns at issue?

9-14. Does the court's approach in *Data Processing* require a consideration of the merits of the case? Is this unavoidable?

9-15. How does the Court in *Data Processing* interpret the APA? Do you agree? Could a plaintiff whose only injury was that the government's actions constituted an ideological affront successfully sue under *Data Processing*? See *Sierra Club v. Morton,* 405 U.S. 727, 735 (1972), holding, in effect, that an ideological interest alone would not be enough to grant standing:

> The impact of the proposed changes in the environment of Mineral King will not fall indiscriminately upon every citizen. The alleged injury will be felt directly only by those who use Mineral King and Sequoia National Park, and for whom the aesthetic and recreational values of the area will be lessened by the highway and ski resort. The Sierra Club failed to allege that it or its members would be affected in any of their activities or pastimes by the Disney development. Nowhere in the pleadings or affidavits did the Club state that its members use Mineral King for any purpose, much less that they use it in any way that would be significantly affected by the proposed actions of the respondents.

Why is that the case? Is it not likely that a foundation established solely to pursue environmental issues will pursue those issues with great vigor in court? Is there any fear of collusion? What are the basic purposes of Article III's "case or controversy" requirements?

9-16. The "zone of interest" test in *Data Processing* was modified and loosened in *Clarke v. Securities Industries,* 479 U.S. 388 (1987), where the

Court noted: "In cases where the plaintiff is not itself the subject of the contested regulatory action, the test denies a right of review if the plaintiff's interests are so marginally related to or inconsistent with the purposes implicit in the statute that it cannot reasonably be assumed that Congress intended to permit the suit. The test is not meant to be especially demanding; in particular, there need be no indication of congressional purpose to benefit the would-be plaintiff." *Id.* at 757. How does this compare to the Court's approach in *Data Processing*? What other limiting factors exist that affect standing? *See also Hazardous Waste Treatment Council v. EPA,* 861 F.2d 277 (D.C. Cir. 1988), and consider the following case.

ALLEN v. WRIGHT

United States Supreme Court
468 U.S. 737 (1984)

JUSTICE O'CONNOR delivered the opinion of the Court.

Parents of black public school children allege in this nationwide class action that the Internal Revenue Service (IRS) has not adopted sufficient standards and procedures to fulfill its obligation to deny tax-exempt status to racially discriminatory private schools. They assert that the IRS thereby harms them directly and interferes with the ability of their children to receive an education in desegregated public schools. The issue before us is whether plaintiffs have standing to bring this suit. We hold that they do not.

I

. . . .

II

A

Article III of the Constitution confines the federal courts to adjudicating actual "cases" and "controversies." As the Court explained in *Valley Forge Christian College v. Americans United for Separation of Church and State, Inc.,* 454 U.S. 464, 471–476, (1982), the "case or controversy" requirement defines with respect to the Judicial Branch the idea of separation of powers on which the Federal Government is founded. The several doctrines that have grown up to elaborate that requirement are "founded in concern about the proper — and properly limited — role of the courts in a democratic society." *Warth v. Seldin,* 422 U.S. 490, 498 (1975).

All of the doctrines that cluster about Article III — not only standing but mootness, ripeness, political question, and the like — relate in part, and in different though overlapping ways, to an idea, which is more than an intuition but less than a rigorous and explicit theory, about the constitutional and prudential limits to the powers of an unelected, unrepresentative judiciary in our kind of government.

Vander Jagt v. O'Neill, 699 F.2d 1166, 1178–1179 (1983) (Bork, J., concurring).

The case-or-controversy doctrines state fundamental limits on federal judicial power in our system of government.

The Art. III doctrine that requires a litigant to have "standing" to invoke the power of a federal court is perhaps the most important of these doctrines. "In essence the question of standing is whether the litigant is entitled to have the court decide the merits of the dispute or of particular issues." Standing doctrine embraces several judicially self-imposed limits on the exercise of federal jurisdiction, such as the general prohibition on a litigant's raising another person's legal rights, the rule barring adjudication of generalized grievances more appropriately addressed in the representative branches, and the requirement that a plaintiff's complaint fall within the zone of interests protected by the law invoked. The requirement of standing, however, has a core component derived directly from the Constitution. A plaintiff must allege personal injury fairly traceable to the defendant's allegedly unlawful conduct and likely to be redressed by the requested relief.

Like the prudential component, the constitutional component of standing doctrine incorporates concepts concededly not susceptible of precise definition. The injury alleged must be, for example, "distinct and palpable," and not "abstract" or "conjectural" or "hypothetical". . . . The injury must be "fairly" traceable to the challenged action, and relief from the injury must be "likely" to follow from a favorable decision. These terms cannot be defined so as to make application of the constitutional standing requirement a mechanical exercise. . . .

Determining standing in a particular case may be facilitated by clarifying principles or even clean rules developed in prior cases. Typically, however, the standing inquiry requires careful judicial examination of a complaint's allegations to ascertain whether the particular plaintiff is entitled to an adjudication of the particular claims asserted. Is the injury too abstract, or otherwise not appropriate, to be considered judicially cognizable? Is the line of causation between the illegal conduct and injury too attenuated? Is the prospect of obtaining relief from the injury as a result of a favorable ruling too speculative? These questions and any others relevant to the standing inquiry must be answered by reference to the Art. III notion that federal courts may exercise power only "in the last resort, and as a necessity," and only when adjudication is "consistent with a system of separated powers and [the dispute is one] traditionally thought to be capable of resolution through the judicial process," *Flast v. Cohen,* 392 U.S. 83, 97 (1968).

B

Respondents allege two injuries in their complaint to support their standing to bring this lawsuit. First, they say that they are harmed directly by the mere fact of Government financial aid to discriminatory private schools. Second, they say that the federal tax exemptions to racially discriminatory private schools in their communities impair their ability to have their public schools desegregated. . . .

This Court has repeatedly held that an asserted right to have the Government act in accordance with law is not sufficient, standing alone, to confer jurisdiction on a federal court. In *Schlesinger v. Reservists Committee to Stop the War,* 418 U.S. 208 (1974), for example, the Court rejected a claim of citizen standing to challenge Armed Forces Reserve commissions held by Members of Congress as violating the Incompatibility Clause of Art. I, § 6, cl. 2, of the Constitution. As citizens, the Court held, plaintiffs alleged nothing but "the abstract injury in nonobservance of the Constitution. . . ." More recently, in *Valley Forge,* we rejected a claim of standing to challenge a Government conveyance of property to a religious institution. Insofar as the plaintiffs relied simply on " 'their shared individuated right' " to a Government that made no law respecting an establishment of religion, we held that plaintiffs had not alleged a judicially cognizable injury. "[A]ssertion of a right to a particular kind of Government conduct, which the Government has violated by acting differently, cannot alone satisfy the requirements of Art. III without draining those requirements of meaning." Respondents here have no standing to complain simply that their Government is violating the law.

Neither do they have standing to litigate their claims based on the stigmatizing injury often caused by racial discrimination. There can be no doubt that this sort of noneconomic injury is one of the most serious consequences of discriminatory government action and is sufficient in some circumstances to support standing. Our cases make clear, however, that such injury accords a basis for standing only to "those persons who are personally denied equal treatment" by the challenged discriminatory conduct. . . .

In *O'Shea v. Littleton,* 414 U.S. 488 (1974), the Court held that the plaintiffs had no standing to challenge racial discrimination in the administration of their city's criminal justice system because they had not alleged that they had been or would likely be subject to the challenged practices. The Court denied standing on similar facts in *Rizzo v. Goode,* 423 U.S. 362 (1976). In each of those cases, the plaintiffs alleged official racial discrimination comparable to that alleged by respondents here. Yet standing was denied in each case because the plaintiffs were not personally subject to the challenged discrimination. Insofar as their first claim of injury is concerned, respondents are in exactly the same position: unlike the appellee in *Heckler v. Mathews,* they do not allege a stigmatic injury suffered as a direct result of having personally been denied equal treatment.

The consequences of recognizing respondents' standing on the basis of their first claim of injury illustrate why our cases plainly hold that such injury is not judicially cognizable. If the abstract stigmatic injury were cognizable, standing would extend nationwide to all members of the particular racial groups against which the Government was alleged to be discriminating by its grant of a tax exemption to a racially discriminatory school, regardless of the location of that school. All such persons could claim the same sort of abstract stigmatic injury respondents assert in their first claim of injury. A black person in Hawaii could challenge the grant of a tax exemption to a racially discriminatory school in Maine. Recognition of standing in such circumstances would transform the federal courts into "no more than a vehicle for the vindication of the value interests of concerned bystanders." *United States v. SCRAP*, 412 U.S. 669, 687 (1973). Constitutional limits on the role of the federal courts preclude such a transformation.

2

It is in their complaint's second claim of injury that respondents allege harm to a concrete, personal interest that can support standing in some circumstances. The injury they identify — their children's diminished ability to receive an education in a racially integrated school — is, beyond any doubt, not only judicially cognizable but, as shown by cases from *Brown v. Board of Education*, 347 U.S. 483 (1954), to *Bob Jones University v. United States*, 461 U.S. 574 (1983), one of the most serious injuries recognized in our legal system. Despite the constitutional importance of curing the injury alleged by respondents, however, the federal judiciary may not redress it unless standing requirements are met. In this case, respondents' second claim of injury cannot support standing because the injury alleged is not fairly traceable to the Government conduct respondents challenge as unlawful.

The illegal conduct challenged by respondents is the IRS's grant of tax exemptions to some racially discriminatory schools. The line of causation between that conduct and desegregation of respondents' schools is attenuated at best. From the perspective of the IRS, the injury to respondents is highly indirect and "results from the independent action of some third party not before the court". . . .

The diminished ability of respondents' children to receive a desegregated education would be fairly traceable to unlawful IRS grants of tax exemptions only if there were enough racially discriminatory private schools receiving tax exemptions in respondents' communities for withdrawal of those exemptions to make an appreciable difference in public-school integration. Respondents have made no such allegation. It is, first, uncertain how many racially discriminatory private schools are in fact receiving tax exemptions. Moreover, it is entirely speculative, . . . whether withdrawal of a tax exemption from any particular school would lead the school to change its policies. It is just as speculative whether any given parent of a child attending such a private school would decide to transfer the child to public school as a result of any changes in educational or financial policy made by the private school once it was threatened with loss of tax-exempt status. It is also pure speculation whether, in a particular community, a large enough number of the numerous relevant school officials and parents would reach decisions that collectively would have a significant impact on the racial composition of the public schools.

The links in the chain of causation between the challenged Government conduct and the asserted injury are far too weak for the chain as a whole to sustain respondents' standing. . . .

The idea of separation of powers that underlies standing doctrine explains why our cases preclude the conclusion that respondents' alleged injury "fairly can be traced to the challenged action" of the IRS. That conclusion would pave the way generally for suits challenging, not specifically identifiable Government violations of law, but the particular programs agencies establish to carry out their legal obligations. Such suits, even when premised on allegations of several instances of violations of law, are rarely if ever appropriate for federal-court adjudication. . . .

. . . When transported into the Art. III context, that principle, grounded as it is in the idea of separation of powers, counsels against recognizing standing in a case brought, not to enforce specific legal obligations whose violation works a direct harm, but to seek a restructuring of the apparatus established by the Executive Branch to fulfill its legal duties. The Constitution, after all, assigns to the Executive Branch, and not to the Judicial Branch, the duty to "take Care that the Laws be faithfully executed." U.S. Const., Art. II, § 3. We could not recognize respondents' standing in this case without running afoul of that structural principle. . . .

The judgment of the Court of Appeals is accordingly reversed, and the injunction issued by that court is vacated.

It is so ordered.

JUSTICE STEVENS, with whom JUSTICE BLACKMUN joins, dissenting. [JUSTICE MARSHALL did not participate in this case and JUSTICE BRENNAN's dissenting opinion is omitted].

Three propositions are clear to me: (1) respondents have adequately alleged "injury in fact;" (2) their injury is fairly traceable to the conduct that they claim to be unlawful; and (3) the "separation of powers" principle does not create a jurisdictional obstacle to the consideration of the merits of their claim.

I

Respondents, the parents of black school children, have alleged that their children are unable to attend fully desegregated schools because large numbers of white children in the areas in which respondents reside attend private schools which do not admit minority children. The Court, JUSTICE BRENNAN, and I all agree that this is an adequate allegation of "injury in fact." . . . This kind of injury may be actionable whether it is caused by the exclusion of black children from public schools or by an official policy of encouraging white children to attend nonpublic schools. A subsidy for the withdrawal of a white child can have the same effect as a penalty for admitting a black child.

II

In final analysis, the wrong the respondents allege that the Government has committed is to subsidize the exodus of white children from schools that would otherwise be racially integrated. The critical question in this case, therefore, is whether respondents have alleged that the Government has created that kind of subsidy.

In answering that question, we must of course assume that respondents can prove what they have alleged. Furthermore, at this stage of the case we must put to one side all questions about the appropriateness of a nationwide class action. The controlling issue is whether the causal connection between the injury and the wrong has been adequately alleged.

An organization that qualifies for preferential treatment under § 501(c)(3) of the Internal Revenue Code, because it is "operated exclusively for . . . charitable . . . purposes," 26 U.S.C. § 501(c)(3), is exempt from paying federal income taxes, and under § 170 of the Code, persons who contribute to such organizations may deduct the amount of their contributions when calculating their taxable income. Only last Term we explained the effect of this preferential treatment:

> Both tax exemptions and tax-deductibility are a form of subsidy that is administered through the tax system. A tax exemption has much the same effect as a cash grant to the organization of the amount of tax it would have to pay on its income. Deductible contributions are similar to cash grants of the amount of a portion of the individual's contributions. . . .

This causation analysis is nothing more than a restatement of elementary economics: when something becomes more expensive, less of it will be purchased. Sections 170 and 501(c)(3) are premised on that recognition. If racially discriminatory private schools lose the "cash grants" that flow from the operation of the statutes, the education they provide will become more expensive and hence less of their services will be purchased. Conversely, maintenance of these tax benefits makes an education in segregated private schools relatively more attractive, by decreasing its cost. Accordingly, without tax exempt status, private schools will either not be competitive in terms of cost, or have to change their admissions policies, hence reducing their competitiveness for parents seeking "a racially segregated alternative" to public schools, which is what respondents have alleged many white parents in desegregating school districts seek. In either event the process of desegregation will be advanced in the same way that it was advanced in *Gilmore* and *Norwood* — the withdrawal of the subsidy for segregated schools means the incentive structure facing white parents who seek such schools for their children will be altered. Thus, the laws of economics, not to mention the laws of Congress embodied in §§ 170 and 501(c)(3), compel the conclusion that the injury respondents have alleged — the increased segregation of their children's schools because of the ready availability of private schools that admit whites only — will be redressed if these schools' operations are inhibited through the denial of preferential tax treatment.

III

Considerations of tax policy, economics, and pure logic all confirm the conclusion that respondents' injury in fact is fairly traceable to the Government's allegedly wrongful conduct. The Court therefore is forced to introduce the concept of "separation of powers" into its analysis. The Court writes that the separation of powers "explains why our cases preclude the conclusion" that respondents' injury is fairly traceable to the conduct they challenge.

The Court could mean one of three things by its invocation of the separation of powers. First, it could simply be expressing the idea that if the plaintiff lacks Article III standing to bring a lawsuit, then there is no "case or controversy" within the meaning of Article III and hence the matter is not within the area of responsibility assigned to the Judiciary by the Constitution. . . . While there can be no quarrel with this proposition, in itself it provides no guidance for determining if the injury respondents have alleged is fairly traceable to the conduct they have challenged.

Second, the Court could be saying that it will require a more direct causal connection when it is troubled by the separation of powers implications of the case before it. That approach confuses the standing doctrine with the justiciability of the issues that respondents seek to raise. The purpose of the standing inquiry is to measure the plaintiff's stake in the outcome, not whether a court has the authority to provide it with the outcome it seeks. . . .

Thus, the " 'fundamental aspect of standing' is that it focuses primarily on the *party* seeking to get his complaint before the federal court rather than on the issues he wishes to have adjudicated." . . . The strength of the plaintiff's interest in the outcome has nothing to do with whether the relief it seeks would intrude upon the prerogatives of other branches of government; the possibility that the relief might be inappropriate does not lessen the plaintiff's stake in obtaining that relief. If a plaintiff presents a nonjusticiable issue, or seeks relief that a court may not award, then its complaint should be dismissed for those reasons, and not because the plaintiff lacks a stake in obtaining that relief and hence has no standing. . . .

Third, the Court could be saying that it will not treat as legally cognizable injuries that stem from an administrative decision concerning how enforcement resources will be allocated. This surely is an important point. Respondents do seek to restructure the IRS' mechanisms for enforcing the legal requirement that discriminatory institutions not receive tax-exempt status. Such restructuring would dramatically affect the way in which the IRS exercises its prosecutorial discretion. The Executive requires latitude to decide how best to enforce the law, and in general the Court may well be correct that the exercise of that discretion, especially in the tax context, is unchallengeable.

However, as the Court also recognizes, this principle does not apply when suit is brought "to enforce specific legal obligations whose violation works a direct harm." . . . Respondents contend that these cases limit the enforcement discretion enjoyed by the IRS. They establish, respondents argue, that the IRS cannot provide "cash grants" to discriminatory schools through preferential tax treatment without running afoul of a constitutional duty to refrain from "giving significant aid" to these institutions. Similarly, respondents claim that the Internal Revenue Code itself, as construed in *Bob Jones,* constrains enforcement discretion. It has been clear since *Marbury v. Madison,* 5 U.S. (1 Cranch) 137 (1803), that "[i]t is emphatically the province and duty of the judicial department to say what the law is." Deciding whether the Treasury has violated a specific legal limitation on its enforcement discretion does not intrude upon the prerogatives of the Executive, for in so deciding we are merely saying "what the law is." Surely the question whether the Constitution or the Code limits enforcement discretion is one within the Judiciary's competence. . . .

I respectfully dissent.

NOTES AND QUESTIONS

9-17. What is the constitutional basis for the causation requirement used by the Court in this case? Does this apply when statutory beneficiaries seek to challenge the government's regulation of third parties on the grounds that it is inadequate? Why does the court deny standing in *Allen v. Wright*?

9-18. Should courts be more willing to entertain suits designed to force the executive branch to carry out its duties more effectively? What are the separation of powers concerns expressed by the majority? Do you agree?

9-19. But for the causation requirement in *Allen,* would petitioners have standing under the *Data Processing* approach? Is the Court relying on certain separation of powers norms to reach its conclusion in *Allen*? What are they? For an analysis of standing and an argument that the use of the causation requirement encourages a private law rather than a public law conception of administrative law, see Sunstein, *Standing and the Privatization of Public Law,* in which Professor Sunstein notes that:*

> The causation requirements present different issues. Standing by themselves, they are natural corollaries of the injury-in-fact requirement and unobjectionable as such. But aside from their manipulability, the central problem is that in the suits in question here, the relevant harms are quite generally probabilistic or systemic. The purpose of the regulatory program is to redress harms of precisely that sort. It would be a large mistake to conclude that such harms are not judicially cognizable. Nineteenth century conceptions of injury should not be used to resolve standing issues in administrative law. Those conceptions have no place in regimes in which the legal injury is often of a different order. A system in which regulatory harms were not judicially cognizable would tend to allow regulated industries, but not regulatory beneficiaries, to have access to court — thus imposing a perverse set of incentives on administrative actors by inclining them against regulatory implementation when it is legally required. Such a result would tend to defeat congressional purposes. Nothing in article III, the APA, or the governing statutes justifies this result.

> In cases brought under the APA, then, courts should generally allow standing to plaintiffs who seek to redress systemic or probabilistic harms. . . .

9-20. What do you think of Justice Stevens' dissent in *Allen*? Would his approach open the floodgates or are there sufficient limiting principles the court can apply? Are these limits better found in doctrines other than standing?

---

* This article originally appeared at 88 COLUM. L. REV. 1432, 1459–61 (1988). Copyright © 1988 by Columbia Law Review. All rights reserved.

PROBLEM 9-1

Consider the following facts from *Intern. Primate Prot. L. v. Administrators of the Tulane Education Fund,* 895 F.2d 1056, 1057–58 (1970):

In 1981, Dr. Edward Taub, the chief of the Behavioral Biology Center of the Institute of Behavioral Research, Inc. ("IBR"), has been conducting experiments at IBR's Silver Spring, Maryland, facility concerning the ability of macaque monkeys to recover use of a limb after nerves in it had been severed. The project had been funded by the National Institutes of Health ("NIH") and was undertaken in a pursuit of benefits for the rehabilitation of human patients suffering from neurological damage.

In September of 1981, Maryland police officers executed a warrant at the facility pursuant to their investigation into the alleged mistreatment of monkeys involved in the experiments. The search resulted in the seizure of 17 macaque monkeys and the arrest and conviction of Dr. Taub on multiple counts of animal cruelty under Article 27, § 59 of the Maryland Code. Pursuant to a court order, NIH was given temporary charge of the monkeys.

Following Dr. Taub's conviction, People for the Ethical Treatment of Animals, Inc. ("PETA"), along with the International Primate Protection League ("IPPL"), the Animal Law Enforcement Association and several named individuals brought suit in Montgomery County, Maryland seeking, *inter alia,* "custody" of the monkeys seized from the facility. The defendants removed to the United States District Court for the District of Maryland, which dismissed the case, finding that none of the claims of the plaintiffs alleged injury sufficient to give them standing to seek possession of the animals.

Although the state court order granting temporary possession to NIH terminated in 1983, NIH has continued to act as keeper of the monkeys with the consent and cooperation of IBR, the monkeys' owners. In response to public clamor and to pressure from members of Congress, NIH transferred a number of the monkeys to Tulane's Delta Regional Primate Center. In December of 1988, NIH announced that they intended to euthanize three of these animals immediately. NIH hopes to gain, through the procedure and subsequent autopsy, knowledge that may lead to improvements in rehabilitation therapy for individuals who have suffered brain or spinal cord damage.

When NIH announced its decision, the present suit was filed in Louisiana Civil District Court asserting various state law claims and seeking possession of the monkeys. The plaintiffs in this suit are IPPL, PETA, Louisiana in Support of Animals and PETA's founder, Alex Pacheco. Named as defendants are NIH, IBR and Tulane. In December of 1989, the court issued a temporary restraining order prohibiting the euthanizing of any of the monkeys. . . .

NIH removed the case, under the authority of 28 U.S.C. § 1442(a)(1), to the United States District Court for the Eastern District of Louisiana.

(a) Assume that you represent NIH and you intend to argue that IPPL and the other plaintiffs have no standing. What are your arguments?

(b) Assume you represent IPPL. How do you respond?

LUJAN v. DEFENDERS OF WILDLIFE

United States Supreme Court
504 U.S. 555 (1992)

JUSTICE SCALIA delivered the opinion of the Court with respect to Parts I, II, III-A, and IV, and an opinion with respect to Part III-B in which THE CHIEF JUSTICE, JUSTICE WHITE, and JUSTICE THOMAS join.

This case involves a challenge to a rule promulgated by the Secretary of the Interior interpreting § 7 of the Endangered Species Act of 1973 (ESA), 87 Stat. 884, 892, as amended, 16 U.S.C. § 1536, in such fashion as to render it applicable only to actions within the United States or on the high seas. The preliminary issue, and the only one we reach, is whether the respondents here, plaintiffs below, have standing to seek judicial review of the rule.

I

The ESA seeks to protect species of animals against threats to their continuing existence caused by man. Section 7(a)(2) of the Act then provides, in pertinent part:

"Each Federal agency shall, in consultation with and with the assistance of the Secretary [of the Interior], insure that any action authorized, funded, or carried out by such agency . . . is not likely to jeopardize the continued existence of any endangered species or threatened species or result in the destruction or adverse modification of habitat of such species which is determined by the Secretary, after consultation as appropriate with affected States, to be critical." 16 U.S.C. § 1536(a)(2).

In 1978, the Fish and Wildlife Service (FWS) and the National Marine Fisheries Service (NMFS), on behalf of the Secretary of the Interior and the Secretary of Commerce respectively, promulgated a joint regulation stating that the obligations imposed by § 7(a)(2) extend to actions taken in foreign nations. The next year, however, the Interior Department began to reexamine its position. . . . A revised joint regulation, reinterpreting § 7(a)(2) to require consultation only for actions taken in the United States or on the high seas, was proposed in 1983, and promulgated in 1986 . . . .

Shortly thereafter, respondents, organizations dedicated to wildlife conservation and other environmental causes, filed this action against the Secretary of the Interior, seeking a declaratory judgment that the new regulation is in error as to the geographic scope of § 7(a)(2), and an injunction requiring the Secretary to promulgate a new regulation restoring the initial interpretation. The District Court granted the Secretary's motion to dismiss for lack of standing. . . . The Court of Appeals for the Eighth Circuit reversed by a divided vote. . . . On remand, the Secretary moved for summary judgment on the standing issue, and respondents moved for summary judgment on the merits. The District Court denied the Secretary's motion, on the ground that the Eighth Circuit had already determined the standing question in this case; it granted respondents' merits motion, and ordered the Secretary to publish a revised regulation. . . . The Eighth Circuit affirmed. We granted certiorari. . . .

II

. . . .

Over the years, our cases have established that the irreducible constitutional minimum of standing contains three elements: First, the plaintiff must have suffered an "injury in fact" — an invasion of a legally-protected interest which is (a) concrete and particularized[1] . . . and (b) "actual or imminent, not 'conjectural' or 'hypothetical,' ". . . . Second, there must be a causal connection between the injury and the conduct complained of — the injury has to be "fairly . . . trace[able] to the challenged action of the defendant, and not . . . th[e] result [of] the independent action of some third party not before the court." . . . Third, it must be "likely," as opposed to merely "speculative," that the injury will be "redressed by a favorable decision." . . .

When the suit is one challenging the legality of government action or inaction, the nature and extent of facts that must be averred (at the summary judgment stage) or proved (at the trial stage) in order to establish standing depends considerably upon whether the plaintiff is himself an object of the action (or foregone action) at issue. If he is, there is ordinarily little question that the action or inaction has caused him injury, and that a judgment preventing or requiring the action will redress it. When, however, as in this case, a plaintiff's asserted injury arises from the government's allegedly unlawful regulation (or lack of regulation) of someone else, much more is needed. In that circumstance, causation and redressability ordinarily hinge on the response of the regulated (or regulable) third party to the government action or inaction — and perhaps on the response of others as well. The existence of one or more of the essential elements of standing "depends on the unfettered choices made by independent actors not before the courts and whose exercise of broad and legitimate discretion the courts cannot presume either to control or to predict," . . . and it becomes the burden of the plaintiff to adduce facts showing that those choices have been or will be made in such manner as to produce causation and permit redressability of injury. . . . Thus, when the plaintiff is not himself the object of the government action or inaction he challenges, standing is not precluded, but it is ordinarily "substantially more difficult" to establish. . . .

---

[1] By particularized, we mean that the injury must affect the plaintiff in a personal and individual way.

III

We think the Court of Appeals failed to apply the foregoing principles in denying the Secretary's motion for summary judgment. Respondents had not made the requisite demonstration of (at least) injury and redressability.

A

Respondents' claim to injury is that the lack of consultation with respect to certain funded activities abroad "increas[es] the rate of extinction of endangered and threatened species." . . . Of course, the desire to use or observe an animal species, even for purely aesthetic purposes, is undeniably a cognizable interest for purposes of standing. "But the 'injury in fact' test requires more than an injury to a cognizable interest. It requires that the party seeking review be himself among the injured." To survive the Secretary's summary judgment motion, respondents had to submit affidavits or other evidence showing, through specific facts, not only that listed species were in fact being threatened by funded activities abroad, but also that one or more of respondents' members would thereby be "directly" affected apart from their "'special interest' in th[e] subject." . . .

With respect to this aspect of the case, the Court of Appeals focused on the affidavits of two Defenders' members — Joyce Kelly and Amy Skilbred. Ms. Kelly stated that she traveled to Egypt in 1986 and "observed the traditional habitat of the endangered Nile crocodile there and intend[s] to do so again, and hope[s] to observe the crocodile directly," and that she "will suffer harm in fact as a result of [the] American . . . role . . . in overseeing the rehabilitation of the Aswan High Dam on the Nile . . . and [in] develop[ing] . . . Egypt's . . . Master Water Plan." Ms. Skilbred averred that she traveled to Sri Lanka in 1981 and "observed th[e] habitat" of "endangered species such as the Asian elephant and the leopard" at what is now the site of the Mahaweli Project funded by the Agency for International Development (AID), although she "was unable to see any of the endangered species"; "this development project," she continued, "will seriously reduce endangered, threatened, and endemic species habitat including areas that I visited . . . [, which] may severely shorten the future of these species"; that threat, she concluded, harmed her because she "intend[s] to return to Sri Lanka in the future and hope[s] to be more fortunate in spotting at least the endangered elephant and leopard." When Ms. Skilbred was asked at a subsequent deposition if and when she had any plans to return to Sri Lanka, she reiterated that "I intend to go back to Sri Lanka," but confessed that she had no current plans: "I don't know [when]. There is a civil war going on right now. I don't know. Not next year, I will say. In the future."

We shall assume for the sake of argument that these affidavits contain facts showing that certain agency-funded projects threaten listed species — though that is questionable. They plainly contain no facts, however, showing how damage to the species will produce "imminent" injury to Mss. Kelly and Skilbred. That the women "had visited" the areas of the projects before the projects commenced proves nothing. . . .

Besides relying upon the Kelly and Skilbred affidavits, respondents propose a series of novel standing theories. The first, inelegantly styled "ecosystem nexus," proposes that any person who uses any part of a "contiguous ecosystem" adversely affected by a funded activity has standing even if the activity is located a great distance away. This approach, as the Court of Appeals correctly observed, is inconsistent with our opinion in *National Wildlife Federation,* which held that a plaintiff claiming injury from environmental damage must use the area affected by the challenged activity and not an area roughly "in the vicinity" of it. 497 U.S., at 887–889. . . . It makes no difference that the general-purpose section of the ESA states that the Act was intended in part "to provide a means whereby the ecosystems upon which endangered species and threatened species depend may be conserved," 16 U.S.C. § 1531(b). To say that the Act protects ecosystems is not to say that the Act creates (if it were possible) rights of action in persons who have not been injured in fact, that is, persons who use portions of an ecosystem not perceptibly affected by the unlawful action in question.

Respondents' other theories are called, alas, the "animal nexus" approach, whereby anyone who has an interest in studying or seeing the endangered animals anywhere on the globe has standing; and the "vocational nexus" approach, under which anyone with a professional interest in such animals can sue. Under these theories, anyone who goes to see Asian elephants in the Bronx Zoo, and anyone who is a keeper of Asian elephants in the Bronx Zoo, has standing to sue because the Director of AID did not consult with the Secretary regarding the AID-funded project in Sri Lanka. This is beyond all reason. . . . It is clear that the person who observes or works with a particular animal threatened by a federal decision is facing perceptible harm, since the very subject of his interest will no longer exist. It is even plausible — though it goes to the outermost limit of plausibility — to think that a person who observes or works with animals of a particular species in the very area of the world where that species is threatened by a federal decision is facing such harm, since some animals that might have been the subject of his interest will no longer exist, *see Japan Whaling Assn. v. American Cetacean Soc.,* 478 U.S. 221, 231, n. 4 (1986). It goes beyond the limit, however, and into pure speculation and fantasy, to say that anyone who observes or works with an endangered species, anywhere in the world, is appreciably harmed by a single project affecting some portion of that species with which he has no more specific connection.

B

. . . .

The most obvious problem in the present case is redressability. Since the agencies funding the projects were not parties to the case, the District Court could accord relief only against the Secretary: He could be ordered to revise his regulation to require consultation for foreign projects. But this would not remedy respondents' alleged injury unless the funding agencies were bound by the Secretary's regulation, which is very much an open question. . . .

Respondents assert that this legal uncertainty did not affect redressability (and hence standing) because the District Court itself could resolve the issue of the Secretary's authority as a necessary part of its standing inquiry.

Assuming that it is appropriate to resolve an issue of law such as this in connection with a threshold standing inquiry, resolution by the District Court would not have remedied respondents' alleged injury anyway, because it would not have been binding upon the agencies. They were not parties to the suit, and there is no reason they should be obliged to honor an incidental legal determination the suit produced. The Court of Appeals tried to finesse this problem by simply proclaiming that "[w]e are satisfied that an injunction requiring the Secretary to publish [respondents' desired] regulatio[n] . . . would result in consultation." . . . We do not know what would justify that confidence, particularly when the Justice Department (presumably after consultation with the agencies) has taken the position that the regulation is not binding. The short of the matter is that redress of the only injury-in-fact respondents complain of requires action (termination of funding until consultation) by the individual funding agencies; and any relief the District Court could have provided in this suit against the Secretary was not likely to produce that action. . . .

IV

The Court of Appeals found that respondents had standing for an additional reason: because they had suffered a "procedural injury." The so-called "citizen-suit" provision of the ESA provides, in pertinent part, that "any person may commence a civil suit on his own behalf (A) to enjoin any person, including the United States and any other governmental instrumentality or agency . . . who is alleged to be in violation of any provision of this chapter." 16 U.S.C. § 1540(g). The court held that, because § 7(a)(2) requires interagency consultation, the citizen-suit provision creates a "procedural righ[t]" to consultation in all "persons" — so that anyone can file suit in federal court to challenge the Secretary's (or presumably any other official's) failure to follow the assertedly correct consultative procedure, notwithstanding their inability to allege any discrete injury flowing from that failure. . . . To understand the remarkable nature of this holding one must be clear about what it does not rest upon: This is not a case where plaintiffs are seeking to enforce a procedural requirement the disregard of which could impair a separate concrete interest of theirs (*e.g.*, the procedural requirement for a hearing prior to denial of their license application, or the procedural requirement for an environmental impact statement before a federal facility is constructed next door to them).[7] Nor is it simply a case where concrete injury has been suffered

---

[7] There is this much truth to the assertion that "procedural rights" are special: The person who has been accorded a procedural right to protect his concrete interests can assert that right without meeting all the normal standards for redressability and immediacy. Thus, under our case-law, one living adjacent to the site for proposed construction of a federally licensed dam has standing to challenge the licensing agency's failure to prepare an Environmental Impact Statement, even though he cannot establish with any certainty that the Statement will cause the license to be withheld or altered, and even though the dam will not be completed for many years. (That is why we do not rely, in the present case, upon the Government's argument that, even if the other agencies were obliged to consult with the Secretary, they might not have followed his advice.) What respondents' "procedural rights" argument seeks, however, is quite different from this: standing for persons who have no concrete interests affected — persons who live (and propose to live) at the other end of the country from the dam.

by many persons, as in mass fraud or mass tort situations. Nor, finally, is it the unusual case in which Congress has created a concrete private interest in the outcome of a suit against a private party for the government's benefit, by providing a cash bounty for the victorious plaintiff. Rather, the court held that the injury-in-fact requirement had been satisfied by congressional conferral upon all persons of an abstract, self-contained, non-instrumental "right" to have the Executive observe the procedures required by law. We reject this view.

We have consistently held that a plaintiff raising only a generally available grievance about government — claiming only harm to his and every citizen's interest in proper application of the Constitution and laws, and seeking relief that no more directly and tangibly benefits him than it does the public at large — does not state an Article III case or controversy. . . .

To be sure, our generalized-grievance cases have typically involved Government violation of procedures assertedly ordained by the Constitution rather than the Congress. But there is absolutely no basis for making the Article III inquiry turn on the source of the asserted right. Whether the courts were to act on their own, or at the invitation of Congress, in ignoring the concrete injury requirement described in our cases, they would be discarding a principle fundamental to the separate and distinct constitutional role of the Third Branch — one of the essential elements that identifies those "Cases" and "Controversies" that are the business of the courts rather than of the political branches. "The province of the court," as Chief Justice Marshall said in *Marbury v. Madison,* 5 U.S. (1 Cranch) 137, 170 (1803) "is, solely, to decide on the rights of individuals." Vindicating the public interest (including the public interest in government observance of the Constitution and laws) is the function of Congress and the Chief Executive. The question presented here is whether the public interest in proper administration of the laws (specifically, in agencies' observance of a particular, statutorily prescribed procedure) can be converted into an individual right by a statute that denominates it as such, and that permits all citizens (or, for that matter, a subclass of citizens who suffer no distinctive concrete harm) to sue. If the concrete injury requirement has the separation-of-powers significance we have always said, the answer must be obvious: To permit Congress to convert the undifferentiated public interest in executive officers' compliance with the law into an "individual right" vindicable in the courts is to permit Congress to transfer from the President to the courts the Chief Executive's most important constitutional duty, to "take Care that the Laws be faithfully executed," Art. II, § 3. It would enable the courts, with the permission of Congress, "to assume a position of authority over the governmental acts of another and co-equal department," *Frothingham v. Mellon,* 262 U.S., at 489, and to become " 'virtually continuing monitors of the wisdom and soundness of Executive action.' " *Allen,* 468 U.S. at 760. . . . We have always rejected that vision of our

> "When Congress passes an Act empowering administrative agencies to carry on governmental activities, the power of those agencies is circumscribed by the authority granted. This permits the courts to participate in law enforcement entrusted to administrative bodies only to the extent necessary to protect justiciable individual rights against administrative

action fairly beyond the granted powers. . . . This is very far from assuming that the courts are charged more than administrators or legislators with the protection of the rights of the people. Congress and the Executive supervise the acts of administrative agents. . . . But under Article III, Congress established courts to adjudicate cases and controversies as to claims of infringement of individual rights whether by unlawful action of private persons or by the exertion of unauthorized administrative power."

Stark v. Wickard, 321 U.S. 288, 309–310 (1944). "Individual rights," within the meaning of this passage, do not mean public rights that have been legislatively pronounced to belong to each individual who forms part of the public. *See also Sierra Club,* 405 U.S., at 740–741, n. 16. . . .

Nothing in this contradicts the principle that "[t]he . . . injury required by Art. III may exist solely by virtue of 'statutes creating legal rights, the invasion of which creates standing.'" *Warth,* 442 U.S., at 500 (quoting *Linda R.S. v. Richard D.,* 410 U.S. 614, 617, n. 3 (1973)). Both of the cases used by *Linda R.S.* as an illustration of that principle involved Congress's elevating to the status of legally cognizable injuries concrete, *de facto* injuries that were previously inadequate in law (namely, injury to an individual's personal interest in living in a racially integrated community, . . .

We hold that respondents lack standing to bring this action and that the Court of Appeals erred in denying the summary judgment motion filed by the United States. The opinion of the Court of Appeals is hereby reversed, and the cause remanded for proceedings consistent with this opinion.

It is so ordered.

JUSTICE KENNEDY, with whom JUSTICE SOUTER joins, concurring in part and concurring in the judgment.

Although I agree with the essential parts of the Court's analysis, I write separately to make several observations.

I agree with the Court's conclusion in Part III-A that, on the record before us, respondents have failed to demonstrate that they themselves are "among the injured." . . .

While it may seem trivial to require that Mss. Kelly and Skilbred acquire airline tickets to the project sites or announce a date certain upon which they will return, this is not a case where it is reasonable to assume that the affiants will be using the sites on a regular basis, nor do the affiants claim to have visited the sites since the projects commenced. With respect to the Court's discussion of respondents' "ecosystem nexus," "animal nexus," and "vocational nexus" theories, I agree that on this record respondents' showing is insufficient to establish standing on any of these bases. I am not willing to foreclose the possibility, however, that in different circumstances a nexus theory similar to those proffered here might support a claim to standing. . . .

I also join Part IV of the Court's opinion with the following observations. As government programs and policies become more complex and far-reaching, we must be sensitive to the articulation of new rights of action that do not have clear analogs in our common-law tradition. Modern litigation has progressed far from the paradigm of Marbury suing Madison to get his commission, *Marbury v. Madison,* 5 U.S. (1 Cranch) 137, or Ogden seeking an injunction to halt Gibbons' steamboat operations. *Gibbons v. Ogden,* 22 U.S. (9 Wheat.) 1 (1824). In my view, Congress has the power to define injuries and articulate chains of causation that will give rise to a case or controversy where none existed before, and I do not read the Court's opinion to suggest a contrary view. . . . In exercising this power, however, Congress must at the very least identify the injury it seeks to vindicate and relate the injury to the class of persons entitled to bring suit. The citizen-suit provision of the Endangered Species Act does not meet these minimal requirements, because while the statute purports to confer a right on "any person . . . to enjoin . . . the United States and any other governmental instrumentality or agency . . . who is alleged to be in violation of any provision of this chapter," it does not of its own force establish that there is an injury in "any person" by virtue of any "violation." 16 U.S.C. § 1540(g)(1)(A).

The Court's holding that there is an outer limit to the power of Congress to confer rights of action is a direct and necessary consequence of the case and controversy limitations found in Article III. I agree that it would exceed those limitations if, at the behest of Congress and in the absence of any showing of concrete injury, we were to entertain citizen-suits to vindicate the public's non-concrete interest in the proper administration of the laws. . . .

An independent judiciary is held to account through its open proceedings and its reasoned judgments. In this process it is essential for the public to know what persons or groups are invoking the judicial power, the reasons that they have brought suit, and whether their claims are vindicated or denied. The concrete injury requirement helps assure that there can be an answer to these questions; and, as the Court's opinion is careful to show, that is part of the constitutional design. . . .

JUSTICE STEVENS, concurring in the judgment.

Because I am not persuaded that Congress intended the consultation requirement in § 7(a)(2) of the Endangered Species Act of 1973 (ESA), 16 U.S.C. § 1536(a)(2), to apply to activities in foreign countries, I concur in the judgment of reversal. I do not, however, agree with the Court's conclusion that respondents lack standing because the threatened injury to their interest in protecting the environment and studying endangered species is not "imminent." Nor do I agree with the plurality's additional conclusion that respondents' injury is not "redressable" in this litigation.

I

In my opinion a person who has visited the critical habitat of an endangered species, has a professional interest in preserving the species and its habitat, and intends to revisit them in the future has standing to challenge agency action that threatens their destruction. Congress has found that a wide variety of endangered species of fish, wildlife, and plants are of "aesthetic, ecological, educational, historical, recreational, and scientific value to the Nation and its people." 16 U.S.C. § 1531(a)(3). Given that finding, we have no license to demean the importance of the interest that particular individuals may have in observing any species or its habitat, whether those individuals are motivated by aesthetic enjoyment, an interest in professional research, or an economic interest in preservation of the species. . . .

The Court nevertheless concludes that respondents have not suffered "injury in fact" because they have not shown that the harm to the endangered species will produce "imminent" injury to them. I disagree. An injury to an individual's interest in studying or enjoying a species and its natural habitat occurs when someone (whether it be the government or a private party) takes action that harms that species and habitat. In my judgment, therefore, the "imminence" of such an injury should be measured by the timing and likelihood of the threatened environmental harm, rather than — as the Court seems to suggest, by the time that might elapse between the present and the time when the individuals would visit the area if no such injury should occur. . . .

JUSTICE BLACKMUN, with whom JUSTICE O'CONNOR joins, dissenting.

I part company with the Court in this case in two respects. First, I believe that respondents have raised genuine issues of fact — sufficient to survive summary judgment — both as to injury and as to redressability. Second, I question the Court's breadth of language in rejecting standing for "procedural" injuries. I fear the Court seeks to impose fresh limitations on the constitutional authority of Congress to allow citizen-suits in the federal courts for injuries deemed "procedural" in nature. I dissent.

I

. . . .

A

To survive petitioner's motion for summary judgment on standing, respondents need not prove that they are actually or imminently harmed. They need show only a "genuine issue" of material fact as to standing. Fed. Rule Civ. Proc. 56(c). This is not a heavy burden. A "genuine issue" exists so long as "the evidence is such that a reasonable jury could return a verdict for the nonmoving party [respondents]." . . .

1

Were the Court to apply the proper standard for summary judgment, I believe it would conclude that the sworn affidavits and deposition testimony of Joyce Kelly and Amy Skilbred advance sufficient facts to create a genuine issue for trial concerning whether one or both would be imminently harmed by the Aswan and Mahaweli projects. In the first instance, as the Court itself concedes, the affidavits contained facts making it at least "questionable" (and therefore within the province of the fact-finder) that certain agency-funded projects threaten listed species. The only remaining issue, then, is whether Kelly and Skilbred have shown that they personally would suffer imminent harm.

I think a reasonable finder of fact could conclude from the information in the affidavits and deposition testimony that either Kelly or Skilbred will soon return to the project sites, thereby satisfying the "actual or imminent" injury standard. . . .

II

The Court concludes that any "procedural injury" suffered by respondents is insufficient to confer standing. It rejects the view that the "injury-in-fact requirement . . . [is] satisfied by congressional conferral upon all person of an abstract, self-contained, non-instrumental 'right' to have the Executive observe the procedures required by law." Whatever the Court might mean with that very broad language, it cannot be saying that "procedural injuries" as a class are necessarily insufficient for purposes of Article III standing.

Most governmental conduct can be classified as "procedural." Many injuries caused by governmental conduct, therefore, are categorizable at some level of generality as "procedural" injuries. Yet, these injuries are not categorically beyond the pale of redress by the federal courts. When the Government, for example, "procedurally" issues a pollution permit, those affected by the permittee's pollutants are not without standing to sue. Only later cases will tell just what the Court means by its intimation that "procedural" injuries are not constitutionally cognizable injuries. In the meantime, I have the greatest of sympathy for the courts across the country that will struggle to understand the Court's standardless exposition of this concept today.

The Court expresses concern that allowing judicial enforcement of "agencies' observance of a particular, statutorily prescribed procedure" would "transfer from the President to the courts the Chief Executive's most important constitutional duty, to 'take Care that the Laws be faithfully executed,' Art. II, sec. 3." In fact, the principal effect of foreclosing judicial enforcement of such procedures is to transfer power into the hands of the Executive at the expense — not of the courts — but of Congress, from which that power originates and emanates.

Under the Court's anachronistically formal view of the separation of powers, Congress legislates pure, substantive mandates and has no business structuring the procedural manner in which the Executive implements these mandates. To be sure, in the ordinary course, Congress does legislate in black-and-white terms of affirmative commands or negative prohibitions on the conduct of officers of the Executive Branch. In complex regulatory areas, however, Congress often legislates, as it were, in procedural shades of gray. That is, it sets forth substantive policy goals and provides for their attainment by requiring Executive Branch officials to follow certain procedures, for example, in the form of reporting, consultation, and certification requirements. . . .

The consultation requirement of § 7 of the Endangered Species Act is a similar, action-forcing statute. Consultation is designed as an integral check on federal agency action, ensuring that such action does not go forward without full consideration of its effects on listed species. . . .

. . . Congress could simply impose a substantive prohibition on executive conduct; it could say that no agency action shall result in the loss of more than 5% of any listed species. Instead, Congress sets forth substantive guidelines and allows the Executive, within certain procedural constraints, to decide how best to effectuate the ultimate goal. . . . The Court never has questioned Congress' authority to impose such procedural constraints on executive power. Just as Congress does not violate separation of powers by structuring the procedural manner in which the Executive shall carry out the laws, surely the federal courts do not violate separation of powers when, at the very instruction and command of Congress, they enforce these procedures.

. . . Here Congress seeks not to delegate "executive" power but only to strengthen the procedures it has legislatively mandated. "We have long recognized that the nondelegation doctrine does not prevent Congress from seeking assistance, within proper limits, from its coordinate Branches." *Touby v. United States,* — U.S. —, —, 111 S. Ct. 1752, 1756, 114 L. Ed. 2d (1991). "Congress does not violate the Constitution merely because it legislates in broad terms, leaving a certain degree of discretion to executive *or judicial actors*" (emphasis added). *Ibid.*

Ironically, this Court has previously justified a relaxed review of congressional delegation to the Executive on grounds that Congress, in turn, has subjected the exercise of that power to judicial review. *INS v. Chadha,* 462 U.S. 919, 953–954, n. 16. . . . The Court's intimation today that procedural injuries are not constitutionally cognizable threatens this understanding upon which Congress has undoubtedly relied. . . .

It is to be hoped that over time the Court will acknowledge that some classes of procedural duties are so enmeshed with the prevention of a substantive, concrete harm that an individual plaintiff may be able to demonstrate a sufficient likelihood of injury just through the breach of that procedural duty. For example, in the context of the NEPA requirement of environmental-impact statements, this Court has acknowledged "it is now well settled that NEPA itself does not mandate particular results [and] simply prescribes the 'necessary process,' but *these procedures are almost certain to affect the agency's substantive decision.*" *Robertson v. Methow Valley Citizens Council,* 490 U.S. 332, 350 (1989) (emphasis added). This acknowledgement of an inextricable link between procedural and substantive harm does not reflect improper appellate factfinding. It reflects nothing more than the proper deference owed to the judgment of a coordinate branch — Congress — that certain procedures are directly tied to protection against a substantive harm. . . .

III

In conclusion, I cannot join the Court on what amounts to a slash-and-burn expedition through the law of environmental standing. In my view, "[t]he very essence of civil liberty certainly consists in the right of every individual to claim the protection of the laws, whenever he receives an injury." *Marbury v. Madison,* 1 Cranch 137, 163.

I dissent.

NOTES AND QUESTIONS

9-21. Why does the majority conclude that plaintiffs failed to establish an injury in fact in this case? Why were plaintiffs' intentions to visit places inhabited by endangered species not sufficient to grant standing? What does "imminent" mean? Why was the interrelated nature of ecosystems not enough for the majority of the Court to find that plaintiffs had standing? What is Justice Stevens' view?

9-22. Why, in the opinion of a plurality of the Court, did the plaintiffs fail to show that their harms could be redressed? Wouldn't the plaintiffs benefit from a decree in their favor by the Secretary of the Interior?

9-23. Justice Scalia's opinion distinguishes between two types of cases: those in which injury arises due to governmental action of which the plaintiff is the object, and those in which the plaintiff's "asserted injury arises from the government's allegedly unlawful regulation (or lack of regulation) of *someone else*. . . ." What constitutional problems do cases in this second category raise so far as Justice Scalia is concerned?

9-24. In an article entitled *The Doctrine of Standing as an Essential Element of the Separation of Powers*, 17 SUFFOLK U. L. REV. 881, 894 (1983),* then-appellate court judge Scalia wrote that:

> [T]he law of standing roughly restricts courts to their traditional undemocratic role of protecting individuals and minorities against impositions of the majority, and excludes them from the even more undemocratic role of prescribing how the other two branches should function in order to serve the interest of the majority itself.

How does this approach play out in *Lujan*? Does it help explain Justice Scalia's application of the injury-in-fact test? Does it help explain why, in Justice Scalia's view, the citizen suit provision in *Lujan* could not confer standing on the plaintiffs in this case? Is it fair to say that Justice Scalia believes that public interest groups might force the executive branch to enforce policies it chooses to ignore? Is that wrong?

9-25. According to Justice Scalia's opinion, whose responsibility is it to vindicate the public interest? What role should courts play in this regard? Why? What approach to this issue is advocated by Justices Kennedy and Souter? Justice Stevens? Are Justice Kennedy and Souter really concurring in Justice Scalia's opinion or modifying it substantially? Do they accept Justice Scalia's ideas about "nexus"? About "redressability"?

9-26. To what extent does Justice Scalia's view of the Take Care Clause dictate the outcome the Court reaches on the issue of citizen standing? What is the relationship of Article II to Article III standing concerns? Consider the

---

* Copyright © 1983 by Suffolk University Law School. All rights reserved.

following in Cass Sunstein, *What's Standing After* Lujan? *Of Citizen Suits, "Injuries," and Article III* [*]:

> *Lujan* seems to be built in key part on the idea that citizen standing — like other legislative interference with the President's power to execute the law — is unacceptable under Article II. Indeed, many of the recent standing cases might be thought to be Article II cases masquerading under the guise of Article III; we may even say that the Article II tail is wagging the Article III dog. But the conflation of Article II and Article III concerns has led to serious confusion. If a plaintiff with a plane ticket can sue under the ESA without offense to Article II, then it makes no sense to say that Article II is violated if a plaintiff lacking such a ticket initiates a proceeding. Beneficiary standing poses no Article II issue. The two articles raise quite different concerns; they should be analyzed separately.
>
> The Court's answer, set out in a brief passage, appears to take the following form. It is one thing for judges to protect "individual rights." Courts can properly engage in this task, which is uniquely theirs. But it is another thing to protect "public rights that have been legislatively pronounced to belong to each individual who forms part of the public." In the end, however, this argument seems to have little to do with the Take Care Clause. Instead, it must rest on the understanding that Article III places a substantive limitation on what sorts of harms can count as legally cognizable injuries.

9-27. Should Congress be allowed to grant standing to citizens? How can they do this after *Lujan*? Can Congress simply use its powers to define what it believes to be an injury, quite apart from what a court might think? What does Justice Kennedy's concurrence suggest in this regard? *See* Sunstein, *supra* at 231, noting that: "Justice Kennedy emphasized that standing need not be based solely on common law-like injuries; his concern was that, in creating the citizen suit, Congress had not even identified the injury it was attempting to redress. Congress can meet this concern by identifying injuries, building on the common law framework to recognize probabilistic, systemic, or regulatory harms." Will this be enough for Justice Scalia?

9-28. If Congress were to grant a cash bounty to all successful citizen plaintiffs, would that satisfy the Court's standing concerns in citizen suits? Is this a good way of ensuring that the laws are enforced? *See* Sunstein, *supra* at 232. Would lawsuits arising under such bounty statutes create the same separation-of-powers concerns that trouble Justice Scalia in *Lujan*? Does it make any difference that Congress would affirmatively have to appropriate the money necessary to pay plaintiffs a cash bounty? If so, why?

---

[*] 91 MICH. L. REV. 163, 213–14 (1992). Copyright © 1992 by Cass R. Sunstein. All rights reserved.

FRIENDS OF THE EARTH, INCORPORATED v. LAIDLAW ENVIRONMENTAL SERVICES (TOC), INC.

Supreme Court of the United States
528 U.S. 167 (2000)

JUSTICE GINSBURG delivered the opinion of the Court.

. . . .

I

A

In 1972, Congress enacted the Clean Water Act (Act), also known as the Federal Water Pollution Control Act, 86 Stat. 816, as amended. Section 402 of the Act, provides for the issuance, by the Administrator of the Environmental Protection Agency (EPA) or by authorized States, of National Pollutant Discharge Elimination System (NPDES) permits. NPDES permits impose limitations on the discharge of pollutants, and establish related monitoring and reporting requirements, in order to improve the cleanliness and safety of the Nation's waters. Noncompliance with a permit constitutes a violation of the Act.

Under § 505(a) of the Act, a suit to enforce any limitation in an NPDES permit may be brought by any "citizen," defined as "a person or persons having an interest which is or may be adversely affected." . . . .

B

In 1986, defendant-respondent Laidlaw Environmental Services (TOC), Inc., bought a hazardous waste incinerator facility in Roebuck, South Carolina, that included a wastewater treatment plant. (The company has since changed its name to Safety-Kleen (Roebuck), Inc., but for simplicity we will refer to it as "Laidlaw" throughout.) Shortly after Laidlaw acquired the facility, the South Carolina Department of Health and Environmental Control (DHEC), acting under 33 U.S.C. § 1342(a)(1), granted Laidlaw an NPDES permit authorizing the company to discharge treated water into the North Tyger River. The permit, which became effective on January 1, 1987, placed limits on Laidlaw's discharge of several pollutants into the river, including — of particular relevance to this case — mercury, an extremely toxic pollutant. The permit also regulated the flow, temperature, toxicity, and pH of the effluent from the facility, and imposed monitoring and reporting obligations.

Once it received its permit, Laidlaw began to discharge various pollutants into the waterway; repeatedly, Laidlaw's discharges exceeded the limits set by the permit. In particular, despite experimenting with several technological fixes, Laidlaw consistently failed to meet the permit's stringent 1.3 ppb (parts per billion) daily average limit on mercury discharges. The District Court later found that Laidlaw had violated the mercury limits on 489 occasions between 1987 and 1995. . . .

On June 12, 1992, FOE filed this citizen suit against Laidlaw under § 505(a) of the Act, alleging noncompliance with the NPDES permit and seeking declaratory and injunctive relief and an award of civil penalties. Laidlaw moved for summary judgment on the ground that FOE had failed to present evidence demonstrating injury in fact, and therefore lacked Article III standing to bring the lawsuit. . . . After examining this evidence, the District Court denied Laidlaw's summary judgment motion, finding — albeit "by the very slimmest of margins" — that FOE had standing to bring the suit. . . .

On January 22, 1997, the District Court issued its judgment. It found that Laidlaw had gained a total economic benefit of $1,092,581 as a result of its extended period of noncompliance with the mercury discharge limit in its permit. The court concluded, however, that a civil penalty of $405,800 was adequate in light of the guiding factors listed in 33 U.S.C. § 1319(d). In particular, the District Court stated that the lesser penalty was appropriate taking into account the judgment's "total deterrent effect." . . .

On July 16, 1998, the Court of Appeals for the Fourth Circuit issued its judgment. The Court of Appeals assumed without deciding that FOE initially had standing to bring the action, but went on to hold that the case had become moot. . . .

We granted certiorari. . . .

II

A

. . . .

Laidlaw contends first that FOE lacked standing from the outset even to seek injunctive relief, because the plaintiff organizations failed to show that any of their members had sustained or faced the threat of any "injury in fact" from Laidlaw's activities. In support of this contention Laidlaw points to the District Court's finding, made in the course of setting the penalty amount, that there had been "no demonstrated proof of harm to the environment" from Laidlaw's mercury discharge violations. ("[T]he NPDES permit violations at issue in this citizen suit did not result in any health risk or environmental harm.").

The relevant showing for purposes of Article III standing, however, is not injury to the environment but injury to the plaintiff. To insist upon the former rather than the latter as part of the standing inquiry (as the dissent in essence does) is to raise the standing hurdle higher than the necessary showing for success on the merits in an action alleging noncompliance with an NPDES permit. Focusing properly on injury to the plaintiff, the District Court found that FOE had demonstrated sufficient injury to establish standing. For example, FOE member Kenneth Lee Curtis averred in affidavits that he lived a half-mile from Laidlaw's facility; that he occasionally drove over the North Tyger River, and that it looked and smelled polluted; and that he would like to fish, camp, swim, and picnic in and near the river between 3 and 15 miles downstream from the facility, as he did when he was a teenager, but would not do so because he was concerned that the water was polluted by Laidlaw's discharges. Curtis reaffirmed these statements in extensive deposition testimony. For example, he testified that he would like to fish in the river at a specific spot he used as a boy, but that he would not do so now because of his concerns about Laidlaw's discharges.

Other members presented evidence to similar effect. CLEAN member Angela Patterson attested that she lived two miles from the facility; that before Laidlaw operated the facility, she picnicked, walked, birdwatched, and waded in and along the North Tyger River because of the natural beauty of the area; that she no longer engaged in these activities in or near the river because she was concerned about harmful effects from discharged pollutants; and that she and her husband would like to purchase a home near the river but did not intend to do so, in part because of Laidlaw's discharges. CLEAN member Judy Pruitt averred that she lived one-quarter mile from Laidlaw's facility and would like to fish, hike, and picnic along the North Tyger River, but has refrained from those activities because of the discharges. FOE member Linda Moore attested that she lived 20 miles from Roebuck, and would use the North Tyger River south of Roebuck and the land surrounding it for recreational purposes were she not concerned that the water contained harmful pollutants. In her deposition, Moore testified at length that she would hike, picnic, camp, swim, boat, and drive near or in the river were it not for her concerns about illegal discharges. CLEAN member Gail Lee attested that her home, which is near Laidlaw's facility, had a lower value than similar homes located farther from the facility, and that she believed the pollutant discharges accounted for some of the discrepancy. Sierra Club member Norman Sharp averred that he had canoed approximately 40 miles downstream of the Laidlaw facility and would like to canoe in the North Tyger River closer to Laidlaw's discharge point, but did not do so because he was concerned that the water contained harmful pollutants.

These sworn statements, as the District Court determined, adequately documented injury in fact. We have held that environmental plaintiffs adequately allege injury in fact when they aver that they use the affected area and are persons "for whom the aesthetic and recreational values of the area will be lessened" by the challenged activity.

Our decision in *Lujan v. National Wildlife Federation*, 497 U.S. 871 (1990), is not to the contrary. In that case an environmental organization assailed the Bureau of Land Management's "land withdrawal review program," a program covering millions of acres, alleging that the program illegally opened up public lands to mining activities. The defendants moved for summary judgment, challenging the plaintiff organization's standing to initiate the action under the Administrative Procedure Act. We held that the plaintiff could not survive the summary judgment motion merely by offering "averments which state only that one of [the organization's] members uses unspecified portions of an immense tract of territory, on some portions of which mining activity has occurred or probably will occur by virtue of the governmental action."

In contrast, the affidavits and testimony presented by FOE in this case assert that Laidlaw's discharges, and the affiant members' reasonable concerns about the effects of those discharges, directly affected those affiants' recreational, aesthetic, and economic interests. These submissions present dispositively more than the mere "general averments" and "conclusory allegations" found inadequate in *National Wildlife Federation*. Nor can the affiants' conditional statements — that they would use the nearby North Tyger River for recreation if Laidlaw were not discharging pollutants into it — be equated with the speculative "'some day' intentions" to visit endangered species halfway around the world that we held insufficient to show injury in fact in *Lujan v. Defenders of Wildlife*, 504 U.S. 555, 564 (1992).

Los Angeles v. Lyons, 461 U.S. 95 (1983), relied on by the dissent does not weigh against standing in this case. In *Lyons*, we held that a plaintiff lacked standing to seek an injunction against the enforcement of a police chokehold policy because he could not credibly allege that he faced a realistic threat from the policy. In the footnote from *Lyons* cited by the dissent, we noted that "[t]he reasonableness of Lyons' fear is dependent upon the likelihood of a recurrence of the allegedly unlawful conduct," and that his "subjective apprehensions" that such a recurrence would even *take place* were not enough to support standing. Here, in contrast, it is undisputed that Laidlaw's unlawful conduct — discharging pollutants in excess of permit limits — was occurring at the time the complaint was filed. Under *Lyons*, then, the only "subjective" issue here is "[t]he reasonableness of [the] fear" that led the affiants to respond to that concededly ongoing conduct by refraining from use of the North Tyger River and surrounding areas. Unlike the dissent, we see nothing "improbable" about the proposition that a company's continuous and pervasive illegal discharges of pollutants into a river would cause nearby residents to curtail their recreational use of that waterway and would subject them to other economic and aesthetic harms. The proposition is entirely reasonable, the District Court found it was true in this case, and that is enough for injury in fact.

Laidlaw argues next that even if FOE had standing to seek injunctive relief, it lacked standing to seek civil penalties. Here the asserted defect is not injury but redressability. Civil penalties offer no redress to private plaintiffs, Laidlaw argues, because they are paid to the Government, and therefore a citizen plaintiff can never have standing to seek them.

Laidlaw is right to insist that a plaintiff must demonstrate standing separately for each form of relief sought. . . . But it is wrong to maintain that citizen plaintiffs facing ongoing violations never have standing to seek civil penalties. . . .

It can scarcely be doubted that, for a plaintiff who is injured or faces the threat of future injury due to illegal conduct ongoing at the time of suit, a sanction that effectively abates that conduct and prevents its recurrence provides a form of redress. Civil penalties can fit that description. To the extent that they encourage defendants to discontinue current violations and deter them from committing future ones, they afford redress to citizen plaintiffs who are injured or threatened with injury as a consequence of ongoing unlawful conduct.

The dissent argues that it is the *availability* rather than the *imposition* of civil penalties that deters any particular polluter from continuing to pollute.

This argument misses the mark in two ways. First, it overlooks the interdependence of the availability and the imposition; a threat has no deterrent value unless it is credible that it will be carried out. Second, it is reasonable for Congress to conclude that an actual award of civil penalties does in fact bring with it a significant quantum of deterrence over and above what is achieved by the mere prospect of such penalties. A would-be polluter may or may not be dissuaded by the existence of a remedy on the books, but a defendant once hit in its pocketbook will surely think twice before polluting again.[1]

We recognize that there may be a point at which the deterrent effect of a claim for civil penalties becomes so insubstantial or so remote that it cannot support citizen standing. The fact that this vanishing point is not easy to ascertain does not detract from the deterrent power of such penalties in the ordinary case. . . .

In this case we need not explore the outer limits of the principle that civil penalties provide sufficient deterrence to support redressability. Here, the civil penalties sought by FOE carried with them a deterrent effect that made it likely, as opposed to merely speculative, that the penalties would redress FOE's injuries by abating current violations and preventing future ones — as the District Court reasonably found when it assessed a penalty of $405,800. . . .

[(JUSTICE STEVENS, concurring opinion is omitted.]

JUSTICE KENNEDY, concurring.

Difficult and fundamental questions are raised when we ask whether exactions of public fines by private litigants, and the delegation of Executive power which might be inferable from the authorization, are permissible in view of the responsibilities committed to the Executive by Article II of the Constitution of the United States. The questions presented in the petition for certiorari did not identify these issues with particularity; and neither the Court of Appeals in deciding the case nor the parties in their briefing before this Court devoted specific attention to the subject. In my view these matters are best reserved for a later case. With this observation, I join the opinion of the Court.

JUSTICE SCALIA, with whom JUSTICE THOMAS joins, dissenting.

. . . .

Typically, an environmental plaintiff claiming injury due to discharges in violation of the Clean Water Act argues that the discharges harm the environment, and that the harm to the environment injures him. This route to injury is barred in the present case, however, since the District Court concluded after considering all the evidence that there had been "no demonstrated proof of harm to the environment," that the "permit violations at issue

---

[1] The dissent suggests that there was little deterrent work for civil penalties to do in this case because the lawsuit brought against Laidlaw by DHEC had already pushed the level of deterrence to "near the top of the graph." This suggestion ignores the District Court's specific finding that the penalty agreed to by Laidlaw and DHEC was far too low to remove Laidlaw's economic benefit from noncompliance, and thus was inadequate to deter future violations. And it begins to look especially farfetched when one recalls that Laidlaw itself prompted the DHEC lawsuit, paid the filing fee, and drafted the complaint.

in this citizen suit did not result in any health risk or environmental harm," that "[a]ll available data . . . fail to show that Laidlaw's *actual* discharges have resulted in harm to the North Tyger River," and that "the overall quality of the river exceeds levels necessary to support . . . recreation in and on the water."

The Court finds these conclusions unproblematic for standing, because "[t]he relevant showing for purposes of Article III standing . . . is not injury to the environment but injury to the plaintiff." This statement is correct, as far as it goes. We have certainly held that a demonstration of harm to the environment is not *enough* to satisfy the injury-in-fact requirement unless the plaintiff can demonstrate how he personally was harmed. In the normal course, however, a lack of demonstrable harm to the environment will translate, as it plainly does here, into a lack of demonstrable harm to citizen plaintiffs. While it is perhaps possible that a plaintiff could be harmed even though the environment was not, such a plaintiff would have the burden of articulating and demonstrating the nature of that injury. Ongoing "concerns" about the environment are not enough, for "[i]t is the *reality* of the threat of repeated injury that is relevant to the standing inquiry, not the plaintiff's subjective apprehensions," *Los Angeles v. Lyons*, 461 U.S. 95, 107, n.8 (1983). At the very least, in the present case, one would expect to see evidence supporting the affidavits' bald assertions regarding decreasing recreational usage and declining home values, as well as evidence for the improbable proposition that Laidlaw's violations, even though harmless to the environment, are somehow responsible for these effects. . . . Plaintiffs here have made no attempt at such a showing, but rely entirely upon unsupported and unexplained affidavit allegations of "concern."

Indeed, every one of the affiants deposed by Laidlaw cast into doubt the (in any event inadequate) proposition that subjective "concerns" actually affected their conduct. Linda Moore, for example, said in her affidavit that she would use the affected waterways for recreation if it were not for her concern about pollution. Yet she testified in her deposition that she had been to the river only twice, once in 1980 (when she visited someone who lived by the river) and once after this suit was filed. Similarly, Kenneth Lee Curtis, who claimed he was injured by being deprived of recreational activity at the river, admitted that he had not been to the river since he was "a kid," and when asked whether the reason he stopped visiting the river was because of pollution, answered "no." As to Curtis's claim that the river "looke[d] and smell[ed] polluted," this condition, if present, was surely not caused by Laidlaw's discharges, which according to the District Court "did not result in any health risk or environmental harm." The other affiants cited by the Court were not deposed, but their affidavits state either that they *would* use the river if it were not polluted or harmful (as the court subsequently found it is not), or said that the river looks polluted (which is also incompatible with the court's findings). These affiants have established nothing but "subjective apprehensions."

The Court is correct that the District Court explicitly found standing — albeit "by the very slimmest of margins," and as "an awfully close call." That cautious finding, however, was made in 1993, long before the court's 1997 conclusion that Laidlaw's discharges did not harm the environment. As we have previously recognized, an initial conclusion that plaintiffs have standing is subject to reexamination, particularly if later evidence proves inconsistent with that conclusion. . . . Laidlaw challenged the existence of injury in fact on appeal to the Fourth Circuit, but that court did not reach the question. Thus no lower court has reviewed the injury-in-fact issue in light of the extensive studies that led the District Court to conclude that the environment was not harmed by Laidlaw's discharges.

. . . By accepting plaintiffs' vague, contradictory, and unsubstantiated allegations of "concern" about the environment as adequate to prove injury in fact, and accepting them even in the face of a finding that the environment was not demonstrably harmed, the Court makes the injury-in-fact requirement a sham. If there are permit violations, and a member of a plaintiff environmental organization lives near the offending plant, it would be difficult not to satisfy today's lenient standard.

II

The Court's treatment of the redressability requirement — which would have been unnecessary if it resolved the injury-in-fact question correctly — is equally cavalier. As discussed above, petitioners allege ongoing injury consisting of diminished enjoyment of the affected waterways and decreased property values. They allege that these injuries are caused by Laidlaw's continuing permit violations. But the remedy petitioners seek is neither recompense for their injuries nor an injunction against future violations. Instead, the remedy is a statutorily specified "penalty" for past violations, payable entirely to the United States Treasury. . . .

A

. . . .

The Court's opinion reads as though the only purpose and effect of the redressability requirement is to assure that the plaintiff receive *some* of the benefit of the relief that a court orders. That is not so. If it were, a federal tort plaintiff fearing repetition of the injury could ask for tort damages to be paid not only to himself but to other victims as well, on the theory that those damages would have at least some deterrent effect beneficial to him. Such a suit is preposterous because the "remediation" that is the traditional business of Anglo-American courts is relief specifically tailored to the plaintiff's injury, and not any sort of relief that has some incidental benefit to the plaintiff. Just as a "generalized grievance" that affects the entire citizenry cannot satisfy the injury-in-fact requirement even though it aggrieves the plaintiff along with everyone else, so also a generalized remedy that deters all future unlawful activity against all persons cannot satisfy the remediation requirement, even though it deters (among other things) repetition of this particular unlawful activity against these particular plaintiffs. . . .

B

As I have just discussed, it is my view that a plaintiff's desire to benefit from the deterrent effect of a public penalty for past conduct can never suffice to establish a case or controversy of the sort known to our law. Such deterrent effect is, so to speak, "speculative as a matter of law." Even if that were not so, however, the deterrent effect in the present case would surely be speculative as a matter of fact.

The Court recognizes, of course, that to satisfy Article III, it must be "likely," as opposed to "merely speculative," that a favorable decision will redress plaintiffs' injury. Further, the Court recognizes that not *all* deterrent effects of *all* civil penalties will meet this standard — though it declines to "explore the outer limits" of adequate deterrence. It concludes, however, that in the present case "the civil penalties sought by FOE carried with them a deterrent effect" that satisfied the "likely [rather than] speculative" standard. There is little in the Court's opinion to explain why it believes this is so. . . .

If the Court had undertaken the necessary inquiry into whether significant deterrence of the plaintiffs' feared injury was "likely," it would have had to reason something like this: Strictly speaking, no polluter is deterred by a penalty for past pollution; he is deterred by the *fear* of a penalty for *future* pollution. That fear will be virtually nonexistent if the prospective polluter knows that all emissions violators are given a free pass; it will be substantial under an emissions program such as the federal scheme here, which is regularly and notoriously enforced; it will be even higher when a prospective polluter subject to such a regularly enforced program has, as here, been the object of public charges of pollution and a suit for injunction; and it will surely be near the top of the graph when, as here, the prospective polluter has already been subjected to *state* penalties for the past pollution. The deterrence on which the plaintiffs must rely for standing in the present case is the marginal increase in Laidlaw's fear of future penalties that will be achieved by adding federal penalties for Laidlaw's past conduct.

I cannot say for certain that this marginal increase is zero; but I can say for certain that it is entirely speculative whether it will make the difference between these plaintiffs' suffering injury in the future and these plaintiffs' going unharmed. In fact, the assertion that it will "likely" do so is entirely farfetched. The speculativeness of that result is much greater than the speculativeness we found excessive in *Simon v. Eastern Ky. Welfare Rights Organization*, 426 U.S. 26, 43 (1976), where we held that denying § 501(c)(3) charitable-deduction tax status to hospitals that refused to treat indigents was not sufficiently likely to assure future treatment of the indigent plaintiffs to support standing. . . .

In sum, if this case is, as the Court suggests, within the central core of "deterrence" standing, it is impossible to imagine what the "outer limits" could possibly be. The Court's expressed reluctance to define those "outer limits" serves only to disguise the fact that it has promulgated a revolutionary new doctrine of standing that will permit the entire body of public civil penalties to be handed over to enforcement by private interests.

C

Article II of the Constitution commits it to the President to "take Care that the Laws be faithfully executed," Art. II, § 3, and provides specific methods by which all persons exercising significant executive power are to be appointed, Art. II, § 2. As Justice Kennedy's concurrence correctly observes, the question of the conformity of this legislation with Article II has not been argued — and I, like the Court, do not address it. But Article III, no less than Article II, has consequences for the structure of our government, and it is worth noting the changes in that structure which today's decision allows.

By permitting citizens to pursue civil penalties payable to the Federal Treasury, the Act does not provide a mechanism for individual relief in any traditional sense, but turns over to private citizens the function of enforcing the law. A Clean Water Act plaintiff pursuing civil penalties acts as a self-appointed mini-EPA. Where, as is often the case, the plaintiff is a national association, it has significant discretion in choosing enforcement targets. Once the association is aware of a reported violation, it need not look long for an injured member, at least under the theory of injury the Court applies today. And once the target is chosen, the suit goes forward without meaningful public control. The availability of civil penalties vastly disproportionate to the individual injury gives citizen plaintiffs massive bargaining power — which is often used to achieve settlements requiring the defendant to support environmental projects of the plaintiffs' choosing. . . . Thus is a public fine diverted to a private interest.

To be sure, the EPA may foreclose the citizen suit by itself bringing suit. This allows public authorities to avoid private enforcement only by accepting private direction as to when enforcement should be undertaken — which is no less constitutionally bizarre. Elected officials are entirely deprived of their discretion to decide that a given violation should not be the object of suit at all, or that the enforcement decision should be postponed. This is the predictable and inevitable consequence of the Court's allowing the use of public remedies for private wrongs. . . .

NOTES AND QUESTIONS

9-29. Does the majority opinion in *Laidlaw* clarify some of the issues in *Lujan*? Are some of the standing hurdles suggested by *Lujan* now reduced in significance?

9-30. Does the Court in *Laidlaw* defer to the legislature's judgments on questions involving actual environmental harm? Do the plaintiff's have to prove actual harm to the environment?

9-31. What about penalties going to the government? Might this constitute redress?

9-32. How does the Court deal with mootness issues in this case? *See* § 9.04 [E], *infra*.

PROBLEM 9-2

The False Claims Act (FCA) authorizes any citizen to sue on behalf of the United States to recover money paid on fraudulent claims submitted to the federal government. The Act authorizes so-called *qui tam* actions. *Qui tam* is short for a Latin phrase that means "who pursues this action on our Lord the King's behalf as well as his own." The Act authorizes treble damages from anyone who has submitted a false claim. The private person initiating the FCA suit — the relator — receives a percentage of the recovery. The relator must notify the Attorney General of its intention to bring such a suit and the AG then has sixty days to decide to intervene or not. If not, the relator conducts the litigation on the government's behalf. The AG may intervene thereafter, but only on a showing of good cause; the relator retains primary control of the case. If the AG intervenes within the sixty day time frame, the AG is in control of the case, but can dismiss the action over the relator's objections only if a court decides the settlement is fair, adequate and reasonable.

(a) Is the FCA constitutional?

(b) Specifically, have the relators incurred any personal injury? If not, is this a case of controversy according to Article III?

(c) Does the Act undermine the President's power to enforce the law? How? *See Vermont Agency of Natural Resources v. United States ex rel. Stevens*, 529 U.S. 765 (2000).

§ 9.04 When Should Judicial Review Occur?

[A] Finality

Courts have developed a number of overlapping doctrines designed to control when judicial review of agency action is appropriate. Three related doctrines, in particular, are relevant: the doctrines of finality, exhaustion and ripeness, which we shall examine below.

Section 704 of the APA provides for judicial review of "final agency action." Why should courts avoid deciding an issue that may not be the agency's final decision? What impact would such decisions have on the administrative process? What impact would they have on the courts? Consider the following case.

FEDERAL TRADE COMMISSION v. STANDARD OIL CO. OF CALIFORNIA

United States Supreme Court
449 U.S. 232 (1980)

JUSTICE POWELL delivered the opinion of the Court.

This case presents the question whether the issuance of a complaint by the Federal Trade Commission is "final agency action" subject to judicial review before administrative adjudication concludes.

I

On July 18, 1973, the Federal Trade Commission issued and served upon eight major oil companies, including Standard Oil Company of California (Socal), a complaint averring that the Commission had "reason to believe" that the companies were violating § 5 of the Federal Trade Commission Act, . . . and stating the Commission's charges in that respect. . . . An adjudication of the complaint's charges began soon thereafter before an Administrative Law Judge, and is still pending.

On May 1, 1975, Socal filed a complaint against the Commission in the District Court for the Northern District of California, alleging that the Commission had issued its complaint without having "reason to believe" that Socal was violating the Act. Socal sought an order declaring that the issuance of the complaint was unlawful and requiring that the complaint be withdrawn. Socal had sought this relief from the Commission and been denied. In support of its allegation and request, Socal recited a series of events that preceded the issuance of the complaint and several events that followed. . . .

The gist of Socal's recitation of events preceding the issuance of the complaint is that political pressure for a public explanation of the gasoline shortages of 1973 forced the Commission to issue a complaint against the major oil companies despite insufficient investigation. The series of events began on May 31, 1973. As of that day, the Commission had not examined any employees, documents, or books of Socal's, although the Commission had announced in December 1971, that it intended to investigate possible violations of the Federal Trade Commission Act in the petroleum industry. . . .

II

The Commission averred in its complaint that it had reason to believe that Socal was violating the Act. That averment is subject to judicial review before the conclusion of administrative adjudication only if the issuance of the complaint was "final agency action" or otherwise was "directly reviewable" under § 10(c) of the APA, 5 U.S.C. § 704. We conclude that the issuance of the complaint was neither.

A

The Commission's issuance of its complaint was not "final agency action." The Court observed in *Abbott Laboratories v. Gardner,* 387 U.S. 136 (1967), that "[t]he cases dealing with judicial review of administrative actions have interpreted the 'finality' element in a pragmatic way." In *Abbott Laboratories,* for example, the publication of certain regulations by the Commissioner of Food and Drugs was held to be final agency action subject to judicial review in an action for declaratory judgment brought prior to any Government action for enforcement. The regulations required manufacturers of prescription drugs to print certain information on drug labels and advertisements. The regulations were "definitive" statements of the Commission's position, and had a "direct and immediate . . . effect on the day-to-day business" of the complaining parties. They had "the status of law" and "immediate compliance with their terms was expected." . . .

By its terms, the Commission's averment of "reason to believe" that Socal was violating the Act is not a definitive statement of position. It represents a threshold determination that further inquiry is warranted and that a complaint should initiate proceedings. To be sure, the issuance of the complaint is definitive on the question whether the Commission avers reason to believe that the respondent to the complaint is violating the Act. But the extent to which the respondent may challenge the complaint and its charges proves that the averment of reason to believe is not "definitive" in a comparable manner to the regulations in *Abbott Laboratories* and the cases it discussed. . . .

Serving only to initiate the proceedings, the issuance of the complaint averring reason to believe has no legal force comparable to that of the regulation at issue in *Abbott Laboratories,* nor any comparable effect upon Socal's daily business. The regulations in *Abbott Laboratories* forced manufacturers to "risk serious criminal and civil penalties" for noncompliance, or "change all their labels, advertisements, and promotional materials; . . . destroy stocks of printed matter; and . . . invest heavily in new printing type and new supplies." Socal does not contend that the issuance of the complaint had any such legal or practical effect, except to impose upon Socal the burden of responding to the charges made against it. Although this burden certainly is substantial, it is different in kind and legal effect from the burdens attending what heretofore has been considered to be final agency action.

In contrast to the complaint's lack of legal or practical effect upon Socal, the effect of the judicial review sought by Socal is likely to be interference with the proper functioning of the agency and a burden for the courts. Judicial intervention into the agency process denies the agency an opportunity to correct its own mistakes and to apply its expertise. Intervention also leads to piecemeal review which at the least is inefficient and upon completion of the agency process might prove to have been unnecessary. Furthermore, unlike the review in *Abbott Laboratories,* judicial review to determine whether the Commission decided that it had the requisite reason to believe would delay resolution of the ultimate question whether the Act was violated. Finally, every respondent to a Commission complaint could make the claim that Socal had made. Judicial review of the averments in the Commission's complaints should not be a means of turning prosecutor into defendant before adjudication concludes.

In sum, the Commission's issuance of a complaint averring reason to believe that Socal was violating the Act is not a definitive ruling or regulation. It had no legal force or practical effect upon Socal's daily business other than the disruptions that accompany any major litigation. And immediate judicial review would serve neither efficiency nor enforcement of the Act. These pragmatic considerations counsel against the conclusion that the issuance of the complaint was "final agency action."

B

Socal relies, however, upon different considerations than these in contending that the issuance of the complaint is "final agency action."

Socal first contends that it exhausted its administrative remedies by moving in the adjudicatory proceedings for dismissal of the complaint. By thus affording the Commission an opportunity to decide upon the matter, Socal contends that it has satisfied the interests underlying the doctrine of administrative exhaustion. The Court of Appeals agreed. We think, however, that Socal and the Court of Appeals have mistaken exhaustion for finality. By requesting the Commission to withdraw its complaint and by awaiting the Commission's refusal to do so, Socal may well have exhausted its administrative remedy as to the averment of reason to believe. But the Commission's refusal to reconsider its issuance of the complaint does not render the complaint a "definitive" action. The Commission's refusal does not augment the complaint's legal force or practical effect upon Socal. Nor does the refusal diminish the concerns for efficiency and enforcement of the Act.

Socal also contends that it will be irreparably harmed unless the issuance of the complaint is judicially reviewed immediately. Socal argues that the expense and disruption of defending itself in protracted adjudicatory proceedings constitutes irreparable harm. As indicated above, we do not doubt that the burden of defending this proceeding will be substantial. But "the expense and annoyance of litigation is 'part of the social burden of living under government.'" . . .

Socal further contends that its challenge to the Commission's averment of reason to believe can never be reviewed unless it is reviewed before the Commission's adjudication concludes. As stated by the Court of Appeals, the alleged unlawfulness in the issuance of the complaint "is likely to become insulated from any review" if deferred until appellate review of a cease-and-desist order. 596 F.2d at 1387. Socal also suggests that the unlawfulness will be "insulated" because the reviewing court will lack an adequate record and it will address only the question whether substantial evidence supported the cease-and-desist order.[11]

---

[11] The Court of Appeals additionally suggested that the complaint would be "insulated" from review because the alleged unlawfulness would be moot if Socal prevailed in the adjudication. These concerns do not support a conclusion that the issuance of a complaint averring reason to believe is "final agency action." To the contrary, one of the principal reasons to await the termination of agency proceedings is "to obviate all occasion for judicial review." . . . Thus, the possibility that Socal's challenge may be mooted in adjudication warrants the requirement that Socal pursue adjudication, not shortcut it.

We are not persuaded by this speculation. The Act expressly authorizes a court of appeals to order that the Commission take additional evidence. Thus, a record which would be inadequate for review of alleged unlawfulness in the issuance of a complaint can be made adequate. We also note that the APA specifically provides that a "preliminary, procedural, or intermediate agency action or ruling not directly reviewable is subject to review on the review of the final agency action," . . . [T]he APA also empowers a court of appeals to "hold unlawful and set aside agency action . . . found to be . . . without observance of procedure required by law." 5 U.S.C. § 706. Thus, assuming that the issuance of the complaint is not "committed to agency discretion by law," a court of appeals reviewing a cease-and-desist order has the power to review alleged unlawfulness in the issuance of a complaint. We need not decide what action a court of appeals should take if it finds a cease-and-desist order to be supported by substantial evidence but the complaint to have been issued without the requisite reason to believe. It suffices to hold that the possibility does not affect the application of the finality rule. . . .

Because the Commission's issuance of a complaint averring reason to believe that Socal has violated the Act is not "final agency action" under § 10(c) of the APA, it is not judicially reviewable before administrative adjudication concludes.[14] We therefore reverse the Court of Appeals and remand for the dismissal of the complaint.

It is so ordered.

JUSTICE STEWART took no part in the consideration or decision of this case. JUSTICE STEVENS concurred.

NOTES AND QUESTIONS

9-33. In *Franklin v. Massachusetts*, 505 U.S. 788 (1992) the Secretary of Commerce delegated census duties to the Bureau of the Census, which included overseas servicepeople in the census counts for the "home[s] of record." The ensuing report was given to the President, who presented it to Congress. The Clerk of the House then sent certificates of eligibility to each State. The Supreme Court held that the informal decision to include servicemembers in the report was shielded from review by the fact that the President actually presented the report to Congress, and that there was no reviewable "final agency action," despite the fact that the whole process depended on the Bureau's report.

9-34. In *Bennett v. Spear*, 520 U.S. 154 (1997), the Supreme Court set forth a two-part test for finality:

---

[14] By this holding, we do not encourage the issuance of complaints by the Commission without a conscientious compliance with the "reason to believe" obligation in 15 U.S.C. § 45(b). The adjudicatory proceedings which follow the issuance of a complaint may last for months or years. They result in substantial expense to the respondent and may divert management personnel from their administrative and productive duties to the corporation. Without a well-grounded reason to believe that unlawful conduct has occurred, the Commission does not serve the public interest by subjecting business enterprises to these burdens.

As a general matter, two conditions must be satisfied for agency action to be "final": First, the action must mark the "consummation" of the agency's decisionmaking process — it must not be of a merely tentative or interlocutory nature. And second, the action must be one by which "rights or obligations have been determined," or from which "legal consequences will flow."

520 U.S. at 177-78.

What has the force of law and what does not often causes a good deal of doctrinal uncertainty. *See, e.g., Air Brake Systems, Inc. v. Mineta*, 357 F.3d 632 (6th Cir. 2004) (opinion letters not final agency action because they did not "directly bind" Air Brake); *Independent Equipment Dealers Ass'n. v. EPA*, 372 F.3d 420 (D.C. Cir 2000) (EPA interpretations of own regulations which it made in a series of letters and statements did not constitute "final agency action").

Consider the following Problem. When can an agency's failure to act constitute "final agency action"?

PROBLEM 9-3

The United States Bureau of Land Management (BLM) manages federally owned forests, mineral resources, grazing land, and deserts. Although much of this land could be exploited for productive use immediately (for example, strip mining), Congress has directed the BLM to manage the land in such a way so as to use some for present productive use, to save some resources for use in the indefinite future, and to exempt some land from any development for use as wildlife refuges. To manage these conflicting priorities, the BLM develops a detailed land use plan for each property that it manages. Federal law requires that the BLM "manage public lands . . . in accordance with the land use plans . . . when they are available." But federal regulations make clear that a land use plan "is not a final implementation decision on actions which require further specific plans, process steps or decisions under specific provisions of law and regulations." The BLM normally does not use the land use plan to make site-specific implementation decisions; instead, an agency regulation says that the plans are "designed to guide and control future management actions and the development of subsequent, more detailed and limited scope plans for resources and land uses."

Under one provision in the one-hundred-fifty page land use plan for the 500,000 acre Green River Prairie, the BLM was to "monitor" the impact that off-road vehicles cause to the Prairie, which had been opened up to such use only five years before. And the plan calls for the BLM to close the Prairie to off-road vehicles "if warranted."

Citizens for a Better Environment has filed suit against the BLM under APA § 706(1), seeking to "compel agency action unlawfully withheld or unreasonably delayed." The complaint alleges that the BLM has failed to comply with the land use plan with respect to a 3,000 acre area of the Green River Prairie known as the San Miguel grassland. Specifically, the group alleges that the BLM 1) has not devised a program to actively monitor damage to the San Miguel Grassland; and 2) has failed to close the Grassland to off-road vehicles, "which are causing immense damage to an environmentally sensitive area." In response, the BLM argues that 1) the group has no cause of action because the land use plan is not a legally binding commitment to take any particular action with respect to the San Miguel Grassland; and 2) implementing an active monitoring program for the San Miguel Grassland would divert critically needed funds that will be used to clean up pollution found in another area of the Green River Prairie. Should the suit be dismissed? On what grounds? If it is not dismissed, what relief can a federal court give the plaintiffs? *See Norton v. Southern Utah Wilderness Alliance*, 542 U.S. 55 (2004).

[B] Exhaustion of Administrative Remedies

How does the doctrine of exhaustion of administrative remedies differ from the need to have "final agency action"? In what ways do these requirements overlap? What policies underlie the doctrine of exhaustion of administrative remedies? Consider the following case.

MYERS v. BETHLEHEM SHIPBUILDING CORP.

United States Supreme Court
303 U.S. 41 (1938)

MR. JUSTICE BRANDEIS delivered the opinion of the Court.

The question for decision is whether a federal district court has equity jurisdiction to enjoin the National Labor Relations Board from holding a hearing upon a complaint filed by it against an employer alleged to be engaged in unfair labor practices prohibited by National Labor Relations Act. . . . First. There is no claim by the Corporation that the statutory provisions and the rules of procedure prescribed for such hearings are illegal; or that the Corporation was not accorded ample opportunity to answer the complaint of the Board; or that opportunity to introduce evidence on the allegations made will be denied. The claim is that the provisions of the act are not applicable to the Corporation's business at the Fore River Plant, because the operations conducted there are not carried on, and the products manufactured are not sold, in interstate or foreign commerce; that, therefore, the Corporation's relations with its employees at the plant cannot burden or interfere with such commerce; that hearings would, at best, be futile; and that the holding of them would result in irreparable damage to the Corporation, not only by reason of their direct cost and the loss of time of its officials and employees, but also because the hearings would cause serious impairment of the good will and harmonious relations existing between the Corporation and its employees, and thus seriously impair the efficiency of its operations.[4]

Second. The District Court is without jurisdiction to enjoin hearings because the power "to prevent any person from engaging in any unfair practice affecting commerce" has been vested by Congress in the Board and the Circuit Court of Appeals, and Congress has declared: "This power shall be exclusive, and shall not be affected by any other means of adjustment or prevention that has been or may be established by agreement, code, law, or otherwise." The grant of that exclusive power is constitutional, because the Act provided for appropriate procedure before the Board and in the review by the Circuit Court of Appeals an adequate opportunity to secure judicial protection against possible illegal action on the part of the Board. No power to enforce an order is conferred upon the Board. To secure enforcement, the Board must apply to a Circuit Court of Appeals for its affirmance. And, until the Board's order has been affirmed by the appropriate Circuit Court of Appeals, no penalty accrues for disobeying it. The independent right to apply to a Circuit Court of Appeals to have an order set aside is conferred upon any party aggrieved by the proceeding before the Board. The Board is even without power to enforce obedience to its subpoena to testify or to produce written evidence. To enforce obedience it must apply to a District Court; and to such an application appropriate defense may be made.

It is true that the Board has jurisdiction only if the complaint concerns interstate or foreign commerce. Unless the Board finds that it does, the complaint must be dismissed. And, if it finds that interstate or foreign commerce is involved, but the Circuit Court of Appeals concludes that such finding was without adequate evidence to support it, or otherwise contrary to law, the Board's petition to enforce it will be dismissed, or the employer's petition to have it set aside will be granted. Since the procedure before the Board is appropriate and the judicial review so provided is adequate, Congress had power to vest exclusive jurisdiction in the Board and the Circuit Court of Appeals. . . .

Third. The Corporation contends that, since it denies that interstate or foreign commerce is involved and claims that a hearing would subject it to irreparable damage, rights guaranteed by the Federal Constitution will be denied unless it be held that the District Court has jurisdiction to enjoin the holding of a hearing by the Board. So to hold would, as the government insists, in effect substitute the District Court for the Board as the tribunal to hear and determine what Congress declared the Board exclusively should hear and

---

[4] It is alleged that in 1934 and 1935 the predecessor of the present National Labor Relations Board instituted somewhat similar action against the Corporation. Although the proceedings were eventually dismissed, the hearings consumed a total of some 2,500 hours of working time of officials and employees and cost the Corporation more than $15,000, none of which could be recovered.

determine in the first instance. The contention is at war with the long-settled rule of judicial administration that no one is entitled to judicial relief for a supposed or threatened injury until the prescribed administrative remedy has been exhausted.[9] That rule has been repeatedly acted on in cases where, as here, the contention is made that the administrative body lacked power over the subject matter.

Obviously, the rules requiring exhaustion of the administrative remedy cannot be circumvented by asserting that the charge on which the complaint rests is groundless and that the mere holding of the prescribed administrative hearing would result in irreparable damage. Lawsuits also often prove to have been groundless; but no way has been discovered of relieving a defendant from the necessity of a trial to establish the fact. . . .

Decrees for preliminary injunction reversed, with direction to dismiss the bills.

Mr. Justice Cardozo took no part in the consideration or decision of this case.

NOTES AND QUESTIONS

9-35. When an agency issues a final decision which can be appealed within the agency, can petitioners challenge that action in court, without exhausting administrative remedies, if the statute is unclear as to whether these remedies must, in fact, be exhausted? Consider *Darby v. Cisneros*, 509 U.S. 137 (1993):

Section 10(c) of the APA bears the caption "Actions reviewable." It provides in its first two sentences that judicial review is available for "final agency action for which there is no other adequate remedy in a court," and that "preliminary, procedural, or intermediate agency action . . . is subject to review on the review of the final agency action." The last sentence of § 10(c) reads:

> "Except as otherwise expressly required by statute, agency action otherwise final is final for the purposes of this section whether or not there has been presented or determined an application for a declaratory order, for any form of reconsideration or, unless the agency otherwise requires by rule and provides that the action meanwhile is inoperative, for an appeal to superior agency authority."

Petitioners argue that this provision means that a litigant seeking judicial review of a final agency action under the APA need not exhaust available administrative remedies unless such exhaustion is expressly required by statute or agency rule. According to petitioners, since § 10(c) contains an explicit exhaustion provision,

---

[9] The rule has been most frequently applied in equity where relief by injunction was sought. . . . But because the rule is one of judicial administration — not merely a rule governing the exercise of discretion — it is applicable to proceedings at law as well as suits in equity. . . .

federal courts are not free to require further exhaustion as a matter of judicial discretion.

Respondents contend that § 10(c) is concerned solely with timing, that is, when agency actions become "final," and that Congress had no intention to interfere with the courts' ability to impose conditions on the timing of their exercise of jurisdiction to review final agency actions. Respondents concede that petitioners' claim is "final" under § 10(c), for neither the National Housing Act nor applicable HUD regulations require that a litigant pursue further administrative appeals prior to seeking judicial review. However, even though nothing in § 10(c) precludes judicial review of petitioners' claim, respondents argue that federal courts remain free under the APA to impose appropriate exhaustion requirements.

We have recognized that the judicial doctrine of exhaustion of administrative remedies is conceptually distinct from the doctrine of finality:

> "[T]he finality requirement is concerned with whether the initial decisionmaker has arrived at a definitive position on the issue that inflicts an actual, concrete injury; the exhaustion requirement generally refers to administrative and judicial procedures by which an injured party may seek review of an adverse decision and obtain a remedy if the decision is found to be unlawful or otherwise inappropriate." *Williamson County Regional Planning Comm'n v. Hamilton Bank of Johnson City*, 473 U.S. 172, 193 (1985).

Whether courts are free to impose an exhaustion requirement as a matter of judicial discretion depends, at least in part, on whether Congress has provided otherwise, for "[o]f 'paramount importance' to any exhaustion inquiry is congressional intent," . . . We therefore must consider whether § 10(c), by providing the conditions under which agency action becomes "final for the purposes of" judicial review, limits the authority of courts to impose additional exhaustion requirements as a prerequisite to judicial review.

. . . .

While some dicta in these cases might be claimed to lend support to respondents' interpretation of § 10(c), the text of the APA leaves little doubt that petitioners are correct. Under § 10(a) of the APA, "[a] person suffering legal wrong because of agency action, or adversely affected or aggrieved by agency action within the meaning of a relevant statute, is *entitled to judicial review thereof.*" 5 U.S.C. § 702 (emphasis added). Although § 10(a) provides the general right to judicial review of agency actions under the APA, § 10(c) establishes when such review is available. When an aggrieved party has exhausted all administrative remedies expressly prescribed by statute or agency rule, the agency action is "final for the purposes of this section" and therefore "subject to judicial review" under the first sentence. While federal courts may be free to apply, where appropriate, other prudential doctrines of judicial administration to limit the scope and timing of judicial review, § 10(c), by its very terms, has limited the availability of the doctrine of exhaustion of administrative remedies to that which the statute or rule clearly mandates.

The last sentence of § 10(c) refers explicitly to "any form of reconsideration" and "an appeal to superior agency authority." Congress clearly was concerned with making the exhaustion requirement unambiguous so that aggrieved parties would know precisely what administrative steps were required before judicial review would be available. If courts were able to impose additional exhaustion requirements beyond those provided by Congress or the agency, the last sentence of § 10(c) would make no sense. To adopt respondents' reading would transform § 10(c) from a provision designed to " 'remove obstacles to judicial review of agency action,' " into a trap for unwary litigants. Section 10(c) explicitly requires exhaustion of all intra-agency appeals mandated either by statute or by agency rule; it would be inconsistent with the plain language of § 10(c) for courts to require litigants to exhaust optional appeals as

[C] Ripeness

How does the doctrine of ripeness differ from the doctrines of finality and exhaustion of administrative remedies? What are the constitutional bases of this doctrine? When is pre-enforcement judicial review possible under this doctrine? Consider the following cases.

ABBOTT LABORATORIES v. GARDNER

United States Supreme Court
387 U.S. 136 (1967)

MR. JUSTICE HARLAN delivered the opinion of the Court.

In 1962 Congress amended the Federal Food, Drug, and Cosmetic Act, to require manufacturers of prescription drugs to print the "established name" of the drug "prominently and in type at least half as large as that used thereon for any proprietary name or designation for such drug," on labels and other printed material. . . . The "established name" is one designated by the Secretary of Health, Education, and Welfare pursuant to § 502(e)(2) of the Act, 21 U.S.C. § 352(e)(2); the "proprietary name" is usually a trade name under which a particular drug is marketed. The underlying purpose of the 1962 amendment was to bring to the attention of doctors and patients the fact that many of the drugs sold under familiar trade names are actually identical to drugs sold under their "established" or less familiar trade names at significantly lower prices. The Commissioner of Food and Drugs, exercising authority delegated to him by the Secretary, published proposed regulations designed to implement the statute. . . . After inviting and considering comments submitted by interested parties the Commissioner promulgated the following regulation for the "efficient enforcement" of the Act, § 701(a):

> If the label or labeling of a prescription drug bears a proprietary name or designation for the drug or any ingredient thereof, the established name, if such there be, corresponding to such proprietary name or designation, shall accompany each appearance of such proprietary name or designation.

21 CFR § 1.104(g)(1).

A similar rule was made applicable to advertisements for prescription drugs, 21 CFR § 1.105(b)(1).

The present action was brought by a group of 37 individual drug manufacturers and by the Pharmaceutical Manufacturers Association, of which all the petitioner companies are members, and which includes manufacturers of more than 90% of the Nation's supply of prescription drugs. They challenged the regulations on the ground that the Commissioner exceeded his authority under the statute by promulgating an order requiring labels, advertisements, and other printed matter relating to prescription drugs to designate the established name of the particular drug involved every time its trade name is used anywhere in such material.

The District Court, on cross motions for summary judgment, granted the declaratory and injunctive relief sought, finding that the statute did not sweep so broadly as to permit the Commissioner's "every time" interpretation. The Court of Appeals for the Third Circuit reversed without reaching the merits of the case. It held first that under the statutory scheme provided by the Federal Food, Drug, and Cosmetic Act pre-enforcement[1] review of these regulations was unauthorized and therefore beyond the jurisdiction of the District Court. Second, the Court of Appeals held that no "actual case or controversy" existed and, for that reason, that no relief under the Administrative Procedure Act, or under the Declaratory Judgment Act, was in any event available. . . .

I.

The first question we consider is whether Congress by the Federal Food, Drug, and Cosmetic Act intended to forbid pre-enforcement review of this sort of regulation promulgated by the Commissioner. The question is phrased in terms of "prohibition" rather than "authorization" because a survey of our cases shows that judicial review of a final agency action by an aggrieved person will not be cut off unless there is persuasive reason to believe that such was the purpose of Congress. . . . Early cases in which this type of judicial review was entertained, . . . have been reinforced by the enactment of the Administrative Procedure Act, which embodies the basic presumption of judicial review to one "suffering legal wrong because of agency action, or adversely affected or aggrieved by agency action within the meaning of a

---

[1] That is, a suit brought by one before any attempted enforcement of the statute or regulation against him.

relevant statute," 5 U.S.C. § 702, so long as no statute precludes such relief or the action is not one committed by law to agency discretion, 5 U.S.C. § 701(a). The Administrative Procedure Act provides specifically not only for review of "[a]gency action made reviewable by statute" but also for review of "final agency action for which there is no other adequate remedy in a court," 5 U.S.C. § 704. The legislative material elucidating that seminal act manifests a congressional intention that it cover a broad spectrum of administrative actions,[2] and this Court has echoed that theme by noting that the Administrative Procedure Act's "generous review provisions" must be given a "hospitable" interpretation . . . [and] that only upon a showing of "clear and convincing evidence" of a contrary legislative intent should the courts restrict access to judicial review. *See also* Jaffe, *Judicial Control of Administrative Action* 336–359 (1965).

Given this standard, we are wholly unpersuaded that the statutory scheme in the food and drug area excludes this type of action. The Government relies on no explicit statutory authority for its argument that pre-enforcement review is unavailable, but insists instead that because the statute includes a specific procedure for such review of certain enumerated kinds of regulations, not encompassing those of the kind involved here, other types were necessarily meant to be excluded from any pre-enforcement review. The issue, however, is not so readily resolved; we must go further and inquire whether in the context of the entire legislative scheme the existence of that circumscribed remedy evinces a congressional purpose to bar agency action not within its purview from judicial review. As a leading authority in this field has noted, "The mere fact that some acts are made reviewable should not suffice to support an implication of exclusion as to others. The right to review is too important to be excluded on such slender and indeterminate evidence of legislative intent." Jaffe, *supra,* at 357. . . .

II.

A further inquiry must, however, be made. The injunctive and declaratory judgment remedies are discretionary, and courts traditionally have been reluctant to apply them to administrative determinations unless these arise in the context of a controversy "ripe" for judicial resolution. Without undertaking to survey the intricacies of the ripeness doctrine it is fair to say that its basic rationale is to prevent the courts, through avoidance of premature adjudication, from entangling themselves in abstract disagreements over administrative policies, and also to protect the agencies from judicial interference until an administrative decision has been formalized and its effects felt in a concrete way by the challenging parties. The problem is best seen in a twofold aspect, requiring us to evaluate both the fitness of the issues for judicial decision and the hardship to the parties of withholding court consideration.

---

[2] *See* H.R. Rep. No. 1980, 79th Cong., 2d Sess., 41 (1946), "To preclude judicial review under this bill a statute, if not specific in withholding such review, must upon its face give clear and convincing evidence of an intent to withhold it. The mere failure to provide specially by statute for judicial review is certainly no evidence of intent to withhold review." . . .

§ 9.04   THE AVAILABILITY AND TIMING OF JUDICIAL REVIEW   895

As to the former factor, we believe the issues presented are appropriate for judicial resolution at this time. First, all parties agree that the issue tendered is a purely legal one: whether the statute was properly construed by the Commissioner to require the established name of the drug to be used *every time* the proprietary name is employed. Both sides moved for summary judgment in the District Court, and no claim is made here that further administrative proceedings are contemplated. It is suggested that the justification for this rule might vary with different circumstances, and that the expertise of the Commissioner is relevant to passing upon the validity of the regulation. This of course is true, but the suggestion overlooks the fact that both sides have approached this case as one purely of congressional intent, and that the Government made no effort to justify the regulation in factual terms.

Second, the regulations in issue we find to be "final agency action" within the meaning of § 10 of the Administrative Procedure Act, 5 U.S.C. § 704, as construed in judicial decisions. . . . The regulation challenged here, promulgated in a formal manner after announcement in the Federal Register and consideration of comments by interested parties is quite clearly definitive. There is no hint that this regulation is informal, or only the ruling of a subordinate official, or tentative. It was made effective upon publication, and the Assistant General Counsel for Food and Drugs stated in the District Court that compliance was expected.

The Government argues, however, that the present case can be distinguished from cases like *Frozen Food Express* on the ground that in those instances the agency involved could implement its policy directly, while here the Attorney General must authorize criminal and seizure actions for violations of the statute. In the context of this case, we do not find this argument persuasive. These regulations are not meant to advise the Attorney General, but purport to be directly authorized by the statute. Thus, if within the Commissioner's authority, they have the status of law and violations of them carry heavy criminal and civil sanctions. Also, there is no representation that the Attorney General and the Commissioner disagree in this area; the Justice Department is defending this very suit. . . .

This is also a case in which the impact of the regulations upon the petitioners is sufficiently direct and immediate as to render the issue appropriate for judicial review at this stage. These regulations purport to give an authoritative interpretation of a statutory provision that has a direct effect on the day-to-day business of all prescription drug companies; its promulgation puts petitioners in a dilemma that it was the very purpose of the Declaratory Judgment Act to ameliorate. As the District Court found on the basis of uncontested allegations, "Either they must comply with the every time requirement and incur the costs of changing over their promotional material and labeling or they must follow their present course and risk prosecution." The regulations are clear-cut, and were made effective immediately upon publication; as noted earlier the agency's counsel represented to the District Court that immediate compliance with their terms was expected. If petitioners wish to comply they must change all their labels, advertisements, and promotional materials; they must destroy stocks of printed matter; and they must invest heavily in new printing type and new supplies. The alternative to compliance — continued use of material which they believe in good faith meets the statutory requirements, but which clearly does not meet the regulation of the Commissioner — may be even more costly. That course would risk serious criminal and civil penalties for the unlawful distribution of "misbranded" drugs. It is relevant at this juncture to recognize that petitioners deal in a sensitive industry, in which public confidence in their drug products is especially important. To require them to challenge these regulations only as a defense to an action brought by the Government might harm them severely and unnecessarily. Where the legal issue presented is fit for judicial resolution, and where a regulation requires an immediate and significant change in the plaintiffs' conduct of their affairs with serious penalties attached to noncompliance, access to the courts under the Administrative Procedure Act and the Declaratory Judgment Act must be permitted, absent a statutory bar or some other unusual circumstance, neither of which appears here. . . .

Finally, the Government urges that to permit resort to the courts in this type of case may delay or impede effective enforcement of the Act. We fully recognize the important public interest served by assuring prompt and unimpeded administration of the Pure Food, Drug, and Cosmetic Act, but we do not find the Government's argument convincing. First, in this particular case, a pre-enforcement challenge by nearly all prescription drug manufacturers is calculated to speed enforcement. If the Government prevails, a large part of the industry is bound by the decree; if the Government loses, it can more quickly revise its regulation.

The Government contends, however, that if the Court allows this consolidated suit, then nothing will prevent a multiplicity of suits in various jurisdictions challenging other regulations. The short answer to this contention is that the courts are well equipped to deal with such eventualities. The venue transfer provision, 28 U.S.C. § 1404(a), may be invoked by the Government to consolidate separate actions. Or, actions in all but one jurisdiction might be stayed pending the conclusion of one proceeding. A court may even in its discretion dismiss a declaratory judgment or injunctive suit if the same issue is pending in litigation elsewhere. . . .

Further, the declaratory judgment and injunctive remedies are equitable in nature, and other equitable defenses may be interposed. If a multiplicity of suits are undertaken in order to harass the Government or to delay enforcement, relief can be denied on this ground alone. . . . The defense of laches could be asserted if the Government is prejudiced by a delay. . . . And courts may even refuse declaratory relief for the nonjoinder of interested parties who are not, technically speaking, indispensable.

In addition to all these safeguards against what the Government fears, it is important to note that the institution of this type of action does not by itself stay the effectiveness of the challenged regulation. There is nothing in the record to indicate that petitioners have sought to stay enforcement of the "every time" regulation pending judicial review. If the agency believes that a suit of this type will significantly impede enforcement or will harm the public interest, it need not postpone enforcement of the regulation and may oppose any motion for a judicial stay on the part of those challenging the regulation. It is scarcely to be doubted that a court would refuse to postpone the effective date of an agency action if the Government could show, as it made no effort to do here, that delay would be detrimental to the public health or safety. . . .

Lastly, although the Government presses us to reach the merits of the challenge to the regulation in the event we find the District Court properly entertained this action, we believe the better practice is to remand the case to the Court of Appeals for the Third Circuit to review the District Court's decision that the regulation was beyond the power of the Commissioner.

Reversed and remanded.

TOILET GOODS ASSOCIATION v. GARDNER

United States Supreme Court
387 U.S. 158 (1967)

MR. JUSTICE HARLAN delivered the opinion of the Court.

Petitioners in this case are the Toilet Goods Association, an organization of cosmetics manufacturers accounting for some 90% of annual American sales in this field, and 39 individual cosmetics manufacturers and distributors. They brought this action in the United States District Court for the Southern District of New York seeking declaratory and injunctive relief against the Secretary of Health, Education, and Welfare and the Commissioner of Food and Drugs, on the ground that certain regulations promulgated by the Commissioner exceeded his statutory authority under the Color Additive Amendments to the Federal Food, Drug and Cosmetic Act. . . . The District Court held that the Act did not prohibit this type of preenforcement suit, that a case and controversy existed, that the issues presented were justiciable, and that no reasons had been presented by the Government to warrant declining jurisdiction on discretionary grounds. . . .

The regulation in issue here was promulgated under the Color Additive Amendments of 1960, a statute that revised and somewhat broadened the authority of the Commissioner to control the ingredients added to foods, drugs, and cosmetics that impart color to them. The Commissioner of Food and Drugs, exercising power delegated by the Secretary, under statutory authority "to promulgate regulations for the efficient enforcement" of the Act, issued the following regulation after due public notice, and consideration of comments submitted by interested parties:

(a) When it appears to the Commissioner that a person has: . . .

(4) Refused to permit duly authorized employees of the Food and Drug Administration free access to all manufacturing facilities, processes, and formulae involved in the manufacture of color additives and intermediates from which such color additives are derived; "he may immediately suspend certification service to such person and may continue such suspension until adequate corrective action has been taken."

The petitioners maintain that this regulation is an impermissible exercise of authority, that the FDA has long sought congressional authorization for free access to facilities, processes, and formulae . . . but that Congress has always denied the agency this power except for prescription drugs. Framed in this way, we agree with petitioners that a "legal" issue is raised, but nevertheless we are not persuaded that the present suit is properly maintainable.

In determining whether a challenge to an administrative regulation is ripe for review a twofold inquiry must be made: first to determine whether the issues tendered are appropriate for judicial resolution, and second to assess the hardship to the parties if judicial relief is denied at that stage.

As to the first of these factors, we agree with the Court of Appeals that the legal issue as presently framed is not appropriate for judicial resolution. This is not because the regulation is not the agency's considered and formalized determination, for we are in agreement with petitioners that under this Court's decisions in *Frozen Food Express v. United States,* 351 U.S. 40 and *United States v. Storer Broadcasting Co.,* 351 U.S. 192 there can be no question that this regulation — promulgated in a formal manner after notice and evaluation of submitted comments — is a "final agency action" under § 10 of the Administrative Procedure Act. . . . Also, we recognize the force of petitioners' contention that the issue as they have framed it presents a purely legal question: whether the regulation is totally beyond the agency's power under the statute, the type of legal issue that courts have occasionally dealt with without requiring a specific attempt at enforcement, . . . or exhaustion of administrative remedies. . . .

These points which support the appropriateness of judicial resolution are, however, outweighed by other considerations. The regulation serves notice only that the Commissioner *may* under certain circumstances order inspection of certain facilities and data, and that further certification of additives *may* be refused to those who decline to permit a duly authorized inspection until they have complied in that regard. At this juncture we have no idea whether or when such an inspection will be ordered and what reasons the Commissioner will give to justify his order. The statutory authority asserted for the regulation is the power to promulgate regulations "for the efficient enforcement" of the Act, § 701(a). Whether the regulation is justified thus depends not only, as petitioners appear to suggest, on whether Congress refused to include a specific section of the Act authorizing such inspections, although this factor is to be sure a highly relevant one, but also on whether the statutory scheme as a whole justified promulgation of the regulation. This will depend not merely on an inquiry into statutory purpose, but concurrently on an understanding of what types of enforcement problems are encountered by the FDA, the need for various sorts of supervision in order to effectuate the goals of the Act, and the safeguards devised to protect legitimate trade secrets. . . . We believe that judicial appraisal of these factors is likely to stand on a much surer footing in the context of a specific application of this regulation than could be the case in the framework of the generalized challenge made here.

We are also led to this result by considerations of the effect on the petitioners of the regulation, for the test of ripeness, as we have noted, depends not only on how adequately a court can deal with the legal issue presented, but also on the degree and nature of the regulation's present effect on those seeking relief. The regulation challenged here is not analogous to those that were involved in *Columbia Broadcasting System, supra,* and *Storer, supra,* and those other color additive regulations with which we dealt in *Gardner v. Toilet Goods Ass'n,* 387 U.S. 167, where the impact of the administrative action could be said to be felt immediately by those subject to it in conducting their day-to-day affairs.

This is not a situation in which primary conduct is affected — when contracts must be negotiated, ingredients tested or substituted, or special records compiled. This regulation merely states that the Commissioner may authorize inspectors to examine certain processes or formulae; no advance action is required of cosmetics manufacturers, who since the enactment of the 1938 Act have been under a statutory duty to permit reasonable inspection of a "factory, warehouse, establishment, or vehicle and all pertinent equipment, finished and unfinished materials; containers, and labeling therein." § 704(a). Moreover, no irremediable adverse consequences flow from requiring a later challenge to this regulation by a manufacturer who refuses to allow this type of inspection. Unlike the other regulations challenged in this action, in which seizure of goods, heavy fines, adverse publicity for distributing "adulterated" goods, and possible criminal liability might penalize failure to comply, *see Gardner v. Toilet Goods Ass'n,* 387 U.S. 167, a refusal to admit an inspector here would at most lead only to a suspension of certification services to the particular party, a determination that can then be promptly challenged through an administrative procedure, which in turn is reviewable by a court. Such review will provide an adequate forum for testing the regulation in a concrete situation. . . .

For these reasons the judgment of the Court of Appeals is affirmed.

Affirmed.

MR. JUSTICE DOUGLAS dissents for the reasons stated by Judge Tyler of the District Court, 235 F. Supp. 648, 651–652.

MR. JUSTICE BRENNAN took no part in the consideration or decision of this case.

MR. JUSTICE FORTAS, joined by THE CHIEF JUSTICE and CLARK J. concurs. . . .

MR. JUSTICE FORTAS, with whom THE CHIEF JUSTICE and MR. JUSTICE CLARK join, concurring in No. 336, and dissenting in Nos. 39 and 438.

I am in agreement with the Court in No. 336, *Toilet Goods Ass'n v. Gardner,* 387 U.S. 158, that we should affirm the decision of the Court of Appeals for the Second Circuit. . . .

I am, however, compelled to dissent from the decisions of the Court in No. 39, *Abbott Laboratories v. Gardner,* 387 U.S. 136, and No. 438, *Gardner v. Toilet Goods Ass'n,* 387 U.S. 167. . . .

The Court, by today's decisions . . . has opened Pandora's box. Federal injunctions will now threaten programs of vast importance to the public welfare. The Court's holding here strikes at programs for the public health.

The dangerous precedent goes even further. It is cold comfort — it is little more than delusion — to read in the Court's opinion that "It is scarcely to be doubted that a court would refuse to postpone the effective date of an agency action if the Government could show . . . that delay would be detrimental to the public health or safety." Experience dictates, on the contrary, that it can hardly be hoped that some federal judge somewhere will not be moved as the Court is here, by the cries of anguish and distress of those regulated, to grant a disruptive injunction.

The difference between the majority and me in these cases is not with respect to the existence of jurisdiction to enjoin, but to the definition of occasions on which such jurisdiction may be invoked. I do not doubt that there is residual judicial power in some extreme and limited situations to enjoin administrative actions even in the absence of specific statutory provision where the agency has acted unconstitutionally or without jurisdiction — as distinguished from an allegedly erroneous action. But the Court's opinions in No. 39 and No. 438 appear to proceed on the principle that, even where no constitutional issues or questions of administrative jurisdiction or of arbitrary procedure are involved, exercise of judicial power to enjoin allegedly erroneous regulatory action is permissible unless Congress has explicitly prohibited it, provided only that the controversy is "ripe" for judicial determination. This is a rule that is novel in its breadth and destructive in its implications as illustrated by the present application. . . . I believe that this approach improperly and unwisely gives individual federal district judges a roving commission to halt the regulatory process, and to do so on the basis of abstractions and generalities instead of concrete fact situations, and that it impermissibly broadens the license of the courts to intervene in administrative action by means of a threshold suit for injunction rather than by the method provided by statute. . . .

Now, with all respect, I submit that this controversy is clearly, transparently and obviously unsuited to adjudication by the courts *in limine* or divorced from a particular controversy. Every reason advanced in No. 336 (the access regulation) is applicable here with equal or greater force to repel this effort to secure judicial review at this stage. . . .

The regulation in No. 39 relates to a 1962 amendment to the Act requiring manufacturers of prescription drugs to print on the labels or other printed material, the "established name" of the drug "prominently and in type at least half as large as that used thereon for any proprietary name or designation for such drug." Obviously, this requires some elucidation, either case-by-case or by general regulation or pronouncement, because the statute does not say that this must be done "every time," or only once on each label or in each pamphlet, or once per panel, etc., or that it must be done differently on labels than on circulars, or doctors' literature than on directions to the patients, etc. This is exactly the traditional purpose and function of an administrative agency. The Commissioner, acting by delegation from the Secretary, took steps to provide for the specification. He invited and considered comments and then issued a regulation requiring that the "established name" appear every time the proprietary name is used. A manufacturer — or other person who violates this regulation — has mislabeled his product. The product may be seized; or injunction may be sought; or the mislabeler may be criminally prosecuted. In any of these actions he may challenge the regulation and obtain a judicial determination.

The Court, however, moved by petitioners' claims as to the expense and inconvenience of compliance and the risks of deferring challenge by noncompliance, decrees that the manufacturers may have their suit for injunction at this time and reverses the Third Circuit. The court says that this confronts the manufacturer with a "real dilemma." But the fact of the matter is that the dilemma is no more than citizens face in connection with countless statutes and with the rules of the SEC, FTC, FCC, ICC, and other regulatory agencies. This has not heretofore been regarded as a basis for injunctive relief unless Congress has so provided. The overriding fact here is — or should be — that the public interest in avoiding the delay in implementing Congress' program far outweighs the private interest; and that the private interest which has so impressed the Court is no more than that which exists in respect of most regulatory statutes or agency rules. Somehow, the Court has concluded that the damage to petitioners if they have to engage in the required redesign and reprint of their labels and printed materials without threshold review outweighs the damage to the public of deferring during the tedious months and years of litigation a cure for the possible danger and asserted deceit of peddling plain medicine under fancy trademarks and for fancy prices which, rightly or wrongly, impelled the Congress to enact this legislation. I submit that a much stronger showing is necessary than the expense and trouble of compliance and the risk of defiance. . . .

. . . Those challenging the regulations have a remedy and there are no special reasons to relieve them of the necessity of deferring their challenge to the regulations until enforcement is undertaken. In this way, and only in this way, will the administrative process have an opportunity to function — to iron out differences, to accommodate special problems, to grant exemptions, etc. The courts do not and should not pass on these complex problems in the abstract and the general — because these regulations peculiarly depend for their quality and substance upon the facts of particular situations. We should confine ourselves — as our jurisprudence dictates — to actual, specific, particularized cases and controversies, in substance as well as in technical analysis. And we should repel these attacks, for we have no warrant and no reason to place these programs, essential to the public interest, and many others which this Court's action today will affect, at the peril of disruption by injunctive orders which can be issued by a single district judge. . . .

NOTES AND QUESTIONS

9-36. In *Reno v. Catholic Social Services*, 509 U.S. 43 (1993), immigration rights groups — Catholic Social Services (CSS) and League of United Latin American Citizens (LULAC) — challenged Immigration and Naturalization Service (INS) regulations pursuant to Title II of the Immigration Reform and Control Act of 1986. Pub. L. 99-603, 100 Stat. 3359. Title II provides a process by which an alien unlawfully present in the United States can apply for temporary resident status and then, after a 1 year interim, for permanent resident status. In each suit, a District Court invalidated the challenged regulation, issuing a remedial order requiring the INS to accept legalization applications beyond the statutory deadline. In its appeals before the Ninth Circuit, the INS argued that the restrictive judicial review provisions of the Act disallowed district court jurisdiction in each case and that the district courts extension of the application deadline violated the substance of the statute, which limits the reach of the courts. After consolidating the appeals, the court of appeals affirmed the district courts' judgments. The Supreme Court considered whether the district courts had jurisdiction to hear the two cases and whether their remedial orders were lawful. The Court vacated and remanded, holding that the record was insufficient to determine all of the jurisdictional issues.

The Court stated that:

> The Reform Act not only sets the qualifications for obtaining temporary resident status, but provides an exclusive scheme for administrative and judicial review of "determination[s] respecting . . . application[s] for adjustment of status" under the Title II legalization program. Section 1255a(f)(3)(A) directs the Attorney General to "establish an appellate authority to provide for a single level of administrative appellate review" of such determinations. Section 1255a(f)(4)(A) provides that a denial of adjustment of status is subject to review by a court "only in the judicial review of an order of deportation under [8 U.S.C. § 1105a]"; under § 1105a, this review takes place in the Courts of Appeals. Section 1255a(f)(1) closes the circle by explicitly rendering the scheme exclusive: "There shall be no administrative or judicial review of a determination respecting an application for adjustment of status under this section except in accordance with this subsection."
>
> . . . .
>
> [An alien] whose application was "front-desked" [or denied by an INS employee before filing] . . . should not [have his challenge] fail for lack of ripeness. Front-desking would also have a further, and untoward, consequence for jurisdictional purposes, for it would effectively exclude an applicant from access even to the limited administrative and judicial review procedures established by the Reform Act. He would have no formal denial to appeal to the Associate Commissioner for Examinations, nor would he have an opportunity to build an administrative record on which judicial review might be based. Hence, to construe § 1255a(f)(1) to bar district court jurisdiction over his challenge, we would have to impute to Congress an intent to preclude judicial review of the legality of INS action entirely under those circumstances. As we stated recently in *McNary*, however, there is a "well-settled presumption favoring interpretations of statutes that allow judicial review of administrative action," *McNary v. Haitian Refugee Center, Inc.*, 498 U.S. 479, 496 (1991) and we will accordingly find an intent to preclude such review only if presented with "'clear and convincing evidence,'" *Abbott Laboratories*, 387 U.S., at 141 (quoting *Rusk v. Cort*, 369 U.S. 367, 379–380 (1962)). *See generally Bowen v. Michigan Academy of*

Family Physicians, 476 U.S. 667, 670–673 (1986) (discussing the presumption in favor of judicial review).

There is no such clear and convincing evidence in the statute before us. . . .

This lack of evidence precludes us from resolving the jurisdictional issue here, because, on the facts before us, the front-desking of a particular class member is not only sufficient to make his legal claims ripe, but necessary to do so. . . . Because only those class members (if any) who were front-desked have ripe claims over which the District Courts should exercise jurisdiction, we must vacate the judgment of the Court of Appeals, and remand with directions to remand to the respective District Courts for proceedings to determine which class members were front-desked.

9-37. In *Ticor Title Insurance Co. v. Federal Trade Commission*, 814 F.2d 731 (D.C. Cir. 1987), an insurance company sought a court injunction to prevent the FTC from adjudicating an unfair trade practice complaint that the agency had issued. The insurance company argued that while it had statutory defenses that it would raise in the hearing before the ALJ, the company sought to have the federal court decide that the enforcement proceedings were unconstitutional because the FTC was not under the direct control and supervision of the president. The district court dismissed the complaint filed in federal court. On appeal, the three-judge panel agreed that the court's dismissal was proper — but the judges could not agree why it was proper. The question of when judicial review should occur evoked three different analyses. What is the focus of each analysis? The parties? The agency? The judiciary?

Judge Edwards thought that the insurance company could not seek judicial intervention until it had exhausted all avenues of relief before the agency. In other words, he though that the insurance company must "raise their nonconstitutional defenses in the pending FTC enforcement proceedings before bringing [its] Constitutional challenge in federal court." The exhaustion doctrine serves two purposes:

> First, the court might be able to avoid the needless decision of a constitutional question, because the plaintiff might prevail on nonconstitutional grounds before the administrative agency. Second, the court would be able to forestall frequent disruptions of administrative proceedings; disruptions that would intolerably interfere with the agency's performance of its assigned task and with the pursuit of the administrative remedy granted by Congress.

The other two judges on the panel that decided this case did not join Judge Edwards's opinion; however, they did both concur in the judgment. Judge Green maintains that the case is not yet "ripe" for judicial review, a doctrine that "requires courts to evaluate both the fitness of the issues for judicial decision and the hardship to the parties of withholding court consideration."

> [U]nder the ripeness doctrine's "fitness of the issues" prong, courts must determine first whether the challenge to the agency's action or proceedings raises purely legal questions (which are presumptively suitable for judicial review) or questions requiring further factual development, and second whether either the court or the agency would benefit from the postponement

of review until the agency action or policy in question has assumed either a final or more concrete form.

Although Judge Green felt that Ticor had met this first prong, it failed, however, to show a hardship beyond the costs of defending itself in a potentially unconstitutional proceeding.

> The Supreme Court has made clear . . . that such a showing of hardship is generally insufficient to warrant the interruption of ongoing agency proceedings. . . . [T]he Court [has] observed that litigation and its accompanying expense and annoyance is one of the costs of living under government, and held that such expense, even if substantial and unrecoupable, does not constitute irreparable injury.

Judge Williams' concurrence, on the other hand, concluded that the district court properly dismissed the complaint because the court lacked jurisdiction under APA § 704, which provides for judicial review of "final agency action[s]." "Administrative orders are final when they impose an obligation, deny a right or fix some legal relationship as a consummation of the administrative process." And for him, the agency's filing of the complaint against Ticor Title Insurance was not a final action, even though Ticor may have to spend time and money defending itself in a proceeding that could ultimately be unconstitutional. While Judge Williams conceded that the doctrines of finality, exhaustion, and ripeness often overlap in the caselaw, he maintains that there are important distinctions among these doctrines.

> First, there is a difference in focus. While exhaustion is directed to the steps a litigant must take, finality looks to the conclusion of activity by the agency. And while ripeness depends on the fitness of issues for judicial review, finality in administrative law plays a role closely akin to the doctrine of the same name restricting interlocutory review of trial courts in the federal system. For our immediate purposes, the more critical distinction is that while exhaustion and ripeness are judge-made *prudential* doctrines, finality is, where applicable, a *jurisdictional* requirement.

[D] Primary Jurisdiction

What is the doctrine of primary jurisdiction? How does it compare to the doctrines reviewed above? What is the legal basis of this doctrine? What policies does it seek to further?

NADER v. ALLEGHENY AIRLINES, INC.

United States Supreme Court
426 U.S. 290 (1976)

MR. JUSTICE POWELL delivered the opinion of the Court.

In this case we address the question whether a common-law tort action based on alleged fraudulent misrepresentation by an air carrier subject to regulation by the Civil Aeronautics Board (Board) must be stayed pending reference to the Board for determination whether the practice is "deceptive" within the meaning of § 411 of the Federal Aviation Act of 1958. We hold that under the circumstances of this case a stay pending reference is inappropriate.

I

The facts are not contested. Petitioner agreed to make several appearances in Connecticut on April 28, 1972, in support of the fundraising efforts of the Connecticut Citizen Action Group (CCAG), a nonprofit public interest organization. His two principal appearances were to be at a noon rally in Hartford and a later address at the Storrs campus of the University of Connecticut. On April 25, petitioner reserved a seat on respondent's flight 864 for April 28. The flight was scheduled to leave Washington, D.C., at 10:15 a.m. and to arrive in Hartford at 11:15 a.m. Petitioner's ticket was purchased from a travel agency on the morning of the flight. It indicated, by the standard "OK" notation, that the reservation was confirmed.

Petitioner arrived at the boarding and check-in area approximately five minutes before the scheduled departure time. He was informed that all seats on the flight were occupied and that he, like several other passenger who had arrived shortly before him, could not be accommodated. Explaining that he had to arrive in Hartford in time for the noon rally, petitioner asked respondent's agent to determine whether any standby passengers had been allowed to board by mistake or whether anyone already on board would voluntarily give up his or her seat. Both requests were refused. In accordance with respondent's practice, petitioner was offered alternative transportation by air taxi to Philadelphia, where connections could be made with an Allegheny flight scheduled to arrive in Hartford at 12:15 p.m. Fearing that the Philadelphia connection, which allowed only 10 minutes between planes, was too close, petitioner rejected this offer and elected to fly to Boston, where he was met by a CCAG staff member who drove him to Storrs.

Both parties agree that petitioner's reservation was not honored because respondent had accepted more reservations for flight 864 than it could in fact accommodate. One hour prior to the flight, 107 reservations had been confirmed for the 100 seats actually available. Such overbooking is a common industry practice, designed to ensure that each flight leaves with as few empty seats as possible despite the large number of "no-shows" reservation-holding passengers who do not appear at flight time. By the use of statistical studies of no-show patterns on specific flights, the airlines attempt to predict the appropriate number of reservations necessary to fill each flight. In this way, they attempt to ensure the most efficient use of aircraft while preserving a flexible booking system that permits passengers to cancel and change reservations without notice or penalty. At times the practice of overbooking results in oversales, which occur when more reservation-holding passengers than can be accommodated actually appear to board the flight. When this occurs, some passengers must be denied boarding ("bumped"). . . .

Board regulations require each airline to establish priority rules for boarding passengers and to offer "denied boarding compensation" to bumped passengers. These "liquidated damages" are equal to the value of the passenger's ticket with a $25 minimum and a $200 maximum. Passengers are free to reject the compensation offered in favor of a common-law suit for damages suffered as a result of the bumping. Petitioner refused the tender of denied boarding compensation ($32.41 in his case) and, with CCAG, filed this suit for compensatory and punitive damages. His suit did not seek compensation for the bumping *per se* but asserted two other bases of liability: a common-law action based on fraudulent misrepresentation arising from respondent's alleged failure to inform petitioner in advance of its deliberate overbooking practices, and a statutory action under § 404(b) of the Act, arising from respondent's alleged failure to afford petitioner the boarding priority specified in its rules filed with the Board under 14 CFR § 250.3 (1975).

The District Court entered a judgment for petitioner on both claims, awarding him a total of $10 in compensatory damages and $25,000 in punitive damages. Judgment also was entered for CCAG on its misrepresentation claim, with an award of $51 in compensatory damages and $25,000 in punitive damages.

The Court of Appeals for the District of Columbia Circuit reversed. . . .

The only issue before us concerns the Court of Appeals' disposition on the merits of petitioner's claim of fraudulent misrepresentation. Although the court rejected respondent's argument that the existence of the Board's cease-and-desist power under § 411 of the Act eliminates all private remedies for common-law torts arising from unfair or deceptive practices by regulated carriers, it held that a determination by the Board that a practice is not deceptive within the meaning of § 411 would, as a matter of law, preclude a common-law tort action seeking damages for injuries caused by that practice. Therefore, the court held that the Board must be allowed to determine in the first instance whether the challenged practice (in this case, the alleged failure to disclose the practice of overbooking) falls within the ambit of § 411. . . .

II

The question before us, then, is whether the Board must be given an opportunity to determine whether respondent's alleged failure to disclose its practice of deliberate overbooking is a deceptive practice under § 411 before petitioner's common-law action is allowed to proceed. The decision of the Court of Appeals requires the District Court to stay the action brought by petitioner in order to give the Board an opportunity to resolve the question. If the Board were to find that there had been no violation of § 411, respondent would be immunized from common-law liability.

A

Section 1106 of the Act, 49 U.S.C. § 1506, provides that "[n]othing contained in this chapter shall in any way abridge or alter the remedies now existing at common law or by statute, but the provisions of this chapter are in addition to such remedies." The Court of Appeals found that "although the saving clause of section 1106 purports to speak in absolute terms it cannot be read so literally." In reaching this conclusion, it relied on *Texas & Pacific R. Co.*

v. Abilene Cotton Oil Co., 204 U.S. 426 (1907). In that case, the Court, despite the existence of a saving clause virtually identical to § 1106, refused to permit a state-court common-law action challenging a published carrier rate as "unjust and unreasonable." The Court conceded that a common-law right, even absent a saving clause, is not to be abrogated "unless it be found that the preexisting right is so repugnant to the statute that the survival of such right would in effect deprive the subsequent statute of its efficacy; in other words, render its provisions nugatory." But the Court found that the continuance of private damages actions attacking the reasonableness of rates subject to the regulation of the Interstate Commerce Commission would destroy the purpose of the Interstate Commerce Act, which was to eliminate discrimination by requiring uniform rates. The saving clause, the Court found, "cannot in reason be construed as continuing in shippers a common law right, the continued existence of which would be absolutely inconsistent with the provisions of the act. In other words, the act cannot be held to destroy itself."

In this case, unlike *Abilene,* we are not faced with an irreconcilable conflict between the statutory scheme and the persistence of common-law remedies. In *Abilene* the carrier, if subject to both agency and court sanctions, would be put in an untenable position when the agency and a court disagreed on the reasonableness of a rate. The carrier could not abide by the rate filed with the Commission, as required by statute, and also comply with a court's determination that the rate was excessive. The conflict between the court's common-law authority and the agency's ratemaking power was direct and unambiguous. The court in the present case, in contrast, is not called upon to substitute its judgment for the agency's on the reasonableness of a rate or, indeed, on the reasonableness of any carrier practice. There is no Board requirement that air carriers engage in overbooking or that they fail to disclose that they do so. And any impact on rates that may result from the imposition of tort liability or from practices adopted by a carrier to avoid such liability would be merely incidental. Under the circumstances, the common-law action and the statute are not "absolutely inconsistent" and may coexist, as contemplated by § 1106.

B

Section 411 of the Act allows the Board, where "it considers that such action . . . would be in the interest of the public," "upon its own initiative or upon complaint by any air carrier, foreign air carrier, or ticket agent," to "investigate and determine whether any air carrier . . . has been or is engaged in unfair or deceptive practices or unfair methods of competition. . . ." Practices determined to be in violation of this section "shall" be the subject of a cease-and-desist order. The Court of Appeals concluded and respondent does not challenge the conclusion here that this section does not totally preclude petitioner's common-law tort action. But the Court of Appeals also held, relying on the nature of the airline industry as "a regulated system of limited competition," and the Board's duty to promote "adequate, economical, and efficient service," "at the lowest cost consistent with the furnishing of such service," that the Board has the power in a § 411 proceeding to approve practices that might otherwise be considered deceptive and thus to immunize carriers from common-law liability.

We cannot agree. No power to immunize can be derived from the language of § 411. And where Congress has sought to confer such power it has done so expressly, as in § 414 of the Act, which relieves those affected by certain designated orders (not including orders issued under § 411) "from the operations of the 'antitrust' laws." When faced with an exemptive provision similar to § 414 in *United States Navigation Co. v. Cunard S.S. Co.*, 284 U.S. 474, this Court dismissed an antitrust action because initial consideration by the agency had not been sought. The Court pointed out that the Act in question was "restrictive in its operation upon some of the activities of common carriers . . . and permissive in respect of others." Section 411, in contrast, is purely restrictive. It contemplates the elimination of "unfair or deceptive practices" that impair the public interest. Its role has been described in *American Airlines, Inc. v. North American Airlines, Inc.*:

> "Unfair or deceptive practices or unfair methods of competition," as used in § 411, are broader concepts than the common-law idea of unfair competition. . . . The section is concerned not with punishment of wrongdoing or protection of injured competitors, but rather with protection of the public interest.

As such, § 411 provides an injunctive remedy for vindication of the public interest to supplement the compensatory common-law remedies for private parties preserved by § 1106.

Thus, a violation of § 411, contrary to the Court of Appeals' conclusion, is not coextensive with a breach of duty under the common law. We note that the Board's jurisdiction to initiate an investigation under § 411 is expressly premised on a finding that the "public interest" is involved. The Board "may not employ its powers to vindicate private rights." 351 U.S. at 83. Indeed, individual consumers are not even entitled to initiate proceedings under § 411, a circumstance that indicates that Congress did not intend to require private litigants to obtain a § 411 determination before they could proceed with the common-law remedies preserved by § 1106.

Section 411 is both broader and narrower than the remedies available at common law. A cease-and-desist order may issue under § 411 merely on the Board's conclusion, after an investigation determined to be in the public interest, that a carrier is engaged in an "unfair or deceptive practice." No findings that the practice was intentionally deceptive or fraudulent or that it in fact has caused injury to an individual are necessary. On the other hand, a Board decision that a cease-and-desist order is inappropriate does not represent approval of the practice under investigation. It may merely represent the Board's conclusion that the serious prohibitory sanction of a cease-and-desist order is inappropriate, that a more flexible approach is necessary. A wrong may be of the sort that calls for compensation to an injured individual without requiring the extreme remedy of a cease-and-desist order. Indeed, the Board, in dealing with the problem of overbooking by air carriers, has declined to issue cease-and-desist orders, despite the determination by an examiner in one case that a § 411 violation had occurred. Instead, the Board has elected to establish boarding priorities and to ensure that passengers will be compensated for being bumped either by a liquidated sum under Board regulations or by resort to a suit for compensatory damages at common law.

In sum, § 411 confers upon the Board a new and powerful weapon against unfair and deceptive practices that injure the public. But it does not represent the only, or best, response to all challenged carrier actions that result in private wrongs.

C

The doctrine of primary jurisdiction "is concerned with promoting proper relationships between the courts and administrative agencies charged with particular regulatory duties." *United States v. Western Pacific R. Co.,* 352 U.S. 59 (1956). Even when common-law rights and remedies survive and the agency in question lacks the power to confer immunity from common-law liability, it may be appropriate to refer specific issues to an agency for initial determination where that procedure would secure "[u]niformity and consistency in the regulation of business entrusted to a particular agency" or where:

> the limited functions of review by the judiciary (would be) more rationally exercised, by preliminary resort for ascertaining and interpreting the circumstances underlying legal issues to agencies that are better equipped than courts by specialization, by insight gained through experience, and by more flexible procedure.

The doctrine has been applied, for example, when an action otherwise within the jurisdiction of the court raises a question of the validity of a rate or practice included in a tariff filed with an agency, particularly when the issue involves technical questions of fact uniquely within the expertise and experience of an agency such as matters turning on an assessment of industry conditions. . . . In this case, however, considerations of uniformity in regulation and of technical expertise do not call for prior reference to the Board.

Petitioner seeks damages for respondent's failure to disclose its overbooking practices. He makes no challenge to any provision in the tariff, and indeed there is no tariff provision or Board regulation applicable to disclosure practices. Petitioner also makes no challenge, . . . to limitations on common-law damages imposed through exculpatory clauses included in a tariff.

Referral of the misrepresentation issue to the Board cannot be justified by the interest in informing the court's ultimate decision with "the expert and specialized knowledge," of the Board. The action brought by petitioner does not turn on a determination of the reasonableness of a challenged practice a determination that could be facilitated by an informed evaluation of the economics or technology of the regulated industry. The standards to be applied in an action for fraudulent misrepresentation are within the conventional competence of the courts, and the judgment of a technically expert body is not likely to be helpful in the 1988 application of these standards to the facts of this case.

We are particularly aware that, even where the wrong sought to be redressed is not misrepresentation but bumping itself, which has been the subject of Board consideration and for which compensation is provided in carrier tariffs, the Board has contemplated that there may be individual adjudications by courts in common-law suits brought at the option of the passenger. The present regulations dealing with the problems of overbooking and oversales were promulgated by the Board in 1967. They provide for denied boarding compensation to bumped passengers and require each carrier to establish priority rules for seating passengers and to file reports of passengers who could not be accommodated. The order instituting these regulations contemplates that the bumped passenger will have a choice between accepting denied boarding compensation as "liquidated damages for all damages incurred . . . as a result of the carrier's failure to provide the passenger with confirmed reserved space," or pursuing his or her common-law remedies. The Board specifically provided for a 30-day period before the specified compensation need be accepted so that the passenger will not be forced to make a decision before "the consequences of denied boarding have occurred and are known." After evaluating the consequences, passengers may choose as an alternative "to pursue their remedy under the common law."

III

We conclude that petitioner's tort action should not be stayed pending reference to the Board and accordingly the decision of the Court of Appeals on this issue is reversed. The Court of Appeals did not address the question whether petitioner had introduced sufficient evidence to sustain his claim. We remand the case for consideration of that question and for further proceedings consistent with this opinion.

It is so ordered.

[Mr. Justice White concurred separately.]

[E] Mootness

In *Friends of the Earth v. Laidlaw Environmental Services, supra* § 9.02, the Court held the issues in contention were not moot, noting:

> The only conceivable basis for a finding of mootness in this case is Laidlaw's voluntary conduct — either its achievement by August 1992 of substantial compliance with its NPDES permit or its more recent shutdown of the Roebuck facility. It is well settled that "a defendant's voluntary cessation of a challenged practice does not deprive a federal court of its power to determine the legality of the practice." *City of Mesquite v. Aladdin's Castle, Inc.*, 455 U.S. 283, 289 (1982). "[I]f it did, the courts would be compelled to leave '[t]he defendant . . . free to return to his old ways.'" *Id.*, at 289, n. 10 (citing *United States v. W.T. Grant Co.*, 345 U.S. 629, 632 (1953)). In accordance with this principle, the standard we have announced for determining whether a case has been mooted by the defendant's voluntary conduct is stringent: "A case might become moot if subsequent events

made it absolutely clear that the allegedly wrongful behavior could not reasonably be expected to recur." *United States v. Concentrated Phosphate Export Assn.*, 393 U.S. 199, 203 (1968). The "heavy burden of persua[ding]" the court that the challenged conduct cannot reasonably be expected to start up again lies with the party asserting mootness.

The Court of Appeals justified its mootness disposition by reference to *Steel Co. v. Citizens for Better Environment*, 523 U.S. 83 (1998), which held that citizen plaintiffs lack standing to seek civil penalties for wholly past violations. In relying on *Steel Co.*, the Court of Appeals confused mootness with standing. The confusion is understandable, given this Court's repeated statements that the doctrine of mootness can be described as "the doctrine of standing set in a time frame: The requisite personal interest that must exist at the commencement of the litigation (standing) must continue throughout its existence (mootness)." *Arizonans for Official English v. Arizona*, 520 U.S. 43, 68, n. 22 (1997) (quoting *United States Parole Comm'n v. Geraghty*, 445 U.S. 388, 397 (1980), in turn quoting Monaghan, *Constitutional Adjudication: The Who and When*, 82 YALE L.J. 1363, 1384 (1973)) (internal quotation marks omitted).

Careful reflection on the long-recognized exceptions to mootness, however, reveals that the description of mootness as "standing set in a time frame" is not comprehensive. As just noted, a defendant claiming that its voluntary compliance moots a case bears the formidable burden of showing that it is absolutely clear the allegedly wrongful behavior could not reasonably be expected to recur. By contrast, in a lawsuit brought to force compliance, it is the plaintiff's burden to establish standing by demonstrating that, if unchecked by the litigation, the defendant's allegedly wrongful behavior will likely occur or continue, and that the "threatened injury [is] certainly impending." *Whitmore v. Arkansas*, 495 U.S. 149, 158 (1990) (citations and internal quotation marks omitted). Thus, in *Los Angeles v. Lyons*, 461 U.S. 95 (1983), as already noted, we held that a plaintiff lacked initial standing to seek an injunction against the enforcement of a police chokehold policy because he could not credibly allege that he faced a realistic threat arising from the policy. *Lyons*, 461 U.S., at 105-110. Elsewhere in the opinion, however, we noted that a citywide moratorium on police chokeholds — an action that surely diminished the already slim likelihood that any particular individual would be choked by police — would not have mooted an otherwise valid claim for injunctive relief, because the moratorium by its terms was not permanent. *Id.*, at 101. The plain lesson of these cases is that there are circumstances in which the prospect that a defendant will engage in (or resume) harmful conduct may be too speculative to support standing, but not too speculative to overcome mootness.

Furthermore, if mootness were simply "standing set in a time frame," the exception to mootness that arises when the defendant's allegedly unlawful activity is "capable of repetition, yet evading review," could not exist. When, for example, a mentally disabled patient files a lawsuit challenging her confinement in a segregated institution, her postcomplaint transfer to a community-based program will not moot the action, despite the fact that she would have lacked initial standing had she filed the complaint after the transfer. Standing admits of no similar exception; if a plaintiff lacks standing at the time the action commences, the fact that the dispute is capable of repetition yet evading review will not entitle the complainant to a federal judicial forum. . . .

Standing doctrine functions to ensure, among other things, that the scarce resources of the federal courts are devoted to those disputes in which the parties have a concrete stake. In contrast, by the time mootness is an issue, the case has been brought and litigated, often (as here) for years. To abandon the case at an advanced stage may prove more wasteful than frugal. This argument from sunk costs does not license courts to retain jurisdiction over cases in which one or both of the parties plainly lack a continuing interest, as when the parties have settled or a plaintiff pursuing a nonsurviving claim has died. But the argument surely highlights an important difference between the two doctrines. . . .

Given the Court's approach to mootness in this case, is it, nonetheless, possible the case could be deemed moot on remand? How? When is it "absolutely clear" that the wrongful behavior will not recur?

§ 9.05 The Proper Forum

Assuming we have the right party filing a law suit at the right time, we must next consider whether it is filed in the right place. The forum for judicial review of agency action is determined by statute. Sometimes, the statute involved is a separate statute that deals explicitly with judicial review of a particular agency's actions. If no such direct or explicit statute governs judicial review of those actions, review usually occurs on the basis of more general jurisdictional statutes such as federal question jurisdiction under 28 U.S.C. § 1331. Review under these general statutes is in federal district court, while review under the more specific statutes governing judicial review of agency actions usually is in the court of appeals. Judicial review under these more specific statutes is called "statutory review." Judicial review under the more general jurisdictional statutes is usually and somewhat misleadingly referred to as "nonstatutory review."

TELECOMMUNICATIONS RESEARCH & ACTION CENTER v. F.C.C.

District of Columbia Court of Appeals
750 F.2d 70 (1984)

Before TAMM, WILKEY and EDWARDS, CIRCUIT JUDGES.

Opinion for the Court filed by CIRCUIT JUDGE HARRY T. EDWARDS.

HARRY T. EDWARDS, CIRCUIT JUDGE:

The Telecommunications Research & Action Center ("TRAC") and several other not-for-profit corporations and public interest groups petition this court for a writ of mandamus to compel the Federal Communications Commission ("FCC" or "the Commission") to decide certain unresolved matters now pending before the agency. The essence of TRAC's claim is that the FCC has unreasonably delayed determining whether American Telephone and Telegraph Company ("AT&T") must reimburse ratepayers for two separate instances of allegedly unlawful overcharges. The first instance relates to the rate of return earned by AT&T and the Bell System on interstate and foreign services furnished during 1978. The second concerns the treatment of expenses incurred by AT&T's manufacturing subsidiary, Western Electric, in its development of "customer premises equipment" ("CPE") during 1980–1982.

The most important question that we face in our consideration of this interlocutory appeal is a threshold jurisdictional issue. . . .

Our jurisdictional inquiry focuses on whether a petition to compel unreasonably delayed agency action properly lies in this court or in the District Court, or whether the two courts have concurrent jurisdiction, when any final agency action in the matter would be directly reviewable only in the Court of Appeals. Although we find the precedent in this circuit to be less than clear on this question, we conclude that, where a statute commits final agency action to review by the Court of Appeals, the appellate court has exclusive jurisdiction to hear suits seeking relief that might affect its future statutory power of review.

On the merits of the instant appeal, we decide that, because the agency has assured us that it is now moving expeditiously to resolve the pending overcharge claims, we need not determine whether the cited delays are so egregious as to warrant mandamus. The court, however, will retain jurisdiction over this case until final disposition by the agency. . . .

II. Jurisdiction

As an initial matter, this case raises two significant and recurrent jurisdictional questions. First, where a statute commits final agency action to review by the Court of Appeals, does that court have jurisdiction to hear suits seeking relief that would affect its future statutory power of review? Second, if the Court of Appeals does have jurisdiction, is that jurisdiction exclusive or concurrent with that of the District Courts?

We recognize that our precedent concerning jurisdiction over interlocutory appeals from agency action (or inaction) is somewhat inconsistent and may be confusing for litigants attempting to select the proper forum for these claims. We are convinced that this state of disarray in which we find the law is the product of innocent inadvertence, sometimes attributable to a desire by the court and parties to promptly resolve claims of unreasonable delay, and sometimes attributable to a failure by the parties to raise or to pursue jurisdictional inquiries. Nevertheless, "[j]urisdiction is, of necessity, the first issue for an Article III court. The federal courts are courts of limited jurisdiction, and they lack the power to presume the existence of jurisdiction in order to dispose of a case on any other grounds." . . . We are therefore obliged to consider and finally resolve the question pertaining to the jurisdiction of the Court of Appeals to hear claims of the sort raised in this case. . . . In deciding this issue, for the reasons hereafter enumerated, we hold that where a statute commits review of agency action to the Court of Appeals, any suit seeking relief that might affect the Circuit Court's future jurisdiction is subject to the *exclusive* review of the Court of Appeals.[24]

A. The Basis of Our Jurisdiction

We think it is clear — and no party disputes this point — that the statutory commitment of review of FCC action to the Court of Appeals, read in conjunction with the All Writs Act, 28 U.S.C. § 1651(a) (1982), affords this court jurisdiction over claims of unreasonable Commission delay. Exclusive jurisdiction over review of final FCC orders is vested in the Court of Appeals by 28 U.S.C. § 2342(1) (1982)[25] and 47 U.S.C. § 402(a) (1982).[26] *See also FCC v. ITT World Communications, Inc. ("ITT")*, 466 U.S. 463 (1984). Here, of course, there is no final order — indeed, the lack of a final order is the very gravamen of the petitioners' complaint. This lack of finality, however, does not automatically preclude our jurisdiction.[27]

The All Writs Act provides that "the Supreme Court and all courts established by an Act of Congress may issue all writs necessary or appropriate in aid of their respective jurisdictions. . . ." 28 U.S.C. § 1651(a). While it is firmly established that section 1651 does not expand the jurisdiction of a court, it is equally well settled that "the authority of the appellate court is not confined to the issuance of writs in aid of jurisdiction already acquired by appeal but extends to those cases which are within its appellate jurisdiction although no appeal has been 'perfected.'" . . . This authority extends to support an ultimate power of review, even though it is not immediately and directly involved. . . . In other words, section 1651(a) empowers a federal court to issue writs of mandamus necessary to protect its prospective jurisdiction. . . . Because the statutory obligation of a Court of Appeals to review on the merits may be defeated by an agency that fails to resolve disputes, a Circuit Court may resolve claims of unreasonable delay in order to protect its future jurisdiction. . . .

The Administrative Procedure Act ("APA") provides additional support for our jurisdiction here. That Act directs agencies to conclude matters presented

---

[24] Because this holding resolves inconsistencies among our prior decisions, this part of our decision has been considered separately and approved by the whole court, and thus constitutes the law of the circuit.

[25] Section 2342(1) provides that: "The Court of Appeals has exclusive jurisdiction to enjoin, set aside, suspend (in whole or in part), or to determine the validity of —

"(1) all final orders of the Federal Communications Commission made reviewable by section 402(a) of title 47. . . ."

[26] Section 402(a) makes reviewable "[a]ny proceeding to enjoin, set aside, annul or suspend any order of the Commission under this Act (except those appealable under subsection (b) of this section). . . ."

47 U.S.C. § 402(b) (1982) narrows review jurisdiction over certain agency actions even further. It provides that certain agency proceedings, not at issue in this case, are appealable only in the Court of Appeals for the District of Columbia.

[27] Although the finality doctrine does limit judicial action, it does not do so in a precise and inflexible way. As the Supreme Court has instructed in *Abbott Laboratories v. Gardner*, 387 U.S. 136, 149–50, 87 S. Ct. 1507, 1515–16 (1967), a federal court should apply the finality requirement in a "flexible" and "pragmatic" way. . . .

to them "within a reasonable time," 5 U.S.C. § 555(b) (1982), and stipulates that the "reviewing court shall . . . compel agency action unlawfully withheld or unreasonably delayed. . . ." 5 U.S.C. § 706(1) (1982). While the APA unquestionably does not confer an independent grant of jurisdiction, . . . section 706(1) coupled with section 555(b) does indicate a congressional view that agencies should act within reasonable time frames and that courts designated by statute to review agency actions may play an important role in compelling agency action that has been improperly withheld or unreasonably delayed. . . .

B. The Exclusivity of Our Jurisdiction

We also conclude that our present jurisdiction over claims that affect our future statutory review authority is exclusive.[30] It is well settled that even where Congress has not expressly stated that statutory jurisdiction is "exclusive," as it has here with regard to final FCC actions, a statute which vests jurisdiction in a particular court cuts off original jurisdiction in other courts in all cases covered by that statute. . . . By lodging review of agency action in the Court of Appeals, Congress manifested an intent that the appellate court exercise sole jurisdiction over the class of claims covered by the statutory grant of review power. It would be anomalous to hold that this grant of authority only strips the District Court of general federal question jurisdiction under 28 U.S.C. § 1331 (1982) when the Circuit Court has present jurisdiction under a special review statute, but not when the Circuit Court has immediate jurisdiction under the All Writs Act in aid of its future statutory review power.[32]

The District Court also lacks jurisdiction under both the All Writs Act, 28 U.S.C. § 1651(a) and the mandamus statute, 28 U.S.C. § 1361 (1982). The All Writs Act is not an independent grant of jurisdiction to a court; it merely permits a court to issue writs in aid of jurisdiction acquired to grant some other form of relief. . . . Because the District Court has no present or future jurisdiction over agency actions assigned by statute to appellate court review, it can contemplate no exercise of jurisdiction that mandamus might aid. The mandamus statute, 28 U.S.C. § 1361 also fails to confer jurisdiction on the District Court to compel agency action. Mandamus is an extraordinary remedy that is not available when review by other means is possible. . . . Because review is available in the Court of Appeals under the special review statute and the All Writs Act, action by the District Court under section 1361 is not.

Nor is District Court review permissible here under section 703 of the APA, which provides for District Court review when statutory review is inadequate.[34] Where statutory review is available in the Court of Appeals it will

---

[30] *See National Advertisers,* 627 F.2d at 1179 (Leventhal, J., concurring). Past suggestions that the District Court has general federal question jurisdiction under 28 U.S.C. § 1331 over some of these claims were in error. . . .

[32] *See* Note, *Jurisdiction to Review Federal Administrative Action: District Court or Court of Appeals,* 88 HARV. L. REV. 980, 983 (1975) ("[t]he rule of exclusivity is [best] justified as promoting the purposes for which Congress adopts special review statutes").

[34] That section reads in pertinent part:

The form of proceeding for judicial review is the special statutory review proceeding relevant to the subject matter in a court specified by statute, or in the absence or inadequacy thereof, any applicable form of legal action, including actions for declaratory judgments or writs of prohibitory or mandatory injunction . . . in a court of competent jurisdiction.

5 U.S.C. § 703 (1982).

rarely be inadequate. We find untenable any suggestion that appellate review of nonfinal agency action may be inadequate due to Courts of Appeals' inability to take evidence. This precise argument was recently rejected by the Supreme Court in *ITT*, where the Court held that, if an agency record is insufficient, the Court of Appeals may either remand the record to the agency for further development or appoint a special master under 28 U.S.C. § 2347(b)(3). *FCC v. ITT*, 466 U.S. 463, 469 (1984).[36]

Furthermore, there are compelling policy reasons for holding that the jurisdiction of the Court of Appeals is exclusive. Appellate courts develop an expertise concerning the agencies assigned them for review. Exclusive jurisdiction promotes judicial economy and fairness to the litigants by taking advantage of that expertise. In addition, exclusive jurisdiction eliminates duplicative and potentially conflicting review, and the delay and expense incidental thereto.

There may be a small category of cases in which the underlying claim is not subject to the jurisdiction of the Court of Appeals (and thus adjudication of the claim in the District Court will not affect any future statutory review authority of the Circuit Court). In such cases, where a denial of review in the District Court will truly foreclose all judicial review, district court review might be predicated on the general federal question jurisdiction statute, 28 U.S.C. § 1331. For example, in *Leedom v. Kyne*, 358 U.S. 184, 79 S. Ct. 180 (1958), the Supreme Court held that, even though there is a statutory prohibition against review of representation orders of the National Labor Relations Board, a District Court has jurisdiction under section 1331 in the very limited circumstance where the Board has clearly violated an express mandate of the statute and the plaintiff has no alternative means of review. . . . However, we need not tarry over this narrow exception because it is in no way implicated in the case before us. The principal point of this decision is to make clear that where a statute commits review of agency action to the Court of Appeals, any suit seeking relief that might affect the Circuit Court's future jurisdiction is subject to the exclusive review of the Court of Appeals. . . .

NOTES AND QUESTIONS

9-38. What legal reasons does the court give for concluding it has exclusive jurisdiction over the claim in this case? What policies underlie these legal reasons?

9-39. The *TRAC* decision deals with adjudication before the F.C.C. Does its reasoning and approach apply to rulemaking and other agencies as well? Are

---

[36] Although *ITT* dealt with final agency action and thus is not fully dispositive of the case at hand, we find its reasoning persuasive and follow it here. It would be highly anomalous for us to hold that remand to the agency or appointment of a special master cannot cure evidence deficiencies in the record of ongoing agency proceedings when the Supreme Court has said they are quite adequate for review of the same issues after final agency order.

there any cases that might be easier for a district court rather than an appellate court to consider? What exceptions does the court in *TRAC* have in mind? For a discussion of these issues and recommendations that the principles set forth in *TRAC* generally be followed in other cases by other agencies, see Sargentich, *The Jurisdiction of Federal Courts in Administrative Cases: Developments,* 41 ADMIN. L. REV. 201 (1989); 1988 ACUS Recommendations and Reports 281. *See also International Union, U.A.W. v. Donovan,* 756 F.2d. 162 (D.C. Cir. 1985) (holding court of appeals has exclusive jurisdiction in a case involving OSHA).

9-40. Even when one has determined the proper court to file a law suit, venue questions arise concerning which district or appellate court is the appropriate one. Some statutes specifically provide for exclusive review for certain kinds of rules in the District of Columbia Court of Appeals. *See, e.g.,* the Clean Air Act, 42 U.S.C. § 7607(b)(i). Others provide for the filing of petitions where "the petitioner resides or has its principal office, or in the [District of Columbia Circuit]." *See, e.g.,* The Administrative Orders Review Act, 28 U.S.C. § 2343. Given the opportunities to file suits in several possible circuits, forum shopping is common. Prior to 1988, there was, quite literally, a race to the courthouse, as venue was determined by filing first in a particular court. In 1988, Congress passed a statute that amended the "first filed" petitions approach. Pub. L. No. 100–236, 101 Stat. 1731 requires that, if within 10 days of the issuance of an agency order, the agency receives petitions for review in two or more courts of appeals, the agency is to notify the Judicial Panel on Multidistrict Litigation. That panel will then use "random selection" to designate a single court of appeals for review of the agency action in question. If only one petition is filed within the 10-day period, the Court of Appeals in which the case is filed will hear the case. A stay may be issued by any Court of Appeals in which proceedings related to an agency order have been filed, but that stay may be modified or revoked by any Court of Appeals to which the proceeding is transferred. Finally, 28 U.S.C. § 2112(a)(3) specifically provides that "for the convenience of the parties in the interest of justice, the court in which the record is filed may thereafter transfer all the proceedings with respect to that order to any other Court of Appeals."

9-41. What if there are multiple petitions filed in one circuit, and only one each filed in other circuits? How should the random selection be made? Assume, as in this case, that the various possible circuits are placed in a drum from which the clerk will draw the "winning circuit." Should there be only one entry per circuit or should there be more, based on the number of parties who have filed in a given circuit?

Chapter 10

OPEN GOVERNMENT

§ 10.01 Open Government — Introduction

Part II has focused on various ways that courts, the legislature and the executive seek to control, or at least influence, the exercise of agency discretion. In addition to the ways we have examined thus far, there are other significant restraints on agency action, including the availability of information regarding their actions, restrictions on information they can acquire, as well as who may advise them, and how public their decisionmaking processes must be and requiring public agency decisionmaking. This chapter briefly will explore these approaches by introducing you to the Freedom of Information Act, the Federal Advisory Committee Act, the Government in the Sunshine Act, and the Privacy Act.

Alfred C. Aman, Jr. and William T. Mayton, ADMINISTRATIVE LAW 631–32 (2d ed. 2001)*

In the late 1960's and throughout the 1970's, Congress passed a number of Acts aimed at increasing the openness with which agencies carried out their regulatory responsibilities. The most important of these was the Freedom of Information Act (FOIA), passed in 1966. It, and its subsequent amendments, establish a liberal disclosure policy regarding public access to information obtained, generated and held by the government. "Any person" is entitled to request and receive identifiable records held by an agency, unless the records in question fall within one of the Act's nine exemptions. . . .

In 1972, Congress passed the Federal Advisory Committee Act (FACA) designed to ensure greater openness with regard to the various boards of experts and advisors which agencies sometimes rely upon for advice. FACA attempts to ensure that the use of such private advisory bodies does not result in private solutions for public matters. Thus, the Act provides, among other things, that advisory board meetings be noticed and take place in public. It also attempts to ensure that there be a wide cross-section of interests represented on the Board.

FACA was the forerunner of the Government in the Sunshine Act passed by Congress in 1976. Just as the Freedom of Information Act established a norm of disclosure for agency records and files, the Sunshine Act established a norm of openness for agency deliberations. The Act requires that most meetings of multimember commissions be noticed in advance and held in public. The title of the Act is derived from a statement by Justice Brandeis and it reflects its basic premises: "Publicity is justly commended as a remedy

---

* Reprinted by permission of Thompson West.

for social and industrial disease. Sunlight is said to be the best disinfectant and electric light the most efficient policeman."

Congress passed the Federal Privacy Act in 1974. Unlike FOIA, FACA and the Sunshine Act, the Privacy Act is more directly concerned with individuals. The basic premise of the Act is that the federal government's ability to use sophisticated information technology, such as computer data banks, greatly magnifies the potential for the harm that can result to individual privacy interests. The Act relies on openness to ameliorate this potential harm. It enables individuals to determine what records pertaining to them are being collected, maintained and used by federal agencies. It seeks to prevent the use of records obtained for one purpose to then be used for an entirely different purpose, without individual consent. And it also seeks to enable individuals to gain access to information pertaining to them and to correct or amend those records if they are wrong.

. . . The common assumption underlying all of this legislation is that open government leads to better government. Open government is in accord with our basic principles of democracy and the need for citizens to know how their government, in fact, functions. This enables the citizenry to make proper evaluations of the wisdom of governmental uses of power. It also, however, is in accord with a healthy sense of distrust of governmental power as well and the need to control agency discretion to ensure that the law is administered properly. In this sense, open government and the publicity that goes along with it provides not only valuable information but a means of effectively constraining government and thus protecting citizens from any potential abuses of governmental power that may exist. Of course, as we shall now see, there are other important interests at stake that often militate in favor of governmental confidentiality, such as when national security interests or the trade secrets of a corporation are at stake. Most of the above statutes thus provide for a number of exemptions to their basic goals of openness and disclosure. Balancing these various policy interests and goals has given rise to a good deal of litigation and case law, especially under the Freedom of Information Act.

We shall begin with an overview of FOIA and examine some typical cases. This Act, in particular, has spawned an enormous volume of litigation. Our treatment, here, can only be introductory in nature.

§ 10.02 The Freedom of Information Act

[A] Overview

A popular Government without popular information, or the means of acquiring it, is but a Prologue to a Farce or a Tragedy; or perhaps both. And a people who mean to be their own Governors, must arm themselves with the power which knowledge gives.

James Madison, 1822.*

The basic purpose of FOIA is to ensure an informed citizenry, vital to the functioning of a democratic society, needed to check against corruption and to hold the governors accountable to the governed.

NLRB v. Robbins Tire Co., 437 U.S. 214, 242 (1978).

. . . FOIA has probably spawned more litigation and increased the cost of government more than any single regulatory program adopted in the past decade.

Robinson, Gellhorn & Bruff, *The Administrative Process* 521 (1980).

When one compares what the Freedom of Information Act was in contemplation with what it has turned out to be in reality, it is apparent that something went wrong.

Antonin Scalia, *The FOIA Has No Clothes*, REGULATION, March/April 1982, p. 16.

Congress passed the Freedom of Information Act (FOIA) in 1966** "to establish a general philosophy of full agency disclosure." Under FOIA, "any person" has the right to request and receive copies of much of the records and information generated or maintained by Federal agencies. Although the Act exempts certain types of information from mandatory release to the public, disclosure is the norm. A requester's motives or her relation to the information she seeks to acquire are irrelevant; the government has the burden of proving that information it withholds is exempt from disclosure. An agency's refusal to disclose requested information is subject to *de novo* judicial review.

The Act was first amended in 1974 in the aftermath of the Watergate hearings. The 1974 amendments provided FOIA with more teeth and greater reach. The Act increasingly has come to symbolize an implicit tenet of democracy: the public's right to know.*** But at the same time, questions

---

* Letter to W.T. Barry, August 4, 1822. Gailand Hunt, ed., *The Writings of James Madison*. Vol. 9, 1910, p. 103, quoted in Sen. Rep. No. 813 (1965).

** Codified as amended at 5 U.S.C. § 552 (1982).

*** See P. Wald, *The Freedom of Information Act. A Short Case Study in the Perils and Paybacks of Legislating Democratic Values*. 33 EMORY L.J. 649, 652 (CITING PRESIDENT JOHNSON: "THIS LEGISLATION SPRINGS FROM ONE OF OUR MOST ESSENTIAL PRINCIPLES: A DEMOCRACY WORKS BEST WHEN THE PEOPLE HAVE ALL THE INFORMATION THAT THE SECURITY OF THE NATION PERMITS"). SEE S. REP. NO. 813, 89TH CONG., 1ST SESS. 3 (1965) ("[I]T IS ONLY WHEN ONE FURTHER CONSIDERS THE HUNDREDS OF DEPARTMENTS, BRANCHES AND AGENCIES WHICH ARE NOT DIRECTLY RESPONSIBLE TO THE PEOPLE THAT ONE BEGINS TO UNDERSTAND THE GREAT IMPORTANCE OF HAVING AN INFORMATION POLICY OF FULL DISCLOSURE").

persist with regard to its scope, its costs compared to its benefits, and its susceptibility to abuse. Critics contend that in practice, FOIA "has turned out to be a far cry from just John Q. Public finding out about how his Government works."* Moreover, computers have triggered a transformation of information services and, more importantly, they have redefined what now qualities as "information." Other critics thus contend that FOIA is outdated and must be revised to take into account the realities of the computer age in which we live.

Consider the following cases. What purposes do you believe FOIA serves, in theory and in practice? If you were to reform the Act, what changes would you propose?

[B] Defining Agency and Agency Records

FORSHAM v. HARRIS

Supreme Court of the United States
445 U.S. 169 (1980)

Mr. JUSTICE REHNQUIST delivered the opinion of the Court.

The Freedom of Information Act, 5 U.S.C. § 552, empowers federal courts to order an "agency" to produce "agency records improperly withheld" from an individual requesting access. § 552(a)(4)(B). We hold here that written data generated, owned, and possessed by a privately controlled organization receiving federal study grants are not "agency records" within the meaning of the Act when copies of those data have not been obtained by a federal agency subject to the FOIA. Federal participation in the generation of the data by means of a grant from the Department of Health, Education, and Welfare (HEW) does not make the private organization a federal "agency" within the terms of the Act. Nor does this federal funding in combination with a federal right of access render the data "agency records" of HEW, which *is* a federal "agency" under the terms of the Act.

I

In 1959, a group of private physicians and scientists specializing in the treatment of diabetes formed the University Group Diabetes Program (UGDP). The UGDP conducted a long-term study of the effectiveness of five diabetes treatment regimens. Two of these treatment regimens involved diet control in combination with the administration of either tolbutamide, or phenformin hydrochloride, both "oral hypoglycemic" drugs. The UGDP's

---

* 1981 Senate Hearings on FOIA (97th Cong., 1st Sess., July-Dec. 1981) (Statement of then Professor, now Justice, Scalia).

participating physicians were located at 12 clinics nationwide and the study was coordinated at the Coordinating Center of the University of Maryland.

The study generated more than 55 million records documenting the treatment of over 1,000 diabetic patients who were monitored for a 5-to 8-year period. In 1970, the UGDP presented the initial results of its study indicating that the treatment of adult-onset diabetics with tolbutamide increased the risk of death from cardiovascular disease over that present when diabetes was treated by the other methods studied. The UGDP later expanded these findings to report a similarly increased incident of heart disease when patients were treated with phenformin hydrochloride. These findings have in turn generated substantial professional debate.

The Committee on the Care of the Diabetic (CCD), a national association of physicians involved in the treatment of diabetes mellitus patients, have been among those critical of the UGDP study. CCD requested the UGDP to grant it access to the raw data in order to facilitate its review of the UGDP findings, but UGDP has declined to comply with that request. CCD therefore sought to obtain the information under the Freedom of Information Act. The essential facts are not in dispute, and we hereafter set forth those relevant to our decision.

The UGDP study has been solely funded by federal grants in the neighborhood of $15 million between 1961 and 1978. These grants were awarded UGDP by the National Institute of Arthritis, Metabolism, and Digestive Diseases (NIAMDD), a federal agency, pursuant to the Public Health Service Act, 42 U.S.C. § 241(c). NIAMDD has not only awarded the federal grants to UGDP, but has exercised a certain amount of supervision over the funded activity. Federal regulations governing supervision of grantees allow for the review of periodic reports submitted by the grantee and on-site visits, and require agency approval of major program or budgetary changes. It is undisputed, however, both that the day-to-day administration of grant-supported activities is in the hands of a grantee, and that NIAMDD's supervision of UGDP conformed to these regulations.

The grantee has also retained control of its records: the patient records and raw data generated by UGDP have at all times remained in the possession of that entity, and neither the NIAMDD grants nor related regulations shift ownership of such data to the Federal Government. . . .

Although no employees of the NIAMDD have reviewed the UGDP records, the Institute did contract in 1972 with another private grantee, the Biometric Society, for an assessment of the validity of the UGDP study. The Biometric Society was given direct access to the UGDP raw data by the terms of its contract with NIAMDD. The contract with the Biometric Society, however, did not require the Society to seek access to the UGDP raw data, nor did it require that any data actually reviewed be transmitted to the NIAMDD. While the Society did review some UGDP data, it did not submit any raw data reviewed by it to the NIAMDD. The Society issued a report to the Institute in 1974 concluding that the UGDP results were "mixed" but "moderately strong."

An additional connection between the Federal Government and the UGDP study has occurred through the activities of the Food and Drug

Administration. After the FDA was apprised of the UGDP results, the agency issued a statement recommending that physicians use tolbutamide in the treatment of diabetes only in limited circumstances. After the UGDP reported finding a similarly higher incidence of cardiovascular disease with the administration of phenformin, the FDA proposed changes in the labeling of these oral hypoglycemic drugs to warn patients of cardiovascular hazards. The FDA deferred further action on this labeling proposal, however, until the Biometric Society completed its review of the UGDP study.

After the Biometric study was issued, FDA renewed its proposal to require a label warning that oral hypoglycemics should be used only in cases of adult-onset, stable diabetes that could not be treated adequately by a combination of diet and insulin. The FDA clearly relied on the UGDP study in renewing this position. . . .

Although this labeling proposal has not yet become final, other FDA regulatory action has been taken. On July 25, 1977, the Secretary of HEW suspended the New Drug Application for phenformin, one of the oral hypoglycemic medications studied by the UGDP. The decision was premised in part on the findings of the UGDP study. . . .

Petitioners had long since initiated a series of FOIA requests seeking access to the UGDP raw data. On August 7, 1975, HEW denied their request for the UGDP data on the grounds that no branch of HEW had ever reviewed or seen the raw data; that the FDA's proposed relabeling action relied on the UGDP published reports and not on an analysis of the underlying data; that the data were the property of the UGDP, a private group; and that the agencies were not required to acquire and produce those data under the FOIA. The following month petitioners filed this FOIA suit in the United States District Court for the District of Columbia to require HEW to make available all of the raw data compiled by UGDP. The District Court granted summary judgment in favor of respondents, holding that HEW properly denied the request on the ground that the patient data did not constitute "agency records" under the FOIA.

The Court of Appeals affirmed on the same rationale. . . . The court found that although NIAMDD is a federal agency, its grantees are not federal agencies. . . . Although HEW has a right of access to the documents, the court reasoned that this right did not render the documents "agency records" since the FOIA only applies to records which have been "created or obtained . . . in the course of doing its work." . . .

II

As we hold in the companion case of *Kissinger v. Reporters Committee for Freedom of the Press*, 445 U.S. 136, it must be established that an "agency" has "improperly withheld agency records" for an individual to obtain access to documents through an FOIA action. We hold here that HEW need not produce the requested data because they are *not* "agency records" within the meaning of the FOIA. In so holding, we reject three separate but related claims of petitioners: (1) the data they seek are "agency records" because they were at least "records" of UGDP, and UGDP in turn received its funds from a federal agency and was subject to some supervision by the agency in its use of those funds; (2) the data they seek are "agency records" because HEW, concededly a federal agency, had sufficient authority under its grant agreement to have obtained the data had it chosen to do so; and (3) the data are "agency records" because they formed the basis for the published reports of UGDP, which in turn were relied upon by the FDA in the actions described above.

Congress undoubtedly sought to expand public rights of access to Government information when it enacted the Freedom of Information Act, but that expansion was a finite one. Congress limited access to "agency records," 5 U.S.C. § 552(a)(4)(B), but did not provide any definition of "agency records" in that Act. The use of the word "agency" as a modifier demonstrates that Congress contemplated some relationship between an "agency" and the "record" requested under the FOIA. With due regard for the policies and language of the FOIA, we conclude that data generated by a privately controlled organization which has received grant funds from an agency (hereafter a grantee), but which data has not at any time been obtained by the agency, are not "agency records" accessible under the FOIA.

A

We first examine petitioners' claim that the data were at least records of UGDP, and that the federal funding and supervision of UGDP alone provides the close connection necessary to render *its* records "agency records" as that term is used in the Freedom of Information Act. Congress did not define "agency record" under the FOIA, but it did define "agency." The definition of "agency" reveals a great deal about congressional intent as to the availability of records from private grantees under the FOIA, and thus, a great deal about the relevance of federal funding and supervision to the definitional scope of "agency records." Congress excluded private grantees from FOIA disclosure obligations by excluding them from the definition of "agency," an action consistent with its prevalent practice of preserving grantee autonomy. It has, for example, disclaimed any federal property rights in grantee records by virtue of its funding. We cannot agree with petitioners in light of these circumstances that the very federal funding and supervision which Congress found insufficient to make the grantee an *agency* subject to the FOIA nevertheless makes its *records* accessible under the same Act.

Under 5 U.S.C. § 552(e) an "agency" is defined as

> "any executive department, military department, Government corporation, Government controlled corporation, or other establishment in the executive branch of the Government . . . , or any independent regulatory agency."

The legislative history indicates unequivocally that private organizations receiving federal financial assistance grants are not within the definition of "agency." In their Report, the conferees stated that they did "not intend to include corporations which receive appropriated funds but are neither chartered by the Federal Government nor controlled by it, such as the Corporation for Public Broadcasting." H. Conf. Rep. No. 93-1380, pp. 14-15 (1974), reprinted in Freedom of Information Act and Amendments of 1974 Source

Book 231–232 (Jt. Comm. Print 1975). Through operation of this exclusion, Congress chose not to confer any direct public rights of access to such federally funded project information.

. . . .

Congress could have provided that the records generated by a federally funded grantee were federal property even though the grantee has not been adopted as a federal entity. But Congress has not done so, reflecting the same regard for the autonomy of the grantee's records as for the grantee itself. Congress expressly requires an agency to use "procurement contracts" when the "principal purpose of the instrument is the acquisition . . . of property or services for the direct benefit or use of the Federal Government . . . ." Federal Grant and Cooperative Agreement Act of 1977, § 4, 92 Stat. 4, 41 U.S.C. § 503 (1976 ed., Supp. II). In contrast, "grant agreements" must be used when money is given to a recipient "in order to accomplish a public purpose of support or stimulation authorized by Federal statute, rather than acquisition . . . of property or services . . . ." § 5, 41 U.S.C. § 504 (1976 ed., Supp. II). As in this case, where a grant was used, there is no dispute that the documents created are the property of the recipient and not the Federal Government. *See* 45 CFR § 74.133 (1979). The HEW regulations do retain a right to acquire the documents. Those regulations, however, clearly demonstrate that unless and until that right is exercised the records are only the "records of grantees." . . .

The fact that Congress has chosen not to make a federal grantee an "agency" or to vest ownership of the records in the Government does not resolve with mathematical precision the question of whether the granting agency's funding and supervisory activities nevertheless make the grantee's records "agency records." Records of a nonagency certainly could become records of an agency as well. But if Congress found that federal funding and supervision did not justify direct access to the grantee's records as it clearly did, we fail to see why we should nevertheless conclude that those identical activities were intended to permit indirect access through an expansive definition of "agency records." Such a conclusion would not implement the intent of Congress; it would defeat it.

These considerations do not finally conclude the inquiry, for conceivably other facts might indicate that the documents could be "agency records" even though generated by a private grantee. The definition of "agency" and congressional policy towards grantee records indicate, however, that Congress did not intend that grant supervision short of Government control serve as a sufficient basis to make the private records "agency records" under the Act, and reveal a congressional determination to keep federal grantees free from the direct obligations imposed by the FOIA. . . .

B

Petitioners seek to prevail on their second and third theories, even though their first be rejected, by invoking a broad definition of "agency records," so as to include all documents created by a private grantee to which the Government has access, and which the Government has used. We do not believe that this broad definition of "agency records," a term undefined in the FOIA, is supported by either the language of that Act or its legislative history. We instead agree with the opinions of the courts below that Congress contemplated that an agency must first either create or obtain a record as a prerequisite to its becoming an "agency record" within the meaning of the FOIA. . . .

We think the foregoing reasons dispose of all petitioners' arguments. We therefore conclude that the data petitioners seek are not "agency records" within the meaning of the FOIA. UGDP is not a "federal agency" as that term is defined in the FOIA, and the data petitioners seek have not been created or obtained by a federal agency. Having failed to establish this threshold requirement, petitioners' FOIA claim must fail, and the judgment of the Court of Appeals is accordingly

Affirmed.

JUSTICES BRENNAN and MARSHALL dissented.

UNITED STATES DEPARTMENT OF JUSTICE v. TAX ANALYSTS

Supreme Court of the United States
492 U.S. 136 (1989)

JUSTICE MARSHALL delivered the opinion of the Court.

The question presented is whether the Freedom of Information Act (FOIA or Act), 5 U.S.C. § 552 (1982 ed. and Supp. V), requires the United States Department of Justice (Department) to make available copies of district court decisions that it receives in the course of litigating tax cases on behalf of the Federal Government. We hold that it does.

I

The Department's Tax Division represents the Federal Government in nearly all civil tax cases in the district courts, the courts of appeals, and the Claims Court. Because it represents a party in litigation, the Tax Division receives copies of all opinions and orders issued by these courts in such cases. Copies of these decisions are made for the Tax Division's staff attorneys. The original documents are sent to the official files kept by the Department.

. . . .

Respondent Tax Analysts publishes a weekly magazine, Tax Notes, which reports on legislative, judicial, and regulatory developments in the field of federal taxation to a readership largely composed of tax attorneys, accountants, and economists. As one of its regular features, Tax Notes provides summaries of recent federal-court decisions on tax issues. To supplement the magazine, Tax Analysts provides full texts of these decisions in microfiche form. Tax Analysts also publishes Tax Notes Today, a daily electronic data base that includes summaries and full texts of recent federal-court tax decisions.

In late July 1979, Tax Analysts filed a FOIA request in which it asked the Department to make available all district court tax opinions and final orders received by the Tax Division earlier that month. The Department denied the request on the ground that these decisions were not Tax Division records. . . .

II

In enacting the FOIA 23 years ago, Congress sought " 'to open agency action to the light of public scrutiny.' " Congress did so by requiring agencies to adhere to " 'a general philosophy of full agency disclosure.' " Congress believed that this philosophy, put into practice, would help "ensure an informed citizenry, vital to the functioning of a democra

The FOIA confers jurisdiction on the district courts "to enjoin the agency from withholding agency records and to order the production of any agency records improperly withheld." § 552(a)(4)(B). Under this provision, "federal jurisdiction is dependent on a showing that an agency has (1) 'improperly' (2) 'withheld' (3) 'agency records.' " Unless each of these criteria is met, a district court lacks jurisdiction to devise remedies to force an agency to comply with the FOIA's disclosure requirements.[1]

In this case, all three jurisdictional terms are at issue. Although these terms are defined neither in the Act nor in its legislative history, we do not write on a clean slate. Nine Terms ago we decided three cases that explicated the meanings of these partially overlapping terms. *Kissinger v. Reporters Committee for Freedom of Press*, 445 U.S. 136 (1980); *Forsham v. Harris*, 445 U.S. 169 (1980); *GTE Sylvania, Inc. v. Consumers Union of United States, Inc.*, 445 U.S. 375 (1980). These decisions form the basis of our analysis of Tax Analysts' requests.

A

We consider first whether the district court decisions at issue are "agency records," a term elaborated upon both in *Kissinger* and in *Forsham*. *Kissinger* involved three separate FOIA requests for written summaries of telephone conversations in which Henry Kissinger had participated when he served as Assistant to the President for National Security Affairs from 1969 to 1975, and as Secretary of State from 1973 to 1977. Only one of these requests — for summaries of specific conversations that Kissinger had had during his tenure as National Security Adviser — raised the "agency records" issue. At the time of this request, these summaries were stored in Kissinger's office at the State Department in his personal files. We first concluded that the summaries were not "agency records" at the time they were made because the FOIA does not include the Office of the President in its definition of

---

[1] The burden is on the agency to demonstrate, not the requester to disprove, that the materials sought are not "agency records" or have not been "improperly" "withheld."

"agency." 445 U.S., at 156. We further held that these documents did not acquire the status of "agency records" when they were removed from the White House and transported to Kissinger's office at the State Department, a FOIA-covered agency:

> "We simply decline to hold that the physical location of the notes of telephone conversations renders them 'agency records.' The papers were not in the control of the State Department at any time. They were not generated in the State Department. They never entered the State Department's files, and they were not used by the Department for any purpose. If mere physical location of papers and materials could confer status as an 'agency record' Kissinger's personal books, speeches, and all other memorabilia stored in his office would have been agency records subject to disclosure under the FOIA."

Forsham, in turn, involved a request for raw data that formed the basis of a study conducted by a private medical research organization. Although the study had been funded through federal agency grants, the data never passed into the hands of the agencies that provided the funding, but instead was produced and possessed at all times by the private organization. We recognized that "[r]ecords of a nonagency certainly could become records of an agency as well," 445 U.S., at 181, but the fact that the study was financially supported by a FOIA-covered agency did not transform the source material into "agency records." Nor did the agencies' right of access to the materials under federal regulations change this result. As we explained, "the FOIA applies to records which have been *in fact* obtained, and not to records which merely *could have been obtained*." (emphasis in original; footnote omitted).

Two requirements emerge from *Kissinger* and *Forsham*, each of which must be satisfied for requested materials to qualify as "agency records." First, an agency must "either create or obtain" the requested materials "as a prerequisite to its becoming an 'agency record' within the meaning of the FOIA." In performing their official duties, agencies routinely avail themselves of studies, trade journal reports, and other materials produced outside the agencies both by private and governmental organizations. To restrict the term "agency records" to materials generated internally would frustrate Congress' desire to put within public reach the information available to an agency in its decision-making processes. As we noted in *Forsham*, "The legislative history of the FOIA abounds with . . . references to records *acquired* by an agency." (emphasis added).

Second, the agency must be in control of the requested materials at the time the FOIA request is made. By control we mean that the materials have come into the agency's possession in the legitimate conduct of its official duties. This requirement accords with *Kissinger*'s teaching that the term "agency records" is not so broad as to include personal materials in an employee's possession, even though the materials may be physically located at the agency. This requirement is suggested by *Forsham* as well, where we looked to the definition of agency records in the Records Disposal Act. Under that definition, agency records include "all books, papers, maps, photographs, machine readable materials, or other documentary materials, regardless of physical form or characteristics, made or received by an agency of the United States Government *under Federal law or in connection with the transaction of public business* . . . ." (emphasis added).[5] . . .

Applying these requirements here, we conclude that the requested district court decisions constitute "agency records." First, it is undisputed that the Department has obtained these documents from the district courts. This is not a case like *Forsham*, where the materials never in fact had been received by the agency. The Department contends that a district court is not an "agency" under the FOIA, but this truism is beside the point. The relevant issue is whether an agency covered by the FOIA has "create[d] or obtaine[d]" the materials sought, *Forsham*, 445 U.S., at 182, not whether the organization from which the documents originated is itself covered by the FOIA.

Second, the Department clearly controls the district court decisions that Tax Analysts seeks. Each of Tax Analysts' FOIA requests referred to district court decisions in the agency's possession at the time the requests were made. . . . Furthermore, the court decisions at issue are obviously not personal papers of agency employees. . . .

For the reasons stated, the Department improperly withheld agency records when it refused Tax Analysts' requests for copies of the district court tax decisions in its files. Accordingly, the judgment of the Court of Appeals is

Affirmed.

JUSTICE WHITE concurs in the judgment.

JUSTICE BLACKMUN, dissenting.

The Court in this case has examined once again the Freedom of Information Act (FOIA), 5 U.S.C. § 552. It now determines that under the Act the Department of Justice on request must make available copies of federal district court orders and opinions it receives in the course of its litigation of tax cases on behalf of the Federal Government. The majority holds that these qualify as agency records, within the meaning of § 552(a)(4)(B), and that they were improperly withheld by the Department when respondent asked for their production. The Court's analysis, I suppose, could be regarded as a fairly routine one.

I do not join the Court's opinion, however, because it seems to me that the language of the statute is not that clear or conclusive on the issue and, more important, because the result the Court reaches cannot be one that was within the intent of Congress when the FOIA was enacted.

---

[5] In *GTE Sylvania, Inc. v. Consumers Union of United States, Inc.*, 445 U.S. 375, 385 (1980), we noted that Congress intended the FOIA to prevent agencies from refusing to disclose, among other things, agency telephone directories and the names of agency employees. We are confident, however, that requests for documents of this type will be relatively infrequent. Common sense suggests that a person seeking such documents or materials housed in an agency library typically will find it easier to repair to the Library of Congress, or to the nearest public library, rather than to invoke the FOIA's disclosure mechanisms. To the extent such requests are made, the fact that the FOIA allows agencies to recoup the costs of processing requests from the requester may discourage recourse to the FOIA where materials are readily available elsewhere.

Respondent Tax Analysts, although apparently a nonprofit organization for federal income tax purposes, is in business and in that sense is a commercial enterprise. It sells summaries of these opinions and supplies full texts to major electronic data bases. The result of its now-successful effort in this litigation is to impose the cost of obtaining the court orders and opinions upon the Government and thus upon taxpayers generally. There is no question that this material is available elsewhere. But it is quicker and more convenient, and less "frustrat[ing]," *see ante*, at 2845, for respondent to have the Department do the work and search its files and produce the items than it is to apply to the respective court clerks.

This, I feel, is almost a gross misuse of the FOIA. What respondent demands, and what the Court permits, adds nothing whatsoever to public knowledge of Government operations. That, I had thought, and the majority acknowledges, was the real purpose of the FOIA and the spirit in which the statute has been interpreted thus far. I also sense, I believe not unwarrantedly, a distinct lack of enthusiasm on the part of the majority for the result it reaches in this case.

If, as I surmise, the Court's decision today is outside the intent of Congress in enacting the statute, Congress perhaps will rectify the decision forthwith and will give everyone concerned needed guidelines for the administration and interpretation of this somewhat opaque statute.

NOTES AND QUESTIONS

10-1. How does the Court in *Forsham* define agency? Why is the definition so important to the function of this Act? What is the significance of the fact that the documents sought were created by an agency exempt from FOIA?

10-2. In 1998 Congress passed the Data Access Act,* commonly referred to as the Shelby Amendment. The Shelby Amendment requires, in part, "[t]hat the Director of OMB [Office of Management and Budget] amends . . . the OMB Circular A-110 to require Federal awarding agencies to ensure that all data produced under an award will be made available to the public through the procedures established under the Freedom of Information Act." In October, 1999, OMB implemented the required changes to Circular A-110. The amended circular provides, in part:

> . . . [I]n response to a Freedom of Information Act (FOIA) request for research data relating to published research findings produced under an award that were used by the Federal Government in developing a regulation, the Federal awarding agency shall request, and the recipient shall provide, within a reasonable time, the research data so that they can be made available to the public through the procedures established under the FOIA.**

---

* Omnibus Consolidated and Emergency Supplemental Appropriations Act, Pub. L. No. 105-277, 112 Stat. 2681–495 (1998).

** 64 Fed. Reg. 54926, vol. 64, No. 195.

Does this adequately implement the intent of Congress expressed in the DAA? Consider the following from Professors Fischman and Meretsky:

The principle that "what the federal government funds, the public is entitled to see" may be fair, but the actual law is considerably less expansive and more complicated. In 1998, Congress sought to ensure that "all data produced" from federal awards of grants be available to the public through the procedures established under FOIA. Buried on page 496 of a 920-page omnibus appropriations bill, the provision, commonly called the "Shelby Amendment," delegates implementation to the OMB through the administrative requirements for federal grants and agreements with non-profit organizations (including universities).

In 1999, the OMB published the new disclosure requirements. In promulgating its interpretation of the legislation, the OMB purported to balance three goals: 1) the advancement of the public interest in widely available information, 2) the maintenance of the traditional scientific process to ensure that research may continue to progress, and 3) the establishment of practical implementation procedures for public access. The most significant concern of the scientific community with the new disclosure condition of federal funding was that researchers would be forced to work in a "fishbowl" that would unveil data and research methods prematurely. The OMB responded to this concern by stressing that the disclosure requirements would protect the confidentiality of data while research is ongoing.

The OMB requirements clarify that the federal government has the right to obtain and use data produced under an award. Such data would then be subject to FOIA. However, if the federal government itself fails to act to obtain the data, the OMB interprets the 1998 legislation to obligate awardees to respond to a FOIA request for "research data relating to published research findings produced under an award that were used by the Federal Government in developing an agency action that has the force and effect of law . . . ." The OMB materials define research data as "recorded factual material commonly accepted in the scientific community as necessary to validate research findings," and specifically exclude "preliminary analyses, drafts of scientific papers, plans for future research, peer-reviews, or communications with colleagues." The OMB requirements bind all federally funded research, even if the federal support is a small proportion of the total research budget. As "faith-based" social programs are now discovering, federal strings come attached to the very first (even if the only) dollar of government money.

The key action triggering disclosure under the OMB requirements is publication. Unless the data requested by a member of the public (including a fellow scientist) are published, researchers have no obligation to disclose. Absent publication, data are unavailable unless: 1) a federal agency obtains them, 2) some other obligation (*e.g.*, in a permit or cooperative agreement) requires disclosure, or 3) the researcher volunteers them. For the purposes of the OMB requirements, data are considered published not only when they appear in a peer-reviewed scientific or technical journal. Data are also considered published when a "[f]ederal agency publicly and officially cites the research findings in support of an agency action that has the force and effect of law."

The question of what constitutes "an action that has the force and effect of law" is one that will likely generate some conflict in the coming years. The OMB interpretive material states that a rule . . . or an administrative order . . . falls within the meaning of the key phrase. In contrast, agency guidance documents fall outside of the agency actions that trigger publication under the OMB requirements. . . .*

How would *Forsham* have been decided under your reading of the DAA? How does it come out in light of OMB's guidelines?

10-3. To what extent has information placed on agency websites obviated the need to file FOIA requests to obtain information? *See* Martin E. Halstuk, *Speed Bumps on the Information Superhighway: A Study on Federal Agency Compliance with the Electronic Freedom of Information Act of 1996*, 5 COMM. L. & POL'Y 423 (2000). *See also* Paul M. Schoenhard, Note *Disclosure of Government Information Online: A New Approach from an Existing Framework*, 15 HARV. J. LAW & TEC. 497 (2002).

10-4. What if an agency file is created by one agency and then given to a private entity? Is it still an agency record? Must the private entity give it up? How does *Tax Analyst* define agency file?

10-5. How would or should computer files be defined under the Act? Are they not "agency files"? On October 2, 1996, President Clinton signed onto law the Electronic Freedom of Information Act Amendments of 1996, P.L. 104-231. In his press release President Clinton stressed the notion that the FOIA may become obsolete as more government documents become available on the Internet. Whether that happens or not remains to be seen, but the Electronic Freedom of Information Act Amendments seek to resolve or clarify several issues which were ambiguous in the FOIA:

1. "Record" under the FOIA now includes any information, in electronic form or otherwise, which would be subject to the FOIA.

2. The extent of any deletion shall be indicated on the portion of the record which is made available or published, unless that indication would harm an interest protected by the exemption. If technically feasible, the amount of the information deleted shall be indicated at the place in the record where such deletion is made.

3. Copies of all records, regardless of form or format, released to any person which have become or are likely to become the subject of subsequent requests and a general index of such records shall be made available to the public. The

---

* Robert L. Fischman & Vicky J. Meretsky, *Endangered Species Information: Access and Control*, 41 WASHBURN L.J. 90, 102-03 (2001). Copyright © 2001 Washburn Law Journal. All rights reserved.

index will be made available by computer by December 31, 1999. All new records (created after November 1, 1996) must immediately be made available by computer or other electronic means.

4. If an agency can readily produce a record in the electronic format requested, the agency shall do so.

5. A Court shall give substantial weight to agency determinations of feasibility and reproducibility.

6. Each agency may promulgate regulations providing for multitrack processing for records based on the amount of work or time (or both) involved in processing individual requests. . . .

8. Agencies can promulgate regulations which allow for expedited processing of requests from persons with compelling needs. Determinations of whether to expedite a request shall be made, and notice of decision sent to the requester, within 10 days of the request.

9. The period for determining whether to comply with a request is changed from ten to twenty days, in recognition of the fact that future requests will be more tedious, as the information requested will probably not be in electronic form in the first instance.

10. Each agency must submit an annual report to the Attorney General outlining the costs of compliance and the statistics on how many requests were honored in a timely fashion, and how many were denied for specific reasons. The Attorney General is required electronically to publish the reports at a central address, and must annually notify the Office of Management and Budget and both the Chairman and minority leader of the House Committee on Government Reform and Oversight and the Chairman and minority leader of the Senate Committees on Governmental Affairs and the Judiciary.

PROBLEM 10-1

Assume that a for-profit corporation, Wackenhut, Inc., now runs many federal prisons. Also assume that the Federal Bureau of Prisons was the primary governmental agency involved in drafting the contract under which the private firm operates. What kind of information can you obtain from Wackenhut with a FOIA request? Does FOIA apply to Wackenhut? What might the Bureau of Prisons be able to provide? Specifically, how would you obtain the following information? Assume no other law would prohibit the release of the information.

- The rules governing prisoner behavior;
- The number and type of infractions that prisoners committed last year;
- The punishments that prisoners received for these infractions;
- Copies of the formal complaints that prisoners filed about the guards or prison conditions;

- Information concerning the ultimate resolution of each complaint;
- The rules governing the qualifications and selection of the prison guard employees;
- The number of patients treated for personal injuries in the prison hospital and a description of the cause of those injuries;
- The number of patients treated for particular diseases in the prison hospital;
- Information concerning medical treatment that a prisoner requested, but did not receive because the treatment was deemed medically inappropriate;
- A copy of the contract between the prison and the government;
- Information concerning the salary of prison employees; and
- Information concerning the recreational, vocational, and educational facilities of the prison — for example, the titles of all of the books available in the prison library.

[C] FOIA Exemptions

KING v. U.S. DEPT. OF JUSTICE

District of Columbia Court of Appeals
830 F.2d 210 (1987)

Before ROBINSON and STARR, CIRCUIT JUDGES, and WRIGHT, SENIOR CIRCUIT JUDGE.

Opinion for the Court filed by CIRCUIT JUDGE SPOTTSWOOD W. ROBINSON, III.

SPOTTSWOOD W. ROBINSON, III, CIRCUIT JUDGE:

In this Freedom of Information Act (FOIA) case, appellant, Cynthia King, seeks production by the Federal Bureau of Investigation (FBI) of documents relating to her deceased mother-in-law, Carol King, a civil rights attorney and activist about whose career appellant is writing a book. The FBI has released many of the documents — most, however, in redacted form. The agency contends that its decision to withhold portions of the requested information is authorized by Exemptions 1 and 7 of the Act, which respectively except from FOIA's disclosure mandate, documents classified for national security reasons and certain other material gathered during investigations for law-enforcement purposes. Appellant challenges the applicability of either exemption in the circumstances presented here.

The District Court denied motions by appellant for summary judgment or in the alternative to compel discovery, rejected appellant's request for in-camera inspection, and granted the FBI's motion for summary judgment. This appeal ensued.

I

The records whose disclosure is here at issue are part of an FBI surveillance file on Carol King compiled during the 1940's and 1950's. She was a prominent civil rights attorney who devoted her practice to defending minorities, aliens, radicals and union members both famous and obscure; and a substantial portion of her practice consisted in representation of aliens facing deportation during the McCarthy era. The nature of Carol King's law practice and her political associations aroused [the] suspicions of the FBI. In 1941, the FBI opened a surveillance file on her, and subjected her to continuous investigation until her death in 1952. The FBI represents that its investigation was devoted exclusively to determining whether Carol King was guilty of political sedition. While the eleven-year investigation amassed a file 1,665 pages in length, no charge was ever made.

Appellant is a writer by profession who intends to publish a biography on her mother-in-law and longtime friend, Carol King. As yet, no significant history of the latter's career has been published. In the course of her research, appellant attempted to obtain information pertaining to Carol King by means of a FOIA request. The FBI eventually responded by releasing to appellant redacted portions of its King investigative file. Ultimately provided were 1,500 pages of the 1,665-page file, and, from most of the 1,500 pages supplied, names and, frequently, substantial passages were deleted.

Contesting the sufficiency of the FBI's response to her FOIA request, appellant filed suit in the District Court, and moved for a *Vaughn* index[16] detailing the grounds for the FBI's exemption claims. Production of the *Vaughn* index was ordered. Thereafter, the FBI submitted the joint declaration of Special Agents Richard C. Staver and Walter Scheuplein, Jr.,[19] and the declaration of John H. Walker of the Immigration and Naturalization Service, attesting to the reasons for excising portions of the King file; it then moved for summary judgment. Appellant in turn moved for summary judgment, or in the alternative to compel a response to outstanding discovery requests.

The District Court granted the FBI's motion for summary judgment. It sustained the Exemption 1 contentions, relying on the Staver-Scheuplein declaration, which it found to set forth with "reasonable specificity of detail rather than mere conclusory statements" an adequate description of the portions of the King file withheld, as well as the national security considerations advanced in support of the FBI's refusal to disclose. Similarly, the

---

[16] *See Vaughn v. Rosen,* 340, 484 F.2d 820 (1973), *cert. denied,* 415 U.S. 977 (1974). [A *Vaughn* index is an itemized index which correlates each withheld document with a specific FOIA exemption and the relevant part of the agency's statement refusing disclosure.]

[19] . . . The declaration consists of two parts: the first, by Special Agent Staver, sets forth the grounds for the FBI's Exemption 1 position and the second, by Special Agent Scheuplein, addresses the FBI's remaining withholding claims, including those under Exemption 7.

District Court deemed the declaration a sufficient foundation for the FBI's claims under Exemptions 7(C) and 7(D) that information withheld was gathered pursuant to an investigation for law-enforcement purposes and that its release would constitute an unwarranted invasion of personal privacy or compromise assurances of source confidentiality.

Appellant urges us to hold that the District Court erred in crediting the FBI's Exemption 1 and 7 arguments, contending that they shield information in contravention of FOIA's broad disclosure mandate. Specifically, appellant asserts that the Staver-Scheuplein declaration presents only a vague and conclusory description of the material excised pursuant to Exemption 1, wholly inadequate for purposes of ascertaining whether the documents in question have in fact been properly classified, or what harm might result from their production. "How," appellant queries, "can release of . . . records of this nature and at this late date possibly damage the national security?" Appellant further contends that the Staver-Scheuplein declaration does not make the threshold showing required for resort to Exemption 7: that the documents in question were compiled for *bona fide* law-enforcement purposes pursuant to an investigation whose relation to the agency's law-enforcement duties is based on information sufficient to support at least a "'colorable claim' of its rationality." And, whether or not a law-enforcement purpose originally animated the investigation, appellant insists no considerations of privacy or confidentiality warrant continued withholding of its fruits. While we reject appellant's challenge to the disposition of the Exemption 7 claims in this case, we believe valid objections to the FBI's showing on the Exemption 1 claims have been raised, and remand in order that the District Court secure a fuller elaboration of the FBI's basis for asserting them.

II

Exemption 1 of the Freedom of Information Act protects from disclosure information that is "specifically authorized under criteria established by an Executive order to be kept secret in the interest of national defense or foreign policy and [is] in fact properly classified pursuant to such Executive order." An agency may invoke this exemption only if it complies with classification procedures established by the relevant executive order and withholds only such material as conforms to the order's substantive criteria for classification. Appellant challenges, on substantive and not procedural grounds, the propriety of the classification decisions underlying the FBI's Exemption 1 claims.

A.

Both appellant and the FBI believe that the directive pertinent to disposition of the Exemption 1 issues in this case is Executive Order 12065, which was in effect when the FBI's classification determinations were made. This order provided that information could be classified only if it concerned:

    (a) military plans, weapons, or operations;

    (b) foreign government information;

    (c) intelligence activities, sources or methods;

(d) foreign relations or foreign activities of the United States;

(e) scientific, technological, or economic matters relating to the national security;

(f) United States Government Programs for safeguarding nuclear materials or facilities; or

(g) other categories of information which are related to national security and which require protection against unauthorized disclosure as determined by the President, by a person designated by the President pursuant to Section 1-201, or by an agency head.

Executive Order 12065 further specified that information concerning any of the enumerated matters was eligible for classification as "confidential," the lowest security designation, only if its "unauthorized disclosure . . . reasonably could be expected to cause at least identifiable damage to the national security." It also established a presumption against classification: "If there is reasonable doubt . . . whether the information should be classified at all . . . the information should not be classified."

Subsequent to the decision to classify the documents involved in this case, and after commencement of this litigation, President Reagan promulgated Executive Order 12356. This order retains all categories of classifiable information enumerated in Executive Order 12065, but diverges from that order in several other significant respects. The new executive order eliminates the prior order's presumption against classification and modifies the standard for classifying information. While the earlier order prohibited an agency from classifying information unless it could be shown that "unauthorized disclosure reasonably could be expected to cause at least identifiable damage to the national security," the new order seemingly commands classification of all material within certain enumerated categories of sensitive information whose "unauthorized disclosure, either by itself or in the context of other information, reasonably could be expected to cause damage to the national security." While the old executive order in some instances required declassification decisions to be made by weighing the need to protect information against the public interest in disclosure, the new executive order eliminates this balancing provision from the declassification calculus. Absent as well from the new order are certain procedures contained in Executive Order 12065 designed to ensure systematic declassification review of older material.

The parties have conformed their arguments regarding the propriety of the classification decisions in dispute to the terms of Executive Order 12065, under which those decisions were made, notwithstanding the fact that Executive Order 12065 is now superseded by Executive Order 12356. Their position finds support in our holding in *Lesar v. United States Department of Justice*, 636 F.2d 472 (D.C. Cir. 1980), that "[o]n review, the court should . . . assess the documents according to the terms of the Executive Order under which the agency made its ultimate classification determination.". . .

Lesar [directs] a reviewing court to assess the propriety of a classification decision purportedly supporting an Exemption 1 claim in terms of the executive order in force at the time the agency's ultimate classification decision is actually made. . . .

B.

Turning to the general principles affecting this appeal, we begin with a reminder that, as in all FOIA cases, the district courts are to review *de novo* all exemption claims advanced, and that the agency bears the burden of justifying its decision to withhold requested information. The agency may meet this burden by filing affidavits describing the material withheld and the manner in which it falls within the exemption claimed; and the court owes substantial weight to detailed agency explanations in the national security context. However, a district court may award summary judgment to an agency invoking Exemption 1 only if (1) the agency affidavits describe the documents withheld and the justifications for nondisclosure in enough detail and with sufficient specificity to demonstrate that material withheld is logically within the domain of the exemption claimed, and (2) the affidavits are neither controverted by contrary record evidence nor impugned by bad faith on the part of the agency. On appeal, the court is to determine, from inspection of the agency affidavits submitted, whether the agency's explanation was full and specific enough to afford the FOIA requester a meaningful opportunity to contest, and the district court an adequate foundation to review, the soundness of the withholding. . . .

The significance of agency affidavits in a FOIA case cannot be underestimated. As, ordinarily, the agency alone possesses knowledge of the precise content of documents withheld, the FOIA requester and the court both must rely upon its representations for an understanding of the material sought to be protected. As we observed in *Vaughn v. Rosen*, "[t]his lack of knowledge by the party seeing [sic] disclosure seriously distorts the traditional adversary nature of our legal system's form of dispute resolution," with the result that "[a]n appellate court, like the trial court, is completely without the controverting illumination that would ordinarily accompany a lower court's factual determination." Even should the court undertake *in camera* inspection of the material — an unwieldy process where hundreds or thousands of pages are in dispute — "[t]he scope of the inquiry will not have been focused by the adverse parties. . . ."

Affidavits submitted by a governmental agency in justification for its exemption claims must therefore strive to correct, however, imperfectly, the asymmetrical distribution of knowledge that characterizes FOIA litigation. The detailed public index which in *Vaughn* we required of withholding agencies is intended to do just that: "to permit adequate adversary testing of the agency's claimed right to an exemption," and enable "the District Court to make a rational decision whether the withheld material must be produced without actually viewing the documents themselves, as well as to produce a record that will render the District Court's decision capable of meaningful review on appeal." Thus, when an agency seeks to withhold information, it must provide "a relatively detailed justification, specifically identifying the reasons why a particular exemption is relevant and correlating those claims with the particular part of a withheld document to which they apply." Specificity is the defining requirement of the *Vaughn* index and affidavit; affidavits cannot support summary judgment if they are "conclusory, merely reciting statutory standards, or if they are too vague or sweeping." To accept an inadequately supported exemption claim "would constitute an abandonment of the trial court's obligation under the FOIA to conduct a *de novo* review."

C.

The District Court examined the affidavits submitted by the FBI in the instant case, and concluded that they substantiated its reliance on Exemption 1. On appeal, then, we are to determine as a threshold matter whether the affidavits in fact provided the District Court with "an adequate basis to decide" the Exemption 1 issues: to ascertain whether the material withheld is within the categories of classifiable information enumerated in Executive Order 12065 and, further, whether its unauthorized disclosure reasonably could be expected to cause the requisite amount of damage to the national security. We turn to the *Vaughn* index and the accompanying declaration prepared by Special FBI Agent, Richard C. Staver.

Staver advised the District Court that "[t]o provide a more workable '*Vaughn* index' format and thus reduce the burden of analyzing Exemption One claims" he was departing from the practice of preparing typed pages separately describing each withheld document, and was submitting instead copies of the documents released pursuant to appellant's FOIA demand with each deletion annotated by means of a four-character code referring in turn to an accompanying code-catalogue. The copy of the redacted documents and the explanatory code-catalogue together comprise the FBI's *Vaughn* filing.

In brief, the system works as follows. For every instance in which information was withheld, the documents released have been marked with the four-character code. The first two characters of the code identify the FOIA exemption assertedly authorizing the withholding — for example, (b)(1); the third character identifies the category in Executive Order 12065 under which the material has been classified — such as Section 1-301(c) (intelligence activities, sources or methods); and the fourth character refers to a statement in the code-catalogue that is offered as a description of the material withheld, intended to demonstrate that it lies within one or more of the classification categories of Executive Order 12065, and to point to the likely harm to the national security attending its release. In sum, the District Court was presented with an intensively redacted and annotated 1500-page reproduction of the requested file, as well as numerous inserts, similarly annotated, representing the remaining 165 pages of the file withheld.

Staver opines that this new method of presentation represents "a vast improvement over previous formats" and that "the required specificity has been enhanced." We regret to differ. The system Staver has adopted imposes a significant burden upon the reviewing court without commensurate benefit. Staver's system of annotation neither adequately describes redacted material nor explains, with sufficient specificity to enable meaningful review, how its disclosure would likely impair national security. . . .

The *Vaughn* index here submitted is, in a word, inadequate — wholly lacking in that specificity of description we have repeatedly warned is necessary to ensure meaningful review of an agency's claim to withhold information subject to a FOIA request. A withholding agency must describe *each* document or portion thereof withheld, and for *each* withholding it must discuss the consequences of disclosing the sought-after information. This requirement, if indeed not explicit in *Vaughn,* is unmistakably implicit in the principles supporting our decision in that case, as our subsequent decisions have made very clear. When, in *Vaughn,* we first insisted that agencies tender an index and affidavits as a precondition to review of exemptions claims, we emphasized the necessity of identifying which exemption was relied upon for each item withheld. In *Mead Data Central v. United States Department of the Air Force,* we elaborated on *Vaughn*'s requirements, explaining that the withholding agency must supply "a relatively detailed justification, specifically identifying the reasons why a particular exemption is relevant and correlating those claims with the particular part of a withheld document to which they apply." As we subsequently reiterated in *Dellums v. Powell, Vaughn*'s call for specificity imposes on the agency the burden of demonstrating applicability of the exemptions invoked *as to each document or segment withheld.*

D.

We conclude that the *Vaughn* index tendered in this case provides an insufficient basis for the *de novo* review that FOIA mandates for Exemption 1 claims. This requires a remand of the case to the District Court for further proceedings. Then, the court may employ any of several measures to acquire enough information to conduct the review requisite.

The District Court may, in its discretion, order production of the excised material or some sample thereof for *in camera* inspection. An opportunity for "first-hand inspection [enables the court to] determine whether the weakness of the affidavits is a result of poor draftsmanship or a flimsy exemption claim," but "the district court's inspection prerogative is not a substitute for the government's burden of proof, and should not be resorted to lightly." Moreover, should the task of *in camera* examination appear too burdensome, the court may allow appellant to engage in further discovery, or order the FBI to supplement its *Vaughn* filings. If so ordered, the FBI must provide on an item-specific basis the maximum amount of information consistent with protection of the interests of national security and the exigencies of forecasting events in this domain.

Whether the District Court proceeds by ordering supplemental affidavits or by *in camera* inspection of documents or samplings, it must ensure that it has an adequate foundation for review of the FBI's withholding claims before giving the agency's expert opinion on national security matters the substantial weight to which it is entitled. At a minimum, the court must secure more information with respect to excisions involving whole documents or substantial parts thereof, where no contextual information is available to supplement and particularize the FBI's code descriptions. Having garnered this additional information on material withheld, the court should then scrutinize afresh the FBI's assessment of the consequences of disclosure, allowing appropriate latitude for opinion but ensuring that the enumeration of alternate consequences presently characterizing the agency's submission reflects predictive uncertainty rather than mere categorical response.

In reviewing the FBI's predictions on disclosure, the court should devote particular attention to the age of the file in this case. It was compiled between 1941 and 1952; all documents it contains are now at least 35 years old. Executive Order 12065 directs declassification "as early as national security considerations permit," and identifies "the occurrence of a declassification event" or "loss of the information's sensitivity with the passage of time" as circumstances sufficient to warrant dissolution of a prior classification determination. . . . [The Court then discussed Exemption 7, upholding the District Court's decision in this regard.]

WOLFE v. DEPARTMENT OF HEALTH AND HUMAN SERVICES

District of Columbia Court of Appeals
839 F.2d 768 (1988)

Before WALD, CHIEF JUDGE, ROBINSON, MIKVA, EDWARDS, RUTH BADER GINSBURG, BORK, STARR, SILBERMAN, BUCKLEY, WILLIAMS, D.H. GINSBURG and SENTELLE, CIRCUIT JUDGES.

Opinion for the court filed by CIRCUIT JUDGE BORK in which STARR, SILBERMAN, BUCKLEY, WILLIAMS, D.H. GINSBURG and SENTELLE, CIRCUIT JUDGES, join.

Dissenting opinion filed by CHIEF JUDGE WALD with whom SPOTTSWOOD W. ROBINSON, III, MIKVA, HARRY T. EDWARDS and RUTH BADER GINSBURG, CIRCUIT JUDGES, join.

Dissenting opinion filed by CIRCUIT JUDGE HARRY T. EDWARDS with whom WALD, CHIEF JUDGE, SPOTTSWOOD W. ROBINSON, III, MIKVA, and RUTH BADER GINSBURG, CIRCUIT JUDGES, join.

Dissenting opinion filed by CIRCUIT JUDGE RUTH BADER GINSBURG with whom WALD, CHIEF JUDGE, SPOTTSWOOD W. ROBINSON, III, MIKVA, and HARRY T. EDWARDS, CIRCUIT JUDGES, join.

BORK, CIRCUIT JUDGE:

The plaintiffs-appellees, members of the Public Citizen Health Research Group, requested access under the Freedom of Information Act ("FOIA"), 5 U.S.C. § 552 (1982), to records which indicate what actions have been completed by the Food and Drug Administration ("FDA") but which await final decision or approval by the Secretary of Health and Human Services ("HHS") or the Office of Management and Budget ("OMB"). HHS refused plaintiffs' requests, contending that the information sought was exempt under FOIA Exemption 5, which shields from disclosure those documents that would not be routinely available in civil litigation with the agency. . . . The government claimed that the information should be exempt under the deliberative process privilege. The district court granted summary judgment for the plaintiffs. A divided panel of this court affirmed the district court. The full court granted review in order to address the proper scope of the deliberative process privilege as it is applied through Exemption 5. We hold that the privilege protects against disclosure of the information requested and therefore reverse the district court.

I.

Plaintiffs filed the instant FOIA request in order to influence decisionmakers more efficiently during predecisional deliberations and in order to locate the cause of what they allege to be unreasonable delay in the issuance of FDA regulations. This case reflects dissatisfaction with the results of the development of formal presidential oversight of executive branch rulemaking. . . . Two developments within the last seven years have sparked this particular attack. First, in 1981 the Secretary of HHS withdrew the delegation of power to the FDA to issue regulations that it deemed in the public interest. Instead, such regulations now must first be reviewed and approved by the Secretary. Second, on February 17, 1981, the President issued Executive Order No. 12,291 which requires all agencies considering issuance of a rule to submit any draft proposed rule and any draft final rule for review by OMB. OMB, insofar as the relevant statutory law permits, reviews the rule for consistency with presidential policies and for net gain as shown by cost benefit analysis. Thus, before a rule can be proposed or promulgated by FDA it must be reviewed and approved first by the Secretary of HHS and then by OMB.

Members of the public are excluded only from the inter-agency stages of the rulemaking process. After FDA, HHS, and OMB have approved a regulatory proposal, members of the public are guaranteed an opportunity to comment on the proposed rule. The APA requires that the FDA publish a general notice specifying the time and place of the rulemaking proceedings, 5 U.S.C. § 553(b)(1) (1982), and guarantees the public the opportunity to comment on the proposed rule. 5 U.S.C. § 553(c) (1982). There may be an opportunity for oral argument. *Id.* Thereafter the FDA is required to consider relevant comments presented to it and to incorporate in any rule adopted a concise and general statement of its basis and purpose. *Id.* The draft final rule is then reviewed by OMB. Plaintiffs, unsatisfied with their statutorily guaranteed input, during the comment period seek the ability to influence the inter-agency stage in the rulemaking process.

In essence, plaintiffs wish to be able to identify, in general, which regulatory actions have been proposed by FDA and to know how long regulatory actions initiated by FDA are spending at each stopping point along the approval route from FDA to HHS to OMB and back to HHS, so that they can identify decisionmakers and contest delays in the consideration of FDA regulations. . . .

Although plaintiffs do not seek access to the specific substance of the proposed rules, they already know the general identity of important regulations and other FDA projects under consideration because "these matters are generally known to those with an interest in the FDA." In addition, as plaintiffs point out, the FDA publishes a semi-annual Regulatory Agenda that lists all current and projected rulemaking being considered by the FDA, all existing FDA regulations presently under review, and all actions that have been completed by the FDA within the prior six months. Thus, if the information requested is made public and shows a transmittal from the FDA to HHS, it is known that the FDA has proposed to regulate a particular subject, and if no transmittal is shown, it is known that the FDA has decided not to recommend such regulation or not to recommend it yet. If no transmittal to OMB is shown, HHS is known to have disapproved the FDA's proposal. If a transmittal is shown but no regulation is put out for notice and comment, OMB is known to have disapproved the regulatory proposal. At oral argument, plaintiffs' counsel conceded that plaintiff was not entitled to information which would reveal that a recommendation to regulate had been made.

The district court ruled that FOIA Exemption 5 did not apply to this case because the information requested does not fall under the deliberative process privilege. The district judge reasoned that none of the policies underlying the privilege would be significantly implicated by disclosure of the requested material and concluded that the mere fact that "a recommendation has been made by one agency to another" is not information "sufficiently 'deliberative' to trigger the protections of the privilege." Accordingly, the district court granted summary judgment for plaintiffs, denied defendant's cross-motion for summary judgment, and ordered disclosure of the requested information within thirty days.

. . . . The full court granted a hearing to determine the scope of the deliberative process privilege. We reverse the judgment of the district court and hold that Exemption 5's deliberative process privilege protects against disclosure of the information requested.

II.

Exemption 5 allows an agency to withhold from the public "inter-agency or intra-agency memorandums or letters which would not be available to a party other than an agency in litigation with the agency." 5 U.S.C. § 552(b)(5) (1982). The common law discovery privilege at issue is the executive or deliberative process privilege. Congress adopted Exemption 5 because it recognized that the quality of administrative decision-making would be seriously undermined if agencies were forced to operate in a fishbowl. As is stated in the legislative history, the purpose of Exemption 5 is to encourage the "frank discussion of legal and policy issues."

In other words, the privilege "rest[s] . . . upon the policy of protecting the 'decisionmaking processes of government agencies.'" However, in accordance with the general disclosure policy of FOIA, Exemption 5 is to be construed "as narrowly as [is] consistent with efficient Government operation."

Thus, the Supreme Court has limited the deliberative process privilege to materials which are both predecisional and deliberative. *EPA v. Mink,* 410 U.S. 73, 88 (1973). Accordingly, the Supreme Court and this court require disclosure of documents which explain an agency's final decision but protect documents which are predecisional. *Renegotiation Bd. v. Grumman Aircraft,* 421 U.S. 168, 184–85 (1975). . . . In the instant case, the materials are unquestionably predecisional. This case turns, therefore, on whether or not the information requested is deliberative — that is "whether it reflects the give-and-take of the consultative process."

It is not possible to resolve whether the information is deliberative by characterizing it, as plaintiffs do, as merely involving a factual request for dates and titles. Exemption 5 disputes can often be resolved by the simple test that factual material must be disclosed but advice and recommendations may be withheld. Indeed the fact/opinion distinction "offers a quick, clear, and predictable rule of decision," for most cases. But "courts must be careful not to become victims of their own semantics." In some circumstances, even material that could be characterized as "factual" would so expose the deliberative process that it must be covered by the privilege. We know of no case in which a court has used the fact/opinion distinction to support disclosure of facts about the inner workings of the deliberative process itself.

The Supreme Court recognized this when it approved the fact/opinion distinction. In *EPA v. Mink* the Court required disclosure of "purely factual material contained in deliberative memoranda" which was "severable from its context," *Mink,* 410 U.S. at 88. These cases illustrate that this court cannot mechanically apply the fact/opinion test. Instead, we must examine the information requested in light of the policies and goals that underlie the deliberative process privilege.

Moreover, in *Grumman,* the Supreme Court specifically noted that the context in which the documents were used itself "serve[d] to define the document." *Grumman,* 421 U.S. at 170, 95 S. Ct. at 1493. Thus the first step in determining whether disclosure would harm the deliberative process is to examine the context in which the materials are used.

Once the information requested is examined within the context of the FDA's predecisional approval process, it becomes clear that it must be protected. The information would disclose that proposals have been made, and that these preliminary recommendations have been accepted or rejected, at various levels of review.

The fact of forwarding is, in each instance, the functional equivalent of an intra-agency or inter-agency memorandum that states, "We recommend that a regulation on this [named] subject matter be promulgated." The fact of a failure to forward from the FDA to HHS, or from HHS to OMB is the equivalent of a memorandum from HHS to FDA that states, "We disapprove of your recommendation that a particular regulation on this [named] subject matter be promulgated."

In addition, the information sought would reveal the timing of the deliberative process and it would indicate the agency in which the deliberative process is at the moment going forward. Thus the information sought will generally disclose the recommended outcome of the consultative process at each stage of that process, as well as the source of any decision not to regulate.

That the information requested does not fully reveal the reasoning of the recommendation but merely memorializes it no more strips it of protection than would a court's sheet memorializing a panel's tentative decision by stating "Reverse; I will write." . . .

It would be impossible for courts to administer a rule of law to the effect that some but not all information about the decisional process may be disclosed without violating Exemption 5. Courts would become enmeshed in a continual process of estimating or, more accurately, guessing about the adverse effects on the decisional process of a great variety of combinations of pieces of information. That would inevitably lead courts on some occasions to undercut legitimate Exemption 5 protections. Indeed, such a procedure would not result in a rule at all. Agencies would have to pass on requests wholly impressionistically, subject to the impressionistic second-guessing of the courts. That is hardly a satisfactory or efficient way of implementing FOIA.

This court has previously noted that the deliberative process privilege embodied in Exemption 5 serves a number of purposes among which are the protection of subordinates' willingness to provide decision-makers with frank opinions and recommendations and the prevention of the premature disclosure of proposed policies before they have been finally formulated or adopted.

Disclosure of the information requested in this case would certainly reveal policies prematurely. The FDA's very decision to regulate in a particular area often embodies a sensitive and important policy judgment, sometimes more sensitive and important than the later decisions concerning the precise extent and nature of the regulation. Decisions to allow AIDS patients to use experimental drugs, or to regulate health claims on food products come to mind as examples. The general views of the decision-maker on whether to regulate at all are often crucially important pieces of information about predecisional recommendations.

When, as in the instant case, subordinates are reporting to superiors, disclosure could chill discussion at a time when agency opinions are fluid and tentative. . . .

Moreover, disclosure would force officials to punch a public time clock. Requests for information at regular intervals would allow plaintiffs, or any other interested group, to attribute delay to FDA, HHS, or OMB. Given plaintiffs' intimate knowledge of these agencies it is likely that plaintiffs would quickly learn to identify and publicize the office or even the person they deem responsible. It strains credulity to believe that such attention would not lead to hasty and precipitous decision-making. Decisional delay is not a fact but an opinion; what plaintiffs or others may identify as delay may be caused by unexpected scientific complications or the difficulties of weighing competing values.

Exemption 5 is manifestly not meant to isolate agency decision-makers from public opinion or to silence public voices. But the statutory framework of the APA allows agencies a space within which they may deliberate. . . . As plaintiffs explicitly admitted in their pleadings, they seek access to the information, in part to issue themselves an invitation to agency deliberations. It is just such a fishbowl that Congress sought to avoid when it enacted Exemption 5. The purposes of Exemption 5 can be adequately served only by permitting HHS to withhold these pre-decisional recommendations.

We reverse the judgment of the district court and remand the case with instructions to enter summary judgment for HHS.

WALD, CHIEF JUDGE, with whom CIRCUIT JUDGES SPOTTSWOOD W. ROBINSON, III, MIKVA, HARRY T. EDWARDS, and RUTH BADER GINSBURG join, dissenting:

While I find this case a close one, I nonetheless agree with my dissenting colleagues and write separately only to underscore my view that the majority has erred in interpreting the facts to which it has applied Exemption 5 law, and that, even so, its opinion must be given a narrow reading, if it is not to work a major disruption in circuit law under FOIA.

I.

The majority opinion states that disclosure of the fact of communications between HHS and OMB as to a proposed rule is tantamount to a memo stating, "We recommend that a regulation on this [named] subject matter be promulgated." As Judge Ginsburg's dissent indicates, this analogy vastly overstates how definitive a message is actually communicated by the mere knowledge of the fact of such a transmittal or nontransmittal.

The majority opinion envisions an FDA-HHS-OMB relationship in which decisionmakers act in lock-step, giving unadorned "yes" or "no" answers to transmittals from below. While information that there has been a transmittal from FDA to HHS about a possible subject of regulation may indeed suggest that the FDA proposes at that point in time to do something about a particular subject, that is all it tells. It sheds no light on what happens later in the process; the FDA may modify or even rescind any of its tentative decisions throughout the process of HHS and OMB review "up until the time when a notice of proposed rulemaking is sent to the Federal Register for publication." Thus, the majority erroneously asserts that if no transmittal from HHS to OMB is shown, it can be surmised that HHS has disapproved of the FDA proposal. Obviously, this is not true; it might be that although HHS approved the regulation, the FDA itself thought better of it and withdrew it. HHS also may have returned the regulation to the FDA for modifications or may have simply not yet taken any action at all. Even actual transmittal from HHS to OMB shows only that some — perhaps drastically altered — version of the original FDA proposal has received HHS approval.

The same argument may be made against the majority's too-facile conclusion that if it becomes known that a transmittal has been made from HHS to OMB, but no regulation is subsequently put out for notice and comment, it is reasonable to conclude that OMB has disapproved of the regulatory proposal. OMB may have rejected the regulation or simply returned it for clarification or refinement. *See* J.A. at 52 (Affidavit of HHS Executive Secretary David A. Rust) (information "might also show, or purport to show, that an action is being delayed by OMB when, in fact, OMB, as part of its review, requested further information from HHS about the matter"). Or OMB may have been on the brink of finally approving the proposal when the FDA itself rescinded its initial decision to act.

In sum, the information requested by the plaintiff — *i.e.,* the date and destination of transmittals to other agencies about rules that the FDA has already revealed are under consideration — discloses neither "the recommended outcome" at each stage nor "the source of any decision not to regulate." The majority assumes a rigidified, and therefore predictable deliberation process that the record and the realities of government decisionmaking do not support.

II.

But even if information regarding the date of a proposal's interagency transmittal did provide a clear signal that a particular agency had given a "thumbs up" or "thumbs down" sign on it, this alone would still not inevitably justify invocation of the deliberative process privilege.

Unlike the case posited by the majority, in which a judge writes a memorandum "Reverse, I will write," a mere "yes" or "no" answer to a proposed regulation, about whose content nothing is initially known other than the subject matter title, will rarely disclose anything about the substance of any agency's recommendation or reasoning. In a judicial appeal, the decision which will be reversed or upheld is a matter of public record and therefore the simple memorandum "Reverse" discloses the reviewing judge's substantive recommendation and a specific line of reasoning that she rejects. But, in the case before us, a "yes" or "no" recommendation is informative only to the degree that the initial proposal itself is known. In many cases, because of the generality of the proposals published in the FDA's Regulatory Agenda or undisclosed FDA policy shifts in the interim, the "yes" or "no" will tell the reader only that something is going forward. The degree to which anything about ongoing deliberations will be revealed will depend, in each situation, on the sum of what was known originally about the FDA's intent and what, in the context of that proposal's history, the transmittal may show additionally.

In my view, to be exempted "inter-agency . . . memoranda or letters" must disclose something meaningful about the substance of an agency's preliminary reasoning or tentative conclusions. 5 U.S.C. § 552(b)(5). In this case, that will depend on how much information a regulation's title discloses. Thus, while a transmittal under the general heading "AIDS" would not alone disclose enough substance, a regulation entitled "Federal Funding for AIDS Education in Public Schools" might. Again, however, exemption should follow only if the transmittal itself reveals the substance of the agency's recommendation. Here, I conclude, this has not been shown. . . .

IV.

The information requested in this case is not deliberative material because it discloses nothing about the substance of agency recommendations or rationales. It does not even show a clear "yes" or "no" agency response to anything in many situations. Finally, there is no independent basis under Exemption 5 for protecting facts about the "deliberative process itself" unless such information discloses an agency's substantive views in a way that may chill candid deliberations. The majority opinion overstates the amount of information disclosed, exaggerates its likely effect on agency deliberations and confuses the appropriate scope of Exemption 5's deliberative memorandum exception as well.

I dissent.

HARRY T. EDWARDS, CIRCUIT JUDGE, dissenting, with whom WALD, CHIEF JUDGE, and SPOTTSWOOD W. ROBINSON, III, MIKVA and RUTH BADER GINSBURG, CIRCUIT JUDGES, join:

I adhere to the views expressed by the majority in the original panel opinion. I would therefore affirm the District Court's judgment in favor of the plaintiffs.

RUTH BADER GINSBURG, CIRCUIT JUDGE, with whom WALD, CHIEF JUDGE, and CIRCUIT JUDGES SPOTTSWOOD W. ROBINSON, III, MIKVA, and HARRY T. EDWARDS join, dissenting:

Like Judge Edwards, I would adhere to the disposition of the original panel; further, I note some respects in which the current court opinion slips from my grasp. First, the current majority opinion reports that "the FDA publishes a semi-annual Regulatory Agenda that lists all current and projected rulemaking being considered by the FDA. . . ." Given that revealing publication, it is not evident to me that "the information requested in this case would certainly reveal policies prematurely."

Second, the current majority opinion appears to envision an FDA-HHS-OMB world in which decisionmakers always say "Yes" or "No," "Approve" or "Disapprove," never "Modify," "Amend," "Explain." Might it not be the case, for example, that "[i]f no transmittal to OMB is shown," HHS may not have "disapproved the FDA's proposal," it may instead have returned the regulation to the FDA for refinement or alteration, if indeed HHS has moved at all.

"Reverse; I will write," *see* court's opinion at 775, seems to me a very different matter from the one here at issue. As it moves along administrative tracks, a proposed regulation may change shape significantly. Nothing in the FOIA request we face seeks the substance of a regulatory proposal at the first or any other administrative stage. But a lower court decision or agency adjudication has a known content; the matter is set out in a public document, displaying the tribunal's reasons. "Reverse; I will write," thus conveys concrete information to the reader, for she knows just what the district court or agency ruled and why.

In sum, I doubt that today's decision construes Exemption 5 "as narrowly as consistent with efficient Government operation," . . . rather, the decision appears to me to stray from the legislature's will.

CENTER FOR NATIONAL SECURITY STUDIES v. U.S. DEPARTMENT OF JUSTICE

United States Court of Appeals, District of Columbia Circuit. 331 F.3d 918 (2003)

Before: SENTELLE, HENDERSON and TATEL, CIRCUIT JUDGES.

Opinion for the Court filed by CIRCUIT JUDGE SENTELLE.

Dissenting opinion filed by CIRCUIT JUDGE TATEL.

SENTELLE, CIRCUIT JUDGE:

Various "public interest" groups (plaintiffs) brought this Freedom of Information Act (FOIA) action against the Department of Justice (DOJ or government) seeking release of information concerning persons detained in the wake of the September 11 terrorist attacks, including: their names, their attorneys, dates of arrest and release, locations of arrest and detention, and reasons for detention. The government objected to release, and asserted numerous exceptions to FOIA requirements in order to justify withholding the information. The parties filed cross-motions for summary judgment. The district court ordered release of the names of the detainees and their attorneys, but held that the government could withhold all other detention information pursuant to FOIA Exemption 7(A), which exempts "records or information compiled for law enforcement purposes . . . to the extent that the production" of them "could reasonably be expected to interfere with enforcement proceedings." 5 U.S.C. § 552(b)(7)(A) (2000). Attorneys filed cross-appeals. Upon *de novo* review, we agree with the district court that the detention information is properly covered by Exemption 7(A); but we further hold that Exemption 7(A) justifies withholding the names of the detainees and their attorneys. . . . We therefore affirm in part, reverse in part, and remand the case to the district court for the entry of a judgment of dismissal.

I. Background

A. The Investigation

Consistent with the mutual decision of the parties to seek resolution to this controversy on summary judgment, the facts are not in serious dispute. In response to the terrorist attacks of September 11, 2001, President George W. Bush ordered a worldwide investigation into those attacks and into "threats, conspiracies, and attempts to perpetrate terrorist acts against United States citizens and interests." The Department of Justice, defendant in this action, has been conducting the investigation in conjunction with other federal, state and local agencies. The investigation continues today.

In the course of the post-September 11 investigation, the government interviewed over one thousand individuals about whom concern had arisen. The concerns related to some of these individuals were resolved by the interviews, and no further action was taken with respect to them. Other interviews resulted in the interviewees being detained. As relevant here, these detainees fall into three general categories.

The first category of detainees consists of individuals who were questioned in the course of the investigation and detained by the INS for violation of the immigration laws (INS detainees). INS detainees were initially questioned because there were "indications that they might have connections with, or possess information pertaining to, terrorist activity against the United States including particularly the September 11 attacks and/or the individuals or organizations who perpetrated them." Based on the initial questioning, each INS detainee was determined to have violated immigration law; some of the INS detainees were also determined to "have links to other facets of the investigation." Over 700 individuals were detained on INS charges. As of June 13, 2002, only seventy-four remained in custody. Many have been deported.

INS detainees have had access to counsel, and the INS has provided detainees with lists of attorneys willing to represent them, as required by 8 U.S.C. § 1229(b)(2) (2000). INS detainees have had access to the courts to file *habeas corpus* petitions. They have also been free to disclose their names to the public.

The second category of detainees consists of individuals held on federal criminal charges (criminal detainees). The government asserts that none of these detainees can be eliminated as a source of probative information until after the investigation is completed. According to the most recent information released by the Department of Justice, 134 individuals have been detained on federal criminal charges in the post-September 11 investigation; 99 of these have been found guilty either through pleas or trials. While many of the crimes bear no direct connection to terrorism, several criminal detainees have been charged with terrorism-related crimes, and many others have been charged with visa or passport forgery, perjury, identification fraud, and illegal possession of weapons. Zacarias Moussaoui, presently on trial for participating in the September 11 attacks, is among those who were detained on criminal charges.

The third category consists of persons detained after a judge issued a material witness warrant to secure their testimony before a grand jury, pursuant to the material witness statute, 18 U.S.C. § 3144 (2000) (material witness detainees). Each material witness detainee was believed to have information material to the events of September 11. The district courts before which these material witnesses have appeared have issued sealing orders that prohibit the government from releasing any information about the proceedings. The government has not revealed how many individuals were detained on material witness warrants. At least two individuals initially held as material witnesses are now being held for alleged terrorist activity.

The criminal detainees and material witness detainees are free to retain counsel and have been provided court-appointed counsel if they cannot afford representation, as required by the Sixth Amendment to the Constitution. In sum, each of the detainees has had access to counsel, access to the courts, and freedom to contact the press or the public at large.

B. The Litigation

On October 29, 2001, plaintiffs submitted a FOIA request to the Department of Justice seeking the following information about each detainee: 1) name and citizenship status; 2) location of arrest and place of detention; 3) date of detention/arrest, date any charges were filed, and the date of release; 4) nature of charges or basis for detention, and the disposition of such charges or basis; 5) names and addresses of lawyers representing any detainees; 6) identities of any courts which have been requested to enter orders sealing any proceedings in connection with any detainees, copies of any such orders, and the legal authorities relied upon by the government in seeking the sealing orders; 7) all policy directives or guidance issued to officials about making public statements or disclosures about these individuals or about the sealing of judicial or immigration proceedings. To support its FOIA request, plaintiffs cited press reports about mistreatment of the detainees, which plaintiffs claimed raised serious questions about "deprivations of fundamental due process, including imprisonment without probable cause, interference with the right to counsel, and threats of serious bodily injury."

In response to plaintiffs' FOIA request, the government released some information, but withheld much of the information requested. As to INS detainees, the government withheld the detainees' names, locations of arrest and detention, the dates of release, and the names of lawyers. As to criminal detainees, the government withheld the dates and locations of arrest and detention, the dates of release, and the citizenship status of each detainee. The government withheld all requested information with respect to material witnesses. Although the government has refused to disclose a comprehensive list of detainees' names and other detention information sought by plaintiffs, the government has from time to time publicly revealed names and information of the type sought by plaintiffs regarding a few individual detainees, particularly those found to have some connection to terrorism.

On December 5, 2001, plaintiffs filed this action in district court seeking to compel release of the withheld information pursuant to the Freedom of Information Act, 5 U.S.C. § 552. Plaintiffs also argued that the First Amendment, as interpreted in *Richmond Newspapers, Inc. v. Virginia*, 448 U.S. 555 (1980) and its progeny, and the common law doctrine of access to public records require the government to disclose the names and detention information of the detainees.

The parties filed cross-motions for summary judgment. In its motion, the government contended that FOIA Exemptions 7(A), 7(C), and 7(F), 5 U.S.C. § 552(b)(7)(A), (C) & (F), allow the government to withhold the requested documents as to all three categories of detainees. These exemptions permit withholding information "compiled for law enforcement purposes" whenever disclosure:

(A) could reasonably be expected to interfere with enforcement proceedings, . . . (C) could reasonably be expected to constitute an unwarranted invasion of personal privacy, . . . or (F) could reasonably be expected to endanger the life or physical safety of any individual.

5 U.S.C. § 552(b)(7)(A), (C), (F). As to the material witness detainees, the government also invoked Exemption 3, 5 U.S.C. § 552(b)(3), which exempts from FOIA requirements matters that are "specifically exempted from disclosure by [other statutes] . . .," contending that Federal Rule of Criminal Procedure 6(e), which limits the disclosure of grand jury matters, bars the release of information concerning material witnesses. . . .

As to Exemption 7(A), the declarations state that release of the requested information could hamper the ongoing investigation by leading to the identification of detainees by terrorist groups, resulting in terrorists either intimidating or cutting off communication with the detainees; by revealing the progress and direction of the ongoing investigation, thus allowing terrorists to impede or evade the investigation; and by enabling terrorists to create false or misleading evidence. As to Exemption 7(C), the declarations assert that the detainees have a substantial privacy interest in their names and detention information because release of this information would associate detainees with the September 11 attacks, thus injuring detainees' reputations and possibly endangering detainees' personal safety. Finally, as to Exemption 7(F), the government's declarations contend that release of the information could endanger the public safety by making terrorist attacks more likely and could endanger the safety of individual detainees by making them more vulnerable to attack from terrorist organizations. For these same reasons, the counterterrorism officials state that the names of the detainees' lawyers should also be withheld.

C. The Judgment

On August 2, 2002, the district court rendered its decision, ruling in part for the plaintiffs and in part for the government. Briefly put, the court ordered the government to disclose the names of the detainees and detainees' lawyers, but held that the government was entitled to withhold all other detention information under Exemptions 7(A) and 7(F).

Addressing the names of the detainees, the court held that disclosure could not reasonably be expected to interfere with ongoing enforcement proceedings, and thus the names were not exempt under 7(A). The court rejected the government's argument that disclosure of detainees' names would deter them from cooperating with the government because terrorist groups likely already know which of their cell members have been detained. Moreover, the court reasoned that the government's voluntary disclosure of the names of several detainees undermined the force of its argument about the harms resulting from disclosure. The court further held that "the government has not met its burden of establishing a 'rational link' between the harms alleged and disclosure" because its declarations provided no evidence that the detainees actually have any connection to, or knowledge of, terrorist activity.

The court next rejected the government's 7(A) argument that disclosure of names would allow terrorist groups to map the course of, and thus impede, its investigation. The government had advanced a "mosaic" argument, contending that the court should consider the aggregate release of the names under 7(A) rather than the release of each in isolation, on the reasoning that the release of the names *in toto* could assist terrorists in piecing together the course, direction and focus of the investigation. The district court rejected this argument, holding, *inter alia*, as a matter of law that FOIA Exemption 7(A) requires an individualized assessment of disclosure, and that the government's mosaic theory could not justify a blanket exclusion of information under Exemption 7(A). In the district court's view, the mosaic theory is only cognizable under Exemption 1, which protects information authorized by Executive Order to be kept secret in the interest of national defense or foreign policy. The court further rejected the government's final 7(A) argument, concluding that there was insufficient evidence that disclosure would enable terrorist groups to create false and misleading evidence.

Turning to Exemptions 7(C) and 7(F), the court rejected the government's claims, holding that the admittedly substantial privacy and safety interests of the detainees do not outweigh the vital public interest in ensuring that the government is not abusing its power. The court noted that plaintiffs have raised "grave concerns" about the mistreatment of detainees and have provided evidence of alleged mistreatment in the form of media reports, and firsthand accounts given to Congress and human rights groups. While rejecting the government's attempt to withhold detainees' names, the court ruled that it would permit detainees to opt out of disclosure by submitting a signed declaration within fifteen days. The court did not address the government's argument that disclosure could harm public safety.

Having rejected the government's Exemption 7 claims, the court further held that Exemption 3 does not bar the release of the names of material witnesses. Specifically, the court held that Exemption 3 does not apply, reasoning Federal Rule of Criminal Procedure 6(e) does not bar the disclosure of the identities of persons detained as material witnesses, but only bars "disclosure of a matter occurring before a grand jury." Fed.R.Crim.P. 6(e)(6). The government's evidence did not establish that any of the detainees were actual grand jury witnesses or were scheduled to testify before a grand jury. Further, the government's disclosure of the identities of twenty-six material witness detainees undercut its argument that disclosure is barred by statute. As to the government's contention that court sealing orders prevent the government from releasing the names of material witnesses, the court ordered the government to submit such orders for *in camera* review or to submit a "supplemental affidavit explaining the nature and legal basis for these sealing orders."

For reasons not unlike its rejection of the government's attempt to withhold the names of detainees, the court also held that the government must reveal the names of the detainees' lawyers.[1] The court determined that the names of the attorneys were not covered by Exemptions 7(A), 7(C), or 7(F) for the same reason it had rejected the government's attempt to withhold the names of detainees; because attorneys have no expectation of anonymity; and because any concerns about physical danger were purely speculative.

Turning to the other information sought by plaintiffs — the dates and locations of arrest, detention, and release — the court granted summary judgment for the government on its claim that such detention information was covered under 7(A) and 7(F). The court credited the counterterrorism officials' judgment that the detention information "would be particularly valuable to anyone attempting to discern patterns in the Government's investigation and strategy," and that disclosure would make detention facilities "vulnerable to retaliatory attacks." Finally, the court rejected plaintiffs' claim that the First Amendment and common law entitle them to the dates and locations of arrest, detention, and release.

The court ordered the government to release the names of detainees and their lawyers in fifteen days, subject to the right of detainees to opt out of disclosure. On August 15, 2002, the district court stayed its order pending appeal. . . .

II. The FOIA Claims

We review *de novo* the district court's grant of summary judgment, and therefore consider anew each of the claims and defenses advanced before the

---

[1] The government has withheld the names of the attorneys for both INS detainees and material witness detainees; it has revealed the names of the attorneys for the criminally charged detainees.

district court. We turn first to the government's claims of exemption from disclosure under FOIA of the names of the detainees and their lawyers.

A. Names of Detainees

"Public access to government documents" is the "fundamental principle" that animates FOIA. "Congress recognized, however, that public disclosure is not always in the public interest." Accordingly, FOIA represents a balance struck by Congress between the public's right to know and the government's legitimate interest in keeping certain information confidential. To that end, FOIA mandates disclosure of government records unless the requested information falls within one of nine enumerated exemptions, *see* 5 U.S.C. § 552(b). While these exemptions are to be "narrowly construed," courts must not fail to give them "a meaningful reach and application," The government bears the burden of proving that the withheld information falls within the exemptions it invokes. 5 U.S.C. § 552(a)(4)(b).

The government invokes four exemptions — 7(A), 7(C), 7(F), and 3 — to shield the names of detainees from disclosure. Upon review, we hold that Exemption 7(A) was properly invoked to withhold the names of the detainees and their lawyers. Finding the names protected under 7(A), we need not address the other exemptions invoked by the government and reserve judgment on whether they too would support withholding the names.

Exemption 7(A) allows an agency to withhold "records or information compiled for law enforcement purposes, but only to the extent that the production of such law enforcement records or information . . . could reasonably be expected to interfere with enforcement proceedings." 5 U.S.C. § 552(b)(7)(A). In enacting this exemption, "Congress recognized that law enforcement agencies had legitimate needs to keep certain records confidential, lest the agencies be hindered in their investigations." Exemption 7(A) does not require a presently pending "enforcement proceeding." Rather, as the district court correctly noted, it is sufficient that the government's ongoing September 11 terrorism investigation is likely to lead to such proceedings.

The threshold question here is whether the names of detainees were "compiled for law enforcement purposes." 5 U.S.C. § 552(b)(7). Because the DOJ is an agency "specializ[ing] in law enforcement," its claim of a law enforcement purpose is entitled to deference. To establish a law enforcement purpose, DOJ's declarations must establish (1) "a rational nexus between the investigation and one of the agency's law enforcement duties;" and (2) "a connection between an individual or incident and a possible security risk or violation of federal law." The government's proffer easily meets this standard. The terrorism investigation is one of DOJ's chief "law enforcement duties" at this time, and the investigation concerns a heinous violation of federal law as well as a breach of this nation's security. Moreover, the names of the detainees and their connection to the investigation came to the government's attention as a result of that law enforcement investigation.

Nonetheless, plaintiffs contend that detainees' names fall outside Exemption 7 because the names are contained in arrest warrants, INS charging documents, and jail records. Since these documents have traditionally been public, plaintiffs contend, Exemption 7 should not be construed to allow withholding of the names. We disagree. Plaintiffs are seeking a comprehensive listing of individuals detained during the post-September 11 investigation. The names have been compiled for the "law enforcement purpose" of successfully prosecuting the terrorism investigation. As compiled, they constitute a comprehensive diagram of the law enforcement investigation after September 11. Clearly this is information compiled for law enforcement purposes.

Next, plaintiffs urge that Exemption 7(A) does not apply because disclosure is not "reasonably likely to interfere with enforcement proceedings." 5 U.S.C. § 552(b)(7)(A). We disagree. Under Exemption 7(A), the government has the burden of demonstrating a reasonable likelihood of interference with the terrorism investigation. The government's declarations, viewed in light of the appropriate deference to the executive on issues of national security, satisfy this burden.

It is well-established that a court may rely on government affidavits to support the withholding of documents under FOIA exemptions, and that we review the government's justifications therein *de novo*, 5 U.S.C. § 552(a)(4)(B). It is equally well-established that the judiciary owes some measure of deference to the executive in cases implicating national security, a uniquely executive purview. *See, e.g., Zadvydas v. Davis*, 533 U.S. 678, 696 (2001) (noting that "terrorism or other special circumstances" might warrant "heightened deference to the judgments of the political branches"); *Dep't of the Navy v. Egan*, 484 U.S. 518, 530 (1988) ("courts traditionally have been reluctant to intrude upon the authority of the executive in military and national security affairs"). Indeed, both the Supreme Court and this Court have expressly recognized the propriety of deference to the executive in the context of FOIA claims which implicate national security.

In *CIA v. Sims*, 471 U.S. 159 (1985), the Supreme Court examined the CIA's claims that the names and institutional affiliations of certain researchers in a government-sponsored behavior modification program were exempt from disclosure under FOIA Exemption 3, 5 U.S.C. § 552(b)(3). The agency claimed that the information was protected from disclosure by a statute charging the CIA to prevent unauthorized disclosure of "intelligence sources and methods," 50 U.S.C. § 403(d)(3). In accepting the CIA Director's judgment that disclosure would reveal intelligence sources and methods, the Court explained that "[t]he decisions of the Director, who must of course be familiar with 'the whole picture,' as judges are not, are worthy of great deference given the magnitude of the national security interests and potential risks at stake." *Sims*, 471 U.S. at 179. The Court further held that "it is the responsibility of the Director of Central Intelligence, not that of the judiciary, to weigh the variety of subtle and complex factors in determining whether disclosure of information may lead to an unacceptable risk of compromising the Agency's intelligence-gathering process."

The same is true of the Justice Department officials in charge of the present investigation. We have consistently reiterated the principle of deference to the executive in the FOIA context when national security concerns are implicated. . . .

Given this weight of authority counseling deference in national security matters, we owe deference to the government's judgments contained in its affidavits. Just as we have deferred to the executive when it invokes FOIA Exemptions 1 and 3, we owe the same deference under Exemption 7(A) in appropriate cases, such as this one. . . .

The need for deference in this case is just as strong as in earlier cases. America faces an enemy just as real as its former Cold War foes, with capabilities beyond the capacity of the judiciary to explore. Exemption 7(A) explicitly requires a predictive judgment of the harm that will result from disclosure of information, permitting withholding when it "could reasonably be expected" that the harm will result. 5 U.S.C. § 552(b)(7)(A). It is abundantly clear that the government's top counterterrorism officials are well-suited to make this predictive judgment. Conversely, the judiciary is in an extremely poor position to second-guess the executive's judgment in this area of national security. We therefore reject any attempt to artificially limit the long-recognized deference to the executive on national security issues. Judicial deference depends on the substance of the danger posed by disclosure — that is, harm to the national security — not the FOIA exemption invoked.

In light of the deference mandated by the separation of powers and Supreme Court precedent, we hold that the government's expectation that disclosure of the detainees' names would enable al Qaeda or other terrorist groups to map the course of the investigation and thus develop the means to impede it is reasonable. A complete list of names informing terrorists of every suspect detained by the government at any point during the September 11 investigation would give terrorist organizations a composite picture of the government investigation, and since these organizations would generally know the activities and locations of its members on or about September 11, disclosure would inform terrorists of both the substantive and geographic focus of the investigation. Moreover, disclosure would inform terrorists which of their members were compromised by the investigation, and which were not. This information could allow terrorists to better evade the ongoing investigation and more easily formulate or revise counter-efforts. In short, the "records could reveal much about the focus and scope of the [agency's] investigation, and are thus precisely the sort of information exemption 7(A) allows an agency to keep secret."

As the district court noted, courts have relied on similar mosaic arguments in the context of national security. In *Sims*, for example, the Supreme Court cautioned that "bits and pieces" of data " 'may aid in piecing together bits of other information even when the individual piece is not of obvious importance in itself.' " Thus, "[w]hat may seem trivial to the uninformed, may appear of great moment to one who has a broad view of the scene and may put the questioned item of information in its proper context." (quotations omitted). Such a danger is present here. While the name of any individual detainee may appear innocuous or trivial, it could be of great use to al Qaeda in plotting future terrorist attacks or intimidating witnesses in the present investigation. Importantly, plaintiffs here do not request "bits and pieces" of information, but rather seek the names of every single individual detained in the course of the government's terrorism investigation. It is more than reasonable to expect that disclosing the name of every individual detained in the post-September 11 terrorism investigation would interfere with that investig

Similarly, the government's judgment that disclosure would deter or hinder cooperation by detainees is reasonable. The government reasonably predicts that if terrorists learn one of their members has been detained, they would attempt to deter any further cooperation by that member through intimidation, physical coercion, or by cutting off all contact with the detainee. A terrorist organization may even seek to hunt down detainees (or their families) who are not members of the organization, but who the terrorists know may have valuable information about the organization.

On numerous occasions, both the Supreme Court and this Court have found government declarations expressing the likelihood of witness intimidation and evidence tampering sufficient to justify withholding of witnesses' names under Exemption 7(A). . . .

For several reasons, plaintiffs contend that we should reject the government's predictive judgments of the harms that would result from disclosure. First, they argue that terrorist organizations likely already know which of their members have been detained. We have no way of assessing that likelihood. Moreover, even if terrorist organizations know about some of their members who were detained, a complete list of detainees could still have great value in confirming the status of their members. For example, an organization may be unaware of a member who was detained briefly and then released, but remains subject to continuing government surveillance. After disclosure, this detainee could be irreparably compromised as a source of information.

More importantly, some detainees may not be members of terrorist organizations, but may nonetheless have been detained on INS or material witness warrants as having information about terrorists. Terrorist organizations are less likely to be aware of such individuals' status as detainees. Such detainees could be acquaintances of the September 11 terrorists, or members of the same community groups or mosques. These detainees, fearing retribution or stigma, would be less likely to cooperate with the investigation if their names are disclosed. Moreover, tracking down the background and location of these detainees could give terrorists insights into the investigation they would otherwise be unlikely to have. After disclosure, terrorist organizations could attempt to intimidate these detainees or their families, or feed the detainees false or misleading information. It is important to remember that many of these detainees have been released at this time and are thus especially vulnerable to intimidation or coercion. While the detainees have been free to disclose their names to the press or public, it is telling that so few have come forward, perhaps for fear of this very intimidation.

We further note the impact disclosure could have on the government's investigation going forward. A potential witness or informant may be much less likely to come forward and cooperate with the investigation if he believes his name will be made public.

Plaintiffs next argue that the government's predictive judgment is undermined by the government's disclosure of some of the detainees' names. The Supreme Court confronted a similar argument in *Sims*, in which respondents contended that "because the Agency has already revealed the names of many of the institutions at which [behavior modification] research was performed, the Agency is somehow estopped from withholding the names of others." In rejecting the argument, the Court stated that "[t]his suggestion overlooks the political realities of intelligence operations in which, among other things, our Government may choose to release information deliberately to 'send a message' to allies or adversaries." We likewise reject the plaintiffs' version of this discredited argument. The disclosure of a few pieces of information in no way lessens the government's argument that complete disclosure would provide a composite picture of its investigation and have negative effects on the investigation. Furthermore, . . . strategic disclosures can be important weapons in the government's arsenal during a law enforcement investigation. The court should not second-guess the executive's judgment in this area. "[I]t is the responsibility of the [executive] not that of the judiciary" to determine when to disclose information that may compromise intelligence sources and methods.

Contrary to plaintiffs' claims, the government's submissions easily establish an adequate connection between both the material witness and the INS detainees and terrorism to warrant full application of the deference principle. First, all material witness detainees have been held on warrants issued by a federal judge pursuant to 18 U.S.C. § 3144. Under this statute, a federal judge may issue a material witness warrant based on an affidavit stating that the witness has information relevant to an ongoing criminal investigation. Consequently, material witness detainees have been found by a federal judge to have relevant knowledge about the terrorism investigation. It is therefore reasonable to assume that disclosure of their names could impede the government's use of these potentially valuable witnesses.

As to the INS detainees, the government states that they were

> originally questioned because there were indications that they might have connections with, or possess information pertaining to, terrorist activity against the United States including particularly the September 11 attacks and/or the individuals and organizations who perpetrated them. For example, they may have been questioned because they were identified as having interacted with the hijackers, or were believed to have information relating to other aspects of the investigation.

"Other INS detainees may have been questioned because of their association with an organization believed to be involved in providing material support to terrorist organizations." Moreover, "[i]n the course of questioning them, law enforcement agents determined, often from the subjects themselves, that they were in violation of federal immigration laws, and, in some instances also determined that they had links to other facets of the investigation." Furthermore, the Watson Declaration speaks of the INS detainees being subject to "public hearings involving evidence about terrorist links," and states that "concerns remain" about links to terrorism, The clear import of the declarations is that many of the detainees have links to terrorism. This comes as no surprise given that the detainees were apprehended during the course of a terrorism investigation, and given that several detainees have been charged with federal terrorism crimes or held as enemy combatants. Accordingly, we conclude that the evidence presented in the declarations is sufficient to show a rational link between disclosure and the harms alleged. . . .

B. Identity of Counsel

We next address whether the government properly withheld the names of the attorneys for INS and material witness detainees under Exemptions 7(A), 7(C), and 7(F). As with the identities of the detainees, we hold that their attorneys' names are also protected from disclosure by Exemption 7(A).

The government contends that a list of attorneys for the detainees would facilitate the easy compilation of a list of all detainees, and all of the dangers flowing therefrom. It is more than reasonable to assume that plaintiffs and amici press organizations would attempt to contact detainees' attorneys and compile a list of all detainees. As discussed above, if such a list fell into the hands of al Qaeda, the consequences could be disastrous. Having accepted the government's predictive judgments about the dangers of disclosing a comprehensive list of detainees, we also defer to its prediction that disclosure of attorneys' names involves the same danger.

C. Other Detention Information

Having held that the government properly withheld the names of the detainees pursuant to Exemption 7(A), we easily affirm the portion of the district court's ruling that allowed withholding, under Exemption 7(A), of the more comprehensive detention information sought by plaintiffs.

As outlined above, plaintiffs sought the dates and locations of arrest, detention, and release for each of the detainees. Even more than disclosure of the identities of detainees, the information requested here would provide a complete roadmap of the government's investigation. Knowing when and where each individual was arrested would provide a chronological and geographical picture of the government investigation. Terrorists could learn from this information not only where the government focused its investigation but how that investigation progressed step by step. Armed with that knowledge, they could then reach such conclusions as, for example, which cells had been compromised, and which individuals had been cooperative with the United States. They might well be able to derive conclusions as to how more adequately secure their clandestine operations in future terrorist undertakings. Similarly, knowing where each individual is presently held could facilitate communication between terrorist organizations and detainees and the attendant intimidation of witnesses and fabrication of evidence. As explained in detail above, these impediments to an ongoing law enforcement investigation are precisely what Exemption 7(A) was enacted to preclude. Accordingly, we affirm the district court and hold that the government properly withheld information about the dates and locations of arrest, detention, and release for each detainee.

III. Alternative Grounds

[The majority rejected plaintiff's alternative grounds for disclosure based on the First Amendment and a common law right of access to government information.]

IV. Conclusion

For the reasons set forth above, we conclude that the government was entitled to withhold under FOIA Exemption 7(A) the names of INS detainees and those detained as material witnesses in the course of the post-September 11 terrorism investigation; the dates and locations of arrest, detention, and release of all detainees, including those charged with federal crimes; and the names of counsel for detainees. Finally, neither the First Amendment nor federal common law requires the government to disclose the information sought by plaintiffs.

Affirmed in part, reversed in part and remanded.

TATEL, CIRCUIT JUDGE, dissenting:

. . . .

I.

I begin with some preliminary observations about the principles that govern this case. First, no one can doubt that uniquely compelling governmental interests are at stake: the government's need to respond to the September 11 attacks — unquestionably the worst ever acts of terrorism on American soil — and its ability to defend the nation against future acts of terrorism. But although this court overlooks it, there is another compelling interest at stake in this case: the public's interest in knowing whether the government, in responding to the attacks, is violating the constitutional rights of the hundreds of persons whom it has detained in connection with its terrorism investigation — by, as the plaintiffs allege, detaining them mainly because of their religion or ethnicity, holding them in custody for extended periods without charge, or preventing them from seeking or communicating with legal counsel. The government claims that the detainees have access to counsel and freedom to contact whomever they wish, but the public has a fundamental interest in being able to examine the veracity of such claims. Just as the government has a compelling interest in ensuring citizens' safety, so do citizens have a compelling interest in ensuring that their government does not, in discharging its duties, abuse one of its most awesome powers, the power to arrest and jail.

Second, while the governmental interests in this case may be uniquely compelling, the legal principles that govern its resolution are not at all unique. The court's opinion emphasizes the national-security implications of the September 11 investigation, but as the government conceded at oral argument, this case is not just about September 11. The law that governs this case is the same law that applies whenever the government's need for confidentiality in a law enforcement investigation runs up against the public's right to know "what [its] government is up to." In all such situations, FOIA fully accommodates the government's concerns about the harms that might arise from the release of information pertaining to its investigations. To be sure, the statute strongly favors openness, since Congress recognized that an informed citizenry is "vital to the functioning of a democratic society, needed to check against corruption and to hold the governors accountable to the governed." But Congress also recognized that "legitimate governmental and private interests could be harmed by release of certain types of information." It therefore "provided . . . specific exemptions under which disclosure could be refused," including the four exemptions relevant to this case. . . . But "'these limited exemptions do not obscure the basic policy that disclosure, not secrecy, is the dominant objective of the Act.'" Accordingly, courts must "narrowly construe []" the exemptions, and "the burden is on the agency to sustain its action." The government may in some situations withhold entire categories of records from disclosure, as it seeks to do here by withholding names and other information pertaining to all terrorism-investigation detainees. In order to sustain its burden, however, the government must demonstrate that "the range of circumstances included in the category 'characteristically support[s] an inference' that the statutory requirements for exemption are satisfied."

The third principle relates to the level of deference we owe the government. Invoking the "heightened deference to the judgments of the political branches with respect to matters of national security," the government refuses to identify the specific categories of information that would actually interfere with its investigation, but rather asks us simply to trust its judgment. This court obeys, declaring that "the judiciary is in an extremely poor position to second-guess the executive's judgment in this area of national security." But requiring agencies to make the detailed showing FOIA requires is not second-guessing their judgment about matters within their expertise. And in any event, this court is also in an extremely poor position to second-guess the legislature's judgment that the judiciary must play a meaningful role in reviewing FOIA exemption requests. Neither FOIA itself nor this circuit's interpretation of the statute authorizes the court to invoke the phrase "national security" to relieve the government of its burden of justifying its refusal to release information under FOIA. . . .

NOTES AND QUESTIONS

10-6. Why should there be a national security exemption to FOIA? How would you draft the exemption, if you believe there should be one? What do you think of the interpretation of this exemption, as expressed by Executive Order 12,065?

10-7. What is the purpose of exemption 7? When does that purpose cease to exist?

10-8. Why were the petitioners interested in obtaining the information sought in *Wolfe v. HHS*? Were they eager to add yet another dimension to a rulemaking record they wished to attack? What is the relationship of this case to the rulemaking process and what is the import of this case in that regard?

10-9. What assumptions do the various opinions make regarding the relationship of HHS, FDA and OMB? Is OMB likely to be the most powerful of these three agencies?

10-10. What should the scope of exemption 5 be? What are its underlying policies and goals? Is Judge Bork true to these goals and purposes? What factors influence his decision? The need to protect brainstorming within an agency? The need to protect executive deliberations? The need to protect executive rulemaking?

10-11. What impact did 9/11 have on the court's reasoning in *Center for National Security Studies*?

10-12. Is the majority's categorical all or nothing approach to Exemption 7(A) justified? Were there any parts of the plaintiff's request that could have been provided?

10-13. How much deference does the majority give to executive determinations of national security? How much deference should it give? On what basis, does the dissent differ in its approach to these issues?

10-14. In the aftermath of the September 11, 2001, attack on the World Trade Center, the federal government has significantly restricted the information it makes available to the public — lest the government provide information that facilitates another terrorist attack. *See generally* Bradley Pack, Note, *FOIA Frustration: Access to Government Records Under the Bush Administration*, 46 ARIZ. L. REV. 815 (2004); Kristen E. Uhl, Note, *The Freedom of Information Act Post-9/11: Balancing the Public's Right to Know, Critical Infrastructure Protection, and Homeland Security*, 53 AM. U. L. REV. 261 (2003).

The Department of Justice has announced that it will defend in court an agency's decision to withhold information so long as the denial has a "sound legal basis or [release of the information] present[s] an unwarranted risk of adverse impact on the ability of other agencies to protect other important records." Memorandum from John Ashcroft, Attorney General, to Heads of All Federal Departments and Agencies re: The Freedom of Information Act (Oct. 12, 2001), available at http://www.usdoj.gov/oip/foiapost/2001foiapost19.htm. This represented a change from the policy under the Clinton administration, which had "adopted the policy that the Justice Department would only defend an assertion of a FOIA exemption by agencies 'in those cases where the agency reasonably foresees that disclosure would be harmful to an interest protected by that exemption.'" William A. Wilcox, Jr., *Access to Environmental Information in the United States and the United Kingdom*, 23 LOY. L.A. INT'L & COMP. L. REV. 121, 215 (2001).

10-15. The Homeland Security Act of 2002, Pub. L. No. 107-296, 116 Stat. 2135, created a new FOIA exemption, the critical infrastructure information exemption, 6 U.S.C. § 133 (2005). It provides as follows:

> § 133. Protection of voluntarily shared critical infrastructure information

(a) Protection

(1) In general. Notwithstanding any other provision of law, critical infrastructure information (including the identity of the submitting person or entity) that is voluntarily submitted to a covered Federal agency for use by that agency regarding the security of critical infrastructure and protected systems, analysis, warning, interdependency study, recovery, reconstitution, or other informational purpose, when accompanied by an express statement specified in paragraph (2) —

(A) shall be exempt from disclosure under section 552 of Title 5 (commonly referred to as the Freedom of Information Act) . . . .

(2) Express statement. For purposes of paragraph (1), the term "express statement", with respect to information or records, means —

(A) in the case of written information or records, a written marking on the information or records substantially similar to the following: "This information is voluntarily submitted to the Federal Government in expectation of protection from disclosure as provided by the provisions of the Critical Infrastructure Information Act of 2002."; or

(B) in the case of oral information, a similar written statement submitted within a reasonable period following the oral communication. . . .

Note that the exemption covers "information" rather than "records," and also note that the exemption does not apply to information that an entity is required to submit to the federal government, 6 C.F.R. § 29.3 (2005).

[D] Reverse FOIA Suits

Given that citizens can seek to obtain information from the Government, can those who submitted that information prevent its disclosure? What are the rights of submitters of information under FOIA? Consider the following case.

CHRYSLER CORP. v. BROWN

United States Supreme Court
441 U.S. 281 (1979)

MR. JUSTICE REHNQUIST delivered the opinion of the Court.

The expanding range of federal regulatory activity and growth in the Government sector of the economy have increased federal agencies' demands for information about the activities of private individuals and corporations. These developments have paralleled a related concern about secrecy in Government and abuse of power. The Freedom of Information Act (hereinafter FOIA) was a response to this concern, but it has also had a largely unforeseen tendency to exacerbate the uneasiness of those who comply with governmental demands for information. For under the FOIA third parties have been able to obtain Government files containing information submitted by corporations and individuals who thought that the information would be held in confidence.

This case belongs to a class that has been popularly denominated "reverse-FOIA" suits. The Chrysler Corp. (hereinafter Chrysler) seeks to enjoin agency disclosure on the grounds that it is inconsistent with the FOIA and 18 U.S.C. § 1905, a criminal statute with origins in the 19th century that proscribes disclosure of certain classes of business and personal information. We agree with the Court of Appeals for the Third Circuit that the FOIA is purely a disclosure statute and affords Chrysler no private right of action to enjoin agency disclosure. But we cannot agree with that court's conclusion that this disclosure is "authorized by law" within the meaning of § 1905. Therefore, we vacate the Court of Appeals' judgment and remand so that it can consider whether the documents at issue in this case fall within the terms of § 1905. . . .

In contending that the FOIA bars disclosure of the requested equal employment opportunity information, Chrysler relies on the Act's nine exemptions and argues that they require an agency to withhold exempted material. In this case it relies specifically on Exemption 4:

"(b) [FOIA] does not apply to matters that are —

. . . (4) trade secrets and commercial or financial information obtained from a person and privileged or confidential. . . ."

Chrysler contends that the nine exemptions in general, and Exemption 4 in particular, reflect a sensitivity to the privacy interests of private individuals and nongovernmental entities. That contention may be conceded without inexorably requiring the conclusion that the exemptions impose affirmative duties on an agency to withhold information sought. In fact, that conclusion is not supported by the language, logic, or history of the Act.

The organization of the Act is straightforward. Subsection (a), 5 U.S.C. § 552(a), places a general obligation on the agency to make information available to the public and sets out specific modes of disclosure for certain classes of information. Subsection (b), which lists the exemptions, simply states that the specified material is not subject to the disclosure obligations set out in subsection (a). By its terms, subsection (b) demarcates the agency's obligation to disclose; it does not foreclose disclosure.

That the FOIA is exclusively a disclosure statute is, perhaps, demonstrated most convincingly by examining its provision for judicial relief. Subsection (a)(4)(B) gives federal district courts "jurisdiction to enjoin the agency from withholding agency records and to order the production of any agency records improperly withheld from the complainant." 5 U.S.C. § 552(a)(4)(B). That provision does not give the authority to bar disclosure, and thus fortifies our belief that Chrysler, and courts which have shared its view, have incorrectly interpreted the exemption provisions of the FOIA. The Act is an attempt to meet the demand for open government while preserving workable confidentiality in governmental decisionmaking. Congress appreciated that, with the expanding sphere of governmental regulation and enterprise, much of the information within Government files has been submitted by private entities seeking Government contracts or responding to unconditional reporting obligations imposed by law. There was sentiment that Government agencies should have the latitude, in certain circumstances, to afford the confidentiality desired by these submitters. But the congressional concern was with the agency's need or preference for confidentiality; the FOIA by itself protects the submitters' interest in confidentiality only to the extent that this interest is endorsed by the agency collecting the information.

Enlarged access to governmental information undoubtedly cuts against the privacy concerns of nongovernmental entities, and as a matter of policy some balancing and accommodation may well be desirable. We simply hold here that Congress did not design the FOIA exemptions to be mandatory bars to disclosure.[14]

III

Chrysler contends, however, that even if its suit for injunctive relief cannot be based on the FOIA, such an action can be premised on the Trade Secrets Act, 18 U.S.C. § 1905. The Act provides:

"Whoever, being an officer or employee of the United States or of any department or agency thereof, publishes, divulges, discloses, or makes known in any manner or to any extent not authorized by law any information coming to him in the course of his employment or official duties or by reason of any examination or investigation made by, or return, report or record made to or filed with, such department or agency or officer or employee thereof, which information concerns or relates to the trade secrets, processes, operations, style of work, or apparatus, or to the identity, confidential statistical data, amount or source of any income, profits, losses, or expenditures of any person, firm, partnership, corporation, or association; or permits any income return or copy thereof or any book containing any abstract or particulars thereof to be seen or examined by any person except as provided by law; shall be fined not more than $1,000, or imprisoned not more than one year, or both; and shall be removed from office or employment."

---

[14] It is informative in this regard to compare the FOIA with the Privacy Act of 1974, 5 U.S.C. § 552a. In the latter Act, Congress explicitly requires agencies to withhold records about an individual from most third parties unless the subject gives his permission. Even more telling is 49 U.S.C. § 1357, a section which authorizes the Administrator of the FAA to take antihijacking measures, including research and development of protection devices.

"Notwithstanding [the FOIA], the Administrator shall prescribe such regulations as he may deem necessary to prohibit disclosure of any information obtained or developed in the conduct of research and development activities under this subsection if, in the opinion of the Administrator, the disclosure of such information —

"(B) would reveal trade secrets or privileged or confidential commercial or financial information obtained from any person. . . ." § 1357(d)(2)(B). . . .

There are necessarily two parts to Chrysler's argument: that § 1905 is applicable to the type of disclosure threatened in this case, and that it affords Chrysler a private right of action to obtain injunctive relief.

A

The Court of Appeals held that § 1905 was not applicable to the agency disclosure at issue here because such disclosure was "authorized by law" within the meaning of the Act. The court found the source of that authorization to be the OFCCP regulations that DLA relied on in deciding to disclose information on the Hamtramck and Newark plants. Chrysler contends here that these agency regulations are not "law" within the meaning of § 1905.

It has been established in a variety of contexts that properly promulgated, substantive agency regulations have the "force and effect of law." This doctrine is so well established that agency regulations implementing federal statutes have been held to pre-empt state law under the Supremacy Clause. It would therefore take a clear showing of contrary legislative intent before the phrase "authorized by law" in § 1905 could be held to have a narrower ambit than the traditional understanding.

The origins of the Trade Secrets Act can be traced to Rev. Stat. § 3167, an Act which barred unauthorized disclosure of specified business information by Government revenue officers. There is very little legislative history concerning the original bill, which was passed in 1864. It was re-enacted numerous times, with some modification, and remained part of the revenue laws until 1948. Congressional statements made at the time of these re-enactments indicate that Congress was primarily concerned with unauthorized disclosure of business information by feckless or corrupt revenue agents, for in the early days of the Bureau of Internal Revenue, it was the field agents who had substantial contact with confidential financial information.

In 1948, Rev. Stat. § 3167 was consolidated with two other statutes — involving the Tariff Commission and the Department of Commerce — to form the Trade Secrets Act. The statute governing the Tariff Commission was very similar to Rev. Stat. § 3167, and it explicitly bound members of the Commission as well as Commission employees. The Commerce Department statute embodied some differences in form. It was a mandate addressed to the Bureau of Foreign and Domestic Commerce and to its Director, but there was no reference to Bureau employees and it contained no criminal sanctions. Unlike the other statutes, it also had no exception for disclosures "authorized by law." In its effort to "consolidat[e]" the three statutes, Congress enacted § 1905 and essentially borrowed the form of Rev. Stat. § 3167 and the Tariff Commission statute. We find nothing in the legislative history of § 1905 and its predecessors which lends support to Chrysler's contention that Congress intended the phrase "authorized by law," as used in § 1905, to have a special, limited meaning.

Nor do we find anything in the legislative history to support the respondents' suggestion that § 1905 does not address formal agency action — *i.e.*, that it is essentially an "antileak" statute that does not bind the heads of governmental departments or agencies. That would require an expansive and unprecedented holding that any agency action directed or approved by an agency head is "authorized by law," regardless of the statutory authority for that action. . . .

In order for a regulation to have the "force and effect of law," it must have certain substantive characteristics and be the product of certain procedural requisites. The central distinction among agency regulations found in the APA is that between "substantive rules" on the one hand and "interpretative rules, general statements of policy, or rules of agency organization, procedure, or practice" on the other. A "substantive rule" is not defined in the APA, and other authoritative sources essentially offer definitions by negative inference. But in *Morton v. Ruiz,* 415 U.S. 199 (1974), we noted a characteristic inherent in the concept of a "substantive rule." We described a substantive rule — or a "legislative-type rule," as one "affecting individual rights and obligations." This characteristic is an important touchstone for distinguishing those rules that may be "binding" or have the "force of law."

That an agency regulation is "substantive," however, does not by itself give it the "force and effect of law." The legislative power of the United States is vested in the Congress, and the exercise of quasi-legislative authority by governmental departments and agencies must be rooted in a grant of such power by the Congress and subject to limitations which that body imposes. As this Court noted in *Batterton v. Francis,* 432 U.S. 416, 425 n. 9:

> "Legislative, or substantive, regulations are 'issued by an agency pursuant to statutory authority and . . . implement the statute, as, for example, the proxy rules issued by the Securities and Exchange Commission. . . . Such rules have the force and effect of law.'"

Likewise the promulgation of these regulations must conform with any procedural requirements imposed by Congress. For agency discretion is limited not only by substantive, statutory grants of authority, but also by the procedural requirements which "assure fairness and mature consideration of rules of general application." The pertinent procedural limitations in this case are those found in the APA.

The regulations relied on by the respondents in this case as providing "authoriz[ation] by law" within the meaning of § 1905 certainly affect individual rights and obligations; they govern the public's right to information in records obtained under Executive Order 11246 and the confidentiality rights of those who submit information to OFCCP and its compliance agencies. It is a much closer question, however, whether they are the product of a congressional grant of legislative authority. . . .

. . . We think that it is clear that when it enacted these statutes, Congress was not concerned with public disclosure of trade secrets or confidential business information, and, unless we were to hold that any federal statute that implies some authority to collect information must grant legislative authority to disclose that information to the public, it is simply not possible to find in these statutes a delegation of the disclosure authority asserted by the respondents here. . . . [The court went on to discuss certain procedural issues under the APA.]

B

We reject, however, Chrysler's contention that the Trade Secrets Act affords a private right of action to enjoin disclosure in violation of the statute. In *Cort v. Ash,* 422 U.S. 66 (1975), we noted that this Court has rarely implied a private right of action under a criminal statute, and where it has done so "there was at least a statutory basis for inferring that a civil cause of action of some sort lay in favor of someone." Nothing in § 1905 prompts such an inference. Nor are other pertinent circumstances outlined in *Cort* present here. As our review of the legislative history of § 1905 — or lack of same — might suggest, there is no indication of legislative intent to create a private right of action. Most importantly, a private right of action under § 1905 is not "necessary to make effective the congressional purpose," for we find that review of DLA's decision to disclose Chrysler's employment data is available under the APA.

IV

While Chrysler may not avail itself of any violations of the provisions of § 1905 in a separate cause of action, any such violations may have a dispositive effect on the outcome of judicial review of agency action pursuant to § 10 of the APA. Section 10(a) of the APA provides that "[a] person suffering legal wrong because of agency action, or adversely affected or aggrieved by agency action . . ., is entitled to judicial review thereof." Two exceptions to this general rule of reviewability are set out in § 10. Review is not available where "statutes preclude judicial review" or where "agency action is committed to agency discretion by law." 5 U.S.C. §§ 701(a)(1), (2). In *Citizens to Preserve Overton Park, Inc. v. Volpe,* 401 U.S. 402, 410 (1971), the Court held that the latter exception applies "where 'statutes are drawn in such broad terms that in a given case there is no law to apply'". . . . Were we simply confronted with the authorization in 5 U.S.C. § 301 to prescribe regulations regarding "the custody, use, and preservation of [agency] records, papers, and property," it would be difficult to derive any standards limiting agency conduct which might constitute "law to apply." But our discussion in Part III demonstrates that § 1905 and any "authoriz[ation] by law" contemplated by that section place substantive limits on agency action. Therefore, we conclude that DLA's decision to disclose the Chrysler reports is reviewable agency action and Chrysler is a person "adversely affected or aggrieved" within the meaning of § 10(a).

Both Chrysler and the respondents agree that there is APA review of DLA's decision. They disagree on the proper scope of review. Chrysler argues that there should be *de novo* review, while the respondents contend that such review is only available in extraordinary cases and this is not such a case.

The pertinent provisions of § 10(e) of the APA, 5 U.S.C. § 706, provide that a reviewing court shall

"(2) hold unlawful and set aside agency action, findings, and conclusions found to be —

"(A) arbitrary, capricious, an abuse of discretion, or otherwise not in accordance with law; . . .

"(F) unwarranted by the facts to the extent that the facts are subject to trial *de novo* by the reviewing court."

For the reasons previously stated, we believe any disclosure that violates § 1905 is "not in accordance with law" within the meaning of 5 U.S.C. § 706(2)(A). *De novo* review by the District Court is ordinarily not necessary to decide whether a contemplated disclosure runs afoul of § 1905. The District Court in this case concluded that disclosure of some of Chrysler's documents was barred by § 1905, but the Court of Appeals did not reach the issue. We shall therefore vacate the Court of Appeals' judgment and remand for further proceedings consistent with this opinion in order that the Court of Appeals may consider whether the contemplated disclosures would violate the prohibition of § 1905.[49] Since the decision regarding this substantive issue — the scope of § 1905 — will necessarily have some effect on the proper form of judicial review pursuant to § 706(2), we think it unnecessary, and therefore unwise, at the present stage of this case for us to express any additional views on that issue.

Vacated and remanded.

[MR. JUSTICE MARSHALL, concurred and raised the issue of the validity of the executive orders involved in this case.]

§ 10.03 The Federal Advisory Committee Act

What role should experts outside an administrative agency play in agency decisionmaking? What might Congress fear from an overly active advisory board? When do public decisions become privatized? Consider the following case.

NATURAL RESOURCES DEFENSE COUNCIL v. HERRINGTON

District of Columbia District Court
637 F. Supp. 116 (1986)

JACKSON, DISTRICT JUDGE.

Plaintiff Natural Resources Defense Council, Inc. ("NRDC"), a non-profit environmental protection organization, invoked the Federal Advisory Committee Act ("FACA" or "Act"), 5 U.S.C. App. II §§ 1–15, to gain admission to all collective activities of six scientist-executives convened last month by the Secretary of Energy to study the safety of a government-owned nuclear reactor currently in operation in the state of Washington. Denied access by the

---

[49] Since the Court of Appeals assumed for purposes of argument that the material in question was within an exemption to the FOIA, that court found it unnecessary expressly to decide that issue and it is open on remand. We, of course, do not here attempt to determine the relative ambits of Exemption 4 and § 1905, or to determine whether § 1905 is an exempting statute within the terms of the amended Exemption 3, 5 U.S.C. § 552(b)(3). Although there is a theoretical possibility that material might be outside Exemption 4 yet within the substantive provisions of § 1905, and that therefore the FOIA might provide the necessary "authoriz[ation] by law" for purposes of § 1905, that possibility is at most of limited practical significance in view of the similarity of language between Exemption 4 and the substantive provisions of § 1905.

defendants, the Secretary and the Department of Energy ("DOE" or "Department"), NRDC now sues to enjoin those activities altogether until its representatives are allowed to attend, and defendants comply with certain other requirements of the Act as well.[1]

The case is presently before the Court on plaintiff's motion for a preliminary injunction and defendants' cross-motion for summary judgment. The material facts appear of record and are not in dispute. For the reasons hereinafter set forth, the Court will deny plaintiff's application for a preliminary injunction, grant defendants' motion for summary judgment, and dismiss the complaint with prejudice.

I.

The litigation was provoked by a DOE initiative in response to the Soviet nuclear disaster at the Chernobyl power station near Kiev in the Ukraine in April, 1986. Before the Chernobyl reactor fire had been extinguished, Secretary Herrington invited six private U.S. citizens, each expert in certain aspects of nuclear physics, engineering, and systems management, to assist DOE in an expedited examination of the safety of its own plutonium production reactor, the N-Reactor, at the Hanford Reservation near Richland, Washington.[2] Like the one at Chernobyl, and apparently unlike any other in the United States, the N-Reactor, built in 1963, moderates the fission reaction of its fuel elements with graphite and cools the reactor core with water.

In a May 5th press release DOE announced that it had "established a special safety review panel" of experts to study the N-Reactor; two days later a DOE Assistant Secretary testified before a Congressional committee that Secretary Herrington had formed an "external panel of independent experts . . . to conduct an analysis and review of the issues raised by the Soviet incident. . . ." DOE then scheduled what it termed "joint briefings" for the experts in Washington, D.C., for May 22nd and 23rd on, principally, general aspects of the Chernobyl incident. Further "joint briefings" are to be given on June 12-13 on the N-Reactor specifically, and a tour of the N-Reactor during shut-down will be conducted on July 1-2. A final "joint briefing," if necessary, will take place in mid-July.

On May 16th NRDC learned of the first "joint briefing" session to occur the following week and, insisting that the "N-Reactor panel" was covered by

---

[1] The Court has subject matter jurisdiction pursuant to 28 U.S.C. §§ 1331, 1361.

[2] In a letter dated May 2, 1986, to two of the experts — the others were contacted orally — Secretary Herrington declared that he had "decided to invite an *ad hoc* group of experts . . . to assist the Department" in "examin[ing] all of the key technical questions and prob[ing] into all the potential safety issues raised by the Soviet incident" as it related to the N-Reactor. "While members of the group will be free to consult with one another in any way they choose," he continued, "it is the individual expertise and . . . advice, from each member, that the Department is seeking. The information and findings developed from the Department's safety reviews of the N-Reactor will, of course, be made available to each member of the group."

The invitees are all pre-eminent academicians or consulting engineers, with many years' technical and executive experience in nuclear power generation. None appears from the record to have any present direct connection with the commercial nuclear power industry. All, moreover, have the requisite security clearances.

FACA, asked to be allowed to send observers. On May 19th DOE refused, prompting the filing of this action on May 20, 1986.

II.

The sole issue raised by defendants' motion for summary judgment is whether or not its ensemble of experts constitutes an "advisory committee" within the meaning of FACA.[4] Section 3 of the Act provides,

> [t]he term "advisory committee" means any committee, board, commission, council, conference, panel, task force, or other similar group . . . which is . . . established or utilized by one or more agencies, in the interest of obtaining advice or recommendations for the President or one or more agencies or officers of the Federal Government. . . .

5 U.S.C. App. II § 3(2)(C).

Read literally, that definition would seem to apply to virtually any convocation of two or more persons from whom any federal official desired information. Although cognizant that such a reading, if it were to import that any curious bystander who wanted to do so be privy to it, would effectively stifle much of the daily intercourse between the government and the rest of the nation, NRDC adverts to certain portions of the legislative history which suggest that Congress nevertheless fully intended as expansive an interpretation as possible be given the definition of "advisory committee," consistent with common sense, to protect federal decision-makers from nefarious influences. . . . The Senate Report, for example, in explaining its version of the bill, stated:

> The intention is to interpret the words "established" and "organized" in their most liberal sense, so that when an officer brings together a group by formal or informal means, by contract or other arrangement, and whether or not Federal money is expended, to obtain advice and information, such group is covered by the provisions of this bill.

NRDC implies that Secretary Herrington proceeded as he did, by way of an informal letter of invitation rather than, with authorization in advance from the President, giving formal notice in the Federal Register of an intent to appoint (as would be required by 5 U.S.C. App. II § 9(a) in the case of a true "advisory committee"), to avoid being bound by the Act and its public access provisions. But there is absolutely no evidence that the Secretary's failure to comply with the Act's requirements was employed as a subterfuge. . . . It appears, rather, that the Secretary had no thought he might be appointing an "advisory committee" at all. He simply wanted the best advice available, public or private, as quickly as possible to avert a repetition of Chernobyl in the United States where conditions seemed most likely to predispose.

NRDC then calls attention to a number of attributes of the "N-Reactor panel" which are characteristic of the sort of formal consultative assembly

---

[4] Section 10 of FACA provides that all advisory committee meetings be open to the public, except where considerations of national security dictate otherwise, and imposes numerous other requirements on the conduct of its business. 5 U.S.C. App. II § 10.

Congress intended should be opened to the public. Not only does DOE itself speak of its creation as a "panel" which it acknowledges it has "established," the "panel" has a "structure" (*i.e.,* a chair and vice-chair), a "charter" (*i.e.,* the Secretary's letter), and a "staff" (*i.e.,* a DOE official assigned by the Secretary to "support" the experts in their work).

DOE asserts that "[a] joint report will neither be sought nor accepted" from the experts, and cites a General Services Administration regulation which states that FACA is inapplicable to "[a]ny meeting initiated by a Federal official(s) with more than one individual for the purpose of obtaining the advice of individual attendees and not for the purpose of utilizing the group to obtain consensus advice or recommendations." The N-Reactor experts are, it says, merely "individual consultants simultaneously retained." As authority for what the Secretary has done, however, the regulation begs the question, for it would provide no sanctuary for the experts' common endeavors outside public view if the statute itself does not permit it.

As a practical matter, DOE says, the appearance of a formal collegial existence for the body is illusory. The "chair" and "vice chair" appointments are merely administrative. No one will be presiding over evidentiary or deliberative proceedings; indeed, there will be none. The experts will work independently and report alone. The "charter" is simply the Secretary's letter explaining why and about what he is asking advice. The "staff" — of one — will function primarily as liaison. The "meetings" (or "joint briefings") will be occasions on which knowledge will be imparted by the government to the experts, not the other way around. Above all, no policy is to be made, save by the Secretary after he has been fully informed about the N-Reactor from sources both within and without the Department.

It serves no purpose here, however, to attempt to distinguish between "advisory committees" subject to the Act and other conclaves for the edification of government officials on the basis of some relative quantum of indicia of formality. It is apparent that the purpose of FACA was to suppress an evil which does not lurk in the circumstances of this particular case. Congress' concern, when it enacted FACA, was with a pernicious species of so-called "advisory" bodies: those dominated by industry leaders and the like with substantial parochial interest in the outcome of the matter under discussion, usually some onerous regulatory or policy proposal. The House Report warns that,

> [o]ne of the great dangers in the unregulated use of advisory committees is that special interest groups may use their membership on such bodies to promote their private concerns. Testimony received at hearings before the Legal and Monetary Affairs Subcommittee pointed out the danger of allowing special interest groups to exercise undue influence upon the Government through the dominance of advisory committees which deal with matters in which they have vested interests.

H.R. Rep. No. 1017, 92d Cong., 2d Sess. 6 (1972), U.S.Code Cong. & Admin. News 1972, pp. 3491, 3496. A Senate staff report submitted for the record by Senator Percy states that,

> [v]iewed in its worst light, the federal advisory committee can be a convenient nesting place for special interests seeking to change and preserve a

federal policy for their own ends. Such committees stacked with giants in their respective fields can overwhelm a federal decision–maker, or at least make him wary of upsetting the status quo.

118 Cong. Rec. 30,276 (1972). . . . *See also Consumers Union v. HEW*, 409 F. Supp. 473, 475 (D.D.C. 1976), *aff'd*, 551 F.2d 466 (D.C. Cir. 1977).[6]

That concern is simply not implicated in the instant case. There is no evidence whatsoever of any selfish advantage to be gained on the part of any of the men chosen by the Secretary to advise him, and none appears from the record to have anything at hazard in the situation. They have not been asked to comment upon nuclear power generally, or the manner of its regulation, but merely to examine, from their several perspectives of technical expertise, whether or not the government ought to allow a single reactor of its own to continue in operation in the immediate future and, if so, under what conditions.

The Court concludes that the six individuals who have been asked for their advice, however their affiliation is termed, are not an "advisory committee" within the meaning of the Act, and their labors may go forward as presently contemplated, and without plaintiff's being in attendance whenever they happen to be together.

III.

. . . In addition to its actual failure of success on the merits, it is unlikely that NRDC will remain for long in doubt as to what the experts will recommend, for their reports will, if not otherwise exempt, be available by way of a request under the Freedom of Information Act, 5 U.S.C. § 552. And, to the extent it wants to be sure that the Secretary acts only upon information which is "thorough and objective," and is fearful that the work of the experts will be neither, it is entitled to give him its own advice, with or without invitation, at any time. Its "injury," therefore, such as it is, is neither substantial nor irreparable, whereas the injury which could be done the Secretary, not to mention the rest of the country, by an indefinite delay of his inquiry while this case proceeds through the courts is too substantial and irreparable to contemplate.

For the foregoing reasons, therefore, it is, this _____ day of June, 1986,

ORDERED, that plaintiff's application for a preliminary injunction is denied; and it is

FURTHER ORDERED, that defendants' motion for summary judgment is granted, and the complaint is dismissed with prejudice.

---

[6] The cases cited by the NRDC in which FACA was held to apply all involved industry "advisors" presumably attempting to ameliorate the impact of what they perceived as excessive or inadequate government regulation.

NOTES AND QUESTIONS

10-16. In 1993, Hilary Clinton headed a committee to explore the potential for and problems of creating a nationalized health plan to cover uninsured and underinsured Americans. The committee held a number of meetings in private. *Association of American Physicians and Surgeons, Inc. v. Clinton*, 997 F.2d 898 (D.C. Cir. 1993) decided whether holding closed meetings for a committee headed by such an influential public figure as the First Lady violated the Federal Advisory Committee Act. The Court held that the President's spouse is a "full-time officer or employee of the federal government" within the meaning of FACA, thereby exempting any committee composed wholly of full-time officers or employees of the federal government from application of the Act.

10-17. In *Public Citizen v. United States Dept. of Justice*, 491 U.S. 440 (1989), the Supreme Court held that FACA did not apply to an American Bar Association standing committee that provided advice to the Justice Department on potential judicial nominees, including Supreme Court nominees. The Court construed FACA to avoid the "formidable constitutional difficulties" that would arise were the Act to interfere with the exercise of the President's Article II appointment powers.

BYRD v. UNITED STATES ENVIRONMENTAL PROTECTION AGENCY

*United States Court of Appeals,
District of Columbia Circuit.
174 F.3d 239 (1999)*

Before: EDWARDS, CHIEF JUDGE, WILLIAMS and HENDERSON, CIRCUIT JUDGES.

Opinion for the court filed by CIRCUIT JUDGE HENDERSON.

Separate opinion concurring in part and dissenting in part filed by CIRCUIT JUDGE WILLIAMS.

KAREN LeCRAFT HENDERSON, CIRCUIT JUDGE:

Appellant Daniel M. Byrd seeks reversal of the district court's grant of summary judgment to the Environmental Protection Agency (EPA) on his claim that EPA violated the Federal Advisory Committee Act (FACA), 5 U.S.C.App. II §§ 1-15. Specifically, Byrd contends that a peer review panel convened by an EPA contractor, the Eastern Research Group (ERG), to update

EPA's interim benzene report constituted a federal "advisory committee" and therefore its proceedings were governed by FACA, with which it admittedly did not comply. Byrd seeks either reversal and a declaration that the panel's proceedings violated FACA or, alternatively, remand for discovery pursuant to Fed. R. Civ. P. 56(f). . . . We affirm for the reasons set forth below.

I. BACKGROUND

In 1985, EPA issued an interim report discussing the carcinogenic effects of benzene. By 1996, EPA had prepared a draft update of its interim benzene report (Benzene Update). Before finalizing the Benzene Update, EPA decided to subject it to external peer review.

Under a contractual arrangement with EPA, ERG, a private environmental consulting firm, convened and conducted the peer review. The contract required ERG to select a panel of qualified experts, organize a public meeting of the panel to discuss the proposed Benzene Update and compile and submit a report to EPA summarizing the panel's assessment. In addition, the contract specified that EPA was to pay ERG a fixed sum and that ERG was to compensate the panel members. The contract also allowed EPA to determine the issues for the panel to evaluate and to comment in writing on ERG's draft final report.

Pursuant to the contract, EPA submitted to ERG for its consideration a list of twenty-four scientists who, in EPA's view, possessed the professional credentials necessary to serve on the peer review panel. From the list, ERG selected four individuals to be panelists. ERG also selected two panelists from its own database of consultants. EPA suggested no modifications to the list of panel members selected by ERG.

On June 27, 1997 EPA held a teleconference with ERG and the selected panelists, during which the panelists were instructed to prepare pre-meeting comments on the draft Benzene Update "specifically addressing a series of questions that [EPA] had provided" to ERG. The panelists circulated their pre-meeting notes among themselves and provided a copy to EPA. On June 30, 1997 EPA gave public notice in the Federal Register of the panel's scheduled meeting. The Federal Register notice explained the purpose of the meeting and noted that the draft was publicly available on the Internet or in writing from EPA. The notice also stated that ERG was to provide "logistical support for the workshop" and that interested persons could attend and participate in the meeting and advised that written comments could be submitted to EPA during a 60-day period ending August 29, 1997.

The panel meeting took place as scheduled on July 16, 1997. "The meeting was managed by ERG. Although several EPA employees who had been involved in developing the draft benzene update attended the meeting and effectively participated . . ., no EPA employee or officer supervised the conduct of the meeting." Byrd, a self-employed "consulting toxicologist and risk assessor," also attended after "learn[ing] about the [July 16, 1997] meeting through EPA's [public notice] in the Federal Register."[1] Byrd participated in

---

[1] Byrd "frequently attend[s], and plan[s] to continue attending, meetings sponsored by [EPA] about the toxicology and risks of specific air pollutants."

the meeting, twice expressing his views to the panel and others present. In addition, because of his concerns regarding the assumptions underlying the Benzene Update and his desire to be more informed, Byrd had earlier sought a copy of the panel members' pre-meeting notes but had been rebuffed three times. Byrd made no additional attempt at the meeting to secure the notes. After the meeting, Byrd timely submitted written comments to EPA on the draft Benzene Update.

On August 22, 1997, Byrd filed this action alleging that the expert panel assembled by ERG was an "advisory committee" within the meaning of FACA.[2] Byrd sought both declaratory relief and a use injunction barring EPA from using the panel's work product. One month later, ERG submitted to EPA its final report, including its analysis of the draft Benzene Update. EPA "did not participate in ERG's preparation of the final report."

On October 10, 1997, almost three months after the meeting, Byrd's counsel wrote a letter to EPA's FOIA officer requesting a copy of the panel's pre-meeting notes. EPA provided all of the requested notes and invited Byrd to submit additional comments. Byrd, however, declined to do so. EPA then moved to dismiss Byrd's complaint or, alternatively, for summary judgment. EPA challenged Byrd's standing and, on the merits, argued that the peer review panel assembled by ERG was not an "advisory committee" under FACA. The district court ruled in favor of EPA. Although it "assum[ed] without deciding" that Byrd had standing, the district court held that a panel convened by a private contractor is not a FACA "advisory committee" as that term has been construed by the Supreme Court and by this Court. Byrd timely filed his appeal.

II. DISCUSSION

[The court held that plaintiff had standing and that the case was not moot.]

C. The Merits

FACA defines an "advisory committee" as

> any committee, board, commission, council, conference, panel, task force, or other similar group, or any subcommittee or other subgroup thereof . . . which is . . . *established* or *utilized* by one or more agencies, in the interest of obtaining advice or recommendations for . . . one or more agencies or officers of the Federal Government.

5 U.S. C. App. II, § 3(2) (emphasis added). Because EPA did not "establish" nor did it "utilize" the panel within the meaning of section 3(2) of FACA, we affirm the district court's grant of summary judgment to EPA. . . .

---

[2] If the benzene panel was in fact an "advisory committee" subject to FACA as defined by 5 U.S. C. App. II § 3(2), both parties agree that the panel functioned in violation of FACA. Among other things, "the records, . . . working papers . . . or other documents which were made available to . . . each advisory committee shall be available for public inspection and copying", FACA, 5 U.S. C. App. II § 10(b), and "[d]etailed minutes of each meeting of each advisory committee shall be kept." *Id.* § 10(c). FACA also stipulates that "[t]here shall be designated an officer or employee of the Federal Government to chair or attend each meeting of each advisory committee." *Id.* § 10(e). "No advisory committee shall conduct any meeting in the absence of that officer or employee." *Id.*

Relying on legislative history, Byrd suggests that "established" and "utilized" should be construed "in their most liberal sense, so that when an officer brings together a group by formal or informal means, by contract or other arrangement . . . to obtain advice and information, such group is covered by [FACA]." The Supreme Court, however, in *Public Citizen v. United States Dep't of Justice*, 491 U.S. 440 (1989), squarely rejected an expansive interpretation of the words, reading "established" and "utilized" narrowly to prevent FACA from sweeping more broadly than the Congress intended. In addition, the Court indicated that an advisory panel is "established" by an agency only if it is actually formed by the agency, and "utilized" by an agency only if it is "amenable to . . . strict management by agency officials." The Court, therefore, held FACA inapplicable to the American Bar Association Standing Committee on the Federal Judiciary, rejecting the argument that that committee had to comply with FACA simply because the Department of Justice regularly sought its input regarding judicial nominees.

We have similarly interpreted "established" and "utilized." . . .

Although this Court has held that an agency "establishes" a committee only if the agency forms the committee, Byrd contends that EPA "effectively created" the panel by "conceiving of the need for" it and implementing it by hiring ERG to handle the logistics. According to Byrd, EPA's actions are unlike those of the FDA in *Food Chemical News v. Young*, 900 F.2d 328 (D.C. Cir. 1990) in that, there, the contractor (not the agency) "proposed using ad hoc groups of knowledgeable experts as a means of carrying out the contract." But our analysis of whether an advisory committee has been "established" does not turn on a determination of who determines the methodology or operation of the peer review. Notably, the contractors in both *Food Chemical News* and here received a "task order" or a "work assignment" from the relevant agency defining the objective, the method and the scope of the studies to be performed. Moreover, because ERG selected the membership of the benzene panel, Byrd cannot show that it was " 'a Government-formed advisory committee' " as required by our narrow interpretation of "established." Byrd nevertheless argues that EPA established the panel because it retained the power to approve ERG's panel member selections. Although EPA provided a list of suggested panel members to ERG, ERG was not required to select its members from that list and two of the panel members were not on the EPA list. Moreover, EPA approved ERG's panel member selections without changes. Finally, ERG, not EPA, paid the panelists from its own funds. Although the contract between ERG and EPA afforded EPA significant potential authority in the panel selection process, EPA never fully exercised it. And there is no reason to assume that the threat of an EPA veto affected ERG's panel selections. The result in this case might have been different if EPA had exercised its authority. The record, however, belies any claim that EPA in fact "established" the panel as required by FACA. The statute describes a panel that "is . . . established," 5 U.S. C. App. II, § 3(2), not one that could have been established by a government agency. Accordingly, EPA did not establish the benzene panel within the meaning of

Byrd also contends that EPA "utilized" the benzene panel because it exercised much more control over it than the agencies in *Food Chemical News* and *Washington Legal Foundation v. Sentencing Comm'n*, 17 F.3d 1446 (D.C. Cir. 1994) exercised over the committees at issue in those cases. But even assuming EPA exercised more influence here than did the FDA or the DOJ in relation to their committees, EPA did not manage and control the benzene panel within FACA's scope, keeping in mind that "the utilized test is a stringent standard, denoting 'something along the lines of *actual management or control* of the advisory committee.'" As we held in *Washington Legal Foundation*, even "significant" influence does not represent the level of control necessary to establish that a government agency "utilized" an advisory panel.

Contrary to Byrd's contention, the record shows that ERG in fact actually managed and controlled the selection of the panel's membership. Moreover, as even Byrd admits,

> The [panel's July 16, 1997 public] meeting was managed by a contractor, ERG. Although several EPA employees who had been involved in developing the draft benzene update attended the meeting and effectively participated . . ., no EPA employee or officer supervised the conduct of the meeting.

Finally, ERG, rather than EPA, prepared the report of the panel's proceedings. Although the contract authorized EPA to receive and comment on the draft report before it was finalized, the district court found "no evidence that EPA's input, if any, resulted in changes being made to the final Expert Panel Report." Because our decision is based on what EPA in fact did, rather than on what it could have done under its contract with ERG, we conclude that EPA's actions regarding the benzene panel do not constitute "actual management and control." Accordingly, the district court correctly determined that the benzene panel was not subject to the constraints of FACA because EPA neither "utilized" nor "established" it.

For the foregoing reasons, the district court's grant of summary judgment to the Environmental Protection Agency is

Affirmed.

STEPHEN F. WILLIAMS, CIRCUIT JUDGE, concurring in part and dissenting in part:

I agree with the majority that we have jurisdiction, albeit on a different theory. On the merits, however, though the case is close, I would reverse. . . .

On the merits, I believe that FACA governs panels established under the challenged policy. Our precedent on this language is rather thin, but appears to say that an agency "establish[es]" a panel if it has real control over its personnel and subject matter at its inception. Thus in *Food Chemical News v. Young*, 900 F.2d 328, 333 (D.C. Cir. 1990), we said that the agency had not "established" the panel because the contractor "proposed" it, "alone selected its members," "set the panel's agenda," "scheduled its meetings," and "would have reviewed the panel's work." Here EPA proposes the use of a panel, submits an initial list of suggested members to the contractor, retains veto power over the final membership, and sets the panel's agenda. (The procedure used for the Benzene Update is evidently representative of EPA's practice.) The veto power is key. That it was not used in the benzene episode does not much help EPA: not only may EPA exercise it in future applications of the policy, but the contractor was and is quite likely to take the fact of veto power into account in its selection decisions. Assuming that contractors will ignore this fact — as the majority appears to do — seems akin to believing that the President takes no account of senators' opinions when he nominates federal judges.

Although the issue of whether EPA "established" the panel is certainly a close one, it seems to me inconsistent with the statute's language and intent to exempt from FACA a panel controlled so closely in membership and purpose.

NOTES AND QUESTIONS

10-18. What is the basis of the majority's conclusion that FACA does not apply to the peer review panel in this case? Could the EPA have controlled this panel more closely if it chose to do so? Is the dissent correct that the panel was "established" by EPA and closely controlled "in membership and purpose"?

10-19. Is OMB correct to conclude, on the basis of this case, that FACA does not apply to peer review?

10-20. Are there other ways to avoid the application of FACA? Consider Sidney Shapiro's analysis in *OMB's Dubious Peer Review Proposals*, 34 ENV. L. REP. 10064 (2004).*

One way that OMB seeks to avoid FACA is by authorizing agencies to "'direct peer reviewers of regulatory information — individually or in a group — to issue a final report detailing the nature of their review and their findings and conclusions.'" According to GSA regulations interpreting FACA, convening a number of people to obtain the advice of each individually (rather than collectively) does not establish an advisory committee. Besides avoiding FACA, OMB's decision to permit peer review by individuals, rather than by a committee, decreases accountability in a second important way. The advantage of conducting peer review by committee is that "each committee member has the opportunity to observe the demeanor of the others and to challenge their evaluations." As a result, "bringing all reviewers together to discuss their opinions can be a powerful shield against favoritism and animus." This shield becomes even more important if OMB succeeds in closing peer review meetings to the public by permitting agencies to avoid FACA by hiring contractors to conduct the peer review.

The other way that OMB seeks to avoid FACA is to permit agencies to hire an outside contractor to oversee the peer review process. OMB claims

---
* Copyright © 2004 by Environmental Law Institute. All rights reserved.

that an agency can avoid complying with FACA if it hires a contractor or consultant, who in turn organizes the peer review. . . .

PROBLEM 10-2

In Chapter 7, § 7.08, we set forth the Data Quality Act in full. Review the text of that Act. Does it support the following OMB regulations, as described in *Developments in Administrative Law and Regulatory Practice 2003-2004*, pp. 161–162 (Jeffrey Lubbers, ed. 2004):*

> On April 28, 2004, OMB published a "Revised Information Quality Bulletin on Peer Review."** Claiming authority not only under the DQA but also under Executive Order 12866 and even the "President's Constitutional authority to oversee the unitary Executive Branch," the Bulletin seeks to impose much more rigorous peer review requirements than most federal agencies have traditionally used, and certainly more uniform approaches than have ever prevailed within the federal government. . . .
>
> The Bulletin leaves no doubt that the expanded peer review requirements are to apply to the rulemaking process. In one passage, the Bulletin makes the observation that traditional APA notice-and-comment cannot provide "an adequate substitute for peer review, as distinguished experts — especially those most knowledgeable in a field — often do not file public comments with federal agencies." The Bulletin accordingly includes the following requirement:
>
>> If an agency relies on influential scientific information or a highly influential scientific assessment subject to the requirements of this Bulletin in support of the regulatory action, it shall include in the administrative record for that action a certification explaining how the agency has complied with the requirements of this Bulletin and the Information Quality Act [DQA].
>
> Just as the DQA has been frequently and roundly criticized by environmental groups and other pro-regulatory interests, so has the new Bulletin on Peer Review. Sticking with the theme that the DQA itself is a recipe for "paralysis by analysis," The environmental and public interest group community claims that the new peer review procedures are nothing more than a "new set of tools to stop regulations," and that they have been "strenuously opposed by the nation's science community."

Do you agree with the assessment of the environmental groups? Why or why not?

---

* Copyright © 2004 by American Bar Association. Reprinted by permission.

** 69 Fed. Reg. 23,230 (Apr. 28, 2004).

§ 10.04 Government in the Sunshine Act

COMMON CAUSE v. NUCLEAR REGULATORY COMMISSION

District of Columbia Court of Appeals
674 F.2d 921 (1982)

Before WRIGHT, WILKEY and GINSBURG, CIRCUIT JUDGES.

Opinion for the court filed by CIRCUIT JUDGE J. SKELLY WRIGHT.

J. SKELLY WRIGHT, CIRCUIT JUDGE:

The Government in the Sunshine Act, 5 U.S.C. § 552b (1976), requires that meetings of multi-member federal agencies shall be open to the public, with the exception of discussions in ten narrowly defined areas. In these cases we must decide an important unresolved issue: whether any of the statutory exemptions from the Sunshine Act apply to agency budget deliberations. Interpreting the statutory language in light of the legislative history and underlying policies of the Act, we conclude that there is no blanket exemption for agency meetings at any stage of the budget preparation process. The availability of exemptions for specific portions of budgetary discussions must be determined upon the facts of each case.

In the proceedings before us the Nuclear Regulatory Commission (Commission) has failed to bear its burden of proving that its budget meetings of July 25, 1981 and October 15, 1981 were lawfully closed or that it may continue to withhold the transcripts of those meetings. We therefore order the Commission to release the transcripts to the public. . . .

I. STATEMENT OF THE CASE

Three interrelated cases have been consolidated in this appeal. Each case turns on the lawfulness of a decision by the Nuclear Regulatory Commission to close a meeting to discuss the agency's budget proposals. In each case the District Court ruled against the Commission. . . .

In July 1980 the Commission scheduled a series of meetings to discuss preparation of the agency's annual budget request for fiscal year 1982, and announced that the sessions would be open to the public. Before the first of the meetings on July 18, 1980, however, the three Commissioners who were present voted unanimously to close all of the budget meetings scheduled to be held within the next 30 days. The Commission relied solely on Exemption 9(B) of the Sunshine Act, which permits closing of meetings if premature disclosure of the discussion would be "likely to significantly frustrate implementation of a proposed agency action." 5 U.S.C. § 552b(c)(9)(B) (1976). A representative of appellee Common Cause, who wished to attend the July 18, 1980 meeting, was excluded. At that meeting the Commissioners received a preliminary briefing from the staff concerning the Commission's budgetary needs and the relationship of each office's budget requests to agency and Office of Management and Budget (OMB) guidelines and previous appropriation levels.

Common Cause filed suit in the District Court on September 15, 1980, seeking a declaratory judgment that closure of the July 18, 1980 meeting had violated the Sunshine Act, an injunction ordering release of the transcript of that meeting, and an order to the Commission to permit Common Cause to attend future Commission meetings "that are similar in nature to the July 18, 1980 meeting(.)" JA 5–8.[5] The parties filed cross-motions for summary judgment. The Commission asserted that Exemption 9(B) permitted closing of the meeting and allowed the transcript to be withheld from the public until the President submitted his budget to Congress in early 1981.

In a memorandum opinion and order issued on July 2, 1981, the District Court granted summary judgment for Common Cause. The court ruled that the Commission had unlawfully closed its July 18, 1980 meeting, which it described as a discussion of "the general proposed budget requests of the NRC and the general relationship between those requests and various budgetary documents." On the basis of its inspection of the transcript the court decided that the Commission had "failed to establish a reasonable likelihood of any harm to future agency actions by opening budget discussion meetings." It therefore found that Exemption 9(B) was inapplicable, and it enjoined the Commission permanently "from closing future meetings of a similar nature." It did not specify the characteristics of the July 18, 1980 meeting which it considered material, nor did it describe with any particularity the future meetings which it ordered to be held in public.

[The court then described the similar factual situations in the other two cases' consolidation appeal.] . . .

III. THE SUNSHINE ACT AND THE BUDGET PROCESS

We turn now to the validity of the District Court's determinations, based on *in camera* inspection of the transcripts, that the Sunshine Act requires the Commission to release the transcripts of its closed meetings held on July 27 and October 15, 1981. *See* 5 U.S.C. §§ 552b(f)(2), 552b(h)(1) (1976).

The Government in the Sunshine Act establishes the policy that "the public is entitled to the fullest practicable information regarding the decisionmaking processes of the Federal Government."[14] Every meeting of a multi-member agency must be open to the public, except that specific portions of a meeting may be closed if the discussion is reasonably likely to fall within one or more of ten narrowly defined exemptions. 5 U.S.C. § 552b(c)(1)–(10) (1976). The Commission contends that these exemptions authorize closing of agency budget discussions. It places primary reliance on Exemption 9(B), which allows an agency to close a meeting or portion of a meeting which is likely to discuss

---

[5] The Sunshine Act gives federal district courts the authority, "having due regard for orderly administration and the public interest, as well as the interests of the parties," to "grant such equitable relief as [they] deem[] appropriate, including granting an injunction against future violations of this section. . . ." 5 U.S.C. § 552b(h)(1) (1976).

[14] Government in the Sunshine Act, ch. 409, 90 Stat. 1241 (1976) (declaration of policy). The section also states, "It is the purpose of this Act to provide the public with such information while protecting the rights of individuals and the ability of the Government to carry out its responsibilities." *Id.*

matters whose "premature disclosure" would "be likely to significantly frustrate implementation of a proposed agency action." *Id.* § 552b(c)(9)(B). The agency also contends that budget meetings may be closed because they encompass information protected under Exemption 2, matters related "solely to the internal personnel rules and practices of an agency," and Exemption 6, material of a personal nature whose disclosure would "constitute a clearly unwarranted invasion of personal privacy." *Id.* §§ 552b(c)(2), 552b(c)(6). In light of the language, legislative history, and underlying purposes of the Sunshine Act, we reject the Commission's proposed interpretations of the Sunshine Act exemptions.

A. The Purposes of the Sunshine Act

Congress enacted the Sunshine Act to open the deliberations of multi-member federal agencies to public view. It believed that increased openness would enhance citizen confidence in government, encourage higher quality work by government officials, stimulate well-informed public debate about government programs and policies, and promote cooperation between citizens and government. In short, it sought to make government more fully accountable to the people. In keeping with the premise that "government should conduct the public's business in public," the Act established a general presumption that agency meetings should be held in the open. Once a person has challenged an agency's decision to close a meeting, he agency bears the burden of proof.[19] Even if exempt subjects are discussed in one portion of a meeting, the remainder of the meeting must be held in open session.[20]

The Act went farther than any previous federal legislation in requiring openness in government. In general the Sunshine Act's exemptions parallel those in the Freedom of Information Act (FOIA),[21] but there is an important difference. Unlike FOIA, which specifically exempts "predecisional" memoranda and other documents on the premise that government cannot "operate in a fishbowl," the Sunshine Act was designed to open the predecisional process in multi-member agencies to the public. During the legislative process a number of federal agencies specifically objected to the Sunshine Act's omission of an exemption for predecisional deliberations. Congress deliberately

---

[19] 5 U.S.C. § 552b(h)(1) (1976); H.R. Rep. No. 94–880 (part 1). . . . With regard to the legality of the decision to close a meeting, the Act establishes a foreseeability standard. The agency must show that it was more likely than not that exempt matters would be discussed at the closed portion or portions of the meeting. . . . The test is different for a retrospective determination of whether the transcripts of a closed meeting should be released. The agency and reviewing court must base their decision on the discussions that actually did occur. If there was in fact no discussion of any exempt material, the entire transcript must be released; if exempt material was discussed, then the specific exempt portions may be deleted. 5 U.S.C. § 552b(f)(2) (1976).

[20] 5 U.S.C. § 552b(c) (1976) refers specifically to "any portion of an agency meeting" where the agency "properly determines that such portion or portions of its meeting or the disclosure of such information" is likely to fall within one of the ten specified exemptions.

[21] . . . Of the nine exemptions to the Freedom of Information Act, seven are included virtually verbatim in the Sunshine Act. The two omitted exemptions are Exemption 5 of FOIA, which allows agencies to withhold documents containing privileged material, including predecisional deliberations, and Exemption 9, which covers specified geological information.

chose to forego the claimed advantages of confidential discussions among agency heads at agency meetings.[23]

Express language in the Sunshine Act also demonstrates that Congress did not intend to follow the FOIA pattern for predecisional discussions at agency meetings. The Sunshine Act applies to all "meetings," which are defined as deliberations which determine or result in "the joint conduct or disposition of official agency business[.]" 5 U.S.C. § 552b(a)(2) (1976). The legislative history demonstrates that "official agency business" means far more than reviewable final action. The Senate report expressly stated:

> The definition of meetings includes the conduct, as well as the disposition, of official agency matters. It is not sufficient for the purposes of open government to merely have the public witness final agency votes. The meetings opened by Section 201(a) are not intended to be merely reruns staged for the public after agency members have discussed the issue in private and predetermined their views. The whole decisionmaking process, not merely its results, must be exposed to public scrutiny. . . .

Notwithstanding the omission of a deliberative process privilege from the Sunshine Act, the Commission asks us to hold that the deliberative process leading to formulation of an agency's budget request is exempt from the Sunshine Act. To resolve this question, we must examine the statutory underpinnings of the budget process and the specific exemptions from the Sunshine Act which the Commission invokes.

B. The Budget and Accounting Act of 1921

The Budget and Accounting Act, 42 Stat. 21 (1921), was designed to centralize formulation of the Executive Branch budget. Previously Congress had received "uncompared, unrelated, and unrevised" estimates from individual departments and agencies, "representing the personal views and aspirations of bureau chiefs[.]" The disadvantages of this uncoordinated system led Congress to delegate to the President exclusive authority to submit budgetary requests on behalf of the Executive Branch. Congress thereby sought to enhance the government's ability to control the overall level of expenditures and to choose among conflicting priorities.

The Commission contends that the Budget and Accounting Act mandates secrecy in the budget formulation process, and that the Sunshine Act must therefore be construed to permit closing of agency budget meetings. We find this statutory argument unpersuasive.

---

[23] The Nuclear Regulatory Commission was one of the federal agencies which criticized the legislation during the committee stage because the bill did not provide any exemption for predecisional deliberations. William Anders, then chairman of the Commission, wrote to Representative Bella Abzug, chairman of the House subcommittee responsible for the Sunshine Act, urging that an exemption similar to FOIA's Exemption 5 should be included in order to protect preparation of budget requests and other matters. . . .

The Federal Trade Commission also objected that the bill did not contain any clear exemption for internal budgetary planning information. The bill's omission of an exemption for predecisional discussions was criticized in letters to the House committee by the Federal Trade Commission, . . . the Federal Communications Commission, . . . the Federal Power Commission, . . . and the Federal Home Loan Bank Board. . . .

The Commission first relies on the President's authority, under the Budget and Accounting Act, to prescribe rules and regulations for preparation of the budget, 31 U.S.C. § 16 (1976), and on the "longstanding practice of confidentiality for Executive Branch discussions leading to the formulation of the President's Budget." The statute, however, makes no reference to confidentiality, nor does it authorize the President to prescribe budgetary rules and regulations without regard to the requirements of other federal statutes. The President's rulemaking authority under 31 U.S.C. § 16 is therefore subject to the specific requirements of the Sunshine Act. Indeed, the OMB directive to agencies, OMB Circular A-10, recognizes that "[c]ertain agencies headed by a collegial body may be required to hold their meetings open to public observation unless the agency properly determines that the matter to be discussed warrants the closing of those meetings for reasons enumerated in the Government in the Sunshine Act. . . ."

Second, the Commission reasons that the congressional goal of centralized budget formulation cannot be achieved without secrecy. If the proposals of individual agencies must be adopted in public, it suggests, development of the presidential budget would be "fragmented" and the President's discretion to choose among alternatives would be impaired. This contention reads too much into the 1921 Act, which simply requires that the President submit a single, unified Executive Branch budget proposal to Congress for consideration. It does not prescribe any method by which he must develop the consolidated budget figures which he submits. Nor does it require that the President's proposals be the only budgetary information available to the public. Even if agencies discuss their budget proposals at public sessions, the President remains capable of revising agency requests and combining them into a unified budget.

Indeed, the Sunshine Act itself affords persuasive evidence that Congress did not intend to allow presidential claims of confidentiality under the Budget and Accounting Act to override the Sunshine Act's specific provisions regarding openness and secrecy. Exemption 3, a provision which received extensive consideration in both houses, allows closing of a meeting or portion of a meeting which would "disclose matters specifically exempted from disclosure by statute," provided that such statute

> (A) requires that the matters be withheld from the public in such a manner as to leave no discretion on the issue, or (B) establishes particular criteria for withholding or refers to particular types of matters to be withheld[.]

5 U.S.C. § 552b(c)(3) (1976). The Budget and Accounting Act of 1921, which contains no explicit references to confidentiality, does not qualify under the strict requirements of Exemption 3.

Therefore, the budget process is exempt from the open meeting requirement, in whole or in part, only if it fits within the terms of other specific Sunshine Act exemptions.

C. No Blanket Exemption for Budget Meetings

Exceptions to the Sunshine Act's general requirement of openness must be construed narrowly. Congress rejected the approach of establishing "functional categories" of agency business whose discussion could automatically be closed to the public. Instead the Sunshine Act provides for an examination of each item of business to ascertain whether it may be closed under the terms of one of ten specific exemptions. Exemptions must be interpreted in light of Congress' intention that agencies must "conduct their deliberations in public to the greatest extent possible." Nevertheless the Commission claims that Exemption 9(B) permits closing of agency budget meetings in their entirety. Exemption 9(B) permits closing of meetings to prevent "premature disclosure" of information whose disclosure would be likely to "significantly frustrate implementation of a proposed agency action." For two reasons, the precept of narrow construction applies with particular force to this exemption, upon which the Commission principally relies. First, as we have seen, Congress decided not to provide any exemption for predecisional deliberations because it wished the process of decision as well as the results to be open to public view. Yet the agencies may attempt to seize upon the language of Exemption 9(B) to avoid the perceived discomfort and inconvenience that are, in the words of one commentary, "inherent in the open meeting principle. . . ." R. Berg & S. Klitzman, *An Interpretive Guide to the Government in the Sunshine Act* 24 (1978). Second, an overly broad construction of Exemption 9(B), which applies to all agencies subject to the Act, would allow agencies to "circumvent the spirit of openness which underlies this legislation." S. Rep. No. 94–354, *supra*, at 20.

The language of the exemption is not self-explanatory; we therefore turn to the legislative history for guidance. The House and Senate committee reports give four concrete examples of Exemption 9(B) situations. First, an agency might consider imposing an embargo on foreign shipment of certain goods; if this were publicly known, all of the goods might be exported before the agency had time to act, and the effectiveness of the proposed action would be destroyed. Second, an agency might discuss whether to approve a proposed merger; premature public disclosure of the proposal might make it impossible for the two sides to reach agreement. Third, disclosure of an agency's proposed strategy in collective bargaining with its employees might make it impossible to reach an agreement. Fourth, disclosure of an agency's terms and conditions for purchase of real property might make the proposed purchase impossible or drive up the price.

We construe Exemption 9(B) to cover those situations delineated by the narrow general principles which encompass all four legislative examples. In each of these cases, disclosure of the agency's proposals or negotiating position could affect private decisions by parties other than those who manage the federal government-exporters, potential corporate merger partners, government employees, or owners of real property. The private responses of such persons might damage the regulatory or financial interests of the government as a whole, because in each case the agency's proposed action is one for which the agency takes final responsibility as a governmental entity.

The budget process differs substantially from the examples given by the House and Senate reports. Disclosure of the agency's discussions would not affect private parties' decisions concerning regulated activity or dealings with the government. Rather, the Commission contends that opening budget discussions to the public might affect political decisions by the President and

OMB. In addition, disclosure would not directly affect "agency action" for which the Commission has the ultimate responsibility. Instead, the Commission fears that disclosure of its time-honored strategies of item-shifting, exaggeration, and fall-back positions would give it less leverage in its "arm's length" dealings with OMB and the President, who make the final budget decisions within the Executive Branch. The Commission argues that it would thereby be impaired in its competition with other government agencies — which also serve the public and implement federal legislation — for its desired share of budgetary resources. It is not clear, however, whether the interests of the government as a whole, or the public interest, would be adversely affected.

Moreover, in the budget context the public interest in disclosure differs markedly from its interest in the four situations described in the committee reports.[41] In those cases disclosure would permit either financial gain at government expense or circumvention of agency regulation. In contrast, disclosure of budget deliberations would serve the affirmative purposes of the Sunshine Act: to open government deliberations to public scrutiny, to inform the public "what facts and policy considerations the agency found important in reaching its decision, and what alternatives it considered and rejected," and thereby to permit "wider and more informed public debate of the agency's policies. . . ."

The budget deliberation process is of exceptional importance in agency policymaking. The agency heads must review the entire range of agency programs and responsibilities in order to establish priorities. According to the Commission, a budget meeting "candidly consider(s) the merits and efficiencies of on-going or expected regulatory programs or projects" and then "decides upon the level of regulatory activities it proposes to pursue. . . ." These decisions, the government contends, have a significant impact on "the Commission's ability to marshal regulatory powers in a manner which insures the greatest protection of the public health and safety with the most economical use of its limited resources."

If Congress had wished to exempt these deliberations from the Sunshine Act — to preserve the prior practice of budget confidentiality, to reduce the opportunities for lobbying before the President submits his budget to Congress, or for other reasons — it would have expressly so indicated. Absent any such statement of legislative intent, we will not construe Exemption 9(B) of the Sunshine Act to allow budget deliberations to be hidden from the public view.

We are not persuaded by the Commission's contention that the separation of powers principle imposes a constitutional requirement that budget meetings be exempt from the Sunshine Act. The Commission suggests that Congress may not require agency budget meetings to be open to the public because openness would interfere with the Commission's role of providing opinions and advice to the President under Article II, Section 2 of the Constitution. But the Supreme Court has recently rejected the contention that separation of

---

[41] To determine whether frustration of agency action would be "significant" or "serious," Congress suggested a balancing test "to determine how the public interest is best served." S. Rep. No. 94–354, *supra* note 1, at 25; H.R. Rep. No.94–880 (part 1), *supra* note 1, at 12.

powers requires "three airtight departments of government[.]" *Nixon v. Administrator of General Services,* 433 U.S. 425, 443, 97 S. Ct. 2777, 2790, 53 L. Ed. 2d 867 (1977). Taking a "pragmatic, flexible" approach, the Court enunciated a functional test of whether separation of powers has been violated: "the extent to which [the challenged legislation] prevents the Executive Branch from accomplishing its constitutionally assigned functions." *Id.* at 442–443, 97 S. Ct. at 2789–90. The Court expressly included the Government in the Sunshine Act among the "abundant statutory precedent for the regulation and mandatory disclosure of [information] in the possession of the Executive Branch," noting that "[s]uch regulation of material generated in the Executive Branch has never been considered invalid as an invasion of its autonomy." *Id.* at 445, 97 S. Ct. at 2791.

We express no view with regard to any constitutional issue of Executive privilege, a question which is narrower than the Commission's general claim based on separation of powers. Only the President, not the agency, may assert the presidential privilege. . . .

D. Particularized Exemptions

The Sunshine Act contains no express exemption for budget deliberations as a whole, and we do not read such an exemption into Exemption 9(B). We recognize, nevertheless, that specific items discussed at Commission budget meetings might be exempt from the open meetings requirement of the Act, and might justify closing portions of Commission meetings on an individual and particularized basis. After examining the transcripts of the Commission's closed meetings of July 27, 1981 and October 15, 1981, however, we conclude that none of the subject matter discussed at either meeting comes within any of the exemptions cited by the Commission. The Commission must therefore release the full transcripts of these meetings to the public. . . .

NOTES AND QUESTIONS

10-21. What are the purposes of the Sunshine Act? Are decisionmakers likely to be as forthcoming in discussions in public as they are in private? Does this matter for purposes of the Act?

10-22. Why was the Commission eager to keep its budget deliberations private? What reasons do they give? Are there any other reasons? Do you think that the Government in the Sunshine Act leads to different decisions than otherwise might have been made? Better decisions? More fully explained decisions?

10-23. How would this case be decided today, in light of the Supreme Court's ruling in *Chevron v. NRDC?*

10-24. What do you think of the Commission's separation of powers argument? How would that issue be decided today in light of the cases you studied in Chapter 7?

§ 10.05 The Privacy Act

Who steals my purse steals trash; 'tis something, nothing;
'twas mine, 'tis his, and has been slave to thousands;
But he that filches from me my good name
Robs me of that which not enriches him,
And makes me poor indeed.

William Shakespeare, *Othello*.

If only it were still so simple. At least Othello did not have to fear the prospect of computers and their ability to invade individual privacy. But Shakespeare knew what he was talking about. Imagine what Iago could have done with a computer.

Some time ago, commentators began noting significant changes in the role played by information in our society:

> Information will [soon] replace manufactured goods as the most valued commodity in the economy. . . . And so inundated will society become with this data deluge that people with the skill to interpret and manage the flood for others will rise to the top of society and perhaps hold it hostage. . . . Even today, as the telecommunications revolution sweeps through the nation's offices and businesses, the very first questions anyone asks are "how safe is my computer?" "Can anyone look into my files?" "Who knows my secret password?" The years ahead will spawn an entire new wave of crime. Indeed, crimes of the 1990s will be radically different from today's concerns. Computer crime in particular — tapping into private electronic files — will soon become the most troublesome crime of the future. And it will trouble foreign governments and domestic corporations as much as the heads of households.*

Law has failed to keep pace with this information explosion. But as technology continues to reveal new uses for — and place a higher premium on** — personal information, the struggle between individuals and government for control of that information will intensify. Information management law promises to be a growth industry.

The Freedom of Information Act and the Privacy Act are the cornerstones of federal information policy, at least to the extent that a formulated "policy" can be discerned. FOIA, discussed *supra,* certainly has its flaws, but it can

---

* Bruce Nussbaum, *The World After Oil, the Shifting Axis of Power and Wealth,* 14–15 (Simon & Schuster, 1983). Copyright © 1983 by Bruce Nussbaum. Reprinted by permission of Simon & Schuster Adult Publishing Group.

** For an economic perspective on the value of privacy in relation to the benefits of information disbursement, *see* Posner, Epstein, Kronman, Easterbrook, et. al., *The Law and Economics of Privacy* (Conference), 9 J. of LEGAL STUD. 621–842 (1980).

also be perceived as a fundamentally sound law in need of fine tuning and reform. The Privacy Act of 1974, however, is an ambitious, seemingly comprehensive statement of federal confidentiality policy. Perhaps owing to its title, the Act gives the impression that individual privacy interests have been addressed and protected, but in today's climate of burgeoning information and instantaneous data transfer, that impression may well be mistaken.

In the novel *Cancer Ward,* Alexander Solzhenitsyn writes:***

> As every man goes through life he fills in a number of forms for the record, each containing a number of questions. . . . These are thus hundreds of little threads radiating from every man, millions of threads in all. If these threads were suddenly to become visible, the whole sky would look like a spider's web, and if they materialized as rubber, banks, buses, trams and even people would all lose the ability to move, and the wind would be unable to carry torn-up newspapers or autumn leaves along the streets of the city. They are not visible, they are not material, but every man is constantly aware of their existence. . . . Each man, permanently aware of his own invisible threads, naturally develops a respect for the people who manipulate the threads.

The Privacy Act of 1974 is a necessary corollary to the Freedom of Information Act. While FOIA provides access by "any person" to most government-held information, it does not deal with the kinds of issues with which the Privacy Act is concerned. The individual's interest in avoiding disclosure of personal matters is at loggerheads with *both* the agencies' need for information and FOIA's mandate to disclose such information to the public. FOIA disclosure of agency-held records which infringe on personal privacy interests may only exacerbate matters. By restricting the types of personal information which an agency can acquire and by giving the individual some control over the accuracy and release of that information by the agency, the Privacy Act seeks to preserve, at least in the realm of agency record-keeping, the constitutionally protected zone of privacy.

Like the 1974 amendments to FOIA, the Privacy Act was crafted in the shadow of the Watergate hearings. The improprieties unearthed at those hearings fueled the active distrust of government during that era, and added to the pressure on Congress to enact some form of privacy legislation. Consider the following case. What do you think the likely effectiveness of this Act really is? How would you change it, if you could?

*** A. Solzhenitsyn, *Cancer Ward,* (copyright © 1968 by Farrar, Straus & Giroux. All rights reserved.) As quoted in Joint Comm. on Gov't Operations, Legis. Hist. of the Privacy Act of 1974: Source Book on Privacy, 94th Cong., 2d Sess. 4 (1976) p. 669 [hereinafter Sourcebook]. The Sourcebook is the single best guide to the legislative history of the Privacy Act.

TIJERINA v. WALTERS

District of Columbia Court of Appeals
821 F.2d. 789 (1987)

MIKVA, CIRCUIT JUDGE:

These actions under the Privacy Act, the Freedom of Information Act (FOIA), and the United States Constitution grow out of a July 1982 incident in which a Deputy Inspector General of the Veterans Administration (VA) wrote an unsolicited letter to the Texas Bar Examiners detailing allegations that one of the appellants had falsified information submitted in support of a loan application. The Examiners later wrote back to request additional details, which the VA also provided. As a result of the disclosures, appellant Lorenzo Tijerina eventually was found morally unfit to take the Texas bar examination. Mr. Tijerina and his wife, Maria Tijerina, brought this action alleging that the VA's two disclosures resulted in violations of the Tijerinas' rights under the Privacy Act and the Constitution. Appellants also alleged that the VA failed to respond properly to their requests for information under FOIA. The district court, on cross-motions for summary judgment, granted the government's motion and dismissed appellants' claims. We reverse the order of summary judgment as to Mr. Tijerina's Privacy Act claims arising out of the July 1982 disclosure, and affirm as to all other claims.

I. Background

In 1980 Maria Tijerina, an Army nurse, and her husband, Lorenzo, at the time a law student at Howard University, applied for a Veterans Administration Home Loan Guaranty. Mr. Tijerina indicated on the application that he was employed by a Mr. Isaac Barfield. The mortgage company sent a verification-of-employment form to the address that Mr. Tijerina gave for Mr. Barfield and received a response, purporting to be from Mr. Barfield, indicating that Mr. Tijerina was in his employ.

Some time after the loan was executed, the VA conducted a random audit of the transaction. In the course of the audit, the agency contacted Mr. Barfield, who denied having completed the verification-of-employment form. The matter was referred to the VA's Office of Inspector General (OIG), which investigated the discrepancy and concluded that Mr. Tijerina had authored the form. The OIG then turned the case over to the office of the United States Attorney. That office declined to prosecute the Tijerinas, for reasons which are the subject of some dispute: appellants contend it was for lack of evidence, while the government maintains it was because the Tijerinas' payments were current and the government had suffered no loss.

During its investigation of the case, the OIG learned that Mr. Tijerina intended to take the Texas bar examination some time in the future and that he already had taken the District of Columbia bar examination. On July 19,

1982, Morris Silverstein, a Deputy Inspector General, wrote an unsolicited letter to the Texas Board of Law Examiners and the Committee on Admissions of the District of Columbia Court of Appeals. Mr. Silverstein told the Bar officials that the OIG had recently completed an investigation into whether Mr. Tijerina had falsified a document in connection with a VA guaranteed home loan. The letter stated that although the U.S. Attorney's office declined to prosecute "due to no established loss to the government," Mr. Silverstein's office had concluded that Mr. Tijerina had falsified the form. The letter then concluded:

> During the course of our investigation, it came to our attention that Mr. Tijerina recently graduated from Howard University Law School and may have plans to practice law in Texas. You are therefore being provided with this information for whatever use you deem appropriate. Should you have any questions regarding this matter, do not hesitate to contact this office. Otherwise, no response to this letter is necessary.

The letter did not mention Maria Tijerina, although it did include a reference number to a VA file that contained information about both appellants.

Mr. Tijerina applied to take the Texas bar examination the following year. On July 13, 1983, the Texas Board of Law Examiners wrote the OIG requesting all information supporting the accusations in Mr. Silverstein's previous letter. Attached to the request was Mr. Tijerina's boilerplate consent authorizing governmental agencies to release information pertaining to him to the Bar Examiners. The OIG responded on July 20 by sending a full copy of the office's investigative report on Mr. Tijerina. The report included biographical information about Mrs. Tijerina as well as joint information that pertained to both appellants, including the couple's assets and liabilities. Neither Mr. nor Mrs. Tijerina was notified that the file had been released.

Three months later, the Texas Board of Law Examiners notified Mr. Tijerina that it had scheduled a hearing to consider the allegation that Mr. Tijerina had obtained a VA guaranteed home loan by means of fraud. The hearing took place on November 22, 1983, and Mr. Tijerina was found morally unfit to sit for the bar examination.

Mr. Tijerina shortly thereafter, on December 25, 1983, wrote the OIG to request his entire file, citing FOIA and the Privacy Act. There was some delay in the agency's response, occasioned in part by Mr. Tijerina's delivery of the letter to the VA's Washington regional office rather than the OIG and in part by the agency's failure to address the request, once it received it, within the ten-day time limit prescribed by FOIA. On January 23, 1984, the Washington office of the VA wrote Mr. Tijerina that it was forwarding his FOIA request to the OIG, but that it had a copy of Mrs. Tijerina's loan file, which it could release to him with his wife's consent. Mr. Tijerina filed the necessary consent, and the VA released the file on February 21. One week later, the OIG responded to Mr. Tijerina's FOIA request by releasing several of the documents in his investigative file and withholding others under claims of various FOIA exemptions. Mr. Tijerina filed an administrative appeal, which the VA decided in October 1984, when it agreed to release nearly all of the requested materials. The agency continued to withhold a litigation report about the instant case, which by this time had been filed, and an FBI report, a copy of which the Tijerinas had by then obtained directly from the FBI.

On July 30, 1984, while the administrative appeal was pending, the Tijerinas filed these actions *pro se* in the United States District Court for the District of Columbia, alleging violations of their rights under the Privacy Act, FOIA, and the equal protection and due process clauses of the Constitution. The Tijerinas charged the government with improper disclosure of information about both of them. Mr. Tijerina also alleged that the VA's records were inaccurately maintained in that they indicate that the reason the government did not prosecute him was that it had suffered no loss, rather than that it lacked sufficient evidence. The complaints also charged the government with violating appellants' rights under FOIA by failing promptly to release all requested material. Finally, the Tijerinas alleged violations of their constitutional rights to due process and equal protection, claiming the government intentionally discriminated against them because they are Mexican-Americans. . . .

II. Discussion

A. The Privacy Act Claims

Among its many other functions, the Privacy Act, 5 U.S.C. § e (1982) (the Act), requires governmental agencies to maintain accurate records and safeguards individuals from capricious dissemination of personal information by the government. Subsection (b) of the Act forbids an agency from disclosing information in its files to any person or to another agency without the consent of the individual to whom the information pertains. This broad prohibition is tempered by a dozen exceptions, one of which is relevant to the instant appeal. The exception permits unconsented disclosure for a "Routine Use," which the Act defines as "the use of such record for a purpose which is compatible with the purpose for which [the information] was collected." 5 U.S.C. § 552a(a)(7). In order to disclose information under this exception, the agency first must have established the Routine Use on which it seeks to rely by publishing a notice in the Federal Register detailing "each routine use [for a given system of records], including the categories of users and the purpose of such use." 5 U.S.C. § 552a(e)(4)(D). In this case, the government seeks to rely on two Routine Uses it previously promulgated for the system of records containing Mr. Tijerina's file. These two uses are Routine Use five, which permits disclosure of information relevant to a suspected violation or reasonably imminent violation of law to another agency charged with investigating the violation, and Routine Use three, which permits the VA to respond to an official request of a state agency by disclosing information relevant to that agency's decision whether to issue a license to an individual.

The principal enforcement mechanism for individuals whose rights under the Privacy Act have been violated is the provision for civil remedies contained in subsection (g). That subsection authorizes an aggrieved individual to bring a civil suit whenever any agency

> (C) fails to maintain any record concerning any individual with such accuracy . . . and completeness as is necessary to assure fairness in any

determination relating to the qualifications, character, rights, or opportunities of, or benefits to the individual that may be made on the basis of such record, and consequently a determination is made which is adverse to the individual; or

(D) fails to comply with any other provision of this section, or any rule promulgated thereunder, in such a way as to have an adverse effect on an individual.

5 U.S.C. § 552a(g)(1)(C) & (D). Subsection (g) further provides for recovery of actual damages, costs, and attorney's fees for a suit brought under (g)(1)(C) or (D) in which the court determines that the agency acted in a manner that was intentional or willful. 5 U.S.C. § 552a(g)(4).

The Act sets out a statute of limitations for actions brought to enforce any liability created under the Act. It provides that actions may be brought "within two years from the date on which the cause of action arises." 5 U.S.C. § 552a(g)(5). Subsection (g)(5) additionally prescribes a more elastic limitations period for cases in which the agency has materially and willfully misrepresented information that is material to establishing its own liability under the Act; in such instances, "the action may be brought at any time within two years after discovery by the individual of the misrepresentation."

Finally, subsection (j) of the Act, entitled "General Exemptions," permits agencies to exempt certain systems of records from some of the constraints established in the Act. Specifically, the subsection provides:

> The head of any agency may promulgate rules, in accordance with the requirements (including general notice) of [other provisions of the Act] to exempt any systems of record from any part of [the Act] except [certain enumerated provisions] if the system of records is:
>
> (1) maintained by the Central Intelligence Agency; or
>
> (2) maintained by an agency or component which performs as its principal function any activity pertaining to the enforcement of criminal laws . . . and which consists of . . . (B) information compiled for the purpose of a criminal investigation, including reports of informants and investigators, and associated with an identifiable individual.

5 U.S.C. § 552a(j). Among the many provisions from which subsection (j) specifically forbids the agency from exempting these systems of records is subsection (b), which governs the agency's duties with regard to disclosure of personal information. Subsection (g), which establishes civil remedies for individuals, is not listed among the enumerated provisions of the Act from which the agency's systems of records may not be exempted.

Having canvassed the relevant provisions of the Act, we turn to their application to the instant suit. We concur with the district court's dismissal of Mrs. Tijerina's Privacy Act claims. Mrs. Tijerina's complaint appears to seek damages only for the government's disclosure of personal information about her. However, Mrs. Tijerina does not allege that she suffered any adverse effect from these disclosures, as required by subsection (g)(1)(D) of the Act. The only harm Mrs. Tijerina mentions is having shared the costs occasioned by Mr. Tijerina's defense before the Texas Board of Law Examiners. These costs arose because of the VA's disclosures about her husband. It is an interesting and, so far as we determine, unresolved question whether Mrs. Tijerina could maintain a suit under (g)(1)(D) alleging that the VA's treatment of a third party — i.e. Mr. Tijerina — failed to comply with the Act in such a way as to have an adverse effect on her. It is clear from the Act, however, that Mrs. Tijerina cannot maintain an action under (g)(1)(D) for improper disclosure of information pertaining to her, because she has failed to demonstrate any adverse effect to her from that governmental conduct.

We also agree that Mr. Tijerina cannot maintain a claim for wrongful disclosure arising out of the July, 1983 disclosure when the OIG sent its file on Mr. Tijerina to the Texas Board of Law Examiners in response to the Board's request. Although the 1983 disclosure may be among the adverse effects caused by the July 1982 letter, the disclosure itself is not actionable under the Act, because Mr. Tijerina consented to it in connection with his application to the Texas Bar, and subsection (b) restricts only disclosures made without the prior written consent of the individual to whom the information pertains. See 5 U.S.C. § 552a(b).

There remains, however, Mr. Tijerina's claims arising out of the July 1982 letter from Mr. Silverstein. Tijerina appears to plead two theories of recovery under the Act: one for wrongful disclosure under subsection (g)(1)(D), and one for injurious failure to maintain accurate records under (g)(1)(C). The second claim is based on Tijerina's allegation that the VA's file failed to reflect that the real reason the U.S. Attorney declined to prosecute him was lack of evidence. The government offers four reasons why it is not liable under the Act on either theory. First, it claims that the VA exempted itself from civil liability with regard to the disclosed records. Second, it argues that the claim was barred by the applicable statute of limitations. Third, it urges that the disclosure was authorized under subsection (b)(3) of the Act because it was for a Routine Use. Fourth, it contends that Mr. Tijerina showed neither adverse effect nor intentional or willful violation, which are required under subsection (g) for recovery of money damages. We address each argument in turn.

1. Exemption

Mr. Tijerina's file apparently was contained in a system of records the OIG maintained to investigate irregularities involving VA regulations and federal laws. Relying on subsection (j), the VA purported to exempt this system of records from a long list of provisions under the Act, including subsection (g). . . . The district court found that subsection (j) of the Act authorizes an agency to exempt itself from the Act's civil remedies provision. The court went on to find that the VA had fulfilled the statutory rulemaking requirements for exemption and therefore had properly exempted itself from civil liability for wrongful disclosure of the material in Mr. Tijerina's file. We agree that the VA followed the procedural steps listed in subsection (j)(2): the OIG has a principal function of law enforcement, the information in Mr. Tijerina's file was compiled for the purpose of a criminal investigation, and the agency included in the announcement of exemption an explanation of the reasons for its action. We find, however, that these efforts were to no avail. We conclude that an agency has no power under the Act to exempt itself from the civil liability provisions of subsection (g). The agency's efforts to elude civil liability for violations of statutory duties which cannot be shirked under the Act contravene the language of the Act and the purpose behind the general exemptions provision.

The government's chief argument is that subsection (j) permits the agency to exempt systems of records from any part of the Act except a list of specific provisions, and subsection (g) is "conspicuously absent" from the list. The government contends that this omission demonstrates that Congress intended agencies to be able to elude civil liability for any violation of the Act. It anchors this position in the well-accepted principle of statutory construction that the starting point for interpreting a statute is the language of the statute itself. The government's position, however, is unfaithful to this rule. The language of the Act does not indicate, as the government contends, that an agency, after following APA requirements, may exempt *itself* from all provisions of the Privacy Act. Subsection (j) only permits an agency to exempt a system of records from the requirements set out in other provisions of the Act. Subsection (g), the Act's civil remedies provision, does not regulate *systems of records*. It is a derivative provision directed not towards agencies but towards courts and aggrieved individuals: the subsection provides a grant of jurisdiction and a waiver of sovereign immunity for suits alleging certain violations under the Act. It simply makes no sense for an agency to use subsection (j) to exempt a system of records from civil liability: records are not subject to civil liability under the Act; the United States is.

In short, an agency can employ subsection (j) in its expertise to adjust certain of its responsibilities under the Act. But liability is not itself among an agency's responsibilities under the Act; it is the result of the agency's failure to meet its duties. One of the agency's duties — and one from which the VA could not exempt itself — is the duty not to make unconsented disclosures of records except under certain circumstances. If the VA violated that requirement in such a way as to have an adverse effect on Mr. Tijerina (and if the government has no available defenses), Congress provided for civil liability to follow as a matter of course.

Besides torturing the language of the Act, the government's interpretation also perverts the purpose behind the Act's general exemptions provision. An examination of subsection (j) against the rest of the Act and its accompanying legislative history demonstrates that the provision is intended principally to permit the government to withhold *access* to certain sensitive information so as not to hamper law enforcement efforts. It specifically is not intended to permit agencies in any way to abridge their responsibilities governing *disclosure*: subsection (j) in fact specifically forbids the agency from exempting records from the Act's many constraints and obligations governing disclosure of personal information, such as subsection (b) (conditions of disclosure), subsections (c)(1) and (2) (accounting of disclosures), and subsection (e)(6) (accuracy of disclosed material). Moreover, the exemptions provision details the kinds of records that may be exempted, and they all relate to law enforcement activities that require a measure of secrecy. As the House Report explained,

> Only records maintained by the Central Intelligence Agency and criminal justice records could be so exempted. Even they would be subject to the

requirements relating to conditions of disclosure. . . . The Committee believes that such a broad [exemption] is permissible for these two types of records because they contain particularly sensitive information. C.I.A. files may include the most delicate information regarding national security. . . . The Committee also wishes to stress that this section is not intended to require the C.I.A. and criminal justice agencies to withhold all their personal records from the individuals to whom they pertain. We urge those agencies to keep open whatever files are presently open and to make available in the future whatever files can be made available without clearly infringing on the ability of the agencies to fulfill their missions.

In fact, the VA itself relied on subsection (j)'s core principle of law enforcement secrecy in explaining its reasons for exempting the system of records containing Mr. Tijerina's file. The agency wrote:

Reasons for exemptions: The exemption of information and material in this system of records is necessary in order to accomplish the law enforcement functions of the Office of Inspector General, to prevent subjects of investigations from frustrating the investigatory process, to prevent the disclosure of investigative techniques, to fulfill commitments made to protect the confidentiality of sources, to maintain access to sources of information and to avoid endangering these sources and law enforcement personnel.

None of the purposes the VA cited is remotely served by allowing the agency to escape civil liability for violations of the disclosure or accuracy requirements of the Act. Rather, the agency's statement of purpose only reaffirms that Congress inserted subsection (j) into the Act in order to permit agencies to shield information whose revelation could impede law enforcement efforts. . . .

2. Statute of Limitations

The district court supplied an alternative ground for dismissing Mr. Tijerina's claims growing out of the July 19, 1982 Silverstein letter. The court found that those claims were barred by the Act's two-year statute of limitations because Mr. Tijerina filed suit two years and 11 days after Silverstein sent the letter. The court apparently concluded that the two-year period automatically begins to run from the time of the contested disclosure, even if the plaintiff has no reason to know of the government's action. On appeal, the government asserts that this is the law, although it cites no authority for that proposition. The government bases its argument on the second part of the Act's statute of limitations (on which appellants do not rely). This section provides that "where an agency has materially and willfully misrepresented any information required under [the Act] to be disclosed to an individual and the information so misrepresented is material to establishment of the liability of the agency to the individual under [the Act], the action may be brought at any time within two years after discovery by the individual of the misrepresentation." 5 U.S.C. § 552a(g)(5). The government contends that this provision makes sense only if Congress intended the normal statutory period to commence at the time of the alleged violation, regardless of whether the potential plaintiff is or should be aware of the agency's action.

We disagree. Although this court has not previously faced the issue of when a cause of action arises for purposes of measuring the statutory limitations period under the Act, other courts that have addressed the question in causes of action similar to the instant case have concluded that "[i]t is necessary . . . for plaintiff to know or have reason to know that the adverse action occurred." . . . Furthermore, this view — which, as far as we can determine, no court has rejected — best accords with Congress's intent in passing the Act, which is our touchstone in determining when the statute begins to run. The Act seeks to provide a remedy for governmental conduct that by its very nature is frequently difficult to discover. An unauthorized, unconsented-to disclosure such as is alleged in this case, for example, is unlikely to come to the subject's attention until it affects him adversely, if then. Mr. Tijerina in fact contends he did not learn of the OIG's disclosure until October, 1983, when the Texas Board of Law Examiners notified him of its impending hearing into his moral fitness. Because possible violations of the Act are often not immediately apparent to the aggrieved individual, Congress's desire to provide a civil remedy would be poorly served if the cause of action could arise before the plaintiff even had reason to know of the violation. We therefore join other courts in holding that in a normal Privacy Act claim, the cause of action does not arise and the statute of limitation does not begin to run until the plaintiff knows or should know of the alleged violation. . . .

3. Routine Uses

Having articulated two distinct bases for granting summary judgment, the district court did not address the government's argument that the Silverstein letter did not violate subsection (b) of the Act, which governs conditions of disclosure, because the disclosure was for a "Routine Use." We find, however, that the Routine Uses that the government cites in this case are unavailing. The government first contends that the Silverstein letter was authorized under Routine Use five, which the VA promulgated to permit disclosure of information relevant to a suspected violation or reasonably imminent violation of law to another agency charged with investigating the violation. The government argues this Routine Use applies to the Silverstein letter because that disclosure helped the Texas Board of Law Examiners investigate a possible violation of the Texas statute that forbids persons from sitting for the bar unless they have demonstrated good moral character. It is not clear, however, that Mr. Tijerina would have violated the Texas statute by taking the bar examination. Even if Mr. Tijerina would have violated Texas law by sitting for the bar examination, the violation was not conceivably "reasonably imminent" at the time of the Silverstein letter; the OIG knew only that Mr. Tijerina might take the Texas bar examination at some time in the future. Routine Use five by its terms does not justify disclosure on the basis of such remote speculation.

The government also attempts to rely on Routine Use three, which permits the VA to respond to an official request of a state agency by disclosing information relevant to that agency's decision whether to issue a license to an individual. Reliance on this Routine Use overlooks one of the most notable aspects of the Silverstein letter: it was unsolicited. The Texas Board of Law Examiners had not requested any information whatsoever. Routine Use three, therefore, like Routine Use five, does not provide a basis for upholding the district court's grant of summary judgment on Mr. Tijerina's wrongful disclosure claim.

4. Adverse Effect and Willful or Intentional Violation

The Act provides a civil remedy when an agency's failure to comply with one of the Act's provisions has an adverse effect on an individual. 5 U.S.C. § 552a(g)(1)(D). The government claims that Mr. Tijerina failed to show that the VA's allegedly unlawful disclosure had an adverse effect on him. According to the government, the real reason Mr. Tijerina was not permitted to take the Texas bar examination was that he had attempted to defraud the government by filing a falsified loan application form, not that the OIG had disclosed this information to the Texas Board. This argument is vacuous. It could be used to justify indiscriminate disclosure of any incriminating information, which Congress clearly did not intend.

The Act further provides for damages, costs, and fees against the government when the court determines that the agency acted in a manner which was intentional or willful. The government contends that to meet this standard, the plaintiff must show that the agency official acted with the actual intent to violate the Privacy Act. The government therefore concludes that Mr. Silverstein's affidavit stating he did not believe he was violating the Act in sending the July 1982 letter disposes of appellant's damages claim. This position misinterprets the intentional-or-willful standard. The standard does not require the official to set out purposely to violate the Act; if the standard were so viewed, damages would be a rare remedy indeed. Rather, as a staff report explaining the compromises between the Senate and House versions of the Act pointed out, the standard "is viewed as only somewhat greater than gross negligence." Inasmuch as there is certainly a genuine issue of material fact as to whether Silverstein acted with something greater than gross negligence in sending out the unsolicited letter, the issue cannot be disposed of on summary judgment. . . .

B. The FOIA Claims

The district court properly dismissed all claims appellants brought under FOIA. The VA's response may have failed to meet FOIA's mandated standards of promptness, but the agency by now has released all nonexempt materials the Tijerinas seek. The only material appellants have not received is the VA's litigation report about the instant case, which is clearly exempt under FOIA. . . .

C. The Constitutional Claims

We affirm the district court's dismissal of appellants' claims that the government violated their constitutional rights to due process and equal protection. Appellants presented no evidence of a racially discriminatory intent or purpose to single them out as a racial minority. Their equal protection claim therefore cannot stand. As for the due process claim, any injury to reputation accompanying the disclosure of the allegation against Mr. Tijerina was not sufficient to trigger due process protection. Although the decision of the Texas Board of Law Examiners preventing Mr. Tijerina from taking the bar examination may have worked an alteration of status sufficient to trigger due process protection, . . . Mr. Tijerina had full notice and opportunity to be heard before that action was taken. Appellants' due process rights therefore were not abridged.

III. Conclusion

The court need not give lengthy consideration to the reasons for Mr. Silverstein's gratuitous submission to the Texas Board of Law Examiners. Whether he was a frustrated government employee trying to find a substitute sanction for the failed criminal prosecution, or merely a good citizen concerned about the character of would-be Texas lawyers, Mr. Silverstein was not a free agent. The Privacy Act was intended to build constraints around the disclosure of information in government files irrespective of the worthiness of the cause for such disclosure. Under those constraints, appellant Lorenzo Tijerina had the right to proceed to trial to test his claims arising out of the July 1982 letter, and if he prevailed, to receive the civil remedies made available in the Act. We reverse the district court's decision to the contrary.

In all other respects the judgment of the district court is affirmed.

It is so ordered.

NOTES AND QUESTIONS

10-25. What are the basic purposes of the Privacy Act? Were they upheld in this case? Does this Act provide any protection against abuses of personal privacy by private corporations?

10-26. How does this Act compare to FOIA? Who can bring suit? Citizens? Non-citizens? Corporate entities?

10-27. The Act defines a "record" to mean "any item, collection or grouping of information about an individual that is maintained by an agency, including, but not limited to his education, financial transactions, medical history and criminal or employment history and that contains his name, or the identifying number, symbol, or other identifying particular assigned to the individual, such as a finger or voice print or a photograph." 5 U.S.C. § 552(a)(4). Is this definition a particularly limiting one? Would sign/in and sign/out sheets at a federal building be a record? Private notes kept to refresh one's memory? Courts have interpreted this provision to require a "system of records" before the Act applies. Does this limit or enhance the Act's effectiveness?

10-28. This case sets forth the civil remedies available to petitioners in this case. Are they likely to be effective? Were they effective in this case? What must be proven before money damages will be awarded?

10-29. What is the future of personal privacy in the information age in which we now live? What changes would you recommend in the law governing these issues?

10-30. Should a federal employee's union have the ability to get the home addresses of union members from the agency under the FOIA or should that type of personal information be protected by the Privacy Act? *See U.S. Dept. of Defense v. Federal Labor Relations Authority*, 510 U.S. 487 (1994).

For a discussion of privacy in general and for an analysis that draws distinctions among citizens, consumers and clients, see Alfred C. Aman, Jr., *Information, Privacy, and Technology: Citizens, Clients or Consumers?* in *Freedom of Expression and Freedom of Information* (Oxford Univ. Press, 2000) (Jack Beatson and Yvonne Cripps, eds.).

10-31. Although individuals are entitled to an award equal to the greater of $1,000 or the amount of actual damages for a willful or intentional violation of the Privacy Act, an individual must prove that she has suffered at least some actual damages in order to qualify for any recovery at all. *See Doe v. Ohio*, 540 U.S. 614 (2004).

Appendix A

THE CONSTITUTION OF THE UNITED STATES OF AMERICA
(Selected Provisions)

Article I

Section 1. All legislative Powers herein granted shall be vested in a Congress of the United States, which shall consist of a Senate and House of Representatives. * * *

Section 7. All Bills for raising Revenue shall originate in the House of Representatives; but the Senate may propose or concur with Amendments as on other Bills.

Every Bill which shall have passed the House of Representatives and the Senate, shall, before it become a Law, be presented to the President of the United States; If he approve he shall sign it, but if not he shall return it, with his Objections to that House in which it shall have originated, who shall enter the Objections at large on their Journal, and proceed to reconsider it. If after such Reconsideration two thirds of that House shall agree to pass the Bill, it shall be sent, together with the Objections, to the other House, by which it shall likewise be reconsidered, and if approved by two thirds of that House, it shall become a Law. * * * If any Bill shall not be returned by the President within ten Days (Sundays excepted) after it shall have been presented to him, the Same shall be a Law, in like Manner as if he had signed it, unless the Congress by their Adjournment prevent its Return, in which Case it shall not be a Law.

Every Order, Resolution, or Vote to which the Concurrence of the Senate and House of Representatives may be necessary (except on a question of Adjournment) shall be presented to the President of the United States; and before the Same shall take Effect, shall be approved by him, or being disapproved by him, shall be repassed by two thirds of the Senate and House of Representatives, according to the Rules and Limitations prescribed in the Case of a Bill.

Section 8. The Congress shall have Power To lay and collect Taxes, Duties, Imposts and Excises, to pay the Debts and provide for the common Defence and general Welfare of the United States; but all Duties, Imposts and Excises shall be uniform throughout the United States; * * *

To regulate Commerce with foreign Nations, and among the several States, and with the Indian Tribes;

To establish an uniform Rule of Naturalization, and uniform Laws on the subject of Bankruptcies throughout the United States; * * *

To constitute Tribunals inferior to the supreme Court; * * *

To make all Laws which shall be necessary and proper for carrying into Execution the foregoing Powers, and all other Powers vested by this Constitution in the Government of the United States, or in any Department or Officer thereof. * * *

Article II

Section 1. The executive Power shall be vested in a President of the United States of America. * * *

Section 2. The President shall be Commander in Chief of the Army and Navy of the United States * * *; he may require the Opinion, in writing, of the principal Officer in each of the executive Departments, upon any Subject relating to the Duties of their respective Offices * * *.

He shall have Power, by and with the Advice and Consent of the Senate, to make Treaties, provided two thirds of the Senators present concur; and he shall nominate, and by and with the Advice and Consent of the Senate, shall appoint Ambassadors, other public Ministers and Consuls, Judges of the supreme Court, and all other Officers of the United States, whose Appointments are not herein otherwise provided for, and which shall be established by Law: but the Congress may by Law vest the Appointment of such inferior Officers, as they think proper, in the President alone, in the Courts of Law, or in the Heads of Departments.

The President shall have Power to fill up all Vacancies that may happen during the Recess of the Senate, by granting Commissions which shall expire at the End of their next Session.

Section 3. He shall from time to time give to the Congress Information of the State of the Union, and recommend to their Consideration such Measures as he shall judge necessary and expedient; * * * he shall take Care that the Laws be faithfully executed, and shall Commission all the Officers of the United States.

Section 4. The President, Vice President and all civil Officers of the United States, shall be removed from Office on Impeachment for, and Conviction of, Treason, Bribery, or other high Crimes and Misdemeanors.

Article III

Section 1. The judicial Power of the United States, shall be vested in one supreme Court, and in such inferior Courts as the Congress may from time to time ordain and establish. The Judges, both of the supreme and inferior Courts, shall hold their Offices during good Behaviour, and shall, at stated Times, receive for their Services, a Compensation, which shall not be diminished during their Continuance in Office.

Section 2. The judicial Power shall extend to all Cases, in Law and Equity, arising under this Constitution, the Laws of the United States, and Treaties made, or which shall be made, under their Authority;—to all Cases affecting Ambassadors, other public Ministers and Consuls;—to all Cases of admiralty and maritime Jurisdiction;—to Controversies to which the United States shall be a Party;—to Controversies between two or more States;—between a State and Citizens of another State; [See Amendment XI]—between Citizens of different States;—between Citizens of the same State claiming Lands under Grants of different States, and between a State, or the Citizens thereof, and foreign States, Citizens or Subjects.

In all Cases affecting Ambassadors, other public Ministers and Consuls, and those in which a State shall be Party, the supreme Court shall have original Jurisdiction. In all the other Cases before mentioned, the supreme Court shall have appellate Jurisdiction, both as to Law and Fact, with such Exceptions, and under such Regulations as the Congress shall make. * * *

Article V

The Congress, whenever two thirds of both Houses shall deem it necessary, shall propose Amendments to this Constitution, or, on the Application of the Legislatures of two thirds of the several States, shall call a Convention for proposing Amendments, which, in either Case, shall be valid to all Intents and Purposes, as Part of this Constitution, when ratified by the Legislatures of three fourths of the several States, or by Conventions in three fourths thereof, as the one or the other Mode of Ratification may be proposed by the Congress; Provided that no Amendment which may be made prior to the Year One thousand eight hundred and eight shall in any Manner affect the first and fourth Clauses in the Ninth Section of the first Article; and that no State, without its Consent, shall be deprived of its equal Suffrage in the Senate.

Article VI

* * *

This Constitution, and the Laws of the United States which shall be made in Pursuance thereof; and all Treaties made, or which shall be made, under the Authority of the United States, shall be the supreme Law of the Land; and the Judges in every State shall be bound thereby, any Thing in the Constitution or Laws of any State to the Contrary notwithstanding.

* * *

Amendment I [1791]

Congress shall make no law respecting an establishment of religion, or prohibiting the free exercise thereof; or abridging the freedom of speech, or of the press; or the right of the people peaceably to assemble, and to petition the government for a redress of grievances.

Amendment IV [1791]

The right of the people to be secure in their persons, houses, papers, and effects, against unreasonable searches and seizures, shall not be violated, and no warrants shall issue, but upon probable cause, supported by oath or affirmation, and particularly describing the place to be searched, and the persons or things to be seized.

Amendment V [1791]

No person shall be held to answer for a capital, or otherwise infamous crime, unless on a presentment or indictment of a grand jury, except in cases arising in the land or naval forces, or in the militia, when in actual service in time of war or public danger; nor shall any person be subject for the same offense to be twice put in jeopardy of life or limb; nor shall be compelled in any criminal case to be a witness against himself, nor be deprived of life, liberty, or property, without due process of law; nor shall private property be taken for public use, without just compensation.

Amendment VI [1791]

In all criminal prosecutions, the accused shall enjoy the right to a speedy and public trial, by an impartial jury of the state and district wherein the crime shall have been committed, which district shall have been previously ascertained by law, and to be informed of the nature and cause of the accusation; to be confronted with the witnesses against him; to have compulsory process for obtaining witnesses in his favor, and to have the assistance of counsel for his defense.

* * *

Amendment IX [1791]

The enumeration in the Constitution, of certain rights, shall not be construed to deny or disparage others retained by the people.

Amendment X [1791]

The powers not delegated to the United States by the Constitution, nor prohibited by it to the states, are reserved to the states respectively, or to the people.

Amendment XI [1798]

The judicial power of the United States shall not be construed to extend to any suit in law or equity, commenced or prosecuted against one of the United States by citizens of another state, or by citizens or subjects of any foreign state.

* * *

Amendment XIV [1868]

Section 1. All persons born or naturalized in the United States, and subject to the jurisdiction thereof, are citizens of the United States and of the state wherein they reside. No state shall make or enforce any law which shall abridge the privileges or immunities of citizens of the United States; nor shall any state deprive any person of life, liberty, or property, without due process of law; nor deny to any person within its jurisdiction the equal protection of the laws.

* * *

Section 5. The Congress shall have power to enforce, by appropriate legislation, the provisions of this article.

Appendix B

FEDERAL ADMINISTRATIVE PROCEDURE ACT

UNITED STATES CODE, TITLE 5
(Selected Provisions)

Sec.

551.	Definitions
552.	Public information; agency rules, opinions, orders, records, and proceedings
552a.	Records maintained on individuals [Privacy Act omitted here, but included in Appendix D.]
552b.	Open meetings [Sunshine Act omitted here, but included in Appendix E]
553.	Rule making
554.	Adjudications
555.	Ancillary matters
556.	Hearings; presiding employees; powers and duties; burden of proof; evidence; record as basis of decision
557.	Initial decisions; conclusiveness; review by agency; submissions by parties; contents of decisions; record
558.	Imposition of sanctions; determination of applications for licenses; suspension, revocation, and expiration of licenses
559.	Effect on other laws; effect of subsequent statute
701.	Application; definitions
702.	Right of review
703.	Form and venue of proceeding
704.	Actions reviewable
705.	Relief pending review
706.	Scope of review
1305.	Administrative law judges
3105.	Appointment of administrative law judges
3344.	Details; administrative law judges
5372.	Administrative law judges
7521.	Actions against administrative law judges

§ 551. Definitions

For the purpose of this subchapter—

(1) "agency" means each authority of the Government of the United States, whether or not it is within or subject to review by another agency, but does not include—

(A) the Congress;

(B) the courts of the United States;

(C) the governments of the territories or possessions of the United States;

(D) the government of the District of Columbia;

or except as to the requirements of section 552 of this title—

(E) agencies composed of representatives of the parties or of representatives of organizations of the parties to the disputes determined by them;

(F) courts martial and military commissions;

(G) military authority exercised in the field in time of war or in occupied territory; or

(H) functions conferred by sections 1738, 1739, 1743, and 1744 of title 12; chapter 2 of title 41; subchapter II of chapter 471 of title 49; or sections 1884, 1891-1902, and former section 1641(b)(2), of title 50, appendix;

(2) "person" includes an individual, partnership, corporation, association, or public or private organization other than an agency;

(3) "party" includes a person or agency named or admitted as a party, or properly seeking and entitled as of right to be admitted as a party, in an agency proceeding, and a person or agency admitted by an agency as a party for limited purposes;

(4) "rule" means the whole or a part of an agency statement of general or particular applicability and future effect designed to implement, interpret, or prescribe law or policy or describing the organization, procedure, or practice requirements of an agency and includes the approval or prescription for the future of rates, wages, corporate or financial structures or reorganizations thereof, prices, facilities, appliances, services or allowances therefor or of valuations, costs, or accounting, or practices bearing on any of the foregoing;

(5) "rule making" means agency process for formulating, amending, or repealing a rule;

(6) "order" means the whole or a part of a final disposition, whether affirmative, negative, injunctive, or declaratory in form, of an agency in a matter other than rule making but including licensing;

(7) "adjudication" means agency process for the formulation of an order;

(8) "license" includes the whole or a part of an agency permit, certificate, approval, registration, charter, membership, statutory exemption or other form of permission;

(9) "licensing" includes agency process respecting the grant, renewal, denial, revocation, suspension, annulment, withdrawal, limitation, amendment, modification, or conditioning of a license;

(10) "sanction" includes the whole or a part of an agency—

(A) prohibition, requirement, limitation, or other condition affecting the freedom of a person;

(B) withholding of relief;

(C) imposition of penalty or fine;

(D) destruction, taking, seizure, or withholding of property;

(E) assessment of damages, reimbursement, restitution, compensation, costs, charges, or fees;

(F) requirement, revocation, or suspension of a license; or

(G) taking other compulsory or restrictive action;

(11) "relief" includes the whole or a part of an agency—

(A) grant of money, assistance, license, authority, exemption, exception, privilege, or remedy;

(B) recognition of a claim, right, immunity, privilege, exemption, or exception; or

(C) taking of other action on the application or petition of, and beneficial to, a person;

(12) "agency proceeding" means an agency process as defined by paragraphs (5), (7), and (9) of this section;

(13) "agency action" includes the whole or a part of an agency rule, order, license, sanction, relief, or the equivalent or denial thereof, or failure to act; and

(14) "ex parte communication" means an oral or written communication not on the public record with respect to which reasonable prior notice to all parties is not given, but it shall not include requests for status reports on any matter or proceeding covered by this subchapter.

§ 552. Public information; agency rules, opinions, orders, records, and proceedings

(a) Each agency shall make available to the public information as follows:

(1) Each agency shall separately state and currently publish in the Federal Register for the guidance of the public—

(A) descriptions of its central and field organization and the established places at which, the employees (and in the case of a uniformed service, the members) from whom, and the methods whereby, the public may obtain information, make submittals or requests, or obtain decisions;

(B) statements of the general course and method by which its functions are channeled and determined, including the nature and requirements of all formal and informal procedures available;

(C) rules of procedure, descriptions of forms available or the places at which forms may be obtained, and instructions as to the scope and contents of all papers, reports, or examinations;

(D) substantive rules of general applicability adopted as authorized by law, and statements of general policy or interpretations of general applicability formulated and adopted by the agency; and

(E) each amendment, revision, or repeal of the foregoing.

Except to the extent that a person has actual and timely notice of the terms thereof, a person may not in any manner be required to resort to, or be adversely affected by, a matter required to be published in the Federal Register and not so published. For the purpose of this paragraph, matter reasonably available to the class of persons affected thereby is deemed published in the Federal Register when incorporated by reference therein with the approval of the Director of the Federal Register.

(2) Each agency, in accordance with published rules, shall make available for public inspection and copying—

(A) final opinions, including concurring and dissenting opinions, as well as orders, made in the adjudication of cases;

(B) those statements of policy and interpretations which have been adopted by the agency and are not published in the Federal Register;

(C) administrative staff manuals and instructions to staff that affect a member of the public;

(D) copies of all records, regardless of form or format, which have been released to any person under paragraph (3) and which, because of the nature of their subject matter, the agency determines have become or are likely to become the subject of subsequent requests for substantially the same records; and

(E) a general index of the records referred to under subparagraph (D);

unless the materials are promptly published and copies offered for sale. For records created on or after November 1, 1996, within one year after such date, each agency shall make such records available, including by computer telecommunications or, if computer telecommunications means have not been established by the agency, by other electronic means. To the extent required to prevent a clearly unwarranted invasion of personal privacy, an agency may delete identifying details when it makes available or publishes an opinion, statement of policy, interpretation, staff manual, instruction, or copies of records referred to in subparagraph (D). However, in each case the justification for the deletion shall be explained fully in writing, and the extent of such deletion shall be indicated on the portion of the record which is made available or published, unless including that indication would harm an interest protected by the exemption in subsection (b) under which the deletion is made. If technically feasible, the extent of the deletion shall be indicated at the place in the record where the deletion was made. Each agency shall also maintain and make available for public inspection and copying current indexes providing identifying information for the public as to any matter issued, adopted, or promulgated after July 4, 1967, and required by this paragraph to be made available or published. Each agency shall promptly publish, quarterly or more frequently, and distribute (by sale or otherwise) copies of each index or supplements thereto unless it determines by order published in the Federal Register that the publication would be unnecessary and impracticable, in which case the agency shall nonetheless provide copies of such index on request at a cost not to exceed the direct cost of duplication. Each agency shall make the index referred to in subparagraph (E) available by computer telecommunications by December 31, 1999. A final order, opinion, statement of policy, interpretation, or staff manual or instruction that affects a member of the public may be relied on, used, or cited as precedent by an agency against a party other than an agency only if—

(i) it has been indexed and either made available or published as provided by this paragraph; or

(ii) the party has actual and timely notice of the terms thereof.

(3)(A) Except with respect to the records made available under paragraphs

(1) and (2) of this subsection, and except as provided in subparagraph (E), each agency, upon any request for records which (i) reasonably describes such records and (ii) is made in accordance with published rules stating the time, place, fees (if any), and procedures to be followed, shall make the records promptly available to any person.

(B) In making any record available to a person under this paragraph, an agency shall provide the record in any form or format requested by the person if the record is readily reproducible by the agency in that form or format. Each agency shall make reasonable efforts to maintain its records in forms or formats that are reproducible for purposes of this section.

(C) In responding under this paragraph to a request for records, an agency shall make reasonable efforts to search for the records in electronic form or format, except when such efforts would significantly interfere with the operation of the agency's automated information system.

(D) For purposes of this paragraph, the term "search" means to review, manually or by automated means, agency records for the purpose of locating those records which are responsive to a request.

(E) An agency, or part of an agency, that is an element of the intelligence community (as that term is defined in section 3(4) of the National Security Act of 1947 (50 U.S.C. 401a(4))) shall not make any record available under this paragraph to—

(i) any government entity, other than a State, territory, commonwealth, or district of the United States, or any subdivision thereof; or

(ii) a representative of a government entity described in clause (i).

(4)(A)(i) In order to carry out the provisions of this section, each agency shall promulgate regulations, pursuant to notice and receipt of public comment, specifying the schedule of fees applicable to the processing of requests under this section and establishing procedures and guidelines for determining when such fees should be waived or reduced. Such schedule shall conform to the guidelines which shall be promulgated, pursuant to notice and receipt of public comment, by the Director of the Office of Management and Budget and which shall provide for a uniform schedule of fees for all agencies.

(ii) Such agency regulations shall provide that—

(I) fees shall be limited to reasonable standard charges for document search, duplication, and review, when records are requested for commercial use;

(II) fees shall be limited to reasonable standard charges for document duplication when records are not sought for commercial use and the request is made by an educational or noncommercial scientific institution, whose purpose is scholarly or scientific research; or a representative of the news media; and

(III) for any request not described in (I) or (II), fees shall be limited to reasonable standard charges for document search and duplication.

(iii) Documents shall be furnished without any charge or at a charge reduced below the fees established under clause (ii) if disclosure of the information is in the public interest because it is likely to contribute significantly to public understanding of the operations or activities of the government and is not primarily in the commercial interest of the requester.

(iv) Fee schedules shall provide for the recovery of only the direct costs of search, duplication, or review. Review costs shall include only the direct costs incurred during the initial examination of a document for the purposes of determining whether the documents must be disclosed under this section and for the purposes of withholding any portions exempt from disclosure under this section. Review costs may not include any costs incurred in resolving issues of law or policy that may be raised in the course of processing a request under this section. No fee may be charged by any agency under this section—

(I) if the costs of routine collection and processing of the fee are likely to equal or exceed the amount of the fee; or

(II) for any request described in clause (ii)(II) or (III) of this subparagraph for the first two hours of search time or for the first one hundred pages of duplication.

(v) No agency may require advance payment of any fee unless the requester has previously failed to pay fees in a timely fashion, or the agency has determined that the fee will exceed $250.

(vi) Nothing in this subparagraph shall supersede fees chargeable under a statute specifically providing for setting the level of fees for particular types of records.

(vii) In any action by a requester regarding the waiver of fees under this section, the court shall determine the matter de novo: Provided, That the court's review of the matter shall be limited to the record before the agency.

(B) On complaint, the district court of the United States in the district in which the complainant resides, or has his principal place of business, or in which the agency records are situated, or in the District of Columbia, has jurisdiction to enjoin the agency from withholding agency records and to order the production of any agency records improperly withheld from the complainant. In such a case the court shall determine the matter de novo, and may examine the contents of such agency records in camera to determine whether such records or any part thereof shall be withheld under any of the exemptions set forth in subsection (b) of this section, and the burden is on the agency to sustain its action. In addition to any other matters to which a court accords substantial weight, a court shall accord substantial weight to an affidavit of an agency concerning the agency's determination as to technical feasibility under paragraph (2)(C) and subsection (b) and reproducibility under paragraph (3)(B).

(C) Notwithstanding any other provision of law, the defendant shall serve an answer or otherwise plead to any complaint made under this subsection within thirty days after service upon the defendant of the pleading in which such complaint is made, unless the court otherwise directs for good cause shown.

[(D) Repealed. Pub.L. 98-620, Title IV, § 402(2), Nov. 8, 1984, 98 Stat. 3357]

(E) The court may assess against the United States reasonable attorney fees and other litigation costs reasonably incurred in any case under this section in which the complainant has substantially prevailed.

(F) Whenever the court orders the production of any agency records improperly withheld from the complainant and assesses against the United States reasonable attorney fees and other litigation costs, and the court additionally issues a written finding that the circumstances surrounding the withholding raise questions whether agency personnel acted arbitrarily or capriciously with respect to the withholding, the Special Counsel shall promptly initiate a proceeding to determine whether disciplinary action is warranted against the officer or employee who was primarily responsible for the withholding. The Special Counsel, after investigation and consideration of the evidence submitted, shall submit his findings and recommendations to the administrative authority of the agency concerned and shall send copies of the findings and recommendations to the officer or employee or his representative. The administrative authority shall take the corrective action that the Special Counsel recommends.

(G) In the event of noncompliance with the order of the court, the district court may punish for contempt the responsible employee, and in the case of a uniformed service, the responsible member.

(5) Each agency having more than one member shall maintain and make available for public inspection a record of the final votes of each member in every agency proceeding.

(6)(A) Each agency, upon any request for records made under paragraph (1), (2), or (3) of this subsection, shall—

(i) determine within 20 days (excepting Saturdays, Sundays, and legal public holidays) after the receipt of any such request whether to comply with such request and shall immediately notify the person making such request of such determination and the reasons therefor, and of the right of such person to appeal to the head of the agency any adverse determination; and

(ii) make a determination with respect to any appeal within twenty days (excepting Saturdays, Sundays, and legal public holidays) after the receipt of such appeal. If on appeal the denial of the request for records is in whole or in part upheld, the agency shall notify the person making such request of the provisions for judicial review of that determination under paragraph (4) of this subsection.

(B)(i) In unusual circumstances as specified in this subparagraph, the time limits prescribed in either clause (i) or clause (ii) of subparagraph (A) may be extended by written notice to the person making such request setting forth the unusual circumstances for such extension and the date on which a determination is expected to be dispatched. No such notice shall specify a date that would result in an extension for more than ten working days, except as provided in clause (ii) of this subparagraph.

(ii) With respect to a request for which a written notice under clause (i) extends the time limits prescribed under clause (i) of subparagraph (A), the agency shall notify the person making the request if the request cannot be processed within the time limit specified in that clause and shall provide the person an opportunity to limit the scope of the request so that it may be processed within that time limit or an opportunity to arrange with the agency an alternative time frame for processing the request or a modified request. Refusal by the person to reasonably modify the request or arrange such an alternative time frame shall be considered as a factor in determining whether exceptional circumstances exist for purposes of subparagraph (C).

(iii) As used in this subparagraph, "unusual circumstances" means, but only to the extent reasonably necessary to the proper processing of the particular requests—

(I) the need to search for and collect the requested records from field facilities or other establishments that are separate from the office processing the request;

(II) the need to search for, collect, and appropriately examine a voluminous amount of separate and distinct records which are demanded in a single request; or

(III) the need for consultation, which shall be conducted with all practicable speed, with another agency having a substantial interest in the determination of the request or among two or more components of the agency having substantial subject-matter interest therein.

(iv) Each agency may promulgate regulations, pursuant to notice and receipt of public comment, providing for the aggregation of certain requests by the same requestor, or by a group of requestors acting in concert, if the agency reasonably believes that such requests actually constitute a single request, which would otherwise satisfy the unusual circumstances specified in this subparagraph, and the requests involve clearly related matters. Multiple requests involving unrelated matters shall not be aggregated.

(C)(i) Any person making a request to any agency for records under paragraph (1), (2), or (3) of this subsection shall be deemed to have exhausted his administrative remedies with respect to such request if the agency fails to comply with the applicable time limit provisions of this paragraph. If the Government can show exceptional circumstances exist and that the agency is exercising due diligence in responding to the request, the court may retain jurisdiction and allow the agency additional time to complete its review of the records. Upon any determination by an agency to comply with a request for records, the records shall be made promptly available to such person making such request. Any notification of denial of any request for records under this subsection shall set forth the names and titles or positions of each person responsible for the denial of such request.

(ii) For purposes of this subparagraph, the term "exceptional circumstances" does not include a delay that results from a predictable agency workload of requests under this section, unless the agency demonstrates reasonable progress in reducing its backlog of pending requests.

(iii) Refusal by a person to reasonably modify the scope of a request or arrange an alternative time frame for processing a request (or a modified request) under clause (ii) after being given an opportunity to do so by the agency to whom the person made the request shall be considered as a factor in determining whether exceptional circumstances exist for purposes of this subparagraph.

(D)(i) Each agency may promulgate regulations, pursuant to notice and receipt of public comment, providing for multitrack processing of requests for records based on the amount of work or time (or both) involved in processing requests.

(ii) Regulations under this subparagraph may provide a person making a request that does not qualify for the fastest multitrack processing an opportunity to limit the scope of the request in order to qualify for faster processing.

(iii) This subparagraph shall not be considered to affect the requirement under subparagraph (C) to exercise due diligence.

(E)(i) Each agency shall promulgate regulations, pursuant to notice and receipt of public comment, providing for expedited processing of requests for records—

(I) in cases in which the person requesting the records demonstrates a compelling need; and

(II) in other cases determined by the agency.

(ii) Notwithstanding clause (i), regulations under this subparagraph must ensure—

(I) that a determination of whether to provide expedited processing shall be made, and notice of the determination shall be provided to the person making the request, within 10 days after the date of the request; and

(II) expeditious consideration of administrative appeals of such determinations of whether to provide expedited processing.

(iii) An agency shall process as soon as practicable any request for records to which the agency has granted expedited processing under this subparagraph. Agency action to deny or affirm denial of a request for expedited processing pursuant to this subparagraph, and failure by an agency to respond in a timely manner to such a request shall be subject to judicial review under paragraph (4), except that the judicial review shall be based on the record before the agency at the time of the determination.

(iv) A district court of the United States shall not have jurisdiction to review an agency denial of expedited processing of a request for records after the agency has provided a complete response to the request.

(v) For purposes of this subparagraph, the term "compelling need" means—

(I) that a failure to obtain requested records on an expedited basis under this paragraph could reasonably be expected to pose an imminent threat to the life or physical safety of an individual; or

(II) with respect to a request made by a person primarily engaged in disseminating information, urgency to inform the public concerning actual or alleged Federal Government activity.

(vi) A demonstration of a compelling need by a person making a request for expedited processing shall be made by a statement certified by such person to be true and correct to the best of such person's knowledge and belief.

(F) In denying a request for records, in whole or in part, an agency shall make a reasonable effort to estimate the volume of any requested matter the provision of which is denied, and shall provide any such estimate to the person making the request, unless providing such estimate would harm an interest protected by the exemption in subsection (b) pursuant to which the denial is made.

(b) This section does not apply to matters that are—

(1) (A) specifically authorized under criteria established by an Executive order to be kept secret in the interest of national defense or foreign policy and (B) are in fact properly classified pursuant to such Executive order;

(2) related solely to the internal personnel rules and practices of an agency;

(3) specifically exempted from disclosure by statute (other than section 552b of this title), provided that such statute (A) requires that the matters be withheld from the public in such a manner as to leave no discretion on the issue, or (B) establishes particular criteria for withholding or refers to particular types of matters to be withheld;

(4) trade secrets and commercial or financial information obtained from a person and privileged or confidential;

(5) inter-agency or intra-agency memorandums or letters which would not be available by law to a party other than an agency in litigation with the agency;

(6) personnel and medical files and similar files the disclosure of which would constitute a clearly unwarranted invasion of personal privacy;

(7) records or information compiled for law enforcement purposes, but only to the extent that the production of such law enforcement records or information (A) could reasonably be expected to interfere with enforcement proceedings, (B) would deprive a person of a right to a fair trial or an impartial adjudication, (C) could reasonably be expected to constitute an unwarranted invasion of personal privacy, (D) could reasonably be expected to disclose the identity of a confidential source, including a State, local, or foreign agency or authority or any private institution which furnished information on a confidential basis, and, in the case of a record or information compiled by criminal law enforcement authority in the course of a criminal investigation or by an agency conducting a lawful national security intelligence investigation, information furnished by a confidential source, (E) would disclose techniques and procedures for law enforcement investigations or prosecutions, or would disclose guidelines for law enforcement investigations or prosecutions if such disclosure could reasonably be expected to risk circumvention of the law, or (F) could reasonably be expected to endanger the life or physical safety of any individual;

(8) contained in or related to examination, operating, or condition reports prepared by, on behalf of, or for the use of an agency responsible for the regulation or supervision of financial institutions; or

(9) geological and geophysical information and data, including maps, concerning wells.

Any reasonably segregable portion of a record shall be provided to any person requesting such record after deletion of the portions which are exempt under this subsection. The amount of information deleted shall be indicated on the released portion of the record, unless including that indication would harm an interest protected by the exemption in this subsection under which the deletion is made. If technically feasible, the amount of the information deleted shall be indicated at the place in the record where such deletion is made.

(c)(1) Whenever a request is made which involves access to records described in subsection (b)(7)(A) and—

(A) the investigation or proceeding involves a possible violation of criminal law; and

(B) there is reason to believe that (i) the subject of the investigation or proceeding is not aware of its pendency, and (ii) disclosure of the existence of the records could reasonably be expected to interfere with enforcement proceedings,

the agency may, during only such time as that circumstance continues, treat the records as not subject to the requirements of this section.

(2) Whenever informant records maintained by a criminal law enforcement agency under an informant's name or personal identifier are requested by a third party according to the informant's name or personal identifier, the agency may treat the records as not subject to the requirements of this section unless the informant's status as an informant has been officially confirmed.

(3) Whenever a request is made which involves access to records maintained by the Federal Bureau of Investigation pertaining to foreign intelligence or counterintelligence, or international terrorism, and the existence of the records is classified information as provided in subsection (b)(1), the Bureau may, as long as the existence of the records remains classified information, treat the records as not subject to the requirements of this section.

(d) This section does not authorize withholding of information or limit the availability of records to the public, except as specifically stated in this section. This section is not authority to withhold information from Congress.

(e)(1) On or before February 1 of each year, each agency shall submit to the Attorney General of the United States a report which shall cover the preceding fiscal year and which shall include—

(A) the number of determinations made by the agency not to comply with requests for records made to such agency under subsection (a) and the reasons for each such determination;

(B)(i) the number of appeals made by persons under subsection (a)(6), the result of such appeals, and the reason for the action upon each appeal that results in a denial of information; and

(ii) a complete list of all statutes that the agency relies upon to authorize the agency to withhold information under subsection (b)(3), a description of whether a court has upheld the decision of the agency to withhold information under each such statute, and a concise description of the scope of any information withheld;

(C) the number of requests for records pending before the agency as of September 30 of the preceding year, and the median number of days that such requests had been pending before the agency as of that date;

(D) the number of requests for records received by the agency and the number of requests which the agency processed;

(E) the median number of days taken by the agency to process different types of requests;

(F) the total amount of fees collected by the agency for processing requests; and

(G) the number of full-time staff of the agency devoted to processing requests for records under this section, and the total amount expended by the agency for processing such requests.

(2) Each agency shall make each such report available to the public including by computer telecommunications, or if computer telecommunications means have not been established by the agency, by other electronic means.

(3) The Attorney General of the United States shall make each report which has been made available by electronic means available at a single electronic

access point. The Attorney General of the United States shall notify the Chairman and ranking minority member of the Committee on Government Reform and Oversight of the House of Representatives and the Chairman and ranking minority member of the Committees on Governmental Affairs and the Judiciary of the Senate, no later than April 1 of the year in which each such report is issued, that such reports are available by electronic means.

(4) The Attorney General of the United States, in consultation with the Director of the Office of Management and Budget, shall develop reporting and performance guidelines in connection with reports required by this subsection by October 1, 1997, and may establish additional requirements for such reports as the Attorney General determines may be useful.

(5) The Attorney General of the United States shall submit an annual report on or before April 1 of each calendar year which shall include for the prior calendar year a listing of the number of cases arising under this section, the exemption involved in each case, the disposition of such case, and the cost, fees, and penalties assessed under subparagraphs (E), (F), and (G) of subsection (a)(4). Such report shall also include a description of the efforts undertaken by the Department of Justice to encourage agency compliance with this section.

(f) For purposes of this section, the term—

(1) "agency" as defined in section 551(1) of this title includes any executive department, military department, Government corporation, Government controlled corporation, or other establishment in the executive branch of the Government (including the Executive Office of the President), or any independent regulatory agency; and

(2) "record" and any other term used in this section in reference to information includes any information that would be an agency record subject to the requirements of this section when maintained by an agency in any format, including an electronic format.

(g) The head of each agency shall prepare and make publicly available upon request, reference material or a guide for requesting records or information from the agency, subject to the exemptions in subsection (b), including—

(1) an index of all major information systems of the agency;

(2) a description of major information and record locator systems maintained by the agency; and

(3) a handbook for obtaining various types and categories of public information from the agency pursuant to chapter 35 of title 44, and under this section.

§ 552a. Records maintained on individuals [Privacy Act omitted]

§ 552b. Open meetings [Sunshine Act omitted]

§ 553. Rule making

(a) This section applies, according to the provisions thereof, except to the extent that there is involved—

(1) a military or foreign affairs function of the United States; or

(2) a matter relating to agency management or personnel or to public property, loans, grants, benefits, or contracts.

(b) General notice of proposed rule making shall be published in the Federal Register, unless persons subject thereto are named and either personally served or otherwise have actual notice thereof in accordance with law. The notice shall include—

(1) a statement of the time, place, and nature of public rule making proceedings;

(2) reference to the legal authority under which the rule is proposed; and

(3) either the terms or substance of the proposed rule or a description of the subjects and issues involved.

Except when notice or hearing is required by statute, this subsection does not apply—

(A) to interpretative rules, general statements of policy, or rules of agency organization, procedure, or practice; or

(B) when the agency for good cause finds (and incorporates the finding and a brief statement of reasons therefor in the rules issued) that notice and public procedure thereon are impracticable, unnecessary, or contrary to the public interest.

(c) After notice required by this section, the agency shall give interested persons an opportunity to participate in the rule making through submission of written data, views, or arguments with or without opportunity for oral presentation. After consideration of the relevant matter presented, the agency shall incorporate in the rules adopted a concise general statement of their basis and purpose. When rules are required by statute to be made on the record after opportunity for an agency hearing, sections 556 and 557 of this title apply instead of this subsection.

(d) The required publication or service of a substantive rule shall be made not less than 30 days before its effective date, except—

(1) a substantive rule which grants or recognizes an exemption or relieves a restriction;

(2) interpretative rules and statements of policy; or

(3) as otherwise provided by the agency for good cause found and published with the rule.

(e) Each agency shall give an interested person the right to petition for the issuance, amendment, or repeal of a rule.

§ 554. Adjudications

(a) This section applies, according to the provisions thereof, in every case of adjudication required by statute to be determined on the record after opportunity for an agency hearing, except to the extent that there is involved—

   (1) a matter subject to a subsequent trial of the law and the facts de novo in a court;

   (2) the selection or tenure of an employee, except a [FN1] administrative law judge appointed under section 3105 of this title;

   (3) proceedings in which decisions rest solely on inspections, tests, or elections;

   (4) the conduct of military or foreign affairs functions;

   (5) cases in which an agency is acting as an agent for a court; or

   (6) the certification of worker representatives.

(b) Persons entitled to notice of an agency hearing shall be timely informed of—

   (1) the time, place, and nature of the hearing;

   (2) the legal authority and jurisdiction under which the hearing is to be held; and

   (3) the matters of fact and law asserted.

When private persons are the moving parties, other parties to the proceeding shall give prompt notice of issues controverted in fact or law; and in other instances agencies may by rule require responsive pleading. In fixing the time and place for hearings, due regard shall be had for the convenience and necessity of the parties or their representatives.

(c) The agency shall give all interested parties opportunity for—

   (1) the submission and consideration of facts, arguments, offers of settlement, or proposals of adjustment when time, the nature of the proceeding, and the public interest permit; and

   (2) to the extent that the parties are unable so to determine a controversy by consent, hearing and decision on notice and in accordance with sections 556 and 557 of this title.

(d) The employee who presides at the reception of evidence pursuant to section 556 of this title shall make the recommended decision or initial decision required by section 557 of this title, unless he becomes unavailable to the agency. Except to the extent required for the disposition of ex parte matters as authorized by law, such an employee may not—

   (1) consult a person or party on a fact in issue, unless on notice and opportunity for all parties to participate; or

   (2) be responsible to or subject to the supervision or direction of an employee or agent engaged in the performance of investigative or prosecuting functions for an agency.

An employee or agent engaged in the performance of investigative or prosecuting functions for an agency in a case may not, in that or a factually related case, participate or advise in the decision, recommended decision, or agency review pursuant to section 557 of this title, except as witness or counsel in public proceedings. This subsection does not apply—

(A) in determining applications for initial licenses;

(B) to proceedings involving the validity or application of rates, facilities, or practices of public utilities or carriers; or

(C) to the agency or a member or members of the body comprising the agency.

(e) The agency, with like effect as in the case of other orders, and in its sound discretion, may issue a declaratory order to terminate a controversy or remove uncertainty.

§ 555. Ancillary matters

(a) This section applies, according to the provisions thereof, except as otherwise provided by this subchapter.

(b) A person compelled to appear in person before an agency or representative thereof is entitled to be accompanied, represented, and advised by counsel or, if permitted by the agency, by other qualified representative. A party is entitled to appear in person or by or with counsel or other duly qualified representative in an agency proceeding. So far as the orderly conduct of public business permits, an interested person may appear before an agency or its responsible employees for the presentation, adjustment, or determination of an issue, request, or controversy in a proceeding, whether interlocutory, summary, or otherwise, or in connection with an agency function. With due regard for the convenience and necessity of the parties or their representatives and within a reasonable time, each agency shall proceed to conclude a matter presented to it. This subsection does not grant or deny a person who is not a lawyer the right to appear for or represent others before an agency or in an agency proceeding.

(c) Process, requirement of a report, inspection, or other investigative act or demand may not be issued, made, or enforced except as authorized by law. A person compelled to submit data or evidence is entitled to retain or, on payment of lawfully prescribed costs, procure a copy or transcript thereof, except that in a nonpublic investigatory proceeding the witness may for good cause be limited to inspection of the official transcript of his testimony.

(d) Agency subpenas authorized by law shall be issued to a party on request and, when required by rules of procedure, on a statement or showing of general relevance and reasonable scope of the evidence sought. On contest, the court shall sustain the subpena or similar process or demand to the extent that it is found to be in accordance with law. In a proceeding for enforcement, the court shall issue an order requiring the appearance of the witness or the production of the evidence or data within a reasonable time under penalty of punishment for contempt in case of contumacious failure to comply.

(e) Prompt notice shall be given of the denial in whole or in part of a written application, petition, or other request of an interested person made in connection with any agency proceeding. Except in affirming a prior denial or when the denial is self-explanatory, the notice shall be accompanied by a brief statement of the grounds for denial.

§ 556. Hearings; presiding employees; powers and duties; burden of proof; evidence; record as basis of decision

[margin note: Formal]

(a) This section applies, according to the provisions thereof, to hearings required by section 553 or 554 of this title to be conducted in accordance with this section. [margin note: Formal rulemaking + Formal adjudication]

(b) There shall preside at the taking of evidence—

   (1) the agency;

   (2) one or more members of the body which comprises the agency; or

   (3) one or more administrative law judges appointed under section 3105 of this title.

This subchapter does not supersede the conduct of specified classes of proceedings, in whole or in part, by or before boards or other employees specially provided for by or designated under statute. The functions of presiding employees and of employees participating in decisions in accordance with section 557 of this title shall be conducted in an impartial manner. A presiding or participating employee may at any time disqualify himself. On the filing in good faith of a timely and sufficient affidavit of personal bias or other disqualification of a presiding or participating employee, the agency shall determine the matter as a part of the record and decision in the case. [margin note: ALJ recusal]

(c) Subject to published rules of the agency and within its powers, employees presiding at hearings may—

   (1) administer oaths and affirmations;

   (2) issue subpenas authorized by law;

   (3) rule on offers of proof and receive relevant evidence;

   (4) take depositions or have depositions taken when the ends of justice would be served;

   (5) regulate the course of the hearing;

   (6) hold conferences for the settlement or simplification of the issues by consent of the parties or by the use of alternative means of dispute resolution as provided in subchapter IV of this chapter;

   (7) inform the parties as to the availability of one or more alternative means of dispute resolution, and encourage use of such methods;

   (8) require the attendance at any conference held pursuant to paragraph (6) of at least one representative of each party who has authority to negotiate concerning resolution of issues in controversy;

   (9) dispose of procedural requests or similar matters;

   (10) make or recommend decisions in accordance with section 557 of this title; and

(11) take other action authorized by agency rule consistent with this subchapter.

(d) Except as otherwise provided by statute, the proponent of a rule or order has the burden of proof. Any oral or documentary evidence may be received, but the agency as a matter of policy shall provide for the exclusion of irrelevant, immaterial, or unduly repetitious evidence. A sanction may not be imposed or rule or order issued except on consideration of the whole record or those parts thereof cited by a party and supported by and in accordance with the reliable, probative, and substantial evidence. The agency may, to the extent consistent with the interests of justice and the policy of the underlying statutes administered by the agency, consider a violation of section 557(d) of this title sufficient grounds for a decision adverse to a party who has knowingly committed such violation or knowingly caused such violation to occur. A party is entitled to present his case or defense by oral or documentary evidence, to submit rebuttal evidence, and to conduct such cross-examination as may be required for a full and true disclosure of the facts. In rule making or determining claims for money or benefits or applications for initial licenses an agency may, when a party will not be prejudiced thereby, adopt procedures for the submission of all or part of the evidence in written form.

(e) The transcript of testimony and exhibits, together with all papers and requests filed in the proceeding, constitutes the exclusive record for decision in accordance with section 557 of this title and, on payment of lawfully prescribed costs, shall be made available to the parties. When an agency decision rests on official notice of a material fact not appearing in the evidence in the record, a party is entitled, on timely request, to an opportunity to show the contrary.

§ 557. Initial decisions; conclusiveness; review by agency; submissions by parties; contents of decisions; record

(a) This section applies, according to the provisions thereof, when a hearing is required to be conducted in accordance with section 556 of this title.

(b) When the agency did not preside at the reception of the evidence, the presiding employee or, in cases not subject to section 554(d) of this title, an employee qualified to preside at hearings pursuant to section 556 of this title, shall initially decide the case unless the agency requires, either in specific cases or by general rule, the entire record to be certified to it for decision. When the presiding employee makes an initial decision, that decision then becomes the decision of the agency without further proceedings unless there is an appeal to, or review on motion of, the agency within time provided by rule. On appeal from or review of the initial decision, the agency has all the powers which it would have in making the initial decision except as it may limit the issues on notice or by rule. When the agency makes the decision without having presided at the reception of the evidence, the presiding employee or an employee qualified to preside at hearings pursuant to section 556 of this title shall first recommend a decision, except that in rule making or determining applications for initial licenses—

(1) instead thereof the agency may issue a tentative decision or one of its responsible employees may recommend a decision; or

(2) this procedure may be omitted in a case in which the agency finds on the record that due and timely execution of its functions imperatively and unavoidably so requires.

(c) Before a recommended, initial, or tentative decision, or a decision on agency review of the decision of subordinate employees, the parties are entitled to a reasonable opportunity to submit for the consideration of the employees participating in the decisions—

(1) proposed findings and conclusions; or

(2) exceptions to the decisions or recommended decisions of subordinate employees or to tentative agency decisions; and

(3) supporting reasons for the exceptions or proposed findings or conclusions.

The record shall show the ruling on each finding, conclusion, or exception presented. All decisions, including initial, recommended, and tentative decisions, are a part of the record and shall include a statement of—

(A) findings and conclusions, and the reasons or basis therefor, on all the material issues of fact, law, or discretion presented on the record; and

(B) the appropriate rule, order, sanction, relief, or denial thereof.

(d)(1) In any agency proceeding which is subject to subsection (a) of this section, except to the extent required for the disposition of ex parte matters as authorized by law—

(A) no interested person outside the agency shall make or knowingly cause to be made to any member of the body comprising the agency, administrative law judge, or other employee who is or may reasonably be expected to be involved in the decisional process of the proceeding, an ex parte communication relevant to the merits of the proceeding;

(B) no member of the body comprising the agency, administrative law judge, or other employee who is or may reasonably be expected to be involved in the decisional process of the proceeding, shall make or knowingly cause to be made to any interested person outside the agency an ex parte communication relevant to the merits of the proceeding;

(C) a member of the body comprising the agency, administrative law judge, or other employee who is or may reasonably be expected to be involved in the decisional process of such proceeding who receives, or who makes or knowingly causes to be made, a communication prohibited by this subsection shall place on the public record of the proceeding:

(i) all such written communications;

(ii) memoranda stating the substance of all such oral communications; and

(iii) all written responses, and memoranda stating the substance of all oral responses, to the materials described in clauses (i) and (ii) of this subparagraph;

(D) upon receipt of a communication knowingly made or knowingly caused to be made by a party in violation of this subsection, the agency, administrative law judge, or other employee presiding at the hearing may, to the extent consistent with the interests of justice and the policy of the underlying statutes, require the party to show cause why his claim or interest in the proceeding should not be dismissed, denied, disregarded, or otherwise adversely affected on account of such violation; and

(E) the prohibitions of this subsection shall apply beginning at such time as the agency may designate, but in no case shall they begin to apply later than the time at which a proceeding is noticed for hearing unless the person responsible for the communication has knowledge that it will be noticed, in which case the prohibitions shall apply beginning at the time of his acquisition of such knowledge.

(2) This subsection does not constitute authority to withhold information from Congress.

§ 558. Imposition of sanctions; determination of applications for licenses; suspension, revocation, and expiration of licenses

(a) This section applies, according to the provisions thereof, to the exercise of a power or authority.

(b) A sanction may not be imposed or a substantive rule or order issued except within jurisdiction delegated to the agency and as authorized by law.

(c) When application is made for a license required by law, the agency, with due regard for the rights and privileges of all the interested parties or adversely affected persons and within a reasonable time, shall set and complete proceedings required to be conducted in accordance with sections 556 and 557 of this title or other proceedings required by law and shall make its decision. Except in cases of willfulness or those in which public health, interest, or safety requires otherwise, the withdrawal, suspension, revocation, or annulment of a license is lawful only if, before the institution of agency proceedings therefor, the licensee has been given—

(1) notice by the agency in writing of the facts or conduct which may warrant the action; and

(2) opportunity to demonstrate or achieve compliance with all lawful requirements.

When the licensee has made timely and sufficient application for a renewal or a new license in accordance with agency rules, a license with reference to an activity of a continuing nature does not expire until the application has been finally determined by the agency.

§ 559. Effect on other laws; effect of subsequent statute

This subchapter, chapter 7, and sections 1305, 3105, 3344, 4301(2)(E), 5372, and 7521 of this title, and the provisions of section 5335(a)(B) of this title that relate to administrative law judges, do not limit or repeal additional requirements imposed by statute or otherwise recognized by law. Except as otherwise required by law, requirements or privileges relating to evidence or procedure apply equally to agencies and persons. Each agency is granted the authority necessary to comply with the requirements of this subchapter through the issuance of rules or otherwise. Subsequent statute may not be held to supersede or modify this subchapter, chapter 7, sections 1305, 3105, 3344, 4301(2)(E), 5372, or 7521 of this title, or the provisions of section 5335(a)(B) of this title that relate to administrative law judges, except to the extent that it does so expressly.

§ 701. Application; definitions

(a) This chapter applies, according to the provisions thereof, except to the extent that—

(1) statutes preclude judicial review; or

(2) agency action is committed to agency discretion by law.

(b) For the purpose of this chapter—

(1) "agency" means each authority of the Government of the United States, whether or not it is within or subject to review by another agency, but does not include—

(A) the Congress;

(B) the courts of the United States;

(C) the governments of the territories or possessions of the United States;

(D) the government of the District of Columbia;

(E) agencies composed of representatives of the parties or of representatives of organizations of the parties to the disputes determined by them;

(F) courts martial and military commissions;

(G) military authority exercised in the field in time of war or in occupied territory; or

(H) functions conferred by sections 1738, 1739, 1743, and 1744 of title 12; chapter 2 of title 41; subchapter II of chapter 471 of title 49; or sections 1884, 1891-1902, and former section 1641(b)(2), of title 50, appendix; and

(2) "person", "rule", "order", "license", "sanction", "relief", and "agency action" have the meanings given them by section 551 of this title.

§ 702. Right of review

A person suffering legal wrong because of agency action, or adversely affected or aggrieved by agency action within the meaning of a relevant statute, is entitled to judicial review thereof. An action in a court of the United States seeking relief other than money damages and stating a claim that an agency or an officer or employee thereof acted or failed to act in an official capacity or under color of legal authority shall not be dismissed nor relief therein be denied on the ground that it is against the United States or that the United States is an indispensable party. The United States may be named as a defendant in any such action, and a judgment or decree may be entered against the United States: Provided, That any mandatory or injunctive decree shall specify the Federal officer or officers (by name or by title), and their successors in office, personally responsible for compliance. Nothing herein (1) affects other limitations on judicial review or the power or duty of the court to dismiss any action or deny relief on any other appropriate legal or equitable ground; or (2) confers authority to grant relief if any other statute that grants consent to suit expressly or impliedly forbids the relief which is sought.

§ 703. Form and venue of proceeding

The form of proceeding for judicial review is the special statutory review proceeding relevant to the subject matter in a court specified by statute or, in the absence or inadequacy thereof, any applicable form of legal action, including actions for declaratory judgments or writs of prohibitory or mandatory injunction or habeas corpus, in a court of competent jurisdiction. If no special statutory review proceeding is applicable, the action for judicial review may be brought against the United States, the agency by its official title, or the appropriate officer. Except to the extent that prior, adequate, and exclusive opportunity for judicial review is provided by law, agency action is subject to judicial review in civil or criminal proceedings for judicial enforcement.

§ 704. Actions reviewable

Agency action made reviewable by statute and final agency action for which there is no other adequate remedy in a court are subject to judicial review. A preliminary, procedural, or intermediate agency action or ruling not directly reviewable is subject to review on the review of the final agency action. Except as otherwise expressly required by statute, agency action otherwise final is final for the purposes of this section whether or not there has been presented or determined an application for a declaratory order, for any form of reconsideration, or, unless the agency otherwise requires by rule and provides that the action meanwhile is inoperative, for an appeal to superior agency authority.

§ 705. Relief pending review

When an agency finds that justice so requires, it may postpone the effective date of action taken by it, pending judicial review. On such conditions as may be required and to the extent necessary to prevent irreparable injury, the reviewing court, including the court to which a case may be taken on appeal from or on application for certiorari or other writ to a reviewing court, may issue all necessary and appropriate process to postpone the effective date of an agency action or to preserve status or rights pending conclusion of the review proceedings.

§ 706. Scope of review

To the extent necessary to decision and when presented, the reviewing court shall decide all relevant questions of law, interpret constitutional and statutory provisions, and determine the meaning or applicability of the terms of an agency action. The reviewing court shall—

(1) compel agency action unlawfully withheld or unreasonably delayed; and

(2) hold unlawful and set aside agency action, findings, and conclusions found to be—

(A) arbitrary, capricious, an abuse of discretion, or otherwise not in accordance with law;

(B) contrary to constitutional right, power, privilege, or immunity;

(C) in excess of statutory jurisdiction, authority, or limitations, or short of statutory right;

(D) without observance of procedure required by law;

(E) unsupported by substantial evidence in a case subject to sections 556 and 557 of this title or otherwise reviewed on the record of an agency hearing provided by statute; or

(F) unwarranted by the facts to the extent that the facts are subject to trial de novo by the reviewing court.

In making the foregoing determinations, the court shall review the whole record or those parts of it cited by a party, and due account shall be taken of the rule of prejudicial error.

§ 1305. Administrative law judges

For the purpose of sections 3105, 3344, 4301(2)(D), and 5372 of this title and the provisions of section 5335(a)(B) of this title that relate to administrative law judges, the Office of Personnel Management may, and for the purpose of section 7521 of this title, the Merit Systems Protection Board may investigate, prescribe regulations, appoint advisory committees as necessary, recommend legislation, subpena witnesses and records, and pay witness fees as established for the courts of the United States.

§ 3105. Appointment of administrative law judges

Each agency shall appoint as many administrative law judges as are necessary for proceedings required to be conducted in accordance with sections 556 and 557 of this title. Administrative law judges shall be assigned to cases in rotation so far as practicable, and may not perform duties inconsistent with their duties and responsibilities as administrative law judges.

§ 3344. Details; administrative law judges

An agency as defined by section 551 of this title which occasionally or temporarily is insufficiently staffed with administrative law judges appointed under section 3105 of this title may use administrative law judges selected by the Office of Personnel Management from and with the consent of other agencies.

§ 5372. Administrative law judges

(a) For the purposes of this section, the term "administrative law judge" means an administrative law judge appointed under section 3105.

(b)(1)(A) There shall be 3 levels of basic pay for administrative law judges (designated as AL-1, 2, and 3, respectively), and each such judge shall be paid at 1 of those levels, in accordance with the provisions of this section.

(B) Within level AL-3, there shall be 6 rates of basic pay, designated as AL-3, rates A through F, respectively. Level AL-2 and level AL-1 shall each have 1 rate of basic pay.

(C) The rate of basic pay for AL-3, rate A, may not be less than 65 percent of the rate of basic pay for level IV of the Executive Schedule, and the rate of basic pay for AL-1 may not exceed the rate for level IV of the Executive Schedule.

(2) The Office of Personnel Management shall determine, in accordance with procedures which the Office shall by regulation prescribe, the level in which each administrative-law-judge position shall be placed and the qualifications to be required for appointment to each level.

(3)(A) Upon appointment to a position in AL-3, an administrative law judge shall be paid at rate A of AL-3, and shall be advanced successively to rates B, C, and D of that level at the beginning of the next pay period following completion of 52 weeks of service in the next lower rate, and to rates E and F of that level at the beginning of the next pay period following completion of 104 weeks of service in the next lower rate.

(B) The Office of Personnel Management may provide for appointment of an administrative law judge in AL-3 at an advanced rate under such circumstances as the Office may determine appropriate.

(4) Subject to paragraph (1), effective at the beginning of the first applicable pay period commencing on or after the first day of the month in which an adjustment takes effect under section 5303 in the rates of basic pay under the General Schedule, each rate of basic pay for administrative law judges shall be adjusted by an amount determined by the President to be appropriate.

(c) The Office of Personnel Management shall prescribe regulations necessary to administer this section.

§ 7521. Actions against administrative law judges

(a) An action may be taken against an administrative law judge appointed under section 3105 of this title by the agency in which the administrative law judge is employed only for good cause established and determined by the Merit Systems Protection Board on the record after opportunity for hearing before the Board.

(b) The actions covered by this section are—

   (1) a removal;

   (2) a suspension;

   (3) a reduction in grade;

   (4) a reduction in pay; and

(5) a furlough of 30 days or less;

but do not include—

    (A) a suspension or removal under section 7532 of this title;

    (B) a reduction-in-force action under section 3502 of this title; or

    (C) any action initiated under section 1215 of this title.

Appendix C

FREEDOM OF INFORMATION ACT
UNITED STATES CODE, TITLE 5, CHAPTER 5

§ 552. Public information; agency rules, opinions, orders, records, and proceedings

(a) Each agency shall make available to the public information as follows:

(1) Each agency shall separately state and currently publish in the Federal Register for the guidance of the public—

(A) descriptions of its central and field organization and the established places at which, the employees (and in the case of a uniformed service, the members) from whom, and the methods whereby, the public may obtain information, make submittals or requests, or obtain decisions;

(B) statements of the general course and method by which its functions are channeled and determined, including the nature and requirements of all formal and informal procedures available;

(C) rules of procedure, descriptions of forms available or the places at which forms may be obtained, and instructions as to the scope and contents of all papers, reports, or examinations;

(D) substantive rules of general applicability adopted as authorized by law, and statements of general policy or interpretations of general applicability formulated and adopted by the agency; and

(E) each amendment, revision, or repeal of the foregoing.

Except to the extent that a person has actual and timely notice of the terms thereof, a person may not in any manner be required to resort to, or be adversely affected by, a matter required to be published in the Federal Register and not so published. For the purpose of this paragraph, matter reasonably available to the class of persons affected thereby is deemed published in the Federal Register when incorporated by reference therein with the approval of the Director of the Federal Register.

(2) Each agency, in accordance with published rules, shall make available for public inspection and copying—

(A) final opinions, including concurring and dissenting opinions, as well as orders, made in the adjudication of cases;

(B) those statements of policy and interpretations which have been adopted by the agency and are not published in the Federal Register;

(C) administrative staff manuals and instructions to staff that affect a member of the public;

(D) copies of all records, regardless of form or format, which have been released to any person under paragraph (3) and which, because of the nature of their subject matter, the agency determines have become or are likely to become the subject of subsequent requests for substantially the same records; and

(E) a general index of the records referred to under subparagraph (D);

unless the materials are promptly published and copies offered for sale. For records created on or after November 1, 1996, within one year after such date, each agency shall make such records available, including by computer telecommunications or, if computer telecommunications means have not been established by the agency, by other electronic means. To the extent required to prevent a clearly unwarranted invasion of personal privacy, an agency may delete identifying details when it makes available or publishes an opinion, statement of policy, interpretation, staff manual, instruction, or copies of records referred to in subparagraph (D). However, in each case the justification for the deletion shall be explained fully in writing, and the extent of such deletion shall be indicated on the portion of the record which is made available or published, unless including that indication would harm an interest protected by the exemption in subsection (b) under which the deletion is made. If technically feasible, the extent of the deletion shall be indicated at the place in the record where the deletion was made. Each agency shall also maintain and make available for public inspection and copying current indexes providing identifying information for the public as to any matter issued, adopted, or promulgated after July 4, 1967, and required by this paragraph to be made available or published. Each agency shall promptly publish, quarterly or more frequently, and distribute (by sale or otherwise) copies of each index or supplements thereto unless it determines by order published in the Federal Register that the publication would be unnecessary and impracticable, in which case the agency shall nonetheless provide copies of such index on request at a cost not to exceed the direct cost of duplication. Each agency shall make the index referred to in subparagraph (E) available by computer telecommunications by December 31, 1999. A final order, opinion, statement of policy, interpretation, or staff manual or instruction that affects a member of the public may be relied on, used, or cited as precedent by an agency against a party other than an agency only if—

(i) it has been indexed and either made available or published as provided by this paragraph; or

(ii) the party has actual and timely notice of the terms thereof.

(3)(A) Except with respect to the records made available under paragraphs (1) and (2) of this subsection, and except as provided in subparagraph (E), each agency, upon any request for records which (i) reasonably describes such records and (ii) is made in accordance with published rules stating the time, place, fees (if any), and procedures to be followed, shall make the records promptly available to any person.

(B) In making any record available to a person under this paragraph, an agency shall provide the record in any form or format requested by the person if the record is readily reproducible by the agency in that form or format. Each agency shall make reasonable efforts to maintain its records in forms or formats that are reproducible for purposes of this section.

(C) In responding under this paragraph to a request for records, an agency shall make reasonable efforts to search for the records in electronic form or format, except when such efforts would significantly interfere with the operation of the agency's automated information system.

(D) For purposes of this paragraph, the term "search" means to review, manually or by automated means, agency records for the purpose of locating those records which are responsive to a request.

(E) An agency, or part of an agency, that is an element of the intelligence community (as that term is defined in section 3(4) of the National Security Act of 1947 (50 U.S.C. 401a(4))) shall not make any record available under this paragraph to—

(i) any government entity, other than a State, territory, commonwealth, or district of the United States, or any subdivision thereof; or

(ii) a representative of a government entity described in clause (i).

(4)(A)(i) In order to carry out the provisions of this section, each agency shall promulgate regulations, pursuant to notice and receipt of public comment, specifying the schedule of fees applicable to the processing of requests under this section and establishing procedures and guidelines for determining when such fees should be waived or reduced. Such schedule shall conform to the guidelines which shall be promulgated, pursuant to notice and receipt of public comment, by the Director of the Office of Management and Budget and which shall provide for a uniform schedule of fees for all agencies.

(ii) Such agency regulations shall provide that—

(I) fees shall be limited to reasonable standard charges for document search, duplication, and review, when records are requested for commercial use;

(II) fees shall be limited to reasonable standard charges for document duplication when records are not sought for commercial use and the request is made by an educational or noncommercial scientific institution, whose purpose is scholarly or scientific research; or a representative of the news media; and

(III) for any request not described in (I) or (II), fees shall be limited to reasonable standard charges for document search and duplication.

(iii) Documents shall be furnished without any charge or at a charge reduced below the fees established under clause (ii) if disclosure of the information is in the public interest because it is likely to contribute significantly to public understanding of the operations or activities of the government and is not primarily in the commercial interest of the requester.

(iv) Fee schedules shall provide for the recovery of only the direct costs of search, duplication, or review. Review costs shall include only the direct costs incurred during the initial examination of a document for the purposes of determining whether the documents must be disclosed under this section and for the purposes of withholding any portions exempt from disclosure under this section. Review costs may not include any costs incurred in resolving issues of law or policy that may be raised in the course of processing a request under this section. No fee may be charged by any agency under this section—

(I) if the costs of routine collection and processing of the fee are likely to equal or exceed the amount of the fee; or

(II) for any request described in clause (ii)(II) or (III) of this subparagraph for the first two hours of search time or for the first one hundred pages of duplication.

(v) No agency may require advance payment of any fee unless the requester has previously failed to pay fees in a timely fashion, or the agency has determined that the fee will exceed $250.

(vi) Nothing in this subparagraph shall supersede fees chargeable under a statute specifically providing for setting the level of fees for particular types of records.

(vii) In any action by a requester regarding the waiver of fees under this section, the court shall determine the matter de novo: Provided, That the court's review of the matter shall be limited to the record before the agency.

(B) On complaint, the district court of the United States in the district in which the complainant resides, or has his principal place of business, or in which the agency records are situated, or in the District of Columbia, has jurisdiction to enjoin the agency from withholding agency records and to order the production of any agency records improperly withheld from the complainant. In such a case the court shall determine the matter de novo, and may examine the contents of such agency records in camera to determine whether such records or any part thereof shall be withheld under any of the exemptions set forth in subsection (b) of this section, and the burden is on the agency to sustain its action. In addition to any other matters to which a court accords substantial weight, a court shall accord substantial weight to an affidavit of an agency concerning the agency's determination as to technical feasibility under paragraph (2)(C) and subsection (b) and reproducibility under paragraph (3)(B).

(C) Notwithstanding any other provision of law, the defendant shall serve an answer or otherwise plead to any complaint made under this subsection within thirty days after service upon the defendant of the pleading in which such complaint is made, unless the court otherwise directs for good cause shown.

[(D) Repealed. Pub.L. 98-620, Title IV, § 402(2), Nov. 8, 1984, 98 Stat. 3357]

(E) The court may assess against the United States reasonable attorney fees and other litigation costs reasonably incurred in any case under this section in which the complainant has substantially prevailed.

(F) Whenever the court orders the production of any agency records improperly withheld from the complainant and assesses against the United States reasonable attorney fees and other litigation costs, and the court additionally issues a written finding that the circumstances surrounding the withholding raise questions whether agency personnel acted arbitrarily or capriciously with respect to the withholding, the Special Counsel shall promptly initiate a proceeding to determine whether disciplinary action is warranted against the officer or employee who was primarily responsible for the withholding. The Special Counsel, after investigation and consideration of the evidence submitted, shall submit his findings and recommendations to the administrative authority of the agency concerned and shall send copies of the findings and recommendations to the officer or employee or his representative. The administrative authority shall take the corrective action that the Special Counsel recommends.

(G) In the event of noncompliance with the order of the court, the district court may punish for contempt the responsible employee, and in the case of a uniformed service, the responsible member.

(5) Each agency having more than one member shall maintain and make available for public inspection a record of the final votes of each member in every agency proceeding.

(6)(A) Each agency, upon any request for records made under paragraph (1), (2), or (3) of this subsection, shall—

  (i) determine within 20 days (excepting Saturdays, Sundays, and legal public holidays) after the receipt of any such request whether to comply with such request and shall immediately notify the person making such request of such determination and the reasons therefor, and of the right of such person to appeal to the head of the agency any adverse determination; and

  (ii) make a determination with respect to any appeal within twenty days (excepting Saturdays, Sundays, and legal public holidays) after the receipt of such appeal. If on appeal the denial of the request for records is in whole or in part upheld, the agency shall notify the person making such request of the provisions for judicial review of that determination under paragraph (4) of this subsection.

(B)(i) In unusual circumstances as specified in this subparagraph, the time limits prescribed in either clause (i) or clause (ii) of subparagraph (A) may be extended by written notice to the person making such request setting forth the unusual circumstances for such extension and the date on which a determination is expected to be dispatched. No such notice shall specify a date that would result in an extension for more than ten working days, except as provided in clause (ii) of this subparagraph.

(ii) With respect to a request for which a written notice under clause (i) extends the time limits prescribed under clause (i) of subparagraph (A), the agency shall notify the person making the request if the request cannot be processed within the time limit specified in that clause and shall provide the person an opportunity to limit the scope of the request so that it may be processed within that time limit or an opportunity to arrange with the agency an alternative time frame for processing the request or a modified request. Refusal by the person to reasonably modify the request or arrange such an alternative time frame shall be considered as a factor in determining whether exceptional circumstances exist for purposes of subparagraph (C).

(iii) As used in this subparagraph, "unusual circumstances" means, but only to the extent reasonably necessary to the proper processing of the particular requests—

(I) the need to search for and collect the requested records from field facilities or other establishments that are separate from the office processing the request;

(II) the need to search for, collect, and appropriately examine a voluminous amount of separate and distinct records which are demanded in a single request; or

(III) the need for consultation, which shall be conducted with all practicable speed, with another agency having a substantial interest in the determination of the request or among two or more components of the agency having substantial subject-matter interest therein.

(iv) Each agency may promulgate regulations, pursuant to notice and receipt of public comment, providing for the aggregation of certain requests by the same requestor, or by a group of requestors acting in concert, if the agency reasonably believes that such requests actually constitute a single request, which would otherwise satisfy the unusual circumstances specified in this subparagraph, and the requests involve clearly related matters. Multiple requests involving unrelated matters shall not be aggregated.

(C)(i) Any person making a request to any agency for records under paragraph (1), (2), or (3) of this subsection shall be deemed to have exhausted his administrative remedies with respect to such request if the agency fails to comply with the applicable time limit provisions of this paragraph. If the Government can show exceptional circumstances exist and that the agency is exercising due diligence in responding to the request, the court may retain jurisdiction and allow the agency additional time to complete its review of the records. Upon any determination by an agency to comply with a request for records, the records shall be made promptly available to such person making such request. Any notification of denial of any request for records under this subsection shall set forth the names and titles or positions of each person responsible for the denial of such request.

(ii) For purposes of this subparagraph, the term "exceptional circumstances" does not include a delay that results from a predictable agency workload of requests under this section, unless the agency demonstrates reasonable progress in reducing its backlog of pending requests.

(iii) Refusal by a person to reasonably modify the scope of a request or arrange an alternative time frame for processing a request (or a modified request) under clause (ii) after being given an opportunity to do so by the agency to whom the person made the request shall be considered as a factor in determining whether exceptional circumstances exist for purposes of this subparagraph.

(D)(i) Each agency may promulgate regulations, pursuant to notice and receipt of public comment, providing for multitrack processing of requests for records based on the amount of work or time (or both) involved in processing requests.

(ii) Regulations under this subparagraph may provide a person making a request that does not qualify for the fastest multitrack processing an opportunity to limit the scope of the request in order to qualify for faster processing.

(iii) This subparagraph shall not be considered to affect the requirement under subparagraph (C) to exercise due diligence.

(E)(i) Each agency shall promulgate regulations, pursuant to notice and receipt of public comment, providing for expedited processing of requests for records—

(I) in cases in which the person requesting the records demonstrates a compelling need; and

(II) in other cases determined by the agency.

(ii) Notwithstanding clause (i), regulations under this subparagraph must ensure—

(I) that a determination of whether to provide expedited processing shall be made, and notice of the determination shall be provided to the person making the request, within 10 days after the date of the request; and

(II) expeditious consideration of administrative appeals of such determinations of whether to provide expedited processing.

(iii) An agency shall process as soon as practicable any request for records to which the agency has granted expedited processing under this subparagraph. Agency action to deny or affirm denial of a request for expedited processing pursuant to this subparagraph, and failure by an agency to respond in a timely manner to such a request shall be subject to judicial review under paragraph (4), except that the judicial review shall be based on the record before the agency at the time of the determination.

(iv) A district court of the United States shall not have jurisdiction to review an agency denial of expedited processing of a request for records after the agency has provided a complete response to the request.

(v) For purposes of this subparagraph, the term "compelling need" means—

(I) that a failure to obtain requested records on an expedited basis under this paragraph could reasonably be expected to pose an imminent threat to the life or physical safety of an individual; or

(II) with respect to a request made by a person primarily engaged in disseminating information, urgency to inform the public concerning actual or alleged Federal Government activity.

(vi) A demonstration of a compelling need by a person making a request for expedited processing shall be made by a statement certified by such person to be true and correct to the best of such person's knowledge and belief.

(F) In denying a request for records, in whole or in part, an agency shall make a reasonable effort to estimate the volume of any requested matter the provision of which is denied, and shall provide any such estimate to the person making the request, unless providing such estimate would harm an interest protected by the exemption in subsection (b) pursuant to which the denial is made.

(b) This section does not apply to matters that are—

(1) (A) specifically authorized under criteria established by an Executive order to be kept secret in the interest of national defense or foreign policy and (B) are in fact properly classified pursuant to such Executive order;

(2) related solely to the internal personnel rules and practices of an agency;

(3) specifically exempted from disclosure by statute (other than section 552b of this title), provided that such statute (A) requires that the matters be withheld from the public in such a manner as to leave no discretion on the issue, or (B) establishes particular criteria for withholding or refers to particular types of matters to be withheld;

(4) trade secrets and commercial or financial information obtained from a person and privileged or confidential;

(5) inter-agency or intra-agency memorandums or letters which would not be available by law to a party other than an agency in litigation with the agency;

(6) personnel and medical files and similar files the disclosure of which would constitute a clearly unwarranted invasion of personal privacy;

(7) records or information compiled for law enforcement purposes, but only to the extent that the production of such law enforcement records or information (A) could reasonably be expected to interfere with enforcement proceedings, (B) would deprive a person of a right to a fair trial or an impartial adjudication, (C) could reasonably be expected to constitute an unwarranted invasion of personal privacy, (D) could reasonably be expected to disclose the identity of a confidential source, including a State, local, or foreign agency or authority or any private institution which furnished information on a confidential basis, and, in the case of a record or information compiled by criminal law enforcement authority in the course of a criminal investigation or by an agency conducting a lawful national security intelligence investigation, information furnished by a confidential source, (E) would disclose techniques and procedures for law enforcement investigations or prosecutions, or would disclose guidelines for law enforcement investigations or prosecutions if such disclosure could reasonably be expected to risk circumvention of the law, or (F) could reasonably be expected to endanger the life or physical safety of any individual;

(8) contained in or related to examination, operating, or condition reports prepared by, on behalf of, or for the use of an agency responsible for the regulation or supervision of financial institutions; or

(9) geological and geophysical information and data, including maps, concerning wells.

Any reasonably segregable portion of a record shall be provided to any person requesting such record after deletion of the portions which are exempt under this subsection. The amount of information deleted shall be indicated on the released portion of the record, unless including that indication would harm an interest protected by the exemption in this subsection under which the deletion is made. If technically feasible, the amount of the information deleted shall be indicated at the place in the record where such deletion is made.

(c)(1) Whenever a request is made which involves access to records described in subsection (b)(7)(A) and—

(A) the investigation or proceeding involves a possible violation of criminal law; and

(B) there is reason to believe that (i) the subject of the investigation or proceeding is not aware of its pendency, and (ii) disclosure of the existence of the records could reasonably be expected to interfere with enforcement proceedings,

the agency may, during only such time as that circumstance continues, treat the records as not subject to the requirements of this section.

(2) Whenever informant records maintained by a criminal law enforcement agency under an informant's name or personal identifier are requested by a third party according to the informant's name or personal identifier, the agency may treat the records as not subject to the requirements of this section unless the informant's status as an informant has been officially confirmed.

(3) Whenever a request is made which involves access to records maintained by the Federal Bureau of Investigation pertaining to foreign intelligence or counterintelligence, or international terrorism, and the existence of the records is classified information as provided in subsection (b)(1), the Bureau may, as long as the existence of the records remains classified information, treat the records as not subject to the requirements of this section.

(d) This section does not authorize withholding of information or limit the availability of records to the public, except as specifically stated in this section. This section is not authority to withhold information from Congress.

(e)(1) On or before February 1 of each year, each agency shall submit to the Attorney General of the United States a report which shall cover the preceding fiscal year and which shall include—

(A) the number of determinations made by the agency not to comply with requests for records made to such agency under subsection (a) and the reasons for each such determination;

(B)(i) the number of appeals made by persons under subsection (a)(6), the result of such appeals, and the reason for the action upon each appeal that results in a denial of information; and

(ii) a complete list of all statutes that the agency relies upon to authorize the agency to withhold information under subsection (b)(3), a description of whether a court has upheld the decision of the agency to withhold information under each such statute, and a concise description of the scope of any information withheld;

(C) the number of requests for records pending before the agency as of September 30 of the preceding year, and the median number of days that such requests had been pending before the agency as of that date;

(D) the number of requests for records received by the agency and the number of requests which the agency processed;

(E) the median number of days taken by the agency to process different types of requests;

(F) the total amount of fees collected by the agency for processing requests; and

(G) the number of full-time staff of the agency devoted to processing requests for records under this section, and the total amount expended by the agency for processing such requests.

(2) Each agency shall make each such report available to the public including by computer telecommunications, or if computer telecommunications means have not been established by the agency, by other electronic means.

(3) The Attorney General of the United States shall make each report which has been made available by electronic means available at a single electronic access point. The Attorney General of the United States shall notify the Chairman and ranking minority member of the Committee on Government Reform and Oversight of the House of Representatives and the Chairman and ranking minority member of the Committees on Governmental Affairs and the Judiciary of the Senate, no later than April 1 of the year in which each such report is issued, that such reports are available by electronic means.

(4) The Attorney General of the United States, in consultation with the Director of the Office of Management and Budget, shall develop reporting and performance guidelines in connection with reports required by this subsection by October 1, 1997, and may establish additional requirements for such reports as the Attorney General determines may be useful.

(5) The Attorney General of the United States shall submit an annual report on or before April 1 of each calendar year which shall include for the prior calendar year a listing of the number of cases arising under this section, the exemption involved in each case, the disposition of such case, and the cost, fees, and penalties assessed under subparagraphs (E), (F), and (G) of subsection (a)(4). Such report shall also include a description of the efforts undertaken by the Department of Justice to encourage agency compliance with this section.

(f) For purposes of this section, the term—

(1) "agency" as defined in section 551(1) of this title includes any executive department, military department, Government corporation, Government controlled corporation, or other establishment in the executive branch of the

Government (including the Executive Office of the President), or any independent regulatory agency; and

(2) "record" and any other term used in this section in reference to information includes any information that would be an agency record subject to the requirements of this section when maintained by an agency in any format, including an electronic format.

(g) The head of each agency shall prepare and make publicly available upon request, reference material or a guide for requesting records or information from the agency, subject to the exemptions in subsection (b), including—

(1) an index of all major information systems of the agency;

(2) a description of major information and record locator systems maintained by the agency; and

(3) a handbook for obtaining various types and categories of public information from the agency pursuant to chapter 35 of title 44, and under this section.

Appendix D

PRIVACY ACT
UNITED STATES CODE, TITLE 5, CHAPTER 5

§ 552a. Records maintained on individuals

(a) Definitions.—For purposes of this section—

(1) the term "agency" means agency as defined in section 552(e) of this title;

(2) the term "individual" means a citizen of the United States or an alien lawfully admitted for permanent residence;

(3) the term "maintain" includes maintain, collect, use, or disseminate;

(4) the term "record" means any item, collection, or grouping of information about an individual that is maintained by an agency, including, but not limited to, his education, financial transactions, medical history, and criminal or employment history and that contains his name, or the identifying number, symbol, or other identifying particular assigned to the individual, such as a finger or voice print or a photograph;

(5) the term "system of records" means a group of any records under the control of any agency from which information is retrieved by the name of the individual or by some identifying number, symbol, or other identifying particular assigned to the individual;

(6) the term "statistical record" means a record in a system of records maintained for statistical research or reporting purposes only and not used in whole or in part in making any determination about an identifiable individual, except as provided by section 8 of title 13;

(7) the term "routine use" means, with respect to the disclosure of a record, the use of such record for a purpose which is compatible with the purpose for which it was collected;

(8) the term "matching program"—

   (A) means any computerized comparison of—

   (i) two or more automated systems of records or a system of records with non-Federal records for the purpose of—

   (I) establishing or verifying the eligibility of, or continuing compliance with statutory and regulatory requirements by, applicants for, recipients or beneficiaries of, participants in, or providers of services with respect to, cash or in-kind assistance or payments under Federal benefit programs, or

(II) recouping payments or delinquent debts under such Federal benefit programs, or

(ii) two or more automated Federal personnel or payroll systems of records or a system of Federal personnel or payroll records with non-Federal records,

(B) but does not include—

(i) matches performed to produce aggregate statistical data without any personal identifiers;

(ii) matches performed to support any research or statistical project, the specific data of which may not be used to make decisions concerning the rights, benefits, or privileges of specific individuals;

(iii) matches performed, by an agency (or component thereof) which performs as its principal function any activity pertaining to the enforcement of criminal laws, subsequent to the initiation of a specific criminal or civil law enforcement investigation of a named person or persons for the purpose of gathering evidence against such person or persons;

(iv) matches of tax information (I) pursuant to section 6103(d) of the Internal Revenue Code of 1986, (II) for purposes of tax administration as defined in section 6103(b)(4) of such Code, (III) for the purpose of intercepting a tax refund due an individual under authority granted by section 404(e), 464, or 1137 of the Social Security Act; or (IV) for the purpose of intercepting a tax refund due an individual under any other tax refund intercept program authorized by statute which has been determined by the Director of the Office of Management and Budget to contain verification, notice, and hearing requirements that are substantially similar to the procedures in section 1137 of the Social Security Act;

(v) matches—

(I) using records predominantly relating to Federal personnel, that are performed for routine administrative purposes (subject to guidance provided by the Director of the Office of Management and Budget pursuant to subsection (v)); or

(II) conducted by an agency using only records from systems of records maintained by that agency;

if the purpose of the match is not to take any adverse financial, personnel, disciplinary, or other adverse action against Federal personnel

(vi) matches performed for foreign counterintelligence purposes or to produce background checks for security clearances of Federal personnel or Federal contractor personnel;

(vii) matches performed incident to a levy described in section 6103(k)(8) of the Internal Revenue Code of 1986; or

(viii) matches performed pursuant to section 202(x)(3) or 1611(e)(1) of the Social Security Act (42 U.S.C. 402(x)(3), 1382(e)(1));

(9) the term "recipient agency" means any agency, or contractor thereof, receiving records contained in a system of records from a source agency for use in a matching program;

(10) the term "non-Federal agency" means any State or local government, or agency thereof, which receives records contained in a system of records from a source agency for use in a matching program;

(11) the term "source agency" means any agency which discloses records contained in a system of records to be used in a matching program, or any State or local government, or agency thereof, which discloses records to be used in a matching program;

(12) the term "Federal benefit program" means any program administered or funded by the Federal Government, or by any agent or State on behalf of the Federal Government, providing cash or in-kind assistance in the form of payments, grants, loans, or loan guarantees to individuals; and

(13) the term "Federal personnel" means officers and employees of the Government of the United States, members of the uniformed services (including members of the Reserve Components), individuals entitled to receive immediate or deferred retirement benefits under any retirement program of the Government of the United States (including survivor benefits).

(b) Conditions of disclosure.—No agency shall disclose any record which is contained in a system of records by any means of communication to any person, or to another agency, except pursuant to a written request by, or with the prior written consent of, the individual to whom the record pertains, unless disclosure of the record would be—

(1) to those officers and employees of the agency which maintains the record who have a need for the record in the performance of their duties;

(2) required under section 552 of this title;

(3) for a routine use as defined in subsection (a)(7) of this section and described under subsection (e)(4)(D) of this section;

(4) to the Bureau of the Census for purposes of planning or carrying out a census or survey or related activity pursuant to the provisions of title 13;

(5) to a recipient who has provided the agency with advance adequate written assurance that the record will be used solely as a statistical research or reporting record, and the record is to be transferred in a form that is not individually identifiable;

(6) to the National Archives and Records Administration as a record which has sufficient historical or other value to warrant its continued preservation by the United States Government, or for evaluation by the Archivist of the United States or the designee of the Archivist to determine whether the record has such value;

(7) to another agency or to an instrumentality of any governmental jurisdiction within or under the control of the United States for a civil or criminal

law enforcement activity if the activity is authorized by law, and if the head of the agency or instrumentality has made a written request to the agency which maintains the record specifying the particular portion desired and the law enforcement activity for which the record is sought;

(8) to a person pursuant to a showing of compelling circumstances affecting the health or safety of an individual if upon such disclosure notification is transmitted to the last known address of such individual;

(9) to either House of Congress, or, to the extent of matter within its jurisdiction, any committee or subcommittee thereof, any joint committee of Congress or subcommittee of any such joint committee;

(10) to the Comptroller General, or any of his authorized representatives, in the course of the performance of the duties of the Government Accountability Office;

(11) pursuant to the order of a court of competent jurisdiction; or

(12) to a consumer reporting agency in accordance with section 3711(e) of title 31.

(c) Accounting of certain disclosures.—Each agency, with respect to each system of records under its control, shall—

(1) except for disclosures made under subsections (b)(1) or (b)(2) of this section, keep an accurate accounting of—

(A) the date, nature, and purpose of each disclosure of a record to any person or to another agency made under subsection (b) of this section; and

(B) the name and address of the person or agency to whom the disclosure is made;

(2) retain the accounting made under paragraph (1) of this subsection for at least five years or the life of the record, whichever is longer, after the disclosure for which the accounting is made;

(3) except for disclosures made under subsection (b)(7) of this section, make the accounting made under paragraph (1) of this subsection available to the individual named in the record at his request; and

(4) inform any person or other agency about any correction or notation of dispute made by the agency in accordance with subsection (d) of this section of any record that has been disclosed to the person or agency if an accounting of the disclosure was made.

(d) Access to records.—Each agency that maintains a system of records shall—

(1) upon request by any individual to gain access to his record or to any information pertaining to him which is contained in the system, permit him and upon his request, a person of his own choosing to accompany him, to review the record and have a copy made of all or any portion thereof in a form comprehensible to him, except that the agency may require the individual to furnish a written statement authorizing discussion of that individual's record in the accompanying person's presence;

(2) permit the individual to request amendment of a record pertaining to him and—

(A) not later than 10 days (excluding Saturdays, Sundays, and legal public holidays) after the date of receipt of such request, acknowledge in writing such receipt; and

(B) promptly, either—

(i) make any correction of any portion thereof which the individual believes is not accurate, relevant, timely, or complete; or

(ii) inform the individual of its refusal to amend the record in accordance with his request, the reason for the refusal, the procedures established by the agency for the individual to request a review of that refusal by the head of the agency or an officer designated by the head of the agency, and the name and business address of that official;

(3) permit the individual who disagrees with the refusal of the agency to amend his record to request a review of such refusal, and not later than 30 days (excluding Saturdays, Sundays, and legal public holidays) from the date on which the individual requests such review, complete such review and make a final determination unless, for good cause shown, the head of the agency extends such 30-day period; and if, after his review, the reviewing official also refuses to amend the record in accordance with the request, permit the individual to file with the agency a concise statement setting forth the reasons for his disagreement with the refusal of the agency, and notify the individual of the provisions for judicial review of the reviewing official's determination under subsection (g)(1)(A) of this section;

(4) in any disclosure, containing information about which the individual has filed a statement of disagreement, occurring after the filing of the statement under paragraph (3) of this subsection, clearly note any portion of the record which is disputed and provide copies of the statement and, if the agency deems it appropriate, copies of a concise statement of the reasons of the agency for not making the amendments requested, to persons or other agencies to whom the disputed record has been disclosed; and

(5) nothing in this section shall allow an individual access to any information compiled in reasonable anticipation of a civil action or proceeding.

(e) Agency requirements.—Each agency that maintains a system of records shall—

(1) maintain in its records only such information about an individual as is relevant and necessary to accomplish a purpose of the agency required to be accomplished by statute or by executive order of the President;

(2) collect information to the greatest extent practicable directly from the subject individual when the information may result in adverse determinations about an individual's rights, benefits, and privileges under Federal programs;

(3) inform each individual whom it asks to supply information, on the form which it uses to collect the information or on a separate form that can be retained by the individual—

(A) the authority (whether granted by statute, or by executive order of the President) which authorizes the solicitation of the information and whether disclosure of such information is mandatory or voluntary;

(B) the principal purpose or purposes for which the information is intended to be used;

(C) the routine uses which may be made of the information, as published pursuant to paragraph (4)(D) of this subsection; and

(D) the effects on him, if any, of not providing all or any part of the requested information;

(4) subject to the provisions of paragraph (11) of this subsection, publish in the Federal Register upon establishment or revision a notice of the existence and character of the system of records, which notice shall include—

(A) the name and location of the system;

(B) the categories of individuals on whom records are maintained in the system;

(C) the categories of records maintained in the system;

(D) each routine use of the records contained in the system, including the categories of users and the purpose of such use;

(E) the policies and practices of the agency regarding storage, retrievability, access controls, retention, and disposal of the records;

(F) the title and business address of the agency official who is responsible for the system of records;

(G) the agency procedures whereby an individual can be notified at his request if the system of records contains a record pertaining to him;

(H) the agency procedures whereby an individual can be notified at his request how he can gain access to any record pertaining to him contained in the system of records, and how he can contest its content; and

(I) the categories of sources of records in the system;

(5) maintain all records which are used by the agency in making any determination about any individual with such accuracy, relevance, timeliness, and completeness as is reasonably necessary to assure fairness to the individual in the determination;

(6) prior to disseminating any record about an individual to any person other than an agency, unless the dissemination is made pursuant to subsection (b)(2) of this section, make reasonable efforts to assure that such records are accurate, complete, timely, and relevant for agency purposes;

(7) maintain no record describing how any individual exercises rights guaranteed by the First Amendment unless expressly authorized by statute or by the individual about whom the record is maintained or unless pertinent to and within the scope of an authorized law enforcement activity;

(8) make reasonable efforts to serve notice on an individual when any record on such individual is made available to any person under compulsory legal process when such process becomes a matter of public record;

(9) establish rules of conduct for persons involved in the design, development, operation, or maintenance of any system of records, or in maintaining any record, and instruct each such person with respect to such rules and

the requirements of this section, including any other rules and procedures adopted pursuant to this section and the penalties for noncompliance;

(10) establish appropriate administrative, technical, and physical safeguards to insure the security and confidentiality of records and to protect against any anticipated threats or hazards to their security or integrity which could result in substantial harm, embarrassment, inconvenience, or unfairness to any individual on whom information is maintained;

(11) at least 30 days prior to publication of information under paragraph (4)(D) of this subsection, publish in the Federal Register notice of any new use or intended use of the information in the system, and provide an opportunity for interested persons to submit written data, views, or arguments to the agency; and

(12) if such agency is a recipient agency or a source agency in a matching program with a non-Federal agency, with respect to any establishment or revision of a matching program, at least 30 days prior to conducting such program, publish in the Federal Register notice of such establishment or revision.

(f) Agency rules.—In order to carry out the provisions of this section, each agency that maintains a system of records shall promulgate rules, in accordance with the requirements (including general notice) of section 553 of this title, which shall—

(1) establish procedures whereby an individual can be notified in response to his request if any system of records named by the individual contains a record pertaining to him;

(2) define reasonable times, places, and requirements for identifying an individual who requests his record or information pertaining to him before the agency shall make the record or information available to the individual;

(3) establish procedures for the disclosure to an individual upon his request of his record or information pertaining to him, including special procedure, if deemed necessary, for the disclosure to an individual of medical records, including psychological records, pertaining to him;

(4) establish procedures for reviewing a request from an individual concerning the amendment of any record or information pertaining to the individual, for making a determination on the request, for an appeal within the agency of an initial adverse agency determination, and for whatever additional means may be necessary for each individual to be able to exercise fully his rights under this section; and

(5) establish fees to be charged, if any, to any individual for making copies of his record, excluding the cost of any search for and review of the record.

The Office of the Federal Register shall biennially compile and publish the rules promulgated under this subsection and agency notices published under subsection (e)(4) of this section in a form available to the public at low cost.

(g)(1) Civil remedies.—Whenever any agency

(A) makes a determination under subsection (d)(3) of this section not to amend an individual's record in accordance with his request, or fails to make such review in conformity with that subsection;

(B) refuses to comply with an individual request under subsection (d)(1) of this section;

(C) fails to maintain any record concerning any individual with such accuracy, relevance, timeliness, and completeness as is necessary to assure fairness in any determination relating to the qualifications, character, rights, or opportunities of, or benefits to the individual that may be made on the basis of such record, and consequently a determination is made which is adverse to the individual; or

(D) fails to comply with any other provision of this section, or any rule promulgated thereunder, in such a way as to have an adverse effect on an individual,

the individual may bring a civil action against the agency, and the district courts of the United States shall have jurisdiction in the matters under the provisions of this subsection.

(2)(A) In any suit brought under the provisions of subsection (g)(1)(A) of this section, the court may order the agency to amend the individual's record in accordance with his request or in such other way as the court may direct. In such a case the court shall determine the matter de novo.

(B) The court may assess against the United States reasonable attorney fees and other litigation costs reasonably incurred in any case under this paragraph in which the complainant has substantially prevailed.

(3)(A) In any suit brought under the provisions of subsection (g)(1)(B) of this section, the court may enjoin the agency from withholding the records and order the production to the complainant of any agency records improperly withheld from him. In such a case the court shall determine the matter de novo, and may examine the contents of any agency records in camera to determine whether the records or any portion thereof may be withheld under any of the exemptions set forth in subsection (k) of this section, and the burden is on the agency to sustain its action.

(B) The court may assess against the United States reasonable attorney fees and other litigation costs reasonably incurred in any case under this paragraph in which the complainant has substantially prevailed.

(4) In any suit brought under the provisions of subsection (g)(1)(C) or (D) of this section in which the court determines that the agency acted in a manner which was intentional or willful, the United States shall be liable to the individual in an amount equal to the sum of—

(A) actual damages sustained by the individual as a result of the refusal or failure, but in no case shall a person entitled to recovery receive less than the sum of $1,000; and

(B) the costs of the action together with reasonable attorney fees as determined by the court.

(5) An action to enforce any liability created under this section may be brought in the district court of the United States in the district in which the complainant resides, or has his principal place of business, or in which the agency records are situated, or in the District of Columbia, without regard to the amount in controversy, within two years from the date on

which the cause of action arises, except that where an agency has materially and willfully misrepresented any information required under this section to be disclosed to an individual and the information so misrepresented is material to establishment of the liability of the agency to the individual under this section, the action may be brought at any time within two years after discovery by the individual of the misrepresentation. Nothing in this section shall be construed to authorize any civil action by reason of any injury sustained as the result of a disclosure of a record prior to September 27, 1975.

(h) Rights of legal guardians.—For the purposes of this section, the parent of any minor, or the legal guardian of any individual who has been declared to be incompetent due to physical or mental incapacity or age by a court of competent jurisdiction, may act on behalf of the individual.

(i)(1) Criminal penalties.—Any officer or employee of an agency, who by virtue of his employment or official position, has possession of, or access to, agency records which contain individually identifiable information the disclosure of which is prohibited by this section or by rules or regulations established thereunder, and who knowing that disclosure of the specific material is so prohibited, willfully discloses the material in any manner to any person or agency not entitled to receive it, shall be guilty of a misdemeanor and fined not more than $5,000.

(2) Any officer or employee of any agency who willfully maintains a system of records without meeting the notice requirements of subsection (e)(4) of this section shall be guilty of a misdemeanor and fined not more than $5,000.

(3) Any person who knowingly and willfully requests or obtains any record concerning an individual from an agency under false pretenses shall be guilty of a misdemeanor and fined not more than $5,000.

(j) General exemptions.—The head of any agency may promulgate rules, in accordance with the requirements (including general notice) of sections 553(b)(1), (2), and (3), (c), and (e) of this title, to exempt any system of records within the agency from any part of this section except subsections (b), (c)(1) and (2), (e)(4)(A) through (F), (e)(6), (7), (9), (10), and (11), and (i) if the system of records is—

(1) maintained by the Central Intelligence Agency; or

(2) maintained by an agency or component thereof which performs as its principal function any activity pertaining to the enforcement of criminal laws, including police efforts to prevent, control, or reduce crime or to apprehend criminals, and the activities of prosecutors, courts, correctional, probation, pardon, or parole authorities, and which consists of (A) information compiled for the purpose of identifying individual criminal offenders and alleged offenders and consisting only of identifying data and notations of arrests, the nature and disposition of criminal charges, sentencing, confinement, release, and parole and probation status; (B) information compiled for the purpose of a criminal investigation, including reports of informants and investigators, and associated with an identifiable individual; or (C) reports identifiable to an individual compiled at any stage of the

process of enforcement of the criminal laws from arrest or indictment through release from supervision.

At the time rules are adopted under this subsection, the agency shall include in the statement required under section 553(c) of this title, the reasons why the system of records is to be exempted from a provision of this section.

(k) Specific exemptions.—The head of any agency may promulgate rules, in accordance with the requirements (including general notice) of sections 553(b)(1), (2), and (3), (c), and (e) of this title, to exempt any system of records within the agency from subsections (c)(3), (d), (e)(1), (e)(4)(G), (H), and (I) and (f) of this section if the system of records is—

(1) subject to the provisions of section 552(b)(1) of this title;

(2) investigatory material compiled for law enforcement purposes, other than material within the scope of subsection (j)(2) of this section: Provided, however, That if any individual is denied any right, privilege, or benefit that he would otherwise be entitled by Federal law, or for which he would otherwise be eligible, as a result of the maintenance of such material, such material shall be provided to such individual, except to the extent that the disclosure of such material would reveal the identity of a source who furnished information to the Government under an express promise that the identity of the source would be held in confidence, or, prior to the effective date of this section, under an implied promise that the identity of the source would be held in confidence;

(3) maintained in connection with providing protective services to the President of the United States or other individuals pursuant to section 3056 of title 18;

(4) required by statute to be maintained and used solely as statistical records;

(5) investigatory material compiled solely for the purpose of determining suitability, eligibility, or qualifications for Federal civilian employment, military service, Federal contracts, or access to classified information, but only to the extent that the disclosure of such material would reveal the identity of a source who furnished information to the Government under an express promise that the identity of the source would be held in confidence, or, prior to the effective date of this section, under an implied promise that the identity of the source would be held in confidence;

(6) testing or examination material used solely to determine individual qualifications for appointment or promotion in the Federal service the disclosure of which would compromise the objectivity or fairness of the testing or examination process; or

(7) evaluation material used to determine potential for promotion in the armed services, but only to the extent that the disclosure of such material would reveal the identity of a source who furnished information to the Government under an express promise that the identity of the source would be held in confidence, or, prior to the effective date of this section, under an implied promise that the identity of the source would be held in confidence.

PRIVACY ACT
D–11

At the time rules are adopted under this subsection, the agency shall include in the statement required under section 553(c) of this title, the reasons why the system of records is to be exempted from a provision of this section.

(l)(1) Archival records.—Each agency record which is accepted by the Archivist of the United States for storage, processing, and servicing in accordance with section 3103 of title 44 shall, for the purposes of this section, be considered to be maintained by the agency which deposited the record and shall be subject to the provisions of this section. The Archivist of the United States shall not disclose the record except to the agency which maintains the record, or under rules established by that agency which are not inconsistent with the provisions of this section.

(2) Each agency record pertaining to an identifiable individual which was transferred to the National Archives of the United States as a record which has sufficient historical or other value to warrant its continued preservation by the United States Government, prior to the effective date of this section, shall, for the purposes of this section, be considered to be maintained by the National Archives and shall not be subject to the provisions of this section, except that a statement generally describing such records (modeled after the requirements relating to records subject to subsections (e)(4)(A) through (G) of this section) shall be published in the Federal Register.

(3) Each agency record pertaining to an identifiable individual which is transferred to the National Archives of the United States as a record which has sufficient historical or other value to warrant its continued preservation by the United States Government, on or after the effective date of this section, shall, for the purposes of this section, be considered to be maintained by the National Archives and shall be exempt from the requirements of this section except subsections (e)(4)(A) through (G) and (e)(9) of this section.

(m)(1) Government contractors.—When an agency provides by a contract for the operation by or on behalf of the agency of a system of records to accomplish an agency function, the agency shall, consistent with its authority, cause the requirements of this section to be applied to such system. For purposes of subsection (i) of this section any such contractor and any employee of such contractor, if such contract is agreed to on or after the effective date of this section, shall be considered to be an employee of an agency.

(2) A consumer reporting agency to which a record is disclosed under section 3711(e) of title 31 shall not be considered a contractor for the purposes of this section.

(n) Mailing lists.—An individual's name and address may not be sold or rented by an agency unless such action is specifically authorized by law. This provision shall not be construed to require the withholding of names and addresses otherwise permitted to be made public.

(o)Matching agreements.—(1) No record which is contained in a system of records may be disclosed to a recipient agency or non-Federal agency for use in a computer matching program except pursuant to a written agreement between the source agency and the recipient agency or non-Federal agency specifying—

(A) the purpose and legal authority for conducting the program;

(B) the justification for the program and the anticipated results, including a specific estimate of any savings;

(C) a description of the records that will be matched, including each data element that will be used, the approximate number of records that will be matched, and the projected starting and completion dates of the matching program;

(D) procedures for providing individualized notice at the time of application, and notice periodically thereafter as directed by the Data Integrity Board of such agency (subject to guidance provided by the Director of the Office of Management and Budget pursuant to subsection (v)), to—

(i) applicants for and recipients of financial assistance or payments under Federal benefit programs, and

(ii) applicants for and holders of positions as Federal personnel,

that any information provided by such applicants, recipients, holders, and individuals may be subject to verification through matching programs;

(E) procedures for verifying information produced in such matching program as required by subsection (p);

(F) procedures for the retention and timely destruction of identifiable records created by a recipient agency or non-Federal agency in such matching program;

(G) procedures for ensuring the administrative, technical, and physical security of the records matched and the results of such programs;

(H) prohibitions on duplication and redisclosure of records provided by the source agency within or outside the recipient agency or the non-Federal agency, except where required by law or essential to the conduct of the matching program;

(I) procedures governing the use by a recipient agency or non-Federal agency of records provided in a matching program by a source agency, including procedures governing return of the records to the source agency or destruction of records used in such program;

(J) information on assessments that have been made on the accuracy of the records that will be used in such matching program; and

(K) that the Comptroller General may have access to all records of a recipient agency or a non-Federal agency that the Comptroller General deems necessary in order to monitor or verify compliance with the agreement.

(2)(A) A copy of each agreement entered into pursuant to paragraph (1) shall—

(i) be transmitted to the Committee on Governmental Affairs of the Senate and the Committee on Government Operations of the House of Representatives; and

(ii) be available upon request to the public.

(B) No such agreement shall be effective until 30 days after the date on which such a copy is transmitted pursuant to subparagraph (A)(i).

(C) Such an agreement shall remain in effect only for such period, not to exceed 18 months, as the Data Integrity Board of the agency determines is appropriate in light of the purposes, and length of time necessary for the conduct, of the matching program.

(D) Within 3 months prior to the expiration of such an agreement pursuant to subparagraph (C), the Data Integrity Board of the agency may, without additional review, renew the matching agreement for a current, ongoing matching program for not more than one additional year if—

(i) such program will be conducted without any change; and

(ii) each party to the agreement certifies to the Board in writing that the program has been conducted in compliance with the agreement.

(p) Verification and opportunity to contest findings.—(1) In order to protect any individual whose records are used in a matching program, no recipient agency, non-Federal agency, or source agency may suspend, terminate, reduce, or make a final denial of any financial assistance or payment under a Federal benefit program to such individual, or take other adverse action against such individual, as a result of information produced by such matching program, until—

(A)(i) the agency has independently verified the information; or

(ii) the Data Integrity Board of the agency, or in the case of a non-Federal agency the Data Integrity Board of the source agency, determines in accordance with guidance issued by the Director of the Office of Management and Budget that—

(I) the information is limited to identification and amount of benefits paid by the source agency under a Federal benefit program; and

(II) there is a high degree of confidence that the information provided to the recipient agency is accurate;

(B) the individual receives a notice from the agency containing a statement of its findings and informing the individual of the opportunity to contest such findings; and

(C)(i) the expiration of any time period established for the program by statute or regulation for the individual to respond to that notice; or

(ii) in the case of a program for which no such period is established, the end of the 30-day period beginning on the date on which notice under subparagraph (B) is mailed or otherwise provided to the individual.

(2) Independent verification referred to in paragraph (1) requires investigation and confirmation of specific information relating to an individual that is used as a basis for an adverse action against the individual, including where applicable investigation and confirmation of—

(A) the amount of any asset or income involved;

(B) whether such individual actually has or had access to such asset or income for such individual's own use; and

(C) the period or periods when the individual actually had such asset or income.

(3) Notwithstanding paragraph (1), an agency may take any appropriate action otherwise prohibited by such paragraph if the agency determines that the public health or public safety may be adversely affected or significantly threatened during any notice period required by such paragraph.

(q)Sanctions.—(1) Notwithstanding any other provision of law, no source agency may disclose any record which is contained in a system of records to a recipient agency or non-Federal agency for a matching program if such source agency has reason to believe that the requirements of subsection (p), or any matching agreement entered into pursuant to subsection (o), or both, are not being met by such recipient agency.

(2) No source agency may renew a matching agreement unless—

(A) the recipient agency or non-Federal agency has certified that it has complied with the provisions of that agreement; and

(B) the source agency has no reason to believe that the certification is inaccurate.

(r) Report on new systems and matching programs.—Each agency that proposes to establish or make a significant change in a system of records or a matching program shall provide adequate advance notice of any such proposal (in duplicate) to the Committee on Government Operations of the House of Representatives, the Committee on Governmental Affairs of the Senate, and the Office of Management and Budget in order to permit an evaluation of the probable or potential effect of such proposal on the privacy or other rights of individuals.

(s) Biennial report.—The President shall biennially submit to the Speaker of the House of Representatives and the President pro tempore of the Senate a report—

(1) describing the actions of the Director of the Office of Management and Budget pursuant to section 6 of the Privacy Act of 1974 during the preceding 2 years;

(2) describing the exercise of individual rights of access and amendment under this section during such years;

(3) identifying changes in or additions to systems of records;

(4) containing such other information concerning administration of this section as may be necessary or useful to the Congress in reviewing the effectiveness of this section in carrying out the purposes of the Privacy Act of 1974.

(t)(1) Effect of other laws.—No agency shall rely on any exemption contained in section 552 of this title to withhold from an individual any record which is otherwise accessible to such individual under the provisions of this section.

(2) No agency shall rely on any exemption in this section to withhold from an individual any record which is otherwise accessible to such individual under the provisions of section 552 of this title.

(u) Data Integrity Boards.—(1) Every agency conducting or participating in a matching program shall establish a Data Integrity Board to oversee and coordinate among the various components of such agency the agency's implementation of this section.

(2) Each Data Integrity Board shall consist of senior officials designated by the head of the agency, and shall include any senior official designated by the head of the agency as responsible for implementation of this section, and the inspector general of the agency, if any. The inspector general shall not serve as chairman of the Data Integrity Board.

(3) Each Data Integrity Board—

(A) shall review, approve, and maintain all written agreements for receipt or disclosure of agency records for matching programs to ensure compliance with subsection (o), and all relevant statutes, regulations, and guidelines;

(B) shall review all matching programs in which the agency has participated during the year, either as a source agency or recipient agency, determine compliance with applicable laws, regulations, guidelines, and agency agreements, and assess the costs and benefits of such programs;

(C) shall review all recurring matching programs in which the agency has participated during the year, either as a source agency or recipient agency, for continued justification for such disclosures;

(D) shall compile an annual report, which shall be submitted to the head of the agency and the Office of Management and Budget and made available to the public on request, describing the matching activities of the agency, including—

(i) matching programs in which the agency has participated as a source agency or recipient agency;

(ii) matching agreements proposed under subsection (o) that were disapproved by the Board;

(iii) any changes in membership or structure of the Board in the preceding year;

(iv) the reasons for any waiver of the requirement in paragraph (4) of this section for completion and submission of a cost-benefit analysis prior to the approval of a matching program;

(v) any violations of matching agreements that have been alleged or identified and any corrective action taken; and

(vi) any other information required by the Director of the Office of Management and Budget to be included in such report;

(E) shall serve as a clearinghouse for receiving and providing information on the accuracy, completeness, and reliability of records used in matching programs;

(F) shall provide interpretation and guidance to agency components and personnel on the requirements of this section for matching programs;

(G) shall review agency recordkeeping and disposal policies and practices for matching programs to assure compliance with this section; and

(H) may review and report on any agency matching activities that are not matching programs.

(4)(A) Except as provided in subparagraphs (B) and (C), a Data Integrity Board shall not approve any written agreement for a matching program unless the agency has completed and submitted to such Board a cost-benefit analysis of the proposed program and such analysis demonstrates that the program is likely to be cost effective.

(B) The Board may waive the requirements of subparagraph (A) of this paragraph if it determines in writing, in accordance with guidelines prescribed by the Director of the Office of Management and Budget, that a cost-benefit analysis is not required.

(C) A cost-benefit analysis shall not be required under subparagraph (A) prior to the initial approval of a written agreement for a matching program that is specifically required by statute. Any subsequent written agreement for such a program shall not be approved by the Data Integrity Board unless the agency has submitted a cost-benefit analysis of the program as conducted under the preceding approval of such agreement.

(5)(A) If a matching agreement is disapproved by a Data Integrity Board, any party to such agreement may appeal the disapproval to the Director of the Office of Management and Budget. Timely notice of the filing of such an appeal shall be provided by the Director of the Office of Management and Budget to the Committee on Governmental Affairs of the Senate and the Committee on Government Operations of the House of Representatives.

(B) The Director of the Office of Management and Budget may approve a matching agreement notwithstanding the disapproval of a Data Integrity Board if the Director determines that—

(i) the matching program will be consistent with all applicable legal, regulatory, and policy requirements;

(ii) there is adequate evidence that the matching agreement will be cost-effective; and

(iii) the matching program is in the public interest.

(C) The decision of the Director to approve a matching agreement shall not take effect until 30 days after it is reported to committees described in subparagraph (A).

(D) If the Data Integrity Board and the Director of the Office of Management and Budget disapprove a matching program proposed by the inspector general of an agency, the inspector general may report the disapproval to the head of the agency and to the Congress.

(6) In the reports required by paragraph (3)(D), agency matching activities that are not matching programs may be reported on an aggregate basis,

if and to the extent necessary to protect ongoing law enforcement or counterintelligence investigations.

[(7) Redesignated (6)]

(v) Office of Management and Budget responsibilities.—The Director of the Office of Management and Budget shall—

(1) develop and, after notice and opportunity for public comment, prescribe guidelines and regulations for the use of agencies in implementing the provisions of this section; and

(2) provide continuing assistance to and oversight of the implementation of this section by agencies.

Appendix E

GOVERNMENT IN THE SUNSHINE ACT
UNITED STATES CODE, TITLE 5, CHAPTER 5

§ 552b. Open meetings

(a) For purposes of this section—

(1) the term "agency" means any agency, as defined in section 552(e) of this title, headed by a collegial body composed of two or more individual members, a majority of whom are appointed to such position by the President with the advice and consent of the Senate, and any subdivision thereof authorized to act on behalf of the agency;

(2) the term "meeting" means the deliberations of at least the number of individual agency members required to take action on behalf of the agency where such deliberations determine or result in the joint conduct or disposition of official agency business, but does not include deliberations required or permitted by subsection (d) or (e); and

(3) the term "member" means an individual who belongs to a collegial body heading an agency.

(b) Members shall not jointly conduct or dispose of agency business other than in accordance with this section. Except as provided in subsection (c), every portion of every meeting of an agency shall be open to public observation.

(c) Except in a case where the agency finds that the public interest requires otherwise, the second sentence of subsection (b) shall not apply to any portion of an agency meeting, and the requirements of subsections (d) and (e) shall not apply to any information pertaining to such meeting otherwise required by this section to be disclosed to the public, where the agency properly determines that such portion or portions of its meeting or the disclosure of such information is likely to—

(1) disclose matters that are (A) specifically authorized under criteria established by an Executive order to be kept secret in the interests of national defense or foreign policy and (B) in fact properly classified pursuant to such Executive order;

(2) relate solely to the internal personnel rules and practices of an agency;

(3) disclose matters specifically exempted from disclosure by statute (other than section 552 of this title), provided that such statute (A) requires that the matters be withheld from the public in such a manner as to leave no

discretion on the issue, or (B) establishes particular criteria for withholding or refers to particular types of matters to be withheld;

(4) disclose trade secrets and commercial or financial information obtained from a person and privileged or confidential;

(5) involve accusing any person of a crime, or formally censuring any person;

(6) disclose information of a personal nature where disclosure would constitute a clearly unwarranted invasion of personal privacy;

(7) disclose investigatory records compiled for law enforcement purposes, or information which if written would be contained in such records, but only to the extent that the production of such records or information would (A) interfere with enforcement proceedings, (B) deprive a person of a right to a fair trial or an impartial adjudication, (C) constitute an unwarranted invasion of personal privacy, (D) disclose the identity of a confidential source and, in the case of a record compiled by a criminal law enforcement authority in the course of a criminal investigation, or by an agency conducting a lawful national security intelligence investigation, confidential information furnished only by the confidential source, (E) disclose investigative techniques and procedures, or (F) endanger the life or physical safety of law enforcement personnel;

(8) disclose information contained in or related to examination, operating, or condition reports prepared by, on behalf of, or for the use of an agency responsible for the regulation or supervision of financial institutions;

(9) disclose information the premature disclosure of which would—

(A) in the case of an agency which regulates currencies, securities, commodities, or financial institutions, be likely to (i) lead to significant financial speculation in currencies, securities, or commodities, or (ii) significantly endanger the stability of any financial institution; or

(B) in the case of any agency, be likely to significantly frustrate implementation of a proposed agency action,

except that subparagraph (B) shall not apply in any instance where the agency has already disclosed to the public the content or nature of its proposed action, or where the agency is required by law to make such disclosure on its own initiative prior to taking final agency action on such proposal; or

(10) specifically concern the agency's issuance of a subpena, or the agency's participation in a civil action or proceeding, an action in a foreign court or international tribunal, or an arbitration, or the initiation, conduct, or disposition by the agency of a particular case of formal agency adjudication pursuant to the procedures in section 554 of this title or otherwise involving a determination on the record after opportunity for a hearing.

(d)(1) Action under subsection (c) shall be taken only when a majority of the entire membership of the agency (as defined in subsection (a)(1)) votes to take such action. A separate vote of the agency members shall be taken with respect to each agency meeting a portion or portions of which are proposed to be closed to the public pursuant to subsection (c), or with respect to any information which is proposed to be withheld under subsection (c). A single vote may be taken with respect to a series of meetings, a portion or portions of which are proposed to be closed to the public, or with respect to any information concerning such series of meetings, so long as each meeting in such series involves the same particular matters and is scheduled to be held no more than thirty days after the initial meeting in such series. The vote of each agency member participating in such vote shall be recorded and no proxies shall be allowed.

(2) Whenever any person whose interests may be directly affected by a portion of a meeting requests that the agency close such portion to the public for any of the reasons referred to in paragraph (5), (6), or (7) of subsection (c), the agency, upon request of any one of its members, shall vote by recorded vote whether to close such meeting.

(3) Within one day of any vote taken pursuant to paragraph (1) or (2), the agency shall make publicly available a written copy of such vote reflecting the vote of each member on the question. If a portion of a meeting is to be closed to the public, the agency shall, within one day of the vote taken pursuant to paragraph (1) or (2) of this subsection, make publicly available a full written explanation of its action closing the portion together with a list of all persons expected to attend the meeting and their affiliation.

(4) Any agency, a majority of whose meetings may properly be closed to the public pursuant to paragraph (4), (8), (9)(A), or (10) of subsection (c), or any combination thereof, may provide by regulation for the closing of such meetings or portions thereof in the event that a majority of the members of the agency votes by recorded vote at the beginning of such meeting, or portion thereof, to close the exempt portion or portions of the meeting, and a copy of such vote, reflecting the vote of each member on the question, is made available to the public. The provisions of paragraphs (1), (2), and (3) of this subsection and subsection (e) shall not apply to any portion of a meeting to which such regulations apply: Provided, That the agency shall, except to the extent that such information is exempt from disclosure under the provisions of subsection (c), provide the public with public announcement of the time, place, and subject matter of the meeting and of each portion thereof at the earliest practicable time.

(e)(1) In the case of each meeting, the agency shall make public announcement, at least one week before the meeting, of the time, place, and subject matter of the meeting, whether it is to be open or closed to the public, and the name and phone number of the official designated by the agency to respond to requests for information about the meeting. Such announcement shall be made unless a majority of the members of the agency determines by a recorded vote that agency business requires that such meeting be called at an earlier date, in which case the agency shall make public announcement of the time, place, and subject matter of such meeting, and whether open or closed to the public, at the earliest practicable time.

(2) The time or place of a meeting may be changed following the public announcement required by paragraph (1) only if the agency publicly announces such change at the earliest practicable time. The subject matter of a meeting, or the determination of the agency to open or close a meeting,

or portion of a meeting, to the public, may be changed following the public announcement required by this subsection only if (A) a majority of the entire membership of the agency determines by a recorded vote that agency business so requires and that no earlier announcement of the change was possible, and (B) the agency publicly announces such change and the vote of each member upon such change at the earliest practicable time.

(3) Immediately following each public announcement required by this subsection, notice of the time, place, and subject matter of a meeting, whether the meeting is open or closed, any change in one of the preceding, and the name and phone number of the official designated by the agency to respond to requests for information about the meeting, shall also be submitted for publication in the Federal Register.

(f)(1) For every meeting closed pursuant to paragraphs (1) through (10) of subsection (c), the General Counsel or chief legal officer of the agency shall publicly certify that, in his or her opinion, the meeting may be closed to the public and shall state each relevant exemptive provision. A copy of such certification, together with a statement from the presiding officer of the meeting setting forth the time and place of the meeting, and the persons present, shall be retained by the agency. The agency shall maintain a complete transcript or electronic recording adequate to record fully the proceedings of each meeting, or portion of a meeting, closed to the public, except that in the case of a meeting, or portion of a meeting, closed to the public pursuant to paragraph (8), (9)(A), or (10) of subsection (c), the agency shall maintain either such a transcript or recording, or a set of minutes. Such minutes shall fully and clearly describe all matters discussed and shall provide a full and accurate summary of any actions taken, and the reasons therefor, including a description of each of the views expressed on any item and the record of any rollcall vote (reflecting the vote of each member on the question). All documents considered in connection with any action shall be identified in such minutes.

(2) The agency shall make promptly available to the public, in a place easily accessible to the public, the transcript, electronic recording, or minutes (as required by paragraph (1)) of the discussion of any item on the agenda, or of any item of the testimony of any witness received at the meeting, except for such item or items of such discussion or testimony as the agency determines to contain information which may be withheld under subsection (c). Copies of such transcript, or minutes, or a transcription of such recording disclosing the identity of each speaker, shall be furnished to any person at the actual cost of duplication or transcription. The agency shall maintain a complete verbatim copy of the transcript, a complete copy of the minutes, or a complete electronic recording of each meeting, or portion of a meeting, closed to the public, for a period of at least two years after such meeting, or until one year after the conclusion of any agency proceeding with respect to which the meeting or portion was held, whichever occurs later.

(g) Each agency subject to the requirements of this section shall, within 180 days after the date of enactment of this section, following consultation with the Office of the Chairman of the Administrative Conference of the United States and published notice in the Federal Register of at least thirty days and opportunity for written comment by any person, promulgate regulations to implement the requirements of subsections (b) through (f) of this section. Any person may bring a proceeding in the United States District Court for the District of Columbia to require an agency to promulgate such regulations if such agency has not promulgated such regulations within the time period specified herein. Subject to any limitations of time provided by law, any person may bring a proceeding in the United States Court of Appeals for the District of Columbia to set aside agency regulations issued pursuant to this subsection that are not in accord with the requirements of subsections (b) through (f) of this section and to require the promulgation of regulations that are in accord with such subsections.

(h)(1) The district courts of the United States shall have jurisdiction to enforce the requirements of subsections (b) through (f) of this section by declaratory judgment, injunctive relief, or other relief as may be appropriate. Such actions may be brought by any person against an agency prior to, or within sixty days after, the meeting out of which the violation of this section arises, except that if public announcement of such meeting is not initially provided by the agency in accordance with the requirements of this section, such action may be instituted pursuant to this section at any time prior to sixty days after any public announcement of such meeting. Such actions may be brought in the district court of the United States for the district in which the agency meeting is held or in which the agency in question has its headquarters, or in the District Court for the District of Columbia. In such actions a defendant shall serve his answer within thirty days after the service of the complaint. The burden is on the defendant to sustain his action. In deciding such cases the court may examine in camera any portion of the transcript, electronic recording, or minutes of a meeting closed to the public, and may take such additional evidence as it deems necessary. The court, having due regard for orderly administration and the public interest, as well as the interests of the parties, may grant such equitable relief as it deems appropriate, including granting an injunction against future violations of this section or ordering the agency to make available to the public such portion of the transcript, recording, or minutes of a meeting as is not authorized to be withheld under subsection (c) of this section.

(2) Any Federal court otherwise authorized by law to review agency action may, at the application of any person properly participating in the proceeding pursuant to other applicable law, inquire into violations by the agency of the requirements of this section and afford such relief as it deems appropriate. Nothing in this section authorizes any Federal court having jurisdiction solely on the basis of paragraph (1) to set aside, enjoin, or invalidate any agency action (other than an action to close a meeting or to withhold information under this section) taken or discussed at any agency meeting out of which the violation of this section arose.

(i) The court may assess against any party reasonable attorney fees and other litigation costs reasonably incurred by any other party who substantially prevails in any action brought in accordance with the provisions of subsection (g) or (h) of this section, except that costs may be assessed against the plaintiff only where the court finds that the suit was initiated by the plaintiff primarily for frivolous or dilatory purposes. In the case of assessment of costs against an agency, the costs may be assessed by the court against the United States.

(j) Each agency subject to the requirements of this section shall annually report to the Congress regarding the following:

(1) The changes in the policies and procedures of the agency under this section that have occurred during the preceding 1-year period.

(2) A tabulation of the number of meetings held, the exemptions applied to close meetings, and the days of public notice provided to close meetings.

(3) A brief description of litigation or formal complaints concerning the implementation of this section by the agency.

(4) A brief explanation of any changes in law that have affected the responsibilities of the agency under this section.

(k) Nothing herein expands or limits the present rights of any person under section 552 of this title, except that the exemptions set forth in subsection (c) of this section shall govern in the case of any request made pursuant to section 552 to copy or inspect the transcripts, recordings, or minutes described in subsection (f) of this section. The requirements of chapter 33 of title 44, United States Code, shall not apply to the transcripts, recordings, and minutes described in subsection (f) of this section.

(l) This section does not constitute authority to withhold any information from Congress, and does not authorize the closing of any agency meeting or portion thereof required by any other provision of law to be open.

(m) Nothing in this section authorizes any agency to withhold from any individual any record, including transcripts, recordings, or minutes required by this section, which is otherwise accessible to such individual under section 552a of this title.

Appendix F

ADMINISTRATIVE DISPUTE RESOLUTION ACT

UNITED STATES CODE, TITLE 5, CHAPTER 5

§ 571. Definitions

For the purposes of this subchapter, the term—

(1) "agency" has the same meaning as in section 551(1) of this title;

(2) "administrative program" includes a Federal function which involves protection of the public interest and the determination of rights, privileges, and obligations of private persons through rule making, adjudication, licensing, or investigation, as those terms are used in subchapter II of this chapter;

(3) "alternative means of dispute resolution" means any procedure that is used to resolve issues in controversy, including, but not limited to, conciliation, facilitation, mediation, factfinding, minitrials, arbitration, and use of ombuds, or any combination thereof;

(4) "award" means any decision by an arbitrator resolving the issues in controversy;

(5) "dispute resolution communication" means any oral or written communication prepared for the purposes of a dispute resolution proceeding, including any memoranda, notes or work product of the neutral, parties or nonparty participant; except that a written agreement to enter into a dispute resolution proceeding, or final written agreement or arbitral award reached as a result of a dispute resolution proceeding, is not a dispute resolution communication;

(6) "dispute resolution proceeding" means any process in which an alternative means of dispute resolution is used to resolve an issue in controversy in which a neutral is appointed and specified parties participate;

(7) "in confidence" means, with respect to information, that the information is provided—

(A) with the expressed intent of the source that it not be disclosed; or

(B) under circumstances that would create the reasonable expectation on behalf of the source that the information will not be disclosed;

(8) "issue in controversy" means an issue which is material to a decision concerning an administrative program of an agency, and with which there is disagreement—

(A) between an agency and persons who would be substantially affected by the decision; or

(B) between persons who would be substantially affected by the decision;

(9) "neutral" means an individual who, with respect to an issue in controversy, functions specifically to aid the parties in resolving the controversy;

(10) "party" means—

(A) for a proceeding with named parties, the same as in section 551(3) of this title; and

(B) for a proceeding without named parties, a person who will be significantly affected by the decision in the proceeding and who participates in the proceeding;

(11) "person" has the same meaning as in section 551(2) of this title; and

(12) "roster" means a list of persons qualified to provide services as neutrals.

§ 572. General authority

(a) An agency may use a dispute resolution proceeding for the resolution of an issue in controversy that relates to an administrative program, if the parties agree to such proceeding.

(b) An agency shall consider not using a dispute resolution proceeding if—

(1) a definitive or authoritative resolution of the matter is required for precedential value, and such a proceeding is not likely to be accepted generally as an authoritative precedent;

(2) the matter involves or may bear upon significant questions of Government policy that require additional procedures before a final resolution may be made, and such a proceeding would not likely serve to develop a recommended policy for the agency;

(3) maintaining established policies is of special importance, so that variations among individual decisions are not increased and such a proceeding would not likely reach consistent results among individual decisions;

(4) the matter significantly affects persons or organizations who are not parties to the proceeding;

(5) a full public record of the proceeding is important, and a dispute resolution proceeding cannot provide such a record; and

(6) the agency must maintain continuing jurisdiction over the matter with authority to alter the disposition of the matter in the light of changed circumstances, and a dispute resolution proceeding would interfere with the agency's fulfilling that requirement.

(c) Alternative means of dispute resolution authorized under this subchapter are voluntary procedures which supplement rather than limit other available agency dispute resolution techniques.

§ 573. Neutrals

(a) A neutral may be a permanent or temporary officer or employee of the Federal Government or any other individual who is acceptable to the parties to a dispute resolution proceeding. A neutral shall have no official, financial, or personal conflict of interest with respect to the issues in controversy, unless such interest is fully disclosed in writing to all parties and all parties agree that the neutral may serve.

(b) A neutral who serves as a conciliator, facilitator, or mediator serves at the will of the parties.

(c) The President shall designate an agency or designate or establish an interagency committee to facilitate and encourage agency use of dispute resolution under this subchapter. Such agency or interagency committee, in consultation with other appropriate Federal agencies and professional organizations experienced in matters concerning dispute resolution, shall—

> (1) encourage and facilitate agency use of alternative means of dispute resolution; and
>
> (2) develop procedures that permit agencies to obtain the services of neutrals on an expedited basis.

(d) An agency may use the services of one or more employees of other agencies to serve as neutrals in dispute resolution proceedings. The agencies may enter into an interagency agreement that provides for the reimbursement by the user agency or the parties of the full or partial cost of the services of such an employee.

(e) Any agency may enter into a contract with any person for services as a neutral, or for training in connection with alternative means of dispute resolution. The parties in a dispute resolution proceeding shall agree on compensation for the neutral that is fair and reasonable to the Government.

§ 574. Confidentiality

(a) Except as provided in subsections (d) and (e), a neutral in a dispute resolution proceeding shall not voluntarily disclose or through discovery or compulsory process be required to disclose any dispute resolution communication or any communication provided in confidence to the neutral, unless—

> (1) all parties to the dispute resolution proceeding and the neutral consent in writing, and, if the dispute resolution communication was provided by a nonparty participant, that participant also consents in writing;
>
> (2) the dispute resolution communication has already been made public;
>
> (3) the dispute resolution communication is required by statute to be made public, but a neutral should make such communication public only if no other person is reasonably available to disclose the communication; or
>
> (4) a court determines that such testimony or disclosure is necessary to—
>
>> (A) prevent a manifest injustice;
>>
>> (B) help establish a violation of law; or
>>
>> (C) prevent harm to the public health or safety,

of sufficient magnitude in the particular case to outweigh the integrity of dispute resolution proceedings in general by reducing the confidence of parties in future cases that their communications will remain confidential.

(b) A party to a dispute resolution proceeding shall not voluntarily disclose or through discovery or compulsory process be required to disclose any dispute resolution communication, unless—

(1) the communication was prepared by the party seeking disclosure;

(2) all parties to the dispute resolution proceeding consent in writing;

(3) the dispute resolution communication has already been made public;

(4) the dispute resolution communication is required by statute to be made public;

(5) a court determines that such testimony or disclosure is necessary to—

(A) prevent a manifest injustice;

(B) help establish a violation of law; or

(C) prevent harm to the public health and safety,

of sufficient magnitude in the particular case to outweigh the integrity of dispute resolution proceedings in general by reducing the confidence of parties in future cases that their communications will remain confidential;

(6) the dispute resolution communication is relevant to determining the existence or meaning of an agreement or award that resulted from the dispute resolution proceeding or to the enforcement of such an agreement or award; or

(7) except for dispute resolution communications generated by the neutral, the dispute resolution communication was provided to or was available to all parties to the dispute resolution proceeding.

(c) Any dispute resolution communication that is disclosed in violation of subsection (a) or (b), shall not be admissible in any proceeding relating to the issues in controversy with respect to which the communication was made.

(d)(1) The parties may agree to alternative confidential procedures for disclosures by a neutral. Upon such agreement the parties shall inform the neutral before the commencement of the dispute resolution proceeding of any modifications to the provisions of subsection (a) that will govern the confidentiality of the dispute resolution proceeding. If the parties do not so inform the neutral, subsection (a) shall apply.

(2) To qualify for the exemption established under subsection (j), an alternative confidential procedure under this subsection may not provide for less disclosure than the confidential procedures otherwise provided under this section.

(e) If a demand for disclosure, by way of discovery request or other legal process, is made upon a neutral regarding a dispute resolution communication, the neutral shall make reasonable efforts to notify the parties and any affected nonparty participants of the demand. Any party or affected nonparty participant who receives such notice and within 15 calendar days does not offer to defend a refusal of the neutral to disclose the requested information shall have waived any objection to such disclosure.

(f) Nothing in this section shall prevent the discovery or admissibility of any evidence that is otherwise discoverable, merely because the evidence was presented in the course of a dispute resolution proceeding.

(g) Subsections (a) and (b) shall have no effect on the information and data that are necessary to document an agreement reached or order issued pursuant to a dispute resolution proceeding.

(h) Subsections (a) and (b) shall not prevent the gathering of information for research or educational purposes, in cooperation with other agencies, governmental entities, or dispute resolution programs, so long as the parties and the specific issues in controversy are not identifiable.

(i) Subsections (a) and (b) shall not prevent use of a dispute resolution communication to resolve a dispute between the neutral in a dispute resolution proceeding and a party to or participant in such proceeding, so long as such dispute resolution communication is disclosed only to the extent necessary to resolve such dispute.

(j) A dispute resolution communication which is between a neutral and a party and which may not be disclosed under this section shall also be exempt from disclosure under section 552(b)(3).

§ 575. Authorization of arbitration

(a)(1) Arbitration may be used as an alternative means of dispute resolution whenever all parties consent. Consent may be obtained either before or after an issue in controversy has arisen. A party may agree to—

(A) submit only certain issues in controversy to arbitration; or

(B) arbitration on the condition that the award must be within a range of possible outcomes.

(2) The arbitration agreement that sets forth the subject matter submitted to the arbitrator shall be in writing. Each such arbitration agreement shall specify a maximum award that may be issued by the arbitrator and may specify other conditions limiting the range of possible outcomes.

(3) An agency may not require any person to consent to arbitration as a condition of entering into a contract or obtaining a benefit.

(b) An officer or employee of an agency shall not offer to use arbitration for the resolution of issues in controversy unless such officer or employee—

(1) would otherwise have authority to enter into a settlement concerning the matter; or

(2) is otherwise specifically authorized by the agency to consent to the use of arbitration.

(c) Prior to using binding arbitration under this subchapter, the head of an agency, in consultation with the Attorney General and after taking into account the factors in section 572(b), shall issue guidance on the appropriate use of binding arbitration and when an officer or employee of the agency has authority to settle an issue in controversy through binding arbitration.

§ 576. Enforcement of arbitration agreements

An agreement to arbitrate a matter to which this subchapter applies is enforceable pursuant to section 4 of title 9, and no action brought to enforce such an agreement shall be dismissed nor shall relief therein be denied on the grounds that it is against the United States or that the United States is an indispensable party.

§ 577. Arbitrators

(a) The parties to an arbitration proceeding shall be entitled to participate in the selection of the arbitrator.

(b) The arbitrator shall be a neutral who meets the criteria of section 573 of this title.

§ 578. Authority of the arbitrator

An arbitrator to whom a dispute is referred under this subchapter may—

(1) regulate the course of and conduct arbitral hearings;

(2) administer oaths and affirmations;

(3) compel the attendance of witnesses and production of evidence at the hearing under the provisions of section 7 of title 9 only to the extent the agency involved is otherwise authorized by law to do so; and

(4) make awards.

§ 579. Arbitration proceedings

(a) The arbitrator shall set a time and place for the hearing on the dispute and shall notify the parties not less than 5 days before the hearing.

(b) Any party wishing a record of the hearing shall—

(1) be responsible for the preparation of such record;

(2) notify the other parties and the arbitrator of the preparation of such record;

(3) furnish copies to all identified parties and the arbitrator; and

(4) pay all costs for such record, unless the parties agree otherwise or the arbitrator determines that the costs should be apportioned.

(c)(1) The parties to the arbitration are entitled to be heard, to present evidence material to the controversy, and to cross-examine witnesses appearing at the hearing.

(2) The arbitrator may, with the consent of the parties, conduct all or part of the hearing by telephone, television, computer, or other electronic means, if each party has an opportunity to participate.

(3) The hearing shall be conducted expeditiously and in an informal manner.

(4) The arbitrator may receive any oral or documentary evidence, except that irrelevant, immaterial, unduly repetitious, or privileged evidence may be excluded by the arbitrator.

(5) The arbitrator shall interpret and apply relevant statutory and regulatory requirements, legal precedents, and policy directives.

(d) No interested person shall make or knowingly cause to be made to the arbitrator an unauthorized ex parte communication relevant to the merits of the proceeding, unless the parties agree otherwise. If a communication is made in violation of this subsection, the arbitrator shall ensure that a memorandum of the communication is prepared and made a part of the record, and that an opportunity for rebuttal is allowed. Upon receipt of a communication made in violation of this subsection, the arbitrator may, to the extent consistent with the interests of justice and the policies underlying this subchapter, require the offending party to show cause why the claim of such party should not be resolved against such party as a result of the improper conduct.

(e) The arbitrator shall make the award within 30 days after the close of the hearing, or the date of the filing of any briefs authorized by the arbitrator, whichever date is later, unless—

(1) the parties agree to some other time limit; or

(2) the agency provides by rule for some other time limit.

§ 580. Arbitration awards

(a)(1) Unless the agency provides otherwise by rule, the award in an arbitration proceeding under this subchapter shall include a brief, informal discussion of the factual and legal basis for the award, but formal findings of fact or conclusions of law shall not be required.

(2) The prevailing parties shall file the award with all relevant agencies, along with proof of service on all parties.

(b) The award in an arbitration proceeding shall become final 30 days after it is served on all parties. Any agency that is a party to the proceeding may extend this 30-day period for an additional 30-day period by serving a notice of such extension on all other parties before the end of the first 30-day period.

(c) A final award is binding on the parties to the arbitration proceeding, and may be enforced pursuant to sections 9 through 13 of title 9. No action brought to enforce such an award shall be dismissed nor shall relief therein be denied on the grounds that it is against the United States or that the United States is an indispensable party.

(d) An award entered under this subchapter in an arbitration proceeding may not serve as an estoppel in any other proceeding for any issue that was resolved in the proceeding. Such an award also may not be used as precedent or otherwise be considered in any factually unrelated proceeding, whether conducted under this subchapter, by an agency, or in a court, or in any other arbitration proceeding.

[(e) Redesignated (d)]

[(f) and (g) Repealed. Pub.L. 104-320, § 8(a)(1), Oct. 19, 1996, 110 Stat. 3872]

§ 581. Judicial review

(a) Notwithstanding any other provision of law, any person adversely affected or aggrieved by an award made in an arbitration proceeding conducted under this subchapter may bring an action for review of such award only pursuant to the provisions of sections 9 through 13 of title 9.

(b) A decision by an agency to use or not to use a dispute resolution proceeding under this subchapter shall be committed to the discretion of the agency and shall not be subject to judicial review, except that arbitration shall be subject to judicial review under section 10(b) of title 9.

§ 582. [Repealed. Pub. L. 104-320, § 4(b)(1), Oct. 19, 1996, 110 Stat. 3871]

§ 583. Support services

For the purposes of this subchapter, an agency may use (with or without reimbursement) the services and facilities of other Federal agencies, State, local, and tribal governments, public and private organizations and agencies, and individuals, with the consent of such agencies, organizations, and individuals. An agency may accept voluntary and uncompensated services for purposes of this subchapter without regard to the provisions of section 1342 of title 31.

Appendix G

NEGOTIATED RULEMAKING ACT
UNITED STATES CODE, TITLE 5, CHAPTER 5

§ 561 Purpose

The purpose of this subchapter is to establish a framework for the conduct of negotiated rulemaking, consistent with section 553 of this title, to encourage agencies to use the process when it enhances the informal rulemaking process. Nothing in this subchapter should be construed as an attempt to limit innovation and experimentation with the negotiated rulemaking process or with other innovative rulemaking procedures otherwise authorized by law.

§ 562. Definitions

For the purposes of this subchapter, the term—

(1) "agency" has the same meaning as in section 551(1) of this title;

(2) "consensus" means unanimous concurrence among the interests represented on a negotiated rulemaking committee established under this subchapter, unless such committee—

   (A) agrees to define such term to mean a general but not unanimous concurrence; or

   (B) agrees upon another specified definition;

(3) "convener" means a person who impartially assists an agency in determining whether establishment of a negotiated rulemaking committee is feasible and appropriate in a particular rulemaking;

(4) "facilitator" means a person who impartially aids in the discussions and negotiations among the members of a negotiated rulemaking committee to develop a proposed rule;

(5) "interest" means, with respect to an issue or matter, multiple parties which have a similar point of view or which are likely to be affected in a similar manner;

(6) "negotiated rulemaking" means rulemaking through the use of a negotiated rulemaking committee;

(7) "negotiated rulemaking committee" or "committee" means an advisory committee established by an agency in accordance with this subchapter and

the Federal Advisory Committee Act to consider and discuss issues for the purpose of reaching a consensus in the development of a proposed rule;

(8) "party" has the same meaning as in section 551(3) of this title;

(9) "person" has the same meaning as in section 551(2) of this title;

(10) "rule" has the same meaning as in section 551(4) of this title; and

(11) "rulemaking" means "rule making" as that term is defined in section 551(5) of this title.

§ 563. Determination of need for negotiated rulemaking committee

(a) Determination of need by the agency.—An agency may establish a negotiated rulemaking committee to negotiate and develop a proposed rule, if the head of the agency determines that the use of the negotiated rulemaking procedure is in the public interest. In making such a determination, the head of the agency shall consider whether—

(1) there is a need for a rule;

(2) there are a limited number of identifiable interests that will be significantly affected by the rule;

(3) there is a reasonable likelihood that a committee can be convened with a balanced representation of persons who—

(A) can adequately represent the interests identified under paragraph (2); and

(B) are willing to negotiate in good faith to reach a consensus on the proposed rule;

(4) there is a reasonable likelihood that a committee will reach a consensus on the proposed rule within a fixed period of time;

(5) the negotiated rulemaking procedure will not unreasonably delay the notice of proposed rulemaking and the issuance of the final rule;

(6) the agency has adequate resources and is willing to commit such resources, including technical assistance, to the committee; and

(7) the agency, to the maximum extent possible consistent with the legal obligations of the agency, will use the consensus of the committee with respect to the proposed rule as the basis for the rule proposed by the agency for notice and comment.

(b) Use of conveners.—

(1) Purposes of conveners.—An agency may use the services of a convener to assist the agency in—

(A) identifying persons who will be significantly affected by a proposed rule, including residents of rural areas; and

(B) conducting discussions with such persons to identify the issues of concern to such persons, and to ascertain whether the establishment of a negotiated rulemaking committee is feasible and appropriate in the particular rulemaking.

(2) Duties of conveners.—The convener shall report findings and may make recommendations to the agency. Upon request of the agency, the convener shall ascertain the names of persons who are willing and qualified to represent interests that will be significantly affected by the proposed rule, including residents of rural areas. The report and any recommendations of the convener shall be made available to the public upon request.

§ 564. Publication of notice; applications for membership on committees

(a) Publication of notice.—If, after considering the report of a convener or conducting its own assessment, an agency decides to establish a negotiated rulemaking committee, the agency shall publish in the Federal Register and, as appropriate, in trade or other specialized publications, a notice which shall include—

(1) an announcement that the agency intends to establish a negotiated rulemaking committee to negotiate and develop a proposed rule;

(2) a description of the subject and scope of the rule to be developed, and the issues to be considered;

(3) a list of the interests which are likely to be significantly affected by the rule;

(4) a list of the persons proposed to represent such interests and the person or persons proposed to represent the agency;

(5) a proposed agenda and schedule for completing the work of the committee, including a target date for publication by the agency of a proposed rule for notice and comment;

(6) a description of administrative support for the committee to be provided by the agency, including technical assistance;

(7) a solicitation for comments on the proposal to establish the committee, and the proposed membership of the negotiated rulemaking committee; and

(8) an explanation of how a person may apply or nominate another person for membership on the committee, as provided under subsection (b).

(b) Applications for membership or [FN1] committee.—Persons who will be significantly affected by a proposed rule and who believe that their interests will not be adequately represented by any person specified in a notice under subsection (a)(4) may apply for, or nominate another person for, membership on the negotiated rulemaking committee to represent such interests with respect to the proposed rule. Each application or nomination shall include—

(1) the name of the applicant or nominee and a description of the interests such person shall represent;

(2) evidence that the applicant or nominee is authorized to represent parties related to the interests the person proposes to represent;

(3) a written commitment that the applicant or nominee shall actively participate in good faith in the development of the rule under consideration; and

(4) the reasons that the persons specified in the notice under subsection (a)(4) do not adequately represent the interests of the person submitting the application or nomination.

(c) Period for submission of comments and applications.—The agency shall provide for a period of at least 30 calendar days for the submission of comments and applications under this section.

§ 565. Establishment of committee

(a) Establishment.—

(1) Determination to establish committee.—If after considering comments and applications submitted under section 564, the agency determines that a negotiated rulemaking committee can adequately represent the interests that will be significantly affected by a proposed rule and that it is feasible and appropriate in the particular rulemaking, the agency may establish a negotiated rulemaking committee. In establishing and administering such a committee, the agency shall comply with the Federal Advisory Committee Act with respect to such committee, except as otherwise provided in this subchapter.

(2) Determination not to establish committee.—If after considering such comments and applications, the agency decides not to establish a negotiated rulemaking committee, the agency shall promptly publish notice of such decision and the reasons therefor in the Federal Register and, as appropriate, in trade or other specialized publications, a copy of which shall be sent to any person who applied for, or nominated another person for membership on the negotiating [FN1] rulemaking committee to represent such interests with respect to the proposed rule.

(b) Membership.—The agency shall limit membership on a negotiated rulemaking committee to 25 members, unless the agency head determines that a greater number of members is necessary for the functioning of the committee or to achieve balanced membership. Each committee shall include at least one person representing the agency.

(c) Administrative support.—The agency shall provide appropriate administrative support to the negotiated rulemaking committee, including technical assistance.

§ 566. Conduct of committee activity

(a) Duties of committee.—Each negotiated rulemaking committee established under this subchapter shall consider the matter proposed by the agency for consideration and shall attempt to reach a consensus concerning a proposed rule with respect to such matter and any other matter the committee determines is relevant to the proposed rule.

(b) Representatives of agency on committee.—The person or persons representing the agency on a negotiated rulemaking committee shall participate in the deliberations and activities of the committee with the same rights and responsibilities as other members of the committee, and shall be authorized to fully represent the agency in the discussions and negotiations of the committee.

(c) Selecting facilitator.—Notwithstanding section 10(e) of the Federal Advisory Committee Act, an agency may nominate either a person from the Federal Government or a person from outside the Federal Government to serve as a facilitator for the negotiations of the committee, subject to the approval of the committee by consensus. If the committee does not approve the nominee of the agency for facilitator, the agency shall submit a substitute nomination. If a committee does not approve any nominee of the agency for facilitator, the committee shall select by consensus a person to serve as facilitator. A person designated to represent the agency in substantive issues may not serve as facilitator or otherwise chair the committee.

(d) Duties of facilitator.—A facilitator approved or selected by a negotiated rulemaking committee shall—

(1) chair the meetings of the committee in an impartial manner;

(2) impartially assist the members of the committee in conducting discussions and negotiations; and

(3) manage the keeping of minutes and records as required under section 10(b) and (c) of the Federal Advisory Committee Act, except that any personal notes and materials of the facilitator or of the members of a committee shall not be subject to section 552 of this title.

(e) Committee procedures.—A negotiated rulemaking committee established under this subchapter may adopt procedures for the operation of the committee. No provision of section 553 of this title shall apply to the procedures of a negotiated rulemaking committee.

(f) Report of committee.—If a committee reaches a consensus on a proposed rule, at the conclusion of negotiations the committee shall transmit to the agency that established the committee a report containing the proposed rule. If the committee does not reach a consensus on a proposed rule, the committee may transmit to the agency a report specifying any areas in which the committee reached a consensus. The committee may include in a report any other information, recommendations, or materials that the committee considers appropriate. Any committee member may include as an addendum to the report additional information, recommendations, or materials.

(g) Records of committee.—In addition to the report required by subsection (f), a committee shall submit to the agency the records required under section 10(b) and (c) of the Federal Advisory Committee Act.

§ 567. Termination of committee

A negotiated rulemaking committee shall terminate upon promulgation of the final rule under consideration, unless the committee's charter contains an earlier termination date or the agency, after consulting the committee, or the committee itself specifies an earlier termination date.

§ 568. Services, facilities, and payment of committee member expenses

(a) Services of conveners and facilitators.—

(1) In general.—An agency may employ or enter into contracts for the services of an individual or organization to serve as a convener or facilitator for a negotiated rulemaking committee under this subchapter, or may use the services of a Government employee to act as a convener or a facilitator for such a committee.

(2) Determination of conflicting interests.—An agency shall determine whether a person under consideration to serve as convener or facilitator of a committee under paragraph (1) has any financial or other interest that would preclude such person from serving in an impartial and independent manner.

(b) Services and facilities of other entities.—For purposes of this subchapter, an agency may use the services and facilities of other Federal agencies and public and private agencies and instrumentalities with the consent of such agencies and instrumentalities, and with or without reimbursement to such agencies and instrumentalities, and may accept voluntary and uncompensated services without regard to the provisions of section 1342 of title 31. The Federal Mediation and Conciliation Service may provide services and facilities, with or without reimbursement, to assist agencies under this subchapter, including furnishing conveners, facilitators, and training in negotiated rulemaking.

(c) Expenses of committee members.—Members of a negotiated rulemaking committee shall be responsible for their own expenses of participation in such committee, except that an agency may, in accordance with section 7(d) of the Federal Advisory Committee Act, pay for a member's reasonable travel and per diem expenses, expenses to obtain technical assistance, and a reasonable rate of compensation, if—

(1) such member certifies a lack of adequate financial resources to participate in the committee; and

(2) the agency determines that such member's participation in the committee is necessary to assure an adequate representation of the member's interest.

(d) Status of member as federal employee.—A member's receipt of funds under this section or section 569 shall not conclusively determine for purposes of sections 202 through 209 of title 18 whether that member is an employee of the United States Government.

§ 569. Encouraging negotiated rulemaking

(a) The President shall designate an agency or designate or establish an interagency committee to facilitate and encourage agency use of negotiated rulemaking. An agency that is considering, planning, or conducting a negotiated rulemaking may consult with such agency or committee for information and assistance.

(b) To carry out the purposes of this subchapter, an agency planning or conducting a negotiated rulemaking may accept, hold, administer, and utilize gifts, devises, and bequests of property, both real and personal if that agency's acceptance and use of such gifts, devises, or bequests do not create a conflict of interest. Gifts and bequests of money and proceeds from sales of other property received as gifts, devises, or bequests shall be deposited in the Treasury and shall be disbursed upon the order of the head of such agency. Property accepted pursuant to this section, and the proceeds thereof, shall be used as nearly as possible in accordance with the terms of the gifts, devises, or bequests.

§ 570. Judicial review

Any agency action relating to establishing, assisting, or terminating a negotiated rulemaking committee under this subchapter shall not be subject to judicial review. Nothing in this section shall bar judicial review of a rule if such judicial review is otherwise provided by law. A rule which is the product of negotiated rulemaking and is subject to judicial review shall not be accorded any greater deference by a court than a rule which is the product of other rulemaking procedures.

TABLE OF CASES

[Principal cases appear in all capital letters; references are to pages.]

A

Abbott Laboratories v. Gardner . . 438; 829; 842; 845; 849; 884; 892; 899
Abdah v. Bush 151
Abing v. Schempp 847
Action on Smoking and Health v. CAB . . . 403
Adams v. Richardson 832
Adoption of (see name of party)
Aeschliman v. NRC 357
AFL-CIO v. Brock 239
Agosto v. INS 735
Air Brake Systems, Inc. v. Mineta 887
Air Transport Association of America v. DOT . . . 406
Al-Anazi v. Bush 151
Al-Joudi v. Bush 151
Al-Marri v. Bush 151
A.L.A. Schechter Poultry Corp. v. United States . . . 522; 540; 556; 569; 572; 578; 637
Alaska Department of Environmental Conservation v. Environmental Protection Agency 801
Allah v. Seiverling 115
Alleged Contempt of (see name of party)
ALLEN v. WRIGHT *851*; 858
ALLISON v. BLOCK *428*; 433
Almurbati v. Bush 152
American Airlines, Inc. v. North American Airlines, Inc. 908
American Association of Exporters and Importers v. U.S 403
American Bus Association v. United States . . 393
American Cyanamid Co. v. FTC 315
AMERICAN HOSPITAL ASSOC. v. BOWEN . . . *388*
American Insurance Co. v. Canter 602
American Mining Congress v. Mine Safety & Health Administration 400; 401
American Postal Workers Union v. United States Postal Service 331
American Power & Light Co. v. SEC 579
American Trucking Assns., Inc. v. United States 472; 635; 636; 740
American Trucking Assns., Inc. v. Atchison, T. & S.F.R. Co. 811
American Trucking Assns., Inc. v. EPA . . . 580
Amos Treat & Co. v. SEC 315
Animal Defense Council v. Hodel 504
Appalachian Power Company v. EPA 375

Appeal of (see name of party)
Appeal of Estate of (see name of party)
Application of (see name of applicant)
Arbitration, In re 492
Arctic Slope Regional Corp. v. FERC 482
Ardastani v. INS 228
Arizona v. California 536
Arizonans for Official English v. Arizona . . 911
Armstrong v. Manzo 77; 202
Arnett v. Kennedy 101; 126; 206
Arnold Tours, Inc. v. Camp 848
Asbestos Information Assoc. v. OSHA 403
Ass'n of Nat'l Advertisers, Inc. v. FTC . . . 377; 380; 383
Associated Industries v. Ickes 849; 850
Associated Industries v. United States Dept. of Labor 366
Association of American Physicians and Surgeons, Inc. v. Clinton 975
ASSOCIATION OF DATA PROCESSING SERVICE ORGANIZATIONS v. CAMP . . . *846*
Association of Data Processing Service Orgs. v. Board of Governors of the Fed. Res. Sys. 736
Atchison, T. & S.F.R. Co. v. Wichita Bd. of Trade 811
ATLAS ROOFING, INC. v. OCCUPATIONAL SAFETY AND HEALTH REVIEW COMM'N *590*; 600
Au Yi Lau v. I.N.S. 296
Automotive Parts & Accessories Ass'n v. Boyd . . 351; 372

B

Babcock v. White 115
Bachowski v. Brennan 831
BAILEY v. RICHARDSON *50*; 58; 100
Bakelite Corp., Ex parte 600
Baker v. Carr 598
BALTIMORE GAS & ELECTRIC CO. v. NRDC *820*
Banks v. Schweiker 265; 266
Barnett; United States v. 164
Barrows v. Jackson 847
Batterton v. Francis 968
Batterton v. Marshall 391
Behrens v. Bertram Mills Circus Ltd. 398
Bell v. Wolfish 109
Bennett v. Spear 886

[Principal cases appear in all capital letters; references are to pages.]

Berkshire Employees Ass'n of Berkshire Knitting Mills v. NLRB 316
BI-METALLIC INVESTMENT CO. v. STATE BOARD OF EQUALIZATION OF COLORADO 8; 14
Bishop v. Wood 100
Bivens v. Six Unknown Narcotics Agents ... 41
Block v. Community Nutrition Institute 845
Block v. Hirsh 593
Bluewater Network v. EPA 824
BLUM v. YARETSKY 190
BOARD OF REGENTS OF STATE COLLEGES v. ROTH 88; 96; 102; 156; 157; 161; 201
Bob Jones University v. United States 854
BOWEN v. GEORGETOWN UNIV. HOSPITAL 323; 800
Bowen v. Michigan Academy of Family Physicians 845; 903
BOWLES v. WILLINGHAM 12
Bowman Transportation, Inc. v. Arkansas-Best Freight System, Inc. 448; 812
Bowsher v. Synar 606; 615; 656; 657; 672; 675
Boyd v. Constantine 262
Bragdon v. Abbott 790
Braniff Airways, Inc. v. CAB 384
Brock v. Cathedral Bluffs Shale Oil Co. ... 394
BROCK v. ROADWAY EXPRESS, INC. ... 199; 208
Brown v. Board of Education 157; 854
Broz v. Schweiker 427
Buckley v. Valeo 526; 527; 612; 638; 647; 662; 675
Burlington Truck Lines, Inc. v. United States ... 441; 812; 814; 815; 819
Burns v. Gleason 398
Burton v. Wilmington Parking Authority ... 195
BUTTREY v. UNITED STATES 231
Byrd v. Raines 625
BYRD v. UNITED STATES ENVIRONMENTAL PROTECTION AGENCY 975

C

Cabais v. Egger 392
Cafeteria and Restaurant Workers Union v. McElroy 66
CAFETERIA & RESTAURANT WORKERS UNION v. McELROY .. 60; 66; 92; 100; 102; 126; 206
CALHOUN v. BAILAR 258
Califano v. Yamasaki 190
Camp v. Pitts 363; 441; 444; 812
Carter v. Carter Coal Co. 522; 583
CASTILLO-VILLAGRA v. IMMIGRATION AND 263
CENTER FOR NATIONAL SECURITY STUDIES v. U.S. DEPARTMENT OF JUSTICE 949
Central Laborers' Pension Fund v. Heinz ... 801
CHEMICAL MANUFACTURERS ASSOCIATION v. NATURAL RESOURCES DEFENSE COUNCIL, INC. 454
CHEMICAL WASTE MANAGEMENT, INC. v. U.S. ENVIRONMENTAL PROTECTION AGENCY 235
Cheney v. United States Dist. 316
Cherokee Nation of Okla; United States v. ... 844
CHEVRON v. NRDC .. 238; 240; 745; 760; 761; 767; 769; 772; 787; 989
Chicago v. Atchison, T. & S.F.R. Co. 848
CHOCOLATE MFRS. ASS'N OF UNITED STATES v. BLOCK 339
Christenson v. Harris County 800
Chrysler Corp v. Brown 964
Chrysler Corp. v. Department of Transportation .. 809
CIA v. Sims 956
CINDERELLA CAREER AND FINISHING SCHOOLS, INC. v. FEDERAL TRADE COMMISSION 312
Cinderella Career & Finishing Schools, Inc. v. FTC 379
Citizen's Awareness Network, Inc. v. NRC .. 243
CITIZENS AWARENESS NETWORK, INC. v. NUCLEAR REGULATORY COMMISSION ... 245
CITIZENS TO PRESERVE OVERTON PARK v. VOLPE 436; 832
City v. (see name of defendant)
City and County of (see name of city and county)
Clarke v. Securities Industries 850
Cleveland Board of Education v. Loudermill 103; 201; 206
CLINTON v. NEW YORK, City of 625
Club Misty, Inc. v. Laski 11
Colgrove v. Battin 595
Commission v. (see name of opposing party)
Commissioner v. (see name of opposing party)
Commissioner of Internal Revenue (see name of defendant)
Commodity Futures Trading Commission v. Schor 607; 608; 668; 675
COMMON CAUSE v. NUCLEAR REGULATORY COMMISSION 982
Commonwealth v. (see name of defendant)
Commonwealth ex rel. (see name of relator)
Communications, Ex Parte 299; 307; 308
Concentrated Phosphate Export Assn; United States v. 911

TABLE OF CASES

TC–3

[Principal cases appear in all capital letters; references are to pages.]

Connecticut Bankers Ass'n v. Board of Governors 242
Connell v. Higginbotham 93
Conservatorship of (see name of party)
Consolidated Edison Co. v. National Labor Relations Board 727
Consolo v. FMC 364
Consumers Union v. HEW 974
Correctional Services Corp. v. Malesko 41
Corrections v. Thompson 107
Cort v. Ash 969
County v. (see name of defendant)
County of (see name of county)
Crowell v. Benson . . . 487; 489; 594; 597; 599; 601; 605; 610; 613; 615; 636
Currin v. Wallace 583
Custody of (see name of party)

D

Daniels v. Williams 180; 182
Darby v. Cisneros 890
Datafin, ex parte 40
Davidson v. Cannon 180
Dellums v. Powell, Vaughn 941
DEPARTMENT OF LABOR v. GREENWICH COLLIERIES *270*
Dep't of the Navy v. Egan 956
Deshaney v. Winnebago County Department of Social Services 177
DEVINE v. PASTORE *491*
Devine v. White 493
Dixon v. Alabama State Board of Education . . 66
Doe v. Ohio 1002
Dole v. United Steelworkers of America . . . 762
Douglas v. Veterans Administration . . . 494; 495
DeSHANEY v. WINNEBAGO COUNTY DEPARTMENT OF SOCIAL SERVICES *177*
Dunlop v. Bachowski 828; 831; 834

E

Edward J. DeBartolo Corp. v. Florida Gulf Coast Building & Construction Trades Council 768
Edwards v. Balisok 115
El Rio Santa Cruz Neighborhood Health Center, Inc. v. U.S. Department of Health and Human Services 824
Envirocare of Utah, Inc. v. NRC 256
ENVIRONMENTAL DEFENSE FUND v. THOMAS *693*
Environmental Defense Fund, Inc. v. Ruckelshaus 432

EPA v. Mink 944; 945
Estate of (see name of party)
Estelle v. Gamble 181
Ethyl Corp. v. EPA 354
Ex parte (see name of applicant)

F

FARMWORKER JUSTICE FUND, INC. v. BROCK *698*
FCC v. ITT 916
FCC v. Pottsville Broadcasting Co. . . . 133; 362
FCC v. Sanders Bros. Radio Station 847
FCC v. Schreiber 356
FDA v. Brown & Williamson Tobacco Corp . . . 464
Federal Power Commission v. New England Power Co. 548
Federal Trade Commission v. Cement Institute . . 520
FEDERAL TRADE COMMISSION v. STANDARD OIL CO. OF CALIFORNIA *883*
Field v. Clark . . . 548; 560; 568; 573; 628; 632
FIRST BANCORPORATION v. BOARD OF GOVERNORS OF THE FEDERAL RESERVE SYSTEM *471*
Flagg Bros., Inc. v. Brooks 193
Flast v. Cohen 846; 852
Fletcher v. Peck 532
Florida East Coast Railway; United States v. . . . 243; 338; 361
Florida Power & Light Co. v. Lorion 448
FOOD AND DRUG ADMINISTRATION v. BROWN & WILLIAMSON TOBACCO CORPORATION *769*
Food Chemical News v. Young 978; 979
Ford Motor Co. v. FTC 420
FORSHAM v. HARRIS *922*; *928*
FPC v. Texaco, Inc. 425;
Franklin v. Massachusetts 842; 886
Freeman United Coal Mining Co. v. Office of Workers' Compensation Programs 271
Freytag v. Commissioner of Internal Revenue . . . 651
FRIENDS OF THE EARTH, INCORPORATED v. LAIDLAW ENVIRONMENTAL SERVICES (TOC), INC. *873*; *910*
Frothingham v. Mellon, 262 U.S., at 489 . . . 865
Frozen Food Express v. United States 898
FTC v. Cement Institute 279; 378; 380
FTC v. Cinderella Career & Finishing Schools, Inc. 314
FTC v. Klesner 830
Fuentes v. Shevin 144

[Principal cases appear in all capital letters; references are to pages.]

Fusari v. Steinberg 129

G

Gardner v. Toilet Goods Ass'n 899
Germaine; United States v. 641; 647; 650
Gherebi v. Bush 149
Gibson v. FTC 297
Gibson Wine Co. v. Snyder 392
Gilligan, Will & Co. v. SEC 315; 379
Goldberg v. Kelly . . . 69; 72; 83; 84; 85; 86; 87;
88; 92; 93; 95; 105; 120; 123; 125;
126; 134; 138; 186; 202
Goss v. Lopez 137; 154; 163; 165
Graf; United States v. 286
Grannis v. Ordean 77
Gray v. Powell 743
Greater Boston Television Corp. v. FCC . . . 806;
818
Green v. McCall 115
Greene v. McElroy 78
GROLIER, INC. v. FEDERAL TRADE COMMISSION *291*
Grutter v. Bollinger 18
GTE Sylvania, Inc. v. Consumers Union of United States, Inc 928
Guantanamo Detainees, In re 149; 150; 151
Guardianship of (see name of party)
Guevara-Flores v. INS 759

H

HAMDI v. RUMSFELD *138*
Hamdi and Mathews v. Eldridge 153
Hampton & Co. v. United States 640
Hardin v. Kentucky Utilities Co. 848
Harris v. McRae 180
Hazardous Waste Treatment Council v. EPA . . .
851
HECKLER v. CHANEY 827; 836; 842
Heckler v. Mathews 853
HECKLER, SECRETARY OF HEALTH AND HUMAN SERVICES v. CAMPBELL *422*
Helvering v. Gregory 783
Helvering v. Mitchell 593
Hemmings v. Barian 401
Hennen, Ex parte 642
Hill v. Smith 272
HOCTOR v. UNITED STATES DEPARTMENT OF AGRICULTURE *396*
Home Bldg. & Loan Ass'n v. Blaisdell 14
Home Box Office, Inc. v. FCC . . 383; 384; 385;
706
Homer v. Richmond 61

Hornsby v. Allen 68
Housing Authority of Omaha v. United States Housing Authority 403
Humphrey's Executor v. United States 644;
645; 652; 659; 663; 667; 673; 678

I

ICC v. Locomotive Engineers 843
ICORE, Inc. v. F.C.C 333
IMMIGRATION AND NATURALIZATION SERVICE v. CARDOZA-FONSECA . . . *757*;
765
IMMIGRATION AND NATURALIZATION SERVICE v. CHADHA . . *522*; 606; 628; 632;
657; 663; 670; 870
Impro Products, Inc. v. Block 333
In re (see name of party)
Independent Equipment Dealers Ass'n. v. EPA . .
887
Independent Ins. Agents of America v. Board of Governors 242
Independent U.S. Tanker Owners Comm. v. Lewis
. 420
INDUSTRIAL SAFETY EQUIPMENT ASS'N INC. v. E.P.A. *329*
Industrial Union Department, AFL-CIO v. American Petroleum Institute 546; 547; 550; 578
INDUSTRIAL UNION DEPARTMENT, AFL-CIO v. HODGSON *366*; 377; 382; 735
Ingraham v. Wright 109; 160; 169; 179
INS v. Stevic 757
Intern. Primate Prot. L. v. Administrators of the Tulane Education Fund 859
International Harvester Co. v. Ruckelshaus . . . . .
343; 354
International Union, United Automobile, Aerospace & Agri v. Donovan 699

J

J. W. Hampton & Co. v. United States 560
Jackson v. Metropolitan Edison Co. . . . 192; 193
Japan Whaling Assn. v. American Cetacean Soc.
. 863
Jewell Ridge Coal Corp. v. Mine Workers . . 749
Johnson v. Robinson 170
Joint Anti-Fascist Refugee Committee v. McGrath
. . . . . . 58; 62; 64; 66; 75; 91; 126
J.W. Hampton, Jr., & Co. v. United States . . 527;
568; 572; 578; 580

K

Kaczmarczyk v. INS 268

TABLE OF CASES

[Principal cases appear in all capital letters; references are to pages.]

Katchen v. Landy 612
Kelly v. Wyman 74
Kent v. Dulles 547
Khalid v. Bush 149
KING v. U.S. DEPT. OF JUSTICE *935*
Kirschbaum Co. v. Walling 785
Kissinger v. Reporters Committee for Freedom of the Press 924; 928
KIXMILLER v. SEC *460*
Knauff v. Shaughnessy, 1950 66
Kwong Hai Chew v. Colding 66

L

Labor Board v. Condenser Corp. 742
Lead Industries Assn., Inc. v. EPA the District of Columbia 575
Leedom v. Kyne 916
Lesar v. United States Department of Justice ... 938
License of (see name of party)
LINCOLN v. VIGIL *840*; 845
Linda R.S. v. Richard D. 866
Local 2578, American Federation of Government Employees v. General Services Administration 493
Lochner v. New York 173
LONDONER v. DENVER, City and County of .. *4*; *9*; *49*
Los Angeles v. Lyons 876; 878; 911
LUJAN v. DEFENDERS OF WILDLIFE .. *860*; 876
Lujan v. National Wildlife Federation 875

M

Marathon Oil Co. v. EPA 230; 234; 239
Marbury v. Madison 867; 870
Marcello v. Bonds 228
Marriage of (see name of party)
MATHEWS v. ELDRIDGE *124*; 134; 137; 138; 142; 143; 147; 150; 154; 163; 166; 174; 176; 189; 198; 202; 208; 288
Matter of (see name of party)
McAulife v. Mayor of New Bedford 58
McCulloch v. Maryland 643
McLouth Steel Prods. Corp. v. Thomas 336
McNary v. Haitian Refugee Center, Inc ... 902
Meachum v. Fano 107; 115; 162
MEAD CORPORATION; UNITED STATES v. .. *787*
Mead Data Central v. United States Department of the Air Force 941
Medical Committee for Human Rights v. Securities and Exchange Commission 461

Medina v. California 288
Menasche; United States v. 828
Mesquite, City of v. Aladdin's Castle, Inc. ... 910
Metropolitan School District v. Davila 400
Meyer v. Nebraska 91; 162
Middendorf v. Henry 288
Missouri v. Horowitz 137
MISTRETTA v. UNITED STATES .. 521; *567*; 579
Morgan; United States v. 282; 378; 441; 520
Morrison v. Olson 581; 617; 636; 645; 670; 671
Morrissey v. Brewer ... 108; 115; 157; 162; 202
Morton v. Ruiz 747; 760; 799; 968
Motor Vehicle Manufacturers Association v. State Farm Mutual 805
MOTOR VEHICLE MFRS. ASSN. v. STATE FARM MUTUAL 766; 777; 782; 805; *807*
Mullins Coal Co. of Va. v. Director, Office of Workers' Compensation Programs 270
Murchison, In re 281
Murray's Lessee v. Hoboken Land & Improvement Co. 62; 487; 599; 603; 614
Muskrat v. United States 847
MYERS v. BETHLEHEM SHIPBUILDING CORP. *888*
Myers v. United States 642; 654; 656; 659; 668; 672

N

NADER v. ALLEGHENY AIRLINES, INC. ... *904*
National Broadcasting Co. v. United States .. 579
National Collegiate Athletic Association v. Tarkanian 42
National Insurance Co. v. Tidewater Co. ... 90; 604
NATIONAL LABOR RELATIONS BOARD v. BELL AEROSPACE COMPANY *417*
National Labor Relations Board v. Columbian Enameling & Stamping Co. 727
NATIONAL LABOR RELATIONS BOARD v. HEARST PUBLICATIONS, INC. *737*
National Labor Relations Board v. Pittsburgh Steamship Co. 726
National Mining Association v. Department of Labor 422
National Tour Brokers Ass'n v. United States ... 342
Nat'l Small Shipments Traffic Conference, Inc. v. ICC 383
Natural Resources Defense Council v. Abraham .. 801

[Principal cases appear in all capital letters; references are to pages.]

NATURAL RESOURCES DEFENSE COUNCIL v. HERRINGTON *970*
Natural Resources Defense Council v. NRC 357
Natural Resources Defense Council v. EPA 503
Neighborhood TV Co., Inc. v. FCC 394
New York v. United States 814
New York Central Securities Corp. v. United States 579
Nixon v. Administrator of General Services 668; 989
Nixon; United States v. 675
NLRB v. Bell Aerospace Co. 473; 796
NLRB v. Hearst 737
NLRB v. Hearst Publications 419; 736; 737
NLRB v. Robbins Tire Co. 921
NLRB v. Transportation Management Corp 273
NLRB v. Walton Mfg. Co. 734
NLRB v. Wyman-Gordon Co. 418
Northern Pipeline Construction Co. v. Marathon Pipe Line Co. 486; 597; 609
Norton v. Southern Utah Wilderness Alliance ... 888
Norwegian Nitrogen Products Co. v. United States 548; 743
NOVA SCOTIA FOOD PRODUCTS CORP.; UNITED STATES v. *346*

O

OFFICE OF COMMUNICATION OF UNITED CHURCH OF CHRIST v. FEDERAL COMMUNICATIONS COMMISSION *250*; 847
Offutt v. United States 520
Ohio Bell Telephone Co. v. Public Utils. Comm'n 265
O'LEARY v. BROWN *721*
O'Shea v. Littleton 853
Overton Park and Camp v. Pitts 444
Owen v. Independence 32

P

Pacific Gas & Electric Co. v. FPC 393
Pacific Legal Foundation v. Department of Transportation 809
Pacific States Box & Basket Co. v. White .. 352; 804
Packard Motor Car Co. v. NLRB 744
Palmore v. United States 486; 602; 604
Panama Refining Company v. Ryan .. 522; 540; 544; 546; 556; 561; 562; 569; 572; 578; 637

Parratt v. Taylor 180
Parsons v. Bedford 595
Parsons v. United States Department of the Air Force 494
Paul v. Davis 104; 105; 169
Penasquitos Village Inc. v. NLRB 734
PENSION BENEFIT GUARANTY CORPORATION v. LTV CORP. *445*
People v. (see name of defendant)
People ex (see name of defendant)
People ex rel. (see name of defendant)
Perkins v. Lukens Steel Co 404
Perry v. Sindermann 95; 102
Petition of (see name of party)
Pharmaceutical Research and Manufacturers of America v. Thompson 801
Phillips v. Commissioner 14
Phillips Petroleum Co. v. Wisconsin 736
Philly's v. Byrne 11
Picciotto; United States v. 402
Pickus v. United States Board of Parole ... 393
PILLSBURY CO. v. FTC *516*; 521
Porter v. Califano 735
Portland Audubon Society v. Endangered Species 312; 711
Portland Cement Association v. Ruckelshaus ... 350; 354
Powell v. Texas 161
Powers v. Russell 272
Preserve Overton Park, Inc. v. Volpe .. 448; 504; 735; 804; 811; 812; 822; 829; 832; 836; 837; 842; 969
Procunier v. Navarette 36
PROFESSIONAL AIR TRAFFIC CONTROLLERS ORG. (PATCO) v. FEDERAL LABOR RELATIONS AUTHORITY *299*; 301
Prometheus Radio Project v. FCC 824
Protect Overton Park v. Volpe 826
Public Citizen v. Steed 702
Public Citizen v. United States Dept. of Justice .. 975; 978

Q

R

Raines v. Byrd 625
Rasul v. Bush 148
Renegotiation Bd. v. Grumman Aircraft ... 944
Reno v. Catholic Social Services 901
Resnick v. Hayes 115
REYNOLDS v. GIULIANI *117*; 122
RFC v. Bankers Trust Co. 612
Rhinehart v. Finch 261

TABLE OF CASES

[Principal cases appear in all capital letters; references are to pages.]

RICHARDSON v. McKNIGHT *30*
Richardson v. Perales 130; 260; 280
Richmond Newspapers, Inc. v. Virginia . . . 952
Rizzo v. Goode 853
Robertson v. Methow Valley Citizens Council . . . 870
Robinson v. California 181
Rochin v. California 80; 180
Roelfs v. Secretary of Air Force 445
Rosenberg, Ingraham v. Wright 169
Rostker v. Goldberg 288
Rowell v. Andrus 343
Ruckelshaus v. Monsanto Co. 484
Rumsfeld v. Padilla 148
Rusk v. Cort 902
Rust v. Sullivan 764
Rutherford; United States v. 772

S

Saginaw Broadcasting v. FCC 724
SANDIN v. CONNER *105*
Sangamon Valley Television Corp. v. United States 384
Scenic Hudson Preservation Conference v. FPC . . 254; 847
Schlesinger v. Reservists Committee 853
Schor v. Commodity Futures Trading Committee .490
SCHWEIKER v. McCLURE *187*; 196
SCRAP; United States v. 854
SEACOAST ANTI-POLLUTION LEAGUE v. COSTLE 228; 234; 239; 241
SEC v. Chenery Corp. 332; 363; 408; 414; 415; 417; 418; 441; 796; 806; 812; 814
Shelley v. Kraemer 192
Shelly v. Buck 834
Sheppard v. Sullivan 336
Sherbert v. Verner 75
Sierra Club v. Costle . . 386; 387; 388; 704; 711
Sierra Club v. Morton 850
Simon v. Eastern Ky. Welfare Rights Organization .880
SKIDMORE v. SWIFT & CO. . . . *784*; 787; 790; 800
Slochower v. Board of Education 75; 92
Small Refiner Lead Phase-Down Task Force v. EPA 344
Snepp v. United States 836
South Chicago Coal & Dock Co. v. Bassett 740
Southern R. Co. v. Seaboard Allied Milling Corp. 828
Speiser v. Randall 75; 97

Springer v. Philippine Islands 641
St. Mary's Hospital v. Blue Cross & Blue Shield Ass'n. 401
Standard Oil Co. of California v. United States . . 517
Stark v. Wickard 848; 866
State v. (see name of defendant)
State ex (see name of state)
State ex rel. (see name of state)
State of (see name of state)
Steadman v. SEC 273
Steel Co. v. Citizens for Better Environment 911
Still v. Lance 100
Stinson v. United States 398; 399
Storer Broadcasting Co.; United States v. . . . 898
SUGAR CANE GROWERS COOPERATIVE OF FLORIDA v. VENEMAN *333*
Sullivan v. Everhardt 762
Sunshine Anthracite Coal Co. v. Adkins . . . 583
Switchmen's Union v. National Mediation Board 849
Synar v. United States 659; 665

T

TC v. Schor 670
TELECOMMUNICATIONS RESEARCH & ACTION CENTER v. F.C.C. *912*
Tennessee Electric Power Co. v. TVA 847
Texaco, Inc. v. FTC 315
THOMAS v. UNION CARBIDE AGR. PRODUCTS CO. *484*; 606; 609
Ticor Title Insurance Co. v. Federal Trade Commission 903
TIJERINA v. WALTERS *992*
TOILET GOODS ASSOCIATION v. GARDNER *897*; 899
Touby v. United States 578; 870
Trust Estate of (see name of party)
Tumey v. Ohio 288
TVA v. Hill 751

U

Union of Concerned Scientists v. U.S. NRC 239
UNITED MUNICIPAL DISTRIBUTORS GROUP v. FERC *478*
United Public Workers v. Mitchell 62
United States v. (see name of defendant)
United States v. Allegheny-Ludlum Steel Corp. . . 355
United States v. Ferreira 641

[Principal cases appear in all capital letters; references are to pages.]

U.S. Dept. of Defense v. Federal Labor Relations Authority 1001
UNITED STATES DEPARTMENT OF JUSTICE v. TAX ANALYSTS *927*
United States Department of Labor v. Kast Metals Corp. 394
United States Lines, Inc. v. FMC 383; 384; 385
United States Navigation Co. v. Cunard S.S. Co. 908
United States Parole Comm'n v. Geraghty . . 911
United States Steel Corp. v. Train 230; 234
UNITED STATES STEELWORKERS OF AMERICA v. MARSHALL *376*
United Technologies Corp. v. EPA 239
UNIVERSAL CAMERA CORP. v. NLRB 723; *726*
USA GROUP LOAN SERVICES, INCORPORATED, USA v. RILEY *502*

V

Valley Forge Christian College v. Americans United for Separation of Church and State, Inc. . . 851
Vander Jagt v. O'Neill 852
Vaughn v. Rosen 939
Vermont Agency of Natural Resources v. United States ex rel. Stevens 882
VERMONT YANKEE NUCLEAR POWER CORP. v. NATURAL RESOURCES DEFENSE COUNCIL *355*; 383; 385; 448; 805; 814
Vigil v. Rhoades 841

W

W. Chicago, City of v. U.S. NRC 241; 248
Walling v. Jacksonville Paper Co. 785
WALTERS v. NATIONAL ASSOCIATION OF RADIATION SURVIVORS *169*
Warth v. Seldin 851
Washington v. Harper 115
Washington Legal Foundation v. Sentencing Comm'n 979
Waters v. Taylor Co. 722
WEBSTER v. DOE *834*; 842; 845

Weinberger v. Hynson 241
WEISS v. UNITED STATES *286*; 652
Western Pacific R. Co.; United States v. . . . 909
White v. Rochford 183
WHITMAN v. AMERICAN TRUCKING ASSOCIATIONS, INC. *575*
Whitmore v. Arkansas 911
Wieman v. Updegraff 62; 92
Wiener v. United States 636; 667; 673
Will; United States v. 611
William v. Luneberg, Retroactivity and Administrative Rulemaking, 1991 332
Williams v. Adams 32
Williamson County Regional Planning Comm'n v. Hamilton Bank of Johnson City 891
Willner v. Committee on Character 92
Willowbrook v. Olech 15
Wisconsin v. Constantineau 104
WITHROW v. LARKIN *277*
WKAT, Inc. v. FCC 311
WOLFE v. DEPARTMENT OF HEALTH AND HUMAN SERVICES *942*; 962
Wolff v. McDonnell. 106; 168
WONG YANG SUNG v. McGRATH *222*; 230; 275; 294; 295; 355; 362
Workmen v. Connally 548
W.T. Grant Co; United States v. 910
WWHT, Inc. v. FCC 834
Wyatt v. Cole 31

X

Y

Yakus v. United States 14; 426; 571; 579
Yates v. Hendon 801
Young v. Community Nutrition Center 751
Youngberg v. Romeo 179; 181
Youngstown Sheet & Tube Co. v. Sawyer . . 145; 640; 641; 667; 679; 681

Z

Zadvydas v. Davis 956

INDEX

[References are to pages.]

A

ADJUDICATORY PROCEEDINGS
ADR techniques (See ALTERNATIVE DISPUTE RESOLUTION (ADR))
Agency non-ALJ presiding officers . . . 243
ALJs (See ADMINISTRATIVE LAW JUDGES/ DECISIONMAKERS)
Burden of proof . . . 270–277
Choosing between rulemaking and adjudication . . . 407–433
Congressional interference . . . 515–521
Decisionmaking restrictions . . . 242
Due Process protections . . . 277–283
    (See also DUE PROCESS PROTECTIONS)
Evidence
    Generally . . . 257–258
    Burden of proof . . . 270–277
    Official notice doctrine . . . 262–270
    Rules of Evidence . . . 258–262
Ex parte communications . . . 299–312
Hearings (See ADMINISTRATIVE HEARINGS)
Informal adjudication (See INFORMAL AGENCY ACTION)
Intervention . . . 250–254
Jury trial, abrogation of right to . . . 590–597
Official notice doctrine . . . 262–270
Parties . . . 250–257
Rules *versus* orders
    Generally . . . 4–17
    Choosing between rulemaking and adjudication . . . 407–433
    Procedural characterization . . . 17–27

ADMINISTRATIVE COMMON LAW
Rulemaking process . . . 354–365

ADMINISTRATIVE EQUITY
Informal agency action . . . 451–466

ADMINISTRATIVE HEARINGS
Clean Water Act . . . 231–235
Deportation proceedings . . . 222–228
Due Process protections (See DUE PROCESS PROTECTIONS)
Evidence
    Generally . . . 257–258
    Burden of proof . . . 270–277
    Official notice doctrine . . . 262–270
    Rules of Evidence . . . 258–262
Federal Water Pollution Control Act . . . 228–231

ADMINISTRATIVE HEARINGS—Cont.
Nuclear Regulatory Commission licensing hearings . . . 241; 245–250
Resource Conservation and Recovery Act . . . 235–240
When unnecessary . . . 241–242

ADMINISTRATIVE LAW JUDGES/ DECISIONMAKERS
Generally . . . 290–291
Ex parte communications . . . 299–312
Independence
    Generally . . . 243–244; 291–299
    Ex parte communications . . . 299–312
    Pre-judgment of case . . . 312–317
Military judges . . . 286–290
Pre-judgment of case . . . 312–317

ADMINISTRATIVE PROCEDURE ACT (APA)
Applicability
    CWA cases . . . 231–235
    Deportation cases . . . 222–228
    FWPCA cases . . . 228–231
    NRC licensing hearings . . . 241; 245–250
    RCRA cases . . . 235–240
Formal adjudication (See ADJUDICATORY PROCEEDINGS)
Informal adjudication (See INFORMAL AGENCY ACTION)
Judicial review exclusions . . . 826–845
New Deal and . . . 216–221
Rulemaking (See RULEMAKING)

AGENCY DECISIONMAKING
(See also GOVERNMENTAL ACTION)
Generally (See ADJUDICATORY PROCEEDINGS)
Judicial review (See JUDICIAL REVIEW)

AGENCY "DISCRETION"
Executive control (See EXECUTIVE POWER)
Judicial control (See JUDICIAL POWER)
Judicial review . . . 827–845
Legislative control (See CONGRESSIONAL AUTHORITY)

AGENCY RULEMAKING (See RULEMAKING)

ALTERNATIVE DISPUTE RESOLUTION (ADR)
Generally . . . 476–477
Arbitration of disputes . . . 483–496
Criticism of . . . 497–500
Mediation . . . 496–497
Mini-trials . . . 496

[References are to pages.]

ALTERNATIVE DISPUTE RESOLUTION (ADR)—Cont.
Negotiated rulemaking . . . 501–509
Settlement of disputes . . . 477–483

APPELLATE REVIEW (See JUDICIAL REVIEW)

APPOINTMENT POWER
Executive authority . . . 638–652

ARBITRATION OF DISPUTES
Generally . . . 483–496

ARTICLE I TRIBUNALS
Judicial authority . . . 597–619

B

BURDEN OF PROOF
Adjudicatory proceedings . . . 270–277

C

COMMON LAW
Administrative . . . 354–365

CONGRESSIONAL AUTHORITY
Article I of the Constitution . . . 521
Delegation doctrine
    Generally . . . 540–549
    Private delegation doctrine . . . 582–586
    Recent revival . . . 550–582
Delegation of authority
    Judicial authority (See JUDICIAL POWER)
    Legislative authority. Delegation doctrine, *above*
Jury trial, abrogation of right to . . . 590–597
Oversight authority . . . 515–521
Private delegation doctrine . . . 582–586
Removal power . . . 657–680
Rulemaking, influence in . . . 704–712
Veto power . . . 522–539

CONTEXT OF PROCESS
Generally . . . 24–27

CORPORATIST THEORY
Generally . . . 26–27

D

DATA QUALITY ACT (DQA)
Executive power and . . . 712–714

DECISIONMAKERS (See ADMINISTRATIVE LAW JUDGES/DECISIONMAKERS)

DELEGATION OF AUTHORITY
Congressional authority (See CONGRESSIONAL AUTHORITY)

DELEGATION OF AUTHORITY—Cont.
Judicial authority (See JUDICIAL POWER)

DELIBERATIVE PROCESS PRIVILEGE
Freedom of information . . . 942–949

DUE PROCESS PROTECTIONS
Adjudicatory proceedings . . . 277–283
Employment discontinuance
    Generally . . . 88–105
    Whistleblower protection . . . 199–209
"Enemy combatant" detainees . . . 138–153
Liberty interests
    "Enemy combatant" detainees . . . 138–153
    Prison regulations . . . 105–116
    Student discipline, *below*
Limiting . . . 154–177
Medicaid patients . . . 190–196
Medicare patients . . . 187–190
Military judges' terms . . . 286–290
Negative rights . . . 177–186
Prison regulations . . . 105–116
Property interests
    Generally . . . 69–72
    Employment discontinuance, *above*
    Public assistance, *below*
    Veterans benefits . . . 169–177
Public assistance
    Discontinuance
    generally . . . 72–88
    disentitlement "reforms" . . . 116–124
    Social Security disability benefits 124–138
    Medicaid patients . . . 190–196
    Medicare patients . . . 187–190
    Privatization reforms . . . 196–198
Public/private distinction . . . 177–209
Right/privilege distinction
    Generally . . . 49–65
    Demise of . . . 65–69
Student discipline
    Corporal punishment . . . 160–169
    Suspensions from school . . . 154–159
Veterans benefits . . . 169–177
Welfare benefits. Public assistance, *above*
Whistleblowers . . . 199–209

E

EMPLOYMENT
Discontinuance (See DUE PROCESS PROTECTIONS)

"ENEMY COMBATANT" DETAINEES
Due Process protections . . . 138–153

EQUITY
Administrative equity . . . 451–466

EVIDENCE
Adjudicatory proceedings (See ADJUDICATORY PROCEEDINGS)
Judicial review of findings of fact . . . 726–736

EXECUTIVE ORDERS
Generally . . . 680–681
OMB-related orders . . . 681–704

EXECUTIVE POWER
Generally . . . 621
Appointment power . . . 638–652
Increase in . . . 622–625
Line item veto . . . 625–638
Office of Management and Budget
    Data Quality Act and . . . 712–714
    Executive orders . . . 681–704
    Privatization and . . . 714–717
    Role of . . . 693–704
Oversight authority
    Executive orders (See EXECUTIVE ORDERS)
    Office of Management and Budget, *above*
Removal power
    Generally . . . 652–657
    Separation-of-powers issues . . . 657–680
Rulemaking
    Ex parte contacts with interested parties . . . 704–712
    Review of agency rulemaking . . . 683–687
Spending power(s)
    Line item veto . . . 625–638
    Office of Management and Budget, *above*

EXHAUSTION OF ADMINISTRATIVE REMEDIES
Judicial review . . . 888–892

EX PARTE COMMUNICATIONS
Administrative Law Judges/decisionmakers 299–312
Agency rulemaking, congressional and executive influence in . . . 704–712

F

FEDERAL ADVISORY COMMITTEE ACT (FACA)
Generally . . . 970–981

FIFTH AMENDMENT (See DUE PROCESS PROTECTIONS)

"FINALITY" OF AGENCY ACTION
Generally . . . 882–888

FINDINGS OF FACT
Judicial review . . . 726–736

FORMAL ADJUDICATION (See ADJUDICATORY PROCEEDINGS)

FOURTEENTH AMENDMENT (See DUE PROCESS PROTECTIONS)

FREEDOM OF INFORMATION ACT (FOIA)
Generally . . . 921–922
"Agency"/"agency records" . . . 922–935
Deliberative process privilege . . . 942–949
Exemptions . . . 935–964
National security information . . 935–942; 949–964
Reverse FOIA suits . . . 964–970

G

GOVERNMENTAL ACTION
Generally . . . 1–3
Procedural characterization . . . 17–27
Public/private distinction
    Generally . . . 27–44
    Due Process protections . . . 177–209
Rules *versus* orders
    Generally . . . 4–17
    Procedural characterization . . . 17–27

GREEN LIGHT THEORIES
Generally . . . 21–24

H

HEARINGS
Clean Water Act . . . 231–235
Deportation proceedings . . . 222–228
Due Process protections (See DUE PROCESS PROTECTIONS)
Evidence
    Generally . . . 257–258
    Burden of proof . . . 270–277
    Official notice doctrine . . . 262–270
    Rules of Evidence . . . 258–262
Federal Water Pollution Control Act . . . 228–231
Nuclear Regulatory Commission licensing hearings . . . 241; 245–250
Resource Conservation and Recovery Act 235–240
When unnecessary . . . 241–242

I

INDIVIDUAL/STATE RELATIONSHIP (See GOVERNMENTAL ACTION)

[References are to pages.]

INFORMAL AGENCY ACTION
Generally . . . 435–436
Administrative equity . . . 451–466
Conditions and commitments . . . 466–476
Judicial review . . . 436–451

INTERVENTION
Adjudicatory proceedings . . . 250–254

J

JUDICIAL POWER
Generally . . . 719–721
Appellate review (See JUDICIAL REVIEW)
Article I tribunals . . . 597–619
Delegation of power
    Generally . . . 586–590
    Article I tribunals, to . . . 597–619

JUDICIAL REVIEW
Generally . . . 825–826
Agency "discretion" . . . 827–845
Agency rules
    Arbitrary and capricious standard 803–804
    "Hard look" doctrine . . . 805–824
    Rational basis test . . . 804–805
APA exclusions . . . 826–845
Deference doctrines . . . 784–803
Exhaustion of administrative remedies . . 888–892
"Finality" of agency action . . . 882–888
Findings of fact . . . 726–736
Informal agency action . . . 436–451
Mootness . . . 910–912
Primary jurisdiction doctrine . . . 904–910
Questions of fact . . . 721–726
Questions of law . . . 736–784
Ripeness doctrine . . . 892–904
Standing to seek . . . 845–882
Substantial evidence standard . . . 726–736
Venue . . . 912–917

JURY TRIAL
Abrogation of right . . . 590–597

L

LAW-ENFORCEMENT INVESTIGATORY INFORMATION
Freedom of information . . . 935–942; 949–964

LEGISLATIVE AUTHORITY (See CONGRESSIONAL AUTHORITY)

LINE ITEM VETO
Executive power . . . 625–638

M

MEDIATION
Generally . . . 496–497

MILITARY JUDGES
Constitutional issues . . . 286–290

MINI-TRIALS
Generally . . . 496

MOOTNESS
Judicial review . . . 910–912

N

NATIONAL SECURITY INFORMATION
Freedom of information . . . 935–942; 949–964

NEGOTIATED RULEMAKING
Generally . . . 501–509

NEW DEAL
APA backdrop . . . 216–221
Monopoly problem and . . . 212–216

NOTICE
Due Process protections (See DUE PROCESS PROTECTIONS)
Official notice doctrine . . . 262–270
Rulemaking (See RULEMAKING)

O

OFFICE OF MANAGEMENT AND BUDGET (See EXECUTIVE POWER)

OFFICIAL NOTICE DOCTRINE
Adjudicatory proceedings . . . 262–270

OPEN GOVERNMENT
Federal Advisory Committee Act . . . 970–981
FOIA (See FREEDOM OF INFORMATION ACT (FOIA))
Privacy Act . . . 990–1002
Sunshine Act . . . 982–989

ORDERS VERSUS RULES
Generally . . . 4–17
Choosing between rulemaking and adjudication . . . 407–433
Procedural characterization . . . 17–27

P

PARTIES
Adjudicatory proceedings . . . 250–257

[References are to pages.]

PRESIDENTIAL POWER (See EXECUTIVE POWER)

PRIMARY JURISDICTION DOCTRINE
Judicial review . . . 904–910

PRISON REGULATIONS
Due Process protections . . . 105–116

PRIVACY ACT
Generally . . . 990–1002

PRIVATE DELEGATION DOCTRINE
Congressional authority . . . 582–586

PRIVATE/PUBLIC DISTINCTION
Generally . . . 27–44
Due Process protections . . . 177–209

PUBLIC ASSISTANCE
Discontinuance (See DUE PROCESS PROTECTIONS)

Q

QUESTIONS OF FACT
Judicial review . . . 721–726

QUESTIONS OF LAW
Judicial review . . . 736–784

R

RED LIGHT THEORIES
Generally . . . 19–21

REMOVAL POWER
Congressional authority . . . 657–680
Executive authority (See EXECUTIVE POWER)

REVERSE FOIA SUITS
Generally . . . 964–970

RIPENESS DOCTRINE
Judicial review . . . 892–904

RULEMAKING
Administrative common law . . . 354–365
Choosing between adjudication and rulemaking . . . 407–433
Congressional *ex parte* contacts with interested parties . . . 704–712
Executive power
    Ex parte contacts with interested parties . . . 704–712
    Review of agency rulemaking . . . 683–687
Hybrid procedures . . . 365–388
Informal processes . . . 339–354

RULEMAKING—Cont.
Negotiated rulemaking . . . 501–509
Notice-and-comment requirements
    Generally . . . 333–337
    Exceptions . . . 388–405
Process requirements
    Generally . . . 337–339
    Administrative common law . . . 354–365
    Exceptions . . . 388–405
    Hybrid procedures . . . 365–388
    Informal processes . . . 339–354
    Notice-and-comment requirements, *above*
Required rulemaking . . . 428–433
What constitutes . . . 329–333

RULES
Descriptive *versus* prescriptive . . . 320–323
Duty to promulgate . . . 428–433
"General policy statements," *versus* . . . 393–394
Interpretive . . . 392–393; 396–405
Judicial review
    Arbitrary and capricious standard 803–804
    "Hard look" doctrine . . . 805–824
    Rational basis test . . . 804–805
Making of (See RULEMAKING)
Orders *versus*
    Generally . . . 4–17
    Choosing between rulemaking and adjudication . . . 407–433
    Procedural characterization . . . 17–27
Procedural . . . 394
Reliance on and use of . . . 422–428
Retroactivity . . . 323–329
What are . . . 319–320

S

SEPARATION OF POWERS
Legislative vetoes . . . 522–539
Removal power . . . 657–680

SETTLEMENT OF DISPUTES
Generally . . . 477–483

SPENDING POWER(S)
Executive authority (See EXECUTIVE POWER)

STANDING
Intervention in proceedings . . . 250–254
Judicial review . . . 845–882

STATE ACTION (See GOVERNMENTAL ACTION)

STUDENTS
Disciplining (See DUE PROCESS PROTECTIONS)

SUNSHINE ACT
Generally . . . 982–989

T

"TERRORIST" DETAINEES
Due Process protections . . . 138–153

V

VENUE
Judicial review . . . 912–917

VETERANS BENEFITS
Due Process protections . . . 169–177

VETO POWER
Congressional authority . . . 522–539
Line item veto . . . 625–638

W

WELFARE BENEFITS
Discontinuance (See DUE PROCESS PROTECTIONS)

WHISTLEBLOWERS
Due Process protections . . . 199–209